Communications
in Computer and Information Science 224

Dehuai Zeng (Ed.)

Applied Informatics and Communication

International Conference, ICAIC 2011
Xi'an, China, August 20-21, 2011
Proceedings, Part I

Springer

Volume Editor

Dehuai Zeng
Shenzhen University
Nanhai Ave 3688, Shenzhen, Guangdong, 518060, China
E-mail: zengdh2008@gmail.com

ISSN 1865-0929 ISSN 1865-0937 (eBook)
ISBN 978-3-642-23213-8 ISBN 978-3-642-23214-5 (eBook)
DOI 10.1007/978-3-642-23214-5
Springer Heidelberg Dordrecht London New York

Library of Congress Control Number: 2011934039

CR Subject Classification (1998): C, D, F, H, I, J.1, J.2

Typesetting: Camera-ready by author, data conversion by Scientific Publishing Services, Chennai, India

Printed on acid-free paper

Springer is part of Springer Science+Business Media (www.springer.com)

Preface

Computers are firmly rooted in nearly all areas of life today. In company life, documents and products are produced by using computers, communication is by e-mail, companies present their commodities and services on the Internet and copious amounts of data are stored in databases. Different application programs are required for all of these processes.

The 2011 International Conference on Applied Informatics and Communication (ICAIC 2011) held during August 20–21, 2011, in Xi'an, China, provided an excellent platform for scientists and engineers of different countries working in various fields to exchange the latest developments and foster world-wide cooperation in the field of applied informatics and communication. Hundreds of experts and scholars from different countries attended ICAIC 2011.

Being crucial for the development of applied informatics and communication, our conference encompasses numerous research topics and applications: from the core fields of information systems and software engineering, manufacturing and automation engineering, computer-based signal processing and image processing to Communications Technology and other related topics. All of the papers were peer-reviewed by selected experts and 451 were selected for the proceedings of ICAIC 2011. We believe that this book provides a valuable reference for researchers in related fields. The papers describe how efficient, user-friendly, secure and upgradeable information technology systems can be designed, built and meaningfully used and operated in practice.

ICAIC 2011 was organized by the Information Engineering Research Institute, USA, and the proceeding are published by Springer. The conference was held in Xi'an. Xi'an, located in central-northwest China, records the great changes of the country just like a living history book. Called Chang'an (meaning the eternal city) in ancient times, Xi'an is one of the birthplaces of the ancient Chinese civilization in the Yellow River Basin area. It is the eastern terminal of the Silk Road and the site of the famous Terracotta Warriors of the Qin Dynasty. More than 3,000 years of history, including over 1,100 years as the capital city of ancient dynasties, have endowed Xi'an with an amazing historical heritage.

We sincerely thank all the members of the ICAIC Organizing Committee, Academic Committee and Program Committee. Moreover, we also express our sincere appreciation to all the referees, staff and volunteers for their tremendous efforts. Finally, we would like to thank all the authors who have contributed to this volume.

We hope that readers will find lots of interesting and useful information in the proceedings.

June 2011

Dehuai Zeng
Jianwei Zhang
Jun Zhang

Table of Contents – Part I

Intelligent Control and System

Target Localization Based on SIFT Algorithm

Lei Bo[1], Jing Yuanping[2], and Ding Jinlei[1]

[1] Science and Technology on Electro-Optic Control laboratory Luoyang 471009, China
[2] Department of Mathematics and physics Luoyang Institute of Science and Technology Luoyang 471003, China
bobolei1980@eyou.com

Abstract. SIFT features are invariant to image scale, translation and rotation, and are shown to provide robust matching across a substantial range of affine distortion, so it is widely used in image matching. This paper presents the SIFT feature extracting process in detail, and the application in image matching and locating. This paper also presents an approach to use SIFT keypoints to calculate the coordinate transforming parameters between two images, and the expressions, finally accomplishing the target locating, which exist in two images together. Simulation results indicate that SIFT features have excellent performance in image matching. It is precision for target locating between two images based on SIFT algorithm.

Keywords: Terms - Image matching, SIFT features, Target locating.

1 Introduction

Usually, we need locating coordinate of the target between two images which one is called based image, another is called real-time image with image matching in precision bombing in operation, which is a fundamental aspect of many problems in computer vision, including object or scene recognition, solving for 3D structure form multiple images, stereo correspondence, and motion tracking.

The task of finding correspondences between two images of the same scene or object is the most import part of image matching, We chose a high level set of natural visual features of the interest point in the image as discrete image correspondences, such as corners, blobs, and T-junctions.

There are many ways to detect interest point in the image. The most widely used detector probably is the Harris corner detector[2], proposed back in 1988, based on the eigenvalues of the second-moment matrix. However, Harris corners are not scale-invariant. Lindeberg introduced the concept of automatic scale selection. This allows to detect interest points in an image, each with their own characteristic scale. He experimented with both the determinant of the Hessian matrix as well as the Laplacian (which corresponds to the trace of the Hessian matrix) to detect blob like structures. Mikolajczyk and Schmid refined this method, creating robust and scale-invariant feature detectors with high repeatability, which they coined Harris-Laplace and Hessian-Laplace[3]. They used a (scale-adapted) Harris measure or the determinant of the Hessian matrix to select the location, and the Laplacian to select the scale.

D. Zeng (Ed.): ICAIC 2011, Part I, CCIS 224, pp. 1–7, 2011.

SIFT was developed by Lowe[4] for image feature generation in object recognition applications. The features are invariant to image translation, scaling, rotation, and partially invariant to illumination changes and affine or 3D projection. These characteristics make them suitable landmarks for robust matching when the cameras are moving around in an environment, as the landmarks are observed from different angles, distances or under different illumination.

The SIFT features are determined by identifying repeatable points in a pyramid of scaled images. Feature locations are identified by detecting maxima and minima in the Difference-Of-Gaussian pyramid. A subpixel location, scale and orientation are associated with each SIFT feature.

Sufficiently distinctive features are required to match scenes in the map. In order to achieve high specificity, a local feature vector is formed by measuring the local image gradients at a number of orientations in coordinates relative to the location, scale and orientation of the feature.

In the next section, we introduce the SIFT algorithm in detail. In section 4, we give a approach of locating target coordinate by SIFT. In section 5, we present simulation results of the proposed method.

2 Interest Point Detector

2.1 Scale-Space Foundations

If we describe some phenomena in different resolution and research them in dynamic resolution, then some cell information will be discovered, which can not be knew in tradition ways. In the field of image processing this method is called Scale-space model.

It has been shown that under a variety of reasonable assumptions the only possible scale-space kernel is the Gaussian function. Therefore, the scale space of an image is defined as a function that is produced from the convolution of a variable-scale Gaussian, as

$$L(x, y, \sigma) = G(x, y, \sigma) * I(x, y). \tag{1}$$

$$G(x, y, \sigma) = \frac{1}{2\pi\sigma^2} e^{-\frac{x^2+y^2}{2\sigma^2}}. \tag{2}$$

Where $I(x, y)$ is an input image, σ is the factor of scale. The discrete function is

$$L(i, j, \sigma) = \sum_{k_1=-m}^{m} \sum_{k_2=-m}^{m} G(k_1, k_2, \sigma) I(i-k_1, j-k_2). \tag{3}$$

Because of the Gaussian function can restrain affect all of image pixels between 3σ, the paper use $m = [4\sigma]$ to simulate so that it can reduce the cost of computation.

To efficiently detect stable keypoint locations in scale space, we can use scale-space extrema in the difference-of-Gaussian function convolved with the image, $D(x, y, \sigma)$, which can be computed from the difference of two nearby scales separated by a constant multiplicative factor k:

$$\begin{aligned} D(x,y,\sigma) &= (G(x,y,k\sigma) - G(x,y,\sigma)) * I(x,y) \\ &= L(x,y,k\sigma) - L(x,y,\sigma) \end{aligned} \quad (4)$$

2.2 Detection of Scale-Space Exterma

Maxima and minima of the difference-of-Gaussian images are detected by comparing a pixel to its 26 neighbors in 3x3 regions at the current and adjacent scales. It is selected only if it is larger than all of these neighbors or smaller than all of them.

C. The Reject Unstable Keypoints

These exterma points are candidate keypoints, which need to be rejected that have low contrast(and are therefore sensitive to noise) or are poorly localized along an edge. we use the Taylor expansion (up to the quadratic terms) of the scale-space function to reject the unstable keypoints:

$$D(\mathbf{x}) = D(x,y,\sigma) = D + \frac{\partial D^T}{\partial \mathbf{x}}\hat{\mathbf{x}} + \frac{1}{2}\mathbf{x}^T \frac{\partial^2 D}{\partial \mathbf{x}^2}\hat{\mathbf{x}}, \quad (5)$$

where

$$D = D(x_0, y_0, \sigma_0), \hat{\mathbf{x}} = (x - x_0, y - y_0, \sigma - \sigma_0)^T.$$

In (5), its derivatives are evaluated at the sample point:

$$\begin{aligned} \frac{\partial D}{\partial \sigma} &= (D(x,y,\sigma_{k+1}) - D(x,y,\sigma_{k-1}))/2, \\ \frac{\partial^2 D}{\partial x^2} &= D(x+1,y,\sigma) + D(x-1,y,\sigma) - 2D(x,y,\sigma), \\ \frac{\partial^2 D}{\partial \sigma^2} &= D(x,y,\sigma_{k+1}) + D(x,y,\sigma_{k-1}) - 2D(x,y,\sigma_k), \\ \frac{\partial^2 D}{\partial x \partial \sigma} &= (D(x+1,y,\sigma_{k+1}) + D(x-1,y,\sigma_{k-1}) \\ &\quad - D(x+1,y,\sigma_{k-1}) - D(x-1,y,\sigma_{k+1}))/4 \end{aligned} \quad (6)$$

Taking the derivative of (5) with respect to $\mathbf{x}$ and setting it to zero, giving:

$$\hat{\mathbf{x}} = -\frac{\partial^2 D^{-1}}{\partial \mathbf{x}^2}\frac{\partial D}{\partial \mathbf{x}}. \quad (7)$$

Then substituting (3) into (2), giving:

$$D(\mathbf{x}) = D + \frac{1}{2}\frac{\partial D^T}{\partial \mathbf{x}}\hat{\mathbf{x}}. \quad (8)$$

$D(\mathbf{x})$ can be used for rejecting unstable extrema with low contrast, which all extrema with a value of $|D(\mathbf{x})|$ less than 0.03 were discarded.

The difference-of-Gaussian function have a strong response along edges, therefore it is needed to reject unstable keypoints of strong response along edges. The eigenvalues of the 2×2 Hessian matrix are proportional to the principal curvatures of $D(\mathbf{x})$. Let α be the eigenvalue with the largest magnitude and β be the smaller one. we can avoid explicitly computing the eigenvalues, as we are only concerned with their ratio. Let r be the ratio, $r = \frac{\alpha}{\beta}$ then:

$$\frac{tr(H)^2}{\det(H)} = \frac{(\alpha + \beta)^2}{\alpha\beta} = \frac{(r\beta + \beta)^2}{r\beta^2} = \frac{(r+1)^2}{r}. \tag{9}$$

Therefore, to check that the ratio of principal curvatures is below some threshold r, we only need to check:

$$\frac{tr(H)^2}{\det(H)} < \frac{(r+1)^2}{r}. \tag{10}$$

The experiments in the paper use a value of $r = 10$, which eliminates keypoints that have a ratio between the principal curvatures greater than 10:

$$\frac{tr(H)^2}{\det(H)} \geq \frac{(r+1)^2}{r} = \frac{(10+1)^2}{10}. \tag{11}$$

Up to now, the stable keypoints have been obtained.

3 Keypoints Matching

A keypoint descriptor is created by first computing the gradient magnitude and orientation at each image sample point in a region around the keypoint location. These are weighted by a Gaussian window, indicated by the overlaid circle, and computed a histogram of local oriented gradients around the interest point and stores the bins in a 128-dimensional vector (8 orientation bins for each of the 4 × 4 location bins). So a keypoint descriptor is a 128-dimensional vector.

Then, the descriptor vectors are matched between different images. The matching is based on a Euclidean distance between the vectors:

$$d = \sqrt{\sum_{i=1}^{128} (\alpha_i - \beta_i)^2}, \tag{12}$$

where α, β is the keypoint descriptor vector of two images, d is the Euclidean distance.

4 Application

When we accomplish image matching between different images, we need locating the target coordinate so that we can implement automated target recognition and track. It can be achieved to compute the transform parameter between two images.

An amount of SIFT keypoints can be detected in the image and the features are invariant of scaling, rotation, translation, so we present a method for computing the transform parameter between two images with SIFT matching keypoints to accomplish locating the target.

It is defined that (x_0, y_0) is the based image coordinate and (x, y) is the real-time image coordinate, so

$$\begin{aligned} x &= T_{11}x_0 + T_{12}y_0 + T_{13} \\ y &= T_{21}x_0 + T_{22}y_0 + T_{23} \end{aligned} . \tag{13}$$

We chose three pairs coordinate of the right match keypoints to computer transform parameter:

$$(x_{01}, y_{01}) \to (x_1, y_1),$$
$$(x_{02}, y_{02}) \to (x_2, y_2),$$
$$(x_{03}, y_{03}) \to (x_3, y_3).$$

The equation (15) and (16) shows the method:

$$\begin{bmatrix} x_1 \\ x_2 \\ x_3 \end{bmatrix} = \begin{bmatrix} x_{01} & y_{01} & 1 \\ x_{02} & y_{02} & 1 \\ x_{03} & y_{03} & 1 \end{bmatrix} \begin{bmatrix} T_{11} \\ T_{12} \\ T_{13} \end{bmatrix}, \tag{14}$$

$$\begin{bmatrix} y_1 \\ y_2 \\ y_3 \end{bmatrix} = \begin{bmatrix} x_{01} & y_{01} & 1 \\ x_{02} & y_{02} & 1 \\ x_{03} & y_{03} & 1 \end{bmatrix} \begin{bmatrix} T_{21} \\ T_{22} \\ T_{23} \end{bmatrix}. \tag{15}$$

5 Simulation and Analysis

We can select two images of 314×235, as shown in figure 1 and figure 2. Obviously, they have translation, rotation, zoom relationship to a certain extent, and little perspective. We select 4 keypoints in figure 1,and we can get 4 targets in figure 2 by SIFT image matching to calculate the transpositional parameter. The simulation result is shown in figure 3.

There are four targets in figure 1, but we only get three in figure 2, because one of the targets in figure 1 does not exist in figure 2.

The simulation result shows that:

1) The target can be located precisely using transpositional parameters calculated by SIFT keypoints. However, the aberration between two images will cause locating error.

2) If there are same areas in both images, targets can be located by our methods.

Fig. 1. Originality image 1

Fig. 2. Originality image 2

Fig. 3. Simulation result

6 Conclusion

This paper presented a method for extracting distinctive features from images, and this can be used to match between images which have translation, rotation, zoom and little perspective relationship. This paper has also presented a method of target locating by SIFT algorithm. The simulation result shows that SIFT keypoints have outstanding matching performance, and can be used for precisely target locating.

References

1. Moravec, H.: Rover Visual obstacle avoidance. In: International Joint Conference on Artificial Intelligence, pp. 785–790 (1981)
2. Harris, C., Stephens, M.: A combined corner and edge detector. In: Fourth Alvey Vision Conference, pp. 147–151 (1988)
3. Bay, H., Tuytelaars, T., Van Gool, L.: SURF: Speeded up robust features. In: ECCV 2006, vol. 1, pp. 404–417 (2006)
4. Lowe, D.G.: Distinctive image features from scale—invariant keypoints. International Journal of Computer Vision 60(2), 91–110 (2004)
5. Helmer, S., Lowe, D.G.: Object recognition with many local Features. In: Workshop on Generative Model Based Vison (GMBV 2004) (2004)
6. Lowe, D.G.: Object recognition from local scale-invariant features. In: International Conference on Computer Vision, pp. 1150–1157 (1999)
7. Se, S., Ng, H.-K., Jasiobedzki, P., Moyung, T.-J.: Vision based modeling and localization for planetary exploration rovers. In: Proceedings of International Astronautical Congress (2004)

Find the Mona Lisa in the Louvre Study on Museum Exhibition Space and Visual Oriented Sign

Min Huang

Department of Design, School of Urban DesignWuhan University
Wuhan, 430072, China
wenmeihuang25@foxmail.com

Abstract. This paper discusses space and visual sign in case of museum exhibition. The topic is drawn from the case of a famous painting, the Mona Lisa, which is collected and long-timely exhibited in the Louvre. The spatial pattern in the Louvre can be summarized as three-dimensional multi-layer spatial pattern. Exhibits are put orderly according to their ages and types. To help people find the Mona Lisa easily, a set of visual signs are well-marked from the entrance hall to the location of the Mona Lisa. The case of space and visual sign in the Louvre arouses our deeply thought. We should adjust measures to local conditions and take more care of evidences' needs.

Keywords: Terms - the Mona Lisa, the Louvre, exhibition, space, visual oriented sign.

1 Introduction

The Louvre, which is located in the Center of Paris, France and north side (right bank) of the Seine River, is one of the world's oldest, biggest and the most famous museums. It has dominated central Paris since the late 12th century. From its beginnings as a royal fortress to the public institution, after 800 years of expansion and rehabilitation, it reaches its today's scale. It celebrates humanity's long journey with the remarkable scope of a collection that spans thousands of years, reaches from America to the borders of India and China, It is worth the saying: the "museum among museums".

Inside the Louvre Museum, there are three priceless famous works. They are the Mona Lisa, known as Leonardo Da Vinci, the Venus de Milo and the Winged Victory of Samothrace. These three works are known as the "three treasures in the Louvre" and highlighting this great museum. Although there are so many famous works in the Louvre, no one who has opportunity to visit there is willingly to miss these three "treasures".

D. Zeng (Ed.): ICAIC 2011, Part I, CCIS 224, pp. 8–15, 2011.

Fig. 1. "Three treasures in the Louvre"

2 Rich Exhibits in the Louvre

The exhibits in the Louvre are extremely rich and complex. The Louvre houses 35,000 works of art drawn from eight departments, 198 exhibition halls, displayed in over 60,000 square meters of exhibition space dedicated to the permanent collections. Explore the works on display, taking a thematic or cross-departmental approach. The eight departments in the Louvre are: the Department of Near Eastern Antiquities, the Department of Egyptian Antiquities, the Department of Greek, Etruscan, and Roman Antiquities , the Department of Islamic Art, the Department of Sculptures, the Department of Decorative Arts, the Department of Paintings, the Department of Prints and Drawings.

The Department of Near Eastern Antiquities is devoted to the ancient civilizations of the Near East and encompasses a period that extends from the first settlements, which appeared more than ten thousand years ago, to the advent of Islam.

The Department of Egyptian Antiquities presents vestiges from the civilizations that developed in the Nile Valley from the late prehistoric era (c. 4000 BC) to the Christian period (4th century AD).

The Department of Greek, Etruscan, and Roman Antiquities oversees works from the Greek, Etruscan, and Roman civilizations, illustrating the art of a vast area that encompasses Greece, Italy, and the whole of the Mediterranean basin, spanning a period that stretches from Neolithic times (4th millennium BC) to the 6th century AD.

The Department of Islamic Art is currently closed, but scheduled to reopen in 2012 in a new gallery in the Cour Visconti. Some two thousand objects will be on display, reflecting the breadth of inspiration and creativity of the Islamic lands over thirteen centuries and three continents.

The Department of Sculptures devoted to "modern" sculpture, opened in 1824, gradually became the Department of Medieval, Renaissance, and Modern Sculpture. Separate collections were founded in 1848 for antiquities and in 1893 for objects' art.

The Department of Decorative Arts presents a highly varied range of objects, including jewelry, tapestries, ivories, bronzes, ceramics, and furniture. The collection extends from the middle ages to the first half of the 19th century.

The Department of Paintings reflects the encyclopedic scope of the Louvre, encompassing every European school from the 13th century to 1848. The collection is overseen by twelve curators, who are among the most renowned experts in their field.

The Department of Prints and Drawings is to the museum's extraordinary collection of works on paper, which include prints, drawings, pastels, and miniatures. These fragile works feature in temporary exhibitions and can also be viewed privately by arrangement, encompassing every European school from the 13th century to 1848. The collection is overseen by twelve curators, who are among the most renowned experts in their field.

3 Spatial Pattern in the Louvre

3.1 Three-Dimensional Multi-layer Spatial Pattern in the Louvre

The spatial pattern and display form of a museum should be planed not only to meet the buildings inside space, but also to meet the audience's physical scales and psychological activities. The audience's path and goals should be put in the first place in exhibition space planning. Therefore, under the premise of traffic function requirement, how to provide a rich and exciting information place to the visitors, and how to give an unforgettable visual experience or psychological experience, becomes the most important goal.

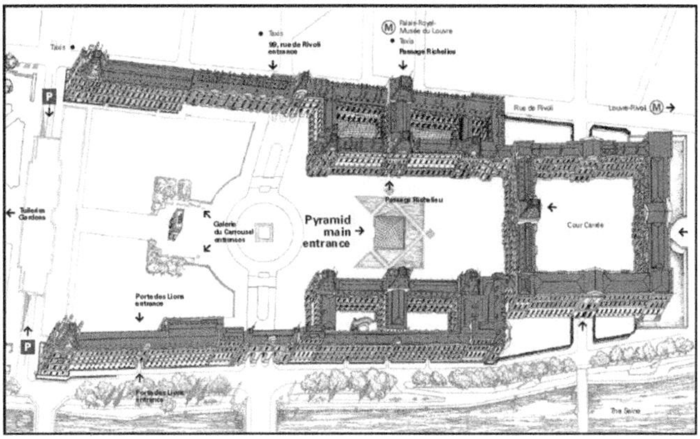

Fig. 2. Overlook of the Louvre

Although exhibits in the Louvre are so rich and so complex, they are arranged properly by three-dimensional and multi-layer spatial pattern. The whole building of Louvre museum is "U" glyph, forming mutually face-to-face letters "p" and "q", ending connection with square hall. According to the shape and inside space of the building, three exhibition parts are first established. They are Sully (a quadrate hall, rounding the quadrate Courtyard), Richelieu (the circle part of the "p", backing against the Rivoli Street), Denon (the circle part of the "q", backing against the Seine). These three parts were distributed into four flours: second floor, first floor, ground floor and lower ground floor. With this kind of three-dimensional multi-layer spatial pattern, exhibits can be arranged properly according to their category, region and age.

3.2 Spatial Function of the Pyramid

To study the space of the Louvre, another important part should not be forgotten. The pyramid, as the main entrance of this huge museum, plays a main role of starting and transition of the exhibition space. This glass pyramid, which was designed by famous Chinese-American architect Ieoh Ming Pei in 1988 to 1989, has many functions without destroying the integrity of the Louvre building. Firstly, the pyramid gives a main entrance, which could accept 15,000 visitors per hour theoretically. Secondly, the underground part of the pyramid gives a collecting and distributing centre connecting the three parts, Sully, Richelieu and Denon, which have been mentioned above. Here audiences can go directly to their favorite part, without having to pass hundreds of miles through several other exhibition halls. So the there is possibility to make the visiting lines more efficiently. Finally, the underground space of pyramid gives sufficient service place. In a modern museum, the area of service facilities is generally about half of the total area. Before the Pyramid was build, only 20% of the area of Louvre had been used for logistics and services. By adding the pyramid building, this museum has enough service space, including the reception hall, ticket offices, canteen, changing rooms, storage rooms, post office, etc,. Therefore, the sectorization of this museum becomes all in readiness.

4 Spatial Sequence of Exhibition and Specialize in the Louvre

4.1 Normal Rule on Spatial Sequence of Exhibition

In order to enhance display effect, a museum exhibition's space plan always follows a spatial sequence. There are four phases as following:

1) Start-up phase: It's the beginning sequence, which indicates that the content will be expanded. This stage should have sufficient attraction and personality.

2) Transitional phase: It's the undertaking stage after the start-up, but also a preparatory for the next climax stage, playing a connecting role in the whole sequence. Transitional phase is a key element which act in guidance, arouse, brewing and attractive.

3) Climax phase: It's the center of the whole series and a full sequence of the essence and purpose. It's also the sequence of the highest artistic expression. The psychological factor after long time looking forward should be considered to meet the emotional push and inspire peak.

4) End phase: It's the last stage of an exhibition; a climax to restore calm. The main task is from the climax to the calm. A good ending helps keeping a long-time recall and memory.

4.2 Spatial Sequence in the Louvre

Different buildings need different layouts of spatial sequences. Different spatial sequences need different artistic sequence organization. In the rich social reality, the methods of spatial sequences cannot accord to a certain model. Sometimes it's needed to break the convention.

In the case of the Louvre museum, exhibits are so complex both on quantity and on type that it's impossible to arrange its exhibition space in only one spatial sequence. Therefore, the space is partitioned first into large areas then into small sectors, layer upon layer.

For example, the Department of Paintings, which is most famous both in the Louvre and in the world, is divided into 35 exhibition halls. These 35 exhibition halls are belonging to the second floor of Sully and Richelieu and the first floor of Denon. On the second floor of Sully, French paintings are distributed according to their ages, that is, French paintings in 14th to 17th century, French paintings in 17th century, French paintings in 18th century, and French paintings in 19th century. A time-basic spatial sequence is adopted here. On the second floor of Richelieu, German, Flemish, Dutch, Belgian, Russian, Swiss and Scandinavian Paintings are orderly distributed.

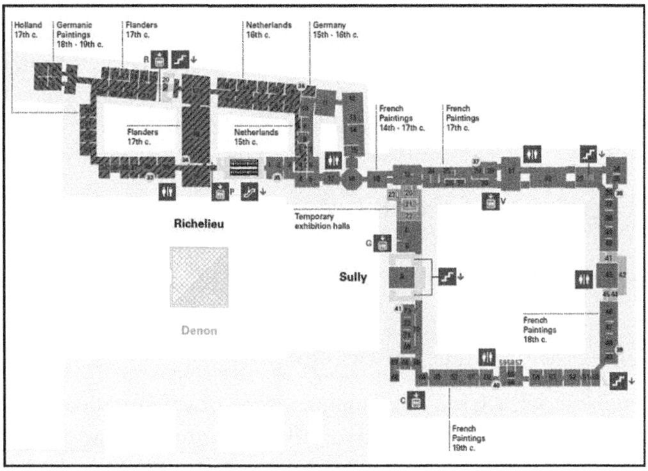

Fig. 3. Plane of second floor of Sully and Richelieu

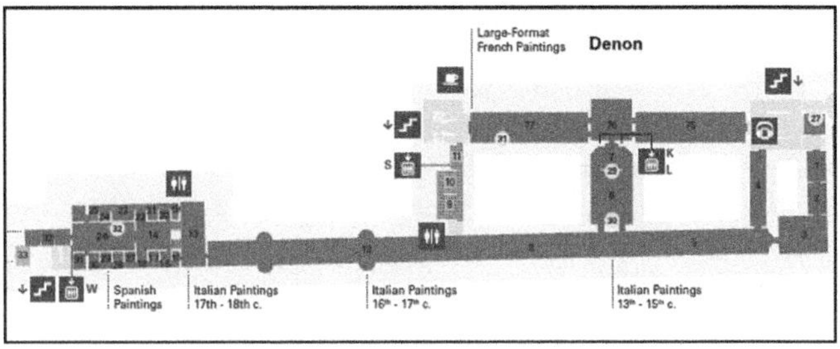

Fig. 4. Plane of first floor of Denon

On the first floor of Denon, there are areas of Large-Format French Paintings, Italian Paintings 13th to 15th century, Italian Paintings 16th to 17th century, Italian Paintings 17th to 18th century, Spanish Paintings and English Paintings. The famous painting the Mona Lisa are placed in a special exhibition hall behind the area of Large-Format French Paintings.

5 Visual Oriented Sign Leading to the Mona Lisa

5.1 Target Audience's Needs

To study exhibition communication, it's important to study target audience's psychology. Audience is a very important and active factor in exhibition communication system. It's also a main key to study the result of exhibition communication. Only when a certain communication in a museum exhibition activity could be accepted by audience, and could arouse some results, the showing process can be declared completed. The audience, as a social group of people, has their certain degree of psychological and physiological features. So in the communication of museum exhibition, it must firstly aim to target audience's heart. The start and result of communication in museum exhibition design are always inseparable from audience's psychology characters and acceptances. There are three main factors that influence the audience's choice of information, that is, audience's needs, audience's attentions and audience's understandings. These three factors are interacting and playing a role together. People pay more attention to the exhibits which they want to know, ending to better understanding of these exhibits.

5.2 Audience's Needs in Case of the Louvre

The Louvre is a huge museum holding rich exhibits and attracting thousands of people every day. Different people visit the Louvre with different expectations and different demands.

To those audiences who visit the Louvre in their first time, yes, they are sightseers attracted by its fame; they want to see those famous works with their own eyes instead of on books or on TV. They are eager to seek for the works which they have heard that now exhibited in the Louvre. Of course, the Mona Lisa is one of the samples. Actuary, they also want to see the grandiose building of the Louvre, to experience the luxuriant ornament inside the Louvre, to study human's culture in this treasure-house. But, if they missed those famous works, they would be regretting forever.

There are also a portion of audiences visiting the Louvre with other demands and appeals. They are schoolchildren, who fortunately live in the Paris city and have their Art lesson in this museum; students, who are from academy of fine arts and copy a master's work in this museum; or ordinary residents of the city, who appreciate the proud of their country in this museum once a month or once a year.

It's difficult to clearly statistics all the audiences' needs, but one fact is obviously , that is, most visitors want to find the Mona Lisa.

5.3 Find Mona Lisa Following the Visual Sign

The Louvre, as we well known, is a real treasure house. People also know that read all the collections will spend at least 2 days and appreciating all the exhibits carefully needs more than 1 month. New comers decide to find famous works, such as the Mona Lisa at first, then others.

Fortunately, a big visual sign with picture of the Mona Lisa and mark of arrow is hung on the wall beside the door of Denon, people can see it easily when they line up for ticket in the big reception hall under the glass Pyramid. People whenever they are from can understand this sign because there is a picture on it. People whether old or young can clearly see it because it's big enough. It' is in well harmony with the environment because the color and font. So the information desk doesn't have to explain which way is to the Mona Lisa over and over again, and the lobbies don't be flooded with blind searchers hurrying back and forth. Visitors can find a similar sign with smaller size in each turning until they stand in front of the great work Mona Lisa.

Fig. 5. Visual sign on the wall beside the door of Denon

Fig. 6. Visual sign in the gallery

Although some of those who stand in front of the Mona Lisa should feel a little disappointed. It was kept off with glass and handrail to prevent touching. The environment light is not so bright that you can hardly appreciate it clearly. The work itself is not as big as you think. Why the color seems a little murky grey? Is this woman beautiful? Is this work valuable to its reputation or price? Ok, that's enough. Please remember that this is a work which is done in the early 16th century. It's more than a painting with special skills and vivid details, which have already been transcended by descendants. Now it is known more like a symbol. On one hand, it is a synonym of fine art, aesthetics, and classics so it is selected as a cover picture on many art books. On the other hand, it is a synonym of change, anti-traditionalism, and even treachery so you may get various pictures when you search the keyword "Mona Lisa" on the web.

Fig. 7. The Mona Lisa and audiences

However, they get their wish to take a glance at that authentic work. Which is the next aim? Is it the Venus de Milo or the Winged Victory of Samothrace? Be in a hurry? The visual signs and guiding plan are ready to help.

References

1. Bitgood: Problems in visitor orientation and circulation. The Educational Role of The Museum. Routledge, London (1994)
2. Edson, G., Dierking.: Understanding the museum experience. The Museum Experience. Whalesback Books, Washington (1992)
3. Philip, J.: Contemporary European Architecture. Tasehen Koln, New York (2000)
4. Min, H., Bing, H.: The world expo's history and principle evolve. Inst. Of Elec. And Elec. Eng. Computer Society 1(1), 1285–1288 (2008)
5. `http://www.louvre.fr/llv/commun/home.jsp`

A Biclustering Technique for Mining Trading Rules in Stock Markets

Qinghua Huang

School of Electronic and Information Engineering
South China University of Technology
Wushan, Tianhe, Guangzhou, P.R. China
qinghuahuang333@tom.com

Abstract. Technical analysis including a large variety of indicators and patterns is widely used in financial forecasting and trading. However, it is difficult to select a combination of indicators that can well capture useful trading points in a specific market. In this paper, we propose a biclustering algorithm to find a subset of indicators with different periodic parameters which produce a similar profitability for a subset of trading points from the historical time series in the stock market. The discovered trading points are grouped into two categories: buy and sell signals. These trading points are applied to both of training and testing periods and the returns are compared with the conventional buy-and-hold trading strategies. We test this algorithm by using the Dow Jones Industry Average Index and Hang Seng Index. The results demonstrate that the trading strategies based on the discovered trading rules using the biclustering algorithm outperform the conventional buy-and-hold strategy.

Keywords: Biclustering, technical analysis, trading rules.

1 Introduction

Technical analysis has been widely used to devise appropriate trading rules in financial markets. It includes a large variety of indicators and patterns which provide dynamic timings for trades according to price fluctuations. According to the "efficient market hypothesis" established in the 1960s and 1970s [1], [2], technical analysis cannot achieve better profit than the overall average returns in the stock market. This hypothesis implies that buy-and-hold or equivalently, random selection trading rule are optimal trading strategies [3]. However, a number of studies since the 1980s have implied that some combinations of technical indicators can successfully detect the reversals of financial market and hence make more profit than a simple buy-and-hold strategy [4]-[8].

In recent years, numerous researches based on expert system and knowledge engineering techniques have worked on technical trading rules that can predict the stock price movement [4]. Gencay and Stengos [5] used a feed-forward neural network (NN) to test the profitability of technical trading rules using the Dow Jones Industrial Average (DJIA) index data and obtained better performance than a buy-and-hold strategy. Chang and Osler [9] conducted a rigorous study of chart patterns

D. Zeng (Ed.): ICAIC 2011, Part I, CCIS 224, pp. 16–24, 2011.

and devised trading rules by identifying head-and-shoulders. Leigh et al. [8] identified "bull flag" using technical charting heuristics. Potvin et al. [10] generated technical trading rules for 14 Canadian companies using genetic programming. Kim and Han [11] used rough sets to extract trading rules from historical price series. Huarng et al. [12] employed a multivariate heuristic model integrated with univariate fuzzy time-series models for financial forecasting. Pruitt and White [6] and Pruitt et al. [7] developed a combination system consisting of cumulative volume, relative strength and moving averages, which is named as CRISMA trading system.

Most of the aforementioned methods demonstrate that one or several predefined technical indicators, e.g. the NN, charting heuristics, daily closing price, moving average or volume, can be incorporated into a trading system. However, it is not always effective for a specified trading signal denoted by one or a specific set of technical indicators in real trading markets. The trading rules based on a combination of several predefined technical indicators may not be able to find potential reversals in financial market. To this end, we propose a biclustering algorithm which is a type of data mining methods to extract reversal patterns containing a subset of technical indicators discovered from a large number of indicators with different periodic parameters. The extracted patterns including a number of typical turning modes are regarded as trading rules (bull and bearish flags) and can be used for making trading decisions in stock markets.

2 A Brief Introduction of Biclustering Algorithms

Given a data matrix, conventional clustering methods classify the data along either the row or the column direction. In biclustering, the data are portioned in both row and column directions to discover local patterns or submatrices in a data matrix. Biclustering is actually a group of data mining algorithms for extracting the local patterns in a two-dimensional data matrix [13]. Cheng and Church [14] proposed a greedy search heuristic which generates a suboptimal bicluster meeting an evaluation criterion called *mean squared residue score* (MSRS). Given a data matrix X with N_r rows and N_c columns, a bicluster is defined as a coherent pattern consisting of a subset of rows and a subset of columns. It can be expressed as a pair (R, C) where $R \subseteq \{1......N_r\}$ is a subset of rows and $C \subseteq \{1......N_c\}$ is a subset of columns. The MSRS is formulated as the following.

$$h(R,C) = \frac{1}{|R| \cdot |C|} \sum_{i \in R, j \in C} \left(e_{ij} - e_{iC} - e_{Rj} + e_{RC}\right)^2,$$

$$e_{iC} = \frac{1}{|C|} \sum_{j \in C} e_{ij}, \; e_{Rj} = \frac{1}{|R|} \sum_{i \in R} e_{ij}, \; e_{RC} = \frac{1}{|R| \cdot |C|} \sum_{i \in R, j \in C} e_{ij} \tag{1}$$

where e_{ij} denotes the element value at the ith row and jth column in the bicluster, δ a homogeneity threshold defining the maximum allowable dissimilarity within the elements of the bicluster, and $h(R,C)$ the value of MSRS for the bicluster. If $h(R,C) \leq \delta$, accept it as a valid bicluster. The homogeneity threshold is set by users according to their respective applications.

In a detailed survey provided in [13], the biclusters have been grouped into four major types: biclusters with constant values, constant values in rows or columns, coherent values, and coherent evolutions. The MSRS can be used for the first two types.

3 Methods

3.1 Data Preparation

For a financial composite index, the historical data in the training period are input into a data matrix where the rows correspond to trading days and the columns correspond to 22 selected technical indicators with different periodic parameters and 12 future returns in subsequent weeks. In this study, we choose 4 popular technical indicators: the moving average (MA), the relative strength indicator (RSI), the Williams' percentage range (%R) and the rate of change (ROC) indicator. For the MA, 7 different time spans are used. For the other three indicators, 5 time spans are used, respectively.

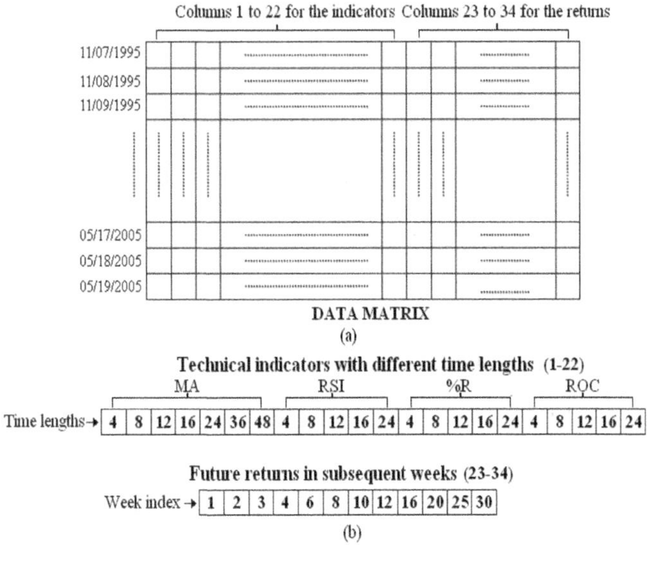

Fig. 1. Data arrangement for a matrix. (a) In the data matrix, the rows correspond to the trading days and the columns are the values of technical indicators with different time lengths. The last 10 columns are the future returns in the subsequent weeks. (b) The time length parameters for the technical indicators and the subsequent week index as shown by the numbers in the panes.

Fig. 1 illustrates the arrangement of rows for trading days and the columns for the indicators and the returns in the subsequent weeks in a data matrix and summarizes the technical indicators and time length parameters used in this study. The values for the elements of the data matrix are set to the values of the corresponding indicators (columns 1 to 22) and the returns in the subsequent weeks (columns 23 to 34) with respect to the trading days (rows). Thus, the data matrix with a width of 34 and a height the same as the number of trading days in the training period can be constructed.

The closing price for each trading day is used in this study. For the columns of the MA and future returns in the subsequent weeks, we replace the element values with the percentage of difference between the closing price of the corresponding trading days and the MA or future returns. This procedure is described by

$$PD_{MA}(i,\theta)=\frac{MA(i,\theta)-CP(i)}{CP(i)}\times 100$$
$$PD_{ret}(i,j)=\frac{CPW(j)-CP(i)}{CP(i)}\times 100 \tag{2}$$

where the $CP(i)$ denotes the closing price at the ith trading day, $MA(i,\theta)$ the moving average with a time length θ at the ith trading day, $CPW(j)$ the closing price for the jth subsequent week with reference to the ith trading day, $PD_{MA}(i,\theta)$ the percentage of difference between $MA(i,\theta)$ and $CP(i)$, $PD_{ret}(i,j)$ the percentage of difference between $CPW(j)$ and $CP(i)$.

Furthermore, values in columns 23 to 34 of future returns are pre-processed. In order to identify the appreciation and depreciation trends well, the values larger than a threshold, T, and smaller than $-T$ are set to 100 and -100, respectively. In this study, T is set to 5 for all of the financial data sets in stock markets. This procedure results in constant future returns that can be well detected by a biclustering algorithm. Because the ranges of the values for the indicators (columns 1 to 22) are quite different, a normalization procedure is applied to each column for converting the data into a range of [0, 1].

3.2 The Proposed Biclustering Algorithm

Apparently, not all types of the biclusters can be used as trading rules. We try to find the biclusters with constant columns since an effective trading rule should be represented by a subset of indicators, each of which has identical values in a subset of trading days, and also produce identical returns in a subset of future weeks. Fig. 2 gives an example illustrating how a bicluster that can be used as a trading rule. The final rule is achieved by averaging each column of technical indicators.

To extract the biclusters with constant columns, we propose a new algorithm. Since each of columns in a bicluster is a group of elements with similar values, we firstly apply an agglomerative hierarchical clustering method using the average linkage with a distance threshold T_{hc} for measuring the proximity of elements to each of the columns of the data matrix. The detected clusters in each column may be potentially part of some biclusters. Thereafter, each of the single column clusters is expanded to the other columns. For a given cluster C_o detected in a single column of the data matrix, another column can be added to it if the expanded bicluster C_e satisfies the criterion of MSRS according to a threshold T_s. This procedure is repeated by adding new column until the final C_e has been the maximal bicluster. The biclustering algorithm is described in Fig. 3.

How to translate a bicluster into a trading rule: An example of buy strategy

1. A bicluster (3×8) detected in the matrix.

$PD_{MA}(12)$*	$PD_{MA}(16)$	$PD_{MA}(24)$	$PD_{MA}(36)$	RSI(16)	ROC(8)	ROC(12)	WEEK(20)
-1.20	-1.23	-1.13	-1.32	54.8	-0.23	-1.08	100
-1.18	-1.31	-1.15	-1.29	52.4	-0.36	-0.98	100
-1.13	-1.30	-1.11	-1.21	53.3	-0.28	-1.06	100

* Indicator (time length), see Eq.(2)

**WEEK(n) denotes the modified percentage of return in the nth subsequent week.

2. After averaging each column of the bicluster, we get the following trading rule:

$PD_{MA}(12)$	$PD_{MA}(16)$	$PD_{MA}(24)$	$PD_{MA}(36)$	RSI(16)	ROC(8)	ROC(12)	WEEK(20)
-1.17	-1.28	-1.13	-1.27	53.5	-0.31	-1.04	100

3. In the testing period, the values of the set of indicators corresponding to those in above trading rule for a specific trading day are listed as follows.

$PD_{MA}(12)$	$PD_{MA}(16)$	$PD_{MA}(24)$	$PD_{MA}(36)$	RSI(16)	ROC(8)	ROC(12)
-1.19	-1.25	-1.16	-1.26	55.1	-0.35	-1.12

It is obvious that the set of values matches the trading rule well (the RMS value is less than T_{rms}, see Eq. (3)). *So we will **buy** in the next trading day.*

Fig. 2. An example for illustrating how a bicluster is translated into a trading rule

The Biclustering Algorithm

Input A data matrix, ***M***.

Output A set of biclusters (*s_bic*)

Let *s_c* = { ϕ } and *s_bic* = { ϕ }.

For each column (*cn*) in ***M***

  Perform a hierarchical clustering algorithm with a distance threshold T_{hc} on all of the values in *cn*. We get a set of clusters in the single column *cn*, denoted as *s_cn*.

  Add *s_cn* into *s_c*.

EndFor

For each cluster (C_o) in *s_c*

  $C_e = C_o$.

  For every column $l \notin C_o$

    Add l into C_e, we get C^*. Calculate the *MSRS* for C^*, denoted as S^*.

    If $S^* < T_S$, **Then** C_e=C^*, **EndIf**

  EndFor

  Add C_e into *s_bic*.

EndFor

Output *s_bic*.

Fig. 3. The biclustering algorithm proposed to find biclusters with constant columns

As mentioned above, the columns of the matrix include two categories, i.e. the technical indicators and the future returns. A valid bicluster should contain columns from both of the two categories, indicating that the detected combination of technical indicators can generate constant profitability in subsequent weeks. We select the N_{bc} largest valid biclusters with respect to the row number and treat them as effective trading rules. If a trading rule generates positive future returns implying an upward trend, it is regarded as a buy signal; otherwise, it is regarded as a sell signal. If a bicluster contains both of positive and negative returns in the subsequent weeks, we consider only the return in the earliest week in the bicluster. All of trading rules are therefore grouped into two classes: buy signal set (S_b) and sell signal set (S_s).

In the testing period, we need to determine whether the combination of technical indicators for a specific trading day well matches any one of trading rules from S_b or S_s. For each trading day, the values for all indicators are calculated. The values of a subset of indicators corresponding to those for a specific trading rule is matched with the indicator values of the trading rule, as illustrated in Fig. 2. The root-mean-square (RMS) of the corresponding indicator differences between the trading rule and the trading day is used to determine whether the indicator values for the trading day belong to the mode of a specific trading rule. The formulation is expressed as

$$RMS = \sqrt{\frac{\sum_{k \in ST} (V_{td}(k) - V_{tr}(k))^2}{n_k}} \quad (3)$$

where the ST denotes the set of technical indicators included in the trading rule, n_k the total number of indicators in ST, $V_{td}(k)$ the kth indicator values in ST for the trading day, and $V_{tr}(k)$ the kth indicator values in ST for the trading rule. If the RMS value is smaller than a predefined value T_{rms}, the corresponding trade (buy or sell) is performed in the next trading day. If the indicator values for a trading day match well with more than one trading rule, the rule with the lowest RMS value is performed.

4 Experimental Results

In this study, we use three trading strategies and compare them with the buy-and-hold strategy. Table 1 describes the three strategies adopted without considering the transaction fee. The daily data for the DJIA and Hang Seng (HSI) indices are tested using the proposed biclustering algorithm in both of the training and testing periods. For the parameters, T_{hc} is set to 0.05 and T_s is set to 0.1. The N_{bc} and T_{rms} are set to 30 and 0.1, respectively. The training period and the testing period defined for the DJIA are 11/07/1995 to 05/19/2005 and 05/20/2005 to 10/08/2007, respectively. The training period and the testing period defined for the HSI are 08/22/1995 to 05/11/2005 and 05/12/2005 to 09/28/2007, respectively.

The proposed algorithm is applied to the training periods and the discovered trading rules are carried out on both of the training and testing periods. Table 2 illustrates the simulation results for the indices using the three investment strategies. The profits are compared with that of the buy-and-hold strategy, which is indicated by the total increase in the training or testing period. It is shown that the strategies 2 and 3 adopted for the indices outperform the buy-and-hold strategy, and the strategy 1 obtains partially better returns. The results demonstrate that the discovered trading rules are capable of making more profits than the buy-and-hold strategy.

In order for demonstrating how the trading rules discovered using the biclustering algorithm perform the buy and sell trades, the trading points are recorded and illustrated in the historical series of the DJIA index, as shown in Fig. 4. As

Table 1. Three trading strategies adopted in this paper

S#	Description
1	*Open a long position when a trading day meets any one of patterns in the set of buy signals. Close the position at the end of the training or testing period*
2	*Open a long position when a trading day meets any one of patterns in the set of buy signals and close the position when a subsequent trading day meets any one of patterns in the set of sell signals. Repeat this trading mode during the training or testing period.*
3	*Open a position when a trading day meets any one of trading signals. Close the position when a reversal signal appears and open a reversal position at the same trading day. Repeat this trading mode during the training or testing period.*

Table 2. The simulation results for the DJIA and HSI indices in both of the training testing periods

Index	Profit in the testing period (in percent)				
	TTt	Ptt	PS1	PS2	PS3
DJIA	38	33.84	34.11	34.69	35.28
HSI	14	94.71	97.91	99.72	101.53

TTt denotes the trade times in the testing period. Ptt denotes the total profit using a buy-and-hold strategy in the testing period. PS1, PS2, and PS3 denote the profits made by the three investment strategies using the trading rules discovered by our algorithm.

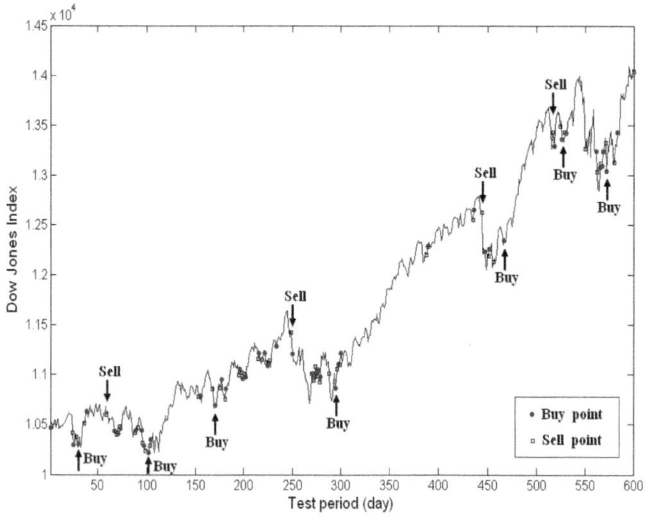

Fig. 4. The example trading records based on the DJIA

indicated by the arrows, it can be observed that the trading rules can successfully detect the buy points at the bottoms and the sell points at the tops in the stock markets.

5 Conclusions

In this paper, a biclustering algorithm is proposed to discover trading rules for stock market. A number of technical indicators with different periodic parameters are considered. The historical series data for the indicators and the future returns are input into a data matrix. The algorithm is designed to extract biclusters with constant columns from the matrix. The extracted biclusters are regarded as trading rules and grouped into buy and sell signals. We have tested the trading rules using two composite indices. The preliminary results demonstrate that the returns using the discovered trading rules outperform the conventional buy-and-hold strategy, confirming the usefulness of the novel trading rule generation method.

However, the number of trading points in both training and testing periods is relatively large and will result in a large amount of transaction fee. Since a specific trading rule is actually effective in short-term or long-term, trading goals will be considered as a factor to avoid highly frequent trades in our future work. We will further apply this algorithm to other financial markets, e.g. foreign exchange rates and futures. More technical indicators, e.g. the candlestick charting, Bolling band, moving average convergence divergence (MACD), etc. will be incorporated into the matrix to discover more powerful trading rules. In conclusion, it can be expected that the proposed biclustering algorithm will be a valuable tool for discovering technical trading rules and guiding profitable financial trades.

References

1. Fama, E.F., Blume, M.E.: Filter rules and stock market trading. J. Bus. 39(1), 226–241 (1966)
2. Jensen, M., Bennington, G.: Random walk and technical theories: some additional evidences. J. Finance 25, 469–482 (1970)
3. Haugen, R.: Modern investment theory. Prentice-Hall, Upper Saddle River (1997)
4. Park, C.H., Irwin, S.H.: What do we know about the profitability of technical analysis? J. Econ. Surveys 21(4), 786–826 (2007)
5. Gencay, R., Stengos, T.: Moving average rules, volume and the predictability of security returns with feedforward networks. J. Forecast. 17(5-6), 401–414 (1998)
6. Pruitt, S.W., White, R.E.: The CRISMA trading system: who says technical analysis can't beat the market? J. Portfol. Manage. 14(3), 55–58 (1988)
7. Pruitt, S.W., Tse, M.K.S., White, R.E.: The CRISMA trading system: the next five years. J. Portfol. Manage. 18(3), 22–25 (1992)
8. Leigh, W., Modani, N., Purvis, R., Roberts, T.: Stock market trading rule discovery using technical charting heuristics. Expet. Syst. Appl. 23(2), 155–159 (2002)
9. Chang, P.H.K., Osler, C.L.: Methodical madness: technical analysis and the irrationality of exchange-rate forecasts. Econ. J. 109(458), 636–661 (1999)

10. Potvin, J.-Y., Soriano, P., Vallée, M.: Generating trading rules on the stock markets with genetic programming. Comput. Oper. Res. 31(7), 1033–1047 (2004)
11. Kim, K., Han, I.: The extraction of trading rules from stock market data using rough sets. Expet. Syst. 18(4), 194–202 (2001)
12. Huarng, K.H., Yu, T.H.K., Hsu, Y.W.: A multivariate heuristics model for fuzzy time-series forecasting. IEEE Trans. Syst. Man Cybern. B Cybern. 37(4), 836–846 (2007)
13. Madeira, S.C., Oliveira, A.L.: Biclustering algorithms for biological data analysis: A survey. IEEE Trans. Comput. Biol. Bioinform. 1(1), 24–45 (2004)
14. Cheng, Y., Church, G.M.: Biclustering of expression data. In: Proc. Eighth Int'l Conf. Intelligent Systems for Molecular Biology (ISMB), pp. 93–103 (2000)

The Design of Image Similarity Tool Based on SCILAB

Jianfeng Sun[*], Xiang Li, and Yuan Zhan

International Department, Beijing University of Posts and Telecommunications
Tucheng 10, West Road, Haidian District, Beijing10086, China
weisun849@gmail.com

Abstract. Nowadays, the plagiarism phenomenon is difficult to solve, due to comparison workload. Dealing with an article, you should consider both of text and image content. In this paper, we designed an open source software to calculate image similarity, especially for the image in the students` paper. We used SCILAB language to calculate data, TCL/TK language to design the interface and C++ language to implement the core algorithm. With each of their features, the software is gorgeous and effective. It is unique to implement the function with the combination of the three programming language.

Keywords: SCILAB, plagiarism, image, similarity.

1 Introduction

In nowadays, the plagiarism phenomenon appears frequently, especially when it comes to students` thesis. Faced with hundreds of pieces of paper, some teacher may judge them by personal experience. Although it may works sometimes, it is not accurate.

Although some softwares only focus on text similarity calculation, it solves part of the problem. For common cases, the thesis may contain not only the text content, but also essential or even important image such as chart. Some students may prefer screenshots instead of typing to make a simple copy, which makes it much more difficult to notice.

At present, the most popular thesis formats are PDF and Doc, whose encoders and decoders are protected by the copyright of their software companies. As a result, only text similarity calculation is not enough to avoid the plagiarism and an image similarity tool is fairly essential to make the accuracy higher. As for the text similarity software, most of them are legitimate edition for the commerce requiring much of money to purchase. Also some other open source software could performance well or even better such as the "Similarity Detector" which award the third prize during the 2010 International SCILAB Contest. Hence an open source image similarity tool may solve the problem better.

[*] Corresponding author.

D. Zeng (Ed.): ICAIC 2011, Part I, CCIS 224, pp. 25–32, 2011.

2 The Design for the Text Similarity Tool Bases on Scilab

2.1 The Architecture of the Tool

SCILAB is an" open source" software developed by the French state information, automation Research Institute (INRIA). Similar to MATLAB, SCILAB is also a kind of scientific and engineering computing software. SCILAB may perform in the same way as MATLAB does, especially for the basic functionalities such as scientific computing, matrix, and graphic displays. However, adopting the open source software SCILAB may avoid spending a lot of money on buying legitimate software MATLAB, therefore using SCILAB as a development platform is a wise choice [1].

Although SCILAB could calculate data effectively, its ability to design the interface is fairly weak. Compared with SCILAB, TCL/TK language can be linked to high-quality picture, which ensures the interface to be attractive. Also, due to the mature technology of the SCILAB interface with TCL/TK, TCL/TK is the most suitable language for the interface.

As for the implementation of the core algorithm, it requires less source codes to use C language than SCILAB. As a result, it strengthens the independence of the software, which is necessary for the software testing period according to the software engineering course [2].

In conclusion, I adopt the following structure, as Fig. 1:

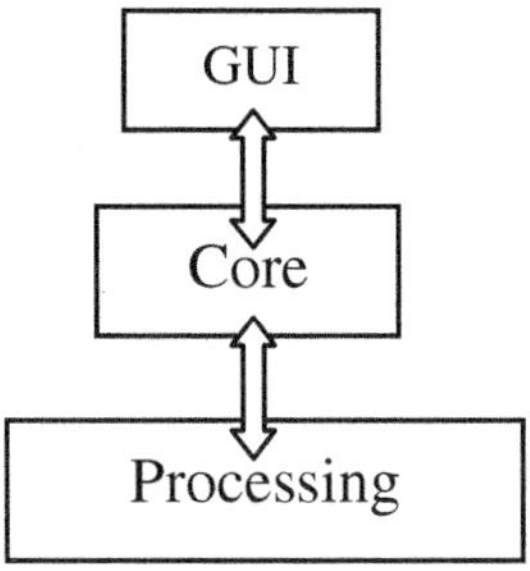

Fig. 1. Software structure

Use TCL/TK to design GUI part, C language to design Processing part which achieves the core algorithm and SCILAB to complete Core part that is responsible for data calculations [3].

2.2 Selection and Analysis of the Algorithm

2.2.1 The Introduction of Algorithm

Our idea is to change two true color bitmap images to Grayscale image, then use Color Histogram to calculate the similarity.

First, bitmap can be regarded as the two-dimensional grid. The image consists of many pixels, whose number equals to the product of the wide and the height of the bitmap. Because bitmap can both show and restore the image perfectly, so it is the most popular image format in daily life. Meanwhile, when we use true color, ie 24bit color (3 bytes), we can get more than 16 million colors, which is close to human eye's resolution.

The 3 bytes in 24bits are used to describe R, G, B color components. Each component ranges from 0 to 255, the higher the value, the bigger the density value. Hence, 255 is the brightest value and 0 is darkest value.

The formula to change a true color pixel to its density value is:

$$Y = 0.299R+0.587G+0.114B$$

In order to make it more accurate, we take the following formula:

$$Y=1000000G+1000R+B$$

Because in the Grayscale map, there are 256 kind of colors, ie, 8 bits color, so the transformed image is 8 bits format. As the palette supports the format mentioned, so we can save the 256 gray colors into the palette. Then we can use Color Histogram to calculate the similarity after we get the gray image [4].

Color Histogram represents the Space-valued distribution of all pixels in an image, as show in Fig. 2, the x axis denotes the distribution of the color channel, y axis denotes the number of pixels fall into the channel. Concretely, suppose the image is I, the image color is made of L level channel, ith of which is Ci(i--1, 2..., L). Number of pixels fall into Ci is hi, then vector H (h1, h2... hL) is the Color Histogram. It appears to be a discrete curve.

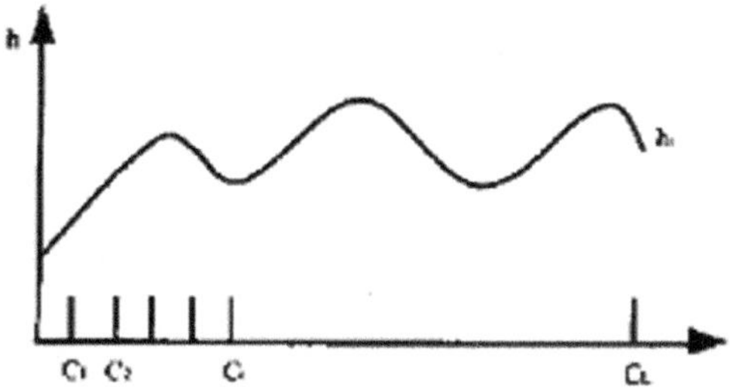

Fig. 2.

According to the principle, for each image I, we can get the Color Histogram H (I) =H (h1, h2... hL) to be the image's Color Feature Index.

Similarity measurement of image is denoted by distance between images. The similarity may be higher as the distance would be. Here, we use Cross-mapping method to calculate the distance, the general expression is:

$$d_x(H,K) = \sum_i \sum_j DISTANCE(h_i, k_j)$$

Where H and K represent the histogram of the two images and the clusters of them are identical, the distance of the corresponding cluster hi and ki is called basic distance [5].

2.2.2 The Reason Why We Choose the Algorithm

Firstly, image color is a relatively straightforward image analysis factors and owns the feature rotation invariance and size invariance. Color histogram method just focuses on the color characteristics of image. If someone only copy other`s image content, they can only add some visual effects, which is really stupid because it is obvious to find changes with human eyes.

Secondly, the algorithm is intuitive and efficient. During the computation process, source codes implement the algorithm with the simplest logical statement, which brings little burden to the CPU.

2.2.3 Pseudo Code of the Algorithm

```
//unify the image format and deal with the image information
int[] imageFormat(Bitmap orginal_image)
{
  declare int[] pixel_infor;
  // to convert the file to 8-bit bitmap format
  Bitmap orginal_image = BitmapConvert(orginal_image,8);
  // to convert the bitmap into the size: IMAGE_WIDTH* IMAGE_LENGTH
  ImageBuffer image_buffer = read(orginal_image);
  if (sizeof(image_buffer)< IMAGE_WIDTH* IMAGE_LENGTH)
  {
  Bitmap temp_image = new Bitmap (original_image, IMAGE_WIDTH,
IMAGE_LENGTH);
  ImageBuffer image_buffer = read (temp_image);
}
// to deal with and get the image information
  for i from 0 to lengthof(image_buffer);
   {
        pixel_infor[i] = (int)image_buffer [i].head*1000*1000+ (int)image_buffer
[i].mid*1000+ (int)image_buffer [i].tail;
}
   return pixel_infor;
}
//compare the two image and get the similarity
int imageCompare(int[] image_infor_1, int[] image_infor_2)
{
  int sum = 0;
  // calculate the differences among the pixels and add them up
 for i from 0 to IMAGE_WIDTH* IMAGE_LENGTH
  {
        Sum +=    abs(image_infor_1[i]-image_infor_2[i]);
}
//sum is the similarity value
return sum;
}
```

2.2.4 Comparison with Other Optional Algorithms

About the image similarity, there are algorithm that uses the shape and eigenvalue. These algorithm can all be used, but with different focus. In our algorithm, we focus on the color. Here we discuss the comparison with other algorithm.

1) The Shape Algorithm
It is more suitable for image matching, while ours focus on finding the difference. Because we judge the thesis by comparing the image content not shape, hence the shape algorithm may lead bias, which is not suitable for our situation.

2) The Eigen value algorithm
It analysis the pictures and find main characteristic of them to compare. It is suitable for pictures that have apparent characters while for a common picture, the algorithm lose it advantage. So we abandon it and choose the more general algorithm using colors [6].

In sum, Color Histogram has advantages in accuracy, efficiency, feasibility and applicability. Hence we finally choose it as our core algorithm.

3 The Result of the Text Similarity Calculation

After run the tool, you should open and load two image files as Fig. 3 and Fig. 4:

Fig. 3. Load and display the first image

Fig. 4. Load and display the second image

Then run the test function to see the similarity between the two images as Fig. 5 and Fig. 6:

Fig. 5. Run the test function

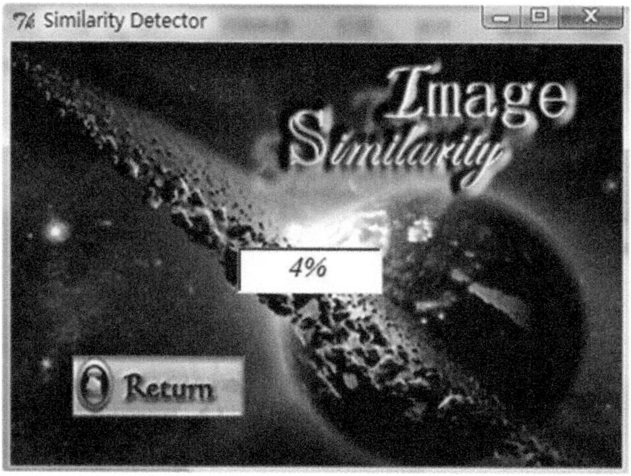

Fig. 6. The result of the similarity between the two images

Also, based on masses of experiment, we supply other statistic as follows:

Image1	Image2	Explain	Similarity
		Compare two different pictures	4% Accurate
		Compare two identical pictures	100% Accurate
		Compare two identical picture with different size	100% Accurate
		Compare a picture with the rotation of itself	99% Accurate
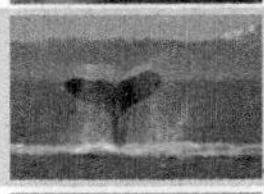	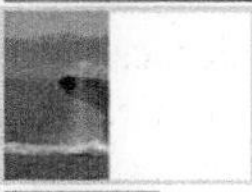	Compare a picture with part of itself covered	41% Accurate
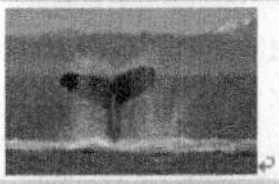	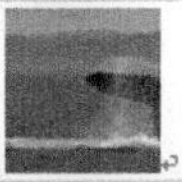	Compare a picture with part of itself cut	100% Not Accurate
		Compare two pictures that has slight difference	98% Accurate
		Compare two pictures that are totally different	0% Accurate

4 Conclusion

The article describes the design and implementation of the image similarity tool based on SCILAB. At present, it will be worthwhile to apply the tool as the aided similarity tool especially in the field of teaching. Also there are rare image similar tools based on Open Source Software. Hence it`s meaningful to develop the tool described in the article.

Innovation of the author of the article is that combination of SCILAB, TCL/TK and C language makes the tool gorgeous, efficient and independent.

Acknowledgements. The authors would like to thank the two anonymous reviewers for their valuable remarks and the time they invested to improve the quality of this survey.

References

1. Campbell, S., Chancelier, J.-P., Nikoukhah, R.: Modeling and Simulation in Scilab/Scicos. Springer, New York (2006)
2. Ousterhout, J.K.: Tcl and the Tk Toolkit. Addison-Wesley, Reading (1994), ISBN 0-201-63337-X

3. Welch, B.B.: Practical Programming in Tcl and Tk, 3rd edn. Prentice Hall, Upper Saddle River (2003), ISBN 0-13-038560-3
4. Shapiro, L.G., Stockman, G.C.: Computer Vision. Prentice Hall, Englewood Cliffs (2003), ISBN 0130307963
5. Wang, X.-Y., Wu, J.-F., Yang, H.-Y.: Robust image retrieval based on color histogram of local feature regions. Springer, Netherlands (2009), ISSN 1573-7721
6. Goshtasby, A.: 2-D and 3-D Image Registration for Medical, Remote Sensing, and Industrial Applications. Wiley Press, Chichester (2005)

Research of Event-Driven Enterprise Application Integration Base on Service Oriented Architecture

Wei Lu [1] and Yanfen Liu[2]

[1] Computer school of Wuhan University, Wuhan China
[2] HuaZhong Normal University, Wuhan China
Wei_Lu2123@163.com

Abstract. The development of informatization in the financial brings the opportunity, but also some new challenges.At present, financial mixed-business management is coming, which will involve financial departments of the bank, securities, insurance, fund, trust and futures and many other services. But now most of the application systems are usually focuses on one business link or management functions, the whole body do not have a high level of communication and integration. Operation of each application system is independent, sharing data is very difficult, therefore inevitably formation Each information island. Because of weak general Design and a lot of repetition , is very difficult, maintenance is very difficult. The successful implementation of integration of the basic functions in whole enterprise is the necessary measure. Financial should provide an open Enterprise Application Integration frame, make the existing applications and database according to implement integrated business, and can add the new application and system quickly. In this case, the enterprise can protect existing investment, integrate the original system according to market and business needs, and create new competitiveness.

Keywords: SOA, EDA, Enterprise application.

1 Enterprise Application Integration

1.1 Introduce of Enterprise Application Integration

Enterprise application integration (EAI), has been proposed and studied in IT field for years. First the concept of EAI is special, only the EAI enterprise interior of interactions between the different application system. Even so, through application integration between data across multiple systems of synchronization and sharing.

The target of EAI is to integrate different application systems, so that, enterprise employees, policymakers and business partners can get data of business and customer easily, and would not have to know these data in what place and which system. In addition, the goal is to integrate further information and business across the enterprise and the inter-organization, including realization transmission flow, data flow and information flow and B2B flow[1]. The flow is, continuous, real-time or quasi real-time data, sent to the users or systems.

D. Zeng (Ed.): ICAIC 2011, Part I, CCIS 224, pp. 33–37, 2011.

1.2 Service Oriented Architecture

The main components of SOA are service, dynamic discovery and messages. Service is the call routines that can access through the network, it introduces interface contracts and a definition of the service behavior. Interfaces are public in center or directory, where the service is provided by different classification. Searching between customer (service) to consumers for specific services accord to different classification by dynamic characteristics, this process is called dynamic service. Now, Consumer or customer service can consume services by messages sending. Because the interface abstracts are independent to platform and language, so that they are usually constructed in XML mode[2].

Roles in SOA includes: ①service users: service users is an application, software module, or a service to another service. It launches the registration of service center through the transmission and executes service function by unbundled service, the executive service according to interface contracts. ② service providers: service provider will be issued to the service and the interface contracts to service centre, they can be found and access by users. It accepts and executes user requests. ③service registration center: service center is the supporter of the service discovery. It contains a service storehouse, and allows the service users find service provider interface.

SOA can be developed based on investing the existing system, and need not to develop completely new systems. If power and resource of the organization be focused on developing service and software based on existing technical or combination of component-based software development methods, there are some advantages: reducing cost, continuous improvement process, shorting the enterprises possess between IT and business.

1.3 Event-Driven Architecture

Event-driven framework (event-driven architecture, EDA) is a kind of design and construction method of application, and event-driven messages transfer in independent Module (they need not to know each other). Event source usually send message to message agent or the middleware, so that subscriber can subscribe this message. Because the messages of events transfer in the way of publishing and subscribing the messages, an event can be send to multiple users. The main difference between EDA and SOA is, in SOA publishers and users is only one-to-one relationship; But in EDA, the event publisher can send the messages to any subscriber who is found in message broker based on the rule.

The main advantage of EDA[3] is that enterprises would be allowed to identify and response to one or more systems by management of events. These events are collected in EDA, can be defined and constructed to relevant information model. In this way, the enterprise can in the real world, real-time response.

The main characteristics[4] of EDA include: (1)asynchronous EDA mainly supports asynchronous activity, once the information is issued, you need not to care about whether it can be received, and also links between the source and destination of a living system need not to be maintained, (2)the publish/subscribe in EDA can support multiple interaction. In EDA, a system about the incident in the network information, many others have subscription and authorization system can receive news and respond to the action, (3)decoupling EDA allows news publishers and subscribers don't know each other. The interactive of information between the two systems, need not to care about the details of the others.

The modules that support the technology of events and messages include the followings: (1) asynchronous information mechanism: structure of systems must ensure that when an event occurs, the relevant department series could send asynchronous messages promptly, and consider that the incident and processing would be temporarily disabled; (2) event management: the architecture must ensure that there is a system used to identify, define and gather events, in this way enterprise data can be in unified management as events and business process Samples. It includes that the event can be accessed in and after occurs, and a series of events can be identified and accessed in particular business scenes.

2 Event-Driven Enterprise Application Integration Base on Service Oriented Architecture

In EAI, the enterprise application system base on SOA can change accord to enterprise business, is a real flexible software system, and it can reduce cost and risk of EAI implementation. SOA is adopted in the underlying framework design in solutions of EAI. According to the SOA, financial business process elements are reformed and packaged for the standardization of financial enterprise service with loose coupling, these services can be easily found, called and managed in this way. So we can gain competitive advantage from quick and efficient response.

We proposed the concept of complete event-driven financial enterprise application integration system architecture based on SOA, as shown in figure 1. Service oriented architecture is a kind of architecture that is flexible and easy to expand common is closed, and it is a breakthrough of designing idea based on functional division, through the design idea based on service of business processes. The key of the ideas focusing on the flow is how to design the process and organizational structure facing changeable business, but not the flow. Cooperation between service and distributed processing model in financial would be expected.

In figure 1, each function is shown in form of service, this is a infrastructure that can apply particular service to specific application. Entity service is a service unit that is a complete closed-loop system and provide specific function.

The system of the service is structured by the following: (1) enterprise service layer Line (enterprise service bus, ESB): this is the basic structure of system in SOA, service access each other through a bus[5]· (2) application service layer: this layer mainly refers to the integration of various financial applications and data storage.(3) bus access Layer: this layer provides adapter services for the access protocol of many popular applications, such as HTTP, JCA/J2C,.net and IBM/CICS, etc. User can visit each application service, access various applications by the mechanism of messages transferring in ESB, and enjoy service in ESB. (4)the core layer: offers a variety of enterprise The necessary service for bus service support, at this layer provides basic services, such as bus News distribution/subscription, queue, directory services and data transfer/mapping services; etc. 5 business support layer: this layer in the business support. Through the general and standard The object and the service model, in this

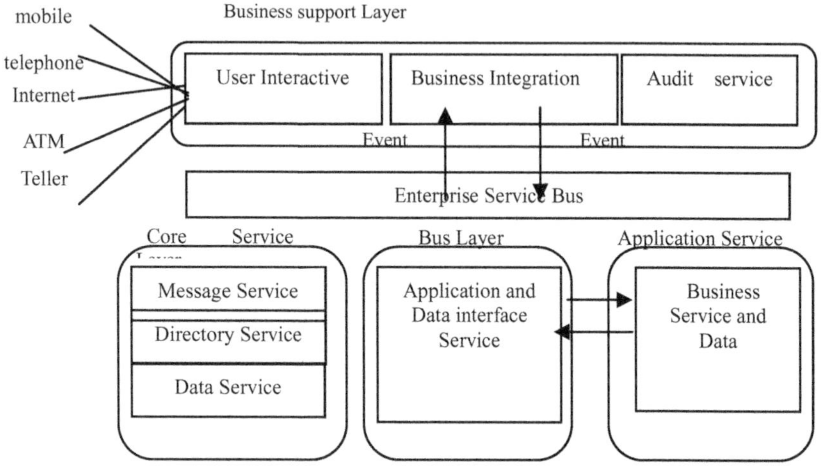

Fig. 1. The event-driven enterprise application integration base on Service Oriented Architecture

layer can be defined based on financial and reusability Industry standard of the business process. At the same time, it also provides the user interaction, unified service Mobile phone bank, the bank of Europe, online banking, self-help bank and traditional bank outlets. Based on the above service bus service can be very small user interaction, and shut Note in their respective interactive characteristic.

The integrated framework based on service-oriented technology, the financial enterprise application is packaged into a integrate service unity through various adapter service, and then it releases the application service to directory service center, and achieve the communication between each application system through the core enterprise service in bus service, such as uniform data format and messages transferring. In the integrated framework, application service can be an existing old application, the integrated platform is the bridge connecting various applications, using it coupling method, any application connected to the system is independent service form. The framework is flexible, simple, quick, and realize "plug and play."

When the framework executes process integration and business integration, it first defines service through the business process, and composites business process chain based on registered application service in certain rules according to the event-driven service model. Business integrated model is achieved by integrated engine invoking the interface of application service to implementation of data accessing, and implementation of business process through the route data transferring between each application service engine.

3 Conclusion

In conclusion, SOA can completely provide a flexible, loose coupling and extensible platform that integrated service to build a foundation, and it also can fully realize data integration and application integration[6]. And then as the event-driven framework involved, we can smoothly build business process modeling and integration, finally achieve the best level of enterprise application integration, namely the process integration.

Service oriented architecture will reduce the time that spend on integrate those completely different department, and swfitly deploy application service by the rapid development and the component reusing. Nowadays, the enterprise application integration is popular in the financial, because in mixed-business management there are some business development factors, such as the requirement of financial to strengthen the relationship with customers and partners, internal business process optimization and shorten the cycle in market of new applications etc. as a result ,EAI become the focus.

References

1. Tan, W.A., Xue, J.S., Wang, J.L.: A Service-Oriented Virtual Enterprise Architecture and its Applications in Chinese Tobacco. Industrial Sector. In: IEEE International Conference on e-Business Engineering (2006)
2. Hammer, K.: Web services and enterprise integration. EAI Journal 11, 12–15 (2006)
3. Global Research Partners Event driven architecture: The next big thing. In: Gartner Application Integration and 6 Services Summit (2004)
4. Linthicum, D.S.: The evolution of adapters. EAI Journal 11, 34–39 (2008)
5. Rouse, W.B.: Enterprises as Systems: Essential Challenges and Approaches to Transformation. Systems Engineering Journal 8, 138–150 (2005)
6. Sushil: Enterprise Flexibility. Global Journal of Flexible Systems Management 2, 53-58 (2006)

Efficient Top-K Query Algorithms Using Density Index

Dongqu Chen[1], Guang-Zhong Sun[1,*],
Neil Zhenqiang Gong[1,**], and Xiaoqiang Zhong[2]

[1] Key Laboratory on High Performance Computing, Anhui Province School of Computer Science and Technology, University of Science and Technology of China, Hefei, Anhui, P.R. China
[2] Power Energy Metering Center, Fujian Electric Power Company Limited, Fuzhou, Fujian, P.R. China
Dong7889@126.com

Abstract. Top-*k* query has been widely studied recently in many applied fields. Fagin et al. [3] proposed an efficient algorithm, the Threshold Algorithm (i.e. TA), to process top-*k* queries. However, in many cases, TA does not terminate even if the final top-*k* results have been found for some time. Based on these, we propose a novel algorithm: Density Threshold Algorithm (i.e. DTA), which is designed to minimize the useless accesses of a top-*k* query, and introduce a novel indexing structure, *Density Index*, to support our algorithms. However, we proved the DTA is not *instance optimal* in Fagin's notion and we also propose an instance optimal algorithm named Selective-Density Threshold Algorithm (i.e. S-DTA). Finally, extensive experiments show that our algorithms have significant improvement on the efficiency, compared with the TA algorithm.

Keywords: Database query processing, Algorithms, Indexes.

1 Introduction

Ranking aware queries, or top-*k* queries, have been widely studied recently in many applied fields such as information retrieval, multimedia databases and data mining. The main reason for such attention is that top-*k* queries avoid overwhelming the user with large numbers of uninteresting answers which are resource-consuming.

A general and simple model proposed by Fagin et al. [3] is that the dataset consists of *m* sorted lists with *n* data items. Under this model, Fagin et al. [3] proposed the efficient Threshold Algorithm (i.e. TA). To measure the optimality of an algorithm, they defined a notion of optimality, *instance optimality* and proved the instance optimality of TA.

However, in many cases, TA does not terminate even if the final top-*k* results have been found for some time, which will bring more cost and delay to the queries. The

---

* Corresponding author.
** Neil Z. Gong is now a postgraduate in EECS, UC Berkeley. This work was completed when Neil Z. Gong was undergraduate student of USTC.

D. Zeng (Ed.): ICAIC 2011, Part I, CCIS 224, pp. 38–45, 2011.

main reason for such useless accesses is the *threshold value* is not low enough to satisfy the terminate condition of TA. To speed up the reduction of the threshold value, U. Güntzer et al. [4] used the reducing speed of the accessed items to predict the speed of the unknown items in the same list. They considered that it could speed up the reduction of the threshold value if the list with the largest predicted value was chosen to be accessed in every step. Our target is similar with U. Güntzer but we reduce the threshold value through choosing the *section* with the largest *lean value* and accessing the lists *section* by *section*, based on the *Density Index* set up in the pre-computing phase.

In this paper, we study the efficient top-*k* queries using pre-computed analysis and indexing method. We propose a novel algorithm: Density Threshold Algorithm (i.e. DTA), and we also turn DTA into an instance optimal algorithm named Selective-Density Threshold Algorithm (i.e. S-DTA). Finally, extensive experiments show that our algorithms have significant improvement on the efficiency, compared with the TA algorithm.

2 Computation Model and TA Algorithm

Our model of the dataset can be described as follows [3]: assume the database D consists of m sorted lists, which are denoted as $L_1, L_2 \ldots L_m$. Each sorted list consists of n data items. We may refer to L_i as list i. Each entry of L_i is of the form $(x, s_i(x))$ where x is an object and $s_i(x)$ is the *ith* local score of x as a positive real number in the interval [0, 1]. Sorted list means that objects in each list are sorted in descending order by the $s_i(x)$ value. For a given object x, x has a total score of $f(x)=f(s_1(x), s_2(x) \ldots s_m(x))$, where the m-dimensional aggregate function f is supposed to be increasingly monotonic:

Definition 2.1 **Aggregate Monotone Function** [3]. *An aggregate function f is monotone iff* $f(a_1, a_2 \ldots a_m) \leq f(a_1', a_2' \ldots a_m')$, *whenever* $a_i \leq a_i'$ *for every i.*

In this paper, we assume the aggregate function is weighted summation function, yielding $f(x)=\sum_{i=1}^{m} w_i s_i(x)$ and $\sum_{i=1}^{m} w_i = 1$ ($w_i \neq 0$), the most common form of aggregate function in applications.

Each data item can be accessed through *sorted access* or *random access*. Sorted access iteratively reads data items sequentially, whereas a random access is a request for a data item in some list given the object's ID. The middleware cost of a top-*k* query algorithm is $a_S c_S + a_R c_R$, where a_S is the number of sorted accesses performed, a_R is the number of random accesses performed, c_S is the cost per sorted access, and c_R is the cost per random access.

Our task is to determine the top-*k* objects, that is, *k* objects with the highest total scores. To solve the top-*k* query described above, Fagin et al. [3] proposed the threshold algorithm (i.e. TA) as described in Fig. 1.

Threshold Algorithm (TA)	
1.	Do sorted access in parallel to each of the m lists. As an object is seen through sorted access in some list, do random access to the other lists to find all its missing local scores, and compute its total score. Maintain a set Y containing the k objects whose total scores are the highest among all the objects seen so far.
2.	For each list L_i, let be $\underline{s_i}$ the bottom score of L_i, which is the last local score seen under sorted access in L_i. Define the *threshold value* to be $\tau = f(\underline{s_1}, \underline{s_2} \ldots \underline{s_m})$.
3.	Halt when $\tau \leq M_k$, where $M_k = \min\{ f(x) \mid x \in Y\}$.

Fig. 1. Threshold Algorithm

3 Density Threshold Algorithm

Before proposing our algorithm, we first introduce an efficient indexing structure, Density Index to support the DTA.

Firstly, we divide each attribute list into b sections and the jth section Sn_j consists of the items whose local scores is in the associated score interval $(1 - j \times (1/b), 1 - (j - 1) \times (1/b)\,]$, where b is a positive integer and $j = 1, 2 \ldots b$. Items with score 0 belong to the bth section Sn_b.

Obviously, a section is a sorted sub-list of one attribute list.

Definition 3.1 **Density.** *For section Sn_j, let size be the number of items in Sn_j. If size is positive, the density of Sn_j is 1/size, denoted as d_j. Sections of zero size do not have density.*

Definition 3.2 **Head Item and Tail Item.** *For section Sn_j, head item is the first item in Sn_j while tail item is the last one.*

Obviously, the head item has the highest local score in the section whereas the tail item is of the lowest score.

Density Index is an indexing structure to remember the density information of every section in every list. It can be m indexing lists corresponding to m attribute lists. Sections of zero *size* are removed from the index.

Now we show the Density Threshold Algorithm in this section.

Definition 3.3 **Availability.** *An item in L_i is available if and only if all the items above it in L_i have been sorted or random accessed before while the item itself has not been sorted accessed before. Similarly we say a section is available if and only if one of its items is available.*

Definition 3.4 **Lean Value.** *For section Sn_j in the ith list and aggregation function $f(x) = \sum_{i=1}^{m} w_i s_i(x)$, the lean value of Sn_j is w_i/d_j.*

Obviously, in order to speed up the reduction of the threshold value, we need to access the available section with the largest lean value. Based on this, we now propose the Density Threshold Algorithm (i.e., DTA), which is described by the pseudo-code in Fig. 2.

Theorem 3.1. *If the aggregation function f is monotone, then DTA correctly finds the top-k answers.*

Proof: Let set Y be the result set DTA returned. According to the algorithm, DTA halts if and only if $Y.size = k$ and $\tau \le M_k$. Hence, for every object $y \in Y$ and every $z \notin Y$:

Density Threshold Algorithm (DTA)

```
Pre-computing Phase:
 Build the Density Index of the given database.
Computing Phase:
1: Y = Ø, τ = 0, M_k = 0, s_i = 1 where i = 1, 2 ...m.
2: while (Y.size < k or τ > M_k) do
3:    Let Sn_j be the section with the largest lean value in the
      available sections according to the Density Index (if
      the largest lean value is reached for more than one
      sections, any of them can be chosen randomly).
4:    for item (x, s_i(x)) = from the head item down to the tail
      item of Sn_j do
5:      s_i = s_i(x).
6:      τ = f (s_1, s_2... s_m).
7:      if object x has not been accessed before then
8:          get the missing local scores of the object x and
            calculate the total score f(x);
9:          if (Y.size < k) then
10:            insert x into Y;
11:            Let t be the object with the lowest total score in Y
               and M_k be its total score;
12:         else
13:            if (f(x) > M_k) then
14:                remove t from Y and insert x into Y;
15:                Let t be the object with the lowest total score
                   in Y and M_k be its total score;
16:            if (τ ≤ M_k) then
17:                go to 20.
18:   end for.
19: end while.
20: Return Y.
```

Fig. 2. Density Threshold Algorithm

Case 1: If z has been seen before DTA halts and finally not in Y, the fact is that there exist at least $Y.size = k$ objects with higher total scores than z.

Case 2: If z has not been seen by DTA and assume that the local scores of z are $s_i(z)$ where $i = 1, 2 \ldots m$, then we have $s_i(z) \le \underline{s_i}$. Therefore, $f(z) \le f(\underline{s_1}, \underline{s_2} \ldots \underline{s_m}) = \tau \le M_k$. Since M_k is the lowest total score in Y, every y has $f(y) \ge M_k \ge f(z)$.

Therefore, z has no chance to be one top-k answer in both cases, as desired. □

4 Selective-Density Threshold Algorithm

To measure the optimality of an algorithm, Fagin et al. [3] defined a notion of optimality, *instance optimality* as following.

Definition 4.1 **Instance Optimality [3].** *We say that an algorithm* $\mathfrak{B}$ *is instance optimal over* **A** *and* **D** *if* $\mathfrak{B} \in$ **A** *and if for every* $\mathcal{A} \in$ **A** *and every* $\mathfrak{D} \in$ **D** *we have* $cost(\mathfrak{B}, \mathfrak{D}) = O(cost(\mathcal{A}, \mathfrak{D}))$*, that is, there are constants c and c' satisfying* $cost(\mathfrak{B}, \mathfrak{D}) \leq c \cdot cost(\mathcal{A}, \mathfrak{D}) + c'$.

We first show an example that demonstrates DTA is not instance optimal.

Table 1. Dataset of Example 1

L_1	L_2
$(R_1, 1.00)$	$(R_n, 1.00)$
$(R_2, 0.95)$	$(R_{n-1}, 0.85)$
...... $(R_i, 0.9 + (n-1-i) \times \frac{0.05}{n-3})$	...... $(R_i, 0.75 + (i-2) \times \frac{0.10}{n-3})$ and $(R_1, 0.80)$ ......
$(R_{n-1}, 0.90)$	
$(R_n, 0.30)$	$(R_2, 0.75)$

Example 1. Assume $m = 2$, $k = 1$, $f(x) = 0.5 \times s_1(x) + 0.5 \times s_2(x)$. The dataset is illustrated in Table 1, where i is from 3 to $n - 2$. Here we set $b = 10$ in DTA.

Obviously the top-1 object is R_1 and TA performs only 4 sorted accesses and 4 random accesses. However, since the lean value of the available section in L_1 is always smaller than that in L_2, L_2 is chosen to be accessed all the time. Therefore, DTA calls $\left\lceil \frac{n-4}{2} \right\rceil + 3$ sorted accesses and as many random accesses. Since n could be arbitrary large, algorithm DTA is not an instance optimal algorithm. □

The reason DTA is not instance optimal is that DTA "selects" some lists to access instead of all lists in parallel like TA. By doing this selection, DTA may do fewer accesses in most databases but may "miss" some important information in some particular databases like Example 1. Nevertheless, we can force DTA to be instance optimal by a little modify of DTA. We call the modified algorithm "Selective-Density Threshold Algorithm (i.e. S-DTA)", which is described by the pseudo-code in Fig. 3.

We note the access cost of S-DTA is at most v times as TA where v is a positive integer. So S-DTA is instance optimal. Since the optimal ratio of TA is $m + m(m-1)c_R / c_S$, the optimal ratio of S-DTA is $v(m + m(m-1)c_R / c_S)$ under some natural assumption [3].

5 Experiments

In this section, we conduct extensive experiments to evaluate the performance of our algorithms. Our algorithms are implemented in C/C++ language. We perform our experiments on a 2-CPU server with 8GB shared memory and each CPU is 4-core Intel Xeon E5430 2.66GHz.

We do experiments on three synthetic datasets and all generated local scores belong to the interval [0, 1]. The three synthetic datasets are produced to model different input scenarios; they are UI, NI and CO, respectively. All of them are generated using the same methodology in [5] [7] [10].

For synthetic datasets, our default settings for different parameters are shown in Table 2. We choose m to be the varying parameter in one of our tests. As a result, the aggregate function $f(x)$ ought to vary with m. Since DTA and S-DTA are designed to determine that which attribute list should be accessed in the query, we should distinguish the attributes with different aggregate weights. Typically, we set .

Selective -Density Threshold Algorithm (S-DTA)

Pre-computing Phase:

Build the Density Index of the given database.

Computing Phase:

```
Y = Ø, τ = 0, M_k = 0, select = 0, s_l = 1 where i = 1, 2 ...m.
while (Y.size < k or τ > M_k) do
  ... // the same as line 3 in DTA.
  for item (x, s_i(x)) = from the head item down to the tail
  item of Sn_j do
    select = select + 1.
    if select mod v == 0 then
        for each l ∈ {1, 2 ... m} do in parallel
            (x, s_l(x)) = Get_next_item (L_1, ... ,L_m).
      // get next item from one of the lists L_1, ... ,L_m in parallel.
            s_l = s_l(x).
            ... // the same as DTA from line 6 to line 17.
        end for.
    else
        ... // the same as DTA from line 5 to line 17.
  end for.
end while.
Return Y.
```

Fig. 3. Selective-Density Threshold Algorithm

the aggregate function with Fibonacci numbers Fi = 1, 1, 2, 3, 5 … :

$$f(x) = \sum_{i=1}^{m} \frac{F_i}{SUM} \cdot s_i(x), \text{ where } SUM = \sum_{i=1}^{m} F_i .$$

As c_R is usually much higher than c_S, we assume $c_R = 10$ and $c_S = 1$ in our tests. Therefore, the access cost of the queries is $a_S + 10a_R$.

Now we show the experimental results in the figures below:

Fig. 4 illustrates the experimental results in which the parameters are set as those in Table 2 except that m, which varies from 6 to 12 with step 2. The results over the databases we considered show us that our algorithms perform more efficient compared with TA as the m becoming larger. This is mainly because the selection on accessing the lists in DTA and S-DTA makes great difference on the efficiency over datasets with many attributes while parallel accessing become weaker as a result of its neglect of the distinction between the attributes. Moreover, we note that the access cost of S-DTA is always higher than DTA and lower than TA. However, over some databases such as Example 1, S-DTA performs much lower than DTA while TA turns out to be the most efficient algorithm in this case. Obviously, since S-DTA selectively calls DTA (mainly) and TA in the query, it combines the efficiency of DTA and the instance optimality of TA. Therefore, the access cost of S-DTA must be between those of TA and DTA.

The experimental results shown in Fig. 5 where the parameter k varies while the others are set as those in Table 2 indicate the access costs of our algorithms are significantly lower than that of TA over the considered datasets. Besides, the access costs increase much more slightly than that when m is the changed parameter. Furthermore, we can also observe that the access cost of S-DTA keeps between those of TA and DTA.

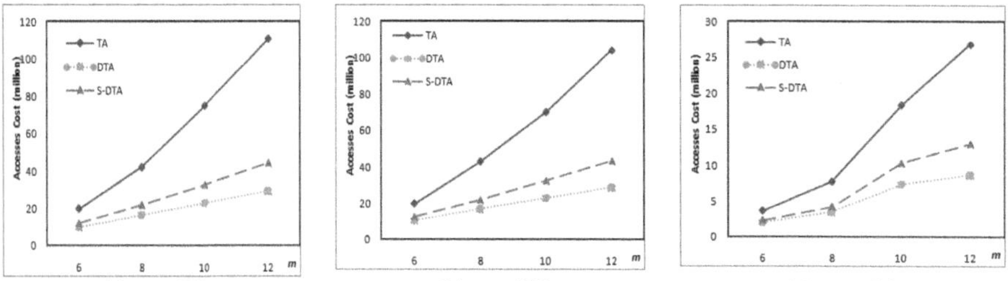

(a) over UI (b) over NI (c) over CO

Fig. 4. Access Cost v.s. m over synthetic datasets, n=1,000,000, k=100, b=1000, v=10

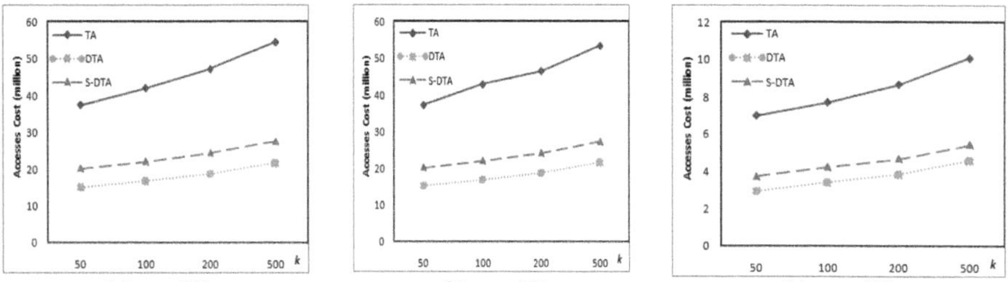

(a) over UI (b) over NI (c) over CO

Fig. 5. Access Cost v.s. k over synthetic datasets, n=1,000,000, m=8, b=1000, v=10

6 Conclusions

Based on the observation on the TA algorithm, we proposed the novel and efficient Density Threshold Algorithm (DTA) to minimize the useless accesses of a top-k query and introduced an efficient indexing structure called Density Index to support our algorithms. Thereafter, we proved the DTA is not instance optimal in Fagin's notion and we also turned the DTA into an instance optimal algorithm named Selective-Density Threshold Algorithm (S-DTA). Finally, we did extensive experiments to compare our algorithms and the TA algorithm. The results showed that our algorithms had significant improvement on the performance of TA algorithm.

Acknowledgment. This work is supported by the National Science Foundation of China under the grant [No. 60873210].

References

1. Ilyas, I., Beskales, G., Soliman, M.A.: A Survey of Top-k Query Processing Techniques in Relational Database Systems. ACM Computing Surveys (2008)
2. Yuan, J., Sun, G.-Z., Tian, Y., Chen, G., Liu, Z.: Selective-NRA Algorithms for Top-k Queries. In: Li, Q., Feng, L., Pei, J., Wang, S.X., Zhou, X., Zhu, Q.-M. (eds.) APWeb/WAIM 2009. LNCS, vol. 5446, pp. 15–26. Springer, Heidelberg (2009)
3. Fagin, R., Lotem, A., Naor, M.: Optimal aggregation algorithms for middleware. In: PODS (2001)
4. Güntzer, U., Balke, W.T., Kie*β*ling, W.: Optimizing Multi-Feature Queries for Image Databases. In: 26th VLDB (2000)
5. Gong, Z., Sun, G.-Z., Yuan, J., Zhong, Y.: Efficient top-*k* query algorithms using *K*-skyband partition. In: Mueller, P., Cao, J.-N., Wang, C.-L. (eds.) INFOSCALE 2009. Lecture Notes of the Institute for Computer Sciences, Social Informatics and Telecommunications Engineering, vol. 18, pp. 288–305. Springer, Heidelberg (2009)
6. Cormen, T.H., Leiserson, C.E., Rivest, R.L., Stein, C.: Introduction to Algorithms. MIT Press, Cambridge (2001)
7. Gong, Z.Q., Sun, G.Z., Chen, D.Q.: Parallel Algorithms for Top-k Query Processing (unpublished)
8. Ilyas, I., Shah, R., Aref, W., Vitter, J., Elmagarmid, A.: Rank-Aware Query Optimization. In: ACM SIGMOD (2004)
9. Fagin, R.: Combining fuzzy information from multiple systems. J. Comput. System Sci. 58(1) (1999)
10. Chen, D.Q., Sun, G.Z., Gong, Z.Q., Yuan, J.: Efficient Approximate Top-k Query Algorithm Using Cube Index (unpublished)
11. Fagin, R., Kumar, R., Sivakumar, D.: Comparing Top K Lists. In: ACM-SIAM SODA (2003)
12. Chaudhuri, S., Dalvi, N., Kaushik, R.: Robust Cardinality and Cost Estimation for Skyline Operator. In: ICDE (2006)

Task Allocation Mechanism Based on Genetic Algorithm in Wireless Sensor Networks

Xiaoqing Hu and Bugong Xu

College of automation science and engineering
South China University of Technology
Guangzhou, China
xiaoqing_hu@21cn.com

Abstract. The main goals of target tracking in WSNs are, through optimizing task allocation on the premise of tracking accuracy, the communication distance can be shortened, the energy consumption can be reduced, and the lifetime of network can be prolonged. We propose a task allocation mechanism of dynamic alliance based on Genetic Algorithm to acquire the balance between the energy consumption and accuracy considered in area sum method. Simulation results show that, the proposed task allocation mechanism is reasonable and effective.

Keywords: WSNs, Target Tracking, Area Sum, Task Allocation, Genetic Algorithm.

1 Introduction

Target tracking play a important role in wireless sensor networks(WSNs)[1]-[2], and the task allocation is the most fundamental problem on target tracking in WSNs, routing strategy, positioning algorithm and data fusion are based on it, only the tracking tasks are assigned to specific nodes to perform, the positioning, routing and data fusion technologies would be implemented. There have so far been several research results on task allocation for multi-target tracking in WSNs, Boukerche[3] only considered the condition of tracking a target and the sensors distribution is a special case of equilateral triangle, constructed a combination of three sensors most close to target to locate for target tracking, not took into account random distribution of sensors, energy consumption in communications and other factors. Zhang Yu[4] proposed a node self-selection method, although the energy factor was considered, but the case of multi-target tracking tasks and the phenomenon of resource competitive conflict were not considered. Nash[5] used the linear programming to allocate sensors. David[6] adopted multi-objective dynamic programming solution to allocate sensors, however optimal multi-sensor allocation for multi-target not only was complex constrained, but also the NP-hard problem of combinatorial explosion, although the traditional mathematical programming method was able to get the optimal solution in theory, often unable to meet the practical requirement due to the dimension constraints of this problem.

Perceiving target information and drawing trajectory curve are basis in the target tracking applications in WSNs, and the two important performance indices are the

D. Zeng (Ed.): ICAIC 2011, Part I, CCIS 224, pp. 46–58, 2011.

accurate sensing information data and lower energy consumption, which always are in opposition to each other. How do establish a proper task allocation mechanism to minimize energy consumption on the premise of tracking accuracy is key problem for target tracking in WSNs.

In this paper, We propose a task allocation mechanism of dynamic coalition based on Genetic Algorithm for multi-target tracking, giving the selection mechanism for the alliance host; using Three-point positioning to locate target, we propose the area sum method to limit the choice of member nodes, which can improve the positioning accuracy; considering a comprehensive performance index function between the energy consumption factor and accuracy factor, we select alliance members by using Genetic Algorithms.

2 Improvement of Dynamic Alliance Mechanism

Many task allocation mechanisms in WSNs are referred to Multi-Agent System(MAS),and some have been implemented such as Contracts, Auction Network, Distributed Constraint Satisfaction, Dynamic Alliance[7]-[11].Task allocation mechanisms based on dynamic alliance can well solve the coordination problem of multi-sensor nodes.

This paper follows the basic concept of dynamic alliance, adequately absorbs advantages of these task allocation mechanisms stated above, abandons their weaknesses, on this basis we propose an improved cooperative task allocation mechanism of dynamic alliance, design a simple and practical selection mechanism for alliance host; and focus on the design of the selection mechanism for alliance members. The specific steps of improved dynamic alliance mechanism are as follow:

1) when a target enters into the perception area from outside, according to the selection mechanism for alliance host, the sensor node firstly sensing the target is chosen as the alliance host, and the host immediately broadcasts the message "target entering" and detection tasks, wakes up nodes around.

2) The nodes receiving the broadcast message are woken up, and give reply message according to task information and their own current state; on the basis of a criteria, the host selects a certain number of nodes as the alliance members in charge of sensing work; once the selected nodes receive the broadcast message, they will determine the status of alliance members, then the alliance succeeds.

3) The members send target detection data to the host, and the host fuses data to obtain the target location according to targeting positioning algorithms, and reports target status to the users.

4) If the distance between the host and target exceeds a certain value β (β can be adjusted according to requirement), then the host can no longer efficiently tracks the target, a new selection operation for the host and members will restart. The former alliance host broadcasts the message of alliance dissolution, then the members stop working after receiving it, the alliance disbands.

3 Selection Mechanism for the Alliance Host

Formatting a dynamic alliance must first determine a host, and how to choose the alliance host? In practice, the sensor node firstly sensing target is chosen as the alliance host. Because the sensor node firstly sensing target are optimal in terms of the distance to target or the aging of sensing target, even the both considered together. How to choose the sensor node firstly sensing target?

When a target doesn't enter the perception area, any sensor is a neither host nor member. If a sensor node firstly senses the target, we select a random number (Its upper limit is the number of sensors around) [12], and beginning to reduce until 0. If the sensor has not yet received the message "target entering" from another sensor until counting to 0, it becomes the host and immediately broadcast the message "target entering" including its own identity and testing tasks to surrounding nodes; but once it has receive the message from another sensor before counting to 0, then it will exit the host selection, give a reply to the host according to the tasks message sent from the host and its current situation, wait for the next selection from the host.

4 Selection Mechanism for the Alliance Members

The proposed task allocation mechanism establishes a comprehensive performance index on basis of the system energy consumption and tracking accuracy, guides the selection of members according to the index, and creates a dynamic alliance. On the one hand it makes the selected members adequately acquire information of the target at each moment, and the host can conveniently use information of these nodes to locate target. On the other hand it ensures that the current generated dynamic alliance consumes less energy on the basis of more adequate information in order to make the system acquire better comprehensive performance. Therefore, this section considers the selection of members from the energy consumption index and the positioning accuracy index below.

In this paper, we assume as follows: a dynamic alliance consists of three sensor nodes; considering capacity constraint, a sensor node can only join a dynamic alliance to track a target.

4.1 Energy Consumption Index

Energy consumption in sensor node generally involves sensing, data processing and communication between nodes, where, the communication is the majority of the energy consumption, and it mainly depends on communication distance. If adopting distributed tracking fusion structure, the total energy consumption of a dynamic alliance can be expressed as follows [13].

$$E = \sum_{n \in \Omega_c} \sum_{k \neq n, k \in \Omega_c} [l_n \varepsilon_{amp} d_{nk}^4 + l_n \varepsilon_{ele}] \tag{1}$$

where Ω_c is the formed dynamic alliance, ε_{amp} is the required energy per bit in Power Amplifier, ε_{ele} is the required energy per bit in filters and other electronic devices,

l_n is the total data amount transferred from node n, d_{nk} is the distance between node n and the selected node k. ε_{amp} , ε_{ele} , l_n can generally be predetermined, only d_{nk} dynamically varies in the process of target tracking, therefore the key point is to make $\sum d_{nk}^4$ minimal in order to get the minimum of communication energy.

Suppose that M targets $T_1, T_2, \cdots T_m, \cdots T_M$ enter the sensor area, then there will be M hosts $H_1, H_2, \cdots H_m, \cdots H_M$.

Taking target T_m for a example ($1 \le m \le M$), its host node is H_m, the woken nodes are $S_1, S_2, \cdots S_n, \cdots S_N$. d_{mn} is the distance between host H_m and the woken node S_n ,letting α_{mn} is the indicated number, if $\alpha_{mn} = 1$,the H_m host chooses the woken node S_n as the alliance member; if $\alpha_{mn} = 0$,the woken node S_n can not be selected as the member.

Therefore in order to minimize the total system communication energy consumption, the task allocation needs to achieve the following energy consumption index [14].

$$\sum_{m=1}^{M} \sum_{n=1}^{N} a_{mn} d_{mn}^4 = \min \tag{2}$$

These constraints in the equation (2) are as follows:

1) A sensor node can only track a target, or sleep to ensure that a sensor only joins a alliance, which can solve the competition conflict of multiple alliances on sensor resources in the case of multiple target tracking. We have

$$\sum_{m=1}^{M} a_{mn} \le 1 \ , \quad n = 1, 2, \cdots, N \tag{3}$$

2) Due to the assumption a dynamic alliance consists of three sensor nodes, one alliance host needs to select two nodes as the alliance members. We have

$$\sum_{n=1}^{N} a_{mn} = 2 \ , \quad m = 1, 2, \cdots, M \tag{4}$$

3) In order to ensure that each target has been allocated , the sum of a_{mn} should satisfy below.

$$\sum_{m=1}^{M} \sum_{n=1}^{N} a_{mn} = 2M \ , \quad m = 1, 2, \cdots, M \ , \quad n = 1, 2, \cdots, N \tag{5}$$

4.2 Positioning Accuracy Index

Target tracking application is built on top of target location, the current location algorithms have the Three-point positioning[15], the maximum likelihood estimation[16] and the minimum maximum method [17],which are commonly used algorithms for calculating target coordinates.

Three-point positioning is the basic way to calculate target coordinates, its main principle is the intersection of three circles centred at the sensor nodes A, B, C and within radiuses of the distance d_1, d_2, d_3 to target M, identifies the coordinates of the target M. This is shown in Fig.1.

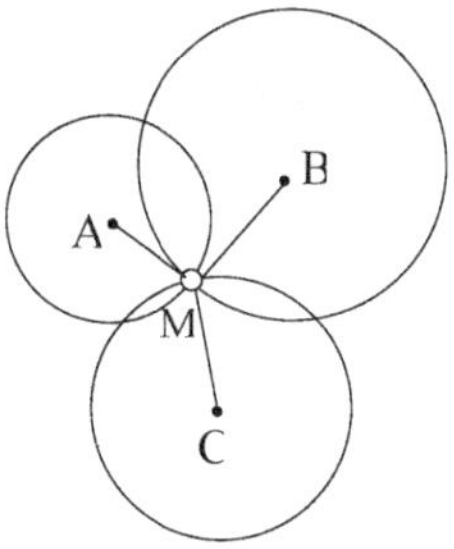

Fig. 1. Three-point positioning

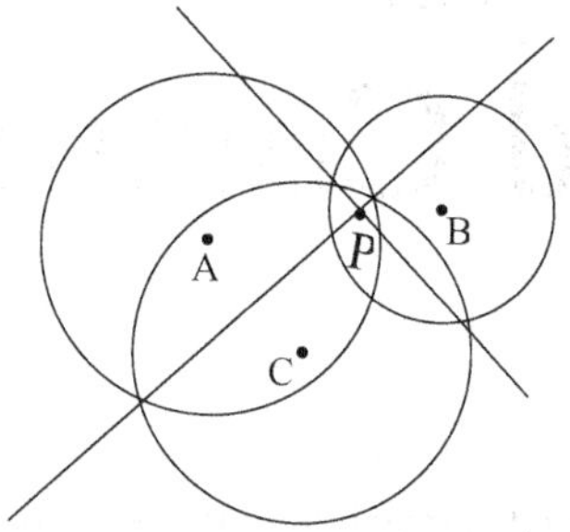

Fig. 2. Three-point positioning under error

However, due to measurement error, the three circles produce overlap region, as is shown in Fig.2.In addition, the intersections of any two circles can define a straight line, and the intersection of any two lines can estimates the target location, so the point P is the final target location. This shows that a point always can be found as an approximate estimated coordinates of the target under any circumstances. Hence, it is proposed to use Three-point positioning to locate in this paper.

We know that the positioning accuracy of Three-point positioning is relative to not only the distance between the nodes and target but also location state between the three nodes and the target; within a certain distance, if the target is surrounded in the triangle range by the three nodes, the positioning accuracy will be higher. We demonstrate the conclusion through simulation experiments below.

Defining the distance between estimated coordinates (x, y) and actual coordinates $(x0, y0)$ of the target as positioning error d, we have

$$d = \sqrt{(x - x0)^2 + (y - y0)^2} \tag{6}$$

Simulation scenario is shown in Fig.3.The coordinates $(x0, y0)$ of Target T1 is (0,0), the host H coordinates $(x1, y1)$ is (4,7), the initial position of the two members is infinitely close to the host H(i.e. the distance almost is equal to 0), the two members start to move down along two lines, the distance between three nodes(it is called the distance of nodes)increases, and the target T1 is slowly surrounded until the end a', b'.

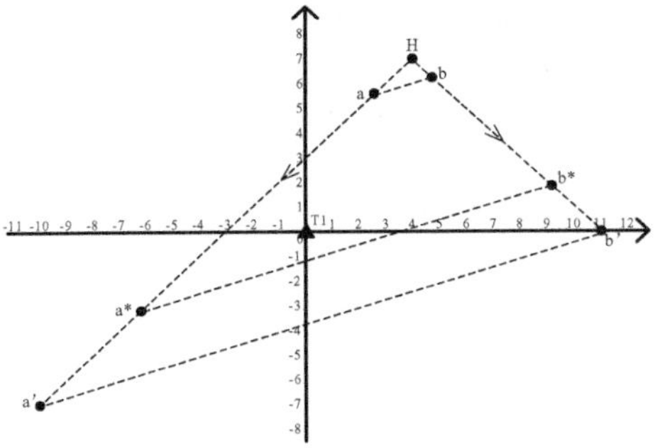

Fig. 3. Simulation scenario

Taking the distance of nodes as the X-axis, the positioning error d as the Y-axis, the simulation result is shown in Fig.4.

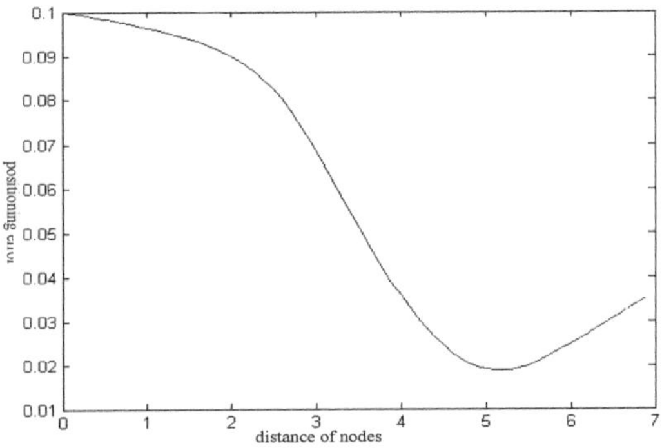

Fig. 4. Positioning error and the distance of nodes

The Fig.4 shows, with the distance of nodes increases from 0, the target is gradually surrounded by the three nodes, and the positioning error is decreasing. When the two nodes move to a^*, b^*, the corresponding distance of nodes is 5.1456, the positioning error is the smallest. If the two nodes continue to move down, the distance between three nodes have been far away from the target, and at this time due to the growing of disruption of measurement data with the distance increasing, the accuracy will reduce, the positioning error begins to increase. That proves that the target is surrounded by three nodes within the triangle range within a certain distance, the positioning error indeed can reduce, the positioning accuracy can also improve, so we will add this constraint to the new Three-point positioning. This can be achieved by area sum method below, as shown in Fig.5.

In Fig.5, if the triangles area sum of PAB, PAC and PBC is equal to the triangle ABC, the point P is in the triangle ABC (including the three sides).The coordinates of the point A,B,C respectively are (A_x, A_y), (B_x, B_y), (C_x, C_y), we obtain the area of the triangle ABC

$$S=\left|(A_x * B_y + B_x * C_y + C_x * A_y - A_y * B_x - B_y * C_x - C_y * A_x)/2\right| \tag{7}$$

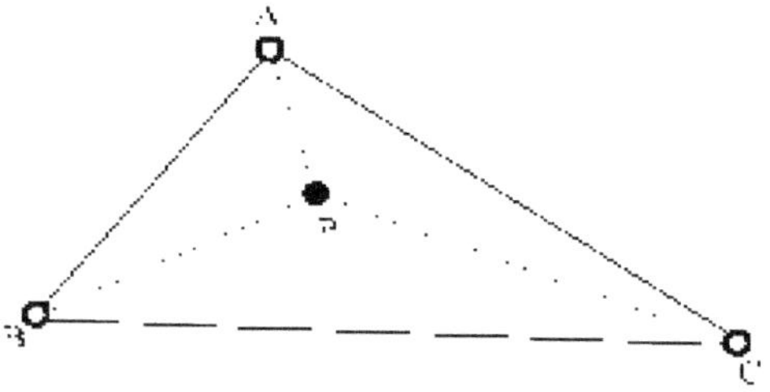

Fig. 5. Schematic diagram of the area sum method

Therefore the area sum method can be shown as follows

$$\begin{aligned}
&\left|(A_x * B_y + B_x * P_y + P_x * A_y - A_y * B_x - B_y * P_x - P_y * A_x)/2\right| \\
&+\left|(A_x * P_y + P_x * C_y + C_x * A_y - A_y * P_x - P_y * C_x - C_y * A_x)/2\right| \\
&+\left|(P_x * B_y + B_x * C_y + C_x * P_y - P_y * B_x - B_y * C_x - C_y * P_x)/2\right| \\
&= \left|(A_x * B_y + B_x * C_y + C_x * A_y - A_y * B_x - B_y * C_x - C_y * A_x)/2\right|
\end{aligned} \tag{8}$$

The equation (8) can be transformed to:

$$\begin{aligned}
\delta=&\left|(A_x * B_y + B_x * P_y + P_x * A_y - A_y * B_x - B_y * P_x - P_y * A_x)/2\right| \\
&+\left|(A_x * P_y + P_x * C_y + C_x * A_y - A_y * P_x - P_y * C_x - C_y * A_x)/2\right| \\
&+\left|(P_x * B_y + B_x * C_y + C_x * P_y - P_y * B_x - B_y * C_x - C_y * P_x)/2\right| \\
&-\left|(A_x * B_y + B_x * C_y + C_x * A_y - A_y * B_x - B_y * C_x - C_y * A_x)/2\right|
\end{aligned} \tag{9}$$

For the equation (9), when $\delta = 0$ the point P is within the triangle ABC; when $\delta > 0$ the point P is not within the triangle ABC, the greater δ, and the farther the point P away from the triangle ABC. In the new Three-point positioning, we ensure that δ is infinitely close to 0, which right stands for the positioning accuracy index in the selection process of members.

4.3 Selection Mechanism for the Alliance Members Based on Genetic Algorithm

To sum up the above arguments, the positioning accuracy index $\delta = 0$ should be satisfied as much as possible, which will be beneficial to locate. But the index

$\delta = 0$ is not suitable as a rigid constraint limit, which should be as a sub-objective function, with another sub-objective function $\sum_{m=1}^{M}\sum_{n=1}^{N} a_{mn} d_{mn}^4 = \min$, constituting Weighted Sum for the comprehensive performance index function.

Letting

$$J_1 = \sum_{m=1}^{M}\sum_{n=1}^{N} a_{mn} d^4{}_{mn} \tag{10}$$

and

$$\begin{aligned} J_2 = \delta = & \left|(A_x * B_y + B_x * P_y + P_x * A_y - A_y * B_x - B_y * P_x - P_y * A_x)/2\right| \\ & + \left|(A_x * P_y + P_x * C_y + C_x * A_y - A_y * P_x - P_y * C_x - C_y * A_x)/2\right| \\ & + \left|(P_x * B_y + B_x * C_y + C_x * P_y - P_y * B_x - B_y * C_x - C_y * P_x)/2\right| \\ & - \left|(A_x * B_y + B_x * C_y + C_x * A_y - A_y * B_x - B_y * C_x - C_y * A_x)/2\right| \end{aligned} \tag{11}$$

We can obtain the comprehensive performance index function J .

$$J = \alpha_1 J_1 + \alpha_2 J_2 = \min \tag{12}$$

where α_1 and α_2 respectively are the weights of J_1 and J_2 ,which can be adjusted to achieve the best tracking performance. In practical applications, the weights can also be adjusted according to the emphasis on energy or accuracy according to application requirements. It proves, the members selection is a process of searching the optimal solution, and the Genetic Algorithm is a class of artificial optimal searching algorithm, which can quickly find the optimal solution or the solution within the error tolerance range [18], therefore this paper will use the Genetic Algorithm to select the alliance members with J as the objective function of Genetic Algorithm.

5 Simulation Results

5.1 Simulation Environment and Programming Steps

In the simulation, there are 100 sampling times and two random moving targets T0 and T1,the perception area is 100m×100m covered by 256 sensors randomly deployed in the field. After establishing two target motion vectors and nodes coordinate vectors, the system begins to select the host according to selection mechanism for the alliance host. Subsequently, finding the two members for each alliance according to selection mechanism for the alliance members based on Genetic Algorithm.

Suppose that the number of individuals(i.e. chromosomes) in the initial population is 100, iteration times is 100. Each node will be coded into 8-bit binary, and then each chromosome has 32 bits. The programming steps are as follows:

*1)*Generating initial population.The initial population is coded into a binary matrix of 100×32, which are chromosomes group of the initial population.

*2)*Decoding.The decoding result is four nodes corresponding to each chromosome.

*3)*Determining whether there is a node repeatedly selected?

*4)*Calculating the objective function (J) and the fitness function (i.e. the reciprocal of the objective function).

*5)*Finding out one of the maximal fitness value in the initial chromosomes.

*6)*Calculating the energy consumption by using (1).

*7)*Calculating the selection probability and cumulative probability.

Letting the fitness value of each chromosome is h_i (i=1,2,...,100),then the selection probability of each chromosome is defined as:

$$p_i = \frac{h_i}{\sum_{i=1}^{100} h_i} \qquad (i = 1, 2, \cdots 100) \tag{13}$$

The Cumulative probability of each chromosome is defined as:

$$T_i = \sum_{j=1}^{i} p_i \quad (\text{i=1, 2, ..., 100}) \tag{14}$$

8) Selecting, crossing and mutating.

①Selecting. Each element (i.e. the cumulative probability) in the cumulative probability matrix of 1×100 subtracts a random value, if the difference is greater than 0, we select the chromosome corresponding to the computed cumulative probability.

②Crossing and mutating. Setting the crossover probability is 0.9, mutation probability is 0.1, when the crossover (mutation) probability is greater than a random value, crossing or mutating; otherwise, neither crossing nor mutating.

*9)*Updating the initial population. After selecting, crossing and mutating, the initial population will be updated until evolution cycle of 100 generations.

*10)*Saving coordinates of the host and members.

*11)*Estimating target location and calculating positioning error. We estimate arriving locations of the two targets using Three-point positioning, draw trajectory curves, and calculate the positioning error at each sampling time.

5.2 Simulation Results and Analysis

The objective function J of Genetic Algorithm takes three different styles. Firstly "without area sum" style only considers the energy consumption index without positioning accuracy index; secondly "rigid constraint limit" style only considers the positioning accuracy index without energy consumption index; thirdly "weighted sum" style considers the comprehensive performance index. These styles are compared in the simulation experiment, the tracking trajectory figures, the energy consumption figures and the positioning error figures under three styles are shown as follows.

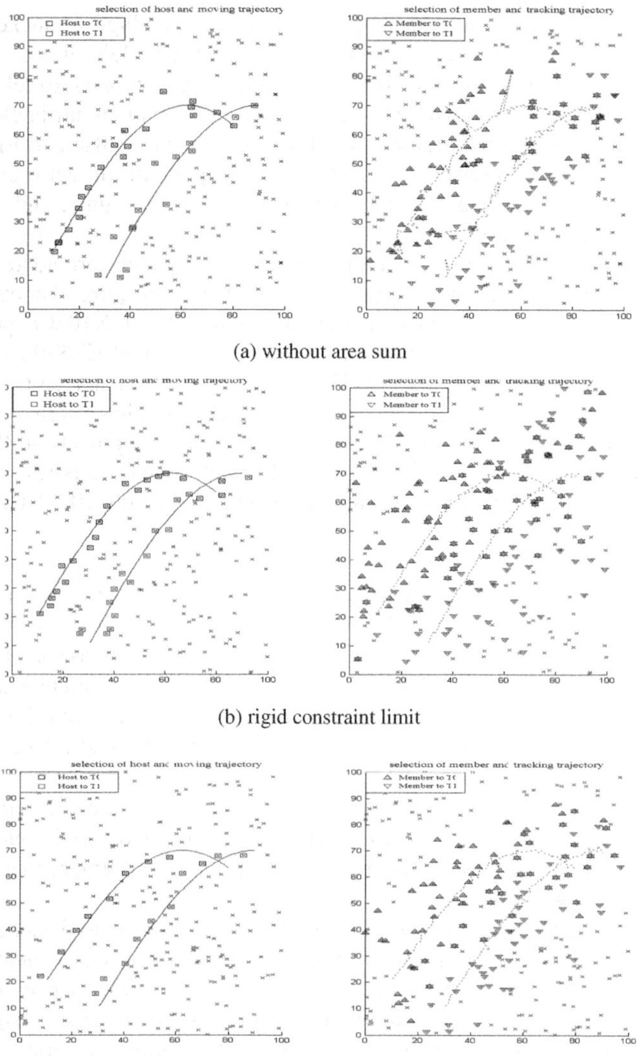

(a) without area sum

(b) rigid constraint limit

(c) weighted sum

Fig. 6. Selection of host and member and the target tracking trajectory

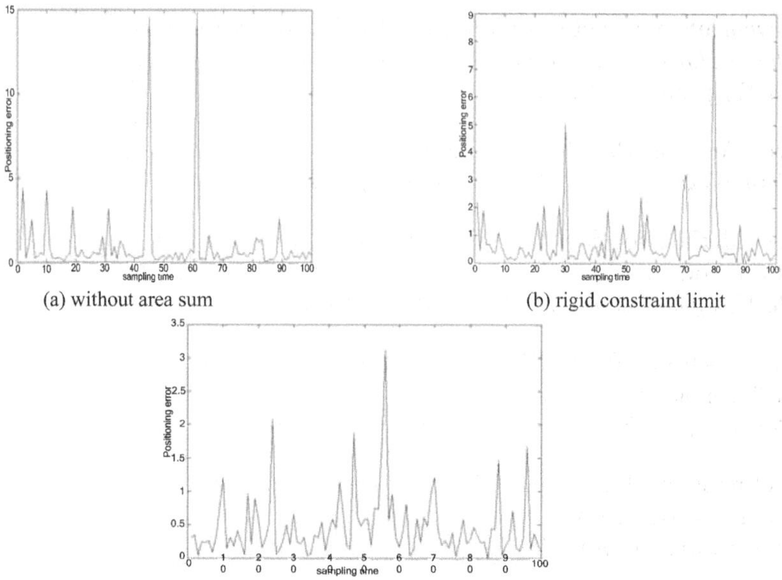

(a) without area sum

(b) rigid constraint limit

(c) weighted sum

Fig. 7. Positioning error to target 0

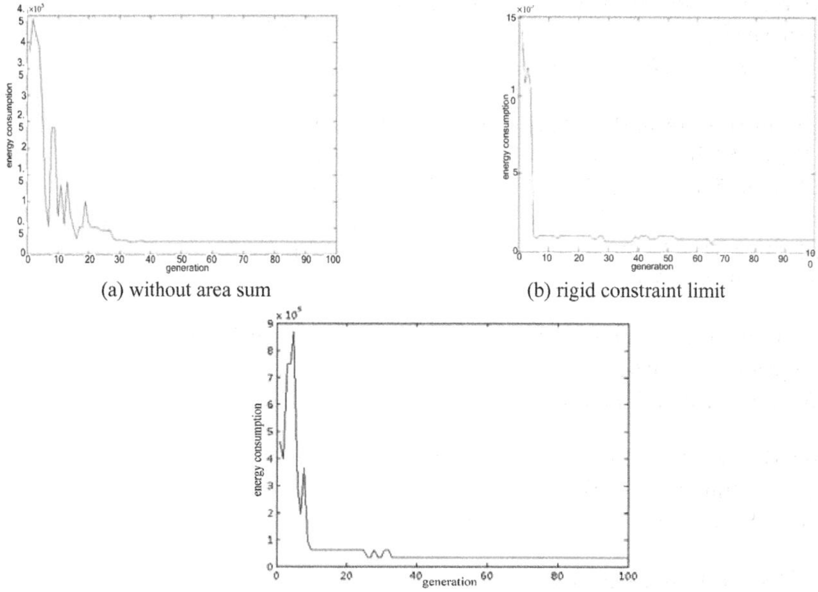

(a) without area sum

(b) rigid constraint limit

(c) weighted sum

Fig. 8. Energy consumption of alliances in every generation

In "weighted sum" style, through debugging, when α_1 is 0.6, α_2 is 0.4 and β is 10m the system can get better tracking effect and balance between the positioning accuracy and energy consumption.

The selection of host and member and the target tracking trajectory is shown in Fig.6. The tracking trajectory under "without area sum" style is not very smooth, some estimation points are far away from the actual point because they can be considered false points, the tracking effect is poor; after adding the area sum method, the tracking results are greatly improved, and the tracking results under "weighted sum" style is better than under "rigid constraint limit" style; Compared with Fig.6-(c),the members are more dispersed in Fig.6-(b), especially in the end of the trajectory curve, the main reason lies in the rigid constraint limit that the target is surrounded by three nodes within the triangle range, which discards nodes close to the target with selecting some nodes that can surround the target, and in this case the positioning accuracy has not increased, but decreased, which may also be shown in Fig.7- (b), (c) .

The positioning error to target 0 is shown in Fig.7.The position error under "without area sum" style is larger. Adding the area sum method, the positioning error significantly reduces, and the positioning error under "weighted sum" style is smaller than under "rigid constraint limit" style.

The energy consumption of alliances every generation at any time (we choose at 100 time) is shown in Fig.8. That is the total system energy consumption of the two alliances consisted of two hosts and four members corresponding to chromosomes of the maximum fitness value in WSNs every generation. Because of only considering the minimal distance of nodes, the energy consumption under "without area sum" style is much smaller. After the adding area sum method, the energy consumption greatly increase, almost six times than the former style, then the energy consumption under "weighted sum" style is a good trade-off ,which is more than under "without area sum" style, although much less than under "rigid constraint limit" style.

It can be also seen in Fig.8, the energy consumption of the alliances corresponding to the members selected by Genetic Algorithm indeed gets smaller and smaller, and the reduction is very significant, which well reaches the aim of greatly saving network energy. This proves that the comprehensive performance index function is reasonable, and member selection based on Genetic Algorithm is effective.

6 Conclusion

The studies on task allocation mechanism for target tracking in wireless sensor networks are relatively weak in this field at present, the proposed task allocation mechanism based on Genetic Algorithm is applied effectively to WSNs for multi-target tracking, but there are a lot of research work needed to be improved, such as the perfect and effective selection mechanism of host remains to be put forward; the selection mechanism of member only considers the two main performance indices of energy and accuracy, the selection mechanism of member involving other more factors remains to be studied further.

References

1. Shen, X., Wang, Z., Sun, Y.: Wireless sensor networks for industrial applications. In: Proceedings of the World Congress on Intelligent Control and Automation (WCICA), vol. 4, pp. 3636–3640 (2004)
2. Sharp, C., Schaffert, S., Woo, A., et al.: Design and implementation of a sensor network system for vehicle tracking and autonomous interception. In: Proceedings of the Second European Workshop on Wireless Sensor Networks, pp. 93–107 (2005)
3. Boukerche, A., Oliveira, H.A.B.F., et al.: Localization systems for wireless sensor networks. IEEE Wireless Communications 14(6), 6–12 (2007)
4. Zhang, Y., Cai, Y.-M., Pan, C.-K., Xu, Y.-Y.: An energy efficient adaptive cooperative node selection scheme in WSN. Dianzi Yu Xinxi Xuebao/Journal of Electronics and Information Technology 31(9), 2193–2198 (2009)
5. Nash, J.M.: Optimal allocation of tracking resources. In: Proceedings of the IEEE Conference on Decision and Control, pp. 1177–1180 (1977)
6. Castaon, D.A.: Approximate dynamic programming for sensor management. In: Proceedings of the 36th IEEE Conference on Decision and Control, pp. 1202–1207 (1997)
7. Liu, J., Reich, J., Zhao, F.: Collaborative in Network Processing for Target Tracking. Journal on Applied Signal Processing (S0941-0635) 23(4), 378–391 (2003)
8. Chen, L., Martin, W., Müjdat, Ç., Willsky, A.S.: Data Association based on Optimization in Graphical Models with Application to Sensor Networks. Mathematical and Computer Modeling, Special Issue on Optimization and Control for Military Applications 43(9-10), 1114–1135 (2006)
9. Makoto, Y.: Distributed Constraint Satisfaction: Foundations of Cooperation in Multi-agent Systems. Springer, Heidelberg (1998)
10. Kahan, J.P., Amnon, R.: Theories of Coalition Formation. Lawrence Erlbaum Associates Publishers, Mahwah (1984)
11. Sha, W., Hu, X.-q.: Predictable Dynamic Alliance Synergistic Mechanism of Tracking. Computer Simulation 27(7), 74–77 (2010)
12. Meng, S.: Analysis and improvement of target tracking applications algorithm based on WSNs. University of Electronic Science and Technology of China (2004)
13. Chen, G.-L., Guo, W.-Z., Chen, Y.-Z.: Research on dynamic alliance of task allocation and its algorithm in wireless sensor network. Tongxin Xuebao/Journal on Communications 30(11), 48–55 (2009)
14. Mei, L., Li, H.-h., Shen, Y.: Research on Task Allocation Technique for Aerial Target Tracking Based on Wireless Sensor Network. Journal of Astronautics 28(4), 960–965 (2007)
15. Guo, S., Li, G., He, Y., Li, X.: The study on precise positioning method of autonomous mobile robot based on three-point location principle. In: 2009 International Workshop on Intelligent Systems and Applications, pp. 1–4 (2009)
16. Takashima, M., Zhao, D., Yanagihara, K., Fukui, K., Fukunaga, S., Hara, S., Kitayama, K.: Location estimation using received signal power and maximum likelihood estimation in wireless sensor networks. Electronics and Communications in Japan, Part I: Communications (English translation of Denshi Tsushin Gakkai Ronbunshi) 90(12), 62–72 (2007)
17. Anthony, B., Goyal, V., Gupta, A., Nagarajan, V.: A plant location guide for the unsure: Approximation algorithms for min-max location problems. Mathematics of Operations Research 35(1), 79–101 (2010)
18. Cai, Z.: Intelligent Control. Publishing house of electronics industry (2004)

Investigation of Multi-view Matching Models for Three-Line-Array Digital Imagery

Dazhao Fan[1,2], Song Ji[2], and Rong Lei[2]

[1] RS & GIS Researching Center, Beijing University, Beijing, China
[2] Institute of Surveying and Mapping, Information Engineering University, Zhengzhou, China
da2763@sina.com

Abstract. Based on redundant image data provided by three-line-array digital imaging systems, the principle, working procedure of multi-view matching models, including GC^3 and MVLL multi-view matching model, were analyzed. Then, similarities and differences between GC^3 and MVLL model were delivered and compared respectively. Based on two ADS40 digital image datasets, multi-view matching experiments were done on both a similar and an occluded feature. The experimental results proved that the two models can synthesize a great number of overlapping images to enhance matching reliability, and compared with traditional single-stereo image matching models, possess great matching superiority.

Keywords: Multi-view, Matching, Three-line-array, GC^3, MVLL.

1 Introduction

As the foreign market of high resolution satellite images is widely opening and ADS40 airborne aerial digital camera is gradually putting into use, the obtaining of three-dimensional spatial information is provided with great data sources[1]. For example, each ADS40 image strip has 3 to 7 overlapping CCD images, and the along-track overlapping ratio of ADS40 camera can reach to 60%[2]. So, a great deal of redundant data is provided for image matching. However, the key problem of the multi-view matching of three-line-array digital images here is how to use these redundant efficiently, and meanwhile, solve the problems existed in traditional matching activities, such as the mismatching of similar or excluded features and so on, to improve the successful rate and precision of image matching[3][4][5].

In this paper, multi-view matching models for three-line-array digital images were introduced briefly, and then, basic principles and working procedure of the models were analyzed. After a comprehensive comparison of the multi-view matching models, experiments were done on ADS40 digital images to verify the advantages of the models.

D. Zeng (Ed.): ICAIC 2011, Part I, CCIS 224, pp. 59–65, 2011.

2 Multi-view Matching Model

2.1 GC3 Multi-view Matching Model

Considering three *ADS40* digital images, which are obtained on the same flight line, the basic principle of Geometrically Constrained Cross-Correlation (GC^3)[4][6] is shown in Fig. 1, where I_0 is selected as reference image, and I_i $(i=1, 2)$ are selected as searching images. Assuming that the orientation parameters of the three images are known (obtained by *GPS/IMU* system or triangulation), for a given ground point p_0, a light ray Cp_0 is obtained, where C is an instantaneous perspective center of point p_0). Through the intersecting of Cp_0 to a plane with a known height Z_0, a ground point $P_0(X_0, Y_0, Z_0)$ is obtained. Since Z_0 is not precise, and has a error of $\triangle Z$, then the precise height position of p_0 lies between $Pmin(Z_0\text{-}\triangle Z)$ and $Pmax(Z_0 + \triangle Z)$. By a certain height step, project these ground points lying on Cp_0 line to the searching images between $Pmin$ and $Pmax$, and then, quasi-epipolar lines of p_0 are determined and denoted as $S_i(Z)(i = 1, 2)$. On the searching images, the precise matching points of p_0 just fall on the quasi-epipolar lines.

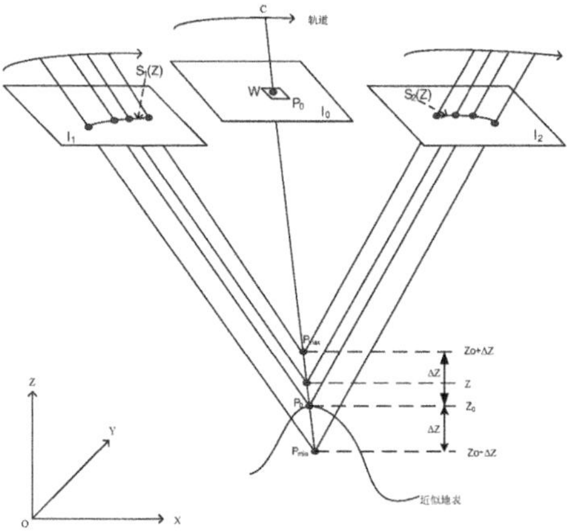

Fig. 1. Basic principle of GC3 model

Based on the above analysis, the matching procedure of GC^3 model can be described as follows[6].

Step1. Selecting reference image I_0 and searching image $I_i(i = 1, 2,\ldots)$. For matching point p_k on image I_0, obtain its approximate height Z_{k0} and height error $\triangle Z_k$ through image pyramid, and obtain the searching step DZ_k through Digital Surface Model (DSM) or the predefined precision of the required final products.

Step2. Using the initial values of Z_{k0}, $\triangle Z_k$, DZ_k and the orientation parameters, determine the quasi-epipolar line $S_i(Z)$ on each searching image I_i and define the size and shape of correlation window W_k.

Setp3. For the light ray p_k, given a height Z_k, compute the plane coordinates (X_k, Y_k). Then, project the coordinated (X_k, Y_k, Z_k) to image I_i to obtain the corresponding image points $p_{ki}(i = 1, 2,\ldots)$.

Step4. Computing the correlation coefficients between image points p_k and $p_{ki}(i = 1, 2,\ldots)$, and then adding the correlation coefficients and obtaining the average value.

Step5. Given a searching step DZ_k, beginning at the height $Z_{k0} - \triangle Z_k$, repeat Step3 and Step 4 unit the height reaching to $Z_{k0} + \triangle Z_k$, and then describing the correlation coefficients by a curve on a coordinate system, where the x axis represents the height and the y axis represents the average correlation coefficient.

Step6. Searching the peak position on the curve, the corresponding height Z is the matching result of point p_k.

Step7. According to the image point of point p_k and its height Z, compute the ground coordinates (X, Y, Z) for point p_k through the imaging model. And then, searching the homogenous points of p_k on each searching images.

Step8. Resetting k (i = 1, 2,...) and repeating the above steps to conduct the matching activities for all the matching points.

2.2 MVLL Multi-view Matching Model

Multiple-view Vertical Line Locus (MVLL) is an improved model of Vertical Line Locus (VLL), whose basic principle is shown in Fig. 2. Similar to Fig. 1, the same three *ADS40* digital images are considered. Assume the orientation parameters of the three images are known, for a given ground point P_0 and its approximate height Z_0, three light rays, including C_0p_0, C_1p_0 and C_2p_0, are obtained, where C_0, C_1 and C_2 are instantaneous perspective centers of point p_0. And the intersecting points of the three light rays on each corresponding image are images points of the ground point P_0.

Since Z_0 is not precise, and has a error of $\triangle Z$, then the precise height position of P_0 lies between $Pmin(Z_0\text{-}\triangle Z)$ and $Pmax(Z_0 + \triangle Z)$. By a certain height step, project these ground points to each image between *Pmin* and *Pmax* gradually, and compute the correlation coefficients between the projected points to obtain the best matching result.

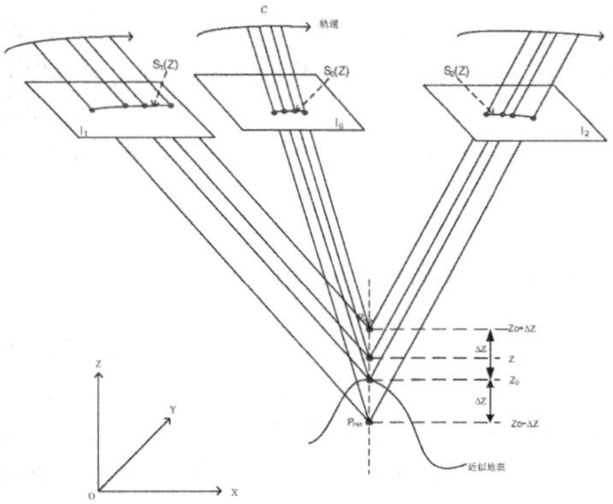

Fig. 2. Basic principle of MVLL model

Based on the above analysis, the matching procedure of MVLL model can be described as follows.

Step1. Given the plane coordinate (X_0, Y_0) of ground point P_0, obtain its approximate height Z_0 and height error $\triangle Z$ through image pyramid, and obtain the searching step DZ through the predefined precision of final products.

Step2. According to the plane coordinate (X_0, Y_0) and the height Z_i, $Z_i = Z_0 - \triangle Z + i*DZ$, ($i$ = 0, 1, 2,⋯), compute the image points (x_{ij}, y_{ij}) (j = 0, 1, 2,⋯, n-1) of P_0 on each matching image.

Step3. Setting (x_{ij}, y_{ij}) (j = 0, 1, 2,⋯, n-1) as the matching center, select a matching window to compute the correlation coefficients between (x_{ij}, y_{ij}) (j =1, 2,⋯, n-1) and (x_{i0}, y_{i0}), and then calculate the average correlation coefficients based on equation (1).

$$m_i = \frac{1}{n-1}\sum_{j=1}^{n-1} m_{ij} \tag{1}$$

Step4. Let $i = i + 1$, repeat Step 2 and Step 3. A correlation coefficient group {m_0, m_1, m_2, ⋯}, namely a correlation coefficient curve, is obtained. If $0 < k < n$ and there is $m_k = max\{m_l, l = 0, 1, 2,\cdots\}$, then the precise height of ground point P_0 is $Z = Z_0 - \triangle Z + k*DZ$.

Step5. According to the precision required by the final DSM product, the ground area corresponding to the overlapping images is divided into grids. Then, repeat the above steps for each grid point to accomplish the matching work.

2.3 Comparison of Multi-view Matching Models

Both GC^3 and MVLL model can synthesize all the information of matching images to obtain correlation coefficient curves, and then obtain matching results through the analysis of the curves. Moreover, all the two models determine the searching area and searching step by image pyramid and approximate DSM respectively. However, there are great differences between the two modes, which are expressed as follows.

1) Different Searching Direction. The searching direction of GC^3 and MVLL model is qusi-epipolar line, but the qusi-epipolar line of GC^3 model is parallel to the flight line of sensors and is easily to overlap with object's edges, while the qusi-epipolar line of MVLL model is a straight line of various directions, and generally expressed as a line through object's top to its bottom.

2) Different Reference Base. For GC^3 model, the downward image is usually used as the reference image, while for MVLL model, there is not any reference image, but the matching widow on the downward image is usually set as the reference matching window.

3) Different Correlation Window Amount. For GC^3 model, the image point is stable, so the there is one correlation window, while for MVLL model, the ground point is stable, and the correlation window on each image is changeable.

4) Different Constraints and Matching Results. The constraint of GC^3 model is qusi-epipolar line, while the constraint of MVLL model is ground plumb line. And the matching results of GC^3 model is DSM cloud of TIN format, while the matching results of MVLL is DSM cloud of regular gird format.

3 Experiments and Analysis

3.1 Experiment Data

Two ADS40 data sets were used in this paper, and the main attributes of the data are shown in table 1.

For dataset ①, the three ADS40 aerial three-line-array digital images were obtained from the LinTong, Xi'an experiment area on 2006-7-30. The average height of the experiment area is 600m, and the three images are of the same flight strip.

For dataset ②, there are six ADS40 aerial three-line-array digital images of two flight lines, where each flight line has three images. The images were obtained from the WaldKrich experiment area of Swiss on 2002-5-16, and the average height of the experiment area is 650m.

Table 1. Main attributes of ADS40 experiment data

Data Set	Level	Focus	GSD	Flight Height	Image Number	Strip Num
①	L 1	62.5mm	0.48m	4800m	3	1
②	L 1	62.5mm	0.21m	2000m	6	2

3.2 Multi-view Matching Experiments and Analysis of Point Features

Through dataset ①, a multi-view matching experiment was done on a similar point feature. During the matching process, the downward image was selected as reference image, and the backward and forward image were selected as searching image. The point feature was selected manually, while in the automatic matching process, point features would be extracted by Foerstner operator. The image pyramid level used in the experiment is two.

As is shown in Fig. 3, there were a few similar features around the selected feature point P, expressed by symbol +. So, there may cause mismatching for feature point P. In the experiment, GC^3 model was used to the feature point and the height searching step was 0.5m. The correlation coefficient curves ρ between the downward image and the forward, backward images were shown in Fig. 3(d) and 3(e). The average correlation coefficient curve was shown in Fig. 3(f). In Fig. 3(a) and 3(c), the lines was qusi-epipolar line, and the × represents the matching result. From Fig. 3(d) and 3(e), it can be seen that there were great local peaks on the curve, so mismatching results must exist on single-stereo matching models, namely traditional matching models, while for GC^3 model, the mismatching was disappear. As was shown in Fig. 3(f), there was only one obvious curve peak, and the corresponding coefficient value was greatly higher than the second local peak coefficient value.

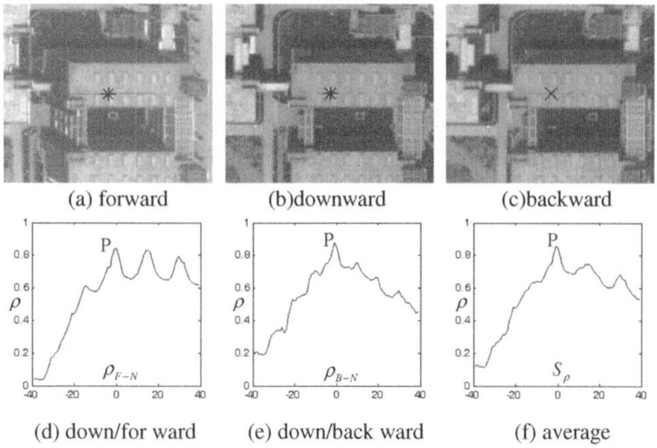

Fig. 3. GC3 multi-view matching of a similar feature

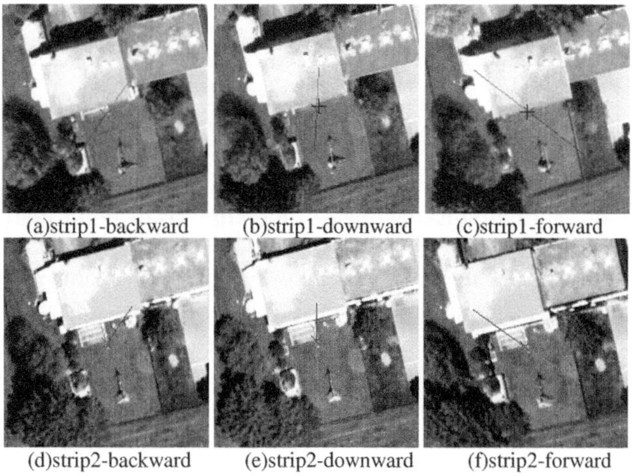

Fig. 4. MVLL multi-view matching of an occluded feature

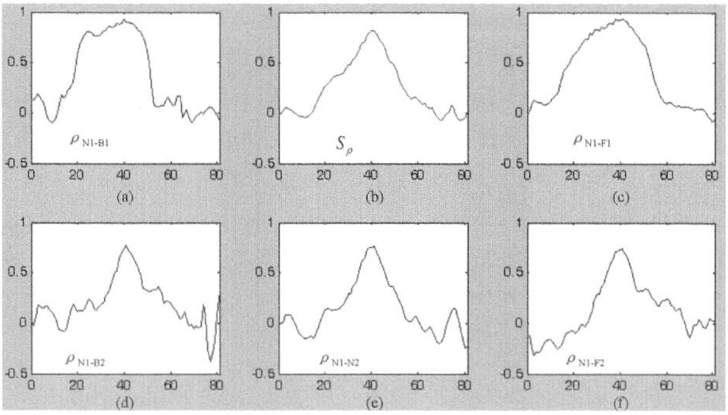

Fig. 5. Correlation Coefficient Curves of MVLL multi-view matching

Through dataset ②, an occluded feature, occluded only in the first image strip, was matched by MVLL model. As is shown in Fig. 4, the initial matching value, expressed imprecisely by symbol +, of the occluded was given by the downward and forward image in the first image strip. The size of correlation window was 31 by 31 pixels, and the searching step was 0.25m. The matching results were shown in Fig. 5.

In Fig. 4, the straight lines were qusi-epipolar lines. Since the feature was occlude in three images of the first image strip, if the downward image of the first image strip was selected as the reference image, another two images of the same image strip had low correlation coefficients with the reference image, as was shown in Fig. 5(a) and 5(c). However, using MVLL multi-view matching model, the average correlation coefficient curve was shown in Fig. 5(b), form which, it can be seen that there was an obvious peak value on the curve. So, a correct matching result, denoted by symbol ×, was obtained and the occluded problem could be greatly solved by MVLL model.

4 Conclusions

From the above analysis, both GC^3 and MVLL multi-view matching model can synthesize all the information of matching images, and under the constraint of qusi-epipolar lines, solve problems existed in traditional single-stereo image matching models, including the mismatching of similar features, occluded features and so on, to improve the reliability and successful rate of matching. Meanwhile, the matching unit of GC^3 and MVLL model is image pixel and ground grid respectively. Therefore, according to the practical production requirements, such as extracting homogenous image points, generating DEM and DSM of various data formats and so on, GC^3 and MVLL model and be combined and synthesized to exert greater application value.

References

1. Zhou, X.L.: The Study on Technology, Method and Application of Ground Processing of Aerial Digital Sensor, Zhengzhou Institute of Surveying and Mapping, Zhengzhou (2007)
2. Liu, J., Zhang, Y.S., Fan, Y.H.: The Photogrammetric Processing and Applications of The ADS40 Airborne Digital Sensor. Journal of Institute of Surveying and Mapping 19(3), 186–188 (2002)
3. Zhang, Z.X.: From Digital Photogrammetry Workstation (DPW) to Digital Photogrammetry Grid (DPGird). Geomatics and Information Science of Wuhan University 32(7), 565–571 (2007)
4. Zhang, L., Gruen, A.: Multi-image matching for DSM generation form IKONOS Imagery. ISPRS Journal of Photogrammetry & Remote Sensing 60, 195–211 (2006)
5. Zhang, Y.S., Fan, D.Z., Ji, S.: Multi-view Matching Algorithm Model for ADS40 Sensor. Journal of Institute of Surveying and Mapping 24(2), 83–86 (2007)
6. Zhang, L.: Automatic Digital Surface Model (DSM) Generation from Linear Array Images, Swiss Federal Institute of Technology Zurich, Zurich (2005)
7. Liu, X.H., Wu, Y.D.: Application of VLL to Obtaining the Elevation of Constructions. Engineering of Surveying and Mapping 15(1), 70–72 (2006)
8. Zhang, Z.X., Zhang, J.Q.: Digital Photogrammetry. Wuhan Surveying and Technical University Press, Wuhan (1996)

Classifying Wetland Vegetation Type from MODIS NDVI Time Series Using Fourier Analysis

Xiaodong Na and Shuying Zang

Key laboratory for remote sensing monitoring of geographic environment
Harbin Normal University
Harbin, Heilongjiang Province, China
Xiaodong1958@qq.com

Abstract. On the basis of multi-temporal MODIS (Moderate Resolution Imaging Spectroradiometer) data, this paper used a kind of supervised classification method to extract wetlands distribution of Sanjiang Plain. The NDVI (normalized difference vegetation index) time series data were got from 16-day MODIS data after processing by Harmonic Analysis of Time Series (HANTS). The shape of NDVI time series, which is diagnostic for certain vegetation phenology, was our primary classifier. A similarity measure based directly on the components of the Discrete Fourier Transform which introduced by J.P. Evans was used to determine a pixels class membership. Based on the difference between vegetation phenology, seven kinds of vegetation had been classified: swamp, meadow swamp, bottomland, paddy field, dry land, bush and woodland. The spatial distribution of natural wetland (swamp, meadow swamp, open water) and manpower wetland (paddy field) were extracted. Validation shows that total classification accuracy is 79.67%, Kappa coefficient is 0.7525. Results indicated that this Fourier component similarity measure produced an objective, computationally inexpensive and rapid method of wetlands classification.

Keywords: wetland, MODIS, NDVI, fourier transform.

1 Introduction

Sanjiang plain is one of the largest wetland in China. It has become an important commodity grain base in China after more than 40 years exploitation. At the same time, the wetland area has decreased sharply. Destruction of wetlands and some environmental problems are attracting more and more attention. To conserve and manage wetland resources, it is important to inventory and monitor wetlands and their adjacent uplands.

Remote sensing allows for the multi-temporal mapping and monitoring of large areas covered with surface water, which may otherwise be inaccessible. Optical remote sensing techniques have been widely used for mapping and monitoring wetlands [1,2]. However, observations over a relatively short time span do not often reflect vegetation features meaningfully, because different plant species may have similar spectral properties in a growing season. Furthermore, leaf structure and

D. Zeng (Ed.): ICAIC 2011, Part I, CCIS 224, pp. 66–73, 2011.

chemistry vary seasonally, resulting in seasonal dynamics of spectral properties [3]. Monitoring seasonal changes in vegetation features and plant phenologies over a long time is essential for us to distinguish vegetation types or determine the stages of ecological succession [4,5]. Over the last decade, different techniques have been developed to determine vegetation dynamics through using the time series NDVI (normalized difference vegetation index) from AVHRR (advanced very high resolution radiometer) and MODIS (moderate resolution imaging spectroradiometer).Ref.[6,7] differentiated rangeland vegetation and assessment of its status using FFCS (fourier filtered cycle similarity) method based on MODIS or SPOT VEGETATION NDVI time series. Ref. [8] defined a Fourier component based similarity measure (FCSM) to indentify the distribution and the fractional cover of species.

The main aim of this study was to determine if a proper indicator reflected different plant phonologies characteristics could be identified to classify wetland vegetation type in Sanjiang Plain. To achieve this goal, we tested and applied a supervised classification method based on FCSM indicator which introduced by Evans and Geerken to NDVI time series of MODIS data covering the Sanjiang Plain in 2005. The classification result was validated based on the field investigation data. This study provided a new method for monitoring the status and dynamics of wetland vegetation for the typical marsh area of China.

2 Study Area

Our study area, the Sanjiang Plain is located at 43°49′ 55″ N ~ 48°27′ 40″ N, 129°11′ 23″ E ~135°05′ 26″ E , and lies in the northeast of the Heilongjiang Province. The regional climate is temperate humid to subhumid continental monsoon. Average temperatures range from -18℃ in January to 21~22℃ in July, with a frost-free period of 120~140 days. Annual precipitation is 500~650 mm, with 80% occurring in May–September. Most of the rivers in the area have riparian wetlands supporting meadow and marsh vegetation. Sedge (Carex spp.) is the dominant plants with Phragmites spp. scattered across some portions [9].

3 Data and Method

3.1 Data Source

Though MODIS sensors on the Terra (EOS AM) and Aqua (EOS PM) satellites theoretically view the entire earth's surface every 1–2 days, it is impossible to acquire reliable earth surface observation data at such an interval, as cloud cover may occur somewhere at the global scale. A 16-day composition was therefore done to optimize the acquisition of cloud-free images, such as the surface reflectance product MOD13Q1. The data used in this study were downloaded from the NASA's Earth Observing System website. 23 NDVI time-series images covering the Sanjiang Plain and spanning one annual cycle from 1 January 2005 to 18 December 2005. All images were transformed from Sinusoidal projection to Albers projection using ERDAS software.

Other ancillary GIS data used in this research were: 1) a digital district map and topographic maps at the scale of 1:250,000 in 1985 from the Heilongjiang Mapping and Surveying Bureau; 2) a vegetation thematic map at the scale of 1:500,000 from the Geography Institution of Changchun, Chinese Academy of Sciences in 1985; 3) For training and testing of the supervised classification and investigating vegetation change and succession, field surveys were conducted in August 2005, collecting real time ground truth reference data, aided by a global positioning system (GPS).

3.2 Study Method

1) Noise filtering and preservation of phenological characteristics: Because the similarity of the annual NDVI cycle is our primary classifier, it is essential to enhance the diagnostic, phonological features while subduing all features that are considered to be noise. The DFT decomposes any complex waveform into sinusoids of different frequencies or so-called harmonics, which together sum up to the original waveform. Once separated into its individual sinusoids, individual frequencies can be filtered or weighted and summed up thereafter to rebuild a complex waveform with the noise frequencies being removed. Preceding the classification, we use this technique to measure and to remove noise from the NDVI layerstack.

As Ref. [7] demonstrated, phenology-related information is generally contained in the first several harmonics. Accordingly, in a scene-wide noise assessment, we assume that all components higher than eight contain only noise, with the total noise being calculated as the sum of harmonics 8–23. For the example of a single NDVI cycle, the separation of signal from noise through Fourier filtering is shown in Fig.1. The weights applied to the individual harmonics to separate the signal from the noise are shown in Fig.2.

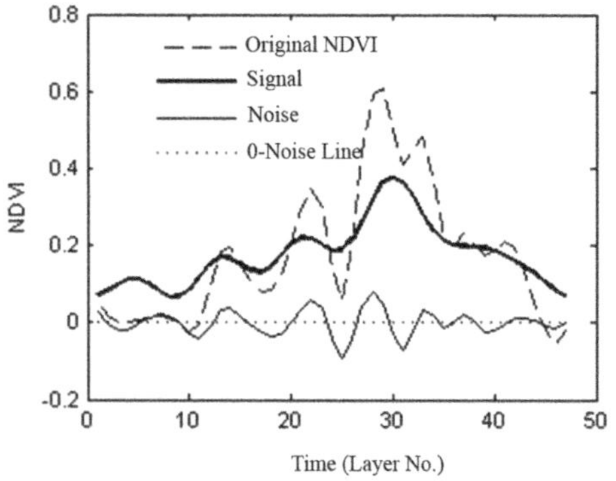

Fig. 1. Original NDVI cycle and after Fourier filtering, showing the cycle's signal component, and its noise component

2) Classification (Fourier component based similarity measure, FCSM): The selection of reference sites for this classification is based on field information. In cases where no field information is available, potential vegetation types can be

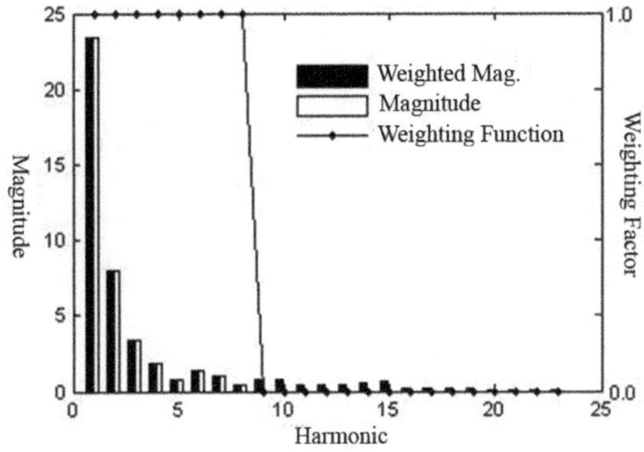

Fig. 2. Weights applied to the individual harmonics to separate the signal from the noise

identified from a color composite that uses the first three Fourier magnitudes (fig. 3). A color composite of the first three Fourier magnitudes is a meaningful and an easy to interpret compression of an NDVI time series. In such color composites, variations in hue indicate differences in vegetation type. 30 reference sites with the cycle shape being diagnostic for each 7 typical vegetation types (swamp, meadow swamp, bottomland, paddy field, dry land, bush and woodland) are selected from fig. 3.

In classifications, the primary classifier should be a quantifiable measure which describes shape similarity between NDVI cycles. The FCSM indicator introduced by Evans and Geerken quantifies the similarity between NDVI cycles of individual pixels and is designed to consider the various dynamics that may influence vegetation growth under different growing conditions. In this regard the algorithm is invariant to

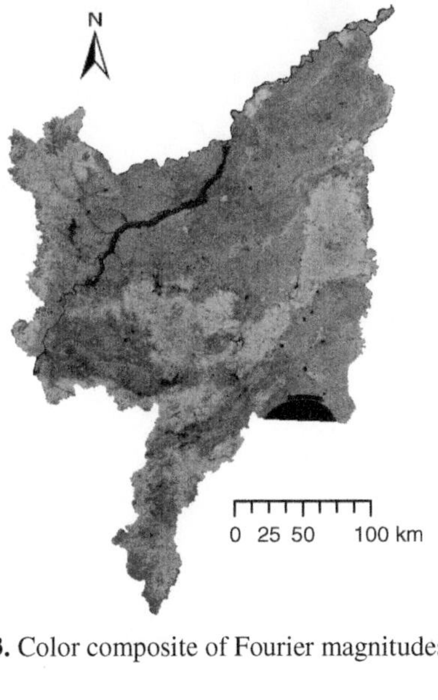

Fig. 3. Color composite of Fourier magnitudes 3, 2, 1

shape transformations including: amplitude scaling; time (phase) translation; amplitude translation; and noise. The similarity measure, ξ, is defined in (1).

$$\xi = 3\sqrt{\sum_{k=1}^{m}(\alpha_k^{ref} - \alpha_k)^2} + \sqrt{\sum_{k=1}^{m}(\theta_k^{ref} - \theta_k)^2} \tag{1}$$

The relative amplitude, α_k, and phase, θ_k, are defined for each harmonic. The relative amplitude is the kth amplitude relative to the first (or annual) amplitude. The relative phase is the cosine of the difference between the first phase and the kth phase, in the kth components phase space.

4 Result

4.1 Classification from MODIS NDVI Time Series

Fig. 4 presents maps of the FCSM for each class. The lower the value the more similar a pixel is to the class reference pixel. Clearly many pixels are assigned FCSM

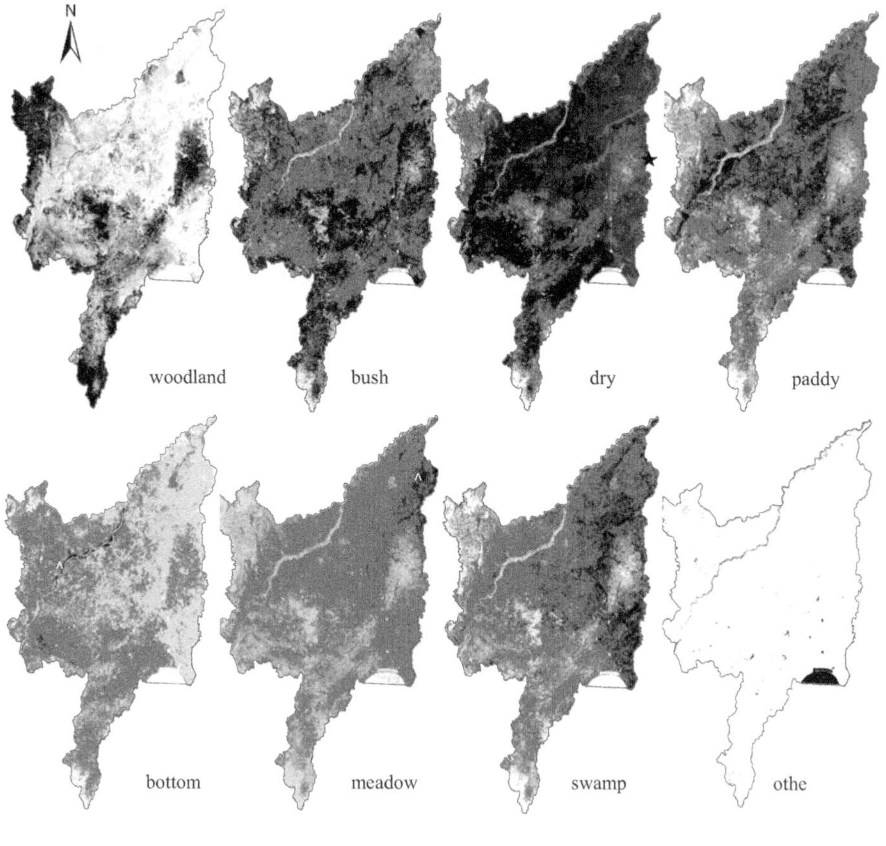

Fig. 4. FCSM maps for each vegetation class of Sanjiang plain

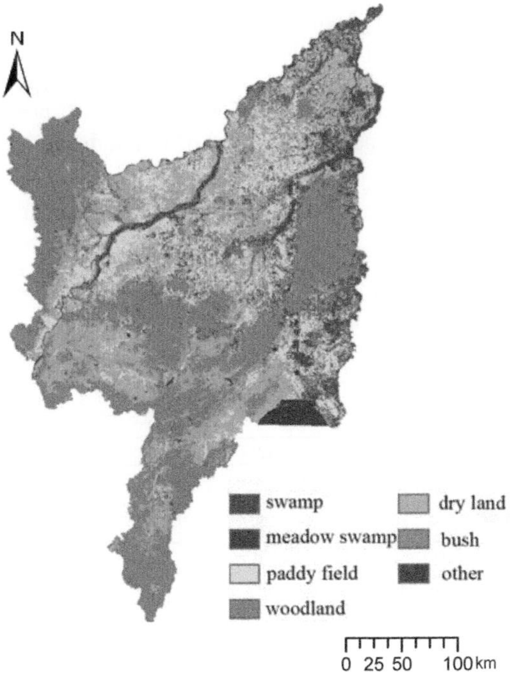

Fig. 5. The distribution of vegetation class in 2005

values for multiple classes reflecting both the similarity of the reference cycles themselves and the fact that 250 m pixels are in general mixtures of land cover types rather than being purely one type. A dominant land cover classification is then produced by assigning each pixel to the class for which it has the lowest FCSM, resulting in the classification shown in Fig. 5. It would also be possible to define classes based on a cutoff value for the FCSM for each class. This is not done here as it introduces a subjective factor which would reduce the reproducibility of results. The distribution of land cover map of Sanjiang plain provides useful distinction of wetland classes (swamp, meadow swamp, bottomland, paddy field).

4.2 Validation of Classification Accuracy

The accuracy of the resultant vegetation maps was assessed with an independent set of 182 test samples in the study area. An error matrix was generated. The producer's accuracy, user's accuracy, overall accuracy, and Kappa coefficients were derived for accuracy assessment. The classification accuracy assessment results of the supervised classification method based on FCSM indicator are shown in Table 1. The % accuracy and Kappa coefficient are 79.67 % and 0.7525 respectively. The classification accuracy is highest for woodland (89.36%) and this is related to its distinct phonological characteristics. In contrast the accuracy for swamp (70%) and meadow swamp (61.53%) is relatively low. This is due to their similar phonological characteristics leading to some lack of discrimination. Although compared with the classification accuracy from high-resolution remote sensing data sources, the accuracy of this study is not preferable. Considering of the advantages of MODIS NDVI series such as real time monitor, small data storage, large covering extend and wildly accessible, the supervised classification method proposed an objective, computationally inexpensive and rapid method of wetlands classification.

Table 1. Vegetation classification confusion matrix

classified data			Reference data				overall	User's accuracy (%)
	swamp	Meadow swamp	paddy field	woodland	dry land	bush		
swamp	21	2	3	2	2		30	70.00
meadow swamp	3	20		3			26	61.53
paddy field		1	20		3		24	83.33
woodland	4			42		1	47	89.36
dry land	2		5	1	23		31	74.19
bush	2	2			1	19	24	79.16
overall	32	25	28	48	29	20	182	
Producer's accuracy (%)	65.62	80.00	71.43	87.5	79.31	95.00		

5 Conclusion and Discussion

This study presents a wetland classification method based on how similar the annual NDVI cycles are. Similarity of the cycles is determined using a similarity measure based on components of the discrete Fourier transform of the NDVI cycle introduced by Evans and Geerken. Land cover classes are defined by the NDVI cycle of a known reference pixel and all pixels are assigned to the class to which they are most similar. This Fourier Component Similarity Measure (FCSM) classification is objective (requiring no user intervention other than the choice of reference pixel), and requires little computation power or user time to create. It demonstrates the ability to successfully differentiate land cover dominated by different wetland vegetation types in the Sanjiang Plain.

The accuracy validation showed that the accuracy for swamp and meadow swamp is relatively low due to their similar phonological characteristics leading to some lack of discrimination. Therefore, future research should pay attention to the phenophases when the differences of NDVI values between swamp and swamp meadow are significant. Assistant data including water depth and terrain would be used to enhance the accuracy for vegetation of swamp and swamp meadow.

Acknowledgement. This research is supported by the National Natural Science Foundation of China (Grant No. 41001243), the Scientific and Technological Projects of Education Department of Heilongjiang Province (China) (Grant No. 11551133) and the Harbin Normal University's Fund for Distinguished Young Scholars (Grant No. 09XBKQ14).

References

1. Phinn, S., Hess, L., Finlayson, C.M.: An assessment of the usefulness of remote sensing for wetland inventory and monitoring in Australia. Techniques for enhanced wetland inventory, assessment and monitoring. Supervising Scientist Report 147. Supervising Scientist Group, Canberra, pp. 44–82 (1999)
2. Davidson, N.C., Finlayson, C.M.: Earth observation for wetland inventory, assessment and monitoring. Aquat. Conserv. 17(3), 219–228 (2007)
3. Zhang, Q.Y., Xiao, X.M., Braswell, B., Linder, E., Ollinger, S., Smith, M.L., et al.: Characterization of seasonal variation of forest canopy in a temperate deciduous broadleaf forest, using daily MODIS data. Remote Sensing of Environment 105(3), 189–203 (2006)
4. Anderson, R.P., Peterson, A.T., Egbert, S.L.: Vegetation index models predict areas vulnerable to purple loosestrife (Lythrum salicaria) invasion in Kansas. Southwest Nat. 51(4), 471–480 (2006)
5. Sakamoto, T., Yokozawa, M., Toritani, H., Shibayama, M., Ishitsuka, N., Ohno, H.: A crop phenology detection method using time-series MODIS data. Remote Sensing of Environment 96(3/4), 366–374 (2005)
6. Geerken, R., Batikha, N., Celis, D., Depauw, E.: Differentiation of rangeland vegetation and assessment of its status: field investigations and MODIS and SPOT VEGETATION data analyses. International Journal of Remote Sensing 26(20), 4499–4526 (2005)
7. Geerken, R., Zaitchik, B., Evans, J.P.: Classifying rangeland vegetation type and coverage from NDVI time series using Fourier Filtered Cycle Similarity. International Journal of Remote Sensing 26(24), 5535–5554 (2005)
8. Evans, J.P., Geerken, R.: Classifying rangeland vegetation type and coverage using a Fourier component based similarity measure. Remote Sensing of Environment 105, 1–8 (2006)
9. Liu, X.T.: Wetland and its rational utilization and conservation in the Sanjiang Plain. In: Chen, Y.Y. (ed.) Study of Wetlands in China, pp. 108–117. Science Press, Beijing (1995)

Application of Hilbert-Huang Transform to Fault Feature Extraction of Offshore Platforms

Chunhong Dou

School of Information and Control Engineering
Weifang University
Weifang, Shandong Province, P.R. China
chunhongdou@yahoo.cn

Abstract. Conventional techniques for feature extraction are based on the stationary process and linear theory, so they are unsuited for processing the non-stationary signals. Hilbert-Huang transform (HHT) has been proposed recently and is specially fit to explore the non-stationary signals. The paper utilizes HHT to analyze the signals from the WZ12-1 platform. First, we employ a simulation signal to measure the performance of empirical mode decomposition (EMD), which is the core of HHT. Next, the HHT method is applied to extract the fault feature from the signals collected from the WZ12-1 platform and successfully reveals the reason causing the excessive vibration of the WZ12-1 platform. The results indicate that HHT could be a helpful method for the fault feature extraction of mechanical systems.

Keywords: feature extraction, Hilbert-Huang transform (HHT), empirical mode decomposition (EMD), offshore platform.

1 Introduction

Feature extraction commonly plays a key role in the fault diagnosis of mechanical systems. Traditional techniques for feature extraction cover time-domain analysis and Fourier transform [1]-[3]. However, these techniques usually assume the process generating signals to be stationary and linear. Unfortunately, the signals collected from defective mechanical systems are ordinarily non-stationary and nonlinear. Used to analyze the signals consisting of faulty information, the traditional techniques unavoidably lead to seriously distorted results. To overcome the deficiency occurring in the traditional techniques, some methods, such as short time Fourier transform, Wigner-Ville distribution, and wavelet transform, have been presented and caused wide concern in recent decade. Nonetheless, all the above methods are still based on Fourier transform and lack the self-adaption for the investigated signals. Empirical mode decomposition (EMD), a novel time-frequency analysis technique, is introduced to process the non-stationary and nonlinear signal and rapidly developed in view of its excellent performance [4]-[6]. EMD can self-adaptively decompose a non-stationary and nonlinear signal into a set of complete and almost orthogonal components named intrinsic mode function (IMF), each of which is assigned truly physical meaning.

D. Zeng (Ed.): ICAIC 2011, Part I, CCIS 224, pp. 74–78, 2011.

The paper employs the EMD method for extracting the fault information from the signals captured from the WZ12-1 platform. As a result, the EMD method effectively overcomes the shortcoming of the traditional techniques, and obtains better results for feature extraction.

2 Hilbert-Huang Transform

The HHT algorithm consists of the EMD algorithm and Hilbert transform, in which EMD is the key part.

2.1 EMD Algorithm

According to the assumption that any signal comprises IMFs of different scales, the EMD method can decompose a signal into a set of IMF components. An IMF is a function that satisfies the following two conditions:(1) in the whole data set, the number of extreme and the number of zero-crossing must either equal or differ at most by one, and (2) at any point, the mean value of the envelope defined by the local maxima and the envelope defined by the local minima is zero [4], [6]. The EMD process of the signal $x(t)$ can be described as follows [4], [6].

(1) Initialize: $r_0=x(t)$, and i=1.
(2) Computer the ith IMF.
 (a) Initialize: $h_{i(k-1)}=r_i$, k=1.
 (b) Find the local maxima and minima of $h_{i(k-1)}$.
 (c) Interpolate the local maxima and the minima to establish the upper and lower envelopes of $h_{i(k-1)}$ using cubic spline function.
 (d) Computer the mean $m_{i(k-1)}$ of the upper and the lower envelopes of $h_{i(k-1)}$.
 (e) Allow $h_{ik}= h_{i(k-1)}-m_{i(k-1)}$.
 (f) If h_{ik} is an IMF, then set $c_i=h_{ik}$ or else return to step (b) with $k=k+1$.
(3) Define $r_{i+1}=r_i-c_i$.
(4) If r_{i+1} has still least two extrema, then return to step (2), or else the decomposition is stopped and r_{i+1} is the final residue of the signal.

Then we get the residue r_i and the collection of l IMFs $c_i(i=1,2,3,\ldots,l)$. Summing up all the IMFs and the final residue r_{l+1}, we can obtain

$$x(t)=\sum_{i=1}^{l} c_i + r_{l+1}. \quad (1)$$

Thus we decompose the signal $x(t)$ into l IMFs and the residue r_{l+1}. The IMFs c_1, c_2, …, c_l represent different frequency components from high frequency to low frequency, while r_{l+1} means the general tendency of the signal $x(t)$. A more detailed description of EMD can refer to [4], [6].

2.2 The Hilbert Spectrum

Having obtained the IMFs, we are easy of applying the Hilbert transform to each component and hence the instantaneous frequency can be calculated. Consequently, the Hilbert spectrum of the signal $x(t)$ can be expressed in the following form:

$$H(\omega,t) = RP\sum_{j=1}^{n} a_j(t)\exp(i\int\omega_j(t)dt), \tag{2}$$

where RP means to select the real part of the sum, $a_j(t)$ indicates the jth instantaneous amplitude, and $\omega_j(t)$ represents the jth instantaneous frequency [4], [6].

After the Hilbert spectrum has been defined, we can continue to give a definition for the Hilbert marginal spectrum:

$$h(\omega) = \int_0^T H(\omega,t)dt, \tag{3}$$

where T is the time length of the signal [4], [6].

3 Simulation Example

To assess the performance of the EMD method, the non-stationary simulation signal shown in Fig. 1 was used as the test signal, which consisted of a continuous sine wave of low frequency and a discontinuous sine wave of high frequency.

Next, the signal was decomposed using the EMD method. The results are shown in Fig. 2. Fig. 2 displays that the EMD method succeeds in decomposing the simulation signal.

Consequently, the simulation confirms that the EMD method is an excellent tool for dealing with the non-stationary signal.

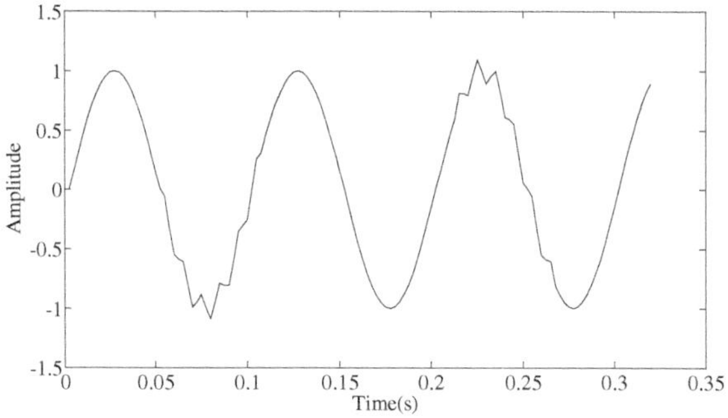

Fig. 1. The simulation signal

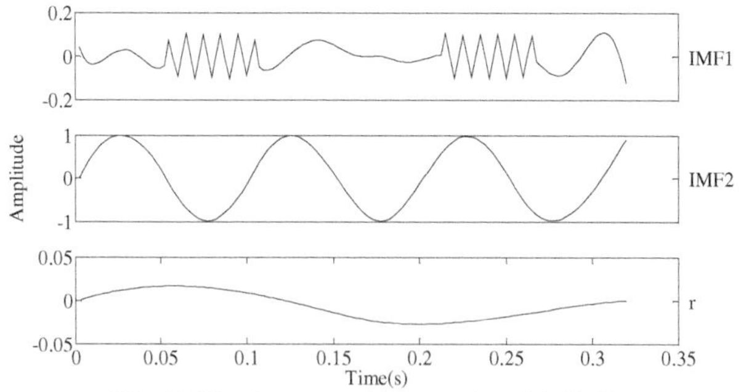

Fig. 2. The decomposition results with EMD

4 Application of Hht to Fault Feature Extraction of Offshore Platform

As stated in previous sections, HHT is suited for exploring the non-stationary and nonlinear signal. Here, the HHT method is applied to extract the fault feature from the signal captured from platforms. After the offshore platform of WZ12-1, a modern platform located in South China Sea, had been working for several years, it was observed that the vibration from the decks of the platform was so acute as to seriously endanger the safety of the platform. By means of the portable data acquisition of DataPAC1500 and the acceleration sensor of MD6301, we successfully acquired the acceleration signal from the deck. The signal is shown in Fig. 3, with the sampling frequency of 1280Hz and the length of 1024. In addition, the signal is explored using HHT and the results are exhibited in Fig. 4; the corresponding Hilbert spectrum is shown in Fig. 5. Fig. 5 clearly displays that the frequency of 16.28Hz almost evenly exists in the whole time domain and other frequencies only occur disorderly. Considering that the rotation frequency of the-natural-gas-compressor on the platform is 16.5 Hz, approaching to 16.28Hz, it seems to be an accepted conclusion that the periodic excitation of the faulty compressor causes the excessive vibration of the WZ12-1 platform. In accordance with the opinion, after the compressor had been repaired, hence the vibration of the WZ12-1 platform again became normal, which further verified the performance of the EMD method.

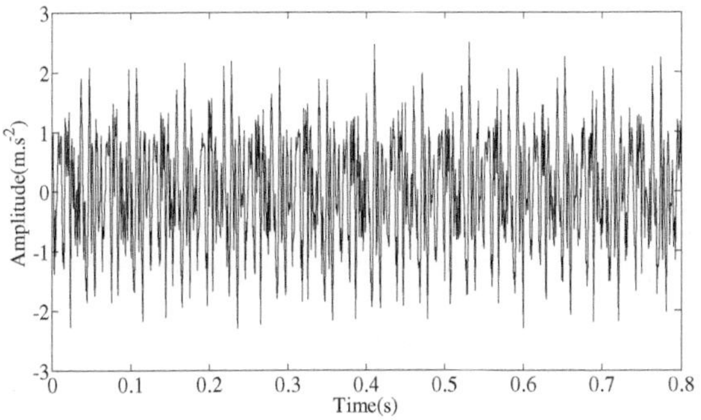

Fig. 3. The acceleration signal from WZ12-1 platform deck

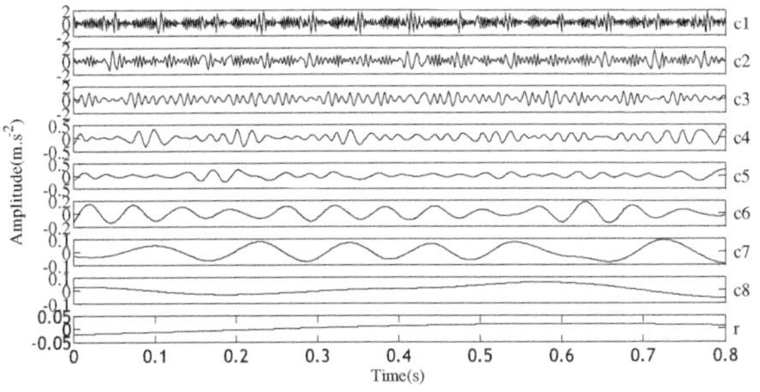

Fig. 4. The decomposition results of the acceleration signal with EMD

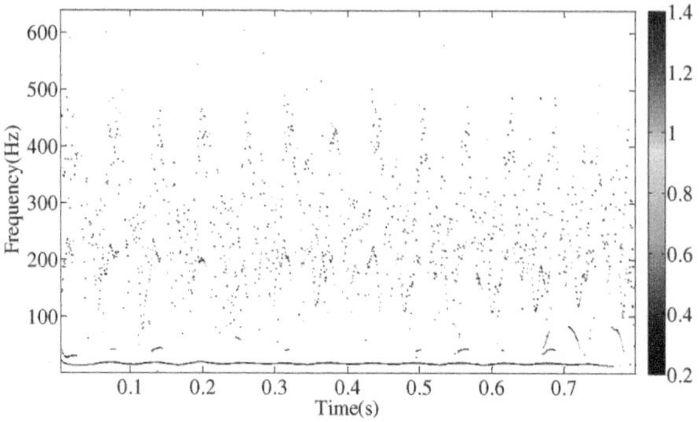

Fig. 5. The Hilbert spectrum of the acceleration signal

5 Conclusions

The HHT method, effectively overcoming the deficiency of conventional techniques, is exploited to extract the fault feature of the WZ12-1 platform. The simulation indicates that the HHT method has the ability to analyze the non-stationary signal. Then the HHT method is applied to extract the fault information from the signal collected from the WZ12-1 platform and succeeds in uncovering the cause resulting in the excessive vibration of the platform. The results show that the EMD-based method is a promising method for the fault feature extraction of mechanical systems.

References

1. Jardine, A.K.S., Lin, D., Banjevic, D.: A rereiw machenical diagnostics and prognostics implementing condition-based maintenance. Mechanical Systems and Signal Processing 20, 1483–1510 (2006), doi:10.1016/j.ymssp.2005.09.012
2. Peng, Z.K., Chu, F.L.: Application of the wavelet transform in mechanical condition monitoring and fault diagnostics: a review bibliography. Mechanical Systems and Signal Processing 18, 199–221 (2004), doi:10.1016/S0888-3270(03)-00075-X
3. Tandon, N., Choudhury, A.: A review of vibration and acoustic measurement methods for the diction of defects in rolling element bearing. Tribology International 32, 469–480 (1999), doi:10.1016/S0301-679X(99)00077-8
4. Huang, N.E., Shen, Z., Long, S.R.: The Empirical mode decomposition and the Hilbert spectrum for nonlinear and non-stationary time series analysis. Proceedings of the Royal Society of London A454, 903–995 (1998)
5. Liu, B., Riemenschneider, S., Xu, Y.: Gearbox fault diagnosis using empirical mode decomposition and Hilbert spectrum. Mechanical Systems and Signal Processing 20, 718–734 (2006), doi:10.1016/j.ymssp.2005.02.003
6. Huang, N.E., Shen, S.S.P.: Hilbert-Huang Transform and Its Applications, vol. 5, pp. 5–14. World Scientific Publishing, Singapore (2005)

A Novel Method of Abnormal Behaviors Recognition

Ruitai Li[1], Chunfang Zhang[1], and Guanghui Zhong[2]

[1] Mathematics and Information Department Hebei Normal University
Shijiazhuang, Hebei Province, China
[2] Department of physics, Hebei Normal University, Shijiazhuang, Hebei Province, China
Ruitai76@ovi.com

Abstract. We propose a hybrid Bag-of-Words model for classifying and recognizing human abnormal behavior, and present an h-pLSA model for semi-supervised learning and classify video and text information simultaneity. The experiments show some encouraging results, which indicate that the method can be a choice for solving the problem described.

Keywords: Abnormal behavior, Interest points, Bag-of-words, Hybrid Probabilistic Latent Semantic Analysis.

1 Introduction

Human motion analysis is one of the most active research topics in the field of computer vision, which has a number of promising applications, ranging from security to augmented reality. One of the powerful instances is wide distribution of Video Surveillance System (VSS). Recognition of the human abnormal behaviour is one of the most significant purposes of VSS [1], It is desirable to find a method of recognition human abnormal motion in different scenarios.

This paper addresses the computing-costly problem with space-time interest points, which reduce the dimensionality of the motion data space without the loss of its features. And it addresses the problem of learning and recognizing abnormal actions in different scenarios through hybrid Bag-of-Words method using standard surveillance cameras.

The paper is organized as follows. In Section 2, we briefly review some related works, which include abnormal behavior method, interest point method, and topic model. Section 3 describes feature denotation. Codebook formation is described in Section 4. Learning and recognizing the object model by h-pLSA is describe in Section 5. An experimental evaluation of the proposed techniques is presented in Section 6, and the paper concludes a discussion and summary in Section 7.

2 Related Work

Some attempts to automatically detect abnormal behaviors have already been performed. One of the pioneers is Ghallab [2], who has proposed a method of

D. Zeng (Ed.): ICAIC 2011, Part I, CCIS 224, pp. 79–86, 2011.

modeling temporal scenarios to be recognized on-line. More work is carried out by Mecocci [3], who introduces the architecture of an automatic real-time video surveillance system, which can autonomously detect anomalous behavioral events. Boiman et al. [4] try to compose a newly observed image region or a new video segment using chunks of data extracted from previous visual examples.

Recent researches on the major existing methods for abnormal detecting are reviewed [5].However, exact reconstruction 3-D from video is still an unsolved or not a well-solved problem. Therefore, we adopt a motion representation method, which is bag of spatial-temporal interest points. In the learning and classifying stage, a topic model is proposed.

2.1 Interest Point Methods

Now a popular approach in object recognition is based on spatial-temporal interest points and local feature descriptors. Schuldt et al. [6,7,8] train a Support Vector Machine classifier based on those spatial-temporal features for recognizing human actions. Dollar et al. [9] propose a space-time interest point detector based on a set of linear filters, and use these local features with k-nearest neighbor classifier for action recognition.

2.2 Topic Models for Visual Recognition

Recently, successes have been made in adopting generative topic models with Bag-of-Words [8, 10] paradigm for solving various recognition problems. Popular topic models include probabilistic Latent Semantic Analysis (pLSA) [11] and Latent Dirichlet Allocation (LDA). Different human actions are captured by the different topics discovered by either pLSA or LDA.

The optimal abnormal behavior detection should detect suspicious events with a minimal description and perform the detection without assumptive scenario [12], and the most important can recognize more abnormal behavior using the same library. For this goal to be achieved, we develop a hybrid Bag-of-Words model, which is described and evaluated in this paper.

3 Feature Representation

In general, spatial-temporal interest points have turned out to be useful in the human motion categorization task, providing a rich description and powerful representation [9].

As the left of Fig.1 shows, we represent each video sequence as a collection of spatial-temporal words by extracting space-time interest points. Among the available interest point detectors for video data, the interest points obtained using the generalized space-time corner detector is too sparse to characterize many complex videos. To solve that, the separable linear filter method [9] is adopted. We will provide a brief review of it. Assuming a stationary camera or a process that can account for camera motion, separable linear filters are applied to the video to obtain the response function as follows:

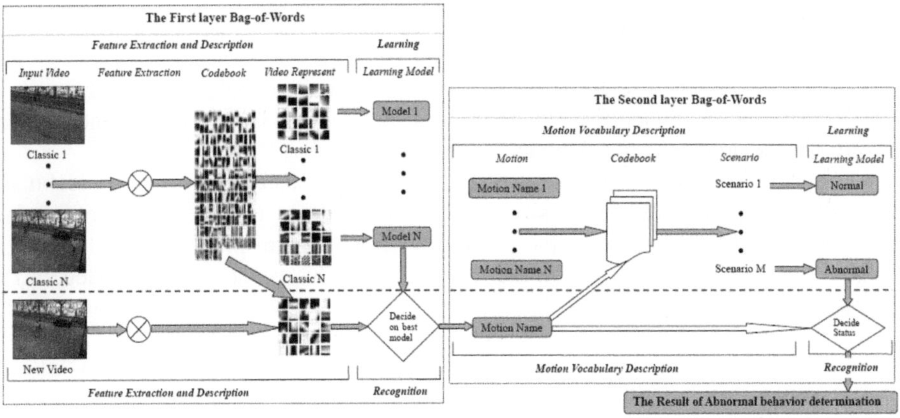

Fig. 1. Flowchart of semi-supervised abnormal action recognition

$$R = (I * g * h_{ev})^2 + (I * g * h_{od})^2 \tag{1}$$

where $g(x, y, t)$ is the 2D Gaussian smoothing kernel, only applied along the spatial dimensions (x, y), h_{ev} and h_{od} are a quadrate pair of 1D Gabor filters applied temporally, which are defined as $h_{ev}(t;\tau,\omega) = -com(2\pi t\omega)\times e^{-t^2/\tau^2}$ and $h_{od}(t;\tau,\omega) = -\sin(2\pi t\omega)\times e^{-t^2/\tau^2}$. The two parameters t and τ correspond to the spatial and temporal scales of the detector respectively. In all the following experiments, we assume $\omega = 4/\tau$, and thus reduce the two number of parameters in the response function R. To handle multiple scales, we must run the detector over a set of spatial and temporal scales. In order to decrease the computation cost, we run the detector using only one scale and rely on the codebook to encode a few changes in scale that are observed in the dataset [13].

Through detecting spatial-temporal interest points, a sparse representation of the video sequences is produced. Small video patches are extracted from each interest point and constitute the local information that is used to learn and recognize object categories. The most important is that the observed local patterns are discriminative enough across object classes, and provide a reasonable feature space, which allows building good human action models. Additionally, this approach relaxes the need of previously common preprocessing steps in global approaches such as background subtraction in [14].

To obtain a descriptor for each spatial-temporal cube, we calculate its brightness gradients in x, y and t three directions. The computed gradients are concatenated to form a vector. The size of the vector is equal to the number of pixels in the cube times the number of smoothing scales times the number of gradients directions. This descriptor is then projected to a lower dimensional space using the principal component analysis dimensionality reduction technique. In the rest of the paper, we will employ results obtained with gradient descriptors [13].

4 Codebook Formation

There are two codebooks in our method. One is video codebook, and the other is text one. All the video sequence words are stored in video codebook, and the motion text words are included in text codebook.

The latent topic models pLSA and LDA rely on the existence of a finite vocabulary of spatial-temporal words with size V. In order to learn the vocabulary of spatial-temporal words, we consider the set of descriptors corresponding to all detected spatial-temporal interest points in the training data. This vocabulary (or codebook) is constructed by clustering using the K -means algorithm and Euclidean distance as the clustering metric. The center of each resulting cluster is defined to be a spatial-temporal word. Thus, each detected interest point can be assigned a unique cluster membership, i.e., a spatial-temporal word, such that a video can be represented as a collection of spatial-temporal words from the codebook. The effect of the codebook size is explored in our experiments. In the text codebook, the latent topic models pLSA and LDA rely on the existence of a finite vocabulary of scenario-motion number with size M .

5 Learning and Recognizing the Anomalous by h-pLSA

We will describe our method for abnormal behavior learning and recognition in different scenarios using hybrid probabilistic Latent Semantic Analysis model (h-pLSA).

5.1 Learning and Recognizing the Text by pLSA

As a practical method for the characterization of word meaning, we know that LSA produces measures of word-word, word-passage and passage-passage relations. The pLSA is a statistical model which has been called aspect model. LSA can be construed in two ways: (1) simply as a practical expedient for obtaining approximate estimates of the contextual usage. (2) as a model of the computational processes and representations underlying substantial portions of the acquisition and utilization of knowledge.

Assume we have a set of $K(k=1,\cdots,K)$ action categories appear in $M(n=1,\cdots,M)$ kinds of different scenarios. The corpus of actions is summarized in an M by K co-occurrence table, where $M(s_i,z_j)$ stores the number of occurrences of an action scenarios word s_i in a video z_j . And there is a latent topic variable r_k associated with each occurrence of a scenario-motion word s_i in a scenario z_j . The topic corresponds to the action abnormal or normal. The joint probability $P(s_i,z_j,r_k)$ is assumed to have the form of the graphical model shown in vertical direction of Fig.2. Nodes are random variables. Shaded ones are observed and other ones are unobserved. The plates indicate repetitions. In the context of human action categorization, k represents action categories, r is recognition abnormal or normal result, and s are scenario-motion categories.

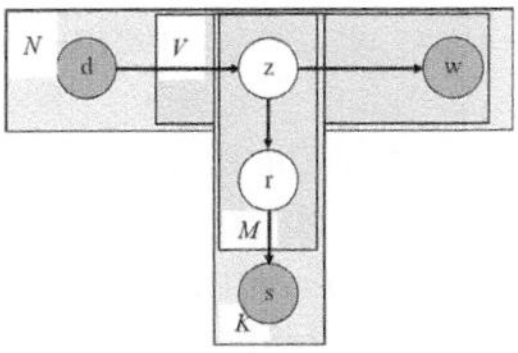

Fig. 2. The h-pLS A model

5.2 Recognizing the Anomalous by h-pLSA

In Fig.2 we assume that the number of action categories in horizontal direction is equal to the number of motion categories in the vertical direction. Finally we draw the conclusion:

$$Result = \arg \max_{m} P(r_m, \frac{P(w_i \mid z_k)P(z_k \mid d_j)}{\sum_{l=1}^{K} P(w_i \mid z_l)P(z_l \mid d_j)}) \qquad (2)$$

6 Experiment

In order to test the feasibility of our approach to abnormal action detection, we experiment with a set of videos recorded by the VSS in five different scenarios, which are meeting room, street, beside the car, lobby, and laboratory.

In the process of building the video codebook, we make use of our algorithm on two datasets: KTH human motion dataset [7], and Weizmann human action dataset [14]. The KTH human motion dataset contains six types of human actions (walking, jogging, running, boxing, hand waving and hand clapping) performed several times by 25 subjects in four different scenarios: outdoors, outdoors with scale variation, outdoors with different clothes and indoors. The Weizmann human action dataset contains 83 video sequences showing nine different people, each performing nine different actions. Representative frames from each datasets are shown in Fig.3.

Fig. 3. Example frame from KTH and Weizmann datasets

We extract interest points and describe the corresponding spatial-temporal patches with the procedure described in Section 3. The detector parameters are set to t =1.5 and τ =2. Each spatial-temporal patch is described with the concatenated vector of its space-time gradients. Then, the descriptors are projected to a lower dimensional space.

In order to build the codebook, we build spatial-temporal codeword using only eight videos of each action thirteen subjects. We keep these sequences out of the training and testing sets to avoid contamination in the data.

Following this, we learn and recognize human action categories using the h-pLSA. In order to test the video codebook efficiency about the combination of the two datasets for the recognition task, we test the two datasets respectively. The confusion matrix of a thirteen-class h-pLSA model using the combination datasets including 3900 codeword is given in Fig.4. Our algorithm automatically assigns each test sequence to one of the action classes that are discovered during training. Each row in the confusion matrix corresponds to the ground truth class, and each column corresponds to the assigned cluster. Also, note that in order to maintain cluster correspondence between columns across different runs, each column is labeled with the majority label of videos that are assigned to the cluster. This test shows we can adopt the combination codebook with other new videos. We also test the effect of the number of combination codeword on recognition accuracy on both two datasets, as illustrated in Fig.5. It shows some dependence of the recognition accuracy on the size of the codebook.

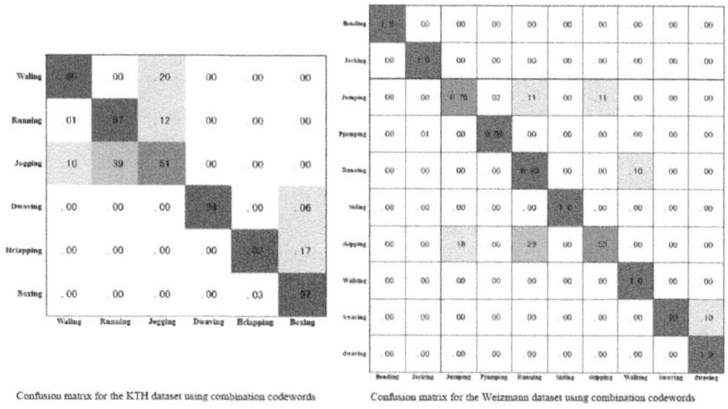

Fig. 4. Confusion matrix for the KTH and Weizmann dataset

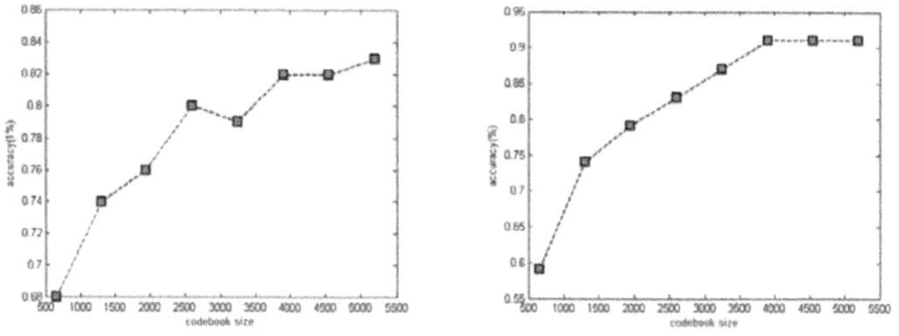

KTH dataset Weizmann dataset

Fig. 5. Classification accuracy vs. combination codebook size

In the text learning and recognizing stage, we learn the knowledge from the surveillance, where the abnormal or normal behavior will be defined. From different scenarios long videos, experts count all kinds of behaviors in a particular scene, at the same time define actions normal and abnormal. In this way, we can get a set of action categories happening.

Being established the video and text codebooks, we test our new surveillance video. We prefer the thirteen actions are corresponding to the probability of normal or abnormal behavior in a special scene, and the other action is represented by the thirteen movements. The result of our method not only can directly recognize the thirteen actions in different scenarios, but also can identify the indirect definition actions. The recognition result in three scenarios is shown in Fig. 6.

scenario	Appear action	Expert conclusion	Our method result	coherence
Meeting room	Walking	Normal	Normal	Yes
	hand clapping	Normal	Normal	Yes
	swaving	Normal	Normal	Yes
	bending	Normal	Normal	Yes
	boxing	Abnormal	Abnormal	Yes
	p-jumping	Abnormal	Abnormal	Yes
	jacking	Abnormal	Abnormal	Yes
	sliding	normal	Abnormal	No
	skipping	Abnormal	Abnormal	Yes
	jogging	Abnormal	Abnormal	Yes
	jumping	Abnormal	Abnormal	Yes
	dwaving	Abnormal	Abnormal	Yes
	running	Abnormal	Abnormal	Yes

Error=1

scenario	Appear action	Expert conclusion	Our method result	coherence
street	Walking	Normal	Normal	Yes
	hand clapping	Normal	Normal	Yes
	swaving	Normal	Normal	Yes
	bending	Normal	Normal	Yes
	boxing	Normal	Abnormal	No
	p-jumping	Abnormal	Abnormal	Yes
	jacking	Abnormal	Abnormal	Yes
	sliding	Abnormal	Abnormal	Yes
	skipping	Normal	Abnormal	No
	jogging	Normal	Normal	Yes
	jumping	Abnormal	Abnormal	Yes
	dwaving	Abnormal	Abnormal	Yes
	running	Normal	Normal	Yes

Error=2

scenario	Appear action	Expert conclusion	Our method result	coherence
beside the car	Walking	Normal	Normal	Yes
	hand clapping	Normal	Normal	Yes
	swaving	Abnormal	Normal	No
	bending	Abnormal	Normal	No
	boxing	Abnormal	Abnormal	Yes
	p-jumping	Abnormal	Abnormal	Yes
	jacking	Normal	Abnormal	No
	sliding	Normal	Abnormal	No
	skipping	Abnormal	Abnormal	Yes
	jogging	Normal	Normal	Yes
	jumping	Abnormal	Abnormal	Yes
	dwaving	Normal	Normal	Yes
	running	Normal	Normal	Yes

Error=4

Fig. 6. The recognition in different scenarios

From the recognition result, we get the 86.2% correct recognition rate. In the general scenes, it is easy to judge the abnormal action, but in some scenes of artificial intelligence (beside a car), the judge of abnormal movements is not very accurate. It is difficult to compare different abnormal action recognition systems. Each system has been designed for a certain purpose. Fig.6 indicates that the hybrid Bag-of –Words method can be a choice for solving the abnormal recognition.

7 Conclusions

In contrast to most contributions to visual gait analysis, we have presented a semi-supervised learning and recognizing approach, i.e., a double-layer Bag-of-Words model for human abnormal action recognition. Experimental results show that the recognition performance using our approach is on par with the current state-of-the-art results obtained by fully supervised training. Our algorithm can also detect multiple actions in complex motion sequences containing multiple actions. The results are promising, though we acknowledge the lack of large and challenging video datasets to thoroughly test our algorithm, which poses an interesting topic for future investigation. Currently, we have been working to demonstrate the applicability and reliability of our abnormal recognition scheme, unconstrained real world settings. In addition, we plan to further investigate the possibilities of using a unified framework by combining generative and discriminative models for human action recognition.

References

1. Chen, Y., Liang, G., Lee, K.K., et al.: Abnormal behavior detection by multi-SVM-based Bayesian network. In: Proc. Int. Conf. Information Acquisition, pp. 298–303 (2007)
2. Ghallab: On Chronicles. Representation “On-line Recognition and Learning”. In: Proc. 5th International Conference on Principles of Knowledge Representation and Reasoning, Cambridge, pp. 597–606 (1996)
3. Mecocci, A., Pannozzo, M., Fumarola, A.: Automatic Detection of Anomalous Behavioural Events for Advanced Real-Time Video Surveilance. In: Proc. International Symposium on Computational Intelligence for Measurement Systems and Applications, Lugano, pp. 187–192 (2003)
4. Boiman, O., Irani, M.: Detecting irregularities in images and in video. In: Proc. IEEE int. conf. Computer Vision, pp. 462–469 (2005)
5. Hu, W., Tan, T., Wang, L., et al.: A survey on visual surveillance of object motion and behaviors. IEEE Trans. System, Man, And Cybernetics 34(3), 334–352
6. Schuldt, C., Laptev, L., Caputo, B.: Recognizing human actions: a local SVM approach. In: IEEE International Conference on Pattern Recognition, pp. 32–36
7. Nowozin, S., Bakir, G., Tsuda, K.: Discriminative subsequence mining for action classification. In: IEEE International Conference on Computer Vision, pp. 1–8
8. Niebles, J.C., Fei-Fei, L.: A hierarchical model of shape and appearance for human action classification. In: IEEE Computer Society Conference on Computer Vision and Pattern Recognition, pp. 1–8
9. Dollar, P., Rabaud, V., Cottrell, G., et al.: Behavior recognition via sparse spatio-temporal features. In: Proc. 2nd Joint IEEE International Workshop on Visual Surveillance and Performance Evaluation of Tracking and Surveillance, pp. 65–72
10. Sivic, J., Russell, B.C., Efros, A.A., et al.: Discovering objects and their location in images. In: Proc. IEEE International Conference on Computer Vision, pp. 370–377 (2005)
11. Hofmann, T.: Probabilistic latent semantic indexing. In: Proc. Twenty-Second Annual International Conference on Research and Development in Information Retrieval, pp. 50–57
12. Duque, D., Santos, H., Cortez, P.: Prediction of abnormal Behaviors for intelligent video surveillance system. In: Proc. IEEE int. conf. Computational Intelligence and Data Mining, pp. 362–367 (2007)
13. Niebles, J.C., Wang, H., Fei-Fei, L.: Unsupervised learning of human action categories using spatial-temporal words. International Journal of Computer Vision 79(3), 299–318
14. Blank, M., Gorelick, L., Shechtman, E., Irani, M., et al.: Actions as space-time shapes. In: Proceedings of the Tenth IEEE International Conference on Computer Vision, pp. 1395–1402

Research and Implementation of the Uniform Authentication Based on Web Service

Songhao Jia[1], Jinliang Guo[1], Cai Yang[1], and Xiaoxia Liu[2]

[1] Department of Computer and Information Technology NanYang Normal University NanYang, Henan Province, China

[2] Department of Information Science and Technology NorthWestern University Xi'an, Shanxi Province, China

song1735@sina.com

Abstract. In order to improve the efficiency of distributed environment in identity authentication, this paper presents a scheme about the unity identity authentication in web service application system. Designment of the scheme adoptes the Cookie, SSL technology and opening interface, provides the user identity authentication between local and remote systems, and ensures user login security at anywhere and gives the access authority. Experimental results shows that the scheme in data transmission of real-time, synchronicity and efficiency, achieves good effect and improves the web application security. This solution will have good practical value and application prospect.

Keywords: web service, the uniform authentication, SOAP, Kerberos protocol.

1 Introduction

Unified identity authentication is a kind of efficient and safe authentication mechanism of network, the user only need login one time in the network of identity authentication, then can access the network resources by unauthorized use of seamless other resources, and don't need to actively participate in subsequent identity authentication[1]. Target of the uniform authentication is unified dispatching user information, just login once can log on to all authorized transparent.

Web Service is a software application through the URL references, the application and the interface which are bound by definition, described with XML, and can achieve very good interactive platform of different information systems[2]. This paper references Web Service and Kerberos bills mechanism design and implement a system which is suitable for the current of the unified identity authentication enterprise management system[3]. Through the Cookie technology and instruments, it provides authentication interface, combining the identity authentication reunification of the original system authentication module. Server system is divided into two parts: server module and agent module. The server module completes user identity authentication and bill of the issuance, and realizes service bills from the service module to acting module securely by RSA encryption. The agent module is

D. Zeng (Ed.): ICAIC 2011, Part I, CCIS 224, pp. 87–92, 2011.

responsible for handling user's request, according to the different requests for interacting with server module.

2 System Design

Without modifying application system (including WEB application system and C/S structure application system), users can freely choose the lead agency and the agent or combination. By simply configuration, the scheme can use uniform identity authentication function. Login process of the unified identity authentication system is shown in figure 1. The process is: 1) Entry module interceptes user access request, inquires the conversation and the URL in user identity information, and judges whether the user has logined. 2) If you can get the correct user information, explaining the user has logged in, then the user can enter directly. 3) If not, will transmit the request to login server processing. 4) The login server receives the request, calls forwarding authentication login module and inquires the login log. 5) If it finds out that user is not login, then turns to the user login module. 6) If the login successfully, the login server will return the request and the user's identity information to application sites. 7) After the application gateway module receives turning request from login server, according to the information temporarily saved in cookie, identifies the identity information true or false, namely, whether is from trustful login server. 8) If the source of information is true, then enters the site, otherwise, to step 3).

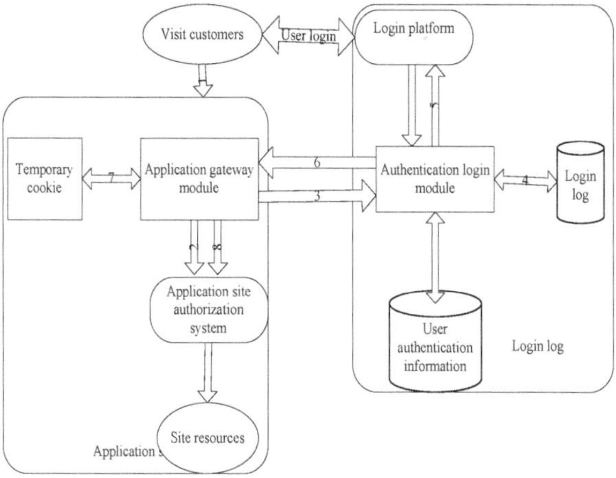

Fig. 1. Unified identity authentication system flowcharts

2.1 Server Module Design

As an independent certification service center, unified identity authentication server provides service to login, and concentrates in this module implements unified authentication[4]. The server is divided into three modules, request processing module, bills licensing services (TGS) module and management module(TMM). TGS authenticates user and issues cookie bills for the legitimate users. And TMM mainly manages and stores the TGT(Ticket Grangting Ticket) and ST(Service Ticket) .

2.2 Ticket's Design

Identity authentication of the unified process is designed to use two kinds of instruments: TGT and ST. These two kinds of instruments are produced by the TMM, managed and stored by the TMM. They are the certificate for client accessing web application. To achieve unified identity login, it will need to keep in communication between the client and the server. Because HTTP is a stateless communications, we use the Cookie of browser to realize the function, and store the simple logo of TGT.

2.3 Agent Module's Design

The agency module interceptes the user request, according to the parameters, decides to communicate with server's some one module, and verifies whether the user protects web resources through server validation. Agent module chart is shown in figure 2.

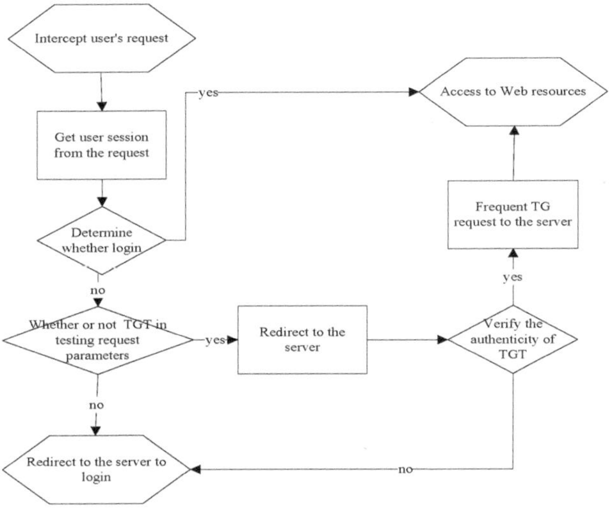

Fig. 2. Agent module working flowcharts

3 System Implementation

3.1 Request Processing Module's Implementation

Request processing module is the entry to the server, all visit to server will pass this module. According to the analysis of the parameters, the request processing module dispatches the request to the appropriate module. The scheme is: design a request of distribution class for the request processing module RequstDispense. In the class, there is a method to deal with all request as the access server's entry. The method is: public void doGet (HttpServletRequest request, HttpServletResponse response).

3.2 TGS Module'S Implementation

TGS module mainly provides a unified identity authentication, combined with the original verification method, and uses the interface technology in Java. The module implements the Authentication class, and it is a interface. The interface defines a method public boolean authenticate (ServletRequest request, String username, String pwd) for realization of the application. The method is used to authenticatethe user identity in web application, successful returns true, otherwise returns false.

3.3 TMM Module'S Implementation

TMM module is used to generate and storage instrument. The scheme designs an abstract class Ticket that represents access services instrument. It contains four methods. The getService ( ) method returns the service of the user requested, namely, the service of the requested URL. The getId ( ) method is used to return ticket service of the logo. The isValid ( ) method is used to verify the effectiveness of the TGT. The CreatTicket ( ) method is used to create the ticket of services.

4 System Security

The data exchanged among authentication services are based on SOAP, a special protocol of Web Service. The SOAP is a kind of XML data formats[5]. The system uses random numbers to avoid replay attack[6]. Processes are as follows: the client does not generate authentication, and directly sends the encrypted bill to the server. The server correctly decrypts bills, then gets proper session decryption key Kc_server. So the client and the server can use Kc_server in request/response mechanism to avoid replay attack. Figure 3 describes the process that the server certificates the client by request/response mechanism.

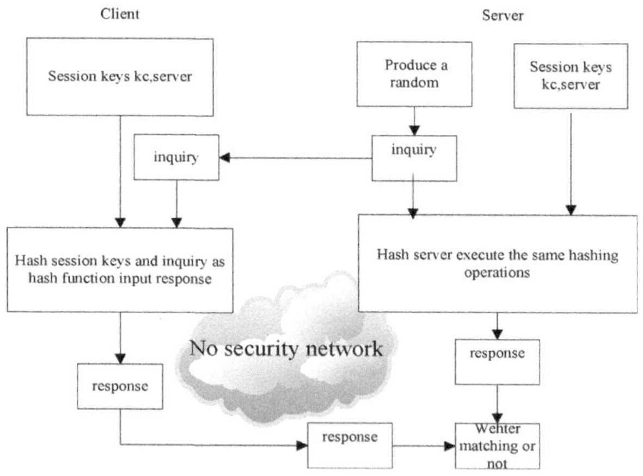

Fig. 3. Avoid replay attack graph based on the random inquiries/response mechanism

Specific process is described as follows: (1) The server creates a random number, and sends to the client as cleartext. (2) After receives inquiries, the client uses the request and session keys Kc_server to calculate with hashing function, and sends the calculating result to the server as a response. (3)The server decryption bills get session key Kc_server, hash calculation random number and Kc_server, then gets the response, same with the client.(4) Compare the two response, if match, then essere certificate.

If the client certificates the server, using similar authentication, the difference between the client and server validation process is that they need exchange position. The client generates random numbers, and the server sends the encryption to the client.

5 System Test

In this system, we establish a remote laboratory between NanYang Nomal University and Northwestern University. And it is realized sharing of the experimental equipment. We put the system to web server, through the two schools of common test results, and feed back the real data of experiment. The test environment is: authentication server, application server, encryption/decryption server, user information database SQL Server2005. Testing results can be seen from table 1, identity authentication need about 0.492 s, if the authentication server and application server has better hardware configuration, will be shorten the time of authentication. Compared with the existing system, this scheme shortens at least half the authentication time. It conforms to the rapid response system requirements, will have great practical value.

Table 1. The identity authentication required time

Test	Authentication server time(ms)	Application Server authentication time(ms)	Finishing authentication time (ms)
1	478	14	523
2	492	14	538
3	523	15	549
4	505	13	550
5	462	14	491
Average	492	14	530

6 Summary

Unified identity authentication system provides uniform certification for users, establishes unified integration platform which based on the role and personalized information access, and improves work efficiency[7]. Refered to Kerberos bills mechanism, this paper presentes a scheme about Web application and service supporting environment of unity identity authentication system. The scheme adopts the Cookie, technology and open SSL and validation of the complex interface to realize the unification, reduces the complexity of the identity authentication system, which makes the system have better robustness. Through the remote test of "NanYang Nomal University - Northwestern University" shows that this plan has a good application prospect.

References

1. Jin, W., Li, P.: Solution Schema for Single Location Invalidation Based on CAS Cluster. Computer Engineering 1, 51–54 (2010)
2. Deng, Y., Cheng, X.: System design of mobile cross-domain single sign-on. Computer Engineering and Design 8, 1667–1672 (2010)
3. Hu, Y., Wang, S.: Research on Kerberos identity authentication protocol based on hybrid system. Journal of Computer Applications 6, 1659–1661 (2009)
4. Ren, Y., Gu, D.: Efficient hierarchical identity based signature scheme in the standard model. Wuhan University Journal of Natural Sciences 6, 665–669 (2008)
5. Sun, S.W., Xia, H.S.: The unified identity authentication system across schools on based Shibboleth and SAML. Microcomputer & Its Applications 5, 65–68 (2010)
6. Chen, T.-y., Xie, D.-q., Yang, X.-h., Yang, H.-t.: Research and implementation of security SSO authentication model based on SAML and XKMS. Application Research of Computers 3, 1019–1021 (2010)
7. Wan, C.-j., Li, C.-y.: Trust-oriented Single Sign-On in Open Network Environment. Computer Engineering 3, 148–151 (2010)

Computer-Aided Composition Method of Children's Song Based on Grammatical Evolution

Zhang Dakun, Zhang Chang, and Jiang Guiyuan

School of Computer Science & Software Engineering Institute
Tianjin Polytechnic University, 300387, Tianjin, China
zhang.dakun0909@gmail.com

Abstract. Computer-aided music creation has become a key research direction. Grammatical Evolution (abbreviation GE) as a new evolutionary computation technique based on formal grammar is applied for composing children's songs. A children's song composition method based on GE is proposed in this paper and proves to be feasible and effective with experiments. This method provides a viable and meaningful idea for computer-aided music creation.

Keywords: computer-aided music creation, grammatical evolution, children's song composition.

1 Introduction to Grammatical Evolution

Grammatical Evolution (abbreviation GE) is a grammar-based form of Genetic Programming. It marries principles from molecular biology to the representational power of formal grammars. In GE, a BNF definition is used to describe the output language to be produced by the system [1]. The genotype is used to map the start symbol as defined in the Grammar onto terminals by reading codons to generate a corresponding integer value, from which an appropriate production rule is selected by using the following mapping function in (1):

$$\text{Rule} = c \mod r \tag{1}$$

where c is the codon integer value, and r is the number of rule choices for the current non-terminal symbol. Consider the following rule from the given grammar, i.e., given the non-terminal <bool>, which describes the set of boolean operators that can be used, there are four production rules to select from. As can be seen, the choices are effectively labelled with integers counting from zero.

```
<biop>::=and     (0)
        |or      (1)
        |xor     (2)
        |nand    (3)
```

D. Zeng (Ed.): ICAIC 2011, Part I, CCIS 224, pp. 93–99, 2011.

If we assume the codon being read produces the integer 6, then 6 mod 4 = 2 would select rule (2) xor. That is, <bool> is replaced with xor. Each time a production rule has to be selected to transform a non-terminal, another codon is read. In this way the system traverses the genome. According to this process, a program, expressions and programs of arbitrary complexity may be evolved [2].

One advantage of GE is that the search space for the problem is narrowed to reflect the problem domain, increasing the speed and accuracy of the algorithm [3].

2 The Design and Implement of Children's Song Composition Algorithm

2.1 General thought

There are structural rules to some extent in oriental and western music. Generative grammars have been used extensively in music theory and analysis. Evolutionary computation for automatic composition has been widely used also, with some successes [4-5]. Therefore, grammatical evolution can be used to composing children's songs. According to features of children's songs, a children's songs composition method based on GE is put forward.

Children's song composition method based on GE is an iterated process, which has 9 basic steps as follows:

1) Defining the BNF reflecting features of children's songs;
2) Designing the fitness function;
3) Deciding generic operations such as selection, crossover and mutation. Setting parameters such as population scale M , maximal number of evolution generation T , crossover probability p_c and mutation probability p_m ;
4) According to the population scale parameter, the initial genotype population is randomly generated.
5) Genotype-phenotype mapping process;
6) Fitness function evaluates phenotypes;
7) Arriving at the maximal number of evolution generation turn to 9), otherwise move to next;
8) Generic operating to genotype, the next generation of population is created;
9) Translating the phenotype into a playable children's song

2.2 Detailed Design

1) Children's song BNF definition

A BNF reflecting features of children's song such as tempo, audio effects and range etc. should be defined firstly. The tempo terminal symbol in this BNF can be replaced with 5 forms: *slow*(50), *medium-speed slower*(100), *medium-speed*(125), *medium-speed faster*(150) and *fast*(200). The audio effect terminal symbol in this BNF can be substituted with 10 forms: *piano*(0), *celesta*(8), *xylophone*(13), *accordion*(21), *violin*(40), *cello*(42), *harp*(46), *trumpet*(56), *oboe*(68) and *bassoon*(70). The tone terminal symbol in this BNF can be replaced with 11 forms: $b(59)$、$c^1(60)$、$d^1(62)$、$e^1(64)$ 、$f^1(65)$、$g^1(67)$、$a^1(69)$ 、$b^1(71)$、$c^2(72)$、$d^2(74)$ 、$e^2(76)$. Consequently, the BNF is defined as follows:

$< composition >::= TEMPO < tempo >< style >$

$< tempo >::= 50 | 100 | 125 | 150 | 200$

$< style >::= STYLE < style >< melody >$

$< style >::= INSTRUMENT < audio >< repeat >$

$< audio >::= 0 | 8 | 13 | 21 | 40 | 42 | 46 | 56 | 68 | 70$

$< repeat >::= true | false$

$< melody >::=< 4Tones >< 4Tones > ENDPHRASE$

$< 4Tones >::=< tone >< tone >< tone >< tone >$

$< tone >::= 59 | 60 | 62 | 64 | 65 | 67 | 69 | 71 | 72 | 74 | 76$

2) Initial genotype population generation and genotype-phenotype mapping process

A group of integer strings as genotype population is randomly generated; each integer string is a genotype individual. According to the BNF and genotype-phenotype mapping process mentioned before, the phenotype of children's song is obtained.

3) Fitness function

An automatic fitness evaluation method is designed in this paper. The fitness function is composed with three parts: E_{tempo}, $E_{tone}(i)$ and E_{melody}. E_{tempo} evaluates the tempo of songs. $E_{tone}(i)$ estimates tones in songs and E_{melody} takes charge of songs' melody. So the definition of fitness function can be represented as in(2):

$$E = E_{tempo} + E_{tone}(i) + E_{melody} \tag{2}$$

a) Definition of E_{tempo}

E_{tempo} represents the evaluation of the songs' tempo with the definition form as in(3):

$$E_{tempo} = TEMPO \bullet W_{tempo} \tag{3}$$

Where TEMPO is song's tempo value and W_{tempo} is tempo's weight.

b) Definition of $E_{tone}(i)$

$E_{tone}(i)$ represents the evaluation of tones in songs in(4), including two parts: one is $E_{Interval}$;the other is $E_{suspend}$.

$$E_{tone}(i) = E_{Interval} + E_{suspend} \tag{4}$$

Where $E_{Interval}$ evaluates intervals between tones and $E_{suspend}$ is responsible for suspended tones in songs.

c) Definition of E_{melody}

E_{melody} represents the evaluation of song's melody in(5).

$$E_{melody} = |\sum_{2}^{n} DIF(i-1,i)| \bullet W_{melody} \quad (5)$$

In (5), i is one tone, n is the number of tones in this song. $|\sum_{2}^{n} DIF(i-1,i)|$ is the absolute value of the sum of pitch difference between two adjacent tones $i-1$ and i .W_{melody} is melody's weight.

4) Genetic operations

There are three operations in this composition method: selection, crossover and mutation. The selection operation is realized with the combination of random tournament selection and simplified elitist selection. The crossover operation is one-point crossover. Taking an integer value to replace a codon in a genotype is mutation. After many experiments, in order to acquire a smooth and steady best-fitness-value curve, the crossover probability is set as 0.9 and mutation probability is set as 0.01. The selection of these two probability values will be discussed in section three.

5) Translation

It has been proved that the maximal number of evolution generation set as 150 can satisfy the convergence of children's song composition method based on GE at faster speed. Hence, before reaching to the maximal number of evolution generation, step2), step3) and step4) loop, and then the final children's song phenotype as follows is obtained:

TEMPO 150 STYLE basic4Bar INSTRUMENT 0.0 13 false 64 72 60 64 69 60 62 74 ENDPHRASE

Translation program divides the whole phenotype into a string consisted a series of tokens. Then, it translates this string by setting song's tempo, audio effect and generating notes until getting a playable children's song.

3 Analysis and Selection of Genetic Parameters

3.1 Analysis of Genetic Parameters

Population scale M and maximal number of evolution generation T have their recommended values, that is, M from 20 to 100, T from 100 to 1000. In order to ensure the running speed of software, population scale M and maximal number of evolution generation T in this algorithm are set as 60 and 150. Besides, crossover probability p_c has its recommended range as 0.4-0.99 and mutation probability p_m also has its range as 0.001-0.1. There are many experiments for getting a group of reasonable crossover and mutation probability parameters. Four of them are listed as follows:

1) Experiment 1 Population scale M is set as 60, maximal number of evolution generation T is set as 150. Crossover probability p_c and mutation probability p_m are smaller values, that is, 0.55 and 0.02. The best-fitness-value curve is shown in Fig.1.

2) Experiment 2 Population scale M is set as 60, maximal number of evolution generation T is set as 150. Crossover probability p_c is a smaller value 0.55, but mutation probability p_m is a bigger value 0.08. The best-fitness-value curve is shown in Fig.1.

3) Experiment 3 Population scale M is set as 60, maximal number of evolution generation T is set as 150. Crossover probability p_c is a bigger value 0.85, but mutation probability p_m is a smaller value 0.02. The best-fitness-value curve is shown in Fig.1.

4) Experiment 4 Population scale M is set as 60, maximal number of evolution generation T is set as 150. Crossover probability p_c and mutation probability p_m are bigger values, that is, 0.85 and 0.08. The best-fitness-value curve is shown in Fig.1.

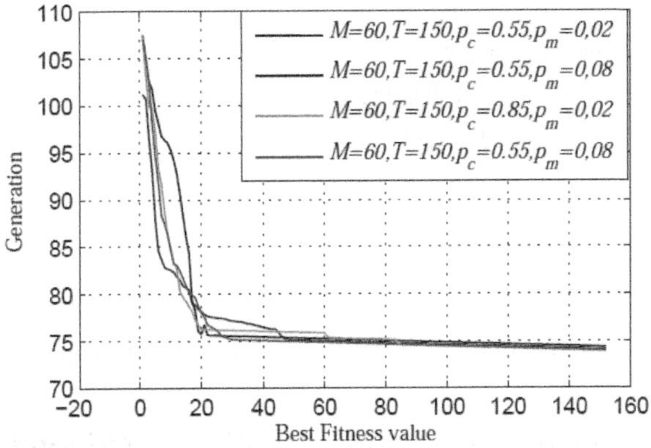

Fig. 1. The best-fitness-value curves in different crossover and mutation probability parameters

3.2 Selection of Genetic Parameters

1) Selection of crossover probability Comparing Fig.1(a) with Fig.1(c), when mutation probability is smaller(0.02), the crossover probability is bigger and the best-fitness-value curve is more smoothly and more steadily; Comparing Fig.1(b) with Fig.1(d), when mutation probability is bigger(0.08), the crossover probability is bigger and the best-fitness-value curve is more smoothly and more steadily. Therefore, in order to obtain a smooth and steady best-fitness-value curve, the crossover probability should be set as a bigger value, for example 0.9.

2) Selection of mutation probability Comparing Fig.1(a) with Fig.1(b), when crossover probability is smaller(0.55), the mutation probability is smaller and the best-fitness-value curve is more smoothly and more steadily; Comparing Fig.1(c) with Fig.1(d), when crossover probability is bigger(0.85), the mutation probability is smaller and the best-fitness-value curve is more smoothly and more steadily.

Therefore, in order to obtain a smooth and steady best-fitness-value curve, the mutation probability should be set as a smaller value, for example 0.01.

From the above, the genetic parameters in this algorithm are set as: Population scale M is 60; maximal number of evolution generation T is 150; crossover probability p_c is 0.9; mutation probability p_m is 0.01.

4 Results and Its Analysis

4.1 Experiment Results

After many experiments, the parameters of method are set as follows: the population scale parameter M is 60, the maximal number of evolution generation parameter T is 150, crossover probability p_c is 0.9, and mutation probability p_m is 0.01. Using Java programming language to realize this method, the software running results is showed in Fig.2.

Fig. 2. Children's song based GE

The Fig.2 indicates that the song generated from GE method is consistent with features of children's song. The interval is reasonable; the range is appropriate and there is less suspended sound. The whole melody is harmonious and stable, which is suitable for children.

4.2 Results Analysis

In the process of evolution, the average and best fitness value turn to be smaller and smaller, given in Fig.3. In this figure, the x-coordinate represents the number of evolution generation; the y-coordinate represents fitness values. Solid line is the best fitness value curve and dotted line is the average fitness value curve.

Fig.3. shows that, before the method runs to tenth generation, that is, the average- and best- fitness-value curves arrive at point A, the average and best fitness value decrease fast as well as their closeness of fit is low. In this process, the convergence speed is fast. From tenth to about fortieth generation, the average- and best-fitness-value curves between point A and B, the average and best fitness value decrease steadily as well as their closeness of fit is better. In this process, the convergence speed is slower. From fortieth to one hundred and fiftieth generations, which is the end condition of the method, the average and best fitness value curves pass point B, the average and best fitness value change smoothly as well as their closeness of fit is the best. In this process, the method is convergent and a satisfactory running result can be obtained.

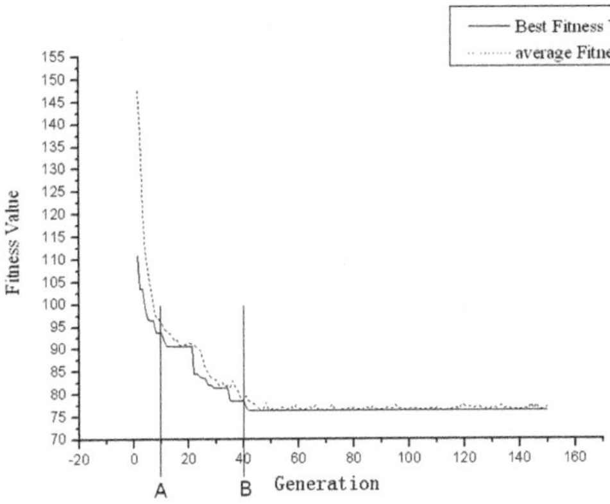

Fig. 3. Average and best fitness value variation curve during evolution

5 Conclusion

In this paper, a children's song composition method based on grammatical evolution is proposed. With analyzing the running result, it has been proved to feasible and effective. In future, some BNF for other music styles can be researched in order to compose corresponding music. Also, a fitness function suitable for evaluating general music can be designed. In addition, grammatical evolution is a new evolutionary computation method, which has good prospects of research and development. It may solve many problems and should be used in other fields.

References

1. O'Neill, M., Ryan, C.: Grammatical evolution:evolutionary automatic programming in an arbitrary language. Kluwer Academic Publishers, Dordrecht (2003)
2. GEVA - Grammatical Evolution in Java (2008), `http://ncra.ucd.ie/geva`
3. O'Neill, M., Brabazon, A.: Recent Adventures in Grammatical Evolution, `http://ncra.ucd.ie/papers/cms2005ge.pdf`
4. Jia, C.: Research and Application of Genetic Algorithm for Computer Aided Musie Composition. Shandong Normal University, Shandong (2007)
5. Yali, G.: Guqin Jiauzi notation Music'Auto Composition Based on Gendic Algorithm. Xiamen University, Fujian (2009)

Decision Making Technique of Processing Technology

Zou Qing-hua

School of Mechanical and Electronic Engineering, Wuhan Textile University,
Wuhan, 430073, China
ZOU7364@126.com

Abstract. Has discussed Decision Making Technique of Processing Technology(DMTPT), apply the theories of both value engineering and operations research, having obtained optimal design indexes for either individual or comprehensive processing technology. The key computer program of Hungary's algorithm for optimal design of technology has been given.

Keywords: technology, optimum, value, function, distribution, Hungary's algorithm.

1 Standard and Steps of Decision Making Technique of Processing Technology(DMTPT)

Decision Making Technique of Processing Technology(DMTPT) is an kind of optimal design of processing technology (ODPT), ODPT is a systematic programming process in which both methods and processes of processing technology are comprehensively applied. It is also one of the important links which we develop and perfect the system of modern industrial production.

ODPT that is executed is to take the maximum value index (VI) of the technology as the standard . VI is equal to the ratio between the function index (Fl) and the cost index (CI), or: VI==FI/CI. Centreing on the analyses with FI, CI and VI, we make ODPT according to the following steps: (1) Work out the technological plans of the workpice, give out both necessary classification of the functions and strict score of the functional importance degree to all processes in the plans, in order that the functions could possess the definite quantified value. (2) Define the technology for the best individual function (TBIF) on the basis of the step (1). (3) Optimize out the technology for the best comprehensive function (TBCF) on the basis of TBIF.

Use illustration 1 as an example for applying the steps above mentioned.

2 Work Out the Technological Plans of the Workpice

Work out the typical technological plans as shown fig 2. By a. b. c. d. e. f. in fig 2 are meant the different machining processes.

D. Zeng (Ed.): ICAIC 2011, Part I, CCIS 224, pp. 100–108, 2011.

a: a_l—Turn (drill and expand centre hole). b: a_l—Drill (drill centre hole). C:Turn(top,.bottom, cylindrical surfaces, drill centre hole)—Drill (4 small holes)—Benchworking(grind, file 4 sides). d: d_l—Turn (drill and expand centre hole).e:e_l—Drill(centre hole). f:e_l—Turn (drill and expand centre hole), a_l. d_l. e_l see table 2.

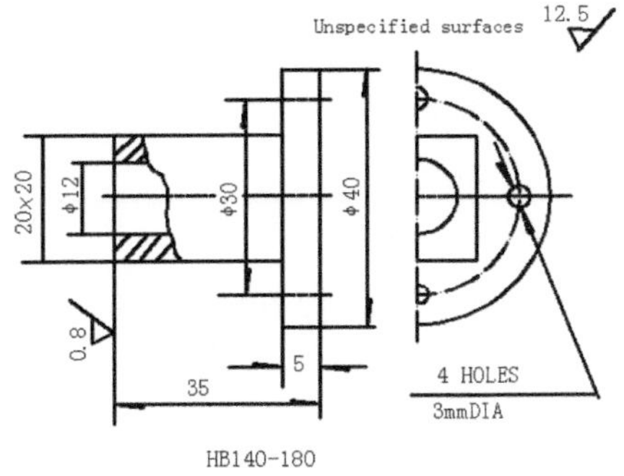

Fig. 1. Pedestal

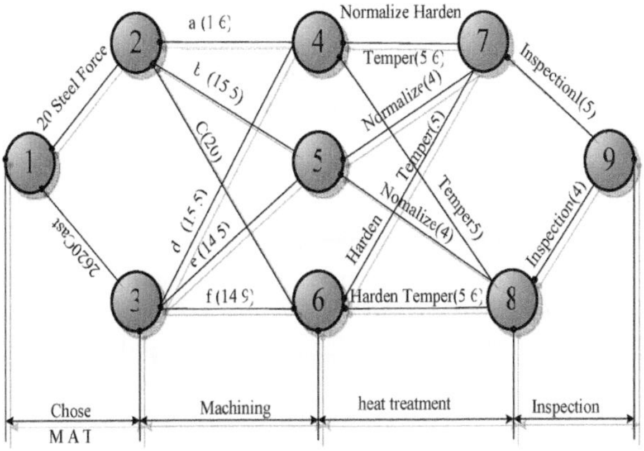

Fig. 2. Process network chart of pedestal The numerals in fig 2 are the production cost (dollar)

3 Importance Degree Index(IDI) of Function

Apply the Force Decision (F.D) method to evaluate IDI(or:wi)

Let it supposed that every technology of the pedestal in fig 1 should satisfy four functions such as the product quality etc., and that the more important functions would score 2 points, the unimportant ones 0 point, the same important ones 1 point by contrasting any one of the functions with the rest one by one each other, resulted score see table 1.

Table 1. Evaluating Importance Degree Index (IDI) of function by F.D.

No. Designation	Method Contrast,	Evaluating points I	II	III	IV	Scored points	Amended points	IDI (Wi)
I	Product		1	2	2	5	6	0.38
II	Production	1		1	2	4	5	0.31
III	Reliability	0	1		2	3	4	0.25
IV	Production	0	0	0		0	1	0.06
Total							16	

4 Optimal Design of Technology for the Best Individual Function (TBIF)

The technological plans in fig 2 could be divided into different sub—Processes, by the sub—process is meant various group processes with different operational sequences. See table 2 (FI table). The number of sub—processes divided might be decided by the requirement in the practical production. The evaluating Points (EP) and scoring points (SP) in table 2 might be obtained by both theory of the time series analysis (TTSA) and the hundred—mark scoring system[1-3]. Analytical procedure of the stochastic evaluating point should be executed by CAD with TTSA, which should be applied into the teaching contents for modern industrial training.

Table 2. Evaluating and Scorting Points of Sub-processes of Component in Fig 1

Evaluating function		Highest quality		Lowest cost		Top reliability		Shortest period		Partial Sum	Total Sum.	Function Index
Importance degree index		0.38		0.31		0.25		0.06		$M_i = \sum W_i S_i$	$\sum M_i$	$F_i = M_i / \sum M_i$
Sub-process designation & SATIS.(Si)		E.P	S.P	E.P	S.P	E.P	S.P	E.P	S.P			
Choose MAT.	Purchased 20	90	34.2	80	24.8	85	21.3	100	6	86.3	255.5	0.34
	ZC20 Cast	65	247	85	264	90	225	70	4.2	77.8		0.31
	20 steel Forge	100	38	80	24.8	95	23.8	80	4.8	91.4		0.36
Heat	Norma	6	24	9	27	6	16	1	6	74.9	251.7	0.3

Table 2. (*continued*)

T.	lize	5	.7	0	.9	5	.3	00				
	Harden. Temper	80	30.4	85	26.4	100	25	80	4.8	86.6		0.34
	Normalize. & Harden. Temper	100	38	80	24.8	95	23.8	60	3.6	90.2		0.36
Machine I	a_1. (See *)	100	38	80	24.8	90	22.5	85	5.1	90.4	260.8	0.35
	d_1.(See *)	90	34.2	85	26.4	95	23.8	90	5.4	89.8		0.34
	e_1. (See *)	65	24.7	95	29.5	85	21.3	85	5.1	80.6		0.31
Machine II	Turn (drill. centre hole)	85	32.3	90	27.9	90	22.5	90	5.4	88.1	253.8	0.35
	Drill (drill. centre hole)	60	22.8	95	29.5	60	15	85	5.1	72.4		0.29
	Turn (drill. & expand centre hole)	100	38	85	26.4	100	25	85	3.9	93.3		0.37

By means of the analysis with network chart in fig 2 , the optimal technological plans for the best individual function have been obtained as below, consult fig 2: E (the bottom production cost):1—3—5—7—9 routing process (r. p). A (the highest product quality): 1—2—4—7—9(r. p). D (the top reliability) : 1—3—4—8—9 (r. p). G (the shortest production period) : Purchase (20 round bar)—dl—Turn (drill centre hole)—Mill (4 small holes)—Normalize (r. p). G has been obtained by the other network chart .

Assuming that the total cost of the sub—processes is made up of production cost (see fig 2) and other costs (equal 20% production cost) , in the meantime consider table 2 ,then table 3 (CI. VI table) is obtained. After make the value indexes of table 3 match respectively the corresponding sub-processes in optimal plans A. D. E. G. above mentioned, table 4 is obtained.

Table 3. C_i & Vi of Sub-process for component in Fig 1

Sub.p class	Sub-process designation	Total cost（dollar）C_i	Total Sum $\sum C_i$	$C_i = \frac{C_i}{\sum C_i}$	$Vi=Fi/Ci$
Choose MAT.	Purchase20 round bar	6（1+20%）=7.2	21	C（P）=7.2/21=0.34	V(P)=0.34/0.34=1
	*ZC*20 Cast	5.5(1+20%)=6.6		C（C）=6.6/21=0.31	V(C)=0.31/0.31=1
	20 steel Forge	6（1+20%）=7.2		C（F）=7.2/21=0.34	V(F)=0.36/0.34=1.06
Heat T.	Normalize	4（1+20%）=4.8	17.5	C（N）=4.8/17.5=0.27	V(N)=0.3/0.27=1.11
	Harden. Temper	5（1+20%）=6		C（H.T）=6/17.5=0.34	V(H.T)=0.34/0.34=1
	Normalize. & Harden. Temper	5.6(1+20%)=7.2		C（(N.H.T）=6.7/17.5=0.3	V(N.H.T)=0.36/0.38=0.95
Machine I	a_1. (See *)	12.6（1+20%）=15.1	43.4	C（a_1）=15.1/43.4=0.35	V（a_1）=0.35/0.3=1
	d_1. (See *)	12.1（1+20%）=14.5		C（d_1）=14.5/43.4=0.33	V(d_1)=0.34/0.33=1.01
	e_1. (See *)	11.5（1+20%）=13.8		C（e_1）=13.8/43.4=0.32	V(e_1)=0.31/0.32=0.97
Machine II	Turn（drill. centre hole))	3.2+(1+20%)=3.8	11.5	C（T）=3.8/11.5=0.33	V(T)=0.35/0.33=1.06
	Drill（drill. centre hole))	3（1+20%）3.6		C（D）=3.6/11.5=0.31	V（D）=0.29/0.31=0.94
	Turn（drill. & expand centre hole)	3.4(1+20%)=4.1		C（D.E）=4.1/11.5=0.387	V(D.E)=0.37/0.357=1.04

* a_1. Mill (top, bottom, sides)—Turn (cylindrical surfaces)—Drill(4 small holes)

e_1. Turn (cylindrical surfaces, ends)—Mill(4 sides)—Drill(4 small holes)

d_1. Shape (top, bottom, sides)—Turn (cylindrical surfaces)—Drill(4 small holes)

It is quite evident that any one of four optimal plans A. D. E. G. might all be adopted, we should make a concrete analysis of concrete conditions. That's all analysis course of optimal design for the best individual function.

Table 4. VI of Sub-process with Optimal Technology for Best Individual Function of Component in Fig 1

Sub.p class & Sub designation	Choose MAT	Heat treatment	Machine I	Machine II	Total Vi, V (i)
A (Highest quality)	1.06	0.95	1	1.04	V (A) =1.01
D (Top reliability)	1.06	1	1.03	1.04	V (D) =1.03
E (Lowest cost)	1	1.11	0.97	0.94	V (E) =1.01
G (Shorest period)	1	1.11	1.03	1.06	V (G) =1.05

5 Optimal Design of Technology for the Best Comprehensive Function (TBCF)

The optimization of the technological plans is usually hoped not only for TBIF but also for TBCF in all respects in the procedure of practical production, for example, the article is hoped not only the higher quality but also the lower cost etc.. Therefore, it is necessary that we take VI of all sub-processes in the optimal plans A. D. E. G. into a comprehensive consideration, trying when which value indexes of the sub-processes are added together (each value index added does not need to be the maximum), we could obtain the maximum of the total value index (MTVI) of the technological plan. This MTVT is just VI of the optimal TBCF. But it is obvious that there are only four optimal value indexes of the sub-processes which are chosen respectively out from every one of the optimal plans A. D. E. G.

First, we make VI numerals in table 4 increase by 100 times for helping the following calculation, then, writting out VI matrix (Cij) by increased VI numerals. To find out MTVI is just to solve the maximum distributive value of matrix (Cij).

Step 1 , writting out (C''ij) == M - (Cij) by the maximum element M=111 in (Cij), assuming that mark each circled element 0 with △, each crossed element 0 with ◎, the concrete calculating steps are [1-2]

$$(C_{ij})=\begin{vmatrix}106 & 95 & 100 & 104\\ 106 & 100 & 103 & 104\\ 100 & 111 & 97 & 94\\ 100 & 111 & 103 & 108\end{vmatrix}\rightarrow(C``_{ij})=\begin{vmatrix}5 & 16 & 11 & 7\\ 5 & 11 & 8 & 7\\ 11 & 0 & 14 & 17\\ 11 & 0 & 8 & 5\end{vmatrix}\begin{matrix}-5\\ -5\\ \\ \\ \end{matrix}$$

$$\xrightarrow{\text{第3步}}\begin{vmatrix}0 & 11 & 6 & 2\\ 0 & 6 & 3 & 2\\ 11 & 0 & 14 & 17\\ 11 & 0 & 8 & 5\\ & & -3 & -2\end{vmatrix}$$

$$\xrightarrow{\text{第4、5、6步}}\begin{vmatrix}-\triangle- & -11- & -3- & -\circledcirc-\\ -\circledcirc- & -6- & -\triangle- & -\circledcirc-\\ 11 & \triangle & 11 & 15\\ 11 & \circledcirc & 5 & 3\end{vmatrix}\xrightarrow{\text{第7步}}\begin{vmatrix}\circledcirc & 14 & 3 & \circledcirc\\ \circledcirc & 9 & \triangle & \circledcirc\\ 8 & \triangle & 8 & 12\\ 8 & \circledcirc & 2 & \triangle\end{vmatrix}\quad\text{得}(X_{ij})=\begin{vmatrix}1 & 0 & 0 & 0\\ 0 & 0 & 1 & 0\\ 0 & 1 & 0 & 0\\ 0 & 0 & 0 & 1\end{vmatrix}$$

Elements △ (or "1 ") in different rows and columns have been come out, thus far, the procedure of finding the solution has been finished, the matrix form of the optimal solving result is (Xij). If (Xij) has still not been come out, the procedure should be executed to return to the step 4 again. Match position "1" in (Xij) with corresponding position in table 4 , the optimal technology for the best comprehensive function (OTBCF) comes out just right:

Forge (20 steel) —Normalize —Turn (cylindrical surface, ends, drill centre hole)— Mill (4 sides) —Drill (4 small holes).

Corresponding VI of OTBCF is; Zmax = (1. 06 + 1. 03 + 1.11 + 1. 06)/4 = 1. 07. Next the routine design will be carried out until the whole design work be finished. Those are the whole analysis course.of the optimal design of OTBCF.

6 Key Computer Program Hungary's Algorithm for Optimal Design of Technology

The computer program of above-mentioned optimal design of technology has been prepared [1].

The key computer program Hungary's algorithm is as follows:

```
// Hungary1.h: interface for the CHungary class.
#if
!defined(AFX_HUNGARY1_H__ACAD425C_9780_4005_BEFF_9A97E0ED2FA7__INCLUDED_)
#define AFX_HUNGARY1_H__ACAD425C_9780_4005_BEFF_9A97E0ED2FA7__INCLUDED_

#if _MSC_VER > 1000
#pragma once
#endif // _MSC_VER > 1000
class CHungary : public CObject
{
public:
    void MoveZero();
    int GetMostLine();
    int GetMostCow();
    BOOL IsOptimlized();
    void Check();
    void OutputData();
    void ProcessData();
    void MakeFlag();
    CHungary();
    void Create(int CowCount, int LineCount);
    void Create(int CowCount, int LineCount, int *pData);
    virtual ~CHungary();
private:
    int FindLowest();
    void ProcessMostZero();
    BOOL IsHaveTwoZero();
    int *m_pData;
    int *m_pDataCopy;
    int *m_pCowFlag;
    int *m_pLineFlag;
    int m_sCowCount;
    int m_sLineCount;
};
```

```
#endif //
!defined(AFX_HUNGARY1_H__ACAD425C_9780_4005_BEFF_9A97E0ED2FA7__INCLUDED_)
// Hungary1.cpp: implementation of the CHungary class.
#include "stdafx.h"
#include "Hungary.h"
#include "Hungary1.h"
#ifdef _DEBUG
#undef THIS_FILE
static char THIS_FILE[]=__FILE__;
#define new DEBUG_NEW
#endif
CHungary::CHungary()
{
}
CHungary::~CHungary()
{
    if(m_pData!=NULL)
            delete [] m_pData;

    if(m_pDataCopy!=NULL)
            delete [] m_pDataCopy;

    if(m_pCowFlag!=NULL)
            delete [] m_pCowFlag;

    if(m_pLineFlag!=NULL)
            delete [] m_pLineFlag;
}
void CHungary::Create(int CowCount, int LineCount)
{
    ASSERT(CowCount!=0 && LineCount!=0);
            m_sCowCount =CowCount;
    m_sLineCount =LineCount;
            m_pCowFlag =new int[m_sLineCount];
    m_pLineFlag =new int[m_sLineCount];
    memset(m_pCowFlag,  0, m_sLineCount*sizeof(int));
    memset(m_pLineFlag, 0, m_sLineCount*sizeof(int));

    int nSize = CowCount* LineCount;
    m_pData = new  int[nSize];
    memset(m_pData, -1, sizeof(int)*nSize);
//  m_pData =pData;
    m_pDataCopy =new  int[nSize];
    memset(m_pDataCopy, -1, sizeof(int)*nSize);
//  m_pDataCopy =pData;
    OutputData();
    return;
}
(omitted)
    OutputData();
    for(i=0;i<m_sCowCount; i++)
            for (j=0; j<m_sLineCount; j++)
            {
                    if(*(m_pDataCopy+ i*m_sLineCount+j)==-1)
                            *(m_pDataCopy+ i*m_sLineCount+j)=0;
            }
    OutputData();
    memset(m_pCowFlag,  0, m_sLineCount*sizeof(int));
    memset(m_pLineFlag, 0, m_sLineCount*sizeof(int));
}
```

7 Conclusion

A .Decision Making Technique of Processing

Technology(DMTPT) is an kind of optimal design of processing technology (ODPT), both the DMTPT (ODPT) of technology for the individual function and the optimization of the technological plans can be systematically-linked by analysis of both value engineering and the operational research model.

An example (the pedestal)for applying the steps above mentioned has been analysesd, which it correspondes with the actual production process.

B. The optimal design of processing technology is a important link which apply, organically and comprehensively, It is a important link both theorical and practical knowleges for processing technology.

C. The key computer program of Hungary's algorithm for optimal design of technology has been given.

Uninterruptedly, develop, improve and perfect this link, make it more stan-dardized, serial and programizing, **so** that make it serve the practical production better,which will be the final aim for the optimal design of Processing technology and will still be one of the basic aim that the system of modern industrial training should achieve.

References

1. Hu, Y.: Operational research, 2nd edn. Tsinghua University Press, Beijing (2003)
2. Ibusuki, U., Kaminski, P.C.: Product development process with focus on value engineering and target-costing: A case study in an automotive company. International Journal of Production Economics 105(2), 459–474 (2007)
3. Arai, T., Shimomura, Y.: Proposal of Service CAD System - A Tool for Service Engineering Manufacturing Technology. Annals of the CIRP 53(1), 397–400 (2004)

Research of Dynamic Priority Improvement Method in μC/OS-II Real-Time Operating System

Xianmin Wei

Computer and Communication Engineering School Weifang University
Weifang, China
Xianmin@live.com

Abstract. This paper analyzes in embedded real-time operating system of μC/OS-II, the shortcomings of achieving the dynamic priority, proposes concepts of the two levels cut-off time and analyzes how to set the two cut-off time and relationship between all of time, and puts forwards getting the dynamic priority method.

Keywords: μC/OS-II, two levels cut-off time, the opportunity time.

1 Introduction

In real-time system, the system output accuracy is a function of operation results, and also a function of the resulting output time. Consequently, the time parameter is an important quota in the real-time operating system performance evaluation,. In a number of time parameters, the task time-limit is one of the most important parameters, the implementation of real-time tasks must be completed within the specified period of time. Otherwise, according to the different applications will result in different degrees of damage.

μC /OS-II real-time operating system is a more comprehensive system. Its kernel is a preemptive kernel, that not only can switch between tasks, but also allows a task in the absence of a resource to continue to run after a certain time sleep; to provide semaphore for shared resource management and for process communications message queue and message mailbox, even to provide memory management mechanism, but the μC / OS-II kernel is still worthy of improvement in some areas, such as the system not supporting time slice scheduling. If there is an infinite loop code in a task, code will execute here for a long time, the scheduler can not control it, and other lower-priority tasks could not be in timely implementation. To solve the low priority task may not running for a long time, we put forward the concept of two levels cut-off time.

2 The Method and Defect of Os-Ii Real Time Operating System to Dynamically Change the Priority

μC/OS-II real-time operating system kernel changes the task priority by calling the user task function INT8U OSTaskChangePrio (INT8U oldprio, INT8U newprio). The

D. Zeng (Ed.): ICAIC 2011, Part I, CCIS 224, pp. 109–112, 2011.

first parameter of this function oldprio is the priority task of the original, the second parameter newprio is the the new priority of task. Function return values may have four froms.

(1) task priority is successfully changed.

(2) in parameters the priority task of the original or new priority is greater than or equal to the maximum priority value (the value smaller, the priority greater), the specified priority is invalid.

(3) the priority of the task parameter already exists.

(4) the original priority of the task parameters does not exist.

Only the return value is the first case of the above four return values, the changing priority function was successfully called.

Using of this function:

```
void taskx（void *data）
{
INT8U err;for(;;){···err=OSTaskChangePrio(10,5) ;...
}
}
```

Defects: the operating system requires users to create tasks to take full account of the requirements of each task, if the user think that the low priority task may not run, it is necessary in the task function to call this function to change to the higher priority. This increases the difficulties for software designers. In addition, the task does not necessarily change the priority every time, so adding the priority changing function in tasks is unreasonable. And the new priorities are set by the user program, if the calling this function, the new priority is fixed, and is not conducive to the expansion of the system. A simple and effective method becomes the key to solving this problem.

3 Two Levels Cut-Off Time

In explaining the two levels cut-off time, we define two concepts to facilitate our further understanding, that are the task validity and the task survival. The task validity is that the task is valid only the task runs to completion in this period of time, the mission succeeds, otherwise the task is removed. The task survival is the period of time from creating the task to finishing the task execution or abandoned (deleted). Under normal circumstances, the task survival is less than the task validity, in the worst case (to be suspended long enough), the task survival is equal to the task validity (if the task is not running completely, abandoned or removed is the same).

The so-called two levels cut-off time, in short, there are two levels cut-off time in tasks running, the first cut-off time and the second deadline. The first cut-off time is defined as the system calls the calculation priority function, to change the moment of the task priority priority. At this time, the taskpriority is improved to the state of higher priority status than all ready tasks, this is only relative to the ready state of the task, not including the task in waiting state and dormant state. Taking into account the μC/OS-II not having the same priority, when we set the priority, we also take into account the priorities not be occupied by any task. The aim is to enable higher-priority tasks still available to run if ready. The second cut-off time is the ultimate moment of the task validity.

we use the formula shows the relationship of every time with time period.

Task period (vp) = the second cut-off time (t2) - the task arrival time (t0) (1)

The task survival (lp) = task completion time or deleted (et) - the task arrival time (t0) (2)

Opportunity time(cp)+the time needed to run(nt)=the second cut-off time(t2)- the first cut-off time(t1) (3)

Opportunity time may be scattered between the first cut-off time and the second cut-off time, it might not be one time, but be multi-segment time, the total opportunity time in terms of a specific task is fixed.

Why set the opportunity time? This is because increasing the task priority is not increased to the highest of all tasks, but rather than at the first cut-off time higher than priority of all the ready state If the arrival of higher priority tasks, this task will be suspended. But if the higher priority task running time is less than the opportunity time, high-priority task is completed, this task can still run. Opportunity time not only to give the chance to the low priority task to run, but also higher-priority operation. If the priority of all tasks mentioned is the highest, while relatively the higher priority task is not fair. This could result in more loss than abandonment of the low priority, so our choice is reasonable and fair.

One notable problem is that if before the arrival of the first cut-off time task is running for a period of time, the first cut-off time defers the same time automatically, this is in the formula (3), why "the time needed to run" rather than the running time.

Setting method of opportunity time is still a relationship with priority, the higher the original priority the opportunity time longer. For example, in μC/OS-II has 64 missions, there are 64 priorities, we can put the highest priority to 0 priority set to 64 time units, 1 opportunity time set to 63 time units, and so on. Depending on the hardware platform unit of time can be different.

4 Ways to Change the Priority

When the first cut-off time is done, using interrupt to call calculation priority function. In this function the first test is if the task is running, if running, then to calculate the remaining run time before the first cut-off time comes, and then interrupt returns; In this case, if the task is not running completely but suspended, at pending time to calculate the next moment of the first cut-off time arrival (the next arrival time = susdended moment + run time before the the first cut-off time), and only in this case, the first cut-off time will come twice. If not then the interrupt service routine continues to run.

The new guidelines of access priority are: (1) a new priority higher than the orginal task priority. (2) the new priority is higher than all priority at ready state. (3) the obtained priority is higher than the lowest original priority (the key is to look at if higher-priority be occupied). (4) the priority selected must not be occupied.

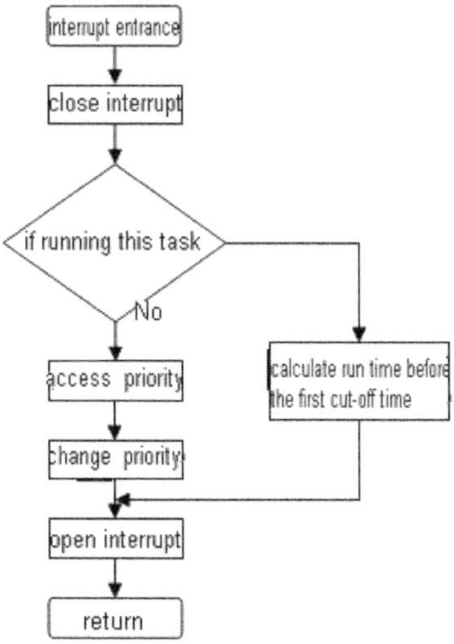

Fig. 1. Interrupt service program flow

In the changing priority function, we only remove the close, open break at the end and at the beginning of the function, to see in Figure 1.

5 Calculation Chance of the First Cut-Off Time

(1) task arrival moments.
(2) the first cut-off time si done wen taskrunning, but later was suspended.

6 Conclusion

The concept introduction of the two levels cut-off time resolves the problem of low-priority task waiting for a long-term and not running. To set the opportunity time not to consider lower-priority tasks, also to consider higher priority tasks, so that the run of the task becomes more fair and reasonable. To maximize the completion of the system tasks. Integration of dynamic access priority function and the priority changing function can dynamically change priorities for tasks, and the operating system is responsible for it, not in system design by system analyst or programmer, and significantly reducing system design difficulties.

References

1. Liu, W.: μC/OS-II embedded operating system of preemptive scheduling strategy. Micro Computer Applications 26(1), 116–117 (2004)
2. Peng, L.: Strong real-time static priority scheduling system schedulability analysis. Computer Engineering and Applications 12, 13–15 (2001)

A New Method of Automatic Monitoring DC Breaker by Using GPRS Technique

Jun Wang[1], Tao Ning[2], Zhihua Li[2], and Wei Chen[2]

[1] Hubei Electric Testing Research Institute
[2] School of Electrical Engineering Wuhan University
Wuhan, Hubei Province, China
jun1839@sina.cn

Abstract. To get the full information of the current in different circuit, a new method is put forward to monitor the D.C. breaker by using the GPRS technique when the breaker is switching of. Also, the software and the hardware of the monitoring system are designed and developed. This system chosen Hall current sensor to measure the signal of reference current in different circuit when DC circuit breaker is in breaking process; By BECKHOFF's CX1020 and EL3702 terminal collecting the signal; Using the KL6001 serial terminal interface module and H7210 GPRS DTU consisting of transport systems and transmitting data via GPRS network; The monitoring center which can receive, display and process the data packet is developed by a VC-based. We build the oscillation circuit to detect the monitoring system in the laboratory. The test result indicates that this system can meet the requirements well for data collecting on real time and transferring in security. The waveform of each loop's current can be displayed in the virtual oscilloscope which provides crucial information to analyze the health state of the breaker.

Keywords: component, GPRS, DC breaker, monitoring, collecting, transmitting, processing, test.

1 Introduction

Since the late 80s, our DC power transmission technology has made the great development. Now we have many DC power transmission projects, such as Sanxia to Changzhou, Sanxia to Guangzhou and Sanxia to Shanghai DC transmission and so on. Our country will plan operate more than 30 DC power transmission project before 2020, simultaneously, to realize and advance "the power transmission from west to east" strategic plan, the country will be advancing vigorously including ±800kV, ±1000kV extra-high DC power transmission project construction [1]. In the future the DC transmission will become the strong intelligence electrical network's important component.

The HVDC breaker is the important electrical equipment in the DC transmission system. Its main task is to clear the line fault and isolate fault equipment in time, and to ensure the normal operation of the non-fault burden of DC system [2].

D. Zeng (Ed.): ICAIC 2011, Part I, CCIS 224, pp. 113–120, 2011.

Through the HVDC breaker's online monitor, using the advanced GPRS wireless transmission technology, we can accumulate the massive real-time performance data in the backstage monitoring system, and form a complete monitor database. Combined the DC breaker's time tentative data and the former examination data, used each kind of numerical analysis and the appraisal method to analyze and determine in time, we can discover and capture equipment's flaw in time, reduce premature or the nonessential power cut overhaul, reduce the maintenance cost, enhance the overhaul pointedness, guarantee the DC breaker work on the safe side, it also obviously proposes the HVDC transmission system's reliability and economical efficiency.

2 GPRS Technology

Along with the wireless communication technology's development, the wireless network operator which provides to realize the long-distance monitoring and the data transmission has been widely applied in each domain. GPRS (General Packet Radio Service) [3-4] is one kind of integrated data bearer service which develops on the existing GSM system, the goal is provide the GSM users with group forms of data services.

The GPRS technology uses with the GSM similar wireless modulation standard, the similar frequency band, the similar sharp-edged structure, the similar frequency-hopping regular as well as the same TDMA frame structure. This kind of new packet data channel is very similar to the current circuit switching's voice feature channel. Therefore, the existing base station subsystem (BSS) may provide the comprehensive GPRS covering surface. The GPRS allows users to transmit and receive data under end-to-end grouping shift pattern, and does not need to use the network resource by circuit switching pattern. Thus it has provided one kind highly effective, low cost packet radio data service, is suitable especially for interrupted, frequent and the few data transmission, is also suitable for the occasional great data size transmission.

The GPRS technology has the following characteristic:

- It uses the transparent double-sided data transmission, and the link maintains automatically;
- The GPRS's theoretical bandwidth may reach 171.2Kb/s, the practical application bandwidth is probably in 40-70Kb/s,and provide the TCP/IP connection on this channel, also may have application in INTERNET connection, data transmission and so on.
- The GPRS uses the block-switch technology; each user may take many wireless channels simultaneously. The identical wireless channel may share by many users, so the resource is used effectively.
- When uses GPRS technology to realize the packet sending and receiving data, the user are forever online. Because charged by flow, the service cost was reduced rapidly.
- The GPRS transmission range is far and has high reliability. Generally, the data packet transmission success ratio is above 99.9%.

3 GPRS Monitoring Systems

3.1 Dc Breaker'S Principle of Work

Figure 1 is the principle diagram of the passive oscillation loop DC breaker [5]. In Gezhou Dam as well as the Fulong convertor station's MRTB is this kind of structure.

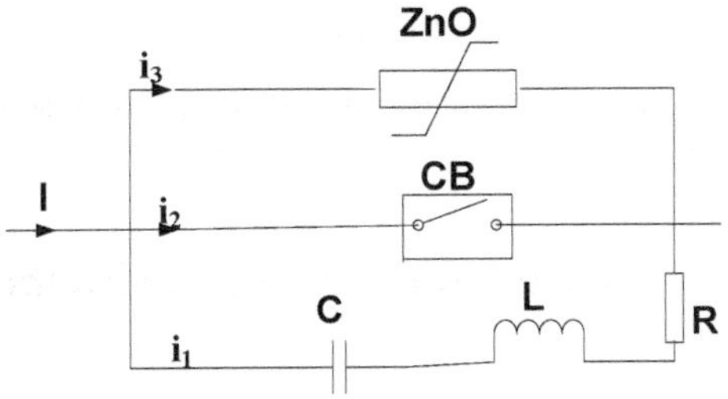

Fig. 1. The principle diagram of the DC breaker

In the Fig1, CB is the contact terminal of DC breaker, L and C respectively are inductance and capacitance of oscillation loop, ZnO is zinc oxide arrester. When CB receives break-brake command, the arc voltage charges up capacitance of oscillation loop. As a result of the arc with instability and the dynatron characteristic, it produces a self-oscillation electric current signal which amplitude increases unceasingly in the oscillation loop. When the amplitude of the electric current signal equals or surpasses steady current of the DC loop, the arc current presents the electric current zero spot, then the arc was put out, and the DC current transfers to the oscillation loop. Because the inductance still stored up the massive energies in the line, it can charge up the capacitance voltage to the operation voltage of ZnO arrester. The arrester group breakover and absorb energy, limit the breaker's voltage to desired value [6-7].

3.2 System Structure

The monitoring system structure is as shown in figure 2, with a signal collecting system installed in oscillation loop of DC breaker, and the signal collecting system is connected with signal transmission system, the monitoring terminal is the data processing center.

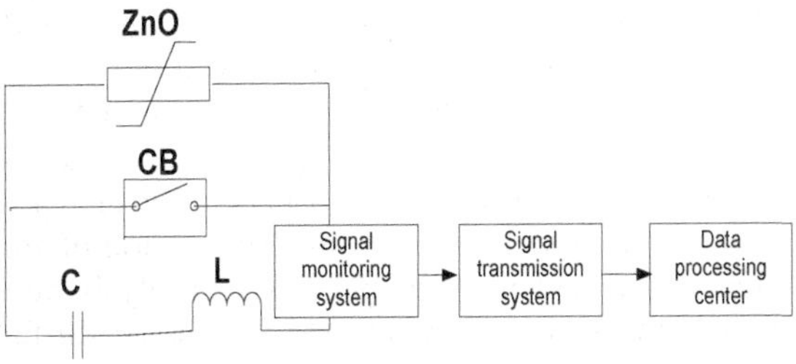

Fig. 2. Picture of system structure

1) Signal acquisition system

The current through the oscillation loop of DC breaker is a high frequency oscillating signal. This system uses Hall current sensor based on Hall effect, compared to traditional CT, it has small volume, big span, wide frequency band, excellent linearity, high accuracy and high sensitivity etc, isolating with the main circuit in electricity, it is qualified in non-contact measurement in situations of ac/dc, pulse and irregular wave current signal [8]. According to the different hall types, the measure current ranges from 50A to 10000A, the output of Hall is a ± 5V voltage signal, and an additional 15V source is need in power supply.

We use an embedded PC terminals acquisition system provided by German company-BECKHOFF with the acquisition terminal to acquire the output voltage signal of Hall element. This system consists of a CPU (CX1020), power supply module (CX1100) and a high-speed data acquisition terminal EL3702 matched with the CX1020. Signals ranged from – 10 V to + 10 V will be managed by analog input terminal module of EL3702. The resolution of digitalized voltage signal is 16, and the signal can be transferred to the up-level automation equipment in the condition electrical isolation. This acquisition terminal input signal satisfies 0 ~ 20 kHz bandwidth, and its maximum sampling frequency can reach 100 KHZ with over-sampling ability

2) Signal transmission system

The transmission system consists of KL6001 serial interface module made by BECKHOFF in Germany and H7210 GPRS DTU product in Shenzhen. KL6001 serial interface can be connected to the equipment with RS232 interface. This interface corresponds to CCITT V. 28 / DIN 66 259-1 standard, the communication rate can reach 19200 baud. Due to the signal processing in electrical isolation, RS232 interface has strong anti-interference ability. H7210 GPRS DTU embedded DDP, PDP, TCP/IP and various communication protocols [9-11], it can realize the distance data transmission and transparent between the on-site equipment and the data center of data, RS232/422/485 or TTL level interface, high-performance, industrial, outer, applicable for all kinds of industrial environments monitor, traffic management meteorology and various applications.

As shown in figure 3, this system uses recording trigger level to detect acquisition in signal collection, EL3702 terminals monitors analog signal, when the analog signals is higher than a certain value, triggering records data. The 200us cycle of acquisition process ensures the speed in recording an integrated data with signal to trigger level. In order to prevent multiple triggered by collecting waveforms, the first record of data shall continue 15ms records later (assuming the sampling time for 15ms), namely 1,500 data, all this are achieved by logic design program. After the completion of data collection, KL6001 serial interface contacts with H7210 DTU, control in sending 150 data per second, namely 300 bytes, to send integrated data to data processing center time after time by GPRS networks through programming.

3) Data processing centre

Its main function is receiving the data sent by GPRS, and processing all kinds of signal, and monitoring the state of HVDC breaker. The communication of data processing centre and GPRS is via dynamic IP and domain name resolution. Once the GPRS data transmit terminal charged, it will forwardly visit the proxy server by the domain name set initially, then the communications link has been set up between proxy serve and surveillance center.

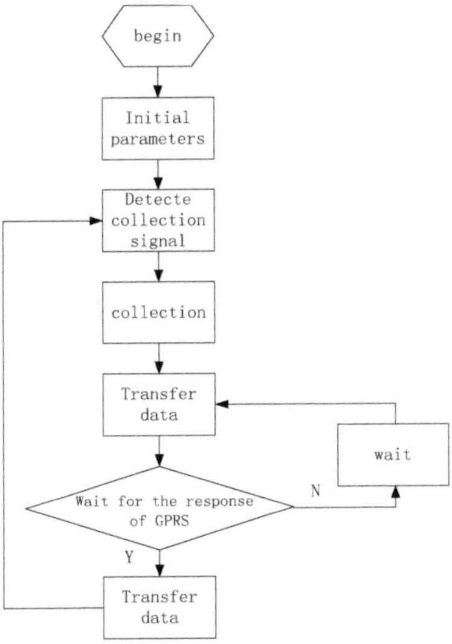

Fig. 3. Data collection and transmission process control charts

The Surveillance center used a monitoring system based on VC which can receive, display, and process data, it was shown in figure 4.The received data will be stored in excel file, and named by the received time which is convenient for query.

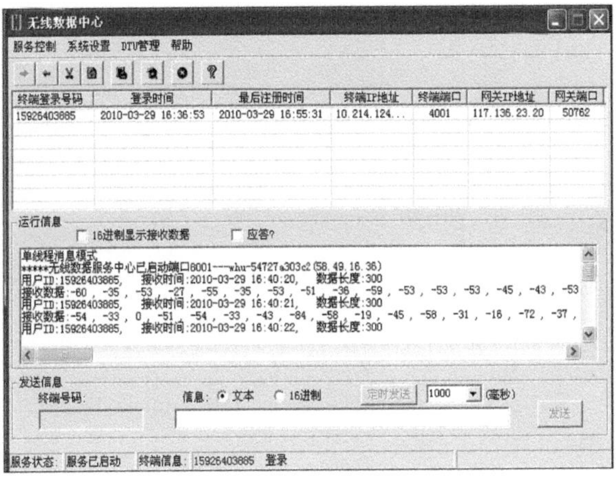

Fig. 4. Monitoring center

When the embedded PC CX1020, GPRS terminal communicate with data processing centre, maybe no response, packet missing, packet damaged would occur, so we have produced a reliable communication scheme which is as illustrated in figure 5.

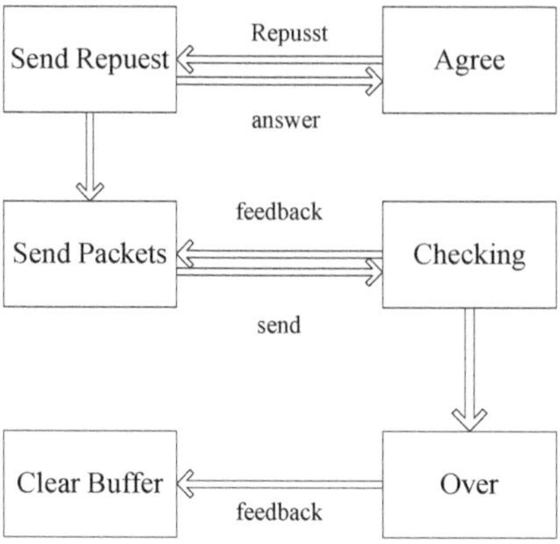

Fig. 5. Flow chart of communication

When CX1020 is going to send data, first CX1020 send a handshaking signal to DSC ,if DSC receive the handshaking signal and the system is normal ,then DSC will also send a handshaking signal to CX1020 which means communication is normal.

After CX1020 receive the handshaking signal, it begin to send package in turn, DSC will check the packet by check code, packets will be send again if packet damaged. When DSC receives all data packets, the counter and data in combuffer will be release, then waiting for the next Data sending.

4 Monitoring Experiment

We build the oscillation circuit to detect the monitoring system in the laboratory. The experimental circuit is as illustrated in figure 6.

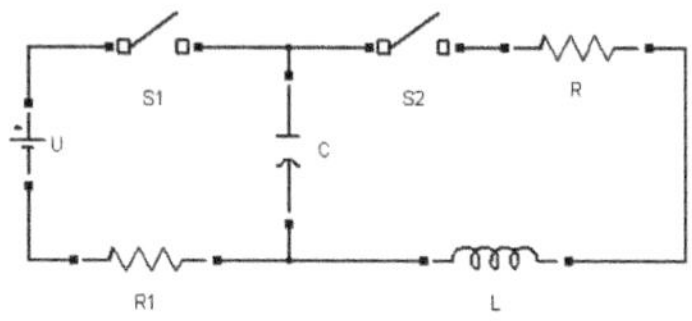

Fig. 6. The schematic diagram of experimental circuit

In the figure 6, U=42V (DC), C=18 μF L=37 μH , first close S1 and open S2, after the capacitance C is charged completely. Second, open S1 and close S2 quickly, then there is a RLC oscillation loop. The current is got by Hall current sensor, the main parameters of Hall current sensor are: rated current 50A, rated output ±3.5V, bandwidth0-100kHz. The voltage of Hall current sensor received by oscilloscope is shown in figure 7.

After the voltage of Hall current sensor signal is collected, it is send to the remote monitoring center by Embedded PC and GPRS terminal., the figure 8 is the signal receive by monitoring center.

From the figure 7 and figure 8, we know that the wave is the same as voltage of Hall current sensor after we checked.

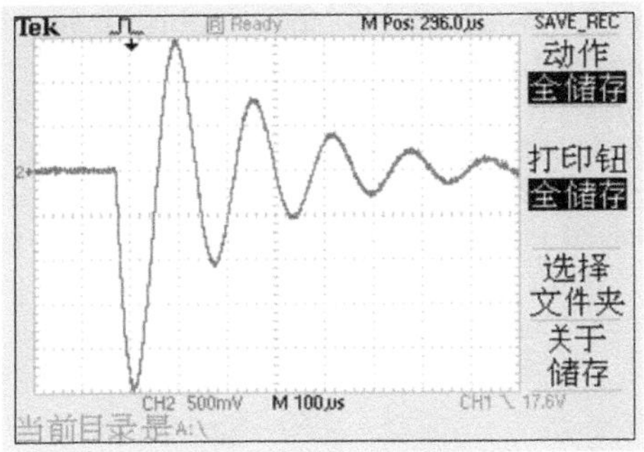

Fig. 7. The output voltage of Hall current sensor

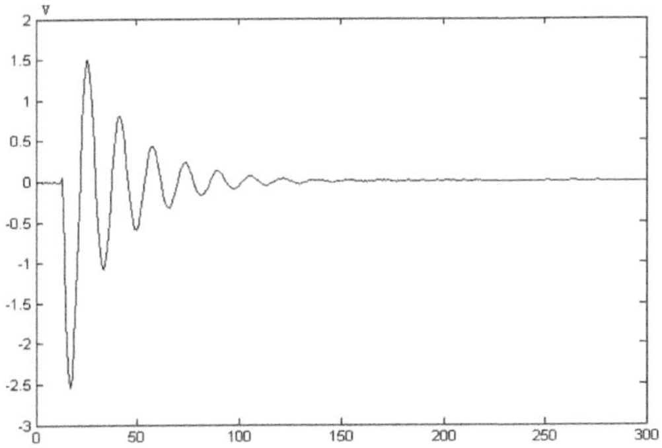

Fig. 8. The signal monitoring center received

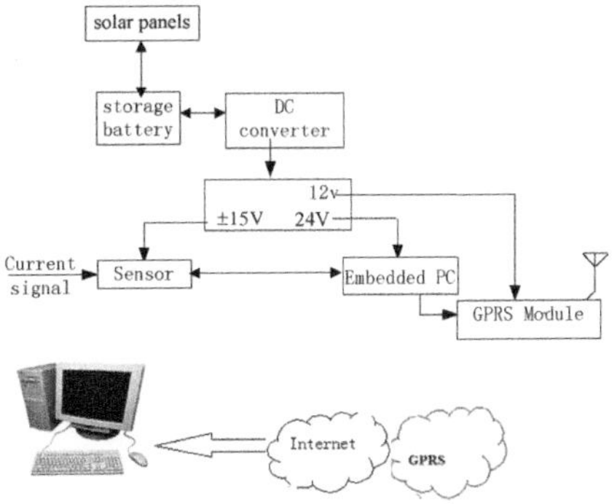

Fig. 9. System diagram

5 Conclusion

It's reliable to monitor the HVDC breaker by the technology of GPRS. From the data and scope received by Data processing center, we can discover and capture equipment's flaw in time, reduce premature or the nonessential power cut overhaul, reduce the maintenance cost, and enhance the overhaul pointedness. It can make sure that the HVDC breaker works safely and reliably, then improving the system's reliability and economical efficiency.

What's more, there are no lines between the monitoring device and the data processing center. Using GPRS technology transmit data is far and has high reliability. The most important is all these devices's power supply is only two storage batteries with solar panels, placed in a chest without electromagnetic interference. As long as these devices and the chest are installed, it can work all the time, the staff's work is only checking the data on the computer screen.

References

1. Han, M.-x., Wen, J.: Principle and application of the HVDC power transmission. Machine Press, Beijing (2008)
2. Zhang, W.-r., Gou, R.-f., Zhao, B.-n., Shang, J.-c.: Study on digital simulation of transfering direct current using DC breakers. High Voltage Apparatus (April 2002)
3. Han, B.-j.: The principle of GPRS. Machine Press, Beijing (2003)
4. Zhao, L., Wang, A., Xu, J.: Remote Monitor and Control System for Wreath Net Cabinet Based on GPRS Technology. In: International Conference on Power SystemTechnology, pp. 1–6 (2006)
5. Liu, G.-y.: The principle and improvement of Gezhou Dam convertor station'DC breaker. China Electric Power, 18–20 (April 1995)
6. Zheng, Z.-f., Zhou, J.-y.: DC Interruption and DC Circuit Breaker. High Voltage Apparatus (December 2006)
7. Bao, M.-d.: Development of HVDC circuit breaker. High Voltage Apparatus (June 1990)
8. Yu, S.-h., Chen, H.-x.: The application of Hall current sensor in series active power filter. The Application of Electrical Devices and Components (October 2008)
9. Oliver, T., Yu, W.: End-to-end adaptive QoS provisioning over GPRS wireless mobile network. Mobile Networks and Applications, 255–267 (August 2003)
10. Andrews, T.: Computer Networks. Prentice Hall International, Inc., Englewood Cliffs (1996)
11. Muthalnlner, M.: TCP/IP: Tutorial and Technical Overview, Upper Saddle River (1998)

Research of Video Transmission System in Wireless Sensor Network

Xu Chunsen, Zhao Yanjuan, and Zhang Yan

School of Information Engineering Northeast Dianli
University JiLin, China
chunsen_xu@yahoo.com.cn

Abstract. In this paper, we introduced a design program of remote video transmission system which is based on the hardware platform of S3C2440 and embedded operating system of Linux. It described the overall structure and implementation of the various parts, and gave the realization of the key features in this software. In the system we used the MPEG-4 video compression algorithm. The system implemented video transmission in wireless local area network, and compared with the traditional video monitoring systems, this system had more advantages, such as small size, low cost, stable and reliable.

Keywords: Wireless Sensor Networks, Video Transmission, Embedded Linux.

1 Introduction

With the development of the "Internet of Things", wireless transmission become to be a hot topic. Because the narrow bandwidth of wireless sensor networks, wireless video transmission become a difficult problem in the wireless transmission. Now video transmission has entered the digital network age. The image which is output from the front capture device is the digital signal. And by the network medium it is transmitted. In this processing, streaming media technology is used to realize multiplex transmission. Therefore, the use of embedded systems for video transmission, in line with network, digital features, and have important practical significance in many industries such as police, security.

2 Problem Description

Usually video transmission or monitoring systems are generally achieved on the platform of PC. This kind of system is bulky, high cost, use of non-flexible. The hardware platform, which we used in this design, is Samsung S3C2440; The Software platform is Linux operating system which the kernel is Linux-2.6.30.4. Because the Linux operating system have the characteristics of open, good proformance for network support and modular structure, it can better meet to the viedo transmission system requirements.

D. Zeng (Ed.): ICAIC 2011, Part I, CCIS 224, pp. 121–126, 2011.

3 The Overall Design of the System

The design of the system used the modular thinking. The system use the CMOS cameras to capture real-time video information, and use MPEG-4 to compress the video information, then it can generate MPEG-4 streams. Through the wireless transmission module the MPEG-4 streams can be transmitted to the receiver. In the receiver the module of wireless sensor receives the MPEG-4 streams, the the receiver displays after the MPEG-4 decoder. Video transmission system architecture diagram shown in Fig 1.

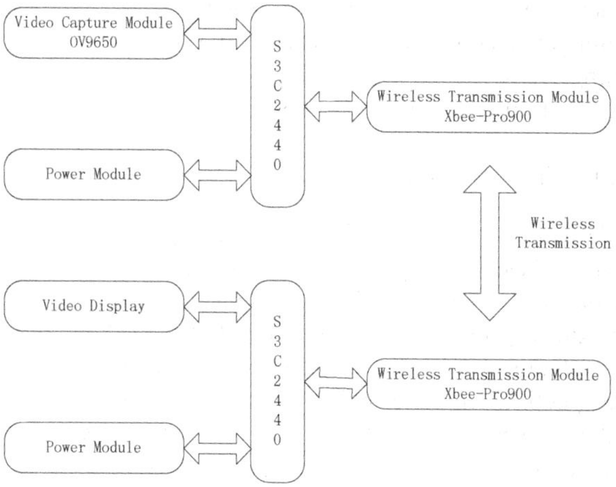

Fig. 1. System block diagram of the overall structure

4 Hardware Design of System

The system is designed to achieve the video transmission in wireless sensor network, it mainly includes video capture module, data processing module, wireless transmitter and receiver module, etc. Hardware mainly includes embedded processor, CMOS image sensors, wireless transmission/receiving module, storage, serial ports, and power management etc.

4.1 The Desing of Data Processing Module

Data processing module is the core module of system, this module will complete encoding and decoding of the collected video. This system is used in Samsung S3C2440 embedded processor, it has ARM920T core and 16/32-bit RISC embedded microprocessor. It mainly has high performance, low power consumption. CPU clock speed 400 MHz, the maximum 533 MHz, to meet the needs of the processing image data. The resources of S3C2440 include LCD controller, SDRAM controller, camera interface, 3-way serial interface, IIC BUS Interface, USB, touch screen interface. Based on the rich resources of the processor, the related expansion also carried out, equipped with onboard 64MB SDRAM, 2MB Nor Flash, 256MB Nand Flash. Under the control of the embedded processor, the collected data of CMOS image sensor (ov9650), is used to copy and storage in the SDRAM after by the frame synchronization signal to trigger an interrupt. The images which are encoded by MPEG-4 encoder, and transmitted by the wireless sensor transmit module, are sent to the receiver, the receiver module receives them, after decoding and then displayed on the LCD. The system block diagram of S3C2440 interfaces is shown in Fig. 2.

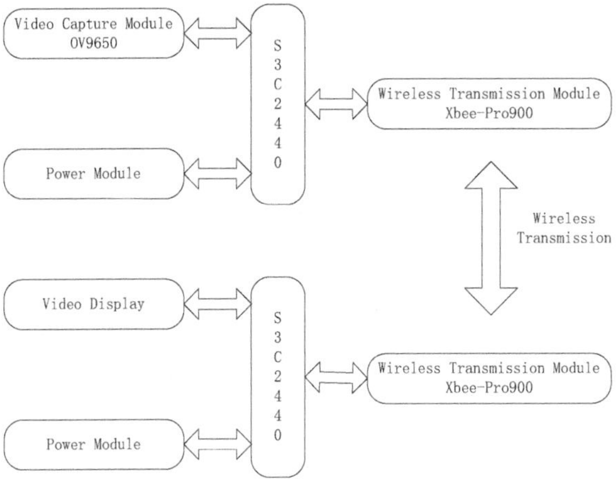

Fig. 2. Block diagram of S3C2440 interfaces

4.2 The Desing of Video Capture Module

The system uses a ov9650 video capture module, ov9650 is COMS camera of OmniVision company, the resolution is 130 million pixel. The video module has 10-bit data interface and standard interface of SCCB (Serial Camera Control Bus), uses CSP - 28 packaging, small volume. Chip supports three data output formats, RGB (4:2:2), YUV (4:2:2), YCrCb (4:2:2). Built-in138 device control register, address respectively from 0x00 ~ 0x8A. Through the SCCB interface can easily set the sensor window size, gain, white balance correction, exposure control, saturation, hue and other parameters. Because the system uses the core of control panel of embedded terminal platform is S3C2440, it was based on Samsung ARM920T core, and it has a dedicated camera interface, CPU can be connected directly image sensor of ov9650. This system can complete the configuration of the video module and the change of associated driven.

4.3 The Design of Wireless Transmitter/Receiver Module

In this system, the use of the wireless transmission module is the Digi's XBee-Pro 900 OEM RF, transmitter frequency is 900MHz, this module provides reliable data transmission between nodes, with high-performance, low power consumption. Indoor transmission distance of this chip is 140m, an outdoor transmission range is up to 3km, the data transfer rate is up to 156.25Kbps, and send power 50mW.It can achieve point to point and multipoint data transmission. In the data collection terminal, the collected information will be processed by the module of data processing, and will be sent to the receiver by the wirless transmission module. Then those information will be received by the wirless transmission module of receiver. This design can send information of wirelessly and long distance.

5 Software Desing of the System

Software platform consists of three parts: the system boot loader, an embedded Linux kernel, file systems and applications. In the design we will transplant u-boot-1.1.6 to the ARM platform to achieve the system boot loader. The uboot not only can boot embedded Linux, but also can easily switch to mode of download and update, and using download of USB to achieve the real-time updates of kernel image and file system. In this paper, the embedded operating system which we used is Linux-2.6.30.4. And the development mode which we used is the most common mode of host development that can compile the kernel and applications on the host, then through the serial port or USB port to download to the target platforms. File system is the largest part of the occupation which is stored in the embedded system software platform. It stores the system configuration files, system programs and system peripheral driver applications. After embedded Linux kernel transplantation, the main work is to write drivers applications in the operating system. Here we focus on the realization of MPEG-4 encoding.

5.1 Mpeg-4 Compression Standard

The number of digital video stream data is huge, to QCIF image (176x144), 20 frames per second, an example, then the amount of data per second is 7.74Mb. Assuming the system has ten road sensor, if the information of digital video stream is not compressed, multiplexed data transmission on the Internet is very difficult. For reliable operation system, this design uses the MPEG-4 compression standard video which has high compression rate. The most significant features of MPEG-4 are content-based coding method. That is, to a video sequence as a different video object VO (Video Object) component, based on the actual situation Encoder can encode the individual video object plane, then the maximum compression ratio up to 100:1.

5.2 Mpeg-4 Implementation and Optimization

There are two way to achieve MPEG-4 encoding, hardware compression and software compression. Hardware compression uses the specialized compression chip for MPEG-4 video signal encoding. And software compression uses the software to encode the video signal. Taking into account the cost of the system, the system uses software encoding and decoding video signals.

Xvid is an open source MPEG-4 multimedia codecs. It is prepared based on OpenDivX. As Xvid is the GNU GPL free software, this means that the software's source code is publicly available. And the programmer can modify the code.

Currently, the system uses the Xvid version Xvid 1.2.2. Download Xvid 1.2.2 source package xvidcore-1.2.2.tar.gz, and unpacke it, cross-compile and transplante to the ARM platform. According to the actual project, compile the following steps:

1) Ensure that the arm-linux-gcc cross compiler tools installed correctly;

2) Uncompress xvidcore source code:

tar xzvf xvidcore-1.2.1.tar.gz

3) Into the directory of "xvidcore / build / generic", you can run ". / Configure -h" to display help information. According to help information, you can set the static link library and the dynamic link library installation path, and configurate the cross compiler. According to the actual situation, you can execute the following commands to configure the software features, and generate the file of "platform.inc".

#./configure build=arm-linux-gcc host=arm-linux –disable -assembly --prefix=/usr/local/arm/3.4.1/arm-linux

4) Manual configuration the file of "platform.inc". Change CC = / usr/local/arm/3.4.1/bin/arm-linux-gcc, then you can run "make", "makeinstall" to compile and install the source code of Xvid.

5) Into the directory of "examples", run the file of "Makefile", compiled xvid_bench, xvid_decraw, xvid_encraw three documents, and download these files to the target board through the serial port, then you can run the three files.

6 System Testing

After debugging and optimized, under the clock speed of 400 MHz, the resolution of QCIF 176 × 144 image is up to 20 f/s encoding speed. And the maximum time delay of image transmission is about 120ms. Then the design basically can meet to the real-time encoding, and can achieve the practical requirements. Outdoor transmission is up to 3km, indoor transmission is up to 140m.Then it can achieve long distance transmission of video information.

Fig. 3. Test results

7 Concluding

In this paper, we achieved the video transmission in wireless sensor network, that is in accord with development trend of digital and networked. And compared with traditional video surveillance solutions this design has the advantageas of simple equipment, small size, low cost. S3C2440 microprocessor is used in the front collected part, use its video interface, the speed of image collection can be achieved requirements of dynamically display (clock frequency in the 400M, display rate of QVGA images is up to 20 f/s). Monitoring client uses the video objects segmentation method which is based on MPEG-4. The system is high cost performance and easy to use.

References

1. Yang, Y., Hu, Y., Lin, Z.: The design of embedded image transmission system based on S3C2410 and Linux. Micro Computer Information (23) (2007)
2. Zhao, Y., Zhang, Y.: Achievement of video image acquisition based on Video4 and Linux. Computer Programming Skills & Maintenance (5) (2006)
3. Hu, D., Zhang, G.: Design and research of digital video surveillance system based on ARM. Electronics 09, 17–19 (2008)
4. Wang, X., Liu, J.: Research of remote video surveillance system based on ARM platform. Micro Computer Information 1(2), 178–180 (2007)
5. Wang, X.: Research an implementation of an MPEG-4 video capture and transmission system. Computer Measurement & Control (2005)
6. Bi, H.: New video compression coding standard H.264/AVC, vol. 3. Posts & Telecom Press (2006)
7. Stevens, W.R.: TCP/IP Illustrated, vol. 1. Machinery Industry Press (2004)
8. Du, M., Chang, C.: The Design Scheme of Streaming Media Syatem based on Mobile Communication Network. Control and Automation Publication Group 8(2), 275–278 (2006)
9. Yang, Q., Zhao, J., Ma, J.: Improvement about H.264 video coding algorithm on DM642. Control and Automation Publication Group 8-2, 269–271 (2006)
10. Han, C., Hu, F.: Optimization of H.264 Encoder Based on TMS320DM642 Platform. Control and Automation Publication Group 3-2, 164–166 (2007)
11. Wang, L., Liao, Y., Zhu, Z.-b., Zhou, H.: Design of H.264 Video Encoder and Motion Estimation algorithm Optimization. Control and Automation Publication Group 3-2, 155–156 (2007)
12. Dai, Y., Li, Q., Zhang, Q.: CC Jay Kuo: SIMD-efficient loop unrolling design for embedded multimedia applications. In: ICME 2004, vol. 126, pp. 1851–1854 (2004)

An Improved Apriori Algorithm

Jianlong Gu[1], Baojin Wang[2], Fengyu Zhang[2], Weiming Wang[1], and Ming Gao[1]

[1] College of Information & Electronic Engineering Zhejiang Gongshang University No.18, Xuezheng Str., Xiasha University Town, Hangzhou, 310018, P.R. China
[2] National Digital Switch System Engineering and Technological R&D Center The PLA Information Engineering University Zhengzhou, 450002, P.R. China
long25246@163.com

Abstract. Association rules mining occupies an important position in data mining. In order to improve the efficiency of mining of frequent itemsets, contrapose the two key problems of reducing the times of scaning the transactional database and reducing the number of candidate item sets, an improved algorithm is presented based on the classic Apriori algorithm. The theoretical analysis and test results show that the improved algorithm is better than Apriori algorithm significantly on efficiency.

Keywords: Data mining, Association rules, Apriori algorithm.

1 Introduction

Data Mining [1] (DM),which is also called Knowledge discover in databases (KDD) [2][3]. It is a process that extraction of implicit beforehand, people do not know, potentially useful information and knowledge from the large, incomplete, noise, and the fuzzy and random data according to the established goal. With the increasing amount of data and people to the relationship between various items of data mining association rules, in data mining is an important status in data mining, and also one of the main tasks.

Problem of mining association rules was presented by Agrawal et in 1993, then the Apriori algorithm come into being in their study,this algorithm has been as a classical association rule mining algorithms have been cited so far. Many studies and improvements are based on the Apriori algorithm started.

2 Description of Apriori Algorithm

The basic idea of the Apriori Algorithm is:

Firstly, the smaller the frequent itemsets L_k produce larger candidate frequently sets L_{k+1}, do this repeatedly,so all the frequency set out. These items set the frequency

D. Zeng (Ed.): ICAIC 2011, Part I, CCIS 224, pp. 127–133, 2011.

of at least appear predefined minimum support as, then by frequency set association rules, these rules generated must meet the minimum support and minimum confidence.

The core of the Apriori algorithm is how togenerate all the frequent itemsets, it uses an iterative approach layer by layer, described as follows in pseudo code[4]:

Import:Data base D; Minimum support threshold min-sup.

Export: Frequent itemsets L in D.

1. L_1 = {large 1-itemsets};

2. for (k = 2; $L_{k-1} \neq \Phi$; k + +) { ;

3.C_k = apriori.gen (L_{k-1} , min.sup) ; / / Generate next candidate item sets of mining;

4. for all transactions $t \in D$ { ;

5. C_t= subset (C_k,t);

6. For all candidates $c \in Ct$;

7. c.count++;

8. };

9. $L_k = \{ c \in C_k \mid c.count \geq min.sup\}$;

10. };

11. return $L = \cup L_k$.

Algorithm called function apriori.gen(L_{k-1}, min.sup) in order to produce k candidates through k-1 frequent itemsets. It uses the following properties[5]:

1.If X is frequent itemsets, any nonvoid proper subsets of X is frequent itemsets;

2.If X is not frequent itemsets, any supersets of X is non-frequent itemsets.

Algorithm described below:

For each itemset $I_1 \in L_{k-1}$

for each itemset $I_2 \in L_{k-1}$

if($I_1[1]=I_2[1]) \wedge (I_1 [2] = I_2 [2]) \wedge \ldots \wedge (I_1 [k-2]= I_2 [k- 2] \wedge (I_1 [k- 1] = I_2 [k-1])$

then {

$c=I_1 \infty I_2$; // Merge: generate candidate set

if has infrequent-subset(c,L_{k-1})

then delete c; / / Pruning process: remove non-frequent itemsets

else insert c to C;

}

return C;

Function called infrequent-subset(c, L_{k-1}) is to judge whether c need to add in the candidate set of k. The Algorithm is:

for each itemsets(k-1).subset s of c

If $s \in L_{k-1}$ then return TRUE;

return FALSE;

Then, the generated frequent itemsets generated rules to meet the minimum confidence to form rule sets and output.

Apriori Algorithm has served as a classical association rule mining algorithm is used. However, there are two significant performance bottleneck[6], namely:

1. The frequent (k-1) - itemsets L_{k-1} that connect to generate large quantities of candidate frequent k-itemsets. The candidate k-itemset C_k generated by L_{k-1} is

growing exponentially, the problem is more serious especially when the two-dimensional candidate sets generated.

2..It needs to scan the entire datebase repeatedly when testing and verifying candidate frequent k-items, that is very time-consuming, and causes great I / O load. For each K cycle, every element in the candidate set C_k must through scanning the database to verify whether it has been added into L_k.

3 The Improved Apriori Algorithm and Its Description

Apriori uses an iterative method called searching step by step, k-item set used to explore (k +1) - itemsets. In order to improve the efficiency of genetaring frequent itemsets step by step, we can use Apriori's nature to compress the search space, namely: all non-empty subset of frequent item sets are must also be frequent.

How to determine the candidate frequent itemsets, how to calculate the support count of itemsets, how to reduce the number of candidate itemsets and how to reduce the times of scaning the transactional database are 4 key technologies in association rules. The improvement based on the set operation presented in this paper contrapose the two key problems of reducing the times of scaning the transactional database and reducing the number of candidate item sets.

Property 1: All nonvoid subsets of the frequent itemset data are frequent.

When mining 2-itemset and k-itemset itemsets (k> 2), all nonvoid subsets of the frequent itemset data are frequent, namely every nonvoid subsets of the frequent itemset may have minimum support. So the Apriori algorithm uses a kind of coupling rule to generate the candidate sets, we usually can define the rule in this way:

$L_k*L_k=\{p \cup q,\ p, q \in L_k,\ p.item1 = q.item1,\ldots,p.itemk\text{-}1 = q.itemk\text{-}1,\ p.itemk<q.itemk\}$

Corollary 1: We can know that the necessary condition of k-D data itemset X_k is frequent itemset is that all its (k-1)-D subitems are frequent items from Property 1,denoted as X_{k-1}.

Corollary 2: K-D data itemset X_k itself isn't the maximum frequent itemset data if any (k-1)-D subitems X_{k-1} of k-D data itemset X_k is not frequent item.

Corollary 3: X_k is k-D frequent itemset, X_k can't be k-D maximum frequent data itemse if the number of (k-1)-D subitem in which is contained in (k-1)-D frequent itemsets less than k-1. The frequent item sets X_k for each element in the (k-1)-D subset C_{k-1}, the number of occurrences is not less than k-1.

Proof: The number of (k-1)-D subitems in data item set X_k is k-1. If the high frequency data item set X_{k-1}, contains the (k-1)-D subitem of X_k is less than the number of k-1, then there exists (k-1)-D subitems X_k is not frequent item sets ,the Corollary 2 showed that k-D data item sets itself is not high frequent data itemset.

The ideas of improving Algorithm:

The improved algorithm in the scanning of the original transaction database to establish a 1-itemsets as the key elements in the set, Tset means the new database table structure of itemset that contains its elements' transaction ordinal, in the calculation of the candidates for the support of the collection, and through such basic operations to reduce found frequently sets the complexity of the calculation process, in order to improve the performance of the algorithm, and also can greatly reduce the space occupying rate.

The basic steps of algorithm:

Scanning the transaction database one by one, resulting in 1-itemset candidate set C_1, when scanning of each transaction, not only count each item, but also record the contained transaction identifier TID. After scanning the database once, in the candidate set C_1, each item set contains a list of corresponded transaction identifier. The structure of C_1 as follows: (itemset Items, supports several sup, transaction identifier set Tset).

Remove the itemsets that don't meet the minimum support from C_1,and get L_1.

L_{k-1} self-connected, generates C_k, in which the affair identifier set of C_k is equal to the intersection of its two L_{k-1}'s affair identifier sets. We can get the count of every itemset in C_k through calculating the number of TID that in the affairs identifier set corresponding to the itemsets in C_k.

The algorithm is being improved mainly contrapose the stage of finding frequent set. The idea of improving algorithm is mainly based on set operations. The formal description of the improved algorithm is given as follows:

```
Import: Data base D; Minimum support threshold min-sup.
Export: Frequent itemsets L.
L1 = {large 1-itemsets};//Here L1 is made up of Itemset 、Tset and support
 number.
     For ( k = 2; Lk-1 ≠ ∅; k++) do begin
      Lk = gen ( Lk-1);     // Generate K-item frequent set
     end
L =∪Lk;
```

In the function gen, the input is L_{k-1},the results can generate k-item frequent sets directly. Function gen is implemented as follows:

```
Import: (k-1)- Frequent itemsets Lk-1
Export: k-Frequent itemsets Lk
gen (Lk-1){
          Ck ={Lk-1.Itemset * Lk-1.Itemset}  // Generate candidate sets
Tk ={Lk-1.Tset ∩Lk-1.Tset}            //Affair-supported sets do intersection
For all candidates c ∈ Ck do
     c.support=Count(c.Tk);           //Calculate each support number
If c.support < minsup then
delete c
end
For each item i∈ 1-itemsets do
i.count=Count(i.c);   // Calculated for
each concentration of an element in the existing number of occurrences of the
candidate
If i.count<k then
     delete c        // Delete the element i contains the candidate set c
end
   return Lk
 }
```

4 Algorithm Testing

The following example to deal with HTTP logs, respectively, the improved algorithm and Apriori algorithm was tested to compare their execution time.

Http logs were selected 200, 500, 1000, 2000, the minimum support is set to 0.1,0.2, respectively, to test, in which the log of the time field to do the preprocessing, the time reduction treatment fields, the day is divided into twenty-four areas, namely:

T_0: 00:00:00-00:59:59
T_1: 01:00:00-01:59:59
T_2: 02:00:00-02:59:59
T_3: 03:00:00-03:59:59
...
T_{21}: 21:00:00-21:59:59
T_{22}: 22:00:00-22:59:59
T_{23}: 23:00:00-23:59:59

Table 1. Algorithm execution time compared Units: s

Data volume	Min-sup=0.1		Min-sup=0.2	
	Improved	Apriori	Improved	Apriori
200	0.8	3.0	0.6	2.6
500	1.1	4.5	1.0	4.1
1000	1.8	9.3	1.5	8.5
2000	2.5	17.6	1.8	16.2

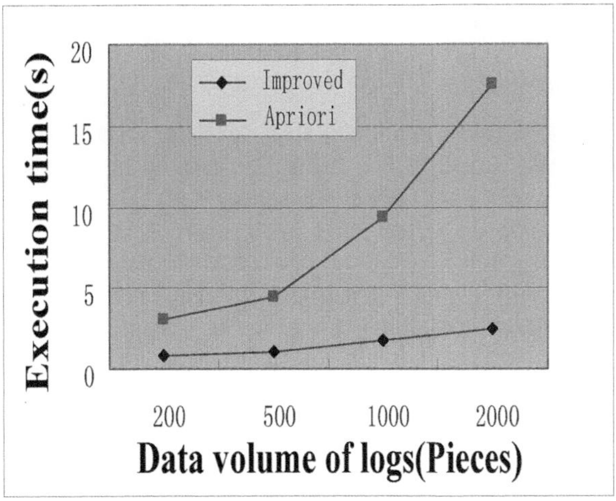

Fig. 1. Compare when min-sup=0.1

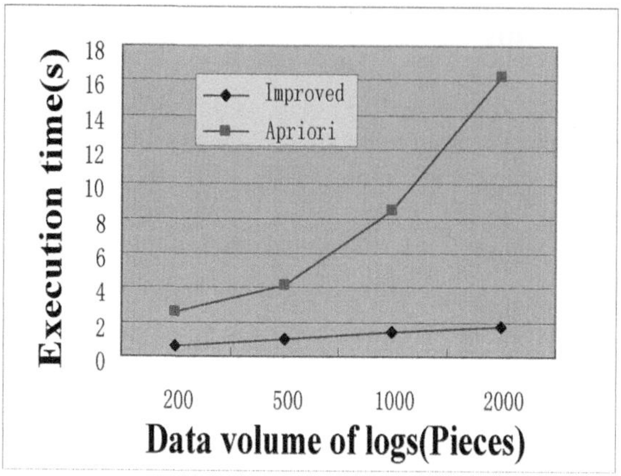

Fig. 2. Compare when min-sup=0.2

The results show that the performance of the improved algorithm is better than Apriori algorithm significantly. When the minimum support is 0.1, with the increase of log data, the improved algorithm can reflect more advantage. When the minimum support increases to 0.2, because of the reducing attributes itemsets, mining time becomes shorter.

5 Conclusions

This paper contraposes the two key problems of reducing the times of scaning the transactional database and reducing the number of candidate item sets,an improved algorithm is presented based on the classic Apriori algorithm. The new algorithm improves the efficiency of mining the frequent itemsets, and then improves the algorithm computing speed.

Acknowlegment. We would like to thank the sponsorship by the National Natural Science Foundation of China under Grant No. 60903214, 60970126, the National High Technology Development 863 Program of China under Grant No. 2008AA01A323, No.2008AA01A325, No.2008AA01Z214, No.2009AA01A334, Zhejiang Provincial NSF China No. Y1080078, Y1090452, and Zhejiang Sci & Tech Project No. 2009C31066, 2009C11050.

References

1. Han, J., Kamber, M.: Data Ming: Concepts and Techniques, 2nd edn. Machinery Industry Press, Beijing (March 2007)
2. Brodley, C.E., Lane, T., Stough, T.M.: Knowledge discovery and data mining. American Scientist 87(1), 54 (1999)
3. Fayyad, U.: Data mining and knowledge discovery in databases. Communications of the ACM 39(11) (1996)

4. Agrawal, R., Srikant, R.: Fast Algorithms for Mining Association Rules in Large Database. ACM, Yark
5. `http://acm.lib.tsinghua.edu.cn` (1996)
6. Brodley, C.E., Lane, T., Stough, T.M.: Knowledge discovery and data mining. American Scientist 87(1), 54 (1999)
7. Palshikar, G.K., Kale, M.S., Apte, M.M.: Association rules mining using heavy itemsets. Data & Knowledge Engineering 61(1), 93–113 (2007)

A Process Modeling Method Based on Cooperation Pattern Research in Airplane Design

Zhou Anning[1] and Liu Yi[2]

[1] College of Aerospace Engineering, Nanjing University of Aeronautics and Astronautics Nanjing, China
[2] College of Aerospace Engineering and Applied Mechanics, Tongji University Shanghai, China
zhouanning001@in.com

Abstract. A process modeling method was raised based on cooperation pattern in airplane design, aiming at the difficulty of complexity and enormous magnitude of airplane design process. By investigating design steps, tools and organization of airplane design experienced, 3 cooperation patterns were summarized. Detailed modeling method based on cooperation pattern and Petri net was described, proven to be less specialized knowledge dependent and convenient.

Keywords: process modeling, airplane design, cooperative design, design process, cooperation pattern.

1 Introduction

Modern plane tends to be more complex and delicate, with increasing variety of onboard equipment, contribution from dozens of disciplines and powerful functions implemented in limited space [1]. Design process of airplane is character- ized by coupling knowledge field, varied partner, intensive conflict, long development cycles and entangled workflow. Thus process optimization and Process Reengineering in airplane design became important and difficult. Especially its design process modeling was hard, considering its enormous magnitude.

Present process modeling method included: directed dia- gram [2,3], IDEF series [4], Petri net [5], and design structure matrix [6,7]. These methods met following difficulties in experience [8]:

1) Process modeling language was complex. And long learn- ing and training time was expended for mastery of it.
2) Subjectivity in modeling effected too much. Individual differences in modeling might be huge.
3) Analyzer must be familiar with the process modeled. Specialized knowledge and running mechanism of enterprize was essential for modeling correctly.

In airplane design, the difficulties tend to be even huger: specialized knowledge was wide edged and profound; staff involved in design was huge, which make it impossible to interview designers one by one.

D. Zeng (Ed.): ICAIC 2011, Part I, CCIS 224, pp. 134–142, 2011.

In present airplane design process, there existed several co- operation patterns. They occurred in different stage, with dif- ferent feature. With the help of cooperation pattern research,design process modeling of airplane might be more objective, decrease the need of specialized knowledge. Cooperation patterns of airplane design were summarized in this paper by investigating working steps, human-human interactions and tools in design-experienced. And a modeling method based on cooperation pattern in airplane was proposed, to overcome above difficulties and advance the research of process optimization and Process Reengineering.

2 Cooperation Pattern in Airplane Design

Present plane was designed in a formal heavy-duty engi- neering design process, in which design activity was divided into several phases linked along specific sequence. Phases include: demonstration phase, scheme phase, engineering de- velopment phase, design typification phase and manufactory typification phase, and each of them might be divided into more detailed phases. Sub system was designed in separate department, and information flow across sub systems must occur through communication pipes between departments. By researching experience in plane design process, 3 cooperation patterns were found to eliminate conflicts: terrace style, companion style, and delivery style. They were combined together in real plane design. Chaos style appeared often in general machinery industry, was rare in plane design.

A. Terrace Style

Sub-systems were designed separately, then they were put together to comprehensively assess for digging conflict out and raising modification resolution, after their design reached a certain completion. This kind of cooperation pattern was defined terrace style.

As demonstrated in Fig. 1, after general parameters were decided, tasks were allocated; interface and boundary be- tween sub-systems were defined. Then structure and equip- ment were designed separately. Functions and performance demands of sub-system itself only were considered during the stage. At last all sub-systems were assembled together and assessed to dig conflict out and find way of eliminating conflict. Above procedure would be iterated until no conflict could be found. Interface and boundary definitions between sub-systems were adjusted, and constrain were added to subsystem before iteration.

This pattern used most often in airplane design. Digital mockup tech was helpful for finding conflict intuitively, weighing effect of conflict solution and eliminating the ambiguity of interface and boundary definitions between sub- systems.

B. Companion Style

In design process of some plane, a designer from partner institute on the fire line was dispatched to resident in the institute responsible for the project. The designer reported the progress of project instantly, especially the portion his institute related. According to the report, partner institute adjusted solution, modify design details to remove conflict, instantly. This cooperation pattern was defined companion style.

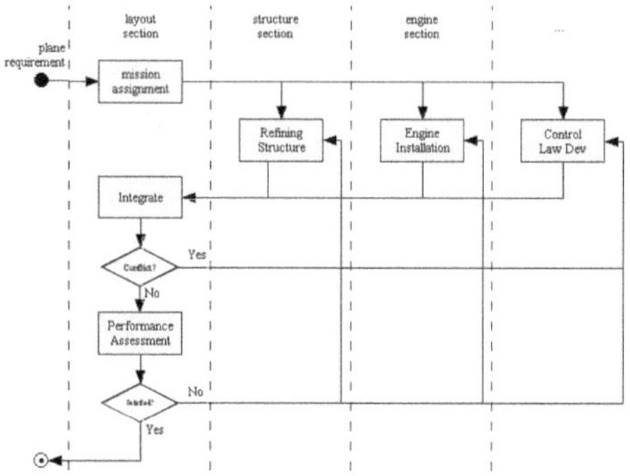

Fig. 1. Terrace Styled Cooperation

As shown in Fig. 2, design of one sub-system kept chang- ing, responding the design improvement of another. Firstly concerned components and features were named in historic custom or some protocol. Dispatched designer observed design process of related components closely, and assessed the effect to his own portion. Once the effect tended to be high, the action was reported to partner institute quickly. Partner institute changed her own design to remove conflict, according to the information newly reported.

The pattern used often either in plane design process. Unified unambiguous naming specification might accelerate transmission of design information.

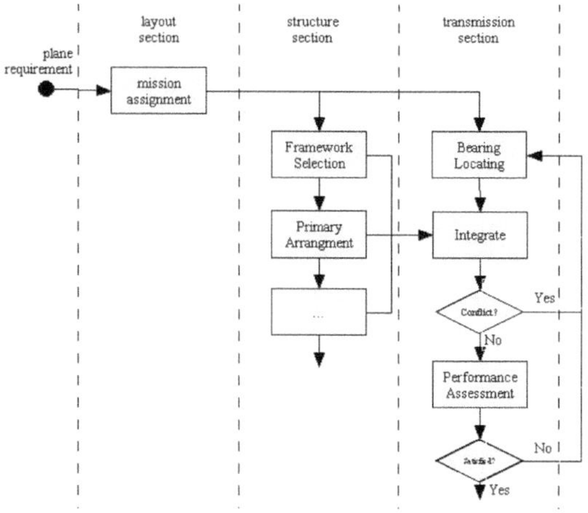

Fig. 2. Companion Styled Collaboration

C. Delivery Style

Delivery style means one part of design act as input for design of another, e.g. cooperation of manufactory design with design typification.

When two tandem design tasks transferred, the former delivered the whole design data, tolerance requirement and special annotation to the latter. Both just concerned the conflict inner itself, without iteration across departments to remove conflict.

Design specifications as DFM and DFA for upstream tasks originate from experience of downstream tasks were quite important for this style. More deeply upstream learned these specifications; more design space might be provided to the downstream.

D. Comparison of Cooperation Patterns

Characteristics of cooperation patterns were shown in table 1. It was outlined that companion style has the best efficiency and effect. While terrace style can support more participants than 2. Delivery style was simple.

Table 1. Comparison of Cooperation Patterns

Patterns	Terrace Style	Companion Style	Delivery Style
Perticipants	n-n	n-1	n-1
Coordination Point	Rare of Iteration	Whole Process	None
Concurrent Degree	High	Very High	Low
Conflict De-bug Rate	High	Very High	Low
Process Complexity	Normal	Complex	Simple
Itertion Times	Many	Few	None

3 Modeling Method Based on Cooperation Pattern

Using cooperation patterns, modeling method might be more convenient and objective. In the method, cooperation sequence was build, representing skeleton of design process.

A. Modeling Procedures

Modeling method includes two parts: cooperation pattern differentiation and analysis; process expression. The former one was executed mainly by airplane designers. And the latter one was modeling experts job.

Cooperation pattern differentiation and analysis was to give detailed cooperation content and sequence. Firstly, all designers wrote down all the cooperation procedures during design of a specific plane type. Time, member, thesis, object, what for, engaging work and then work representation in each procedure should be recorded. After that, records cross designers was reconsidered synthetically, focusing on uniting records with same time segment, designer involved, thesis and reason. Cooperation patterns of records were identified. Every cooperation patterns were analyzed in detail, to give participants, themes, duration and relationship between de- sign object. All cooperation patterns were collected, coded and sorted. Hierarchical and nesting relations between objects were revealed either. Cooperation sequence was built by linking cooperation patterns along time line.

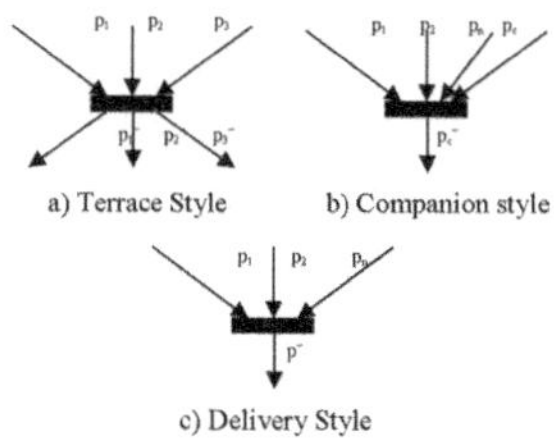

Fig. 3. P/T Representations of Cooperation Patterns

Process expression was to model the process, according to the cooperation sequence. Sequence of cooperation patterns was described with P/T net. The net was mapped to a abstract model net. By analyzing the net morphism, iterating and singleton segment was discovered, so that P/T net was simpli- fied, shaping ultimate process model net. Detailed design task was filled between cooperation. Actors might be traced either. Most complicated transition information was listed. And the dependency between tasks was clear. It became much easier for modeling expert to express the design process with certain modeling language.

By polishing in designs of several plane types, a mature, stable, generalized design process model might come into being.

B. Analyze with Net Morphism

Net morphism involve 2 P/T net: Cooperation connection net and Abstract model net.

Cooperation connection net N was defined as a P/T net (P, T, F) of cooperation sequence, among which:

P represents real design object, assigned new identifier once modified;

T represents cooperation, assigned new identifier each time; F represents dependence between cooperation and design object.

Cooperation patterns were described by transfer demon- strated in Fig. 3. Terrace style involved design objects p1,p2,..., pn, and-leads to modification requirement of objects p1 , p2 ,...., pm ; in companion style, object pc accomplished several modification p1, p2,..., pn of object p, and reached pc ; delivery style-get p , after p1, p2,..., pn was submitted.

Abstract model net N' was another P/T net (P', T, F'), among which:

P' represents abstract design object, whose identifier won't change after cooperation modification;

T represents cooperation;

F' represents connection between P' and T, assigned by replacing P elements in F with corresponding P', one direction presenting once.

Morphism $f: N \rightarrow N'$ was defined with:

$\forall p \in P, f(p) \in P'$ equals to abstract object of p;

$\forall t \in T, f(t) = t$;

$\forall \mathrm{f} \in F, f(\mathrm{f}) \in F'$ equals to corresponding abstract direction.

Obviously f implemented map modes in Fig. 4, so compromised definition of net morphism[9]. Besides, $f(P) = P'$, $f(T) = T$, $f(F) = F'$, $f(P \cup T) = P' \cup T$ show f is homomorphic mapping.

As sub-net of N, $N_1 = (P_1, T_1, F_1)$ and $N_2 = (P_2, T_2, F_2)$, were repeating/iterating procedure, if the fol- lowing was satisfied.

For $\forall x \in P_1$, $\exists y \in P_2$, so that $f(x) = f(y)$.

For $\forall x \in T_1$, $\exists y \in T_2$, so that $f(^o x) = f(^o y)$.

For $\forall x \in T_1$, if $\exists p_1 \in {}^o x$ and $x_1 \in {}^o p_1$, then $\exists y \in {}^o T_2$, $p_2 \in {}^o y$, $y_1 \in {}^o p_2$, made $f(^o x) = f(^o y)$ and $f(^o x_1) = f(^o y_1)$.

Each cooperation corresponds to some design tasks, which modified or initiated design objects. So cooperation proce- dure represented transferring of design task. Design object in plane design, was stated as node of product structure. Product structure was hierarchical tree formed, while the design ob- ject in real design was specific leaf. So it might imply upper level node in design task. Searching of repeating/iterating procedure should be executed either, after design object was fold into upper level node.

As important reference of modeling, repeating/iterating procedures founded in analyze should be commented with reason of acceptation/ abandon in detail.

Fig. 4. Map Modes of Net Morphism

C. Use Case

Use case involved a segment in design of some plane on a section. As shown in table 2, the design included 7 cooperation procedure: one delivery style, one companion style and 5 terrace style.

Cooperation connection net N=(P,T,F)was build, among which:

P={p1:Hydraulic, p2:Bottom Board, p3:Hydraulic.1, p4: Bottom Board.1, p5:Wire, p6:Wire.1, p7:Left Board, p8:Fuel Tank, p9:Left Board, p10:Hydraulic, p11:Left Board.2, p12:Wire.2, p13:Section 091104, p14:Pipe, p15:Pipe.1};

T={t1, t2, t3, t4, t5, t6, t7};

F={(p1,t1), (p2,t1), (t1,p3), (t1,p4), (p4,t2), (p1,t2), (p5,t2), (t2,p6), (p7,t3), (p8,t3), (t3,p9), (p9,t4), (p3,t4), (t4,p10), (p10,t5), (p9,t5), (t5,p11), (t5,p12), (p4,t6), (p11,t6), (t6,p13), (p14 ,t7), (p2 ,t7), (p4 ,t7), (t7,p15)}.

Abstract model net N′=(P′,T,F′), including:

P′={ p1′: Hydraulic, p2′: Bottom Board, p5′:wire, p7′: Left Board, p8′:Fuel Tank, p13′:Section 091104, p14′:Pipe}; F′={(p1′,t1), (p2′,t1), (t1,p1′), (t1,p2′), (p2′,t2), (p1′,t2), (p5′,t2), (t2,p5′), (p7′,t3), (p8′,t3), (t3,p7′), (p7′,t4), (p1′,t4), (t4,p1′), (p1′,t5), (p7′,t5), (t5,p7′), (t5,p5′), (p2′,t6), (p7′,t6), (t6,p13′), (p14′,t7), (p2′,t7), (p2′,t7), (t7,p14′)}.

Net morphism m: P→P′ was defined as shown in table 3.

No repeating sub-net could be found.

Table 2. Coordination During a Design Segment

ID	Pattern	Participant	Thesis	Time
t1	Terrace Style	Hydraulic & Structure	Hydraulic installing	2009-09-25
t2	Terrace Style	Hydraulic & Structure	Hydraulic Plugging Wire	2009-10-12
t3	Terrace Style	Fuel Hydraulic & Structure	Setup Breathe Hole	2009-10-20
t4	Terrace Style	Hydraulic & Structure	Re-laying Components	2009-10-25
t5	Terrace Style	Hydraulic & Structure	Hydraulic Plugging Wire	2009-10-29
t6	Delivery style	Structure & Overall	Freezing 091104	2009-11-05
t7	Companion style	Structure & Pipe	Hydraulic Piping	2009-09-25

Table 3. Morphismm

P	p1	p2	p3	p4	p5	p6	p7	p8
m(p)	p1′	p2′	p1′	p2′	p5′	p5′	p7′	p8′
P	p9	p10	P11	p12	p13	p14	P15	
M(p)	p7′	p1′	P7′	p5′	p13′	p14′	p14′	

When design object was elevated to upper product structure node, cooperation connection net was transformed to N1= (P1, T, F1), among which:

P1= {p11: Hydraulic, p12: Section, p13: Hydraulic.1, p14: Section.1, p15: Wire, p16: Wire.1, p17: Section.2, p18: Fuel Tank, p19: Section.3, p110: Hydraulic.2, p111: Section.4, p112: Wire.2, p113: Section 091104, p114: Pipe, p115: Pipe.1};

F1={(p11,t1), (p12,t1), (t1,p13), (t1,p14), (p14,t2), (p11,t2),(p15,t2), (t2,p16), (p17,t3), (p18,t3), (t3,p19), (p19,t4),(p13,t4), (t4,p110), (p110,t5), (p19,t5), (t5,p111), (t5,p112), (p14,t6), (p111,t6), (t6,p113), (p114 ,t7), (p12 ,t7), (p14 ,t7), (t7,p115)}.

Abstract model net became N′=(P1′,T,F1′), among which:

P1′={p11′:Hydraulic, p12′:Section, p15′:Wire, p18′:Fuel Tank, p114′:Pipe};
F1′={(p11′,t1), (p12′,t1), (t1,p11′), (t1,p12′), (p12′,t2), (p11′,t2), (p15′,t2), (t2,p15′), (p12′,t3), (p18′,t3), (t3,p12′), (p12′,t4), (p12′,t4), (t4,p11′), (p11′,t5), (p12′,t5), (t5,p12′), (t5,p15′), (p12′,t6), (p12′,t6), (t6,p12′), (p114′,t7), (p12′,t7), (p12′,t7), (t7,p114′)}.

Net morphism m1: P1→P1′ was defined as shown in table 4.
Sub-nets: ({p11, p12, p13, p14, p15, p16}, {t1, t2}, {(p11, t1), (p12, t1), (t1, p13), (t1, p14), (p14, t2), (p11, t2), (p15, t2), (t2, p16)}) and ({p13, p19, p110, p111, p112}, {t4, t5}, {(p19, t4), (p13, t4), (t4, p110), (p110, t5), (p19, t5), (t5, p111), (t5,p112)}) were searched out to be repeating procedure.

Since the sub-net represents design process of hydraulic system installing inside airframe, it could be used in folding and simplifying cooperation connection net. Folding was realized by replacing sub-net with a transfer tf. All element of sub-net was removed, and outer links was transferred to tf. Then N turned to Nf=(Pf, Tf, Ff), among which:

Pf={ pf1:Hydraulic, pf2:Section, pf3:Hydraulic.1, pf5:Wire,

Table 4. Morphismm1

P	p11	P12	P13	P14	P15	P16	P17	P18
M1(p)	p11′	P12′	P11′	P12′	P15′	P15′	P12′	P18′
P	P19	P110	P111	P112	P113	P114	P115	
M1(p)	P12′	P11′	P12′	P15′	P12′	P114′	P114′	

pf6:Wire.1, pf7:Section.2, pf8:Furl Tank, pf9:Section.3, pf11:Section.4, pf12:Wire.2, pf13:Section 091104, pf14:Pipe, pf15:Pipe.1};
Tf={tf1, t3, tf2, t6, t7};
Ff={(pf1,tf1), (pf2,tf1), (pf1,tf1), (pf5,tf1), (tf1,pf3), (tf1,pf6), (pf7,t3), (pf8,t3), (t3,pf9), (pf9,tf2), (pf3,tf2), (tf2,pf11), (tf2,pf12), (pf4,t6), (pf11,t6), (t6,pf13), (pf14,t7, (pf2,t7), (pf4,t7), (t7,pf15)}.
Design process model was demonstrated in Fig. 5.

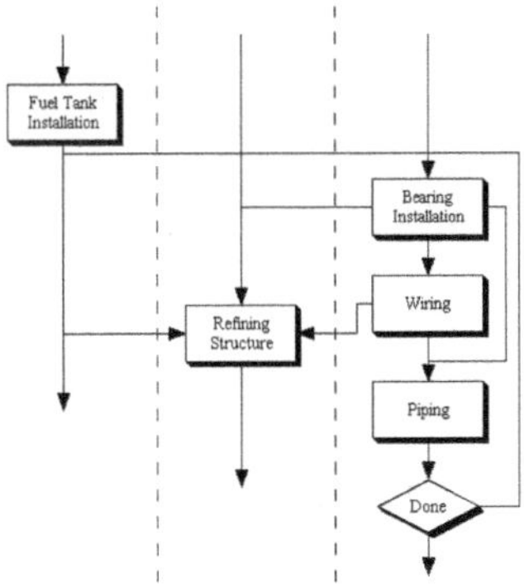

Fig. 5. Compartment of Some Plane Design Process

By identification and verification of cooperating activity, information about design and its track were recorded objectively. First part of modeling method was executed by designers together, so contradictory and ambiguous situation might be excluded by mutual proving. This part was quite objective. Using Petri net based general analyze method, process model might be deducted, which proved to be an objective operation. So the modeling method tends to be more objective. Moreover, expertise requirement on plane design and modeling skill were separated and executed by separated expert in the method, which decreased difficulty of plane design process modeling greatly. The method matches the design process of massive complex equipment with profound domain specific knowledge, and long term design cycle. Comprehensive documentation system and formal human resource management were good to the application of the method. And Petri net analyze show more value when flow of process tend to be sophisticated.

4 Conclusion

Cooperation patterns in airplane design made full use of mature engineering technology, upheld carrying out design of airplane, satisfying function and performance requirements. By investigating these patterns, process model of airplane might be built up more easily. Specialist knowledge was peeled off in form of cooperation patterns, and processed by designer. Only description and expression of model was left to modeling expert. Knowledge requirement for modeling was deduced, and modeling process tended to be more objective.

With convenient modeling method, process optimization and Process Reengineering in airplane design might be ad- vanced more smoothly.

References

1. Gu, S.F., Xie, S.S.: Airplane Overall Design. Press of Beihang University, BeiJing (2000)
2. Zhao, T.Q., Chen, Y.L.: Study on Workflow Modeling and Its Dy- namic Scheduling Based on Activity Analysis. System Engineering- Theory & Practice 22(3), 40–45 (2002)
3. Eppinger, S.D., Whitney, D.E., Smith, R.P.: A model based method for organizing tasks in product development. Research in Engineering Design 6(1), 1–13 (1994)
4. Lin, T., Zhang, Z.H., Li, H.C.: Process models in workflow management system. Computer Application 22(6), 13–18 (2002)
5. Fan, Y.S.: Fundamentals of Workflow Management Technology. Tsinghua University press, Beijing (2001)
6. Browning, T.R.: Applying the DSM to system decomposition and integration problems: a review and new directions. Engineering Management 48(3), 292–306 (2001)
7. Yassine, A., Falkenburg, D., Chelst, K.: Engineering design manage- ment: an information structure approach. International Journal of Production Research 37(13), 2957–2975 (1999)
8. Kong, J.L., Jia, G.Z.: The Study of Process Modeling Method Based on Process Mining. China Management Informationization 11(21), 58–61 (2008)
9. Yuan, C.Y.: Petri Net Theory and Application. Publishing House of Electronics Industry, Beijing (2005)

Present Research Status and Future Trends of Microbial Enhanced Oil Recovery*

Songyuan Liu[1] and Shuang Liang[2]

[1] School of Life Sciences Fudan University Shanghai, China
[2] School of Petroleum Engineering Northeast Petroleum University Daqing, Heilongjiang Province, China
song1715@sina.com

Abstract. In this paper, we introduced the application status of microbial enhanced oil recovery technology at home and abroad, illustrated the basic concept, mechanism and application method, the advantages and problems of the technology were also discussed, on this basis, we discussed the trend of microbial enhanced oil recovery technology, and concluded that the MEOR is one of the most important way to enhanced oil recovery.

Keywords: microbe. oil recovery technique, research status, active mechanism, trend.

1 Introduction

Oil is a non-renewable energy, through primary exploitation and secondary oil recovery, there is still 60% -70% of the crude oil can not be mined in the formation, how to enhance oil recovery by utilizing tertiary oil recovery(TOR) is always a subject that has been studied in many countries [1].

MEOR is a technique of TOR after thermal drive, chemical flooding, polymer flooding, and a pioneering application of biological engineering technology in the oil field development [2]. MEOR has been developed for half a century, but it is not formed a large-scale application in the world. First, enhanced oil recovery technologies such as chemical flooding developed rapidly, people focus main effort on the study of these technologies in the petro-states, but less in MEOR; second, the mechanism of MEOR is complex, and there are some issues have not been researched systematically, some defective technologies are still existent. However, it is proved that from preliminary research and testing, the MEOR with the advantages such as low cost, widely applicability and environmental protection is feasible, in the past ten years, the development speed of MEOR is obviously fast. In April 2009, "World Petroleum Microbial Technology Conference" has been held in Nigeria, MEOR has been concerned further around the world, and it showed a good development foreground.

* This work is partially supported by the National Natural Science Foundation of China Grant #50174035 to Shuang Liang.

D. Zeng (Ed.): ICAIC 2011, Part I, CCIS 224, pp. 143–149, 2011.

2 Appliaction Status of Meor

MEOR means that inject the microorganisms bacterium fluid which is fostered isolated in surface and nutrient solution in the reservoir, or simply inject the nutrient solution in the reservoir to activate the micro-organisms, make it grow and reproduce in the reservoir, produce metabolites to enhance oil recovery.

As early as 1926, Beckman, an American proposed the assumption that use the microbial activity and its metabolites to enhance oil recovery. In 1940, American Petroleum Research Institute proceeded a series of microbiological experiments, confirmed that microbes can produce the metabolite which is similar to chemical flooding enhanced oil recovery. In 1943-1953, the project of "Plan 43A" organized by the API had concentrated the systematic research on how micro-organisms influence on the oil origin and components, established a theoretical foundation for MEOR. The United States has conducted a pilot test in many fields in the 1980s, studied that MEOR can be used in paraffin precipitation, broken down and scale removal, single well huff and puff, profile modification, etc [3]. The past 20 years, the U.S. Department of Energy has funded at least 47 research projects of microbial enhanced oil recovery, the findings and field experiment showed that oil recovery can be increased by 16% at the later stage of water flooding [4]. The research and field application of indigenous microbial enhanced oil recovery technology are well-developed in Russian. At present, the technology has entered the stage of industrial application, has made 55×10^4t production increasing in old oil fields such as the Romanshkinian and Bashkir, and has extended the development life of the reservoir. In a variety of microbial enhanced oil recovery methods, the technology developed jointly by the Russian and German experts has been expanded in oil production, which is based on the process of injecting clostridium or bacillus, molasses with sugar content not less than 40% and inorganic additives into formation [4]. In the 1990s, the MEOR has been developed extensively in England, including technology analysis of microbial enhanced oil recovery, studies of reservoir simulator and effectiveness prediction [5]. Statoil has proceeded MEOR field test successfully in Norne field in the North Sea. At present, MEOR has been studied in Canada, Romania, Netherlands and Japan, the technology is increasingly sophisticated [6].

MEOR started late in China, the technology has been introduced from the United States and Canada. At the end of 1980s, two single wells have proceeded huff and puff field test in the Daqing oil field, and achieved good results, the oil production increased, water content decreased by about 10%. From 1990s, the pilot tracey of MEOR has been developed successfully in 14 oilfields, including Daqing, XinJiang, Shengli ect and achieved good effect. The first oil Microbial Technology Research Center has been built in Shengli Oilfield in China. At the late of 1990s, the research from a single well to block, the cumulative oil has overtaken 6×10^4t. In 1995, Jinzhou Oil Production Plant of Liaohe taked the lead in microbiological manipulation which is used in the research of gum and asphaltene in heavy oil [8].Since 2001, microbial oil field application test has been developed in Kongdian oil field of Dagang Oilfield, in 2004, the test expanded to three blocks, has enhanced cumulative production about 2.2×10^4t, the ratio of input-output is 1:13.2, achieved a better economic returns. The accomplishments of fungus compatibility research is obviously in Daqing oilfield. In 2008, microbial enhanced oil recovery technology has acquired new breakthrough in the Daqing Oilfield Exploration and Development Institute, by using microbial surfactants instead of part of synthetic surfactants, 30% cost of the active agent has been reduced. In China, we have gained achievements and experiences in the aspect of selection and evaluation of fungus, the production of fungus, design and monitoring of field application.

3 Mechanism and Method of Meor

3.1 Mechanism of MEOR

Microorganism can self-reproduced, underground reservoir is a highly efficient biological fermentation plant, in appropriate conditions, a bacillus can produce 4×10^9-7×10^9 a day and night, the capacity of drive oil is the result of bacteria synergistic effects. The mechanism of MEOR is complex, it can be briefly summarized into two aspects as followings [9,10]:

1) Microorganism Can Improve Oil Composition

a)Microbe can degrade high molecular weight hydrocarbons, include alkane, alicyclic hydrocarbons and aromatic side chains, which can reduce the oil viscosity or freezing point, and improve liquidity.

b)The enzyme that released from the grown of microorganism can degrade crude oil, change crude oil from the high-carbon chain to low-carbon chain, reduce heavy constituent, increase light component, make freezing point and viscosity low, which improve the liquidity of the crude oil in reservoir, and improve the quality of crude oil.

c)Microbe can produce the low molecular weight organic solvents such as alcohols, ketones, esters and others, which are dissolved in oil, reduce the viscosity of crude oil, or improve liquidity as a cosurfactant.

2) Microbe Changes the Flooding Environment

*a)*Microbe produce surface-active substances which can reduce interfacial tension, change the wettability of rock surface, make the film strip from the rock surface, improve washing oil ability of the flood water, the surface substances can make crude oil disperse and emulsify heavy oil to improve the heavy oil recovery.

b)Microbe produce low molecular weight organic acids, which can dissolute carbonate or inorganic mineral scale of rock surface and improve the formation permeability.

c)Microbe produces gases such as carbon dioxide, methane, nitrogen, which increase the formation pressure and reduce the viscosity of crude oil, carbon dioxide also can dissolve carbonate minerals, increase permeability.

d)Microbe produces biopolymer, which can increase the viscosity of injected water, improve the mobility ratio, seal off high permeability layer, deep profile and improve the sweep efficiency of water.

e)The relict body of bacteria can seal off high permeability layer, change the direction of flow, improve water flooding effect.

The key of MEOR is to create a specific environment in the reservoir, in which bacteria or beneficial indigenous bacteria can reproduce multiply, produce metabolites which are benefit for increasing oil.

3.2 The Method of MEOR

MEOR is mainly four methods [11]:

1) Microbial Huff Production: Inject the microbial fermentation liquor and nutrient solution into the production wells, shut-in for a period of time (range from days to weeks), make microbial fermented, then open wells to product, and so on.

2) Microbial Profile: The technology is to inject micro-organisms which can produce ploymer into the formation, make it reproduced highly in high permeability layer, and thus micro-organisms will play a role in blocking the high permeability zone. It is more effective than the injection of the synthetic organic polymer or gel, and it will not cause permanent damage formation.

3) Microbial Wax-removing Technology: Microbial wax-removing technology can replace the role of solvent and dispersant, and it can largely replace the hot oil treatment method.

4) Microbial Water Flooding: The technology is inject a mixture of bacteria and nutrient solution into the target stratum, produce active substances by physical and chemical effects such as surfactants, acids, alcohols, gases and others, which can release crude oil adsorbed at the surface of rock, make the oil not flow originally in the form of oil-water emulsion inject into the water flooding production wells, then be picked out from production wells.

4 The Advantages and Problems of Meor

4.1 The Advantages of MEOR

Compared with other TOR technologies, MEOR has its advantages [9,12]:

1) Low Cost: Injected microorganisms and culture medium are low-cost and not impacted by the prices of crude oil, strain formula can be adjusted flexibly by the reservoir.

2) The Required Equipment is Simple: The conventional flooding ground equipment can meet the construct requirements.

3) Wide Application: It can be used for various types of crude oil, including heavy oil and light oil.

4) Good Ecological Characteristics : Because microbes can move independently in oil reservoirs with underground fluid, without pressure, no harmful for formation, it will not cause significant problems of scaling and corrosion, and the product of MEOR is biodegradable, it will not cause environmental pollution.

5) Small Size and Strong Migration: Microorganisms can enter the corners and cracks of the reservoir that other technology can not reach, it only breed in oil and produce metabolites, avoiding blindness of the surfactant injecting and viscosity plugging.

Certain environmental conditions will be required for the growth of microorganisms, microbial enhanced oil recovery must choose appropriate reservoir conditions, such as temperature, pressure, salinity, pH and permeability, not all reservoirs are suitable for microbial enhanced oil recovery technology, which also determines the limitations of its own.

4.2 Problems of MEOR

MEOR technology developed rapidly, but there are still some problems [2,13]:

1) The Limitations of MEOR: Firstly, micro-organisms can be destroyed easily under reservoir conditions such as higher temperature, higher salinity and high content of heavy metal ions; secondly, cultivation conditions of microorganisms is not easy to grasp; thirdly, MEOR technology is not constructed easily in winter. In order to overcome these limitations, you need use genetic engineering, computer technology and genetic testing for MEOR.

2) Mechanism is Indistinct: Enhanced oil recovery mechanism under different formation conditions and concrete migration of microbial in the reservoir have not been thoroughly investigated, for example the contribution of different microbial metabolic products for EOR can't be quantified.

3) Field Process Optimization of MEOR is Difficult: Microbiological test blocks are often in the production tail and the situation in the ground is very complicated, which make the ground simulation extremely difficult. In the process of optimization, there are two problems, firstly, activator and microorganisms will be adsorbed by porous medium in the process of migration, the adsorption capacity of various components is difficult to determine; secondly, the total alternation of microorganisms in growth and reproduction is affected by reservoir conditions and nutritional concentration, there is not mature numerical simulation to determine the number of variations.

4) The Recognition and Emphasis of MEOR is Not High: The MEOR development is short, people are lack of knowledge, and the attention is insufficient, the development plan of MEOR has not yet formed in the country.

5 The Trend of MEOR

After nearly a century, the MEOR has been matured, obtained satisfied effect of simulation and dropping cost, especially for the exploitation of heavy oil, the methods is unmatched by others. Nowadays, the majority of our oil fields have entered the stage of tertiary oil recovery, the water content of produced fluid is more than 90%, meanwhile the distribution of heavy oil resources is wide, geological reserves is about 16.4×10^8t, the land-based heavy oil resources accounts for 20% of the total oil, the heavy oil riched in gum and bitumen accounts for about 7% of the total crude oil production, which provided the microbial enhanced oil recovery technology with broad application prospects.

MEOR will become one of the main technology of enhanced oil recovery in future. In order to achieve the goal of industrialized MEOR in China, the development trend of MEOR mainly focused on the following aspects in the future [12]:

1) Exploratory Study of Oil Engineering Microbial Bacteria: Using modern biological engineering technology, we can make feasible evaluation on microbial oil recovery engineering bacteria technology and the problem of economic and environment.

2) Screening and Training Bacteria Strain and Establishing Strains Library: We will establish the initial scale oil production microbial strains library in China.

3) The Study of MEOR Mechanism: Determine the main factors which to improve oil recovery directly in the process of microbial flooding, establish computer expert system which can determine microbial strains under reservoir conditions, achieve the intelligentization of screening MEOR reservoir and matching candidate species.

4) The Study of MEOR Numerical Simulation Software: We will develop the MEOR numerical simulation software which has intellectual property rights, achieves scientific scheme design and production operation of MEOR.

5) Draw Up Evaluation Index System, Evaluation Methods and Evaluation Standards of MEOR: In view of different reservoir conditions, such as heavy oil reservoirs, high water reservoirs, chemical flooding oil reservoirs, we will study evaluation index, evaluation methods and evaluation criteria of MEOR.

The application of MEOR is a complicated systematic project, in view of its comprehensiveness, complexity and multi-disciplinary, in order to achieve the above objects, we need work with the experts on microbiology, petroleum engineering, petroleum geology and organic geochemistry, and requires integrated use of intelligent computer expert system.

6 Conclusion

1) MEOR is TOR technology which follows the thermal flooding, chemical flooding, polymer flooding, it is one of the important ways to enhance oil recovery.
2) The study and field use of MEOR achieved significant results in oil companies at home and abroad, the technology has entered the stage of industrial application.
3) MEOR enhanced oil recovery mainly by improving components of crude oil and changing the flooding environment.
4) Methods of MEOR include extraction method, profile method, paraffin method and water displacement method.
5) Compared with other tertiary oil recovery technology, MEOR has advantages of low cost, simple equipment requirement, wide range of application and good ecological characteristics.

MEOR has broad development prospects, but there are still many problems on its applicability and application capability of people, so it is a long way to realize the industrialization of MEOR.

References

1. Chen, w., Hu, r., He, q.: Microbial enhanced oil recovery (MEOR) and oversea research progress in its application. Journal of Xi'an Petrolum University (Natural Science Edition) 24(4), 57–64 (2009)
2. Dou, q.: Advances in researches and outlook for microbial enhanced oil recovery. Natural Gas Industry 15(5), 559–563 (2004)

3. Liu, l.: Advances in Researching the Techniques of Microbial Enhanced Oil Recovery and Their Application Prospects. Sino-Global Energy 14(3), 41–45 (2009)
4. Mokhatab, S., Giangiacomo, L.: A Microbial enhanced oil recovery techniques improve production. World Oil 227(10), 6 (2006)
5. Sen, R.: Biotechnology in petroleum recovery: The microbial EOR. Progress in Energy and Combustion Science 34(6), 714–724 (2008)
6. Aksel, H., Krista, K.: Microbial enhanced oil recovery Mechanism. In: International Symposium of the Society of Core, Analysts, Canada, September 2007, pp. 10–13 (2007)
7. Lei, g.: The research and appliaction of microbial enhanced oil recovery. Acta Petrolei Sinica 22(2), 56–61 (2001)
8. Zhang, z., Li, q., Wang, h.: Advances in Researches on Field Trials for Microbial Enhanced Oil Recovery. Oilfield Chemistry 18(4), 383–388 (2001)
9. Chang, y.: The principle and applications of indigenous microbial enhanced oil recovery technology. Science & Technology Information (13), 109 (2006)
10. Lai, f., Cen, f., Huang, z., Xu, j.: Summary of microbial enhanced oil recovery technology development. Resources & Industries 8(2), 60–62 (2006)
11. Wu, r., Huang, x., Zhang, h.: Development of microbial enhanced oil recovery research. Inner Mongolia Petrochemical (10), 9–10 (2008)
12. Lu, j., Li, m.: Status and prospects of microbial enhanced oil recovery. Inner Mongolia Petrochemical (4), 24–25 (2006)
13. Peng, y., Ji, h.: Field of Microbial Enhanced Oil Recovery. Petroleum Industry Press (1997)

The Algorithm Design and Application of the Neural Network*

Junping Shi

Jishou University, Jishou Hunan, China
junpingshi@hotmail.com

Abstract. In order to improve oil and gas production, taking advantage of advanced neural network tools to design an appropriate algorithm to predict the extent of oil and gas damage and then to protect the oil and gas layer provided a strong guarantee of promoting oil and gas production. The application in Karamay Oilfield shows that combining neural network toolbox of Matlab with the sample data of the oil and gas layer training and establishing a set of mathematical models to predict the damage extent of oil and gas layer provides a powerful help to protect the oil and gas layer. The neural network prediction model has played a positive role in promoting the oil and gas production and enhancing the application of neural network system in oil and gas forecasting.

Keywords: Oil and gas damage, Algorithms, Neural networks, Modeling.

1 Introduction

Oil and gas layer damage is always a serious and common problem which troubled the production of oil industry. In recent years, oil and gas layer protection technology has become an important technology in oil and gas exploration and development of the whole process of each production in international. It has become a complex engineering problem which involved in multi-disciplinary, multi-disciplinary. According to the characteristics of reservoir bed, it has successfully applied a well drilling, well completion system which is compatible with each reservoir bed and support with each other, well completion methods, and a variety of measures to increase production. Neural network system in recent years is one of the world's advanced intelligent information processing technology, which is an intelligent information processing system developed on the basis of artificial intelligence theory and computer application science. The difference between Neural network system and general information system is that it's able to complete some works of reasoning with the thinking method which is similar to human mind; in some specific areas, it is able to make judgments and decisions as well as human experts or even better. Subsequently, Feigenbaum, a professor of the United States Stanford University, put forward the concepts of neural network system, well drilling and completion technology which is aimed at protecting the oil and gas layer from contamination achieved a rapid development in this period[1].

* Hubei Provincial Department of Education Science and Technology Research Project(B20101304): BP neural network prediction analysis in cleft lip surgery research.

D. Zeng (Ed.): ICAIC 2011, Part I, CCIS 224, pp. 150–155, 2011.

2 Assessment of the Oil and Gas Damage

There are seven evaluation methods of oil and gas layer sensitivity, namely: speed-sensitivity, water sensitivity, salt sensitivity, alkali sensitivity, acid sensitivity, stress sensitivity, temperature sensitivity[2]. Among which, the sensitivity test formula of speed-sensitivity, water sensitivity, salt sensitivity, alkali sensitivity, acid sensitivity is: $\frac{k_{i-1}-k_i}{k_{i-1}}\times 100\% \geq 5\%$ The corresponding penetration rate of the previous flow of Qi-1 is Ki-1, the corresponding penetration rate of Qi is Ki, then Qi-1 is called critical flow. When the measured values of degrees of damage are at different stages, its water sensitivity level is also different, as shown in Table 1.

Table 1. Water-sensitive level of evaluation criteria

Varying degrees of damage	≤5 %	5%~30 %	30%~7 0%	70%~90%	≥90%
Degree of water-sensitiv e	An hydrous Min	Jo-shui -min	Mediu m water-sensit ive	High water sensitivity	Highly water-sensiti ve

The calculation formula of damage extent can also be recorded as follows: $\frac{K_{\max}-K_{\min}}{K_{\max}}\times 100\%$. But we can not access to these parameters directly in the production practice. In view of this, through large number of production practice, we can get, the main factors that affected the damage of oil and gas layer are: montmorillonite content, illite content and kaolinite content, chlorite content, porosity, total salinity, clay content, particle The median particle size, oil viscosity, oil and gas ratio, permeability, etc., and the parameter value of these factors can be obtained by direct measurement. In the wellblock, because the geological structure is similar, so we can firstly obtain the sensitivity data of some kind of well through experiment, and then take these data as the training samples of neural network system to study, predict and analyze. Before prediction and analysis, firstly do three-dimensional reconstruction for testing samples through testing programs, the software flow chart is shown in Figure 1.

After the sample data is trained, we can get a prediction target data, by which, we can test the effect of training samples. Re-design a neural network system; obtain the final forecast data through the design of related algorithms and analysis. The main program is as follows.

```
function [Resulat]=testarray(TrainIn,TrainOut,TestIn)

P =TrainIn;

P=P';

T=TrainOut;

T=T';
```

```
net=newff(minmax(P),[17,2],{'tansig','purelin'},'trainlm');
net.trainParam.epochs=50;
net.trainParam.goal=0.001;
net.trainparam.show=NaN;
net=train(net,P,T);
P_test=TestIn;
Y = sim(net,P_test);
Y=Y';
Resulat=Y;
end
```

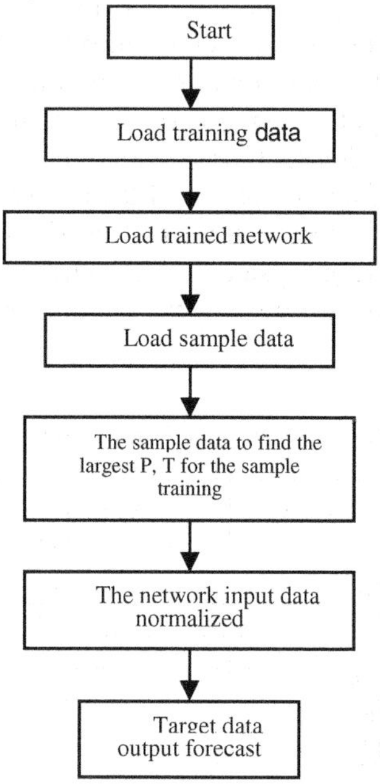

Fig. 1. Flow diagram of training samples program

In the neural network system, we comprehensively compare the effect of oil and gas evaluation by designing four sets of algorithms: descent algorithm of momentum gradient traingdm, Fletcher-Powell reverse algorithm of conjugate gradient traincgf; descent algorithm of adaptive learning rate of gradient traingda; using Levenberg-Marquardt method trainlm and so on.

3 Application of Neural Network System in Evaluation if Oil and Gas Layer Damage in the Xinjiang Oil Field

According to the design of neural network algorithm, we here take water sensitivity as an example. Firstly, through testing measured parameter values of a variety of data that sample wells affected water sensitivity indexes, take these tested data as training sample data, as which is shown in Table 2. Table 2 is the sample wells data that we measured in Karamay Xinjiang.

Table 2. Affect the Oil and Gas Major Factor in the Damage Layer of Data Like Wells

Pound	Montmorillonite (%)	Illite (%)	Kaolinite(%)	Chlorite (%)	Porosity	Total mineralization (mg/L)	Muddy(%)	Median particle size (mm)	Viscosity of crude oil (mPa·s)	Gas-oil ratio	$[K^{+}+Na^{+}]$(mg/L)	Permeability (μm^2)	Water-sensitive index
Zao-1	63.3	7.09	25.17	3.09	0.857143	601.76	0.15072	0.096	62.77	1	0.10216	0.2972	0.77
Zao-43	63	7.09	25.07	2.3	0.857143	516.671	0.21112	0.0965	3.34	0.75	0.089541	0.241352	0.8
Zao-12	63	7.09	25.07	2.3	0.857143	516.671	0.18536	0.096	9.4	0.75	0.089541	0.2482	0.68
Zao-1286	63	7.09	25.07	2.3	0.857143	516.671	0.19336	0.097	85.49	0.75	1	0.28024	0.82
Zao-116	63	7.09	25.07	2.3	0.857143	516.671	0.6264	0.096	16.85	0.75	1	0.832	0.35
F29-19	63.3	7.09	25.17	3.09	0.857143	384.102	0.7568	0.096	55.21	0.55	0.275176	0.136088	0.61
Zao-40-2	63.3	7.09	25.17	3.75	0.857143	404.108	0.15976	0.096	135.2	0.65	0.877214	0.68	0.56
F37-17	58.5	7.09	25.17	3.09	0.81	277.407	0.16936	0.096	65.77	0.317	0.213055	0.1448	0.79
Zao-1141	63	7.75	28	3.09	0.81	277.407	0.17296	0.096	89.45	0.317	0.204562	0.1712	0.65
F30-15	63.3	7.75	25.17	2.3	0.857143	516.671	0.258804	0.097	43.07	0.75	0.404271	0.169806	0.82
F33-1	63.3	7.75	25.07	2.3	0.857143	384.102	0.340531	0.096	134.6	0.55	0.245814	0.415399	0.35
F10-1	63.3	7.09	25.07	2.3	0.857143	384.102	0.351661	0.097	68.55	0.55	0.275176	0.209271	0.61
F15-5	63.3	7.09	25.07	3.09	0.857143	273.406	0.196844	0.098	46.9	0.275	0.069401	0.376054	0.56
Zao-1236	63.3	7.09	25.17	3.09	0.857143	535.609	0.1	0.15	126.57	0.8	0.136375	0.404555	0.79

In table 2, water sensitivity index is measured through testing. Take these data as sample data of neural network system training. In the neural network system, text the data in table 2 through four different training algorithms under the environment of matlab 6.5, we get Figure 2.

We can get from Figure 2, if we demand forecast accuracy reach 10-5, the algorithm Levenberg-Marquardt can achieve the required accuracy after 5 times. The descent algorithm of adaptive learning rate gradient traingda has not yet reached the required accuracy after 1000 times. Fletcher-Powell reverse algorithm of conjugate gradient traincgf Reverse achieved the requirements of the training accuracy after trained for 300 times. The descent algorithm of momentum gradient traingdm has also not yet reached the required accuracy after 1000 times. Analysed according to this, we have chosen Levenberg-Marquardt method trainlm as the preferred method for this network systems. Using this algorithm models to build prediction system and then to forecast the he water sensitivity index of five producing wells nearby, we can get the results shown in Table 3.

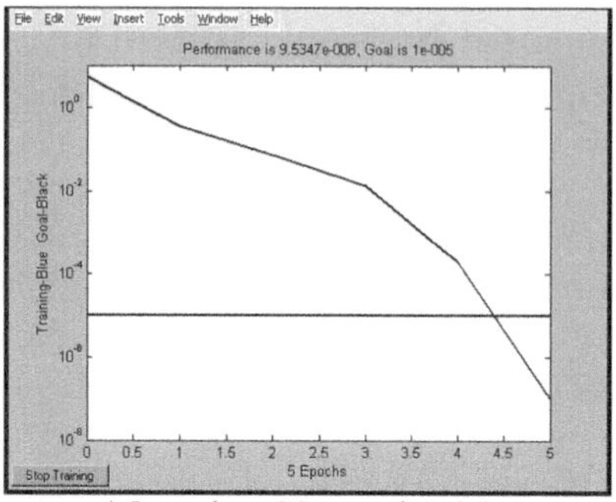

A Levenberg-Marquardt trainlm

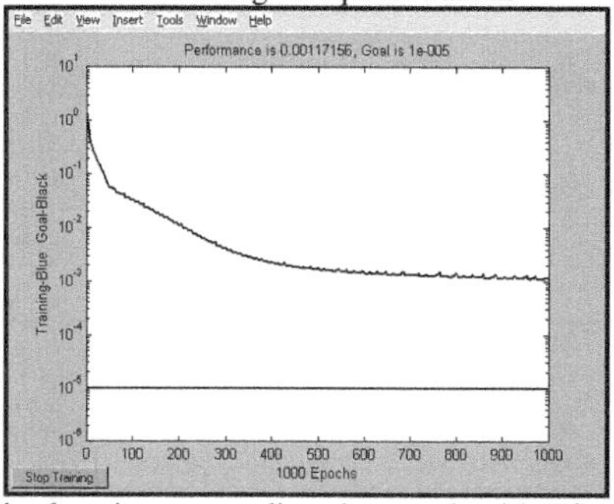

B Adaptive learning rate gradient descent algorithm for traingda

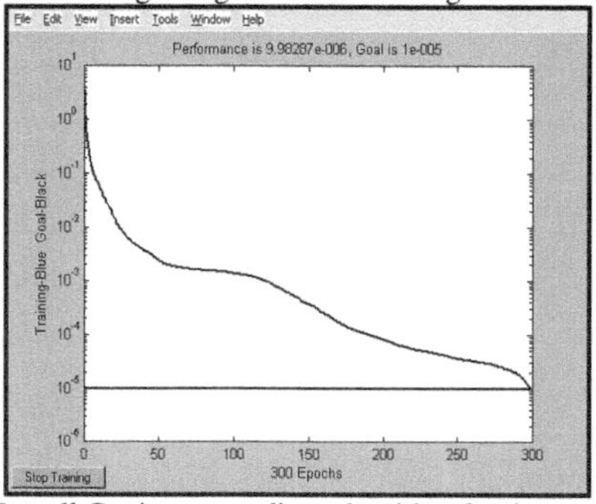

C Fletcher-Powell Conjugate gradient algorithm for the reverse traincgf

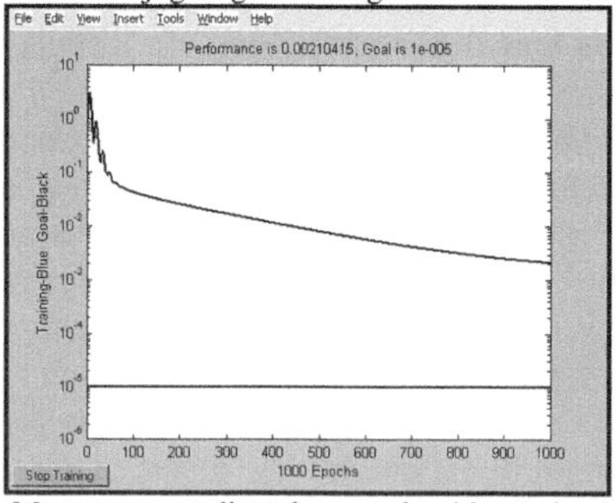

D Momentum gradient descent algorithm traingdm

Fig. 2. Result schematic diagram about four different algorithms of neural network system on data processing

Table 3. Comparison of Forecast Data with the Measured Data

Pound	Measured water-sensitive index	Predicted water-sensitive index
Zao-132 0	0.89	0.88
Zao-40- 21	0.86	0.87
Zao-30- 6	0.79	0.80
Zao-21	0.86	0.82

When predicted oil and gas layer data again for other wells in Karamay wellblock, the predicted results that we used this neural network is very close to the forecast results, the predicted accuracy has reached 90%. It can meet our requirements of production practices, played an active role in the protection of oil and gas layer and improved the production efficiency.

4 Conclusions

Neural network system is currently the most active subject in artificial intelligence research [3], which is also the crystallization of production and practice of human, scientific research, artificial intelligence and computer technology development, ,and have successfully applied in some areas. It has been widely extended to other research and applications areas. Because the neural network system united theory knowledge with expert experience, it greatly enhanced the accuracy of diagnosis and prediction, more and more widely used in oil and gas layer damage aspect, especially has a positive significance for the oil and gas exploration sensitivity prediction of wells exploration[4]. The technology's applying the neural network model to prediction of oil and layer damage improved monitoring of the oil and gas damage, played an important role in the oil and gas exploration, which is an innovation of oil and gas layer assessment.

References

1. Lu, S., Liu, L., Shek, L., Li, Y.: Based on automated reasoning in intelligent planning method. Journal of Software, Nian 05, 1226–1238 (2009)
2. Chen, M.: The Tactics Analysis about Early Phase Ends of the Partial Distortion Search. IEEE, Los Alamitos (2008), doi: 10.1109/WGEC, 17, 324-327
3. Jiang, Q.: The Realization of the Passive Caller Resumption about Mobile System Core Pool. IEEE, Los Alamitos (2008), doi: 10.1109/WGEC.2008.17, 487-490
4. Zhou, Z., Chen, S.: Neural network integration. Journal of Computers, Nian 01, 1–8 (2002)

Parameter Estimation of High-Voltage Circuit Breaker Based on Genetic Algorithms

Tao Jin[1], Wei Chen[2], Tao Ning[2], and Zhihua Li[2]

[1] Hubei Electric Power Test and Research Institute
[2] School of Electrical Engineering Wuhan University
Wuhan, Hubei Province, P.R. China
taotao48@yahoo.com

Abstract. A method of parameter estimation of High-Voltage circuit break based on genetic algorithms is proposed in order to estimate the parameters of capacitance, inductance and resistance in oscillation circuit DC circuit breaker and then properly assess the performance of DC circuit breaker. In this paper A genetic algorithm is introduced and applied in parameter estimation of High-Voltage circuit breaker and then compare it with the traditional MATLAB curve fitting, the result clearly reveal the advantages of genetic algorithm.

Keywords: Genetic algorithm, DC circuit breaker, parameter estimation.

1 Introduction

In recent years, research and development of HVDC transmission technology have achieved great development, and HVDC grid will become an important component of the strong grid of our country in the future.

In a DC Power Transmission Project, the DC Circuit-Break's main task is to clear the line fault and isolate fault equipment in time, and to ensure the normal operation of the non-fault burden of DC system, at the same time, it can also be applied to compose radiated-type ,ring-netted-type or radiant-type multi-terminal DC power transmission system[1]. Currently the most wide application of DC circuit breaker is in two-terminal HVDC transmission system, it mainly play the role of changing the DC operating mode, and the typical application include the metallic return transfer breaker (MRTB), ground loop switch (GRTS) and neutral bus switch(NBS).

Dc circuit breaker is one of the most important electrical equipments in DC converter stations. Its operational conditions will directly affect the operation of HVDC system, thus the regular overhaul and maintenance is of great importance. In contract with lots of deficiencies as for heavy workload in measurement, many of influence factors and no real-time result of off-line measurement, this paper propose an on-line parameter estimation method for DC circuit breaker oscillation circuit, which can give a on-line parameters estimation of capacitor, reactor and resistance of DC circuit break by calculating the collected current data of the oscillation circuit.

D. Zeng (Ed.): ICAIC 2011, Part I, CCIS 224, pp. 156–164, 2011.

2 Dc Circuit Breaker

2.1 Active Oscillation Circuit Dc Circuit Breaker

This article selects active oscillation loop DC circuit breaker as research object which is one of the forced through zero type widely applied currently. Active oscillation loop DC circuit breaker composed by breaking loop, oscillation loop and absorbing loop, the principle diagram is shown in Fig. 1.

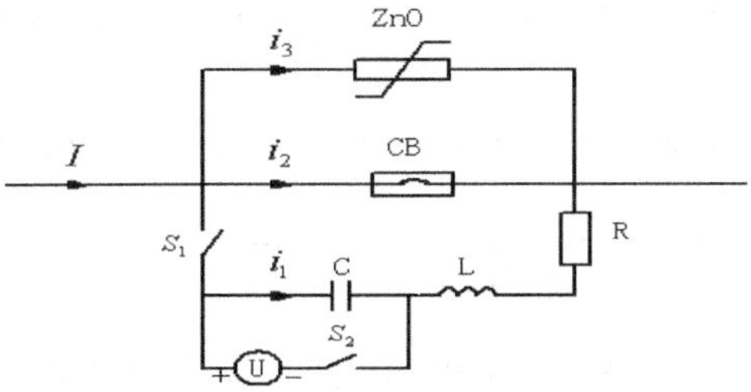

Fig. 1. Principle Diagram of Active Oscillation Loop DC Circuit Breaker

The active oscillation loop DC circuit breaker set with a dc pre-charging device in the oscillation loop. When the circuit breaker (CB) receives break-brake command, the switch S1 is turned on, and the pre-charged capacitor C begin to discharge, the high frequency reverse current caused by the oscillation circuit superimpose with the direct current and generate current zero, the arc goes out at this point. When the fracture's transient recovery voltage achieves the Zinc oxide (ZnO) arrester's action voltage, the arrester conduction energy absorption, the fracture voltage is limited to the desired value[1][2][3]. Active DC circuit breaker highly requires a time coordination on auxiliary switches, so more auxiliary equipments are needed and the control systems are more complicated, but compared with passive-type DC circuit breaker, it can generate a sufficiently large amplitude oscillation current and the breaking time is normally shorter, its breaking capacity of high-current is greater [4]. Currently active DC circuit breakers are widely used in HVDC transmission projects.

2.2 Simulation and Field Test of Oscillation Circuit Parameters

A MRTB simulation circuit is built as shown in Fig. 2, the capacitor pre-charging voltage E=5kV, the oscillation circuit switch S1 closed at 0.1 second, the total simulation time is 0.5 second, the breaking components have been in closed state during simulation process, the other parameters of the circuit remain unchanged.Current simulation waveform of oscillation circuit is shown in Fig. 3. It can be seen that the capacitor discharge of the oscillation loop does not exceed the total time of 0.03s, the current flows through the breaking device quickly return to the initial DC value. In addition, the total current flow through the DC circuit breaker has remained the same, which does not affect the running state of the DC transmission system.

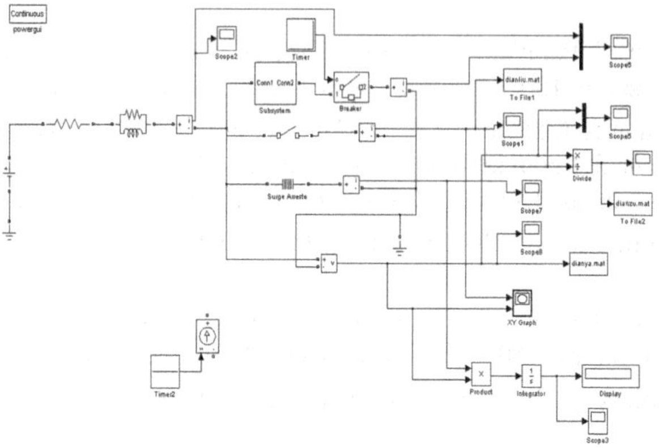

Fig. 2. MRTB Simulation Circuit

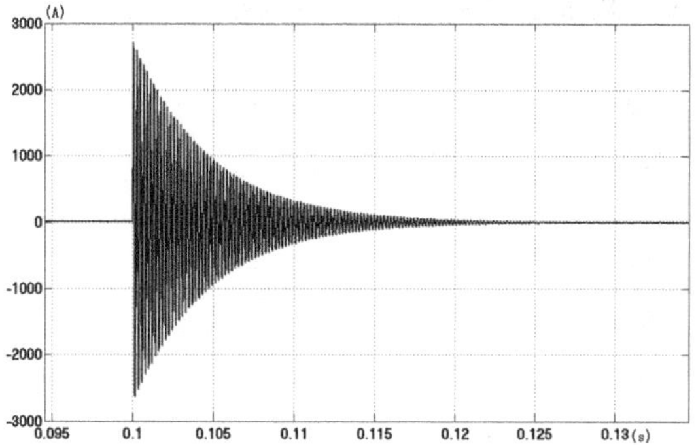

Fig. 3. Current Waveform of Oscillation Circuit

3 Online Parameter Estimation of HVDC Oscillation Circuit

3.1 Traditional Online Parameters Estimation of Oscillation Circuit Based on Matlab

From the equivalent circuit the following differential equation of the oscillation circuit can be obtained

$$LC\frac{d^2u_C}{dt^2}+RC\frac{du_C}{dt}+u_C=0$$

So the oscillation circuit current can be found as

$$i=\frac{U_0}{\omega L}e^{-\delta t}\sin\omega t$$

And the oscillation frequency can be obtain as

$$f = \frac{1}{2\pi\sqrt{LC}} \tag{1}$$

The peak values (include the trough values which should take their absolute values) satisfy the following equation

$$i' = i_0 e^{-\delta t}$$

$$i_0 = \frac{U_0}{\omega L} \tag{2}$$

$$\delta = \frac{R}{2L} \tag{3}$$

The fitting curve is shown as the dotted line waveform in Fig.4 By taking several times and the corresponding peak current values, using MATLAB's curve fitting toolbox, the mathematical fitting equations can be obtained , and the parameters i_0 and δ can be easily get. Consequently substitute the pre-charging voltage value of the capacitor to equations (1)(2)(3), the R,L,C values of the oscillation circuit can be accurately estimated.

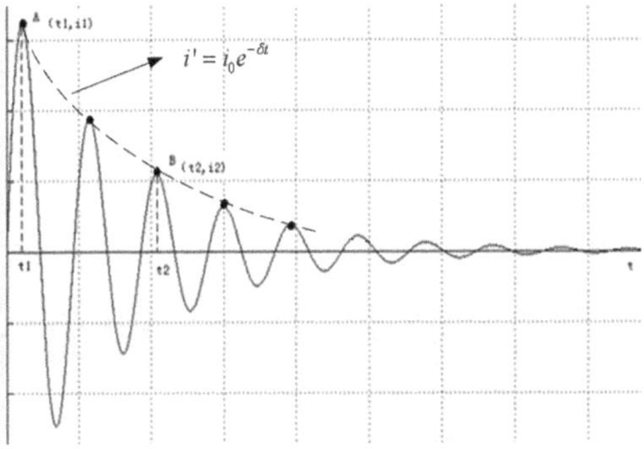

Fig. 4. Fitting curve of the peak current values

3.2 Online Parameters Estimation Based on Genetic Algorithm

Genetic algorithm is a kind of random search method which takes reference of the biological laws of evolution. It was first proposed by professor J. Holland of the United States in 1975, its main features are to directly operate on structure objects, there is no limitations of derivative and continuity of function; and it has inherent implicit parallelism and better global optimization ability; more ever, by using probability-oriented optimization methods, guidance can be automatically optimized for the search space and the search direction adaptively adjusted, no more other rules are needed [5] [6]. Fig.5 is a flow chart of genetic algorithm, the steps of genetic algorithm will be outlined below.

1) Steps of genetic algorithm [7]

Step 1 Coding and Decoding As the genetic algorithm cannot directly deal with the data of the solution space, so the solution space variable must be encoded as a string of genetic structure of the genotype space --- gene sequence data. Use a binary gene string to represent the individual groups, the allele is represented by (0, 1).The initial group of genes in each individual series are generated by random number [8].

000000 ...... 000000=0 X_{min}
000000 ...... 000001=1 $X_{min}+\delta$
⋮ ⋮
111111 ...... 111111=2^{k-1} X_{max}
And $\delta = (X_{max}-X_{min})/2^{k-1}$

Decoding (Calculate Object Value): The corresponding parameter of $b_k b_{k-1} b_{k-2} \ldots b_2 b_1$ can be decoded as

$$X_{min} + (\sum_{i=1}^{k} b_i * 2^{i-1}) * \frac{X_{max} - X_{min}}{2^k - 1}$$

Step 2 Calculate Fitness Value During the search evolution process, the only basis for future genetic manipulation is the fitness value which can be used to evaluate the merits of the individual or the solution, so the fitness value determines the degree of adaptability to the environment.

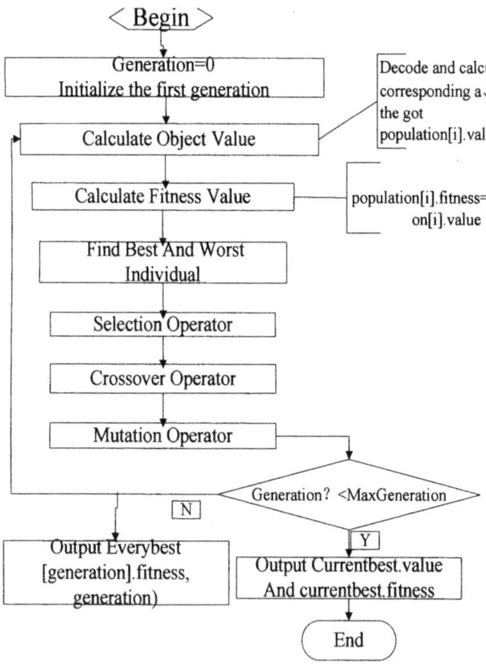

Fig. 5. Flow Chart of Genetic Algorithm

Step 3 Find Best and Worst Individual Find out the Best and Worst Individual according to its fitness value.

Step 4 Selection Operator Just simulate the function of natural selection and in accordance with principle of the higher fitness value the individual is, the greater probability it will is selected, better individuals are retained from the current group to breed.

Step 5 Crossover Operator Crossover operation is the most important operation. The groups been selected for breeding next offspring randomly pair off and select crossover point i, at which point two genes exchange the right part of their strings and create new individuals, the new individuals inherent the advantages of their parents.

Step 6 Mutation Operator Randomly select some individuals with certain probability to change their genetic values of a character string.

Step 7 Convergence judgment According to the maximum evolution generation, if current generation is less than the maximum evolution generation, then continue to start from the second step of calculating the fitness of new individuals and evaluating the individual merits and so on, the new generations gradually accumulated good genes, so the average fitness value and the best individual's fitness value increase and optimal solution converge continuously. If current generation is greater than or equal to the maximum evolution generation, terminate iteration and output the required parameters.

2) Breaker parameter estimation of genetic algorithm

For the oscillation circuit current equation

$$i = \frac{U_0}{\omega L} e^{-\delta t} \sin \omega t$$

Suppose $a = U_0 / \omega L$, $b = \delta$. Taking into account the actual waveform is not collected from zero and zero drift of the Hall sensor, two variables θ and c are added, then the oscillation circuit current equation changes to

$$i = ae^{-bt} \sin(\omega t + \theta) + c$$

Step 1 Encode parameters a, b ,θ , c with 10 length binary code individually, and a initial group with forty allele on every chromosome is obtained;

Step 2 Decode the initial group;

Step 3 Calculate the fitness value;

$$F_{fitness} = 1 / \sum_{i=1}^{n} (fabs(a * \exp(-b * X[i]) * \sin(X[i] * 2 * pi / T + \theta) - Y[i])$$

Step 4 Selection operation, crossover operation and mutation operation;

Step 5 Terminate program by setting the maximum evolution generation, after the end of the program output the corresponding individual coding of maximum fitness and decode it to have parameters a, b ,θ , c.

4 Practical Example

Take a lot of oscillation parameters tests on high-voltage DC circuit breaker of Gezhouba HVDC Converter Station as an example. Before experiment the capacitance inductance and resistance are measured by the Japanese HIOKI 3532-50 LCR tester, here are the measuring results: C=17.559μF, L=39.861μH, R=0.450Ω. All tests, just like the traditional test methods in the past, are carried out offline. The field test circuit diagram is shown in Fig.6. Choose the data when DC charging voltage is 60V for the following algorithm calculations.

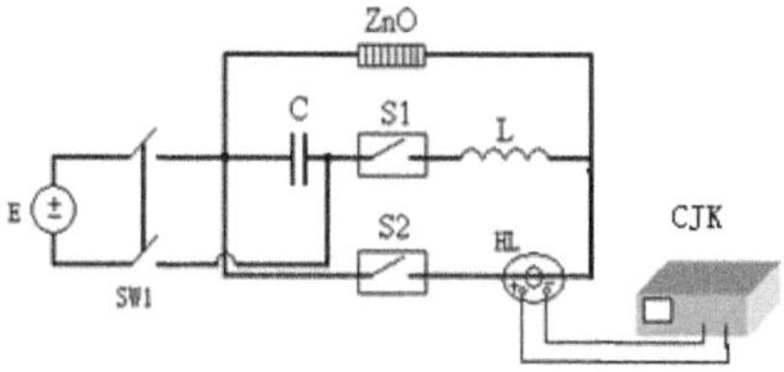

Fig. 6. Field Test Circuit Diagram

The data collected by the data acquisition card with frequency of 100K are as follows

Y[50]=[-4456,-6699,-7820,-7808,-6716,-4939,-2975, -823, 1216, 2929, 3998, 4458, 4185, 3404, 2143, 765, -657,-1760,-2568,-2887,-2789,-2218,-1414, -437, 502, 1307, 1886, 2112, 2054, 1659, 1113, 415, -246, -853,-1249,-1474,-1414,-1222, -789, -340, 160, 566, 925, 1069, 1102, 947, 674, 397, 13, -254]

X[50]=[1:1:50]

From the data above there are 16.8 points in every collection period on average, and the interval of two points are 10μs, so the oscillation period T = 168μs.

4.1 Traditional Online Parameters Estimation of Oscillation Circuit Based on Matlab

Apply MATLAB Curve Fitting Toolbox to the peak value of current waveform. Set curve fitting objective function as

f(x) = a*exp(-b*x)

And the fitting result is

a = 8988(8062, 9915)

b = 0.05347(0.04498 0.06196)

So $$i_0 = \frac{U_0}{\omega L} = \frac{U_0 T}{2\pi L} = \frac{a}{32767/10} * \frac{50}{3.5} \tag{4}$$

And from $\delta t = bx$

So $$\delta = \frac{bx}{t} = \frac{b}{10*10^{-6}} = \frac{R}{2L} \tag{5}$$

Simultaneous with the equation

$$T = 2\pi\sqrt{LC} = 0.000168 \tag{6}$$

Following parameters can be obtained R=0.4378Ω, L=4.094e-005, C=1.7463e-005.

4.2 Online Parameters Estimation Based on Genetic Algorithm

There are four parameters need to be pre-set in basic genetic algorithm: PopSize, MaxGeneration, Pc and Pm. PopSize as population size, that is, the number of individuals contained in the group, generally taken to be 20~ 100; MaxGeneration is the termination number of genetic algorithm evolution, generally taken to be 100~5000; Pc is crossover probability of genetic algorithm, generally taken to be 0.4~0.99; and Pm for the mutation probability, generally taken to be 0.001~0.05 [8]. This program set PopSize, MaxGeneration, Pc, Pm, as 100, 5000, 0.05, 0.02 respectively. Run the program and the results were as follows:111001111110001100001111000111000000 1010 0.000137 9061.583578 0.054741 2.969619 9.775171

That means the best individual is 1110011111100011000011110001110000001010, which have a best fitness of 0.000137, a=9061.583578, b=0.054741, θ=2.969619 c=9.775171. According to the above equations (4) (5) (6), the parameters can be obtained as: *R*= 0.44458, *L*=4.061e-005, *C*=1.76046e-005

4.3 Error Analysis

Table 1 shows the relative error of oscillation circuit parameters.

Table 1. Oscillation Circuit Parameter Estimates and Error Analysis

Parameter	Measuring value	MATLAB Fitting		Genetic Algorithm	
		Fitting value	error%	calculating value	error%
L (μH)	39.861	40.94	2.71	40.61	1.88
C (μF)	17.559	17.463	0.55	17.60	0.23
R (Ω)	0.450	0.4378	2.71	0.4445	1.22

1. Traditional method of using MATLAB curve fitting tool adopts the basic principle of the least square method. It applies the fitting function y = a * exp (-b * t) to fit the peak of the current waveform, since acquisition frequency is 100K, then every cycles collected 16.8 points on average, this card cannot guarantee to collected maximum points of the actual waveform, in fact the actual collection of data is low which affects the calculation of parameter a, thus parameter a is smaller in MATLAB fitting. The farther the collection point is from the corresponding peak point, the greater the possible error result in. And the greatest possible error occur when $Y(X_n) = Y(X_{n+1})$;

2. Traditional method of MATLAB curve fitness tool only use little part of the collection points (6-8 peak values), the amount of information is not comprehensively enough; But genetic algorithm nearly use all the valid data during the break of the DC circuit break, which will certainly get a better result;

3. Genetic algorithm takes into account that the acquisition may not start from zero, so adjust the angle by introducing a variable θ; also it take into account the Hall sensor zero drift phenomenon, and introducing one up and down adjustment of the variable c, so the consideration is more comprehensive and reduced the possible error to the best.

Moreover test wiring, instrument reading, calculations can also cause some errors.

5 Conclusion

The method of parameter estimation of High-Voltage circuit break based on genetic algorithms can accurately estimate the parameters of capacitance, inductance and resistance in oscillation circuit DC circuit breaker and then properly assess the performance of DC circuit breaker. Compared with traditional MATLAB curve fitting the result reveal the advantages of genetic algorithm.

References

1. Zhen, Z.-f., Zou, J.-y.: DC breaking and DC circuit breaker. High Voltage Apparatus (December 2006)
2. Zhang, W.-r., Gou, R.-f.: Simulation of the DC transfer process by DC circuit breaker. High Voltage Apparatus (April 2002)
3. Bao, M.-z.: Development of HVDC circuit breaker. High Voltage Apparatus (June 1990)
4. Andersson, D., Henriksson, A.: Passive and Active DC Breakers in the Three Gorges-Changzhou HVDC Project. In: ICPS 2001 Conference, Wuhan, China (2001)
5. Huang, S.-f., Jin, J.-l., Duan, J.-j.: New method of variogram parameter estimation on geostatistics. Geology and Exploration, 41–43 (July 1999)
6. Li, M.-q., Kou, J.-s., Lin, D.: The basic theory of genetic algorithm and application. Science Press of Beijin (2002)
7. Zou, W.-j., Wei, L.-d., Xu, W.-y.: Based on genetic algorithm analysis of slope stability, pp. 19–21. Guangxi University of Technology (April 2003)
8. Zhang, S.-w., Liu, J.-d., Han, X.-b.: A data fitting method based on genetic algorithm. Natural Science, Air Force Engineering University, 66–68 (August 2007)

Development of an Implanted Neural Prostheses*

Hongyun Liu[1], Weidong Wang[2,**], and Zhengbo Zhang[2]

[1] Department of Biomedical Engineering
[2] Department of Medical Engineering and Supply Center
General Hospital of Chinese PLA, Beijing, China
Hong7386@126.com

Abstract. To research and design a type of implantable functional electrical stimulator for restoring the injured peripheral nervous system. The crucial circuits of the implantable neural prosthesis were designed based on the digital signal processor TMS320VC54x and programmable logic device XC95144XL, corresponding program were developed and an experiment was carried on for verifying the system. Results show that the prototype realized the bi-directional wireless communication between the implantable simulator and the external controller. The output of stimulation pulse width, duration and some other parameters are controllable. This low power and system integrated implantable neural prosthesis stimulator could generate biphasic stimulating pulses, which after improving and optimizing could be used for repairing injured nerve system.

Keywords: Neural prostheses, Functional electrical stimulation, Cochlear implant, Biphasic stimulus.

1 Introduction

Peripheral or central nervous system dysfunction, trauma, or unpredictable disease can leave persons with severe and life threatening motor or sensory disabilities that can compromise the ability to control basic vital functions[1-6]. Persons with neurological impairments often depend on artificial assistants to facilitate their essential activities and daily life. Implanted neural prostheses are highly effective methods for restoring function to individuals with neurological deficits by functionally electrical stimulating the peripheral or central nervous systems[7-8]. Methods and techniques exist to selectively activate axons of any size and location within a nerve or fascicle, making it possible to preferentially target small sensory fibers or reconstruct natural motor unit recruitment order to alleviate fatigue and classify the strength of a stimulated muscular contraction. Apart from stimulating the peripheral or central nervous system, the appropriate current waveform and configuration of electrodes can block nerve impulse conduction and restrain action potential transmission. Thus, in principle any end organ normally under neural control is a candidate for neural prosthetic control[4-5].

* This work is partially supported by NNSF Grant #60571005 to W.D. Wang.
** Corresponding author.

D. Zeng (Ed.): ICAIC 2011, Part I, CCIS 224, pp. 165–171, 2011.

Implanted neural stimulation in the therapy of nervous diseases and nerve injury rehabilitation function plays an important role. With the development of microelectronic technology, Micro-nano technology and bio-technology, neural stimulation has been transformed the progressive development stage from a traditional transcutaneous electrical stimulation to implantable electrical stimulation. Compared to transcutaneous electrical stimulation, implantable neural electrical stimulation has outstanding advantages. Implanted neural prostheses in the treatment of Parkinson's disease, epilepsy, chronic pain, incontinence, audio visual barriers has made substantial progress, other issues such as spinal cord stimulation, electrical stimulation of gastrointestinal, and through electrical stimulation treatment of spastic, spasmodic torticollis, senile dementia. and other analgesic drug also has tempting prospect[1-4].

One specific example of implanted neural stimulation is to regulate cardiac functions and hemodynamic performance by delivering electrical stimulation pulses to locations of the autonomic nervous system[4-6]. Also, cochlear implant is another successful example of functional electrical stimulation for restoring partial hearing to sensorineural hearing loss person[5]. Implanted neural stimulation has been the subjects of a number of studies and has been proposed for many therapies. Implanted neural prostheses have been successfully applied to sensory and motor systems, as well as to the viscera and central nervous system. In this paper, a prototype of implanted neural prostheses is designed and implemented for experimental research.

2 Materials and Methods

2.1 Principle and Structure of Neural Prostheses

Implantable neural prostheses are used to deliver neural stimulation. A typical implantable neural stimulation system includes an implantable neural stimulator that delivers electrical stimulation pulses through a plurality of stimulation electrodes[9-12]. According to the location of the nerve fiber to be stimulated, the stimulation electrodes may be incorporated onto the implantable neural stimulator and connected to the implantable neural stimulator using one or more implantable leads. In practice, the desirable stimulation sites may not be in location with anatomical structure allowing for easy implantation of the stimulator of easy access by the leads. The stimulator also includes a controller, which is used to receive corresponding neurological or physiological signal or data, and to control the implanted neural stimulator to generate desirable electrical pulses. According to various embodiments, the presented implanted neural stimulator also includes a sensing circuit adapted to be connected to at least one sensor, the at least one sensor adapted to monitor target neurological or physiological activity. Figure 1 is the block diagram of the presented implanted neural prostheses.

As shown in Fig.1, sensing circuits monitor and pick up neurological or physiological signals of interests, the signals are then processed through signal conditioning circuit, after selection of switch circuit, the processed data are presented to the digital signal processor TMS320VC54x to encode. Corresponding useful information are collected and wirelessly transmitted through Si472x/nRF2401. The implanted neural stimulator communicate with external controller based on

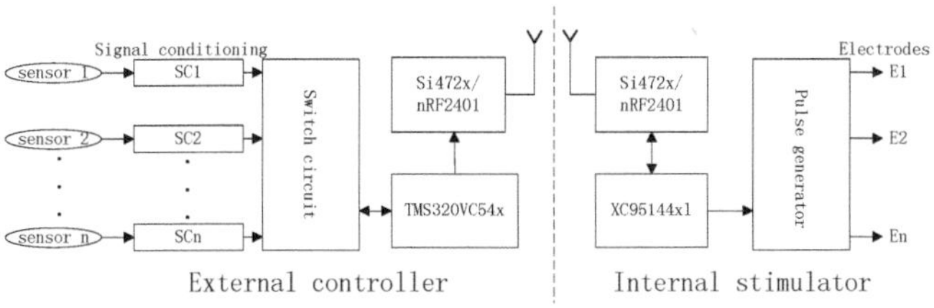

Fig. 1. Block diagram of implantable neural prostheses

Si472x/nRF2401 system that propagates signals using radio frequency carriers. The wirelessly received data signals are presented to a microcontroller, which may be any programmable device or devices suitable for controlling the neural prostheses, and may include one or more application specific integrated circuits, as well as external volatile memory to support the operation. In this paper, a complicated programmable logic device XC95144XL is used to decode corresponding data signals. The decoded signals are applied to the pulse generator circuit to generate pulse or pulse trains, which are delivered to the target location of nerve or muscle through electrodes.

2.2 Biphasic Current Controlled Stimulation

To avoid any adverse long-term effects such as pH shift, ionic charges near the implanted electrodes, and erosion of the electrode material [13-15], researchers usually apply a charge-balanced, biphasic stimulus through implanted electrodes or leads to stimulate peripheral or central nerve fibers. The first (cathodal) phase of the stimulus depolarizes the cell membrane, thus initiating an action potential. The second (anodal) pulse brings the net charge balance in the electrode to zero.

Precise current configure is necessary in the current driver design. High accuracy and linearity are crucial design and implement considerations. According to the variable characteristics of the load impedance, the output impedance of the current driver has to be high in order to generate a constant current under a wide range of conditions, this must be taken into consideration in the process of circuit design.

There are many methods and approaches to setting the output current of the current drive circuit. The specific example is to use a voltage controlled resistor, whose threshold voltage is determined by the voltage mode DAC[8-9]. In this paper, current controlled stimulation was implemented due to the control it provides over the charge delivered to the tissue. The pulse generator is developed to supply biphasic stimulation current to the tissue with certain impedance as illustrated in Fig.2.

As shown in Fig.2(a), during the cathodal phase $\phi 1$when IO74 output high level and IO73 output low level, the antistatic Q2 and Q4 are conducted, the current is flowing from electrode E1a to electrode E1r and then to the ground. During the anodal phase $\phi 2$, IO73 output high level and IO74 output low level, the current is flowing from electrode E1r to electrode E1a. The four diodes construct over current protection circuit to protect the pulse generator. The amplitude and duration of the current pulses during the two phases need not be the same. As long as the area under the two waveforms is the same the charge that was delivered to the tissue is retracted from the tissue. The stimulator is fully programmable and the amplitude and the duration of each pulse can be set independently.

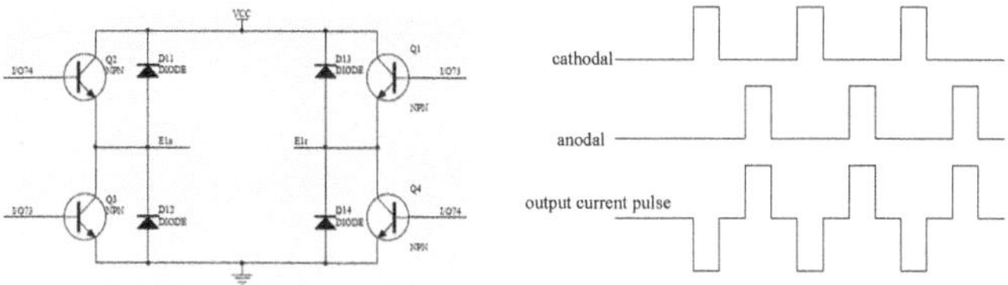

(a) Circuit of current pulse generator (b) block diagram of output current

Fig. 2. Implementation of biphasic stimulation

2.3 Software Design Flow of Implanted Neural Prostheses

Since the hardware circuits of implant neural prostheses are designed and implemented, the software programme which is the crucial part of the system is planned as shown in Fig.3. Firstly, the implanted system is initialized, including RF module, XC95144XL, and pulse generator initialize. After initializing, the RF module gets ready for receiving wirelessly transmitted data. Secondly, while there are data received, the microcontroller XC95144XL decodes the data. The decoded data, which contain information of channel, amplitude, stimulating last time, pulse width, frequency of pulse and so on, are used to control the pulse generator to generates desirable stimulating pulses.

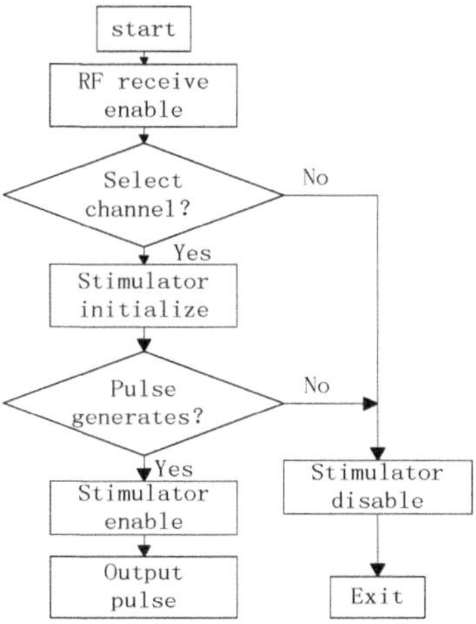

Fig. 3. Software Design Flow of crucial circuits

The microcontroller and the pulse generator are constructed entirely from low-powered hardware circuits and components, which could consistently generate a user-selected and user-programmable charge-balanced pulse waveform, would eliminate the need for processing components to control pulse parameters. This would not only increase device portability but also minimize power requirements, thus making it valuable in many functional electrical stimulation applications. The creation of such a device was the subject of this work.

3 Experimental Results

A prototype of the implanted neural prostheses for restoring partial hearing to sensorineural hearing loss person was implemented. Corresponding wires were properly attached to the voltage regulator and the two channel digital oscilloscope (DPO2012, Tektronix). In the experiment, a piece of Chinese sentence shown in Fig.4 was picked up by a microphone, the phrase was then processed and encoded before transmitting. As shown in Fig.4, waveform in top pan is the original signal and the waveform in bottom pan is wirelessly received signal. The encoded data was wirelessly received and decoded to control the pulse generator. Corresponding current pulse generated through pulse generator flow a resistor and the voltage waveform collected. To evaluate the stimulator limits without the restriction imposed by subject pain-threshold, a 3KΩ-load resistor R_{skin} was initially fixed. Stimulation rates is determined by original signal itself. Note that in this particular instantiation of the basic circuit design, fixed values for the timing resistors were used. Continuous, coupled control of pulse duration could be achieved. Stimulation waveform of one channel is shown in Fig.5.

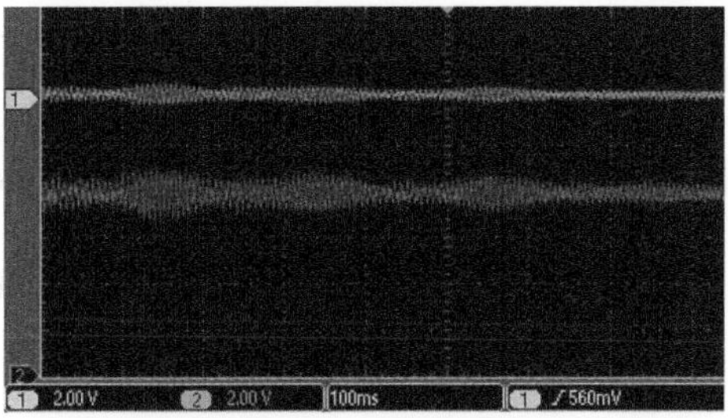

Fig. 4. Speech signal for experiment

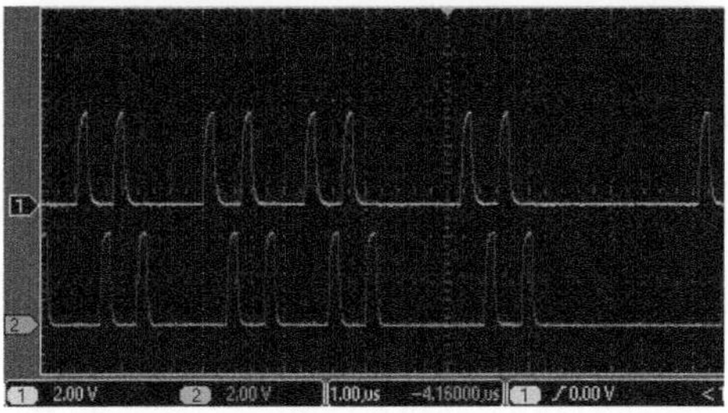

Fig. 5. Stimulation waveform of one channel

Based on the measurements presented in Fig.5, for the given fixed 3KΩ-load resistor Rskin and detected voltage about 3.3V, the calculated current pulse value is about 1-2mA with worst ripple about 7.34%. So a larger values of capacitor was used to decrease the ripple, at expense of higher overall consumption. The pulse width and pulse-pulse duration are determined by the specific speech coding strategy, these parameters will be varied for different speech coding strategy. As shown in Fig.5, the frequency of stimulation pulse is not fixed, it varies with the change of original speech signal. In general, pulse rates are usually set as relatively low as possible, which aims to reduce the system power consumption.

4 Discussion and Conclusion

The characteristics of this implanted neural prostheses circuitry make it proper for applications in which stimulation pulse parameters are flexible and it is necessary that the stimulating device draw minimum power. The programmable and controllable duration period between the positive and negative pulses allows the user to setting when necessary. This is important in many applications to ensure proper stimulation of the target region of human body.

In neural prosthetic applications, pulse parameters such as amplitude, pulse width, interphase between positive and negative pulses are established initially, and need not change throughout the stimulation process. Only the frequency of stimulation is varied for response to the change of original signal. Also microcontroller used in this kind of implanted neural prostheses is an ultralow power consumption chip, which makes the designed prototype operate in low-power consumption mode.

Although the prototype of the implanted neural prostheses is designed for cochlear implants, the proposed topology can be applied to other ranges of central or peripheral nerve stimulators. Its small number of components and low consumption make it valuable for low-cost and remote applications.

Acknowledgment. This work was supported financially by the National Natural Science Funds .We thank all the people who participated in the research work. The authors are grateful to Prof. S.Y YU of department of Neurology, for his kind and constructive proposals.

References

1. Tehovnik, E.J.: Electrical stimulation of neural tissue to evoke behavioral responses. Journal of Neuroscience Methods 65, 1–17 (1996)
2. Lanmuller, H., Ashley, Z., Unger, E., et al.: Implantable device for long-term electrical stimulation. Med. Biol. Eng. Comput. 43(5), 35–40 (2005)
3. Jalilian, E., Onen, D., Neshev, E., Mintchev, M.P.: Implantable neural electrical stimulator for external control of gastrointestinal motility. Med. Eng. Phys. 29(2), 38–52 (2009)
4. Thurgood, B.K., Warren, D.J., Ledbetter, N.M., Clark, G.A., Harrison, R.R.: A wireless integrated circuit for 100-channel charge-balanced neural stimulation. IEEE Transactions on Biomedical Circuits and Systems 3(6), 405–414 (2009)
5. Jandial, R., Aryan, H.E., Hughes, S.A., Levy, M.L.: Effect of vagus nerve stimulator magnet on programmable shunt settings. Neurosurgery 55(62), 7–9 (2004)
6. Dhillon, G.S., Horch, K.W.: Direct neural sensory feedback and control of a prosthetic arm. IEEE Trans. Neural Syst. Rehabil. Eng. 13(4), 68–72 (2005)
7. Coulombe, J., Sawan, M., Gervais, J.F.: A highly flexible system for microstimulation of the visual cortex: Design and implementation. IEEE Transactions on Biomedical Circuits and Systems 1(4), 258–269 (2007)

8. Hart, D.J., Taylor, P.N., Chappell, P.N., Wood, D.E.: A microcontroller system for investigating the catch effect: functional electrical stimulation of the common peroneal nerve. Med. Eng. Phys. 28(4), 38–48 (2006)
9. Williams, J.C., Hippensteel, J.A., Dilgen, J., Shain, W., Kipke, D.R.: Complex impedance spectroscopy for monitoring tissue responses to inserted neural implants. Journal of Neural Engineering 4, 410–423 (2007)
10. Thurgood, B.K., Warren, D.J., Ledbetter, N.M., Clark, G.A., Harrison, R.R.: A wireless integrated circuit for 100-channel charge-balanced neural stimulation. IEEE Transactions on Biomedical Circuits and Systems 3(6), 405–414 (2009)
11. Jandial, R., Aryan, H.E., Hughes, S.A., Levy, M.L.: Effect of vagus nerve stimulator magnet on programmable shunt settings. Neurosurgery 55(62), 7–9 (2004)
12. Liu, X., Demosthenous, A., Donaldson, N.: An integrated implantable stimulator that is fail-safe without off-chip blocking capacitors. IEEE Transactions On Biomedical Circuits and Systems 2(3), 231–244 (2008)
13. Ilic, M., Vasiljevic, D., Popovic, D.B.: A programmable electronic stimulator for FES systems. IEEE Trans. Rehabil. Eng. 2(23), 4–9 (2004)
14. Constandinou, T.G., Georgiou, J., Toumazou, C.: A partial-current steering biphasic stimulation driver for vestibular prostheses. IEEE Transactions On Biomedical Circuits and Systems 2(2), 106–113 (2008)
15. Lee, J., Rhew, H., Kipke, D., Flynn, M.: A 64 channel programmable closed-loop deep brain stimulator with 8 channel neural amplifier and logarithmic ADC. In: IEEE Symposium on VLSI Circuits, pp. 76–77 (June 2008)

Image Feature Extraction Method Based on Shape Characteristics and Its Application in Medical Image Analysis

Jianhua Liu[1] and Yanling Shi[2]

[1] Department of Sofeware Institute
[2] Department of Information Engineering
North China University of Water Resources and Electric Power Zhengzhou, Henan Province, China
jianhualiu64@gmail.com

Abstract. With the continuous development and perfection of computer-aided diagnosis technology, image feature extraction methods are more and more used in medical image analysis, which increase diagnostic accuracy and work efficiency of doctors. In this article, common image shape features and their characteristics are introduced. Methods of shape characteristics are summarized, and their applications in medical image analysis are introduced.

Keywords: Image Analysis, Feature Exaction, Shape Characteristics, Recognition.

1 Introduction

The process of extracting features which can express things better from original image is called image feature extraction. Broadly speaking, feature extraction is a process of transformation. That is, using the low-dimensional space of image sample express the high-dimensional space of image sample through transform, in order to achieve the purpose of dimension reduction [1]. Image feature extraction is the foundation and prerequisite of pattern recognition, which can directly influence the classifier design of classifier and classification accuracy. So far, many domestic and foreign scholars put forward many valuable image feature extraction methods from different angles. These methods are widely applied in medical image analysis, including. microscopic image processing; the analysis and counting of red blood cell and white blood cell; analysis of eggs slice and biopsy; recognition of cancer cell; visceral size, shape, and anomaly detection, etc. However, because of the complexity of medical images, methods of feature extraction in medical image analysis applications have some limitations. On the one hand, in the case of limited sample, it is unreasonable to design classifiers using a large number of features according to the calculation of cost and performance of classifiers. On the other hand, it is not linear for the relation between features and classifiers performance. However, the number of features, if allowed to increase to an excessive degree, the performance of classifiers will become worse [2].

D. Zeng (Ed.): ICAIC 2011, Part I, CCIS 224, pp. 172–178, 2011.

2 The Representation and Characteristics of Image Features

Image features are the most fundamental attributes or characteristics used to recognize an image. The properties of one image can be used to distinguish it with other images. The task of the feature extraction is to extract the image properties which can distinguish this image from others. In the feature extraction methods, there are four types of image features often used: color (gray) image features, texture features, shape features and spatial relations.

Through the image feature extraction, features should be able to describe objects abstractly and concretely, so as to provide a reliable basis for subsequent classification. Good features should have the following characteristics [3]:

1) Uniqueness: Each individual object must have its own unique representation which can be used to distinguish it from other objects.

2) Integrity: The algorithm can describe the characteristics of object in whole.

3) Invariance under the geometric structure: Generated features should not change with the changes of position, size, and rotation direction, in order to avoid results were affected.

4) Agility: Descriptive methods can easily reflect the differences between similar objects.

5) Abstractness: The useful of feature information can be extracted from many image details. The description of objects is simple and effective.

Image feature representation and feature extraction are the basic step in image analysis. Good features can fully identify the object which required to be identified. Effective feature extraction method can accurately extract the features so that the design of classifiers can be simplified and more accurate classification results can be got.

3 Shape-Based Feature Extraction Methods

Visual features of objects are called the shape characteristics or visual features. For example, circular object or triangular objects or other shapes, perimeter boundary of the object, the diameter of the border and so on. The visual features showed intuitively are all belongs to shape features. Shape features can be divided into two categories, one is based on the characteristics of the border, and the other is based on regional characteristics. Accordingly, the methods of image shape feature extraction are also divided into boundary-based feature extraction methods and region-based feature extraction methods. As the intuitiveness and understandability of shape features, targets in images can be identified very well. However, this approach lacks a sound mathematical model. When target is out of shape, the result is not reliable. The demand for calculation consumption and store consumption is high when the target is describing comprehensively. The target shape information reflected from many of the objectives is not exactly the same as human intuition. The accuracy of the shape feature extraction result depends on the pre-segmentation effect.

3.1 The Shape Feature Extraction Methods Based on the Boundary

1) Some Simple Descriptors

a) Perimeter of the Boundary

The perimeter of the boundary is the length of the smallest outer boundary contour of the connected region. The number of pixels around a boundary means its length[4]. Calculated[3] as follows:

First, the thinning method. Refine the outline of connected regions by morphological methods. Then calculate the length of the outline directly. In the X, Y direction, the length of path point distance set to 1. And the length of diagonal distance set to $\sqrt{2}$. The computing speed of this approach is fast.

Second, the chain code method. Calculate the contour length of connected region outside by chain code. When the chain code of outer contour is even, set its number to M. When the chain code of outer contour is odd number, set its number to N. So that, the perimeter of the connected region is $P=M+\sqrt{2}N$. The operation of this way is complex and the speed is slow.

Third, the boundary tracing method. When the outer contour is unknown, its length can be calculated by the boundary tracing method. The program design of this method is complex and the operation speed is medium.

b) Diameter of Boundary

The longest distance between two points on the border is called diameter of bounder. The diameter of a boundary B is defined as

$$Diam(B) = \max_{i,j}[D(p_i, p_j)] \tag{1}$$

Where D is a distance measure which is any of Euclidean distance, block distance and chessboard distance, and p_i and p_j are points on the boundary. The value of the diameter and the orientation of a line segment major axis of the boundary are useful descriptors of a boundary.

c) Eccentricity

The line segment whose the two endpoints connect diameter of the boundary is called major axis. The minor axis of a boundary is defined as the line perpendicular to major axis. The ratio of the major to the minor axis is called the eccentricity of the boundary.

d) Curvature

In the continuous case, the curvature means the rate of change of slope. In the discrete space, the curvature means the rate of the total number of the border (the border perimeter) pixels to the number of boundary pixels whose boundary direction change significantly.

2) Fourier Descriptors

The basic idea of Fourier shape descriptors is that using the Fourier transform of object boundary shape characteristic function describes the shape. Fourier transform can access the characteristics of the object through changing the sensitivity and direct representation into the frequency domain. Frequency domain characteristics are not easily affected by small changes and noise. Discrete Fourier transform expression of the boundary can be used as the basis of characteristic parameters which describe the shape of the border quantitatively. The Fourier descriptors are insensitive to translation, rotation, scale changes and the starting point [5].

3) Statistical Moments

Statistical moment is a statistical form of the image pixel. Shape of boundary segments can be described quantitatively by using simple statistical moments, such as the mean, variance, and higher-order moments. Moment is calculated by pixel, and it is affected little by noise.

To describe the amplitude of g as discrete variable v, and form histogram on $p(v_i)$, i=0,1,2,…,A-1. Here, A is the number of discrete amplitude values. $p\ (v_i)$ is the probability valuation of generate value v_i. So that the first n-mean estimate is[4]

$$\mu_n(v) = \sum_{i=0}^{A-1} (v_i - m)^n p(v_i) \tag{2}$$

In the formula: m is the mean of v, μ_2 is its variance.

$$m = \sum_{i=0}^{A-1} v_i p(v_i) \tag{3}$$

3.2 Shape Feature Extraction Methods Based on Region

1) Some Simple Descriptors

a) Regional Area

In the digital image, the area of a region is defined as the number of pixels in the region. Mark the pixels within the region as f(x,y)=1,outside the region as f(x,y)=0.

The area can be calculated[4] as:

$$A = \sum_{(x,y)\in R} 1 \tag{4}$$

b) Roundness

Roundness is also known as compactness. It is used to describe the degree of regional shape close to circular. With the size of interest region unchanged, the regional area and the length of the border often used to describe the shape of target. For fixed area images, the smaller the perimeter, the closer target to the circle is. The longer the perimeter is, graphic surface is less smooth and more complex. Using roundness measure the shape degree the graphics tend to circle. Formula of roundness is:

$$C=(4\pi A)/P2 \tag{5}$$

In the formula, P is the perimeter of regional bounder, A is the regional area. When the region is circular, C takes the maximum value 1. When the region is long and thin strip or more complex, C value is smaller.

c) Regional Focus

Regional focus is also a kind of shape characteristics. The coordinates calculated according to all the points belonging to the region are the coordinates[4] of the regional focus.

$$\bar{x} = \frac{1}{A}\sum_{(x,y)\in R} x \quad \bar{y} = \frac{1}{A}\sum_{(x,y)\in R} y \tag{6}$$

In formula, x,y is the points within the region, A is the regional area.

2) Topological Descriptors

Topological features are useful for the overall description of the image plane region. The commonly used topological descriptors are the number of the holes H, connected components C and the Euler number E.

$$E=C-H \tag{7}$$

These features have simple calculations and they are insensitive to translation, rotation and scale changes.

4 Applications of Shape Feature Extraction Methods in Medical Image Analysis

Shape feature extraction methods have been widely used in medical image analysis. Accuracy and efficiency of doctors diagnosis were improved. As the complexity of medical images, features were often selected combining with clinical expertise of doctors. Image shape feature extraction methods were widely used in leucocyte image feature extraction, CT brain tumor image extraction, edge extraction head CT, lung cancer liver cancer medical image feature extraction, the extraction of human parasite eggs in the image recognition and so on. Sometimes, the required high recognition rate of the results can't be reached only using the image shape features. Texture features were often combined with to make up for the shortage, so as to achieve better results.

4.1 Application of Shape Feature Extraction Methods

Shape feature extraction methods in blood leukocyte classification have been applied very well. Abnormal white blood cells can be identified[7] by feature extraction of morphological, measurement and statistical analysis. Diagnostic recognition rate is as high as 80%. The shape features applied in the paper are the cell size, number of nucleus, shape, and rule level of contour and so on. Shape features extraction was excellent applied to classification and recognition of lymphocytes [8]. The study provided a reliable diagnosis of medical pathology parameters and improved diagnostic accuracy. Shape feature extraction of lymphocytes included the cell geometry described through cell area, perimeter, equivalent diameter, shape factor, boundary Fourier description of factors and the regional geometry described through cell number, cell area within the region, the measured size of the area, area percentage of cells in the region. Shape feature extraction is the key to achieve identification of helminth eggs in the computer classification[9] and diagnostic. The problem that observation accuracy was low and instable according to human experience was solved though the shape feature extraction, analysis and recognition of Helminth Eggs [9]. Shape features applied in human helminth eggs images analysis were perimeter, area, roundness. The application of image feature extraction is useful for doctors making effective diagnosis of the patient's lesions.

4.2 Application of Combining the Shape Feature Extraction Methods and Texture Feature Extraction Methods

The diagnostic recognition rate was 80% only using shape feature extraction methods in the classification of blood leukocytes[7]. The main reason of error identification was due to the classification of granular cells. The extraction combing with shape features and texture features can make up for the shortage, so the overall recognition rate improved as high as 90%. Texture features applied in the paper involved gray variance correlation matrices, gray gradient correlation matrices and neighbor variance gray correlation matrices. In the lung cancer[10] and liver cancer CT images of the computer-aided diagnosis researches, shape features and texture features were extracted combing with the shape feature extraction methods and texture feature extraction methods. The data was analysis comprehensively and diagnosis rate was improved.

5 Conclusions

Feature extraction is an important link of the image analysis, which received extensive attention. In this paper, the shape characteristics of the image are introduced. Two types of image shape feature extraction methods, feature extraction methods based on boundary and feature extraction methods based on region, are summarized. The applications of shape feature extraction method in medical image analysis are reviewed. In medical image feature extraction, the methods of shape feature extraction were used widely. Doctors' diagnostic accuracy and work efficiency were greatly increased. Although there are many feature extraction methods, these methods still have some limitations in solving practical problems. At present, how to combine with the current methods and how to propose new methods for specific issues are the important research direction of the medical image feature extraction methods.

References

1. Zhang, X., Bian, Z.: Pattern Recognition. Tsinghua University Press, Beijing (August 2004)
2. Wang, J., Linlin, C.l., Yao, K.: A Survey of Feature Selection. Computer Engineering and Science 27(12), 68–71 (2005)
3. Jiang, X.: Digital Image Pattern Recognition Engineering Software Design. China Water Power Press, Beijing (2008)
4. Gonzalez, R.C., Woods, R.E.: Digital Image Processing, pp. 643–665. Electronic Industry Press, Beijing (2007)
5. Miao, J.: Research of Image Retrieval Technology based on Shape feature. Chang Chun University of Technology (March 2009)
6. Zhang, Y.: Image Engineering-Image Processing and Analysis. Tsinghua University Press, Beijing (1999)
7. Yang, X., Luo, L.: Study of Leukocyte Features in Peripheral Blood for Automatic Classification. Journal Of Applied Sciences 12(2), 120–126 (1994)

8. Nin, X., Tang, J.: Cell morphology Extraction and Identification Technology. Laser Journal 26(4), 95–97 (2005)
9. Peng, S.: Engineering Research on the Features Extraction and Recognition of Image of Human Helminth Egg. Hunan University, pp. 16-20 (2005)
10. Zhu, J.: Automated Detection System of Peripheral Pulmonary Carcinoma in CT Images. Sichuan University, pp. 48-51 (2007)

Study on the Traverse Mechanism with Rotary Wings*

Zhang Xu[1,2], Wei Jian[1,2], Du Lijuan[2], Zhao Ming[2], and Li Tianwei[3]

[1] Department of Mechanical Engineering Donghua University Shanghai, China
[2] College of Aviation Transportation Shanghai University of Engineering Science Shanghai, China
[3] Shanghai Erfangji Co Ltd Shanghai, China
zhang18309@sina.com

Abstract. Traverse mechanism with rotary wings is a new generation mechanism, which moves the filament back and forth continuously by a pair of blades rotating in opposite direction and conduces to increasing the winding speed further. The internal connections of structure parameters can be determined through the geometrical relations of mechanism parts, the variational regularity of reciprocating velocity of filament can be analyzed in accordance with composition theorem of velocities. Thus, the operation property can be perfected and the reciprocating velocity of filament can be uniformed by regulating the structure parameters, and the requirement of winding the cylinderical package can be satisfied. And the theoretical foundation and implementing means are provided for rational machine design of traverse mechanism with rotary wings.

Keywords: winding, traverse mechanism, rotary wing, blade, machine design.

1 Introduction

As the winding speed of spinning machine increases, the reciprocating velocity of filament for winding must be increased correspondingly. When the winding speed reaches 6000 *m/min* and the winding angle is 7°, the reciprocating speed of filament will reach 730 *m/min*. The reciprocating frequency will at least come up to 3000 times every minute if the traverse stroke is 120 *mm*. However, the groove cam rotating speed may be up to 12,000 revolutions per minute as for the traditional traverse mechanism with groove cam. Owing to the traverse guider slides rapidly in the cam groove, the wear and tear will be generated violently, and the vigorous impulse damage and great noise will be cause by changing the direction of traverse guider in cam groove. from and structure has been modified many times. Although the material has been replaced and in several decades, the weight of traverse guider has been lightened from more than 10 grams to less than 1 *gram*, the service life of traverse guider is still very shortness and it is a vulnerable part always requiring exchange. This not only increases the workload of the operation and the cost of production, but also decreases the efficiency of the machine. Therefore, the traverse mechanism with groove cam has become a major technical bottleneck of further improving the speed of spinning.

* This topic has received the subsidization from Shanghai Dawn Plan Item (2000SG48).

D. Zeng (Ed.): ICAIC 2011, Part I, CCIS 224, pp. 179–189, 2011.

The traverse mechanism with rotary wings, which moves the filament back and forth continuously by a pair of blades rotating in opposite direction, has thoroughly changed this situation. With the same speed of winding, the rotating speed of wings has been decreased to less than 1500 *r/min*. In addition, there is no parts undergoing the reciprocation within the whole mechanism, which break through the insurmountable technical obstacles caused by the traverse mechanism with groove cam. This new generation of traverse mechanism has become a forerunner that leads the winding to high-speed further.

Because of the filament is wound into a cylindrical package in spinning machine, so the filament must be moved on uniform reciprocating motion by the traverse mechanism. In the traverse mechanism with groove cam, the uniform motion is guaranteed by the cam curve. As for the traverse mechanism with rotary, the motion is ensured by the blades and leading plate. Since there is little research about the traverse mechanism with rotary wings, this paper takes the widely used dual-blades mechanism as an example to determine the structure parameters of mechanism along with their interrelations through the geometrical relations, analysis the variational regularity of reciprocating velocity of filament as well as search for the method of uniforming velocity according to the composition theorem of velocities starting from the simp lified model.

2 The Concentric Mechanism

The concentric mechanism is a simplified model with a pair of two counter rotary wings to be situated at same axis, some basic characteristics of traverse mechanism with rotary wings could be obtained trough analysis of this model.

2.1 The Structure Parameters

Generally speaking, traverse stroke of filament is known as $2S$. As for the dual-blades mechanism, the central angle must be 90° for a blade moving from one side to the other side of the stroke. As shown in Fig.1, set point O as the origin of coordinates, abscissa x is parallel with the stroke line, while ordinate y is perpendicular to the stroke line. Now the distance OC (from the central point O to the stroke line) equals to: $OC = AC = CB = S$ .So, theoretical working length of the blade r_0 is: $r_0 = OA = OB = \sqrt{2}S$.

2.2 The Reciprocating Velocity of Filament

Traverse mechanism with rotary wings move the filament back and forth continuously by a pair of blades rotating in opposite direction. But the locus of the reciprocating motion is in random. Only fixed with a special designed leading plate, the reciprocating motion of filament could be uniformed along the direction of package axis.

In order to facilitate the discussion, the filament is considered as infinitely fine linear material which is a geometry point in the mechanism schematic (as point E shown in Fig.1).

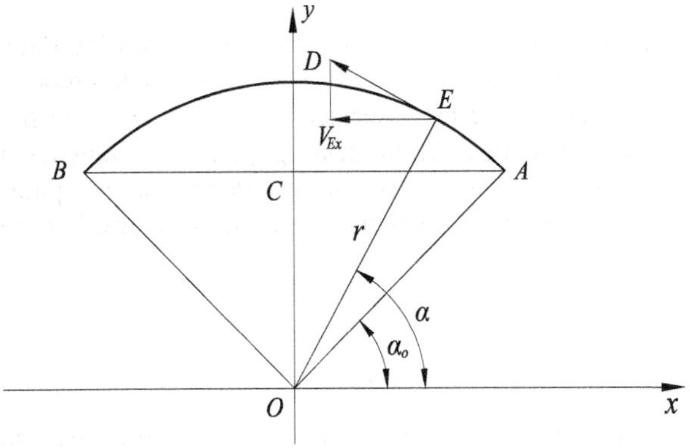

Fig. 1. The schematic diagram of concentric mechanism with an arc leading plate

1) The Arc Leading Plate

In Fig.1, $\widehat{ADB}$ is A section of arc whose center is point O and radius is $OA = OB$, the reciprocating velocity of filament in arbitrary point E equals to:

$$V_{Ex} = r\omega \sin\alpha = \sqrt{2}S\omega \sin\alpha \tag{1}$$

Where r is the working radius OE of point E, $r = r_0$, ω is the angular velocity of blade, α is the rotating angle of blade, α_0 is the initial angle of blade(as for dual-blade mechanism, $\alpha_0 = 45^\circ$), the reciprocating velocity of filament is $V_{Ax} = V_{Bx} = S\omega$ at point A and point B. And $V_{Dx} = \sqrt{2}S\omega$ at point D, which means that the reciprocating velocity of filament is the maximum at point D but the minimum at the ends of stroke. The package winding with the arc leading plate will be taken the shape of saddle.

2) The Rectilinear Leading Plate

In Fig.2, line AB is expressed as the rectilinear leading plate. The arbitrary point E is a point on leading plate, moreover, the point E may be regarded as a point on filament as well as on blade. The point E as a point on filament is moved along blade OE with relative motion and along line AB with absolute motion ,the relative velocity is V_r and the absolute velocity is V_a, the point E as a point on blade is known as converted point and revolved round the center O, the converted velocity is V_e [3]. In the vector triangle of velocity, the reciprocating velocity V_{Ex} of filament is:

$$V_{Ex} = \frac{S\omega}{\sin^2\alpha} \tag{2}$$

At point A and B, the reciprocating velocity of filament is $V_{Ax} = V_{Bx} = 2S\omega$, and at point C is $V_{Cx} = S\omega$, which means that the velocity is the maximum at both ends of stroke but the minimum at point C. The package winding with the rectilinear leading plate will be taken the shape of waist drum.

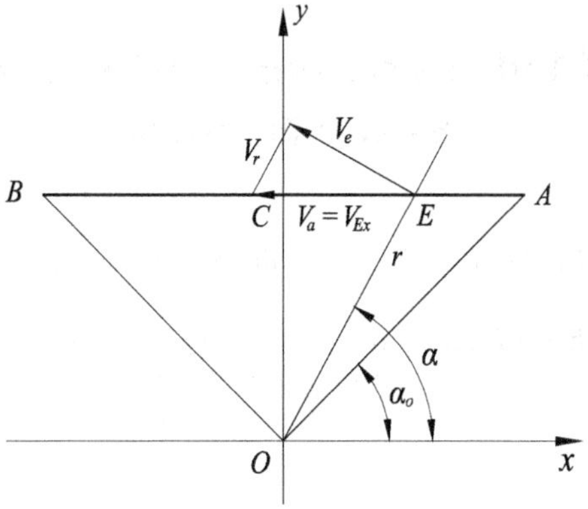

Fig. 2. The schematic diagram of concentric mechanism with a rectilineal leading plate

3) The Curved Leading Plate

It is impossible to wind the cylindrical package neither by applying arc leading plate nor arc rectilinear leading plate. It has no difficulty in comjecting that there exists a leading plate made by a certain curvilinear which could wind the filament into cylindrical package, and which could be expressed by a curve [1, 2].

As for the sake of calculating easily, here $2S$ could be taken as the radius, the working surface of leading plate is drawn from a curve around the centre P on the ordinate y as shown in Fig.3.

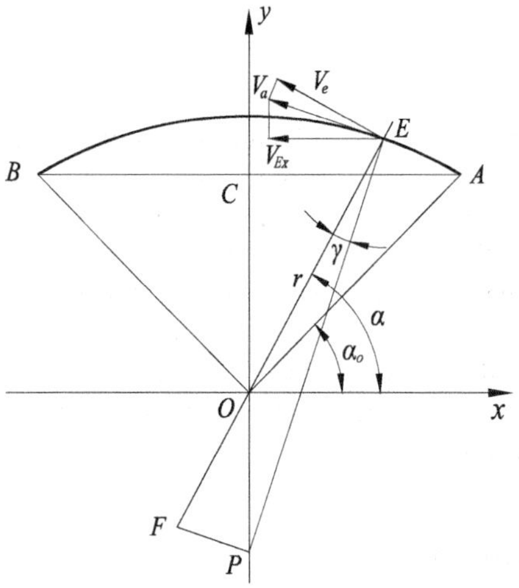

Fig. 3. The schematic diagram of concentric mechanism with a curved leading plate

At the arbitrary point E, the absolute velocity of filament along the curve V_a is:

$$V_a = \frac{r\omega}{\cos\gamma}$$

Where r is the instantaneous working radius of the blade, then:

$r=\overline{OE}=\sqrt{\overline{EP}^2-\overline{FP}^2}-OF=\left[\sqrt{4-[(\sqrt{3}-1)\cos\alpha]^2}-(\sqrt{3}-1)\sin\alpha\right]S$ And γ is the angle between the working radius of the blade and the curve radius,here

$$\gamma=\sin^{-1}\frac{FP}{EP}=\sin\frac{(\sqrt{3}-1)\cos\alpha}{2}$$

So (reciprocating velocity of filament) V_{Ex} is:

$$V_{Ex}=\frac{r\omega}{\cos\gamma}\sin(\alpha+\gamma) \tag{3}$$

Take $2S=120\,mm$, the reciprocating velocity of filament at various rotating angle between initial angle 45° and end angle 135° can be obtained, the variationol regularity of reciprocating velocity of filament is shown in Fig.4, that is to say, the maximum difference rate is only 0.768%, the requirement for winding the cylindrical package can be satisfied completely.

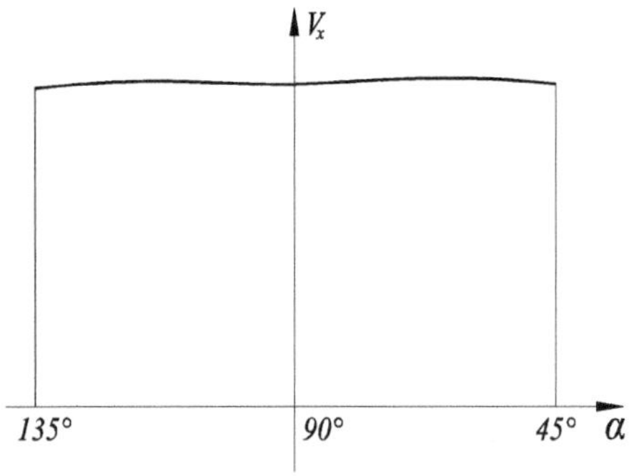

Fig. 4. The velocity distribution diagram of concentric mechanism with a curved leading plate board

3 The Eccentric Mechanism

3.1 The Structure Parameters

In the concentric mechanism, the actual working length of the blade must be a little longer than that of the theoretical in order to catch the filament, that is $\overline{OA_1}=\overline{OA}+(3\sim5)\,mm$. In this case, the filament is not easy to slip out of former blade when one blade arriving from point A at point B turns the filament over to other blade rotating in opposite direction. The only solution is to apply the eccentric mechanism, in which rotating centers of two blades are deviated a small distance e from the ordinate Y separately. At this moment, the vertical distance O_1C_1 between the centre O_1 and the reciprocating stroke AB as shown in Fig.5 is: $O_1C_1=\sqrt{(S-e)(S+e)}$

The initial working radius of the blade O_1A and the end working radius O_1B are:

$$O_1A = \sqrt{2S(S-e)}$$

$$O_1B = \sqrt{2S(S+e)}$$

So the catching length l is:

$$l = O_1B - O_1A = \sqrt{2S(S+e)} - \sqrt{2S(S-e)}$$

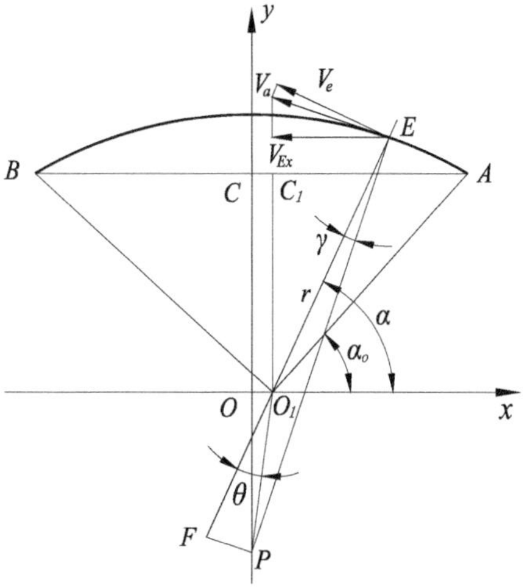

Fig. 5. The schematic diagram of eccentric mechanism with a curved leading plate

Similarly, take $2S$ as the curve radius of the leading plate, then the distance b between centre O_1 and the curved centre P is:

$$b = O_1P = \sqrt{\left(\sqrt{\overline{AP}^2 - \overline{AC}^2} - \overline{O_1C_1}\right)^2 + \overline{OO_1}^2} = \sqrt{4S^2 - 2\sqrt{3}\sqrt{(S-e)(S+e)}S}$$

3.2 The Reciprocating Velocity of Filament

At the arbitrary point E, the absolute velocity of filament along the curve V_a is:

$$V_a = \frac{r\omega}{\cos\gamma}$$

$$\gamma = \sin^{-1}\frac{b\sin\theta}{2S}$$

Where r is the instantaneous working radius of the blade, then

$$r = \sqrt{4S^2 - (b\sin\theta)^2} - b\cos\theta$$

In where

$$\theta = \cos^{-1}\frac{e}{b} - \alpha$$

The reciprocating velocity of filament V_{Ex} is

$$V_{Ex} = \frac{r\omega}{\cos\gamma}\cos(90 - \alpha - \gamma) \quad (4)$$

Take $2S = 120$ mm and $2e = 5$ mm as an example, the reciprocating velocity of filament at each rotating angle of the blade could be calculated. The velocity is $74.1\times10^{-3}\omega$ at point A and $78.2\times10^{-3}\omega$ when the rotating angle is 120°, besides, the velocity is $78.1\times10^{-3}\omega$ at the point B, difference rate is as high as 5.2%. So far as individual blade is concerned, the reciprocating velocity is a great deal of difference. The coil is dense where the velocity is low and vice versa. But in light of accomplishing a reciprocating process by two counter rotary blades, the reciprocating velocity can be compensation each other, which means that the coil density of every layer of filament is consistent on the whole.

This eccentric mechanism has been applied to industry. Structure parameters can be modified to meet the needs of moving the filament more smoothly and reciprocating velocity of filament more uniformly. One of the most efficiency solution is to design a working surface of blede which is not passed through the centre O but has a vertical distance from it, the size of vertical distance can be selected according to requirement.

4 The Eccentric Mechanism Carrying Vertical Distance

4.1 The Structure Parameters

Take $2S$ as the stroke, $2e$ as the centre distance and $2S$ as the curve radius of leading plate, then

$$O_1C_1 = \sqrt{(S-e)(S+e)}$$

$$O_1A = \sqrt{S(S-e)}$$

$$O_1B = \sqrt{S(S+e)}$$

$$\alpha_0 = \cos^{-1}\frac{S-e}{\sqrt{2S(S-e)}}$$

$$b = O_1P\sqrt{4S^2 - 2\sqrt{3}\sqrt{(S-e)(S+e)}S}$$

In Fig.7, the angle θ is:

$$\theta = \cos^{-1}\frac{e}{b} - \alpha_0 + \varphi$$

Where:

$$\varphi = \sin^{-1}\frac{h}{O_1B}$$

In where h is the vertical distance.

Therefore, when the rotating angle of blade is α_0, the instantaneous working radius of the blade is:

$$r_0 = O_1E_0 = \sqrt{\overline{E_0H}^2 + h^2}$$

Where :

$$E_0H = \sqrt{4S^2 - (b\sin\theta + h)^2} - b\cos\theta$$

The hand-over course of filament between the two counter rotary blades is more complicated since there is a vertical distance h. When the blade O_1A is of the position shown in Fig.6, the intersecting point of working surface of blade and leading plate has removed form point A to point E. When the working surface of blade O_1A and leading plate intersect at point A (not shown), the blade arrives at working area. But intersecting the point of working surface of the other blade O_2B (not shown) and the leading plate has not arrived at point A, the filament is still controlled by blade O_2B. In this case, the blade O_1A begins to work really and moves the filament to the left when the working surface of blades O_1A, O_2B and leading plate $\overset{\frown}{AB}$ intersect together, but the blade O_2B will still continue working and move the filament to the right before it arrives at point A. In extreme short duration,a hand-over transitional period to move the filament simultaneously by two counter rotary blades is appeared.

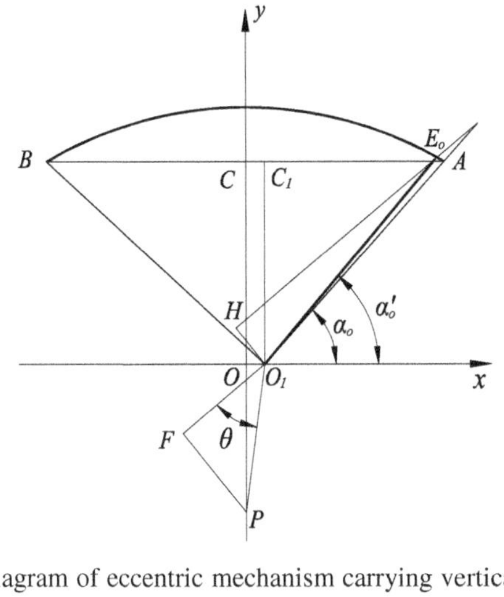

Fig. 6. The structural diagram of eccentric mechanism carrying vertical distance with a curved leading plate

4.2 The Reciprocating Velocity of Filament

As shown in Fig.7, at arbitrary point E, the instantaneous working radius r of blade is:

$$r = O_1E = \sqrt{\overline{EH}^2 + h^2}$$

Where :

$$EH = \sqrt{4S^2 - (b\sin\theta + h)^2} - b\cos\theta$$

$$\theta = \cos^{-1}\frac{e}{b} + \varphi - \alpha$$

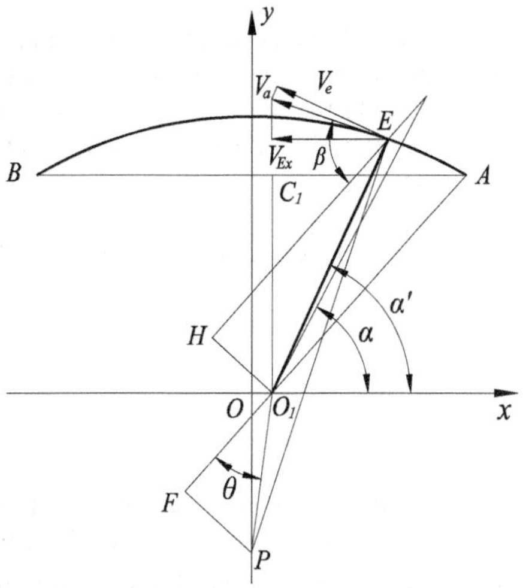

Fig. 7. The schematic diagram of eccentric mechanism carrying vertical distance with a curved leading plate

In where α is the rotating angle of the blade. Then the working angle of the blade α' is:

$$\alpha' = \alpha + (90 - \varphi) - \cos^{-1}\frac{h}{r}$$

The included angle γ between curve radius and instantaneous working radius of blade is:

$$\gamma = \cos^{-1}\frac{e + r\cos\alpha'}{2S} - \alpha'$$

The absolute velocity of filament along the curve V_a at point E is:

$$V_a = \frac{r\omega}{\sin\beta}\sin(\beta + \gamma)$$

Where:

$$\beta = 90 - (\gamma + \sin^{-1}\frac{h}{r})$$

The reciprocating velocity of filament V_{Ex} is:

$$V_{Ex} = V_a \sin(\alpha' + \gamma) \quad (5)$$

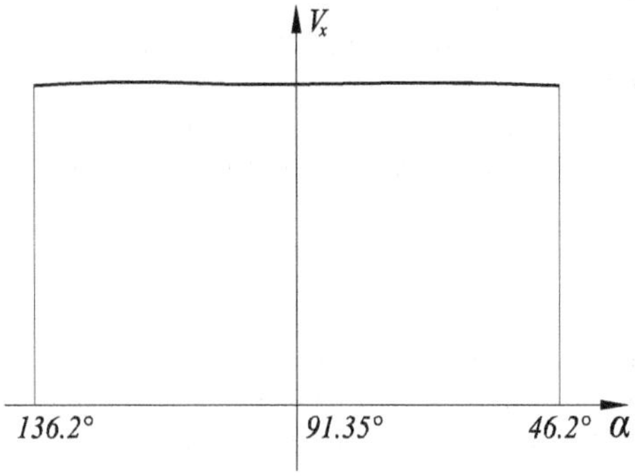

Fig. 8. The velocity distribution diagram of eccentric mechanism carrying vertical distance with a curved leading plate

Take $2S = 120\,mm$ as the stroke, $2e = 5\,mm$ as the centre distance and $h = 9.5\,mm$, then the reciprocating velocity of filament at each rotating angle of the blade can be calculated. The variational regularity of reciprocating velocity of filament is shown in Fig.8, the velocity is $75.95\times10^{-3}\omega$ at point A, $76.56\times10^{-3}\omega$ at 120° and $75.97\times10^{-3}\omega$ at point B, the maximum difference rate of reciprocating velocity is reduced to 0.79%.

Therefore, selecting the suitable vertical distance of working surface of blade can reduce the difference rate of the reciprocating velocity and improve its uniformity significantly.

5 Conclusions

The rotating blades of traverse mechanism move the filament and cause it to produce reciprocating motion, the outmoded conventions using the reciprocating parts to move the filament and cause it to produce reciprocating motion is broken down and a completely new machine design concept is provided.

Beside some processing parameters such as the winding velocity and winding angle, there are only two parameters, the traverse stroke $2S$ and the centre distance $2e$, need to be preset for design of the traverse mechanism with rotary wing.

Concentric mechanism with a curved leading plate can produce uniform reciprocating motion of filament, however, certain difficulty is appeared during hand-over of filament between the two counter rotary blades. Though eccentric mechanism overcomes this difficulty, the reciprocating velocities of filament rise up progressively from lower to higher, so it is not an uniform motion as to individual blade, but in light of working of two counter rotary blades, there are compensation each other, the coil density of every layer of filament is basically constants, the shape of package is still cylindrical.

Eccentric mechanism carrying vertical distance uses vertical distance as the adjust parameter, which leads to the reciprocating velocity of filament uniformly and the reduction in difference rate of the reciprocating velocity, and the working performance of the traverse mechanism with rotary wing can be further improved.

This article conducts a thorough analysis and study on the traverse mechanism with rotary wing, which contributes to understand the working performance of different type mechanisms as well as the variational regularity of reciprocating velocity. The solution of informing the reciprocating velocity with adjusting the structure parameters and the theoretical basis for the rational design and correct use of the traverse mechanism with rotary wing are provided.

Traverse mechanism with rotary wing is not only applied in winding of synthetic filament, but also winding the pure and blended yarn, such as cotton, wool, silk and ramie.

References

1. Yan, Y.: Design Theory of Traverse Mechanism with Rotary Wing. Journal of China Textile University 2(17), 22–29 (1991) (in Chinese)
2. Zheng, X., Xie, S.: Design Research on Traverse Mechanism for Winding Machine of PS-4 type. Journal of Textile 17(1), 31–33 (1996) (in Chinese)
3. Hua, D.: Theory of Machine, 2nd edn., pp. 28–34. Higher Education Press, Beijing (1997) (in Chinese)

Analytic Invariant Curves in a Two Dimensional Complex Discrete Dynamical System

Lingxia Liu

Department of Mathematics, Weifang University,
Weifang, Shandong 261061, P.R. China
lkantadey@yahoo.com

Abstract. In this paper, we are concerned with the existence of analytic invariant curves of a 2-D mapping in the complex field $\mathbb{C}$. Employing the method of majorant series, we need to discuss the eigenvalue α of the mapping at a fixed point. We discuss not only these α at the hyperbolic case $0<|\alpha|<1$ and resonance, i.e., at a root of the unity, but also those α near resonance (i.e., near a root of the unity) under Brjuno condition.

Keywords: Invariant curves, iterative equation, majorant series, Diophantine condition, Brjuno condition.

1 Introduction

Invariant curves of the area preserving maps play an important role in the theory of periodic stability of discrete dynamical systems. A common and useful method to understand behaviors of a discrete dynamical system generated by the iteration of a self-mapping is to find a simple structures in its phase space and to describe the dynamics in terms of the effect caused by the presence of these structures. In particular, invariant curve, in dimension two, is one of such structures. P.M. Diamond researched the existence of invariant curves for a class of map of the form

$$\begin{cases} x_1 = x + y, \\ y_1 = y(1+\beta x^k) + F(x,y) \end{cases}$$

in [1]. For an investigation of other related problems the interested reader is referred to [2]-[6]. The purpose of this paper is to find invertible and linearizable invariant analytic curves of the 2-D complex map

$$T:\mathbb{C}^2 \to \mathbb{C}^2, (z,w) \mapsto (z_1, w_1),$$

defined by

$$\begin{cases} z_1 = p(z) + q(w), \\ \omega_1 = v(z) + h(w). \end{cases} \tag{1}$$

Throughout the paper, we assume that $p(z), q(z), v(z)$ and $h(z)$ are analytic in a neighborhood of the origin , and $p(0) = q(0) = v(0) = h(0) = 0,\ p'(0) = \xi,\ \ h'(0) = \eta,$

D. Zeng (Ed.): ICAIC 2011, Part I, CCIS 224, pp. 190–201, 2011.

$v'(0)=\mu,\ q'(0)=\zeta\neq 0, \xi\eta-\zeta\mu\neq 0.$ Clearly, map T has a fixed point $O=(0,0)$ with the Jacobian matrix

$$A=DT(0)=\begin{pmatrix}\xi & \zeta\\ \mu & \eta\end{pmatrix}$$

at O. It's characteristic polynomial is

$$P_A(\lambda)=\alpha^2-(\xi+\eta)\alpha+\xi\eta-\zeta\mu.$$

As is well known that a curve $\omega=f(z)$ is said to be an invariant curve of T if $\omega_1=f(z_1)$. Thus, we see that map T has an invariant curve $\omega=f(z)$ if and only if f satisfies the functional equation

$$f\{p(z)+q[f(z)]\}=h[f(z)]+v(z),\quad z\in\mathbb{C}. \tag{2}$$

Since $q(0)=0$ and $q'(0)=\zeta\neq 0$, function q is invertible near zero. If we denote the inverse function of q by g, then g is analytic in a neighborhood of the origin and $g(0)=0$, $g'(0)=\frac{1}{\zeta}:=s\neq 0.$ Let $\psi(z)=p(z)+q(f(z))$, then equation (2) can be written equivalently as the iterative equation

$$g\{\psi[\psi(z)]-p[\psi(z)]\}=h\{g[\psi(z)-p(z)]\}+v(z),\quad z\in\mathbb{C}. \tag{3}$$

As in [7]-[9], our strategy remains to reduce equation (3) with the conjecture transformation $\psi(z)=\phi(\alpha\phi^{-1}(z))$, to another functional equation

$$g\{\phi(\alpha^2 z)-p[\phi(\alpha z)]\}=h\{g[\phi(\alpha z)-p(\phi(z))]\}+v[\phi(z)],\ z\in\mathbb{C}, \tag{4}$$

which called the auxiliary equation of (3), in which iteration of the unknown function is not involved but an indeterminate complex α needs to be discussed. In this paper, the complex α in (4) is chosen in $\sigma(A):=\{\lambda\in\mathbb{C}\mid P_A(\lambda)=0\}$ and satisfies the following hypotheses:

(H1) $0<|\alpha|<1$.

(H2) $\alpha=e^{2\pi i\theta}$, where $\theta\in\mathbf{R}\backslash\mathbf{Q}$ is a Brjuno number ([10]-[11]), i.e., $B(\theta)=\sum_{k=0}^{\infty}\frac{\log q_{k+1}}{q_k}<\infty$, where $\{p_k/q_k\}$ denotes the sequence of partial fraction of the continued fraction expansion of θ, said to satisfy the Brjuno condition.

(H3) $\alpha=e^{2\pi iq/p}$ for some integers $p\in\mathbf{N}$ with $p\geq 2$ and $q\in\mathbf{Z}\backslash\{0\}$ and $\alpha\neq e^{2\pi il/k}$ for all $1\leq k\leq p-1$ and $l\in\mathbf{Z}\backslash\{0\}$.

Observe that α is the inside of the unit circle S^1 in the case of (H1) but on S^1 in the rest cases. More difficulties are encountered for α on S^1, as mentioned in the so-called ``small-divisor problem'' (seen in [12] p.22 and p.146 and [13]). Under Diophantine condition: $|\mu|=1$, *$\mu$ is not a root of unity, and* $\log\frac{1}{|\mu^n-1|}\leq T\log n$, $n=2,3,\cdots$ *for some positive constant* $T$, the number $\alpha\in S^1$ is ``far'' from all roots of the unity and was considered in different settings [7,8,9]. In [14] the case of (H3), where α is a root of the unity, was also discussed for a general class of iterative equations. Since then, we have been striving to give a result of analytic solutions for those α ``near'' a root of the unity, i.e., neither being roots of the unity nor satisfying the Diophantine condition.

The Brjuno condition in (H2) provides such a chance for us. As stated in [15], for a real number α, we let $[\theta]$ denote its integer part and $\{\theta\}=\theta-[\theta]$ its fractional part. Then every irrational number θ has a unique expression of the Gauss' continued fraction $\theta=a_0+\theta_0=a_0+\frac{1}{a_1+\theta_1}=\ldots$, denoted simply by $\theta=[a_0,a_1,\ldots,a_n,\ldots]$, where a_j 's and θ_j 's are calculated by the algorithm: **(a)** $a_0=[\theta]$, $\theta_0=\{\theta\}$ and **(b)** $a_n=\left[\frac{1}{\theta_{n-1}}\right], \theta_n=\left\{\frac{1}{\theta_{n-1}}\right\}$ for all $n\geq 1$. Define the sequences $(p_n)_{n\in\mathbb{N}}$ and $(q_n)_{n\in\mathbb{N}}$ as follows:

$q_{-2}=1, q_{-1}=0, q_n=a_nq_{n-1}+q_{n-2}$; $p_{-2}=0, p_{-1}=1, p_n=a_np_{n-1}+p_{n-2}$. It is easy to show that $p_n/q_n=[a_0,a_1,\ldots,a_n]$. Thus, for every $\theta\in\mathbf{R}\backslash\mathbf{Q}$ we associate, using its convergence, an arithmetical function $B(\theta)=\sum_{n\geq 0}\frac{\log q_{n+1}}{q_n}$. We say that θ is a Brjuno number or that it satisfies Brjuno condition if $B(\theta)<+\infty$. The Brjuno condition is weaker than the Diophantine condition. For example, if $a_{n+1}\leq ce^{a_n}$ for all $n\geq 0$, where $c>0$ is a constant, then $\theta=[a_0,a_1,\ldots,a_n,\ldots]$ is a Brjuno number but is not a Diophantine number. So, the case (H2) contains both Diophantine condition and a part of μ ``near'' resonance.

In this paper, considering the Brjuno condition instead of the Diophantine one, we discuss not only the case (H1) and (H3) but also (H2) for analytic invariant curves of the mapping T defined in (1).

2 Auxiliary Equation Case (H1)

Theorem 1. Assume that $\alpha\in\sigma(A)$ and (H1) holds. Then for any $\tau\in\mathbf{C}$ equation (4) has an analytic solution $\phi(z)$ in a neighborhood of the origin such that $\phi(0)=0$, and $\phi'(0)=\tau$.

Proof. Fix an $\tau\in\mathbb{C}$. If $\tau=0$, then (4) has a trivial solution $\phi(z)\equiv 0$. Assume that $\tau\neq 0$. Let

$$p(z)=\sum_{n=1}^{\infty}a_nz^n,\quad a_1=\xi, \tag{5}$$

$$h(z)=\sum_{n=1}^{\infty}c_nz^n,\quad c_1=\eta, \tag{6}$$

$$g(z)=\sum_{n=1}^{\infty}g_nz^n,\quad g_1=s, \tag{7}$$

and

$$v(z)=\sum_{n=1}^{\infty}v_n z^n,\quad v_1=\mu. \tag{8}$$

Since $p(z)$, $h(z)$, $g(z)$ and $v(z)$ are analytic in a neighborhood of the origin, there exists a constant $\rho>0$ such that

$$|a_n|\le\rho^{n-1},|c_n|\le\rho^{n-1},|g_n|\le\rho^{n-1},|v_n|\le\rho^{n-1},\quad n=2,3\cdots.$$

Introducing new functions

$$\tilde{\phi}(z)=\rho\phi(\rho^{-1}z),\ \tilde{p}(z)=\rho p(\rho^{-1}(z)),$$
$$\tilde{h}(z)=\rho h(\rho^{-1}(z)),\ \tilde{g}(z)=\rho g(\rho^{-1}(z)),\ \tilde{v}(z)=\rho v(\rho^{-1}(z)).$$

From (4) we see $\tilde{\phi}(z)$ satisfies

$$\tilde{g}[\tilde{\phi}(\alpha^2 z)-\tilde{p}(\tilde{\phi}(\alpha z))]=\tilde{h}[\tilde{g}(\tilde{\phi}(\alpha z)-\tilde{p}(\tilde{\phi}(z)))]+\tilde{v}[\tilde{\phi}(z)],\quad z\in C,$$

the same form of (4) but

$$\tilde{p}(z)=\rho p(\rho^{-1}(z))=\xi z+\sum_{n=2}^{\infty}a_n\rho^{1-n}z^n,$$

$$\tilde{h}(z)=\rho h(\rho^{-1}(z))=\eta z+\sum_{n=2}^{\infty}c_n\rho^{1-n}z^n,,$$

$$\tilde{g}(z)=\rho g(\rho^{-1}z)=sz+\sum_{n=2}^{\infty}g_n\rho^{1-n}z^n,$$

and

$$\tilde{v}(z)=\rho v(\rho^{-1}z)=\mu z+\sum_{n=2}^{\infty}v_n\rho^{1-n}z^n,$$

where obviously the coefficient $|a_n\rho^{1-n}|\le 1, |c_n\rho^{1-n}|\le 1,$ $|g_n\rho^{1-n}|\le 1,$ $|v_n\rho^{1-n}|\le 1, n=2,3,\ldots$. Without loss of generality , we assume that

$$|a_n|\le 1,\quad |c_n|\le 1,\quad |g_n|\le 1,\quad |v_n|\le 1,\quad n=2,3,\ldots. \tag{9}$$

Let

$$\phi(z)=\sum_{n=1}^{\infty}b_n z^n \tag{10}$$

be the expansion of a formal solution of equation (4). Substituting (5), (6), (7), (8) and (9) into (4) and comparing coefficients, we get

$$\begin{aligned}\alpha^n\sum_{\substack{n_1+n_2+\cdots+n_i=n\\ i=1,2,\cdots,n}}g_i[\prod_{k=1}^{i}(b_{n_k}\alpha^{n_k}-\sum_{\substack{l_1+l_2+\cdots+l_t=n_k\\ t=1,2,\cdots,n_k}}a_t b_{l_1}b_{l_2}\cdots b_{l_t})]\\ =\\ =\sum_{\substack{n_1+n_2+\cdots+n_i=n\\ i=1,2,\cdots,n}}c_i\prod_{j=1}^{i}[\sum_{\substack{m_1+m_2+\cdots+m_V=n_j\\ V=1,2,\cdots,n_j}}g_V\prod_{k=1}^{V}(b_{m_k}\alpha^{m_k}-\sum_{\substack{l_1+l_2+\cdots+l_t=m_k\\ t=1,2,\cdots,m_k}}a_t b_{l_1}b_{l_2}\cdots b_{l_t})]\\ +\sum_{\substack{l_1+l_2+\cdots+l_t=n\\ t=1,2,\cdots,n}}v_t b_{l_1}b_{l_2}\cdots b_{l_t},\quad n=1,2,\cdots.\end{aligned} \tag{11}$$

By a simple computation, we obtain

$$P_A(\alpha)b_1=0, \tag{12}$$

$$P_A(\alpha^n)b_n = \zeta \sum_{\substack{l_1+l_2+\cdots+l_t=n \\ t=2,3,\cdots,n}} [(\alpha^n-\eta)sa_t+v_t]b_{l_1}b_{l_2}\cdots b_{l_t}$$

$$-\zeta(\alpha^n-\eta)\sum_{\substack{l_1+l_2+\cdots+l_t=n \\ t=2,3,\cdots,n}} g_t\prod_{k=1}^{t}[(\alpha^{l_k}-\xi)b_{l_k}-\sum_{\substack{m_1+m_2+\cdots+m_v=l_k \\ v=2,3,\cdots,l_k}} a_v b_{m_1}.b_{m_2}\cdots b_{m_v}]$$

$$+\zeta\sum_{\substack{l_1+l_2+\cdots+l_t=n \\ t=2,3\cdots,n}} c_t\prod_{k=1}^{t}\{\sum_{\substack{m_1+m_2+\cdots+m_j=l_k \\ j=1,2,\cdots,l_k}} g_j\prod_{i=1}^{j}[(\alpha^{m_i}-\xi)b_{m_i}-\sum_{\substack{n_1+n_2+\cdots+n_l=m_i \\ l=2,3,\cdots,m_i}} a_l b_{n_1}b_{n_2}\cdots b_{n_l}]\},$$

$$n=2,3,\cdots. \tag{13}$$

Since $\alpha\in\sigma(A)$, we know that the coefficient of b_1 in (12) is equal to zero. Hence we can choose $b_1=\tau\neq 0$. On the other hand, when $0<|\alpha|<1$, we have $\lim_{n\to\infty}\frac{1}{|P_A(\alpha^n)|}=\frac{1}{|\xi\eta-\zeta\mu|}$. Thus, there exists a positive number M such that, for any integers $n\geq 2$ and $0<|\alpha|<1$, $|\frac{|\zeta|[(1+|\eta|)|s|+1]}{P_A(\alpha^n)}|\leq M$, $|\frac{|\zeta|(1+|\eta|)}{P_A(\alpha^n)}|\leq M$, $|\frac{|\zeta|}{P_A(\alpha^n)}|\leq M$. Therefore, from (8) and (13) we obtain

$$|b_n|\leq M[\sum_{\substack{l_1+l_2+\cdots+l_t=n \\ t=2,3\cdots n}} |b_{l_1}|.|b_{l_2}|\cdots|b_{l_t}|$$

$$+\sum_{\substack{l_1+l_2+\cdots+l_t=n \\ t=2,3,\cdots,n}}\prod_{k=1}^{t}((1+|\xi|)|b_{l_k}|+\sum_{\substack{m_1+m_2+\cdots+m_v=l_k \\ v=2,3,\cdots,l_k}}|b_{m_1}|.|b_{m_2}|\cdots|b_{m_v}|)$$

$$+\sum_{\substack{l_1+l_2+\cdots+l_t=n \\ t=2,3,\cdots,n}}\prod_{k=1}^{t}\sum_{\substack{m_1+m_2+\cdots+m_j=l_k \\ j=1,2,\cdots,l_k}}\prod_{i=1}^{j}((1+|\xi|)|b_{m_i}|+\sum_{\substack{n_1+n_2+\cdots+n_l=m_i \\ l=2,3,\cdots,m_i}}|b_{n_1}|.|b_{n_2}|\cdots|b_{n_l}|)],$$

$$\leq M[\sum_{\substack{l_1+l_2+\cdots+l_t=n \\ t=2,3,\cdots,n}} |b_{l_1}|.|b_{l_2}|\cdots|b_{l_t}|$$

$$+\sum_{\substack{l_1+l_2+\cdots+l_t=n \\ t=2,3,\cdots,n}} N^t\prod_{k=1}^{t}(|b_{l_k}|+\sum_{\substack{m_1+m_2+\cdots+m_v=l_k \\ v=2,3,\ldots,l_k}}|b_{m_1}|.|b_{m_2}|\cdots|b_{m_v}|)$$

$$+\sum_{\substack{l_1+l_2+\cdots+l_t=n \\ t=2,3,\cdots,n}}\prod_{k=1}^{t}\sum_{\substack{m_1+m_2+\cdots+m_j=l_k \\ j=1,2,\cdots,l_k}} N^j\prod_{i=1}^{j}(|b_{m_i}|+\sum_{\substack{n_1+n_2+\cdots+n_l=m_i \\ l=2,3,\ldots,m_i}}|b_{n_1}|.|b_{n_2}|\cdots|b_{n_l}|)],$$

$$n=2,3,\cdots, \tag{14}$$

where $N=1+|\xi|$. In order to construct a governing series of (10), we consider the implicit functional equation

$$W(z)=|\tau|z+M\{\frac{[W(z)]^2}{1-W(z)}+\frac{[V(z)]^2}{1-V(z)}+\frac{[U(z)]^2}{1-U(z)}\}, \tag{15}$$

where $V(z)=\frac{NW(z)}{1-W(z)}$, $U(z)=\frac{V(z)}{1-V(z)}$, i.e.,

$$W=|\tau|z+M\{\frac{W^2}{1-W}+\frac{N^2W^2}{(1-W)[1-(1+N)W]}$$

$$+\frac{N^2W^2}{[1-(1+N)W][1-(1+2N)W]}\}.$$

Define the function

$$F(M,\tau,z,W)=W-|\tau|z-M\{\frac{W^2}{1-W}+\frac{N^2W^2}{(1-W)[1-(1+N)W]}+\frac{N^2W^2}{[1-(1+N)W][1-(1+2N)W]}\}$$

for (z,W) in a neighborhood of $(0,0)$. Then $F(M,\tau,0,0)=0$, $F_{W'}(M,\tau,0,0)=1\neq 0$. Thus, there exists a unique function $W(M,\tau,z)$, analytic in a neighborhood of zero, such that $W(M,\tau,0)=0$, $W_{z'}(M,\tau,0)=-\frac{F_z'(M,\tau,0,0)}{F_W'(M,\tau,0,0)}=|\tau|$ and $F(M,\tau,z,W(M,\tau,z))=0$. So $W(M,\tau,z)$ can be expanded into a convergent power series

$$W(M,\tau,z)=\sum_{n=1}^{\infty}B_n z^n,\quad B_1=|\tau|. \tag{17}$$

Replacing (17) into (15) and comparing coefficients, we obtain that $B_1=|\tau$ and

$$\begin{aligned}B_n=M[&\sum_{\substack{l_1+l_2+\cdots+l_t=n\\ t=2,3,\cdots,n}}B_{l_1}B_{l_2}\cdots B_{l_t}\\ &+\sum_{\substack{l_1+l_2+\cdots+l_t=n\\ t=2,3,\dots,n}}N^t\prod_{k=1}^{t}(B_{l_k}+\sum_{\substack{m_1+m_2+\cdots+m_v=l_k\\ v=2,3,\cdots,l_k}}B_{m_1}B_{m_2}\cdots B_{m_v})\\ &+\sum_{\substack{l_1+l_2+\cdots+l_t=n\\ t=2,3,\cdots,n}}\prod_{k=1}^{t}\sum_{\substack{m_1+m_2+\cdots+m_j=l_k\\ j=2,3,\cdots,l_k}}N^j\prod_{i=1}^{j}(B_{l_i}+\sum_{\substack{n_1+n_2+\cdots+n_l=m_i\\ l=2,3,\cdots,m_i}}B_{n_1}B_{n_2}\cdots B_{n_l})],\quad n=2,3,\cdots.\end{aligned} \tag{18}$$

Furthermore,

$$|b_n|\le B_n,\ n=1,2,\cdots. \tag{19}$$

In fact, $|b_1|=|\tau|=B_1$. For inductive proof we assume that $|b_j|\le B_j, j\le n-1$. Observe that in (14) $|b_{l_j}|\le B_{l_j}$, $j=1,2,\cdots,k$, because $1\le l_1,l_2,\cdots,l_k\le n-1$. From (18) we know $|b_n|\le B_n$ and (19) is proved. By the convergence of (17) and the inequality (19) , we see that the series (10) is convergent in a neighborhood of the origin. This completes the proof of Theorem 1.

3 Auxiliary Equation in Case (H2)

When α is on the unit circle but not a root of unity, the analysis of the convergence of (10) is complicated since it will appear the small divisor $\alpha^{n-1}-1$ in (13). In [8]-[9], the related questions as α satisfies Diophantine condition were discussed. In this section, we will consider the existence of analytic solution for the equation (4) under the Brjuno condition which is weaker than the Diophantine condition. To do this, we need to introduce Davie's Lemma. First, we recall some facts in [16] briefly. Let $\theta\in \mathbf{R}\backslash\mathbf{Q}$ and $(q_n)_{n\in\mathbb{N}}$ be the sequence of partial denominators of the Gauss's continued fraction for θ as in the Introduction. As in [15], let

$$A_k = \{n \ge 0 \mid \| n\theta\| \le \frac{1}{8q_k}\},\ E_k = \max(q_k, \frac{q_{k+1}}{4}),\ \eta_k = \frac{q_k}{E_k}.$$

Let A_k^* be the set of integers $j \ge 0$ such that either $j \in A_k$ or

for some j_1 and j_2 in A_k, with $j_2 - j_1 < E_k$, one has $j_1 < j < j_2$ and q_k divide $j - j_1$. For any integer $n \ge 0$, define

$$l_k(n) = \max\left((1+\eta_k)\frac{n}{q_k} - 2,\ \ (m_n\eta_k + n)\frac{1}{q_k} - 1\right),$$

Where $m_n = \max\{j \mid 0 \le j \le n,\ j \in A_k^*\}$. We then define function $h_k : \mathbf{N} \to \mathbf{R}_+$ as follows:

$$h_k(n) = \begin{cases} \dfrac{m_n + \eta_k n}{q_k} - 1, & \text{if } m_n + q_k \in A_k^*, \\ l_k(n), & \text{if } m_n + q_k \notin A_k^*. \end{cases}$$

Let $g_k(n) := \max\left(h_k(n), \left[\dfrac{n}{q_k}\right]\right)$, and define $k(n)$ by the condition $q_{k(n)} \le n \le q_{k(n)+1}$. Clearly, $k(n)$ is non-decreasing. Then we are able to state thefollowing result:

Lemma 1. (Davie's Lemma [16]) Let

$$K(n) = n\log 2 + \sum_{k=0}^{k(n)} g_k(n)\log(2q_{k+1}).$$

Then

(a) there is a universal constant $\gamma > 0$ (independent of n and θ) such that $K(n) \le n\left(\sum_{k=0}^{k(n)} \dfrac{\log q_{k+1}}{q_k} + \gamma\right)$,

(b) $K(n_1) + K(n_2) \le K(n_1 + n_2)$ for all n_1 and n_2, and

(c) $-\log|\alpha^n - 1| \le K(n) - K(n-1)$.

Now we state and prove the following theorem under Brjuno condition.

Theorem 2. Suppose that $\alpha \in \sigma(A)$, (H2) holds and $|\xi + \eta| > 2$. Then for any $\tau \in \mathbf{C}$ equation (4) has an analytic solution $\phi(z)$ in a neighborhood of the origin such that $\phi(0) = 0$ and $\phi'(0) = \tau$.

Proof. Clearly, (4) has a trivial solution $\phi(z) \equiv 0$ if $\tau = 0$. Assume $\tau \ne 0$. As in the proof of Theorem 1, we seek a power series solution of (4) of the form (10). For chosen $b_1 = \tau$, using the same arguments as above we can determine a sequence $\{b_n\}_{n=2}^{\infty}$ by (13) recursively. Since $P_A(\alpha) = 0$, i.e. $\xi\eta - \zeta\mu = (\xi + \eta)\alpha - \alpha^2$, we have $P_A(\alpha^n) = (\alpha^n - \alpha)(\alpha^n + \alpha - \xi - \eta)$. Thus, $|P_A(\alpha^n)| \ge |\alpha^{n-1} - 1|(|\xi + \eta| - 2) > 0$. Put $M = \max\{\dfrac{|\zeta|[(1+|\eta|)|s|+1]}{|\xi+\eta|-2}, \dfrac{|\zeta|(1+|\eta|)}{|\xi+\eta|-2}\}$ for convenience.

From (13) we have

$$
\begin{aligned}
|b_n| \le \frac{M}{|\alpha^{n-1}-1|}[& \sum_{\substack{l_1+l_2+\cdots+l_t=n\\ t=2,3,\cdots,n}} |b_{l_1}|.|b_{l_2}|\cdots|b_{l_t}| \\
& + \sum_{\substack{l_1+l_2+\cdots+l_t=n\\ t=2,3,\cdots,n}} N^t \prod_{k=1}^{t} (|b_{l_k}| + \sum_{\substack{m_1+m_2+\cdots+m_v=l_k\\ v=2,3,\cdots,l_k}} |b_{m_1}|.|b_{m_2}|\cdots|b_{m_v}|) \\
& + \sum_{\substack{l_1+l_2+\cdots+l_t=n\\ t=2,3,\cdots,n}} \prod_{k=1}^{t} \sum_{\substack{m_1+m_2+\cdots+m_j=l_k\\ j=1,2,\cdots,l_k}} N^j \prod_{i=1}^{j} (|b_{m_i}| + \sum_{\substack{n_1+n_2+\cdots+n_l=m_i\\ l=2,3,\cdots,m_i}} |b_{n_1}|.|b_{n_2}|\cdots|b_{n_l}|)],
\end{aligned}
\tag{20}
$$

$n = 2, 3, \cdots,$

where N is defined in (14).

To construct a governing series we consider the implicit functional equation

$$F(M,\tau,z,\Psi)=0, \tag{21}$$

where F is defined in (16). Similarly to the proof of Theorem 1, using the implicit function theorem we can prove that (21) has a unique analytic solution $\Psi(M,\tau,z)$ in a neighborhood of the origin such that $\Psi(M,\tau,0)=0$ and $\Psi'_z(M,\tau,0)=|\tau|$. Thus $\Psi(M,\tau,z)$ in (21) can be expanded into a convergent series

$$\Psi(M,\tau,z)=\sum_{n=1}^{\infty} C_n z^n, \quad C_1=|\tau|, \tag{22}$$

in a neighborhood of the origin. Replacing (22) into (23) and comparing coefficients we obtain that $C_1=|\tau|$ and

$$
\begin{aligned}
C_n = M[& \sum_{\substack{l_1+l_2+\cdots+l_t=n\\ t=2,3,\cdots,n}} C_{l_1}C_{l_2}\cdots C_{l_t} + \sum_{\substack{l_1+l_2+\cdots+l_t=n\\ t=2,3,\cdots,n}} N^t \prod_{k=1}^{t} (C_{l_k} + \sum_{\substack{m_1+m_2+\cdots+m_v=l_k\\ v=2,3,\cdots,l_k}} C_{m_1}C_{m_2}\cdots C_{m_v}) \\
& + \sum_{\substack{l_1+l_2+\cdots+l_t=n\\ t=2,3,\cdots,n}} \prod_{k=1}^{t} \sum_{\substack{m_1+m_2+\cdots+m_j=l_k\\ j=2,3,\cdots,l_k}} N^j \prod_{i=1}^{j} (C_{l_i} + \sum_{\substack{n_1+n_2+\cdots+n_l=m_i\\ l=2,3,\cdots,m_i}} C_{n_1}C_{n_2}\cdots C_{n_l})],
\end{aligned}
\tag{23}
$$

$n=2,3,\cdots.$

Note that the series (22) converges in a neighborhood of the origin. Hence there is a constant $T>0$ such that

$$C_n \le T^n, \quad n=1,2,\cdots. \tag{24}$$

Now, we can deduce, by induction, that $|b_n| \le C_n e^{K(n-1)}$ for $n \ge 1$, where $K:\mathbf{N}\to\mathbf{R}$ is defined in Lemma 1. In fact $|b_1|=|\eta|=C_1$. For inductive proof we assume that $|b_j| \le C_j e^{K(j-1)}, j \le n-1$. From (20) and Lemma 1 we know

$$
\begin{aligned}
|b_n| \le \frac{M}{|\alpha^{n-1}-1|}[& \sum_{\substack{l_1+l_2+\cdots+l_t=n\\ t=2,3,\cdots,n}} C_{l_1}C_{l_2}\cdots C_{l_t} e^{K(l_1-1)+\cdots+K(l_t-1)} \\
& + \sum_{\substack{l_1+l_2+\cdots+l_t=n\\ t=2,3,\cdots,n}} N^t \prod_{k=1}^{t} (C_{l_k} e^{K(l_k-1)} + \sum_{\substack{m_1+m_2+\cdots+m_v=l_k\\ v=2,3,\cdots,l_k}} C_{m_1}C_{m_2}\cdots C_{m_v} e^{K(m_1-1)+\cdots K(m_v-1)}) + \sum_{\substack{l_1+l_2+\cdots+l_t=n\\ t=2,3,\cdots,n}} \prod_{k=1}^{t} \sum_{\substack{m_1+m_2+\cdots+m_j=l_k\\ j=1,2,\cdots,l_k}} N^j \prod_{i=1}^{j} (C_{m_i} e^{K(m_i-1)} \\
& + \sum_{\substack{n_1+n_2+\cdots+n_l=m_i\\ l=2,3,\cdots,m_i}} C_{n_1}C_{n_2}\cdots C_{n_l} e^{K(n_1-1)+\cdots+K(n_l-1)})] \\
\le \frac{M}{|\alpha^{n-1}-1|} e^{K(n-2)} [& \sum_{\substack{l_1+l_2+\cdots+l_t=n\\ t=2,3,\cdots,n}} C_{l_1}C_{l_2}\cdots C_{l_t}
\end{aligned}
$$

$$+\sum_{\substack{l_1+l_2+\cdots+l_t=n\\ t=2,3,\cdots,n}} N^t\prod_{k=1}^{t}(C_{l_k}+\sum_{\substack{m_1+m_2+\cdots+m_v=l_k\\ v=2,3,\cdots,l_k}} C_{m_1}C_{m_2}\cdots C_{m_v})$$

$$+\sum_{\substack{l_1+l_2+\cdots+l_t=n\\ t=2,3,\cdots,n}}\prod_{k=1}^{t}\sum_{\substack{m_1+m_2+\cdots+m_j=l_k\\ j=1,2,\cdots,l_k}} N^j\prod_{i=1}^{j}(C_{m_i}+\sum_{\substack{n_1+n_2+\cdots+n_l=m_i\\ l=2,3,\cdots,m_i}} C_{n_1}C_{n_2}\cdots C_{n_l})] \quad =\frac{e^{K(n-2)}}{|\alpha^{n-1}-1|}C_n .$$

Note that

$$K(l_1-1)+K(l_2-1)+\cdots+K(l_t-1)\le K(n-2)\le K(n-1)+\log|\alpha^{n-1}-1|.$$

Then $|b_n|\le C_n e^{K(n-1)}$ as required. Note that $K(n)\le n(B(\theta)+\gamma)$ for some universal constant $\gamma>0$. Then $|b_n|\le T^n e^{(n-1)(B(\theta)+\gamma)}$,

That is, $\limsup_{n\to\infty}(|b_n|)^{1/n}\le\limsup_{n\to\infty}(T^n e^{(n-1)(B(\theta)+\gamma)})^{1/n}=Te^{B(\theta)+\gamma}$. This implies that the convergence radius of (10) is at least $(Te^{B(\theta)+\gamma})^{-1}$. This completes the proof.

4 Auxiliary Equation Case (H3)

In case (H3) the constant α is not only on the unit circle in **C** but also a root of unity. In such a case, the resonant case, both Diophantine condition and Brjuno condition are not satisfied.

Let $\{D_n\}_{n=1}^{\infty}$ be a sequence define by $D_1=|\tau|$ and

$$D_n=\Gamma M[\sum_{\substack{l_1+l_2+\cdots+l_t=n\\ t=2,3,\cdots,n}} D_{l_1}D_{l_2}\cdots D_{l_t}+\sum_{\substack{l_1+l_2+\cdots+l_t=n\\ t=2,3,\cdots,n}} N^t\prod_{k=1}^{t}(D_{l_k}+\sum_{\substack{m_1+m_2+\cdots+m_v=l_k\\ v=2,3\cdots l_k}} D_{m_1}D_{m_2}\cdots D_{m_v})$$

$$+\sum_{\substack{l_1+l_2+\cdots+l_t=n\\ t=2,3,\cdots,n}}\prod_{k=1}^{t}\sum_{\substack{m_1+m_2+\cdots+m_j=l_k\\ j=2,3,\cdots,l_k}} N^j\prod_{i=1}^{j}(D_{l_i}+\sum_{\substack{n_1+n_2+\cdots+n_l=m_i\\ l=2,3,\cdots,m_i}} D_{n_1}D_{n_2}\cdots D_{n_l})],$$

$$n=2,3,\ldots,$$

where $\Gamma=\max\{1,|\alpha^i-1|^{-1}: i=1,2,\ldots,p-1\}$, N and M are defined in Theorem 2.

Theorem 3. Suppose that (H3) holds, $\alpha\in\sigma(A)$, $|\xi+\eta|>2$ and p is given as above. Let $\{b_n\}_{n=1}^{\infty}$ be determined recursively by $b_1=\tau$ and

$$(\alpha^n-\alpha)(\alpha^n+\alpha-\xi-\eta)b_n=\Theta(n,\alpha),\quad n=2,3,\cdots, \tag{26}$$

where

$$\Theta(n,\alpha)=\zeta\sum_{\substack{l_1+l_2+\cdots+l_t=n\\ t=2,3,\cdots,n}}[(\alpha^n-\eta)sa_t+v_t]b_{l_1}b_{l_2}\cdots b_{l_t}$$

$$-\zeta(\alpha^n-\eta)\sum_{\substack{l_1+l_2+\cdots+l_t=n\\ t=2,3,\cdots,n}} g_t\prod_{k=1}^{t}[(\alpha^{l_k}-\xi)b_{l_k}-\sum_{\substack{m_1+m_2+\cdots+m_v=l_k\\ v=2,3,\cdots,l_k}} a_v b_{m_1}.b_{m_2}\cdots b_{m_v}]$$

$$+\zeta\sum_{\substack{l_1+l_2+\cdots+l_t=n\\ t=2,3,\cdots,n}} c_t\prod_{k=1}^{t}\{\sum_{\substack{m_1+m_2+\cdots+m_j=l_k\\ j=1,2,\cdots,l_k}} g_j\prod_{i=1}^{j}[(\alpha^{m_i}-\xi)b_{m_i}-\sum_{\substack{n_1+n_2+\cdots+n_l=m_i\\ l=2,3,\cdots,m_i}} a_l b_{n_1}b_{n_2}\cdots b_{n_l}]\}.$$

If $\Theta(vp+1,\alpha)=0$ for all $v=1,2,\cdots$, then equation (4) has an analytic solution $\phi(z)$ in a neighborhood of the origin such that $\phi(0)=0, \phi'(0)=\tau$, and $\phi^{vp+1}(0)=(vp+1)!\tau_{vp+1}$, where all $\tau_{vp+1}s$ are arbitrary constants satisfying the inequality $|\tau_{vp+1}| \le D_{vp+1}$ and the sequence $\{D_n\}_{n=1}^{\infty}$ is defined in (25). Otherwise, if $\Theta(vp+1,\alpha) \ne 0$ for some $v = 1,2,\cdots$, then equation (4) has no analytic solutions in any neighborhood of the origin.

Proof. Clearly, (4) has a trivial solution $\phi(z) \equiv 0$ if $\tau = 0$. Assume $\tau \ne 0$ and seek a power series solution of (4) of the form (10) as in the proof of Theorem 2, where the equality in (13) or (26) is indispensable. If $\Theta(vp+1,\alpha) \ne 0$ for some natural number v, then the equality in (26) does not hold for $n = vp+1$ since $\alpha^{vp+1} - \alpha = 0$. In such a circumstance equation (4) has no formal solutions.

When $\Theta(vp+1,\alpha) = 0$ for all natural number v, for each v the corresponding b_{vp+1} in (26) has infinitely many choices in **C** that is, the formal series solution (10) defines a family of solutions with infinitely many parameters. Choose $b_{vp+1} = \tau_{vp+1}$ arbitrarily such that

$$|\tau_{vp+1}| \le D_{vp+1}, \quad v = 1,2,\cdots, \tag{27}$$

where D_{vp+1} is defined by (25). In what follows we prove that the formal series solution (10) converges in a neighborhood of the origin. Observe that $|\alpha^{n-1} - 1|^{-1} \le \Gamma$ for $n \ne vp+1$. It follows from (26) that

$$\begin{aligned} |b_n| \le \Gamma M[&\sum_{\substack{l_1+l_2+\cdots+l_t=n\\ t=2,3\cdots n}} |b_{l_1}|.|b_{l_2}|\cdots|b_{l_t}| \\ &+ \sum_{\substack{l_1+l_2+\cdots+l_t=n\\ t=2,3,\cdots,n}} N^t \prod_{k=1}^{t} (|b_{l_k}| + \sum_{\substack{m_1+m_2+\cdots+m_v=l_k\\ v=2,3,\cdots,l_k}} |b_{m_1}|.|b_{m_2}|\cdots|b_{m_v}|) \\ &+ \sum_{\substack{l_1+l_2+\cdots+l_t=n\\ t=2,3,\cdots,n}} \prod_{k=1}^{t} \sum_{\substack{m_1+m_2+\cdots+m_j=l_k\\ j=1,2,\cdots,l_k}} N^j \prod_{i=1}^{j} (|b_{m_i}| + \sum_{\substack{n_1+n_2+\cdots+n_l=m_i\\ l=2,3,\cdots,m_i}} |b_{n_1}|.|b_{n_2}|\cdots|b_{n_l}|)], \end{aligned} \tag{28}$$

for all $n \ne vp+1, v = 1,2,\ldots$. Thus $b_n^{'}s$ are estimated by (27) and (28). Let

$$G(\Gamma M,\tau,z) = \sum_{n=1}^{\infty} D_n z^n, \quad D_1 = |\tau|. \tag{29}$$

It is easy to check that (29) satisfies the implicit functional equation

$$F(\Gamma M,\tau,z,G) = 0, \tag{30}$$

where F is defined in (16). Moreover, similarly to the proof of Theorem 1, we can prove that (30) has a unique analytic solution $G(\Gamma M,\tau,z)$ in a neighborhood of the origin such that $G(\Gamma M,\tau,0) = 0$ and $G_z'(\Gamma M,\tau,0) = |\tau|$. Thus (29) converges in a neighborhood of the origin. Moreover, It is easy to show that, by induction, $|b_n| \le D_n$, $n = 1,2,\ldots$ Therefore, the series (10) converges in a neighborhood of the origin. This completes the proof.

5 Analyticity of Invariant Curves

In this section, we will state and prove our main result.

Theorem 4. Suppose one of the conditions in Theorem 1-3 are fulfilled. Then equation (2) has a solution of the form

$f(x)=g\{\phi[\alpha\phi^{-1}(z)]-p(z)\}$ in a neighborhood of the origin such that $f(0)=0,\ f'(0)=\frac{1}{\zeta}(\alpha-\xi)$, where $g(z)=q^{-1}(z)$ and $\phi(z)$ is an analytic solution of equation (4).

Proof. By Theorems 1-3, we can find an invertible analytic solution ϕ of the auxiliary equation (4) in the form of (10) such that $\phi(0)=0$ and $\phi'(0)=\tau\neq 0$. Let $f(z)=g\{\phi[\alpha\phi^{-1}(z)]-p(z)\}$, which is also analytic in a neighborhood of the origin. From (4), it is easy to see

$$\begin{aligned} f\{p(z)+q[f(z)]\} &= f[\phi(\alpha\phi^{-1}(z))] \\ &= g\{\phi(\alpha\phi^{-1}(\phi(\alpha\phi^{-1}(z))))-p[\phi(\alpha\phi^{-1}(z))]\} \\ &= h\{g[\phi(\alpha\phi^{-1}(z))-p(z)]\}+v(z)=h[f(z)]+v(z), \end{aligned}$$

and $f'(z)=g'\{\phi[\alpha\phi^{-1}(z)]-p(z)\}\left(\alpha\phi'(\alpha\phi^{-1}(z))(\phi^{-1})'(z)-p'(z)\right)$. Thus, we have $f(0)=g\{\phi[\alpha\phi^{-1}(0)]-p(0)\}=0$ and

$$\begin{aligned} f'(0) &= g'\{\phi[\alpha\phi^{-1}(0)]-p(0)\}\left(\alpha\phi'(\alpha\phi^{-1}(0))(\phi^{-1})'(0)-p'(0)\right) \\ &= g'(0)(\alpha\phi'(0)(\phi^{-1})'(0)-p'(0))=\frac{1}{\zeta}(\alpha-\xi). \end{aligned}$$

The proof is complete.

References

1. Diamond, P.M.: Analytic invariants of mappings of two variables. J. Math. Anal. Appl. 27, 601–608 (1969)
2. Birkhoff, G.D.: Dynamical systems with degrees of freedom. Trans. Amer. Math. Soc. 18, 199–300 (1917)
3. Birkhoff, G.D.: Surface transformations and their dynamical applications. Acta. Math. 43, 1–119 (1920)
4. Moser, J.: The analytic invariants of an area-preserving mapping near a hyperbolic fixpoint. Comm. Pure Appl. Math. 9, 673–692 (1956)
5. Moser, J.: On invariant curves of area-preserving maps of an annulus. Nachr. Akad. Wiss. Gottingen 1, 199–226 (1962)
6. Siegel, C.L., Moser, J.K.: Lecture on celestial mechanics. Springer, CA (1971)
7. Si, J.: On an pp.alytic solutions of the equation of invariant cures. C. R. Math, Rep. Acad. XVII, 49–52 (1995)
8. Si, J., Wang, X.-P., Zhang, W.: Analytic invariant curves for a planar map. Appl. Math. Letters 15, 561–573 (2002)
9. Si, J., Zhang, W.: Analytic solutions of a functional equation for invariant curves. J. Math. Anal. Appl. 259, 83–93 (2001)
10. Bjuno, A.D.: Analytic form of differential equations. Trans. Moscow Math. Soc. 25, 131–288 (1971)

11. Marmi, S., Moussa, P., Yoccoz, J.-C.: The Brjuno functions and their regularity properties. Comm. Math. Phys. 186, 265–293 (1997)
12. Berger, M.S.: Nonlinearity and Functional Analysis. Academic Press, London (1977)
13. Siegel, C.L.: Vorlesungenuber Himmelsmechanik. Springer, Berlin (1956)
14. Si, J., Zhang, W.: Analytic solutions of a nonlinear iterative equation near neutral fixed points and poles. J. Math. Anal. Appl. 283, 373–388 (2003)
15. Carletti, T., Marmi, S.: Linearization of Analytic and Non-Analytic Germs of Diffeomorphisms of $(\mathbb{C},0)$. Bull. Soc. Math. France 128, 69–85 (2000)
16. Davie, A.M.: The critical function for the semistandard map. Nonlinearity 7, 219–229 (1994)

Improvements of Genetic Algorithm to the Knapsack Problem

Zhang Haibo, Cai Liwen, Gao Shenyong, Cheng Jianguo, Yu Feng, and Li daqing

Zhejiang Water Conservancy and Hydropower College, Hangzhou 310018
zhanghaibo05@hotmail.com

Abstract. This paper constructs a Genetic Algorithm to the Knapsack Problem and makes several modifications to improve the algorithm. By keep the group of best chromosomes the best solutions can be improved step by step. Adaptive hybrid probability and mutation probability are applied when more duplicated answers appears, constantly increasing hybrid probability and mutation probability can enlarge the searching horizon base on the preliminary results. Multi-point crossover can also make searching scope larger and conducive to better outcomes. A roulette function is defined that provides a comparative series of probabilities, by which definitly priority of chromosomes at front position is achieved. This paper also provides contrastive results to show the effect of these improvements. the measures of keeping top chromosomes and the new roulette function is new.

Keywords: GA, Knapsack Problem, Improvements.

1 Introduction

Knapsack problem is a NP-complete combinatorial optimization, which can be described as given a set of items and each them has its own weight and price, the total weight of a limited, how to choice these items to make the maximum total price of goods. This kind of problems often arise in business, combinatorial mathematics, computational complexity theory, cryptography and applied mathematics and other fields.

The following data is from the paper "Genetic Algorithm of Good Point Set" published in the Chinese Journal of Computers by Professor Zhang Ling and Zhang Bo:

Weight:
80,82,85,70,72,70,66,50,55,25,50,55,40,48,50,32,22,60,30,32,40,38,35,32,25, 28,30,22,50,30 ,45,30,60,50,20 ,65,20,25,30,10 ,20,25,15,10,10,10,4, 4, 2,1

Corresponding values:

220,208,198,192,180,180,165,162,160,158,155,130,125,122,120,118,115,110, 105,101,100,100,98,96,95,90,88,82,80,77,75,73,72,70,69,66,65,63,60,58,56,50,30,20, 15,10,8,5,3,1

The result of the article is 3103 which is the best answer of the problem, these data is used to research algorithm so that we can make comparison.

D. Zeng (Ed.): ICAIC 2011, Part I, CCIS 224, pp. 202–206, 2011.

2 Construction of the Genetic Algorithm

2.1 Encoding

We use conventional encoding mode, the code contains a 50-bit binary digital as a gene sequence, in which one bit is 1 means the corresponding item is selected, and this can easy decoding and fitness process.

2.2 Construction of the Fitness Function

Fitness function of knapsack problem is simple, by directly calculating of the sum of the value of selected items the fitness can be easily gained, but for we have to specifically treat those total weight exceeds the limit (1000) by simply set the fitness to 0 so that the chromosome can be removed facilitate.

2.3 Roulette Function

In order to achieve the priorities of the good chromosomes that participate crossing process, a roulette function is defined, the basic requirements are as follows:

$$\begin{cases} \sum_{i=1}^{N} f(i) = 1 \\ f(i) > f(i+1) \end{cases}$$

Based on the above considerations, a comparative series is constructed, the ratio is less than 1, 0.9 for example, the general term is:

$$aq^i$$

Where a is first term, q is the ratio, because

$$\sum_{i=1}^{N} aq^i = 1$$

According the summary formula of comparative series, a is about 1-q:

$$\mathbf{a \approx 1 - 0.9 = 0.1}$$

This function can give every individual chromosome a suitable chance to participation the crossing process, compare with usual roulette functions this function is more fixed, and can provide definitly priority of chromosomes at front position in the queue, furthermore, it can avoid some small number of prominent chromosomes have too much probability of hybrid.

At first choose one chromosome of the hybrids, determine the other chromosome by a random number rnd that is in [0,1], add each term from i=0 to summary value until rnd is larger than it, the value of I is the order the other parent, we also take measures to prevent any chromosome crosses with itself.

The design reduces computation and ensures the chromosome with good fitness get more opportunity to involve in hybridization.

2.4 Ending Conditions

The ending condition of knapsack problem is difficult to determine and there can be a variety of standard. Because of the characteristics of the knapsack problem, the good chromosomes may be damaged by crossover and mutation and resulting outcome fall back, so it is not definite that better results can come from more iterations. One of the standard is convergence of finesses, when the finesses come to similar then end the iterations, another one is end iteration at certain rounds.

Determined these key issues, the algorithm can be realized and after 400 iterations an ideal outcomes can be got, most of the fitness of theses outcome are above 3090 which is close to the best result.

3 Improvement of the Traditional Genetic Algorithm

Above algorithm can solve this kind of problem, but there are also several problems, the course of convergence is dilatory, the best result of each generation is volatile because in some cases the best fitness setbacks for the best chromosome is broken by crossing and mutation. So we make the following step to improve the algorithm:

1. Originally the first 100 chromosomes are produced by random, then a pool of chromosomes is set to store the 400 new chromosomes generated by acrossing and mutation that can provide enough items to be selected as the next generation, then mutation is processed to these 400 chromosomes, finally 100 best chromosomes is selected from the pool to form the new generration of codes.
2. The best several chromosomes (5 e.g.) is kept by islated from crossing and mutation process, this can protect the best chromosomes to avoid degeneration by crossing and mutations, and then join in the queue in pool to be selected to make new generation. This machiniusm can esure the best solutions be improved constantly.
3. As the best five chromosomes have be retained, in order to prevent premature convergence, the probability of crossover and mutation can be increased to make chromosomes change more frequently, this can reduce premature convergence risk and increase the probability of getting good chromosome. Actually the hybrid probability used is 0.4, mutation probability is 0.03 that are significantly larger than commonly used 0.3 and 0.01.

Based on these improvements, the highest fitness increased, so the convergence condition is changed to no more better solution during 200 iterations.

Compare with traditional GA this algorithm of Knapsack Problem become very stable, the contract result show in table 1, in order to make comparation, all the result is the best answer of the 100 generations.

The result of new algorithm can be improved significantly by increase the number of iterations, improved algorithm have much more 3103 which is the best result of the problem than traditional GA for 200 generations, there is more than 60% trails is 3103 show it have very good precious and stability; however, traditional GA are not so stable because its best result can be destroy by crossing and mutation other than be retained, this can reduce the speed of convergence, there is no 3103 of 10 trails and all the results are all between 3076 and 4094.

Table 1. Results of two algorithms

ID	Traditional algorithm		Improved algorithm	
	weight	price	weight	price
1	1000	3067	1000	3091
2	997	3069	998	3093
3	1000	3081	999	3090
4	1000	3093	1000	3103
5	1000	3067	1000	3083
6	1000	3070	1000	3088
7	1000	3088	999	3099
8	999	3094	1000	3089
9	1000	3057	1000	3095
10	1000	3094	1000	3092
average	999.6	3078	999.6	3092.3
variance	0.84	167.4	0.44	29.01

4 Further Improvements

Although the above algorithm improved the stability and the convergence rate, there also emerge a large number of duplicated chromosomes during the iteration process that lingers process at its later stage, the quality of the solutions are not good enough and need to be improved, therefore, the following attempts are implemented:

1. Improved hybrid performance by using multi-point crossover, The traditional way of coding may produce duplicate the individual chromosomes, multi-point crossover can increase searching scope and reduce duplication of chromosomes by provide more diversity. The new chromosome is produced by taking the corresponding bits from the parent in accordance to the set probability, this achieves the multi-point crossover.
2. Using the adaptive probability of crossover and mutation. When too many same codes are produced, the probabilities are gradually increased to increase the searching horizon so that the better solutions can appear more possible.

Above improvements can slow convergence of the algorithm, but the stability and accuracy of results have significantly improved, ten trail's results of 200 iterations are shown in Table 2, which shows that the robustness of the results improved, the average and variance of the results.

Table 2. Results after further improvements

1	3103
2	3096
3	3103
4	3092
5	3091
6	3096
7	3093
8	3092
9	3092
10	3097
average	3095.5
variance	19.83333

5 Conclusion

Knapsack problem has a significant representation, as a classical method of adaptive search genetic algorithm is simple and efficient. Improved algorithm can undertake more extensive search and get better results. By retaining a set of best chromosomes we can make the best results improved step by step, adaptive crossover and mutation probability increase searching scope on the basis of early results and increased the probability of good solutions.

Acknowledgment. The authors gratefully acknowledge the contributions of DING Jian-Li,Chen Zeng-Qiang, Yuan Zhu-ZHi, Zhang Wei, Li Shouzhi, Gao Feng, Andreas Bortfeldt, Hermann Gehring, D.Y.He and J.Z.Cha for their work on the original version of this document.

References

1. Ding, J.-L., Chen, Z.-Q., Yuan, Z.-Z.: On the combination of Genetic Algorithm and Ant Algorithm. Journal Of Computer Research and Development 40(9), 1351–1356 (2003)
2. Zhang, W., Li, S., Gao, F.: Comparative Study of Several Intelligent Optimization Algorithms. In: Proceedings of the 24th Chinese Control Conference, Guangzhou, P.R. China, July 15-18, pp. 1316–1320 (2005)
3. Bortfeldt, A., Gehring, H.: A Hybrid Genetic Algorithm for The Container Loading Problem. European Journal of Operational Research 131, 143–161 (2001)
4. He, D.Y., Cha, J.Z.: Research on Solution to Complex Container Loading Problem Based on Genetic Algorithm. In: The First International Conference on Machine Learning and Cybernetics, Beijing-China, pp. 78–82 (2002)

Polarity Analysis Based on an Improved Feature Selection Algorithm

Tian Weixin[1], Zheng Sheng[2], and Wang Anhui[1]

[1] College of Computer and Information Technology China Three Gorges University Yichang, China
[2] College of Science China Three Gorges University Yichang, China
Tian1817@yeah.net

Abstract. Polarity analysis is a technique that analyzes text according to the attitude implied from it. Since the correspondence between the attitude and surface word features is subtle, the ordinary methods for topical text analysis are not sufficient for polarity analysis. This paper proposed a classification method combined with feature selection algorithm to the problem. Firstly, all possible feature schemas are designed and features are collected. Then a feature selection algorithm named improved SIMBA is used to distill the candidate features. In the last, the selected features are used as clues for a standard classifier. Experiment shows that the performance is better than that of previous method on the same dataset.

Keywords: sentiment analysis, polarity classification, feature selection, SIMBA.

1 Introduction

With the development of Internet and the technology of wireless access, more and more subjective text such as emotions, comments, reviews and etc. swell in the community, blogs or other shopping sites of the web. The opinions, preferences or stands in the subjective text are useful for many purposes. For example, the government can use the information to track the folk reactions to events; someone can get useful information from what others think before deciding to do something. Opinion mining or sentiment analysis, which devotes to extract and analyze subjective information from the web text, has been drawn more and more attention in recent years.

Compare with the factual text analysis, sentiment analysis is believed to be more difficult for the two characteristics of it. One is semantic relevance. The subjectivity is related to the meaning of surface words or phrases of text, and the presence or frequency of words, which is often used in the factual text analysis, is not enough to present the subjectivity. The other is locality. The subjective text such as opinions, reviews is usually bound to certain objects. Many objects often overlap in paragraphs. So the local bound of subjectivity should be confirmed before analyzing.

This paper addresses an important subtask of sentiment analysis named polarity analysis. The goal of the polarity analysis is to determine whether the attitude implied in given text is positive or negative. We start with having extracted the text to be

D. Zeng (Ed.): ICAIC 2011, Part I, CCIS 224, pp. 207–214, 2011.

determined from sentences and don't distract our focus to the process of acquiring the unit of subjectivity, which is narrated in another paper. The methodology adopted in our paper is machine learning, which supposes that the polarity of a piece of text completely depends on the text itself. So the adequate features from the text are collected more fully, the precision is higher. However, there is a paradox in this methodology. Because with the growth of the features, the noise and the time consumption are also growing, and thus lower the precision and cut down the applicability of the method. To solve this problem, we apply an improved feature selection algorithm in the front of the machine learning to distill the features. The experiment shows that the method proposed in the paper exceeds other methods on the same test data in precision.

The rest of the paper is organized as follow. Section 2 is the related works that are relevant to our study. Section 3 is about the grammar and collocation features and the method to get them. Section 4 is about the improved feature selection algorithm. We proposed an improve SIMBA algorithm and use it to integrate the multiple features. Section 5 is the experiment and section 6 is the conclusion of the paper.

2 Related Works

The polarity analysis has been research topic for several years and many methods have been proposed by researchers. Generally, these methods can be put into three classes: the supervised learning method, induction from lexicon method and Bootstrapping method.

The supervised learning method developed from the topic classification. For example, Pang applied Naïve Bayes, SVM, Maximum Entropy respectively on the movie review dataset to classify text according to implied sentiment polarity. The result showed that the performance is lower than that of same methods applied to the topical classification [1]. Airoldi etc. used a heuristic method named Tabu-Search enhanced Markov Blanket Classifier to the polarity classification. The method can obtain proper amount or relevant lexicon automatically and the learning process has linear complex [2]. Dave etc. collected the rating data from product review sites, used Naïve Bayes classifier and Laplace smoothing algorithm to classify and preprocess the data. They scored a higher precision than the baseline [3]. Gamon used the linear SVM to analyze the user feedback data from the web, which contains much more noise than general data. The result showed that the performance is satisfying after eliminating the redundant features and it's helpful to add deep linguistic analysis to the normal N-grams features [4]. Kudo etc. introduced a Boosting method based on weak learning, using the subordinate dependency tree as the features. They did experiment on the PHS review data collected from web by themselves and got a score equal to that by SVM. The precision gotten by their method is between that using bag of word and n-grams [5].

The induction from lexicon method doesn't need the learning process. The method first creates a list of sentiment words using unsupervised learning and then determines the polarity of sentences by functions induced from the polarity of words in the lexicon. Following are the representative researches. Hatzivassiloglou etc. proposed a logistic linear classifier to determine the grade of adjective polarities. Their method used the comparative or superlative degree of the adverbs or phrases that often modify adjectives, or the morphology of the comparative or superlative degree of the adjectives as indication. Then they defined logistic function on the indication and determined the grade according to the function value and the thresholds predefined [6]. Turney proposed a method to determine the polarity through the average semantic orientations of the adjectives or adverbs in the phrases. The semantic orientation of a word can be obtained by the difference between the mutual information of the word and "excellent" and the mutual information of the word and "poor". The mutual information of two words means logarithm of the concurrence of two words dividing by the two logarithm of occurrence of the single word. To PMI-IR, the mutual information is computed by the amount of relevant documents returned by the search engine while making the two words as keywords [7]. Other researches use existing lexicons such as WordNet, HowNet as basis of computing. For example, Kamps proposed a method using WordNet, which determined a word by the difference of the distance to "good" and the distance to "bad"[8]. Kim etc. first collected few sentiment seed words and expanded the words set by adding the synonym or antonym of the seed words in WordNet [9].

The idea of bootstrapping method is to get training data by an initial classifier and use the training data to create a classifier to separate the final data. For example, Wang etc. took a weak supervised learning method to determine the polarity of sentiment words in Chinese corpus. In the condition of using no word-segment, a bootstrapping method which computes the polarity of words by the relation between the templates and the return words was adopted. In the condition of using word-segment, scores were assigned to the words by the relation between the word and the approving and derogatory words in lexicon. The two ways fuse to a universal method in the end [10].

The idea of our method is same to that of [4], while the method that we used is an improved feature selection algorithm, and the features that we considered are richer than theirs.

3 Base Method and Features

We consider the polarity analysis as binary classification and solve the problem using supervised learning method.

3.1 Problem Setup

Our method to analyze polarity of sentences is divided into three steps. Firstly, we prepare a collection of sentences which have been labelled as whether the attitude is positive or negative beforehand. Then we design algorithm to get sorts of features from sentences and train a Naïve Bayes classifier. While training, we use an improved feature selection algorithm to adjust the weight of each of the features. In the end, we use the Naïve Bayes classifier together with the adjusted feature weights to classify the sentences. Lets begin with the definition of the problem.

Let $S_u = \{s_1, s_2, ...s_n\}$ is the subjective sentences set to be analyzed, $Y = \{-1, 1\}$ is the label set that represent the classes of s_n, S_l is the labelled dataset i.i.d. to S_u, given training set $Tr = \{< s_i, y_i >\}, 1 \le i \le m$, $s_i \in S_l$ 。 The goal is to get the function $z : S_u \to Y$ 。

To get the function z, Lets $F = \{f_1, f_2 \dots f_l\}$ be the features set, let H be the l dimension space expanded by F , $g : S_u + S_l \to H, v : H \to Y$ is the function from $S(S_u + S_l)$ to H , H to Y respectively, then $z = v \bullet g(S_u)$ 。

3.2 Features

For the map from sentences to the features set, several feature presentations can be taken such as character sequence, word sequence, language model and so on. The performances of different presentations are sensitive to the application domain and characteristic of the sentences. With the hypothesis of having no knowledge of the domain in this paper, we adopt different feature presentations as much as possible at the same time. The features will be integrated late. Following are the features used in this paper.

Word. Word is an often used feature in text analysis task. To get words in sentences is an easy task in English. We use presence and frequency to represent words. For Chinese text, a word segment process is applied.

Phrase. Phrase is fix collocation that usually composes with two or more characters or words. The component words can be disjoined and separated by other words. Because the sparseness of phrase occurrence, we use presence only to represent phrases. To get the Phrases, we first compile a list of phrases and count the presence according to the list.

Syntax. Syntax is language feature in grammar level such as voice, sentential form, tense and so on. We utilize the morphology and position to get the syntax features.

Sentiment words. Sentiment words are important clues when analyzing sentiment. We determine whether a sentence comprises sentiment words by looking up a pre-compiled sentiment words lexicon. The grade of sentiment words is ignored and all the words are of equal effect. We use the frequency to present sentiment words feature without making a distinction among different words.

4 Feature Selection

In the above section, we collect all sorts of candidate features as much as possible. If these features are all used equally to train classifier, they will spend much unnecessary computing time and generate much noise. Feature selection is a technique to get a subset from given feature set, while the subset can totally stand for the prediction property of the superset. Feature selection can help wipe out the unnecessary features and thus reduce the dimension of the whole matrix.

Feature selection algorithms can be divided into two models: wrapper model and filter model. The wrapper model combines with the classifier and optimises its performance directly. The filter model adopts preprocessing procedure, which maximizes a predefined evaluation function to get the eligible features.

Simba is a filter model feature selection algorithm based on margin measurement. It shows good performance in before experiment [11]. There are two problems when applying origin SIMBA to the subjectivity detection domain. The one is in that the iteration times of origin SIMBA is fixed and it is hard to choose appropriate times; the other is in that the origin SIMBA selects the instances randomly and can't avoid the high similarity among them, thus the weight vector w may sink into local vertex and the selected features can't represent the object document well.

To address the above problems, we improve the origin SIMBA as follow. First, we use the difference of w between the current round and last round to control the iteration times. The iteration will terminate when the difference is less than a threshold. Second, after randomly selecting the instances, we omit the instances which are high similar to the exist instances to avoid output the instance set that will expose the process to the risk of falling into local vertex. The improved SIMBA is listed in algorithm 1.

Algorithm 1

IMPROVED SIMBA ALGORITHM

1.Initiate l-dimension row vector $w = (1,1,...1), \Delta = w$, Initiate sentence set $S_{sel} = Empty$

2. while $\max|\Delta_i| > \varepsilon$ *do* 3, 4

3.Randomly select s_i from Tr

4. If $Sim(S_{sel}, s_i) < 0$ *then* 5, 6, 7

5. $S_{sel} = S_{sel} \cup \{s_i\}$

6. calculate nearmiss($g(s_i)$) and nearhit($g(s_i)$) with respect to $g(Tr - s_i)$.

7. *for* $i = 1$ *to* l *do* a, b

a. $$\Delta_i = \frac{1}{2}\left(\frac{(x_i - nearmiss(x)_i)^2}{\|x - nearmiss(x)\|_w} - \frac{(x_i - nearhit(x)_i)^2}{\|x - nearhit(x)\|_w}\right) w_i$$

b. $w = w + \Delta$

8. $w \leftarrow w / \|w^2\|_\infty$

Where $Sim(S_{sel}, s_i)$ compares s_i with each s in the S_{sel} , it will return -1 when every similarity is less than threshold, and return 1 otherwise. The similarity between two sentences is calculated by first setting up vector space model according to the presence of the characters in sentence through calculating the product of the two vectors. The threshold is ascertained through experiment on some sentences that the similarities were known before.

The method first defines weight vector w for every dimension of the feature set and initiates the vector as unit vector to stand for the equal importance of the initial weight w. Then margin-based measure function is defined and iteratively calculated on each instance in the training set to determine the variation of the w. When the function is maximized, the weight vector w tells the importance of the corresponding feature and the feature set can be chosen according to the threshold.

Margin. Margin is an important concept in machine learning to evaluate the effectiveness of algorithm. A good algorithm should ensure the maximum of the distance between the different classes after classification. This feature selection algorithm in this paper adopts the margin as the criterion. There are two types of margin. One is margin of instances, calculating by the distance between the instances in different classes. The other is hypothesis margin, while calculating by the distance between one instance and its nearest instance and the distance between one instance and its furthest instance. The second margin type is used in the paper. Follow is the equation.

$$\theta_P^w = \frac{1}{2}(\|x - nearmiss(x)\|_w - \|x - nearhit(x)\|_w)$$
$$where\ \|z\|_w = \sqrt{\sum_i w_i^2 z_i^2}\ . \tag{1}$$

Measurement function. The measurement of a feature weight vector is gotten by calculating hypothesis margin of each instance and sums them up. The equation is as follow.

$$e(w) = \sum_{x \in S} \theta_{s\backslash x}^w(x) \tag{2}$$

Calculating process. Utilizing the smoothing of $e(w)$, we can maximum the $e(w)$ by iteratively calculating the gradient. The equation is as follow.

$$\begin{aligned}(\nabla e(w))_i &= \frac{\partial e(w)}{\partial w_i} = \sum_{x \in S} \frac{\partial e(w)}{\partial w_i} \\ &= \frac{1}{2}\left(\frac{(x_i - nearmiss(x)_i)^2}{\|x - nearmiss(x)\|_w} - \frac{(x_i - nearhit(x)_i)^2}{\|x - nearhit(x)\|_w}\right) w_i\end{aligned} \tag{3}$$

In every round, method calculates $(\nabla e(w))_i$, normalizes and updates the w, until the gradient decreases to the threshold.

5 Experiment and Results

We test our method on movie review dataset [1] and hotel review dataset[12]. movie review dataset was collected by Pang etc. It consists of 752 negative and 1301 positive reviews, which were given out by 144 reviewers. Hotel review dataset is collected by Tan. 1000 negative and 1000 positive reviews were selected for experiement. Precison is used as measurement.

Feature selection. We implement the improved SIMBA on Matlab, and get the weight vectors respect to the original feature. The threshold to select final feature is set to 0.05. The features of which the threshold is less than 0.05 are filtered out and we use the final features to train and test.

Training and test. The process of training is to calculate the decision function. For each dataset, we use half data to train and test respectively.

Experiment and result. We design two set of experiment to test our method. One is the features fusion experiment to test the performance of improved SIMBA. We use the standard NB classifier but adopt different features to get the results. The different features are word only(W-NB), phrase only(P-NB), syntax only(SYN-NB), sentiment word only(SENT-NB) and integrated features(ISIMBA-NB). We use the accuracy to evaluate the performance. The other set of experiment is to compare our fusion based method with the baseline. The baseline is presented by Pang[1], which is conducted on the same dataset. The results is list in Table I, the figure in each cell is the average value of 4 runs.

Table 1 shows that the accuracy of integrate features using ISIMBA is better than that of single type of features, and the performance of our method is also higher than the baseline.

Table 1. Accuracy of Different Features Schema And Baseline

SCHEMA	ACC_MOVIE	ACC_HOTEL
WORD-NB	0.7824	0.7653
PHRASE-NB	0.7511	0.7983
SYN-NB	0.7213	0.7462
SENT-NB	0.7983	0.8011
ISIMBA-FUSION	0.8637	0.8724
BASELINE	0.8290	0.8413

6 Conclusion and Future Works

Polarity analysis is an important task for many applications. While there are no explicit clues in text and thus makes the task much difficult. This paper proposes a data-driven method, utilizing an improved feature selection method SIMBA to fuse all sorts of possible features. The accuracy is higher than that using single type of features only and achieves higher performance than the published result on same dataset as well. In subsequent research, the match between the sentiment words and selected features will bear watching. Active-learning or heuristic method will be good approaches to try.

Acknowledgement. This paper is supported by NSF with No.60855009.

References

1. Pang, B., Lee, L., Vaithyanathan, S.: Thumbs up? Sentiment classification using machine learning techniques. In: Proceedings of the Conference on Empirical Methods in Natural Language Processing (EMNLP), pp. 79–86 (2002)
2. Airoldi, E.M., Bai, X., Padman, R.: Markov blankets and meta-heuristics search: Sentiment extraction from unstructured texts. In: Mobasher, B., Nasraoui, O., Liu, B., Masand, B. (eds.) WebKDD 2004. LNCS (LNAI), vol. 3932, pp. 167–187. Springer, Heidelberg (2006)

3. Dave, K., Lawrence, S., Pennock, D.M.: Mining the peanut gallery: Opinion extraction and semantic classification of product reviews. In: Proceedings of WWW, pp. 519–528 (2003)
4. Gamon, M.: Sentiment classification on customer feedback data: noisy data, large feature vectors,and the role of linguistic analysis. In: Proceedings of the International Conference on Computational Linguistics (COLING) (2004)
5. Kudo, T., Matsumoto, Y.: A Boosting Algorithm for Classification of Semi-Structured Text. In: Proc. of 9th EMNLP, pp. 301–308 (2004)
6. Hatzivassiloglou, V., Wiebe, J.: Effects of adjective orientation and gradability on sentence subjectivity. In: Proceedings of the International Conference on Computational Linguistics (COLING) (2000)
7. Turney, P.: Thumbs up or thumbs down? Semantic orientation applied to unsupervised classificationof reviews. In: Proceedings of the Association for Computational Linguistics (ACL), pp. 417–424 (2002)
8. Kamps, J., Marx, M., Mokken, R.J., de Rijke, M.: Using WordNet to measure semantic orientation of adjectives. In: LREC (2004)
9. Kim, S.-M., Hovy, E.: Determining the sentiment of opinions. In: Proceedings of the International Conference on Computational Linguistics, COLING (2004)
10. Wang, B., Zhang, S., Zhang, Q.: Detecting Chinese sentiment words. In: Proceedings of first first Chinese Opinion Analysis Evaluation (2008)
11. Gilad-Bachrach, R., Navot, A., Tishby, N.: Margin Based Feature Selection: Theory and Algorithms. In: International Conference on Machine Learning, ICML (2004)
12. songbo, T.: `http://www.searchforum.org.cn/tansongbo/corpus-senti.htm`

A New Method for Stochastic Simulation of Macromolecule Conformation*

Hu Shu-yong, Zhang Lie-hui, and Yao Heng-shen

State Key Laboratory of Oil and Gas Reservoir Geology and Exploitation
Southwest Petroleum University
Chengdu, Sichuan Province, China
xiaohutuxianhu@gmail.com

Abstract. The conformation statistics of single chain of polymer is a most basic and important problem in polymer science. Common polymer chain could do internal rotation around its chemical bond because thermal motion, this makes polymer chain's form change ceaselessly. Because the molecular weight of macromolecule is very large, the number of polymer conformation is too large to be resolved using the common mathematical methods. This paper researches the free rotation chain conformation in non-lattice chain of high molecule. Through setting-up mathematical model, a new method is proposed to simulate the polymer chain. Simulation result shows the polymer conformation in microcosmic and reflects the characteristic "random coil" of polymer chain actually. These results provide an important basis for further quantitative analysis and optimal design.

Keywords: Macromolecule Chain, Mathematical Model, Stochastic Simulation, Conformational Analysis.

1 Introduction

There is a wide application prospect of association polymer in the fields of petroleum project and other production technologies because of its peculiar performance. According to different use and demand in production practices, need optimization design of association polymer, so it's necessary to make a overall, deep research on the series of basic problems such as polymer conformation, association reaction course, reliance relation of association reaction on its influence factors, etc., so that the polymer association finds more extensive application in these fields. The conformation statistics of high molecular chain is also a most basic and important problem in polymer science. The most basic characteristic of high molecule lies in its molecular weight is very enormous, thus the quantity of conformation, which results from high molecular chain's internal rotation around its single chemical bond, is nearly infinite. So it's a very difficult problem of researching conformation and characteristic of polymer chain[1,2]. The most important work of researchers is to

* The research is supported by CNPC Innovation Fund, the projects for State Key Laboratory of Oil and Gas Reservoir Geology and Exploitation in P.R.C.

D. Zeng (Ed.): ICAIC 2011, Part I, CCIS 224, pp. 215–222, 2011.

look for new method constantly to make effective statistics of polymer chain conformation, such as Monte Carlo method[5,6,7,8,9], which is successfully applied in this field. Based on this purpose, the article utilizes the already matured mathematical theory and technology, combines with some commonly used matured basic theory and method in polymer science, makes every effort to simulate polymer chain from a new direction, analyzes the conformation and characteristic of polymer chain.

2 Conformational Model of Macromolecule Chain

In high molecular conformation study, many models have been proposed, and chain model is very common. Chain model is divided into non-lattice chain and lattice chain model.The former model can reflect the structure and conformation of high molecular chain more truly in a great deal of respects[3,4,5,10], and it has many kinds of models. Here we only research the association polymer, which is widely used in petroleum industry and any other production fields. Its single chain belongs to free rotation chain, every monomer unit length l=1.53 $\mathring{A}$, the included angle of two adjoin monomer unit $\omega = 109^{o}28^{'}$, now suppose one monomer unit is fixed and the next one can rotate freely, namely mean on the plane which regards the monomeric unit direction as its normal direction, any arbitrary radial vector can be the projection of the next monomeric unit if the vector starts from perpendicular foot. In easy words, any point in the circle whose centre of circle is perpendicular foot Q and radius $r = l\sin 70^{\circ}32^{'}$ may be end point of the next monomer unit, the next one's perpendicular foot is in the prolonged line of the front one and the distance from it to the front monomeric unit's end point (M) $|MQ| = l\cos 70^{\circ}32^{'}$. The model shows in Fig. 1.

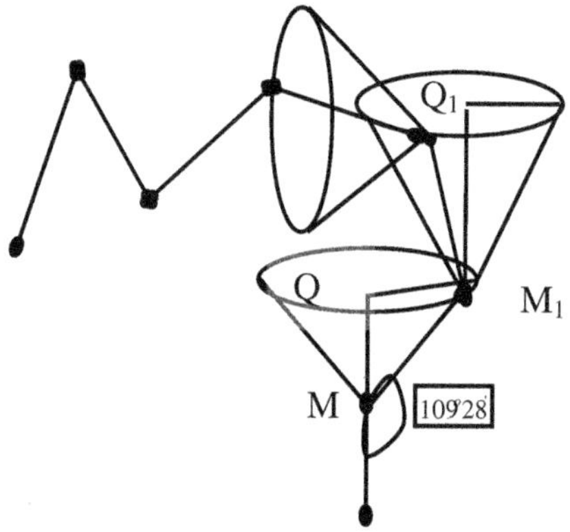

Fig. 1. Free rotation chain model

According to the above assumptions, the conformational characteristics are simulate, such as the crimp rule of polymer chain, mean square end to end distance, polymer coil's diameter, etc.

3 Establishment of Mathematics Model

Suppose the direction of monomeric unit 0 is coincident with the negative semi-axis of Z in three dimensional rectangular coordinate system, the end point is origin. In this coordinate system, the end point position of monomer unit i is marked as $M_i=(x_i, y_i, z_i)$, $i=0,1,2,\ldots n$, n is the length of polymer chain; the cosine of monomeric unit i $M_{i-1}M_i$ is marked as ($\cos\alpha_i$, $\cos\beta_i$, $\cos\gamma_i$). Suppose a radial vector is perpendicular with $M_{i-1}M_i$, and mark its cosine as ($\cos\varphi_{i+1}$,$\cos\Psi_{i+1}$,$\cos\theta_{i+1}$), because the free rotation of the next monomer unit compared with the front one, it's necessary to suppose ϕ_i as an average distribution random number in the interval $[0,2\pi)$. For example, to make sure the coordinate of the end point M_1 (x_1,y_1,z_1) of the monomer unit 1. First, in the plane, which contains point $Q_1=(x=u_1=0,\ y=v_1=0,\ z=w_1=l\cos\theta_1=l\cos 70°32')$ and perpendicular with axis Z, draw a circle with origin Q_1, radius $r= l\sin\theta_1$. Arbitrarily select a point $M_1=(x_1, y_1, z_1)$ in the circle at random of equal probability and M_0M_1 is the position of monomer unit 1. So it's necessary to bear random number ϕ_1 average distributed in the interval $[0,2\pi)$ firstly, then to get $\cos\phi_1$ by ϕ_1, and:

$$\cos\psi_1 = \pm\sqrt{1-\cos^2\phi_1 - \cos^2\theta_1} = \pm\sqrt{1-\cos\phi_1}\,,\left(\theta_1 = \frac{\pi}{2}\right) \tag{1}$$

When $0 \le \phi_1 < \pi$, the front of radical sign is positive sign; when $\pi \le \phi_1 < 2\pi$, the front is negative sign.

The position of point M_1 is determined by the following equation:

$$\begin{aligned} x_1 &= l\sin 70^\circ 32'\cos\phi_1 \\ y_1 &= l\sin 70^\circ 32'\cos\psi_1 \\ z_1 &= l\sin 70^\circ 32' \end{aligned} \tag{2}$$

Generally, after determining the point $M_i=(x_i, y_i, z_i)$,the cosine in direction $\overrightarrow{M_{i-1}M_i}$ is calculated:

$$\begin{aligned} \cos\alpha_i &= \frac{x_i - x_{i-1}}{l} \\ \cos\beta_i &= \frac{y_i - y_{i-1}}{l} \\ \cos\gamma_i &= \frac{z_i - z_{i-1}}{l} \end{aligned} \tag{3}$$

And then the coordinate of origin Q_{i+1} in plane i+1:

$$\begin{aligned} u_{i+1} &= x_i + l_0\cos\alpha_i \\ v_{i+1} &= y_i + l_0\cos\beta_i \\ w_{i+1} &= z_i + l_0\cos\gamma_i \end{aligned} \tag{4}$$

The plane equation through point Q_{i+1} and perpendicular with $\overrightarrow{M_{i-1}M_i}$ is

$$\cos\alpha_i(x-u_{i+1})+\cos\beta_i(y-v_{i+1})+\cos\gamma_i(z-w_{i+1})=0 \tag{5}$$

Given the average distribution random number ϕ_{i+1} in interval $[0,2\pi)$, through the equation group:

$$\begin{cases}\cos\alpha_i\cos\phi_{i+1}+\cos\beta_i\cos\psi_{i+1}+\cos\gamma_i\cos\theta_{i+1}=0\\ \cos^2\phi_{i+1}+\cos^2\psi_{i+1}+\cos^2\theta_{i+1}=1\end{cases} \tag{6}$$

$\cos\theta_{i+1}$ and $\cos\psi_{i+1}$ are soluted:

$$\cos\theta_{i+1}=\frac{-\cos\alpha_i\cos\phi_{i+1}\cos\gamma_i\pm|\cos\beta_i|\sqrt{\cos^2\beta_i+\cos^2\gamma_i-\cos^2\phi_{i+1}}}{\cos^2\beta_i+\cos^2\gamma_i} \tag{7}$$

The front of radical sign in numerator may be positive or negative sign and the respective probability is 1/2:

$$\cos\psi_{i+1}=\pm\sqrt{1-\cos^2\phi_{i+1}-\cos^2\theta_{i+1}} \tag{8}$$

When $0\le\phi_{i+1}<\pi$, the front of radical sign is positive sign, when $\pi\le\phi_{i+1}<2\pi$, the front of radical sign is negative sign. And then we can figure out:

$$\begin{aligned}x_{i+1}&=u_{i+1}+r\cos\phi_{i+1}\\ y_{i+1}&=v_{i+1}+r\cos\psi_{i+1}\\ z_{i+1}&=w_{i+1}+r\cos\theta_{i+1}\\ M_{i+1}&=(x_{i+1},y_{i+1},z_{i+1})\end{aligned} \tag{9}$$

In sum, the mathematical model of free rotation chain is set up as follow.

Solute $M_i(x_i,y_i,z_i)$, $x_i=u_i+r\cos\phi_i$, $y_i=v_i+r\cos\psi_i$, $z_i=w_i+r\cos\theta_i$, where:

$$\begin{cases}u_i=x_{i-1}+l_0\cos\alpha_{i-1}\\ v_i=y_{i-1}+l_0\cos\beta_{i-1}\\ w_i=z_{i-1}+l_0\cos\gamma_{i-1}\\ \cos\alpha_{i-1}=\dfrac{x_{i-1}-x_{i-2}}{l}\\ \cos\beta_{i-1}=\dfrac{y_{i-1}-y_{i-2}}{l}\\ \cos\gamma_{i-1}=\dfrac{z_{i-1}-z_{i-2}}{l}\\ \cos\theta_i=\dfrac{-\cos\alpha_{i-1}\cos\phi_i\cos\gamma_{i-1}\pm|\cos\beta_{i-1}|\sqrt{\cos^2\beta_{i-1}+\cos^2\gamma_{i-1}-\cos^2\phi_i}}{\cos^2\beta_{i-1}+\cos^2\gamma_{i-1}}\\ (\cos\phi_i\ \textit{is given at random})\\ \cos\psi_i=\pm\sqrt{1-\cos^2\phi_i-\cos^2\theta_i}\\ (\cos\psi_i>0, \textit{when}\ 0\le\phi_i<\pi, \cos\psi_i<0, \textit{when}\ \pi\le\phi_i<2\pi\\ r=l\sin70^\circ32', l_0=l\cos70^\circ32\end{cases} \tag{10}$$

Calculate the solution of the model through the method mentioned above, namely calculate the points $M_i \to Q_{i+1} \to M_{i+1}$ in turn, get all points M_i, i=1, 2, …, n, then according to give M_i position coordinate in three dimension rectangle coordinate system, we can simulate a polymer conformation of n long chain, and M_i is end point of monomeric unit. In output, we can select a suitable k and output the coordinate of the end point M_i every 10^k monomeric units. For instance, k=3, output one point M_i every 1000 monomer units, and show the result in 3D picture to observe the polymer conformation directly.

In addition, the simulation method can be applied in the following too:

(1) Calculate the mean square end to end distance of high molecule whose chain is n long

$$S = \sqrt{x_n^2 + y_n^2 + z_n^2}$$

(2) Calculate the diameter of chain coil

$$\begin{aligned} d_n &= \max_{1\le i\le n} \max_{1\le j\le n} \left|\overrightarrow{M_i M_j}\right| \\ &= \max_{1\le i\le n} \max_{1\le j\le n} \sqrt{(x_j - x_i)^2 + (y_j - y_i)^2 + (z_j - z_i)^2} \end{aligned}$$

, and record i_0, j_0, fulfill $\left|\overrightarrow{M_{i_0} M_{j_0}}\right| = d_n$.

(3) Show the projection of high molecule in three planes consisted of coordinate axis.

4 Simulation Algorithm

According to the above deduce course, the simulation algorithm of polymer conformation is obtained.

(1) Initialization: the length of a monomer unit is l, number of chain segment is n, step number $count$=0

(2) Bear the average distribution random number ϕ_1 in $[0,2\pi)$, confirm that $\cos\psi_1 = \pm\sqrt{1-\cos\phi_1}$, so that $x_1 = l\sin 70^\circ 32'\cos\phi_1$, $y_1 = l\sin 70^\circ 32'\cos\psi_1$ and $z_1 = l\sin 70^\circ 32'$, draw point $M_1(x_1, y_1, z_1)$, $count = count+1$

(3) $\cos\alpha_1 = \frac{x_1}{l}$, $\cos\beta_1 = \frac{y_1}{l}$, $\cos\gamma_1 = \frac{z_1}{l}$, $l^* = l + l\cos 70^\circ 32'$, so $u_2 = l^*\cos\alpha_1$, $v_2 = l^*\cos\beta_1$, $w_2 = l^*\cos\gamma_1$

(4) Bear random number ϕ_2, calculate $\cos\phi_2$ and $\cos\psi_2$, so $x_1 = u_2 + r\cos\phi_2$, $y_1 = v_2 + r\cos\psi_2$, $z_1 = w_2 + r\cos\theta_2$, draw point $M_1(x_1, y_1, z_1)$, $count = count+1$

(5) If $count > n$, continue step (6), otherwise return to step (3)

(6) Calculate the distance from start to end point $S = \sqrt{x_n^2 + y_n^2 + z_n^2}$

(7) Calculate the diameter of chain coil,

$d(i) = \max_{1 \le j \le n} \left| \overrightarrow{M_i M_j} \right| = \max_{1 \le j \le n} \sqrt{(x_j - x_i)^2 + (y_j - y_i)^2 + (z_j - z_i)^2}$, and record $j_0^{(i)}$, until satisfy $\left| \overrightarrow{M_i M_{j_0^{(i)}}} \right| = d(i)$, i=1,2,…,n, then calculate $d_n = \max_{1 \le i \le n} d(i)$, and record i_0, j_0: $\left| \overrightarrow{M_{i0} M_{j0}} \right| = d_n$, in this formula $j_0 = j_0^{(i)}$

(8) Give the projection of polymer coil in three planes consisted of three coordinate axis

(9) Show 3D picture: Give the space position of point column $\{M_{10^k \cdot i}\}, i = 1,2,\ldots,n/10^k$.

5 Problem and Improvement

① When calculating $\cos\theta_{i+1}$, if the algebraic expression under radical sign $\cos^2\beta_i + \cos^2\gamma_i - \cos^2\phi_{i+1}$<0 is true, bear random number ϕ_{i+1} is needed again, until $\cos^2\beta_i + \cos^2\gamma_i - \cos^2\phi_{i+1} \geqslant 0$, so as to make sure the value $\cos\theta_{i+1}$ is in interval [-1, 1], if $|\cos\theta_{i+1}|>1$, need bear random number ϕ_{i+1} again, until $|\cos\theta_{i+1}| \leqslant 1$;

② In the course of producing polymer chain, some monomeric units may parallel with x, y, z axis, here, $\phi_{i+1} = 0$, $\pi/4$ or other value, not be average distribution random number in $[0,2\pi)$ anymore, so it maybe $1 - \cos^2\phi_{i+1} - \cos^2\theta_{i+1} < 0$, the settlement for this problem is bear random number ϕ_{i+1} again, until $1 - \cos^2\phi_{i+1} - \cos^2\theta_{i+1} \ge 0$.

③ When using this sample method to study the characteristics of polymer conformation, because don't differentiate low-energy conformation and high-energy conformation, all conformation's probability is the same, it isn't accord with Boltzmann distribution, so leads to deviation between calculated sample and practical sample. This can be improved by:

a. Use importance sampling method to judge accept or reject through energy when add a new chain joint.

b. Maintain the method above, create a chain, then use metropolis[4] sample method to make chain move, and make statistic of multi-conformation's statistical average after certain steps.

6 Results

Utilizing the above mathematical model, program of simulation with computer is designed to show the born and evolutional course of polymer chain in microcosmic, get the following results.

(1) Fig. 2 is free rotation chain model with 10000 monomeric units, could see obvious random coil characteristics though the model.

(2) Table 1 provides diversified statistical values of free rotation chain with 500 monomer units. As seen from table 1, the error of free rotation chain's diversified statistical value between simulation result and experiment result is acceptable.

(3) Fig. 3 is the simulation of free rotation chain with 50 monomeric units, there are 3D graph and projection in three planes in this figure, and can see the rough shape of free rotation chain.

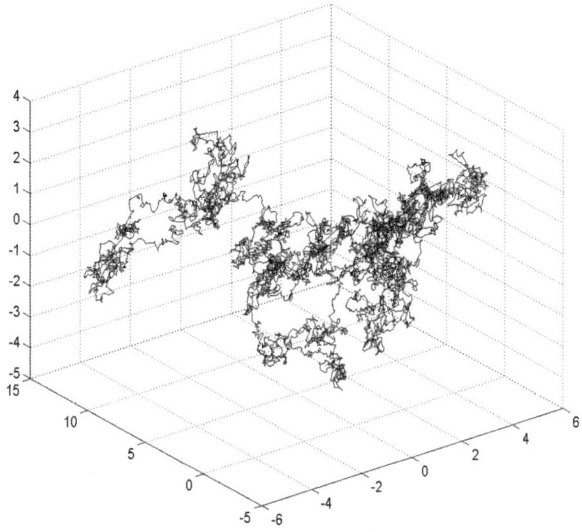

Fig. 2. Free rotation chain

Table 1. Statistic Value When Monomer Unit Is 500

Statistic value	Standard value	Free rotation chain	explanation
$\langle R^2 \rangle$	1001	1225	Approximate distance between start and end point
$\langle S^2 \rangle$	166.74	162.7799	Approximation of $\langle S^2 \rangle$
$\langle L_1^2 \rangle : \langle L_2^2 \rangle : \langle L_3^2 \rangle$	/	1:2.6:11.4	
$\langle A \rangle$	/	0.3962	

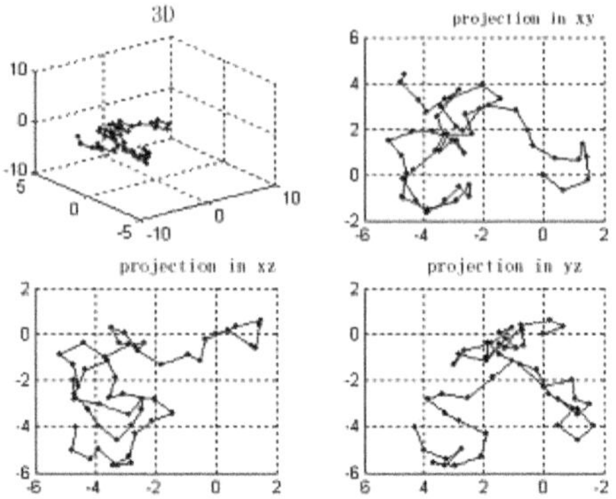

Fig. 3. Free rotation chain

References

1. Yamakawa, H.: Modern Theory of Polymer Solution. Happer & Row, New York (1971)
2. Flory, P.J.: Principles of Polymer Chemistry. Cornell Univ. Press, Ithica (1953)
3. Wu, D.: Introduction for conformation analysis of macromolecule. Sichuan educational Press, Chengdu (1985)
4. Flory, P.J.: Statistical Mechanics of Chain Molecules. Wiley-Intersciencek, New York (1969)
5. Frenkel, S.: Molecule simulation——from arithmetic to application (translated by Wang, W., et al). Chemistry Industry Press, Beijing (2002)
6. Allen, M.P., et al.: Computer Simulation of Liquids. Clarendon Press, Oxford (1987)
7. McCrackin, F.L.: Configuration of isolated polymer molecules adsorbed on solid surfaces studied by Monte-Carlo computer simulation. J. Chem. Phys. 47, 1980–1986 (1967)
8. Verdier, P.H., Ibid: Monte Carlo studies of lattice-model polymer chains.II.end to end length. J. Chem. Phys. 45, 2122–2128 (1966)
9. Rosenbluth, M.N., Rosenbluth, A.W.: Monte Carlo calculation of the average extension of molecular chains. J. Chem. Phys. 23, 356–359 (1955)
10. Volkenstein: Configurational Statistics of Polymeric Chains; Translated from the Russian: Timasheff, S. N., Timasbeff, M. J. (ed.) Interscience, New York (1963)

An Approach for IPSecVPN Network Topology Discovery Based on Layer 3 Topology*

Dancheng Li, Tianyi Yin, Cheng Liu, Chunyan Han, and Yixian Liu

Software College Northeastern University
Shenyang 110004, Liaoning, P.R. China
dancheng_56@foxmail.com

Abstract. Network topology discovery is crucial to auto network management system. In research area, the reseach of Layer 3 topology discovery uses ipRouteTable [1,2], which efficiency is slow. This paper proposes a improved approach to Layer 3 discovery algorithm. Then, this paper gives the time complexity of algorithm analysis. And this paper proposes a approach to discover IPSecVPN protocol topology based on Layer 3 topology. In addition, the architecture of topology discovery module proposed is helpful to further topology discovery. Those alogrithms relied on SNMP MIB information have been implemented in Java and tested in several enterprises network. The discovering results demonstrate that it is accurate and efficient to discover Layer 3 topology and IPSecVPN protocol topology.

Keywords: Network Topology Discovery, SNMP, OSPF, IPSec VPN.

1 Introduction

With the continuous development of IT and VPN technology gradual advance, more and more enterprises deploy VPN to built Secure network environment. In traditional high-quality IT Service management, the emergence of new technologies VPN, enterprises have new business needs. It is well known that in a complex network environment, fast and accurate discovery of network topology is the foundation of providing high quality network service management. In addtion, it is the foundation of achieving new business VPN service management.

Network topology discovery is aimed to keep track of the existence of network elements and their interconnections. Network elements include routers, switches, hosts and subnets. Their interconnections include physical connections and logical connections. Some business management is builted on the top of the specific protocol connection. Protocol connection is more helpful based on the top of the logical connection. The network environment is very complex in enterprises network. For this reason, this paper proposes an automatic network topology discovery algorithm.

The remainder of this paper is organized as follows. Secion 2 briefly presents the related works followed by section 3 which presents the system architecture. In section 4, the proposed algorithm is described in detail. The comparison of algorithm is shown in section 5. Finally, section 6 gives the conclusinos and further works.

* This reseach work is supported by "Natural Science Foundation of LiaoNing Province" (20092006).

D. Zeng (Ed.): ICAIC 2011, Part I, CCIS 224, pp. 223–232, 2011.

2 Related Works

In the field of Network topology discovery, domestic and foreign scholars and corporate R & D personnel have done many research. In foreign country, there are already some advanced commerical network management software, such as CiscoWork 2000 series, HP OpenView NNM, IBM TivoliNetView and open source OPENNMS, and so on . But only for specific network vendosr, their discovery right rate is relatively high. In paper[3], David T.Stott[3] only collects ipRouteTable MIB to discover Layer 3 topology , without considering the Heterogeneity of the network. And the discovery algorithm is not efficient. In paper[4,5,6], the writers proposed approaches to find large Layer 3 network topology based on OSPF agent servers. However, the OSPF agent servers should be deployed in every OSPF domain. That results in the difficulty of achieving in network management software. Paper[7,8] do some research on VPN network management and the design of VPN gateway. Paper[9,10,11,12] propose the architecture of automatic topology discovery and introduce the discover process. All of these papers are based on SNMP protocol supported in each routers and managed switches.

Nowadays SNMP is more and more applied to the network management. Taking into account the characteristics of enterprise-claass network and further need for topology discovery, this paper proposes some algorithms which can accurately and effectively discovery the layer 3 physical topology and IPSec VPN protocol topology connections. At the same time, the system architecture can adapt to the further need for topology discovery.

3 System Architecture

Considering the emergence of further new demand network, this paper designs the system architecture of network topology discovery. The architecture consists of five modules as illustrated in Figure 1.

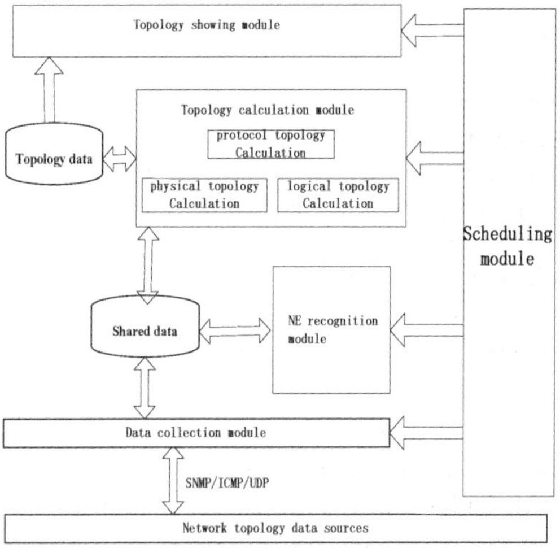

Fig. 1. The Architecture Of Topology Discovery Module

This paper is only focused on NE recognition module and topology calculation module .The remainder paper descries NE recognition module and topology calculation module in detail.

4 Algorithms Used

Before calculating network topology, the first step is to probe and detect acitve devices in the range of the enterprise network. It is neccesary to find out network device type and manufacturer type. The IP addresses range and the SNMP authentication information will be provided before probing and detecting. And this paper gives the following definition:

Definition 1. Network Elements: Network elements are included routers, Layer 3 switches, Layer 2 switches, and hosts.

Definition 2. Equipment Dictionary: Equipment dictionary is defined that it is a collection which key is the value of sysObjectID(OID: 1.3.6.1.2.1.1.2) and which value is the device type.

Definition 3. Device Collection: there are 3 collection, according to device type.

RouterQueue=($R_1, R_2,..., R_i$), R_i as router

L3SwitchQueue=($S_1, S_2,.. S_i$), S_i as Layer 2 switch

L2SwitchQueue=($S_1, S_2,..S_i$), S_i as Layer 3 switch

4.1 Network Element Recogntion

The seed files include the IP addresses range and the SNMP authentication information. Management center use thoes information to communicate with network elements and find out the device type by running network element recogntion algorithm. The device collection is the foundation of network topology calculation. So this paper proposes a improved algorithm of network equipment recogntion.

The first setp is to synchronously probe and detect acitve devices.The thread of sending probing and detecting PDU reads the value of sysUpTime (OID as 1.3.6.1.2.1.1.3) under the system group of MIB-II. The thread sends an asynchronous request PDU to all nodes. If the thread of receiving PDU has successed receiving the request PDU,it can extract from the source IP address from requesting PDU.IP address will be added to the managed device set R.

The second step is to recognise network elements. We collect device data value of sysObjectID (OID as 1.3.6.1.2.1.1.2) and match with equipment dictionary. If the match fails, we collect device data value of $sysServices$ (OID as 1.3.6.1.2.1.1.7) . It is expressed the form of $sysServices=\sum_{i=1}^{Li} 2^{(Li-1)}$. (Li is the ith layer of OSI seven layer model. If the device is to provide services in the i-layer, then the corresponding layers of Li). We make the value of sysServices phase 6.If the result is 2,the device is layer 2 switch. If the result is 4, the device is router. If the result is 6,the device is layer 3 switch. Based on the above discussion, network element recogntion algorithm is defined as following algorithm 1.

Algorithm 1. Algorithm of network equipment identification

```
Input: managed device set R, Equipment dictionary T
Output: RouterQueue,L3SwitchQueue,L2SwitchQueue
Foreach device a in R
  get sysObjectID value
      If sysObjectID in T
         get a device's type
      End if
      get sysObjectID value
      i= sysObjectID&6
      If i = = 2
         a ∈ L2SwitchQueue
      End if
      If i = = 4
         a ∈ RouterQueue
      End if
      If i = = 6
         a ∈ L3SwitchQueue
      End if
      End for
```

4.2 Network Node Discovery

Network nodes are directly connected to the router, so those nodes can be determined from the values in the ipAdEntAddr and ipAdEntNetMask columns in the table IPAddrTable (OID as 1.3.6.1.2.1.4.20) .Network nodes can be determined by putting ipAdEntAddr phase wtih ipAdEntNetMask. In other words, network nodes are the subnet. However, the table IPAddrTable may include some special IP addresses, such as "127.0.0.1", "0.0.0.0", "255.255.255.255". Those IP addresses are helpless to calculate network nodes.

Table 1. IPAddrTable (OID as 1.3.6.1.2.1.4.20)

Variable name	Variable OID
ipAdEntAddr	1.3.6.1.2.1.4.20.1.1
ipAdEntIfIndex	1.3.6.1.2.1.4.20.1.2
ipAdEntNetMask	1.3.6.1.2.1.4.20.1.3

4.3 OSPF Layer 3 Topology Discovery

The connections among layer 3 network topology include Router to Router Link(RRL) and Network to Router Link(NRL).They can be abstracted into model like Figure 2.

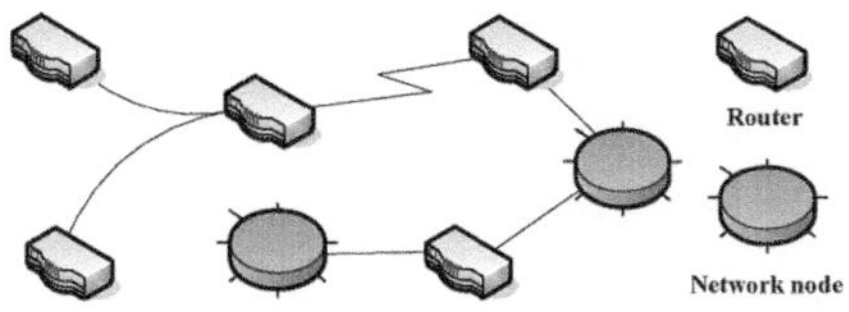

Fig. 2. Layer 3 model of network topology

This paper proposes a improved layer 3 topology discover algorithm. For the routers which open OSPF server, we can get the connections by analyzing the table ospfIfTable (OID as 1.3.6.1.2.1.14.10) like table 2.and ospfNbrTable (OID as 1.3.6.1.2.1.14.7) like table 3.For the routers which do not open OSPF server, we can get the connections by analyzing the table ipRouteTable. We can determine by collecting ospfAdminStat (OID as 1.3.6.1.2.1.14.1.2) in IP group of SNMP MIB-II.

Table 2. ospfIfTable（OID as 1.3.6.1.2.1.14.10）

name	OID
ospfIfIpAddress	1.3.6.1.2.1.14.7.1.1
ospfAddressLessIf	1.3.6.1.2.1.14.7.1.2
ospfIfType	1.3.6.1.2.1.14.7.1.4
ospfIfAdminStat	1.3.6.1.2.1.14.7.1.5
ospfIfState	1.3.6.1.2.1.14.7.1.12
ospfIfDesignatedRouter	1.3.6.1.2.1.14.7.1.13

Table 3. ospfNbrTable（OID as 1.3.6.1.2.1.14.7）

name	OID
ospfNbrAddr	1.3.6.1.2.1.14.10.1.1
ospfNbrAddressLessIndex	1.3.6.1.2.1.14.10.1.2
ospfNbrRtrId	1.3.6.1.2.1.14.10.1.3

4.3.1 NRL Calculation

NRL can be expressed as NRL<N, P1, P2, …, Pn>，N is the Network node, P is the router expressed as(RouterID，IfIndex). For the routers which open OSPF server, NRL calculation process is described in Figure 3.

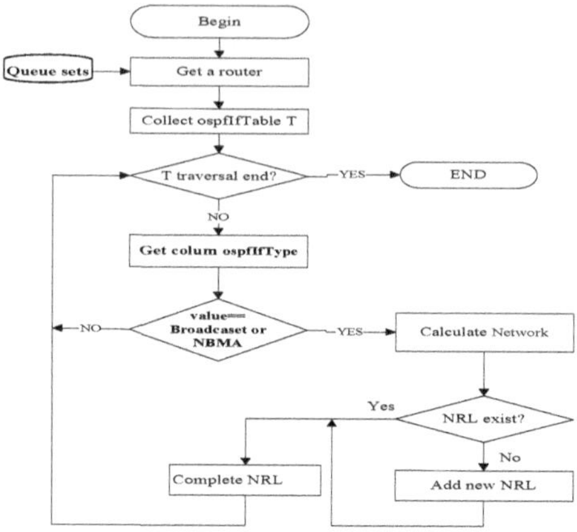

Fig. 3. NRL discover Process

When column ospfIfType is equal to broadcaset or nbma, ospfIfDesignatedRouter is the IP address of the network of corresponding interface to the router. Then, we can get the corresponding value of if Index for interfaces by finding in the table IPAddrTable in the column value ospfIfIp Address. For the routers which do not open ospf server, what need to be done is to analyze the table ipRouteTable like table 4.The columns which column ipRouteType is equal to direct should be filtered.

Table 4. ipRouteTable (OID 1.3.6.1.2.1.4.21)

Variable name	Variable OID
ipRouteDest	1.3.6.1.2.1.4.21.1.1
ipRouteIfIndex	1.3.6.1.2.1.4.21.1.2
ipRouteNextHop	1.3.6.1.2.1.4.21.1.7
ipRouteType	1.3.6.1.2.1.4.21.1.8
ipRouteMask	1.3.6.1.2.1.4.21.1.11

4.3.2 RRL Calculation

RRL can be expressed as <RtID_Src, RtID_Dest, IfIndex_Src, IfIndex_Dest>. RtID_Src is the RouterID of the connected source router. IfIndex_Src is the port of the connected source router.Using the <RtID_Src, RtID_Dest, IfIndex_Src, IfIndex_Dest>,we can uniquely identify Router to Router Link.We traversal the table ospfNbrTable of the source router to get RRL<RtID_Src, RtID_Dest, ?,

IfIndex_Dest>. Then we can complete RRL by traversaling the table ospfNbrTable of the destinational router. For the routers which do not support OSPF server, what need to be done is to combine the column ipRouteNextHop which column ipRouteType is equal to inDirect. We get RRL<RtID_Src, RtID_Dest, IfIndex_Src,?>.We compelte RRL by traversaling the table ipRouteTable of NextHop node.

This algorithm has been deployed and tested in an enterprise network. There are more than 30 router devices in the enterprise network. It costs 3 minutes in layer 3 topology discovery. The result is shown in Figure 4.

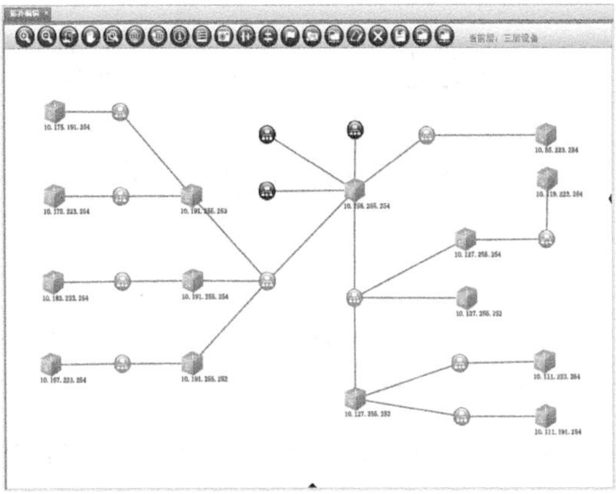

Fig. 4. Three-layer topology discovery diagram of an enterprise

The figure is conformed with the enterprise network.We can clearly identify the routers connectivity and grasp characteristic of the network topology to deploy enterprise features.

4.4 IPSecVPN Protocol Topology Discovery

The aim of IPSecVPN Protocol Topology Discovery is to find out router to router logic link(RRLL) which the routers open IPSec VPN server. RRLL can be expressed as <RtID_Src, RtID_Dest, IfIndex_Src, IfIndex_Dest>.

This paper proposes a IPSec VPN protocol topology discovery algorithm: multithreads probe and detect asynchronously the devices which open IPSec VPN server includeing static IPSecVPN and dynamic IPSecVPN.The second step is to calculate RRLL which the routers open IPSec VPN server.For Cisco devices,we can determine SVPN by collecting cipSecMibLevel(OID as 1.3.6.1.4.1.9.10.62.1.1.1.0). DVPN can be determined by collecting cikeTunnelTable (OID as 1.3.6.1.4.1.9.9.171.1.2.3). RRLL can be calculated by gathering cipsStaticCryptomapTable like Table 5 and cikeTunnelTable like Table 6.

Table 5. cipsStaticCryptomapTable

Variable name	Variable OID
cipsStaticCryptomapPriority	1.3.6.1.4.1.9.10.62.1.2.3.3.1.1
cipsStaticCryptomapPeer	1.3.6.1.4.1.9.10.62.1.2.3.3.1.5

Table 6. cikeTunnelTable

Variable name	Variable OID
Index	1.3.6.1.4.1.9.9.171.1.2.3.1.1
cikeTunLocalValue	1.3.6.1.4.1.9.9.171.1.2.3.1.3
cikeTunRemoteValue	1.3.6.1.4.1.9.9.171.1.2.3.1.6

The topology discovery algorithm is implemented in Java.In an enterprise network, the IPSec VPN topology discovery result is as following in Figure 5.

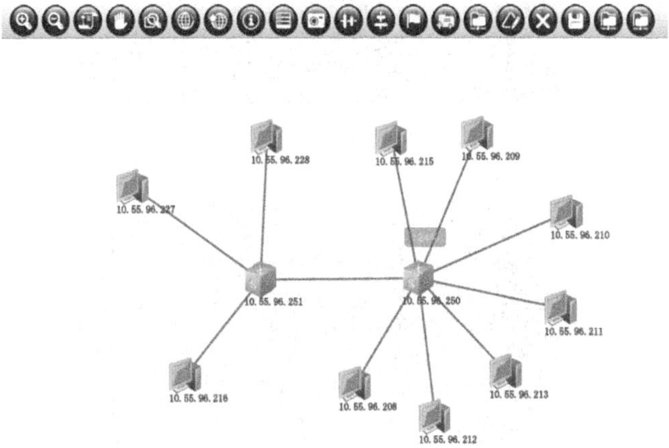

Fig. 5. IPSec VPN Topology

5 Algorithm Comparison

The imporved layer 3 topology discovery algorithm does not have to gather all the table ipRouteTable. Besides there is no heavy network load problem caused by gathering LSA[5]. We give the following definitions in Table 7.

Table 7. Notation

$R1, R2, ..., Ry$	Router Sets
n	The number of the routers which open OSPF serever
Mi	The row number of router Ri in table ipRouteTable
Ni	The row number of router Ri in table ospfIfTable and ospfNbrTable
X	The cost time of gathering a row data
y	The cost time of traditional algorithm
z	The cost time of improved algorithm

In an enterprise network, The row number of router in table ipRouteTable is nearly a thousand entries or more. However, The row number of router in table ipRouteTable is less. So the value of Mi is far greater than Ni. After calculating, we can get that

$$y = \sum_{i=1}^{y} NiX, z = \sum_{i=1}^{n} MiX + \sum_{i=1}^{y-n} NiX \tag{1}$$

$$y - z = \sum_{i=1}^{n} (Mi - Ni)x \tag{2}$$

Our algorithm is tested in a enterprise network.The test result is as following: R=7,n=6,{ $M1, M2, ..., M7$ }={708,711,647,638,787,788,621}, $\{N1, N2, ..., N6\}$={38,42,48,46,28,32}, { $N1$ }={621x}.

According to previous reasoning, we can get that y=4113x ,Z=855x.We draw function images in Matlab software as following Figure 6.

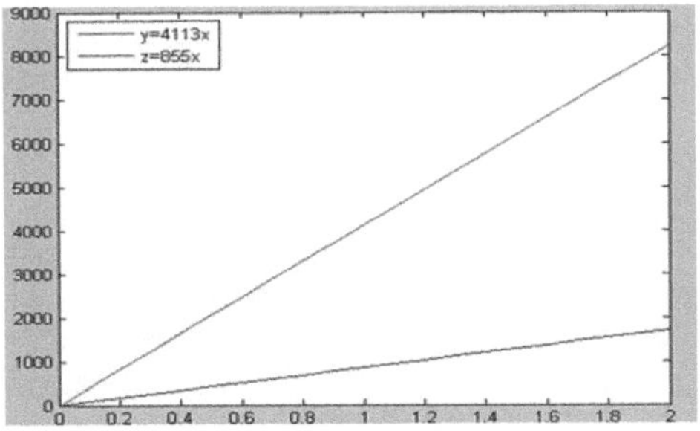

Fig. 6. Function images

It can be obviously seen that the improved algorithm is more efficient.

6 Conclusions and Further Work

Network topology discovery plays an import role in network management system software. Heterogeneity and complexity of the network make more difficulty discovering network topology accurately and efficiently. In addtion, emergence of new technologies raise new network topology discovery needs. So this paper presents an improved algorithm for discovering Layer 3 topology of the network. And this paper presents a algorithm for discovering IPSecVPN protocol topology of the network. The main work in the following areas:

a. study the process of topology discovery
b. design the Architecture of topology discovery
c. propose a algorithm for Layer 3 topology
d. present a algorithm for IPSecVPN protocol topology based on Layer 3 topology

The algorithm has been implemented and tested in several enterprise-level networks, and the results demonstrate that it discovers the network topology accurately and efficiently. Further work is to study and verify those algorithms in IPV6 network, study Layer 2 topoogy based on VLAN and research diversity of VPN protocol topology discovery.

References

1. Nazir, F.: An Efficient Approach Towards IP Network Topology Discovery for Large Multi-subnet Networks (NIIT). IEEE, New York (2006), 0-7695-2588-1/06
2. Lin, H.-C., Lai, S.-C., Chen, P.-W.: An Algorithm for Automatic Topology Discovery of IP Networks. Department of Computer Science National Tsing Hua University HsinChu, Taiwan, R.O.C. IEEE, New York (1998)
3. Stott, T.: Snmp-based layer-3 path discovery. Tech. Rep. ALR-2002-005, Avaya Labs Research, Avaya Inc., Basking Ridge, NJ (2002)
4. Xu, J., Deng, Y., Ding, S.: OSPF Server Based Network Topology Discovery. Computer Applications 24(8), 88–100 (2004)
5. Shaikh, A., Goyal, M.: An OSPF Topology Server: Design and Evaluation. IEEE Journal on Selected Areas in Communications 20(4), 746–755 (2002)
6. Xu, J., Deng, Y., Ding, S.: OSPF Server Based Network Topology Discovery. Computer Applications 24(8), 88–100 (2004)
7. Linqing: VPN network management research and implement based on IPSec, TP393.08 (2004)
8. Yang, W.: Design and impelment of VPN Gateway Based IPSec, TP393.08 E233-39 (2008)
9. Jiang, Y., Fang, B.X., Hu, M.Z., Yun, X.: A Distributed Architecture for Internet Router Level TopologyDiscovering Systems. In: The Fourth International Conference (2003)
10. Jiang, Y., Hu, M.Z., Fang, B.X., Zhang, H.L.: An Internet router level topology automatically discovering system. Joumal on Communications 23(1,2), 54–62 (2002)
11. Guan, Y., Wang, X.J., Lu, J.D.: An Improved SNMP based Network Topology Discovery Algorithm. Microelectronics & Computer 23(6), 172–175 (2006)
12. Paxson, V., Mahdavi, J., Adams, A., Mathis, M.: An architecture for large—scale Internet measttrement". IEEE Communication 36(8), 48–54 (1998)

Protecting Flow Design for DoS Attack and Defense at the MAC Layer in Mobile Ad Hoc Network

Jian Su[1] and Huining Liu[2]

[1] Guangxi Science & Technology Project Evaluation Center, 530022 Nanning, China
[2] Guangxi Science & Technology Department, 530012, Nanning, China
Jian58546@163.com

Abstract. This paper discusses possible DoS attacks induced by IEEE 802.11 in wireless Ad hoc networks. The protecting flow based solutions are emphatically analyzed with respect to CCA(Colluding adversaries attack) DoS attack at MAC layer. This paper proposes the principles of protecting flow design. By placing protecting flows in different positions, we compared the throughput and delay of these flows being attacked. Simulation results show that the design rule of protecting flow is effective and applicable.

Keywords: Ad Hoc Networks, MAC Layer, DoS attack, Protecting Flow.

1 Introduction

Wireless Ad hoc networks is widely used in the military field and civil mobile communications, where fixed communications infrastructures (such as base station) are not available and each node works as a router to forward the packets of other nodes. It reflects the mobility and flexibility of wireless network perfectly.

Denial of service (DoS) attack has brought great threats to current wireless networks. Generally speaking, any means that make users cannot connect to networks can be called DoS attack. The simplest way to launch a DoS attack is to consume the resources of the host by using the vulnerabilities of the protocol, then the host will not be able to offer services to other users.

IEEE 802.11 is a standard MAC protocol widely used for MANET. The 802.11 Distributed Coordination Function (DCF) standard combines Carrier Sense Multiple Access/Collision Avoidance (CSMA/CA) with a Request to Send/Clear to Send (RTS/CTS) handshake to avoid collisions.

2 The Analysis of Dos Attack in Manet

A MANET could be attacked from the physical, media access control (MAC), or network layer. Even though various MANET network layer security mechanisms have been proposed, little research has been done on MAC layer security. While the attacks toward physical and MAC layer can cause great threats to the survivability or information security of network (including confidentiality, integrity and

D. Zeng (Ed.): ICAIC 2011, Part I, CCIS 224, pp. 233–240, 2011.

non-repudiation). The DoS attack at the MAC Layer can be divided into two styles bellow:

Single adversary attack (SAA): The attacker intrudes into the network and sends a large number of data to the legal nodes to consume its resource, at the same time occupy the channel.

Colluding adversaries attack (CAA): By using the unfairness of 802.11 protocols, two or more attackers send a large number of data to each other directly to occupy the channel nearby, so that other nodes cannot communicate normally.

Gupta [1] simulated and analyzed several SAA scenarios. They proposed a fair MAC protocol to mitigate attacks but at the cost of overall throughput degradation. Yihong Zhou [2] proposed a packet-by-packet authentication scheme to counter SAA attacks but at the cost of transmission efficiency and energy consumption. To mitigate CAA attacks, one of the methods Yihong Zhou [2] proposed is that by using protecting flow, but she didn't verify its feasibility. This paper had a deep research on CAA, and selectively analyzed protecting flow based solution, proposed the rules and the ways to design the protecting flow, at last, verified the way that how to design protecting flow by simulation.

3 The Unfairness of 802.11 Protocol and the Principle of Protecting Flow

The unfairness is caused by two mechanisms in the 802.11 MAC protocol: the difs/eifs timing scheme, and the exponential backoff mechanism. They are explained in the following sections

difs/eifs Timing Scheme:

To realize different channel access priorities, 802.11 uses three interframe spaces: the short interframe space (sifs), the DCF interframe space (difs), and the extended interframe space (eifs). They are defined by the following equations:

$$\text{difs=sifs+2*SlotTime} \tag{1}$$

$$eifs = sifs + \frac{ACK_{framesize}}{BasicRate} + difs \tag{2}$$

Sifs is the time delay introduced by the physical layer hardware. Difs and eifs are the period of duration for a node to determine the channel status. Obviously, eifs is much longer than difs, and difs is longer than sifs. Therefore, a node that waits for a period of sifs duration to transmit the next frame has the highest channel access priority, while a node that waits for a period of eifs duration to transmit the next frame has the lowest channel access priority.

Exponential Backoff mechanism:

The exponential backoff mechanism, used for resolving collisions in the 802.11 MAC protocol, is another source of the unfairness problems. Exponential backoff occurs when the sender does not receive a CTS or an ACK from the receiver. Therefore, the sender retransmits its RTS or data packet with an exponentially increasing backoff window, which leads to lower and lower chances of accessing the channel.

Accord to the above unfairness in 802.11 protocol, Yihong Zhou[1] pointed out that the best position to launch a DoS is at the edge of the network, so we only analyze the attacks launched at the edge of the normal communicating flow in this paper. While the protecting flow we proposed in this paper also used the above unfairness, it will launch an attack to attacking flow, so as to make the attacking flow cannot communicate normally, and at the same time get the effects of protecting normal communicating flow out from being attacked. We will define two parameters first:

$$R_t = \frac{\text{The throughput before adding in protecting flow}}{\text{The throughput after adding in protecting flow}} \quad (3)$$

$$R_t = \frac{\text{The delay before adding in protecting flow}}{\text{The delay after adding in protecting flow}} \quad (4)$$

In the simulation of this paper, routing protocol is AODV, attacking flow uses UDP protocol, normal communicating flow and protecting flow use TCP protocol, communicating time of normal communicating flow is 1-300s, attacking time is 20-240s, and protecting time of the protecting flow is 30-240s. Firstly, we will verify the feasibility of the protecting flow.Fig.1 gives one of the topology after adding in protecting flow.

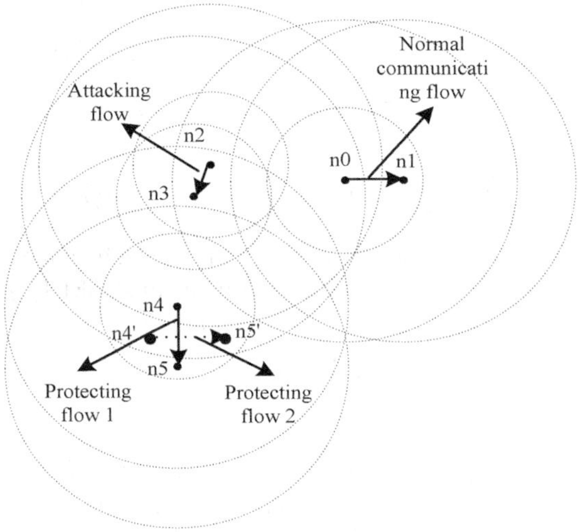

Fig. 1. The topology after adding arbitrary protecting flow

In Fig. 1, n0->n1 is a normal communicating flow, attacking flow launched a DoS attack at its sender sides, normal communicating flow will be suppressed because of the difs/eifs timing scheme. n4->n5 and n4'-> n5' are protecting flow 1 and protecting flow 2. In this scenario, attacking flow is in the interference of n0 and n4, but out of that of n1 and n5, so n0 and n4 can detect from the signal from attacking flow, but n1 and n5 cannot. n4' and n5' of protecting flow 2 can detect the signal of the whole attacking flow n2->n3. The performance of normal communicating flow after adding in protecting flow 1 and protecting flow 2 respectively is shown in TABLE 1.

We can see from the comparisons of throughput and delay in TABLE 2

Table 1. Performance After Adding in Different Protecting Flow

Parameters / Protecting flow	Throughput comparison R_t	Delay comparison R_d	Protecting effect
Protecting flow 1	0.506	1.102	bad
Protecting flow 2	3.671	0.869	good

that protecting flow 1 suffered the attack from attacking flow, while after adding in protecting flow 2, the throughput and delay of normal communicating flow improved a lot. So the position of protecting flow should be designed properly.

4 Position Analysis of Protecting Flow

The adding in of protecting flow is to defend against the attack from attacking flow, so the position of protecting flow should be the place that can launch an attack toward attacking flow.

There are two scenarios that attacking flow launches an attack:

Attacking flow at the sender side of the normal communicating flow

Attacking flow at the receiver side of the normal communicating flow

This section aims at verifying the inference above, at the same time draw the conclusion that how to improve the feasibility of protecting flow. According to the analysis above, we will analyze the problem in two occasions below:

4.1 Attacking Flow Launches an Attack at the Sender Side of Normal Communicating Flow

When attacking flow launches an attack at the sender side of normal communicating flow, difs/eifs timing scheme is used. To mitigate this kind of attack, we can use either difs/eifs timing scheme at the sender side of attacking flow, or exponential backoff mechanism at the receiver side of the attacking flow to launch an attack, then normal communicating flow is protected.

The topology that attacking flow launches an attack at the sender side of normal communicating flow is shown in Fig. 2, and topology a) is the one that adding in protecting flow at the sender side of attacking flow, while topology b) is the one that adding in protecting flow at the receiver side of attacking flow.

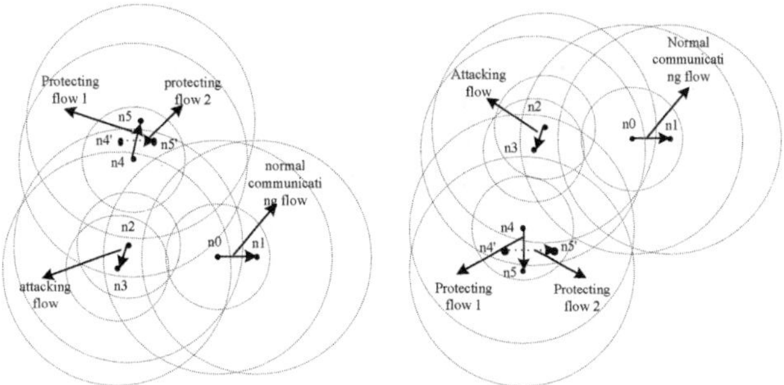

(a) Protecting flow at the sender side of attacking flow

(b) Protecting flow at the receiver side of attacking flow

Fig. 2. The topology that attacking flow at the sender side of normal communicating flow

In Fig. 2 a) and b), n0->n1 is a normal communicating flow, attacking flow launches an attack at its sender side n0, n0 will have less opportunity to access the channel because of difs/eifs timing scheme. n4->n5 and n4'->n5' are protecting flow 1 and protecting flow 2. Attacking flow is in the interference of n0 and n4, but out of that of n1 and n5. In topology a), n4' and n5' of protecting flow 2 only cover sender side n2 of attacking flow. In topology b), n4' and n5' of protecting flow 2 only cover receiver side n3 of attacking flow. The performance comparisons of normal communicating flow after adding in protecting flow 1 and protecting flow 2 respectively are shown in Fig. 3.

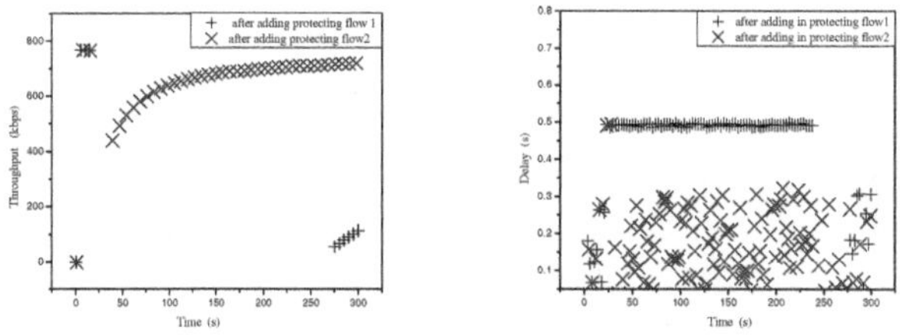

(a) Throughput comparison in Fig.2a (b) Delay comparison in Fig.2a

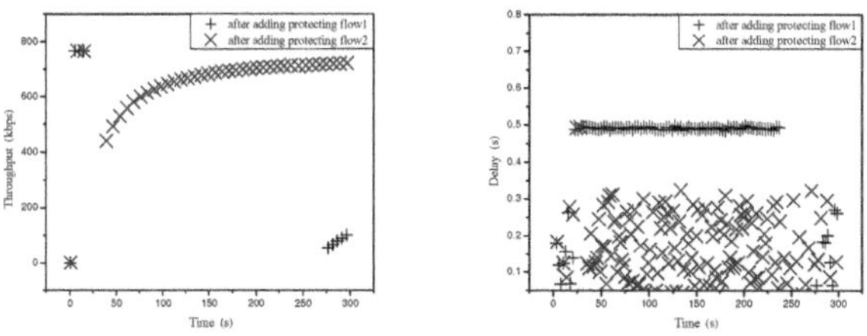

(c) Throughput comparison in Fig.2b (d) Delay comparison in Fig.2b

Fig. 3. Performance comparison of normal communicating flow in Fig.2

In Fig.3, (a) and (b) are the performance comparisons after adding in protecting flow 1 and protecting flow 2 respectively at the sender side of attacking flow. (c) and (d) are the performance comparisons after adding in protecting flow 1 and protecting flow 2 respectively at the receiver side of attacking flow. In topology a) of Fig. 2, performance comparisons of normal communicating flow after adding in protecting flow 1 are R_t =0.506, R_d =1.102. While after adding protecting flow 2 they are R_t =3.671, R_d =0.869. In topology b) of Fig. 2, performance comparisons of normal communicating flow after adding in protecting flow 1 are R_t =0.506, R_d =1.102. While after adding protecting flow 2 they are R_t =3.673, R_d =0.438. We can see from the comparison results that protecting flow 2 in topology a) and b) of Fig. 2 can defend against the attack from attacking flow, while protecting flow 1 cannot.

4.2 Attacking Flow Launches an Attack at the Receiver of Normal Communicating Flow

When attacking flow launches an attack at the receiver side of normal communicating flow, exponential backoff mechanism is mainly used. To mitigate this kind of attack, we can use either difs/eifs timing scheme at the sender side of attacking flow, or exponential backoff at the receiver side of the attacking flow to launch an attack, then normal communicating flow is protected.

The topology that attacking flow launches an attack at the receiver side of normal communicating flow is shown in Fig. 4, and topology a) is the one that adding in protecting flow at the sender side of attacking flow, while topology b) is the one that adding in protecting flow at the receiver side of attacking flow.

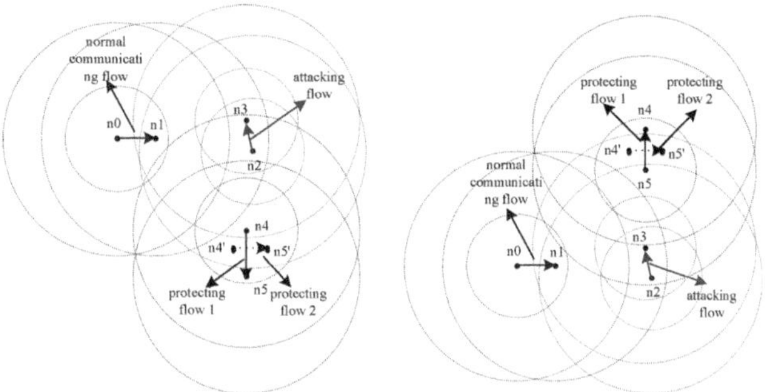

(a) Protecting flow at the sender side of attacking flow (b) Protecting flow at the receiver side of attacking flow

Fig. 4. The topology that attacking flow at the sender side of normal communicating flow

In Fig. 4 a) and b), n0->n1 is a normal communicating flow, attacking flow launches an attack at its receiver side n1, n0 will have less opportunity to access the channel because of exponential backoff mechanism. n4->n5 and n4 ' -> n5 ' are protecting flow 1 and protecting flow 2. Attacking flow is in the interference of n1 and n4, but out of that of n0 and n5. In topology a), n4 ' and n5 ' of protecting flow 2 only cover sender side n2 of attacking flow. In topology b), n4 ' and n5 ' of protecting flow 2 only cover receiver side n3 of attacking flow. The performance comparisons of normal communicating flow after adding in protecting flow 1 and protecting flow 2 respectively are shown in Fig. 5.

In Fig. 5, (a) and (b) are the performance comparisons after adding in protecting flow 1 and protecting flow 2 respectively at the sender side of attacking flow. (c) and (d) are the performance comparisons after adding in protecting flow 1 and protecting flow 2 respectively at the receiver side of attacking flow. In topology a) of Fig. 4, performance.

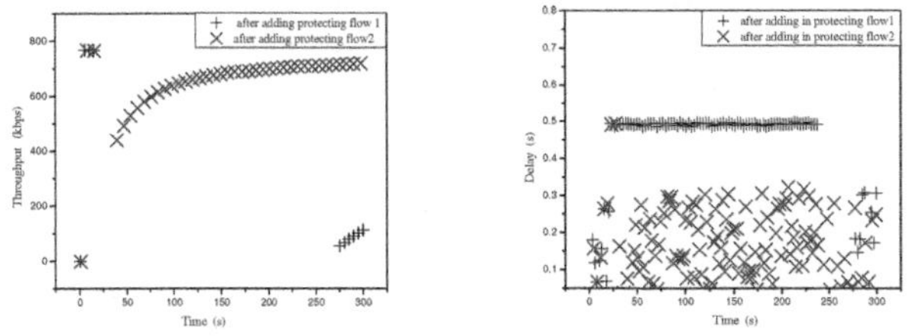

(a) Throughput comparison in Fig.2a (b) Delay comparison in Fig.2a

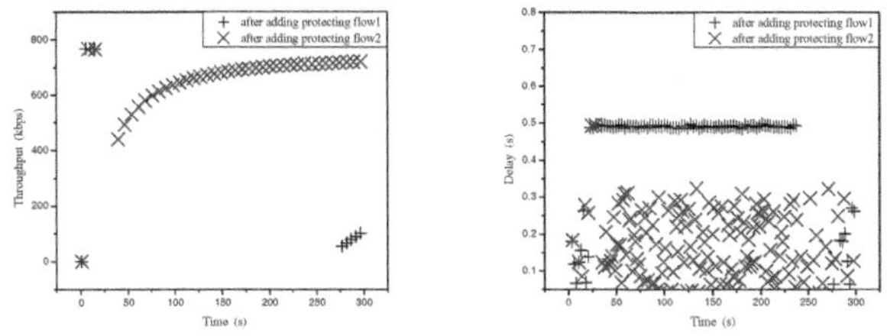

(c) Throughput comparison in Fig.2b (d) Delay comparison in Fig.2b

Fig. 5. Performance comparison of normal communicating flow in Fig.4

We can draw the conclusion from the analysis that: when attacking flow launches an attack near normal communicating flow, no matter which mechanism is used, if one side of protecting flow can cover the whole attacking flow, while another side cannot cover any of attacking flow.

5 Conclusion

This paper analyzed and simulated CAA at the MAC layer in MANET. It is pointed out how to design the proper position of protecting flow by analyzing the throughput and delay of normal communicating flow pre and post adding in protecting flow. Simulation results show that the DoS attack can be defended by adding in protecting flow at proper position.

References

1. Gupta, V.: Denial of service attacks at the MAC Layer in wireless Ad Hoc networks. In: Proceedings of MILCOM, vol. 2, pp. 7–10 (2002)
2. Zhou, Y., Wu, D., Nettles, S.M.: On MAC-layer denial of service attacks in IEEE 802.11 ad hoc networks: analysis and counter measures. International Journal of Wireless and Mobile Computing 1(3/4), 268–275 (2006)

3. Tran, T.M.C., Scheuermann, B., Mauve, M.: Detecting the presence of nodes in MANETs. In: Proc. of the ACM MOBICOM 2007, New York, USA, pp. 43–50 (2007)
4. Mahajan, R., Rodrig, M., Wetherall, D.: Analyzing the MAC level Behavior of Wireless Networks in the Wild. In: ACM SIGOCOM 2006, Pisa, Italy (September 2006)
5. Wei, R., Tenghong, L., Hai, J.: Congestion-Based RoQ DDoS Attacking and Defense Scheme in Mobile Ad Hoc Networks. Journal of Computer Research and Development 43(11), 1927–1932 (2006)

Research of Weighted Frequent Patterns Algorithm Based on Web-Log Mining*

Lixia Zou[1] and Haiyan Xue[2]

[1] Department of Computer Science and Technology Henan Radio & Television University
Zhengzhou, Henan, 450015 China
[2] Department of Computer Science and Application
Zhengzhou Institute of Aeronautic Industry Management
Zhengzhou, Henan, 450015 China
lixiazou@eyou.com

Abstract. Web log mining is one of web mining. The process of the Web log mining is introduced. This paper proposes the WFPM algorithm which is improved according to FP-Growth and uses it to mine the weblogs. The new algorithm can find the weighted frequent patterns between pages in the webs, and then helps web managers or companies to improve the web designs or business decisions. The experiments show that in the process of using WFPM algorithm is more efficient in time and space.

Keywords: web log mining, weighted frequent Patterns, weighted support, weighted confidence.

1 Introduction

Web log mining is also called the Web using patterns mining, that is, using data mining technology analyzes large Web users and other relevant data which is composed of datasets to get valuable site conditions. The main target of Web log mining is to extract interesting patterns[1] from the Web access records. The web server logs have entire structure. When information users are access to Web sites, log records all the information of relevant pages, time, user ID, so it is feasible to make information mining. In the process of mining, the log data is first imaged various relationships information which is pretreated in general, including clearing its irrelated information, etc. Using the method of association rules for to mine these preprocessing data and get the visiting association rules between pages can help understand users' behaviour and improve the site structure and provide personalized service.

* This work is partially supported by Henan Science and Technology Development Plan Project #092300410040.

D. Zeng (Ed.): ICAIC 2011, Part I, CCIS 224, pp. 241–247, 2011.

2 The Data Preprocessing from Web Log

Due to the local caching, proxy server, firewall, make web log data is not accurate, direct mining there may be incorrect results. Only to log data preprocessing, data of a server logs can be accurately reflect user access to web sites, the mining association rules is really useful. The data preprocessing generally includes four steps: data cleaning, users identification, conversation identification, path compensation. Calculate user retention time in each page according to user's access time in data preprocessing.

3 Questions

Association rules mining finds out all association rules meeting minimum support and confidence from known database. Association rules mining can be decomposed into two questions: first, find all the frequent itemsets meeting minimum support from the database, and then produce association rules that can satisfy the minimum confidence using the frequent itemsets.

Apriori algorithm [3] and FP-Growth algorithm [4] are classical algorithm mining frequent itemsets. There is a default hypothesis in their thought: the importance of each item in the database is the same and average. Therefore, the classical algorithms deal with various projects in the database in equal and unanimous ways. However, web log mining mainly mines the rules between user access pages. Each page is a project. Sometimes a high access page frequency cannot represent user interest. Although some access pages frequency is not very high , but users are interested in them. High frequency access pages contain the pages hyperlink interesting users, so users frequently enter through this page. In this kind of circumstance , the access time is generally very short while the access of the pages interesting users is long. Therefore, the importance of each page is not the same and unevenly distributed. In order to solve this problem, many researchers proposed weighted association rules and mining weighted frequent itemsets algorithm [5-10]. This paper introduced the concept of weighted value given for each page.

Second, many algorithms research mining association rules from frequent itemsets, but the generating association rules efficiency was not researched too much . The main problems for FP-Growth method - when mining frequent itemsets, it needs to produce condition FP-Tree recursively. When support threshold is less, even for small database, hundreds of thousands of frequent patterns will be also produced, dynamic generation and the release of hundreds of thousands of condition FP-Tree will spend a lot of time and space. In addition, the FP-Tree and the condition FP-Tree need to be produced from top to down while frequent patterns mining needs to be dealed with from bottom up. Because condition FP-Tree is produced recursively, FP-Tree and the condition FP - Tree must be traversed two-way. The nodes of FP-Tree and condition of FP-Tree just need more pointers, which need more memory space to save.

According to the above questions of algorithm FP-Growth and the characteristics of association rules applied in personalized recommendation, this paper uses the storage structure thought by Ying Yan [11] and improves FP-Growth algorithm, makes weighted FP-Tree and designs WFPM(Weighted Frequent Pattern Mining) algorithm which produces the frequent patterns sets.

4 Basic Concepts

After data cleaning, users identification and conversational identification of web log, user access records will be divided into a single session, whose data form is formed by multiple pages. For example, $Si=\{[i_1,time_{i1}],[i_2,time_{i2}]...[i_n, time_{in}]\}$, in represents the nth page , $time_{in}$ represents the stay time on the nth page.

In page set $I = \{i_1 , i_2 , ..., i_n \}$, every page i_j is weighed $w(i_j)$ which represents the importance of i_j when it's visited .Weights computation formula is as follows:

$$w(i_j)=\frac{ATime(i_j)}{\sum_{j=1}^{n} ATime(i_j)} \quad (1)$$

$ATime(i_j)$ is the average access time of i_j, and $\sum ATime(i_j)$ is the sum of all pages average access time, $0\le w(i_j)\le 1$, $j=\{1, 2, \cdots, n\}$. After the data item has weight, subordinate data itemsets have corresponding weights. In the itemset , $X,Y\subseteq I$,X weight W(X) is defined as:

$$W(X)=MAX(w(x)) \quad (x\in X) \quad (2)$$

Apparently ,$0\le W(X) \le 1$. A weighted support WSup(X) of itemset X is defined as:

$$WSup(X) = W(X) \times Sup(X) \quad (3)$$

The weighted confidence WConfidence(X ==> Y) is the probability of a itemset Y appearing after a itemset X appears:

$$WConfidence(X \Rightarrow Y) = \frac{WSup(X \cup Y)}{WSup(X)} \quad (4)$$

Here Sup(X) is support of Boolean association rules [1]. Project supported Number is named for sup_count, the minimum support threshold of input by users is named minsup_count, the minimum weighted support threshold is named wminsup. If $WSup(X)\ge wminsup$, X is considered as weighted frequent itemsets. When the weighted frequent itemsets X contains k projects, X is called weighted frequent k itemsets. Lk is considered as all weighted frequent k itemsets collection. All the weighted frequent itemsets collection is considered as L.

Nature suppose weighted frequent itemsets $X=\{i_1 , i_2 , ..., i_k\}$, $k>1$, $Y\subseteq X$,so:

(1) if $W(Y) \ge W(X)$,Y is the weighted frequent itemsets.
(2) if $W(Y) < W(X)$,Y is not necessarily the weighted frequent itemses.

Proof. Suppose X is frequent itemsets $Y\subseteq X$. From the formula (1) (2) and weighted frequent itemsets definition $WSup(X) = W(X) \times Sup(X) \ge wminsup$ is concluded. $Y\subseteq X$, so $Sup(Y) \ge Sup(X)$. And because $WSup(Y) = W(Y) \times Sup(Y)$, if $W(Y) \ge W(X)$,

WSup(Y) ≥W(X) ×Sup(X) ≥ wminsup , Y is the weighted frequent itemsets, otherwise Y is not necessarily the weighted frequent itemsets.

Theorem. Suppose weighted frequent K-itemsets X={i_1 , i_2 , …, i_k}, if W(X) =w(i_j),(1≤j ≤k), ∀Y⊆X, and i_j ∈Y, Y must be the weighted frequent itemsets.

Proof. Because the weighted frequent K-itemsets X={i_1 , i_2 , …, i_k},W(X) = w(i_j),(1≤j ≤k), so WSup(X) = w(i_j)×Sup(X) ≥ wminsup. And because Y⊆X and i_j ∈Y, WSup(Y) = w(i_j) ×Sup(Y) ≥ w(i_j), ×Sup(X) ≥ wminsup,Y is the weighted frequent itemsets.

Conclusion Suppose the weighted frequent K-itemsets X={i_1 , i_2 , …, i_k},W(X) = w(i_j),(1≤j≤k),if 2 - itemsets Z={i_j, z}, z∈X and∈ z≠ ij, then

Z must be weighted frequent.

A collection of all the single point contained in X itemsets is completely equal to a collection of all the single point contained in 2-itemsets Z.

5 Weighted Frequent Patterns Algorithm

The weighted frequent patterns mining algorithm is given and the algorithm is described as follows:

Input: transaction database; minsup_count is the minimum support number; wminsup is the minimum weighted support threshold; wminconf is the minimum confidence threshold; n is the maximum qianxiang length of produced association rules.

Output: the collection of all weighted frequent itemsets S.

Methods:

The first step is as follows, constructing weighted FP - Trees:

(1) Scan transaction database D once. Collect all the 1- itemsets collection C_1 meeting minsup_count ,calculate their weighted support, and pick out weighted frequent item sets collection of 1, L_1, to get candidate item sets collection C_2.

(2)Scan transaction database twice, calculate weighted support of each item sets in C_2, get all the weighted frequent 2-itemsets. Finally, all the single point set contained in the weighted frequent 2-itemsets make up a set as L in accordance with the descending order of weighted support.

(3) Create a weighted FP-Tree root node marked as "null". Process each transaction in D. Specific methods are as follows: Select the projects contained in the affairs and collection L and order them in accordance with the L. Suppose the result after sorting as[p/P], p is the first element, and P is the collection of the remaining element. Call insert_tree([p/P],T). The execution process of function insert_tree([p/P],T)is : if T have children N, N.item_name=p.item_name, N count is added one. Otherwise, create a new node N count is set one, and linked to its parent node T, and through the node chain structure linked to nodes having the same item_name nodes. If the P is non-empty ,recursively call insert_tree(P,N).

Second, call FP –Mine to mine weighted FP-Tree. Storage structure:

Freq-Set-Tree is a tree structure and used to store frequent itemsets of i-size and (i+1)-size (i=1,2,3…,n).Tree node is divided into five fields, including id as stored itemsets name;Support is support of itemsets; wsupport is the weighted support of weighted frequent itemsets $\{p_1,p_2 \ldots p_{(i-1)}, p_i\}$;Left and right are two pointers.left points to the node id which is one more than itself; The right has the same length of node id another itemsets corresponding node .

Realizing process is as follows:

```
FP-Mine()
{
  Using FP - trees head table size; establish 1-size node;
for(i=1;i<=n;i++)
{ for each item in i-size
P_Insert()/*Generate the Freq-Set-Tree of i-size and (i+1)-size and the corresponding association rules*/
release all i-size nodes from the Freq-Set-Tree
delete (i+1)-size nodes of Freq-Set-Tree that do not meet the minimum weighted support;
}
release all (n+1)-size nodes from the Freq-Set-Tree
  }
process P_Insert(Freq-Set-Tree, FP-Tree,S)
 {
  for all i-size nodes∈Freq-Set-Tree
 {
  take the first i1 in node.id,
  get the corresponding record named i1 at the FP-Tree head table.
find the corresponding node named P according to the records of node_link,
 repeat
{
find a branch containing i−size nodes according to sequence in node.id by the node P matched downward in FP-Tree;
suppose the corresponding node as q referring to the last item of node.id in i-size node;
find (i+1)-size itemsets formed by 1-size itemsets subsequent name using q child pointer
its support is the minimum count in each 1-size node which makes up (i+1)-size itemsets
accumulate support of the same item
P=P.nodelink;/* Search the next nodes with the same name */
}
Until P=NULL;;
the msupport of (i+1)-size itemsets is equal to the result that the maximum weight in each 1-size itemsets which makes up (i+1)-size itemsets multiply the support of the (i+1)-size itemsets
the weighted confidence of (i+1)-size itemsets is equal to the result that the msupport of (i+1)-size itemsets divides the msupport of i-size itemsets
if the msupport of (i+1)-size itemsets meets the minimum weighted support threshold and the weighted confidence satisfies the minimum weighted confidence threshold
```

then (i+1)-size weighted frequent itemsets are put into the collection of S

insert (i + 1)-size node into Freq-Set-Tree through node.left and node.right pointers;

}

}

6 Experiments and Performance Analysis

Experimental environment is IBM R52, main frequency is 1.73MHz , memory is 512MB, operating system is Windows XP, program by Visual c + + 6.0. Experimental data uses test data to make comparison in the same standard. Following several principles in the process of concrete operating:

(1) support threshold is consistent;
(2) data structure is consistent;
(3) the same function is realized with the same function;
(4) minimum confidence thresholds are consistent

The performance of FP-Growth algorithm and WFPM algorithm is tested. Testing results are shown in figure 1. Results show that the efficiency of WFPM algorithm is improved a lot compared with FP-Growth algorithm.

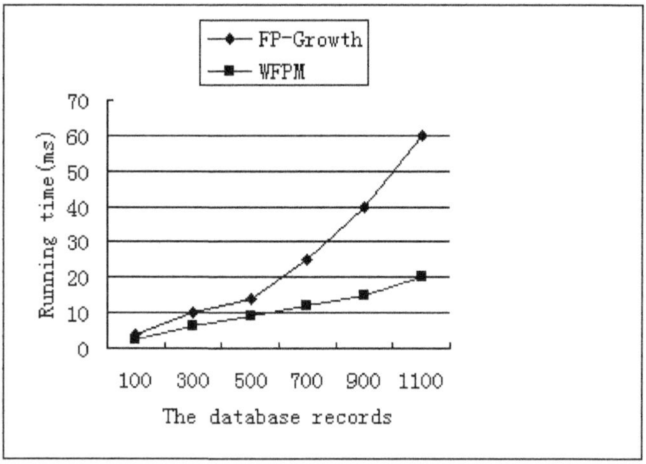

Fig. 1. Running time contrast figure between WFPM algorithm and FP-Growth algorithm

7 Conclusions

Analyse the preprocessed Web log data,generate weighted frequent itemsets, and then mine weighted association rules. These behaviors improve the site structure, help web manager understand users' behaviour and offer personalized services to users.

References

1. Cooley, R.: Web Usage Mining: Discovery and Application of Interesting Patterns from Web data. PhD thesis, Dept. of Computer Science, University of Minnesota (May 2000)
2. Lin, W., Alaverz, S.A., Ruiz, C.: Efficient Adaptive-Support Association Rule Mining for Recommendation Systems. Data Mining and Knowledge Discovery 6, 83–105 (2002)
3. Agrawal, R., Srikant, R.: Fast algorithms for mining association. In: Proc. of the 20th Int' l Conf. on Very Large Database, pp. 487–499 (1994)
4. Han, J., Pei, J., Yin, Y.w.: Mining frequent patterns without candidate generation. In: Proceedings of the 19 th ACM SIG MOD, ACM SIG MOD 2000, Dallas, TX, USA, pp. 1–12 (2000)
5. Cai, C.H., Fu Ada, W.C., Cheng, C.H., et al.: Mining association rules with weighted items. In: Proc. of the Int' l Database Engineering and Applications Symposium, pp. 68–77 (1998)
6. Weimin, O., Cheng, Z., Qingsheng, C.: Database, the development of the weighted association rules. Journal of Software 12(4), 612–619 (2001)
7. Zhang, W., Lu, J.: Weighted Boolean type of association rules. Computer Engineering 29(9), 55–57 (2003)
8. Yu, G., Sen, W., Adon, Y.: Weighted association rules, etc. Of the improved algorithm. Computer Engineering and Application 40(22), 177–179 (2004)
9. Wang, Y., Jiang, B., Song, J.: A new weighted association rule model. Computer Engineering and Application 42(5), 162–164 (2006)
10. Yang, J., Liu, N., Lan, T.: Weighted maximum frequent itemsets. Mining algorithm. Computer and Microelectronics 25(6), 123–126 (2008)
11. Yan, Y., Daling, W.: Support personalized recommendation Web page algorithm for mining association rules. Computer Science and Engineering 31(1), 79–81 (2005)

Research on Method of Bezier Triangular Curved Highway Surface 3D Restructure

Weiyong Ji[1], Jianjun Cui[1], and Shaohua Zhang[2]

[1] College of Geology Engineering and Geometrics Chang'an University Shaanxi Xi'an, China, 710054
[2] Information Engineering University of the People's Liberation Army HeNan Zhengzhou, China, 450052
Weiyong53@ovi.com

Abstract. This paper mainly deals with general process and method of route 3D model in highway exploration and design. We use Delaunay triangular grid to construct the ground model. On the basis of these, we further use triangular Bezier curved surface and effectively solve the problem of large quantity of 3D restructure data and unsmooth facet.

Keywords: Bezier triangular curved surface, discrete data, close in, curved surface restructure.

1 Introduction

The new method for highway exploration and design, which use 3D technology to restructure the highway surface terrain, has aroused extensive attention of internal and foreign experts. Its main significance lies in that the highway 3D ribbon entity could be shown in form of either traditional two dimensional schemes (horizontal, longitudinal, and crosspiece scheme), or furthermore computer assisted 3D scheme. As a result, the decision maker and designer could have a direct 3D vision of the route design and thus form a more scientific judge about the geometry line of route, horizontal, longitudinal, and crosspiece adjustment in general, test on visible distance of driving, and scene adjustment, etc.

In the process of 3D modeling display, we usually regard the discrete data as the basis of the data. After TTN is generated, we use the mass triangular facets generated by grids recursive and fine sorted method to meet the requirement of ground surface modeling. Theoretically speaking, the denser the triangular grids are, the closer the modeling result is to the original curved surface. On one hand, it results in the large quantity of triangular data used to show the ground surface. On the other hand, because of the limitation of the measure method, the number of the measure points are limited, so that triangular grids could not be close to the original curved surface limitlessly. On the basis of triangular grids division, it is very necessary to approximately imitate the original curved surface by triangular curved surface.

D. Zeng (Ed.): ICAIC 2011, Part I, CCIS 224, pp. 248–253, 2011.

According to the previous problem, by using Delaunay triangular grids to construct ground curved surface model and using Bezier curved surface to construct 3D model of the design surface, we could not only ensure the precision of ground surface model and smoothness of the design surface, but also effectively solve the problem of smoothness in surface combination.

2 Triangular Bezier Curved Surface

The theory of Bezier triangular curved surface was advocated by French learner deCastiljau in 1959. After its value is discovered in 1975, it has aroused extensive attention of the learners concerned. Besides, because it may be inserted in any border discrete points, it has been attached great importance by CAD field and develops at a fast pace. It is one of the most effective ways to construct terrain models by fitting the earth's surface.

2.1 Basic Formula

Bezier triangular curved surface is a primary function which keeps contact with a controlling peak. A piece of Bezier triangular curved surface's number of n times is defined by $(n+1)(n+2)/2$ controlling peak $p_{ijk}(i,j,k \ge 0, i+j+k=n)$ constructed by triangular array. As a result, the equation of Bezier triangular curved surface is defined as follows:

$$P(u,v,w) = \sum_{i=0}^{n} \sum_{j=0}^{n-i} P_{i,j,k} B^{n}_{i,j,k}(u, v, w) \quad u,v,w \in [0,1]$$

$$u+v+w=1 \ \text{且} \ u,v,w \ge 0$$

Among these: $$B^{n}_{i,j,k}(u,v,w) = \frac{n!}{i!j!k!} u^i v^j w^k \quad u,v,w \in [0,1]$$

is double variant defined on the triangular area, and the number of n times is Bernstein primary function. In the formula, u, v, and w is the triangular areal coordinate of P respectively.

2.2 Calculation of Areal Coordinate

In the formula of Bezier triangular curved surface, the reference u, v, w are the areal coordinates of triangle, shown as Figure 1:

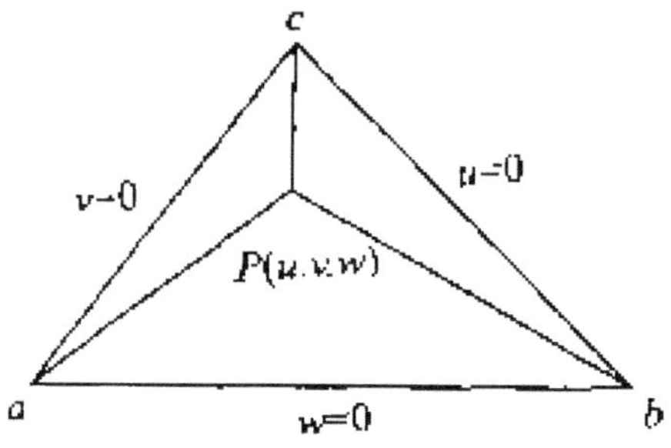

Fig. 1. Triangular areal coordinates

To the point P in the triangle, its areal coordinates are u, v, w and could be calculated by following formula:

$$u = \frac{\text{area}(Pbc)}{\text{area}(abc)},\quad v = \frac{\text{area}(aPc)}{\text{area}(abc)},\quad w = \frac{\text{area}(abP)}{\text{area}(abc)}$$

In it, the reference $u, v, w \geq 0, \quad u + v + w = 1$.

2.3 Approximate Curved Surface

In the process of approximate calculation, we put the measure points into many groups and each group of data is approximated three times respectively by triangular Bezier curved surface. All the three times of approximate of triangular Bezier curved surface need 10 controlling points which are marked as

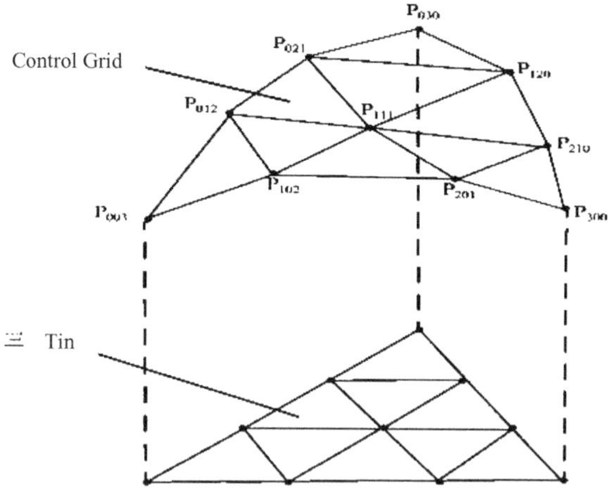

Fig. 2. Three times triangular Bezier curved surface controlling grids

$p_{ijk}(i, j, k \geq 0, i+j+k=10)$. If we use the line to link the controlling points according to the following diagram, the curving controlling grid is formed. It is made up of triangles, and the peaks of grids is corresponding to the nodes of triangles respectively. Figure 2 gives us an example of three times of triangular Bezier curved surface.

Assume that the set points of measure points constructed by a group of flat triangular grid is Qs (s=0……10). As a fitting point, curved surface controlling point Pijk is calculated reversely. The corresponding 3 points in Qs are considered as three known controlling peak of the curved surface as P003, P030, and P300. Then the triangular Bezier curved surface should meet the following conditions:

$$\sum_{i=0}^{n}\sum_{j=0}^{n-i} P_{i,j,k} B^{n}_{i,j,k}(u, v, w) = Q_s \quad s = 0 \cdots 10$$

If we put the set points Qs into the previous formula, we may get all the unknown controlling peak data, that's to say, the curved surface is made sure.

2.4 Curved Surface Combination

In order to keep GC1 in a row, each Bezier triangular is subdivided and staged, and GC1 is modified. Finally, we can get the compound curved surface formed by a piece of three times triangular grid's four times Bezier triangular curved surfaces. The exact process is as follows:

- Subdivide the two next three times Bezier curved surface on the nodes of (1/3, 1/3, 1/3) respectively. We may get 6 pieces of 3 times Bezier triangular curved surfaces shown as Figure 3:

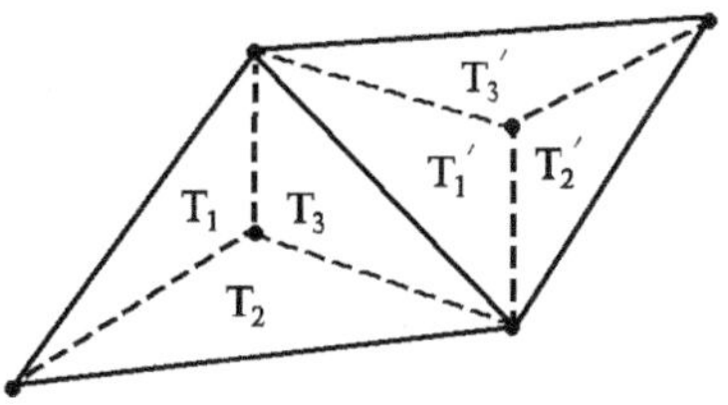

Fig. 3. Combination of two next curved surfaces

- Lift the stage of T3 curved surface to be 4 times Bezier curved surface.
- Combine T3 after its stage is lifted and T' 1 together.
- Lift the stage of T' 1 to be 4 times Bezier curved surface.
- G1 modify the combined curved surface.

3 The Test and Its Result

We carried out our test by using DEM in areas of Haiyuan and Delong etc., in Shaanxi. The following diagram on the left is the restored terrain model by using the method mentioned in this paper. And the diagram on the right is restored terrain model by the usual method. We may find from the two diagrams that the restored model on the left is obviously better than the one on the right. (Here we need to add two 3D restored models with highways, and they should not be the same and the differences are easily found. So we can know the application advantage of the method mentioned in this paper in reconstruction of highway by the example of the two diagrams.)

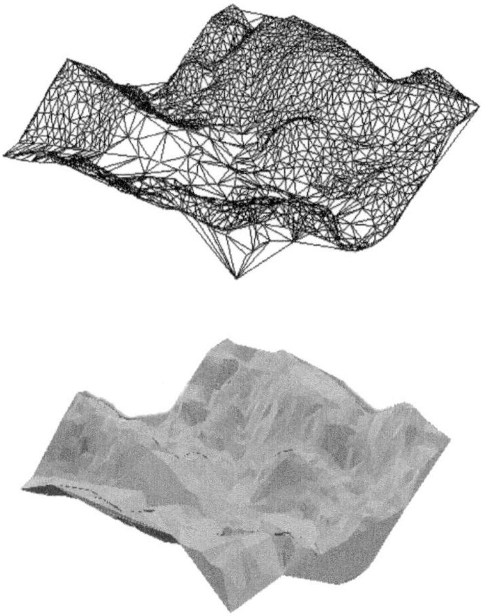

Fig. 4. Terrain surface (triangular grid and restored curved surface)

4 Conclusion

On the basis of using Delaunay triangular grids to construct the terrain model, we approximate the terrain surface by Bezier triangular curved surface. As compared with the traditional method of terrain modeling, the amount of calculation is basically the same, but quantity of data is obviously less than that of the traditional method. Besides, it is not necessary to import too much data structure and to consider the problem of multi-layer resolving capability. Moreover, different resolving capability can use different fitting step length, which results in smooth and handsome curved surface. The result of the test shows that the method has better closer of the discrete points and smoothness of the curved surface, which has very good application effect in the practical reverse work.

References

1. Xu, Q.: Terrain 3D Visualization Technology. Topography Publishing House, Beijing (2000)
2. Zhu, X.: Free Curved Surface Modeling Technology. Science Publishing House, Beijing (2000)
3. Liu, Z., Huang, C.: Reverse Engineering Technology. Mechanical Engineering Publishing House, Beijing (1993)
4. Ron, G.: Pyramid Algorithms: A Dynamic Programming Approach to Curver and Surfaces for Geometric Modeling. Elsevier Science, USA (2003)
5. Ke, Y., Xiao, Y., Li, J.: The Research of several algorithms to triangulation Bezier curved surface. Tsinghua Science and Technology (Natural Sciences) 41(7) (2001)

Study on the Method of Matching with Cartoon Sequence Graphics on the Base of Character's Centroid

Baoyin Zhang[1], Jianjun Cui[2], and Weiyong Ji[2]

[1] Xi'an Surveying and Mapping Institute Shaanxi. Xi'an 710054, China
[2] College of Geology Engineering and Geometrics Chang'an University Shaanxi. Xi'an 710054, China
bao18376@sina.com

Abstract. This paper aim at the common problem that adopting the artificial operation way to control the corresponding relationship among the original paintings in the process of the animation production at present, putting forward the Series graphics matching based on the centroid of the character, it efficiently solve the problem which the inconsistence of the original graphic object in numbers during the matching process and then obtain a well effect.

Keywords: cartoon, sequence graphics, character, centroid, matching.

1 Introduction

The key issue to conduct the cartoon animation production with computer is to solve the problem about the interpolation. That is generating the medium animation through interpolation with two or more than two original paintings. The core is to reconfirm the matching relationship among the original drawings. In order to reconfirm this corresponding relationship, the common method at present is that the animator should draw the original drawing according to the content of the graph and the order of the previous drawing. That is control the corresponding relationship among the original drawings through artificial operation. However, this approach will increase the workload of the animation production by double when you make the high-quality animation, especially the animation with great variation on their movement. So whether we can establish the mutual corresponding relationship of the original drawings rapidly and intellectually has became a key issue about the digitization of the cartoon animation.

2 Basic Idea

Actually, cartoon animation is a exaggerating demonstration of the real world, so the character in the cartoon animation will not surpass the relational change of the reality. So, there bound to be some relationships among the graphs which constitute the cartoon character, and this relationship will not change with the change of the character's act, even if it has changed, this change has its regularity. So we can make

D. Zeng (Ed.): ICAIC 2011, Part I, CCIS 224, pp. 254–261, 2011.

full use of the internal information (the mutual positioning information among the polygons of the character),of the cartoon sequence, according to the regularity which the position of the centroid of the polygons in the character has the continuous regularity, then finding the matching relationship of the every polygons in the adjacent frame. The Calculating proves take as follow:

(1) Calculating the centroid of the every polygons.

(2) finding the solution to the quantity in accordance with the area of the polygon.

(3) Taking the character as the entirety of the centroid position which constitute of the every polygons with their quality, calculating the position of the communal centroid of this character.

(4) Taking the centroid of the polygon and communal centroid as the matching prerequisite to finish the matching work among the every polygon.

3 The Mathematical Foundation

3.1 The Centroid of the Polygon

There are several polygons in one character, represented as S(z)={Cti,i=0, 1,…,N-1 }, S(z)denote as the Z'th polygon, Ns is the number of the polygon of this character. for every polygon Cti find solution for the centroid Ci=(xi,yi,zi) respectively, and we get the set C(z)= {Ci,i=0,1,…,Ns-1} of the centroid points. The algorithm of the centroid shows as following:

We use the function f(x, y) to represent the polygon, the value is 1 when f(x, y) in the polygon, under all the other conditions the value is 0. The moment set of the function f(x, y) defined as:

$$M_{jk} = \int_{-\infty}^{\infty}\int_{-\infty}^{\infty} x^j k^k f(x,y)dxdy$$

In the formula, j and k are non-negative integer value. Its first and zeroth moment is:

$$M_{10} = \int_{-\infty}^{\infty}\int_{-\infty}^{\infty} x^j f(x,y)dxdy$$

$$M_{01} = \int_{-\infty}^{\infty}\int_{-\infty}^{\infty} y^k f(x,y)dxdy$$

$$M_{00} = \int_{-\infty}^{\infty}\int_{-\infty}^{\infty} f(x,y)dxdy$$

Obviously, M00 is the area of the polygon. The coordinates of the centroid of this polygon is:

$$\bar{x} = \frac{M_{10}}{M_{00}} \qquad \bar{y} = \frac{M_{01}}{M_{00}} \tag{1}$$

3.2 The Quantity of the Polygon

Taking the every polygons in the character as a object, when the quality and the density of the object On behalf of the polygons are same, the quantity of the centroid of the polygon is in direct proportion to its area (on the condition that we have the prior knowledge can also let the different polygons have their weigh to represent the difference of the density).so its mi can be represented as following:

$$m_i = \Delta_i A_i \tag{2}$$

The Δ_i is the density of the polygon Ct_i , A_i is the area of the polygon.

The approach we usually employ to calculate the acreage of the polygon is the arc-acreage calculation. The polygon is comprised of one or more than one arc. The every arc sector of the polygon can be represented as y=f (x) , [a,b]is the interval of the arc sector, so the arc sector y=f(x)、x=a、x=b constitute the closed area with X axle, showing in the graph 1.suppose the right of the forward direction is the direction of the area, the acreage of this area is:

$$A_{arc} = \int_a^b f(x)dx \tag{3}$$

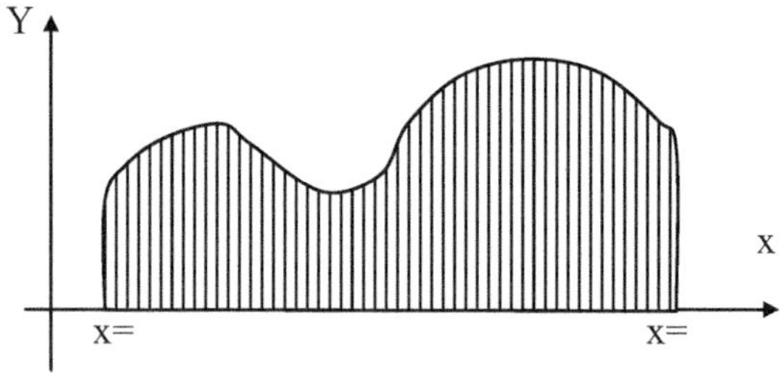

Fig. 1. Integral of the curve segment's area

The f(x)dx in the Eq.[3] is the area element in the rectangular coordinate system , it denote the area of the rectangle which height is f(x) and bottom is dx.

Generally, the curve segment of the graph is denoted as the discreet Coordinate string (x1,y1), (x2,y2) ... (xn,yn),we can use the x to divide the curve segment into some narrow curved Trapezoidal. The Eq.[2] can be transformed as follow using the Trapezoid area calculation to:

$$A_{arc} = \int_a^b f(x)dx = \frac{1}{2}(y_1+y_2)\Delta x + \frac{1}{2}(y_2+y_3)\Delta x + \cdots \frac{1}{2}(y_{n-1}+y_n)\Delta x \tag{4}$$

In the Eq.(4), $\Delta x = x_{i+1} - x_i$, we can transform it to:

$$A_{arc} = \frac{1}{2}\sum_{i=1}^{i=n}(y_{i+1} + y_i)(x_{i+1} + x_i)$$

Suppose the polygon is constituted of m strip curve segment, so the area of the polygon is:

$$A_{polygon} = A_{arc1} + A_{arc2} + \cdots + A_{arcm} \quad (5)$$

3.3 The Communal Centroid of the Character

After finding the area of every polygons in the character with the help of Eq.[5], then calculating the quantity of the centroid of the every polygons with the help of Eq.[2], finding the solution for the centroid of the polygon with Eq.[1].When all the quantity of the centroid of the polygons in the character are obtained, we can calculating the position of communal centroid of this character cg(z),as showing in Fig.2

Fig. 2. The common centroid of character

We can get the cg(z)from the following equation:

$$c_g(z) = \left[\frac{\sum_{i=0}^{N_s-1} m_i x_i}{\sum_{i=0}^{N_s-1} m_i}, \frac{\sum_{i=0}^{N_s-1} m_i y_i}{\sum_{i=0}^{N_s-1} m_i}, \quad z \right] \quad (6)$$

We suppose Cu={Ciu,i=0,1,…,Nu-1} represent the centroid of the every polygons of the previous frame, and the Ciu= (xiu, yiu,ziu) ,the communal centroid is cgu; the Cl={Cil,i=0,1,…,Nl-1} represent the centroid of the every polygons of the next frame, and the Cil= (xil, yil,zil) ,the communal centroid o is Cgl, Nu and Nl are respectively the number of the polygon of the previous and next frames in the character.

For the reason that the position of the communal centroid in the character will influence the matching effect directly, so besides to judge and calculate the communal centroid in terms of angle, we should also make further amendment in the aspect of the distance. That is, calculating the distance between the centroid of every polygons and the communal centroid of the current character, to calculate the communal centroid with the weighted method on the Eq.[6], the more distance are, the less the weight is, this will decrease the great offset of the communal centroid in the adjacent frame when the distance of the communal centroid is far away from polygons that take great variation. This paper is searching the matching relationship of the cartoon series from the character with more polygons to the character with less polygons, so we can let the $Nu \geq Nl$, ,otherwise , to reverse the order of the adjacent frame as what the following describe.

4 Matching with the Cartoon Sequence

When calculating the matching with the cartoon sequence, three problems should be mainly considered:

(1) To the every polygons Ctiu in the character of the previous frame, we convert the coordinate x,y (xiu,yiu) of it's centroid to the common centroid's polar coordinates (ρiu, φiu), similarly, for the every polygons Ctjl in the character of the next frame, we also convert the coordinate x,y (xjl,yjl) of it's centroid to the common centroid's polar coordinates (ρjl, φjl), so for coordinate (ρiu, φiu)of the centroid of the every polygons in the character of the previous frame ,there must exist a polygon Ctjl in the next frame, if the polar coordinate of the centroid of this polygon get closest with the Ctjl, meanwhile if it's area get closest ,we consider this pair of polygons are matched.

So, we can Convert above-mentioned method to below three conditions:

- The semi-diameter of the polar coordinate of the centroid is closest to each other.
- The angular of the polar coordinate of the centroid are closest to each other.
- The area of the polygons are closest to each other.

Obviously, the polygons which angular have great difference can not matching ,(the polygon A as show in the Fig.3(a) ,can not match with the polygon C' in the drawing Fig.3(b)),so we just find the matching relationship from the polygons which in the contiguous character and it's argument difference within cetain limits. We suppose the PMi={Cti1l,Cti2l,…,Ctinl} contained in the polygons of the character in the next frame, it's angular of the polar coordinate of the centroid and that's in the character of the previous frame have the difference within the threshold θ(as showing in the polygon A of the Fig.3(a) ,it corresponded to the polygons set in the sector of the Fig.3(b)).

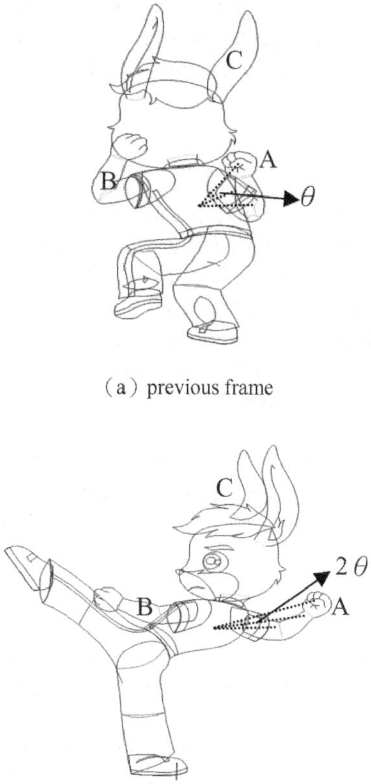

(a) previous frame

(b) next

Fig. 3. The schematic diagram of the matching between consecutive frame

(2) Designing a metric function f(i,j) to measure the possibility that polygon Ctiu match the every cartoon sequence in the PMi:

$$f(i,j)=\left|\rho_i^u-\rho_j^l\right|+\alpha\left|\varphi_i^u-\varphi_j^l\right|+\beta\left|\gamma_i^u-\gamma_j^l\right|.\ j=i_1,i_2,\ldots,i \qquad j=i_1,i_2,\ldots,i$$

α and β respectively is the regulator factor to regulate the three proportions of the items, the definite value can be fixed through the experiment. The 3 items of the aforementioned equation correspond to the 3 factors required to be considered, the first item is used to measure the difference of the semi-diameter of the coordinate, the second item is used to measure the difference of the angular of the coordinate, the third one is used to measure the similarity of the polygon. So in the PM , a polygon Ctisl which make f(i,j) satisfied the minimal value ,is the Ctiu which matches the polygon Ctm(i)l in the character of next frame.

For the reason that there can be some movements of the communal centroid of the character in the adjacent frame , so to the polygon that is near to the communal centroid (as showing in the polygon B and B'of the Fig.3), its angular will take great change in the adjacent frame, in that case, the method which only the polygon have little difference in angular can matching is not work as aforementioned, the solution is to set a threshold Ω,then the aforementioned method can be used to the polygon which the distance larger than the Ωof the centroid of the polygon to the communal centroid; on the other hand ,for the polygon which the distance smaller than the Ωof the centroid of the polygon to the communal centroid, we can find the optimal matching polygon.

So, we can confirm the matching relationship with every polygons in the consecutive frames, the obvious merit of this method is: it have favourable globally, plenitudinous using the information of polygons in the identical character, it is simple, faster, and good practicability.

5 The Outcome of the Experiment and Analysis

This paper employs the aforementioned method matching and interpolating the two drawings which with great variation . The outcome show in the following.

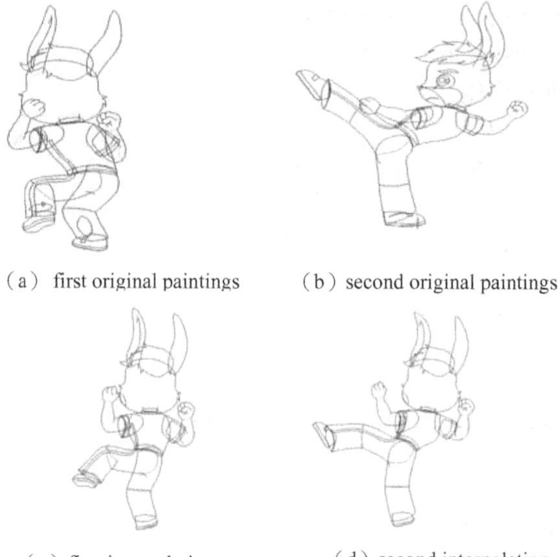

(a) first original paintings (b) second original paintings

(c) first interpolation (d) second interpolation

Fig. 4. The effect of the matching and interpolating

In Fig.4,(a) and (b) are two original paintings, (c) and (d) are the animation interpolated from (a) and (b), the result shows that take this method will realize the matching among the original paintings greatly, the matched graphic object will interpolate a well animation effect.

6 Conclusion

This paper aim at the key issue in the process of animation production assisted by the computer, conducting the deeper research on the mathematical notation of the graph and the regularity of the character change in the animation, putting forward the centroid-based matching of cartoon sequence and the experiment we did afterwards shows that this approach efficiently solve the problem about establish the mutual corresponding relationship among the original paintings in a speedy and automatic way, and this will improve the efficiency of animation production assisted by the computer.

References

1. Wang, C.: Graph theory. Beijing Institute of Technology Press (1997)
2. Yang, H.: Graph theory commonly used algorithm Selected. China Railway Publishing House (1998)
3. Zhang, B.: Vectorization expressof the Graph picture with time sequence. Surveying and Mapping Institute Journal of liberation army (February 2001)
4. Wu, G., Yang, J., Li, D.: Research on the Identify method on the base of object invarient. Computer Science (February 2000)

Fuzzy Rees Hypercongruences on Hypersemigroups

Fei Gao and Xiang-Yun Xie

School of Mathematics and Computation Science
Wuyi University
Jiangmen, Guangdong, 529020, P.R. China
FeiGao002@126.com

Abstract. Fuzzy Rees congruences on semigroups have been introduced and studied by Xie. In this paper, Rees hypercongruences and fuzzy Rees hypercongruences on hypersemigroups are studied. Moreover, we generalize a homomorphism theorem of Davvaz in [Bull. Malays Math. Soc. 23(1)(2000), 53-58].

Keywords: Rees hypercongruences, Fuzzy Rees hypercongruences, fuzzy hyperideal, hypersemigroups.

1 Introduction

Hyperstructure theory was born in 1934 when Marty [10] defined hypergroups as a generalization of groups. This theory has been studied in following decades by many researchers. There are widely applications of hyperstructures containing groups, rational algebraic functions, hypergraphs, lattices, fuzzy sets and rough sets, artificial intelligence [1,2].

Zadeh [16] introduced the notion of a fuzzy subset of a non-empty set X, as a function from X to $[0, 1]$. There are many papers devoted to fuzzify the classical mathematics into fuzzy mathematics. Algebraic structures play a prominent role in mathematics with wide ranging applications in many disciplines such as theoretical physics, computer sciences, control engineering, information sciences, coding theory, topological spaces and so on. This provides sufficient motivations for researchers to review various concepts and results from the realm of abstract algebras to a broader framework of fuzzy sets. Rosenfeld [12] presented first the concept of fuzzy group.

In 1971, Zadeh [16] introduced the concept of fuzzy relations. Further, fuzzy congruence relations on semigroups appeared in [13]. In 1999, Xie [15] introduced fuzzy Rees congruences on semigroups.

In [3,4,5,6,7,8,9], Davvaz applied the concept of fuzzy set theory in the algebraic hyperstructures, in particular in Davvaz [6] defined the concept of fuzzy hyperideals in semihypergroups and in Davvaz [6] introduced the concept of a fuzzy strongly regular relation on a semihypergroup.

Here, we introduce and study Rees hypercongruences and fuzzy Rees hypercongruences on hypersemigroups.

D. Zeng (Ed.): ICAIC 2011, Part I, CCIS 224, pp. 262–269, 2011.

2 Preliminaries

Let S be a emptyset set, $P^*(S)$ be the family of all nonempty subsets of S and "$\circ$" a hyperoperation or join operation (For exampe, see [1]), that is , "$\circ$" is a mapping from S to $P^*(S)$. If $(a, b) \in S \times S$, then its image under "$\circ$" is denoted by $a \circ b$ or ab. A emptyset S with hyperperation "$\circ$", that is, the algebraic hyperstructure $(S, \circ)$ is called a *hypergroupoid.* A hypergroupoid $(S, \circ)$, which is associative, that is, $x \circ (y \circ z) = (x \circ y) \circ z, \forall x, y, z \in S$ is called a *semihypergroup* (in view of the theory of semigroups, we call it a *hypersemigroup* in this paper)[?]. In a hypersemigroup S, if $z \circ x = x \circ z = \{x\}$ for all $z \in S$, x is called a *zero element* of S. A hypersemigroup $(S, \circ)$ is called a hypergroup if it satisfies that [2]

$$x \circ S = S \circ x = S, \forall x \in S.$$

Let $(S, \circ)$ be a hypersemigroup. A nonempty subset A of S is called a *hypersubsemigroup* of S if $A \circ A \subseteq A$. The subset A is called a *right hyperideal* of S if $A \circ S \subseteq S$. Similarly a subset A of S is called a *left hyperideal* of S if $S \circ A \subseteq S$. If a subset A of S is both a left hyperideal and a right hyperideal, it is called a *hyperideal* of S [4]. Let ρ be a congruence on a hypersemigroup $(S, \circ)$, A and B nonempty subsets of S. We call $(A, B) \in \rho$ if for every $a \in A$, there exists $b \in B$ such that $(a, b) \in \rho$. A congruence ρ on a hypersemigroup S is called a *hypercongruence* on S if $(a \circ c, b \circ d) \in \rho$, for all $a, c \in A, b, d \in B$ [14].

A fuzzy subset μ of S is called a *fuzzy subhypersemigroup* of S if $min\{\mu(x), \mu(y)\} \leq inf\{\mu(z)/z \in (x \circ y)\}$ for every $x, y \in S$. The fuzzy subset μ is called a *fuzzy right hyperideal* of S if $\mu(x) \leq inf\{\mu(z)/z \in x \circ y\}$ for every $x, y \in S$. Similarly a fuzzy subset of S is called a *fuzzy left hyperideal* of S if $\mu(y) \leq inf\{\mu(z)/z \in x \circ y\}$ for every $x, y \in S$. If a fuzzy subset μ of S is both a fuzzy left hyperideal and a fuzzy right hyperideal, it is called a *fuzzy hyperideal.*

Let $F(S)$ denote the set of all fuzzy sets in S. A fuzzy set f of a hypersemigroup S is called a *fuzzy point of* S if there exists $x \in S$ and $\lambda \in [0, 1]$ such that $f = x_\lambda$, where x_λ is defined as

$$x_\lambda(y) = \begin{cases} \lambda, & \text{if } x = y \\ 0, & \text{otherwise.} \end{cases}$$

Clearly, for any $f \in F(S)$, $f = \bigcup_{x \in suppf} x_{f(x)}$.

3 Fuzzy Rees Hypercongruences on Hypersemigroups

Definition 3.1[4]. Let $(S_1, \circ)$, $(S_2, \circ)$ be hypersemigroups. A function $\phi : S_1 \to S_2$ is called an *inclusion homomorphism* if $\phi(x \circ y) \subseteq \phi(x) \circ \phi(y)$, for all $x, y \in S_1$. The function ϕ is called a *strong homomorphism* if $\phi(x \circ y) = \phi(x) \circ \phi(y)$, for all $x, y \in S_1$.

Theorem 3.2[4]. *Let $(S, \circ)$ and $(H, \circ)$ be hypersemigroups, $\phi : S \to H$ be strong homomorphism. Then*

$$ker\phi = \{(a, b) \in S \times S \mid a\phi = b\phi\}.$$

is a hypercongruence on S.

Theorem 3.3[4]. *Let ρ be hypercongruence on $(S, \circ)$. We define the hyperoperation "$\circ$" on S/ρ as follows:*

$$x\rho \circ y\rho := (x \circ y)\rho = \{c\rho : c \in x \circ y\}.$$

Then $(S/\rho, \circ)$ is a hypersemigroup.

Lemma 3.4[4]. *Let I be a hyperideal of a semihypergroup S. We consider the Rees relation ρ_I on H as follows:*

$$a\rho_I b \Longleftrightarrow a = b \quad or \quad a \in I, b \in I.$$

Then ρ_I is a hypercongruence on S.

Theorem 3.5. *Let A be a hyperideal and B a hypersubsemigroup of a hypersemigroup $(S, \circ)$, $A \cap B \neq \emptyset$. Then the hypersemigroups $(A \cup B)/\rho_A$ and $B/\rho_{(A\cap B)}$ are isomorphism.*

Proof. It is clear that $(B, \circ)$ and $(A \cup B, \circ)$ are hypersubsemigroups , A and $A \cap B$ are hyperideals of $A \cup B$ and B respectively. Let ϕ is a mapping defined as follows:

$$\phi : B \to (A \cup B)/\rho_A \mid b \hookrightarrow b\rho_A,$$

for all $b \in B$. Then ϕ is an isomorphic mapping. In fact:

(1) ϕ is onto. For each $x\rho_A \in (A \cup B)/\rho_A$, we have $x \in A$, or $x \in B$. If $x \in A$, since $A \cap B \neq \emptyset$, then there exists $b \in (A \cap B)$ such that $x\rho_A = b\rho_A$. If $x \in B$, it is clear.

(2) ϕ is strong homomorphism. In fact:

$$(b_1 \circ b_2)\phi = (b_1 \circ b_2)\rho_A = b_1\rho_A \star b_2\rho_A = b_1\phi \star b_2\phi,$$

for every $b_1, b_2 \in B$.

(3) ϕ is an isomorphism. In fact:

$$\begin{aligned} ker\phi &= \{(b_1, b_2) \in B \times B \mid b_1\phi = b_2\phi\} \\ &= \{(b_1, b_2) \in B \times B \mid b_1\rho_A = b_2\rho_A\} \\ &= \{b_1 = b_2\} \cup \{b_1 \in A \cap B \text{ and } b_2 \in A \cap B\} \\ &= \rho_{A\cap B}. \end{aligned}$$

Then $B/\rho_{A\cap B} \cong (A \cup B)/\rho_A$.

Corollary 3.6. *Let A and B be hyperideals of a hypersemigroup $(S, \circ)$. Then the hypersemigroups $(A \cup B)/\rho_A$ and $B/\rho_{(A\cap B)}$ are isomorphism.*

Proof. Since A and B be hyperideals of a hypersemigroup $(S, \circ)$, we have $A \cap B \neq \emptyset$. By Theorem 3.5, the hypersemigroups $(A \cup B)/\rho_A$ and $B/\rho_{(A\cap B)}$ are isomorphism.

Remark 3.7. The Theorem 3.5 and Corollary 3.6 are generalizations of the Theorem 3.6 in [5].

Definition 3.8. (Murali [11]) Let A be a non-empty set. A function μ from $A \times A$ into the unit interval $[0, 1]$ is called a *fuzzy relation* on A. A fuzzy relation μ on A is called *fuzzy reflexive* if $\mu(x, x) = 1$ for all $x \in A$, it is called *fuzzy symmetric* if $\mu(x, y) = \mu(y, x)$ for all $x, y \in A$, and is called *fuzzy transitive* if $\mu(x, y) \geq \mu \circ \mu(x, y) = sup\{min\{\mu(x, z), \mu(z, y)\}/z \in A\}$ for all $x, y \in A$.

A fuzzy relation μ on a set A is called a *fuzzy equivalence relation* on A if it is fuzzy reflexive, fuzzy symmetric, and fuzzy transitive.

Definition 3.9. A fuzzy equivalence relation μ on a hypersemigroup S is called *fuzzy right compatible* if for all $x, y, c \in S$,

$$\mu(x, y) \leq inf\{\mu(a, b)/a \in x \circ c, b \in y \circ c\},$$

A fuzzy equivalence relation μ is called *fuzzy left compatible* if for all $x, y, c \in S$,

$$\mu(x, y) \leq inf\{\mu(a, b)/a \in c \circ x, b \in c \circ y\}.$$

Definition 3.10. A fuzzy equivalence relation μ on a hypersemigroup S is called *fuzzy weak right compatible* if for all $x, y, c \in S$, there exist $a \in x \circ c, b \in y \circ c$ such that $\mu(x, y) \leq \mu(a, b)$. A fuzzy equivalence relation μ is called *fuzzy weak left compatible* if for all $x, y, c \in S$, there exist $a \in c \circ x, b \in c \circ y$ such that $\mu(x, y) \leq \mu(a, b)$.

Definition 3.11. A fuzzy equivalent relation μ on a hypersemigroup S is called *fuzzy hypercongruence* on S if it is fuzzy right and left compatible.

Definition 3.12. A fuzzy equivalent relation μ on a hypersemigroup S is called *fuzzy weak hypercongruence* on S if it is fuzzy weak right and weak left compatible.

Theorem 3.13[6]. *A fuzzy equivalent relation μ on a hypersemigroup S is fuzzy hypercongruence on a hypersemigroup $(S, \circ)$ if and only if for all $a, b, c, d \in S$,*

$$\mu(a, b) \wedge \mu(c, d) \leq inf\{\mu(x, y)/x \in a \circ c, y \in b \circ d\}.$$

Definition 3.14. For any fuzzy equivalence relations ρ and θ of a hypersemigroup S, the product $\rho \circ \theta$ is defined by:

$$\rho \circ \theta(x, y) = sup_{z \in S}\{min\{\rho(x, z), \theta(z, y)\}\}.$$

A hypersemigroup $(S, \circ)$ is called a *strong hypersemigroup* if $a, b \in a \circ b$, for all $a, b \in S$.

Proposition 3.15. If ρ and θ are the fuzzy hypercongruence on a strong hypersemigroup S, then $\rho \circ \theta$ is also a fuzzy hypercongruence on S.

Proof. Let x, y, z and c be any element of H, then

$$\begin{aligned}
& inf\{\rho \circ \theta(a,b)/a \in c \circ x, b \in c \circ y\} \\
&= inf\{sup_{z \in S} min\{\rho(a,z), \theta(z,b)/a \in c \circ x, b \in c \circ y\} \\
&\geq sup_{z \in S} inf\{\{min\{\rho(a,z), \theta(z,b)/ \\
& a \in c \circ x, b \in c \circ y\}\} \\
&\geq sup_{z \in S} min\{\{\rho(a,z), \theta(z,b)\}/a \in c \circ x, b \in c \circ y\} \\
&\geq sup_{z \in S} min\{\rho(x,z), \theta(z,y)\},
\end{aligned}$$

thus we have

$$inf\{\rho \circ \theta(a,b)/a \in c \circ x, b \in c \circ y\} \geq \rho \circ \theta(x,y).$$

It implies that $\rho \circ \theta$ is fuzzy left compatible, similarly we can prove that $\rho \circ \theta$ is fuzzy right compatible. Then $\rho \circ \theta$ is the fuzzy hypercongruence on S.

In [15], the author defined fuzzy Rees congruences on semigroups, we consider the following definition now.

Definition 3.16. Let μ be a fuzzy hyperideal of a hypersemigroup S. Then we can define a fuzzy relation θ_μ on S defined as follows:

$$\theta_\mu(x,y) = \begin{cases} min\{\mu(x), \mu(y)\}, & \text{if } x \neq y, \\ 1, & \text{if } x = y. \end{cases}$$

Proposition 3.17. *Let μ be a fuzzy hyperideal of a hypersemigroup S. Then θ_μ is a fuzzy weak hypercongruence on S.*

Proof. By definition of θ_μ, it is obvious that θ_μ is reflexive and symmetric. For all $x, y \in S$, we consider the following two cases:

(1) If $x = y$, then

$$\begin{aligned}
& sup\{min\{\theta_\mu(x,z), \theta_\mu(z,x)\}\} \\
&= sup_{z \in S}\{\theta_\mu(x,z)/z \in S\} \\
&= \theta_\mu(x,x) = 1.
\end{aligned}$$

(2) If $x \neq y$, then

$$\begin{aligned}
& sup_{z \in S}\{min\{\theta_\mu(x,z), \theta_\mu(z,y)\}\} \\
&= sup\{sup_{z \in S-\{x,y\}}\{min\{\theta_\mu(x,z), \theta_\mu(z,y)\}\}, \\
& min\{\theta_\mu(x,x), \theta_\mu(x,y)\}, min\{\theta_\mu(x,y), \theta_\mu(y,y)\}\} \\
&= sup\{\theta_\mu(x,y), sup_{z \in S-\{x,y\}}\{min\{\mu(x), \\
& \mu(z), \mu(z), \mu(y)\}\} \\
&\leq sup\{\theta_\mu(x,y)\}, sup_{z \in S-\{x,y\}}\{min\{\mu(x), \mu(y)\}\} \\
&= sup\{\theta_\mu(x,y), \theta_\mu(x,y)\} = \theta_\mu(x,y).
\end{aligned}$$

By (1) and (2), θ_μ is fuzzy transitive. Furthermore, θ_μ is fuzzy left compatible. In fact: For any $x, y, c \in H$, if $c \circ x = c \circ y$. Thus for $a \in c \circ x = c \circ y$, $\mu(a, a) = 1 \geq \mu(x, y)$.

If $c \circ x \neq c \circ y$, then $x \neq y$. Thus

$$\begin{aligned}\theta_\mu(x, y) &= min\{\mu(x), \mu(y)\} \\ &\leq min\{inf\{\mu(a)/a \in c \circ x\}, inf\{\mu(b)/b \in c \circ y\}\} \\ &= inf\{min\{\mu(a), \mu(b)\}/a \in c \circ x, b \in c \circ y\}\} \\ &\leq inf\{min\{\mu(a), \mu(b)\}/a \in c \circ x, b \in c \circ y, a \neq b\}\} \\ &\leq \theta_\mu(a, b).\end{aligned}$$

In the same way, we can also prove that θ_μ is fuzzy weak right compatible.

The fuzzy congruence defined in Definition 3.16 is called *fuzzy Rees weak hypercongruence* on S.

Lemma 3.18. *A emptyset I be a hyperideal of a hypersemigroup S if and only if χ_I is a fuzzy hyperideal of S.*

Proof. $\Rightarrow$. Let I be a hyperideal of a hypersemigroup S. For any $x, y \in S$, if $x \notin I$, then $inf\{\chi_I(z)/z \in x \circ y\} \geq 0 = \chi_I(x)$; if $x \in I$, since I is a right hyperideal of S, we have $x \circ y \subseteq I$, for all $y \in S$. Thus $inf\{\chi_I(z)/z \in x \circ y\} = \chi_I(x) = 1$. Therefore, χ_I is a right fuzzy hyperideal of S. Similarly we can prove that χ_I is a left fuzzy hyperideal of S since I is a left hyperideal of S.

$\Leftarrow$. Let χ_I be a fuzzy hyperideal of a hypersemigroup S. For any $x, y \in S$, if $x \in I$, since χ_I is a right fuzzy hyperideal of S, then $inf\{\chi_I(z)/z \in x \circ y\} \geq \chi_I(x) = 1$. Thus $\chi_I(z) = 1$ for all $z \in x \circ y$, it implies that $x \circ y \subseteq I$ for all $y \in S$, that is , I is a right hyperideal of S. Since χ_I is also a left fuzzy hyperideal of S, by the same way, we can obtain that I is a left hyperideal of S.

Proposition 3.19. *Let I be a hyperideal of a hypersemigroup S, and let ρ be the Rees relation on S. Then the characteristic function χ_ρ of ρ is fuzzy Rees weak hypercongruence.*

Proof. Assume that $a = b$, then $a\rho b$, and so $\chi_\rho(a, b) = 1$. If $a \neq b$, we consider the following cases:

(1) If $a \in I$, and $b \in I$, then $(a, b) \in \rho$. Thus $\chi_I(a) = \chi_I(b) = \chi_\rho(a, b) = 1$.

(2) If $a \in I$, and $b \notin I$, then $(a, b) \notin \rho$. Thus $\chi_I(a) = 1, \chi_I(b) = 0$ and $\chi_\rho(a, b) = 0$.

(3) If $a \notin I$, and $b \in I$, then then $(a, b) \notin \rho$. Thus $\chi_I(a) = 0, \chi_I(b) = 1$ and $\chi_\rho(a, b) = 0$.

(4) If $a \notin I$, and $b \notin I$, then $(a, b) \notin \rho$. Thus $\chi_I(a) = \chi_I(b) = \chi_\rho(a, b) = 0$.

By summarizing all cases as above, we obtain that if $a \neq b, \chi_\rho(a, b) = min\{\chi_I(a), \chi_I(b)\}$. If $a = b, \chi_\rho(a, b) = 1$. Therefore χ_I is a fuzzy Rees weak hypercongruence on S determined by χ_I.

Definition 3.20. A hypersemigroup S is called *fuzzy Rees weak hypercongruence semigroup* (abbr. $FRWH$-semigroup) if every fuzzy hypercongruence on S is a fuzzy Rees weak hypercongruence.

Let elements ∇_s and $\triangle_s$ be fuzzy congruences on a hypersemigroup S defined by $\nabla_s(x,y) = 1$ for all $x, y \in S$, and $\triangle_s(x,y) = 0$ if $x \neq y$ and $\triangle_s(x,y) = 1$, if $x = y$, then it is clear that ∇_s and $\triangle_s$ are all fuzzy hypercongrences on S and are the greatest element and least element respectively among all fuzzy hypercongruences on S.

Theorem 3.21. *Let S be a $FRWH$-semigroup. Then*

(1) S has a zero element.

(2) If θ is a fuzzy hypercongruence on S, then $\theta_\mu = \theta$, where $\mu(x) = \theta(x,0)$ for all $x \in S\backslash\{0\}$, and 0 is the zero element of S.

Proof. To prove (1), observe that $\triangle_s$ is a fuzzy hypercongruence on S. Since S is a $FRWH$-semihypergroup, there exists a fuzzy hyperideal μ ($\neq 0$) of S such that $\triangle_s = \theta_\mu$. Since $\mu \neq 0$, we have $\mu(x) \neq 0$ for some $x \in S$. Then for any $y \in S$ such that $y \neq x$, we have $\triangle_s(y,x) = \theta_\mu(x,y) = min\{\mu(x), \mu(y)\} = 0$. Thus, $\mu(y) = 0$. Since μ is a fuzzy hyperideal of S, for all $z \in S$, we have $inf\{\mu(a)/a \in z \circ x\} \geq \mu(x), inf\{\mu(b)/b \in x \circ z\} \geq \mu(x)$, this implies that $z \circ x = x \circ z = \{x\}$. This proves that x is a zero element of S.

To prove (2), let θ be a fuzzy hypercongruence on S. Then, by hypothesis, there exists a fuzzy hyperideal $\mu(\neq 0)$ such that $\theta = \theta_\mu$. Let $(\forall x \in S)$, $\nu(x) = \theta(x,0)$, where 0 is a zero element of S by (1). Then for all $y \in S$,

$$\begin{aligned}
&inf\{\nu(c)/c \in y \circ x\} \\
&= inf\{\theta(c,0)/c \in y \circ x\} \geq \theta(x,0) = \nu(x), \\
&inf\{\nu(c)/c \in y \circ x\} \\
&= inf\{\theta(c,0)/c \in y \circ x\} \geq \theta(y,0) = \nu(y), \\
&\nu(0) = \theta(0,0) = 1.
\end{aligned}$$

Thus, ν is a fuzzy hyperideal of S. Moreover, we have $\nu = \mu$ for all $x \in S\backslash\{0\}$. In fact, since for any $y \in S$ such that $y \neq 0$, $\nu(y) = \theta(y,0) = \theta_\mu(y,0) = min\{\mu(y), \mu(0)\} = \mu(y)$. Then, we have $\mu = \nu$ for all $x \in S\backslash\{0\}$.

4 Conclusion

Using the concept of Rees congruences on semigroups and fuzzy sets presented by Zadeh, we have investigated in this paper the Rees hypercongruences and fuzzy Rees hypercongruences on a hypersemigroups, we also introduce fuzzy Rees weak hypercongruences hypersemigroups and give characterizations of hypercongrences on $FRWH$-semigroups. Further study will be needed to establish whether the notations put forth in this paper may lead to a fruitful theory, for example, the theory of hypercongruences extensions on hypersemigroups.

Acknowledgment. The authors would like to thank the anonymous referees for their interest in our work. The work is supported by the National Natural Science Foundation (No. 10961014), and by the Science and technology projects in Guangdong Province (2010B010600039).

References

1. Corsini, P.: Prolegomena of hypergroup theory, 2nd edn. Aviani editor, Udine (1993)
2. Corsini, P., Leoreanu, V.: Applications of Hyperstructure Theory, Advances in Mathematics. Kluwer Academic Publishers, Dordrecht (2003)
3. Davvaz, B.: Fuzzy H_v-groups. Fuzzy Sets Syst. 101, 191–195 (1999)
4. Davvaz, B.: Fuzzy hyperideals in semihypergroups. Italian J. Pure Appl. Math. 8, 67–74 (2000)
5. Davvaz, B.: Some results on congruences in semihypergroups. Bull. Malays Math. Soc. 23(1), 53–58 (2000)
6. Davvaz, B.: Strong regularity and fuzzy strong regularity in semihypergroups. Korean J. Comput. Appt. Math. 7(1), 205–213 (2000)
7. Davvaz, B.: Fuzzy H_v-submodules. Fuzzy Sets Syst. 117, 477–484 (2001)
8. Davvaz, B.: A study on the structure of H_v-near-ring modules. Indian J. Pure Appl. Math. 34(5), 693–700 (2003)
9. Davvaz, B.: $T_H$and S_H-interval-valued fuzzy subhypergroups. Indian J. Pure Appl. Math. 34(1), 61–69 (2004)
10. Marty, F.: Sur une generalization de la notion de groupe. In: 8th Congress Math. Scandianaves, Stockholm, pp. 45–48 (1934)
11. Murali, V.: Fuzzy equivalence relations. Fuzzy Sets and Systems 30, 155–163 (1989)
12. Rosenfeld, A.: Fuzzy groups. J. Math. Anal. 35, 512–517 (1971)
13. Samhan, M.A.: Fuzzy congruences on semigroup. Inform. Sci. 74, 165–175 (1993)
14. Sen, M.K., Ameri, R., Chowdhury, G.: Fuzzy hypersemigroups. Soft Computing 12, 891–900 (2008)
15. Xie, X.Y.: Fuzzy Rees congruences on semigroups. Fuzzy Sets Syst 102, 353–359 (1999)
16. Zadeh, L.A.: Fuzzy Sets. Infom. and Control 8, 338–353 (1965)
17. Zadeh, L.A.: Similar relations and fuzzy ordering. Inform. Sci. 3, 117–200 (1971)

The Application of the Pseudo Vector Multiplication in the Image Encryption Algorithm

Xiang Liu[1] and Zongying Li[2]

[1] Network Center Linyi Normal University Shandong Linyi 276000, China
[2] School of Science Linyi Normal University Shandong Linyi 276000, China
Xiang7283@sohu.com

Abstract. In this paper, we first designed one kind of the pseudo vector multiplication on the digital image pixel gray value, then introduced a novel digital image encryption algorithm, which is based on the 2D Arnold transformation and the pseudo vector multiplication. At last, the large number of simulation results and analysis have both shown that the proposed algorithm has very good diffusion properties and is a very good encryption algorithm.

Keywords: Image correlation, Image encryption, His-togram, Sensitivity, The pseudo vector multiplication.

1 Introduction

With the development of information society, particularly the rapid development of the Internet and the multimedia technology, The security of transmitted digital image [1]-[3] information through a channel, against passive or active attacks, becomes more and more important. At present, many researchers proposed different image encryption schemes to overcome image encryption [4]–[11], such as the classic Arnold transformation, affine transformation, Peanon curve transformation and magic transformation and the encryption algorithm based on the chaotic theory and so on. However, these traditional image encryption algorithm may still be improved.

In this paper, we presents a whole novel digital image encryption algorithm based on the 2D Arnold transformation and the pseudo vector multiplication, and all the experimental results and analysis have both shown that the algorithm can achieve the goal of better encryption effect.

2 The Proposed Scheme

2.1 The 2D Arnold Transformation

The digital images can beviewed as a matrix when they are displayed on the computer screen, where the matrix element is located in the rows and columns are called pixel coordinates, the numeric value of the element is the pixel grayscale for a digital image, to change the location of the matrix element or value, it will become another

D. Zeng (Ed.): ICAIC 2011, Part I, CCIS 224, pp. 270–277, 2011.

image transformation based on the location of the element to change to achieve image scrambling.

The Arnold transformation can be regarded as the process of tensile, compression, folding and stitching. The general 2D Arnold transformation [4] is an invertible chaotic map, which may be described by:

$$\begin{pmatrix} x_{n+1} \\ y_{n+1} \end{pmatrix} = \begin{pmatrix} 1 & 1 \\ 1 & 2 \end{pmatrix} \begin{pmatrix} x_n \\ y_n \end{pmatrix} \bmod N \tag{1}$$

And its reversible form can be described by:

$$\begin{pmatrix} x_n \\ y_n \end{pmatrix} = \begin{pmatrix} 2 & -1 \\ -1 & 1 \end{pmatrix} \begin{pmatrix} x_{n+1} \\ y_{n+1} \end{pmatrix} \bmod N \tag{2}$$

The Arnold map is known to be chaotic, when N =1, the formula(1) is a standard Arnold transform, and with geometrical explanation shown in Fig.1, from which one can see that a units quare is first stretched by the linear transform and then folded by the modular operation, which is abbreviated as mod.

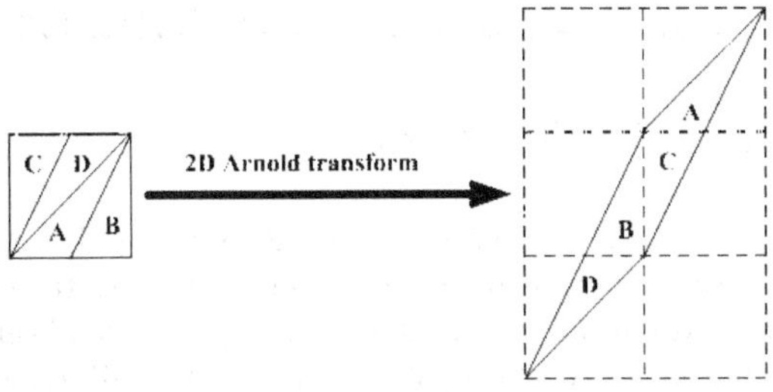

Fig. 1. Geometrical explanation of the generalized discrete 2D Arnold map

The above 2D Arnold transformation can be generalized by introducing two control parameters a and b as follows:

$$\begin{pmatrix} x_{n+1} \\ y_{n+1} \end{pmatrix} = \begin{pmatrix} 1 & a \\ b & ab+1 \end{pmatrix} \begin{pmatrix} x_n \\ y_n \end{pmatrix} \bmod N \tag{3}$$

where a, b, N are positive integer and such that $a, b < N$.

2.2 The Pseudo Vector Multiplication

If we only permutate the location of the image pixel by the two-dimensional Arnold transformation when we want to encrypt one digital image, we can't change the statistical histogram of the image. Therefore, we must apply the diffusion function to change the statistical histogram of the image in order to improve the capability of encryption scheme.

The gray value of the adjacent pixels of the pixel (x,y) are expressed as:

$$f(x-1, y-1), f(x-1, y), f(x-1, y+1), f(x, y+1),$$
$$f(x+1, y+1), f(x+1, y), f(x+1, y-1), f(x, y-1)$$

Then we split them into the diagonally adjacent pixels set and the linear adjacent pixels set as following:

The diagonally adjacent pixels set D:

$$\{f(x-1,y-1), f(x-1,y+1), f(x+1,y+1), f(x+1,y-1)\}$$

And the linear adjacent pixels set L:

$$\{f(x-1,y), f(x,y+1), f(x+1,y), f(x,y-1)\}$$

In the paper, we calculate the vector multiplication between vector D and L':

$$\begin{aligned} D\times L' = {} & f(x-1, y-1)\times f(x-1, y) \\ & + f(x-1, y+1)\times f(x, y+1) \\ & + f(x+1, y+1)\times f(x+1, y) \\ & + f(x+1, y-1)\times f(x, y-1) \end{aligned} \tag{4}$$

To ensure that the form of calculation is simple, we redefine the addition operation and the multiplication operation as the following form:

$$\begin{aligned} D \otimes L' = {} & f(x-1, y-1) \otimes f(x-1, y) \\ & \oplus f(x-1, y+1) \otimes f(x, y+1) \\ & \oplus f(x+1, y+1) \otimes f(x+1, y) \\ & \oplus f(x+1, y-1) \otimes f(x, y-1) \end{aligned} \tag{5}$$

where the symbol $\otimes$ and $\oplus$ are defined as below:

$$a \otimes b = \mathrm{mod}(a+b, 256)$$
$$a \oplus b = bitxor(a,b)$$

Let $f_{value} = D \otimes L'$, and regard it as the gray value of one fictitious pixel corresponding to the pixel at the grid (x, y).

The expression is given as follow:

$$f(x, y) = (f(x, y) + f_{value}) \bmod 256 \tag{6}$$

where $f(x, y)$ means the gray value of the pixel at the grid (x, y), and f_{value} means the gray value of its corresponding fictitious pixel.

We name formula (6) as the diffusion equation based on the pseudo vector multiplication, and it's obvious a reversible transformation.

2.3 The Encryption Algorithm Steps

The novel digital image encryption algorithm is presented which is based on the 2D Arnold transformation and the pseudo vector multiplication, the integrated image encryption scheme consists of the following four steps of operations:

Step1: Select the encryption iteration rounds k.

Step2: Using the discrete 2D Arnold transformation to the image pixel position of scrambling.

Step3: For every image pixel, the previously formula (6) is used to get a newly transformed image with the corresponding fictitious pixel which is given by formula (5).

Step4: After each round of scrambling, operations from Step2 to Step3 are interleaved for k rounds to satisfy the requirement of security. finally get the information data output.

2.4 The Decryption Algorithm Steps

The deciphering procedure is similar to that of the enciphering process illustrated above, and consists of the following steps of operations:

Step1: Select the encryption iteration rounds k.

Step2: To take advantage of the reversible diffusion equation to process the encrypted image.

Step3: Using the reversible form of the 2D Arnold map to the digital image which is generated from Step2.

Step4: Repeat Step2 and Step3 operating k times, at last we will get a new digital image which is the original image.

3 The Experimental Result Sanalysis

In order to investigate the quality of encryption, a large number of digital simulations are performed. The simulation results and performance analysis of the proposed image encryption scheme are provided in this section.

3.1 The Correlation of Adjacent Pixels

In general, adjacent pixels of most plain images are highly correlated. However, one of the requirements of an effective image cryptosystem is the generation of a cipher image with sufficiently low correlation of adjacent pixels. To analyze the effectiveness of our cryptosystem in this aspect, the correlations [4]–[11] between two adjacent pixels along horizontal, vertical and diagonal directions are calculated.

The correlation coefficient is defined as follows:

$$r_{xy} = \frac{con(x, y)}{\sqrt{D(x)}\sqrt{D(y)}} \tag{7}$$

Where

$$E(x) = \frac{1}{N}\sum_{i=1}^{N} x_i$$

$$D(x) = \frac{1}{N}\sum_{i=1}^{N} \left(x_i - E(x)\right)^2$$

$$con(x, y) = \frac{1}{N}\sum_{i=1}^{N} \left(x_i - E(x)\right)\left(y_i - E(y)\right)$$

In the paper, we randomly select 3000 pairs of two-adjacent pixels from the plain images and encrypted images along the direction of the horizontal, vertical and diagonal. And their corresponding results are shown in Fig.2 and listed in TABLE 1. The results imply that the proposed encryption algorithm can effectively make the adjacent pixels uncorrelated in the original image after fifthen cryption round.

Table 1. Correlation of the adjacent pixels

	horizontal	vertical	diagonal
Original Image	0.9642	0.9793	0.9615
Encrypted Image	0.0492	0.0078	0.0235

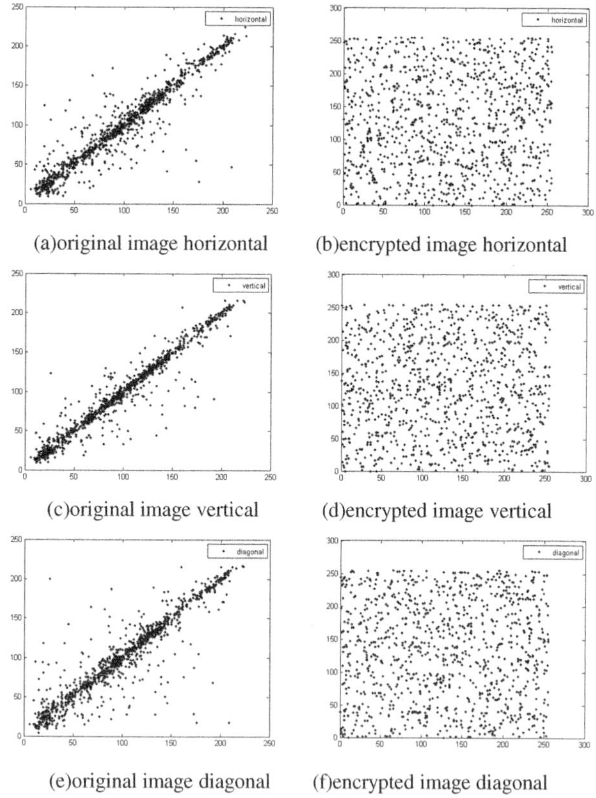

(a)original image horizontal (b)encrypted image horizontal

(c)original image vertical (d)encrypted image vertical

(e)original image diagonal (f)encrypted image diagonal

Fig. 2. Correlation of the neighboring pixels

3.2 Histogram Analysis

Intensity transformation functions based on information extracted from image intensity histograms [1]–[3] play a basic role in image progressing.

In this paper, the original image Lena of size 256×256 and 256 gray levels is employed. It is shown in Fig.3(a) while its histogram is given in Fig.3(b). After fifteen rounds of the confusion process, the ciphered image obtained is shown in Fig.3(c), its corresponding histogram found in Fig.3(d). As we can see, the histogram of the ciphered image is fairly uniform and significantly different from that of the original image.

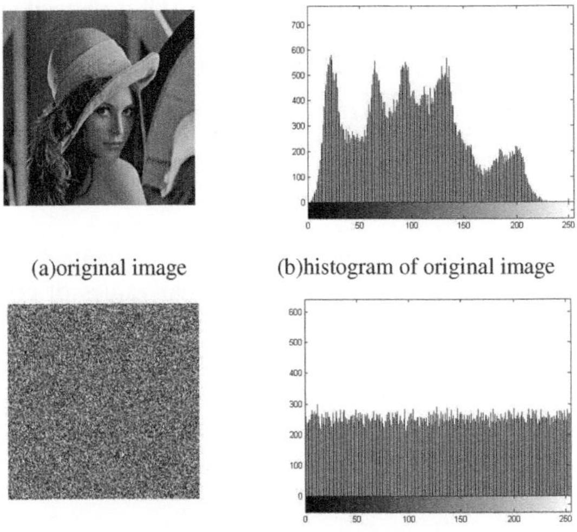

(a)original image (b)histogram of original image

(c)encrypted image (d)histogram of encrypted image

Fig. 3. image and its histogram

3.3 The Original Image Sensitivity

In differential attacks, some original images with little difference may be selected to analyze the according difference between their encrypted forms. In this way, opponent maybe able to find out arrelationship between the original image and its encrypted form. Thus, much difference between encrypted forms is expected in order to keep high security. The original image sensitivity is the most analyzed by NPCR and UACI [4]–[11].

The number of pixel change rate (NPCR) stands for the number of pixels changed in the encrypted form when only one pixel value is changed in original image. The larger the NPCR is, the higher sensitivity the original image has and the more difficult the system's security against differential attack is. Let two encrypted images of the same size be A and B, where A has only one pixel difference. Then NPCR is defined as:

$$NPCR = \frac{\sum_{i,j} D(i,j)}{W \times H} \times 100\% \tag{8}$$

where W and H are the width and the height of images and $D(i,j)$ is bipolar array defined as:

$$D(i,j) = \begin{cases} 0 & A(i,j)=B(i,j) \\ 1 & A(i,j)\neq B(i,j) \end{cases}$$

The UACI measures the average intensity of the differences between the original image and the ciphered image. The larger the UACI is, the more resistant to the differential attack the system will get. And the UACI is defined as:

$$UACI = \frac{1}{W \times H}\left[\sum_{i,j} \frac{\left|A(i,j) - B(i,j)\right|}{255}\right] \times 100\% \tag{9}$$

Where the expression $A(i,j)$ or $B(i,j)$ means the pixel in the position (i,j) of the image.

When we test the original image sensitivity, we changed grayscale value of pixel at the grid (150,191) from 81 to 82. And the real values of NPCR and UACI in the different encryption round are given in Fig.4 and TABLE 2.

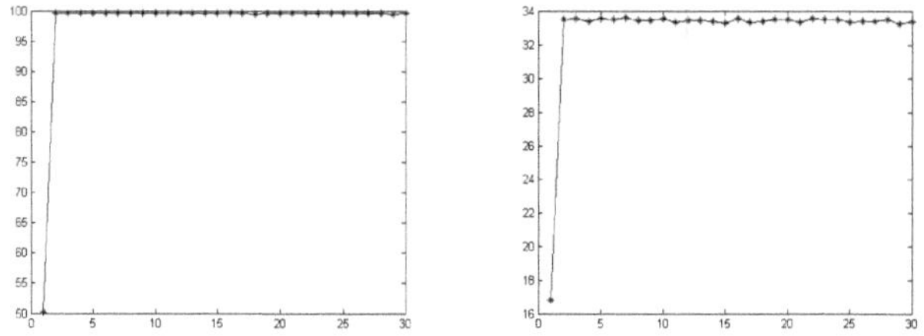

(a)NPCR vs. encryption rounds (b)UACI vs. encryption rounds

Fig. 4. NPCR,UACI vs. encryption rounds

Table 2. Relationship between encryption rounds and NPCR,UACI

rounds	1	2	3	4	5
NPCR(%)	50.1758	99.5992	99.6549	99.6528	99.5842
UACI(%)	16.7975	33.4738	33.5627	33.4051	33.5723
rounds	10	15	20	25	30
NPCR(%)	99.6614	99.5692	99.6592	99.5863	99.6013
UACI(%)	33.5397	33.3036	33.5262	33.3308	33.4048

The results in Fig.4 and TABLE 2 have both shown that the NPCR and UACI are high enough to confirm that the two images are very different. It is obvious that the proposed encryption algorithm is resistant against differential attacks only after second encryption round.

4 Conclusion

In this article, a new digital image encryption algorithm is proposed. And a large number of simulation experiments were carried out, all the experimental results show that the proposed encryption algorithm has very good diffusion properties, is sufficient for practical usage in terms of security, and is a very effective encryption algorithm.

References

1. Castleman, K.R.: Digital Image Processing. Prentice Hall, Inc., Englewood Cliffs (1996)
2. Gonzalez, R.C., Woods, R.E.: Digital Image Processing, 2nd edn. Electronic Industry Press (2003) (in Chinese)
3. Gonzalez, R.C., Woods, R.E., Eddins, S.L.: Digital Image Processing Using MATLAB. Electronic Industry Press (2004)
4. Chen, G.R., Wang, X.F.: Dynamical Systems Chaos Theory, Methods and Applications, pp. 80–105. Shanghai Jiaotong University Press (2006) (in Chinese)
5. Qi, D.X., Zou, J.C., Han, X.Y.: A New Class of Scrambling Transformation and Its Application in the Image Information Covering. Science in China(Series E) 43(3), 304–312 (2000)
6. Zhang, Y.W., Wang, Y.M., Shen, X.B.: A chaos-based on image encryption algorithm using alternate structure. Science in China(Series F) 50(3), 334–341 (2007)
7. Giesl, J., Vlcek, K.: Image encryption based on strange attractor. ICGST-GVIP Journal 9(2), 19–26 (2009)
8. Tian, Y., Xie, Y.B., Liu, J.: Based on block and chaotic network of image scrambling method. Image and Graphics 12(1), 56–60 (2007) (in Chinese)
9. Zhao, L.L., Fang, Z.L., Gu, Z.C.: A new digital image-based cube transform scrambling encryption algorithm. Optoelectronics. Laser 19(1), 131–134 (2008) (in Chinese)
10. Jastrzdeþski, K., Kotulski, Z.: On Improved Image Encryption Scheme Based on Chaotic Map Lattices. Engng. Trans. 57, 69–84 (2009)
11. Awad, A., Awad, D.: Efficient Image Chaotic Encryption Algorithm With No Propagation Error. ETRI Journal 32(5), 774–783 (2010)

Innovation Pattern Recognition of Equipment Manufacturing Industry Based on Jing You Method*

Hou Xi-lin[1], Zhang Li-li[1], Liu Sen[2], and Zhao Xi-nan[2]

[1] School of Business Administration University of Science and Technology LiaoNing Anshan, Liaoning 114051, China

[2] School of Business Administration University of Northeastern Shenyang, liaoning Province, 110004, China

houxilin2525@qq.com

Abstract. Innovation pattern recognition of equipment manufacturing has been attached great importance to scholars and practitioners. Based on the analysis of primary pattern recognition methods, choose match better conforming to rules method to recognize each type of equipment manufacturing industry innovation pattern. It is a quantitative recognition method, which relies on ideal solution evaluation method, the innovation pattern is expressed by weight structure which can show the industry performs better or not from every recognition indicator's perspective, according to the innovation recognition indicator system constructed and the relevant data of each type, the innovation pattern characteristic of each type included in the industry is analyzed specifically and hierarchically. Countermeasures and suggestion are put forward based on the analysis result.

Keywords: equipment manufacturing industry, technological innovation, pattern recognition, structure characteristic.

1 Introduction

Equipment manufacturing industry is the general term of enterprises which provides technical equipment for national economy and national security, and is the industry which manufactures various kinds of technical equipment to meet the development need from each department of national economy. With the pace of economic globalization continuing to accelerate and international economic competition becomes increasingly fierce, technological innovation plays a decisive role in enhancing international competitiveness and enterprise's survival and development. There are seven types of equipment manufacturing enterprises, recognition innovation pattern of equipment manufacturing industry for each type is important for the relevant management departments to give the right guide for the development.

Aiming at the pattern recognition problem of equipment manufacturing industry with innovation characteristics, a pattern recognition method based on match better

* This work is partially supported by NSF Grand#70971016 and Liaoning province society science fund Grand#2009A367.

D. Zeng (Ed.): ICAIC 2011, Part I, CCIS 224, pp. 278–285, 2011.

conforming to the natural rule model is put forward. According to the indicator data of equipment manufacturing industry, relying on the ideal solution evaluation model, data mining each individual equipment manufacture innovation characteristics. The calculation result can provide some support for decision making.

2 Literature Review

The pattern recognition is theory of research classification recognition and the method and is a comprehensive and overlapping discipline. As pattern recognition becomes more and more popular in modern economics and management research, lots of papers research on this field, not only from the perspective of recognition method, but also from the perspective of analyzing one specific industry. For example, on one hand, SHI Xiao-jun (2005) put forward a development pattern analysis method based on FA-DEA clustering, which consists of three key steps: model classification; model comparison and model evolution analysis[1]. ZHAO Xi-nan etal(2009) on the basis of identifying individual advantage characteristic of the regional scientific and technical capability, an analytic method of regional science and technology development pattern is proposed. From individual value—orientation in society system, individuals were put up the hierarchical cluster and democracy proxy evaluation, and all patterns were analyzed. Scientific and technical development patterns of 31 provincial regions in China in 2002-2004 were analyzed by this method. On the second perspective[2]. Zhang Shao-jie Tang Zhong-bin(2007) research on enterprise knowledge innovation dynamic model with four-dimensional based on porter's five forces model[3]. Tang Jun(2006) researched on automotive industry innovation pattern based on indigenous development, he studies on the background and the significance of industrial innovation pattern in our country's automotive industry. It analyzed Japan and Korea[4]. ZHANG Cheng-hu etal(2007) aiming at money laundering through financial institutions, the combination of intelligence information technology and KYC Standard provides a new way for anti-money laundering work to increase the recognition rate of suspicious client to apply the pattern recognition technology to anti-money laundering field, a clustering based method for client transaction behavior pattern recognition is proposed to identify the suspicious client who has the abnormal transaction behavior through judging whether the client transaction behavior pattern is normal[5]. And XU Xiao- min (2009) analyses complexity of social, economic and engineering problem, defines the pattern from some sides of theory, method and technology and points out that the aim of research is to enhance the validity of applying pattern further[6].

Nowadays, quantitative methods for identifying innovation pattern of equipment manufacturing industry are quite few, they tool lack analysis capability, can only recognize single layer innovation pattern characteristics. Furthermore, the analysis may be not in great detail and specific, and it may lose lots of useful information. Recognition innovation pattern based on qualitative methods is difficult to reach a consensus, since the conclusions always vary from person to person, which are hard to reach a consensus.

This paper applies match better conforming to the natural rules recognition method, equipment manufacturing industry innovation pattern is identified. It is a quantitative analysis method, which can data mine individual and group structure characteristics hierarchically through the expression of weights to help managers and analysts identify and to classify their focus of business innovation pattern. And seven types of equipment manufacturing industry recognition show that the method is more efficient than human recognition and other quantitative method. This research contributes to a better understanding of how equipment manufacturing industry innovation, which innovation indicator paid more attention, and which less, it can also identify the difference between different type of equipment manufacturing industry.

3 Innovation Pattern Recognition Model of Different Type of Equipment Manufacturing Industry Based on Ideal Solution Evaluation Method

Summarizing the industry evolution progress, it is not difficult to find that industry develops and makes progress as enterprises actively exploring and acting in accordance with evolution rules. However, the complexity of the development rule and subjectivity of cognition inevitably bring different feelings, views and handling ways to different enterprises with the innovation problem. So from the perspective of encouraging innovation, according to the situation of different type of equipment manufacturing industry has different internal and external environment, the recognition method had better not have the function of comparing between different types of equipment manufacturing industries. Based on the above analysis, this paper applies the ideal solution evaluation method to recognize innovation pattern.

Considering most of the recognition indicator system is hierarchical structure, supposing the recognition indicator structure is as following:

1)from the point of view of the ith type of equipment manufacturing industry, middle level indicator k to its basic level pattern recognition model:

$$\begin{aligned} &\min_{\lambda} d_{ik}^2(\vec{x}_i,\vec{x}^*) = \sum_{j=1}^{p_k} \lambda_{ikj}^2 \left(x_{ikj}^* - x_{ikj}\right)^2 \\ &s.t: \sum_{j=1}^{p_k} \lambda_{ikj} = 1 \\ &\lambda_{ikj} \geq 0 \quad j=1,2,\cdots p_k \end{aligned} \tag{1}$$

2)from the point of view of the ith type of equipment manufacturing industry, top to middle level innovation pattern recognition model:

$$\begin{aligned} &\min_{\mu} d_i^2(\vec{y}_i,\vec{y}^*) = \sum_{k=1}^{m} \mu_{ik}^2 (y_{ik} - y_{ik}^*)^2 \\ &s.t: \sum_{k=1}^{m} \mu_{ik} = 1 \\ &\mu_{ik} \geq 0, k = 1,2,..., m \end{aligned} \tag{2}$$

$y_{ik}^{2} = \sum_{j=1}^{p_k} (\lambda_{ikj}^{*})^{2} (x_{ikj}^{*} - x_{ikj})^{2}$. y_{ik}^{*} is the ideal value of the kth indicator, and $x_{ikj}^{*} = x_{ikj}$, $y_{ik}^{*} = 0$.

错误！未找到引用源。. INNOVATION PATTERN RECOGNITION OF EQUIPMENT MANUFACTURING INDUSTRY

The evaluation index system follows "systematic, scientific, comparability, guidance, feasible principle" and so on, further more, at the process of constructing the index system, relevant research and policies also be considered, taking all factors into consideration, the scientific and technological innovation ability evaluation index system of sub-province cities are determined. According to the previous researches[7], equipment manufacturing innovation index system can be expressed as the following:

(1)y_1:guarantee and support capability of innovation.

It includes:

x_{11}:total number of people for scientific and technological activities(ten thousand people);

x_{12}: gross industrial output(billion yuan);

x_{13}: the ratio of micro-electronics control equipment original price to production and management original price(%);

(2)y_2: innovative resources investment capacity:

x_{21}: the ratio of R&D people to total employed person (%);

x_{22}: the ratio of R&D expenditure to sales revenue (%);

x_{23}: the ratio of scientific and technological activities expenditure to sales revenue (%);

x_{24}: the ratio of enterprises with scientific research institution to total enterprises (%);

x_{25}:the ratio of new-product development expenditure to sales revenue (%);

(3)y_3: conversion of science and technology into real productivity capability;

x_{31}: the ratio of digestion and absorption expenditure to of technology introduced expenditure (%);

x_{32}:the ratio of technological transformation expenditure to sales revenue (%);

x_{33}: the ratio of new product development project number to scientific and technological activities project number (%) ;

y_4: scientific and technological output capability:

x_{41}: number of patent for invention per ten thousand employed persons;

x_{42}: the ratio of new-product sales revenue to total sales revenue (%);

y_5: scientific and technological innovation environmental protection capability:

x_{51}: output value of the integrated energy million(tce);

x_{52}: attainment rate of the industrial waste water(%);

x_{53}: comprehensive utilization rate of industrial solid wastes (%).

There are seven types of equipment manufacturing industry, the name is shown in table 1:

Table 1. Seven types of equipment manufacturing enterprises

Code	Type
I_1	metal product industry
I_2	ordinary machinery
I_3	special equipment manufacturing industry
I_4	transport Equipment
I_5	electric mechanism and equipment manufacture
I_6	manufacture of communication equipment, computers and other electronic equipment
I_7	instrumentation and culture, office machinery manufacturing

According to model(1) and (2), the innovation pattern can be obtained in the following table2-table6.

Table 2. z innovation pattern recognition

	Y_1	Y_2	Y_3	Y_4	Y_5
I_1	0.00	0.00	0.00	0.50	0.50
I_2	0.02	0.41	0.34	0.03	0.20
I_3	0.00	0.50	0.50	0.00	0.00
I_4	0.50	0.00	0.00	0.50	0.00
I_5	0.00	0.50	0.50	0.00	0.00
I_6	0.20	0.20	0.20	0.20	0.20
I_7	0.00	0.02	0.18	0.56	0.24

Table 3. y_1 innovation pattern recognition

	X_{11}	X_{12}	X_{13}
I_1	0.33	0.35	0.33
I_2	0.63	0.18	0.19
I_3	0.55	0.24	0.21
I_4	1.00	0.00	0.00
I_5	0.51	0.28	0.20
I_6	0.00	0.50	0.50
I_7	0.30	0.29	0.41

Table 4. y_2 innovation pattern recognition

	X_{21}	X_{22}	X_{23}	X_{24}	X_{25}
I_1	0.20	0.20	0.20	0.20	0.20
I_2	0.09	0.25	0.37	0.15	0.15
I_3	0.00	0.00	0.33	0.33	0.33
I_4	0.92	0.02	0.03	0.03	0.01
I_5	0.00	1.00	0.00	0.00	0.00
I_6	1.00	0.00	0.00	0.00	0.00
I_7	0.37	0.14	0.09	0.31	0.09

Table 5. y_3 innovation pattern recognition

	X_{31}	X_{32}	X_{33}
I_1	0. 22	0. 60	0. 18
I_2	0. 01	0. 76	0. 23
I_3	0. 00	1. 00	0. 00
I_4	0. 03	0. 91	0. 06
I_5	1. 00	0. 00	0. 00
I_6	0. 00	0. 00	1. 00
I_7	0. 00	0. 01	0. 99

Table 6. y_4 innovation pattern recognition

	X_{41}	X_{42}	X_{43}	X_{44}
I_1	1.00	0.00	0.00	0.00
I_2	0.13	0.52	0.16	0.20
I_3	0.35	0.43	0.10	0.12
I_4	0.00	1.00	0.00	0.00
I_5	0.44	0.35	0.09	0.13
I_6	0.00	0.00	0.50	0.50
I_7	0.01	0.00	0.00	0.99

Table 7. y_5 innovation pattern recognition

	X_{51}	X_{52}	X_{53}
I_1	0. 00	0. 00	1. 00
I_2	0. 10	0. 89	0. 01
I_3	0. 81	0. 09	0. 09
I_4	0. 06	0. 94	0. 00
I_5	0. 80	0. 19	0. 01
I_6	0. 50	0. 50	0. 00
I_7	0. 84	0. 16	0. 00

Relying on the strategy of "rejuvenating our country through science and education", every type of equipment manufacturing industry performs actively, cultivates science and technology innovation ability according to the need of building the innovative country and integrate the characteristic of itself. And every type has its own distinguishing innovation pattern features.

(1) Analysis of the top grade indicator based on the second grade indicators' performance

From the perspective of obtaining the best result for each field of equipment manufacturing enterprises, the first indicator result expressed by second grade indicators innovation pattern characteristics is shown in Table 1, According to the calculation result, metal product industry pays attention on both "scientific and technological output capability" and "attainment rate of the industrial waste water(%)", but performs relatively poor on "guarantee and support capability of innovation", "innovative resources investment capacity" and "conversion of science and technology into real productivity capability". Ordinary machinery performs best on "innovative resources investment capacity", better on "conversion of science and technology into real productivity capability", performs normally on "scientific and technological innovation environmental protection capability", but performs not quite well on "scientific and technological output capability" or "guarantee and support capability of innovation". Along the same lines, other three fields of industries innovation pattern can be analyzed.

(2) Analysis of the basic grade indicators
According to table 2, from the point of view of "guarantee and support capability of innovation", metal product industry performs equally on "x_{11}:total number of people for scientific and technological activities(ten thousand people)", "x_{12}: gross industrial output(billion yuan) " and "x_{13}: the ratio of micro-electronics control equipment original price to production and management original price(%)". Different from the innovation pattern of "metal product industry", "ordinary machinery" attach more attention on " total number of people for scientific and technological activities(ten thousand people)", but performs relatively poor on "the ratio of R&D expenditure to sales revenue (%)" and "the ratio of micro-electronics control equipment original price to production and management original price(%)".the innovation pattern of the other fields can be analyzed following the same way.

The innovation pattern of "the ratio of digestion and absorption expenditure to of technology introduced expenditure (%)", "scientific and technological output capability" and "scientific and technological innovation environmental protection capability" can be analyzed in the same way.

4 Conclusions and Suggestions

Science and technology innovation ability means the ability to transform science and technology into new products, techniques and services. It is important for cultivating core competency of equipment manufacturing industry. Takes the thought of match better conforming to natural rule as a guide[8], serving for the system with indicators of hierarchical structure, an equipment manufacturing industry innovation pattern recognition model based on each type of equipment manufacturing industry individual advantage value parameters as indicator weights is built up. It is helpful to recognize equipment manufacturing innovation pattern, improving the way of analyzing by decision makers, providing analysis method support for relevant strategies.

References

1. Shi, X.-j.: A Development Pattern Analysis Method Based on FA-DEA Clustering with its Application in China Software Parks Research. Mathematics in Practice and Theory 35(4), 140–148 (2005)
2. Zhao, X.-n., Wang, Y.-m., Jing, K.: Individual Advantage Characteristic Identifying-Based Patterns of Regional Science and Technology Development and Its Application. Chinese Journal of Management 6(4), 541–545 (2009)

3. Zhang, S.-j., Tang, Z.-b.: Research on four-dimensional dynamical enterprises knowledge innovation pattern based on Five Competitive Forces of Porter Model. Journal of Information 26(8), 25–27 (2007)
4. Tang, J.: Research on Automotive Industry Innovation Pattern Basing on Indigenous Development. Wu Han University of Technology Press (2006)
5. Zhang, C.-h., Yue, X., Yue, H.: Client transaction behavior pattern recognition based on clustering method. Computer Engineering and Applications 43(10), 195–198 (2007)
6. Zhang, C.-h., Yue, X., Yue, H.: Client transaction behavior pattern recognition based on clustering method. Computer Engineering and Applications 43(10), 195–198 (2007)
7. Wang, Z.-b., Sun-chen: Research on equipment manufacturing industry technology innovation ability based on PCA. Journal of Industrial Technology Economics 26(12), 63–68 (2007)
8. Zhao, X.-n., Liu, B.-d., Xu, H.-m.: A Study on the Impact of the Thought of Conforming to the Natural Rule on the Progress of Human Society. Chinese Journal of Science, Technology and Dialectics 23(2), 32–35 (2006)

Face Recognition Using Discrete Cosine Transform and Fuzzy Linear Discriminant Analysis*

Qi-wen Zhang, Wen-xia Du, Liu-qing Yuan, and Ming Li

School of Computer and Communication LanZhou University of Technology
LanZhou, China
qi17262@sina.com

Abstract. In order to solve the problem of uncertainty that occurred in the field of face recognition because of the variations of the facial expressions, illuminations and poses as well, a new feature extraction method for face recognition is proposed in this paper. The method combines the DCT with FLDA. Firstly, DCT is performed on the entire face image to obtain all the components in the frequency domain. Due to the energy compaction, only the lower frequency components will be retained and thus, the dimension reduced features are obtained, then FLDA is employed to extract the most discriminating features. Finally, the nearest neighbor classifier is employed for classification. The results of experiments conducted on Olivetti Research Laboratory (ORL) database show that the proposed method is better than other methods in terms of accurate recognition rate.

Keywords: Face Recognition, Feature Extraction, Discrete Cosine Transform, Fuzzy Linear Discriminant Analysis.

1 Introduction

Face recognition is a challenge task in biometrics, pattern recognition field and computer vision communities. It has been an active research area in the past few years because of its potential applications in areas such as security systems, identify authentication, video telephony, medicine, and so on. In face recognition, feature extraction is one of the most important steps, and it performs the reduction of high dimensional image data into low dimensional feature vectors. The popular feature extraction techniques most frequently used with face recognition are principal component analysis (PCA), linear discriminant analysis (LDA), independent component analysis (ICA), and so on. These methods extract features in image domain. In recent years, some researchers have investigated the possibility of extracting features in frequency domain, such as the space obtained by performing discrete cosine transform (DCT) [1,2,3]. The results have shown that it is feasible and promising to extract discriminatory frequency components for classification. Hafed and Levine [1] used DCT for face recognition. They pointed out that DCT obtains the

* This work is partially supported by Natural Science Foundation of Gansu Province (0803RJZA025) and Science Foundation of Gansu Education Department (0803-07).

D. Zeng (Ed.): ICAIC 2011, Part I, CCIS 224, pp. 286–293, 2011.

optimal performance of Karhunen-Loeve Transform (KLT) in facial information compression and the performance of DCT is superior to conventional transforms. But DCT is based on statistical characterization, it is not to effectively use the class information of samples. LDA can use the priori class information, and extract the optimal discriminant features. So the combination of DCT and LDA is proposed by YH. Zhang et al. [4], they claim that a more robust face recognition system can be obtained by the combination of these well-known appearance based techniques. They firstly use the DCT to achieve dimension reduction, then LDA transform is performed on the lower space to extract features. But LDA is based on binary classification criterion. While in face recognition, distribution of face samples is often affected by illumination, expression, and pose et al., performance of LDA may degenerate. Thus, fuzzy theory is introduced by Kwak et al. [5], they propose a fuzzy linear discriminant analysis (FLDA) for face recognition, which makes full use of the distribution of samples. Samples distribution information is represented by fuzzy membership degree corresponding to every class.

In this paper, we propose a feature extraction method to enhance the image classification information and improve the recognition results. The proposed method combines the DCT with FLDA. The organization of this paper is as follows: In Section 2, we briefly review the DCT and FLDA face recognitions techniques. In Section 3, we present the proposed method. In Section 4, experiments with face images data are presented to demonstrate the effectiveness of the new method. Conclusions are summarized in Section 5.

2 Overview of DCT and FLDA Based Methods

2.1 Discrete Cosine Transform (DCT)

The DCT [6] is a popular technique in image and video compression, which transforms signals from the spatial representation into a frequency representation. The 2D-DCT for an input $M \times N$ image is defined by

$$C(u,v) = a(u)a(v)\sum_{x=0}^{M-1}\sum_{y=0}^{N-1} f(x,y) \times \cos\frac{(2x+1)u\pi}{2M}\cos\frac{(2y+1)v\pi}{2N} \tag{1}$$

where $u = 0,1\cdots,M-1$, $v = 0,1\cdots,N-1$ and the function $a(u)$, $a(v)$ are defined by

$$a(u) = \begin{cases} \sqrt{1/M}, & u = 0 \\ \sqrt{2/M}, & u = 1,2\cdots,M-1 \end{cases} \tag{2}$$

$$a(v) = \begin{cases} \sqrt{1/N}, & v = 0 \\ \sqrt{2/N}, & v = 1,2\cdots,N-1 \end{cases} \tag{3}$$

For an $M \times N$ face image, we have an $M \times N$ DCT coefficient matrix covering all the spatial frequency components of the image. Fig. 1 shows the application of the DCT on one of the face images obtained from the ORL database and zig-zag pattern. Fig. 1(a) displays a 92×112 8-bit image, and Fig. 1(b) displays the result of applying the DCT on the face image. From Fig. 1(b), it can be observed that most information or energy of the image is concentrated in the upper-left corner of the DCT coefficient matrix. Accordingly, we can scan the DCT coefficient matrix in a zig-zag pattern as shown in Fig. 1(c), starting from the upper-left corner and subsequently convert it to a one-dimensional vector. We select the largest m coefficients to reconstruct the original image. References[7] has been proved that the reconstructed image maintained the main facial features such as outline of hair and face, position of eyes, nose and mouth. These facial features are more stable than the variable high-frequency facial features.

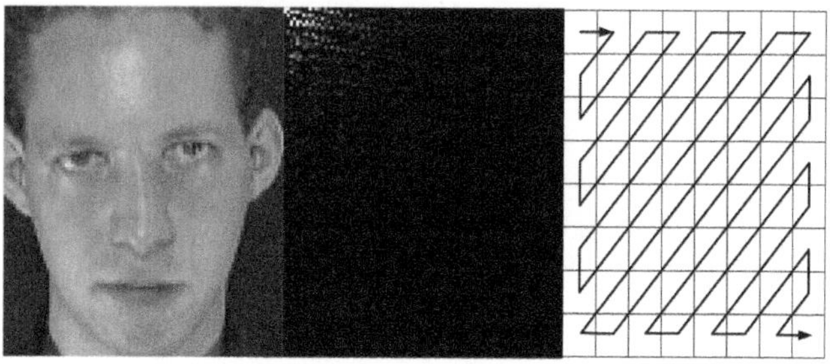

(a)92×112 face image (b)its DCT coefficients (c)zig-zag pattern

Fig. 1. Face image and its DCT coefficients

2.2 Fuzzy Linear Discriminant Analysis (FLDA)

1) Linear Discriminant Analysis (LDA)

LDA is one of the powerful tools used for feature extraction and dimensionality reduction in most of pattern recognition applications [8]. The objective of LDA is to find the optimal projection so that the ratio of between-class scatter and the within-class scatter is maximized.

Suppose there are L known pattern classes $w_1, w_2, \cdots, w_L$ and N number of n-dimensional training samples. $X = \{x_i^j \mid i = 1, \cdots, L; j = 1, \cdots, N_i\}$ is a set of samples. x_i^j is the jth sample of class i. N_i is the number of training samples of class i and satisfies $N = \sum_{i=1}^{L} N_i$. $u_i = \frac{1}{N_i} \sum_{j=1}^{N_i} x_i^j$ is the mean image of class w_i, $u = \frac{1}{N} \sum_{i=1}^{L} \sum_{j=1}^{N_i} x_i^j$ is the mean image of all samples.

Then, the between-class scatter matrix is define as

$$S_b = \frac{1}{N} \sum_{i=1}^{L} N_i (u_i - u)(u_i - u)^T. \tag{4}$$

the within-class scatter matrix is define as

$$S_w = \frac{1}{N}\sum_{i=1}^{L}\sum_{j=1}^{N_i}\left(x_i^j - u_i\right)\left(x_i^j - u_i\right)^T. \tag{5}$$

and total-class scatter matrix is define as

$$S_t = S_b + S_w \tag{6}$$

Now, the optimal projection W_{LDA} is

$$W_{LDA} = \arg\max_W \frac{\left|W^T S_b W\right|}{\left|W^T S_w W\right|} = \left[w_1, w_2, \cdots, w_d\right] \tag{7}$$

where $w_1, w_2, \cdots, w_d$ are satisfied $S_b w = \lambda_i S_w w$.

2) Fuzzy Linear Discriminant Analysis (FLDA)

Classical linear discriminant analysis is based on binary classification criterion. That is to say, to be assigned sample, hard criterion is adopted and the sample belongs to one class or another class strictly. This condition can be not application in some circumstances. Thus, fuzzy linear discriminant analysis via fuzzy technology to overcome the limitation of classical LDA.

Suppose $Z_j\left(j = 1, 2, \cdots, N\right)$ is a set of feature vectors, and the membership matrix is $U = \left[u_{ij}\right]$, $i = 1, 2, \cdots, L$, $j = 1, 2, \cdots, N$, where L is the number of class, N is the number of training samples, u_{ij} is the membership grade of jth sample in the ith class satisfying the following two constraints: $\sum_{i=1}^{C} u_{ij} = 1$ and $0 < \sum_{i=1}^{N} u_{ij} < 1$, and u_{ij} can be gained through FKNN[9] algorithm, the steps are as follows:

Step1: Compute the Euclidean distance matrix between pairs of feature vectors in training samples.

Step2: Set diagonal elements of this Euclidean distance matrix to infinity.

Step3: Sort the distance matrix (treat each of its columns separately) in an ascending order. Collect the corresponding class labels of the patterns located in the closest neighborhood of the pattern under consideration (as we are concerned with '*k*' neighbors, this returns a list of '*k*' integers).

Step4: Compute the membership degree to class '*i*' for *j*th pattern using the expression proposed in the literature [5]

$$u_{ij} = \begin{cases} 0.51 + 0.49 \times \left(n_{ij}/k\right) & \text{If } i \text{ is the same as the label of the } j\text{th pattern} \\ 0.49 \times \left(n_{ij}/k\right) & \text{If } i \text{ is not the same as the label of the } j\text{th pattern} \end{cases} \tag{8}$$

where n_{ij} stands for the number of the neighbors of the jth pattern that belong to the ith class.

Therefore, the fuzzy membership matrix U can be achieved with the result of FKNN. Taking into account the fuzzy membership degrees, the mean vector of each class is

$$fm_i = \sum_{j=1}^{N} u_{ij}^p Z_j \Big/ \sum_{j=1}^{N} u_{ij}^p \tag{9}$$

Then, the membership degree of each sample (contribution to each class) should be considered and the corresponding fuzzy within-class scatter matrix S_{FW} , fuzzy between-class scatter matrix S_{FB} and fuzzy total scatter matrix S_{FT} can be redefined as follow [10]:

$$S_{FW} = \sum_{i=1}^{L} \sum_{Z_j \in w_i} u_{ij}^p \left(Z_j - fm_i\right)\left(Z_j - fm_i\right)^T. \tag{10}$$

$$S_{FB} = \sum_{i=1}^{L} \sum_{j=1}^{N} u_{ij}^p \left(fm_i - \overline{Z}\right)\left(fm_i - \overline{Z}\right)^T \tag{11}$$

$$S_{FT} = S_{FB} + S_{FW}. \tag{12}$$

where $\overline{Z}$ is the mean of all samples. p is a constant which controls the influence of fuzzy membership degree. In this paper, we take p=2.

The optimal fuzzy projection W_{FLDA} of FLDA follows the expression:

$$W_{FLDA} = \arg\max_{W} \frac{\left|W^T S_{FB} W\right|}{\left|W^T S_{FW} W\right|} = \left[w_1, w_2, \cdots, w_d\right] \tag{13}$$

3 The Proposed Method

In this section we present our methodology for combining two appearance-based (or statistical) methods for face recognition: the DCT and the FLDA. In the method, DCT is first of all applied to the face image and the DCT coefficient matrix is calculated and then we scan the DCT coefficient matrix in a zig-zag pattern, starting from the upper-left corner and subsequently convert it to a one-dimensional vector. We retain the largest m coefficients. This is done to reduce the dimensionality. Second, FLDA transform is used to extract the optimal discriminant features on DCT domain. After acquiring feature vectors with FLDA, the next step is to classify an unknown face image. In this paper, a Nearest Neighbor (NN) classifier is used to decide the class of an unknown face image. The main steps of our method can be summarized as follows:

Step1: Perform DCT on the images of the training samples and retain the largest m coefficients in the upper-left corner as the coefficient vectors Z .

Step2: Perform FKNN on the coefficient vectors Z . The fuzzy membership degree matrix U and the mean vector of each class fm can be got by using Eq. 8 and Eq. 9.

Step3: Compute the scatter matrices S_{FW}, S_{FB}, and S_{FT} respectively.

Step4: Compute the optimal set of discriminant vectors W_{FLDA} using Eq. 13.

Step5: Perform DCT on the images of the testing samples and get the coefficient vectors, then project coefficient vectors into the obtained optimal discriminant vectors and classification.

4 Experimental Results and Analysis

The experiment uses ORL (Olivetti Research Laboratory) face database to demonstrate the efficiency of our method. It is composed of 400 individual images of 40 persons. For each person, there are 10 images with various in illumination, pose, facial expression and accessories. They are gray-scale images and the resolution of each image is 92×112. Fig.2 shows ten images of one person in the ORL database.

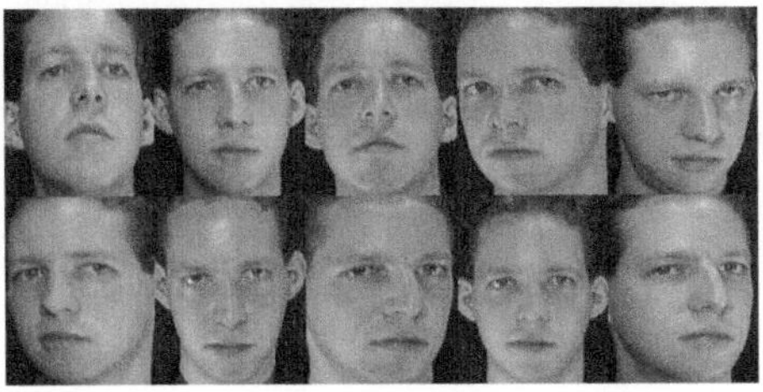

Fig. 2. Ten images of one person in the ORL database

The first experiment was performed using 5 images per class for training and the remaining 5 images for testing. In the experiment, we preserve 39 feature vectors. The recognition rate with the different number of DCT coefficients is shown in Fig.3.

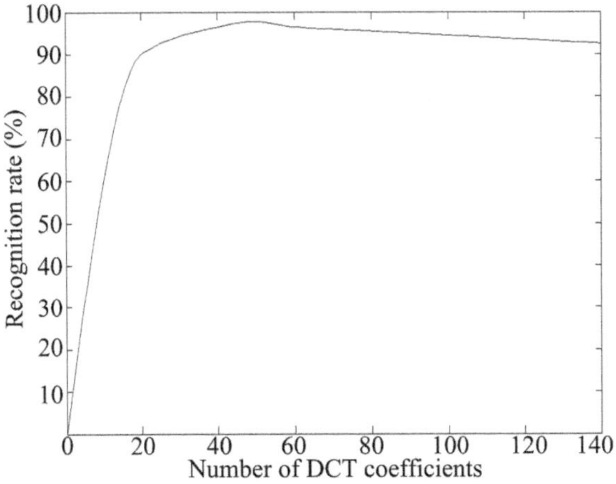

Fig. 3. Recognition rate with the different number of DCT coefficients

From Fig.3, we can see that the recognition rate is highest when the number of DCT coefficients extracted is about 50. This is because DCT coefficients extracted are the low-frequency coefficients of the larger values and the main facial features such as outline of hair and face, position of eyes, nose and mouth contained in the low-frequency coefficients. However, the removed coefficients are the high-frequency coefficients of the small values, which are sensitive to illumination, expression and pose variations. So more coefficients do not increase recognition rate. Instead it will introduce much unfavorable information and recognition effect will be bad.

In the second experiment, recognition rates with different number of training samples are tested. *K* images of each person are randomly selected for training and the remaining images for testing, where $3 \le k \le 9$. We select 49 DCT coefficients and preserve 39 feature vectors for the experiment. The experiment is carried 20 times for each *K* and the average result is show in Table 1.

Table 1. Recognition rates with different number of training samples (%)

K	*PCA+FLDA*	*DCT+LDA*	*Our method*
3	89.50	91.05	93.70
4	91.55	93.85	95.85
5	92.50	96.50	97.85
6	92.85	96.85	98.15
7	93.65	97.50	98.35
8	95.40	98.05	98.60
9	95.75	99.00	99.00

From Table 1, we can see that the proposed method outperforms PCA+FLDA and DCT+LDA methods. Why can our method outperform other methods? First, PCA is the optimal representation under the least mean square error, but the optimal representation contains some irrelevant and redundant information such as illumination, expression and poses variations. While DCT effectively discards the high-frequency information, and the remaining information are not sensitive to face expression, pose and illumination. Second, FLDA makes full use of the distribution of samples and samples distribution information is represented by fuzzy membership degree corresponding to every class. So the proposed method outperforms other methods.

5 Conclusion

A new feature extraction method for face recognition has been proposed in this paper. The proposed method combines the DCT with FLDA. The main advantage of the DCT transform is that it can be used as a dimensionality reduction step and it has speeded up computational. FLDA makes full use of the distribution of samples and considers the fuzzy membership degree in the scatter matrix. So the combination of DCT and FLDA enhances the discriminatory power and reduces the computational speed. The results of experiments on the ORL database show that the proposed method is effective and outperforms other methods.

References

1. Hafed, Z.M., Levine, M.D.: Face recognition using the discrete cosine transform. International Journal of Computer Vision 43, 167–188 (2001)
2. Er, M.J., Chen, W.L., Wu, S.Q.: High-speed face recognition based on discrete cosine transform and rbf neural networks. IEEE Transactions on Neural Networks 16, 679–691 (2005)
3. Liu, N., Wang, H.: Feature selection in frequency domain and its application to face recognition. In: 2008 International Joint Conference on Neural Networks (IJCNN 2008), pp. 3967–3972 (June 2008)
4. Zhang, Y.K., Liu, C.Q.: Efficient face recognition method based on DCT and LDA. Journal of Systems Engineering and Electronics 15, 211–216 (2004)
5. Kwak, K.C., Pedrycz, W.: Face recognition using a fuzzy fisherface classifier. Pattern Recognition 38, 1717–1732 (2005)
6. Yin, H.T., Fu, P., Qiao, J.Q.: Face recognition based on DCT and 2DLDA. In: Second International Conference on Innovative Computing, Information and Control, pp. 581–584 (2007)
7. Chen, Y.H., Zhao, Y.: Face recognition using DCT and hierarchical RBF model. In: Intelligent Data Engineering and Automated Learning, pp. 355–362 (2006)
8. Belhumeur, P.N., HesPanha, J.P., Kriegman, D.J.: Eigenfaces vs. Fisherfaces: Recognition using class specific linear projection. IEEE Transaction on Pattern Analysis and Machine Intelligence 19, 711–720 (1997)
9. Keller, J.M., Gray, M.R., Givens, J.A.: A fuzzy k-nearest neighbor algorithm. IEEE Transactions on Systems, Man, and Cybernetics 15, 580–585 (1985)
10. Yang, W.K., Wang, J.G., Ren, M.W., Zhang, L., Yang, J.Y.: Feature extraction using fuzzy inverse FDA. Neurocomputing 72, 3384–3390 (2009)

Morbidity Research on Grey Forecast Model

Ying Wei

Computer Department, Wuhan Polytechnic
wuhan, Hubei, China
Yingying1970@live.cn

Abstract. This paper researches on the morbidity problem for the GM(1,1) model with the accumulating method based on the condition number theory. It proves that we can get a new healthier model by make a multiple transformation on the initial data, and the transformation doesn't affect the precision of the model. Therefore, morbidity problem for the GM(1,1) model with the accumulating method is resolved well.

Keywords: morbidity, GM(1,1) model, Accumulating method, multiple transformation.

1 Introduction

The grey system has been applied extensively. However, the morbidity has been existed in the core model of GM(1,1). The tiny changes of the initial data and numerical round-off can result in the estimation and parameter errors. How to overcome the morbidity and guarantee the reliability and stability of the model has become an important aspect in the reconstruction and improvement of the core GM(1,1) model[1].

Accumulating method is a new kind of curve fitting technical that appeared in the resent years with which we make use of it in the establishment of accumulating method GM(0,N) [2]. But this newly modeling methodology has no more research on its morbidity and accuracy.

This paper has analyzed the morbidity problem in accumulating method GM(1,1) model basing on the condition number Theorem, it proves that we can easily resolve the morbidity problems only if we make a multiple transformation on the primitive data and as a result this kind of the data changes would not affect on the accuracy of the model.

2 Preliminaries

Definition 1. Suppose $A \in R^{n\times n}$, $\| \ \|$ is operator norm and $cond(A) = \|A^{-1}\|\|A\|$, $cond(A)$ (or it can be recorded as $k(A)$) is regarded as the condition number of *A*. we define

$$\|A\| = \|A\|_1 = \max_{1\le j\le n} \sum_{i=1}^{n} |a_{ij}|$$

D. Zeng (Ed.): ICAIC 2011, Part I, CCIS 224, pp. 294–298, 2011.

Definition 2. Any of norms of matrix of $R^{n\times n}$ is equivalence with others. That is to say when we analyze and estimate the norm of matrix, the selection of norm would not make any material difference on the conclusion.

Practically, it is generally regarded as that: If $0 < k(A) < 10$, then A is absolutely well- conditioned; If $10 \le k(A) < 100$, then A is well- conditioned; If $100 \le k(A) \le 1000$, then A is medium or mighty ill-conditioned. If $k(A) > 1000$, then A is seriously ill-conditioned [5].

Accumulating method has an excellent result on the parameter estimation of econometrics. And now we give the parameter estimation in the model of GM(1,1) with accumulating method. We provide the accumulative operator to the equation of the GM(1,1), supposed that the highest rank of the accumulative operator is r, and for the cause of the modeling parameter having 2, so r mustn't be less than 2. Practically we usually define r equalize to 2.

$$\sum_{k=2}^{n} {}^{(1)}x^{(0)}(k) + a\sum_{k=2}^{n} {}^{(1)}z^{(1)}(k) = u\sum_{k=2}^{n} {}^{(1)}$$

$$\sum_{k=2}^{n} {}^{(2)}x^{(0)}(k) + a\sum_{k=2}^{n} {}^{(2)}z^{(1)}(k) = u\sum_{k=2}^{n} {}^{(2)}$$

We denote:

$$X_r = \begin{pmatrix} \sum_{k=2}^{n} {}^{(1)}z^{(1)}(k) & -\sum_{k=2}^{n} {}^{(1)} \\ \sum_{k=2}^{n} {}^{(2)}z^{(1)}(k) & -\sum_{k=2}^{n} {}^{(2)} \end{pmatrix}$$

$$Y_r = \begin{pmatrix} -\sum_{k=2}^{n} {}^{(1)}x^{(0)}(k) \\ -\sum_{k=2}^{n} {}^{(2)}x^{(0)}(k) \end{pmatrix}$$

So the equation can be expressed as a matrix form

$$X_r \hat{a} = Y_r$$

Then we have

$$\hat{a} = X_r^{-1} Y_r$$

3 The Morbidity Analysis

Theorem 1. The condition number of the coefficient matrix by the GM(1,1) model with the accumulating method in the parameter estimation is

$$cond(X_r)_1 = \frac{[0.5(n+2)(n-1)+\beta](\alpha+\beta)}{(n-1)[0.5(n+2)\alpha-\beta]}$$

where

$$\alpha=\sum_{k=2}^{n} {}^{(1)}z^{(1)}(k) \ ,$$

$$\beta=\sum_{k=2}^{n} {}^{(2)}z^{(1)}(k) \ .$$

The Theorem 1 may be proved by a similar process of Ref. [1].

Theorem 2. If we make multiple transformation on primitive sequence of number in GM(1,1) model

$$\overline{x}^{(0)}(k)=\rho x^{(0)}(k)\ ,\quad k=1,2,\cdots,n\ ,$$

where

$$0<\rho<\frac{(n-1)\left[99(n+2)\alpha-(n+202)\beta\right]}{2\beta(\alpha+\beta)}$$

Then establishing GM(1,1) model with accumulating method, we can get a condition number of the coefficient matrix in parameter estimation

$$0<k(\overline{X}_r)<100\,.$$

Proof. After the multiple transformation,

$$\overline{x}^{(1)}(k)=\sum_{m=1}^{k}\overline{x}^{(0)}(m)=\sum_{m=1}^{k}\rho x^{(0)}(m)=\rho x^{(1)}(k)$$

$$\begin{aligned}\overline{z}^{(1)}(k)&=0.5\overline{x}^{(1)}(k)+0.5\overline{x}^{(1)}(k-1)\\&=0.5\rho x^{(1)}(k)+0.5\rho x^{(1)}(k-1)\\&=\rho z^{(1)}(k)\end{aligned}$$

$$\overline{\alpha}=\sum_{k=2}^{n} {}^{(1)}\overline{z}^{(1)}(k)=\sum_{k=2}^{n} {}^{(1)}\rho z^{(1)}(k)=\rho\alpha$$

$$\overline{\beta}=\sum_{k=2}^{n} {}^{(2)}\overline{z}^{(1)}(k)=\sum_{k=2}^{n} {}^{(2)}\rho z^{(1)}(k)=\rho\beta$$

The coefficient matrix of parameter estimation which comes from the newly established sequence of number with accumulation method GM(1,1) model is:

$$\overline{X}_r=\begin{pmatrix}\rho\alpha & -(n-1)\\ \rho\beta & 1-0.5n(n+1)\end{pmatrix}$$

Its condition number is:

$$cond(\overline{X}_r)_1=\left\|\overline{X}_r^{-1}\right\|_1\bullet\left\|\overline{X}_r\right\|_1=\frac{[0.5(n+2)(n-1)+\rho\beta](\alpha+\beta)}{\left|(n-1)[\beta-0.5(n+2)\alpha]\right|}$$

Now we define

$$cond(\overline{X}_r)<100\,,$$

Then we have

$$0<\rho<\frac{(n-1)\left[99(n+2)\alpha-(n+202)\beta\right]}{2\beta(\alpha+\beta)}$$

From the Theorem 2, it should be for us to make multiple transformation on primitive sequence of number and in the meanwhile the condition number is controlled less than 100, therefore the formal ill-conditioned matrix will be turned into well-conditioned.

4 Characteristic Analysis

From Theorem 2, we have made a conclusion that the morbidity problem of GM(1,1) model can easily be settled through a multiple transformation. But both the characteristics of the new model and its accuracy are needed to be analyzed for more. This kind of the analyses is intended to keep the estimation model of grey system in high accuracy.

Theorem 3. We define the parameter of GM(1,1)model with accumulating method $\bar{a},\bar{u}$ only after the multiple transformation. The parameter is a,u before the transformation and we can get that

$$\bar{a} = a,$$
$$\bar{u} = \rho u$$

Proof. Through the modeling process of GM(1,1) with accumulating method , so we can get:

$$a = \frac{-[1-0.5n(n+1)]\sum_{k=2}^{n} {}^{(1)}x^{(0)}(k) - (n-1)\sum_{k=2}^{n} {}^{(2)}x^{(0)}(k)}{|X_r|}$$

$$u = \frac{\beta\sum_{k=2}^{n} {}^{(1)}x^{(0)}(k) - \alpha\sum_{k=2}^{n} {}^{(2)}x^{(0)}(k)}{|X_r|}$$

where

$$|X_r| = [1-0.5n(n+1)]\alpha + (n-1)\beta$$

Now we make multiple transformation to the primitive sequence of number, the expression method is similar with the Theorem 2. That is

$$\bar{x}^{(0)}(k) = \rho x^{(0)}(k)\ , k = 1,2,\cdots,n$$

After the transformation, we can get those below through the proof of Theorem 2

$$\bar{X}_r = \begin{pmatrix} \rho\alpha & -(n-1) \\ \rho\beta & 1-0.5n(n+1) \end{pmatrix},$$

$$\bar{Y}_r = \begin{pmatrix} -\rho\sum_{k=2}^{n} {}^{(1)}x^{(0)}(k) \\ -\rho\sum_{k=2}^{n} {}^{(2)}x^{(0)}(k) \end{pmatrix}$$

So we have

$$\bar{a} = \frac{-[1-0.5n(n+1)]\rho\sum_{k=2}^{n} {}^{(1)}x^{(0)}(k) - (n-1)\rho\sum_{k=2}^{n} {}^{(2)}x^{(0)}(k)}{\rho|X_r|}$$

$$= a$$

$$\bar{u} = \frac{\rho^2\beta\sum_{k=2}^{n} {}^{(1)}x^{(0)}(k) - \rho^2\alpha\sum_{k=2}^{n} {}^{(2)}x^{(0)}(k)}{\rho|X_r|}$$

$$= \rho u$$

From Theorem 3, we can make a conclusion: multiple transformation does not effect on the development coefficient. Whereas development coefficient has reflected the trends of estimation value and so it effects on the accuracy of the modeling. From those we know that this kind of modeling can guarantee the model in a high accuracy.

5 Conclusions

This paper is emphasized on the modeling method with accumulating of GM(1,1) that it can easily overcome the defects and shortcoming which condition number is too larger in the coefficient matrix that is companied by the traditional one. Moreover, modeling method with accumulating of GM(1,1) not only can evade the complicated calculation in the matrix, but also can reduce the quantities of the calculation. As a whole, it can ensure the stability and reliability of the estimation in high quality in the grey system and it is certain that the GM(1,1) model has a good application future indeed.

References

1. Zheng, Z., Wu, Y.: The Morbidity Problems in the GM(1,1) Model. Management Science of China 9(5), 38–44 (2001)
2. Li, F., Wang, Z.: The New Methodology in the Parameter Estimation in the GM(0,n) Model. The Journal of Wuhan University of Technology(Edition of Traffic Science and Engineering) 26(1), 625–627 (2002)
3. Cao, D., Zhang, S.: The Theory of Accumulating Method. Science Publishing House, Beijing (1999)
4. Wang, N.: The Concise Courses to the Numeric Value Analysis. High Education Publishing House, Beijing (1984)
5. Chen, X., Wang, S.: The Modern Regression Analysis. Anhui Education Publishing House, Hefei (1987)
6. Xiao, X., Deng, L., Zha, J.: The Grey System Analysis and Its Application. Marine University of Dalian Publishing House, Dalian (1997)
7. Chao, J., Hang, S.: The High Rank of GM(1,1) Model Basing on the Space of Greyness Generation. The Journal of Fushan College of Science and Technology, Fushan 20(1), 9–12 (2002)
8. Xiao, X., Tong, S.: Research on Iii- Conditioned Problem in Grey Prediction Control Model. In: Proceedings of the Third International Conference on Machine Learning and Cybernetics, pp. 2010–2013 (August 2004)

Distributed Range-Free Localization Algorithm for 3D Wireless Sensor Networks under Irregular Radio Propagation Model*

Jianping Xing, Dehua Wang, and Yang Liu

School of Information Science and Engineering Shandong University
Jinan 250100, China
jianpingxing@yahoo.com.cn

Abstract. This paper presents a novel Distributed Range-free Localization Algorithm(3D-DRL) for three-dimensional wireless sensor networks under irregular radio propagation environment. In the scheme, the sensing space is divided into cubic cells with resolution a and each anchor, equipped with Global Positioning System (GPS), votes for each cubic cell. Each unknown node averages the COG (center of the gravity) of cells with highest votes as its estimated location. The scheme eliminates the requirement for specific positioning hardware, avoids the need for any interaction between the individual unknown nodes, and is independent of node densities and network topologies. Simulation results indicate that the average localization error is below 3 meters, when DOI(Degree of Irregularity)=0.1, ANR(Anchor to Node Range Ratio)=2.5 and all nodes are randomly deployed in 100×100×100 m3 scenarios. Especially, all unknown nodes can localize themselves by adjusting ANR.

Keywords: wireless sensor network, three-dimensional localization, range-free, Degree of Irregularity, grid-based representation.

1 Introduction

The wireless sensor network (WSN) is a kind of self-organized network, composed of large amount of sensor nodes by means of wireless communication technology. In recent years, WSN is succeeding in being used in many fields such as military surveillance, medical care, environmental monitoring, public service and home automation applications [1]. In many applications, for example forest fire pre-warning, each sensor node is required to report not only its sensing data but also its current location. Therefore, localization has become a critical problem in WSN and also received additional consideration.

Although various localization algorithms have been proposed for two-dimensional WSN, there are relatively few localization schemes for three-dimensional WSN. The

* This work is supported by State Key Program of National Natural Science of China (Grant No. 60532030), Program for New Century Excellent Talents in University (Grant No. NCET-08-0333) and Civil Aviation Open Foundation (2008BUAA04) to JP.Xing.

D. Zeng (Ed.): ICAIC 2011, Part I, CCIS 224, pp. 299–306, 2011.

self-localization of WSN deployed in three-dimensional Scenario has recently attracted massive attentions from both academia and industry. Liang et al. [2] proposed a localization approach for WSN in Constrained 3-D spaces, which is efficient on several different network structures with cuboid or cone profile and layered or random node distributions. Ou et al. [3] presented a three-dimensional localization algorithm based on flying anchors, which have bean implemented in the real wireless sensor network environment.

This paper presents an effective distributed range-free localization algorithm for three-dimensional wireless sensor network(3D-DRL). The accuracy of the estimation can be easily adjusted by changing some system parameters, which makes it flexible. Furthermore, the scheme eliminates any interaction between unknown nodes, which helps to save energy and extends the life time of the network. Most significantly, the scheme is range-free and is independent of node density and network topologies.

2 Review of 3D-DRl

In our scheme, Anchors, occupying a very small proportion, can obtain their accurate position through GPS devices. The unknown nodes can localize themselves according to the beacon information of anchors.

2.1 Problem Description

When the localization scheme starts, each anchor broadcasts its location beacon periodically, which contains the ID of the anchor, the absolute position (X,Y,Z), power level L, and the additional propagation range (R_{L-1},R_L). What an unknown node to do is to listen to the signals from anchors, stores the useful information into local table， and calculates its location.

Anchors have the ability to control the transmitted power. When an unknown node listens to several signals with different power levels from an anchor, the unknown node just saves the signal with the lowest power level.

2.2 Related Definitions

(1) AH(Anchors Heard): The average number of anchors in one hop transmission range.

(2) BJT(Beacons Judging Threshold): In the scheme, each anchor will broadcast its beacon periodically and the unknown node may receive some of them. The beacons will be judged to be true, only when the number of received beacons from the same anchor is above BJT.

(3) S: S=DT/AH. DT(Decision Threshold) is the threshold by which the unknown node decides whether the correct beacons are sufficient enough to localize itself. AH may be different for unknown nodes, accordingly, unknown nodes may have different value of DT. Thus, it's not practical to set a specific value of DT for each unknown node. A better alternative is using the system parameter S, which is more flexible. The default value is 0.5.

2.3 Grid-Based Representation

The grid-based representation of the location area is widely used in range-free localization schemes [4, 5] for Wireless Sensor Network. 3D-DRL also adopts a grid-based representation of the sensing space.

In our scheme, having deployed the network and just before voting, each unknown node will establish its own grid, and perform initialization. The implementation is as follows: After the hearing stage, the unknown node assumes the Centroid of all anchors heard by itself as the coordinate origin $O(x_0, y_0, z_0)$, takes the latitude line going over centre O as abscissa axis X, the longitude line going over centre O as Y-axis, and builds the relative orthogonal coordinate system in the sensing space. Then the terrain $\{ x, y, z) / |x - x_0| < R, |y - y_0 < R|, |z - z_0| < R, (x, y, z) \in \Delta\}$ (R denotes the transmission range of anchors and $\triangle$denotes the sensing space) is divided into many cubic grid cells(length of the grid side is a, called grid resolution). With this method, the initialization terrain can be reduced effectively, which results in less computation, and more efficiency. Thus, each unknown node maintains a table of the terrain represented in grid cells, with initialized value to be zero.

During localization, anchors will vote for each cell within its transmission range. The value of a cell reflects the agreement of anchors that this cell is a likely position of the unknown node. The higher the value, the more anchors agree that this cell is a likely location of that unknown node. Finally, 3D-DRL averages the COG of cells with highest votes as the estimated location of that unknown node.

2.4 Radio Model

As demonstrated in [4, 5, 6], radio propagation patterns are not isotropic. Thus, to get a result close to that in real situation, we adopt the DOI(Degree of Irregularity) [9] model in our simulation. The DOI model has been proposed to approximate a realistic radio propagation pattern in a two-dimensional plane. Our simulation extends the DOI concept to the three-dimensional space. If the DOI is zero, the radio propagation is assumed to be a perfect sphere, and an increasing value of the DOI represents an increasing degree of radio irregularity.

$$RSS_{real} = Random[(1 - DOI)RSS, (1 + DOI)RSS] \tag{1}$$

where RSS_{real} denotes the real received signal strength and RSS represents the received signal strength under perfect spherical radio model. $Random(a,b)$ denotes a uniformly distributed random function between a and b. The DOI range is [0,1].

In the scheme, we eliminate any statistical models to calculate the actual distance and use RSS to indicate the relative distance between anchors and unknown node. So the proposed scheme is range-free.

2.5 Algorithm Description

Step1. Anchors broadcast their beacons, including anchor's ID, the absolute position of the anchor (X,Y,Z), power level L, and the additional propagation range (R_{L-1}, R_L).

Step2. The unknown node receives the beacons of anchors. Then decide whether the number of beacons from anchors is above BJT. If it's true, store the information into local table, otherwise discard that beacon. The local table of each unknown node contains the information of every received anchor, just as follows:

(1) AH: The average number of anchors heard by unknown nodes.

(2) Beacon[1…n]: The beacons of neighboring anchors for each unknown node, where n equals to AH.

Step3. Execute the Grid-based Representation of the sensing space, as described in section 3.3.

Step4. Judging that a cell is within its communication range, the anchor will vote for it, otherwise the anchor does not vote.

Step5. After voting of all anchors, if the highest vote is larger than DT, then we take the COG of cells with highest votes as the estimated location of that unknown node. Otherwise, the unknown node will send a requirement of re-localization and repeat step1.

2.6 Handling Radio Irregularity

In 3D-DRL, we set several system parameters (S , DT and BJT) to accommodate this irregularity.

When the unknown node receives too much incorrect beacons due to the radio irregularity, the highest votes may be lower than DT. Then, the unknown node will request anchors to rebroadcast their beacons. This scheme is helpful for correct localization under radio irregularity.

Fig.1 demonstrates such characteristic clearly. The default value of S is 0.5. The unknown node receives three beacons from anchor X, anchor Y and anchor Z. Thus, DT=S×AH=1.5. However, due to the radio irregularity, the unknown node receives an error beacon from anchor Z, and the highest vote in all cells is 2 instead of 3, which is higher than DT, so this unknown node can be localized.

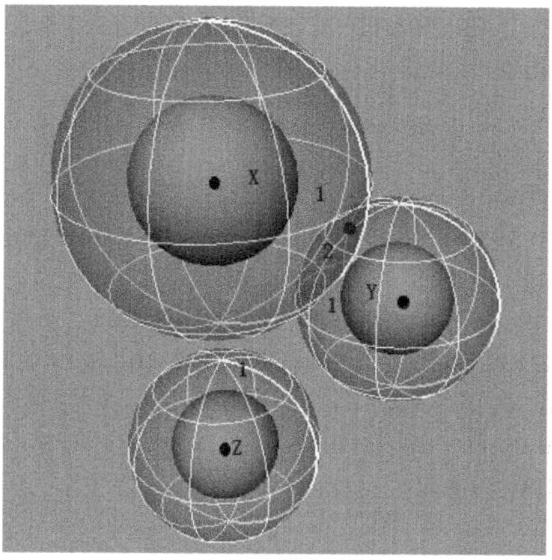

Fig. 1. An example of handling radio irregularity

Finally, we assume the centroid of the cells, with the highest value 2, as the estimation location of this unknown node. As a result, the error beacon from anchor Z is not taken into account in the calculation. Further simulation results in section 4 show that the re-broadcasting scheme can also help to handle radio irregularity.

3 Simulation Results and Analysis

In this section, we present some computer simulation results using MATLAB to show the performance of the proposed algorithm. We consider two performance metrics: the average location error and the location ratio. In our scheme, the location ratio equals to 100% by adjusting ANR(Anchor to Node Range Ratio). In all simulations, the sensing space is 100×100×100m3 and contains totally 500 randomly deployed sensor nodes, with a transmission range of 50 meters. And yet, only ten percent anchors, also randomly deployed in the sensing space, are used.

3.1 Parameters and Performance Measurements

In our simulation, several system parameters that directly affect the accuracy of 3D-DRL are considered. The relevant system parameters are listed below:

(1) ANR(Anchor to Node Range Ratio): The average transmission range of anchors divided by the average transmission range of the unknown nodes.

(2) ND(Node Density): The average number of sensor nodes in one hop transmission range.

(3) Grid resolution (a)

(4) AH(Anchors Heard)

(5) DOI(Degree of Irregularity)

(6) BJT(Beacons Judging Threshold)

Additionally, the following parameter should be set before localization:

(7) S: S=DT/AH.

(8) RLPL(Range of Lowest Power Level): The range that anchors with lowest power level can reach. And the range that the anchors with N power level can reach is N×RLPL. The default value is 25 meters.

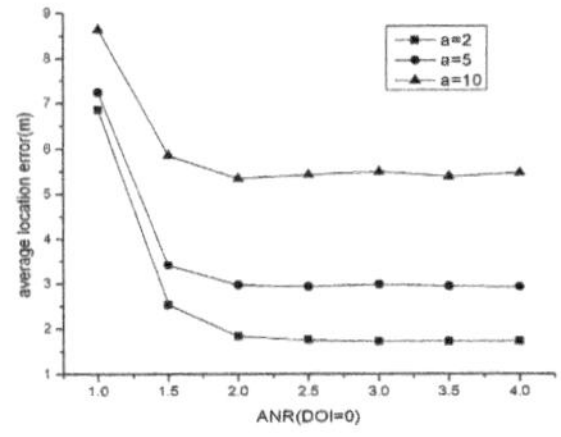

Fig. 2. The average location error vs. ANR with DOI=0

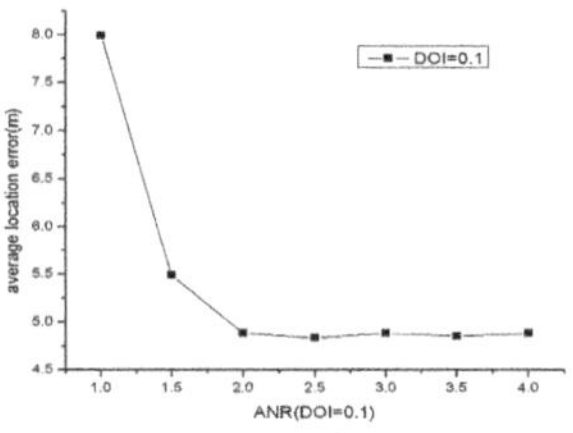

Fig. 3. The average location error vs. ANR with DOI=0.1

3.2 Simulation Results

a. Varying a:

Fig.2 reveals that in a perfectly spherical radio propagation model (DOI=0), decreasing the grid resolution can reduce the estimation error. In the scheme, the smaller size of a, the more calculation overhead and the higher accuracy we get. Therefore, we should select a proper value of a to make a trade-off between calculation overhead and location accuracy. As demonstrated in Fig.2, when a=5 and ANR=2, the location error can be reduced to less than 3m, with 100 percent location ratio.

b. Varying ANR:

Fig.2 also demonstrates that, once given the value of a, increasing ANR(DOI=0) will reduce the estimation error till the best accuracy. The reason is that increasing ANR will increase the number of audible anchors for each unknown node, and more anchors will vote for the unknown node. Thus, the votes of the cells near the unknown node will get a much higher value, generating a more accurate estimation.

However, as shown in Fig.3, under the DOI model (DOI=0.1), with the increase of ANR, the average location error decreases first and oscillates around a fixed value. Under the DOI model, increasing ANR has two effects: on the one hand the number of anchors heard increases; on the other hand more incorrect votes will be generated. When ANR is small, the first reason plays the major role, and accordingly the average location error reduces. When ANR is large enough, both factors can affect the location accuracy and bring about the oscillation.

c. Varying AH and ND:

Fig.4 reveals that increasing AH can reduce the average location error and as mentioned in 4.3.2, increasing ANR will increase the location error. With the increase of AH, each unknown node can hear more anchors and the cells near the node will get a higher value of votes, thus resulting in a higher accuracy. When AH>35, the location error can be reduced to 5.5m, which is acceptable for most applications of WSN.

As shown in Fig.5, along with ND increasing, the average location error oscillates around a fixed value. The reason is that there is no interaction between unknown nodes. Thus, the scheme is independent of node density (ND) and robust to the network topology.

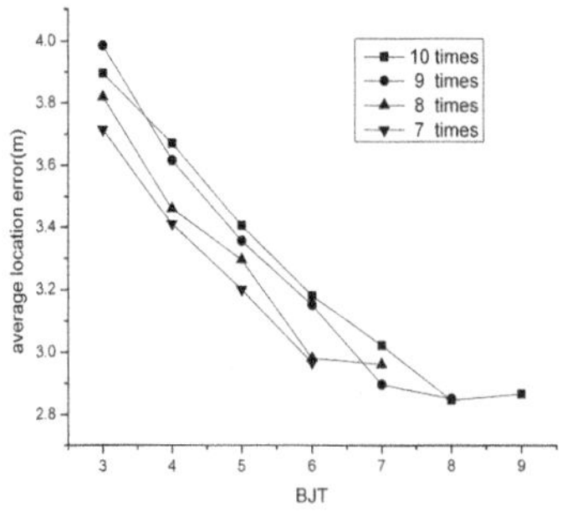

Fig. 4. The average location error vs. AH with DOI=0.1

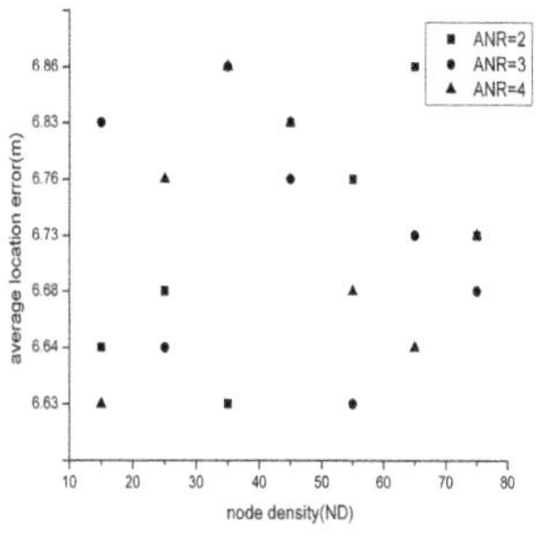

Fig. 5. The average location error vs. ND with DOI=0.1, AH=20

d. Varying DOI and varying BJT

Fig.6 illustrates that the average location error increases with increasing DOI. This is because the lager DOI brings about the lager variation along different directions. Therefore, more incorrect votes might be generated.

Fortunately, as observed in Fig.7, increasing BJT helps reduce the influence of radio irregularity, resulting in a higher accuracy. In our simulation, each anchor re-broadcasts its beacon for K times. The simulation result indicates that when BJT equals to K-1, we get the best accuracy. For example, when K=9 and BJT=8, the minimum location error is 2.85m, close to the accuracy with DOI=0.

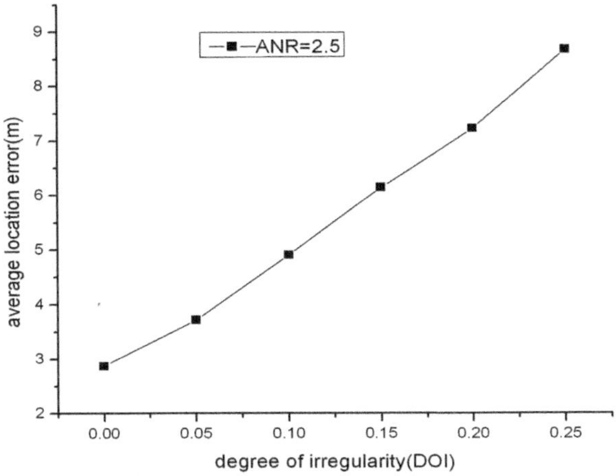

Fig. 6. The average location error vs. DOI with ANR=2.5

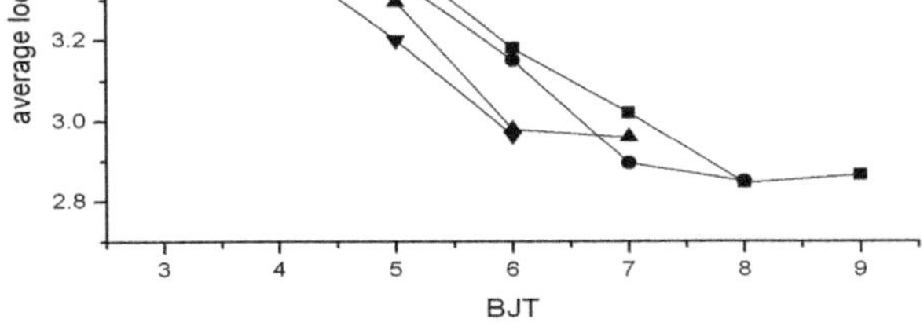

Fig. 7. The average location error vs. BJT with DOI=0.1, ANR=2.5

4 Conclusion

This paper presents a range-free localization algorithm(3D-DRL) for three-dimensional wireless sensor network. The scheme eliminates the requirement for specific positioning hardware, avoids any interaction between the unknown nodes and is independent of network densities and topologies.

Simulation results indicate that even under the irregular radio propagation model, the scheme also performs well in terms of high average location error and 100 percent location ratio. Therefore, the accuracy provided by the proposed scheme is sufficient to support various applications in wireless sensor networks with low complexity.

Acknowledgment. Authors wish to thank the project was funded by CNS/ATM Labs, CAAC and partly supported by the State Key Program of National Natural Science of China(Grant No. 60532030),the project supported by Program for New Century Excellent Talents in University (Grant No. NCET-08-0333),the project supported by Shandong Province Natural Science Foundation (Grant No.Y2007G10).We also wish to thank the help of Navigation Communication Co-system Engineering Center of Shandong Province.

References

1. Akyildiz, I.F., Su, W., Sankarasubramaniam, Y., et al.: A survey on sensor networks. IEEE Communications Magazine 40(8), 102–114 (2002)
2. Zhang, L., Zhou, X., Cheng, Q.: Landscape-3D: A Robust Localization Scheme for Sensor Networks over Complex 3D Terrains. In: Proceedings of the 31st IEEE Int'l Conf. Local Computer Networks (LCN 2006), pp. 239–246 (2006)
3. Ou, C.H., Ssu, K.F.: Sensor Position Determination with flying anchors in three-dimensional wireless sensor networks. IEEE Transactions on Mobile Computing 7(9), 1084–1097 (2008)
4. He, T., Huang, C.D., Blum, B.M., et al.: Range-free localization schemes for large scale sensor networks. In: Proceedings of the ninth annual international conference on Mobile computing and networking (MobiCom 2003), San Diego, California, pp. 81–95 (2003)
5. Qi, Y., Tan, S.K., Yu, G., et al.: An area localization scheme for large wireless sensor networks. In: IEEE 61st Vehicular Technology Conference, pp. 2835–2839 (2005)
6. Gang, Z., Tian, H., Sudha, K., et al.: Impact of radio irregularity on wireless sensor networks. In: International Conference on Mobile System, Application and Services, pp. 125–138 (2004)

HCI Using a Robust Hand Tracking Method

Shilin Zhang and Hui Wang

Faculty of Computer Science, Network and Information Management Center
North China University of Technology, Beijing, China
shiyutoi@163.com

Abstract. The interaction between man and computer has become an important topic as it can generalize the use of computers, robots and other intelligent machines. For active H/R interaction scheme, the computer needs to detect human faces in its vicinity and then interpret canonical gestures. In this paper, we firstly present a method to track the hands robustly in videos recorded by a camera, and then by compute the similarity of the trajectories of the hands' motion, we can interact with computer by some simple sign languages. An efficient color segmentation on the skin-like colored pixels is used. Then we locate the hands by a fast optic flow method which is computed only by the skin-like image blocks. At the last stage, we get the hand motion trajectory and map it to a string. By String Edit Distance method, we can compute the similarity of the string representing input hand command with some template strings denoting sign language pre-trained and stored in database. We can let the computers or some other machines recognize some simple words like "UP","DOWN","OK","LEFT","RIGHT" and etc. Results of tracking and recognition are illustrated in the paper and show the process robustness in cluttered environments and in various light conditions. The limits of the method and future works are also discussed.

Keywords: Hand Tracking, String Edit Distance, Human-Machine Interaction.

1 Introduction

Man-machine interaction has become an important topic in the artificial intelligent community. In this context, advanced robots or TV set must integrate capabilities to detect humans' presence in their vicinity and interpret their motion. For an active interaction, the robot must also be able to interpret gestures performed by the tracked person. As for robotics, this person should have been beforehand identified among all the possible robot tutors, and then granted the right to interact with the robot; as for a TV set, it is not necessary to grant the rights to interact with the machines. In the first scenarios, a face recognition step is required; in the second scenarios, just face detection is needed. In the case where the person is recognized, his/her hand location and posture are used as symbols to communicate with the robot. The visual functions of our system are depicted in Fig. 1 and detailed in the paper.

D. Zeng (Ed.): ICAIC 2011, Part I, CCIS 224, pp. 307–314, 2011.

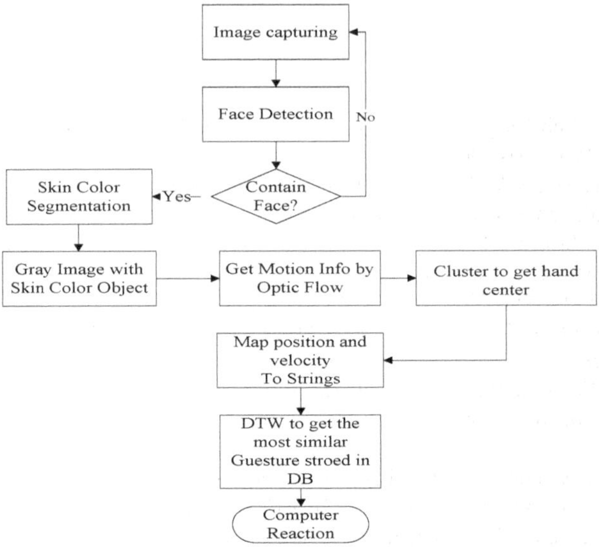

Fig. 1. The workflow of the Human-Machine Interaction Scheme by hand tracking

Human limbs (especially the hands) are highly deformable articulated objects with many degrees of freedom and can, through different postures and motions, be used to express information. General tracking and accurate 3D pose estimation require elaborate 3D articulated rigid [1] or even deformable [4] models with difficult initialization and time-consuming updating procedures. Some other hand tracking systems need magnetic sensors [6], and hand tracking with bare hands is rarely reported in literature. The aim here is to track a number of well-defined hand postures that represent a limited set of commands that the users can give to the robot with bare hands. To use a simple view-based shape representation, face and hand are therefore represented by coarse 2D rigid models, e.g. their silhouette contours, which are modeled by spines [5]. These models, although simplistic, permit to reduce the complexity of the involved computations and remain discriminatory enough to track a set of known hand postures in complex scenes as will be shown later. The purpose of this paper is to show how a real-time system for face/hand tracking and hand posture recognition can be constructed combining color and optic flow cues. This is done by using color segmentation and optic flow method, which enables face detection and simultaneous tracking and posture recognition of the hand. One reason for choosing optic flow method as the tracking engine comes from its capability to work with the non-Gaussian noise models required to represent cluttered environments.

The face detection and color segmentation process will be described in section 2. Section 3 depicts the well-known optic flow formalism and how to combine shape and color cues in a new measurement model dedicated to this tracker. K-means cluster method is also introduced to get the hands center. Considerations about and string edit distance method are described in section 4. Applications of real-time face/hand tracking and hand posture recognition with bare hands for active H/R interaction context are also presented and illustrated. Section 5 gives some experiment results.

Finally, the last part of the paper summarizes this approach and opens the discussion of future works.

2 Face Detection and Skin Color Segmentation

As for a frame captured from the camera, the first task is to detect the face, and record the face location. If we do not find the face, the image can be ignored and continue to process the next frame. By Haar-like feature provided by OpenCV source library [1], it is easy to locate the face. After the face is located, we can construct polar coordinate system and the point below the face center 0.5 times face radius from the face center is as the origin. Fig.2.

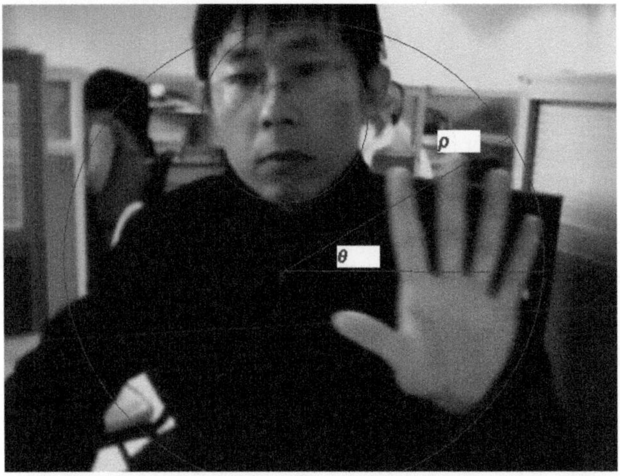

Fig. 2. The face detection and the polar coordinate system

Most of the skin detection techniques discussed in literature [2] are used a preprocessor for face detection and tracking systems. Though skin color analysis often produces high TPRs, it also produces high FPRs when the image contains cluttered background and shadows. To improve the accuracy of the classifier, various other features such as shape, spatial and motion information can be used along with skin-color information. In the past decade significant advancement has been made in skin detection using color information in the visual spectrum. However, to build an accurate classifier which can detect all the skin types under different illuminations, shadows, cluttered backgrounds and makeup is still an unsolved problem. In this paper, skin color detection method is used as a preprocessor to track the hands motion. So, some TPRs or FPRs do not affected the overall hand tracking and the optic flow method used in the next step which can make up that deficiency. The human skin colors of different individuals cluster in a small region in color space provided that the images are taken under illumination controlled environments. Hence, one of the easiest and often used methods is to define skin-color cluster decision boundaries for different color space components. Single or multiple ranges of threshold values for each color space component are defined and the image pixel values that fall within these predefined range(s) for all the chosen color components are defined as skin pixels.

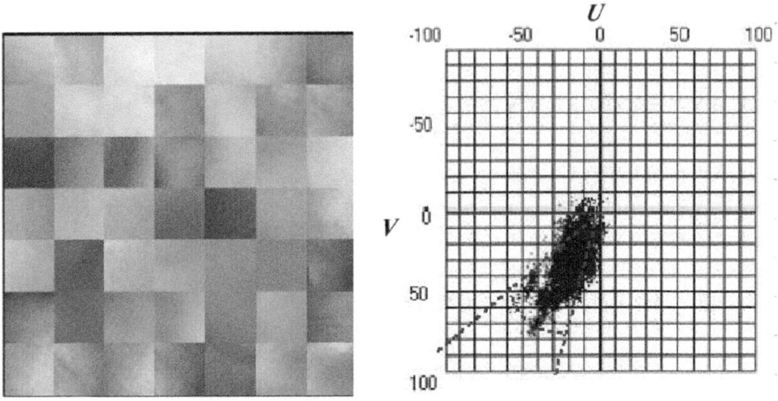

Fig. 3. Every skin color in 50k pixels and skin color distribution in UV color space

As can be seen in Fig.3, images firstly is transformed into YUV color space and further mapped into UV color space in 2-dim.In UV space, skin color has a good cluster attribute which is shown by formula (1) and (2).

$$\begin{aligned} &0.261\pi \le \tan^{-1}\left(\frac{u}{v}\right) \le 0.3111\pi \\ &43 \le \sqrt{u^2+v^2} \le 78 \end{aligned} \tag{1}$$

$$\begin{aligned} &0.25\pi \le \tan^{-1}\left(\frac{u}{v}\right) \le 0.3161\pi \\ &0 \le \sqrt{u^2+v^2} \le 70 \end{aligned} \tag{2}$$

Through the above method, we can get the hands position and shape by and large which is shown in Fig.4.

Fig. 4. Skin color segmentation result

3 Optical Flow Method and K-Means Cluster

3.1 Optical Flow Method

In order to track the hands motion, just skin color is not enough to accomplish the robustly hand tracking. So camshift (Continuously Adaptive Mean Shift) and some other method is put forward [3].In the Human-Machine Interaction scene, only the moving gesture is meaningful, so the static face or other static skin color like subject needs to be avoided. The optical flow [2] is just fit the situation and it can also solve the problem of overlap of the face and hands. In this literature, we use the optical flow to track the hands motion. The optical flow computation is time consuming in general, but in our experiment, the computation is just over gray images after skin color segmentation. So it can be computed real-time.We proceed by providing a general framework for the basic constraint equation which describes the one-dimensional motion components of single spatial frequencies. If I is the attribute value that is constant at corresponding points, then

$$I(x+u\delta t, y+v\delta t, t+\delta t) = I(x,y,t) \tag{3}$$

Where t represents time and x and y represents two different Cartesian coordinates. The letters u and v represent the x and y components of the flow u, respectively. Of course, our observations of these derivatives are inevitably going to be highly noisy but that fact is incorporated in our noise model. The mathematical issue of whether these derivatives exist is not a real issue. Both in the real world and the image domain, we smooth or average a small amount before we do anything else.

At time $t+\delta t$, the point moves to $(x+\delta x, y+\delta y)$,where $\delta x = u\delta t$, $\delta y = v\delta t$. If $I(x,y,t)$ is smooth, then we can expand the above (1) as:

$$I(x,y,t) + \delta x\frac{\partial I}{\partial x} + \delta y\frac{\partial I}{\partial y} + \delta t\frac{\partial I}{\partial t} + e = I(x,y,t) \tag{4}$$

$$\frac{\partial I}{\partial x}\frac{dx}{dt} + \frac{\partial I}{\partial y}\frac{dy}{dt} + \frac{\partial I}{\partial t} = 0 \tag{5}$$

The above (5) represents the relation between the temporal component, spatial component and the velocity component.There are three primary classes of methods for computing optical now: gradient-based methods, frequency-domain methods, and correlation methods. Gradient-based and frequency-domain methods derive optical now in two separate stages: first, information about the one-dimensional motion components of local edges or single spatial frequencies is obtained; then, the individual measurements within some neighborhood are combined into an estimate of optical now. These two classes of methods are faced with similar noise issues and thus can be given a very similar mathematical analysis. Correlation techniques perform region-based matching and in general cannot be separated into one-dimensional and two-dimensional components. Thus, they will be given a separate analysis that is somewhat different, but not very different. Lucas [12] proposes a method to estimate optical flow using weighted least-squares. In a small neighborhood space Ω , the optical flow error is defined as (**W(x)** represents the window weighing function):

$$\sum_{(x,y)\in\Omega} W^2(\mathbf{x})(I_x u + I_y v + I_t)^2 \tag{6}$$

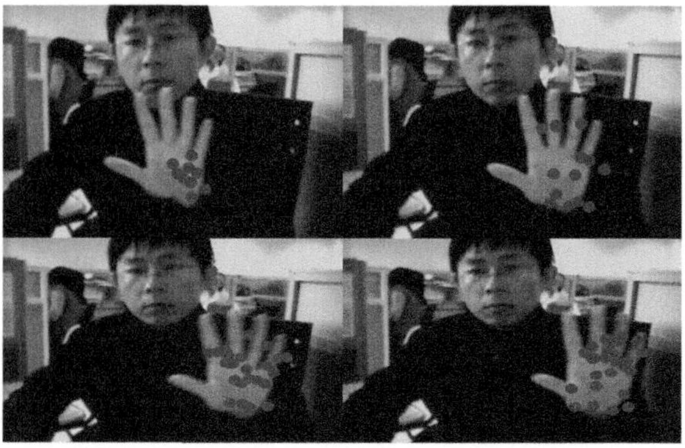

Fig. 5. Finding the hand motion by optical flow method

In Fig.5 above, the four pictures demonstrate the motion estimation using optical flow method computed only on skin color like image blocks. The velocity and the Ω width can be adjusted to capture enough red dotted blocks. In the next step, we will cluster the red points to one class as for one hand, and to two classed as for double hands.

4 Polar Coordinates Construction and Feature Expression

4.1 Polar Coordinates Construction

We will construct polar coordinates in the above captured images which already have the hands' center.

In Fig 7, the hands motion features are represent by left hand's velocity and motion angle, and right hand's velocity and motion angle. So we can get the time serial feature by analyzing the video frames.

Table 1. Hand Features extracted from Frames in "turn left" gesture

Frame number	ρ	θ	v	α
70	0.4624	4.3267	0.8254	3.4523
76	0.1123	2.8975	0.2536	5.2434
77	0.5234	5.3421	0.9231	4.3475
78	0.2897	1.3452	0.5346	1.9806

In Tab 1, ρ represents the distance to center in polar coordinates which is normalized in (0, 1) and θ represents the angle to center in polar coordinates which in (0,2 π). V represents the left hand' motion velocity normalized in (0, 1) and α represents the motion angle in (0,2 π). The first column represents the frame number of every frame of videos. The right hand' feature is the same and is not listed in above table.

Table 2. Accuracy of the Gesture recognition

Gesture	Train Set	Test Set	Accuracy	%
Turn left	23	50	50	100%
Turn right	57	50	50	100%
Turn own	45	50	50	100%
circle	53	50	49	98%

5 Conclusion and Future Works

It is very difficult to perform hand tracking using only shape or skin color information. By introducing color segmentation and optical flow make the tracker more robust in cluttered environment and in various light conditions. In order to analysis the motion information of the images, the optical flow speed and Ω can be adapted so as to capture enough moving blocks. K-means clustering guarantees that we can get the hands center correctly. In our experiment, the hand center number can be set 2, and it can robustly capture two hands motion information. By computing string edit distance, we can compare the input string and the template strings stored in database. So, according to the distance, we can recognize the user's gesture meaning. Furthermore, we want to adapt our tracker to be able to track multiple users simultaneously.

References

1. OpenCv library, `http://www.sourceforge.net/projects/opencvlibrary`
2. Kakumanu, P., Makrogiannis, S., Bourbakis, N.: A survey of skin-color modeling and detection methods. Pattern Recognition 40, 1106–1122 (2007)
3. Funkunage, K., Hostetler, L.: The estimation of the gradient of a density function with applications in pattern recognition. IEEE Trans. Information Theory 21, 32–40 (1975)
4. Huttenlocher, D.P., Noh, J.J., Rucklidge, W.J.: Tracking Non-rigid Objects in Complex Scenes. In: Int. Conf. on Computer Vision (ICCV 1993), pp. 93–101 (1993)
5. Hjelmas, E.: Face Detection, a Survey. Int. Journal of Computer Vision and Image Understanding, CVIU 2001, 236–274 (2001)
6. Mitobe, K., Kaiga, T., Yukawa, T., Miura, T., et al.: Development of a motion capture system for a hand using a magnetic three dimensional position sensor. In: ACM SIGGRAPH, p. 102 (2006)
7. Hsieh, J.W., Yu, S.L., Chen, Y.S.: Motion-Based Video Retrieval by Trajectory Matching. IEEE Trans. on Circuits and Systems for Video Technology 16(3) (2006)
8. Chen, L., Oŝu, M.T., Oria, V.: Symbolic Representation and Retrieval of Moving Object Trajectories. In: MIR 2004, New York, pp. 15–16 (2004)

9. Ahmad, A., Dey, L.: A k-mean clustering algorithm for mixed numeric and categorical data. Data & Knowledge Engineering 63, 503–527 (2007)
10. Pang, Y.W., Li, X.L., Yuan, Y.: Fast Haar Transform Based Feature Extraction for Face Representation and Recognition. IEEE Transactions on Information Forensics and Security 14(3), 441–450 (2009)
11. Ristad, E.S., Yianilos, P.N.: Learning string-edit distance. IEEE Transactions on Pattern Analysis and Machine Intelligence 20, 522–532 (1998)
12. Lucas, B.D., Kanade, T.: An iterative image registration technique with an application to stereo vision. In: Proceedings of Imaging Understanding Workshop, pp. 121–130 (1981)

A Hybrid Genetic Algorithm to Solve Zero-One Knapsack Problem

Qing Chen[1,2] and Yuxiang Shao[3]

[1] Hubei Province Key Laboratory of Intelligent Robot Wuhan Institute of Technology
[2] School of Computer Science & Engineering Wuhan Institute of Technology
Wuhan, China
[3] School of Computer Science & Engineering China University of Geosciences
Wuhan, China
qing19328@sina.com

Abstract. In order to overcome the disadvantages of the traditional genetic algorithm and improve the speed and precision of the algorithm, the author improved the selection strategy, integrated the greedy algorithm with the genetic algorithm and formed the hybrid genetic algorithm. The paper discussed the basic idea and method to solve the zero-one knapsack problem using this hybrid genetic algorithm. The experiments prove the feasibility and validity of the algorithm.

Keywords: Zero-One Knapsack, Hybrid Genetic Algorithm, Optimization.

1 Introduction

A knapsack problem is a combinatorial optimization problem and it is known as a NP-hard problem; there is no algorithm, which can find an exact optimal solution within a practical limited time. Around it has various methods to solve it, such as dynamic in designated, branch-and -bound. These methods are all index level, not to solve the practical problems. Solving the knapsack problem has extensive application prospects. In the academic, it can solve the zero-one integer designed problems or as a category which can be summed up to the zero-one knapsack problem; in the production, it will directly affect the efficiency of its social productivity. So it is always a hot topic to explore this issue [1][2].

When the items number n is very large, the recursive backtracking method is not practical to solve the zero-one knapsack problem. Moreover, using the greedy method to solve the problem can't guarantee the satisfying results. Simple genetic algorithm usually adopts penalty method to deal with non-feasibility and lack use of knapsack load-bearing. However, with the increasing of the items number n, the effect of penalty method is not ideal.

In allusion to the shortages of the algorithm, this paper designed a hybrid genetic algorithm, which firstly improved the selection strategy of genetic algorithm, then used greedy algorithm to improve crossover and mutation operator and convert them to

D. Zeng (Ed.): ICAIC 2011, Part I, CCIS 224, pp. 315–320, 2011.

normal coding individuals. Vast experiments show that this algorithm is better able to deal with non-feasibility and lack use of knapsack load-bearing problem so that the genetic algorithm gets rapid convergence. Thus, the speed and precision of the algorithm is increased effectively [3][4].

2 Zero-One Knapsack Problem

2.1 Problem Description

The zero-one knapsack problem involves filling a knapsack, which has a weight capacity c, with a number of items numbered 1,2,···, n one by one. Each item has an associated weight w_i, and profit v_i. The aim is to find a combination of items whose weight does not exceed the knapsack's capacity and to maximize the overall profit. Each item has only two choices namely encasing and non-encasing knapsack and item i can't be encased repeatedly or partly [5].

2.2 Mathematical Model

Mathematically,given $C > 0, w_i > 0, v_i > 0, 1 \le i \le n$, the zero-one knapsack problem can be represented by a vector of binary values $x_1, x_2, \cdots, x_n$, $x_i = 0\ or\ 1$, $1 \le i \le n$, ($x_i = 1$ means encasing, $x_i = 0$ means non-encasing). The aim is to find a vector which satisfies the constraint $\sum_{i=1}^{n} w_i x_i \le C$ and maximizes the total profit $\sum_{i=1}^{n} v_i x_i$.

The mathematical model is $\max \sum_{i=1}^{n} v_i x_i$

The restrictions is $\begin{cases} \sum_{i=1}^{n} w_i x_i \le C \\ x_i = 0 or 1, 1 \le i \le n \end{cases}$

3 Hybrid Genetic Algorithm for Solving Zero-One Knapsack Problem

3.1 Basic Idea

During each iterative process, the hybrid genetic algorithm for solving the zero-one knapsack problem executes, firstly, the improved selection operator, then, the crossover and mutation operator, furthermore greedy operator to ensure that each individual in population satisfies the restrictions. Thereby, the problem can be solved successfully. Thus, a new hybrid genetic algorithm is formed [6].

3.2 Algorithm Flow

1) Gene coding and initial group

Genetic code of zero-one knapsack problem is composed of ordinal x_i values, of which the number is n. Specifically, $X=(x_1,x_2,\cdots,x_n), x_i=0$ or 1. $x_i=1$ represents putting item i into the knapsack. $x_i=0$ represents not putting item i into the knapsack. For example, "110001100000000⋯ ⋯0000000011" is a solution which means that the items numbered 1、2、6、7、⋯、$n-1$、n will be put into the knapsack and others not. This paper generated the initial group in completely random way [7~9].

2) Fitness function

As the fitness value is the unique deterministic index of the individual to achieve the survival opportunity, the fitness function directly determines the group behavior evolution. In genetic algorithm, in order to associate the fitness function and the pros and cons degree of individual in group, the fitness must be non-negative and always the bigger the better in any case. This article used target function as fitness function when evaluated the individual fitness, namely, $F(X)=f(x_1,x_2,\cdots,x_n)=\sum_{i=1}^{n} v_i x_i$.

3) Operator selection

Different selection strategy has great influence on algorithm performance. Roulette wheel method is a selection strategy in common use, but can bring biggish sample error. Relevant improvement measurements are such as breeding pool selection, Boltzmann selection etc. But these strategies are based on adapted value proportion selection, and often bring precocity convergence. However non-linear arrangement avoids this problem, superfluity calculated quantity is bigger when colony size is great. The text puts forwards one kind of new selection strategy, namely improved roulette wheel selection strategy.

Firstly, sort every chromosome from small to big, according to the adaptability of environment;

Secondly, choose 2/5 of the great adaptive chromosome in cluster copy to the filial generation straight;

Thirdly, produce a random value for the odd 3/5 of every chromosome out of population, and sort the random value, then choose 1/3 of that get into the filial generation by the compositor. The intention is to avoid precocity convergence and stagnant phenomenon, and at the same time assured the multiplicity of population. By the selection, the filial generation obtains 3/5 of the previous generation chromosome, but gets the 2/5 chromosome of the leaving filial generation by crossbreeding.

4) Hybrid reproduction operator

Reproduction operator usually includes crossover operator C and mutation operator M to generate the new group, in which maybe contain more satisfactory individuals, based on the current group. However, for some gene coding clusters, the individuals generated through crossover operator (such as one point crossover) and mutation operator (such as point mutation) not always meet the restrictions and express the feasible solution. Thus, the article improved the reproduction operator with the idea of greedy algorithm.

Import greedy transform $G:\{0,1\}^n \to \{0,1\}^n$, for any $X = x_1, x_2, \cdots, x_n$, set $G(X) = y_1, y_2, \cdots, y_n$, where, $y_n (i = 1, 2, \cdots, n)$ is defined as follows:

①For all the items $x_i = 1$, order them by their value density v_i / w_i to form the queue $b(i)$, where, $b(1)$ is the serial number of the item with the first value density, $b(2)$ is the serial number of the item with the second value density, and so on;

②Set $k = 1$;

③Compute $c_k = \sum_{j=1}^{k} w_{b(j)}$;

④If $c_k \leq c$, then set $y_{b(k)} = 1$, namely putting the item which serial number is $b(j)$, set $k = k + 1$ and go to ③ ; else go to ⑤;

⑤ For each serial number j in $\{1, 2, \cdots, n\}$, however not in $\{b(1), b(2), \cdots, b(k)\}$, set $y_j = 0$.

This paper compounded greedy transform with basic crossover operator (one point crossover) and mutation operator (point mutation) respectively, so formed hybrid one point crossover operator C_h and hybrid point mutation operator M_h : $C_h = G \circ C, M_h = G \circ M$.

3.3 Algorithm Parameters

In this article, for the genetic algorithm, the group number M , the terminating evolution generation T , crossover probability P_c and mutation probability P_m are supposed to be M =100, T =100, P_c =0.5 and P_m =0.05.

3.4 Experiments and Analyses

Experiment 1 [10][11]:

n=10, C=269, W={95, 4, 60, 32, 23, 72, 80, 62, 65, 46}, V={55, 10, 47, 5,4, 50, 8, 61, 85, 87}

Experiment 2: n=20, C =878,

W={92, 4, 43, 83, 84, 68, 92, 82, 6, 44, 32, 18, 56, 83, 25, 96, 70, 48, 14, 58},

V={44, 46, 90, 72, 91, 40, 75, 35, 8, 54, 78, 40, 77, 15, 61, 17, 75, 29, 75, 63}

Experiment 3: n=50, C= 1000,

W={220, 208, 198, 192, 180, 180, 165, 162, 160, 158, 155, 130, 125, 122, 120, 118, 115, 110, 105, 101, 100, 100, 98, 96, 95, 90, 88, 82, 80, 77, 75, 73, 72, 70, 69, 66, 65, 63, 60, 58, 56, 50, 30, 20, 15, 10, 8, 5, 3, 1},

V={80, 82, 85, 70, 72, 70, 66, 50, 55, 25, 50, 55, 40, 48, 50, 32, 22, 60, 30, 32, 40, 38, 35, 32, 25, 28, 30, 22, 25, 30, 45, 30, 60, 50, 20, 65, 20, 25, 30, 10, 20, 25, 15, 10, 10, 10, 4, 4, 2, 1}.

Experiment 4 [12]: n=100, C =4995,

W={108, 98, 95, 107, 98, 100, 96, 105, 93, 112, 95, 105, 91, 96, 100, 103, 91, 96, 105, 90, 101, 110, 108, 95, 99, 96, 108, 101, 102, 100, 111, 88, 99, 112, 101, 105, 94, 113, 87, 101, 108, 96, 91, 89, 102, 99, 98, 93, 98, 99, 106, 112, 90, 100, 92, 94, 98, 97, 99, 95, 112, 108, 100, 98, 117, 98, 100, 98, 99, 113, 94, 111, 102, 99, 97, 87, 97, 103, 97, 89, 96, 94, 93, 104, 92, 109, 97, 109, 100, 88, 92, 108, 97, 106, 97, 97, 99, 94, 102, 95}

V={117, 113, 113, 113, 112, 112, 112, 112, 112, 111, 110, 110, 109, 109, 108, 108, 108, 108, 108, 108, 108, 107, 106, 106, 105, 105, 105, 105, 104, 103, 102, 102, 102, 101, 101, 101, 101, 100, 100, 100, 100, 100, 100, 99, 99, 99, 99, 99, 99, 99, 99, 98, 98, 98, 98, 98, 98, 98, 98, 97, 97, 97, 97, 97, 97, 97, 97, 96, 96, 96, 96, 96, 96, 95, 95, 95, 95, 95, 94, 94, 94, 94, 94, 93, 93, 93, 92, 92, 92, 91, 91, 91, 90, 90, 89, 89, 88, 88, 87, 87}.

Greedy algorithm (GA), standard GA (SGA) and HGA did ten times according to the above four experiments with the results shown in table 1.

Table 1. Comparison Table by GA, SGA and HGA

	Greedy algorithm(GA)	Standard genetic algorithm(SGA)		Hybrid genetic algorithm (HGA)	
	The best result	*The best result*	*genetic generation*	*The best result*	*average genetic generation*
N=10	295/269	295/269	37	295/271	5
N=20	1024/871	1037/874	100	1042/877	18.65
N=50	3077/999	3103/1000	100	3112/1000	20.72
N=100	5372/4992	5365/4991	100	5375/4996	31.91

From Table 1, we can analyse as follows:

(1) To the knapsack problem with 10 items, the greedy algorithm, standard genetic algorithm, and hybrid genetic algorithm all got the best result. HGA not only has high convergence, but also has rapid convergence speed. HGA can get the optimal solution when the average genetic generation is 5.

(2) To the knapsack problem with 20 items, the SGA got good result. However, HGA got better result. Not only is the convergence of HGA quite high, but also the convergence speed is quite rapid. HGA can get the optimal solution when the average genetic generation is 16.65.

(3) To the knapsack problem with 50 items, both of the SGA and HGA succeed. Nevertheless, HGA is superior to the SGA in precision and convergence speed. HGA can get the optimal solution when the average genetic generation is 15.72.

(4) To the knapsack problem with 100 items, HGA is superior to SGA in precision (The worst precision of HGA is higher than the average precision of SGA. Meanwhile, the SGA precision is worse than that of GA sometimes.) Moreover, the convergence speed of HGA is faster than that of SGA (HGA can get the optimal solution when the average genetic generation is 21.91. However, that of SGA is 100).

The above examples prove that the computing result of HGA is smartly superior to GA and SGA. The reason is that the greedy transform makes HGA have higher probability to get excellent coding chromosome. Thereby, using HGA to solve the zero-one knapsack problem will achieve better effect.

4 Conclusions

On the basis of improving the selection operator of genetic algorithm, this paper integrated genetic algorithm with greedy algorithm and presented the hybrid genetic algorithm enhancing the searching ability of genetic algorithm. The hybrid genetic algorithm quickens the searching speed, increases the precision and overcomes the disadvantage of the traditional algorithm effectively which is easily running into local optimization. The experiment shows that the hybrid genetic algorithm is effective for solving the zero-one knapsack problem.

Acknowledgment. The Project was Supported by the Special Fund for Basic Scientific Research of Central Colleges, China University of Geosciences (Wuhan) (No. CUGL090237) and the 863 Program of China (No. 2008AA121602).

References

1. Qin, P.P., Yan, Q.P., Huang, D.M.: Railway Passenger Volume Forecast by Means of Feed-Forward Neutral Network Method. Railway Transport and Fconomy 12, 95–98 (2005)
2. Wang, Z., Wang, Y.H., Jia, L.M., Li, P.: The Application of Improved BP Neural Network in the Prediction of Railway Passenger. Volume Time Serial 26(2), 127–131 (2005)
3. Gao, A.X., Chen, Y.Y., Rong, J.: The Road Section Actual Capacity Based on the BP Neural Network. Journal of Beijing University of Technology 30(4), 462–465 (2004)
4. Liu, Z. J., Ji, L., Ye, Y.L., Geng, Z.M.: Study on Prediction of Railway Freight Vol umes Based on RBF Neural Network. Journal of the China Railway Society 28(5), 1–5 (2006)
5. Zhou, X., Zhu, X.Y., Wen, C.Y., et al.: Base on hereditary learn arithmetic and BP arithmetic nerve network application in the mining pit surge water capacity account (1999)
6. Qian, A., Shrestha, G.B.: An ANN-based load model for fast transient stability calculations. Elec. Power. Sys. Res 76, 217–227 (2006)
7. Yarlagadda, P.K.D.V., Chiang, E.C.W.: A neural network system for the prediction of process parameters in pressure die casting. Mater. Proc. Technol. 89-90, 583–590 (1999)
8. Yia, J.Q., Wang, Q., Zhao, D.B., et al.: BP neural network prediction-based variable-period sampling approach for networked control systems. Applied. Math. Comput. 185, 976–988 (2007)
9. Chang, P.C., Chen, S.H., Liu, C.H.: Sub-population genetic algorithm with mining gene structures for multiobjective flow shop scheduling problems. Expert Sys. 33, 762–771 (2007)
10. Wu, X., Chu, C.H., Wang, Y.F., Yan, W.L.: A genetic algorithm for cellular manufacturing design and layout. Euro J. Opera Res. 181, 156–167 (2007)
11. Srinivas, V., Ramanjaneyulu, K.: An integrated approach for optimum design of bridge decks using genetic algorithms and artificial neural networks. Adv. Eng. Sof. 38, 475–487 (2007)
12. Jenkins, W.M.: Neural network weight training by mutation. Comput. Struct. 84, 2107–2112 (2006)

Research on the Authenticated Encryption Technology in CCSDS

Gong Chang-Qing and Yang Ya-Hui

College of Computer Shenyang Aerospace University
Shenyang, Liaoning Province, China
Gongyouth@21cn.com

Abstract. U.S. NASA, European ESA, Japanese NASDA and other institutions all have adopted the CCSDS as space communication standards; CCSDS has shown the latest technological developments in space communication system. This paper analyzed security threats in space communications system. The TC data protection methods were summarized firstly, then the performance of several encryption algorithms used in TC protocol was compared. SCPS-SP protocol and SCPS-SP data security process were introduced also. At last, an interoperation method between SCPS –SP and IPSec will be put forward.

Keywords: CCSDS, SCPS-SP, Authentication, Encryption.

1 Introduction

Space communications system is an effective platform for using space resources to send, transmit, receive and analyze spatial information. At present, China's space activities are mainly used for scientific research and national defense construction, and the security of data related to country's military, political and economic. As the development of electronic reconnaissance and electronic warfare technology and the openness of space communications systems, the spatial data transmission faces a great number of threats.

In 1982, the Consultative Committee for Space Data Systems (CCSDS) has been established by 8 space agencies in U.S. and international (eg NASA, ESA, etc.). In the early 1980s, Telemetry Protocol [1] is proposed by CCSDS. In the packet telemetry systems, spatial data sources grouped as a united to transmit by a fixed length transmission frame format. Shortly, CCSDS published the Telecommand Protocol [2] and the Advanced Orbiting System Standard (Advanced Orbiting System) [3] .AOS protocol extends packet telemetry standard for transferring files, audio, video and other documents. In 1990s, under the help of the DoD/NASA, CCSDS has developed the Space Communications Protocol Specification (Space Communication Protocol Specification, SCPS), which including SCPS-NP [4], SCPS-SP [5], SCPS-TP [6], and SCPS-FP [7].

D. Zeng (Ed.): ICAIC 2011, Part I, CCIS 224, pp. 321–329, 2011.

2 Security Threats, Security Requirements and Security Classification of the Space Communication System

Security threats that Space communication systems facing can be divided into passive and active attack threat; passive attack threat can be divided into data confidentiality threat and the confidential threat of flow; active attack threat includes tampering information data, attack of denial service and spoofing attack. The security requirement of Space communication systems includes confidentiality, integrity and authentication of information. According to the different missions of space communications, it can be divided into high, medium and low level of security, representing by A, B and C [8]. Security level A is major to provide protection for government, military space mission, to provide telecommand data confidentiality, integrity, access control and authentication services; to provide confidentiality, integrity, authentication services for telemetry data; to provide data confidentiality, integrity, access control and authentication services for terrestrial systems. Security level B is mainly to protect commercial, meteorology, telesensing and other space missions, to provide confidentiality (optional), integrity, authentication services for telecommand data; to provide confidentiality and integrity services for telemetry data; to provide the integrity of system data and certification services for ground. Security level C is to provide protection for other space missions, it provides confidentiality of data (optional), integrity, certification services for telecommand data; for telemetry data and ground system, just certification service is provided. This paper mainly research on space communications protocol stack telecommand protocol of link layer and the SCPS-SP protocol of network layer.

3 Security Research of Telecommand Protocol

Telecommand is the data transmission system to meet the need of the Recommendation for space communications system which is raised by Consultative Committee for Space Data Systems. In the telecommand system, different source's data and data of different rates is packaged as independent data Collection, which constitutes the standard format data packets, it can be transmitted through the uplink channel. As telecommand standard has been accepted by the major aerospace countries (Organization), so the countries (regions) can support each other by means of the earth station [9].

3.1 The Protection of Telecommand Data

The introduction of telecommand data brings great benefits to space communications systems, while also security issues is worrying. Because the nature of space communication system itself makes unauthorized users can access, analyze, forged spatial data, therefore a method need to be proposed so that unauthorized users can not access the data, decryption of spatial data in an open environment. The security requirement in telecommand system of CCSDS includes the confidentiality, integrity and authentication of telecommand data.

1) Encryption and Authentication: Any unauthorized user can not forge or modify message from authorized source, the message receiver can confirm the source of the data.

2*) Data Encryption*: the message can not be decrypted by any unauthorized user.

3) Data Integrity: The message receiver can verify whether the data is modified, and any non-authorized user can not replace the legal data by forged data.

3.2 The Introduction of Authenticated Encryption Algorithm in Telecommand System

In 2006, CCSDS has developed Security Threats against Space Mission and The Application of CCSDS to Secure System proposal. Applying different cryptographic algorithm into the telecommand system of CCSDS is becoming a key point of research in nearly two years. The ESA authenticated encryption algorithm [10] was first used in sublayer of telecommand system by S. Susanna from Italy. It provide encryption and authentication protection for telecommand data. Traditionally, we use the method of "first signed and then encrypted" to achieve the combination of encryption and signature. The computing and transferring cost of this method usually is the sum of encrypting and signing, and this traditional method always using public key encryption and signature algorithm. The speed of computing is slow and it is expensive also. In 1994, Horster, Michels and Petersen proposed a HMP authenticated encryption scheme [11] which is based on message that can be recovery according signature, and the cost of achieving authentication and encryption is lower. In 1995, Lee and Chang give a modified HMP scheme-LC scheme [12], which is characterized by not using Hash function. In 1999, Chen also proposed a modified scheme-Chen scheme [13]. Hash function is not be used in the scheme, but this scheme uses Redundancy function to verify the validity of the message. In 1997, Zheng proposed a called signcryption (signcryption) idea to achieve both authenticated and encryption [14], which symmetric encryption and digital signature is combined in a logical step to achieve both authentication and encryption, but it also using Hash function. Currently, Authenticated encryption algorithms which are used include OCB, CCM [15], EAX [16], GCM [17] and CWC [18] and so on.

GCM's design motivation is for the high transmission rate for network applications. It has features of high efficiency achieved by the hardware, good performance, and provable security. Its design idea is very similar to CWC, compared with the CWC, and GCM is a dual pan-Domain Hash computing, while CWC is a 127 bit integer operating on integer domain. Therefore, the cost of GCM hardware implementation is small, and the computing speed is fast, and it can be achieved by using software much easier. GCM algorithm uses AES encryption algorithm. The following table describes performance comparison of the amount of data which the processor can handled per clock cycle 1000 according to the different algorithm when they are executed in software and hardware, (based on AES-128), GCM (64k), GCM (8k), GCM (4k), GCM (256) represent the storage space of each GCM state is 64k, 8k, 4k and 256.

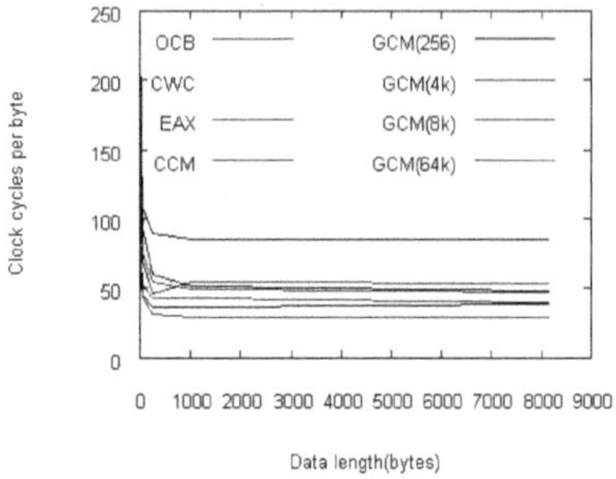

Fig. 1. Comparison of AEAD algorithms

Through comparing and analyzing, OCB algorithm has some speed advantages, which is due to the impact of the underlying block cipher. OCB algorithm speed advantages will be offset by other advantages of GCM, at the same time, OCB algorithm is also lack of intellectual property restriction. Therefore, the using of GCM authenticated encryption algorithm in telecommand system of CCSDS can meet the requirements of high data processing and low overhead of the system. The question of the processing of on-board computer is limited and high request of real-time can be solved also.

4 Protection of Spatial Data in Space Communications Security Protocol

CCSDS (the Consultative Committee for Space Data Systems) specification provides a set of non-connected end to end security services space communications protocol specification - Security Protocol (SCPS-SP). SCPS-SP is the security protocol standard of CCSDS in network layer. The SCPS-SP pursuit of the best bits of efficiency, with minimal communication overhead, to provide data protection for space communication missions, and it can provide an effective end to end confidentiality, integrity, authenticity of data service, or the combination of these services.

4.1 Scps-Sp and the Data Protection

SCPS-SP supports a variety of options of authentication, integrity, confidentiality and access control which is used for the exchange of spatial data. Space communications systems has characteristics of a large data transmission delay, high error rate, large differences in uplink and downlink, the limitation of CPU data processing capacity, small available memory and traffic-free cycle, so it pursues optional bit efficiency, to provide protection for the communication data of space missions with the smallest communication overhead.

SCPS-SP packages transport layer protocol data unit (T-PDU) into a security protocol data unit (S-PDU), through T-PDU encryption and integrity check to provide confidentiality and integrity service. SCPS-SP is designed to achieve approximative optimal bit rate, guaranteed less bit overhead, which is the difference of SCPS-SP from other security protocols. SCPS-SP protocol makes the head of network layer, link layer and physical layer is plaintext, the transport layer header, users data and integrity check value is ciphertext, SCPS-SP protocol also add SCPS-SP a plain header and a encrypted header.

4.2 The Comparison between Terrestrial Networks Ipsec and Scps-Sp

RFC [RFC 2401 ~ 1411] [W-IPsec] which is published in November 1998 described the IP security architecture [RFC 2041] and described to provide IPsec protocol suite [RFC 2411] also. IPsec ESP protocol (Encapsulation Security Payload) provides data confidentiality, data integrity or authentication, and through the AH protocol (Authentication Header) provides only authentication or data integrity, and it does not provide data confidentiality. From the security side, SCPS-SP has the same function with the IPsec ESP protocol. However, IPsec ESP is a heavyweight protocol that each IP packet adds at least 10Byte. SCPS-SP protocol provides the same security services as IPsec ESP services, but more efficiently. By comparison, SCPS-SP is fit for the environ-ment of low bandwidth and short connection times, small overhead, SCPS-SP only increases 2Byte each packet costs, including populated and identification information.

4.3 Improved Multi-level Security Adaptive Scps-Sp

The main feature of SCPS-SP is the smallest bits of communication overhead and optimal efficiency to provide data protection for space communications system, whose value is reflected by the applications which is used in the space communication environment of limited bandwidth and CPU processing capacity. With the development of space communications technology, now space communication bandwidth has been increased rapidly. NASA study predicts [19], LEO, GEO satellite communications capability can be achieved to 1Gbit / s in 2010 from 150Mbit / s in 2004 if the new physical layer technologies emerge. In 2020, this number will reach to 20Gbit / s. The link communication capacity between Earth and Mars is also expected increased to 5 Mbit / s in 2010. In this case, the system should consider the compatibility and the diversity of functional, rather than how to compress byte overhead.

The primary advantage of SCPS-SP is to provide end to end security, but it allows the data unit header from the lower layer is plaintext. Middle system can relay the SCPS-SP protocol data unit, the shortcoming is that traffic analysis can not be provided, encrypted data may be intercepted by unauthorized users. As the influence of communication channel bandwidth to the constraints of space communications gradually reducing, for the SCPS-SP shortcoming that it can not providing protection against traffic analysis, drawing on the ground in Internet security protocol IPsec tunnel mode, some corresponding protocol data can be added into SCPS-SP protocol data packet to design a space communications security protection Tunneling Protocol with the traffic analysis protection [20].

As the security classification of the space task mentioned above, First, define the level of security in SA (Security Association), and establish security services of each level and encryption algorithm used by, by adding a logo in SCPS-SP's protected

HDR to select the security option selected service, and then define a header in the protection of security options to choose optional services which is identified in the field. Compared with the original agreement, SCPS-SP protocol data added protection security options in the protected HDR, and optional services to provide security services. Protocol data unit format is shown as below.

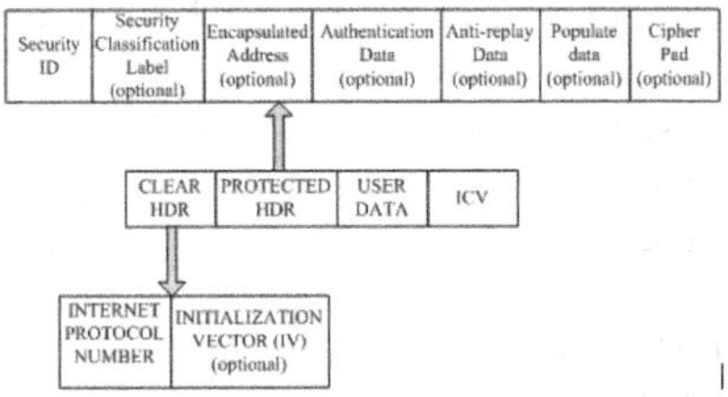

Fig. 2 Data units of multi-level security improved SCPS-SP

Security ID: The sender can choose the type of security services, such as data confidentiality, integrity, authentication, anti-replayed protection, protection against traffic analysis, and the receiver can determine security measures used by sender according to the security ID to take corresponding processing.

Security Classification Label: Data security is used to indicate the security level, which is specified in the SA. In the process of establishing security alliance by communicating parties, both sides have set a security level security options range, according to communications security, environment, communications requirements and security requirements of space missions needs to select the appropriate level of security which is settled before.

Encapsulated Address: it includes encryption source and destination address field, and sender's identification can be identified by using it.

Anti-replay Data: For the purpose of message freshness and resisting replayed attack, additional data field is needed to store the fresh information. A common method is to increase a stamp or a replayed counter. Sender can encrypt the message with a fresh factor after the data field to resist anti-replayed attack and the receiver decrypt data and verify the fresh factor to resist replayed attack.

Populate data: In order to prevent unauthorized users analyzing spatial data, this protocol data unit can be filled with some invalid data, so unauthorized user can not analyzes useful information through the account of data.

4.4 Interoperability of SCPS-SP and IPsec

When the data is transported between space network and ground network, because of the difference of protocols, in the space network, data needs to meet the CCSDS standard, but in the terrestrial network, the data needs to comply with Internet standards. It is needed to be transformed to each other. A trusted network gateway is needed also to establish a secure tunnel between these two networks [21]. The main operation of the gateway is to encrypt, decrypt SCPS-SP and the IPsec data, converse these two kinds of data forma to each other. Unencrypted data can be seen in this area, therefore the gateway must be trusted. According to 3.3 Improved SCPS-SP, the

SCPS-SP protocol can be instead by improved SCPS-SP protocol during interoperating.

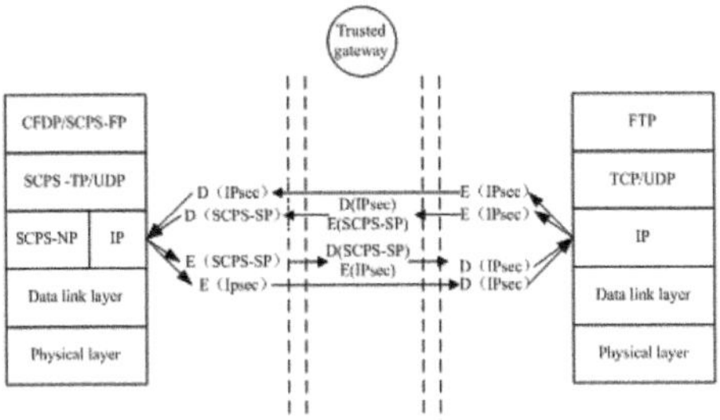

Fig. 3. Trusted gateway of interconnected network between air and Ground

The specific operations of the gateway: a) if data is transmitted from ground network to space network, IP data is encrypted first at the source end by IPsec, then sends the encrypted data into ground link, after the data arriving at the security gateway, the gateway decrypts IPsec first, and then encrypts SCPS-SP, and sends the data into space link, the destination end decrypts SCPS-SP, at last packages the data in the form of SCPS-NP and sends it to space network user. b) if data is transmitted from space network to ground network, SCPS-NP of data encrypted first at the source end by SCPS-SP, then sends the encrypted data into space link, when it reaches the trusted gateway, the gateway decrypts SCPS-SP, and then encrypts IPsec, and then sends the data into ground link, the destination decrypts the IPsec, packages the data in the form of IP and sends it to the terrestrial network user. c) When the space user sends or receives data in the network layer in the form of IP, the trusted gateway does not decrypt the encrypted data packet; just transmit the data packet received. The gateway is not visible for terrestrial network users and space network user. In order to achieve the interoperability between SCPS-SP and IPsec, IPsec and SCPS-SP use security database which must include two security associations (SA): one SA for a network user from the ground, suspended in space network user data; another SA for a space network user, suspended in the ground network user data. SA sets up security parameters for secure communication between two communication entities.

5 Conclusion

This paper researches the space communication system security issues. First, the security agreement in the telecommand is analyzed and the security needs of telecommand protocol are discussed also. With the introduction of cryptography, according to the requirements of space communication environment, the encryption authentication algorithm is introduced into space communication system. Some authentication encryption algorithms are compared; GCM encryption authentication algorithm is proved the much fit for space communications system by comparing. Furthermore, this article also researches on network layer security protocol which involved in space communication security, it was compared with IPSec which is used in terrestrial network. This paper has proposed an improved multi-level security adaptive SCPS-SP, and a method was proposed to solve the problem of traffic analysis that space communication is facing. Finally, a concept of trusted gateway is given for the interoperability between SCPS-SP and IPSec, space communication can be more safely through the trusted gateway.

References

1. CCSDS 132.0-B-1 TM space data Link protocol, Recommendation for Space Data System Standards. Blue Book, Issue 1, Washington, DC, CCSDS (September 2003)
2. CCSDS 132.0-B-1 TC space data Link protocol, Recommendation for Space Data System Standards. Blue Book, Issue 1, Washington, DC, CCSDS (September 2003)
3. CCSDS 732.0-B-2 AOS Space Data Link protocol, Recommendation for Space Data System Standards. Blue Book, Issue 2, Washington, DC, CCSDS (July 2006)
4. CCSDS 713.0-B-1 Space Communications Protocol Specification(SCPS)-Network protocol(SCPS-NP), Recommendation for Space Data System Standards. Blue Book, Issue 1, Washington, DC, CCSDS (May 1999)
5. CCSDS 713.5-B-1 Space Communications Protocol Specification(SCPS)-Security protocol(SCPS-SP), Recommendation for Space Data System Standards. Blue Book, Issue 2, Washington, DC, CCSDS (July 2006)
6. CCSDS 714.0-B-2 Space Communications Protocol Specification(SCPS)- Transport protocol(SCPS-TP), Recommendation for Space Data System Standards. Blue Book, Issue 2, Washington, DC, CCSDS (July 2006)
7. CCSDS 717.0-B-1 Space Communications Protocol Specification (SCPS)-File Protocol (SCPS-FP), Recommendation for Space Data System Standards. Blue Book, Issue 1, Washington, DC, CCSDS (May 1999)
8. CCSDS 350.0-G-1 the Application of CCSDS Protocols to Secure Systems, Report concerning space data System standards. Green Book, Issuel, Washington DC, CCSDS, (March 1999)
9. CCSDS 232.0.B-l,TC Space data link protocol. Washington, USA, National Aeronautics Space Administration (2003)
10. Spinsante S, Chiaraluce F, Gambi E. New Perspectives in Telecommand Security: The Application of EAX to TC Segment s. In: Proc. Data Systems in Aerospace (DASIA), Naples, Italy (2007)
11. Horster, P., Michels, M., Petersen, H.: Authenticated encryption schemes with low communication costs. Electronics Letters 30(15), 1212–1213 (1994)
12. Lee, W., Chang, C.: Authenticated encryption scheme without using a one-way function. Electronics Letters 31(19), 1656–1657 (1995)
13. Chen, K.: Signature with message recovery. Electronics Letters 34(20), 1934 (1998)
14. Zheng, Y.: Digital signcryption or how to achieve cost (Signature & encryption) < < cost(Signature) + cost(Encryption). In: Kaliski Jr., B.S. (ed.) CRYPTO 1997. LNCS, vol. 1294, pp. 165–179. Springer, Heidelberg (1997)
15. Whiting D, Housley R, and Ferguson. Counter with CBC-MAC (CCM). IETF Network working Group, Request For Comments, 3610 (September 2003)
16. Bellare, M., Rogaway, P., Wagner, D.: The EAX mode of operation. In: Roy, B., Meier, W. (eds.) FSE 2004. LNCS, vol. 3017, pp. 389–407. Springer, Heidelberg (2004)

17. McGrew, D.A., Viega, J.: The security and performance of the galois/Counter mode (GCM) of operation. In: Canteaut, A., Viswanathan, K. (eds.) INDOCRYPT 2004. LNCS, vol. 3348, pp. 343–355. Springer, Heidelberg (2004)
18. Kohno, T., Viega, J., Whiting, D., The, C.W.C.-A.E.S.: dual-use mode. Internet Draft, Cryto Form Research Group (May 20, 2003) (work in progress)
19. Huang, Z., Li, L., Mi, X.-m., Gu, X.-m.: Space Communication Protocol Specification (SCPS) and Application: Status, Problem and Prospect. Telecommunication Engineering 47(06), 8–11 (2007)
20. Duan, X.-f., An, H.-z., Xie, S.-m.: Space Communi-cation Security Protocols. Communications Technology 42(12), 101–102 (2009)
21. Liu, Y., Dong, Y., Li, Z.-h.: Discussion of Data Security about Space-Earth All-in-One Networking and Analysis of CCSDS SCPS. Chinese Space Science and Technology 1, 35–36 (2004)

Quality Assessment in Virtual Surgical Training*

Hui Liang and Minyong Shi

Communication University of China University of Springfield Beijing, China
hui7728@yeah.net

Abstract. Simulation-based surgical training is beginning to be recognized by medical society with its apparent benefits. As an important function of virtual surgical training system, providing systemic and competitive surgical quality assessment to trainees is still a brand new field. In this paper, we present several metrics and their corresponding measurement methods used in our surgical training system designed for UK's Royal Bournemouth Hospital to assess trainees' task accomplishing quality. Classification algorithm and evaluation result of the training record is concisely discussed at the end of the paper.

Keywords: quality assessment, virtual surgical training, simulation.

1 Introduction

The extensive potential benefits of realistic virtual surgery training system: cutting in cost, objective assessment of surgical skill and decreased risk to patients are strong attractions to modern hospitals and institutes. Although up till now, several training simulators have been developed by medical companies designed to reproduce with high fidelity the human body, such simulators are scarcely designed to provide any constructive information to trainees to point out their limitations in surgical technique. And this feedback in training is very important in helping trainees to remedy mistakes efficiently and make progress accordingly. There are a very few simulators begin to include some basic surgical skill metrics such as time to completion and wall collisions to provide evaluation. However these metrics can only give a rather incomplete assessment of user's performance and some of them even have been explicitly demonstrated to be a poor measure of skill [1], let along provide systemic and comprehensive assessment.

In our virtual surgery training system [2] developed for the UK's Royal Bournemouth Hospital [3] to conduct interactive surgical training and surgery planning, we constructed a surgical technique evaluation model consisting of static structure and dynamic process, as well as a compositive surgery performance evaluation index system [4]. This evaluation index system is devised based on Bournemouth Hospital's experienced surgeons' intuitive descriptions of good technique in their discipline. Their domain expertise is certainly an extremely useful resource and can facilitate the development of highly relevant and successful metrics.

* This work is supported by the Project of State Administration of Radio Film and Television (SARFT) Grant #2007-07.

D. Zeng (Ed.): ICAIC 2011, Part I, CCIS 224, pp. 330–337, 2011.

All the metrics can be objectively evaluated from the following three categories of surgical skills: *Efficiency* (it refers to the metric that measures the time trainee spends to complete the task and the metric that presents how many redundant fabrics are used), *Safety* (it refers to such task parameters that present the performance of safe operations during the virtual training procedure, such as the ability of avoiding the unwanted collisions between instruments and nerves or blood vessels.) and *Quality* (it refers to such parameters that measure how well trainees performed the task).

The European Working Time Directive (EWTD) has placed serious constraints upon medical education. Before becoming a senior surgeon, a trainee should be expected to work over 30,000 hours before the instruction of EWTD [5]. Even thought the Royal College of Surgeons calculates that this will now fall to 8,000 hours, there is no doubt that the surgical proficiency is vital to surgeons. Therefore, the quality assessment of training task accomplishment, which could provide constructive feedback to trainees to facilitate independent learning and improvement, is essential to the development of virtual training systems. In this paper, we mainly talk about the quality metrics and the corresponding measurement methods. The classification algorithm and analysis of evaluation result based on the trainees performance records is also be concisely introduced.

2 Quality Metrics

Generally speaking, evaluating trainees' task accomplishing quality is difficult, because it involves all aspects of surgical skills during the complex procedure of virtual surgery. Beside these, an important consideration increasing the challenge of giving comprehensive assessment is that in the traditional "apprenticeship" surgical training model, assessment of proficiency is based on the subjective impression of the surgical educator. And this traditional model still dominates the surgical proficiency evaluation now. Since the economics, efficiency, reliability, effectiveness, degree of responsibility, and ethics of this traditional "apprenticeship" model have come into question in recent years [6], objective and standardized assessment tools should be put forward and take responsibility for providing objective evaluation in surgical training. As the first step of this, we should make clear that which evaluation metrics should be included and how these metrics form a unified whole to make a full understanding of trainee's task accomplishing quality. The problem needs to be resolved by setting up a competitive index system with hierarchy structure rather than providing some basic metrics only.

As has been mentioned, the index system constructed thus far in our training system is devised based on experienced surgeons' outstanding professional skill and at the same time, the development of highly relevant and successful metrics also requires us a lot of cleverness and manual labor, and must, at least in part, be repeated for each new procedure that is simulated.

As an important component of our evaluation index system, the task accomplishing quality metrics are divided into three grades (as shown in Table 1). The first grade index presents the level of task accomplishing quality and the other two grades are composed by subsets of concrete metrics. From the second grade index, we can see that the task accomplishing quality can be objectively evaluated from the following three categories of assessing metrics: Drilling & Cutting Technique, Suctioning Technique and Suture Technique. And almost all the normal concrete standards usually used for evaluation in hospital's training course are included in the last grade.

Table 1. Training Task Accomplishing Quality Metrics

Quality	Drilling/Cutting Technique	Drilling/*Cutting Length*
		Drilling/*Cutting Depth*
		Drilling/*Cutting Region*
		Drilling/*Cutting Angle*
		Jump Frequency
		Instrument Selection
	Suctioning Technique	*Distance between Drill/Scalpel and Suction*
		Executive Dust Time
	Suturing Technique	*Distance between insertion points*
		Distance between insertion point and wound edge

3 Measurement of Quality Metrics

It is common that an open surgery requires incisions in the patient's body. The surgeon often has direct visual and tactile contact with the region of interest. The accomplishing quality of cutting surface skin, drilling enlarged bone, using suction to remove bone dust and body fluid brought by cutting and drilling, and finally suturing wound is tested in our training system.

For example, in a virtual bone spur removal surgery, as shown in Figure 1, the enlarged bone spur narrows the spinal canal (marked in yellow) and poses a great threat to the nearby never roots (marked in red). The training task is removing the enlarged parts of the vertebra by using virtual drill (shown in bottom of Figure 1 and marked in gray) with high quality. The exact procedure will depend upon the location and severity of the spur. It will also depend on the surgeon performing the operation, which covers all the metrics we listed above including drilling and cutting, suctioning bone dust, and suturing wound. As the data base of further classification of trainees' proficiency level and analysis of evaluation results, the trainees' performance should be measured and recorded during the simulation trials.

3.1 Drilling/Cutting Technique

Due to the lack of space, the measurement methods of all the "Drilling/Cutting Technique" metrics could not be detailed and only the testing of "drilling angle" is presented as an example.

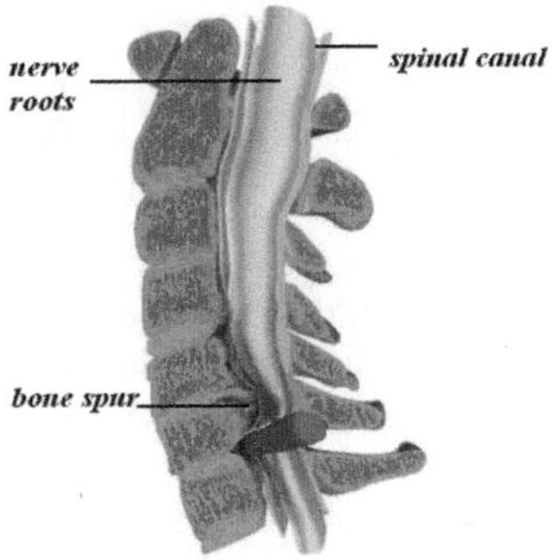

Fig. 1. Vertebra with bone spurs which shoud to be removed by drill

As the spherical drill burr ratates, the flumes are spinning much faster along the equator than at the tip, making it more efficient to drill using the side of the burr. And at the same time, the way in which the great circle of the drill dig into the bone also makes for more reliable control when drilling in this way. See Figure 2 for examples of good and poor technique according to this criterion. As shown in Figure 2-a, the tip of the burr is being used, with the drill perpendicular to the bone surface, resulting in inefficient bone removal and more difficult handing. And the angle θ between the primary drill axis vector and the force vector is near 0 degree. In Figure 1-b, the side of the burr is being used, making bone removal more efficient and handing easier. The angle θ is close to 90 degrees.

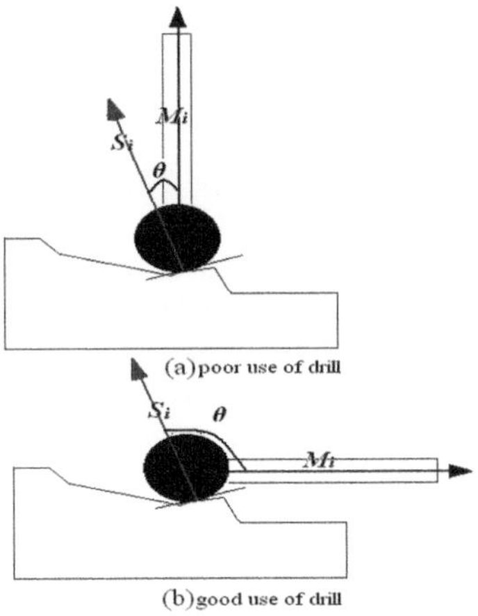

Fig. 2. Computing drill angles

The angle θ between the primary drill axis (direction vector M_i) and the generated force vector S_i is calculated by taking the arccosine of the dot product of these two normalized vectors, shown in the next formula:

$$Cos\theta = \frac{M \bullet S}{\|M\| * \|S\|}$$

3.2 Suctioning Technique

When drilling, to keep a clear visibility of the bone surface in surgical field, good technique in the use of the suction involves removing bone dust timely created by drilling enlarged bone spur. In our simulator, particles of bone dust are generated as bone is removed by drilling, and a suctioning device held in the opposite hand as the drill is used as a second haptic device to remove these particles.

1) Executive Dust Time
"Executive Dust Time" is included to denote for how long time the trainees have drilled while more than a specified number of dust particles obscured the surgical field. The particle number can be tracked by the bone dust generator and updated once particles are generated or removed. The algorithm is consists of a sequence of steps:

Step 1: When collision between bone and drill is detected, dust generator begins to produce dust particles and the particle number increases.

Step 2: When using suctioning device, the nearby dust particles perish and the particle number decreases.

Step 3: Update the dust particle number and calculate it's density in surgical field at a certain time interval.

Step 4: Once the density of dust particle is greater than a critical density, which will obstruct the view of trainees, the timer of "Executive Dust Time" is triggered and begins to accurate the duration time until the dust density is lower than the critical value. Record this duration time, reset the timer and wait for the next trigger.

Step 5: Accumulate all the duration time recorded when training finishing.

2) Distance between Drill and Suction
The coordination of the drill and the suction is an important element of good "two handed technique". The suction should be kept near the drill when removing the bone to prevent bone dust accumulating and also to properly cool the drilling surface by irrigating. Therefore, the "Distance between Drill and Suction" metric identifies the didtance between the drill and suction to make sure that the suction is moving along with the drill in a specified distance which is specified distance is specified by the configuration of suction's power. "Distance between Drill and Suction" can be simply get by calculating the distance of the tip points of the burr and suction.

3.3 Suturing Technique

To evaluate the suturing technique is somewhat complex, which involves: 1) *choosing of suturing materials* -when we select a suture material, there are two variables to consider: the suture thread (type and gauge) and needle (type and size); 2) *Method of suturing*-there are many methods of suturing, the most common of which includes: simple interrupted, vertical mattress, horizontal mattress, continuous over and over, half-buried horizontal, subcuticular and so on; 3) *Tying of a suture*-a suture is tied to just appose the wound adages and a tight suture will result in wound edge ischemia, necrosis with increased scarring and suture marks; and 4) *Removal of the wound*.

We only include two basic suturing techniques: "Distance between insertion points" and "Distance between insertion point and wound edge", which are most commonly used for simple skin or soft tissue wound closure.

"Distance between insertion points" measures the distance between two neighborhood needle insertion points. "Distance between insertion point and wound edge" tests the distance from the needle insertion point to the edge of wound. If needle insertion points are too close from the edge of the wound, the suture will tear the soft tissue instead of suturing the incision together when the tension applied on the pierced nodes beyond a preset threshold. If too sparse, suturing will have no effect and wound will not heal.

As shown in Figure 3-b, the distance between two adjacent insertion points (red points) l_p can be calculated as follows:

- Step 1: Record the individual 3D coordinates of all points contacted as needle pierces into the skin surface, where n is the contacted pointer number and P_i is the ith insertion point. So the 3D coordinate of P_i can be presented as (P_{ix}, P_{iy}, P_{iz}).
- Step 2: Supposing that the distance between two adjacent insertion points (P_i and P_{i+1}) presented as D_{pi}, where the range of i is from 1 to $n-1$, we can calculate the ith distance as following:

$$D_{pi} = \sqrt{(P_{(i+1)x} - P_{ix})^2 + (P_{(i+1)y} - P_{(i-1)y})^2 + (P_{(i+1)z} - P_{iz})^2}$$

- Step 3: Having the $n-1$ distances, we can calculate the mean and standard deviation of l_p as following:

$$\mu_{p=} \frac{1}{n-1} \sum_{i=1}^{n-1} D_{pi}$$

$$\sigma_p = \sqrt{\frac{1}{n-1} \sum_{i=1}^{n-1} (D_{pi} - \mu_p)^2}$$

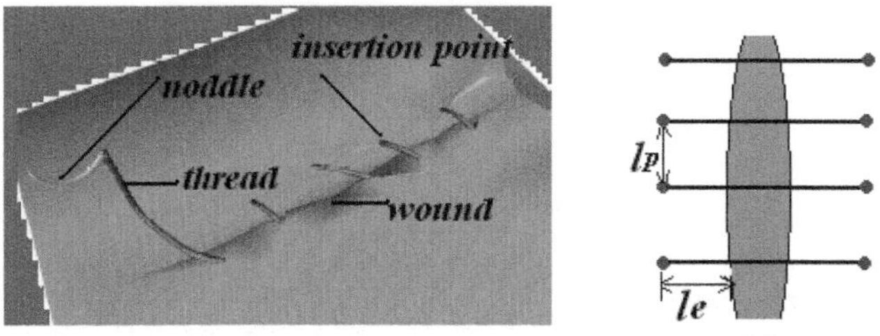

(a) (b)

Fig. 3. Distance between insertion points (l_p) and distance between insertion point and wound edge (l_e)

The calculation of distance between insertion point and wound edge l_e is similar to the calculation of l_p. The only difference is we should not only record both the distance between the insertion point and the edge of the wound but also record the distance between the pull-out point (on which the needle is put out for a next new insertion) and the edge of the wound.

4 Discussions and Conclusion

On the base of the trainee's performance recorded and calculated during runs of our virtual surgery training, we applied machine learning algorithm-Hidden Markov Models [7] to recognize and classify of metric values as data streams, to recognize the "pattern" of the user and classify his/her level of expertise.

We recorded a series of virtual operation performed on our training system by fifteen subjects. Data were sampled ten times per second, with a 25 millisecond sliding window smoothing the original data sampled at one millisecond intervals. Using a seven-state HMM, the number of experts and novices (out of each) correctly classified for each of ten trials (with different random initializations) is shown in Table 2. We can find that 85% of experts and 85% of novices were correctly classified.

Table 2. NUMBER of correct classification for each trial

	Experts	*Novices*
Trail 1	6	7
Trail 2	7	7
Trail 3	7	7
Trail 4	7	6
Trail 5	7	7
Trail 6	7	7
Trail 7	6	6
Trail 8	7	7
Trail 9	7	6
Trail 10	7	8
Mean	6.8	6.8
StdDev	0.4	0.6
Pct	85%	85%

To valid our evaluation model, besides the automatic evaluating by our training system, we also invited some experienced surgeons to assess the trainee's skill in our experiences and found that the metrics correlated reasonably well with subjective assessments of performance by these experts.

The implementation of Fuzzy Logic recognizing algorithm and the application of Rough Set theory in the analysis of derived importance will be the important part of our next work, which will surely help trainees a lot by providing useful instructional feedback and indicating their insufficiency in surgical skills to make further improvements.

References

1. Ritter, E.M., McClusky, D.A., Gallagher, A.G., Smith, C.K.: Real-time objective assessment of knot quality with a portable tensiometer is superior to execution time for assessment of laparoscopic knottying performance. Surg. Innov. 12, 233–237 (2005)
2. Liang, H., Shi, M.: Design of Virtual Abdominal Surgery System for the UK's Royal Bournemouth Hospital. In: Proc. IEEE The First International Conference on Knowledge and Systems Engineering (KSE 2009), pp. 39–43. IEEE Press, Los Alamitos (2009)
3. UK's Royal Bournemouth Hospital, `http://www.rbch.nhs.uk/`
4. Liang, H., Shi, M.: Surgical Skill Evaluation Model for Virtual Surgical Training. In: Proc. IEEE Global Congress on Science Engineering (GCSE 2010). IEEE Press, Los Alamitos (2010) (in press)
5. Hanly, D.: Report of the National Task Force on Medical Staffing. Department of Health and Children, Stationery Office, Dublin (2003)
6. Sidhu, R.S., Grober, E.D., et al.: Assessing competency in surgery: where to begin? Surgery 135, 6–20 (2004)
7. Mackel, T.R., Rosen, J.: Markov Model Assessment of Subjects' Clinical Skill Using the E-Pelvis Physical Simulator. Proc. IEEE Transactions on Biomedical Engineering 54(12), 33–41 (2007)

The Deceptive Effect of Blinking Decoys on ARMs

Dong Wen-feng[1,2], Liu Quan[1], Cheng Zhong-kuan[2], and Pan Zi-kai[2]

[1] School of Information Engineering, Wuhan University of technology
Wuhan 430070, China
[2] AFRA,Wuhan 430019, China
dongxinanu@foxmail.com120

Abstract. The idea of blinking operation of decoyed radar system is presented and its deceptive mechanism to ARM PRS (passive radar seeker) is analyzed. Several kinds of blinking modes are put forward. The simulation shows that blinking mode is one of the important operation modes of decoyed radar system, which can provide much more possibilities for the safety of radar confronting threat from ARM.

Keywords: ARM, PRS, radar, decoys, blinking modes.

1 Introduction

Because of the broad view field and relatively weak angle resolution, ARMs are possibly deceived confronting multi-active-source (decoy) system [1,2] which has the same frequency and almost the same waveforms for all sources. Blinking jamming is a kind of effective operation mode to counter radar-guided missile[4], and its idea may provide a kind of good choice for countering ARM by decoyed radar system. In blinking mode, two or more radiators of the same kind are switched on and off according to given pattern or almost randomly, which interferes with the aiming process of ARM PRS and force the ARM to turn right or left consequently so that the ARM will be unable to trace its target, the radar.

2 The Blinking Modes of Anti-arm Decoys

In a multi-active-source decoyed system, the radar and decoys can operate simultaneously[5], alternatively, or randomly, which forms blinking EM (Electromagnetic) fields to ARM PRS in space, and lead the ARMs not to attack any source. The blinking modes can be divided into to basic types, synchronous blinking mode and asynchronous blinking mode.

2.1 Synchronous Blinking Mode

In synchronous blinking mode, the operation waveforms of radiating sources in the multi-source decoying system are kept synchronous in time sequence. A simple pattern

D. Zeng (Ed.): ICAIC 2011, Part I, CCIS 224, pp. 338–347, 2011.

of synchronous blinking mode is shown in Fig.1 (a), when two radiators are modulated by square wave $f_1(t)$ and $f_2(t)$ respectively. There is only one radiating at any moment, and the blinking period is $T_M = \sum_{i=1}^{n} \tau_i$, where τ_i (i=1,2,3, ···) is the transmitting duration of each radiator.

2.2 Asynchronous Blinking Mode

In asynchronous blinking mode, each radiator transmits according its own way, as shown in Fig.1(b). Accordingly, there may exists four cases randomly as follows.

1) *Case 1:* Radiator 1 transmits and radiator 2 stops, therefore, the PRS of ARM will aim at radiator 1;
2) *Case 2:* Radiator 2 transmits and radiator 1 stops, therefore, the PRS of ARM will aim at radiator 2;
3) *Case 3:* Both radiators stop, therefore, the PRS of ARM will lose target signal sources;
4) *Case 4:* Both radiators transmit simultaneously, therefore, the PRS of ARM will aim at somewhere according to the amplitude and phase relationship between the radiating signals from different sources[1,2].

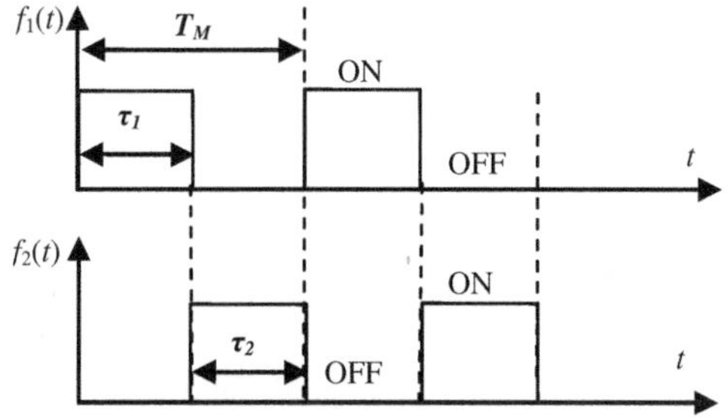

(a) Synchronous blinking mode

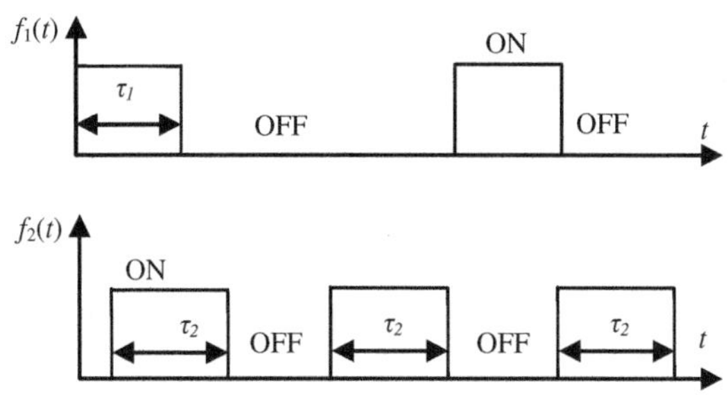

(b) Asynchronous mode

Fig. 1. Waveforms of blinking modes

3 The Response of Angle Tracking Circuit of Arm Prs

The angle tracking circuit of ARM PRS consists generally of antennas and feed, receivers and antenna servo system. It enables the PRS antennas to trace target signal direction, receive stable signal so that the ARM will be supplied with navigating signal to turn to the signal source direction automatically. Among automatic tracking techniques, proportional guidance is widely employed in flying system[3]. The principle of proportional guidance in ARM system is depicted in Fig.2, where the change of line of sight of radar to ARM, q, is proportion to the change of aiming angle of PRS, θ, *i.e.*,

$$dq/dt = \varpi = k \cdot d\theta/dt\ t \tag{1}$$

where ϖ is the maneuver angular rate of ARM towards radar.

Its schematic diagram is shown in Fig.3 [4], where, θ is the error angle between signal direction and the current aiming direction of PRS; $G(s)=k_1/T_1s+1$ is the transfer function of the PRS receiver, k_1 is the transfer coefficient of PRS receiver, T_1 is inertial constant, and s is Laplace operator; k_2 is the transfer coefficient of the stable circuit; $1/s$ realizes integral; V is the error voltage out of the circuit.

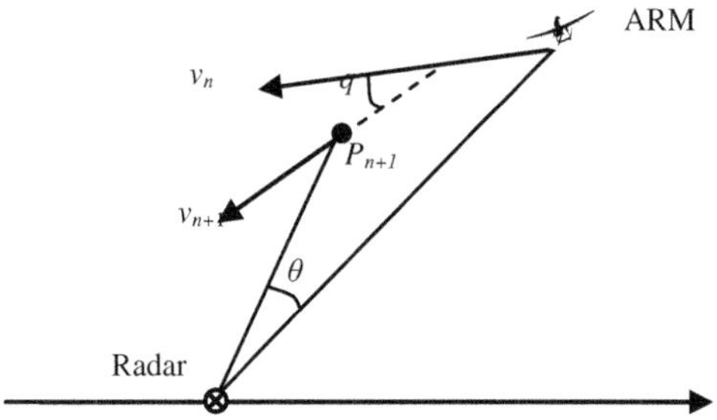

Fig. 2. The principle of proportional guidance in ARM

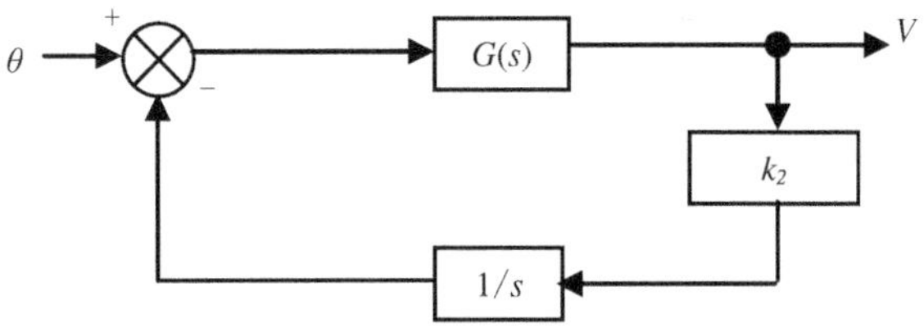

Fig. 3. Block diagram of angle tracking circuit

The transfer function of the angle tracking circuit is often a second-order one, which has the advantage of response smoothly to the input signal. According to the feature of ARM PRS, the transfer function can be designed as band-pass or low-pass forms. It can be expressed as follows

$$H(s)=\frac{V}{\theta}=\frac{G(s)}{1+\frac{k_2}{s}G(s)}=\frac{k_1 s}{T_1 s^2+s+k_1 k_2}=\frac{\omega_1^2 s}{s^2+2\xi\omega_0 s+\omega_0^2} \tag{2}$$

Where, $\xi=\sqrt{1/k_1k_2T}/2$ is called the damp coefficient of the system, $0<\xi<1$; $\omega_1=\omega_0/k_2$; $\omega_0=\sqrt{k_1k_2/T_1}=2\pi f_0$, f_0 is inherent resonant frequency of the circuit. By adjusting ξ and f_0, the characteristics of the circuit can be improved.

The Laplace response of the error voltage can be deduced as

$$V(s)=H(s)\theta(s)=\frac{\omega_1^2 s\theta(s)}{s^2+2\xi\omega_0 s+\omega_0^2} \tag{3}$$

Form Eq.(3), the error voltage V is a response of error angle θ, in fact, it is proportion to θ. Assuming proportional coefficient k=1 in Eq.(1),for simplicity's sake, the voltage can be proportion to $\varpi(t)$, the angular rate of line of sight change. By inverse Laplace transformation of $V(s)$, $\varpi(t)$ can be deduced as

$$\varpi(t)=\frac{\omega_1^2\theta}{\omega_0\sqrt{1-\xi^2}}e^{-\xi\omega_0 t}\sin(\omega t) \tag{4}$$

$$\omega=\omega_0\sqrt{1-\xi^2} \tag{5}$$

Where, ω is the inherently damp resonant frequency of $\varpi(t)$. By setting ξ and f_0, the characteristics of $\varpi(t)$ can be controlled. Fig.4 gives the curve of angular rate $\varpi(t)$ against damp coefficient ξ. It shows that the curve is oscillatory, with slow amplitude attenuation rate when ξ is small, *e.g.* , ξ=0.1, and shift amplitude decrease when ξ is large, *e.g.* ξ=0.7, which reaches to near zero within one period.

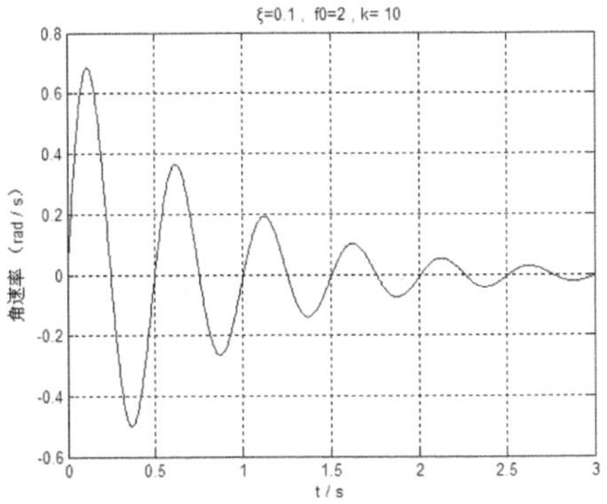

(a)

Fig. 4. The curve of $\varpi(t)$ against ξ

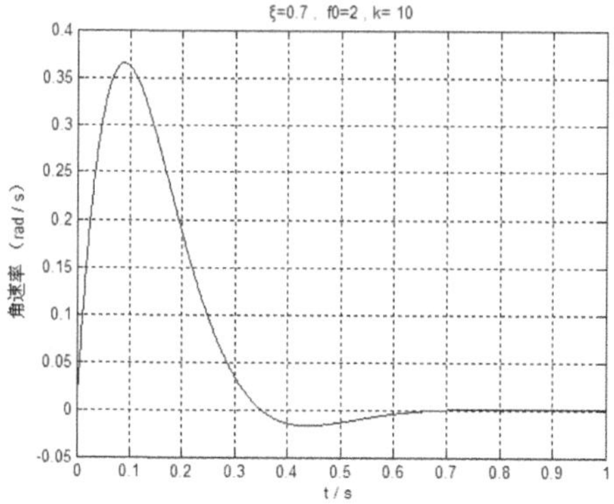

(b)

Fig. 4. (*continued*)

4 The Influence of Blinking Decoy Systems on Prs Aiming at Radiators

4.1 The Influence of Blinking Frequency on Prs Aiming

Taking two synchronous decoys blinking system as an example, as shown in Fig.1(a), the influence of blinking frequency on PRS aiming is investigated by simulation. According to Eq.(3), the change of ϖ, the angular rate of target line of sight, can be depicted in Fig.5, with the alternative transmission of blinking decoys at different frequency. When the blinking frequency is 1Hz, whose period is greater than the time constant of the angle tracking circuit, the aiming direction of PRS can switch between the two decoys with their transmission although ϖ is changing. When PRS is stably aiming at a decoy, ϖ reaches zero, as shown in Fig.5(a). In Fig.5(b) when the blinking frequency is 2.5Hz, PRS will swing between the two decoys because the blinking period is less than the time constant of angle tracking circuit so that the circuit can not respond completely to the input error voltage. In this case, ϖ can rise to a rather high rate. When the blinking frequency increases to 5 Hz, the angle tracking circuit is more difficult to follow the shift of input error voltage so that it appears low pass feature, as shown in Fig.4(c). In this case, ϖ is quite small and the PRS will almost aim at the "energy center" of the two decoys[1]. When ARM moves to the discriminating angle(normally 60°), it will fly to either decoy randomly. However, it is too close to ground now to turn to the decoy before it strikes ground.

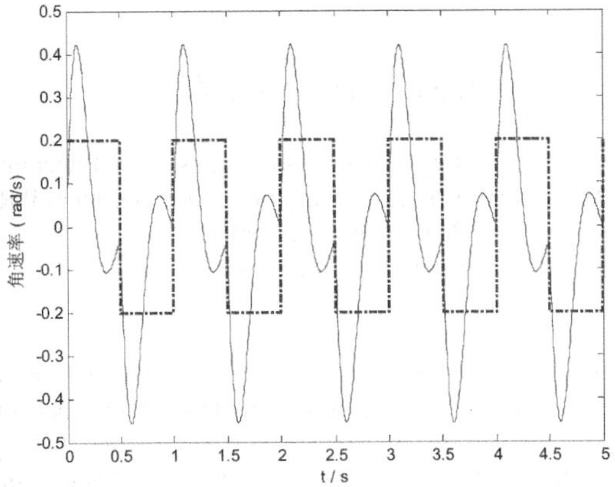

(a) Blinking frequency: 1Hz

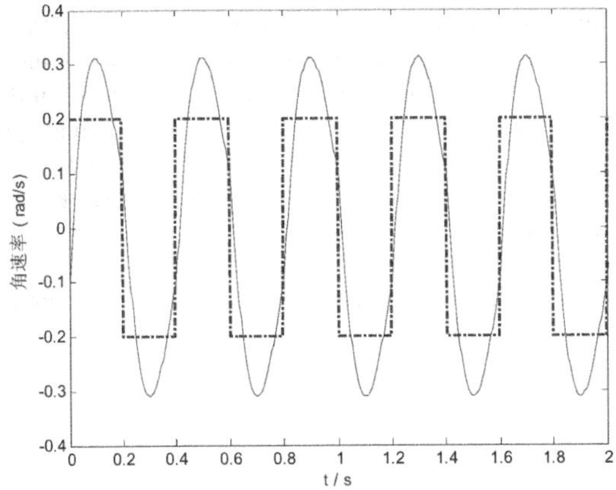

(b) Blinking frequency: 2.5Hz

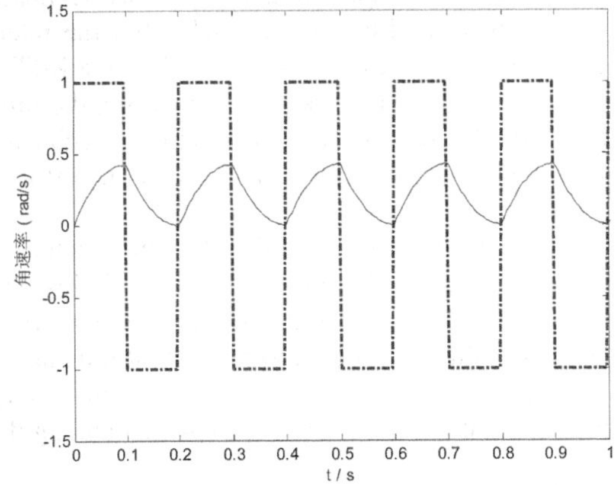

(c) Blinking frequency: 5Hz

Note: Solid curve---Angular rate of line of sight to signal source;
Dashed line---Blinking signal entering PRS receivers

Fig. 5. Angular rate of line of sight to signal source at different blinking frequency

4.2 Result Analysis

With rather high blinking frequency, the angle tracking circuit of PRS displays low-pass filter feature. Therefore the output angular rate of line of sight of source to ARM is small, and the PRS is not able to adjust its aiming direction in time owing to inertial. On the other hand, with rather low blinking frequency, the circuit will generate complete response to reach a stable tracking state, which means the PRS can aim at the transmitting decoy in the blinking period and a decoyed system can not tolerate this fact.

5 The Influence of Time Sequence of Blinking Decoy Signals on Prs Direction Finding Characteristics

ARM PRS is often designed to sample at the rising edge, falling edge, or middle of received radar pulses. Once a signal is locked, PRS will measure the direction of the radar, and generate navigation signal for ARM to aim at the radar. In order to protect the radar from ARM attack from all possible direction, decoy signals must have the same waveform as radar's and cover radar signals at any time and position.

5.1 Time Sequence Models of Decoyed Radar System

From energy point of view, in order to deceive ARM PRS, the pulse width of decoys is a little wider than that of radar at transmission, as shown in Fig.6(a).

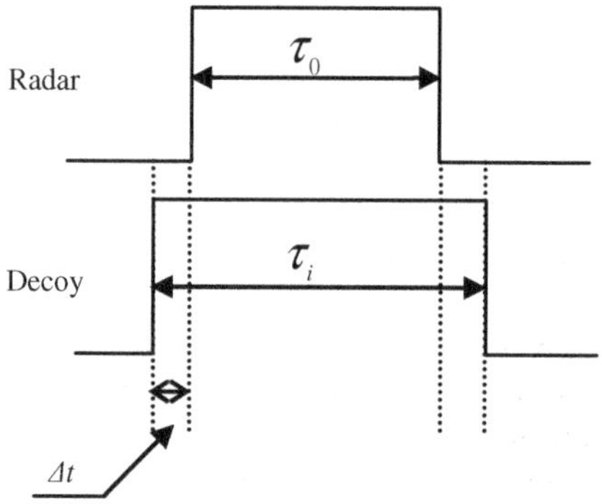

(a) Radar and decoy pulse width

Fig. 6. Time sequence of radar and decoy pulses

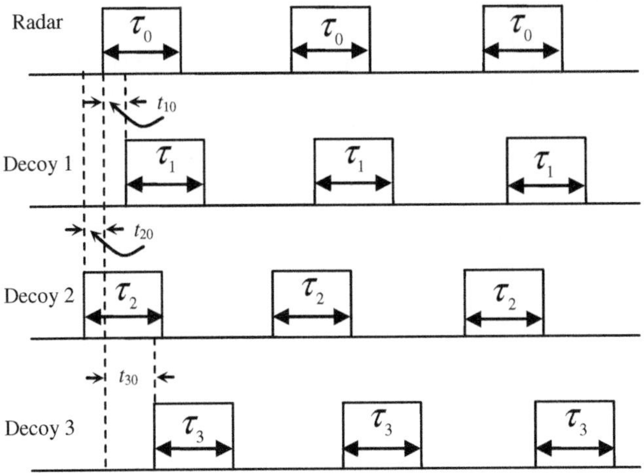

(b) Time sequence of radar and decoy pulses at PRS position owing to transmission delay and propagation delay

Fig. 6. (*continued*)

Normally, the difference between pulse width of decoys and radar's meets the following relationship:

$$\tau_i \geq \tau_0 + 2d_i/c \tag{6}$$

Where, τ_0 is pulse width of radar; τ_i is the pulse width of the *i*th decoy, *i*=1,2,3,⋯; d_i is the distance between radar and the *i*th decoy; *c* is light speed.

Owing difference of distance to PRS from radar and decoys, the propagation of EM wave will generate different extra time delay, as shown in Fig.6(b).

With the help of ARM warning equipment, the radar system can determine the position of ARM and adjust the transmission time of radar and decoys so that their pulses will reach PRS simultaneously and mislead the ARM to a place ('energy center') away from any radiators[2].

5.2 Time Sequence among Pulses of Blinking Decoys and Radar

There are many cases of blinking laws in a decoyed radar system to form different blinking EM field distribution in space where ARM appears, and to force the ARM to maneuver randomly away from radar.

1) *Case 1:* single decoy pulses covering radar pulses in space at any moment

In synchronous blinking mode, three decoys can blink with each other while any of their pulses cover the radar pulses at PRS position at any position in space and any moment, as shown if Fig.7. In this case, the combined EM fields at PRS is changing with the blinking law of decoys and will cause the PRS to generate randomly changing direction angle to guide the ARM.

2) *Case 2:* more decoy pulses covering radar pulses in space at any moment

Fig.8 shows another kind of decoy blinking law, where the radar pulses are covered by pulses from one or two decoys at any moment. It provides rather complicated

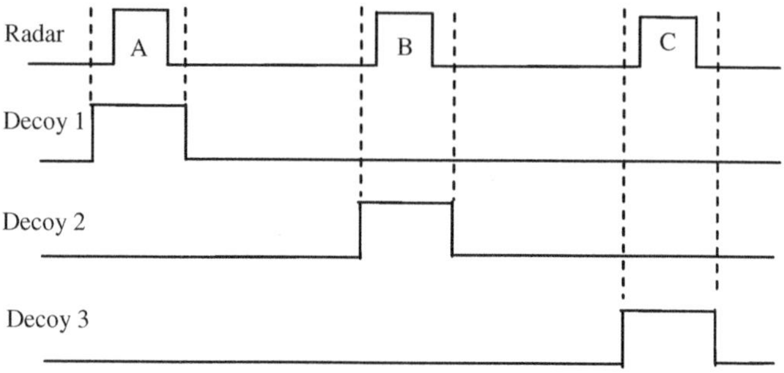

Fig. 7. Single decoy pulses covering radar pulses

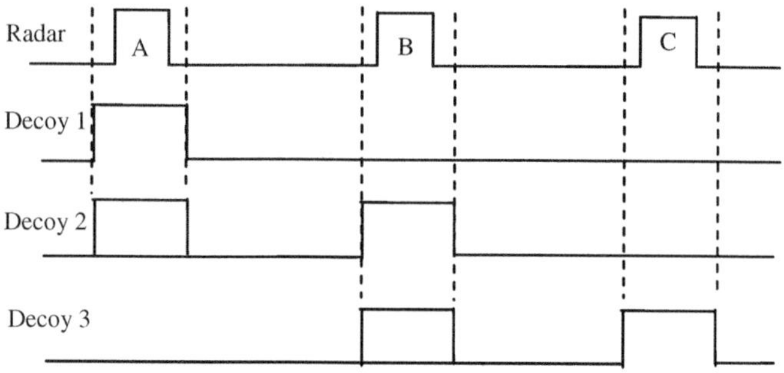

Fig. 8. Pulses from one or two decoys covering radar pulses in space

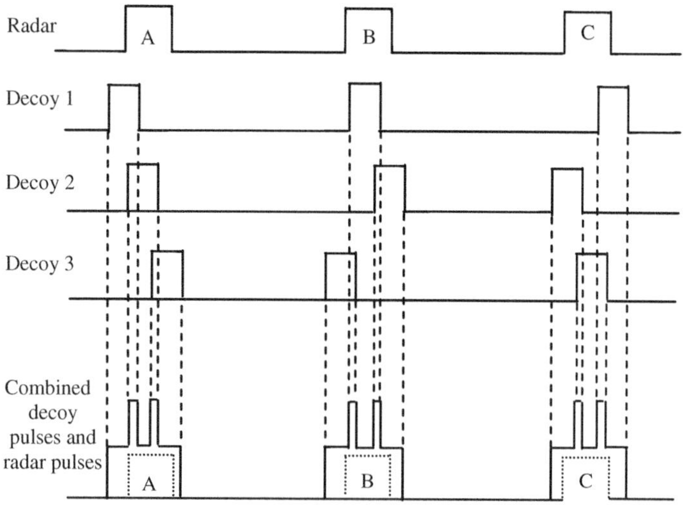

Fig. 9. Three blinking decoy pulses covering radar pulses

variation of EM environment in ARM space. In Fig.9, all decoy pulses take part in the protection of radar pulses, where the time sequence of decoy pulses changes all the time and the combined waveform at PRS is much more complicated. In this case, even a PRS employing special technique to sample the rising edge, falling edge, or the middle of pulses can not discriminate the right direction of any radiators since the determination of radiator direction is directly related to the amplitude and phase of EM field at PRS position. As a result, the ARM will be misguided by the random direction information given by PRS, and maneuver in a random trajectory missing any radiators.

6 Conclusion

Based on the deception principles of decoys in a decoyed radar system, the idea of blinking operation is presented and its deceptive mechanism to ARM PRS is analyzed. Several kinds of blinking modes are put forward. The simulation shows that blinking mode is one of the important operation modes of decoyed radar system, which can provide much more possibilities for the safety of radar confronting threat from ARM. On the other hand, the ARM PRS has to search new approaches to find the real radar direction so as to guide the ARM attack it.

References

1. Yang, L., Wu, Y., Fan, X.: Analysis of Countermeasure Techniques to Anti-radiation Missile. Journal of Detection & Control 23(2), 53–56 (2006)
2. Zhou, W., Luo, J., Wang, H.: The Deceptive Effect of Combined Field from Multi-source on ARM. Acta Electronica Sinica 36(6), 1193–1197 (2008)
3. Ma, L., Liu, X.: Study on the Infrared Angle Track Loop of the Seeker in rolling Airframe Missile. Aerospace Control 26(6), 8–11 (2008)
4. Liao, S.: A Research on Maximum Rate of Step Response of Second-order Oscillating System. Journal of Southwest University for Nationalities (Natural Science Edition) 29(4), 445–448 (2003)
5. Yan, X.-p., Li, P., Geng, X.-m.: Study on Blinking Frequency Selection in Synchronous Non-Coherent Blinking Jamming. Transactions of Beijing Institute of Technology 28(6), 553–556 (2008)

Design of Virtual Reclosing System

Qian Zhang[1] and Qun Mei[2]

[1] Science Division Yanshan University Qinhuangdao, Hebei Province, China
[2] Library Yanshan University Qinhuangdao, Hebei Province, China
qian1827@sina.com

Abstract. Adaptive auto-reclosure has many advantages over the conventional approach. For the single-phase grounding fault, two-phase grounding fault, two-phase fault, this paper analyzes the characteristic of post-fault voltage. And this paper distinguishes the transient faults and permanent faults on transmission lines using voltage criterion. The concept of virtual instruments is also introduced in this paper, and the virtual reclosing system is developed which takes the graphical programming software LabVIEW as software development platform. This system is excellent for friendly interface and simple operation. It can be applied to the test research and lab teaching of the new method of adaptive auto-reclosure with practical significance.

Keywords: adaptive auto-reclosure, virtual instruments, fault type, transient faults, permanent faults.

1 Introduction

In the power system component, the transmission line's fault rate is the highest. After transmission line's fault, utilizing the adaptive re-closure strategy plays an important role in enhancing the power supply reliability. However, the auto-reclosure is blind in general. If switching onto permanent fault, the system will be impacted again by the fault, bringing great harm to the system. Therefore, correctly differentiating transient fault and permanent fault and realizing adaptive auto-chosure are of great importance.

Virtual Instruments (VI) technology is a reform in the development history of measuring instrument. Essentially, it's the combination of measuring technology and computer technology. On the basis of analyzing the adaptive auto-reclosure approach, this paper adapts the thought of virtual instrument, fully utilizes the modern computer technology and designs a set of adaptive auto-reclosure system. The experiment proves that this system moves and functions reliably.

2 Adaptive Auto-reclosure Approach

2.1 Research Condition of Reclosing

At present, the single-phase adaptive auto-reclosure research based on the discrimination of transient faults and permanent faults has achieved practical criterion and the corresponding apparatus is developed, which has made great progress for

D. Zeng (Ed.): ICAIC 2011, Part I, CCIS 224, pp. 348–355, 2011.

adaptive separated phase auto-reclosure and adaptive three phases auto-reclosure. However, now its research still pauses in the stage of theory. There is also a long way to go for the practical application. [1]

On the basis of the current research fruits, this paper analyzes adaptive auto-reclosure and adapts virtual instrument technology to conduct experiment analysis for this approach.

2.2 Analysis of Adaptive Auto-reclosure Approach

The key of distinguishing adaptive auto-reclosure from the traditional auto-reclosure is that it can make an effective distinction between transient fault and permanent fault. Therefore, it's the key of adaptive auto-reclosure to find the proper criterion to distinguish transient fault and permanent fault.

The circuit model is as shown in Figure 1. Now analyze the criterion of transient fault and permanent fault under different types of fault.

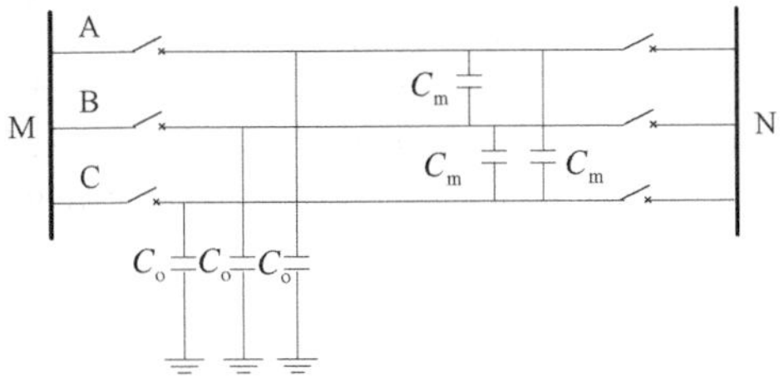

Fig. 1. Circuit Model

When the single-phase grounding fault occurs to the circuit, because the transmission line has the property of distribution parameter, there are coupling interaction among each single-phase. Therefore, no matter the fault is transient or permanent, after the circuit breaker breaks at each ends of the single-phase circuit, both ends of the fault still have voltage. Suppose A phase occurs single-phase grounding fault, and each side's circuit breaker breaks, at this time the voltage of the broken phase's two sides is composed of two parts: capacitive coupling voltage U_y and inductive coupling voltage U_{x1}. When the transient fault happens to the circuit, the terminal voltage of the fault phase is composed of two parts: capacitive coupling voltage U_y and inductive coupling voltage U_{x1}. When the permanent fault happens to the circuit, earth capacity discharges steadily, so $U_y = 0$ or smaller, fault phase voltage only depends on inductive coupling voltage.

Thus it can be seen that when transient fault occurs, fault phase voltage is bigger than the terminal voltage of fault phase when permanent fault occurs. When single-phase grounding fault occurs, the voltage criterion of adaptive auto-reclosure is expressed as

$$C_V = \left|\frac{U}{U_{x1}}\right| = \left|\frac{U}{I_0(Z_0 - Z_1)L}\right| \tag{1}$$

In this formula, U is the voltage of fault phase's two ends after fault breaking. The movement condition of criterion is when $C_V \geq 1$, it's transient fault and allows reclosing; when $C_V < 1$, its permanent fault and shuts reclosing. [2]

When two-phase grounding fault occurs, after the two fault phases jumping, capacitive coupling voltage of the broken phase's two ends is bigger when transient fault occurs than when permanent fault occurs. From that the voltage criterion of adaptive auto-reclosure is constructed when there is two-phase grounding short circuit. When meeting the criterion, it's that transient fault allows reclosing; on the contrary, three phases trip and shut the reclosing. The criterion of this voltage is

$$|U - U_{x1}| \geq KU_{zd1} \quad (2)$$

In formula, U is the measure voltage of the broken phase in two ends' phase. K is reliable coefficient, setting 0.8~0.9. U_{x1} is that the sound phase forms the induced voltage for fault phase according to fault distance. In it U_{zd1} is threshold value, setting as 0.1~0.12U_N according to operating condition.

When two-phase grounding short circuits, short circuit fault is eliminated after one fault tripping, because keeping two phase operating is better for stability than keeping one phase operating. After tripping one fault phase, if it's permanent fault, the voltage of tripping phase is nearly equal to the voltage of untripping fault phase; if it's transient fault, the voltage of two phase has great difference. Accordingly the voltage criterion of distinguishing transient fault and permanent fault is constructed. When meeting the criterion, it's judged that transient fault allows reclosing; on the contrary, the reclosing is shut. The criterion is : $|U_{fault1} - U_{fault2}| > U_{zd2}$ (3)In formula, U_{fault1}、U_{fault2} are two ends' measure voltage of two faults respectively. U_{zd2} is threshold value, setting as 0.2~0.3U_N according to operating condition[3].

According to the criterion type of adaptive auto-reclosure under the above-mentioned different types of fault, the flow chart of adaptive auto-reclosure can be achieved as shown in Figure 2.

3 VIRTUAL Instrument Technology

3.1 Concept

Virtual instrument is taking the computer as the hardware platform and is designed by the user with virtual panel. Software is the key of the whole instrument, namely "software is instrument". Just because of the flexibility of virtual instrument, it can be widely used in each field and is called the third generation instrument.

3.2 Development Environment of Virtual Instrument

LabVIEW is the most successful and most widely-used virtual instrument software development environment at present. This programming has the advantages of more vivid and flexible interface and more reliable property; and its orientation is the user without programming experience, but not experts, especially suitable for scientists and engineer technical personnel engaging in the scientific research and development. It's honored as the language of engineer and scientists [4].

4 Virtual Reclosing System Design

Virtual reclosing can provide an experiment platform for adaptive auto-reclosure. On this platform, the user can or not as to conduct revision. Besides, in university power lab,traditional instrument to realize reclosing, it's hard for every student to have the opportunity to do it themselves. If replacing the traditional instrument by virtual

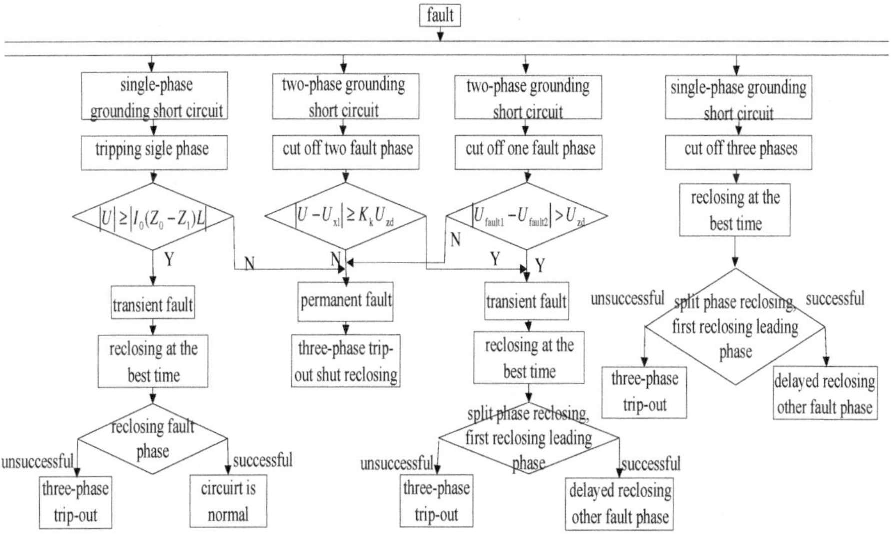

Fig. 2. Adaptive Auto-Reclosure Flow Chart

reclosing system, it can not only solve the above-mentioned problem, but make the students program and debug themselves, which does better to deepen the students' understanding of learned knowledge and enhance their ability in each aspect.

4.1 System Structure and Parameter

The system adapts the structure in Figure 1, the parameter is as following: $Z_1 = 0.0246 + j0.2504\Omega / km$, $U_N = 220kV$, $Z_0 = 0.0253 + j0.27564\Omega / km$, $K = 0.85$, $L = 20km$ 。

4.2 Signal Producing and Collection Filtering

Analog signal in this system comes from signal out of relay protection experiment platform in the lab. This signal is input the computer by data acquisition card to carry out analysis processing. The system adapts USB2003 data acquisition card of A ER Tai Company. The card is the data acquisition card of bus compatible with small volume, supporting hot plug, plug and play, doing without external power supply. It can provide 32 circuits signal-ended analog signal and 16circuits switch quantity switch signal input and output. The maximum sampling rate: 100 kb/s. the electric signal collected by data acquisition card often has harmonic component and dc component current. In order to avoid that these components make an impact on the judgment result in the process of judging, before analysing and calculating, the signal needs to be filtered. In the system digital filter is adapted and fundamental component is extracted from signals through program.

4.3 Judgment of Fault Type

Because different types of fault corresponds to different voltage criterion, when the fault happens to the system, first judging the type of fault. There are many diagnostic methods of fault types, such as voltage sequence component method, current component sequence method, and phase current. This system judges the type of fault through sequence component. The software design flow chart is as following in Figure 3.

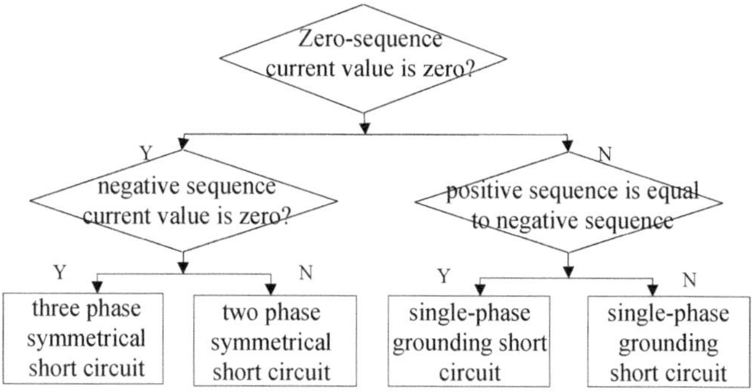

Fig. 3. Judgment of Fault Type

4.4 Adaptive Auto-reclosure Approach Reclosing Way

Adaptive auto-reclosure approach reclosing way is as following:

1) When single-phase grounding short circuits, single phase trips, then judges the types of fault. If it's permanent fault, three-phase trip-out no longer reclosing; if it's transient fault, it will reclosing at the best time under the condition of transient fault. If the reclosing is unsuccessful, the three-phase will trip.

2) When short circuit occurs to two-phase grounding, two fault phases trip. Then the type of fault is judged by the broken capacitive coupling voltage. If it's permanent fault, three-phase trip-out no longer reclosing; if it's transient fault, it will split phase reclosing at the best time under the condition of transient fault. If the reclosing is unsuccessful, the three-phase will trip.

3) When there is two-phase un-grounding short circuit (interphase short circuit), one of the two fault phases trips, then whether the fault is permanent fault is judged by whether the voltage of the two fault phase are equal. If it's permanent fault, three-phase trips; if it's transient fault, it will reclosing at the best time under the condition of transient fault. If the reclosing is unsuccessful, the three-phase will trip.

4) When three-phase short circuit occurs, three phases all trip. According to the best reclosing time under the condition of permanent fault, split phase reclosing, if any phase reclosing is unsuccessful, three phases trip.

4.5 Reclosing Time of Adaptive Auto-reclosure

Traditional auto-reclosure is calculating reclosing time on the basis of ensuring system stability, considering fault quenching of arc time and insulating medium. This time delay is certain value with great blindness. If at the moment of reclosing, voltage is on wave crest and trough, it will do harm to the life of component in the system. Now determine reclosing time according to adaptive auto-reclosure theory. Reclosing time criterion is that to make the voltage of circuit breaker's two ends are zero, that is: $\begin{cases} U_k = 0 \\ dU_k / dt < 0 \end{cases}$, in it, U_k is the voltage of circuit breaker's two ends, however if the reclosing wants to be successful, it must have $\begin{cases} t < t_1 \\ t < t_2 \end{cases}$, in it, t_1 is the necessary minimum time of ensuring fault point arc; t_2 is the maximum reclosing time required by system stability.

5 Virtual Reclosing Experiment Platform Design Example

5.1 Experiment Platform Front Panel

The software program of utilizing LabVIEW to write includes two parts: front panel and flow chart. It's composed of module which can finish certain function and the module connects through connecting line. Virtual reclosing system front panel which is designed by utilizing LabVIEW is as shown in Figure 4. From Figure 4, we know, this virtual instrument front panel is composed of 4 parts: operating button, stop button, parameter setting area and display area. System adapts USB2003 data acquisition card, it transforms the collected analog signal into digital signal and outputs to the computer as to conduct processing and analysis for signal in computer. The collected parameter needs the common setting of software and hardware. In the parameter setting area of front panel, the collected parameters of needing to set are first channel, last channel, sample frequency, and range. Filtering adapts bateosi low pass digital filter. It filters the higher harmonic from signal and only keeps fundamental components. The usage of this digital filter is easy. It only needs to set filtering order and end frequency in the area of filtering parameter. In the display area, the user can observe the state of circuit, the type of fault, fault property and whether it needs reclosing and reclosing which phase.

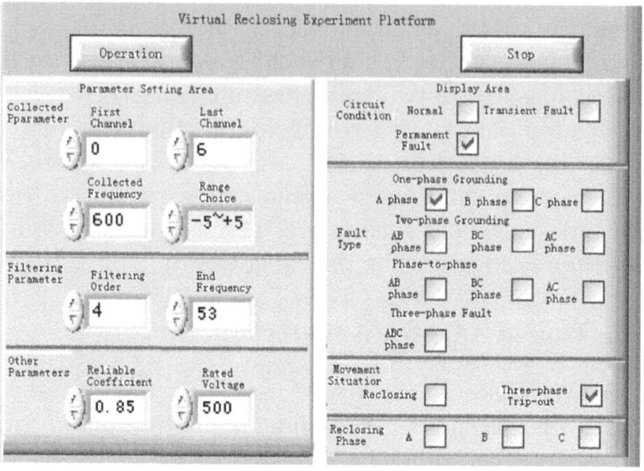

Fig. 4. Virtual Reclosing System Front Panel

5.2 Experiment Platform Program Flow Chart

Flow chart is the software program part. In order to enhance the programming efficiency, it can write subprogram. These subprograms can be employed in the main program. Virtual reclosing system program flow chart is as shown in Figure 5. The collected driver includes the following parts: creating equipment, initializing equipment, reading equipment, releasing initial resources, releasing equipment. When reading data, the acquisition card transforms the analog signal into digital signal as to conduct processing, analysis and calculation for signal. The active window in Figure 5 is the window when reading data. After through filtering, the collected data judges the type of fault (the judgment of fault type adapts subprogram module) and fault property. The program of A phase transient fault is displayed in the figure.

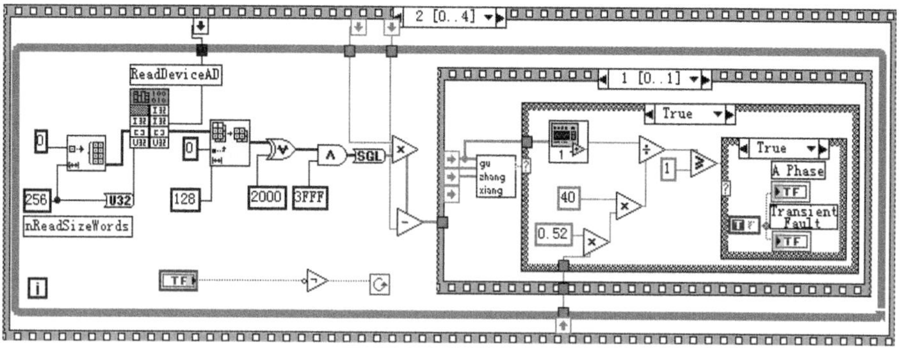

Fig. 5. Virtual Reclosing System Program Flow Chart

5.3 Experiment Steps

The steps of using this virtual reclosing system for experiment is as following: (1) connect data acquisition card with output signal and computer, and open computer power; (2) open system front panel, and set corresponding parameter in parameter setting area; (3) click operating button, system conducts analysis for circuit condition and displays the result on front panel; (4) experiment ending, first close signal input terminal, and close the computer.

6 Conclusion

As one of effective measures to ensure power system's safe power supply, reclosing has been widely applied in power system. However in actual power system, adapting the traditional reclosing didn't distinguish transient fault and permanent fault. When switching onto permanent fault, it brings great harm to the system. Through the analysis of analysing power system's research current situation, this paper proposes adaptive auto-reclosure approach by utilizing the current voltage reclosing criterion, adaptive auto-reclosure time and split phase reclosing technology, and develops virtual reclosing system combing with virtual instrument technology. The experiment proves that this adaptive auto-reclosure system can overcome the defect of traditional reclosing; in the meanwhile, virtual instrument technology can create an experimental environment for new theory method, which can avoid the risk brought by experiment and unnecessary power failure.

References

1. Song, G.-b., Suonan, J.-l., Sun, D.-d.: A Survey on Methods to Distinguish Permanent Faults from Instantaneous Faults in Transmission Lines. Power System Technology 30(18), 75–80 (2006)
2. Chen, S., Zhang, H., Chen, Y.: Study on Adaptive Single-Phase Reclosure Based on Intelligent Control. Automation of Electric Power Systems 26(6), 62–64 (2002)
3. Li, B., Li, Y., Huang, Q., Zhai, Y., Zeng, Z., Ma, Z., He, J.: Study ON Phase Criterion For Single-Pole Adaptive Reclosure. Automation of Electric Power Systems 27(22), 41–44 (2003)
4. Yan, H., Pan, W.: Virtual Instrument Technology and its Application in Electrical Experiment. East China Electric Power 30(12), 78–79 (2002)

Emulation of Dynamic Secondary Cooling and Soft Reduction in Continuous Slab Casting

Peng Rui[1], Zhang Xiao Long[1], and Zhang Hua[2]

[1] School of Computer Science and Technology Wuhan University of Science and Technology Wuhan, Hubei Province, China

[2] School of Materials and Metallurgy Wuhan University of Science and Technology Wuhan, Hubei Province, China

pengrui315@sohu.com

Abstract. Aiming at dealing with the center segregation, center porosity and slab crack in the steel-making process. We propose a continuous casting slab soft reduction and two cooling control method. This method is implemented in a software system. Through the establishment of two-dimensional unsteady heat transfer model for discretization draw reasonable temperature field distribution model, cold water model and pressing position prediction model. The experimental results show that the proposed method appears to be better accuracy.

Keywords: simulation, continuous casting, secondary cooling water, soft reduction, heat transfer model.

1 Introduction

Continuous casting is the important link in steel-rolling. How to reduce the production cycle and to improve product quality as well as the manufacturing process are the major problems to the iron and steel enterprises. As there is an obviously unsteady state in the casting process, the casting speed, the casting temperature, the environment temperature, the temperature of the cooling water, the quantity of the second cooling water and the raw materials component will affect the quality of products [1].

Research and improvement to the production process technique of continuous casting is of great significance to the steel technology. Currently the foreign continuous casting production of automation has been highly developed. In order to learn advanced technology and experience, some domestic steel companies have introduced the Siemag or VAI secondary control system [2]. However, production practice shows that the second dynamic process of secondary cooling water control is a lag and complex system [3]. It often delays the dynamic secondary cooling water ratio. Before calculating the quantity of the two cooling water under in the current loop, the slab has been moved to the next area, affecting the results. If the result is not precise enough, it will directly affect the depressed position identified and reduce product quality.

D. Zeng (Ed.): ICAIC 2011, Part I, CCIS 224, pp. 356–364, 2011.

Different from the previous general casting simulation software, the system modeling and simulation analysis based on the continuous casting metallurgy standards are used to predict the continuous casting production. And the finite difference method is used to establish a slab solidification heat transfer model of two-dimensional non-steady state. This method can compare the target temperature curve with the actual temperature. Experiments and simulations are carried out, and the results show the proposed method is applicable.

2 Two-Dimensional Unsteady Heat Transfer Model

Heat transfer model mainly includes the establishment of the solidified differential equation and discrete solution of the difference equation. The former is mainly based on heat transfer characteristics of physical to establish the mathematical modeling. The latter uses the finite difference method to discrete mathematical equations.

2.1 Establishment of Solidification Heat Transfer Differential Equations

The establishment of solidification heat transfer equations is the basic of simulation system Research on the solidification heat transfer model accumulated a great deal of experience. The purpose is to obtain better temperature distribution curve. The strand outflow from the mould moves down through the meniscus into the secondary cooling zone, air-cooled area. There are three main heat transfer mode:

1) Heat conduction: the heat is transferred from high temperature to the adjacent low temperature areas. Such as the heat transferred in the center of the cast and the heat transferred between the nip roller and surface of the slab shell.

2) Heat convection: heat exchange caused by the relative movement of the parts of the fluid of different temperature. For example, the strand flowing in the mould will bring about heat transfer and the heat exchange between the secondary cooling water and slab.

3) Thermal radiation: the objects with temperature spontaneously emit energy in the form of electromagnetic waves. In the production of the casting, there is always the heat emission around the slab surface.

Therefore, the casting solidification heat transfer is three-dimensional unsteady heat transfer process accompanied by heat conduction, convection and radiation at the same time [4]. Heat transfer differential equation is:

$$\rho C \partial T / \partial t = \nabla(\lambda \nabla T + q) + \phi \tag{1}$$

In the formula(1), ρ stand for slab density, C stand for heat, $\partial T / \partial t$ stand for the derivation of slab temperature to conduction time , λ is the thermal conductivity, q is latent heat release, ϕ is steel viscous dissipative term, ∇ is Hamilton operator, $\nabla \equiv \vec{i}\partial / \partial x + \vec{j}\partial / \partial y + \vec{k}\partial / \partial z$ 。

As shown in Fig.1, coordinate system is established by its center of slab O, its width direction X axis, its thickness direction Y axis, its casting direction Z axis. Because the width and thickness of slab is far less than the length of the slab, casting speed is much greater than the conduction velocity in direction of the casting. So the thermal convection in the casting direction can be ignored, and the influence of the latent heat release and steel viscous dissipative term can not be taken into account. Three-dimensional solidification heat transfer equations can be simplified to two-dimensional differential equation:

$$\rho C \partial T / \partial t = \lambda \partial^2 T / \partial x^2 + \lambda \partial^2 T / \partial y^2 \tag{2}$$

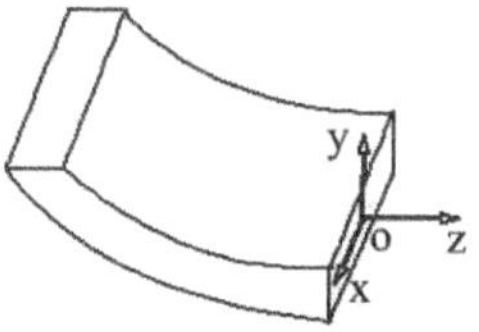

Fig. 1. Casting Slab

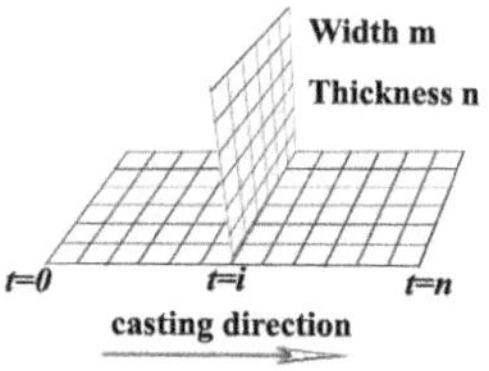

Fig. 2. Casting Grid

2.2 Discrete Solution of Differential Equation

After the process of casting solidification and heat transfer was analyzed, it can be summed up as the problems-solving of partial differential equations [5]. As the heat transfer process changes with time, the partial differential equations can be described as: If the initial time t= t_0 is given, the solution to equations of the time t> t_0 depends entirely on the initial conditions and boundary conditions. The essence of the finite difference method is to begin with the initial value and find the approximate solution of differential equations gradually along the direction of time increasing by the method of difference schema [6]. The solution procedure is divided into two steps:

1) Using the difference equations to instead the differential equations. The continuous variables will be display the discrete variables. Fig.2 illustrates the process of the difference method. Through the grid partition method, the width of the slab section is set to be m, the thickness n. Along the x, y direction the section is divided into $m \times n$ cells and the time zone is divided into $[0, t_n]$ in the casting direction. Suppose a temperature function $T(x, y)$, x is continuous variables defined in the width area $[0, m]$, y is continuous variables defined in the thickness area $[0, n]$, disperse the area $[0, m]$, $[0, n]$ on step length $h = \Delta x$ $h = \Delta y$, the temperature of node (i, j) can be expressed as:

$$T(x_i, y_j) = T(0 + i\Delta x, 0 + j\Delta y) = T(i\Delta x, j\Delta y) \tag{3}$$

Obviously, the step length is smaller, the number of cells will be larger and the accuracy of approximate solutions will be higher.

2) Establishing the differential equations. Considering the stability and convergence of the difference equations as well as the facilitation of difference scheme and the convenience of the solution, we select forward difference quotient and intermediate difference quotient to replace the derivative of differential equation.

$$(\partial T / \partial t)^t_{i,j} = (T^{t+1}_{i,j} - T^t_{i,j}) / \Delta t \tag{4}$$

$$(\partial^2 T / \partial x^2)^t_{i,j} = (T^t_{i+1,j} - 2T^t_{i,j} + T^t_{i-1,j}) / (\Delta x)^2 \quad (5)$$

$$(\partial^2 T / \partial y^2)^t_{i,j} = (T^t_{i,j+1} - 2T^t_{i,j} + T^t_{i,j-1}) / (\Delta y)^2 \quad (6)$$

Import the formula (4), (5), (6) into formula (2).The target surface temperature at any point on the slab along the casting direction in secondary cooling zone can be expressed as:

$$T^{t+1}_{i,j} = T^t_{i,j} + \Delta t[\lambda(T^t_{i+1,j} - 2T^t_{i,j} + T^t_{i-1,j})/(\Delta x)^2 + \lambda(T^t_{i,j+1} - 2T^t_{i,j} + T^t_{i,j-1})/(\Delta y)^2]/\rho C$$

3 Implementation of Soft Reduction Model

This model has been implemented with Java. Mysql is used as database. And Jdbc is used as database connection. The graphical output of data invokes the JfreeChart that resolves the current graphics needs [7].

3.1 Architecture Design

The system of three layers technical architecture, It includes:

1) Access layer: Using graphical user interface (GUI) as the front of the visit, the system receives data like cast machine parameters and environmental parameters.

2) Application layer: including system processing logic, and interfaces to the access layer and the data layer. All of the business logic process is in the application layer. Calculation, aggregate, analyze, print, update, and add new features of all function stored in the application layer. It is mainly responsible for the establishment of a two-dimensional unsteady heat transfer model, the temperature field model, secondary cooling water model, and the soft reduction model. The layer will calculate the results stored in the collection of data, then output, print and save the data in the form of chart.

3) Data layer: the database management system (DBMS) is responsible for the reading and writing of data, which includes the function of adding, deleting, updating, and the preservation of simulation results.

3.2 System Functions

The system is implemented by the object-oriented technology with two-dimensional display function. As shown in Fig.3, the main function is analog simulation: according to the boundary conditions in continuous casting process, effective heat transfer difference equations of two-dimensional unsteady state can be established. With the distribution of the target surface temperature of slab in the secondary cooling zone along the direction of casting for constraint, the essential process can be replicated that the continuous casting is based on the function of the temperature field model, secondary cooling water model, and the soft reduction model. Through the simulating, the location of the soft reduction can be forecasted. Thus, the simulation results of the different production process parameters can be contrasted and analyzed. A theoretical support to improve the casting production technology is provided. The functions of the system are:

1) Input modeling, the graphical modeling construction.

2) Run simulation test. Calculate the temperature of exact location on the slab.

3) Simulating the existing production environment, computing the impact of casting speed,the amount of cold water and several others process parameters on the slab.

4) Determine two-phase region and pressing position according to the calculated results.

5) Data analysis and optimize action of the results.

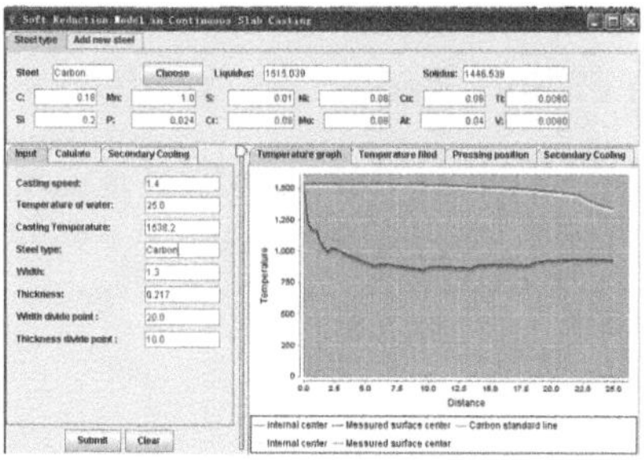

Fig. 3. UI of the System

3.3 The Basic Model Design

The system is developed base on the two-dimensional unsteady heat transfer model. It includes the temperature field model, secondary cooling water model and the soft reduction model.

1) The temperature field model

The temperature field model relies on the two-dimensional transient heat transfer model. The heat transfer process is described in Fig.4.

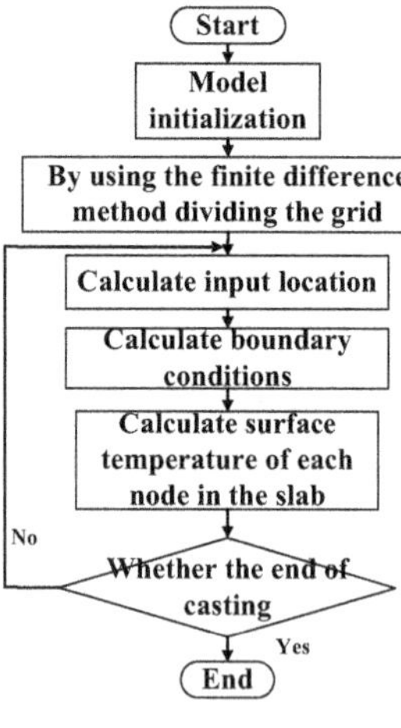

Fig. 4. Temperature field program flowchart

a) Select material, set initialization modeling process parameters. Divide the slab section to the grid by the finite difference method.

b) After the completion of the modeling. First, calculate input location, and then load the initial temperature, degree of superheat, etc; finally calculate the boundary conditions. Since solidification process of the slab along direction of casting mainly passes through three areas: mould, secondary cooling zone, air cooling area. Different area has different boundary conditions. Therefore when temperature field model calculating the boundary conditions, it should be divided three regions using the finite difference method.

c) Output the parameters to solve the slab surface temperature distribution.

d) Judge whether the slab arrived along the direction of casting to the end? If reach the end, the model calculates terminates.

2) Secondary cooling water model

Secondary cooling water model is mainly based on target temperature algorithm; calculate the amount of water in each loop of secondary cooling zone. Detailed explanation of this model is: In the case of steel selected to determine the process parameters. Suppose the amount of water in each loop has been given, computes the heat transfer coefficients corresponding to the each loop. According to the temperature field model, the system calculates slab surface temperature in each loop, and compared with the target temperature. Then by using the method of dichotomy, adjusting the amount of secondary cooling continuously in each loop until the slab temperature and target temperature are roughly the same. Thus the amount of secondary cooling water in each loop can be calculated. The algorithm process for:

a) Determine the input of steel, the section size, casting speed, casting temperature, ambient temperature, cooling water temperature, the surface of different steel target temperature and other parameters.

b) Set the initial amount of water in each loop of secondary cooling zone, the maximum and minimum amount of water, distribution coefficient of Outside the arc and within the arc in each loop, And the maximum allowed absolute error between the calculate temperature and the target temperature.

c) Update the amount of water in current position loop, use temperature field model to calculate slab surface temperature.

d) Calculating the slab surface temperature in the current loop, then compare with the target temperature. And return to the step (3) to calculate the amount of water until the slab temperature and the target temperature are equal.

e) Get the target amount of water in current loop. According to the proportion of each loop inside the arc and outside the arc, the amount of water is calculated.

f) Judge the position of the slab in the secondary cooling zone. If the slab reaches the end of secondary cooling zone, output the result with the graphical form. Otherwise return the step (b).

g) End algorithm.

3) Soft Reduction Model

The essence of the soft reduction is: Giving a pressure nearby the end of slab liquid core, produce a certain amount of pressure to compensate for its solidification shrinkage. Finally reduce or even eliminate center segregation and center porosity. This method is to first identify the process parameters such as overheat, casting sections, casting speed, etc. Then with the temperature field model, calculate the temperature curve, liquidus, solidus, and the position of the two-phase region. This process can be detailed as:

To begin with, determine the terminal location of liquidus and solidus. Then identify the scope of Solid fraction: f_s =0.6~0.85. Select f_s accord to physical properties of the slab in the two-phase. Therefore the starting position of soft reduction should not at the beginning of the two-phase region. Therefore $f_s \geq 0.6$ is more appropriate. To the end position of pressure, with the increase of solid fraction in the center of slab, the narrow face of the slab becomes uniform. This process also consider avoiding brittle area near the solidus, and reduce the trend of the inter crack of the slab. At the end position, $f_s \leq 0.85$ is appropriate.

4 Results and Validation

Some experiments have carried out to identify the system as shown in the Fig.5. Simulation uses low carbon material, and the initial casting speed is 1.4 m/min.

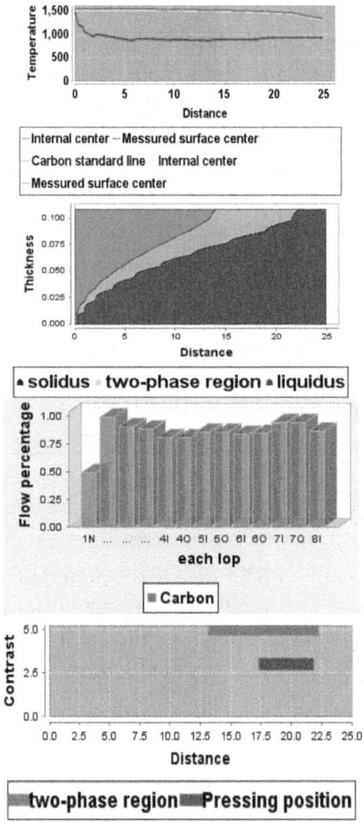

Fig. 5. Simulation experiment results

1) In the first graph, we using the infrared scanner import the data that is from the process of a factory production. The results indicate that under the same production process the deviation between the measured actual temperature curve and the target temperature curve is less than 1.6 per cent. Analysis results are accurate with the high reference value.

2) As the second graph shows, the liquid's, solidus, and the two-phase region change significantly with the casting speed. The initial casting speed of 1.4 m/min, and the horizontal distance of liquidus is 13.487m. Then raise the speed to 1.5 m/min, and the horizontal distance of liquidus will be 14.8m. The liquidus region increases evident.

3) As the third graph shows, the secondary cooling water simulation based on the target temperature algorithm finds the relationship between the casting speed and flow percentage in each loop. The results showed that with the increase of casting speed the flow percentage will change. Calculation and analysis also indicates that with the increase of casting speed, the amount of water in each loop will increase.

4) As the fourth graph shows, in order to achieve the expected effect avoid the center segregation and center porosity. The program calculate the position of two-phase region based on the temperature field model, and use the solid fraction $0.6 \le fs \le 0.85$ this program indentifies the pressing position providing the theoretical support to the practical production.

5 Conclusions

We have developed a simulation system which is based on one slab caster and two-dimensional unsteady heat transfer model. The program can simulate under the different production processes. It also analyzes the simulation results, and optimizes the results. The simulation calculations show that the method is effective. It provides a good support for improving the Continuous Casting Process.

Acknowledgment. This work was supported in part by Project (2008TD04) from Science Foundation of Wuhan University of Science and Technology, and Open Foundation of State Key Laboratory of Bioelectronics, Southeast University, and Project (No. 2008CDB344, 2009CDA034) from Hubei Provincial Natural Science Foundation, P.R. China, as well as National Natural Science Foundation of P.R. China (60975031).

References

1. Qian, G., Ruan, X.: Cause for central segregation of CC bloom from bearing steel and countermeasures. Iron & Steel 37(5), 17–18 (2002)
2. Zheng, Q.: Development and research of new technique in slab caster. Shanghai Baosteel Engineering Design 3, 15–21 (2001)
3. Zhang, L., Cai, C.: Secondary Cooling Control of Continuous Casting Based on BP Networks. Computer and Modernization 158(10), 66–69 (2008)
4. Bouhouche, S., Lahreche, M., Bast, J.: Control of heat transfer in continuous casting process using neural networks. Acta Automatica Sinica, 701–706 (2008)

5. Feng, K., Liao, J.-y., Cheng, D.-f.: Research of secondary cooling heat transfer model in Continuous casting. Journal Of The Chinese Rare Earth Society 18, 247–250 (2000)
6. Sun, H.-y., Wang, Z.-m.: Analyze of finite difference method for two-dimension heat transfer and development of currency program. Chemical Engineer 125, 17–18 (2006)
7. Wang, Z.-q.: Drawing charts with jfreeChart development package. Journal of Xingtai Polytechnic College 24(1), 30–41 (2007)

Gaussian Process Machine Learning Model for Forecasting of Karstic Collapse

Yan Zhang, Guoshao Su, and Liubin Yan

School of Civil and Architecture EngineeringUniversity of Guangxi
Nanning, Guangxi Province, China
yan72816@sina.com

Abstract. Aiming to the fact that it is still difficult to reasonably forecasting the karstic collapse, the model based on GP machine learning is proposed for forecasting of karstic collapse. According to few learning samples, the nonlinear mapping relationship between karstic collapse and its influencing factors is established by GP model. The model was applied to a real engineering. The results of case study show that GP model is feasible, effective and simple to implement for forecasting of karstic collapse. Compared with artificial neural networks and support vector machine, it has attractive merits of self-adaptive parameters determination and excellent capacity for solving non-linear small samples problems.

Keywords: Karstic collapse, Gaussian process, Machine learning, Forecast.

1 Introduction

China is one of the most karst developed countries in which karstic areas are widely distributed. In the last few years more and more engineering projects have been constructed in karstic areas with the sustained and rapid development of economy, so geological disaster caused by these projects become obviously severe and frequent. Karstic collapse is a typically geological disaster usually occurred in these regions. It normally causes great damage to projects. For examples, the freeway is cut off and the building is destroyed (Fig.1). It is necessary to find effective ways to reduce the damage of karstic collapse [1].

Fig. 1. Photos of damage for karstic collapse to freeway and building

D. Zeng (Ed.): ICAIC 2011, Part I, CCIS 224, pp. 365–372, 2011.

Because karstic collapse often occurs unexpectedly and hiddenly, the prediction before the construction is the key tache ensuring the safety of engineering construction. However, karstic collapse is affected by many natural and human factors most of which express fuzziness and randomness, it is difficult to forecast of karstic collapse. Predictions of karstic collapse are studied by a number of researchers [2-3]. Currently, it is well accepted that machine learning methods such as Grey method [4], artificial neural networks (ANN) [5] and support vector machine (SVM) [6] can reveal underlying evolution law between karstic collapse and its influencing factors. However, there are some open issues for above-mentioned methods, which are very hard to overcome. For examples, ANN is always difficult to find an appropriate network topology and the optimum hyperparameters. In addition, ANN is limited in solving for small sample problem. SVM cannot escape from the blindness which is the common phenomenon in man-made choice of kernel function and its parameters [7]. It is necessary to develop a novel effective method to solve the problems.

Gaussian process (GP) is a newly developed machine learning technology based on strict theoretical fundamentals and Bayesian theory [8-11]. In recent years GP has attracted much attention in the machine learning community because it has excellent merits of dealing with high dimensions, small samples and nonlinear complex problems [12-14]. Compared with ANN and SVM, GP is simple to implement and its hyperparameters are obtained by self-adaption. In this paper, we propose a new model of karstic collapse prediction using GP.

For the purpose to establish a GP model for forecasting of karstic collapse, this paper is subdivided 6 sections. After introducing the theory of GP in section 2, a new model for forecasting of karstic collapse is proposed in section 3. Section 4 addresses the application and section 5 discusses the influence of different covariance functions. Finally, the conclusions are drawn in Section 6.

2 Theory of GP

GP is regarded as one of machine learning technology based on gaussian stochastic process and Bayes' learning theory. In this section we provide a brief introduction of Gaussian process. More details about GP can be seen in the work by Rasmussen and Williams [15].

Gaussian process is a collection of random variables, any finite set of which has a joint Gaussian distribution and is completely specified by its mean function $m(\boldsymbol{x})$ and the covariance function $k(\boldsymbol{x},\boldsymbol{x}')$:

$$f(\boldsymbol{x}) \sim GP(m(\boldsymbol{x}), k(\boldsymbol{x},\boldsymbol{x}')) \tag{1}$$

There is a training set $\boldsymbol{D}$ of n observations, $\boldsymbol{D}=\{(\boldsymbol{x}_i, y_i) \mid i=1,\ldots n\}$, where $\boldsymbol{x}$ denotes an input vector, y denotes a scalar output or target. The column vector inputs for all n cases are aggregated in the $\boldsymbol{D} \times n$ design matrix $\boldsymbol{X}$, and the targets are collected in the vector $\boldsymbol{y}$.

The goal of Bayesian forecasting is to compute the distribution $p(y_*|\boldsymbol{x}_*,\boldsymbol{D})$ of output y_* given a test input $\boldsymbol{x}_*$ and a set of training points $\boldsymbol{D}$. Using Bayesian rule, the posterior distribution for the Gaussian process outputs y_* can be obtained. By conditioning on the observed targets in the training set, the predictive distribution is Gaussian:

$$y_*\big|\boldsymbol{x}_*, \boldsymbol{X}, \boldsymbol{y} \sim N(\hat{y}(\boldsymbol{x}_*), \hat{\sigma}(\boldsymbol{x}_*)) \tag{2}$$

where the mean and variance are given by:

$$\hat{y}(\boldsymbol{x}_*) = \boldsymbol{k}_*^T(\boldsymbol{K} + \sigma_n^2\boldsymbol{I})^{-1}\boldsymbol{y} \tag{3}$$

$$\hat{\sigma}(\boldsymbol{x}_*) = k(\boldsymbol{x}_*, \boldsymbol{x}_*) - \boldsymbol{k}_*^T(\boldsymbol{K} + \sigma_n^2\boldsymbol{I})^{-1}\boldsymbol{k}_*^T \tag{4}$$

where, a compact form of the notation setting for matrix of the covariance functions are: $\boldsymbol{k}_* = \boldsymbol{K}(\boldsymbol{X}, \boldsymbol{x}_*)$, $\boldsymbol{K} = \boldsymbol{K}(\boldsymbol{X}, \boldsymbol{X})$, σ_n^2 is the unknown variance of the Gaussian noise.

Gaussian process has some covariance functions such as:

Squared exponential covariance function:

$$k_y(x_p, x_q) = \sigma_f^2 \exp\left(-\frac{1}{2l^2}\left(x_p - x_q\right)^2\right) + \sigma_n^2\delta_{pq} \tag{5}$$

Matern covariance function:

$$k_y(x_p, x_q) = \sigma_f^2\left(1 + \frac{\sqrt{3(x_p - x_q)^2}}{l}\right)\exp\left(-\frac{\sqrt{3(x_p - x_q)^2}}{l}\right) + \sigma_n^2\delta_{pq} \tag{6}$$

Neural network covariance function:

$$k_y(x_p, x_q) = \sigma_f^2.\arcsin\left(\frac{x_p.x_q}{l\sqrt{(l^2 + x_p{}^2)(l^2 + x_q{}^2)}}\right) + \sigma_n^2\delta_{pq} \tag{7}$$

Linear covariance function:

$$k_y(x_p, x_q) = \frac{x_p x_q}{l^2} + \sigma_n^2\delta_{pq} \tag{8}$$

These functions express the idea that the cases with nearby inputs will have highly correlated outputs. The covariance is denoted k_y as it is for the noisy targets y rather than for the underlying function f. GP employs a set of hyperparameters $\boldsymbol{\theta}$ including the length-scale $\boldsymbol{l}$, the signal variance σ_f^2 and the noise variance σ_n^2 . $\boldsymbol{\theta}$ can be optimized based on log-likelihood framework:

$$\log p(\boldsymbol{y} \mid \boldsymbol{X}, \boldsymbol{\theta}) = -\frac{1}{2}\boldsymbol{y}^T(\boldsymbol{K} + \sigma_n^2\boldsymbol{I})^{-1}\boldsymbol{y} - \frac{1}{2}\log\left|\boldsymbol{K} + \sigma_n^2\boldsymbol{I}\right| - \frac{n}{2}\log 2\pi \tag{9}$$

Hyperparameters $\boldsymbol{\theta}$ are initialized to random values (in a reasonable range) and then use an iterative method, for example conjugate gradient, to search for the optimal values of $\boldsymbol{\theta}$.

We initialize the hyperparameters to random values (in a reasonable range) and then use an iterative method, for example conjugate gradient, to search for optimal values of the hyperparameters. We found that this approach is sometime susceptible to local minima. To overcome this drawback, we randomly selected a number of starting positions within the hyperparameters space.The fundamental principles of GP can been seen in Fig.2.

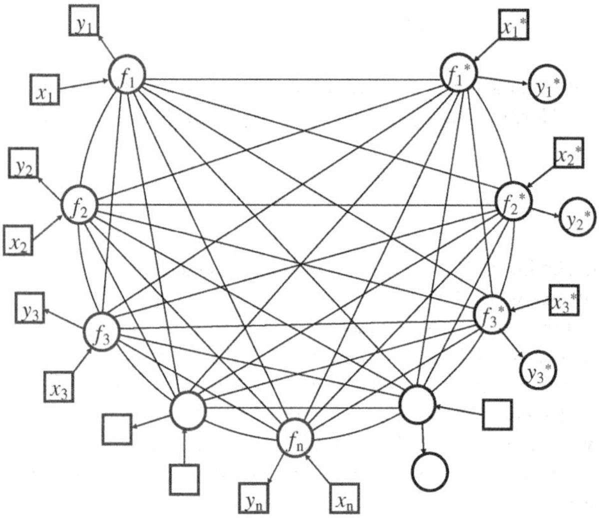

Fig. 2. The fundamental principles of GP

3 GP Model Forecasting of Karstic Collapse

3.1 Determine the Major Influencing Factors

Karstic collapse is influenced by various factors. The major factors should be analyzed according the conditions of engineering. According to many cases from Guilin [6], 6 coefficients including rock quality coefficient (RQC), rock mass structure coefficient (RMSC), ground water coefficient (GWC), soil stratum coefficient (SSC), landform physiognomy coefficient (LPC) and environment condition coefficient (ECC) are determined as the major influencing factors.

3.2 Establish the Forecasting Model

GP model for karstic collapse prediction is established as following steps:

Step 1: Historical cases (total number is n) are collected as training samples for GP machine learning. Import sample couples for GP is noted: $(\boldsymbol{x}_i, y_i)$, i=1, 2, ...n. Where, $\boldsymbol{x}_i$ is n-dimension input vector, which represent some quantitative control influencing factors of karstic collapse.y_i is the threshold value for the level of karstic collapse.

Step 2: Train GP model. The training samples are learned by GP. The hyperparameters $\boldsymbol{\theta}$ can be optimized based on log-likelihood framework by (8). Then, the nonlinear relationship between the factors and karstic collapse is established by GP.

Step 3: Predict with GP model. Use (3) to predict the threshold value of karstic collapse under novel conditions.

In order to implement the model proposed above, a MATLAB based program was developed.

4 Case Study

Cases from real engineering located in Guilin [6] are collected as samples. Randomly arrange the 13 samples, treat the first 9 samples as training samples and the rest of 4 samples as prediction samples (Table 1). Simultaneously, intensity of karstic collapse is divided into five levels judging by threshold values: 1.00 (no collapse), 2.00 (light collapse), 3.00 (medium collapse), 4.00 (easy collapse), 5.00 (violent collapse). After learning the training sample using GP model whose covariance function is squared exponential, the optimum hyperparameters of GP model are obtained self-adaptively: l=(743.53, 689.46, 827.23, 3.46, 3.20, 2.56), σ_f=1.69, σ_n =0.33.

Table 1. The Training and Prediction Samples for GP Model

No.	The major influencing factors						Threshold values
	RQC	RMSC	GWC	SSC	LPC	ECC	
1	1.80	1.95	0.81	0.83	0.90	1.25	5.00
2	0.50	1.55	1.07	1.06	0.90	1.00	5.00
3	0.90	1.45	1.18	1.45	0.90	1.00	5.00
4	0.90	1.40	0.48	1.09	0.90	1.00	5.00
5	1.80	1.85	0.36	0.86	0.70	0.00	3.00
6	0.50	1.25	0.36	0.46	0.40	0.00	2.00
7	1.80	1.90	0.41	0.89	0.90	0.30	4.00
8	0.30	1.20	0.36	0.42	0.40	0.00	1.00
9	0.50	1.20	0.36	0.60	0.90	0.00	3.00
10	1.50	1.50	1.20	1.67	0.90	1.00	5.00
11	1.50	1.80	1.16	1.70	0.90	1.00	5.00
12	1.60	1.89	1.16	1.67	0.90	1.00	5.00
13	1.80	1.85	0.46	0.83	0.70	0.00	3.00

The prediction results using GP model are shown in Table□.The results show that the prediction accuracy of the new model is good. The maximum relative error is only 3.12%, and the average relative error is only 0.86%. Furthermore, we use ANN model with 6-n-1 to predict the karstic collapse that n is obtained by regularization adjust method [16]. The maximum relative error is 6.73%, and the average relative error is

2.52%. The SVM model [6] is also compared with the GP model. The comparative results among different models can be seen in Table 2. Obviously, the GP model can provide more high precision of prediction results comparing to ANN and SVM model. Moreover, the parameters for GP model are determined by self-adaption that overcomes the questions of ANN and SVM determined by man-made.

Table 2. Comparison among the Prediction Results Using Different Models

No.	Threshold values	GP model		SVM model		ANN model	
		Prediction	Relative error (%)	Prediction	Relative error (%)	Prediction	Relative error (%)
10	5.00	5.002	0.04	5.146	2.92	4.663	6.73
11	5.00	4.988	0.24	5.148	2.96	4.923	1.53
12	5.00	5.002	0.04	4.759	4.82	4.926	1.49
13	3.00	2.907	3.12	3.258	8.60	2.990	0.34

5 Influence of Different Covariance Functions

Covariance function is the crucial ingredient in the GP model. In this paper, the influence of different covariance functions is discussed based on the case study.

The prediction results using different covariance functions for GP model are shown in Table 3. The choice of covariance function really affect the prediction accuracy for GP model. For example, the maximum relative error is 9.86% and the average relative error is 4.95% for GP model using linear covariance function, while the maximum relative error is 4.95% and the average relative error is 2.56% for GP model using neural network covariance function. The GP model using squared exponential covariance function has the best prediction accuracy.

Table 3. Comparison among The GP Forecasting Results Using Different Covariance Function

No.	Threshold values	Squared exponential		Matern		Neural network		Linear	
		Prediction	Relative error (%)	Prediction	Relative error (%)	Prediction	Relative error (%)	Prediction	Relative error (%)
10	5.00	5.002	0.04	5.025	0.50	5.247	4.95	5.143	2.87
11	5.00	4.988	0.24	5.045	0.89	4.977	0.47	4.843	3.14
12	5.00	5.002	0.04	5.029	0.59	4.937	1.26	4.803	3.95
13	3.00	2.907	3.12	3.213	7.10	3.106	3.54	2.704	9.86

6 Conclusion

A feasible and effective GP model is developed for predicting karstic collapse. Results of case study show that the GP model can get higher precision prediction results without complicated mechanic calculation and analysis. Moreover, GP model processes unique goodness, that is, self-adaptive parameters determination, which overcomes the open questions of other models. Based on the overall performance of GP model goodness, different covariance function has influence to the prediction accuracy. In a real project, compare the prediction results using different covariance function and choose the best one can improve the prediction accuracy for GP model.

Acknowledgment. This work is supported by the National Natural Science Foundation of China under Grant No. 50809017 and No.51069001, Special Research fund of State Key Laboratory of Geohazard Prevention and Geoenvironment Protection (Chengdu University of Technology) under Grant No. SKLGP2010K014.

References

1. Zhang, L.-F., Zeng, X.-S., Yao, Y.-S., Liao, W.-L.: Review on karst collapse in China. The Chinese Journal of Geological Hazard and Control 18(3), 126–130 (2007)
2. Liu, Z.-K., Liang, J.-C.: The influence on construction site for karst cave and soil cave in the karst area. The Geological Press, Beijing (2006)
3. Qin, L.-W., Shi, J.: Evaluation and prediction of karst collapse in Guangxi. The Chinese Journal of Geological Hazard and Control 8(suppl.), 43–53 (1997)
4. Qiu, X.-R.: Grey fuzzy synthetic assessment for stability of karst collapse. Hydrogeology & Engineering Geology 31(4), 58–61 (2004)
5. Bao, H.-M., Hu, C.-S.: Neural network prediction of karstic ground collapse. Journal of Engineering Geology 10(3), 299–304 (2002)
6. Lai, Y.-B., Qiao, C.-S.: Intelligent model of karstic collapse prediction based on SVM. Journal of Beijing Jiaotong University 32(1), 36–39, 43 (2008)
7. Xiong, Z.-H., Zhang, J.-C., Shao, H.-H.: GP-based soft sensor modeling. Journal of System Simulation 17(4), 793–794 (2005)
8. Seeger, M.: Gaussian processes for machine learning. International Journal of Neural System 14(2), 69–106 (2004)
9. Girolami, M., Rogers, S.: Variational Bayesian multinomial probit regression with Gaussian process priors. Neural Computation 18(8), 1790–1817 (2006)
10. Sofiane, B.-B., Amine, B.: Gaussian process for nonstationary times series prediction. Computational Statistics & Data Analysis 47(4), 705–712 (2004)
11. Gramacy, R.-B.: tgp: An R package for Bayesian nonstationary, semiparametric nonlinear regression and design by treed Gaussian process models. Journal of Statistical Software 19(19), 1–46 (2007)
12. Su, G.-S., Song, Y.-C., Yan, L.-B.: A new method for forecasting of blasting effect in rock mass. Chinese Journal of Rock Mechanics and Engineering 26(suppl. 1), 3509–3514 (2007)
13. Zhang, Y., Su, G.-S., Yan, L.-B.: Study on Gaussian process machine learning method for identifying the distribution structure of reservoir. Advances in Science and Technology of Water Resources 29(2), 13–15 (2009)

14. Su, G.-S., Zhang, Y., Zhang, X.-F.: Application of Gaussian Process machine learning to the prediction of groundwater level. China Rural Water and Hydropower 54(12), 48–50 (2008)
15. Rasmussen, C.-E., Williams, C.-K.-I.: Gaussian Processes for Machine Learning. The MIT Press, Cambridge (2006)
16. Wen, X., Zhou, L., Li, X.: MATLAB neural network simulation and application. Science Press, Beijing (2002)

Study of a Scheme of Bid Evaluation by Experts Based on Chinese Remainder Theorem

Xiaohan Sun

Department of Computer Science Weinan Teachers University
Weinan, 714000, Shaanxi Province, P.R. China
Xiao2828@yeah.net

Abstract. Bid evaluation, the most important link during a tender phase, is easily influenced negatively by human factors. A method based on Chinese Remainder Theorem is proposed, by which all the experts who grade tender documents are anonymous, all the scores are unknown before they are submitted to a bid invitation unit, and any score is not associated with the identification of an expert. If there are any dishonest behaviors during a bid evaluation, the scores given by dishonest experts can be deleted from the results.

Keywords: Bid Evaluation, Chinese Remainder Theorem, Zero knowledge proof.

1 Introduction

In China, the government began to implement the system of public bidding for project from the early of 1980s and passed "The Bidding Law" in 1998. However, there are still some problems to be solved in the process of bid and tender. Bid evaluation is the most important link during tendering. Presently, the major method to evaluate a tender document is an expert evaluation method, by which experts evaluate and grade the tender documents based on their knowledge and experience. The fair and impartial tender result depends on the experts' fair and impartial bid evaluation. The anonymity ensures that the experts are impervious to the winds of opinion and evaluate and grade tender documents independently. If an expert is dishonest in the process of bid evaluation, his anonymity will be cancelled compulsorily and the scores he gave will be deleted from the results [5, 7].

2 Initialization of System

The scheme includes three entities: Experts E, Bid Invitation Unit B and Key Center K, whose public keys and private keys are expressed by P_{UE_i}, P_{RE_i}, P_{UB}, P_{RB}, P_{UK} and P_{RK} respectively.

D. Zeng (Ed.): ICAIC 2011, Part I, CCIS 224, pp. 373–377, 2011.

2.1 Initialization of Bid Invitation Unit

The initialization is on the basis of Mignotte sequence.

B chooses the identification $\mathrm{ID}_i (i = 1, 2, \cdots, k)$ for each expert.

B chooses $m (m > k)$ random integer numbers $x_i \in Z (i = 1, 2, \cdots, m)$. They must satisfy: (1) $x_1 < x_2 < \cdots < x_m$; (2) $\gcd(x_i, x_j) = 1$ when $i \neq j$, where gcd() refers to the greatest common divisor function; and (3) $\prod_{i=m-t+2}^{m} x_i < \prod_{i=1}^{t} x_i (k < t \leq m)$ [1,2].

B chooses secret D which satisfies $\prod_{i=m-t+2}^{m} x_i < D < \prod_{i=1}^{t} x_i$ and computes $D \equiv I_i (\bmod x_i)(i = 1, 2, \cdots, m, m \geq k + t)$. Congruent system of equations is thus obtained: $\begin{cases} x \equiv I_1 (\bmod x_1) \\ x \equiv I_2 (\bmod x_2) \\ \cdots\cdots \\ x \equiv I_m (\bmod x_m) \end{cases}$ [3,4]

B chooses randomly k numbers from $(I_1, I_2, \cdots I_m)$. Suppose they are $I_1, I_2, \cdots I_k$ [1].

B chooses randomly $t-1$ pairs of (I_i, x_i), which are represented as $(I_i, x_i)_{t-1}$, from the pairs of (I_i, x_i) which are not chosen.

At last, B encrypts $I_1, I_2, \cdots I_k$ with its private key and E's public key and sends respectively $P_{UE_i}(P_{RB}(I_i, ID_i, (I_i, x_i)_{t-1}))$ to each expert.

2.2 Initialization of Key Center

The initialization is on the basis of Chinese Remainder Theorem.

K chooses randomly two big prime numbers p and q and computes $n = pq$. Then K chooses $e \in Z_n$ and computes d which satisfies $ed \equiv 1 (\bmod \phi(n))$ in which $\phi(n)$ is an Euler function [4,6].

K chooses k different integer numbers $y_i \in Z_n (i = 1, 2, \cdots k)$, any two of which satisfy $\gcd(y_i, y_j) = 1$ when $i \neq j$ [4, 6].

K solves the congruent system of equations:

$$\begin{cases} e \equiv f_1 (\bmod y_1) \\ e \equiv f_2 (\bmod y_2) \\ \cdots\cdots \\ e \equiv f_k (\bmod y_k) \end{cases}$$

2.3 Initialization of Experts

E chooses two secret numbers $g, e_i \in Z$ and computes d_i which satisfies $e_i d_i \equiv 1 (\mathrm{mod}\, g)$.

E grades a tender document. The score that E gave is represented as $m_i (i = 1, 2, \cdots k)$. E computes $m_i^{e_i} (\mathrm{mod}\, g)$. Then $m_i^{e_i}$ is encrypted with E's private key and K's public key. E sends $P_{UK}(ID_i P_{RE_i}(ID_i \| m_i^{e_i}))$ to K in the end.

3 Evaluation by Experts

3.1 Blind Signature by Key Center

K decrypts $P_{UK}(ID_i P_{RE_i}(ID_i \| m_i^{e_i}))$ and compares the ID_i decrypted with its private key with the ID_i decrypted with its private and E's public key. If the two of ID_i are same, the identification ID_i is legal. Then K computes $((m_i^{e_i}))^d$ and encrypts it with its private key and E's public key and sends $P_{UE_i}(P_{RK}(f_i, ((m_i^{e_i}))^d))$ to E.

E decrypts $P_{UE_i}(P_{RK}(f_i, ((m_i^{e_i}))^d))$ to obtain $((m_i^{e_i}))^d$. Then E computes $((m_i^{e_i})^d)^{d_i} (\mathrm{mod}\, n) = m_i^d (\mathrm{mod}\, n)$.

B. Zero Knowledge Proof by Experts

E chooses two public number $g_1, g_2 \in Z^*$, a public hash function $H_1(\bullet)$ and a secret number $a_i \in Z$. It then computes $hp = g_1 g_2^{a_i}$ and $hw = hp^{a_i^{-1}}$ and makes a zero knowledge proof about the secret a_i. The proof is $V = PROOF((hw / g_2), g_1) = (c, s)$ in which $c = H_1(hw / g_2) \| g_1 \| (hw / g_2)^r$, $s = r - ca_i$, and r is a random number[8,9].

3.2 Recovery of the Secret D

According to $P_{UE_i}(P_{RB}(I_i, ID_i, (I_i, x_i)_{t-1}))$ received from B, E computes $X = \prod x_i$ which includes all the x_i received, $X_i = X / x_i$, and $X_i X_i^{'} = 1 (\mathrm{mod}\, x_i)$ and recovers the secret D based on the formula $D = \sum I_i X_i X_i^{'}$ [1,2].

E sends $P_{UB}(D, hw, V, f_i, m_i^d, a_i ID_i)$ to B.

4 Computation of the Scores of Tender Documents

4.1 Confirmation of Identifications of Experts

1) Verification of the Secret D

B verifies whether the secret D is right, according to which the legal identification of E is confirmed.

2) Verification of V

The verification of V is as follows:

$$c = H_1((hw/g_2) \| g_1 \| (hw/g_2)^s g_1^c)$$

$$(hw/g_2)^s g_1^c = (hp^{a_i^{-1}} / g_2)^s g_1^c = ((g_1 g_2^{a_i})^{a_i^{-1}} / g_2)^s g_1^c \text{ [9]}$$

$$= (g_1^{a_i^{-1}})^{r-ca_i} g_1^c = g_1^{a_i^{-1} r} = (hw/g_2)^r$$

After V is verified, B believes E has the secret number a_i.

4.2 Determination of the Unit Who Wins the Tender

1) Computation of the Scores of Tender Documents

The steps to compute the resulting score is as follows:

Step 1, B computes $e = \sum_{i=1}^{k} f_i F_i F_i^{'}$ in which $F = \prod_{i=1}^{k} f_i$, $F_i = F / f_i$ and $F_i F_i^{'} \equiv 1 (\bmod f_i)$ [6].

Step 2, B computes $(m_i^{\ d})^e (\bmod n) = m_i (\bmod n)$.

Step 3, B computes $M = \frac{\sum_{i=1}^{k} m_i}{k}$ as the result of a tender document.

2) Determination of the Unit Who Wins the Tender

B compares the scores of all tender documents and determines the unit who wins the tender.

4.3 Deletion of the Score Given by a Dishonest Expert

If an expert E_l is dishonest in the process of bid evaluation, B will require imperatively E_l submit his secret number a_l, compute $a_l ID_l$ to find the score m_l given by E_l and calculate $M^{'} = \frac{Mk - m_l}{k-1}$ as a new score.

5 Analysis of Security

5.1 Anonymity of Experts

The identifications of experts are unknown to B. when each expert submits the score he gave to a tender document, his identification ID_i is multiplied by a secret number a_i. B cannot derive the expert's identification ID_i from $a_i ID_i$ with a_i unknown to B.

B confirms E's legal identification based on whether E can recover the secret D that can not reveal E's identification.

5.2 Confidentiality of Scores

Before all the scores are submitted to B, they are unknown. The score submitted by E to K is $m_i^{e_i}$, through which the initial score m_i can not be derived. The score submitted by E to B is m_i^d, by which m_i can not be derived unless e has been known. e can not be computed until all of f_i are collected.

References

1. Hou, Z., Han, J.: Resaerch of(t, n) secret sharing scheme against active cheating. Journal of Zhejiang University (Science Edition) 34(6), 633–635 (2007)
2. Yang, Y., Hou, Z.: Weighted threshold secret sharing scheme based on Mignotte sequence. Application Research of Computers 27(4), 1505–1507 (2010)
3. Zou, F.: Verifiable secret sharing scheme based on the Mignotte sequence. Journal of Shandong University of Technology(Natural Science Edition) 22(2), 14–16 (2008)
4. Zhang, J., Ru, X.: Threshold Multiple Secret Sharing Scheme. Computer Engineering and Applications 42(36), 134–135 (2006)
5. Wang, X.: A secure electronic tender protocol in Internet. Journal of Jinan University(Natural Science) 26(3), 345–349 (2005)
6. Shamir, A.: How to share a secret. Communications o f the ACM 22(11), 612–613 (1979)
7. Lei, l., Tan, Y.: A Research on Applicability of Evaluating Methods of Inviting Bidding. Journal of Air Force Engineering University(Natural Science Edition) 4(3), 87–91 (2003)
8. Wang, S., Wang, Y., Wang, X., Qin, B.: A zero-knowledge proof scheme of possessing a RSA digital signature. Journal of China Institute of Communications 25(1), 30–33 (2004)
9. Li, M., Yang, Y.: Revocable anonymous off-line E-cash scheme without TTP. ACTC Electronic SINICA 33(3), 456–458 (2005)

Converting Digital Image to SVG for User Interaction*

Qiang Wei, Dancheng Li, Cheng Liu, Binsheng Liu, and Zhiliang Liu

Software College University of Northeastern ShenYang, LiaoNing Province, China
qiang23709@163.com

Abstract. This paper presents a novel method to convert digital image to be Scalable Vector Graphic (SVG) format using the similar features of pixel, and make the converted SVG file becomes interactive. For example, we have a panoramic digital image of a school. There is lots of buildings and roads on it, and now we are going to construct a map application with this digital image for the school. This application ought to have functions, such as clicking to show building's information, searching for road by road name etc. It must be a big job to repaint an interactive image for the school. This paper introduces a method that aims at solving this problem. First, we directly convert digital image to SVG file through the way of one pixel of digital image to one rectangle of SVG. Then it allows user to select one or more 'seed' SVG pixels by which program can find a region with similar pixel feature. Finally, it can also detect the edge of the region and allows user to add event listener to the region.

Keywords: svg, digital image, image to svg, svg conversion.

1 Introduction

Scalable Vector Graphics (SVG) [1] language is now a W3C approved standard, and provides a new planar network image format based on XML (eXtensible Markup Language) features of two-dimensional graphics format for Web user. SVG is an effective combination graphic, raster image and text, it can display various kinds of high quality vector graphics on the web page, and it can inherit all features of XML[2].SVG offers an embed script mechanism to interact with web page and an event listener mechanism to interact with user such as mousedown listener, mousehover listener ect. The above ability of SVG is beyond the digital image's capacities.

But sometimes making image hold the ability of interaction is necessary. Taking Google map as example, we know that Google map allows user to click on a place and tell user where it is. A pure digital image cannot do that, but SVG is the opposite. So we wish to take use of SVG rather than digital image to construct application with user interaction. If we only have a digital image (In most of the cases, it always happens), and how we can build a SVG? Repainting one seems not to be a good solution because it is an undoubted big job. So we just wish to use computer to

* This research work is supported by "Natural Science Foundation of LiaoNing Province" (20092006).

D. Zeng (Ed.): ICAIC 2011, Part I, CCIS 224, pp. 378–385, 2011.

convert digital image to SVG file at first, and then make use of some algorithms to indicate key objects on SVG file so that we can make those objects interactive. That is what this paper wants to purpose.

The paper is structured as follows: Section 2 introduces the architecture of solution method. Section 3 reports the details of converting digital image to SVG file. Section 4 is devoted to the steps of selecting seed pixel points. Section 5 conducts to achieve the region of key object by seed pixel and add listener to the region for user interaction. Section 6 shows the experiment result for this paper. The final section closes the paper tracking also directions for future works.

2 Solution Overview

Our architecture has two sub-systems; one is for converting digital image to SVG (we call it Convert Tool), and the other one is for detecting regions of key objects to add interactive features (we call it Region Tool). Architecture is shown as follow.

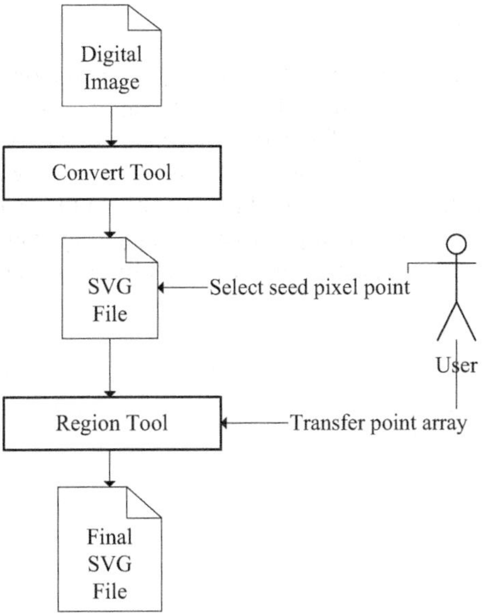

Fig. 1. Solution architecture

As shown in Fig.1, the main image processing steps is listed below.

1) Convert Digital Image To SVG: The converted SVG file allows user to click on it and return the position information of the clicked point which is called seed pixel point. A seed pixel should be a representative one of the region pixels.

2) Detect Regions: After transferring the seed pixel point array and SVG file generated in Step 1 into Region Tool, the regions of key object in SVG can be detected. The region is represented with polygon in SVG specification.

3) Add Interactive Feature: We can add listeners to the region of key objects in SVG so as to make SVG file interactive.

3 Conversing

We can simply understand digital image as a two-dimensional matrix, and each element in matrix is pixel. A pixel contains three values of color attributes, and they represent respectively red, green, blue which is also called RGB. If we magnify the digital image, we will find that every pixel is a square and it has only one color. That is why we recognize the pixel as the unit of an image. According to characteristics of digital image, we design the converting method shown as Fig 2.

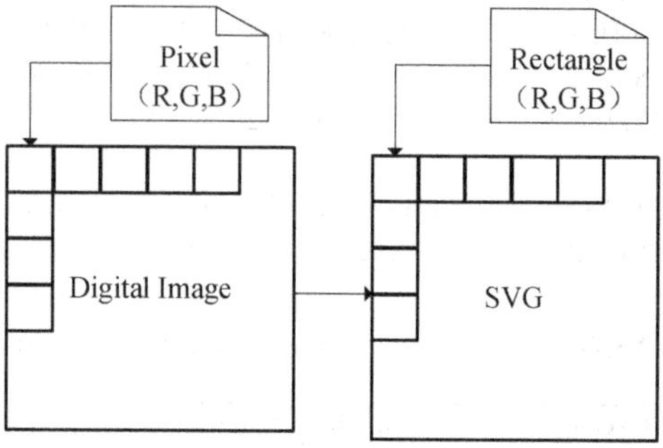

Fig. 2. Relation between digital image and SVG

In SVG specification, we can take use of *<rect>* element to create a square which is just like the pixel in digital image. Convert Tool will traverses the matrix of digital image and reads out the RGB from each pixel, then creates *<rect>* element whose width is one unit for each pixel. The *<rect>* element has the same RGB as the pixel in the same relative position of digital image. The created *<rect>* element's content is just similar with "*<rect height="1" width="1" style="fill:rgb(26,72,29);stroke-width:0;" x="10" y="2"/>*". At the end of traversing, a SVG image which looks same as the original digital image will be generated.

4 Seed Pixel Point Selection

After the conversion, we want to find the key objects on SVG. The key objects can interact with user. For people, it is very easy to find the key objects by human's eyes. So we let user to select seed pixel points which may be located in the middle or four corners of the key object region. Then the program will keep extending a segment that starts as one seed pixel until the segment contains the whole region of key object. To explain this process, paper offers Fig 3 as below.

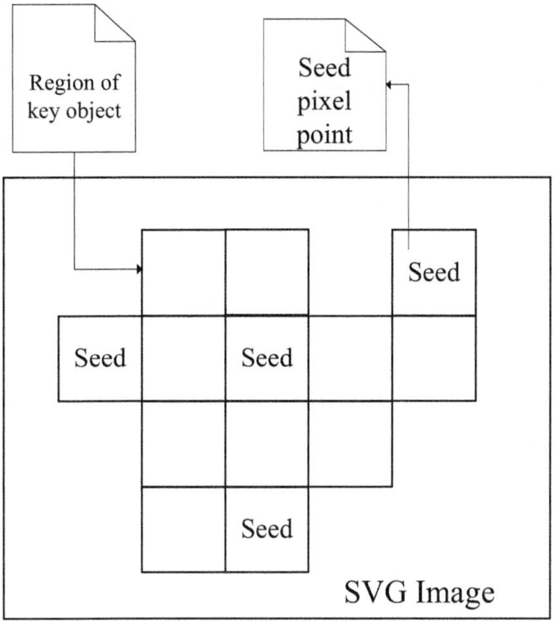

Fig. 3. Seed and Region

On the above SVG image, key object region contains some pixels. There should be more pixels of one key object region in actual application. We can not let user select all pixels of one region. So we just let user select some seed pixels as Fig 3 illustrated. Though different people have different selection, but there is rule user must comply with, that those seed pixels must place in the region scope. It should not be difficult for user to do that by his eyes. After the selection, program will transfer the array of seed pixel and SVG file to the Region Tool.

5 Detect and Active Region

In this part, we will take use of some algorithms to detect the key object region by seed pixels.

5.1 Step 1

We first define a function F: **G**ray = $0.299R + 0.587G + 0.114B$, to get the gray value of one pixel (0.299, 0.587 and 0.114 is best weight in test) , an appropriate threshold **T** and a segment **S** that starts as only one seed pixel, **(1)**then make seed pixel compare to its 8-connected neighbors: eight neighbors of the seed pixel. If **G**s - **G**n <= **T** (**G**s represents the gray value of seed pixel, and **G**n is neighbor's), then we can regard current checked neighbor is in the same region scope and than put it into segment S. Back to step **(1)** to continue verifying the neighbors of the recently added pixel of **S** until **S** increases no more. Finally we will get S containing key object region. The best is that **S** is exactly the same as key object region, but we still tolerate some error as long as there is not too much difference.

5.2 Step 2

Suppose we have got a satisfactory segment **S** to represent the region of key object. The next we should do is to add listener to the segment **S** so that it can interact with user. It will dramatically increase the SVG file size if we add listener to every <rect> element of **S**. so we must find a way to detect the edge of **S**, so we can construct a polygon to surround it. The key of edge detection for image is to detect more edge details, reduce the noise impact to the largest degree [3]. Solution method is shown below: Traverse all <rect> elements of **S**, and for each element, judge whether it at least has one border not connected to other <rect> element also in **S** or not. If the answer is yes, we regard it as an edge element and the end points of the unconnected borders will be added into the polygon of **S**. The schematic diagram is just shown in Fig 4 as below.

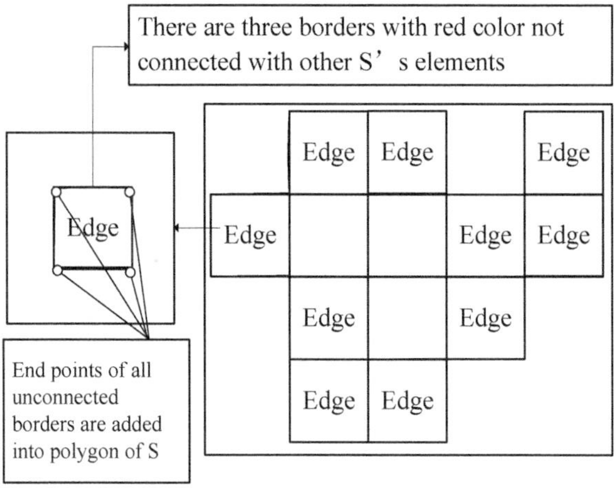

Fig. 4. Seed and Region

The final SVG file should contains elements like Fig5.

On the Fig 5, the polygon [4] is a generated SVG element to represents the region of key object. In the event handler, programmers can do anything they want to interact with user. Still taking map application as a sample, polygon maybe represents a building. When user clicks on the building, application will popup an information dialog about this building. The code for click event handling should be written in red part of Fig 5 [5]. Then we finally realize the user interaction. By language of JavaScript, SVG can be much easy to interact with web browser and web user [6].

```
<script type="text/javascript">
<![CDATA[
function mouseClick(evt)
{
        var target = evt.target;
        //do something
}
]]>
</script>
<polygon points="x1, y1 x2, y2 x3, y3 ..."
onclick="mouseClick(evt)"/>
...
```

Fig. 5. Region polygon

6 Experiment Result

In order to assess the performance of the proposed approach, a set of experiments is carried out on a test dataset of digital images. More than 100 pictures have been tested by those algorithms introduced in this paper. The results are gratifyingly uncontroversial. This paper will demonstrate the result by an example of a flower picture. The source picture of the flower is shown in Fig 6.

Fig. 6. Source picture

We make use of Convert Tool to change source image into SVG file, and open it with web browser. The SVG file shown on browser is just like Fig 7.

Fig. 7. SVG file on browser

As shown in Fig 7, the generated SVG is identical with the original picture, and thus has no distortion. Then user can select some points on the flower, such as some petal points and bud points. Since the Convert Tool has appended click listener to every <rect> element. As user click on picture, the dialog with position information about clicked point will popup. The result is shown in Fig 8 as below.

Fig. 8. Seed pixel selection

Take notes of those points and transfer them to the Region Tool. Then the generation of final SVG file is finished in no time. Open it with web browser and click any point of the picture, a dialog of what you have pointed will popup. The result is shown in Fig 9 and Fig 10.

Fig. 9. Click on petal region

Though we just selected some seed points of petal region, the final SVG file supports the check of whole petal region scope.

Different region has different information. We need to choose different seed points and event handler for different region of key object.

According to experiment, it will be easy to realize application just like map application. Spatial information of SVG can be displayed by JavaScript, and Showing detail message about SVG is necessary for almost all SVG applications [7]. Not only simple event listener can be added into SVG, but also animation can be made use to render SVG.

Fig. 10. Click on bud region

7 Conclusions

The purpose of this paper is to describe the process of converting digital image to SVG and making SVG interactive. It proposes a series of algorithms to achieve the goal. It has some features. For example, the conversion has no distortion and Region Tool can accurately detect the edge of key object region. But this mechanism is still not perfect, and it has some defects. The final SVG file is little too big and it is inefficiency. The conversion mechanism makes the final SVG file lose vector characteristic. More test and optimization are needed. Overall, we still have a long way to go.

Acknowledgment. This research work is supported by "Natural Science Foundation of LiaoNing Province" (20092006).

References

1. Scalable Vector Graphics (SVG) 1.2 W3C Working Draft (October 27, 2004), `http://www.w3.org/TR/2004/WD-SVG12-2004-10-27/`
2. Yuan, J., Huang, J.: Converting Real Images to SVG Based on XML
3. Yan, W., Shen, S.: An Edge Detection Method for Chromosome Images. In: iCBBE 2008 (2008)
4. How to create polygon in svg, `http://www.w3schools.com/svg/svg_polygon.asp`
5. How to add script to SVG, `http://www.w3.org/TR/SVG/script.htm`
6. Gao, F., Tang, J.: The Use of Javascript in Map Application Based on SVG. Academic Journal of Normal University in Jiangxi Province China 3, 262–265 (2004)
7. Wang, H., Zhu, J.: Science of Test, vol. 4, pp. 90–91 (July 2006)

Research on the Customer Consumption Classification Model Based on RS-NN

Wan Yinghong[1,2], Cao Xiaopeng[1], Yue Ying[1], and Hu Wanping[1]

[1] School of management, Xi'an Jiaotong University
[2] Experiment Center for Management Teaching & Learning, Xi'an Jiaoton University (Demo-Center at State Level for Experiment Teaching)
Xi'an, China
wan0837@tom.com

Abstract. Since customer consumption attributes are multi-dimensional, related and uncertain, this paper proposed a customer consumption classification model based on rough set and neural network (RS-NN). Due to the rough set characteristics of customer consumption classification, the research framework of this paper was constructed by preprocessing knowledge space, establishing classification model and applying the classification model. Besides, based on RS, this paper also described consumption attributes reduction, classification rule extraction, and original topology of RS-NN construction, network model training and testing. Then a case study on telecom customers shows that RS-NN is better than BP-NN in construction, classification efficiency and prediction accuracy, which means RS-NN is an effective and practical new method for customer classification.

Keywords: Customer consumption attributes, RS-NN, customer classification model, telecom customers.

1 Introduction

Classification of customer consumption in customer relationship management includes: establishing classification model, regulations and knowledge or experience, classifying customers and predicting consumer behavior by certain classification model. Therefore, how to adopt advanced and practical consumption model to classify customers and make proper marketing strategies are significant for enterprises. Widely-used classification methods based on data mining are naïve Bayesian classification, decision tree, logistic regression and neural network (NN). In specific applications, decision tree can easily be converted into classification rules, however, it is too inflexible to deal with large training sets; Although Bayesian classification is a statistical method, the prediction accuracy will be affected when the independent hypothesis of the classes lack accurate probability distribution; logistic regression is based on the hypothesis that classification variables and attribute values have significant liner relationship; then, the typical advantages of artificial neural network (ANN) are self-learning, self-adaptive and fault-tolerant, and with the known-type samples, ANN establishes complex nonlinear relationship between classes and

D. Zeng (Ed.): ICAIC 2011, Part I, CCIS 224, pp. 386–396, 2011.

attributes. Therefore, ANN is better than other methods in reflecting nonlinear relationship.

With deep research on characteristics impacting customer consumption (CC), CC characteristic variables have been expanded from the basic and static characteristics at a certain time to dynamic characteristics in a certain period. And customer consumption data is presented in quantitative/qualitative, precise/fuzzy and other forms. Customer classification model based on NN have the following problems: (1) how to judge and determine the input nodes, hidden layers and hidden nodes; (2) classification features are multi-dimensional and correlated with different importance and certain redundancy, which will lead to complex model structures and learning inefficiency, as well as weaken explanatory power of knowledge classification without retrench and selection; and (3) due to inaccurate, uncertain and incomplete data characteristics, it is difficult for classification model to preprocess the input data.

Rough Set Theory (RS), first described by Zdzislaw I. Pawlak, is analytic methods dealing with indiscernibility relations. RS is used to: (1) process incomplete, inaccuracy and uncertain quantitative data, (2) identify and evaluate the dependent relationship between condition attributes and decision attributes implied in accumulative data; (3) remove redundant attributes and their values, and simplify knowledge expression space on premise of keeping key information. Therefore, RS and NN can be integrated to solve the problems existing in customer consumption classification models mentioned above.

For CC classification, RS-NN model proposed in the paper simplifies CC characteristics by RS to obtain the smallest train set on the premise of keeping the key information; obtains the simplest network classification model with fault tolerant and anti-interference abilities by self-learning, self-organizing and self-adjusting of NN.

2 Related Works

2.1 CC Attributes and Classification

Maslow's hierarchy of needs indicates that needs decided by customer characteristics and external environments stimulate customers to take actions to achieve specific purposes. Specific to consumption subjects, consumption are achieved by selection of specific products, consumption behavior and outcomes.

CC classification model is to classify known-type customer samples to identify characteristic attributes of each customer type, and establish corresponding relationships between customer classes and consumption attributes, in order to distinguish new customers based on these characteristics. Classification problems analysis, model establishment and model application are three key elements for CC model researches. Current researches and applications usually adopt advanced technology and methods, such as data mining, statistics, intelligent learning technologies, to utilize historical customer data to discover rules, relationships and patterns of customer behaviors.

Variables used to analyze, observe and predict customer consumptions have been extended from static characteristics at a certain time (i.e. demographic variables) to dynamic characteristics in a certain period (i.e. trend of consumption behavior, adjustment parameters for product selection). And characteristics reflecting customer consumptions include basic characteristics, consumption environment, product selection etc. In specific industry or market, each consumption attributes has corresponding semantic and data characteristics, including qualitative/quantitative, precise/fuzzy and continuous/discrete forms.

Due to multi-dimension, correlation and imprecise statue, customer consumption characteristics and classification couldn't be reflected by simple classification rules. For example, customer groups with same consumption condition attribute values have different decision attributes, while customer groups with different consumption condition attribute values have the same decision attributes. Besides, most consumption attributes are not equally important for classification and some are even redundant. In this sense, before finding the relationship between customer classes and consumption characteristics and establishing classification model, on premise of keeping key information, it is necessary to select key attributes to retrench knowledge expression space, in order to decrease classification resource waste, such as large storage space, high cost for information access and efficiency decrease of modeling.

2.2 RS Characteristics of Customer Classification Universe

This section applies RS theory to identify relevant concepts in this research.

1) Consumption decision table and RS characteristics

A two -dimensional table is used to express customer data, in which row records a customer object, and column describes condition attributes of consumption and decision attributes of given classes.

Definition 1: Assign Consumption Classification Table $S=<U, C, D, V, f>$, where U is a nonempty finite set of objects (universe); C is a consumption attribute set; D is a decision attribute set($D \neq \varnothing$) ;V is a range set of all attributes. Assign O=C∪D, f: U×O→V is an information function, and set a value for each attribute, i.e. $\forall o \in O$, $x \in U$, $f(x, o) \in V$.

In RS theory, decision table is the knowledge space reflecting the nature of classification, using equivalence relation for interpretation. And each attribute corresponds to an equivalence relation. The table can be treated as a collection of equivalence relations. Therefore, if R is equivalent to customer object in universe U, $X_i=[x]_R$ represents equivalence class for R, U/R={X_1, X_2,..., X_n} represents all equivalence classes for R; All equivalence classes of R consist of a partition block, corresponding to equivalence classes.

Definition 2: For the universe of CC decisions U, X⊆U, and R is equivalent. If X is the union set of R categories, so X is definable for R, called R precise set; or X is indefinable for R, called R rough set. Customer object X and equivalence relation *IND (R)*, as well as largest definable set included in X and smallest definable including X can all be determined by R, and the former is called lower approximation set of X, donated by R_(X), while the latter is called upper approximation set of X, donated by $R^{-}(X)$, which can be expressed as follows:

$$R\_(X)=\cup\{x\in U \mid IND(R)\subseteq X \}$$

$$R^{-}(X)=\cup \{x\in U \mid IND(R)\cap X \neq\varnothing\}$$

So, $BN_R(X) = R^-(X) - R\_(X)$ is called R boundary of X; $POS_R(X)=R\_(X)$ is called R positive region of X; $NEG_R(X) = U - R^-(X)$ is called R negative region of g. Among attributes of classification universe reflected by customer consumption data, most distributes in the scope of $BN_R(X)$, $R\_(X) \neq R^-(X)$, which has the typical characteristics of RS.

Table 1. Consumption decision table

Rules	Objects	Condition Attributes				Decision Attributes
		C_1	C_2	…	C_n	D
1	t_1	a_{11}	a_{12}	…	a_{1n}	b_1
…	…	…	…	…	…	…
m	t_m	a_{m1}	a_{m1}		a_{mn}	b_n

2) Consumption attributes reduction

Consumption attribute reduction in RS theory refers to use some necessary condition attribute from the condition attribute set, substituted for all condition attributes, in order to make the same classification. Decision attributes are distinction variables for classes, so we need to reduce these attributes in the consumption decision table.

Definition 3: Assign consumption classification decision table S. For consumption attribute set $A \subseteq C$, D is equivalent to U set; If $r \in A$, $POS_{\{A-\{r\}\}}(D) = POS_A(D)$, consumption attribute r in A is dispensable for D. Otherwise attribute r in A is indispensable for D.

Reduction algorithm for reducing consumption attributes is adopted based on discernibility matrix and logical operation in this paper. According to reduction algorithm, we obtain new CC decision table, see table 1. All attribute values are core values in this table, and all records can derive the simplest rule (named Rule) of CC classification and reliability of Rule (see Definition 5).

Definition 4: Supposing S is a consistent consumption decision table, when customer records have the same consumption attribute values, their decision attribute values are also equal. In other words, decision rules derived from table S are determined. If S is a inconsistent consumption decision table, at least two customer objects have the same values in consumption condition attribute set, but different decision attribute values. So there must be undetermined rules in the inconsistent decision table.

Definition 5: According to RS, rules can be expressed as: $Rule_m$: if A then B。A is a consumption condition subset, $A = a_{11} \wedge a_{12} \cdots \wedge a_{1n}$, while B is decision attribute b1. The reliability of Rule is:

$$CF(Rule) = CF(B, A) = \frac{|Y \cap [x]_R|}{[x]_R}$$

Where, Y is a record set of decision table satisfying decision conclusion B; and x is any record satisfying consumption condition attribute A, so equivalence class $[x]_R$ represents record set all satisfying consumption attribute A, obviously $0 \leq CF(B, A) \leq 1$.

2.3 Initial Topology of RS-NN

NN is an approach with the idea of nonlinear mapping and parallel process, which expresses implicit function of input and output knowledge with network structure. For customer consumption classification, the basic idea for rough set and neural network (RS-NN) technology is as follows: based on BP network and classification rules derived from RS, we construct initial topology of RS-NN.

Layer 1: Input Layer. The core attributes processed by consumption attributes reduction are used as an input. The input vector $X=(x_1,x_2,...x_n)^T$ is corresponding to a set of core attributes, and the values of these core attributes are derived from new learning samples preprocessed and reduced from the given sample database.

Layer 2: Rough Membership Layer. The neuronal connection between this layer and layer 1 refers to the conditions for consumption classification rules. The i_{th} neuron in layer 1 connects with r_i neurons in this layer (r_i is discrete intervals). Assign the function of neurons in this layer $j=\sum r\_i$ (i=1..n) as rough membership function [13], and the output as $N_{ji}=\mu_{Aji}(x_i)=\mu_{ij}$, where N_{jr} means the j_{th} equivalent class for the i_{th} component, and A_{ji} as connection weight of rough membership function between x_t and N_{ji}, which means the equivalent class presented by j_{th} class.

Layer 3: Classification Rule Layer. Each neuron represents a rule, and acquisition and description of rules are based on RS theory. The neuronal relationship among this layer, layer 2 and layer 4 is decided by classification rules. Assuming there are m ($m \leq n$) classification rules, fitness calculation of rules can be completed by neurons in this layer, and the output of the t_{th} neuron R_t is

$$\pi_t = \mu_{1t} \bullet \mu_{2t} ... \mu_{nm} = \prod \mu_{jt}, (t = 1...m, j = 1...\sum r_i) \cdot$$

Where, μ_{1t} is the output of j_{th} neuron in layer 2 connecting with the t_{th} neuron in this layer.

Layer 4: Output Layer. Set one output node as the classification variable. Assign the initial value for connection weight to each node in layer 3 ωi as the crediability of each rule c*ft. The output of the node in this layer is:

$$y = \sum c \bullet f_t \bullet \pi_t, (t = 1...m) \cdot$$

3 Methodology

3.1 Research Framework

CC classification model based on RS and NN consists of three subsystems, preprocess of knowledge space reduction, establishing consumption classification network model, and classification model application. Research framework is shown in Figure 1.

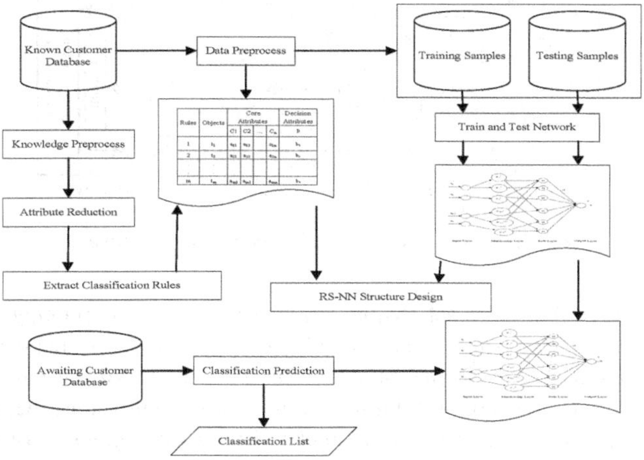

Fig. 1. Classification model based on RS-NN

1) Subsystem 1: preprocess of knowledge space reduction

The main task for this phase is to establish the smallest knowledge space (learning sample set) for classification model and corresponding classification rules:

a) Data preprocess. Most types of CC attribute data are continuous numeric, whereas RS processes discrete data only. Therefore, these data should be converted to discrete ones. Equal frequency methods for unsupervised discretization are adopted in this paper, and the processes are as follows: according to ascending sort of m objects, ask experts to determine the number of intervals k, and divide m object records into k segments in average. We get m/k object records in each segment and k break point sets. Finally, customer consumption classification sheet is formed with discrete data.

b) Consumption attributes reduction. With consumption attributes reduction based on discernibility matrix and logical operation, consumption attribute set A =C∩D, according to data sheet for customer consumption classification S=< U, A, V, f >, in which C is consumption attribute set, and D is decision attribute set. So identify discernibility as

$$C_{ij}=\begin{cases} a \mid a\in C,\ f(x_i,a)\neq f(x_j,a),(x_i,x_j)\notin IND(D) \\ 0, others \end{cases}$$

The approaches for consumption attributes reduction are as follows:

- Calculate discernibility matrix for customer consumption classification sheet C_D。
- For element *q* in nonzero and nonempty set of discernibility matrix, establish corresponding disjunctive logic expression Lij, and make $L_{ij}=\bigcup_{a_i\in C_{ij}} L_{ij}$.
- Conduct conjunctive calculation to all disjunctive logic expressions, to obtain conjunctive paradigm L, and make $L=\bigcap_{C_{ij}\neq 0, C_{ij}\neq\varnothing} L_{ij}$. Convert paradigm L into disjunctive paradigm $L'=\bigcup_i L_i$.

- Output the results of attributes reduction. Each item in disjunctive paradigm is corresponding to a result of attribute reduction, and attributes in each item forms the reduced attribute set.

c) Extract classification rules. Based on attributes reduction, attribute value reduction is an optional step. Same as attributes reduction, a new table is obtained by reduction, and all attribute values are core-values in this table. Finally the simplest rules of consumption classification and reliability for rules can be obtained.

2) Subsystem 2: establish classification network model

This subsystem is to generate and test RS-NN model for CC classification, and main processes are as follows.

Design initial topology of RS-NN and initialization. Based on knowledge expression space reduced from samples, assign numbers of input and output neuron nodes in neural network, hidden layers and hidden nodes, as well as functions and initial values for connecting weights, then establish initial topology construction of RS-NN.

Preprocess learning samples. To avoid the influences from differences of each variable to the accuracy of network training, normalize all the inputs by the formula $xi = \frac{xi - x_{min}}{x_{max} - x_{min}}$, and divide learning samples into training samples (80%) and test samples (20%).

Train RS-NN. As used in common BP-NN model, Tangsig function is selected for the transfer function. BP-NN algorithm iterates to train sample data. In self-learning and self-adjusting processes of connecting weights, parameters of weights, class centers of equivalence classes c_{ij} and variance δ_{ij} in the network are needed to adjust. Then, mapping model reflecting the relationship of input space and output space for classification network can be obtained. Generalized δ rule is adopted for error calculation.

Test and evaluate RS-NN. The method is to test the input model for samples, and then compare the prediction results with the actual classification. If the prediction accuracy is larger than 85%, deviation is within the acceptable range, indicating the model passes the test.

3) Subsystem 3: classification prediction application

With classification model, we can classify new customers and forecast their behaviors according to their consumption attributes. The main steps are:

a) Extract and convert data from different database (such as basic characteristics of customers, product transactions), and generate CC attribute sheet.

b) Classify values of inputs from customer consumption attribute sheet to obtain the consumption classes that customers belong to.

c) Generate forecasting report for consumption class, as a basis for marketing strategy decision-making.

3.2 Modeling Software Tools

Rosetta V1.4.41 is adopted, which is a software based on GUI and developed for RS by Norwegian University with functions for decision table introduction, data discretization, attributes reduction, rules extraction, classification and so on. Matlab is also selected, in order to construct a software platform for classification model.

4 Empirical Case Study

4.1 Samples, Consumption Attribute Variables and Data Preprocess

X is a subcompany of China Telecom, which aims to conduct customer relationship management. The expert team selects 2100 customers (in a certain industry) for classification, and the data comes from the data sheet of customer consumptions from June to September in 2008, 2008. The table structure includes 22 consumption attribute items and 1 decision attribute. By testing the redundancy and ommition of data, we delete 113 records. Equal frequency interval method and discretization method for continuous attribute data are used and converted customer consumption decision table can be obtained, seeing Table 2.

4.2 Consumption Attributes Reduction and Classification Rule Extraction

With Rosetta V1.4.41, we reduce redundant consumption attributes, and get 8 core attributes (total cost, trend of local cost, trend of toll call, cost of local call, cost of toll call, fluctuation of total cost, fluctuation of toll call, occupy of toll call), and generate consumption classification decision table. Then reduce classification rules and get 9371 attributes and 893 classification rules, and choose the rules whose reliability is larger than 0.65. Finally, 53 classification rules are got and corresponding learning sample set is generated.

4.3 CC Classification Model Establishment

1) Initial topology of CC model based on RS-NN

We identify RS-NN model as a four layer neural network structure with 8 neurons in the Input Layer, 40 neurons in the Rough Membership Layer (according to discrete intervals for attribute values), 53 neurons in the Rule Layer (according to reduced 53 classification rules), 1 neuron in the Output Layer and the output variable is discriminate value for customer class.

2) Parameter selection for training function, transfer function and other functions

We adopt tansig function for transfer function, and advanced BP algorithm for training function. The algorithm selects Momentum Gene as learning rule and self-learning rate for learning rate. The training parameters are: target error as 0.01, learning rate as 0.1 and training times as 1000.

3) Model training and accuracy test

The system randomly selects 200 samples as test data from 1987 learning samples, while remaining 1787 samples as training samples. 8 core consumption attributes of training samples are inputted into the Input Layer of the model for training the network. After 350 iterations, the network is convergent, see Figure 2. When the mapping rules are extracted, classification model is determined.

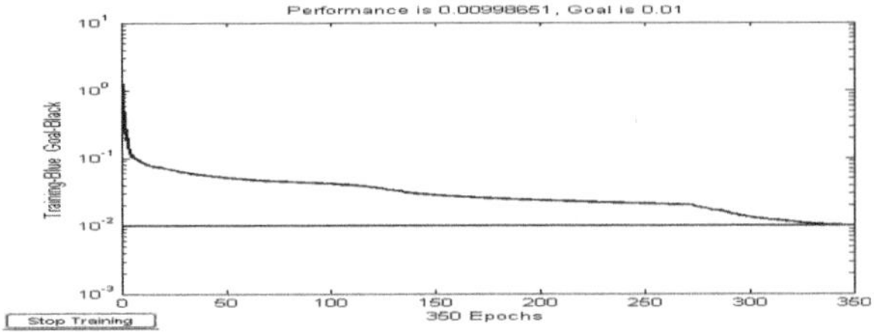

Fig. 2. Training performance

Afterwards, the random 200 test samples are inputted to the network model to test the accuracy of the model. With Matlab, the errors between forecast values and the actual values are converted s into Figure 3. Most errors are around 0, and there are only 6 samples whose errors are larger than 1. Classification accuracy reaches 97%, which indicates the classification model has a high accuracy consistent with the actual statues.

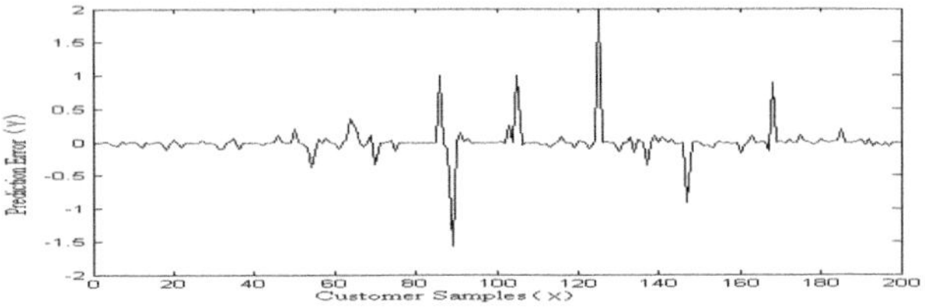

Fig. 3. Prediction error

Table 2. X-company consumption decision table

	Variables	1	2	3	4	5
Customer basic characteristic variables	Customer Recognition types	Attribute values are discrete.				
	Industry					
	Customer access types					
	Preferential types					
	Consumption duration	[*,16)	[16,45)	[45,46)	[46,59)	[59,*)
Customer Relationship characteristic variables	Total cost	[*,57.2)	[57.2,101.69)	[101.69,164.82)	[164.82,327.42)	[327.42,*)
	Local call cost	[*,4.97)	[4.97,20.65)	[20.65,50.94)	[50.94,141.39)	[141.39,*)
	Monthly rent	[*,18)	[18,35)	[35,36)	[36,72)	[72,*)
	Toll cost	[*,4.97)	[4.97,20.65)	[20.65,50.94)	[50.94,141.39)	[141.39,*)
	Website cost	[*,0.03)	[0.03,8.5)	[8.5,29.38)	[29.38,96.32)	[96.32,*)
Customer demand derived variables	Fluctuation of total cost	[*,0.05)	[0.05,0.11)	[0.11,0.18)	[0.18,0.29)	[0.29,*)
	Fluctuation of local cost	[*,0.09)	[0.09,0.20)	[0.20,0.31)	[0.31,0.51)	[0.51,*)
	Fluctuation of toll cost	[*,0.01)	[0.01,0.31)	[0.31,0.54)	[0.54,0.83)	[0.83,*)
	Fluctuation of website cost	[*,0.01)	[0.01,0.16)	[0.16,0.48)	[0.48,0.78)	[0.78,*)
	Rate of monthly rent	[*,0.1)	[0.1,0.18)	[0.18,0.32)	[0.32,0.57)	[0.57,*)
	Rate of local call cost	[*,0.07)	[0.07,0.21)	[0.21,0.36)	[0.36,0.58)	[0.58,*)
	Rate of toll cost	[*,0.01)	[0.01,0.09)	[0.09,0.22)	[0.22,0.41)	[0.41,*)
	Trend of total cost	[*,-9.27)	[-9.27,-0.69)	[-0.69,0.96)	[0.96,10.4)	[10.4,*)
	Trend of monthly rent	[*,0)	[0,1)	[1,3)	[3,9)	[9,*)
	Trend of local cost	[*,-4.11)	[-4.11,-0.16)	[-0.16,0.52)	[0.52,6.14)	[6.14,*)
	Trend of toll cost	[*,-3.53)	[-3.53,-0.01)	[-0.01,0.03)	[0.03,7.2)	[7.2,*)
	Trend of website cost	[*,-0.01)	[-0.01, 0.01)	[0.01,5.9)	[5.9,23.09)	[23.09,*)

4.4 Models Comparison

In order to analyze the performance of RS-NN model, we compare it with BP-NN model. With the same training accuracy, BP-NN, which uses initial samples as training samples has obviously more training steps than RS-NN; While RS-NN, which uses reduced samples as training samples has much faster training speed. With the same training samples and test samples, the accuracy of RS-NN is higher than the accuracy of BP-NN, which illustrates that RS-NN is more efficient, shown in Table 3.

Table 3. Comparision of RS-NN and NN

Input Vector of Neural Network	Network Structures			Training Steps	Training Time (min)	Training Accuracy Rate
	Nodes in Input Layer	Nodes in Hidden Layer	Training Accuracy			
Samples after learning (RS-NN)	8	53	0.01	350	5	97%
Initial samples (BP-NN)	24	100	0.01	650	25	95%

5 Conclusions

CC classification issue is a hot topic in customer relationship management. Classification based on data mining and historical data is efficient, but the bottleneck in practice is obvious as (1) how to identify and analyze consumption attributes, avoid attribute redundancy, and select core attributes, in order to reduce complexity of classification models and improve the explanatory power; (2) consumption attributes and consumption classification are indiscernible and inconsistent, while traditional classification methods couldn't solve these problems.

This paper proposes a RS-NN based method to establish a CC classification model, and the key processes are: conduct attributes reduction to obtain core consumption attributes, in order to solve attribute redundancy and classification insistency problems existing in CC classification; extract customer classification rules to obtain rule knowledge for classification, in order to solve the classification insistency problem; by integrating classification rules into neural network and initialization of classification model and parameters, reduce complexity of the model and training time, and improve the learning ability, inference ability and classification ability to realize customer dynamic classification. By a case analysis, it is found that CC model based on RS-NN is better than those based on RS or NN. RS-NN model not only solves redundancy of classification variables, but also improves the efficiency and accuracy of classification models. Therefore, RS-NN is an efficient and practical customer classification method.

From the perspective of customer lifetime, customers in different stages of lifetime have different transactions, consumption behavior, preference and profits for enterprises. The future research on customer classification model should bring lifetime stages, preference variables and industrial background into the framework. And our future research can shed further light on this issue.

Acknowledgement. This work was supported by the National Natural Science Foundation of China (70471036, 70771086).

References

1. Zeng, H.: Intelligent computing - on the rough set theory, fuzzy logic, neural network theory and its application. Chongqing University Press (2004)
2. Wei, J.: The knowledge discovery based on rough sets and its application in CRM, Harbin Engineering University (March 2006)
3. Qi, J., Wan, Y.: Customer relationship management theory and method. China Water Power Press & Intellectual Property Press (2006)

4. Zhu, Y.: Customer segmentation model research based on consumer behavior. Sichuan Normal University (May 2007)
5. Lingras, P.: Comparison of neo fuzzy and rough neural networks. Information Sciences 110(3-4), 207–213 (1998)
6. Banerjee, M., Mitra, S., Pal, S.K.: Rough fuzzy MLP: knowledge encoding and classification. IEEE Transactions on Neural Networks 9(6), 1203–1216 (1998)
7. Peters, J.F., Han, L., Ramanna, S.: Rough neural computing in signal analysis. Computational Intelligence 17(3), 493–513 (2001)
8. Gu, X.P., Tso, S.K.: Applying rough-set concept to neural-network-based transient-stability classification of power system. In: Proceedings of the 5th International Conference on Advances in Power System Control, Operation and Management, pp. 400–404. IEEE, Hong Kong (2000)
9. Ahn, B.S., Cho, S.S., Kim, C.Y.: The integrated methodology of rough set theory and artificial neural network for business failure prediction. Expert Systems with Applications 18(2), 65–74 (2000)
10. Pedrycz, W., Han, L., Peters, J.F., et al.: Calibration of software quality: fuzzy neural and rough neural network computing approaches. Neural-Computing 36(1-4), 149–170 (2001)
11. Xue, F., Lin, K.: Rough sets – Application of neural network system in five level classification of commercial bank loan. Systems Engineering Theory & Practice 1, 40–45 (2008)
12. Wang, G.: Rough set theory and knowledge acquisition. Xi'an Jiaotong University Press, Shaanxi (2001)
13. He, M., Feng, B., Ma, Z., Fu, X.: A rough network construction method based on rough
14. Dai, J.: Rough set theory and its application in knowledge discovery research. PhD thesis, Wuhan University (March 2003)
15. Hu, S., He, Y.: Rough decision theory and Its application. Beijing University of Aeronautics and Astronautics Press, Beijing (2006)
16. Ahn, B.S., Cho, S., Kim, C.: The integrated methodology of rough set theory and artificial neural network for business failure prediction. Expert Systems with Applications 18(2), 65–74 (2000)

Influencing Factors of Sports Consumption: Provincial Evidence in China

Hua Chen and Xinke Yin

Department of Physical Education
Xiamen University
Xiamen, China
huachen00@eyou.com

Abstract. This paper made qualitative analysis about influencing factors of sports consumption using of mathematical methods, and makes empirical analysis based on China's provincial data of sports consumers from 31 provinces, municipalities and autonomous regions in 2009. The results show that, both material and cultural factors can impact sports consumption. The income level is the main factor and it basically determines the sports consuming behavior of the residents. And other factors, such as basic sports facilities, leisure time and cultural values of consumption, are associated with residents' decision-making on sports consumption, but they all have very little effects.

Keywords: sports consumption, material factors, cultural factors.

1 Introduction

With the growth in the social productivity and living standards, consumption structure of society, people's consumer awareness and consumer habits have undergone significant changes, and sports consumption has become an important part in modern consumption life. Under the stimulation of booming global sport market, sports consumption is constantly extension. Sports consumption in the social composition of the consumption structure is also growing. As an important part of modern consumption, the rational expansion of sports consumption has great significance to the change of consumption structure and consumption pattern. It also has a positive effect for the enhancement of the quality and improvement of community sport and promoting of the social productive forces.

There are a lot of research on sports, and they can be divided into the following categories: First, the methods of physical training, mainly for competitive sports, many coaches have systematically summed up the physical training methods; Second, the sports industry report, in order to promote the development of sports industry, sports associations, sports industry has done a lot consume and demand survey analysis in the sports industry, use detailed market data on real sports industry to analyzed; three, research on sports health, mainly medical staff during the sports industry, for example, SHEN Yi, Wa Ying sinks diagnosis of rotator cuff injuries of the shoulder MRI and physical examination is belong to this category; four, sports economics, Jiang Guojun, Cai dashu studied on Hubei financial investment model, Wang used the method of

D. Zeng (Ed.): ICAIC 2011, Part I, CCIS 224, pp. 397–403, 2011.

input-output economics, predictive analysis about the Yangtze River in Jiangsu Province, Zhejiang Province, Shanghai Sports Development inputs (capital investment, human input) and outputs (athletes, the whole operation will score and medals).

Most of the research on sports consumption have stayed on the qualitative description. This paper uses economic mathematical methods, and takes into account both material and cultural factors to analyze the factors that affect the sports consumption. After qualitative description of the results of various factors, we use the data from 31 provinces, municipalities and autonomous regions to make empirical analysis to verify the results of qualitative analysis.

2 Qualitative Analysis

Sports consumption is a higher level of consumer behavior which through participation in sports or watch sports competitions to use and consume sports resource in order to meet the needs of a variety of sports. Sports consumption needs to have a foundation: First, the material basis, that is the level of social and economic development; Second, cultural foundation, that is the community education process. As China's social and economic development, people's living standard's improve, the improvement and perfection of the market economy, people are becoming more conscious of sports consumption, more and more people want to further improve their quality of life, and gradually realized that the importance of the health and physical exercise, but less leisure time, the traditional concept of culture and consumption, local sports venues, he quantity and poor quality of sports conditions and other reasons t lead the lack of sports spending, but its market potential is huge.

Sports consumption are affected by various factors involved in income levels, cultural factors, educational factors, leisure time, basic sports facilities and many other issues. This paper divided the factors that impact of sports consumption into two parts: inside and outside factors, thus emphasizing sports consumption is the result of both internal and external factors, reflecting the complexity that impact of sports consumption decisions.

2.1 Material Factors

The amount of sports consumption(C) is positive correlated with the local sports infrastructure(I, personal income level(Income Level, IL) and spare time(ST) . The functional relationship between these variables is,

$$C = F(I, \; IL, \; ST) \tag{1}$$

The function has the following properties:

1. Because the sport is a higher level of consumption behavior, when the economic level is very poor, personal free time is very little, and there is almost no infrastructure, the amount of sports consumption will be close to 0, that is, when I, IL, ST value is very small, C approaches 0;

2. When the basis of sports facilities is better, higher levels of personal income, more leisure time, the amount of sports consumption will also increase, that is, the first

derivative F_I 、 F_{IL} 、 F_{ST} , are greater than 0, but sports consumption can not unlimited subsequent growth, the growth rate will reach a certain size then slow down as conditions improve, that is the second derivative is less than 0.

2.2 Cultural Factors

Cultural factors are the most far-reaching and one of the most extensive environmental factors on people's sports culture consumer behavior. As a social and cultural phenomenon, Sports has long been integrated into people's lives. Every society has its unique system of consumption habits and ideas, these habits and ideas through family, school and social education, so that members of society, consciously and unconsciously, to accept the social behavior patterns from an early age. The Come apart of School Physical Education and lifelong Sports, can not meet public health needs, which undoubtedly will affect the students' sports-loving habits during and after school, prevent the establishment of lifelong development of sports consciousness, and the concept of sports consumption and behavior will be restricted. This paper consider the amount of sports consumption (Consumption, C) ,the Chinese traditional culture (Traditional Culture, TC), consumer attitudes (Consumer Attitudes, CA) and education (Education, E), but due to cultural factors can not be quantified, and differences in terms of each individual is also very large, It is difficult to describe the specific function of the relationship between them, the paper will use the age composition of residents of an area to distinguish the cultural differences between different groups, attitudes of different ages of consumer in sports difference is very significant, if culture is a culture that contains a variety of variable factors, the sports consumption function is:

$$C = F(culture) \tag{2}$$

3 Empirical Analysis

3.1 Data Collection

The samples that we use for empirical analysis are from 31 provinces, municipalities and autonomous regions in 2009. The selected data is from the China Statistical Yearbook 2010 and the web site of Chinese National Bureau of Statistics.

3.2 Variable Definition

According to the analysis of earlier in this article, sports consumption of many factors, some factors more easily separated, and relatively easy to quantify, on the contrary that some factors (such as cultural influences, consumer attitudes, etc.) is difficult to quantify, in order to facilitate the analysis, also taking into account data collection problems, the paper selected as the per capita consumption expenditure Sports explanatory variables, per capita disposable income, basic sports facilities, leisure time and cultural factors as explanatory variables, the variable name and the meaning described in Table 1.

Table 1. Variable Definition

Variable name	Meaning
Consumption	Sports consumption expenditure per capita (yuan)
Income	Disposable income per capita (yuan)
Infrastructure	Basic sports facilities
Spare Time	Instead pf Gross Dependency Ratio1
Culture	Cultural Factors

3.3 Empirical Analysis

To ensure that the linear model is reasonable, we firstly examine the relationship between the dependent variable and independent variables through simple correlation analysis. Based on sports consumption data of urban residents from 31 provinces, municipalities and autonomous regions in Chinese mainland, the correlation coefficient matrix among each variable is as shown in Table 2.

Table 2. The Correlation Coefficient Matrix

	CONSUPTION	Income	Infrastr-ucture	Spare Time	Culture
CONSUPTION	1.0000	0.9301	0.4842	-0.4496	0.4673
Income	0.9301	1.0000	0.5492	-0.5177	0.5317
Infrastructure	0.4842	0.5492	1.0000	-0.4496	0.4678
Spare Time	-0.4496	-0.5177	-0.4496	1.0000	-0.9979
Culture	0.4673	0.5317	0.4678	-0.9979	1.0000

From the correlation coefficient matrix and Figure 2 to Figure 4 in Appendix, we can see that,

- Although sports consumption and sports infrastructure have not a high degree of linear relationship, but there is stronger positive correlation between them.

[1] **Gross Dependency Ratio:** also called gross dependency coefficient, refers to the ratio of non-working-age population to the working-age population, express in %. Describing in general the number of non-working-age population that every 100 people at working ages will take care of, this indicator reflects the basic relation between population and economic development from the demographic perspective. The gross dependency ratio is calculated with the following formula:

$$GDR = \frac{P_{0-14} + P_{65^+}}{P_{15-64}} \times 100\%$$

Where: GDR is the gross dependency ratio, P0-14 is the population of children aged 0-14, P65+ is the elderly population aged 65 and over, and P15-64 is the working-age population aged 15-64.

- With the change of social gross dependency ratio, Sports consumption expenditure changes relatively a little, and the key still lies in the income level. If the social gross dependency ratio is high, the residents'
- Less leisure time will be less, and its corresponding sports spending will be less too. The two have a strong negative correlation, but there is no linear relationship between them.
- Population age structure and sports consumption expenditures have a strong positive correlation, which indicates that residents between 15 to 64 years-old is the main sports consumption population.

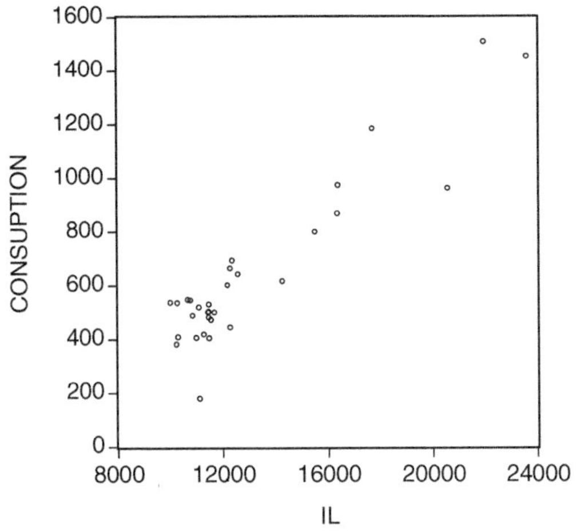

Fig. 1. Scatter plot of the relationship between sports consumption expenditure and Disposable income per capita

There is a strong linear relationship between sports consumption expenditure per capita and disposable income per capita. We get the estimation result by OLS (Ordinary Least Square) as follows.

$$Consumption = -396.4169 + 0.078785 Income$$
$$(-5.055169) \quad (13.63543) \qquad (3)$$
$$R^2 = 0.865069, \bar{R}^2 = 0.860416, D.W. = 1.779682$$

4 Conclusions

There are various factors that affect sports consumption level, include both physical constraints and cultural factors, according to the analysis summarized in this article before; we can get the conclusions as follows.

- Income level is a major an most fundamental factor that can effect sports consumption
- The foundation sports facilities have a positive impact on sports consumption.

- Too little spare time have a negative impact on sports consumption.
- Population age structure will affect consumer attitudes, thus will affect the sports consumption.

In addition to these factors above, there are many factors affect the sports consumption in China, such as the geographical environment, climatic conditions, economic imbalance between rich and poor will affect the sports consumer, but the key point is increase the level of economic development and improve people's income level, the main measures are conduct the national physical education, strengthen the consciousness of national bodybuilding. With China's sustained and rapid economic development, health and sports needs will continue to improve, sports consumer market will certainly expand and develop, and the sports industry will be referred to as a “sunrise industry.”.

Acknowledgment. Our work is sponsored by Sports Philosophy and Social Science Research Projects, General Administration of Sport of China. (Research of Sports Consumption of Urban and Rural Residents).

References

1. Jiang, G., Cai, D.: Financial Investment Model of Sports in Hubei. Policy Research 12, 36–39 (2003)
2. Chen, X., Xu, C., Wang, X.: Research on Life Quality and Sports Investment of Graduate Students in University. Sports Science 25(2), 59–63 (2005)
3. Huang, B.-h., Yin, x.-k.: An empirical analysis of the consumption function of China's rural residents. In: 2009 International Conference on Future Computer and Communication, FCC 2009, pp. 179–181 (2009), doi:10.1109/FCC.2009.36
4. Sun, H.: All-people Body Building and the Current Situation Analysis and Research of Junior Middle School Students Sports Investment. The Border Economy and Culture 4, 157–159 (2009)
5. Tang, H.-g.: An Inquiry into Urban Resident Sports Consumption Level in Wuhan City. Journal of Wuhan Institute of Physical Education 1, 7–11 (1997)
6. Zhang, Y., Zhang, S., Li, Z.: Sports Economic Research. Jilin People's Press, Jilin (1990)

Appendix

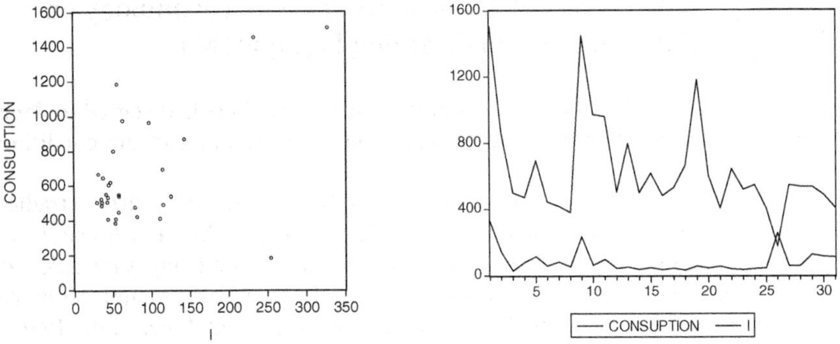

Fig. 2. Scatter plot and linear graph of the relationship between sports consumption expenditure and investment in infrastructure

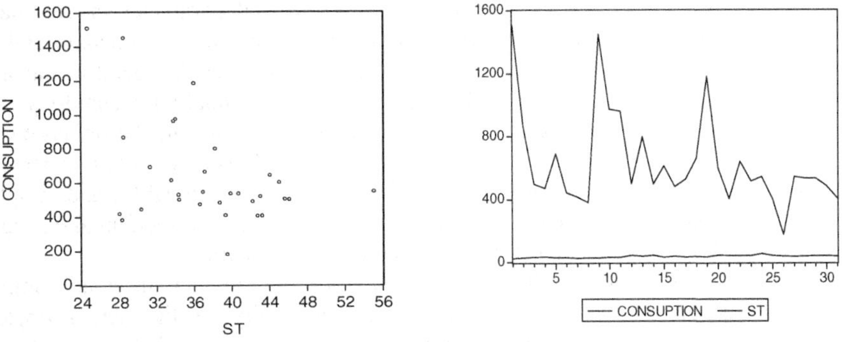

Fig. 3. Gross Scatter plot and linear graph of the relationship between sports consumption expenditure and Gross Dependency RatioDependency Ratio ependency Ratio

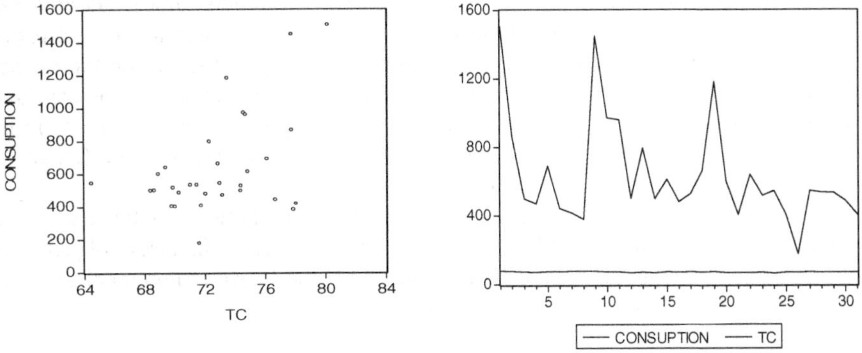

Fig. 4. Scatter plot and linear graph of the relationship between sports consumption expenditure and population age structure

Study on Security Architecture for Internet of Things*

Hui Li[1] and Xin Zhou[2]

[1] School of Computer Science Beijing University of Posts and Telecommunications
[2] The first Research Institute Ministry of Public Security of P.R.C
Haidian, Beijing, China
Huiyingh@live.com

Abstract. The development of Internet of Things(IoT) will bring a new ubiquitous computing and communication era. Due to the lack of security mechanisms in the early Internet, we had to build patches to improve the security of it, which leads to that the Internet security is always a big risk. To avoid the same thing happened in building IoT, the security of IoT should be systematically studied from the beginning design of the IoT. In this paper, based on the studies on the IoT architecture and the analysis on the secure threats in IoT, the security architecture of the IoT is presented on the basis of the secure architecture of the information system, the related secure problems in the IoT are analyzed from the aspect of the secure service, secure domain and network layer. In addition, the limitation and the hardness work for the future are pointed out in this field.

Keywords: Internet of Things, security architecture, RFID, wireless sensor network.

1 Introduction

Internet of Things(IoT) is set up through immanent network techniques, which is a new wave of information industry and technology field after the Internet and mobile network. The term Internet of Things (IoT) was invented by the MIT Auto-ID Center in 2001[1]. Generally, IoT refers to a network of objects using the information sensor hardware, which includes RFID, sensors and GPS and can achieve intelligentized identification, orientation, trace, inspection and management by information exchange and communication technologies.

Having every 'thing' connected to the global future Internet and 'things' communicating with each other, especially through various wireless techniques, many security and privacy problems arise, e.g., confidentiality, authenticity, and integrity of data sensed and exchanged by 'things', as well as privacy of humans, localization and tracking[2]. How to ensure the security of IoT has caught many attentions of researchers recently. Several achievements have been gained among the field of RFID and sensor networks.

In the aspect of RFID security, a lot of attentions have been paid on the information security and human privacy. Because the design cost of RFID should be

* This work is partially supported by NSFC Grant # 61070207.

D. Zeng (Ed.): ICAIC 2011, Part I, CCIS 224, pp. 404–411, 2011.

low, the complex and high level security algorithms cannot run on it, which makes researchers constantly improve the security protocol under the hardware limitations in order to enhance the security of RFID system. The representative achievements are Hash-lock[3,4], Hash chains[5] and distributing challenge and response protocol[6], etc. But most existing RFID protocols have drawbacks, which have been pointed out in [7].

In the aspect of sensor network security, many secure schemes have been proposed, which include authentication, encryption and key management scheme, such as Localized Encryption and Authentication Protocol, hierarchical sensor network authentication scheme[8], Identity-based encryption for sensor networks [9], dynamic key management scheme based on ID-based symmetric keying[10] and the schemes based on exclusion-based systems (EBSs)[11-13],etc.

Nowadays, the study on the security in IoT just begins, and it is short of systemic and thorough researches on the security of IoT. In this paper the secure threats among IoT is analyzed based on the network architecture for IoT, and the security architecture for IoT is presented on the basis of the secure architecture of information system, the related secure problems in the IoT are analyzed from the aspects of the secure service, network layer and secure domain.

The rest of this paper is organized as follows: section 2 describes the network structure of IoT, and analyzes the security threats of IoT. Section 3 presents the security architecture of IoT, and describes the secure problem and main secure mechanisms from the aspects of the secure service, network layer and secure domain. Section 4 presents the conclusion and future works.

2 Architecture and Security Threats of IoT

Now IoT is an extension of Internet in most cases. Market researchers anticipate that by year 2012 20% of all sold phones will be NFC enabled. With 300 million NFC phones sold in year 2012, mobile phones will become the largest infrastructure of RFID readers world-wide.[14] It is very possible that the converged network of mobile networks and internet networks will be the information exchange platform for IoT, so the IoT is an extention of future network and its architecture is shown in Fig. 1.

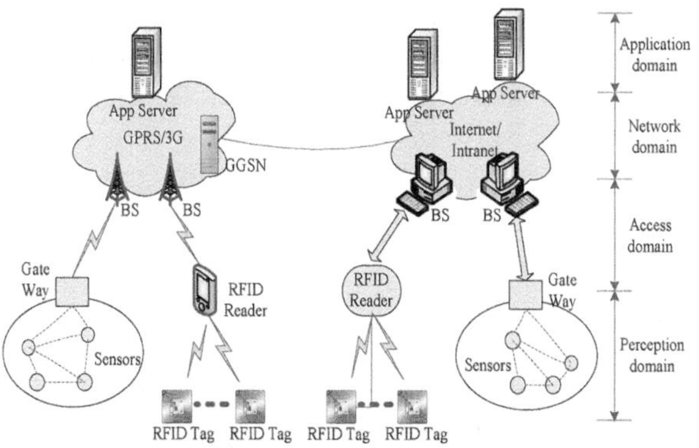

Fig. 1. Architecture of IoT

The architecture for IoT includes four domains: the first one is the perception domain, which can fulfill the function of information collection by the readers or the gateway. The reader can read the information sent by the RFID tag, which is sticked to the 'things', while the gateway can receive the signal sent by the sensors, then the existence of the 'things' or the change of the environment will be known. The techniques of smartcard, RFID tag, identification code or sensors can be used in this domain. The next one is the access domain, in which the reader or gateway head sends the information of 'things' or the environment to the access point, which maybe a base station or a gateway station, and the access point will then send those information to the network domain. The network domain takes on the responsibility of information transmission and exchange. The form of network is possible for any existing network, such as wlan, mobile network, Internet or broadcast and television network. The last domain is the application domain, which can implement the recognition and apperception between 'things' and 'things' or between 'things' and person, and at last the function of intelligent traffic or intelligent home can be achieved. Small scale of IoT may only include some of the domain, such as perception domain and application domain.

Similar to the Internet, there are a lot of inherent security threats in the IoT. Since there are such wireless devices as RFID, infrared sensors, GPS etc. in the perception domain, the following attacks are much easier to be implemented in IoT:

1) Spoofing attack, including fake domain name, IP address spoofing and MAC spoofing. For example, the attacker may broadcast a false Electronic Product Code(EPC) in RFID system.

2) Eavesdropping attack, information transferred in the IoT has more possibilities to be eavesdropped than other networks because of the use of wireless techniques.

3) Insert attack, which refers to the insertion of system command when it needs for input data. For example, a system instruction rather than a good data(such as EPC) is stored in the tag data storage

4) Replay attack, which means that the attcker can get the valid data from the RFID signal trasferred between tag and reader, store those data and send them to the reader later. Because the data is valid, the system will receive and deal with those data.

5) Denial of Service(DoS) attack, one kind of DoS is named as RF jamming, which means that RF will be jammed when RF signal is submerged by noise signal. The other kind of DoS can make the system lose the ability to deal with right data. The result of DoS can make RFID system invalid.

Besides, some other security threats also exist in the application domain such as:

1) Privacy attack, for example, the information in RFID tag of IoT may be related to the person, and the human being's privacy right cannot be ensured when these information are obtained by the attacker.

2) Location tracking attack, the illegal user can track with the tag through many methods and then recognize the actions of the 'things'.

The threats faced by the access domain and network domain are the same as the existing network[15]. If no security mechanisms are applied in IoT, the applications of intelligent traffic, intelligent medical treatment, public safety of city, logistics management and intelligent production process management based on IoT will cause many security problems and the development of the IoT will be delayed.

3 Security Architecture of IoT

There are many research achievements in the field of security architecture for information system. One is a security architecture frame in open systems interconnection basic reference model [16], which defines five security services: authentication, confidentiality, integrality, access control and non-repudiation etc. The other is an information security architecture based on OSI reference model[17], which is a three-dimensional matrix composed of security attributes, OSI protocol layers and system components. Based on the above-mentioned security architectures, a security architecture with three-dimensional matrix of IoT based on the characteristics of the network architecture of IoT described in section 2 of this paper is presented and shown in fig. 2.

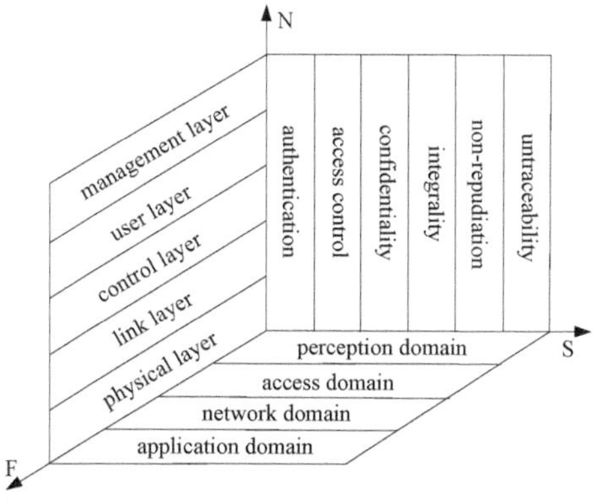

Fig. 2. Security architecture of IoT

In Fig. 2 S axis represents security service which has six elements, i.e. authentication, access control, confidentiality, integrality, non-repudiation and untraceability, while the relationship of each element is hierarchical. N axis describes the network layer, consisted of five layers, i.e. physical layer, link layer, control layer, user layer and management layer referring to the layers of OSI reference model and mobile network. Security domain, which is represented by axis F, is made up with different security domains, which can be divided by the specific security policy. The security domain of IoT can be divided as perception domain, access domain, network domain and application domain, just as the division of the domains in the network architecture of the IoT. Any security mechanism in the IoT may be mapped to a point in the three-dimensional matrix, and can be explained as the security service provided in one of the security domain in IoT to meet the requirement in certain layer.

The rest of Section 3 describes the security elements and their logical relationship, as well as the security techniques from the aspects of security services, network layer and security domain.

3.1 Security Services

Security services of IoT include authentication, access control, confidentiality, integrality, non-repudiation and untraceability etc. There is hierarchical relationship for each kind of security service, and only one security service cannot meet the secure requirements of IoT. The hierarchical relationship of the security services in IoT is shown in Fig. 3.

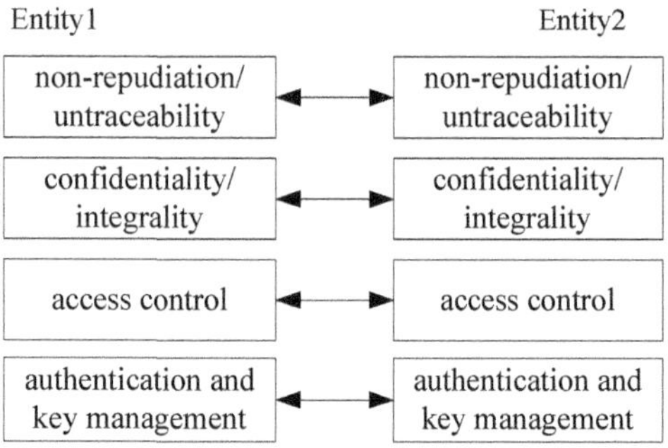

Fig. 3. Hierarchical relationship model of security services

The entity 1 and 2 in Fig. 3 represent different components in different security domains in IoT. For example, they may be RFID tag and reader in logistics network built with RFID techniques in perception domain, they also may be sensors and gateway note in WSN. But entity 1 and 2 stand for mobile terminal and base station in access domain, as well as base station and digital switch in network domain or security module and mobile terminal in user domain.

All security services should be setup upon the usability of IoT, which makes IoT work as the pre-established rules, and can prevent denial of service attack in certain ways. The other security services depend on the identification and authentication between the subject and the object, as well as the key management. The main security technologies of the authentication and key management are light-weight authentication and key management protocol for RFID or WSN, mutual authentication protocol between system and terminal, smart card supported PKI, etc. The access control is the core of the whole security system, whose aim is to prevent any unauthorized access to resources and it is useful for data confidentiality and integrity. Confidentiality and integrity ensure that the data cannot be tampered with and eavesdropped; they are also important guarantees for the validity of authentication and access control. The general method to gain confidentiality and integrity is to use encryption or hash algorithm. Non-repudiation and untraceability are necessary for some special applications.

3.2 Network Layer

As what is mentioned before, N axis is divided into physical layer, link layer, control layer, user layer and management layer, which refers to the layers of OSI reference model and mobile network. Each layer has some security requirements in every domain. More detailed analysis shows:

1) Management layer: Management layer is the upmost layer in the proposed model, which takes the responsibilities for the whole information security in IoT. In the management layer, the security threats are analyzed and managed, and protected resources will be recognized, as well as the secure techniques to be used will be decided. Besides, the reasonable management standards will be established in IoT.

2) User layer: User layer provides end to end security of transaction processing in user layer, which is the basic requirement for the high security level M2M applications. Because IoT is composed of large number of devices (RFID, sensor, etc.), and the devices are seldom inspected by human being, so how to distribute and manage the large number of keys in the M2M applications of IoT requires deeper study. The non-repudiation and untraceability are required in this layer for special applications in IoT.

3) Control layer: Control layer is responsible for the network process. The security service of authentication and user management is implemented in control layer.

4) Link layer: Link layer ensures the correctness and security for data transferred in wired links or wireless links. Generally, the frame synchronization, interleaving and de-interleaving, channel coding, error protection, encryption and other techniques are used to achieve the security in link layer.

5) Physical layer: There are almost all kinds of physical techniques in IoT, which includes timing structure and the radio frequency channel, etc. The main purpose is to prevent damage of physical access, the eavesdropping of the physical path and attack interference, which is more difficult because of the same reason mentioned in section 2.

3.3 Security Domain

There are four security domains in IoT, i.e. perception domain, access domain, network domain and application domain. The corresponding secure requirements and techniques required in each security domain are:

1) Perception domain: The main task of perception domain is the security access services within the domain. There are different requirements for RFID and wireless sensor networks. In RFID network, the required security functions are identification and authentication of tags, confidentiality and integrity of data transferred between the tag and the reader, and non-tracking of tags. In wireless sensor networks, apart from the above requirements, certain robustness is required. The reason is that wireless sensor networks deals with network topology changes, loss of or add to the core node. Wireless sensor networks should be more adaptive for various security attacks, when a particular attack succeeds, this characteristic can minimize its impact. The main methods can be used in this domain are authentication, encryption, self-testing, intrusion detection, redundant routing etc. Otherwise, since the hardware devices in the region, such as labels or sensors have the characteristics of limited resources, it requires the proper design of security mechanisms in order to ensure the availability and provide security services.

2) Access domain: Access domain provides secure access services in the access domain, which includes identity confidentiality of the equipment used as RFID reader or gateway, authentication, confidentiality and integrity of the data transferred in network access channel, identification of mobile devices, etc. Those security requirements are fulfilled mainly through the temporary identification; mutual authentication protocol based on symmetric key algorithm and key agreement protocol for encryption key and integrity key.

3) Network domain: The main security mechanisms in this domain are authentication between network entities (such as switches and base stations, switches and switches), confidentiality and integrity of data transmission, and monitoring on the attack information.

4) Application domain: The security relative to the special applications of IoT should be solved in application domain. It is not difficult to understand that the security requirements are different for different applications. It is important to set proper security mechanisms for each application of IoT. For example, the security mechanisms to protect the human privacy must be concerned in the IoT for medical applications. And end to end security functions should be used in the high-level IoT applications, which is difficult for key management when concerning the huge number of objects.

4 Conclusions

In this paper, the security issues for the Internet of Things are studied, and a security architecture of IoT is provided. The security elements of IoT are analyzed from three dimensions, i.e. the security services, network layer and security domain. Study shows that the perception domain of IoT can be regarded as the end of the entire network, which is responsible for collecting basic information about objects or the environment. The security mechanism is limited by equipment capacity constraints, the security technologies in the perceived domain of Internet of Things should be studied more deeply in the future. In addition, as noted, end to end security technological research for the IoT is another important and difficult issue.

References

1. Brock, D.L.: The Electronic Product Code (EPC), A Naming Scheme for Physical Objects. MIT AUTO-ID CENTER (2001)
2. Mayer, C.P.: Security and Privacy Challenges in the Internet of Things. Electronic Communications of the EASST 17, 1–12 (2009)
3. Sarma, S.E., Weis, S.A., Engels, D.W.: RFID systems and security and privacy implications. In: Kaliski Jr., B.S., Koç, Ç.K., Paar, C. (eds.) CHES 2002. LNCS, vol. 2523, pp. 454–469. Springer, Heidelberg (2003)

4. Sarma, S.E., Weis, S.A., Engels, D.W.: Radio frequency identification: Secure risks and challenges. RSA Laboratories Cryptobytes 6(1), 2–9 (2003)
5. Ohkubo, M., Suzuki, K., Kinoshita, S.: Hash-chain based forward secure privacy protection scheme for low-cost RFID. In: Proceedings of the 2004 Symposium on Cryptography and Information Security (SCIS 2004), Sendai, pp. 719–724 (2004)
6. YunLim: Symmetric encryption in RFID authentication protocol for strong location privacy and forward-security. In: 2006 International Conference on Hybrid Information Technology (ICHIT 2006), vol. 2, pp. 718–723 (November 2006)
7. Zhou, Y.-b., Feng, D.-g.: Design and analysis of cryptographic protocols for RFID. Chinese Journal of Computers 29(4), 581–589 (2006)
8. Zhu, S., Satia, S., Jajodia, S.: LEAP: Efficient Security Mechanisms for Large-scale Distributed Sensor Networks. In: Proceedings of ACM Conference on computing and Communication Security, pp. 72–72. ACM Press, New York (2003)
9. Oliveira, L.B., Dahab, R., Lopez, J., et al.: Identity-based encryption for sensor networks. In: Proceedings of 5th Annual IEEE International Conference on Pervasive Computing and Communications Workshops, White Plains, NY, pp. 290–294 (2007)
10. Jolly, G., Kuscu, M.C., Kokate, P., Younis, M.: A low-energy key management protocol for wireless sensor networks. The 8th IEEE International Symposium on Computers and Communication, ISCC 2003 (June 2003)
11. Eltoweissy, M., Wadaa, A., Olariu, S., Wilson, L.: Group key management scheme for large-scale wireless sensor network. J. Ad Hoc Networks, 796–802 (September 2005)
12. Younis, M., Ghumman, K., Eltoweissy, M.: Location-aware combinatorial key management scheme for clustered sensor networks. IEEE Trans. Parallel and Distrib. Sys. (2006)
13. Eltoweissy, M., Moharrum, M., Mukkamala, R.: Dynamic key management in sensor networks. IEEE Communications Magazine, 122–130 (April 2006)
14. Wiechert, T., Thiesse, F., Michahelles, F., Schmitt, P., Fleisch, E.: Connecting mobile phones to the Internet of things: A discussion of compatibility issues between EPC and NFC. Presented at the Americas Conf. Inf. Syst. (AMCIS), Keystone, CO (2006)
15. Li, H., Yang, Y.-x.: Analysis on the Security Threads of TETRA System. Mobile Communications 3(29), 22–25 (2005)
16. ISO IS 7498-2. Information Processing Systems - Open Systems Interconnection Basic Reference Model-Part: Security Architecture. ISO Geneva, Switzerland (1989)
17. Department of Defense. Trusted Computer System Evaluation Criteria. Standard 5200.28-STD. (December 1985)

Emotion Recognition from Physiological Signals Using AdaBoost*

Bo Cheng[1,2]

[1] School of Economics and Management Chongqing Three Gorges University Chongqing 404000, China
[2] Department of Computer Science and Engineering Nanjing University of Aeronautics and Astronautics, Nanjing 210016, China
bo82719@tom.com

Abstract. Emotion recognition is one of the key steps towards emotional intelligence in advanced human-machine interaction. This paper adopted principal component analysis (PCA) to dimensionality reduction and combined AdaBoost algorithm to be served as classifier. Experimental result shows that the classifier performance was effective and steady. Emotion recognition impression was fairish and reasonable for special affective state groupings.

Keywords: emotion recognition, physiological signals, Adaboost, PCA.

1 Introduction

Emotion recognition is one of the key steps towards emotional intelligence in advanced human-machine interaction. Although many efforts have been taken recently to recognize emotions using facial expressions, speech and physiological signals [1][2][3][4][5], current recognition systems are not yet advanced enough to be used in realistic applications. Particularly little attention has been paid so far to physiological signals for emotion recognition compared to audiovisual emotion channels. Reasons are some significant limitations resulting from the use of physiological signals for emotion recognition. The main difficulty lies in the fact that it is very hard to uniquely map physiological patterns onto specific emotion types and that physiological data are very sensitive to motion artifacts. On the other hand, physiological signals have considerable advantages. We can continuously gather information about the users' emotional changes while they are connected to biosensors. Moreover, physiological reactions should be more robust against possible artifacts of human social masking since they are directly controlled by the human autonomous nervous system. Work done in psycho physiology provides evidence that there is a strong relationship between physiological reactions and affective states of humans. Furthermore, bodily signals can be recorded and analyzed based on algorithmic or auto inference models that do not require human intervention [6].

* This work is supported by Chongqing Three Gorges University Foundation (2008-sxxyqn-29), China.

D. Zeng (Ed.): ICAIC 2011, Part I, CCIS 224, pp. 412–417, 2011.

Principal component analysis (PCA) is a well-known technique of multivariate linear data analysis. PCA has been applied to many fields including data compression, image analysis, visualization, pattern recognition, regression, and time-series prediction. Due to higher dimensional original physiological signal data, the data wasn't directly input into the classifier to run. In this paper, PCA was used for feature extraction and dimensionality reduction. AdaBoost is a very popular classification algorithm on machine leaning. AdaBoost is a very efficient mechanism; it can elect a very small part of the diversity and the excellent classifier. In this paper, AdaBoost was used for classifier. In this paper, physiological signals data sets come from University of Augsburg, Germany [7]. This paper adopted electromyogram (EMG), skin conductivity (SC) and respiration change (RSP) as original feature. Twenty five recordings (25 days) for each emotion were collected. The length of the recordings depends on the length of the songs. It included four emotion classes, joy, anger, sadness and pleasure. Experimental result shows that the approach about dimensionality reduction based on principal component analysis (PCA) and classifier using AdaBoost algorithm was very effective and potential for the practical application of emotion recognition.

2 Feature Extraction and Classification

2.1 Dimensionality Reduction by PCA

Try Principal component analysis (PCA) is a well-known technique of multivariate linear data analysis. The central idea of principal component analysis (PCA) is to reduce the dimensionality of a data set consisting of a large number of interrelated variables, while retaining as much as possible of the variation present in the data set. This is achieved by transforming to a new set of variables, the principal components (PCs), which are uncorrelated, and which are ordered so that the first few retain most of the variation present in all of the original variables. Using this idea, PCA has been applied to many fields including data compression, image analysis, visualization, pattern recognition, regression, and time-series prediction.

PCA is usually regarded as a descriptive multivariate technique which does not have any statistical model in contrast to FA [8]. It is formulated by the spectral decomposition of the covariance matrix Σ expressed by

$$\Sigma = \Gamma \Lambda \Gamma^{\mathrm{T}} \tag{1}$$

Where

$$\Lambda = diag(\lambda_{1,} \cdots, \lambda_p), \qquad \Gamma = (\gamma_1, \cdots, \gamma_p)$$

λ_j and γ_j indicating the j th largest eigenvalue and the associated eigenvector of Σ, respectively. We regard Eq. (1) as an explicit PCA model, where the covariance matrix has a structural model which consists of the eigenvalues and eigenvectors.

Due to higher dimensional original physiological signal data, the data wasn't directly input into the classifier to run. This paper adopted electromyogram (EMG) signal, skin conductivity (SC) signal and respiration change (RSP) signal as original feature. Original feature of each signal is 3840. Therefore, dimensionality reduction with principal component analysis (PCA) was used for feature extraction. After dimensionality reduction with PCA, the dimensionality of original signal was decrease to 10.

2.2 Adboost Classifications

AdaBoost algorithm use Boosting algorithm [9] to learn some weak classification, and then combined into a strong Classifier base on a series of Haar-like Features. Its basic idea is as follows:

1) Give Each sample a weight.

2) AdaBoost calls a given weak learning algorithm repeatedly in a series of rounds t= 1,…., T (Number of weak classifiers) to extract in each iteration one classifier with the minimum error of misclassification.

3) The algorithm selects a parameter α that measures the importance that is assigned to the weak classifier and its power of classification over the training set.

Selected T weaker Classifiers after studying, then Cascade the Classifiers according to their weights. The number of the Cascade Classifiers dependents on the error rate and the rate of recognition. Any machine learning methods can be used for training a function classification through learning if it is given collections which include positive samples and negative samples.

AdaBoost is a very popular and important classification algorithm on machine leaning. AdaBoost algorithm was served as classifier and applied to image retrieval and facial expression recognition widely. This paper adopted AdaBoost algorithm to serve as classifier. Original physiological signals feature matrixes with the PCA dimensionality reduction approach was classified by the AdaBoost algorithm. The physiological signals data set was divided into training sample sets and test sample sets randomly. The classifier was trained and tested repeatedly. The classification performance was evaluated by the average accuracy.

3 Experimental Results

The data set of physiological signals is the University of Augsburg: a corpus containing physiological data of a single user in four different emotional states and a corpus containing physiological data recorded from a single user under varying stress [7]. The dimensionality of physiological signals data was reduced by principal component analysis (PCA). After dimensionality reduction with principal component analysis (PCA), the dimensionality of original signal was decrease to 10. As a result, the feature vector dimension with inputting into the AdaBoost classifier is 30.

Table1 is a recognition rate of four emotions group with dimensional reduction. During the experiment, the four affective states (joy, anger, sadness and pleasure) were divided into four groups. Each group included two affective states. The physiological signals data set was divided into training sample sets and test sample sets randomly. The classifier was trained and tested repeatedly. After repeated experiments, the classifier recognition rate was that the classifier was trained and tested by fifty times. The details were listed on table1. In Table1, groups of joy versus sadness and groups of anger versus pleasure have a well recognition effect, whereas the groups of joy versus anger(J vs A) and the groups of sadness versus pleasure(S vs P) recognition effect is less good recognition effect. This shows that affective states were identified by physiological signals with groups of joy versus sadness(J vs S) and groups of anger versus pleasure(A vs P), but the groups of joy versus anger and the groups of sadness versus pleasure recognition effect is less.

Table 1. Recognition rates of four emotions group with dimensional reduction

Emotions	the worst	the best	the average
J vs A	0.7500	0.9167	0.8750
S vs P	0.7500	0.9000	0.8333
J vs S	0.9167	1	0.9500
A vs P	0.9167	1	0.9444

Table2 is a recognition rate of two emotions group with valence and arousal. Valence groups are anger and sadness versus joy and pleasure. Arousal groups are joy and anger versus sadness and pleasure. In table2, according to the arousal to grouping emotions, the classifier has a well recognition effect, but according to the valence to grouping emotions, recognition effect of the classifier is less. This shows that affective states were identified by physiological signals with the arousal, the groups with the valence recognition effect is less.

Table 2. Recognition rates of two emotions group with valence and arousal

emotions	the worst	the best	the average
Valence	0.7778	0.8833	0.8333
Arousal	0.8889	1	0.9545

Table3 and table4 is a classifier performance with training times (tr_number) and division ratio indications. In table3, the data set division ratio is fixed, but the training times of classifiers is variation. The classifier was trained ten, thirty, fifty and one hundred times. The variance is the average recognition rate variance of each emotions group. The classifiers have a well recognition effect when the classifier was trained and tested by fifty times. The classifiers recognition effect is less when the training times of classifiers is far away fifty times. In table3, the variance of each emotions group is wee. This shows that the classification performance of classifiers is stabilization when the training times of classifiers is in a certain range. In table4, the classifier has a well recognition effect when the division ratio of emotions group with valence is 10/40. Whereas the division ratio of remaining emotions group is 12/38, the classifier can obtain a well recognition effect. The variance is the average recognition rate variance of each emotions group. According to the average recognition rate variance of each emotions group, the classification performance of classifiers (Joy vs Anger, Sadness vs Pleasure and Valence emotions group) is less when the division ratio of data sets is 20/30. In table4, the variance of each emotions group is wee. This shows that the classification performance of classifiers is stabilization when the division ratio of data sets is in a certain range.

Table 3. Recognition rates of six emotions group with different training number of times

tr_number	J vs A	S vs P	J vs S	A vs P	Valence	Arousal
10	0.8333	0.8000	0.9275	0.9167	0.8333	0.9167
30	0.8333	0.8333	0.9444	0.9500	0.8333	0.9500
50	0.8750	0.8333	0.9500	0.9444	0.8333	0.9545
100	0.9000	0.8000	0.9167	0.9167	0.8000	0.9444
variance	0.0011	0.0004	0.0002	0.0003	0.0003	0.0003

Table 4. Recognition rates of six emotions group with different division of data set

Division Ratio	J vs A	S vs P	J vs S	A vs P	Valence	Arousal
12/38	0.8570	0.8333	0.9500	0.9444	0.8000	0.9545
10/40	0.8570	0.8000	0.9444	0.9375	0.8333	0.9375
8/42	0.8750	0.8333	0.9167	0.9375	0.7857	0.9286
20/30	0.7500	0.7222	0.9444	0.9444	0.7333	0.9375
16/34	0.8143	0.7843	0.9375	0.9375	0.7250	0.8929
variance	0.0025	0. 0021	0.0002	0.000014	0. 0021	0.0005

4 Conclusions

Experimental result shows that the approach about dimensionality reduction based on principal component analysis (PCA) and classifier using AdaBoost algorithm was very effective and potential in the practical application of emotion recognition. Correct-classification ratio was advanced by improving dimensionality reduction approach and AdaBoost algorithm. The improving dimensionality reduction approach and AdaBoost algorithm is a future work.

References

1. Cowie, R., Douglas-Cowie, E., Tsapatsoulis, N., Votsis, G., Kollias, S., Fellenz, W., Taylor, J.G.: Emotion recognition in human computer interaction. IEEE Signal Process. Mag. 18, 32–80 (2001)
2. Healey, J.A.: Wearable and Automotive Systems for Affect Recognition from Physiology, PhD thesis. MIT, Cambridge (May 2000)
3. Picard, R.W., Vyzas, E., Healey, J.: Toward Machine Emotional Intelligence: Analysis of Affective Physiological State. IEEE Transactions Pattern Analysis and Machine Intelligence 23(10), 1175–1191 (2001)
4. Haag, A., Goronzy, S., Schaich, P., Williams, J.: Emotion Recognition Using Bio-Sensors: First Step Towards an Automatic System. In: Affective Dialogue Systems, Tutorial and Research Workshop, Kloster Irsee, Germany, June 14-16 (2004)
5. Nasoz, F., Alvarez, K., Lisetti, C.L., Finkelstein, N.: Emotion Recognition from Physiological Signals for Presence Technologies. International Journal of Cognition, Technology and Work, Special Issue on Presence 6(1) (2003)
6. Leon, E., Clarke, G., Sepulveda, F., Callaghan, V.: Optimised attribute selection for emotion classification using physiological signals. In: 26th Annual International Conference of the IEEE, Engineering in Medicine and Biology Society, IEMBS 2004, vol. 1, pp. 184–187 (2004)

7. Wagner, J., Kim, J., André, E.: From Physiological Signals to Emotions: Implementing and Comparing Selected Methods for Feature Extraction and Classification. In: IEEE International Conference on Multimedia & Expo (ICME 2005) (2005)
8. Everitt, B.S., Dunn, G.: Applied Multivariate Data Analysis, 2nd edn. Arnold, London (2001)
9. Schapire, R.E.: The strength of weak learnability. Machine Learning (1990)

Search on Security of Wireless Sensor Network in Facilities on Sports Venues

Liu Bin[1], Wang Long[2], and Zhang Guo-Feng[2]

[1] College of Electronic and Informational Engineering, Hebei University, Baoding 071002, China
[2] Physical department, Hebei University, Baoding 071002, China
liuhao01@sohu.com

Abstract. Security issue of sensor networks is greatly different from that of conventional networks. In this paper, the characteristics analysis of wireless sensor network(WSN) has been carried out firstly, through analysis, the security architecture of sensor networks is proposed, trying to outline a general illustration on this area, and then security defense on the wireless sensor network security issues has been implemented secondly, finally the pairwise keying algorithm has been described and analyzed ,from above all, the ultimate security solution of wireless sensor network has been proposed.

Keywords: wireless sensor network, security, key algorithm.

1 Introduction

General network of wireless sensor networks nurtured a new information acquisition and processing techniques. A typical sensor network has hundreds to millions of sensor nodes[1], each sensor node is typically low-cost, limited in computation and information storage resources, highly power constrained, and communicates over a short-range wireless network interface[2]. These described features ensure a wide range of applications for sensor networks.

However, it seems that the security issue of sensor networks has not been considered as sufficiently as it should be.Sensor networks compared with the traditional networks have the following characteristics[3]: the node distributions are dense, the node resources are very limited, most of the nodes are static, from above,the high security of the sensor networks is very difficult.

2 Wireless Sensor Network Characteristics and Security Analysis

2.1 Wireless Sensor Network Charateristics and Composition

WSN is a large-scale distributed networks, often deployed in the no maintenance, poor conditions of the environment, and in most cases, sensor nodes are one-time use.it is characterized mainly reflected in the following aspects:(1)Energy is limited; (2)computing power is limited; (3)The storage capacity is limited; (4)The

D. Zeng (Ed.): ICAIC 2011, Part I, CCIS 224, pp. 418–423, 2011.

communication range is limited. In addition, most sensor network topology can not be predicted, while the entire network topology, sensor nodes in the network are constantly changing and a lot of network parameters and keys are after deployment formed after consultations. Based on the above analysis we can see wireless sensor networks are vulnerable to variety of threats and attacks.

The infrastructure of a WSN can be described as a combination of two parts. Data acquisition network and Data dissemination network[4].

(1) Data acquisition network: It is a collection of sensor nodes and the base station. The base station collects the information from the motes and forwards control data to the network environment.

(2) Data dissemination network: It is a collection of wired and wireless networks that provides an interface of the data acquisition network to a user.

The security model we expect to encounter in current WSN applications need to consider two kinds of security namely Inside Security and Outside Security, respectively,in two different network parts (in Data acquisition network and Data dissemination network).

(1) Inside Security: Since data acquisition network part of WSN use a shared wireless communication medium, authentication is necessary to enable both the sensor nodes and BS(Base Station), for detecting themessage that was injected with a malicious intent. This authentication prevents the attacker from injecting/spoofing packets. We call these security schemes as Inside Security, since it secures the mote–mote, mote–BS and BS–mote communication.

(2) Outside Security: This security concentrates on the data dissemination network part of the WSN. In this place, threats may arise from either side i.e., illegitimate users retrieve information from the network, or a malicious node forces the legitimate user to accept the false information. The security solution to countermeasure these threats is referred as Outside Security as it involves the (outside) user and WSN.

2.2 Security Requirements and Analysis

Various security requirements on wireless sensor networks are presented in almost all the related papers. As a summary, we classify those requirements into three security levels[5]:

(1) Message-Based level. Similar with that in conventional networks, this level deals with data confidentiality, authentication, integrity and freshness. Symmetric key cryptography and message authentication codes are necessary security primitives to support information flow security. Also data freshness is necessarily required as lots of content-correlative information is transmitted on a sensor network during a specific time.

(2) Node-Based level. Situations such as node compromise or capture are investigated on this level. In case that a node is compromised, loaded secret information may be improperly used by adversaries.

(3) Network-Based level. On this level, more network-related issues are addressed, as well as security itself. A major benefit of sensor networks is that they perform in-network processing to reduce large streams of raw data into useful

aggregated information. Protecting it is critical. The security issue becomes more challenging when discussed seriously in specific network environments. Firstly, securing a single sensor is completely different from securing the entire network, thus the network-based anti-intrusion abilities have to be estimated. Secondly, such network parameters as routing, node's energy consumption, signal range, network density and etc., should be discussed correlatively. Moreover, the scalability issue is also important with respect to the redeployment of node addition and revocation.

3 Security Components of Wireless Sensor Network

Security components include the following four phases[6].

3.1 Pre-deployment Phase

Before the deployment the BS chooses a secret S_x. Then it distributes an identity (IDS_k) and a distinguished secret key $SK_k = H(IDS_k \oplus S_x)$ to each (k th) sensor node.Where, H is a strong one way hash function.

3.2 Registration Phase

Each user needs to register under BS to access for the services in future. User sends its identity ID_i and registration request for this purpose. BS computes a secret token (S_i) using its secret S_x as $S_i = H(ID_i \oplus S_x)$. Then, it returns the computed S_i to the corresponding user via a secure channel.

3.3 Authentication and Group Key Establishment Phase

A user stands some where in the network, and broadcasts its identity (ID_i) as a request for service. The motes in its proximity provides the confidential information in their hand after authenticating the user.

Step1 :Let m nodes in the user's periphery. Each sensor node (with identity IDS_k) generates a random nonce N_{Ik}, and sends E_{SK_k} $(N_{ik} \| ID_i \| IDS_k)$, IDS_k to BS. Where, $E_{Sk_k}(.)$ is the symmetric key encryption with key SK_k. Each individual node IDS_k keeps N_{ik} corresponding to ID_i for a valid time period in its buffer.

Step2: BS selects $p(p \le m)$ first arrived message and decrypts($D_{sk_K}(E_{SK_k}(N_{ik} \| ID_i \| IDS_k))$) to obtain N_{Ik}, ID_i, IDS_k using the secret key ($SK_k = H(IDS_k \oplus S_x)$). If IDS_k computed after decryption does not match with that received (in non-encrypted form), BS rejects that nonce. If those two matches, BS computes $(n_1, ..., n_{p-1}, n_p^{'})$ using.

$$(n_1,....,n_p) = RCA_p^q(N_{i1},....,N_{ip}) \tag{1}$$

$$n_p^{'} = n_p \oplus S_i \tag{2}$$

Finally, BS sends $n_1,....,n_{p-1},n_p^{'}$ along with the corresponding sensor node identities $<IDS_1,...., IDS_p>$ to the user ID_i.

Step3: The user reverse computes the nonce values $(N_{i1},....,N_{ip})$ using its assigned secret token as in

$$n_p = n_p^{'} \oplus S_i \tag{3}$$

$$(N_{ip},....,N_{i1}) = RCA_p^q(n_p,....,n_1) \tag{4}$$

The user uses these nonce values as session key with the corresponding sensor nodes. To proof its identity, the user sends $E_{N_{ik}}(ID_i)$ (the encrypted identity with the nonce (N_{ik}) as key) to the corresponding sensor with identity IDS_k.

Step 4: Each sensor node (IDS_k) accesses the nonce value (N_{ik}) corresponding to ID_i from its buffer. Decrypts the received information using N_{ik}. If ID_i is obtained as result, sensor node (IDS_k) authenticates the user (ID_i).

The next phase (secured response phase) needs to be executed only for legitimate users. Node IDS_k discards the information and close the communication.

3.4 Secured Response Phase

This phase maintains confidentiality of responses resisting node capturing attack. For this reason, it has been assumed that each mote has partial information that to be provided to the user. The correct answer can be determined using at least s partial correct answers.

4 Key Algorithm Scheme

Key algorithm plays a very key role in deploying security strategies of wireless sensor networks[7][8][9], In this section, two different kinds of key algorithms are presented: Probabilistic key distribution and polynomial pool-based key distribution.

4.1 Probabilistic Key Distribution

Probabilistic key distribution scheme is designed to make sure that at least a key-shared path exists in "almost certain" situation. This algorith scheme picks a random pool (set) of keys S out of the total possible key space. For each node, m keys are randomly selected from the key pool S and stored into the node's memory. This set of m keys is called the node's key ring. The number of keys in the key pool $|S|$ is chosen such that two random subsets of size m in S will share at least one key with some probability p.

We abstract a sensor network as a random graph $G(n, p)$, with the wireless communication rang limit n', where n denotes the number of sensor nodes, p the probability that a link exists between any two nodes. Given a desired global probability P_c for graph connectivity, $p=\frac{\ln(n)-\ln(-\ln(P_c))}{n}$ is held.

4.2 Polynomial Pool-Based Pairwise Key Predistribution

As addressed above[10][11], a bivariate $t$degree polynomial is used to generate keys. However, this polynomial-based key pre-distribution scheme can only tolerate no more than t compromised nodes, and the value of t is limited due to the memory constraints of sensor nodes. The idea of a pool of multiple random bivariate polynomials is desirable. The basic idea of the polynomial pool-based scheme can be considered as the expansion on the meaning of "key". That is, this scheme is also based on the concept of "key pool", whereas keys are expressed as different polynomials.

5 Conclusions

Wireless sensor network security has become a hotspot of current research. Although research on wireless sensor networks security has achieved many notable results as addressed above, more challenges arise due to the continuous change of requirements. The next step is to improve the existing limitations in order to better meet the communication security of wireless sensor networks.

Acknowledgment. This paper is supported by Natural Science Foundation of Hebei Province and project of science and technology of Hebei Province.

References

1. Perrig, A., Szewczyk, R., Wen, V., Culler, D., Tygar, J.: SPINS: Security protocols for sensor networks. In: Proc. of the 7th Annual Int'l Conf. on Mobile Computing and Networks, pp. 189–199. ACM Press, Rome (2001)
2. Akyildiz, I.F., Su, W., Sankarasubramaniam, Y., Cayirci, E.: Wireless sensor networks: A survey. Computer Networks 38(4), 393–422 (2002)
3. Zhu, S., Setia, S., Jajodia, S.: LEAP: Efficient security mechanisms for large-scale distributed sensor networks. In: Proc. of the 10th ACM Conf. on Computer and Communications Security (CCS 2003), Washington, D.C, pp. 62–72 (2003)
4. Deng, J., Han, R., Mishra, S.: Defending against path-based DoS attacks in wireless sensor networks. In: Proc. ACM Workshop on Security of Ad Hoc and Sensor Networks, SASN, 2005, pp. 89–96 (2005)

5. Manzo, M., Roosta, T.: Time synchronization attacks in sensor networks. In: Proc. ACM Workshop on Security of Ad Hoc and Sensor Networks (SASN 2005), pp. 107–116 (2005)
6. Zhang, W., Cao, G.: Group rekeying for filtering false data in sensor networks: A predistribution and local collaboration-based approach, `http://www.cse.psu.edu/~wezhang/papers/paper-infocom05.pdf`
7. Malan, D.J., Welsh, M., Smith, M.D.: A public-key infrastructure for key distribution in Ting OS based on elliptic curve cryptography, `http://airclic.eecs.harvard.edu/publications/secon04.pdf`
8. Chan, H., Perrig, A., Song, D.: Random key predistribution schemes for sensor networks. In: Proc. of the IEEE Symp. on Research in Security and Privacy, pp. 197–213. IEEE Computer Society, Oakland (2003)
9. Du, W.L., Wang, R.H., Ning, P.: An efficient scheme for authenticating public keys in sensor networks. In: Proc. of the 6th ACM Int'l Symp. on Mobile Ad Hoc Networking and Computing (MobiHoc 2005), pp. 58–67. ACM Press, Urbana-Champaign (2005)
10. Eschenauer, L., Gligor, V.D.: A key-management scheme for distributed sensor networks. In: Proc. of the 9th ACM Conf. on Computer and Communications Security, pp. 41–47. ACM Press, Washington DC (2002)
11. Chadha, A., Liu, Y., Das, S.K.: Group key distribution via local collaboration in wireless sensor networks. In: Proc. IEEE SECON 2005, pp. 46–54 (2005)

Realization of the Minimum Cost Spanning Tree's Storage and Optimization in Prim Algorithm *

Pan Da-zhi[1,2], Liu Zhi-bin[2], Chen You-jun[1], and Ding Xian-feng[2]

[1] College of Mathematic and Information China West Normal University
Nanchong 637009, China
[2] School of Sciences Southwest Petroleum University Chengdu 610050, China
panpyewr@163.com

Abstract. This paper designs a special data structure for vertices in the network. the storage of edges in minimum cost spanning tree(for short, MCST) has been realized by the vertex array ,which is created by the special data structure. Through the vertex array, the vertices in V-U set constitute a static bi-directional circular linked list, so Prim algorithm realizes truly operation selecting the shortest side though the V-U set, by which the Prim algorithm is optimized to improve the efficiency of the operation. For the same vertex lying in U and V-U at the different moments, the special data structure makes storage space to be fully used and improves space utilization.

Keywords: network, Prim Algorithm, minimum cost spanning tree, bi-directional circular linked list, static linked list.

1 Introduction

For a given network, it has great practical significance to find the MCST [1]. For example, in real life, the communication system between the cities can be expressed as a graph, and its vertices represent cities, and its edges represent communication lines between cities, and the weight of the edge represent the cost which the lines have been set up. Since the difference of the distance and location between cities, the cost of setting up lines is also different. In order to let the cities communicate with each other, and get the lowest cost, we have to find the network's MCST.

In many implementations of the MCST's Prim algorithms, they did not deal with the MCST's storage, see, for example ,[2,3,4,5,6]. The process of their implement is: select a edge and output the edge. There are double problems in this process:

First, it is very inconvenient for the actual problems that need to use the topology of the MCST;

Second, for the selecting edge operation between the U and V-U, it has not been realized according to the V-U set, but has been realized through dealing with all vertexes.

* This work is partially supported by Scientific Research Fund of Sichuan Education Department (10ZB018).

D. Zeng (Ed.): ICAIC 2011, Part I, CCIS 224, pp. 424–431, 2011.

For realization the MCST's storage and real implementation the operation of selecting shortest edge based on V-U, we design special data structure for the vertex in the network. Though the data structure and adjacent matrix, we implement really the Prim algorithm and realize the MCST's storage, which makes the following operation of the MCST convenient.

2 Prim Algorithm Ideal

For the convenience of following description, we introduce the ideal of the Prim algorithm. Let G=(V, E) be a connected network with N vertexes, and T=(U, TE) be a MSCT of G, where U is the vertex set of T, TE is the edge set of T, and the initial values of U and TE are empty set. Let edge $(v_i, v_j) \in E$ which means the edge between v_i and v_j, and w_{ij} be the weight of the edge. The basic ideal of Prim algorithm is as follows:

(1) initialization of T: $U := \phi, TE := \phi$;

(2) let the vertex v0 be the root of MCST and enter U, that is, $U := \{v_0\}$;

(3) if(U==V)then goto(6) else goto (4);

(4) select edge (v_k,v_m) such that
$w_{km} = \min\{w_{ij} \mid (v_i, v_j) \in E, v_i \in U, v_j \in V - U\}$;

(5) execute merge operation such that
$U := U \cup \{v_m\}, TE := TE \cup \{(v_k, v_m)\}$,goto (3);

(6) gain the MCST of G : T ,the algorithm is over.

3 The Design of the Vertex Data Structure

For optimization of the Prim algorithm and the storage of the MCST, in the section, we have designed the special data structure of the network's vertex. A definition is as follows:

Definition 1. (extracting edge) let (v_i, v_j) be the shortest edge among the edges between U and V-U, where v_i is in U and v_j is in V-U, the edge (v_i, v_j) is called the extracting edge of v_i.

3.1 The Vertex Data Structure

The special data structure of the vertex is as follows:

```
struct V_node{
  int min_v;
  int pre;
  int next;
};
V_node V_array[N+1];
```

Where min_v field means the adjacent vertex that of the corresponding vertex, which the edge between the double vertexes is the shortest edge between the corresponding vertex to V-U, and means whether the vertex is in U; pre field means the precursor of the corresponding vertex in the V-U constructed static linked list when the vertex is in V-U, and is used to make the static linked list of vi's extracting edge when the vertex is in U, where v_i leads the corresponding vertex into U; next field means the successor of the corresponding vertex in the V-U constructed static linked list when the vertex is in V-U, and means the first pointer of the static linked list of the corresponding vertex's extracting edge; V_array is used to storage the vertexes and its subscript is looked as the number of the vertex.

3.2 Explain the Data Structure

In the special data structure, we realize two kinds static linked lists, they are as follows:

First, the vertexes in V-U have been constructed static double circular linked list, with the pre and next fields of the vertexes in V-U. As selecting the shortest edge between U and V-U, we can select really the vertex from V-U by the linked list and optimize the Prim algorithm.

Second, the extracting edges of each vertex in U have been constructed respective extracting edge static linked list. For the vertexes in U, each vertex v_i forms respective linked list, which has been constructed by the v_i's next field and the pre fields of other vertexes that have been introduced in U. with each vertex's extracting edge static linked list, the MCST has been stored.

For each vertex v_i in V, its current state is reflected by its min_v field. the meaning of the min_v field is as follows:

First, as min_v>0, there is $v_i \in V - U$ and min_v is number of the vertex which is v_i's adjacent vertex of the shortest edge form v_i to U. In the state, v_i's pre and next fields are used to constructed static double circular linked list.

Second, as min_v=0 , there is $v_i \in U$,and v_i's pre and next fields are used to constructed respective extracting edge static linked list.

3.3 Example Analysis

We describe the vertex's array based on the example from [1]. The network is given in figure 1, and the vertex data structure is designed as shown in figure 2. Let the tree's root v0 be 3,and three vertexes 3,1 and 6 be introduced in U and two edges (3,1) and (1,6) be added in TE, the state of vertex's array is given in figure 3.

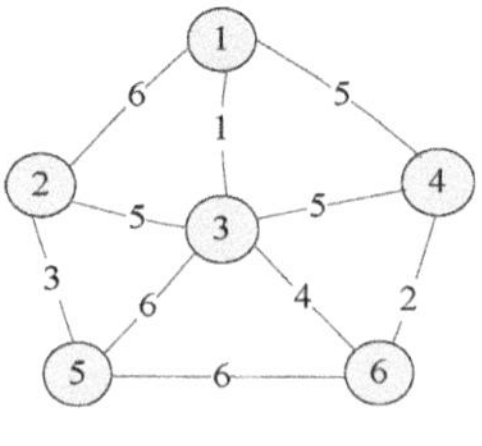

Fig. 1. Network

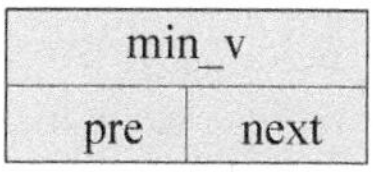

Fig. 2. The structure of V node

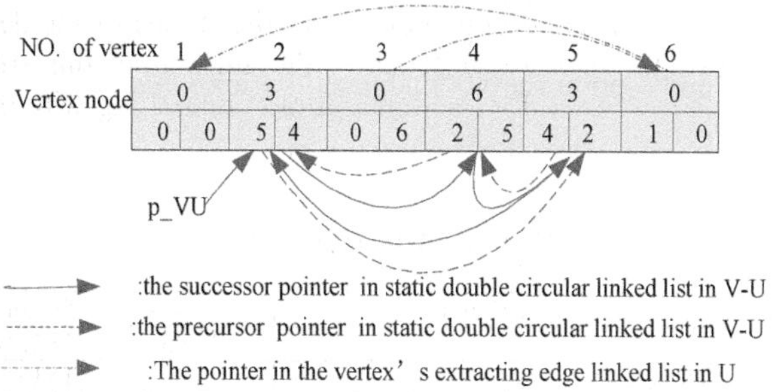

Fig. 3. The vertex array after vertex 3,1,6 has been placed in U

In figure 3, p_VU is the head pointer of static double circular linked list. According to figure 3, two vertexes 1 and 6 have been introduced in U by vertex 3, and the vertex 3 has two exacting edges: (3,1) and (3,6), so the static linked list has been created through the next field of vertex 3 and the pre fields of two vertexes 1 and 6;because two vertexes 1 and 6 have not extracting edge, their next fields are null.

4 Extension of the Prim Algorithm

In the section , we will realize the storage of MCST and optimize the selecting edge operation between U and V-U through extending the Prim algorithm.

4.1 Data Structure in Algorithm

Some data structures are as follows:

First, the adjacent matrix of the network: G. its element g_{ij} means the weight of the edge between v_i and v_j; if there is not a edge between v_i and v_j ,g_{ij} is assigned Max value(Max is bigger than any edge's weight).

Second, vertex array:V_array. Its index is as the number of the corresponding vertex.

Third, the head pointer of static double circular linked list formed by the vertexes in V-U: p_VU. its value is the list head's number.

Four, the pointer that points the shortest edge between U and V-U: p_minV. Its value is the number of the corresponding vertex.

4.2 Extension of the Prim Algorithm

The extended Prim algorithm is as follows:

(1) Initialization: obtain the network's data, form G, and determine the MCST's root v0, there is U={v0};
(2) Form V_array, and fix each vertex data fields, the process is as follows:
  (2.1) For the vertex v0 :
    V_array[v0].min_v:=0,
    V_array[v0].pre:=0,v_array[v0].next:=0;
  (2.2)for the vertexes in V-U: construct the static double circular linked list, let p_VU point the list head and place v0 in the min_v field of each vertex in V-U ; at the same time , let p_minV point the v0's adjacent vertex which forms the shortest from v0 to V-U with v0;
(3) If (U==V)then goto(5);
    else
     if((U≠V)&&
       (G[V_array[p_minV].min_v][p_minV])==Max)
     then goto(6); else goto(4);
(4) Select the shortest edge and modify the vertex's state and p_VU linked list and p_minV, these operations are as follows:
  (4.1)Modify p_VU linked list: cut the vertex ,which p_minV is pointing, from p_VU linked list and let temporary pointer t_minV point it; because the vertex will be put in U, we usually judge whether the min_v field of each vertex in V-U need modify and get the new p_minV value;
  (4.2) Put the edge (V_array[t_minV].min_v, t_minV) into TE:
     V_array[t_minV].pre:=
         V_array[V_array[t_minV].min_v].next;
     V_array[t_minV].next:=0;
     V_array[V_array[t_minV].min_v].next:=t_minV;
  (4.3) Put the vertex pointed by t_minV into U:
    V_array[t_minV].min_v=0;
  (4.4) goto (3);
(5) The algorithm is over;
(6) The network is not connected, we can't form MCST, and the algorithm is over.

C. The algorithm obtaining the MCST's edges

The edges of the MCST are saved by the vertex's pre data field and next data field, the algorithm is as follows:

(1) Let the pointer p_vode point the first vertex: p_Vnode:=1;
(2) If(p_Vode>N) then goto (8) else goto (3);
(3) Set the pointer p_Enode's initial value:
    p_Enode:=V_array[p_Vnode].next;
(4) If(p_Enode==0) then goto(7) else goto (5);
(5) Gain the edge (p_Vnode,p_Enode),and put out it;
(6) Let p_Enode point the next exacting edge of p_Vnode:
    p_Enode:=V_array[p_Enode].pre; goto(4);
(7) Let p_Vnode point next vertex:
    p_Vnode:=P_Vnode+1;goto (2);
(8) The algorithm is over.

5 The Algorithm'S Code

We have implemented the extended Prim algorithm and the obtained the MCST'sedge algorithm with C++ program.

5.1 The Code of the Extended Prim Algorithm

```
void Prim_Ex( )
{
int k,p_minV,t_minV,p_VU,t_Vnode,v0;
v0=create_Net( );/*create_Net function :obtain the
    network's data,create G and get v0 */
V_array[v0].min_v:=0,V_array[v0].pre:=0;
v_array[v0].next:=0;//initialize v0
  p_VU= (v0==1?2:1);
t_Vnode=p_minV=p_VU;//initialize _VU,p_minV,t_Vnode
  for(k=1;k<=N;k++)
 /*let the vertexes in V-{v0}form the static double circular linked list*/
 if(k!=v0)
 {
    V_array[k].min_v=v0;
    V_array[k].pre=t_Vnode;
    V_array[t_Vnode].next=k;
    if(g[v0][k]<g[v0][p_minV])
        p_minV=k;
     t_Vnode=k;
  }
V_array[p_VU].pre=t_Vnode ;
V_array[t_Vnode].next=p_VU;
  for(k=1;k<N;k++)//select N-1edges and form CMST
  {
 t_minV=p_minV;
 if(p_VU==p_minV)//p_minV is list head of p_VU
   p_VU=V_array[p_minV].next;
 V_array[V_array[p_minV].pre].next=
        V_array[p_minV].next;//cut the p_minV from list
   V_array[V_array[p_minV].next].pre=
        V_array[p_minV].pre;
   t_Vnode=p_VU;p_minV=p_VU;
  /*modify the shortest edge form each vertex in V-U to U, and get the new value
   of p_minV*/
  while(V_array[t_Vnode].next!=p_VU)
   {
    if(g[t_minV][t_Vnode]< g[V_array[t_Vnode].min_v][t_Vnode])
      V_array[t_Vnode].min_v=t_minV;
   if(g[V_array[t_Vnode].min_v][t_Vnode]<
         g[V_array[p_minV].min_v][p_minV])
```

```
            p_minV=t_Vnode;
        }
        V_array[t_minV].pre=
        V_array[V_array[t_minV].min_v].next;
           //put the edge into TE
        V_array[t_minV].next=0;
        V_array[V_array[t_minV].min_v].next=t_minV;
        V_array[t_minV].min_v=0;
          //put thevertex t_minV into U
      }
   }
```

5.2 The Code of Algorithm Obtained the MCST's Edges

```
   void get_Edge( )
   {
 int p_Vnode,p_Enode;
      /*obtain edges form each vertex */
 for(p_Vnode=1;p_Vnode<=N+1;p_Vnode++)
     {
  p_Enode=V_array[p_Vnode].next
  /* output the current vertex's exacting edge */
  while(p_Enode!=0)
   {
     cout<<"("<<p_Vnode<<","<<p_Enode<<")"<<endl;
      p_Enode=V_array[p_Enode].pre;
    }
   }
   }
```

6 Conclusion

Through the vertex's special data structure, we have divided the vertexes into tow sets: U and V_U. with the data structure, the storage of the MCST's edges is realized, that makes the following operation easy; with the data structure, two linked lists are constructed and realize really the edge's selecting operation from U to V_U, that enhances the algorithm's time efficiency; because the vertex's data fields have different means in different time, the storage space is used fully, that improves the space efficiency.

References

1. Yan, W.M., Wu, W.M.: Data Structure. Tsinghua University Press, Beijing (2001)
2. Sun, Q., Sheng, J.H., Gu, Z.J.: Algorithm for Finding All the Shortest Paths from One Node to Another in A Graph. Computer Engineering 28(2), 134–136 (2002)

3. Hou, L.P., Li, W.S.: Minimum Spanning Tree Algorithm Based on Extended Double List Storage Structure. Journal of Beijing Jiaotong University 27(2), 93–95 (2003)
4. Wan, K.X., Enslow, H., Pan, Q.J.: the New Algorithm of CMST Problem. Chinese Journal of Computers 14(9), 34–37 (1991)
5. Lai, W.G., Li, O., Cheng, J.: A Novel Genetic Algorithm for Degree Constrained Minimum Spanning Tree Problem. Computer Simulation 25(8), 162–165 (2008)
6. Li, H.B., Chen, J.: Dynamic optimum of minimum span tree's algorithm devised by Prim. Computer Engineering and Applications 43(12), 69–73 (2007)

Object Tracking Based on Unmanned Aerial Vehicle Video*

Xiong Tan, Xuchu Yu, Jingzheng Liu, and Weijie Huang

Institute of Surveying and Mapping Information Engineering University
Zhengzhou City, Henan Province, China, 450052
xiong281@tom.com

Abstract. The video sequence images about the ground targets of dynamic information are obtained from the high speed unmanned aerial vehicle, the camera movement has brought some difficulties to the target detection, object tracking. With the characteristics of displacement of the background in UAV video sequences images, the moving target detection and tracking technology is divided into three parts: motion estimation, target detection, object tracking. Because of the target smaller, lower resolution in the UAV video sequences image, so a region-based tracking algorithm is proposed. The computation of method, the speed of computational meets the needs of real-time tracking, experiment and achieved good results.

Keywords: sequential imagery, motion estimate, target detection, object tracking.

1 Introduction

Currently, the moving target detection and tracking is a focus field of computer vision research, the moving target detection and tracking technology are many ways, such as the theory of knowledge-based algorithms[1],region-based algorithm[2][3],feature-based algorithm[4][5],and contour-based algorithm[6]. However, these algorithms are rarely used in the processing of UAV video tracking. The reasons of the object deformation, illumination changes, occlusion and others makes the implementation of a fast moving target detection and tracking robustness is still a huge challenge.

The general algorithm for moving target detection and tracking is not suitable for moving target detection and tracking in UAV video, mainly in the following reasons:

1) The computation time is large, not suitable for real-time applications. The UAV video analysis and processing needs of a fast track multiple moving targets, and therefore must consider the real-time tracking and the robustness of the algorithm.
2) The algorithm versatility. Most of the algorithm is carried out under the ideal conditions, such as the camera is stationary, the image quality is very good, very clear objectives, targets move is slowly and simply background.

* This article is supported by the Innovation fund of the dissertation of Master degree of Surveying and Mapping Institute.

D. Zeng (Ed.): ICAIC 2011, Part I, CCIS 224, pp. 432–438, 2011.

However, The UAV equipped with visible light or infrared camera move fast, the target in video may move quickly. Therefore, the resolution of the target in UAV video is relatively low, the background is complex, brings some difficulties to the video processing.

3) The target characteristics. For general targets in the UAV video, have very obvious features or boundaries. However, for some point object in the UAV video, only constitute of several number of pixels, the size is very similar with the noise, so detecting and tracking a small target will be difficult.

In order to solve these problems, this paper presents a fast moving target based on UAV video tracking algorithm.

2 Proposed Method

Mentioned in the previous article, a variety of UAV video tracking algorithm can not be used for target tracking, mainly because these methods do not apply to handle small target detection and tracking as well as large amount of calculation is not suitable for real-time tracking. Compared with other tracking methods, region-based tracking more suitable for UAV video tracking target tracking. We improve the tracking algorithm based on region. we divide object tracking into three steps: motion estimation; target detection; object tracking. The proposed algorithm is depicted in Figure 1:

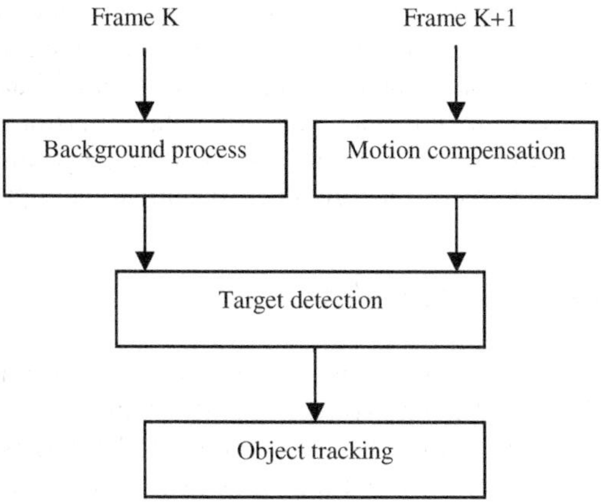

Fig. 1. Tracking algorithm

It contains three steps: compensation of the image displacement by the camera moving; detect the movement of image area in each frame; tracking the moving regions in time. The global motion compensation included estimate the motion parameters between two consecutive frames of video images; The moving targets are detected by the spatiotemporal change detection algorithm; tracking is that segmenting the target region in the subsequent frames of the video sequence and establishing a model, then finding the correspondence region in the next video sequence image.

2.1 Motion Estimation and Global Motion Compensation

UAV video data is obtained about the dynamic information of the target in the condition of the high speed moving UAV. To detect and track the moving object in the background of image, the first considered thing is that cancel the displacement between two frames caused by moving camera which also called global motion compensation. Removing the impact of the background, eliminating error, and thus extracting the moving objects, tracking targets more accurate, Motion estimation and motion compensation for subsequent detection and tracking of moving targets laid the foundation.

I_0 , I_1 is denoted illumination of two consecutive frames, the geometric parameters align I_0 and I_1 can be estimated using a motion model. The most commonly used models include affine transformation model and the quadratic approximation model of the motion. Here we use three-parameter model[7] to estimate the background displacement caused by moving camera.

$$I_1(x,y)=I_0(x\cos\theta-y\sin\theta+d_x, y\cos\theta+x\sin\theta+d_y) \tag{1}$$

Where, d_x , d_y , θ denote the horizontal displacement, vertical displacement and rotation angle. When the rotation angle θ is very small, we can approximate instead the $\sin\theta$, $\cos\theta$,with θ and 1. by use of Taylor series expansion, The"(1)"becomes:

$$I_1(x,y)\approx I_0(x,y)+(d_x-y\theta)g_x(x,y)+(d_y-x\theta)g_y(x,y) \tag{2}$$

$$g_y(x,y)=\frac{\partial I_0(x,y)}{\partial y} \qquad g_x(x,y)=\frac{\partial I_0(x,y)}{\partial x}$$

The error function is:

$$E(d_x,d_y,q)=\Sigma[I_1(x,y)-I_0(x,y) \tag{3}$$

$$-(d_x-yq)g_x(x,y)-(d_y-xq)g_y(x,y)]^2$$

We can estimate the three motion parameters by minimizing the error function. The parameter estimation is solved as:

$$\begin{bmatrix} d_x \\ d_y \\ \theta \end{bmatrix} = \begin{bmatrix} \Sigma g_x^2 & \Sigma g_x g_y & \Sigma g_x g_{xy} \\ \Sigma g_x g_y & \Sigma g_y^2 & \Sigma g_y g_{xy} \\ \Sigma g_x g_{xy} & \Sigma g_y g_{xy} & \Sigma g_{xy}^2 \end{bmatrix}^{-1} \times \begin{bmatrix} \Sigma g_x g_t \\ \Sigma g_t g_y \\ \Sigma g_t g_{xy} \end{bmatrix} \tag{4}$$

where $g_{xy}=xg_y-yg_x$, $g_t=I_1-I_0$.

We can get motion estimation sub-pixel accuracy by the least square method. However, this accuracy is obtained only for the assumption that a small translation and rotation angle. To improve the accuracy, iterative method is used. First we calculate the motion parameters from"(4)",and then warp I_1 toward I_0 using the motion parameters, repeat the iteration until the motion parameters is less than a certain threshold. In most cases, this approach will soon converge. Another in the motion estimation if all the pixels involved in the calculation would be very time consuming. Here we use the sub-sampling the image, only with a subset of the image can be used to sacrifice a small amount of pixel precision to save a lot of computing time.

In the motion estimation, in order to get accurate motion parameters, we should try to select the background pixels to avoid target pixels. After obtaining the three motion parameters, I_1 is registered to I_0 with a bilinear interpolation, and the target motion detection can be done in two sequence image.

The experiment data is used the download UAV video data, In figure (2) :(a) (b) is two successive frames of video images, (c) is the result of the image obtained after motion compensation. In order to show the effect of background motion compensation, comparing the two differential images. The results is shown in figure (d) and (e).

The experimental results showed that: Because the influence of moving background, the result of direct differential is not very satisfactory, the target appeared empty and redundant. After background motion compensation, we can get the broad contours of target clearly. We acquired the better results, this could conducive to the subsequent target detection and object tracking.

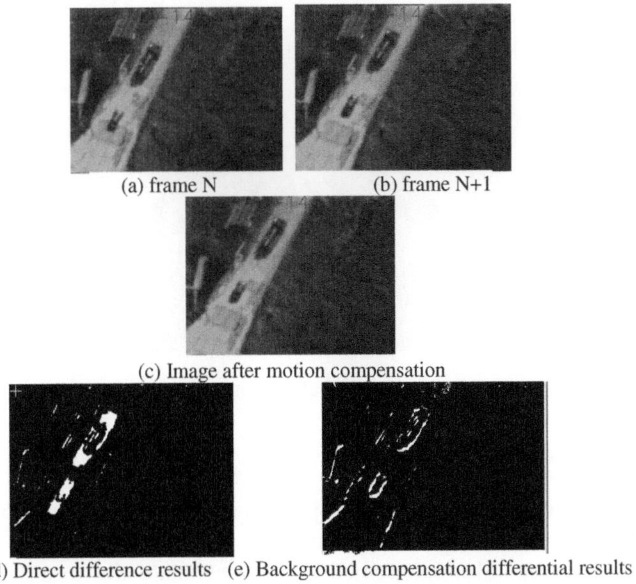

Fig. 2. Video sequence image Global Motion Compensation

2.2 Moving Target Detection

Because eliminate the background of the displacement after the global motion compensation, simply we can directly subtract the two video sequences images, after threshold transformation, and get the moving target area. Here $I_n(x, y), I_{n+1}(x, y)$ are two successive frame, The binary difference image is expressed as:

$$D_n(x, y) = I_{n+1}(x, y) - I_n(x, y) \tag{5}$$

$$DP_n(x, y) = \begin{pmatrix} 1 & |D_n(x,y)|>T \\ 0 & \text{其它} \end{pmatrix} \tag{6}$$

Where T is a threshold. If the two image pixels corresponding to the absolute difference greater than the threshold T (T = 60), it indicates that the pixels is moving target pixel, set the value to 1; if less than the threshold, it indicates that is the pixels background pixels, set value to 0. This binary image is $DP_n(x, y)$.

In reality, the background of active images can not be completely eliminated, as shown in Figure 2 (e). Although the moving object can be detected significantly, but there was some noise such as road boundary. To eliminate the noise, the methods of the corrosion and expansion morphology filter can be used. Figure 3 is the experimental results obtain by using the corrosion and expansion method with the binary image. We can see from the figure that we can get a more complete target area though difference calculation, morphological filtering operation. The differential method has the advantage: it can detect the basic shape of the object after the movement of the background is eliminated, and the method is simple and fast. It is more suitable for real-time detection.

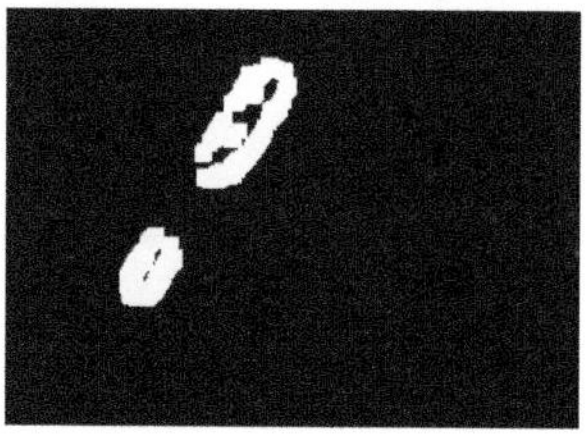

Fig. 3. The binary image after morphology of operation

2.3 Region-Based Target Tracking

The essential of the tracking moving objects is to establish the relationship between the image and model. It including two steps: target detection and target motion orientation prediction. Motion prediction is to estimate the location of the target appeared in the next frame, the moving target detection accuracy direct influence the video tracking accuracy.

A fast and efficient object tracking method is region-based. Region-based tracking is actually a template matching process. After the completion of target detection, you can get target location, size, shape and other information. Taking the target as a template to obtain an area from the image, calculate correspondence between the region and the template block pixel correlation coefficient. The advantages of this method are: when the target is not obscured, the accuracy is high, tracking is more stable.

We make the experiment by region-based object tracking method for 2 group videos. It can be seen from Figure 4 that we get very good experiment results, tracking more accurate, faster calculation. The image in figure 5 is taken by the UAV video images, moving target is smaller and the targets characteristics is not obvious, in this case, the algorithm also can accurately tracking objects.

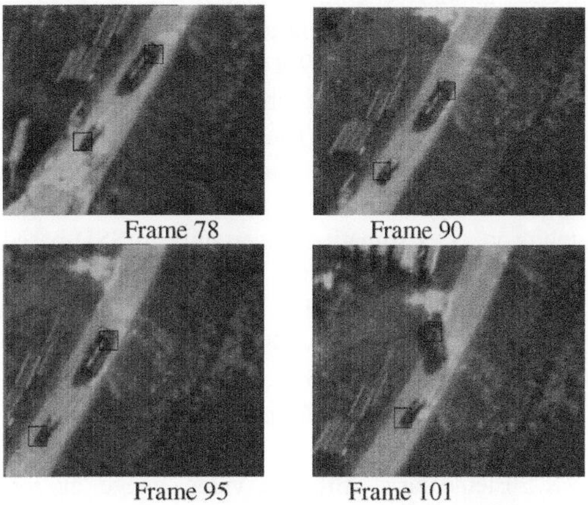

Fig. 4. The results of object tracking (1)

Fig. 5. The results of object tracking (2)

3 Conclusion

In this paper, we mainly describe quickly object tracking in the UAV videos. The tracking is divided into three steps: motion estimation, target detection, object tracking. To the displacement of the background of the image sequence, we use the model of rotational translation to estimate the motion and compensate the global motion to eliminate the background displacement; after eliminate the displacement, a simple frame difference method to segment the moving object; Finally, we use region-based tracking algorithm to calculate the target position in each frame to achieve target tracking. The entire tracking process is computationally inexpensive, faster and has good experimental results, to satisfy the demand of a fast real-time UAV video object tracking.

References

1. Cohen, I., Medioni, G.: Detecting and tracking moving objects for video surveillance. In: Computer Vision and Pattern Recognition, pp. 2319–2325 (1999)
2. Meyerf, B.: Region-based tracking using a fine motion models in long image sequences. CVCIP. Image Understanding 60(2), 119–140 (1994)
3. Basele, B., Deriehe, R.: Region tracking through image sequences. In: Proceedings of IEEE International Conference of Computer Vision, pp. 302–307 (1995)
4. Tissainayagam, P., Suter, D.: Objeet tracking image sequences using point feature. Pattern Recognition 38(1), 105–113 (2005)
5. Niekels, K., Hutehinson, S.: Estimating uncertainty in SSD-based feature tracking. Image and Vision Computing 20(1), 47–58 (2002)
6. Peterfreund, N.: Robust tracking of position and velocity with kalman snakes. IEEE Trans. Pattern Anal. Mach. Intell. 21, 564–569 (1999)
7. Hardie, R.C., Barnard, K.J., Bognar, J.G., et al.: High-Resolution image reconstruction from a sequence of rotated and translated frames and its application to an infrared imaging system. Opt. Eng. 37, 247–260 (1998)
8. Zhang, P., Yu, X.: Elementary. Airborne video image motion detection and tracking techniques. Surveying and Mapping 24(6) (2007)
9. Jia, Y.: Machine Vision. Science Press, Beijing (2004)

Design and Implimentation of Rural New Energy Source Gis System Based on Kml

Li Tan*, Lu Wang, ChongChong Yu, and Jie Liu

School of Computer and Information Engineering
Beijing Technology and Business University, 10048
Beijing, China
litan003@gmail.com

Abstract. Upon analysis and summery of the theory and technical research of new energy in rural area, this paper achieved rural new energy GIS system based on B/S structure applying Microsoft's NET as the development platform and C# as the programming language. With the energy statistics and planning program as the core of process and analysis module, this system builds up a solid document management and functional module on GUI display applying the key technology such as KML and Web-GIS, which eventually enable the display of the energy information on Google Earth and Google Maps. In addition, a test case prefecture has been taken to test on the system's main modules preliminarily. The result indicates that the system realized the function of energy statistics and planning effectively, with a good interaction and convenient performance.

Keywords: rural new energy, KML, GIS system, Web-GIS.

1 Introduction

For items not addressed in these instructions, The main thesis of this paper is based on field investigated data of energy structure and consumption of 543 typical villages trough out the country, and by applying Google Earth and Google Maps based on KML (Keyhole Markup Language) to accomplish displaying and management of data statistics and calculation of the existing regular energy and renewable energy structure and application based on which further analyzing their potential laws. Employ regulation and case base method to predict the future energy consumption trend and feasibility of replacing regular energy with renewable energy under various evaluation targets. Further more, adopting NET as a development platform with Visual Studio 2008 and SQL Server 2005 as the main developing instruments to design and develop the rural new energy GIS system.

* Corresponding author.

D. Zeng (Ed.): ICAIC 2011, Part I, CCIS 224, pp. 439–447, 2011.

2 Kml

2.1 Figures and KML General Description

KML (Keyhole Markup Language) is a kind of symbol language based on grammatical and documental form of XML (eXtensible Markup Language). It is principally to describe and store geographical information such as point, line, area and 3Dmodel etc[1-3]. KML absorbed and made use of OGC (Open Geospatial Consortium) formulated GML (Geography Markup Language) criteria based on which deleted description of topological relations in the geographical models, simplified description element, to describe geographical information with a tag grammatical form. At present, KML is mainly applied in geographical information description in Google Earth which is a virtual globe software developed by Google Company that arranged satellite photos, navigation chart and GIS together in the 3Dimension model of the globe and is an information carrier with space identifier. On the Google Earth, massive geographical information is integrated through placemark with which communications between the client and server with photos, pictures and KML documents, but not with direct space data.

2.2 KML Expressions

KML is the main data carrier in the system operation. On the one hand, it is to receive data that inquired from the bottom data layer, and on the other, it is the only distinguishing symbol language of the front terminal of Google Earth and Google Maps displaying module, hence it is the key technology serving as a link between the front and the following, that plays an irreplaceable role in the whole system[4].

In the whole course of KML data processing, beginning from the inquiry of client side to the final inquired data displaying, is guided by data. The process is shown in the following Fig.1.

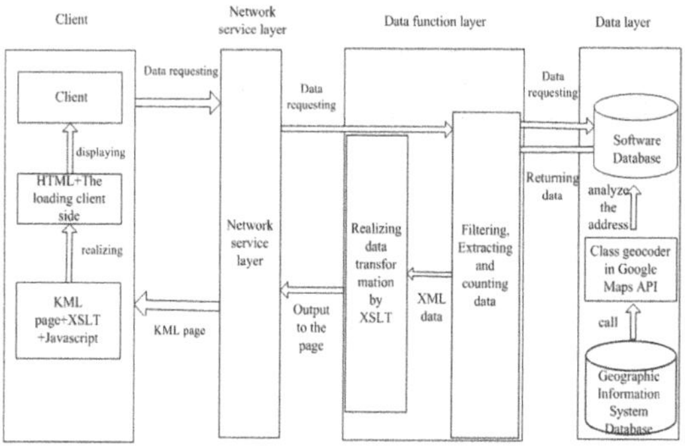

Fig. 1. Framework of KML Data Processing

The key technology is that to analyze the address with geocoder through Google API, to realize data transformation from XML to KML with the assistance of XSLT as well as to display KML on the client side with the placemark details through Google Maps[5].

3 Design of the System

The original data source of the system is composed up with three parts of data, i.e. 1) the investigated data of new energy utilization and the local natural resources of the 543 villages from various climatic zones through out the country; 2) data obtained with Google Earth and other auxiliary instruments; 3) authorized data by standard coal transform coefficient and that are obtained by the climatic zone authority. Discarding those obviously untrue disturbing data by data filtering algorithm, then statistic and calculate with energy statistic algorithm, the result would be taken as partial energy planning input parameters, retrieve corresponding regulations in regulation bank, thus obtain energy planning result with reasoning machine, finally display it on the picture interface sub-system. The whole process is developed around data processing and the data shown as in Fig.2 like a pyramid from more at bottom and getting less on the top, from complicated to simple and from general to concrete.

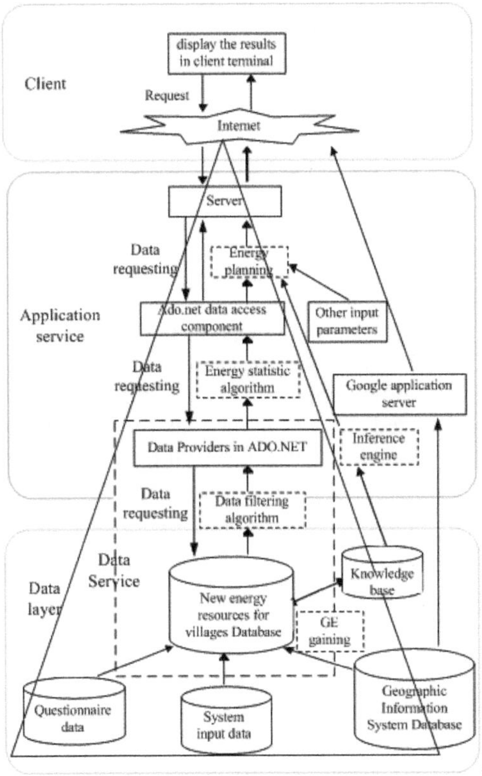

Fig. 2. Structure of the System

3.1 Question Bank Management

In the system, an automatic composition of questionnaire function is designed for question bank management around the process of "Question Bank—Questionnaire---

Investigation Table". The same is true as the function is also the most important part in the data layer of the pyramid structure, for it shoulders the task of obtaining investigated data on the one hand, and to store them in XML form on the other.

The reasons why the investigated data are stored by XML form are that XML technology relatively to data bank technology possesses the privileges of inter-platform and easy expression etc. in data application.

As for investigation data display, that is controlled by integration of XSLT (eXtensible Style Language Transformation) and JavaScript. XSLT possesses the superiority in information display and processing, for the same XML data documents are analyzed through different XSLT documents would have displayed in different forms that enable the system to have the separate characteristics from one another for data express, operation and display. The XML+XSLT+JaavaScript data display form greatly improves logic and effectiveness of the system.

The automatic composition of questionnaire function embodied in investigation table that may select at random questionnaire which again could freely select questions from the question bank and in addition the questions possess the function of addition, modification and deletion etc.

3.2 KML Expressions

The purpose of the energy planning and processing module is to realize the energy planning function in the top layer of the pyramid structure and regulations are the core of energy planning. The energy planning and processing module is chiefly composed of knowledge bank and case base, and the knowledge showing of the knowledge bank is based on regulations, the normal expression is : If [(condition 1) o (condition 2) o …o (condition n)] Then (conclusion).

From condition 1 to n are the input parameters in the energy planning process; while conclusion of regulations is the corresponding planning result, "o" is the logic relationship among all conditions[6].

In the energy planning and processing module, the task of reasoning machine is to match the initial condition and planning result in the knowledge bank as regulations. Upon the reasoning and matching process of the reasoning machine, the final result would be our energy planning conclusion[7-8]. The flow sheet of the whole energy planning and processing module is shown as Fig.3.

3.3 Energy Source Statistic Algorithm

Purposefully on the basis of field investigation on rural energy utilization of the five climatic zones of severe cold, cold, hot in summer and cold in winter, hot in summer but warm in winter and mild warm, from which extraction, statistics and transform calculation of currently typical rural energy utilization data were done by the system. Consequently the local energy structures as well as proportion of renewable energy utilization in the energy consumption system have been obtained and the result simultaneously taken as partial rural new energy planning input parameters that are all the preliminaries of the energy planning.

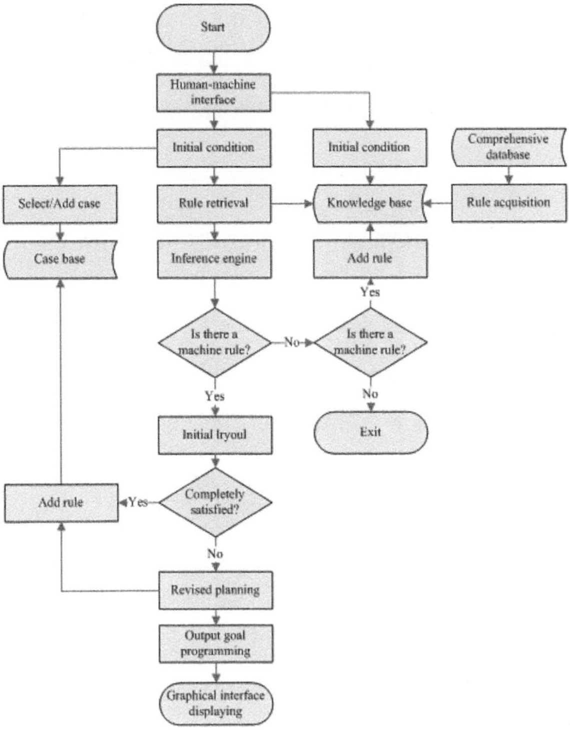

Fig. 3. Flow Sheet of Energy Planning and Processing Module

With the purpose to get the present rural energy consumption structure, renewable energy and the local economic status, statistics were conducted over per capita average energy consumption of various energy, total energy per capita average consumption, energy consumption structure, utilization rate of renewable energy and average income per capita etc.

- Per capita average energy consumption of Energy X , E_{xp} =Energy X total annual energy consumption E_x^* standard coal transform rate (refer to Table 1) ρ_x , permanent residential population P .

$$E_{xp} = E_x^* * \rho_x / P . \tag{1}$$

- Total energy per capita average consumption $E_{tp} = \sum_{i=1}^{n}$ energy i per capita average consumption $E_{ip}(\mathrm{i} = 1,2,\ldots,\mathrm{n})$.

$$E_{tp} = \sum_{i=1}^{n} E_{ip} (\mathrm{i} = 1,2,\ldots,\mathrm{n}) . \tag{2}$$

- Energy consumption structure: Energy i ratio between per capita average consumption to the total p_i=energy i per capita average energy consumption E_{ip} / total energy per capita average energy consumption E_{tp}.

$$p_i = E_{ip} / E_{tp} . \tag{3}$$

The above obtained group of p_i value must satisfy the following conditions:

$$\sum_{i=1}^{n} p_i = 1 (i = 1,2,...,n) \tag{4}$$

- Renewable energy consumption rate rp =total renewable energy per capita average consumption E_{rtp} / total energy per capita average consumption E_{tp}

$$rp = E_{rtp} / E_{tp} . \tag{5}$$

Among the above total renewable energy per capita average consumption $E_{rtp} = \sum_{j=1}^{m}$ renewable energy j per capita average consumption $E_{rjp} (j = 1,2,..,m)$.

$$E_{rtp} = \sum_{j=1}^{m} E_{rjp} (j = 1,2,...,m) \tag{6}$$

- Per capita average annual income M_p =annual household total income M_t / permanent residential population P .

$$M_p = M_t / P . \tag{7}$$

Table 1. Energy to Standard Coal Transform Coefficient

Code No.	Commonly used Coefficient	Unit	Coefficient Value
1	Power to standard Coal	Kgce/kwh	0.404
2	Low quality coal to std coal	Kgce/Kg	0.7143
3	Chart coal to std coal	Kgce/Kg	1.1616
4	Liquid gas to std coal	Kgce/Kg	1.7143
5	Natural gas to std coal	Kgce/m3	1.2143
6	Stalks to std coal	Kgce/Kg	0.5
7	Straw to std coal	Kgce/Kg	0.4282
8	Firedamp to std coal	Kgce/m3	0.629
9	Solar energy to std coal	Kgce/MJ	29.3076

4 Development and Implimentation of the System

NET is the development platform for the system, the main instruments are Visual Studio 2008 SQL Server 2005 and C#, JavaScript is the developing language, the second development is carried out to the software system by exploiting Google Earth API and Google Maps API. The system is composed of data layer, data processing and net interface layer as well as the service layer: a) On the sever side data in the data layer are stored with Server2005 and XML documents; b) the medium part is the data processing and net interface layer; c) on the client side, data are displayed by XSLT+JavaScript+XML+Ajax. The following Fig.4 and Fig.5 shows some function test that was carried out to the system with living cases of Cangzhou Prefecture of Hebei Province.

Fig. 4. The Main Interface of the System

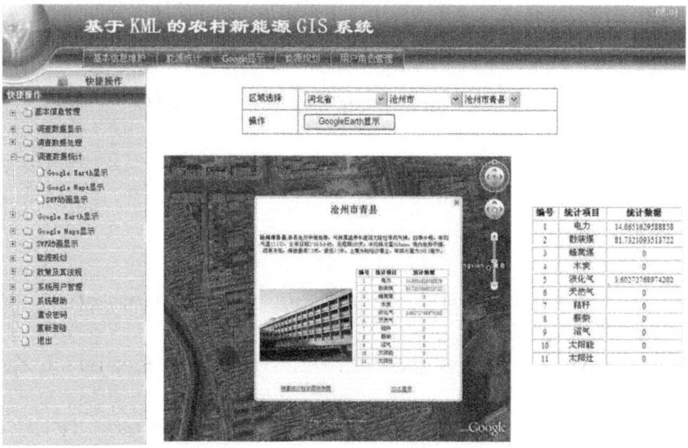

Fig. 5. Displaying of Energy Structure Google Earth of the System

5 Conclusion

Upon analysis of working principle and way of implementation of the present rural new energy system in this paper, the design program for rural new energy GIS system based on KML was established, given out the structural pattern of the system and the detailed specifications of its core technology of the main functional module from working principle to execution process. The system possesses the following features to compare with previous energy planning and Web-GIS systems.

1) **Convenience and Science of investigation:**Work out different designs of investigation table to various regions and make timely necessary modification through the automatic composition function.
2) **Vividness and straightness of display:** SWF, Google Earth and Google Maps technology have been applied in display by the system that not only enable the display of information in a vivid picture, but also fix them to specific geographical location.
3) **Practicability and effectiveness of energy statistics and planning:**The investigated data are obtained through field investigation of questionnaire and net inquiry etc., finally the corresponding result was achieved through statistics and planning algorithm.

Eventually, as Web-GIS and KML technology have been adopted in the rural new energy GIS system based on KML, in one aspect it is capable to analyze, predict the trend of energy consumption of the locality and reasonably resolve the energy shortage by making full use for renewable energy, for such regions would be taken as models by the system to encourage and popularize in the other.

Acknowledgment. The involved project is funded by National Science-Tech Tackle Key Project, 'Rural New Energy Sources Developing-and-Saving Key Technology Project-Rural Living Energy Consumption Standard' (No.2006BAJ04B01 -2), is Supported by the Research Foundation for Youth Scholars of Beijing Technology and Business University.

References

1. Jiang, K., Gong, X.: Google API Development Elaboration: Google Maps and Google Earth, pp. 242–380. Publishing House of Electronics Industry (2008) (in Chinese)
2. Google Inc., KML2.1 Reference (2007), http://www.google.com/earth/index.html
3. Yuan, M., Yu, C., Nie, J.: Distributed WebGIS model based on ArcSDE and SVG. Application Research of Computers 26(3), 939–941 (2009) (in Chinese)
4. Yao, Q., Yu, C., Liu, J.: Design and implementation of automatically generating questionnaire based on XML. Computer Engineering and Design 30(10), 2538–2540 (2009) (in Chinese)
5. Du, Y., Yu, C., Liu, J.: A Study of GIS development based on KML and Google Earth. In: 2009 Fifth International Joint Conference on INC, IMS and IDC, pp. 1581–1585 (2009)

6. Tan, L., Gong, D.: Research and Development of Parame terized Control System. Process Automation Instrumentation 26(5), 20–22 (2005) (in Chinese)
7. Liu, S., Yang, X., Jiang, W., Cao, K.: Decision support system for crop diseases and insect pests prevention and control based on GIS[J]. Transactions of The Chinese Society of Agricultural Engineering 19(4), 147–150 (2003) (in Chinese)
8. Gao, L., Chen, J., Yu, X., Wang, C., Hu, B.: Research and development of the expert system platform for forecast and prediction of agricultural pests. Transactions of the Chinese Society of Agricultural Engineering 22(10), 154–156 (2006) (in Chinese)

Development of Real-Time Register System for Printing Press Based on μCOS-II

Guodong Sun and Daxing Zhao

School of Mechanical Engineering
Hubei University of Technology
Wuhan, Hubei Province, China
guodong027@126.com

Abstract. The fundamental composition and operating principle of color register system for printing press have been studied. Base on deep analyzing the characteristic of register system at home and abroad, a real-time monitoring system for printing press registration control has been proposed based on multitask real-time operating system μCOS-II. Using Data Flow Diagram analysis method, the register system is divided into five basic tasks. Assigning these tasks' priorities properly and designing inter-task communication and synchronization mechanism, the system performance has been optimized. Finally, its efficiency has been proved by an example.

Keywords: register system, real-time monitoring, multitask, μCOS-II.

1 Introduction

With the development of computer, network, laser and digital technology, the printing technology has presented the following trends: network printing workflow, CTP technology (Computer to Plate), green printing, highly automated, high precision, high speed and shaft less technology. To respond to these new changes, all countries have invested large amounts of financial and human resources to study printing technology. At present, printing methods commonly used include digital printing, offset printing, flexo printing and gravure printing. No matter what printing method, the registration is one of the critical systems to ensure the printing quality, speed, high stability, and wide adaptation, especially for high speed color printing presses.

Compared to international advanced level, less domestic register system could meet the requirements of high quality printing machine, which has become a bottleneck restricting domestic printing press update. And most of printing presses rely on imports. Therefore, it is one of the most cost-effective means to upgrade domestic printing machine by improving the performance of the register system.

2 Basic Composition and Principle of Register System

The register means two or more printed images are accurately aligned with each other. When printing color images, firstly the color images are divided into a number

D. Zeng (Ed.): ICAIC 2011, Part I, CCIS 224, pp. 448–455, 2011.

of monochrome images and each plate is make respectively in a certain order, and each printing unit is responsible for one color, at last the exquisite color image is compounded by overlapping all the monochrome images. Printing machines generally include 6~12 color units that could print 6~12 colors on the print surface. The entire printing process and register system are showed in Fig. 1.

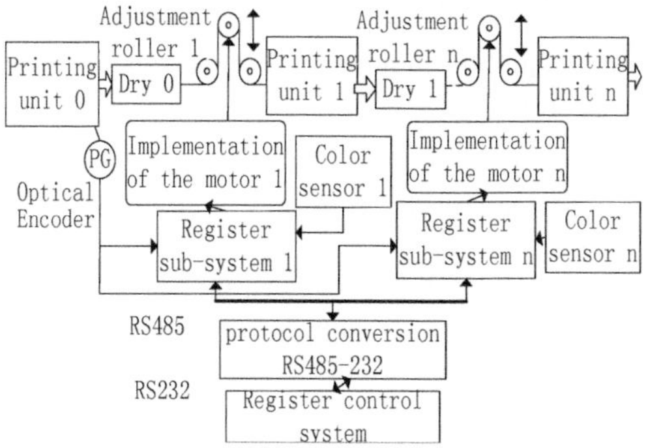

Fig. 1. Process flow and composition of printing register system

When the print passing the first color unit, printing could start from anywhere, but after the first color, printing location must register with the former one. In order to ensure accurate registration of the various colors' printing so as to form a clear image, the register error detection and control are necessary for color printing. The register precision of high-end printing machine is no more than 0.10mm.

In order to detect the register error timely, the mark consisted of color code and "+" line is tagged in the specified location when plate-making. When printing, the marks are printed on the margin of print, with the overlapping of all "+" lines and 20mm intervals of each color code. The "+" lines are used for static measurement, while the color codes are used for automatic detection. After the second color group, each color printing unit is equipped with the color code sensors to scan the moving color codes. The sensor counts the pulses between the two color codes, counting starts when the front color code arrival, and stops when the rear arrival. By the count value the size and direction of the register error can be determined. Assuming when the pulse count value is N, the distance of adjacent color codes is 20mm, the register error is zero. If the pulse count value is n, and the difference between n and the standard value N is δ, then the absolute value of δ is proportional to the register error, the positive or negative of δ corresponds to the direction of register error. When the error is detected, the register system would emanate the corresponding signal to actuate the electrical motor, and then fine-tuning adjustment roller would change small displacement between the printing units to eliminate register error [1].

3 Analysis of Register Control System and Development Platform

In order to shorten the development cycle and save cost, stable industrial panel PC is adopted as the host computer. The monitoring software installed in the panel PC is responsible for the management and monitoring of lower computers.

3.1 Function Analysis of Register Monitoring System

Register control system generally monitors 1~12 register subsystems of printing units. Its main functions are as follows:

1) **Parameter Setting:** Set the system parameters of the register subsystems, included the original parameters of the printing units (such as circumference of the plates, the order of color codes, etc) and the control parameters of register subsystems (such as control mode, control precision, alarm threshold, etc). These parameters are transmitted via RS485 to their register subsystems which run according to the setting.

2) **Data Analysis and Show:** Make unified management of the real-time data uploaded by each register subsystem, then analyze and show them to the operator by combination of graphics and number. The displayed contents include register error of single printing unit, comprehensive register error, dynamic curve of signal register error, dynamic curve of comprehensive register error and the connection status, etc.

3) **Warning Prompt:** When the register error existed in the printing units is more than corresponding threshold set in register subsystem or the system works abnormally, monitoring system will alert the users by sounds and graphics.

4) **Human-Computer Interaction:** According to the real-time running status, the operational parameters of register subsystems will be modified at any time. All operations on the register subsystems could be completed conveniently by the monitoring system.

5) **Reliable Network Communications:** monitoring host computer and register subsystems communicate by RS485 protocol, which provides efficient transmission of the set parameters and the upload real-time data.

3.2 Development Platform of Monitoring System

Compared with other real-time operating systems, DOS system requires little disk space, has the advantages of good real-time performance and high stability, short interruption response time, being free to use, and abundant development tools and information. Although DOS is a single-tasking operating system and has no ability of multi-task scheduling, there have already been a large number of real-time scheduling kernels and transplantation examples, which are recognized in stability and real-time performance after the long-term practice tests. The μCOS- II is recognized as an embedded RTOS, and its real-time kernel is open source.

Therefore, the multi-task scheduling of register real-time monitoring system is achieved by transplanting μCOS- II on DOS7.1 version, where Borland C++ integrated development environment is adopted.

4 Multi-task Design of Real-Time Monitoring System Based on μCOS- II

In traditional software design, the system is often divided into various sub-modules, and then broken them down into functions. While in embedded application software design the system is divided into a number of concurrent tasks, which communicate one another. The traditional design method is not suited to the concurrent design pattern, thus the DARTS [2] (Design and Analysis of Real-Time System) design method which provides the basic way of task division as an extension of structure analysis and design, is adopted in this monitoring software development. Several key issues on real-time multi-task design are discussed as following.

4.1 Tasks Division

The tasks division is the basis for real-time multi-tasking; the task division strategy has a direct impact on the load balance, synchronization and communication complexity, dependencies between tasks, etc. Reasonable task division will not only simplify the system design and facilitate software debugging, but also enhance the real-time performance and stability.

General principle of the tasks division is based on the functional module, at the same time considering the real-time performance and execution efficiency to reduce the system call time. The relatively independent tasks should be compressed into a single task in order to reduce the scheduled burden of multi-tasking kernel. But for these tasks which are closely related and require more processing time, if their priority is higher and they once occupy the CPU, it is very difficult to respond other tasks in real time. Therefore, these tasks should be divided into some simple tasks according to the actual situation and efficiency, and the interoperability of these simple tasks is achieved by synchronization or communication mechanism of μCOS- II.

The DFD (Data Flow Diagram) is a good graphical analysis tool, which gets rid of the physical contents, precisely describes the system functions, input, output and storage. According to the system DFD, the tasks could be constructed from different profiles, such as I/O functions, internal functions, task internal cohesion, task priorities [3]. For every profile, there are some principles used to determine whether a transform should compose a task separately or together with other transforms. But each principle just illustrates in a certain aspect, when there is a conflict between the principles, the optimal division should be selected based on the actual situation. Fig. 2 is the data flow diagram of the register control software. In accordance with the DFD and the relevant principles, register control system is divided into five tasks:

1) Receive and Save(TaskRxSave) : When receiving the data, firstly determine the validity of them, then analyze the data, at last dispatch these analysis results to the corresponding data processing module.

2) Input and Save(TaskInputSave) : Achieve human-computer dialogue. The task detects the data input of the operator, and analyzes them in appropriate way, then sends them to the lower computers utilizing TaskTx task. At the same time, the analysis results are sent to TaskDisplayAlarm task to show the running status.

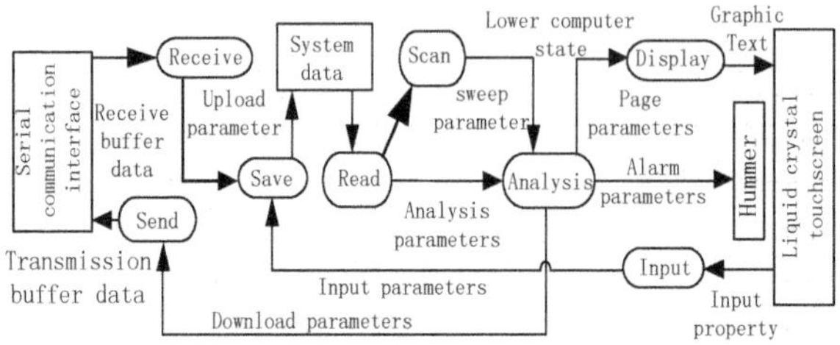

Fig. 2. Data flow diagram of register system software

3) Display or Alarm(TaskDisplayAlarm) : Monitor the running status of the lower computers. The display contents fall into two categories: real-time data and system parameters. The real-time data such as the location of various color codes, register error, printing speed, printing length, the pulse count values measured by PG and so on, are processed for show in the mean of reasonable graphics or texts. At the same time, the system parameters are collected in the appropriate interface to facilitate the operators to know the running status of the whole system and take appropriate measures. If the register error exceeds the set thresholds, the alarm will occur through the interface animations and buzzer.

4) Send(TaskTx) : Firstly analyze the data which will be sent, then connect to the specified lower computer on the basis of the analysis results, at last call the corresponding module to send data.

5) Scan(TaskScanAll) : Mainly test connection status of various lower computers to realize the lower computers' dynamic linking. If the lower computers are connected correctly, then the real-time data and modified system parameters will be uploaded. If the connection is abnormal, then the connection state will be changed.

4.2 Task Priority Assignment

μCOS-II is a real time operating system based on the priority, and identifies the tasks by priority. Every task must be assigned the different priority; otherwise the tasks could not be distinguished. The highest priority task in the ready state will occupy the CPU firstly, and only after the usage right of CPU is transferred, other tasks can be executed. Therefore, the setting of the task priority has a significant impact on the real-time performance [4, 5].

There are at most 64 tasks indicated by numbers 0 to 63 in μCOS-II, the smaller the value is, the higher its priority is. Among them, the system reserves the lowest priority task; it is suggested to keep four of the highest and four of the lowest priority tasks for the upgrade of μCOS-II version. Therefore, there are 56 application tasks for the users. At the same time, there is an interval of the certain priority between two tasks with the adjacent priorities, so as to add more application tasks without readjusting the whole system priority when upgrading and adding functions in the future. However the priority interval cannot be too large, otherwise it will be at the expense of hardware resources. With comprehensive analysis and the actual debugging, the interval of two priorities is set.

On the basis of the DFD in Fig. 2 and the above analysis, the priorities of five basic tasks order as follows: the priority of TaskTx is 5, TaskDsiplayAlarm is 8, TaskRxSave is 11, TaskInputSave is 14, TaskScanAll is 17.

4.3 Synchronization and Communication between Tasks

1) Synchronization between Tasks: When multiple tasks in register system need to be synchronized, it can realize easily by the semaphore of μCOS-II. TaskInputSave and TaskRxSave need synchronize with TaskDisplayAlarm, TaskInputSave and TaskScanAll need synchronize with TaskTx. Therefore, two synchronous semaphores are created in the system: the semaphore for display is SemSynDisplay waited by TaskDisplayAlarm, and the semaphore for sending is SemSynTx waited by TaskTx.

2) Communication between Tasks: The easiest way for communication between tasks is sharing data structure. Especially when all tasks are at the same address space, the variables (such as global variables, pointers, buffers, linked lists and cyclic buffers, etc) can achieve the sharing data structure, and simplify the communication between tasks. However, it must ensure the exclusivity when each task deals with sharing data, so as to avoid the competition and data destruction. It's the very easy way of exclusive access sharing data to lock or open the interrupt, μCOS-II provides two macro calls for on/off interrupt: OS_ENTER_CRITICAL ( ) and OS_EXIT_CRITICAL ( ).

Therefore, the sharing global data structures are adopted for the communication between tasks in this register control system software, with the on/off interrupts to realize the legal access of sharing data. Among the five basic tasks, TaskTx and TaskDisplayAlarm need to read the global variables, TaskInputSave and TaskRxSave need to write the global variables, and TaskScanAll need to read and write the global variables.

TaskDisplayAlarm and TaskTx need sync signal to enter the running state, i.e. they do not completely run concurrently, and they have the highest priority, no other tasks can deprive their right of using CPU. Therefore, their access to global variables will not cause data corruption. Because the global variable scopes accessed by TaskInputSave and TaskScanAll are different, the switch of these two tasks will not destroy the global data. Although the global variables accessed by TaskRxSave and TaskScanAll have overlapping, once TaskScanAll begins scanning, it will send sync signal to make TaskTx run, only after the corresponding lower computer receives and responds the orders sent by TaskTx, TaskRxSave will receive and process the data. Therefore, TaskScanAll controls system's orderly execution with the help of TaskTx.

However, the priority of TaskInputSave is higher than TaskRxSave, and most of the global variables accessed by them are overlapping, when TaskRxSave depriving the right of using CPU from TaskInputSave, it may result in data corruption. Therefore, only TaskInputSave really needs the on/off interrupt to access global variables.

5 Software Structure of Register System

In summary, the final software structure of register system is shown in Fig. 3, which illustrates five basic tasks scheduling by μCOS- II multi-task real-time kernel, synchronization and communication between tasks, the interface of tasks and peripheral devices. Among it, solid arrows represent the task synchronization, the appropriate synchronization semaphores are indicated above the arrows; hollow arrows represent the global variable access, and the task which needs on/off the interrupt to protect the global variables is labeled; shaded hollow arrows represent the interfaces of system software and peripheral devices.

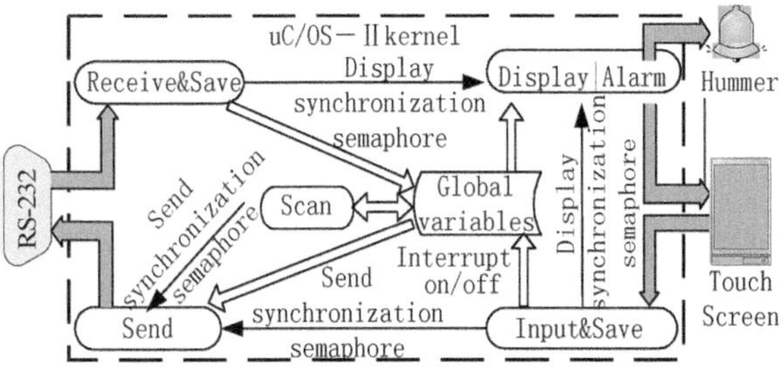

Fig. 3. Software architecture of register monitoring system

In order to achieve a clear program structure, a temporary task called TaskStart is created in the main program. TaskStart is only responsible for initialization and creation five basic tasks above, then it will do nothing, real-time kernel will not dispatch it again.

6 System Operation and Conclusion

This real-time register monitoring system needs to communicate with the lower computers, so the real-time performance is closely related to the software and hardware of lower computers. Considering the existing printing equipment and the cost, the low-grade lower computers were equipped in this system.

After field testing, when the printing speed is less than 150m/min the register accuracy is up to ±0.1mm, which satisfies the register monitoring request of mid-range printings. The monitoring system can continuously and stably operate for 7 × 24 hours without being out of control and crash faults.

Furthermore, the register monitoring interface is friendly and humane, the operator can real-time adjust the parameter setting with the interface shown in Fig. 4. Among them, the right-most twelve buttons represent printing units (lower computers) symbols, current printing unit is U2 (pressed); the top five graphic buttons are for switching control interfaces, the current is system parameter setting interface (pressed). Various display forms provide alternative monitoring interface for the operators to adapt different occasions. Fig. 5 shows the register error of current printing unit by cursor, the operator can move the cursor to complete the register operation.

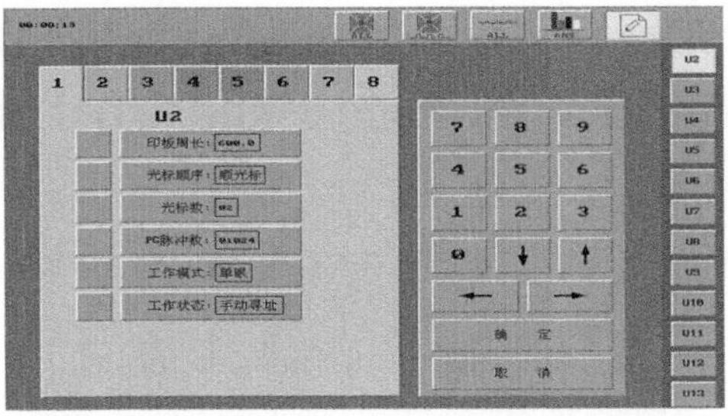

Fig. 4. System operating parameters setting

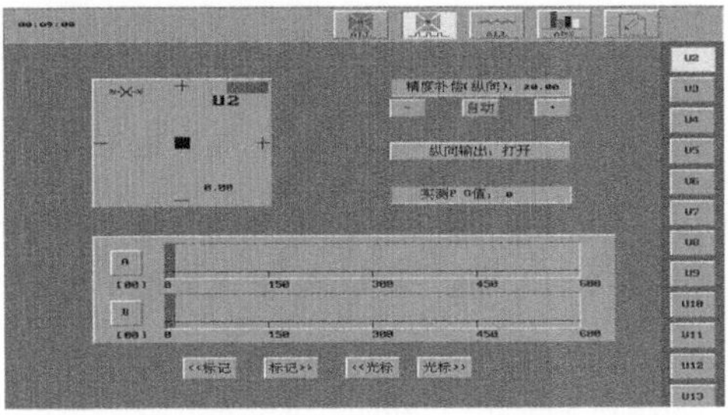

Fig. 5. Register error comprehensive monitoring

Actual operating results have proved the rationality and practicality of the whole system design. This proposed register monitoring system has good stability, high real-time performance, and being easy to implement, which meets the needs of mid-range register system, and introduces a new solution for high-end register system.

References

1. Jing, J., Kang, X., Fei, L.: A method of register error detection based on pattern recognition. In: Pro. Int. Conf. Model. Simul., ICMS, United Kingdom, vol. 7, pp. 38–42 (2009)
2. Sangyeoll, K., Dean, A.G.: DARTS: Techniques and tools for predictably fast memory using integrated data allocation and real-time task scheduling. In: Real-Time Technology and Applications – Proceedings, pp. 333–342 (2010)
3. Jeong, J., Chang, P.: A task-priority based framework for multiple tasks in highly redundant robots. In: IEEE/RSJ Int. Conf. Intelligent Rob. Syst., IROS, pp. 5886-5891 (December 2009)
4. Villen-Altamirano, M.: Response time optimization by task priority assignment. Electr. Commun. 62(3-4), 280–287 (1988)
5. Jin, H., Wang, H., Wang, Q., Dai, G.: Integrated design method of task priority. Journal of Software 14(3), 376–382 (2003)

Locally Optimum Detection of a Noise Model Based on Generalized Gaussian Distribution*

Yanqing Dai**, Gang Tang***, and Taiyue Wang†

College of Mathematics and Physics, Huangshi Institute of Technology, Huangshi, Hubei Province, 435003, P.R. China
wangch318@yahoo.cn

Abstract. In order to optimize signal detection in non-Gaussian environments, the work is addressed to provide realistic modeling of a generic noise probability density. The model depends on few parameters which can be estimated quickly and easily, and so general to be able to describe many kinds of noise such as symmetric or asymmetric. To this end, a new model is introduced, which derives from the generalized Gaussian function, and depends on there parameters: kurtosis, for representing variable sharpness, left variance and right variance, for describing deviation from symmetry. The model is applied in the design of a locally optimum detection test.

Keywords: asymmetry generalized Gaussian distribution, locally optimum detection, higher-order statistics.

1 Introduction

The work is addressed to modeling in a realistic way generic background noise, in order to optimum signal detection in non-Gaussian environments. Detection is dealt with as binary hypothesis testing in the context of statistical inference[1]: the purpose is to decide between the two hypotheses of presence H_1 or the absence H_0 of a transmitted deterministic signal $s_i, i = 1,\cdots,k$, on the basis of acquired observations $x_i, i = 1,\cdots,k$, the noise $n_i, i = 1,\cdots,k$ corrupting the signal during the propagation is assumed additive, stationary, independent and identically distributed, and generally non-Gaussian. For designing a detector, it is characterized by: ① high performances in the case of weak signals. ② easy applicability to real case, that is,

---

* **Foundation item:** Supported by national science foundation of China under Grant No: 60672048.

** **Yanqing Dai** , Born in 1967, male, he is associate professor, His research interests include signal processing and watermarking.

*** **Gang Tang** , Born in 1962, male, he is associate professor, His research interests include signal processing and wavelet analysis.

† **Taiyue Wang,** Born in 1977 male, he is lecturer, His research interests include GGD signal processing.

D. Zeng (Ed.): ICAIC 2011, Part I, CCIS 224, pp. 456–462, 2011.

easy and realistic estimation of needed parameters realistic noise modeling, and robustness to variable boundary conditions. ③ algorithmical simplicity.

For satisfying condition ①, the statistical testing method selected is a locally optimum detector(LOD). In order to condition ② and ③,the investigation is addressed to express generalized noise probability density function models, usually depending on parameters difficult to be estimated from real data samples, in terms of higher-order statistics(HOS)[2] parameters. HOS parameters are very easy and quick to be extracted from data and particularly suitable for quantifying deviation from Gaussian in terms of asymmetry and variable sharpness. As conventional signal processing algorithms based on second-order statistics, optimized in presence of Gaussian noise, may decay in non-Gaussian environments, various works used HOS theory [2] as signal processing basis for noise analysis and detection optimization. However, some approaches work only with non-Gaussian noise [3][4] or only in Gaussian noise[5][6], some methods only under specifically assumptions of noise distributions[7], the others means are complicated[8].

To come first in, in the paper, generalized Gaussian function,then, the asymmetry generalized Gaussian function[9] is introduced. It derives from the combination of the generalized Gaussian probability density function and of the asymmetric Gaussian model. The first model is symmetric and depends on a shape parameter α, which is not easy to estimate from data. Nevertheless, shape parameter α presents a physical meaning, as linked with the probability density function sharpness. The HOS parameter which better describes sharpness variability is the kurtosis k. Hence the analytical relationship between α and k is introduced. The resulting symmetric function based on kurtosis k has the characteristics of generalized Gaussian probability density function. In order to introduce also possible deviation from symmetry, the resulting kurtosis-based function is modified by taking into account the asymmetric Gaussian model [10]. It directly derives from the Gaussian shape, but is asymmetric and depends on two second-order parameters: the left and right variances. By introducing these two parameters in kurtosis-based generalized Gaussian function, so, the asymmetric generalized Gaussian model can be obtained. The new model is compared with the generalized Gaussian and the asymmetric Gaussian probability density functions. It is widely applied in the design of a LOD test, image processing, watermarking detection and so on. Promising experimental results are presented which derive from the application of test for detecting signals corrupted by real underwater acoustic noise radiated by ship traffic [11].

2 Generalized Gaussian Model and Its Property

In the context of noise modeling, one of the most noticeable ways in which estimated noise distributions deviate from Gaussian is in kurtosis k, i.e., the ratio of the fourth and the square of the second central moments; it is expressed by the following formula:

$$k=\frac{EX^4}{(EX^2)^2} \tag{2.1}$$

It is equal to 3 in the Gaussian case; the sharpness of a probability density function shape is higher (lower) than the corresponding Gaussian function as k is large (smaller) than 3, a good model for general probability density function has variable sharpness. One of the well-known symmetric probability density function, which has as follows of form[12]:

$$p_{gG}(x) = \left[\frac{\alpha}{2\beta\Gamma(1/\alpha)}\right] e^{\left[-\left|\frac{x-\mu}{\beta}\right|^{\alpha}\right]} \tag{2.2}$$

Where $\beta = \sqrt{\frac{\sigma^2\Gamma(1/\alpha)}{\Gamma(3/\alpha)}} = \sigma\sqrt{\frac{\Gamma(1/\alpha)}{\Gamma(3/\alpha)}}$ $\sigma > 0$, $\Gamma(z) = \int_0^{\infty} e^{-t} t^{z-1} dt$

is gamma function, $\mu, \sigma^2, \alpha, \beta$ ismean, variance, shape parameter, scale parameter, respectively. Zero mean Gaussian distribution and Laplacian distribution is its especial form, note that for $\alpha = 2$, this density reduces to the Gaussian density and for $\alpha = 1$,it becomes the Laplacian density. But α cannot be directly estimated from data samples, hence the relationship between k and α is introduced. It derives from the k definition and is expressed by the following formula:

$$\text{k} = \frac{EX^4}{(EX^2)^2} = \frac{\Gamma(5/\alpha)\Gamma(1/\alpha)}{\Gamma^2(3/\alpha)} \tag{2.3}$$

the relations between kurtosis k and shape parameter α is shown as Fig.1.

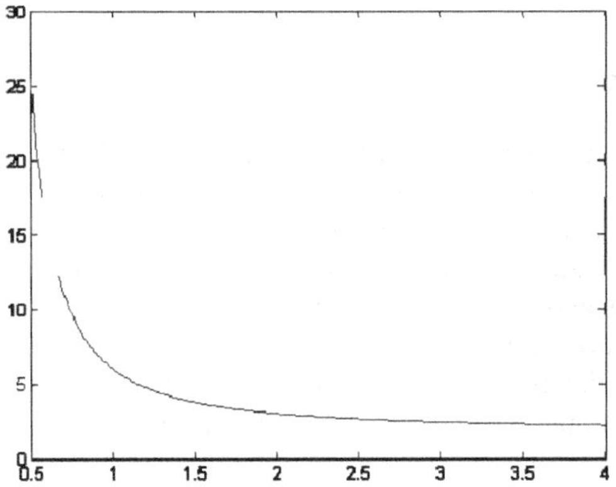

Fig. 1. The relations between kurtosis k and shape parameter α

Expressing exactly α in terms of k is not possible because of the presence of the gamma function. That is why asuitable analytical approximation of the function $\alpha = \alpha(k)$ was found:

$$\alpha = \alpha(k) = \sqrt{\frac{5}{k - 1.865}} - 0.12 \tag{2.4}$$

So this formula allows one to express $p_{gG}(x)$ in terms of k. The validity is confirmed by observing that for $k > 3$,there sulting probability density function has heavy tails, for $k < 3$ the distribution is sub-Gaussian distribution, the relations between generalized Gaussian probability density and kurtosis is shown as Fig.2

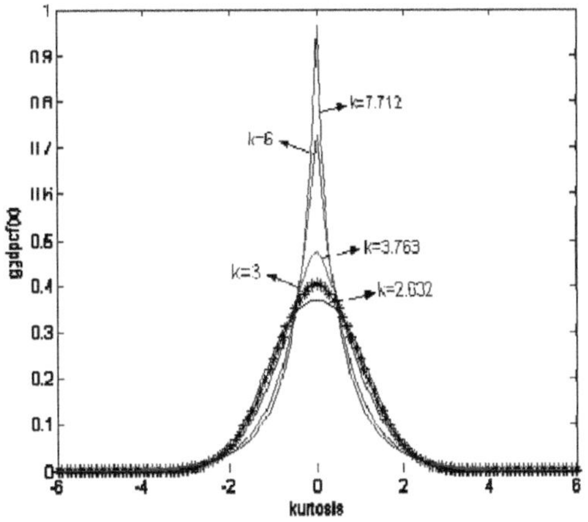

Fig. 2. PDF of generalized Gaussian ($u = 0, \sigma = 1$)

3 The Asymmetric Generalized Gaussian Model

In order to generalize this model so that it can be also suit for asymmetry. The asymmetric Gaussian model is taken into account. It depends on two second-order parameters which derives from the definition of variance, σ_l^2 and σ_r^2 , called respectively lift variance and right variance, and estimated from finite sequences of process $\{x\}$ according to the following terms:

$$\sigma_l^2 = \frac{1}{N_l - 1} \sum_{k=1, x_k < \mu}^{N_l} (x_k - \mu)^2,$$

$$\sigma_r^2 = \frac{1}{N_r - 1} \sum_{k=1, x_k > \mu}^{N_r} (x_k - \mu)^2$$

where N_l and N_r is the respectively number of samples $x_k < \mu$ and $x_k > \mu$, the model can expression follows:

$$f_{aG}(x) = \begin{cases} \dfrac{2}{\sqrt{2\pi}(\sigma_l + \sigma_r)} e^{-\frac{(x-\mu)^2}{2\sigma_l^2}} & x < \mu \\ \dfrac{2}{\sqrt{2\pi}(\sigma_l + \sigma_r)} e^{-\frac{(x-\mu)^2}{2\sigma_r^2}} & x \geq \mu \end{cases} \tag{3.1}$$

In same way, it is analytically simple and easy to be estimated if some data sequences are available. Notice that in the case of $\sigma_l = \sigma_r$, the expression coincides with the function, it is shown as Fig.3

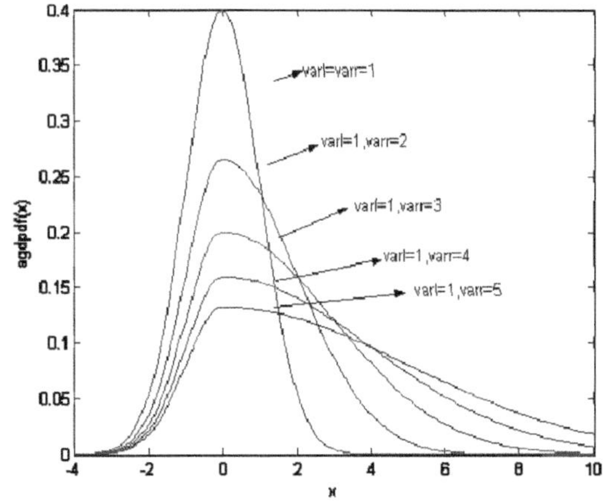

Fig. 3. PDF of asymmetric generalized Gaussian ($u = 0$)

As the left and right variances were replaced to the variance in the Gaussian probability density function for building the asymmetric Gaussian model, in a similar way, these two parameters are introduced in the kurtosis-based generalized Gaussian function probability density function, the following asymmetric generalized Gaussian model:

$$f_{agG}(x) = \begin{cases} [\dfrac{2\alpha}{\beta_a \Gamma(1/\alpha)}] e^{-\left[\frac{-(x-\mu)^\alpha}{\beta_l^\alpha}\right]} & x < \mu \\ [\dfrac{2\alpha}{\beta_a \Gamma(1/\alpha)}] e^{-\left[\frac{(x-\mu)^\alpha}{\beta_r^\alpha}\right]} & x \geq \mu \end{cases} \tag{3.2}$$

with $\beta_a = (\sigma_l + \sigma_r)\sqrt{\dfrac{\Gamma(1/\alpha)}{\Gamma(3/\alpha)}}$, $\beta_l = \sigma_l \sqrt{\dfrac{\Gamma(1/\alpha)}{\Gamma(3/\alpha)}}$, $\beta_r = \sigma_r \sqrt{\dfrac{\Gamma(1/\alpha)}{\Gamma(3/\alpha)}}$; which is easy to know that if $\sigma_l = \sigma_r$, it coincides with the generalized Gaussian model and it is symmetric; if $\sigma_l = \sigma_r$ and $k = 3$, then it coincides with the Gaussian model. A family of the probability density functions of asymmetric generalized Gaussian is shown as Fig.4.

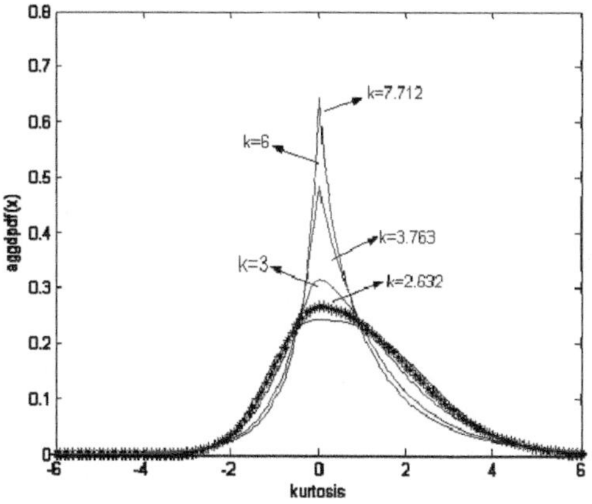

Fig. 4. PDF of asymmetric generalized Gaussian ($u = 0$)

4 Experiment and Analysis

The detection performances of LOD test developed on the basis of the asymmetric generalized Gaussian model are analysis by means of experimental curves of the detection probability P_D as the ratio of signal to noise (SNR) varies. Given the value of the probability of false alarm $P_{FA} = 0.05$, the results derive from the application of the test for the detection of known deterministic signals corrupted by ship-traffic-radiated noise. Noise was analyzed and characterized by the estimated parameters $\sigma_l = 1860, \sigma_r = 150$ and $k = 2.44$. The probability of detection for different values of SNR is shown as Fig.5

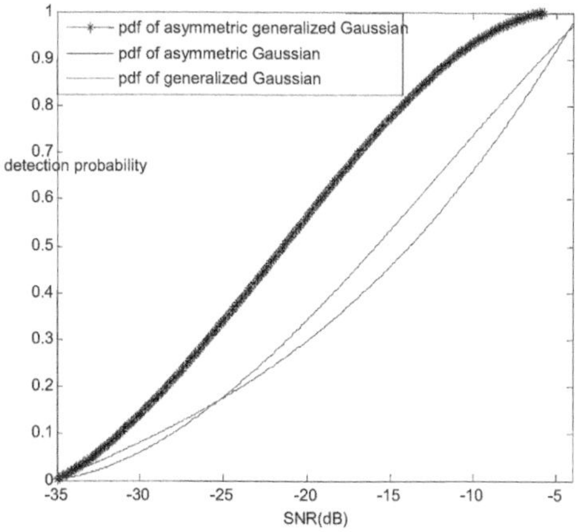

Fig. 5. Comparison of LOD test performances

In the diagram the performances obtained by using the new probability density function model which depends on the kurtosis and on the left and right variance are compared with those provided by a generalized Gaussian model or an asymmetric Gaussian model which depends on the left andright variances. The performance improvement is mainlyassociated to the capability of now probability density function to model non-Gaussian noise in a more realistic way, so it should be better filtered.

References

1. Kassam, S.A.: Signal Detection in Non-Gaussian Noise. Springer, Berlin (1998)
2. Nikes, C., Mendel, J.: Signal Processing with Higher-order spectra. IEEE SP Magazine, 10–37
3. Hench, M.J., Wilson, G.R.: Detection of Non-Gaussian Signals in Non-Gaussian Noise Using the Bispectrum. IEEE Trans. on ASSP 38(3), 1126–1131 (1990)
4. Barni, M., Bartolini, De, F., Piva, R.M.: A new decoder for the optimum recovery of nonadditive watermarks. IEEE Trans. on Image Processing 10(5), 755–765 (2006)
5. Sangfelt, E., Persson, L.: Experimental Performance of Some Higher-Order Cumulant Detectors for Hydro acoustic Transients. In: Proc. of IEEE HOS Workshop, pp. 182–186 (June 2005)
6. Zhao, J., Kunder, E.: Embedding Robust Labels into Image for Copyright Protection. Image and Signal Processing 143, 251–256 (2004)
7. Tesei, A., Thomas, J.B.: Signal Detection in Non-Gaussian Noise by a Kurtosis-Based ProbabilityDensity Function Model. In: Tesei, A., Thomas, J.B. (eds.) IEEE Workshop on HOS, pp. 162–165. 162-165 (2005)
8. Webster, R.J.: Ambient Noise Statistics. IEEETrans. on SP 41(6), 229–236 (2004)
9. Miller, J.H., Thomas, J.B.: Detector for Discrete-Time Signal in Non-Gaussian Noise. IEEE Trans. on IT 18(2), 241–250 (1972)
10. Joshi, R.J., Fischer, T.R.: Comparison of generalized Gaussian and Laplacian modeling in DCT image coding. IEEE Trans. on signal Processing Letters 2(5), 81–82 (1995)
11. Regazzoni, C.S., Tesei, A., Tacconi, G.: A Comparison Between Spectral and Bispectral Analysis for Ship Detection from Acoustical Time Series. In: Proc. of ICASSP 2006, pp. 289–292 (April 2006)
12. Kamran, S., Alberto, L.: Estimation of Shape Parameter for Generalized Gaussian Distribution in Subband Decompositions of Video. IEEE Trans on Circuits and Systems for Video Technology 5(1), 52–56 (1995)

New Development of Simulation Methods on Refrigeration and Air Conditioning Equipments

Cao Wensheng

College of Mechanical Engineering University of Jimei
Xiamen 361021, China
wenshengcao@sina.cn

Abstract. Development status of classical simulation technology and application status of artificial intelligence on refrigeration and air conditioning equipments were introduced. The new concept of intelligence simulation was also primarily introduced, and the further development direction of simulation and optimization was put forward lastly. The modern artificial intelligence technology (fuzzy-neural network method) improving on the traditional numerical simulation has theoretic and practical inevitability. Only the combination of the fuzzy-neural network method and the traditional simulation model is likely to get the optimal general simulation effect. The intelligence simulation method of refrigeration and air conditioning equipments has well application foreground.

Keywords: refrigeration and air conditioning equipments, artificial intelligence, fuzzy-neural network, intelligence simulation, new development.

1 Introduction

It is the pursuing aim to improve the performance and reduce power consumption of refrigeration and air conditioning equipments (refrigerator, freezer, air-condition, etc.). The refrigeration and air conditioning equipments are faced with how to re-matching after using the new refrigerants in the big background of CFCs substitute. So the research is imperative that how to use advanced methods to accomplish the optimal matching of equipments so as to save energy and materials.

The existing development mode of refrigeration and air conditioning products may generalize "academic forecast + experiment + experience", and "experiment + experience" is main part. The reliability of experience and rule is affected by various factors and the effective applying range is restricted more often. Although experiment is direct and reliable, mass tests result in high cost and long period of product development. The introduction of computer simulation methods replacing experiment offers an effective approach for the design modernization of refrigeration and air conditioning products. At present, the simulation technology of refrigeration and air conditioning systems has been developing considerably, but the simulation precision and adjustability are still short in the face of diversity and complicacy of actual equipments. In order to improve more the simulation precision and adjustability and practicality, it is needed to bring into play the advantage of interdisciplinary subjects,

D. Zeng (Ed.): ICAIC 2011, Part I, CCIS 224, pp. 463–468, 2011.

such as introducing artificial intelligence technology into the simulation of refrigeration and air conditioning systems.

2 Development Status of Classical Simulation Technology on Refrigeration and Air Conditioning Equipments

From late 1970s to early 1980s, some international researchers had started to develop the simulation work of system performance on refrigeration and air conditioning equipments.

The development of classical simulation research was enslaved to the contradiction between model accuracy and calculation complexity first. In the early research work, it mostly was algorithm to solve differential equations. For being sure calculation stability and not very long calculation time, very small time step (dynamic simulation) and simple lumped parameter model (low precision) were used. Later in the 1980s, an implicit difference scheme was adopted to improve calculation stability and increase time step. It was possible to consider establishing distributed parameter model to enhance the description ability of actual object of study. But many deemed relative subordinate factors were ignored out of consideration of calculation speed and actual effect. In the 1990s, the lumped parameter and distributed parameter models had developed to a certain extent. The research started to transform to practicality and a lot of works to different actual objects had been done such as refrigerator, car air conditioning and air-condition etc. Although the above simulation technology on refrigeration and air conditioning equipments based on numerical calculation has been developing comparatively nowadays, the more practicality falls across unprecedented resistance. The complicacy of model and arithmetic affects practicality, and simple model can not ensure precision and applicability. So it is needed to seek breakthrough and innovation in the study means for more simulation practicality.

The development of simulation research on refrigeration and air conditioning equipments is restricted to the model description ability to the actual object characteristic yet. At present, many phenomena can not be expounded accurately in theory such as two-phase flow. Moreover, many research issues are very sensitive to environment conditions (such as manufacturing technics, term of use etc.), and theoretic perfect research results are hard to apply to actual objects such as heat transfer coefficient equation. In the former studies, researchers almost adopted the method of "select best", namely chose the one which was closest to the test result after comparing calculation and test results through one by one tryout on the former foundation research outcomes (sometimes the outcome of certain hypothesis and experience). But the outcomes of various researches may be inconsistent so as to be difficult to get the universal conclusion such as the choice of vacuole coefficient on refrigeration and air conditioning equipments.

Selecting simple model and arithmetic is good for simulation practicality, at the same time being sure the model has good description ability to the actual object. The classical numerical simulation is difficult to meet the above two requirements, so it is needed to look for way out from the crossed subjects.

3 Application Status of Artificial Intelligence in Refrigeration and Air Conditioning Industry

The modern artificial intelligence technology (expert system, artificial neural network and fuzzy theory are representative) has been primarily applied in recent years. We can see from these research statuses:

1) Adopting the modern artificial intelligence technology to study actual application questions which are hard to resolve by the traditional theory may get better actual effect. The classical theory is short of accurate description ability to actual objects that is difficult to adapt the complicated task requirements due to the characteristics of complicacy, time change and high nonlinearity of refrigeration and air conditioning equipments. Resolving these questions is just the advantage of intelligence method. The artificial intelligence is mainly applied in the following aspects: ①intelligent control; ②fault diagnosis and monitoring; ③load forecast.

2) The researchers basically bypassed the traditional theory and directly apply the artificial intelligence technology in dealing with the relationship of the traditional theory and the modern artificial intelligence technology. This type of application is unlikely to all questions. Some actual questions are lucubrated on academic study, but there is some difference between theory and fact that is hard to accordant modification for theory model is always based on perfect hypothesis. In this case, it is not the best way to resolve the question adopting the artificial intelligence technology completely that bypasses the traditional theory because the formative process of artificial intelligence needs continuous study and adjustment and there is the question of efficiency and effect in existence. Furthermore, the sheer artificial intelligence model only reflects the outside behavior of the study object and it's difficult to analyze the inside characteristic deeply.

3) The artificial intelligence technology is under development. Although it can overcome the shortages of the classical simulation in some aspects, the function of comparative parts of artificial intelligence can not meet the existing effect of the classical simulation. The new concept of the classical simulation combined with the artificial intelligence may learn from other's strong points to offset one's weakness. The two aspect study results of the classical simulation and the artificial intelligence laid a solid foundation for the combination of both sides.

4 The Raise of the Intelligence Simulation Method on Refrigeration and Air Conditioning Equipments

At a word, the integration of the traditional numerical simulation theory and the modern artificial intelligence technology comes into being the intelligence simulation method on refrigeration and air conditioning equipments. The main reason of studying the intelligence simulation method is that it is provided with the function of self-learning, self-adapting and self-organizing. There is a very large difference between the mathematical tool of the intelligence simulation study and the traditional simulation method. The mathematical tool of the traditional simulation theory is numerical calculation method essentially. But, the one of the artificial intelligence is mainly symbolic reasoning and first-order predicate logic etc. The mathematical tool of the intelligence simulation study is cross and combination of the above two sides. This combination expresses diverse forms including the most active neural network theory and fuzzy set theory recently. The neural network theory implements complicated function relationship through many simple relations which is nonlinear dynamics system that does not depend on models. The fuzzy set theory utilizes formulae to logic reasoning, but its logic value is continuous change from 0 to 1 which is processed by numerical method instead of symbolic method. These two methods are like with the artificial intelligence in some aspects such as logic relationship and being independent of models, and alike with usual numerical method of the traditional simulation theory in other aspects such as running value and nonlinear dynamics characteristic. So they are the mathematical tools between the both and the main study tool of the intelligence simulation for the future.

Because adopting pure fuzzy-neural network method has limitation, it is needed to combine the traditional numerical simulation and the fuzzy-neural network method to form the intelligence simulation method of refrigeration and air conditioning equipments based on the traditional theory model. On the one hand, the correctional fuzzy-neural network model coupling with the traditional theory model using the fuzzy-neural network method makes the simulation forecast result more close to the actual test data through self-learning and self-adapting. On the other hand, the supply of part input values of the fuzzy-neural network model using excellent qualitative simulation performance of the traditional theory model may effectively lessen learning capacity and improve learning speed. For the traditional theory model covers the key input parameters of configuration etc, the input parameters of the fuzzy-neural network model could be simplified, as well as the fuzzy-network frame that are good for the frame optimization of refrigeration and air conditioning equipments. Moreover, the very complicated, experienced and uncertain parts of the traditional theory model may come under the fuzzy-neural network model to simplify the traditional model and to improve robustness of simulation calculation. From the more thought, how to make the traditional theory model and the fuzzy-neural network model to accomplish optimal matching is a farther requisite research matter.

Fig.1 is elementary structure of the intelligence simulation on refrigeration and air conditioning equipments. The integrated models of the traditional theory mode (TTM) and the fuzzy-neural network model (FNNM) have multifold combination modes, such as Fig.2 and Fig.3 shown. The proper combination mode should be chosen to improve overall efficiency.

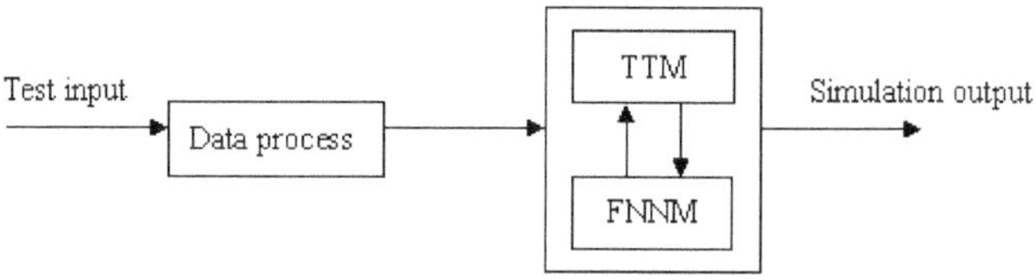

Fig. 1. Elementary structure of the intelligence simulation on refrigeration and air conditioning equipments

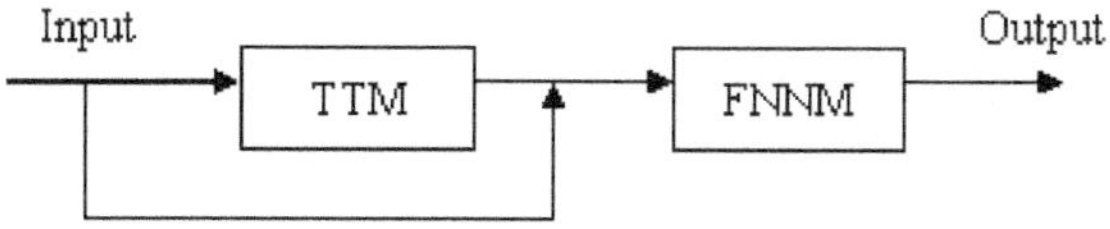

Fig. 2. Combination mode 1 of the intelligence simulation

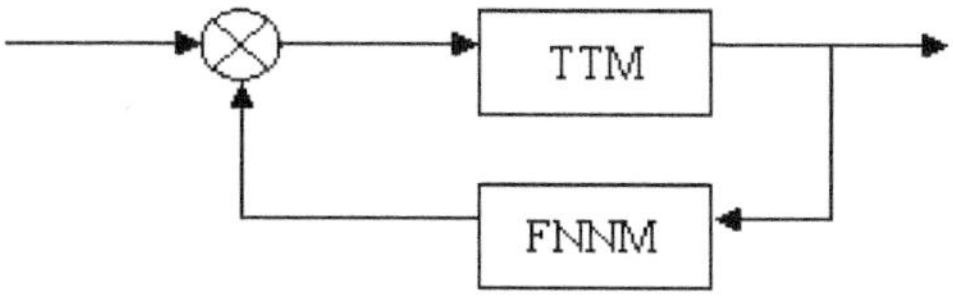

Fig. 3. Combination mode 2 of the intelligence simulation

From Fig.1 we can see, the raise of the intelligence simulation method on refrigeration and air conditioning equipments has enhanced the test study corresponding to simulation a higher level that has never been reached before. The main aim of the test work is to sampling the key characteristic parameters of run process and to transform the required learning sample and test sample of parts and system model after standardization data process and analysis. And it is needed to research how to design and accomplish "the least capacity test", namely using the least capacity test to complete the standard function of simulation. The intelligence simulation on refrigeration and air conditioning equipments causes incorporation from theory to test and from test to theory again, and creates condition for more practicability of simulation technology.

5 Conclusions

1) The modern artificial intelligence technology (fuzzy-neural network method) improving on the traditional numerical simulation has theoretic and practical inevitability. It will blaze a new effective way in refrigeration and air conditioning equipments to more practicability.

2) Only the combination of the fuzzy-neural network method and the traditional simulation model is likely to get the optimal general simulation effect.

3) The intelligence simulation method on refrigeration and air conditioning equipments has well application foreground.

Acknowledgment. This paper is supported by the doctor research fund of Jimei University.

References

1. Ding, G., Zhang, C.: Simulation and optimization of refrigeration and air conditioning equipments. Science press (June 2001)
2. Zhang, C., Ding, G.: Approximate analytic solutions of adiabatic capillary tube. Int. J. Refrig. 27, 17–24 (2004)

3. Sami, S.M., Maltais, H.: Numerical modeling of alternative refrigerants to HCFC-22 through capillary tube. Int. J. Energy Res. 24, 1359–1371 (2000)
4. Cho, C.H., Norden, N.: Computer optimization of refrigeration plants. Int. J. Refrig. 5, 289–294 (1980)
5. Ahrens, F.W.: Heatpump modeling simulation and design. Wisconsin, USA (1981)

Assessing Dynamic Neural Networks for Travel Time Prediction

Luou Shen[1] and Min Huang[2]

[1] School of Civil and Transportation Engineering, South China University of Technology
Guangzhou, Guangdong 510641, China
[2] School of Environmental and Civil Engineering, Wuhan Institute of Technology
Wuhan, Hubei 430073, China
luoushen999@qq.com

Abstract. Ularly suitable for predicting variables like travel time, but has not been adequately investigated. This study compares the travel time prediction performance of three dynamic neural network topologies with different memory settings. The results show that the time-delay neural networks out-performed the other two topologies. This topology also performed slightly better than the multilayer perceptron neural networks.

Keywords: Advanced Traffic Information System, Travel Time Prediction, Detector Data, Dynamic Neural Networks.

1 Introduction

Providing travellers with accurate and reliable traffic information allows them to make more informed decisions and avoid congestion, yielding not only benefits for the individual travellers but also potentially reducing the traffic congestion for the entire transportation network. Traffic management centre (TMC) also needs such information to better evaluate and manage the surface traffic.

Most existing advanced traveller information systems (ATIS) use instantaneous travel times estimated based on the current measurements, assuming traffic conditions will not change from the measured conditions in the near future. For more effective applications, it has been proposed that ATIS should use travel times predicted for short-term future conditions rather than the instantaneous travel times measured or estimated for current conditions. A number of approaches have been used to predict travel time. These approaches can be classified as model-based approaches or data-driven approaches.

The model-based travel time prediction methods predict traffic conditions based on traffic flow theory or real-time traffic simulation. Examples of these methods are the use of DYNAMIT in [1], DYNASMART in [2], and CORSIM in [3]. The predictive quality is strongly influenced by the quality of the input data, the used model, and the model calibration.

Data-driven methods predict travel times based on current and past real-world detector data. The quality of the data, and the parameters used in the development and implementation of the model influence the quality of prediction.

D. Zeng (Ed.): ICAIC 2011, Part I, CCIS 224, pp. 469–477, 2011.

Two of the most popular data-driven methods for travel time prediction are the time series and the Neural Networks (NNs). Time series forecasting uses a statistical model to forecast future events based on known past events. The time series approach was used for travel time prediction in references [4] and [5].

Previous studies illustrated that NNs can provide an accurate and robust approach to travel time prediction. NNs' applications to travel time prediction have included the use of simple Multilayer Perceptron (MLP) in [6], modular neural networks in [7]), and spectral basis neural networks in [8] and [9]. Reference [10] applied fuzzy logic to NNs for dynamic travel time estimation to compress the input data dimension and reduce the model complexity. It was reported in these studies that NNs out-perform other travel time prediction techniques, including the regular time series and Kalman filtering approaches.

Dynamic neural networks (DNNs) as a sub-class of NNs, are particularly suitable for travel time prediction. DNNs take into account spatial and temporal information about traffic conditions simultaneously, and consider travel time from past time intervals as well as the current time interval. However, DNNs have not been adequately explored for travel time prediction. Based on the previous literature, only a sub-class of DNNs called state-space neural networks (SSNNs) has been used for travel time prediction in [11], [12] and [13]. Another important type of NNs referred to as time-delayed neural networks (TDNNs) has been investigated for traffic volume prediction in [14] and [15], but not for travel time prediction. In these studies, TDNNs were shown to have the potential to be superior to MLP for traffic volume prediction.

This paper investigates the ability of a number of DNN topologies with different parameters to predict travel time and compares the performance of these models with the basic MLP.

2. Dynamic Neural Network

Most of the NNs used in previous studies have used travel time information for the current time step. Due to the dynamic nature of traffic conditions, future travel time may also be correlated with traffic conditions at previous time steps. Few of the studies have considered this correlation when developing NNs for travel time prediction.

A DNN model has a short-term memory, in which it stores previous outputs of the network or hidden neuron activities as described in [16]. Thus, it can account for traffic information from previous time steps in its prediction. The DNN model receives input signals from the current time instants and combines these with signals from its memory to make prediction. DNN varies in how the short-term memory is built and how it is applied to the network.

2.1 Short-Term Memory

The simple short-term memory is the time delay (also called time lag), which can be implemented at the synaptic level inside the network or at the input layer of the network. There are two types of delay have been used: tapped delay line memory (TM) and Gamma delay memory (GM). TM is the simplest and commonly used form. With the help of the *z*-transform, which is also called the unit delay operator, the current input signal can be transformed to a previous signal for the next time-step; that is, when z^{-1} operates on $x(t)$, it yields its delayed version $x(t-1)$. In Figure 1-(a), the z^{-1} operator is applied p times, resulting in p unit delays. As indicated in Figure 1-(b), with GM, the output of a junction has combined information from the current inputs (with weight of μ) and the unit delay inputs (with weight of $1-\mu$).

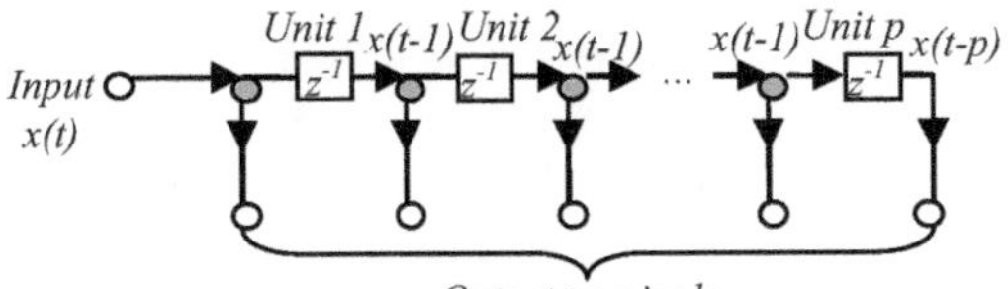

(a) Tapped Delay Line Memory

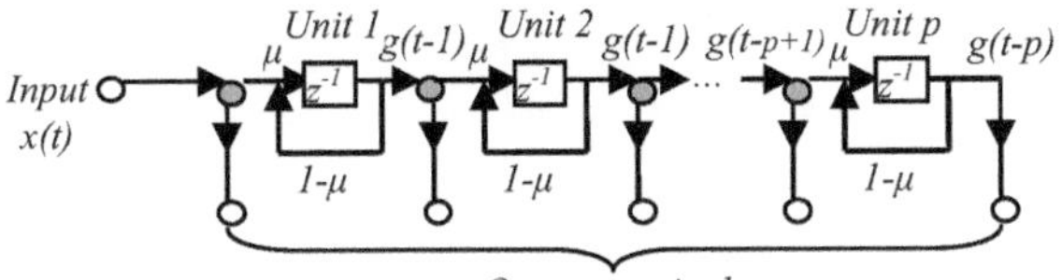

(b) Gamma Memory

Fig. 1. Short-Term Memories

2.2 Feedback Application

There are two basic ways of applying feedback to NNs: local feedback at a single neuron inside the network and global feedback encompassing the entire network. Given a multilayer perceptron as the basic building block, local feedback can be applied to the input layer, at which the previous inputs are combined with the current instant input information which is called time-delayed neural network. The NNs with global feedback is referred to as a recurrent neural network (RNN). The use of global feedback has the potential to reduce the required memory significantly compared to normal NNs solutions. The simplest RNN is the state-space neural network, which includes feedbacks from the hidden layer to the input layer but it allows the inclusion of only one time lag memory. However, a more generalized SSNN model allows various time lags.

This study investigates the use of both TDNN and generalized SSNN models. In addition, this study investigates the use of a third structure refer to as the “fully RNN.” This structure allows the implementation of a memory with various time lags both on the input layer and the hidden layer which referred to fully RNN. The three structures are demonstrated in Figure 2.

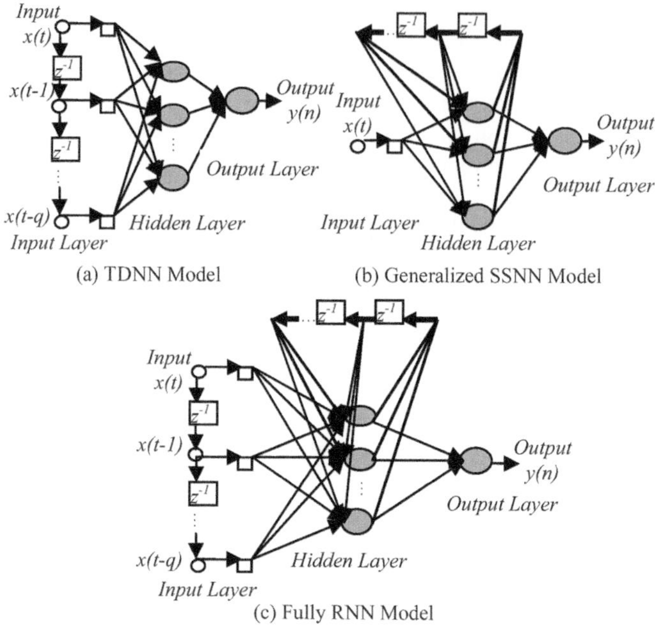

Fig. 2. DNN Model Topologies

3 Scope of the Study

The qualities of the predicted travel times using the explored DNN models were compared with the MLP model, and the estimated instantaneous travel time.

In addition to the above, this study investigates the influences of an important parameter of travel time prediction, the rolling step, which defines the temporal resolution of input data in terms of the time interval at which the historical travel time data is aggregated. The current predicted travel time can be displayed on dynamic message signs (DMSs) that disseminate travel time information to vehicles passing by them.

4 Methodology

In this study, travel time prediction using DNNs was investigated using traffic detector data collected from an 8.25-mile stretch of southbound I-95 segment in Broward County, Florida. These detectors are placed approximately one-half mile apart along the corridor. The detectors capture traffic data such as speed, traffic flow, and occupancy at a 20-second interval.

Target data is needed for NNs training before the learned network can be used for prediction. The trajectory method from a previous study of [17] was used to produce the target travel time from the training input data which is the detector data: speed and traffic flow. This travel time estimation method has been proved to be performing very well with a low average error of 2.8%.

The training traffic detector data were collected along the study segment between 6:00 AM and 9:00 PM which covers the AM, MD and PM peak periods. The study dataset includes three month's worth of data from June to August 2007. The June and July data were used for NNs training, while the August data were used for model testing. To investigate the effect of the length of the rolling step, the training and testing processes were conducted separately for each rolling step from 1 minute to 5 minutes.

The performance measures used were the mean absolute error (MAE) and mean absolute percentage error (MAPE), calculated using the following formulas:

$$MAE = \frac{1}{n}\sum_{i}|O_i - D_i| \tag{1}$$

$$MAPE = \frac{1}{n}\sum_{i}\frac{|O_i - D_i|}{D_i} \tag{2}$$

where O_i is the model output value and D_i is the desired value.

With the software of NeuroSolutions, the NN structure such as the number of neurons in the hidden layer was automatically optimized using the imbedded genetic algorithm function. And the performances of the optimized networks for different models are presented in the following section with comparison.

The testing of the developed models was carried out first for the entire daytime period using data from three weekdays of August during the testing process. Meanwhile, testing was performed separately for selected periods that exhibit considerable congestion. Four intervals were identified that were particularly congested in the three days. These periods were from 3:02 PM to 6:04 PM of the first day, from 7:52 AM to 9:14 AM and from 12:30 PM to 6:45 PM of the second day, and from 11:13 AM to 12:27 PM of the third day. According to the incident information, lane blockage incidents occurred for the first three of the four peaks mentioned above. The duration of these lane blockages were 91, 32, and 59 minutes, respectively. The fourth peak also represents a non-recurrent congestion condition, although no incident could be identified based on the incident management database. Conducting separate testing for the congested periods that include lane-blockage incidents allows for better examination of the performance of the model, which is more challenging and useful than the prediction in the other low traffic periods.

5 Results

The performance measures for the optimized DNN models and MLP model, compared to the instantaneous travel time are shown in Figure 3 for both the entire daytime period and congestion period.

The results presented in Figure 3 indicate that the predictions using the DNN models and MLP model out-perform the instantaneous travel time estimation. The MAPE was reduced by 40% for predicted travel time for daytime conditions and about 25% for the congestion conditions, compared to the instantaneous travel time. As can be seen, the performance of the travel time prediction during the congested conditions of all tested networks was not as good as that during daytime conditions.

Figure 4 shows that the best performing DNN model works better than the MLP model, particularly for congested/incident conditions. It is determined that up to 16%

improvement in the prediction for congested conditions and 10% improvement for daytime conditions for the DNN model compared to the MLP model.

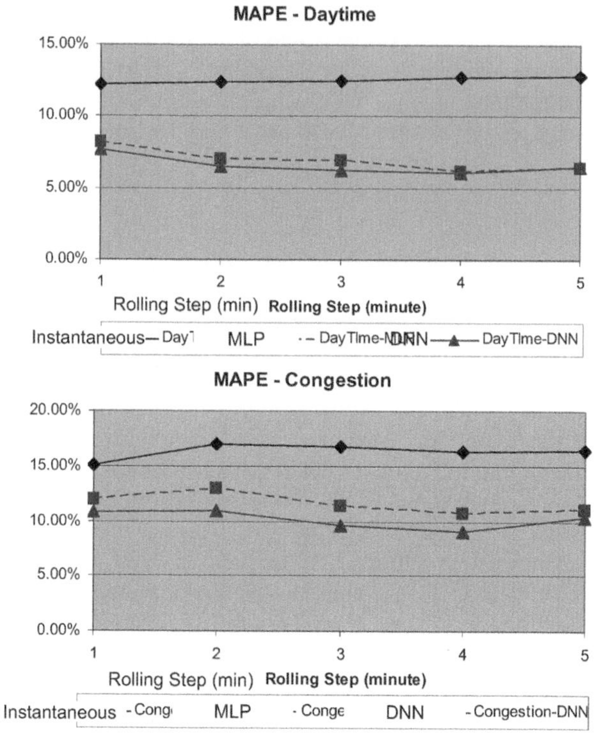

Fig. 3. MAPE of DNN and MLP Prediction Compared to Instantaneous Prediction

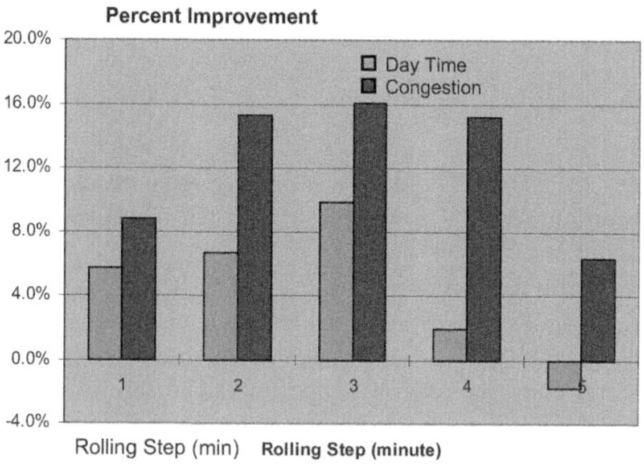

Fig. 4. Performance Improvement of DNN Compared to MLP

The performances of the DNN structures are shown in Table 1. Since the trend of the performances is similar for all the five rolling steps, only the results of the 4-minute rolling step are presented which has the best performance compared to other rolling steps.

Table 1 shows that MLP model performed close to or better than most of the investigated DNN models for all rolling steps. This indicates that the travel time estimated based on the current time step data is an important determining factor for future travel time prediction. Only the TDNN model was found to perform better than the MLP model for all aggregation time intervals. This means that the use of the immediate past traffic conditions is also correlated with the future travel time and can improve travel time prediction accuracy.

Table 1. Prediction Results of DNN Models Compared to the MLP Model

Rolling Step	Model	Daytime (6AM~9PM)		Congestion Time	
		MAE	MAPE	MAE	MAPE
4-minute	MLP	0.53	6.18%	0.92	10.7%
	TDNN-TM-1 lag	**0.52**	**6.0%**	**0.78**	**9.1%**
	TDNN-TM-2 lag	0.70	8.1%	1.28	14.9%
	TDNN-GM-1 lag	0.56	6.5%	1.08	12.6%
	TDNN-GM-2 lag	0.59	6.8%	1.11	13.0%
	Generalized SSNN-1 lag	0.67	7.8%	1.46	17.1%
	Generalized SSNN-2 lag	0.72	8.5%	1.33	15.5%
	Fully RNN-TM-1 lag	0.69	8.0%	1.39	16.3%
	Fully RNN+TM-2 lag	0.69	8.0%	1.35	15.7%
	Fully RNN+GM-1 lag	0.74	8.7%	1.53	17.9%
	Fully RNN+GM-2 lag	0.76	8.9%	1.55	18.1%

Note: MAE units is minute

The TDNN model with tapped delay line memory worked better than other DNN models. The TDNN model with local feedback worked better than the generalized SSNN model with global feedback and the fully RNN model that includes both local and global feedback. In most cases, the TDNN models that worked best had only one time lag, and a few have two time lags. Thus, it can be concluded that only the very near past information can be useful for prediction for the investigated transportation system. The best performance was achieved when a TDNN model was used with one time lag and a 4-minute rolling step (MAPE equal to 9.1%). The best performance achieved with the MLP was also with the 4-minute rolling step (MAPE equal to 10.7%).

6 Conclusion

Based on the results presented in this paper, it can be concluded that both TDNN model and MLP model were able to produce better predictions of travel time compared to the use of instantaneous travel time. The prediction results in increasing the accuracy of travel time by about 40% for the daytime conditions and by 25% for the congestion periods. The TDNN topology with 2-, 3-, and 4-minute rolling steps and tapped delay time memory was found to out-perform various configurations of MLP model, Generalized SSNN model, and fully RNN model. However, the improvement in the prediction with the use of TDNN model compared to the use of MLP model was relatively small for the investigated transportation system. The better performance of TDNN model compared to Generalized SSNN model and Fully RNN model indicates that local feedback works better than global feedback. The TDNN model with only one time lag performed the best among the investigated time lags, indicating that only the information from the immediate past time step is useful for travel time prediction.

The above findings may be affected by the size of the system under consideration. For example, if data are available from detectors located long distances upstream of the segment for which travel time prediction is needed, the information from previous time lags will be more relevant to the estimation and the DNN structures are expected to become more effective compared to MLP model. It is recommended that an additional investigation be made of the effect of the size of the freeway network and the location of upstream detectors on travel time prediction to determine how these factors will affect the conclusions from this study.

References

1. Ben-Akiva, M., Cuneo, D., Hasan, M., Jha, M., Yang, Q.: Evaluation of freeway control using a microscopic simulation laboratory. Transportation Research Part C: Emerging Technologies 11(1), 29–50 (2003)
2. Hu, T.Y.: Evaluation framework for dynamic vehicle routing strategies under real-time information. Transportation Research Record, 1774, Transportation Research Board, Washington, DC, pp. 115–122 (2001)
3. Liu, Y., Lin, P.-W., Lai, X., Chang, G.-L., Marquess, A.: Developments and Applications of Simulation-Based Online Travel Time Prediction System: Traveling to Ocean City, Maryland. Transportation Research Record, 1959, Transportation Research Board, Washington, D.C, pp. 92–104 (2006)
4. D'Angelo, M., Al-Deek, H., Wang, M.: Travel time prediction for freeway corridors. Transportation Research Record 1676, 184–191 (1999)
5. Ishak, S., Al-Deek, H.: Performance evaluation of short-term time-series traffic prediction model. Journal of Transportation Engineering 128(6), 490–498 (2002)
6. Innamaa, S.: Short-term prediction of travel time using neural networks on an interurban highway. Transportation 32, 649–669 (2005)
7. Park, D., Rilett, L.R.: Forecasting multiple period freeway link travel times using modular neural networks. Transportation Research Record, 1617, Transportation Research Board, Washington, DC, pp. 163–170 (1998)
8. Park, D., Rilett, L.R., Han, G.: Spectral basis neural networks for real-time link travel times forecasting. Journal of Transportation Engineering 125(6), 515–523 (1999)
9. Rilett, L.R., Park, D.: Direct forecasting of freeway corridor travel times using spectral basis neural networks. Transportation Research Record, 1752, Transportation Research Board, Washington, DC, pp. 140–147 (2001)
10. Palacharla, P.V., Nelson, P.C.: Application of fuzzy logic and neural networks for dynamic travel time estimation. International Transactions in Operational Research 6, 145–160 (1999)

11. Van Lint, J.W.C., Hoogendoorn, S.P., Van Zuylen, H.J.: Freeway travel time prediction with state-space neural networks -modeling state-space dynamics with recurrent neural networks. Transportation Research Record, 1811, Transportation Research Board, Washington, DC, pp. 30–39 (2002)
12. Van Lint, J.W.C.: Reliable real-time framework for short-term freeway travel time prediction. Journal of Transportation Engineering 132(12), 921–932 (2006)
13. Liu, H., Van Zuylen, H., Van Lint, H., Salomons, M.: Predicting urban arterial travel time with state-space neural networks and Kalman filters. Transportation Research Record, 1968, Transportation Research Board, Washington, D.C, pp. 99–108 (2006)
14. Lingras, P., Sharma, S., Zhong, M.: Prediction of recreational travel using genetically designed regression and time-delay neural networks model. Transportation Research Record, 1805, Transportation Research Board, Washington, DC, pp. 16–24 (2002)
15. Ishak, S., Kotha, P., Alecsandru, C.: Optimization of dynamic neural networks performance for short-term traffic prediction. Transportation Research Record, 1836, Transportation Research Board, Washington, DC, pp. 45–56 (2003)
16. Haykin, S.: Neural networks – A comprehensive foundation, 2nd edn. Prentice-Hall Inc., Englewood Cliffs (1999)
17. Shen, L., Hadi, M.: Estimation of Segment Travel Time Based on Point Traffic Detector Measurements. In: Proceeding of Transportation Research Board 88th Annual Meeting, Washington, DC (2009)

Fault Feature Extraction of Gearboxes Using Ensemble Empirical Mode Decomposition

Jinshan Lin

School of Mechanical and Electronic Engineering
Weifang University
Weifang, Shandong Province, P.R. China
jinshanlinwf@126.com

Abstract. The paper employs ensemble empirical mode decomposition (EEMD) to extract the fault information from the signal collected from a defective gearbox. In view of the shortcoming of the mode mixing which empirical mode decomposition (EMD) fails to overcome, the EEMD method is used to decompose the signal captured from the defective gearbox and successfully separate the different components from high frequency to low frequency. Then, the first four intrinsic mode functions (IMFs), containing the most energy of the signal, are extracted; by analyzing the spectrum of the first four components, we succeed in uncovering the reason causing the fault of the gearbox. The results show that the EEMD method could be feasible to diagnose the fault of the gearbox.

Keywords: feature extraction, gearbox, emsemble empirical mode decomposition(EEMD), intrinsic mode function(IMF).

1 Introduction

Gearboxes usually serve a fundamental role in mechanical systems, and their condition monitoring and fault diagnosis have been drawing widespread interests [1]. When gearboxes malfunction, the vibration signals captured from them are non-stationary [2]. Unfortunately, because of the absence of proper techniques for analyzing the non-stationary signals, the vibration signals from defective gearboxes have been usually processed as the stationary signals. Empirical mode decomposition (EMD), a novel method for signal processing, has been proved to be fit for analyzing the non-stationary and nonlinear signal [3]. However, one of the main deficiencies occurring in the EMD method is the mode mixing, which limits the practical applications of the EMD method to some extent.

Ensemble EMD (EEMD), fully taking advantage of the uniformly statistical feature of the white noise, adds the white noise with the limited amplitude to the signal and effectively overcomes the mode mixing existing in the EMD method [4]. The paper exploits the EEMD to extract the fault information from a defective gearbox. The proposed scheme successfully alleviated the mode mixing, enhanced the frequency resolution and was effective for the fault diagnosis of the gearbox.

D. Zeng (Ed.): ICAIC 2011, Part I, CCIS 224, pp. 478–483, 2011.

2 Ensemble Empirical Mode Decomposition

Being considered as a consequence of signal intermittency, the mode mixing, whose definition is that an individual intrinsic mode function (IMF) holds dramatically disparate scales, or some scale signal is split into different IMF components, is one principal drawback of the EMD; it leads to the serious aliasing in the plane of time-frequency distribution as well as the unclear physical meaning of individual IMF [4].

A new noise-assisted method named the ensemble EMD (EEMD) is introduced to relieve the mode mixing problem of the EMD. The EEMD obtains the true IMF components by averaging the overall trials, each of which comprises the signal plus a white noise with finite amplitude. The ensemble method can clearly separate the natural scales of a signal without beforehand selecting any a subjective criterion [4].

The EEMD algorithm can be stated as follows [4], [5]:

(1) Initialize the ensemble number M and the amplitude of the added white noise, let $M = 1$.

(2) Implement the mth trial for the signal added the white noise.

(a) Add the white noise series with the given amplitude to the investigated signal, that is

$$x_m(t) = x(t) + n_m(t) \tag{1}$$

where $n_m(t)$ represents the mth added white noise, and $x_m(t)$ indicates the noise-added signal of the mth trial.

(b) Decompose the signal $x_m(t)$ into l IMFs c_{im} (i=1,2,…,l, m=1,2,…,M) using the EMD method, where c_{im} indicates the ith IMF of the mth trial; l is the number of IMFs and M means the number of the ensemble.

(c) If $m<M$, then let $m=m+1$and iterate the step (a) and (b) until $m=M$, but with different white noise each time.

(3) Compute the ensemble mean $\overline{c_i}$ of the M trials for each IMF, and we obtain

$$\overline{c_i} = \frac{1}{M}\sum_{m=1}^{M} c_{i,m}. \tag{2}$$

(4) Consider the mean $\overline{c_i}$ (i=1,2,…,l) of l IMFs as the final ith IMF.

The above section has illustrated the EEMD algorithm and its specific operating steps. In addition, before employing the EEMD, we need to set two parameters: the number of the ensemble and the amplitude of white noise. Next, we will discuss how to choose these two parameters.

The effect of the added white noise ought to comply with the following statistical rule [4]:

$$e_n = \frac{a}{\sqrt{N}}, \tag{3}$$

where N is the number of the ensemble, a indicates the amplitude of the added white noise, and e_n means the standard deviation of error, which is the discrepancy between the input signal and the corresponding IMFs [4].

To make the EEMD effective, the amplitude of the added white noise must be large enough to cause the change of extrema that the EMD depends on. Although the added white noise may result in some errors, it only causes the little effect as long as the ensemble number is large enough. Generally, an ensemble number of a few hundreds will produce an exact result, and the remaining noise would cause no more than a fraction of one percent of error if the added noise has the amplitude that is a fraction of the standard deviation of the investigated signal [4].

Being an improved dyadic filter, the EEMD decomposition is a noise-friendly method. Within a certain range of noise amplitude, the decomposition results of the EEMD have a small sensitivity to the noise amplitude; thus the decomposition results are hardly changed with the increase of the noise amplitude and the ensemble number if the amplitude of the added noise is moderate and the ensemble number is large enough. However, to effectively lower the contribution of the added noise to the decomposition results, the ensemble number should increase with the increment of the noise amplitude. Different from the decomposition results of the EMD, those of the EEMD are unique and robust. It is suggested that the proper amplitude of the added noise be about 0.2 time of the standard deviation of the investigated signal. Nevertheless, it is not always proper for any case since there is not a specific guide to choose the noise amplitude. Consequently, we have to evaluate different noise levels for picking out the relatively appropriate one [4].

3 Applications of eemd to Fault Feature Extraction of Gearboxes

The gearbox to be investigated is double-stage driving and has three shafts; besides, an additional mass fixed on the flywheel of the output shaft is used to simulate the misalignment of the output shaft. The tooth numbers of the first pair of gears are 25 and 42, respectively; those of the second pair of gears are 23 and 55, respectively. According to the input rotation speed of 1130 r/m, we can obtain the rotation frequencies of the three shafts, which are 18.77Hz, 11Hz, and 4.67Hz, respectively; similarly, we can obtain the mesh frequencies of the two pairs of gears, which are 469Hz and 257Hz, respectively.

Fig. 1 demonstrates the time waveform of the acceleration signal in the vicinity of bearing of the output shaft. To further survey the fault occurring in the gearbox, we used the EEMD method to decompose the signal. According to [4], the amplitude of the added white noise is 0.2 time of the standard deviation of the investigated signal

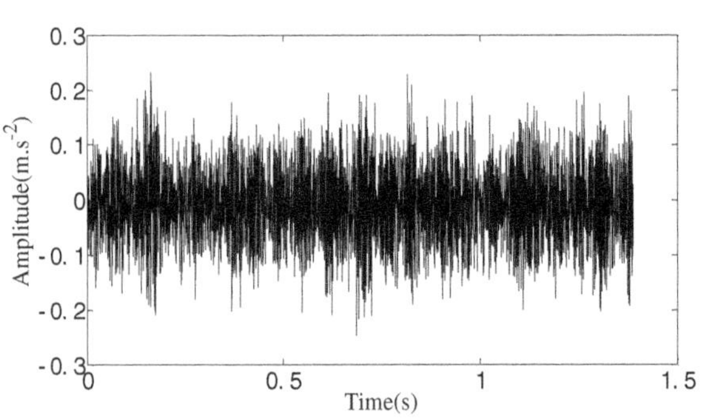

Fig. 1. The time waveform of the acceleration signal

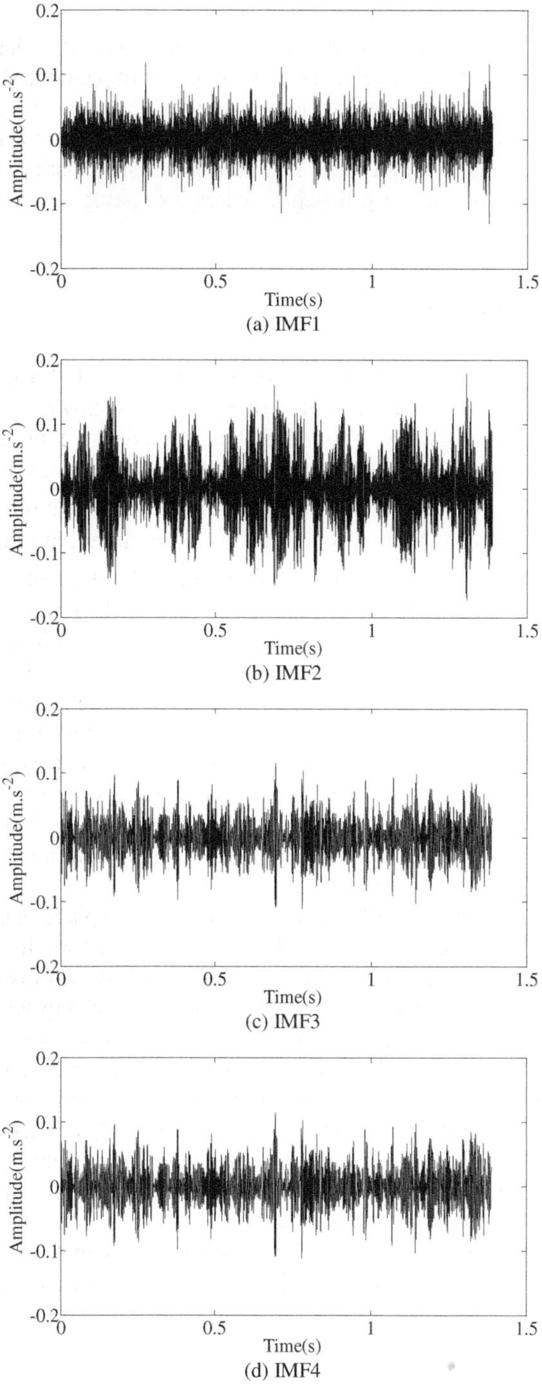

Fig. 2. The first four IMFs from EEMD

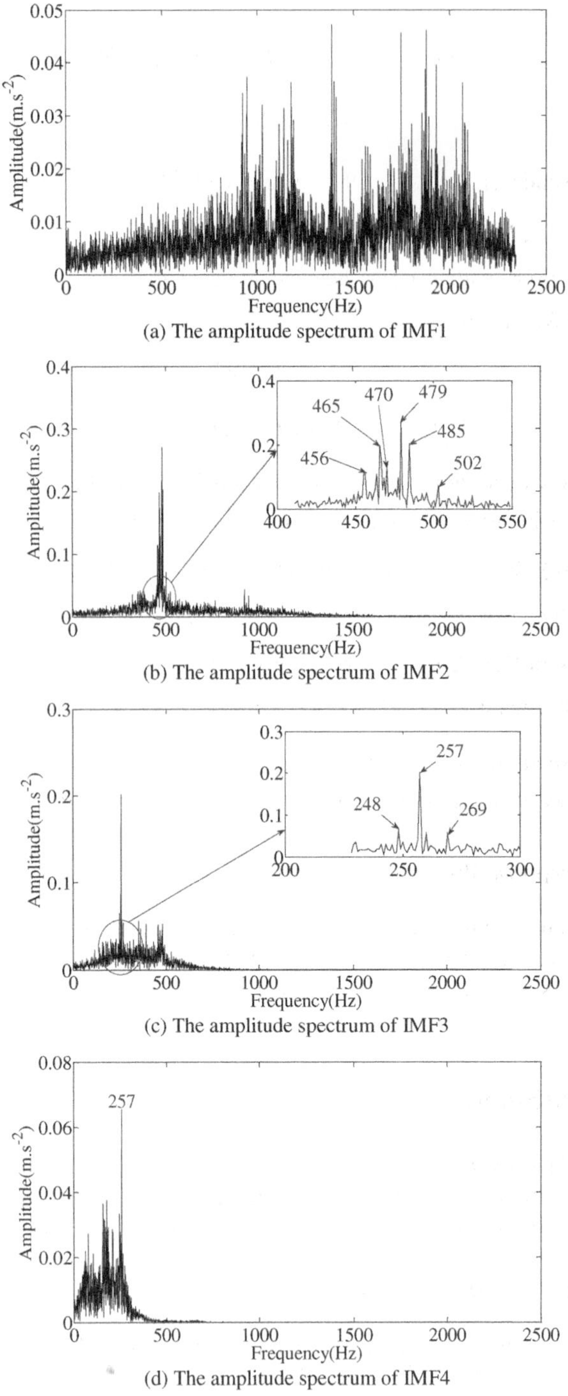

(a) The amplitude spectrum of IMF1

(b) The amplitude spectrum of IMF2

(c) The amplitude spectrum of IMF3

(d) The amplitude spectrum of IMF4

Fig. 3. The amplitude spectrum of the first four IMFs

and the ensemble number is 100. As a result, a group of eleven IMFs were obtained and, here, we only examined the first four IMFs, which contained the most energy of the signal. The time signals of the first four IMFs are illustrated in Fig. 2 and the amplitude spectrum in Fig. 3.

Fig. 3 indicates that the components of IMF1-IMF4 are obviously separated from high frequency to low frequency, which implies that the EEMD method successfully relieves the mode mixing problem appearing in the EMD method. Fig. 3(b) reveals that the frequencies close to the multiplication of the rotation frequency of the input shaft occur on either side of the mesh frequency of the first pair of gears. Fig. 3(c) exhibits that the frequency close to the double of the rotation frequency of the output shaft appears on the either side of the mesh frequency of the second pair of gears. Generally, Fig. 3 presents that either of IMF2 and IMF3 is characterized by the modulation in which the mesh frequencies of the two pairs of gears are the carrier frequency and the rotation frequency of the output shaft as well as its frequency multiplication is the modulation frequency. In accordance with [2], we could conclude that there occurs a misalignment of the output shaft in the investigated gearbox, which suggests the EEMD method successfully uncovers the fault existing in the gearbox.

4 Conclusions

Given the deficiency of the mode mixing appearing in the EMD, the paper utilizes the EEMD method to decompose the signal from a defective gearbox. The first four IMFs are extracted, holding the most energy of the signal. Next, by analyzing the spectrum of the first four components, the paper is successful in revealing the fault of the gearbox. The used method effectively alleviates the mode mixing and heightens the accuracy of fault diagnosis. The results show that the EEMD is feasible to diagnose the fault of the gearbox and the paper seems to provide a novel scheme for the fault diagnosis of gearboxes.

Acknowledgment. This project is supported by Key Subject Research Foundation of Shandong Province.

References

1. Bartelmus, W., Zimroz, R.: A new feature for monitoring the condition of gearboxes in non-stationary operating conditions. Mechanical system and signal processing 23, 1528–1534 (2009), doi:10.1016/j.ymssp.2009.01.014
2. Ding, K., Li, W., Zhu, X.: The practical technology of fault diagnosis for gears and gearbox, pp. 10–27, 96–97. China Machine Press, Beijing (2005)
3. Huang, N.E., Shen, S.S.P.: Hilbert-Huang Transform and Its Applications, vol. 5, pp. 5–14. World Scientific Publishing, Singapore (2005)
4. Wu, Z.H., Huang, N.E.: Ensemble empirical mode decomposition: a noise-assisted data analysis method. Advances in Adaptive Data Analysis 1, 1–41 (2009), doi: 10.1142/S1793536909000047
5. Lei, Y., He, Z., Zi, Y.: Application of the EEMD method to rotor fault diagnosis of rotating machinery. Mechanical system and signal processing 23, 1327–1338 (2009), doi:10.1016/j.ymssp.2008.11.005

Data Mining Method for Incident duration Prediction

Luou Shen[1] and Min Huang[2]

[1] School of Civil and Transportation Engineering South China University of Technology
Guangzhou, Guangdong 510641, China
[2] School of Environment and Civil Engineering Wuhan Institute of Technology
Wuhan, Hubei 430073, China
luoushen999@qq.com

Abstract. Traffic incident management and information dissemination strategies will benefit from the prediction of incident duration in real time. This study investigates the development of an incident duration prediction model based on a detailed historical incident database. A data mining technique, namely the Bayesian Network was applied to develop the prediction models. The analysis results suggest that the Bayesian Network model is advantageous in terms of accurate prediction and the convenience of application.

Keywords: Incident Management, Incident Duration Prediction, Data Mining, Bayesian Network.

1 Introduction

Incidents are a major contributor to traffic congestions. As reported by Lindley in reference [1], up to 60% of all traffic congestion on freeways is caused by incidents. An important aspect of incident management is to inform travelers about traffic congestion and alternative routes using dynamic message signs, highway advisor radios, advanced traveler information telephone and website. The incident management and information dissemination strategies mentioned above will benefit from the prediction of incident durations in real-time. This prediction will allow making better incident management response strategies and providing more accurate and reliable information to travelers.

The incident management is a time sequential process. At the beginning of an incident, when the traffic management center is first notified that an incident has occurred, there is limited information available. The availability of closed circuit television cameras at the incident site would provide some additional information about the incident type, incident severity, and location during the verification stage. If incidents have been verified, response vehicle will be dispatched. Once a response vehicle arrives at the incident scene, more information about the incident can be obtained such as vehicle type, levels of any injuries, extent of damages, number of lanes closed, and nature of any hazardous material spill. This indicates that at the initial stages of the incident, the incident duration prediction may not be accurate based on the amount and quality of information available. More accurate incident duration prediction will become possible as more information become available at the

D. Zeng (Ed.): ICAIC 2011, Part I, CCIS 224, pp. 484–492, 2011.

Traffic Management Center (TMC), particularity when response vehicle arrived at incident location.

The purpose of this paper is to provide an effective and practical method for predicting incident duration based on the time sequence stage when incidents were verified by the TMC and response vehicle arrived at incident location. A data mining technique: Bayesian Network (BN) was investigated in this study. Prediction model was developed based on data stored in the SMART SunGuide incident management database maintained by Florida Department of Transportation (FDOT) District 4. This database includes detailed and comprehensive information about freeway incidents and management activities. This paper begins with a review of previous research, followed by a description of data preprocessing tasks. The BN is then applied for modeling, and an example is given to demonstrate the application of the developed BN model. At the end, conclusions and recommendations were drawn.

2 Previous Research

There has been some research exploring a number of techniques for predicting incident duration. Some studies have attempted to capture the influence of most of the causal and non-causal factors that are expected to affect incident duration. These factors include operational characteristics such as response times and whether a heavy wrecker was used, incident characteristics such as injuries and number of vehicles involved and number of lanes blocked, and environmental conditions such as weather and visibility.

The time sequential characteristic of the incidents was widely accepted by researchers, and many papers have aimed at developing sequential incident duration prediction models.

In reference [2], Giuliano identified 12 factors affecting incident durations and introduced a duration function using a series of ANOVA tables derived from a highly categorized incident database. Regression model generated from the incident clearance data was developed by Ozbay and Kachroo's in [3]. Reference [4] developed time sequential truncated regression models of incident durations using data provide by the Illinois Department of Transportation (IDOT) on Chicago area freeways. Garib et al. in [5] also developed a multiple regression model to predict incident clearance duration using 205 incidents occurring over a two-month period in Oakland, California.

Hazard-based duration models were first applied by Nam and Mannering in [6] to statistically evaluate the time taken to detect/report, respond to, and clear incidents using highway incident data collected between 1994 and 1995 in Washington State. Following that, Qi and Teng in reference [7] proposed a time sequential procedure based on a hazard-based duration regression model with different variables representing the available information.

Another popularly used method is the classification model. K. Smith and B. Smith in [8] developed a classification tree model. Naïve Bayesian classifier was developed by Boyles et al. in [9] to predict incident duration class in different time point using incident records from the Georgia Department of Transportation. Jiyang et al. in [10] has used Bayesian method-based decision tree to classify incident data recorded in

Shanghai. Rule-based tree model was applied to predict the incident duration by Kim et al. in [11]. Furthermore, artificial neural networks models were created by Wei and Lee in [12] to sequentially forecasting of incident duration.

3 Methodology

Regression models, hazard-based duration models, and decision tree models except for neural network models require inputs of all independent variables to make a prediction. In practice, this data is often incomplete. While, interpolation or data filling maybe a method to handle this problem, this will affect the prediction accuracy.

Almost all duration prediction models used in previous studies are deterministic and output a duration length or class. Considering the large variance characteristic of incident duration, probabilistic predictions are becoming necessary and more useful for decision-makers to select appropriate incident management strategies.

The Bayesian Network model estimates the probabilities of a given instance belongs to each prediction class. The probability estimates allow predictions to be ranked, and their expected cost to be minimized by incorporating utilities functions for each class. Furthermore, the BN model has the advantage of using whatever information is available to make useful predictions regardless of the incomplete information.

The BN is a useful tool for prior knowledge representation and inferential exploration. A BN represents the cause-effect relationships and conditional dependencies between variables of interest by a directed acyclic graph and local conditional probability distribution for each node that defines the joint probability distribution. According to David's tutorial in [13], BN models have the following advantages when applied to data analysis:

They can handle situations of missing data for encoding the dependencies among all variables.

1) They can learn causal relationships and gain an understanding regarding a problem domain.

2) They comprise an ideal method for combining prior knowledge and data with causal and probabilistic semantics.

3) They can prevent over-fitting of data.

In 1763, Bayes' theorem was published in an essay that appeared in Philosophical Transactions of the Royal Society of London and can be expressed as the following equation:

$$P(A \mid B) = \frac{P(B \mid A) \times P(A)}{P(B)} \tag{1}$$

By defining **X** as the variable set, X_i as the variable of node I, and Pa_i as the parents of node I in the structure. Following Bayes' theorem, once the structure is known, the joint probability distribution for **X** is given by:

$$p(X) = \prod_{i=1}^{n} P(x_i \mid Pa_i) \tag{2}$$

The joint probabilities can be Bayesian or physical depend on whether the structure is leaned from prior knowledge or from data.

Expert knowledge can provide the structure of the network using domain knowledge. However, the structure can also be learned directly from historical data, which enables the extraction of unknown, useful, and understandable knowledge from data.

The way to construct a learning algorithm for BN is to define two components: an assessment function for evaluating a given network based on the data and a searching method through the space of possible networks as described in reference [14].

The quality of a given network is measured by the probability of the data given the network. Here, the sum of logarithms of the probabilities (log-likelihood) accords to each instance of the network is used. Some measures for evaluating the quality of the network in practice include Akaike Information Criterion (AIC), MLD principle, and Bayesian metric.

Regarding the searching method, some heuristic search algorithms including K2, Hill Climbing, Tabu Search, Simulated Annealing, and Genetic Algorithm method have already adopted in structure learning.

Once a BN structure is constructed by means of structural learning, we need to determine the probabilities of any given instances. This is known as probability inference. Since the BN has determined a joint probability distribution, in principle we can use the network to compute any probabilities of interest. This can be handled using the probabilities tables based on the Bayes' theorem. However, for problems with many variables, the direct approach is not practical. Fortunately, probabilities can be calculated by probabilistic inference algorithms that are implemented in some software packages such as WEKA.

The BN can't handle continuous variables. Therefore, it is necessary to define discrete categories for the continuous incident duration variables. This might coincide with local incident management policy. When an incident occurs, the BN predict the probability of the incident duration category or interval, and the appropriate policy could be chosen based on what duration class is most likely.

Reporting the probability for each duration category provides information about the certainty of the prediction to incident management staff in an intuitive manner. Additionally, by classifying all incidents into broad categories, the resulting model is robust with respect to outliers.

4 Data Acqusition and Preprocession

The FDOT District 4's Fort Lauderdale Traffic Management Centre manages 57.73 centreline miles of limited access facilities. Incident data is stored in an Oracle database called the SMART SunGuide database. In this study, incident records from January 3rd, 2005 to October 31st, 2006 were used to develop the incident duration prediction model.

The raw incident data are usually incomplete, inconsistent and contain errors and outliers. Hence, data preprocessing is required. In the SMART SunGuide database, there are a total of 208,763 incident records. At the first data filtering step, only those "valid" and "closed" incidents were extracted. Furthermore, those incidents occurred on local road were excluded for this study due to this study is focusing on freeway incident management.

Furthermore, in this study, only incidents involving lane blockages were included in the analysis considering that lane blockage incidents have the most significant impacts on freeway operations. The lane blockage incident dataset with the exclusion of the erroneous data comprised 2,722 records. Table 1 presents the distribution of lane-blockage incidents by types. As can be seen from the table, most of the lane blockage incidents are accidents, followed by disabled vehicles and debris on the roadway. Due to the very small percentages of other types of incidents and most of them are special events, they are excluded in the analysis of this study. At the end, only 2,629 incidents were used for incident duration modelling with the three types of accident, disabled vehicle, and debris on roadway.

Table 1. Incident Type Distribution

Incident Type	Description	Number	Percent	Included?
1	Accident	2,143	78.73%	Yes
2	Disabled Vehicle	433	15.91%	Yes
3	Abandoned Vehicle	4	0.15%	
5	Debris on Roadway	53	1.95%	Yes
8	Road Work – Emergency	14	0.51%	
10	Police Activity	43	1.58%	
13	Other	17	0.62%	
14	Emergency Vehicles	5	0.18%	
15	Vehicle Fire	4	0.15%	
16	Off Ramp Backup	2	0.07%	
17	Weather	4	0.15%	
Total		2,629	100%	

Most of the variables in the incident duration dataset are nominal variables except the incident durations including the response, clearance, and to total incident durations. The numerical variables need be discretized to nominal variables. A number of discretization strategies were considered for this purpose. The FDOT's current practice of duration is as follows:

1) Level 1: Impact on traffic is estimated to be less than 30 minutes, with minor lane blockage or no lane blockage.

2) Level 2: Impact on traffic is estimated to be more than 30 minutes but less than 2 hours.

3) Level 3: Impact on traffic is estimated to be more than 2 hours, or may include complete road closure in any single direction where significant area-wide congestion is expected.

Reference [9] used three categories for incident duration: less than 30 minutes, 30 to 60 minutes, and more than 60 minutes. Here, the incident duration was discretized into four categories, clearance duration into three categories, and arrival time into four categories as presented in Table 2. Table 2 also shows the percent of the analysed incidents in each category.

Table 2. Incident Duration Discretization

Category	Incident Duration		Clearance Duration		Arrival Time	
	Duration	%	Duration	%	Duration	%
Short	<=30	37.0	<=30	62.8	<=10	41.5
Median	[30, 60]	37.9	(30, 60]	24.3	(10, 20]	32.7
Long	[60, 90]	16.4	>60	12.9	(20, 30]	21.3
Very long	>90	8.8	---	---	>30	4.5

Through discretization, all the attributes are classified into nominal variables. The final data attributes used in this study are listed in Table 3.

Table 3. Data Attributes Description

#	Factor Name	Description
1	INCIDENT DURATION	"Short", "Median", "Long", "Very long"
2	CLEARANCE DURATION	"Short", "Median", "Long"
3	ARRIVE TIME	"Short", "Median", "Long", "Very long"
4	ROADWAY	I-95, I-595, I-75
5	TOTALLANE	Total lanes of freeway section
6	INCIDENT TYPE	Accident, Disabled-Vehicle, Debris
7	NOTIFIER	First notify TMC about the incident: 911, TMC, Other
8	AGENCY	Agencies response to incident: FHP, Road anger, SIRV, Other
9	VEHICLETYPE	Car, Truck, Trailer, Tanker, Bus, Motorcycle, Other, Unknown
10	VEHICLECOUNT	Vehicles involved: One, Two, Three, Four/More, Unknown
11	LANESCLOSE	One, Two, Three, Four/More
12	SEVERITY	Four levels: Level1, Level2, Level3, level4
13	INJURY	Five types: None, Minor, Major, Fatal, Unknown
14	HAZMAT	HAZMAT or not
15	FIRE	Fire or not
16	ROLLOVER	Rollover or not
17	PAVEMENT CONDITION	Three types: dry, wet, unknown
18	RAINY	Rainy or not
19	DAYLIGHT	Light on or not
20	TIME	Time interval: MP(7-8), DOP(9-15), AP(16-18), NOP(19-21), NIGHT(22-6)
21	WEEKDAY	Weekend or not

5 Model Development and Application Example

In this study, the BN model was developed in WEKA, a collection of machine learning algorithms for data mining tasks that was developed at the University of Waikato in New Zealand. The BN model was developed for the stage when response vehicle arrives at incident location. The BN model was constructed with Bayes score metric and Tabu Search. The variables in Table 3 are used as inputs into WEKA, and the dependent variable is the clearance class due to the fact that the response time has passed. Table 4 and Figure 1 comprise the model performance and model structure graph.

The overall classification accuracy is 72.6% which is reasonably good for field application. Furthermore, we can see that the prediction precision for short class is 81.8% which means a very reliable prediction. However the prediction precision of median and long class is 54.2% and 49.8% relatively which reveal a fact that incident duration becoming more varied with duration increases.

Table 4. Model Prediction Accuracy

Clearance time	TP Rate	FP Rate	Precision
Short class	88.4%	33.3%	81.8%
Median class	52.9%	14.4%	54.2%
Long class	32.2%	4.8%	49.8%
	Total:		72.6%

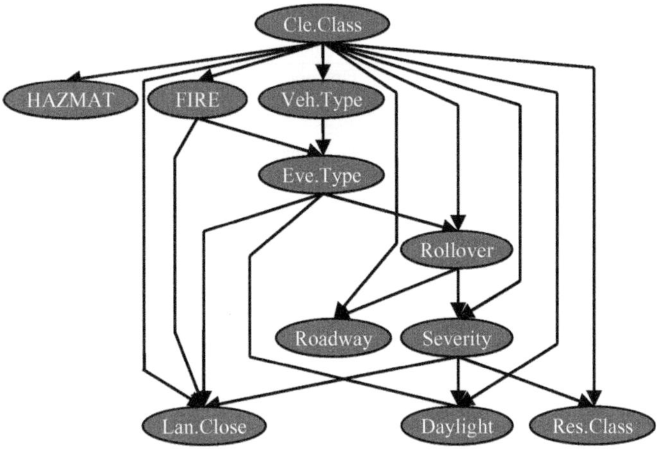

Fig. 1. Learned Bayesian Network

Each node in Figure 1 has a distribution table including all the conditional probabilities. The following example shows how the probability of each prediction class was calculated. When missing data occurred for one or several specific nodes, the BN will be pruned by simply removing those nodes and the edges connected to it. The pruned NB can still be used to produce prediction as one of the advantages of the BN.

An example incident was used to demonstrate how BN calculates the probabilities of each clearance classes. Based on the BN structure and probability table for each node, we can calculate the product probabilities for each duration class. The calculated probabilities are presented in Table 5, and the example incident is classified as the "Short" class.

Table 5. Bayesian Network Prediction Example

ClearanceTimeClass	Long	Median	Short
VehicleType=Unknown	0.206	0.223	0.158
HAZMAT=FALSE	0.990	0.995	1.000
FIRE=FALSE	0.966	0.929	0.957
Rollover=FALSE	0.753	0.793	0.930
EventType=Accident	0.763	0.763	0.763
Roadway=I-95	0.672	0.700	0.802
Severity=Level1	0.002	0.001	0.584
LanesClosed=Two	0.250	0.250	0.263
Daylight=NoLight	0.500	0.500	0.829
ResponseTimeClass=Median	0.250	0.250	0.332
Probability	0.0005%	0.0003%	0.3638%
Relative Probability	0.13%	0.07%	99.79%
Class			Yes

6 Conclusions and Recommendations

In this paper, we proposed a probability model of Bayesian Network to predict the incident clearance duration. Several advantages of the Bayesian Network are: it is capable in accommodating incomplete information, it outputs probabilities for each duration classes considering the large varying nature of incident duration, and it is more robust to outliers by classifying incidents into broader categories according to some field applications.

The Bayesian Network model can provide applicable prediction accuracy. Furthermore, the probability results of the Bayesian Network model are straightforward and the calculation process is very direct and can be easily implemented in computer. However, the highly variable nature of incident duration is noted as that reported in previous studies.

References

1. Lindley, J.: Urban freeway congestion: quantification of the problem and effectiveness of potential solutions. ITE Journal 57, 27–32 (1987)
2. Giuliano, G.: Incident characteristics, frequency, and duration on a high volume urban freeway. Transportation Research Part A 23, 387–396 (1989)
3. Ozbay, K., Kachroo, P.: Incident Management in Intelligent Transportation Systems. Artech House, Boston (1999)
4. Khattak, A.J., Schofer, J.L., Wang, M.: A simple time-sequential procedure for predicting freeway incident duration. IVHS Journal 2, 113–138 (1995)
5. Garib, A., Radwan, A.E., Al-Deek, H.: Estimating magnitude and duration of incident delays. Journal of Transportation Engineering, ASCE 123, 459–466 (1997)
6. Nam, D., Mannering, F.: An exploratory hazard-based analysis of highway incident Duration. Transportation Research Part A 34(2), 85–102 (2000)
7. Qi, Y., Teng, H.: An information-based time sequential approach to online incident duration prediction. Journal of Intelligent Transportation Systems 12, 1–12 (2008)

8. Smith, K., Smith, B.: Forecasting the clearance time of freeway accidents. Publication STL-2001-012. Center for Transportation Studies, University of Virginia (2002)
9. Stephen, B., David, F., Travis, W.S.: Naïve Bayesian Classifier for Incident Duration Prediction. In: Proceeding of Transportation Research Board 86th Annual Meeting, Transportation Research Board, Washington D.C (2007)
10. Jiyang, B., Zhang, X., Sun, L.: Traffic incident duration prediction grounded on Bayesian decision method-based tree algorithm. Journal of Tongji University (Natural Science) (2008)
11. Kim, W., Natarajan, S., Chang, G.: Empirical analysis and modeling of freeway incident duration. In: Proceeding of 11th International IEEE Conference on Intelligent Transportation System, Beijing, pp. 453–457 (2008)
12. Wei, C., Lee, Y.: Sequential forecast of incident duration using Artificial Neural Network models. Accident Analysis and Prevention 399, 44–954 (2007)
13. David, H.: A tutorial on learning with Bayesian networks. Report: MSR-TR-95-06, Microsoft Research (1995)
14. Witten, I.H., Frank, E.: Data Mining Practical Machine Learning Tools and Techniques, 2nd edn. Morgan Kaufmann Publishers, San Francisco (2005)

Research and Application of Credit Score Based on Decision Tree Model

Jiang Wei-Li

College of Finance, The University of Zhejiang Gongshang
1194109591@qq.com

Abstract. In order to timely and properly analyse the customer credit assessment, and to speed up the decision-making speed, here introduced the application of data mining technology used in the bank on the users" evaluation, and establish a decision tree model of customer credit evaluation which is aimed at improving the credit rating quality . And introduced the basic process of decision tree algorithm. Bank customer's credit is classified as background. Using the decision tree algorithm C4.5 as the most classic tools, specific studies of business understanding, data understanding, data preparation, modeling, evaluation and implementation of aspects of publishing have been done. Customer credit, using the decision tree classification algorithm, obtained a series of decision rules with which a bank to make the right decisions.

Keywords: credit rating, data mining, decision tree, C4.5 algorithm.

1 Introduction

Overdraft amount in the credit card business has a huge amount of small features single, which makes data mining technology of an inevitable in the credit card business. data mining technology have been widely used by Foreign credit card issuers for the development of the credit card business to achieve a comprehensive performance management. Since 1985, China issued the first credit card, then the credit card business has been great progress. it helped to accumulated a huge amount of data with which data mining in credit card business has gain growing importance as show.

In other countries, levels of credit card industry information is higher. as the database retains a large number of data resources, using data mining technology to build the different models in the implementation of credit card business is very successful. Currently, domestic credit card issuer firstly establish an application using data mining scoring model, as the first step in credit card business. many card-issuing banks have their own historical data to establish a customized application scoring models. Overall, the application of data mining in credit card business of China is still in its early stages. In domestic credit card market, the difficulty lies in quality issues of data mining and business model which is difficult to construct. Along with various domestic or issuing bank has established a data warehouse, where the data is

D. Zeng (Ed.): ICAIC 2011, Part I, CCIS 224, pp. 493–501, 2011.

collecting from different operational sources to a centralized storage environment with appropriate cleaning and conversion, the data mining operation which provide a good platform for data mining will bring a variety of convenience and functionality. People's Bank personal credit information system has also been on the line, forming a nationwide personal credit data set. based on the improving of the internal and external environment, data mining in credit card business will have an increasingly broad application prospects.

2 Data Mining

Data mining is a process to extract potential, valuable knowledge (model or rule) from the stored in databases, data warehouses or other information storage medium in a large number of random actual data. which is to extract from a large number, incomplete, noisy, ambiguous, practical application of random data, information and knowledge (people do not know in advance, but potentially valuable) implicit in them. Data Mining absorb mathematical statistics, a large number of databases and artificial intelligence technology in the process of self-development. It combines database, statistics, machine learning and artificial intelligence and other fields of theory and technology. The specific data mining methods include multivariate statistical analysis, decision trees, neural networks and etc. The common used specific data mining methods include multivariate statistical analysis, decision trees, neural networks and etc. Data mining is an application-oriented technology, it is a process of extraction, transformation, analysis, and other treatment models , extracted crucial date which can supporting critical business decisions for enterprise business from a large number of databases data. Now most companies have accumulated a large amount of sales data, the task of data mining is to found useful data which can help to evaluate customer credit in huge amounts of data. Transform the assessment of customer credit data into decision rules through a mining algorithm. Finally, use these rules to help companies to make the right decisions in the sales process.

3 The Decision Tree Algorithm

Decision tree is a potential way of mining classification rules of data mining. It is higher than neural networks, multivariate statistical methods such as discriminant analysis in a fast, high precision, easy to use build model, and is widely used in data mining. The data were analyzed using the decision tree, the first analysis of variables need to specify a variable as the target variable (dependent variable) and other relevant variables as input variables (independent variables); and the data collected by the appropriate training were randomly divided into sample set and test sample set. And then generate the decision tree training set, target variables obtained on the classification of each input variable prediction rule; and through the testing sample set and the optimization of decision tree classification of predicted effects on the test. Decision tree process is ongoing on the training set by the process From the root node represents the entire training set start step by step on the training set divided, so that the resulting sample of each leaf node in the distribution of the target variable values as concentrated. Decision tree algorithm used fork on the number and the like CART Algorithm is the binary tree obtained.[1] Again, if half of the binary tree can also be multi-branch tree. In Decision Tree, for each non-leaf nodes, are required to select from multiple input variables one of the best classification variables and values from the classification of the many variables in selecting an optimal segmentation threshold, so that out by the nodes in the distribution of sample values of the target variable focus as much as possible, and each node target variable values between different samples as large as possible.

3.1 The Theoretical Basis of the Decision Tree

Decision tree concept first appeared in Hunt's CLS (Concept Learning System) in 1986. JR Quinlan proposed the ID3 method, and he improved ID3 algorithm called C4.5 in 1993. C4.5 algorithm is a better edition of ID3 Algorithm, generally recognized by the industry, often be regarded as a reference standard in research and analysis of [2]Category questions. Commercial applications of the C4.5 algorithm to improve the computing speed and accuracy, called C5.0. Decision tree, ID3, C4.5,C5.0 are analysis models build on information entropy . In general, the probability of small probability events is larger than the large amount of information, such as "911" which is certainly better than the crash of a more general information. Information theory proposed by Shannon to address the problem of the size of metric information in 1948.now illustrate it with credit classification background. Event Gi is defined as the amount of information $\inf o(G_i)$, where $p(Gi)$ indicated that the probability of event Gi occurs.

$$\inf o(G_i) = -1bP(G_i) \tag{1}$$

Suppose G is a corporate credit rating to take a finite number of different credit ratings, G_1 G_2 , ,· · · , G_n variables, the amount of information through its information entropy $E(G)$ can be measured.

$$E(G) = -\sum_{i=1}^{n} p(Gi)1bP(Gi) \tag{2}$$

equation (2) provides the time when the $P(Gi) = 0$, $-p(Gi)1bp(Gi) = 0$.

In the number of classification decisions, assuming that S is the training sample set, $|S|$ is the number of training samples, the sample has been divided into n different classes $G_1, G_2, G_3 \ldots G_n$,and the size of these classes are denoted $|G_1|, |G_2|, |G_3| \ldots |G_n|$ Then the probability of A random sample of S belongs to class G,

$$p(S_i) = \frac{|G_i|}{|S|} \tag{3}$$

According to equation (3), the average information entropy

$$E(S) = -\sum_{i=1}^{n}\left[\frac{|G_i|}{|S|}1b\frac{|G_i|}{|S|}\right] \tag{4}$$

can be defined in classification of a given sample.

In decision-making classification, assuming that A is a finite number of different values obtained $a_1, a_2, a_3, \ldots, a_m$ attribute, the value of the training set can be divided into m sub-set of $\{S_1, S_2, \ldots, S_m\}$, the attribute information

$$E(\mathrm{A}) = -\sum_{j=1}^{m} p(S_j) 1bp(Gi / S_j) \tag{5}$$

$$E(S / \mathrm{A}) = -\sum_{j=1}^{m} p(S_j) \sum_{i=1}^{n} p(G_i / S_J) 1bp(Gi / S_j) \tag{6}$$

In the equation, $p(S_j) = |G_i| / |S|$;

P is the probability of subset S which is belonging to the class G.

Suppose that $|S_{ij}|$ is the number of samples of class G in subset S. then $p(G_i / S_J) = |S_{ij}| / |S|$.

Entropy of sample classification change. property A provided information on the classification, and the change in entropy is called information attribute A for the classification of gain.

$$\Delta E(S, A) = E(S) - E(S / A) \geq 0 \tag{7}$$

As a result, information gain ratio is defined as follows

$$R_{\Delta E}(S, A) = \frac{\Delta E(S, A)}{E(A)} \tag{8}$$

3.2 C4.5 Introduction to the Core Algorithmables

One of regular use of data mining process is to classify, the purpose of classify is to construct a classification function or model (also known as classification) based on the characteristics of data set, the model can map the unknown sampling of a given category one. Decision tree algorithm is frequently used classification of data mining technology, which is a kind of example-based inductive learning algorithm, provides similar in the "what and under what conditions will get value" method of such rules can be used to analyze data and make predictions. Three generation is the core of the decision tree algorithm, all data are in the root node in the beginning, then select the test attribute based on the set standard, the test properties in different data splitting recursively. A decision tree is constructed to form a training set of the classification process, it can be completed in the classification process to obtain the target extraction strategy and rule extraction. Most of the developed decision tree learning algorithm is a variant of ID3 algorithm. the algorithm uses statistical tests to determine a separate category for each instance of the property. The ability to sample and classification capability is selected as the best properties of the root of the tree test. Then the root node attribute values of each possible branch, and to arrange training samples in the appropriate branch. under repeated the whole process associated with each branch node, to select the training sample to be tested at that point with[3] best attribute, enable the decision tree structure from top to bottom. The decision tree generated for each internal node which represents a test of a property. the branch on behalf of each of the test results, and each leaf node in the tree represents a category. the core issue of C4.5 algorithm is the classification capability the best metrics standard of attribute, it selects one standard called "information gain" standard to measure the properties of a given ability to distinguish between the training sample. C4.5 algorithm using the standard information gain attributes from the candidates and select properties in every step of the tree growth. In order to precisely define the information gain, use the entropy metric to describe the purity of any sample set. If the target attribute has c different values, then the sample set S relative to c-state classification entropy is defined as:

$$Entropy(s) \equiv \sum_{i=1} -p_i \log_2 p_i \tag{9}$$

Where P is the proportion of S which is belonging to class i ratio. Information gain of an attribute is resulting from the sample entropy expectation decrease caused by the use of this property split. That is, the information gain $Gain(S, A)$ of S and an attribute A relative to the sample set is defined as:

$$Gain(S, A) \equiv Entropy(S) - \sum_{v \in value(A)} \frac{|S_v|}{|S|} \bullet Entropy(S_v) \tag{10}$$

Which, Values (A) is the attribute set of all possible values of A, Sv is the subset of attribute A with the value of v .The first is the entropy of the original set S, the second is the entropy S after A classification , that is, the weighted sum of the entropy of each subset, the right value is $\frac{|S_y|}{|S|}$,the proportion of Sv sample of their original sample S.

3.3 Improved C4.5 Algorithm

Algorithm used information gain ratio to ensure that a high branch and property will not be selected, prevent a node tree from being loose because of too much branches which will make the decision tree branches over-reliance on a property. In this way , bovercomes the lack of ID3 algorithm. However, only giving the sheer rate of information gain can not consider the amount of information of the property, and will make it conducive that the classification properties can not occur earlier[4]. Therefore, this article, consider the information gain ratio R mainly in the selected node attributes, taking into account information gain $\Delta E(S, A)$ the size of a certain level based on certain improvements in the classical C4.5 algorithm.

1) The decision tree

Step 1 according to formula (4) ,Calculate the total requirements for customer credit classification information entropy $E(S)$.

Step 2 according to formula (5) the conditions calculated for each attribute classification information entropy $E(S / A)$

Step 3 According to formula (7), (8), to calculate the properties of the information gain $\vartriangle E(S,A)$ and the information gain ratio.

Step 4 Select $R\vartriangle E(S,A)$ the largest and $\vartriangle E(S,A)>(1/3)\vartriangle E$ which is corresponsive to the property (if absence of such property selected , by the size of the order of $\vartriangle E(S,A)$ as a test property to the property as nodes. Each of distribution of property leads to a branch, plan accordingly $(1/3)$ sub-samples. Where, $\vartriangle E(S,A)$ is the gain value of the top 3positions in descending sort of all attributes of $\vartriangle E(S,A)$.

Step 5 to determine whether all nodes in the same class for all samples, and if so, then change the node into leaves and to mark the leaves of the credit category. Step 6 and so on, until the subset of data records in the main attribute values are the same, or no longer available properties for division can be used recursively to form the initial decision tree T.

2) The decision tree T is converted into a converted set of rules R, each leaf node from the root to the path corresponds to a rule, it is the first item on this path all the property values of the conjunction of the test. After entry is a leaf node to determine their respective levels of credit.

3) C4.5 decision tree pruning algorithm to solve the over-fitting, and isolated points [5] by the noise caused by data anomalies branch pruning algorithm is adopted. C4.5 with a backward pruning method and using pessimistic estimates to determine a node whether need for pruning. The idea is to be assigned to a node such as n instance of the node by the node to determine the m months after the miscarriage of justice, self-observation of the node while the pessimistic error rate estimated that the m / n, such cases, the error rate should be at least (m +0.5+se) / 2

which $se=\sqrt{\frac{(m+0.5)\times[n-(m+0.5)]}{n}}$ is standard deviation. If the rate of error caused after the cut a node is not more than pessimistic error rate, the pruning process makes sense. Then, tectonic subset of classification rules

4) because after pruning the rule set is no longer mutually exclusive. Of the R, to be a contradiction which met the first condition of rules will be selected in terms for instance of a training. If all the rules, are not met, it will be a default rule that met.

5) The model assessment and the results published

Model assessment means to make a good result after the evaluation of their model and explain the meaning and value. Results release refers to, spreading the results of the model in a certain way. Only in this way can the models be ultimately applied to the business environment.

After the model being built and validated, it can be provided to analysis, for reference or to apply the model to different data sets.

4 Case Study

By using the c4.5 algorithm, taking a bank's customer credit data on bank customers as an example to analyse the data to classify the customer. Specific mining analysis process is as follows:

1) Business Analysis and Data Understanding

In this case the data source is excel table. Table structure consists of 11 fields, and a total of 10276 data. The following is the data table structure and data in the table. Figure :

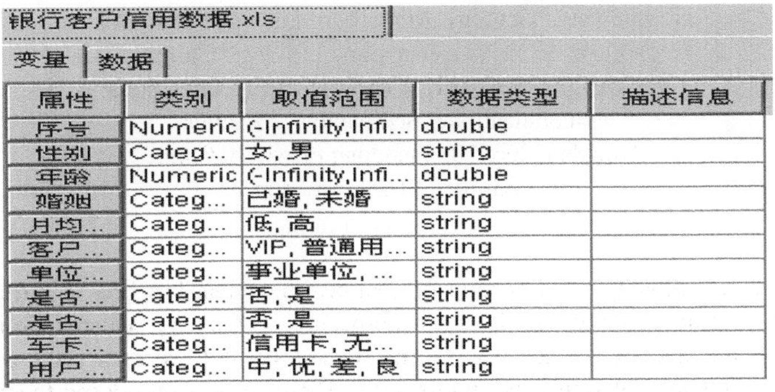
银行客户信用数据.xls

变量 | 数据

属性	类别	取值范围	数据类型	描述信息
序号	Numeric	(-Infinity,Infi...	double	
性别	Categ...	女, 男	string	
年龄	Numeric	(-Infinity,Infi...	double	
婚姻	Categ...	已婚, 未婚	string	
月均...	Categ...	低, 高	string	
客户...	Categ...	VIP, 普通用...	string	
单位...	Categ...	事业单位, ...	string	
是否...	Categ...	否, 是	string	
是否...	Categ...	否, 是	string	
车卡...	Categ...	信用卡, 无...	string	
用户...	Categ...	中, 优, 差, 良	string	

Fig. 1. credit data of bank customers

2) data preprocessing

Data preprocessing, including conversion of the property set and property transform(in this case discrete), as shown:

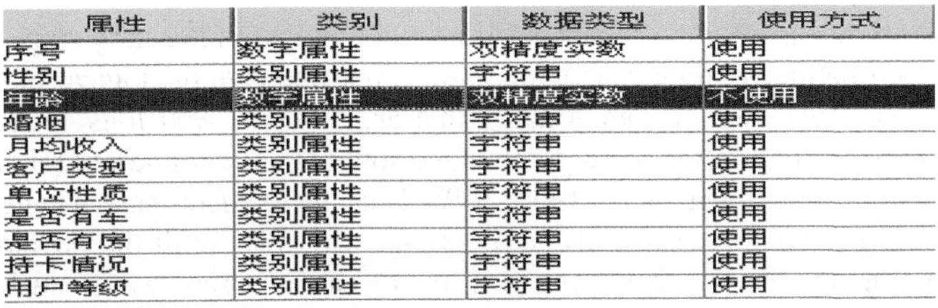

属性	类别	数据类型	使用方式
序号	数字属性	双精度实数	使用
性别	类别属性	字符串	使用
年龄	数字属性	双精度实数	不使用
婚姻	类别属性	字符串	使用
月均收入	类别属性	字符串	使用
客户类型	类别属性	字符串	使用
单位性质	类别属性	字符串	使用
是否有车	类别属性	字符串	使用
是否有房	类别属性	字符串	使用
持卡情况	类别属性	字符串	使用
用户等级	类别属性	字符串	使用

Fig. 2. Data property

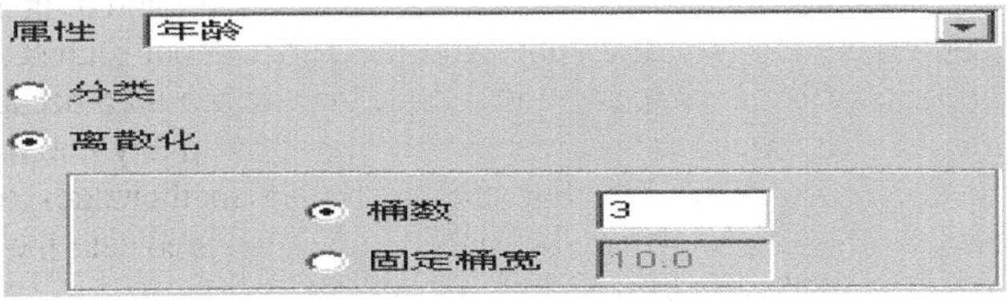

Fig. 3. Data Discretization

3) build models and assumptions

Threshold can be set on the decision tree, as shown:

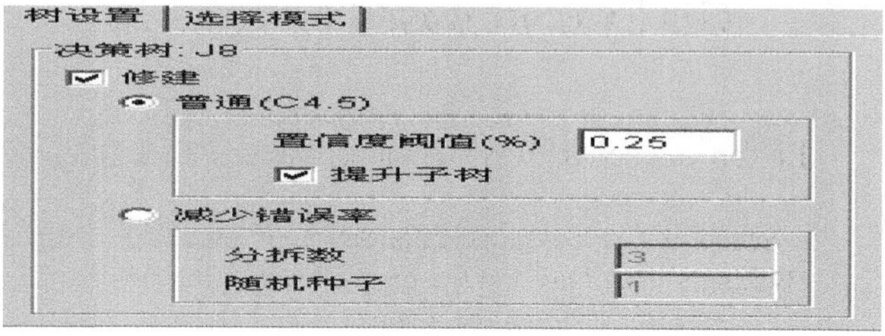

Fig. 4. Threshold settings

The tree view of mining results can be view when running the C4.5 algorithm, such as view map, rules, views, etc. As shown in figure:

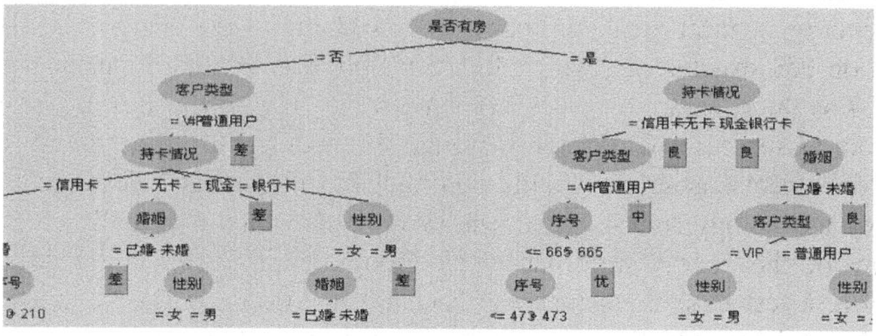

Fig. 5. Viewmap

4) The mining results score

First load test data, then uses the test data generated on the classification of trainin samples for testing, then run algorithm, as shown:

年龄	序号	性别	婚姻	客户类型	是否有房	持卡情况	用户等级	预测类	置信度(%)
(16,66]	11	女	已婚	VIP	是	银行卡	优	优	100
(16,66]	12	男	未婚	VIP	是	信用卡	良	良	71.429
(16,66]	13	女	未婚	VIP	否	现金	差	差	58.824
(16,66]	14	男	已婚	VIP	是	信用卡	优	良	71.429
(16,66]	15	女	未婚	VIP	是	无卡	优	良	55.063
(16,66]	16	女	已婚	VIP	否	无卡	差	差	35.052
(16,66]	17	男	已婚	VIP	是	无卡	良	良	55.063
(16,66]	18	女	已婚	普通用户	是	现金	良	良	54.054
(16,66]	19	男	未婚	VIP	否	信用卡	中	中	85.714
(16,66]	20	男	已婚	普通用户	否	信用卡	差	差	78
(16,66]	21	女	已婚	普通用户	是	现金	良	良	54.054
(16,66]	22	男	已婚	普通用户	否	无卡	中	差	78
(16,66]	23	女	未婚	普通用户	否	无卡	差	差	78
(16,66]	24	女	未婚	普通用户	否	无卡	差	差	78
(16,66]	25	女	未婚	普通用户	否	银行卡	差	差	78
(16,66]	26	女	未婚	普通用户	是	无卡	优	良	55.063
(16,66]	27	女	未婚	VIP	是	无卡	良	良	55.063
(16,66]	28	女	已婚	VIP	是	无卡	良	良	55.063
(16,66]	29	男	已婚	VIP	否	现金	差	差	58.824
(16,66]	30	男	已婚	VIP	是	现金	良	良	54.054
(16,66]	31	男	已婚	普通用户	是	无卡	良	良	55.063
(16,66]	32	女	已婚	VIP	是	信用卡	中	良	71.429
(16,66]	33	女	未婚	VIP	否	信用卡	中	中	85.714
(16,66]	34	男	未婚	VIP	否	信用卡	中	中	85.714

Fig. 6. Rating mining results

The "user grade" credit rating test.xls field is the user level of the user table to the test data. Input the test data to the classifier to carry out excavation. "predicted_ user rating" is the classification of the categories of users. The results of experiments has shown that the classifier is connected with higher accuracy.

5 Conclusions

Taking the example of bank customer data using the C4.5 decision tree algorithm demonstrated the technology in customer credit analysis. Customer credit used decision tree technology for effective and persuasive analysis to arrive at a more standardized and professional customer transactions to determine the rules, so that customer transactions such as audits and customers can maintain a more professional management based on the enhanced operability, to avoid the past, mainly relying on personal experience to determine the status of customer credit, to some extent reduce the risk of the transaction. Experimental results show that the algorithm has high precision.

References

1. Chye, K.H., Chin, T.W., Peng, G.C.: Credit scoring usingdata mining techniques. Singapore Management Review 26(2), 26–47 (2004)
2. Hyman, F., Garg, S., Harrison, S.: Oracle Internet File Syst Installation Guide Release 9.0.1.1.0 for Microsoft Windo NT/2000[EB/ OL] (September 2001), http://www.oracle.com
3. Ruggieri, S.: Efficient C4. 5. IEEE Transactions on Knowledge and Data Engineering 14(2), 438–444 (2002)
4. Li, H., Setiono, R.: Feature Selection via Discretization. IEEE Transactions on Knowledge and Data Engineering 9(4), 642–645 (1997); Quinlan, J R.: Induction of decision tree. Machine Learning 1, 81–106 (1986)
5. Stokes, A., Dawson, D.: Oracle Internet File System Develop Reference Release 9. 0. 1. 1. 0 Oracle 9iFS and Oracl database documentation sets[EB/OL] (September 2001), http://www.oracle.com

Rank and Kernel of a Binary Code

Xiaoyan Zhang

School of Mathematics and Computation Science
Huangshi Institute of Technology
Huangshi, 435003, P.R. China

Abstract. Given two binary codes of length n, we construct a code of length $2n$. The construction works for linear and nonlinear codes. For the linear codes, we obtain that the dimension of the final code is $2k_1 + k_2 - dim(C_1 \cap C_2)$, which $dim(C_1) = k_1$, and $dim(C_2) = k_2$. In this paper, we get that both parameters are the relation of the corresponding ones of the starting codes.

Keywords: $(u_1|u_2 + v)$-construction, rank, kernel, codes.

1 Introduction

A binary code of length n is a subset of $\mathbb{Z}_2^n$, its elements are called codewords. The Hamming distance between codewords $x, y \in C$, denoted $d(x, y)$, is the number of coordinates in which x and y differ. The minimum distance of a code C is the minimum of the distance between pairs of different codewords. Let C be a binary code. If C is a subspace of $\mathbb{Z}_2^n$, then we say that C is a $[n, k, d]$ linear code, where k is the dimension of C and d is its minimum distance. If C is not a subspace, we say that is a nonlinear $(n, |C|, d)$ code (see[1],[2]).

The following definition can be found in [2].

Definition 1.1 Given a binary code C, the rank of C is defined as the dimension of the linear span of C, i.e., $rank(C) = dim < C >$. The Kernel of a binary code, $Ker(C)$, is the set of vectors that leave C invariant under translation, i.e., $Ker(C) = \{x \in \mathbb{Z}_2^n \mid C + x = C\}$.

The following remark is easy to see.

Remark1. If c contains the all-zero vector $\mathbf{0} = (0, 0, \cdots, 0)$, then $Ker(C)$ is a linear subcode of C.

Obviously, if C is a linear code, then the rank and the dimension of the Kernel are simply the dimension of the code.

Definition 1.2 Let C_1 and C_2 be two binary codes of length n. We can construct a binary code C of length $2n$ by terms of C_1 and C_2 with the following construction:

$$C = \{(u_1|u_2 + v) : u_1, u_2 \in C_1, v \in C_2\}, \tag{1.1}$$

where $'|'$ denotes concatenation. Such construction is called $(u_1|u_2 + v)$ -construction.

In particular, $C' = \{(u|u + v) : u \in C_1, v \in C_2\}$ is a Plotkin construction and was first stated by Plotkin in 1960[3]. Note that C' is a subcode of code C.

D. Zeng (Ed.): ICAIC 2011, Part I, CCIS 224, pp. 502–506, 2011.

2 Rank and Kernel

we begin with two Lemma.

Lemma 21. *If C_1 and C_2 are linear $[n, k_1, d_1]$ and $[n, k_2, d_2]$ codes, then C in a linear $[2n, 2k_1 + k_2 - dim(C_1 \cap C_2), min\{d_1, d_2\}]$ code.*

Proof. Let $w_1, w_2, \cdots, w_s$ be a basis of $C_1 \cap C_2$. We extend $w_1, w_2, \cdots, w_s$ for

$$w_1, w_2, \cdots, w_s, u_1, u_2, \cdots, u_t,$$

and

$$w_1, w_2, \cdots, w_s, v_1, v_2, \cdots, v_r,$$

such that

$$w_1, w_2, \cdots, w_s, u_1, u_2, \cdots, u_t$$

is a basis of C_1,and

$$w_1, w_2, \cdots, w_s, v_1, v_2, \cdots, v_r$$

is a basis of C_2.

Then we claim that
$(w_1|0), (w_2|0), \cdots, (w_s|0), (0|w_1), (0|w_2), \cdots, (0|w_s), (u_1|0), (u_2|0), \cdots, (u_t|0), (0|u_1), (0|u_2), \cdots, (0|u_t), (0|v_1), (0|v_2), \cdots, (0|v_r)$
is a basis of C.

To prove claim, for any $a_1, a_2 \in C_1, v \in C_2$, suppose

$$a_1 = l_1^{(1)} w_1 + \cdots + l_s^{(1)} w_s + e_1^{(1)} u_1 + e_2^{(1)} u_2 + \cdots + e_t^{(1)} u_t,$$

$$a_2 = l_1^{(2)} w_1 + \cdots + l_s^{(2)} w_s + e_1^{(2)} u_1 + e_2^{(2)} u_2 + \cdots + e_t^{(2)} u_t,$$

and

$$v = g_1 w_1 + \cdots + g_s w_s + h_1 v_1 + \cdots + h_k v_k.$$

Then we have

$$\begin{aligned}
(a_1|a_2 + v) &= (a_1|0) + (0|a_2) + (0|v) \\
&= l_1^{(1)}(w_1|0) + l_2^{(1)}(w_2|0) + \cdots + l_s^{(1)}(w_s|0) \\
&+ e_1^{(1)}(u_1|0) + e_2^{(1)}(u_2|0) + \cdots e_t^{(1)}(u_t|0) \\
&+ l_1^{(2)}(0|w_1) + l_2^{(2)}(0|w_2) + \cdots + l_s^{(2)}(0|w_s) \\
&+ e_1^{(2)}(0|u_1) + e_2^{(2)}(0|u_2) + \cdots e_t^{(2)}(0|u_t) \\
&+ g_1(0|w_1) + g_2(0|w_2) + \cdots g_s(0|w_s) \\
&+ h_1(0|v_1) + h_2(0|v_2) + \cdots h_k(0|v_k).
\end{aligned}$$

In the following, we will demonstrate $(w_1|0), (w_2|0), \cdots, (w_s|0), (0|w_1), (0|w_2)$ $, \cdots, (0|w_s), (u_1|0),$
$(u_2|0), \cdots, (u_t|0), (0|u_1), (0|u_2), \cdots, (0|u_t), (0|v_1), (0|v_2),$
$\cdots, (0|v_r)$
are linear independent.
Indeed,

$$\begin{aligned}
&p_1(w_1|0) + p_2(w_2|0) + \cdots + p_s(w_s|0) + p_1'(0|w_1)\\
&+ p_2'(0|w_2) + \cdots + p_s'(0|w_s)\\
&+ q_1(u_1|0) + q_2(u_2|0) + \cdots + q_s(u_s|0) + q_1'(0|u_1)\\
&+ q_2'(0|u_2) + \cdots + q_t'(0|u_t)\\
&+ r_1(0|v_1) + r_2(0|v_2) + \cdots + r_k(0|v_k)\\
&= 0.
\end{aligned}$$

Then we have $(p_1w_1 + \cdots + p_sw_s + q_1u_1 + \cdots + q_tu_t|p_1'w_1 + \cdots + p_s'w_s + q_1'u_1$ $+ \cdots + q_t'u_t + r_1v_1 + \cdots + r_kv_k) = (0|0)$.
Hence,

$$p_1w_1 + \cdots + p_sw_s + q_1u_1 + \cdots + q_tu_t = 0, \tag{2.2}$$

and

$$p_1'w_1 + \cdots + p_s'w_s + q_1'u_1 + \cdots + q_t'u_t + r_1v_1 + \cdots + r_kv_k = 0. \tag{2.3}$$

The equation (2-2) and the assume of $w_1, \cdots, w_s$, $u_1, \cdots, u_t$ implies

$$p_1 = \cdots + p_s = q_1 = \cdots = q_t = 0.$$

We will turn equation (2-3) into the version of

$$\begin{aligned}
&p_1'w_1 + \cdots + p_s'w_s + q_1'u_1 + \cdots + q_t'u_t\\
&= -(r_1v_1 + \cdots + r_kv_k) \in C_1 \cap C_2.
\end{aligned}$$

Therefore, there exist $p_1'', p_2'', \cdots, p_s''$ such that

$$-(r_1v_1 + \cdots + r_kv_k) = p_1''w_1 + \cdots + p_s''w_s,$$

i.e.,

$$p_1''w_1 + \cdots + p_s''w_s + r_1v_1 + \cdots + r_kv_k = 0.$$

Since $w_1, w_2, \cdots, w_s, v_1, v_2, \cdots, v_s$ is a basis of C_2, we have

$$p_1'' = p_2'' = \cdots = p_s'' = r_1 = r_2 = \cdots = r_k = 0.$$

Thus, the equation (2-4) change to

$$p_1'w_1 + \cdots + p_s'w_s + q_1'u_1 + \cdots + q_t'u_t = 0.$$

By assumption, $w_1, w_2, \cdots, w_s, u_1, u_2, \cdots, u_s$ is a basis of C_1, hence

$$p'_1 = p'_2 = \cdots = p'_s = q'_1 = q'_2 = \cdots = q'_t = 0$$

as required.

To check the minimum distance of C, let us consider any vector $u \in C$. Vector u can be represented by $u = (u_1|u_2 + v)$, where $u_1, u_2 \in C_1$, and $v \in C_2$. Since C is a binary linear code, it is enough to show that the weight of u is at least $d = min\{d_1, d_2\}$.

If $v = 0$, then $w(u) = w(u_1|u_2) \geq w(u_1) \geq d_1$.

If $v \neq 0$, by using the triangle inequality we immediately obtain

$$w(u) = w(u_1) + w(u_2 + v) \geq w(v) \geq d_2.$$

Hence, $d \geq min\{d_1, d_2\}$. The equality holds because taking the specific vector $u_1 \in C_1$ with minimum weight d_1 and $v \in C_2$ with minimum weight d_2 we obtain $w(u_1|0) = d_1$ and $w(0|v) = d_2$.

The following Lemma is obvious.

Lemma 22. *If C_1 and C_2 are nonlinear $[n, |C_1|, d_1]$ and $[n, |C_2|, d_2]$ codes, then C in a nonlinear $(2n, \leq |C_1|^2 \cdot |C_2|, min\{d_1, d_2\})$ code.*

Theorem 23. *Let C_1 and C_2 be binary codes of length n, $0 \in C_1, 0 \in C_2$, and let C be the binary code built from them via construction (1-1). Then*

(1) $Ker(C) = \{(x_1|x_2 + y) : x_1, x_2 \in Ker(C_1), y \in Ker(C_2)\}$;

(2) $< C >= \{(x_1|x_2 + y) : x_1, x_2 \in < C_1 >, y \in < C_2 >\}$.

Proof. (i) For any $x_1, x_2 \in Ker(C_1), y \in Ker(C_2), (u_1|u_2 + v) \in C$. We obtain

$$(x_1|x_2 + y) + (u_1|u_2 + v) = (x_1 + u_1|(x_2 + u_2) + (y + v)) \in C.$$

Thus $(x_1|x_2 + y) \in Ker(C)$.

Conversely, suppose $(x_1|x_2+y) \in Ker(C)$. For any $u_1, u_2 \in C_1$, and $v \in C_2$, we have $(u_1|u_2+v) \in C$, and $(x_1|x_2+y)+(u_1|u_2+v) = (x_1+u_1|(x_2+u_2)+(y+v)) \in C$. By construction, $x_1 + u_1 \in C_1$, and therefore $x_1 \in Ker(C_1)$. To prove that $x_2 \in Ker(C_1)$, we consider $u \in C_1$ and the codeword $(x_1|u+v) \in C$. Then, since

$$(x_1|x_2 + v) + (x_1|u + v) = (0|(x_2 + u) + 0) \in C.$$

We conclude that $x_2 + u \in C_1$ and $x_2 \in Ker(C_1)$.

In the following, let $v \in C_2$ and codeword $(x_1|x_2 + 0) \in C$. Then, since

$$(x_1|x_2 + y) + (x_1|x_2 + v) = (0|0 + (y + v)) \in C.$$

We have $y + v \in C_2$ and $y \in Ker(C_2)$.

(ii) Let $x_1 = \sum_{i=1}^{s} u'_i \in < C_1 >, x_2 = \sum_{k=1}^{t} u''_k \in < C_1 >$, and $y = \sum_{j=1}^{r} v_j$, where, $u'_i \in C_1$, for $i = 1, 2, \cdots, s, u''_k \in C_1$, for $k = 1, 2, \cdots, t$, and $v_j \in C_2$, for $j = 1, 2, \cdots, r$.

Then

$$(x_1|x_2+y)=\sum_{i=1}^{s}(u_1'|0)+\sum_{k=1}^{t}(0|u_i'')+\sum_{j=1}^{r}(0|v_j)\in<C>.$$

Finally, if $(x_1|x_2+y)\in<C>$, then

$$(x_1|x_2+y)=\sum_{i=1}^{t}(u_i'|u_i''+v_i)=(\sum_{i=1}^{t}u_i'|(\sum_{i=1}^{t}u_i'')+(\sum_{i=1}^{t}v_i)),$$

where $x_1=\sum_{i=1}^{t}u_i'\in<C_1>, x_2=\sum_{i=1}^{t}u_i''\in<C_1>$, and $y=\sum_{i=1}^{t}v_i\in<C_2>$.

Theorem 24. *With the same conditions as in Theorem2.3.*
(1) $dim(Ker(C))=2dim(Ker(C_1))+dim(Ker(C_2))-dim(Ker(C_1)\cap Ker(C_2))$*;*
(2) $rank(C)=2rank(C_1)+rank(C_2)-rank(C_1\cap C_2)$*.*

Proof. (i) Straightforward from the Lemma2.1 and Theorem 2.3(i). (ii) It is easy to check that

$$<C_1>\times<C_1>\times<C_2>\longrightarrow<C>,$$
$$g:(x_1,x_2,y)\longrightarrow g(x_1,x_2,y)=(x_1|x_2+y)$$

are subjection, and $Ker(g)=\{(0,x,-x)|x\in<C_1\cap C_2>\}$.
Hence, we have

$$<C_1>\times<C_1>\times<C_2>/Ker(g)\cong<C>.$$

Therefore, $|<C>|=|<C_1>|^2\cdot|<C_2>|/|Ker(g)|=|<C_1>|^2\cdot|<C_2>|/|<C_1>\cap<C_2>|$, and

$$\begin{aligned}rank(C)&=dim(<C_1>\times<C_1>\times<C_2>/Ker(g))\\&=dim(<C_1>\times<C_1>\times<C_2>)\\&-dim(Ker(g))\\&=2rank(C_1)+rank(C_2)-rank(C_1\cap C_2).\end{aligned}$$

References

1. MuWilliams, F.J., Sloane, N.J.A.: The Theory Error-Correctiory Codes. North-Holland, Amsterdam (1997)
2. Fernndez, C., Pujol, J., Villanueva, M.: On Rank and Kernel of Z_4-linear codes. LNCS, pp. 46–55
3. Plotkin, M.: Binary codes with specificial minimum distance. IEEE Fans. Inform. Theory 6, 445–450 (1960)

Analysis and Research for Multi-mode Identity Authentication of E-Commerce

Ge XiaoMin and Wu CuiHong

Shanghai Second Polytechnic University
Shanghai, China, 201209
ge_xiaomin@sohu.com

Abstract. With the continuous speed-up of society informatization, the action of E-commerce is more and more extensive. Meanwhile safety troubles increase steadily, it severely restrict the development of E-commerce. How to handle and keep away the safety problems is becoming the vita points of Internet trading. This paper is mainly to investigate the identity authentication technology in commerce, analyse the advantage & disadvantage of identity authentication technology based on PKT and identity authentication technology based on biometric characters. Consequently it integrates these two technologies and puts forward the protection password of biometric authentication. Via the password protection of biometric authentication, it settles the identity authentication in E-commerce trust management thoroughly.

Keywords: E-commerce, Internet trading, trust management, identity authentication.

1 Introduction

Online trading is more and more prevailing owing to the popularity of Internet. Also the trading activity via Internet is creasing. Comparing with traditional business, E-commerce offers the advantage of economic, convenient, non space limits, etc. According to the *The 24th statistics report for China Internet developing situation* issued by China Internet Network Information Center (CNNIC), up to 30th June, 2009, the netizen in China was 338 million, popularity rate reached 25.5%. Compared with the quantity in the end of 2008, the rate of increment in half year was 13.4%. And the scope of China netizen keeps the trend of increasing. Furthermore, from data of *Research Report for 2009 China Network Trading Market*, up to June 2009, the quantity of internet trading user in China reached 87.88 million. The users increase 24.59 million, the yearly rate of increment was 38.9%.

Although the E-commerce has huge netizen foundation and internet trading proportion raises greatly, most netusers still keep the wait-and-see attitude. For the netusers who attended the E-commerce trading, they mainly focus on the low price trading zone such as clothes, makeup, books considering the security troubles. The extent and depth of the E-commerce development don't reach the due level. The caused

D. Zeng (Ed.): ICAIC 2011, Part I, CCIS 224, pp. 507–513, 2011.

reason is most netusers don't trust the gradual complex and jumbled E-commerce trading circumstance adequately. However trust is the precondition for occurrence of the trading in E-commerce.

2 Trust Relation in E-Commerce

Trust is one of cognitive phenomena in human society. In the relationships of human society, trust relation is the core in interpersonal relationship and the base of social relations; also it is the basic tool for establishment of social order. In E-commerce, the core content of E-commerce security field is how to manage the trust. It need fulfil the trust management from two aspects. Firstly make sure to manage the trust of each sidentity authenticatione of trading scientificly and reasonably based on technology. Secondly make great efforts to establish a good trust environment based on social culture. In detailed practices of E-commerce, it should keep comprehensive balance and no prejudice in two aspects of technology & social culture. This paper mainly researchs the trust problems in E-commerce from technology aspect.

In this virtual network environment of E-commerce, the technical framework of trust management is mainly consisting of establishment of trust relation, transmission of trust relation and the evaluation of entitative trust degree. See Fig.1

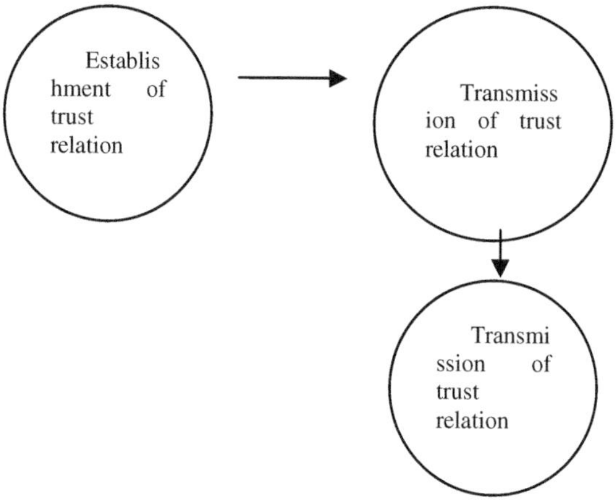

Fig. 1. Technical framework of trust management in E-commerce

In the whole framework of E-commerce trust management, it is mainly to set up trust relation via identity authentication, transfer the trust relation via PKI certificate chain and evaluate trust relation via trading activities. So pass the identity authentication is the fist link in trust management. Trust relation is set up based on the entitative identity authentication which is the entity identity authenticationentity can be authenticated exactly and without the risk of imitation by others, i.e. the real subject in real world can be traced according to the network identity authentication information. At present the common technologies are identity authentication based on PKI and identity authentication information based on biometric characters.

3 Identity Authentication Based on Pki

PKI (Public Key Infrastructure) is a universal security fundamental facility, it can fulfil and supply security service by using public key algorithm principle and technology. One of its core services is identity authentication. The components of PKI are Security Strategy, Certificate Authority (CA), Registration Authority(RA), Certificate Management System, Hardware & Software System, and PKI Application Interface, etc.

Certificate Authority (CA) is an authority which issues the certificate according to the certificate management strategy strictly. It is the core of PKI and the credible third authority. Due to the security requirement, CA extends the online checkup subsystem for user registration as the user interface, that is the Registration Authority(RA). The functional responsibility of certificate management system is mainly consisting of creation & issuance of digital certificate, receiving & handling the certificate update request of end-user, receiving & handling the certificate withdraw request and creating & issuing withdraw list, receiving & handling the certificate and CRL inquire request, and so on.

In the usage of identity authentication based on PKI, users should firstly apply the own personal digital certificate and then log in E-commerce system to identity authenticationentify it with the certificate. See Fig.2

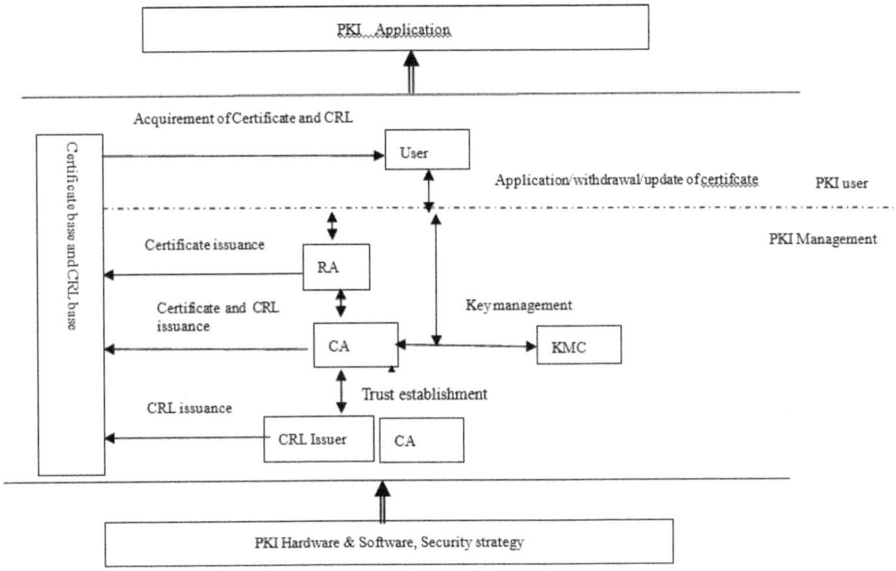

Fig. 2. PKI frame system structure

During the course of identity authentication based on PKI, it is subjectively thought that the end user will keep his private key well, ie the holder of private key is the real owner of the key. But in practical application, this assumption is difficult to come into existence. For common user, it's not easy do security protection for private key. And user's private key may be stolen owing to the improper protection thus it results the private key owner is not real owner. Aiming to this situation, identity authentication system based on PKI can't distinguish the true or false for the user, that means identity authentication based on PKI only transfer the trust relation.

4 Identity Authentication Based on Biometric Character

Biometric authentication uses the human biometric characters to handle the identity authentication. In theory, biometric identity authentication has the function of uniqueness, stability, catholicity and easy to collect, so it can fulfil identity authentication. The human biometric character is consisting of static character and dynamic character. Recently the useful static characters which can be identity authenticationentify the personal identity authentication are fingerprint, iris, retina, hand shape, face type and palm veins diagram etc; the dynamic characters are sound, signature, etc.

A typical biometric identity authentication is mainly dividentity authenticationed into registration stage and authentication stage. See Fig.3 and Fig.4.

The identity authentication principle of various biometric characters is basicly same except data acquisition ways are different. Although the biometric identity authentication can solve the identity authentication problems for the truth of user identity authentication, there is still some problems in appling directly in E-commerce field. Firstly biometric authentication is suitable for the local identity authenticationentity authentication, E-commerce is cross-region long-distance business way which is often used in local users apply for the identity authentication of long-distance busniess system. If the biometric identity authentication can be applied to E-commerce field directly, during the transmission of biometric characters data, it might be attacked via many ways such as "juggled", "reject to service","intermediator" and "playback" etc. So it is not suitable for long-distance identity authentication authentication. Secondly, biometric authentication is suitable for single field identity authentication. If the user want to fulfil identity authentication in multiple systems, the user's own image of biometric character should be submitted in every application system during registration. So biometric authentication is not suitable for the cross-domain identify authentication.

5 Identity Authentication Based on Multi-mode

Through above analyses for the identify authentication based on PKI and based on biometric authentication, it is found that either application is not the safest method. So we consider induct the PKI technology and biometric authentication simultaneously, combine the both and learn from others's strong points to offset one's weakness. To protect the password via biometric authentication and to protect biometric character via password, thus it not only solves the password protection problem in PKI identify authentication but also achieve the goal of pass everywhere by only on authentication. Consequently it solves the identify authentication in E-commerce trust management completely.

Surely for the combination of both, it may have different ways. Herein we investigate the combination way for using the biometric authentication to protect the user's private key. That is when the user want to use own private key, he should firstly apply the biometric character to ensure the owner of the private key is the real owner. So the user need to register the available account number, besides to enter distinguishable user name, password and other necessary information, the user should offer his own biometric image via the relevant hardware of user terminal to create the data templet of biometric character and save it in safe way. Then CA system create the private key and digital certification for the use, and associate the biometric characteristic data templet with the user's private key. See Fig.5

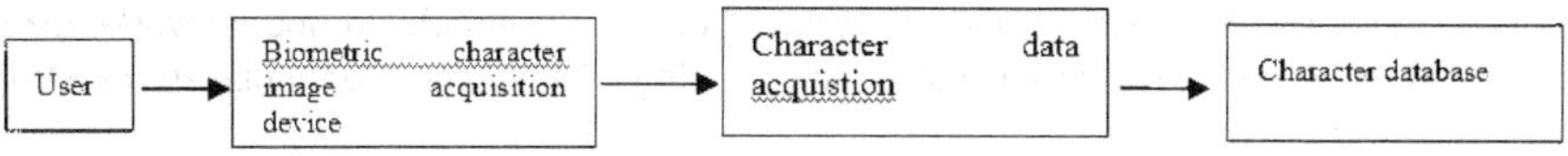

Fig. 3. Biometric registration stage

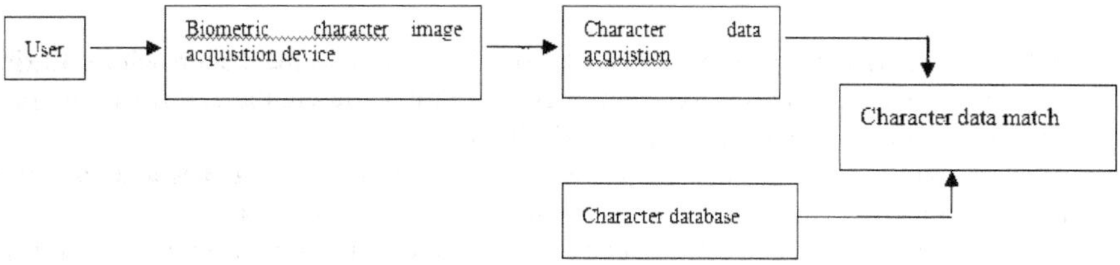

Fig. 4. Biometric authentication stage

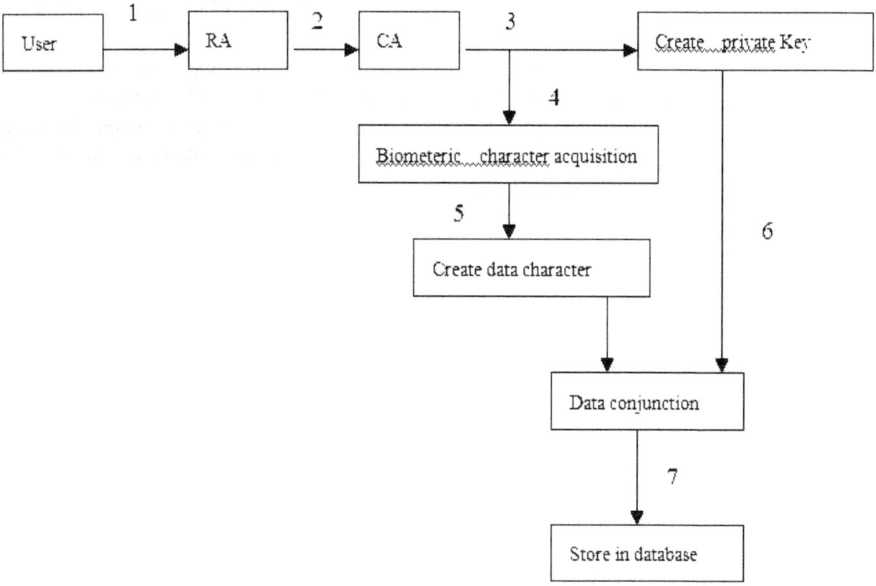

Fig. 5. Registration Stage

1: User downloads the digital application form from RA firstly, then fills in the form with relevant information and submits the information form to RA.

2: RA receives user's information form and checkups the privilege, if yes, the system will sign with its own private key for the user information then submit to CA.

3: CA creates the private key for the user and sign with CA signature key for user public key information, thus create digital certificate. Then CA transmits the digital certificate to RA which approved the user. RA conveys the digital certificate and private key to user. The transmission of private key must be guaranteed by the safe way.

4: User acquires biometric character via biometric image acquisition device under the supervision of supervision organizaation.

5: Create biometric character data.

6: Establish the association between the user biometric character data and identity digital certificate.

7: Store the data in USBKey or CA database.

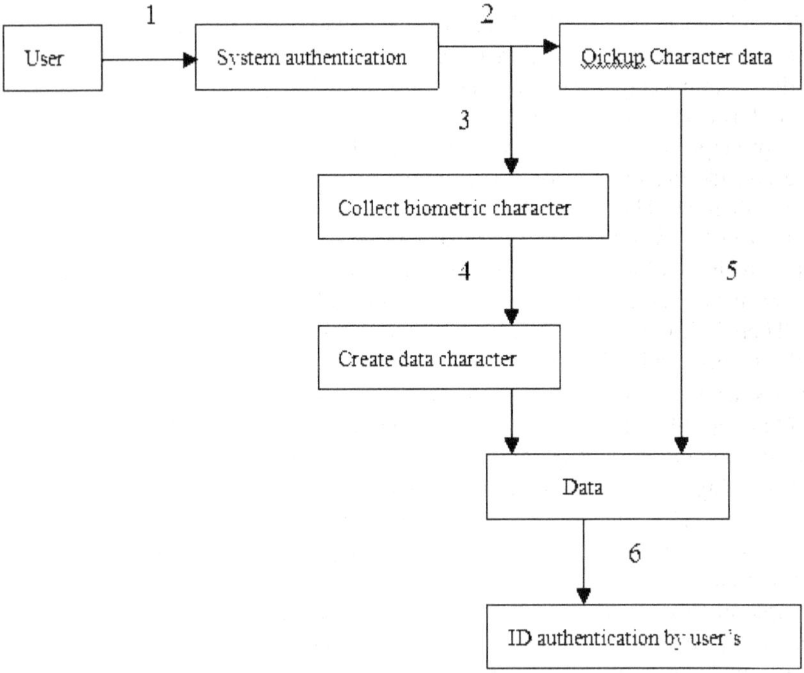

Fig. 6. Authentication Stage

1: User puts forward the application for identity authentication to application servicer.

2: Application system picks up the user biometric character data from template library.

3: User supplies own biometric image on line under the clue of application system. Application system acquire the user biometric image.

4: System handles the user's biometric image digitally and create the data.

5: System matches the acquired biometric image and picked biometric character data from template library. If they are same, the identity authentication is pass. Otherwise it is failed.

6: User does safe services such as long-distance cross authentication with own private key or do digital signature.

6 Conclusion

With the continuous speed-up of society informatization, the action of E-commerce is more and more extensive. Meanwhile safety troubles increase steadily, it severely restrict the development of E-commerce. How to handle and keep away the safety problems is becoming the vita points of Internet trading. This paper is mainly to investigate the identity authentication technology in commerce, analyse the advantage & disadvantage of identity authentication technology basked on PKT and identity authentication technology basked on biometric characters. Consequently it integrates these two technologies and puts forward the protection password of biometric authentication. Via the password protection of biometric authentication, it settles the identity authentication in E-commerce trust management thoroughly.

References

1. Qian, X., Du, J.M.: A safe trust mode of P2P in E-commerce. Extracted from Computer Science 33(9), 52–54 (2006)
2. Zhang, J.: Discussing of uniform identity authentication based on reliable compute flatform. Extracted from Technology Trend 22 (2009)
3. Xie, T., Luo, L., Zhang, Z.L.: Unify identity authentication to secure the safe data. Extracted from China Education Network 12 (2009)
4. Zhang, C.R., Ren, P.: Design and Realization of multi system identity authentication based on certification. Extracted from Computer Engineering and Design 18 (2009)
5. Wang, Y., Mu, Z.C., Xu, Z.G.: Summary of the development of multi mode biometric characters technology. Extracted from Computer Application and Software 2 (2009)
6. This paper is subsidized by the university talents training construction project of Shanghai Municipal Education Commission

Study of Key Technology for Laser Scanner Based Measurement of Railway Complete Profile

Yumei Zhang and Hongmei Shi

School of Mechanical, Electronic and Control Engineering
Beijing Jiaotong University, Beijing, China
YumeiZhang001@163.com

Abstract. To know well of the railway complete profile dimensions and its variation trend is an effective measure to guarantee rail traffic safety. This paper probes into key technology for dynamic measurement of railway complete profile based on laser scanner, proposes corresponding solutions, including the calibration of the laser scanner, the application of laser rangefinder in train positioning system, the algorithm of adjacent line spacing and contact line height detecting. At the end, gives a brief introduction of the software system for railway complete profile detection.

Keywords: complete profile, laser scanner calibration, positioning, adjacent line spacing, contact line height.

1 Introduction

To guarantee the smooth and safety of rail traffic, avoiding the deformation, invading phenomenon occurs to infrastructure like track, bridge, tunnel that caused by geological deformation, facilities protrudes, fallen stuff and so on, mastering the railway complete profile dimensions and its variation trend timely and accurately proves to be efficient safe measures.

The main content of railway complete profile detection includes bridge and tunnel profile, adjacent line spacing, contact line height, track bed profile and other railway clearance dimensions. As the rapid development of railway transportation, daily inspection, periodical comprehensive examine combined with real-time static monitor of few key spots, which is the traditional detection way, couldn't meet the detection requirement of rail infrastructure, so vehicle-borne high-speed dynamic measurement technology has received wide attention. There are mainly two way to detect railway complete profile. The photography method based on triangulation principle, which is susceptible to external environment, and the detection content incomplete, measurement range short, can hardly meet the measure requirement of various line environment. As the development of electro-optical technology, the laser scanner based on light propagation principle is used for vehicle-borne railway profile detection, because of its easy data processing, high precision, strong anti-jamming capability, and low influence on normal line operation.

D. Zeng (Ed.): ICAIC 2011, Part I, CCIS 224, pp. 514–521, 2011.

The vehicle-borne dynamic detection of railway traffic line complete profile this paper talks about is based on laser scan sensor; it obtains the line profile by the laser scanner borne on inspection car. To reduce the affect to the vehicular-borne measure caused by car vibrate, compensating the profile data with car attitude got by Strap down inertial navigation system is necessary and effective. Combined with the velocimetry and positioning system of inspection car, the profile data are recorded in accordance with time as well as the mileage, to facilitate the playback and variation trend analysis of line profile, and ultimately performs the inspection of line condition.

In the line complete profile dynamic detection system, the profile data measured by laser scanner is to be transformed into the external measurement reference coordinate system. The laser emitted by laser scanner is invisible and discontinuous, which makes the calibration of laser sensor become to one of the key problem of the system. One of the system features is to analyze the variation trend of the line profile, to ensure the accuracy of the analysis, the positioning system of the inspection car should be of high precision and good repeatability, so the positioning is one of the key problems of the system. And another key point of the system is the detection of the adjacent line spacing and the contact line height. There will be detailed discussion and analysis about these problems.

2 The Calibratioin of the Laser Scanning Sensor

The line complete profile dynamic detection system uses the LMS200 as profile detection equipment, which is based on light propagation principle and of pulsatile, and the scanner measure the distance with the obstacle by calculate the time span between the emission and reflection of laser. The emission angle of the sensor can

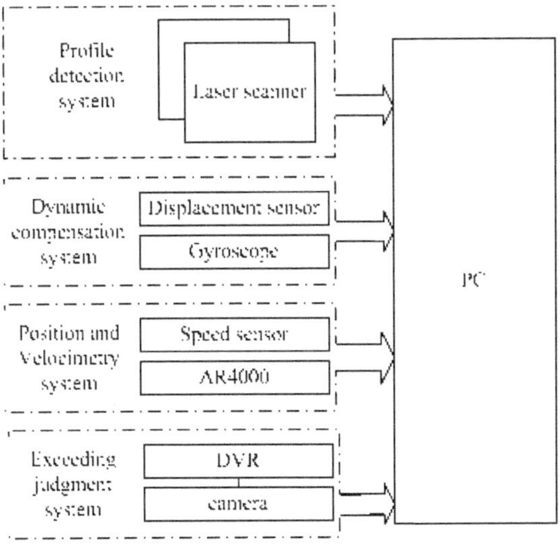

Fig. 1. The system frame structure

varies at the range of 180 degree, and the minimum angle interval is 0.5 degree. Since one scanner can get the profile data of its corresponding range, we can install 2 to 4 scanners which are synchronized to get the line complete profile.

The profile data get from the laser scanner is in the sensor coordinate system, to directly and conveniently observe the line profile as well as judge the exceeding point, the profile data have to be transformed into the external measurement reference coordinate system where the rail plane are in. The transform need to get the transformation matrix between two coordinate systems by calibrating the laser sensor.

Usually, the 3D measurement system use standard template to perform calibration. In the standard template method, sensor measures the known points on the standard template and gets their coordinates in sensor coordinate system, and the transform matrix can be calculated by combining the points' coordinates in two coordinate systems.

Suppose the sensor coordinate system is OSUVW, the external measurement reference coordinate system is OTXYZ, and then we can transform the sensor coordinate system to the measurement reference system by rotating and translation. For example, we can first rotate the OSUVW through an angle α about OSW, then rotate through θ about OSV, rotate through angle β about OSU; at last with the simple translation we can get the reference coordinate system. The process of transformation can be expressed as a formula:

$$\begin{bmatrix} X \\ Y \\ Z \end{bmatrix} = \begin{bmatrix} \cos\alpha\cos\beta - \sin\alpha\sin\theta\sin\beta & \sin\alpha\cos\beta + \cos\alpha\sin\theta\sin\beta & -\cos\theta\sin\beta \\ -\sin\alpha\cos\theta & \cos\alpha\cos\theta & \sin\theta \\ \cos\alpha\sin\beta + \sin\alpha\sin\theta\cos\beta & \sin\alpha\sin\beta - \cos\alpha\sin\theta\cos\beta & \cos\theta\cos\beta \end{bmatrix} \begin{bmatrix} U \\ V \\ W \end{bmatrix} + \begin{bmatrix} x^0 \\ y^0 \\ z^0 \end{bmatrix}$$

This can be simplified as

$$X = \begin{bmatrix} r_{11} & r_{12} & r_{13} \\ r_{21} & r_{22} & r_{23} \\ r_{31} & r_{32} & r_{33} \end{bmatrix} \begin{bmatrix} U \\ V \\ W \end{bmatrix} + \begin{bmatrix} r_{14} \\ r_{24} \\ r_{34} \end{bmatrix} = \begin{bmatrix} r_{11} & r_{12} & r_{13} & r_{14} \\ r_{21} & r_{22} & r_{23} & r_{24} \\ r_{31} & r_{32} & r_{33} & r_{34} \end{bmatrix} \begin{bmatrix} U \\ V \\ W \\ 1 \end{bmatrix} = Ru \qquad (1)$$

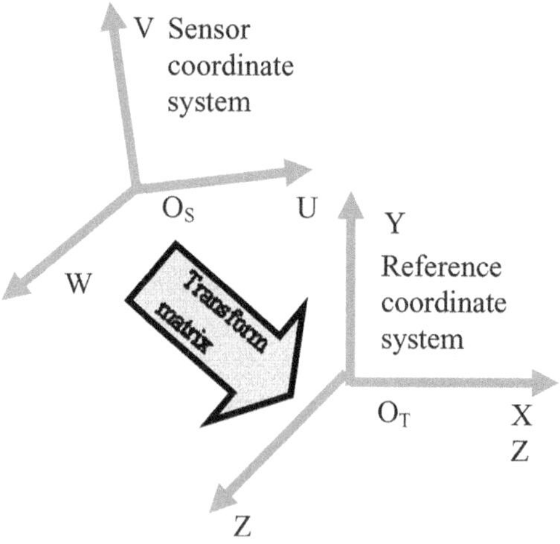

Fig. 2. The schematic diagram of the coordinate transform

In above formula, X and u are the coordinates in the external measurement reference coordinate system and sensor coordinate system separately; the process of sensor calibration is calculating the transformation matrix according to {X， u} and formula (1). We can see from the formula that the calculation needs at least four measured points to obtain the transformation matrix. In reality application, it usually by measuring more points to improve the accuracy of calibration. Suppose that the measured points' measurement values are random variable of IID, then the transformation matrix can get by least square method, the formula is

$$R = (A^T A)^{-1} A^T X \tag{2}$$

In which

$$R = [r_1 \quad r_2 \quad r_3]^T, \quad r_i = [r_{i1} \quad r_{i2} \quad r_{i3} \quad r_{i4}],$$

$$A = [Diag(u_1,3)) \quad Diag(u_2,3) \quad \ldots \quad Diag(u_N,3)]^T{}_{3N\times 12}$$

$$Diag(u_i,3) = \begin{bmatrix} u_i & 0 & 0 \\ 0 & u_i & 0 \\ 0 & 0 & u_i \end{bmatrix}, \quad u_i = [U_i \quad V_i \quad W_i \quad 1]^T$$

Because the laser emitted by laser scanner is invisible and discontinuous, since we can't precisely know the measured points' coordinate in external measurement reference system, using the standard template method could not satisfy the precision requirement of system, so a one-dimensional calibration method is proposed. In the one-dimensional calibration method, a flat plate is used as the template, when it is placed horizontally or vertically, one coordinates of the measured points on the template can be precisely known. The precision of the sensor calibration can be improved largely by just make the known one coordinate participate the least square calculating, while the other two not.

In the one-dimensional calibration method, first adjust the attitude of the template to make it perpendicular to the X axis of the measure reference coordinate system, and then we can precisely measure its horizontal distance with the original point. Find out the points of the flat plate from the laser data as a group of calibration points, substitute their coordinates into formula (1) and only preserve the equation about X coordinate. Change the plate's position and measure three times then we can get three groups of calibration points. The Y coordinate can get three groups of calibration points and their corresponding equations. According to the calibration points and the least square calculation equation (2) calculates the corresponding coefficient of the transformation matrix. The data of Z coordinate have coupled into X and Y coordinates, so there is no need to do calibration and set its coefficient to zero.

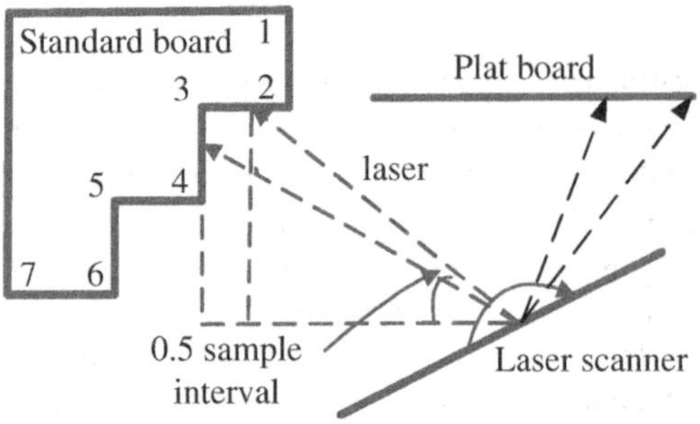

Fig. 3. The standard template method and one-dimensional calibration method schematic diagram

3 The Application of Laser Range Finder in the Positioning of the Car

The detection system measures the line complete profile, meanwhile, the velocimetry and positioning system gains the car's mileage relative to the starting position. The profile data was recorded in accordance with the time as well as the position to facilitate the line profile's playback and variation trend analysis. Because the profile data of different location dose not have comparability, and the trend analysis is nonsense, so the velocimetry and positioning system must be of high accuracy and have good repeatability.

In the vehicular detection system, the velocimetry and positioning of the detection car is performed by speed sensor, which is usually photoelectric speed sensor. By scanning the slotted disk that synchronized with the axel, the sensor outputs square-wave signal that linearly proportional to the speed. Then the speed can get by counting the pulse number in unit time, and when accumulated we can get the distance of the car relative to its start position. Because of the slippage and counting error of the pulse during the running of the car, there will be accumulation error in the running distance. To eliminate the accumulation error of the car position, we can use some reference object and their information in external environment, by recognizing the external reference stuff to ascertain the current position of the car, and adjust the car position get by speed sensor.

The reorganization of the line environment should be based on certain measurement data, and in our system we use the laser range finder AR4000 to get the measurement data. The AR4000 range finder applies the principle of reflection time difference, it emits modulated collimation laser bean, which will be reflected on surface of measured object and the reflection light will be received by laser receiver that homocentric with the emitter. By recording the time difference, which is proportional to the distance between the laser and the object, the range finder can get the measured distance by multiplying the time span with the light speed. Its measure results are outputted via RS232 or RS422 interface, and it can measure as far as 16.45m, while its accuracy can reach 2.54mm and repeatability 0.0197in, the maximum sample rate of AR4000 is 50 KHz.

The key point of the application of AR4000 in car positioning is the recognition of the reference object, while the recognition can be divided into the build of the pattern, the pick-up of the features and the match of the features. The first step of the recognition is the build of the model of the line. The laser range finder is equipped on the detection car with the laser emitter downward to scan the line information. When the car runs along the line the range finder measures at a fixed distance interval, we can get a group of measurement data that represent the space distribution information of the track. Record the data in accordance with the mileage as the line model. Once the line model is built, we can perform the positioning of the car using AR4000.

The next step is the features extraction and matching, which is transforming and processing the measurement data of the object, forming the recognition feature of the object and matches them with the model data. During the running of the detection car the laser range finder collects the height data. Do correlation analysis with the measurement data and the model data when the height information satisfies the recognition condition; consider the point where the correlation coefficient is the biggest to be the same point, and then we can acquire the current mileage.

4 The Calculation of Adjacent Line Spacing and Contact Line Height

Adjacent line spacing is the distance between the adjacent lines' track centers. When the running speed of train on rail reaches 200km/h, the aerodynamics problem of the train is particularly outstanding and important, while among the main line standard adjacent line spacing is the only standard that closely relate to it. The catenary is the key part of the power supply system in electrification railway; the electric locomotive obtains energy through catenary. The geometric parameters of the contact line directly influence the current collection quality, so the detection of the height and other parameters of the contact line have significant sense to keep good dynamic performance of the catenary.

The detection of the adjacent line spacing and contact line height uses the image processing technology; it extracts relevant feature points from the complete profile image measured by laser scanner and calculate the detection parameters through certain algorithm. Because the thought of the algorithm of the adjacent line spacing and contact line height detection is the same, so we only introduce the detection process of the adjacent line spacing.

The key point of the adjacent line spacing is extracting the positions of the two rails of adjacent line from the profile image. Because the profile data is centered about the track centerline, so the adjacent line spacing is the average of the two rails' position. The width of the rail is very small so that the scanning point of the rail top in one pack of profile data is quite few; we overlap several data packs together to be used for processing. To eliminate the influence of the isolated points, which are formed by disruptors in background environment , we use the median filter algorithm to smooth away the noise point in the profile image. And then is the judge of the rail position. In vertical direction, the profile data is oriented from the plane the rail top is in, so the coordinates of the rail top in profile image is near original. In general, the width of the rail top is 80mm, and the height is 40mm, find out the points that the Y coordinates are near the origin and the X coordinates are one gauge off-center, centered around the highest point, calculating the average position of its neighboring points as the central position of the rail. And the average of the positions of the two rails is the adjacent line spacing.

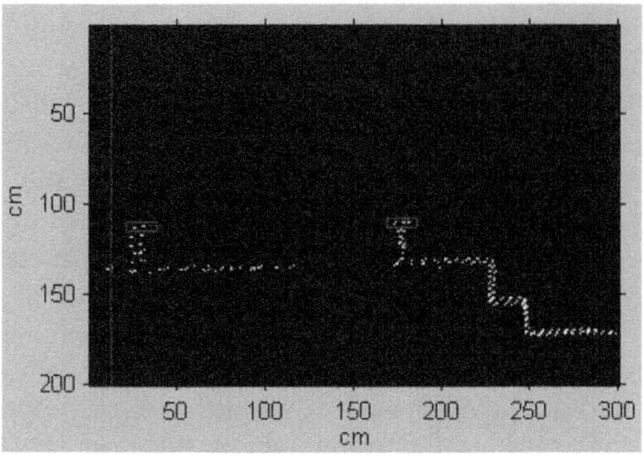

Fig. 4. The calculation of adjacent line spacing

5 Introduction of the Software System

The software system of the vehicular-borne line complete profile dynamic detection, which is developed in the Microsoft Visual C++6.0 integrated development environment, is based on multithreading and database technology. The software system is mainly made up of complete profile detection and information management two part. The part of complete profile detection realizes the sampling processing and display of various sensors information, the calculation of the adjacent line space and the contact line height, as well as the judgment of clearance exceeding. While the information management part completes the save, query and playback of measurement data and the profile variation trend analysis.

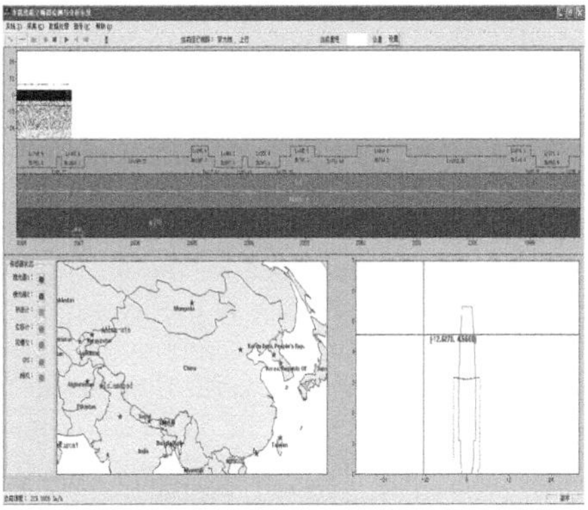

Fig. 5. The software system

The information of various sensors needs to be collected at the same time, but the data protocol and communication interface of each sensor are different, and the required sample rate varies as well. So we apply multithreading technology to perform all sensors' collection and transform process. The profile data collection thread is the main thread, in which the samples laser data are transformed from polar coordinate into Cartesian coordinate after coordinate transfer, and then reduced into measurement reference coordinate system. The profile data are dynamically compensated use the car attitude that got by inertial navigation system. The calculation of adjacent line spacing and contact line height are both based on the measurement data of laser scanner.

The complete profile detection system will produce a lot of data each time. Efficient and unitive data save and management is the base of making the data effectively used in query and analysis, so considering applying database technology to realize the management of the detection data. After comparison we choose the oracle database, which supports the object-oriented feature and distributed application, and use ADO method to access the database. The effect of the software is as shown in Fig 5.

Acknowledgment. This paper is supported by the National Natural Science Foundation of China (60972092) and the Scientific Foundation of Beijing Jiaotong University (2009JBZ005-3) and Haidian District Scientific Foundation (K20100086X).

References

1. Wang, H.: The introduction of standard setting basis of line circular curve, transition curve length and adjacent line spcaing. Railway Standard Design, 33–36 (July 2004)
2. Peng, C., Gao, X., Wang, L.: Portable detection system of contact line geometry parameters. Electric Railway. 4th ed., Beijing, pp. 26–28 (2007)
3. Yu, Z., Yang, Y.: Study on calibration method for 3-D laser scanning system. Journal of Electronic Measurement and Instrument 21, 31–35 (2007)

Path Planning for Mobile Robot Based on Fuzzy Control

Tongxiang He, Peng Li, and Ningqing Han

School of Control and Computer Engineering, North China
Electric Power University,
Baoding 071003, China
tongxianghe@gmail.com

Abstract. A path planning for mobile robot is studied. An algorithm based on fuzzy control is presented and a reasonable and applicable fuzzy control table is constructed. In view of deadlock problem that the local path planning has, the deadlock prevention mechanism is established. When the robot detects dangerous obstacle field which possible causes deadlock, the robot will travel along the edge of the obstacle to escape from the obstacle through the deadlock prevention mechanism, and thus deadlock is avoided. When deadlock can't be avoided in some complex environments by the deadlock prevention mechanism, the deadlock resolution strategy would be adopted to eliminate the deadlock. The algorithm offers a new idea of the solution of deadlock. Simulation results in several kinds of environments prove the effectiveness and feasibility of the algorithm.

Keywords: Mobile robot, path planning, fuzzy logic controller, deadlock prevention mechanism, solution of deadlock.

1 Introduction

Path planning is an indispensable part of the mobile robot technology and it demands a robot searches an optimal or approximate optimal collision-free path from a starting point to a target point according to some performance index. Path planning can be divided into two types according to the degree that a robot knows about the environment in which it travels: one type is the environment that is known, and we call it global path planning; the other type is the environment that is globally unknown or partially unknown, and we call it local path planning [1]. This paper studies the mobile robot path planning in globally unknown environments based on fuzzy control method, it requires the robot chooses its path autonomously, avoids obstacles and successfully reaches the target point.

The path planning based on sensor information can realize real-time control for the robot. However, when the robot travels in some types of obstacles, it would fall into a local minimum and could not escape from the obstacle trap, we call the phenomenon deadlock. The most typical obstacle trap is U-type obstacle. The traditional solution of deadlock model is taking strategies to eliminate the deadlock such as moving following the edge of obstacle method [2-3] and virtual target method [2, 4] after the

D. Zeng (Ed.): ICAIC 2011, Part I, CCIS 224, pp. 522–531, 2011.

robot is judged fell into deadlock. However, the effect of path planning based on the model is not ideal because the robot has taken a roundabout route when deadlock occurs. This paper presents a new algorithm to overcome the defect of the traditional solution of deadlock model. In the new algorithm, the deadlock prevention mechanism is established. When the robot detects dangerous obstacle field which possible causes deadlock, the robot can travel along the edge of the obstacle to escape from it by the deadlock prevention mechanism rather than solving deadlock after deadlock occurred. The algorithm highlights the prevention link, thus the robot effectively avoids deadlock and makes the path optimized. When faced with more complex obstacle such as the semi-closed double U-type obstacle, the robot couldn't not avoid deadlock by the deadlock prevention mechanism and the deadlock resolution strategy would be adopted to eliminate the deadlock. The new path planning algorithm is composed of deadlock prevention mechanism and the deadlock resolution strategy, and offers a new idea of the solution of deadlock.

2 Design of the Fuzzy Logic Controller

2.1 Input and Output Variables

In the mobile robot path planning, the fuzzy logic controller is a two inputs and one output system. The inputs are d and θ [5-7], d is the distance between the robot and the frontal obstacle and θ is the direction angle between the forward direction of the robot and the target point, which are as shown in Fig.1. The output is the steering angle φ. The robot moves a fixed value step after each planning.

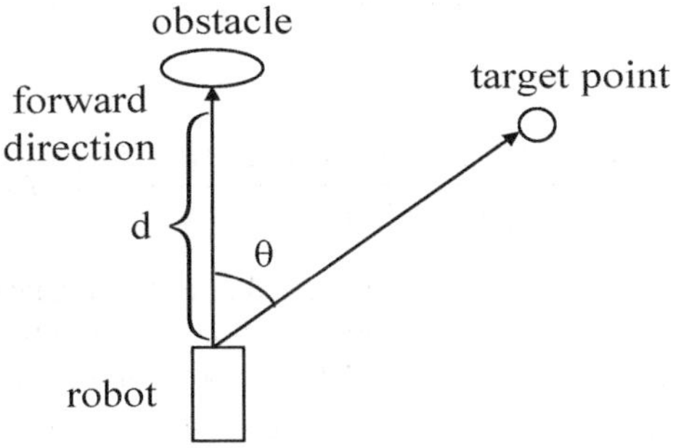

Fig. 1. Inputs of the fuzzy logic controller

2.2 Define the Linguistic Variables and Fuzzy Set for the Inputs and Outputs

We uniformly quantize the range of the ranging sensor to the interval [0, 8], so the discrete universe of discourse of d is [0, 1, 2, 3, 4, 5, 6, 7, 8]. We define the fuzzy set of d is {VS: very small, S: small, M: Middle, B: big, VB: very big}. The scope of θ is the interval (-∞, +∞) and it is non-uniformly quantized to the interval [-4, 4] (the interval [-60°, 60°] is uniformly quantized to [-4, 4], (60°, +∞) is quantified as 4, and (-∞, -60°) is quantified as -4), so the discrete universe of discourse of θ is [-4, -3,

-2, -1, 0, 1, 2, 3, 4]. The fuzzy set of θ is {RB: right big, RS: right small, Z: zero, LS: left small, LB: left big}. The scope of φ is [-60°, 60°] and it is uniformly quantized to the interval [-4, 4], so the universe of discourse of φ is [-4, -3, -2, -1, 0, 1, 2, 3, 4]. The fuzzy set of φ is {TRB: turn right big, TRS: turn right small, TZ: turn zero, TLS: turn left small, TLB: turn left big}. We stipulate that when the target point on the left (right) side of the forward direction of the robot, θ is positive (negative); and when φ is positive (negative), the robot is set to turn left (right). The membership functions for the sets d, θ and φ are shown in Figs. 2-4 [7].

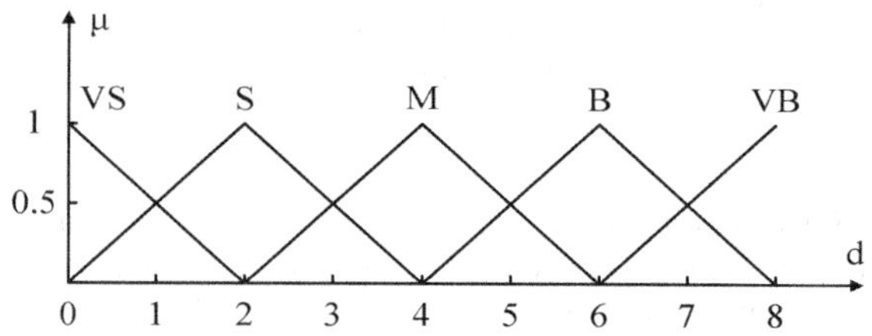

Fig. 2. The membership function for the set "d"

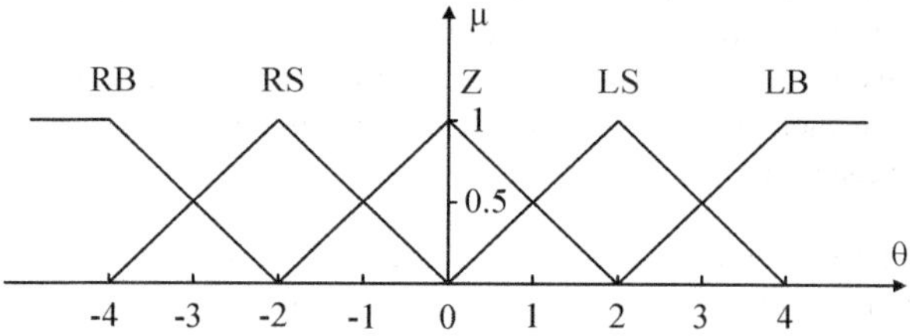

Fig. 3. The membership function for the set "θ"

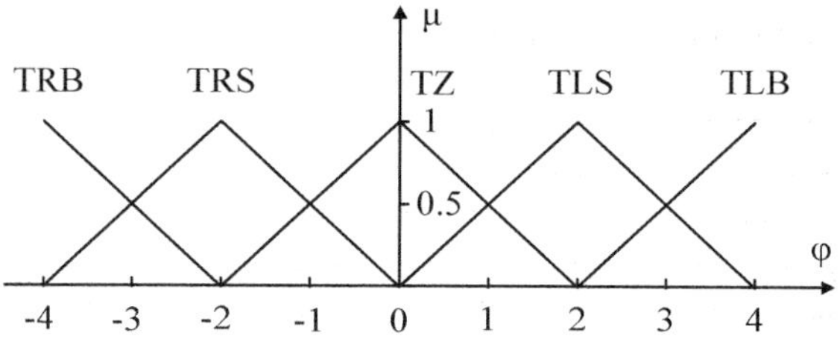

Fig. 4. The membership function for the set "φ"

2.3 Define the Fuzzy Rules

The basic idea of the obstacle avoidance is as follows: ensuring the robot to avoid obstacles, meanwhile, to toward target. When the target point on the left (right) side of the robot, it turns left (right). When the frontal obstacle distance is small and the target point is in the rear of the obstacle, the robot turns left or right based on the left obstacle distance and the right obstacle distance: if the left obstacle distance is greater than or equal the right obstacle distance, the robot chooses to turn left, because left is safer, otherwise to turn right. It corresponding to two rules, that is, when d is VS or S and θ is Z, φ is TRB or TLB. The obstacle avoidance fuzzy rules are shown in Table 1.

Table 1. Fuzzy rules

	RB	RS	Z	LS	LB
VS	TRB	TRB	TRB or TLB	TLB	TLB
S	TRB	TRB	TRB or TLB	TLB	TLB
M	TRS	TRS	TZ	TLS	TLS
B	TRS	TZ	TZ	TZ	TLS
VB	TRS	TZ	TZ	TZ	TLS

2.4 Fuzzy Reasoning and Defuzzification

Fuzzy reasoning is the core of the fuzzy controller. This paper uses Mamdani fuzzy reasoning method and the result of the fuzzy reasoning is defuzzified using the Centroid method also known as Centre of Area (COA) method [8]. In order to ensure the real-time control for the robot, we use the off-line calculation and online lookup method for fuzzy control. The crisp output values are obtained by the off-line calculation and the fuzzy control table (shown in Table 2) is constructed through the experimental test and modification for crisp output values. The fuzzy control for the obstacle avoidance is completed through the robot looks up the control table directly, so the online computational complexity is very small. In the fuzzy control table, VAR is a variable. The meaning of the VAR is as follows: when the left obstacle distance is greater than or equal the right obstacle distance, φ=4.0 that makes the robot turn left big, otherwise φ=-4.0 that makes the robot turn right big. The crisp values in the control table are needed to convert into the actual output steering angle through the scale transformation. This paper adopt the linear transformation and the scale transformation factor is k=60°/4=15°.

Table 2. Fuzzy control table

	-4	-3	-2	-1	0	1	2	3	4
0	-4.0	-4.0	-4.0	-4.0	VAR	4.0	4.0	4.0	4.0
1	-3.5	-3.5	-3.5	-3.5	VAR	3.5	3.5	3.5	3.5
2	-3.5	-3.5	-3.5	-3.5	VAR	3.5	3.5	3.5	3.5
3	-2.5	-2.5	-2.5	-1.5	VAR	1.5	2.5	2.5	2.5
4	-2.0	-2.0	-2.0	-1.0	0.0	1.0	2.0	2.0	2.0
5	-2.0	-1.0	-1.0	-1.0	0.0	1.0	1.0	1.0	2.0
6	-2.0	-1.0	-1.0	-0.5	0.0	0.5	1.0	1.0	2.0
7	-2.0	-1.0	-1.0	-0.5	0.0	0.5	1.0	1.0	2.0
8	-2.0	-1.0	-1.0	-0.5	0.0	0.5	1.0	1.0	2.0

3 The Basic Idea of Deadlock Prevention Mechanism

3.1 The Progress of the Robot Moves

According to the values of the inputs d and θ, the output steering angle φ is determined by looking up the fuzzy control table. But the robot does not move forward a fixed step immediately after it turned the angle φ, because the robot does not know the frontal obstacle distance in the new direction, if it moves, it is likely to hit obstacle. So after the robot turned the angle φ it must to detect obstacle distance again. If the obstacle distance is greater than a fixed step, the robot moves forward a fixed step, otherwise the robot doesn't, then the robot needs to turn δ degrees one or more times according to a certain direction (for example, turns left) until it finds a safe path, and then moves forward a fixed step. We define the process is the secondary obstacle avoidance. The process of the secondary obstacle avoidance is shown in Fig. 5.

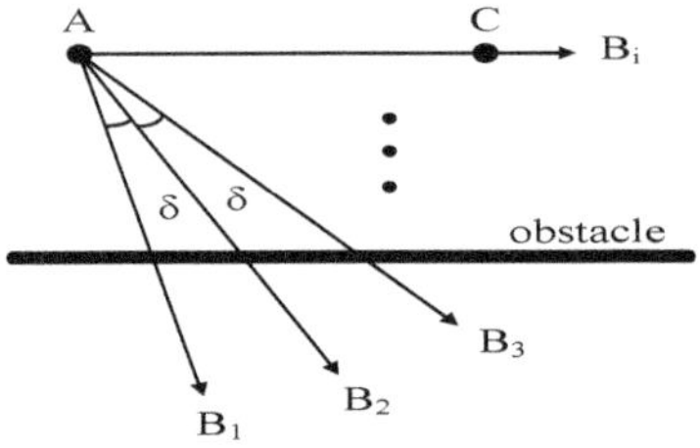

Fig. 5. The secondary obstacle avoidance

In Fig. 5, A is the position of the robot and AB_1 is the new forward direction after the robot turned the output φ. Through detection, the obstacle distance is less than a fixed step in AB_1 direction, then the robot turns left (assumption) δ degrees and the direction becomes AB_2. Detecting again, the obstacle distance is still less than a fixed step in AB_2 direction, then the robot turns left δ degrees again. The robot will continue to do so until it finds a safe direction $AB_{i,}$ then the robot moves forward a fixed step to C. In this paper δ is set to 15°, that is, the robot turns 15° every time in the secondary obstacle avoidance. The robot turns left or right in the secondary obstacle avoidance is decided by the turning sign T: if T=1, the robot turns left every time in the secondary obstacle avoidance, and if T= -1, the robot turns right every time.

3.2 Deadlock Prevention Mechanism

The algorithm uses the deadlock prevention mechanism to avoid deadlock. This is the deadlock prevention mechanism: when the robot detects the dangerous field, it will combine the fuzzy obstacle avoidance with the secondary obstacle avoidance through setting the value of T, so the robot can travel along the edge of the obstacle to escape from the obstacle, thus the robot effectively avoids deadlock. The operation of the deadlock prevention mechanism is decided by the deadlock prevention sign P: P=0 represents robot does not in the state of deadlock prevention and P=1 represents the robot in the state of deadlock prevention. Any of the following two conditions appears is considered the robot moves into the dangerous field: one condition is P=0 and the robot need the secondary obstacle avoidance to move a step; the other condition is P=0 and φ is VAR. If any of the above conditions appears, P is set to 1 and T is set to 1 or -1, and then the deadlock prevention mechanism is started. The value of T is decided by the positive and negative of the present φ, if φ is positive, T is 1, otherwise T is -1.

3.3 Free from the State of Deadlock Prevention

When the robot escapes from the dangerous obstacle, the mission of deadlock prevention mechanism is completed, and then the deadlock prevention mechanism should exit. The condition of the robot frees from the deadlock prevention mechanism is as follows: if T=1, the right side sensors don't find obstacle and $\theta<60°$, then the robot is considered has escaped from the dangerous obstacle and P is set to 0; if T=-1, the left side sensors don't find obstacle and $\theta>-60°$, and P is set to 0.

3.4 Path Planning Simulations in VC++

The simulation program is developed in VC++6.0. Figs. 6-10 show five simulations of the robot path planning in various environments. Fig. 6 shows the robot travels in the U-type obstacle field.

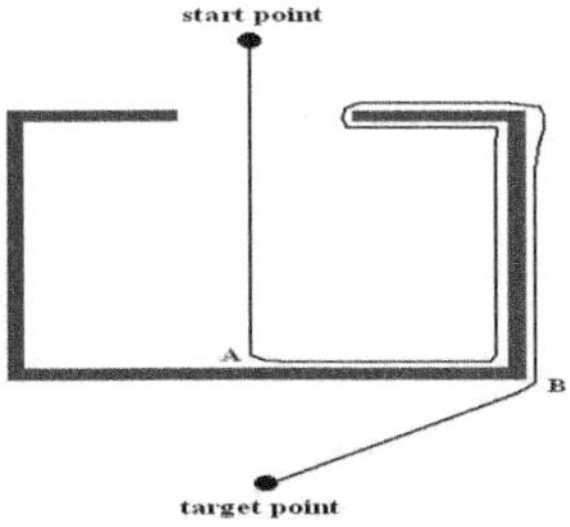

Fig. 6. Travel in the U-type obstacle field

In Fig. 6, when the robot moves to position A, d is VS or S and θ is Z, and the output φ is VAR by looking up the fuzzy control table. The condition that the robot moves into the dangerous field is satisfied, so the deadlock prevention mechanism is started and P is set to 1. According to the definition for VAR, because at A the left obstacle distance is greater than or equal the right obstacle distance, φ=4.0; and because $\varphi>0$, T is set to 1. The robot travels along the edge of the obstacle from A to B by the deadlock prevention mechanism. At B, the right side sensors of the robot don't find obstacle and $\theta<60°$, so the condition of the robot frees from the deadlock prevention mechanism is satisfied, the deadlock prevention mechanism exits, P is set to 0. The robot escapes from the U-type obstacle and reaches the target point successfully.

Fig. 7 shows the robot travels in the double U-type obstacle field. Fig. 8 shows the robot travels in the multi-obstacles field. Fig. 9 shows the robot travels in the high density obstacles field. Fig. 10 shows the robot travels in the labyrinth obstacle field.

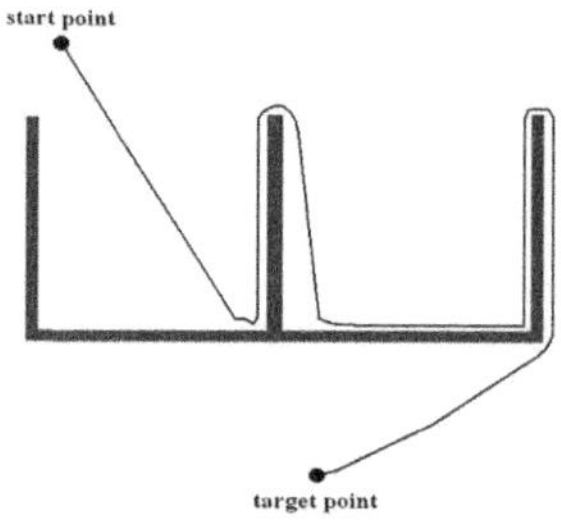

Fig. 7. Travel in the double U-type obstacle field

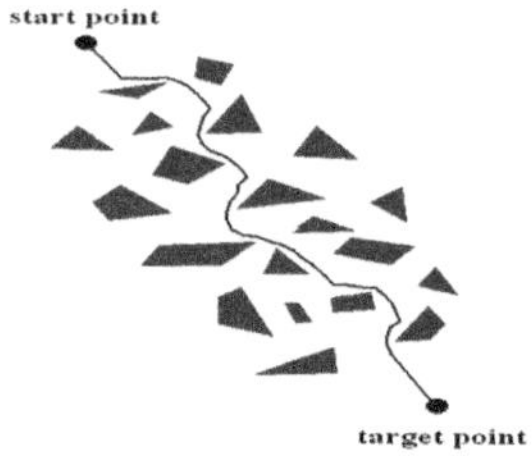

Fig. 8. Travel in the multi-obstacles field

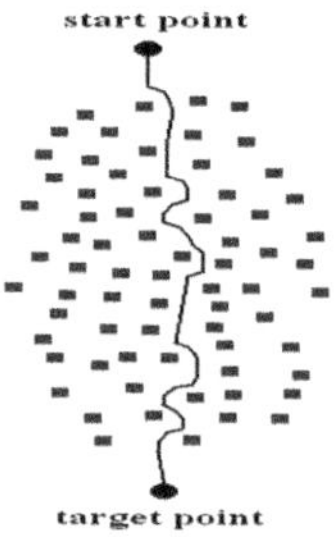

Fig. 9. Travel in the high density obstacles field

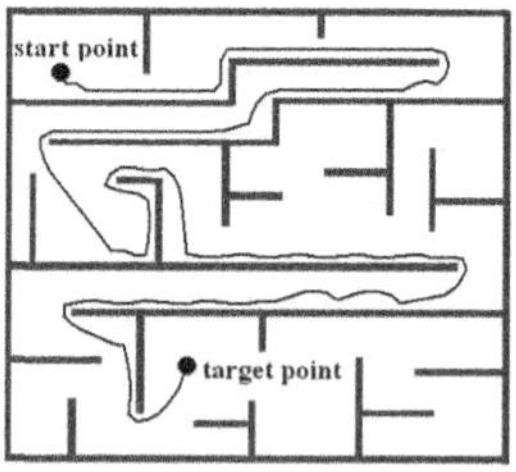

Fig. 10. Travel in the labyrinth obstacle field

From the simulation results in various environments can be seen, the effect of the path planning is better and no deadlock occurs.

4 Deadlock Problem

The robot can effectively avoid deadlock by the deadlock prevention mechanism. But when the robot faces with more complex obstacle environment such as the semi-closed double U-type obstacle, the robot can not avoid deadlock by the deadlock prevention mechanism, it would adopt the deadlock resolution strategy to eliminate the deadlock. The deadlock resolution strategy is composed of deadlock judgment, solution of deadlock and judgment whether deadlock is eliminated or not.

4.1 Deadlock Judgment

Judging whether the robot in the state of deadlock or not correctly is the most important condition to solve the deadlock problem. We adopt a grid method to judge deadlock: Firstly, we divide the whole robot workspace into several grid regions of the appropriate and the same size. If the robot in the state of deadlock prevention and the grid region where the robot is passing has not a mark, then the robot makes a mark and its value equals the value of T; and if the robot in the state of deadlock prevention and passes a marked grid region, then the robot will judge deadlock: if T doesn't equal the mark of the grid region, we consider that a deadlock occurs and the robot begins to solve the deadlock; if T equals the mark of the grid region, the deadlock couldn't occur and the robot deals with nothing. The process of deadlock occurrence is shown in Fig. 11.

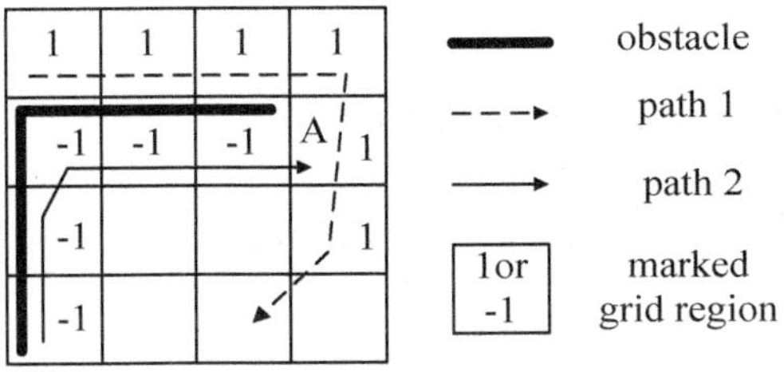

Fig. 11. The process of deadlock occurrence

In Fig. 11, the dashed line is the path which the robot in state of deadlock prevention passed previously and the value of T is 1 at that time, so the marks of the grid regions which the dashed line passes through are set to 1. The solid line is the path in which the robot in the state of deadlock prevention is passing now and the value of T is -1, so the marks of the grid regions which the solid line passes through are set to -1. When the robot travels the grid region A, it finds that the region has been marked and the mark is 1, unluckily, the value of T at the present doesn't equal the value of the mark, so a deadlock occurs at A.

4.2 Solution of Deadlock

After the deadlock occurred, the method for solving deadlock would be adopted to make the robot free from the deadlock. The method is as follows: the robot turns toward the target point, and T is set to the opposite value of it; when the robot starts the deadlock prevention mechanism again, T is not set to new value and still keeps the present value and the output φ is set to T*60°.

4.3 Deadlock Elimination Judgment

When the robot starts the deadlock prevention mechanism again after a deadlock occurred, the robot begins to eliminate the deadlock. The condition of deadlock elimination is as follows: the robot continuously passes three unmarked grid regions. When meeting the condition of deadlock elimination, the robot frees from the deadlock.

4.4 Simulation

Fig. 12 shows the robot travels in the semi-enclosed double U-type obstacle field. In the obstacle field a deadlock occurs.

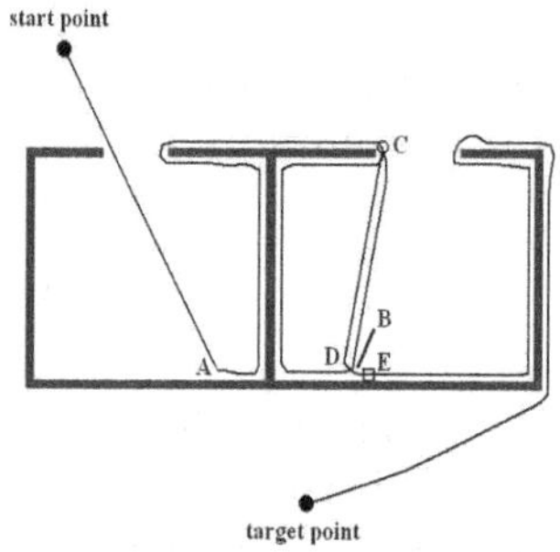

Fig. 12. Travel in the semi-enclosed double U-type obstacle field

At A, the robot starts the deadlock prevention mechanism and turns left (see from the robot angle). T is set to 1, so the grid regions which the robot passes through from starting the deadlock prevention mechanism to exiting the mechanism are marked 1. At B, the robot starts the deadlock prevention mechanism the second time and turns right. T is set to -1, so the unmarked grid regions which the robot passes through are marked -1 until the deadlock prevention mechanism exits. When the robot travels along the edge of the second U-type obstacle to C, it finds the grid region where C locates has a mark and its value is 1, and the present T doesn't equals the mark, so a deadlock occurs at C. The robot begins to eliminate the deadlock: the robot turns toward the target point, and T is set to the opposite value of it, that is T=1; at D, the robot starts the deadlock prevention mechanism again, according to the solution of deadlock, T is not changed and φ is set to T*60°, that is T=1 and φ=60°, then the robot turns left; when the robot travels to E, the robot already has continuously passed three unmarked grid regions, so the condition of deadlock elimination is satisfied and the robot frees from the deadlock. The robot continues to travels along the edge of the obstacle, and finally escapes from the obstacle and reaches the target point successfully.

5 Conclusions

This paper studies the mobile robot path planning in globally unknown environment based on fuzzy control. The fuzzy rules are established according to the human driving experience and fuzzy control table is constructed by the fuzzy reasoning and defuzzication. This paper presents the path planning algorithm composed of the deadlock prevention mechanism and the deadlock resolution. The algorithm offers a new idea of the solution of deadlock and achieves the goal that the robot can find a non-collision path successfully from the start point to the target point in the unknown obstacle environment and the effect of the path planning is better.

References

1. Wang, Y.: Robot Intelligence Control Engineering. Science Press, Beijing (2004)
2. Lu, Y.: A on-line self-organizing dynamic fuzzy Q-learning algorithm and its application in the real-time path planning for mobile robot. Doctor Thesis, University of Science and Technology of China, Hefei, China (2005)
3. Su, Z., Lu, J.: A study on the path planning of mobile robot with the fuzzy logic method. Transactions of Beijing Institute of Technology 23(3), 290–294 (2003)
4. Fu, Y., Gu, X., Wang, S.: A fuzzy control based path planning strategy for autonomous robot. Robot 26(6), 548–552 (2004)
5. Wen, S., Zhu, Q., Zhang, X.: Simulation of the path planning of mobile robot based on the fuzzy controller. Applied Science and Technology 32(4), 31–33 (2005)
6. Fayad, C., Webb, D.P.: Optimized fuzzy Logic based on algorithm for a mobile robot collision avoidance in an unknown environment. In: Proceedings of the 7th European Congress on Intelligent Techniques and Soft Computing, Aachen, Germany, pp. 13–16 (September 1999)
7. Li, P., Wen, S.: Realization of the Path Planning Algorithm Based on Fuzzy Control. Journal of Hangzhou Dianzi University 27(6), 82–86 (2007)
8. Durkin: Expert Systems: Design and Development, Macmillan Publishing Company, New York (1994)

No-Model Tracking by Data-Driven Method Using BP Networks

Jin Xue-bo[1], He Hai-ran[1], Wang Ya-ming[1], and Yuan Meng-yang[2]

[1] College of Informatics and Electronics
Zhejiang Sci-Tech University, Hangzhou, China
[2] College of Informatics and Electronics
SIAS International University, Zhengzhou, China
xuebojin2011@hotmail.com

Abstract. In the model-driven tracking approach, the tracking performance is mainly based on the system model. But the accurate model is difficult to obtain, while data-driven tracking approach can't depend on the accuracy of system model and it can tracking by the measurement data. This paper use BP net to develop a data-driven tracking. The BP net is trained by system measurement and prediction get by Kalman filter and the tracking as the output data. The simulation has shown that the data-driven tracking by BP net can obtain good performance even when the moving target is different.

Keywords: model-driven tracking, data-driven tracking, Kalman filter, BP net, video tracking.

1 Introduction

The target tracking system consists of a system dynamic/process model (predictor) unit of the object being tracked, a set of sensor model units, a set of sensor validation units, a set of data fusion units and a filter/correction unit. The process model is the key to estimation because it will decide the predicted state from the process model unit, which is used as the reference datum for the sensor model units to generate the predicted sensor data according to the characteristic of each sensor used in the system.

Several system models have been developed for tracking. The CV model and AC model assume the disturbance of velocity and acceleration as Gaussian white noise. But in the actual tracking problem these assumptions are often incorrect. In Singer model, the target acceleration is described as the correlation function. But the parameters should be selected carefully, or else the model still can not be consistence to maneuvering target.

In practice, it's very difficult to described maneuvering target model by a single model. In the multiple model approach it is assumed that the system obeys one of a finite number of models. A Bayesian framework is used: Starting with prior probabilities of each model being correct (i.e., the system is in a particular mode), the corresponding posterior probabilities are obtained. This will result in the static MM

D. Zeng (Ed.): ICAIC 2011, Part I, CCIS 224, pp. 532–540, 2011.

estimator. While the mode that is in effect stays fixed, each model has its own dynamics, so the overall estimator is dynamic.

Recently data-driven tracking approach has received a great deal of attention. Data plays an important role in simulation. Relevant and correct data is needed to formalize the model and its environment, including parameter fitting, calibration and validating of the model, so we can have meaningful and credible simulation results.

The concept is that DDDAS applications dynamically incorporate data from on-line measurements of the actual systems, to refine the original models that are driven at execution time by dynamic inputs 23. Large quantities of data which are get by sensors and detectors can model the system, which can be used to estimate parameters for simulation studies. As data are processed, simulation models are adjusted in DDDAS to best agree with known measurements 4.

Reference 5 and 6 are discussed multiscale interpola-tion and parameter updating using an objective function. It's concluded that frequent updating of the sensor data in the sim-ulations can significantly improve the prediction results. 7 proposes a dynamic data-driven approach to improve the ada-ptability of the model which can be fed with data derived from different scenarios, from decision variations or from real-time measurements to accomplish accurate and automated model calibration.

In this paper, we try to use the BP network in data-driven tracking problem. The remaining of the paper is organized as follows. In next section, we describe the basis theory of BP net. The data-driven tracking approach is shown by simulations in Section 3 and Section 4 is developed to the conclusions.

2 BP Netmork

As an important tool of studying nonlinear phenomenon and complex system, the neural net algorithm has essential parallelism and intelligent features such as self-organizing, self-adapting and self-study, BP network has simple structure, good stability, and strong nonlinear mapping ability. A standard BP network consists of one input layer, one output layer and one or more hidden layers. Each layer contains a number of nodes, Connections exist only between the nodes of two successive layers. The functions animating the network are the same for all hidden layers and output layer;

$$o_{pi}^{(k)} = f\left(I_{pi}^{(k)}\right) = 1/\left(1+\exp(-I_{pi}^{(k)})\right) - 1/2iKp \qquad (1)$$

$$I_{pi}^{(k)} = \sum_{j=1}^{n(k-1)} \left(W_{ij}^{(k)} o_{pj}^{(k-1)}\right) + bias_i^{(k)} \qquad (2)$$

where $o_{pi}^{(k)}$ is the output of node i in layer κ, the subs-cript p denotes the order of arrangement of the training patt-erns used in the training phase, $W_{ij}^{(k)}$ is the corresponding wei-ght between the node j in layer k-1 and the node i in la-yer K, $bias_i^{(k)}$ $bias_i^{(k)}$ is the bias for the node i in layer K, and $n(k-1)$ is the number of nodes in layer $k-1$. The output value of each node ranges over -0.5 to 0.5. BP networks are usually trained by following delta rule with a momentum term:

$$\Delta W_{ij}^{(k)}(n) = -\frac{1}{n_p}\eta_{ij}^{(k)}(n)\sum_p \frac{\partial E_p(n)}{\partial W_{ij}^{(k)}} + \beta\Delta W_{ij}^{(k)}(n-1) \tag{3}$$

$$\Delta bias_i^{(k)}(n) = -\frac{1}{n_p}\eta_i^{(k)}(n)\sum_p \frac{\partial E_p(n)}{\partial bias_i^{(k)}} + \beta\Delta bias_i^{(k)}(n-1) \tag{4}$$

where $E_p(n)$ is the square error function of the pattern after n-th iteration and n_p is the number of training patterns. At (n+l)th iteration during training, the update of connection weight $\Delta W_{ij}^{(k)}$ is based on two components. The first component is a function of the error gradient. The second component is proportional to the amount of weight change in the previous iteration. p is the momentum factor which helps prevent the oscillation problem near the solution point. β denotes the learning rate which can be modified in each training epoch as follows:

$$\text{If} \quad \sum_p \frac{\partial E_p(n)}{\partial W_{ij}^{(k)}} \sum_p \frac{\partial E_p(n-1)}{\partial W_{ij}^{(k)}} \geq 0 \quad \text{then} \quad \eta_{ij}^{(k)}(n) = \eta^+ \eta_{ij}^{(k)}(n-1) \tag{5}$$

$$\text{If} \quad \sum_p \frac{\partial E_p(n)}{\partial W_{ij}^{(k)}} \sum_p \frac{\partial E_p(n-1)}{\partial W_{ij}^{(k)}} < 0 \quad \text{then} \quad \eta_{ij}^{(k)}(n) = \eta^- \eta_{ij}^{(k)}(n-1) \tag{6}$$

where η^+ and η^- are positive constants for which the values are slightly higher than or lower than 1 respectively. The adjustment rule of $\eta_i^{(k)}$ is similar to that of $\eta_{ij}^{(k)}$.The adaptive modification of learning rate can considerably speed up the training. Essentially, the learning algorithm described above is a kind of conventional BP algorithm.

3 Simulation

3.1 Tracking Target by Kalman Filter

We have got a series of video images shown as in Fig. 1. In the video, the ball as a target does free fall. The centroid data of ball have been obtained by image process approach and been used as the measurement data of target for tracking.

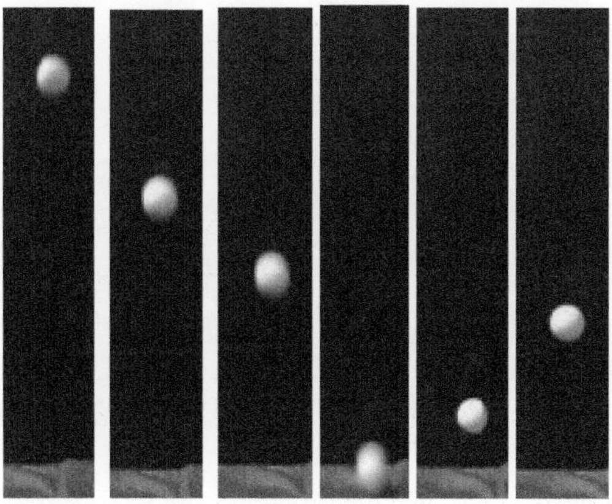

Fig. 1. The tracked video

The following CV model is used:
State equation:

$$x(k+1) = \Phi_{CV} x(k) + w_{CV}(k) \tag{7}$$

and

$$\Phi_{CV} = e^{A_{CV}T} = \begin{bmatrix} 1 & T \\ 0 & 1 \end{bmatrix} \tag{8}$$

$$w_{CV}(k) = \int_0^T e^{A_{CV}(T-\tau)} \Gamma_{CV} \omega(kt+\tau) d\tau = \int_0^T \begin{bmatrix} T-\tau \\ 1 \end{bmatrix} \omega(kt+\tau) d\tau \tag{9}$$

State covariance is

$$Q_{CV}(k) = \int_0^T \begin{bmatrix} T-\tau \\ 1 \end{bmatrix} \sigma^2 \begin{bmatrix} T-\tau & 1 \end{bmatrix} d\tau = \begin{bmatrix} \frac{1}{3}T^3 & \frac{1}{2}T^2 \\ \frac{1}{2}T^2 & T \end{bmatrix} \tag{10}$$

T is the sampling interval. Theresults by Kalman filter have shown in Fig. 2.1

where $Q = 1000 \times \begin{bmatrix} 10 & 0 \\ 0 & 10 \end{bmatrix}, R = 20^2$

and Fig. 2.2, where $Q = 10 \times \begin{bmatrix} 10 & 0 \\ 0 & 10 \end{bmatrix}, R = 15^2$.

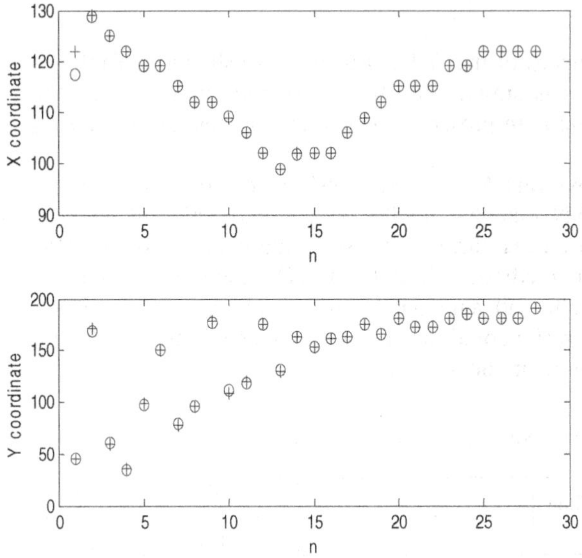

Fig. 2.1. Tracking by Kalman filter. "O" the track estimated by Kalman filter; "+" the real track

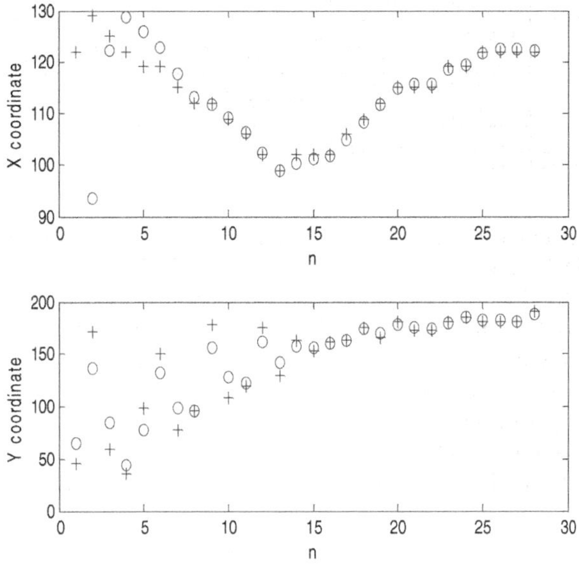

Fig. 2.2. Tracking by Kalman filter. "O" the track estimated by Kalman filter; "+" the real track

From the Fig 2.1 and Fig. 2.2, we can see the variance of process and measurement noise is very important to the performance of tracking. But in practice, the accurate model of target is difficult to get. The inaccurate model need higher robust of estimation algorithm, which will result the more complex algorithms. So in the tracking or estimation problem, the system model has been always key and difficult.

3.2 Tracking Target by BP

We believe the system model is hidden in the input and output data of system. By the BP net, we study the estimation of Kalman filter. The BP net is shown as in Fig.3, where the input data are the measurement and prediction, the output data is the estimation of tracking.

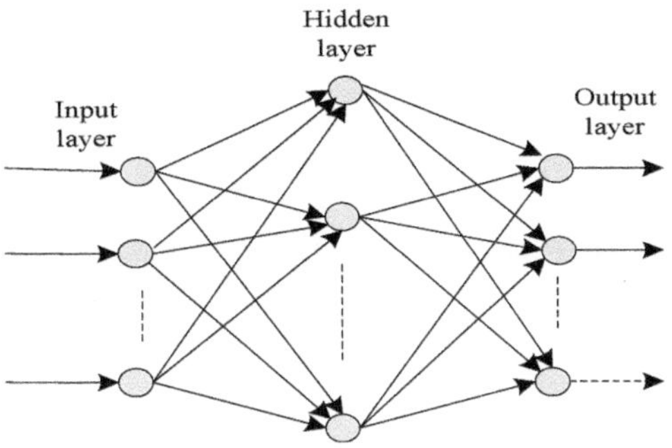

Fig. 3. BP net

We use the tracking results of Kalman filter shown in Fig.2 to training BP net, then the trained net is used for tracking. The tracking results are shown in Fig. 4 where "O" is the tracking results get by Kalman and "+" is the results get by BP net. Fig. 5 shows the difference of tracking by the Kalman and BP. The another video is tracked by the trained BP net and Kalman filter (with $Q = 1000 \times \begin{bmatrix} 10 & 0 \\ 0 & 10 \end{bmatrix}, R = 20^2$). The tracking results is shown in Fig. 6 and Fig. 7.

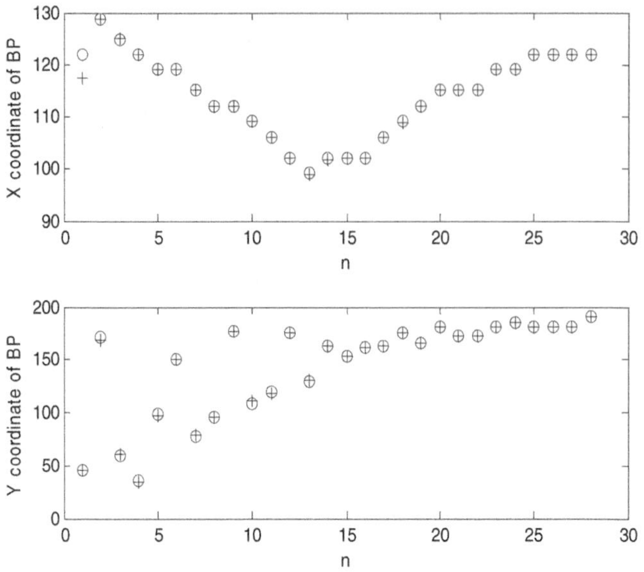

Fig. 4 The tracking results of BP; "O" Kalman, "+" BP net

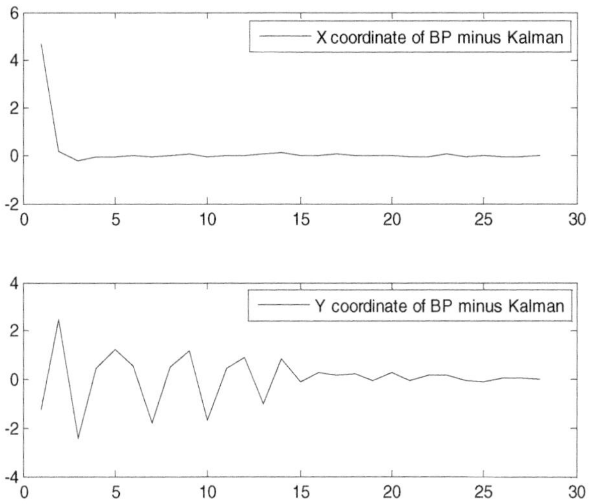

Fig. 5 The difference tracking by BP and Kalman filter

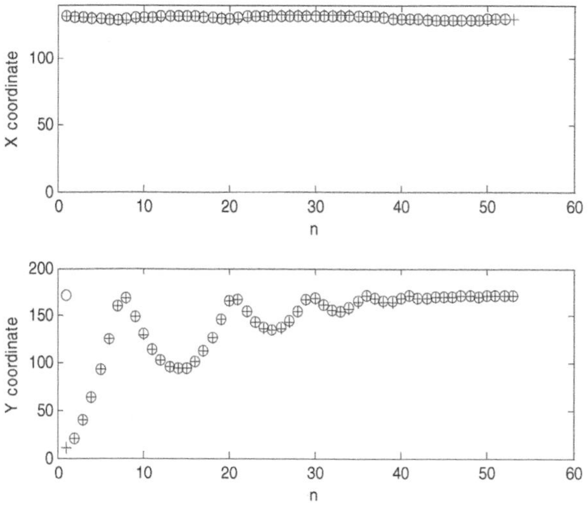

Fig. 6. The video tracked by BP net; "O" Kalman filter, "+" BP net

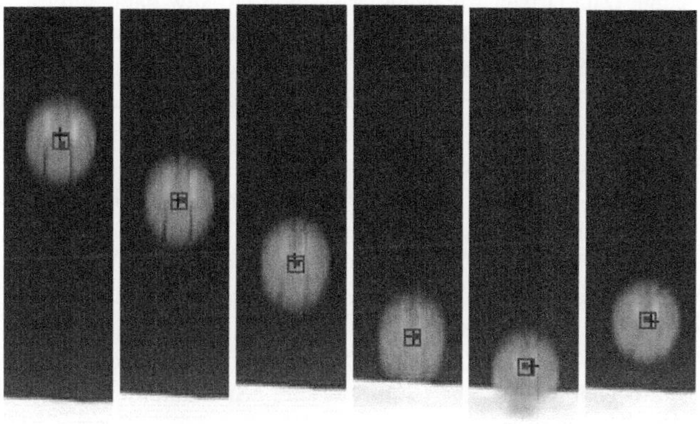

Fig. 7. The video tracked by Kalman filter and BP net; "square"Kalman filter, "small square" real track,"+" BP net

From the results, it's shown that the trained BP net can get a perfect tracking performance, and needn't the accurate system parameter, such as the variance of noise Q and R.

4 Conclusion

Tracking target has been used for lots of applications in many occasions. The system model is one of the key factors to the performance of tracking. This paper uses BP net to deal with tracking problem by data-driven method. The tracking results have shown that the trained BP net can obtain a good performance for different video.

The work of this paper is a beginning, as the target moves as free fall movement. The following work will focus on maneuvering target, and the BP net maybe developed new structure, too.

Acknowledgment. This work was supported by the National Natural Science Foundation of China under Grants No. 60971119, 60873020 and 61070063, Foundation of Science and Technology Department of Zhejiang Province of China No. 2009C34017 and Zhejiang Provincial Natural Science Foundation of China grants No. Z1080702.

References

1. DDDAS Workshop Groups, Creating a dynamic and symbiotic coupling of application/simulations with measurements/experiments. NSF DDDAS 2000 Workshop (2000), `http://www.nsf.gov/cise/cns/dddas/` (accessed March 20, 2009)
2. DDDAS Workshop Groups, Dynamic Data Driven Application Systems Workshop Report, NSF DDDAS 2006 Work-shop (2006), `http://www.nsf.gov/cise/cns/dddas/` (accessed March 20, 2009)
3. Darema, F.: Dynamic Data Driven Applications Systems: A New Paradigm for Application Simulations and Measurements. In: Bubak, M., van Albada, G.D., Sloot, P.M.A., Dongarra, J. (eds.) ICCS 2004. LNCS, vol. 3038, pp. 662–669. Springer, Heidelberg (2004)
4. Douglas, C.C.: Dynamic Data Driven Applications Systems – DDDAS 2008. In: Bubak, M., van Albada, G.D., Dongarra, J., Sloot, P.M.A. (eds.) ICCS 2008, Part III. LNCS, vol. 5103, pp. 3–4. Springer, Heidelberg (2008)
5. Douglas, C.C., Efendiev, Y., Ewing, R., Ginting, V., Lazarov, R.: Dynamic DataDriven Simulations in Stochastic Environments. Computing 77(4), 321–333 (2006)
6. Douglas, C.C., Efendiev, Y., Ewing, R.: Interpolation and Update in Dynamic Data-Driven Application. NATO Security through Science Series C: Environmental Security, pp. 235–246. Springer, Berlin (2007)
7. Huang, Y.L., Verbraeck, A.: A Dynamic Data-Driven Approach For Rail Transport System Simulation. In: Proceedings of the 2009 Winter Simulation Conference (WSC), pp. 2553–2562 (2009)

A Controlled Seismic Emulator: Regenerating Earthquakes via a Robot

Guangyu Liu[1,*], Feng Song[2], Jiang-Feng Tao[3], and Guang Ma[4]

[1] School of Automation Hangzhou Dianzi University, Hangzhou, China
guangyu_liu@126.com
[2] Department of Design, Suzhou Auto Technology Co., Ltd
[3] School of Mechanical Engineering Shanghai Jiao Tong University
[4] College of Mechanical and Electrical Engineering
Wenzhou University, Wenzhou, China

Abstract. In recent years, earthquakes have caused the collapse of numerous constructions and buildings, and killed thousands of people. A small scale seimic emulator is designed to regenerate seismic waves, which can be used to evaluate the performance of a scaled buidling or construction in civil engineering. The emulator is a robot device that consists of a plate movable in a planar plane, two DC servo motors with built in quadrature encoders for acutation and sensing, and a NI CompactRIO for control signal. A control strategy based on inverse dynamics and feedback is used to track the recorded seismic waves.

Keywords: seismic emulator, inverse dynamics, feedback.

1 Introduction

Earthquakes are an unstoppable and unpredictable act of nature that can result in the destruction of buildings and even fatalities [1]. For example, the death tolls due to the building destruction have hit 200,000 in Haiti earthquake, 2010 and 80,000 in Chinese Wenchuan earthquake, 2008. The only control we have over earthquakes is to design and construct buildings in a way that damage can be minimised, if not totally avoided. A shake table can be used to simulate the ground movement of an earthquake, which can be used for controlled testing of structures subjected to earthquakes [2]. New concepts are often tested on shake tables before implementation in real buildings to see if they respond as predicted. This makes shake tables a valuable tool in designing buildings against earthquake damage.

Most shake tables are uni-axial and built on large scales which produce a unidirectional, sinusoidal movement [3]. These facilities are not easily accessible for civil engineers or students to study the interaction of earthquake dynamics and building structures. More importantly, these tables cannot reproduce the actual seimic waves that are more complex than the unidirectional, sinusoidal movemnt although

* Corresponding author.

D. Zeng (Ed.): ICAIC 2011, Part I, CCIS 224, pp. 541–549, 2011.

the latter is easy to operate and interprete. To this end, a few small scale seismic motion simulators that support tuning gains [4] and tracking functions [5, 6] were built at some institutes.

The objective of this study is to provide a new small scale two degrees of freedom robotic shake table where a novel control strategy is implemented to reprodue the destructive planar L-waves. Here, the less destructive vertical P-waves are ignored becaenuse buildings are built to withstand the pull of gravity and able to withstand substantial accelerations in the vertical direction [7]. This robotic table is not only a good educational tool but also a practical exiciter for testing new concepts of scaled building structures.

2 Mechatronic Design

The objective of mechanical parts is to have an aluminum platform that could move within a planar area of within an area of 460×520 mm as shown in Fig. 1. Two pairs of low friction polymer coated aluminum linear guides are used to support the platform and constrain its movements in x and y directions respectively. The guides in x direction are fixed to two aluminium base plates that remain on a wooden base. The guides in y direction are fixed to two alumimium base plates that are free to slide in x direction. A synchromesh cable and pulley transmission system is to provide easy transmission of the rotational motion of pulleys into the desired linear motion of the platform. Two pulleys are the drive pulleys, each of which is on the shaft of a 12V brushed DC servo motor capable of 4700 rpm in Fig. 2. All pulleys as well as motors are mounted on the still aluminum bases. The synchromesh design of the cable engages with the helical grooves of the drive pulleys on the motor shafts, ensuring no slippage. Also, as they physically engage with the drive pulley there is no need for large tensions required if a flat belt were used and low tension is sufficient to provide zero backlash. Also, the low inertia cable allows for maximum accelerations. These characteristics are essential to maintain accurate positioning of the platforms through the earthquake motion emulation.

The objective of electronic parts is to measure linear displacements and velocities of the platform and provide control control signals to DC motors. In Fig. 2, the angles and angular velocities of the drive pulleys are measured by two quadrature encoders attached to two DC motors which have an algebriac relationship with linear motions of the platform and, hence, provide output feedback information for the control system. An advanced embedded control and data acquisition system, a standard NI CompactRIO with a NI 9505 full H-bridge brushed DC servo drive module, a NI 9411 digital input module and a power supply in Fig. 3, is used to implement a controller to supply a varying voltage driving the motors. Four limit switches are placed at close to the extremes of the linear guides to trigger the cotroller to stop the platform from travelling further outside the designated area.

LabVIEW RT 8.6 is used as a platform for software design to implement a control algorithm that generates FPGA codes deployed directly onto the CompactRIO FPGA. The host computer is not compulsory once the codes are run in CompactRIO.

Finally, a robotic planar shaker table is built up in Fig. 4, where electronic design and software design are relatively standard and handy since NI products are commerical hardware and software.

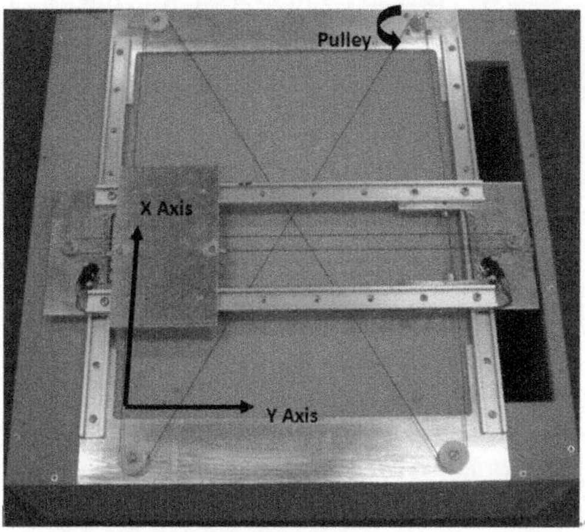

Fig. 1. Shaker table assembly

Fig. 2. A brushed DC motor with a quadrature encoder that is mounted in a guide rail

Fig. 3. A Standard NI CompactRIO Control Unit

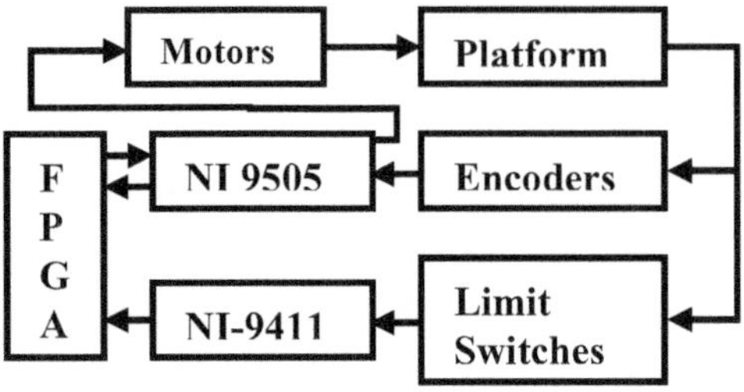

Fig. 4. Schematic set-up of the rototic shaker table

3 Trajactory Tracking Controller Design

Recall that the robotic device is to reproduce real seismic L-wave acclerations. Here, we assume that the mechatronic design satisfy the design specifications. Then, the objective of control design is to derive a cross voltage signal for each motor based on an arbitrary L-wave (including a sinusoid) for reference and sensory feedback information. Because the shaker table movement is decoupled into x and y directions, we deal only with one of decoupled systems in sequel and the same procedure applies to another. Let DC motors with armature's moment of inertia J_a, armature ristance R_a, torque constant K_t, and back emf constant K_e.

We suppose that $\ddot{x}_r(t)$ be a desirable reference signal for $x(t)$ in x direction. Applying Newtonian's second law leads to a feedforward linear control force

$$f_{x,r}(t) = M_x \ddot{x}_r(t) \tag{1}$$

where M_x is the total movable mass in x direction. Define ρ be a radius of the drive pulley. The induced load torque exerted on the shaft is

$$\tau_{x,L,r}(t) = \rho f_{x,r}(t) = \rho M_x \ddot{x}_r(t) \tag{2}$$

Applying Euler's equation for deriving the angular dynamics of the rotor gives

$$J_a \ddot{\theta}_{x,r}(t) = \tau_{x,r}(t) - \tau_{x,L,r}(t) \tag{3}$$

where $\theta_{x,r}(t)$ is the reference signal of the armature's angle $\theta_x(t)$ corresponding to x direction, $\tau_{x,r}(t)$ is the desirable emf torque and $\tau_{x,L,r}(t)$ is the load introduced in Eq. (2). The mechanical design implies a fixed relationship

$$\frac{d^j \theta_{x,r}(t)}{dt^j} \equiv \frac{1}{\rho} \frac{d^j x_r(t)}{dt^j}, \quad j = 0,1,2 \tag{4}$$

Based on Ohm's law, the desirable emf torque $\tau_{x,r}(t)$ relates to the desirable cross voltage $v_{x,r}(t)$

$$\begin{aligned}\tau_{x,r}(t) &= K_t \frac{v_{x,r}(t) - K_e \dot{\theta}_{x,r}(t)}{R_a} \\ &= K_t \frac{v_{x,r}(t) - \dfrac{K_e}{\rho}\dot{x}_r(t)}{R_a}\end{aligned} \tag{5}$$

On the other hand, according to Eq (2) to Eq (3), the desirable emf torque $\tau_{x,r}(t)$ also satisfies

$$\begin{aligned}\tau_{x,r}(t) &= J_a \ddot{\theta}_{x,r}(t) + \rho M_x \ddot{x}_r(t) \\ &= \left(\frac{J_a}{\rho} + \rho M_x\right)\ddot{x}_r(t)\end{aligned} \tag{6}$$

Comparing Eq (5) and Eq (6) gives

$$\left(\frac{J_a}{\rho} + \rho M_x\right)\ddot{x}_r(t) = K_t \frac{v_{x,r}(t) - \dfrac{K_e}{\rho}\dot{x}_r(t)}{R_a} \tag{7}$$

Rearranging Eq (7) gives the desirable feedforward control voltage for the DC motor

$$v_{x,r}(t) = \frac{R_a}{K_t}\left(\frac{J_a}{\rho} + \rho M_x\right)\ddot{x}_r(t) + \frac{K_e}{\rho}\dot{x}_r(t) \tag{8}$$

Remark 3.1 Eq. (8) is named as the inverse dynamics of this specific robotic shaker given that the linear motions of the movable platform are known as a priori. From another point view, Eq. (8) is also the norminal dynamics of the shaker in x direction.

Dropping off the subscript r from Eq. (8) gives us the robot's nominal dynamics in x direction

$$v_x(t) = \frac{R_a}{K_t}\left(\frac{J_a}{\rho} + \rho M_x\right)\ddot{x}(t) + \frac{K_e}{\rho}\dot{x}(t) \tag{9}$$

Define $e_{x,1}(t) = x(t) - x_r(t)$, $e_{x,2}(t) = \dot{x}(t) - \dot{x}_r(t)$, and $u_x(t) = v_x(t) - v_{x,r}(t)$. We have a state space equation in state space form is

$$\begin{bmatrix} \dot{e}_{x,1}(t) \\ \dot{e}_{x,2}(t) \end{bmatrix} = A \begin{bmatrix} e_{x,1}(t) \\ e_{x,2}(t) \end{bmatrix} + Bu_x(t) \tag{10}$$

with $A = \begin{bmatrix} 0 & 1 \\ 0 & -\frac{K_t K_e}{R_a(J_a+\rho^2 M_x)} \end{bmatrix}$ and $B = \begin{bmatrix} 0 \\ \frac{K_t \rho}{R_a(J_a+\rho^2 M_x)} \end{bmatrix}$.

Lemma 3.1. Consider the nominal dynamics Eq. (9) of the implemented robotic shaker. Assume that $v_x(t) \equiv v_{x,r}(t)$, where $v_{x,r}(t)$ is given by Eq. (8), $x(0) = x_r(0)$, and $\dot{x}(0) = \dot{x}_r(0)$. Then, $x(t) \equiv x_r(t)$ and $\dot{x}(t) \equiv \dot{x}_r(t)$ hold for $t \in (0, \infty)$.

Proof. In this case, we obtain an autonomous linear dynamical system

$$\begin{bmatrix} \dot{e}_{x,1}(t) \\ \dot{e}_{x,2}(t) \end{bmatrix} = A \begin{bmatrix} e_{x,1}(t) \\ e_{x,2}(t) \end{bmatrix}$$

whose solution is

$$\begin{aligned} \begin{bmatrix} e_{x,1}(t) \\ e_{x,2}(t) \end{bmatrix} &= \begin{bmatrix} e_{x,1}(0) \\ e_{x,2}(0) \end{bmatrix} \exp(At) \\ &= \begin{bmatrix} 0 \\ 0 \end{bmatrix} \exp(At) \\ &= \begin{bmatrix} 0 \\ 0 \end{bmatrix}. \end{aligned}$$

Therefore, $x(t) = x_r(t)$ and $\dot{x}(t) = \dot{x}_r(t)$ hold for $t \in (0, \infty)$.

Remark 3.2. The feedforward controller Eq. (8) performs a role of the guidance control action such that the trajectory of the controlled system Eq. (9) tracks exactly the given reference trajectory if the initial condition of Eq. (9) also satisfies the given reference trajectory. However, this nice property is easily violated if the actual dynamics has discrepancies from Eq. (9), for example, disturbance, unmodelled dynamics, and different initial conditions.

The feedforward action alone could not ensure the convergence of the error signals in Eq. (10). To this end, we design a feedback controller to Eq. (10), e.g., a PD controller

$$u_x(t) = -K_{x,1}e_{x,1} - K_{x,2}e_{x,2} \tag{11}$$

such that the matrix $A-BK$ with $K=(K_{x,1} \quad K_{x,2})$ is Hurwitz [8]. Then, the controlled system Eq. (10) with the controller Eq. (11) has a solution

$$\begin{bmatrix} e_{x,1}(t) \\ e_{x,2}(t) \end{bmatrix} = \begin{bmatrix} e_{x,1}(0) \\ e_{x,2}(0) \end{bmatrix} \exp((A-BK)t)$$

where $\exp((A-BK)t) \to 0$ as $t \to \infty$. Hence, $(e_{x,1}(t) \quad e_{x,2}(t))^T \to 0$ as $t \to \infty$ for any given initial condition.

Remark 3.3. The feedback controller Eq. (11) guarantees the convergence of the actual trajectory to the reference trajectory even though the initial condition has discrepancies. Moreover, the controller is able to reject the disturbance and improve the robustness of the controlled system.

Remark 3.4. In fact, Eq. (11) implies the feedforward control action Eq. (8) because the actual controller is a cascaded design of a feedforward action and a feedback action, that is, $v_x(t) = u_x(t) + v_{x,r}(t)$.

Combining Eqs (8) and (11) gives the final controller in x direction

$$\begin{aligned} v_x(t) = & -K_{x,1}(x(t)-x_r(t)) - K_{x,2}(\dot{x}(t)-\dot{x}_r(t)) \\ & + \frac{R_a}{K_t \rho}\left(J_a + \rho^2 M_x\right)\ddot{x}_r(t) + \frac{K_e}{\rho}\dot{x}_r(t) \end{aligned} \tag{12}$$

Similarly, we can obtain a controller in y direction

$$\begin{aligned} v_y(t) = & -K_{y,1}(y(t)-y_r(t)) - K_{y,2}(\dot{y}(t)-\dot{y}_r(t)) \\ & + \frac{R_a}{K_t \rho}\left(J_a + \rho^2 M_y\right)\ddot{y}_r(t) + \frac{K_e}{\rho}\dot{y}_r(t) \end{aligned} \tag{13}$$

Eqs (12) and (13) are the designed control voltage outputs of NI CompactRio system and the inputs of the motor controlled platform, where $x(t)/\rho$, $\dot{x}(t)/\rho$, $y(t)/\rho$, and $\dot{y}(t)/\rho$ are measured by encoders, and $x_r(t)$, $\dot{x}_r(t)$, $y_r(t)$, and $\dot{y}_r(t)$ as a priori are given by an emulation task. Eqs (12) and (13) contain both feedback and feedforward, where feedforward performs as a guidance control law and feedback performs as a disturbance rejection control law. Therefore, the controlled robot must create a planar movement the same as the reference trajectory in principle.

Admittedly, Eqs (12) and (13) are derived from the nominal dynamics of the real system. It is not a surprise that the real trajectory has discrepancies from the reference one.

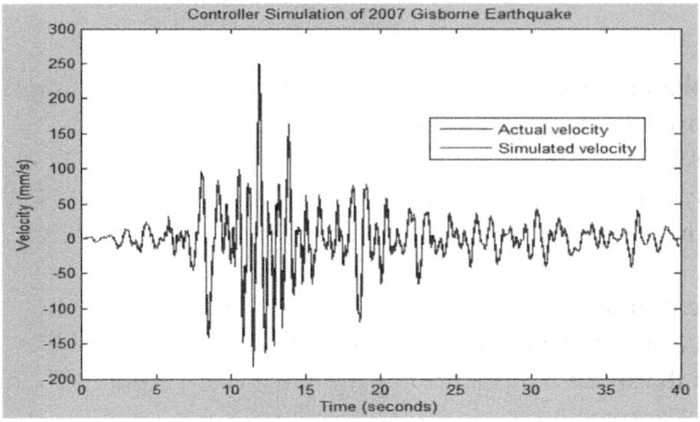

Fig. 5. Emulated earthquake wave regenerates a real seismic wave

4 Emulated Earthquake Waves

Seismic L-wave data is provided for the acceleration, velocity and displacement of the 2007 Gisborne earthquake which measured 6.87 on the Richter scale with a maximum displacement of 32.986 mm, maximum velocity of 250.28 mm/s and maximum acceleration of 2623.5 mm/s^2 in New Zealand [9]. The plot of this earthquake waves can be found in [10]. This earthquake caused roofs to collapse, power lines to fall and created a hole in one of the main roads in the city. Fig. 5 shows that the planar earthquake wave is regenerated by the feedback control system.

5 Conclusion

A small scale seismic emulator is built to reproduce seismic L-waves in a horizontal plane. The robic emulator is a mechatronic device that comprises mechanical parts, electronic parts, and software. The proposed trajectory tracking controller is very effective to reproduce an earthquake wave.

Acknowledgement. The authors thank A. Patterson and B. Baylis for their contribution to the mechatronic design.

References

1. Hough, S.: Earthshaking Science: What We Know (and Don't Know) about Earthquakes. Princeton University Press, Princeton (2002)
2. Dyke, S., Nepote, B., Caicedo, J., Johnson, S., Oware, E.: Earthquake Engineering Education: A Modern Approach. In: Proc. of the ASEE Annual Meeting, June 18–21, 2000, St. Louis, Missouri (2000)
3. Calvi, G., Pavese, A., Ceresa, P., Dacarro, F., Lai, C., Beltrami, C.: Design of a large-scale dynamic and pseudo-dynamic testing facility. In: ROSE Monograph, p. 192. IUSS Press, Pavia (2005)

4. Trombetti, T., Conte, J., Durrani, A.: Actuator-foundation-specimen interaction in a small shaking table. In: Proc. of 12th Engineering Mechanics Conference, American Society of Civil Engineers, Reston, VA, pp. 770–773 (1998)
5. Newell, D., Dai, H., Sain, M., Quast, P.P., Spencer, B.: Nonlinear modelling and control of a Hydraulic seismic simulator. In: Proc. of American Control Conference, Seattle, WA, pp. 801–805 (1995)
6. Crewe, A., Taylor, C., Mouzakis, H., Vougioukas, E., Franchioni, G.: The performance of the shaking table control systems at the National Technical University of Athens, Bristol University and ISMES, Italy. In: Proc. of 10th International Seminor on Earthquake Prognostics, Cairo (1996)
7. Bolt, B.: Earthquakes. W.H. Freeman, New York (1993)
8. Goodwin, G., Graebe, S., Salgado, M.: Control System Design. Prentice Hall, New Jersay (2000)
9. `ftp://ftp.geonet.org.nz/strong/processed/Proc/2007/12_Prelim/2007-12-20_075516/Vol2/data/20071220_075516_GISS.V2A` (last visit in June 22, 2009)
10. `ftp://ftp.geonet.org.nz/strong/processed/Proc/2007/12_Prelim/2007-12-20_075516/Vol2/plots/20071220_075516_GISS.PDF` (last visit in June 22, 2009)

The Location of the WSN-Nodes Based on RSSI *

Jiachun Zheng

School of Information Engineering,
Jimei University, Xiamen 361021, China
jc_zheng@sohu.com

Abstract. Particular introduced the ranging theory, the correction technology and the location algorithm of the WSN's ranging location based on the RSSI (Received Signal Strength Indication). For the problem of the nonlinear equations need to be solved in the location algorithm, this paper uses the UKF (Unscented Kalman Filter) algorithm, uses the algorithm's nonlinear model, applys a minimal sample point-group to approximate the distribution function of system function. This sample group can really obtain the mean value and variance of system state. When according to the actual evolution of nonlinear model, it can be well carrying on fitting to the posterior mean value and variance of nonlinear function. The simulation results indicated that the node location's estimation accuracy is within 5% for using the UKF algorithm. Visually , it has better tracking function and filtering consequence to solve the problem of the nonlinear maneuvering objective tracking.

Keywords: Wireless sensor networks, localization, RSSI, UKF, beacon.

1 Introduction

For the sensor nodes, especially the movable nodes, we must to know their true position, then we know that " what happened in a specific position or area ",[1] and achieve the location or track to these nodes. So , the problem of node location is one of the main problem of system. The location's method can use the global position system(GPS), but there have many factors' restriction using GPS in the WSNs, such as: the price, the volume ,the power and so on. So we don't use GPS location system in general. To the WSN location, many node location algorithms had been proposed in recently. [2]- [7] They can be divided into two kinds: the Range-Based and the Range-Free algorithm. According to the requirements of the high accuracy location in navigation marks, and their distribution in the sea, the Range-Based algorithm is better for this application. among them the range based on the RSSI is the common method for the location of WSNs. Now there are many related researches. For example, in [8] using the method of weight and mean value to eliminate the measurement influence of RSSI by environment factors, the ranging accuracy is 2

* This work is partially supported by Technology Project of Fujian Province under Grant No. 2008H0032, supported by Fujian Province education department under Grant No.JA08144.

D. Zeng (Ed.): ICAIC 2011, Part I, CCIS 224, pp. 550–559, 2011.

meters in the distance of 15 meters. In [9] it separately calculates the estimation distance of the two decline cure of RSSI and LQI, and calculating the final estimation value by dynamically optimization. In [10] takes the Gauss model to reduce ranging error. Its accuracy is 2 meters when the distance is less then 20 meters. For the influence of the radio wave diffraction and the multi-path transmission in natural environment, the location accuracy of traditional RSSI is low. In order to improve the location accuracy, we proposed a new algorithm using UKF(Unscented Kalman Filter) to process the goal node's location and tracking after the comprehensive analysis of the existing algorithms. This algorithm will be introduced as follow.

2 Ranging of Based on Rssi

2.1 Ranging Theroy

The fundamentals of the ranging based on RSSI is that: according to the signal intensity of the beacon node and the signal intensity which had been received by the receiving node, calculate the loss of the signal in the transmitting proc-ess, and then applies a signal model of theory or experiences to translate the transmitting loss to distance.

Supposed, (x_{si}, y_{si}) is the plane coordinates of the beacon node i, (x, y) is the moveable node's, and d_i is the distance between the two nodes. Then the signal intensity which the moveable node receive from node i can be discribed as formula (1).

$$RSSI_i = P + G - (PL(d_0) + 10 \cdot n \cdot \log_{10}(d_i / d_0)) + v_i \tag{1}$$

Where:P is the transmitting power of the beacon node I;G is the antenna gain of beacon node i; d_1 (m)is the distance betwe-en transmitter and receiver;d_0 (m) is the reference distance, it usually is 1 meter;$RSSI_i$ (dBm) is the signal power received by the receiver; v_i (dBm) is a Gauss random variable , the mean value of it is zero, it shows the variation of receiving signal power when the distance is a constant; n is the index number of the path loss, which is related to the communi-cation channel environment; $PL(d_0)$ is the power loss of transmission path (dBm) at the point of the reference distan-ce , it is related to the operating frequency f (GHz). Considering the environment on the sea, the model of the transmission path loss can adopt the model of the sea. The model is $PL(d_0) = 32.44 + 10 \cdot n \cdot \log_{10}(d_0) + 10 \cdot n \cdot \log_{10}(f)$.

According to the ZigBee technology, the working frequency is selected the ISM frequency of 2.4 GHz which is not to regesiter, and considering the work environment on the sea ,the n is selected 2, then we can get that the $PL(d_0)$ is equal 40(dBm). As the P and G are constant , the formula (1) can be rewritten as follow:

$$RSSI_i = PL_0 - 10 \cdot n \cdot \log_{10}(d_i / d_0) + v_i \tag{2}$$

Where:PL_0=P+G-$PL(d_0)$ (dBm), it is the receiving signal power of receiver when the communication distance is the reference distance. According to the formula (2), we can conclude that there is a certain relation between RSSI and the distance of wireless signal transmittion. In the actually environment, the measurement of RSSI has repeatability and exchangeability, the variation of RSSI also has some regula-tions. So using the measured values of the RSSI we can directly compute the distance between nodes.

2.2 Correction Technology

In the actually environment, some uncertainly factors, such as multi-path, diffraction, obstacle, weather, temperature, wetness and so on, affect the wireless signal's transmittion, cause the deduce of the RSSI's measured accuracy and reliability. So we must take some effective measures to correct the actual measurement value. Two correction model are decribed as follow.

2.2.1 Correction Model of the Statistics Average

The model of statistics average is that the unknown nodes collect a group (the number is m) value of RSSI, and then compute the average :

$$\overline{\mathrm{RSSI}} = \frac{1}{m}\sum_{i=1}^{m} RSSI_i \tag{3}$$

Where: m is the number of collection data, we can adjust the value of m to balance the real time and accuracy. When m is very big, the randomness of the location data can be solved effectively, but the correspondence cost will increase correspondingly. While the model has some disadvantages in handling the big perturbation.

2.2.2 Correction Model Based on the Distances of Beacon Nodes

When we compute the distance between the unknown node and beacon node, we take the distance of a couple of beacon nodes and the RSSI value of measurement as the reference, and take the distance of beacon nodes and the receiving signal intensity to correct the model of measurement.

In Fig.1 ,we supposed $\overline{\mathrm{RSSI}}_{12}$、$\overline{\mathrm{RSSI}}_{13}$、$\overline{\mathrm{RSSI}}_{23}$ separately indicated the RSSI average value (dBm) that the beacon node B1 has received beacon node B2 , the beacon node B1 has received beacon node B3,and the beacon node B2 has received beacon node B3. d_{12}、d_{13}、d_{23} separately express the distance between the beacon node B1 and the beacon node B2, between beacon the node B1 and the beacon node B3, and between the beacon node B2 and the beacon node B3. According to the Eq. (2), we have:

$$RSSI_{12} = PL_0 - 10 \cdot n \cdot \log_{10}(d_{12} / d_0) \tag{4}$$

$$RSSI_{13} = PL_0 - 10 \cdot n \cdot \log_{10}(d_{13} / d_0) \tag{5}$$

$$RSSI_{23} = PL_0 - 10 \cdot n \cdot \log_{10}(d_{23} / d_0) \tag{6}$$

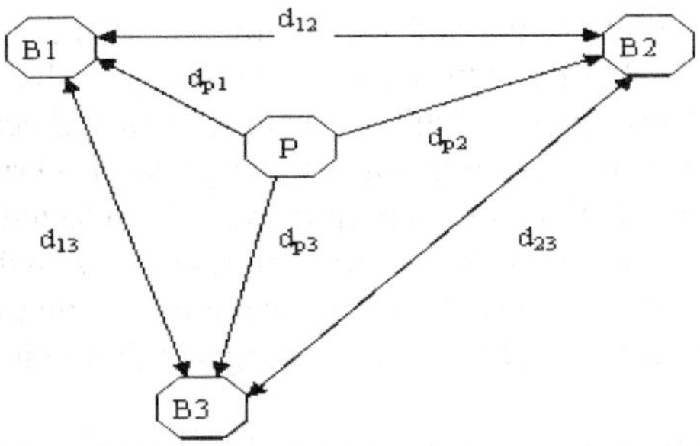

Fig. 1. The correction model based on the distance between beacon nodes

Eq.(4) subtract Eq.(5), then get n_1, n_2, n_3.And then the optimal path loss index number $\overline{n}$ is:

$$\overline{n} = \frac{n_1 + n_2 + n_3}{3} \tag{7}$$

Substituting Eq.(7) into Eq.(4), Eq.(5), Eq.(6), the distance between node P and node B1 described as :

$$d_{p1} = d_0 \times 10^{0.1\times(\overline{RSSI}_{p1} - \overline{PL}_0 - \xi)/\overline{n}} \tag{8a}$$

To the beacon node B2 and B3, we have:

$$d_{p2} = d_0 \times 10^{0.1\times(\overline{RSSI}_{p2} - \overline{PL}_0 - \xi)/\overline{n}} \tag{8b}$$

$$d_{p3} = d_0 \times 10^{0.1\times(\overline{RSSI}_{p3} - \overline{PL}_0 - \xi)/\overline{n}} \tag{8c}$$

3 Location Algorithm

In Fig.1, we supposed that the coordinates of the beacon node B1、B2、B3 are separately as (x_{B1}, y_{B1})、(x_{B2}, y_{B2})、(x_{B3}, y_{B3}), and the coordinates of the unknown position's node is (x_P, y_P).Then we can get:

$$(d_{P1}^2 - d_{P2}^2 + x_{B2}^2 - x_{B1}^2 + y_{B2}^2 - y_{B1}^2)/2 = (x_{B2} - x_{B1})\cdot x_P + (y_{B2} - y_{B1})\cdot y_P \tag{9}$$

$$(d_{P1}^2 - d_{P3}^2 + x_{B3}^2 - x_{B1}^2 + y_{B3}^2 - y_{B1}^2)/2 = (x_{B3} - x_{B1})\cdot x_P + (y_{B3} - y_{B1})\cdot y_P \tag{10}$$

$$(d_{P2}^2 - d_{P3}^2 + x_{B3}^2 - x_{B2}^2 + y_{B3}^2 - y_{B2}^2)/2 = (x_{B3} - x_{B2})\cdot x_P + (y_{B3} - y_{B2})\cdot y_P \tag{11}$$

The solution of the nonlinear equation set is the estimation coordinates value of the unknown node P. Now there are many kinds of algorithm to solve this hyperbolic equation set which have the different accuracy and the complexity of calculation. They have different requirements to the error feature of the RSSI, and also have different complexity of calculation. On the various RSSI noise, those algorithms can separately achieve the optimal solution or sub-prime solution of the location estimation. This kind of method is used to transform the nonlinear state equations and the observation equation to the linearity.The typical algorithm is the Extended Kalman Filter (EKF). It is simply and easily to realization, but the tracking feature is not better when the environment is strong nonlinear and non-Gauss, and even the filter divergence will appear. Unscented Kalman Filter (UKF) adopts the determined sample points, and uses the sample set with the weights to approximate goal's state posterior Probability Density Function(PDF).It can avoid the tracking error which caused by the linearization. So, we adopt UKF to filter and optimize for improving the location accuracy.

4 Model Based on Ukf Algorithm

4.1 State Equation

As the navigation mark's WSN nodes layout on the sea. So we can use the plane rectangular coordinates to indicate its location. We established the state variables as follow:

$$X = [x \quad y \quad v_x \quad v_y] \tag{12}$$

Where: (x,y) is the position coordinates of the unknown position's node;(v_x, v_y) separately indicate the corresponding velocity component of the x,y-axis. Then the system's state equation can be write as:

$$X_{k+1} = AX_k + W_k \tag{13}$$

Supposed T is the monitoring interval, so the one step transition matrix is

$$A = \begin{bmatrix} 1 & 0 & T & 0 \\ 0 & 1 & 0 & T \\ 0 & 0 & 1 & 0 \\ 0 & 0 & 0 & 1 \end{bmatrix} \tag{14}$$

Where : W is the disturbance vector, defined as

$W_k = [0 \quad 0 \quad w_{xk} \quad w_{yk}]^T$; w_{xk} w_{yk} separately indicates the velocity disturbance error of x direction, y direction at k moment. We supposed they obey the uniform distribution from –a to +a, then the variance is $\sigma_w^2 = \frac{a^2}{3}$, the covariance Q is

$$Q = \begin{bmatrix} 0 & 0 & 0 & 0 \\ 0 & 0 & 0 & 0 \\ 0 & 0 & \frac{a^2}{3} & 0 \\ 0 & 0 & 0 & \frac{a^2}{3} \end{bmatrix} \tag{15}$$

4.2 Observation Equation

From the Eq.(8a), Eq.(8b) and Eq.(8c),we can get

$$\overline{RSSI_{p1}} = PL_0 - 10 \cdot n \cdot \log_{10}(d_{p1} / d_0) + \xi \tag{16}$$

$$\overline{RSSI_{p2}} = PL_0 - 10 \cdot n \cdot \log_{10}(d_{p2} / d_0) + \xi \tag{17}$$

$$\overline{RSSI_{p3}} = PL_0 - 10 \cdot n \cdot \log_{10}(d_{p3} / d_0) + \xi \tag{18}$$

Then the observation equation is decribed as:

$$Z_k = \left[\overline{RSSI_{p1}} \quad \overline{RSSI_{p2}} \quad \overline{RSSI_{p3}}\right]^T \tag{19}$$

4.3 Steps of Ukf Algorithm

(1) Algorithm's Initialization

$$\overline{X} = E[X_0] \tag{20}$$

$$P_x = E[(X_0 - \overline{X})(X_0 - \overline{X})^T] \tag{21}$$

(2) The Sigma Points at K Monent X_k

$$\mathrm{X}_0 = \overline{X} \tag{22}$$

$$\mathrm{X}_i = \overline{X} + (\sqrt{(L+\lambda)P_x})_i \quad , \ i=1,\ 2,\ \ldots,\ L \tag{23}$$

Where : $(\sqrt{(L+\lambda)P_x})_i$ =the matrix square root's i column.

$$\mathrm{X}_i = \overline{X} - (\sqrt{(L+\lambda)P_x})_{i-L} , \ i=L+1,\ L+2,\ \ldots,\ 2L \tag{24}$$

$$X_k = [\mathrm{X}_0, \ \mathrm{X}_i, \ \mathrm{X}_i] \tag{25}$$

Then the forecast's state is

$$\hat{X}_{k/(k-1)} = AX_k \tag{26}$$

(3) Predicted State'S Mean Value and Variance

Sample mean value's weight:

$$\omega_0^{(m)} = \frac{\lambda}{L+\lambda}, \omega_i^{(m)} = \frac{1}{2(L+\lambda)} \quad , \ i=1,2,\ldots,2L$$

$$W^{(m)} = [\omega_0^{(m)}, \omega_i^{(m)}] \tag{27}$$

Variance weight is:

$$\omega_0^{(c)} = \frac{\lambda}{L+\lambda} + (1-\alpha^2+\beta), \lambda = \alpha^2(L+\gamma) - L = L(\alpha^2-1), \beta = 2,$$

$$\omega_i^{(c)} = \frac{1}{2(L+\lambda)}, \quad i=1,2,\ldots,2L$$

$$W^{(c)} = [\omega_0^{(c)}, \omega_i^{(c)}] \tag{28}$$

State prediction value's mean value:

$$\overline{X}_{k/k-1} = \sum_{i=0}^{2L} \omega_i^{(m)} (\hat{X}_{k/k-1})_i = \hat{X}_{k/k-1} \bullet W_i^{(m)T} \tag{29}$$

State prediction error's variance matrix:

$$\begin{aligned} P_{k/k-1} &= \sum_{i=0}^{2L} \omega_i^{(c)} [(\hat{X}_{k/k-1})_i - \overline{x}_{k/k-1}][(\hat{X}_{k/k-1})_i - \overline{x}_{k/k-1}]^T + Q_k \\ &= [\hat{X}_{k/k-1} - \overline{x}_{k/k-1}] \bullet W_i^{(c)T} \bullet [W_i^{(c)} \bullet [(\hat{X}_{k/k-1})_i - \overline{x}_{k/k-1}]^T] + Q_k \end{aligned} \tag{30}$$

(4) Observation Value's Prediction Value and Variance
Prediction's observation value:

$$(\hat{Z}_{k/k-1})_i = h((\hat{X}_{k/k-1})_i), \quad i=0,1,2,\ldots,2L \tag{31}$$

Observation value's predicted mean value:

$$\overline{Z}_{k/k-1} = \sum_{i=0}^{2L} \omega_i^{(m)} (\hat{Z}_{k/k-1})_i = \hat{Z}_{k/k-1} \bullet W_i^{(m)T} \tag{32}$$

Observation value's predicted variance: $P_{\hat{z}\hat{z}} = \sum_{i=0}^{2L} \omega_i^{(c)} [(\hat{Z}_{k/k-1})_i - \overline{Z}_{k/k-1}][(\hat{Z}_{k/k-1})_i - \overline{Z}_{k/k-1}]^T + R_k$

$$= [\hat{Z}_{k/k-1} - \overline{Z}_{k/k-1}] \bullet W_i^{(c)T} \bullet [W_i^{(c)} \bullet [(\hat{Z}_{k/k-1})_i - \overline{Z}_{k/k-1}]^T] + R_k \tag{33}$$

$$\begin{aligned} P_{\hat{x}\hat{z}} &= \sum_{i=0}^{2L} \omega_i^{(c)} [(\hat{X}_{k/k-1})_i - \overline{X}_{k/k-1}][(\hat{Z}_{k/k-1})_i - \overline{Z}_{k/k-1}]^T \\ &= [\hat{X}_{k/k-1} - \overline{X}_{k/k-1}] \bullet W_i^{(c)T} \bullet [W_i^{(c)} \bullet [(\hat{Z}_{k/k-1})_i - \overline{Z}_{k/k-1}]^T] + R_k \end{aligned} \tag{34}$$

(5) Kalman GAIN

$$K = P_{\hat{x}\hat{z}} P_{\hat{z}\hat{z}}^{-1} \tag{35}$$

Filter value is

$$\overline{X}_k = \overline{X}_{k/k-1} + K(Z_k - \overline{Z}_{k/k-1}) \tag{36}$$

Where : Z_k = the observation value at k moment

Filter error matrix:

$$P_k = P_{k/k-1} - KP_{\tilde{z}\tilde{x}} K^T \tag{37}$$

At k+1 moment the process is repeated from (2) to (5).

5 Algorithm Simulation

According to the scene of Fig.1, we supposed that the coordinates of the three beacon nodes B1,B2,B3 separately is(0, 0) 、(50, 500) 、(200, 250). The initial position coordinates of the target node is(100,0) , and forward's speed is two meters per second. By simulation we get this node's motion trail showed at Fig.2.

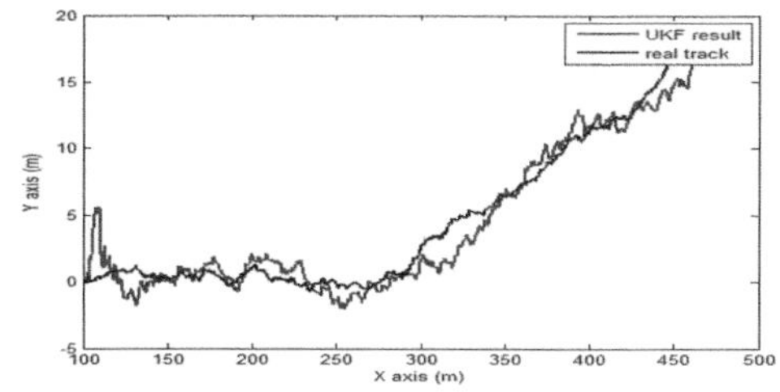

Fig. 2. Node's motion trail

Fig.2 shows that the result of using UKF filter is good at obtaining the tracking goal's actual position. Fig.3 shows the estimated error of the target's position.

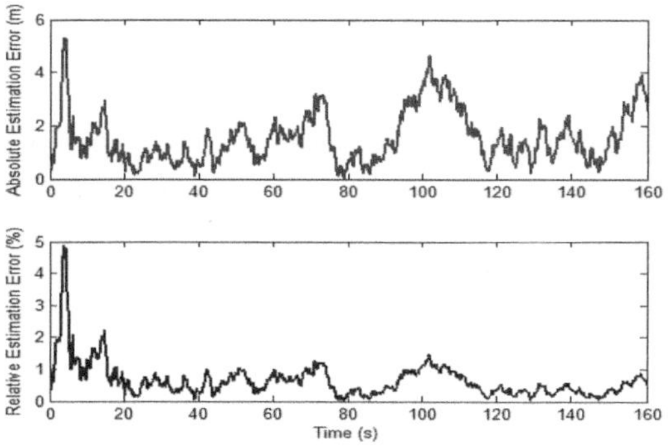

Fig. 3. Node position's estimation error

From the Fig.3 ,we can see that the absolute estimation error is less than 6 meters, and the relative estimation error is less than 5%.

Fig.4 shows the maximum estimation error under different measurement variance. It indicates that with the increase of measurement variance , the estimation error also increases. When the measurement variance is more than 10, the estimation error increases to more than 50 meters. As the requirement of navigation mark application on sea location error is less than 20 meters, so the measurement variance should be controlled less than 2.5.

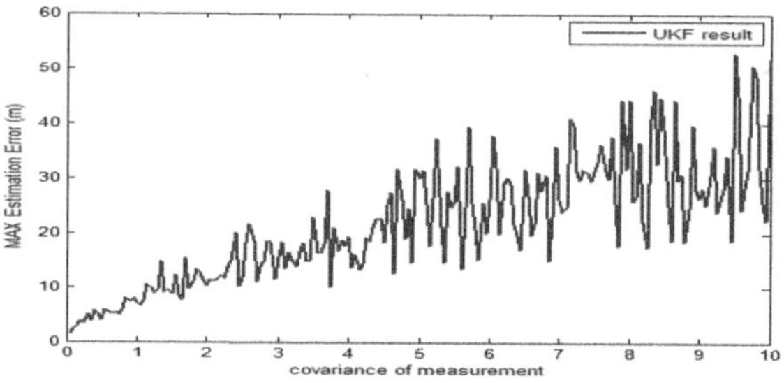

Fig. 4. Maximum estimation error under different measurement variance

Fig.5 shows relationship curve between the attenuation coefficient and estimation error. As the figure illustrates, under the premise that the signal can be received reliably, the estimation error decreases with the increase of attenuation coefficient.

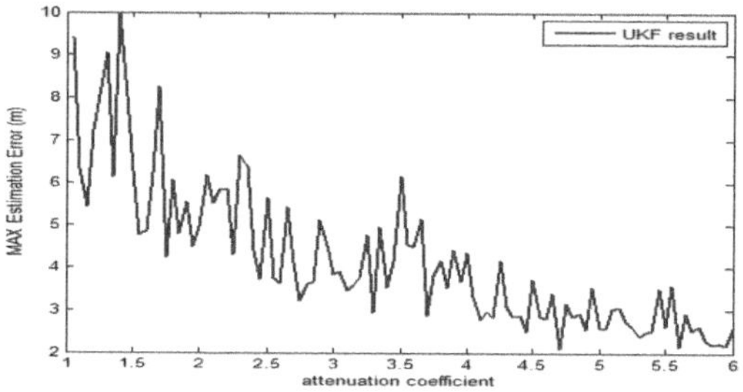

Fig. 5. Relationship between attenuation coefficient and estimation error

6 Conclusion

The RSSI-based ranging location is one of the most commonly used methods in WSN location, but its location algorithm should solve the nonlinear equation set. This paper adopts UKF algorithm, uses the actual nonlinear model, and uses a minimal set of sample points which can actual get the mean value and variance of the system to approximate the system state's distribution function. When the actual evolution of the nonlinear model is taken, we can be well fitting the posterior mean value and variance of the nonlinear function. This algorithm takes advantage of each sensor measurement's information and then further optimizes the measurement error. The result of simulation shows that compared to other algorithms for nonlinear problems, the UKF algorithm has a better tracking performance and filter results on solving the problem of nonlinear maneuvering target tracking.

References

1. Rabacy, J.J., Ammer, M.J., da Silva Jr, J.L., et al.: Picorodio supports ad hoc ultra low power wireless networking. Computer 33(7), 42248 (2000)
2. Zhang, Q.g., Huang, J.w., Wang, J.h., Jin, C.: Novel Node Localization Algorithm for Wireless Sensor Networks. Journal of Chinese Computer Systems 30(3), 460–465 (2009)
3. Wang, F., Shi, L., Ren, F.: Self Localization systems and algorithms for wireless sensor networks. Journal of Software 16(5), 857–868 (2005)
4. Savvides, A., Han, C.C., Srivastava, M.: Dynamic fine grained localization in ad-hoc networks of sensors (C/OL). In: Proc. Of the 7th Annual Int'l Conf. On Mobile Computing and Networking, pp. 166–179. ACM Press, Rome (2001)
5. Shang, Y., Rum, L.W., Zhang, Y., et al.: Localization from mere connectivity (C/OL). In: Proc. of the 4th ACM Int'l Symp.on Mobile Ad Hoc Networking & Computing, pp. 201–212. ACM Press, Annapolis (2003)
6. Bergamo, P., Mazzini, G.: Localization in sensor networks with fading and mobility[C/OL]. In: Proc. of the 13th IEEE Int'l Symp. On Personal, Indoor and Mobile Radio Communications, vol. 2, pp. 750–754. IEEE Communications Society, Lisbon (2002)
7. Savarese, C., Rabay, J., Langendoen, K.: Robust positioning algorithms for distributed ad-hoc wireless sensor networks (C/OL). In: Ellis, C.S. (ed.) Proc. of the USEN IX Technical Annual Conf., pp. 317–327. USENIX Press, Monterey (2002)
8. Zhen, F., Zhan, Z., Peng, G., Yuguo, Z.: Analysis of Distance Measurement Based on RSSI. Chinese Journal of Sensors and Actuators 20(11), 2526–2530 (2007)
9. Zhang, J., Sun, M., Wang, X.: Dynamic distance estimation method based on RSSI and LQI. Electronic Measurement Technology 30(2), 142–145 (2007)
10. Zhao, Z., Chen, X.: An Improved Localization Algorithm Based on RSSI in WSN. Chinese Journal of Sensors and Actuators 22(3), 391–394 (2009)

Lithology Recognitions of Coal-Bearing Strata on BP-ANN in Qiongdongnan Basin, Sea of South China*

Lv Dawei[1,2], Ding Xigui[1], Li Zengxue[2], Liu Haiyan[2], and Chen xiaoyan[2]

[1] Key Laboratory of Marine Hydrocarbon Resources and Environmental Geology, Ministry of Land and Resources
Qingdao, 266071, Shandong Province, China
[2] Shandong Provincial Key Laboratory of Depositional Mineralization& Sedimentary Minerals
Qingdao, 266510, Shandong Province, China
lvdawei11@sohu.com

Abstract. Lithology identification of coal-bearing Strata has been a difficult problem in the geology for a long time, especially in the deep sea area. So it is very significance for us to study the mathematics way to recognize the coal-bearing lithology of well logs. In this paper, BP-ANN was introduced to apply to the predicate the lithology. And take the Qiongdongnan Basin as an example, the Yc13-1-a1well samples was used. By the study of it, the result was found correctly. So this way is useful and may be popularized.

Keywords: coal-bearing strata, BP ANN, Qiongdongnan Basin, training.

1 Introduction

There are many means to identify the coal-bearing lithology. In the early stage, the means are mainly the qualitatively analysis which are formal indications, logical judgment and so on. All these ways have a commonality that are used the well logs' shapes such as middle-high resistivity, high gamma gamma and low natural gamma ray (Huang.., *et al*, 1982, 1984, 1985, 1987; Pan..,*et al*, 1990, 1998; Liu.., 1991). But these means have their limitations and inaccuracy, especially in a complicated area. With the development the coal-geology, many experts had proposed many mathematics ways, such as fuzzy mathematics (Huang.., 1987; Liu..,*et al*, 1993), volume model(Huang.., 1987), Grey Clustering Evaluation Model(Zhuang.., 1995). All these means were effective to analyze the coal-bearing lithology by the shape of one kind of well log in the land exploration (less 2000m of burial depth). Nowadays, coal-formed gas explored in sea area has become a main prospect research hot spot. And the burial depth almost is more than 2000m. It is difficult for us to forecast strata lithification in sea area because there is a high burial depth and less wells can be cored. And there are many chemical elements which influence the accuracy of well log. So the former mathematics ways can not predicated accurately. So it is of great significance for us to predicate the coal-bearing strata exactly using the mathematics ways.

* This work is partially supported by Key Laboratory of Marine Hydrocarbon Resources and Environmental Geology, Ministry of Land and Resources(.MRE201010).

D. Zeng (Ed.): ICAIC 2011, Part I, CCIS 224, pp. 560–565, 2011.

By the nonlinear dynamic system formed by a large number of simple Neurons processing unit, artificial neural net can realize the information processing capability such as studying, distinguishing and memory et al, and the ability of self-study, self-organization, fault-tolerance, high nonlinearity, associative memory function and sense of functional reasoning et al. The paper cited artificial neural net technique by many kinds of well logs to predicate the coal-bearing lithology is applied practically, which provides references for coal-formed exploration.

2 The Overview of Bp Ann

Nowadays, BP network model is the mostly used and ANN is broadly applied. It is put forward by Rumelhart *et al* in PDP group in 1985, and the construction is shown in Fig. 1. BP(Back Propagation) network model can change the group of samples input to a nonlinear optimization problem. It uses the most common gradient descent algorithm in optimization, solve the right by the iterative calculations, and add the hidden node to increase the adjustable parameters, which is the process to approach the exact approach.

BP network is composed of input layer, output layer and the hidden layer, and one or several hidden layers. Every layer has many neurons. The neuron is linked to those of adjacent layer, not of their own layer, and has no feedback among the neurons. The input information first spreads to the hidden nodes, the output information spreads to the output nodes after the transformation function, and output result is gained after the process. The node transformation function commonly chooses the sigmoid model function. Generally, the hidden layer adopts S model logarithm function or tangent activation function, and the output layer uses the linear activation function.

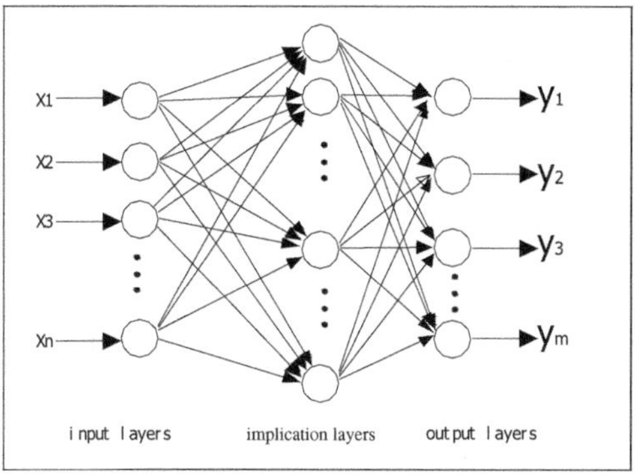

Fig. 1. Structure of Back Propagation (BP) ANN

3 An Forecasting Example of Yacheng Formation in Qiongdongnan Basin

3.1 The Geological Setting of Qiongdongnan Basin

Qiongdongnan basin lies in the Southeastern Waters area, Hainan Islands China, the Northern South China Sea of the Northwestern Part of continental margin. It is the

NE—trending extensional basin formed in Cenozoic. And the west is adjacent to Yinggehai basin (Fig. 2).

Yacheng formation is a major coal-bearing strata in Qiongdongnan Basin, which was mainly made up of coarse clastic rocks such as conglomeratic coarse sandstone, grit sandstone, midium-sandstone as well as mudstone, caustobiolith(coal) and so on. The main types of sandstone are feldspathic-quartz sandstone and feldspathic litharenite, which include unstable components rich in feldspar, lithic fragment and mica. Mudstones are mostly rich in plant debris and organic components. The underlying strata of Yacheng formation is Eocene Lingtou formation, which was mainly made up of interbeddings of light brown red sandstone and light gray conglomeratic coarse sandstone. The overlying strata is Lingshui formation, which the bottom sediments were mainly deposited in transitional environment but the top and middle parts were mainly formed in marine environment and some areas formed in bathyal environment. So this study mainly works on the Yacheng Formation.

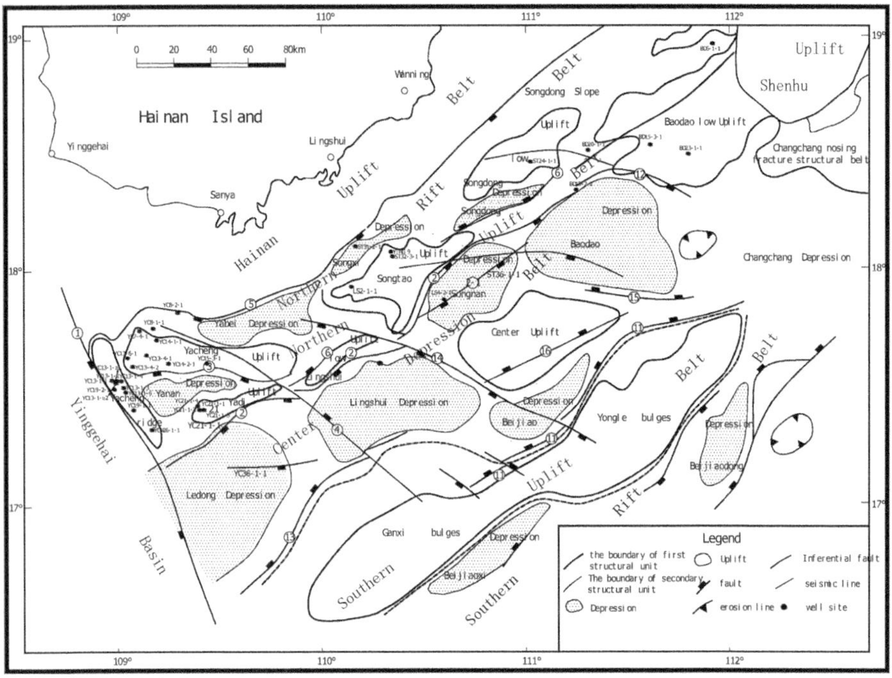

Fig. 2. Secondary depression and tectonic sketch of Qiongdongnan Basin

3.2 The Stages of Research

The identification of coal-bearing strata in Yacheng Formation, Qiongdongnan Basin is completed. And the stages were as follows (Fig.3): Firstly, the data of well log is collected. Then the samples of strata lithology can be concluded. And learning factors and the number of layer are found. By the study of work, four kind of lithology in Yacheng Formation of Qiongdongnan Basin can be concluded, which are conglomerate, coarse sandstones, sandstone, mudstone, carbonaceous mudstone and coalbed. Other lithology can be classified into upper four kinds of lithology. For example, coarse sandstone with gravel can be defined in coarse sandstone, sandstone with mud can be thought as sandstone. Then the number of input layers is four. And four lithology can be identified after learning. So we can define the matrix form of result. When the result of well logs identification is conglomerate, the result matrix form is [1, 0, 0, 0, 0, 0]. When it is sandstone, the result matrix form is [0, 0, 1, 0, 0, 0]. The rest can be done in the same manner. Secondly, the input matrix can be insured. In this research, four kinds of well log can be used to construct the origin data matrix. Four kinds of well logs are as follows: SGR ,RHOB, DT, RT and so on. Thirdly, BP training net can be constructed. Then error is revised. Finally, the lithology of coal-bearing strata can be forecasted. And coal seams can be found. Based on the principles, we can defined the input layer number is six, output layers number is six and the implication layers is twelve.

3.3 The Result of Study

498 samples of the core Yc13-1-a2 can be used to train according to the practice. In Matlab, use the toolbox of BP, 1086 cycles can be trained (Fig.4). Compared to the coring lithology, results are mainly accuracy(Fig.5) . So this way can be used to forecast the lithology in the small scale geology area where the geology environment is almost not changed or little. But many samples should be gained and the little difference of geology environment between samples data and unknown data in order to succeed to forecast the lithology. So this way still has a limitation.

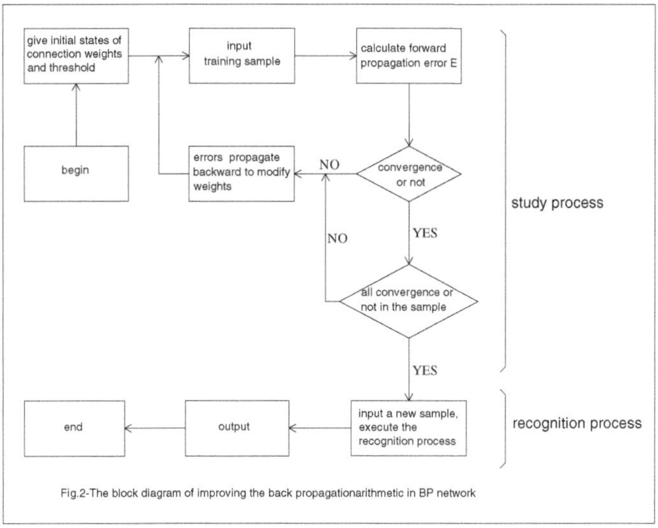

Fig. 3. Identification stages

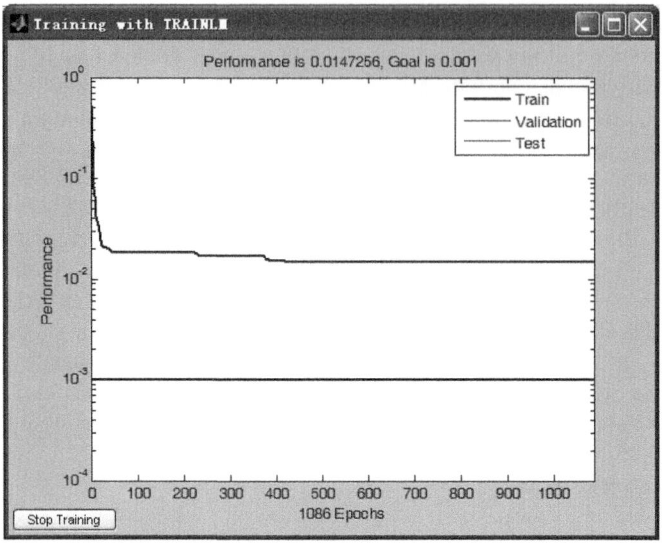

Fig. 4. Training process

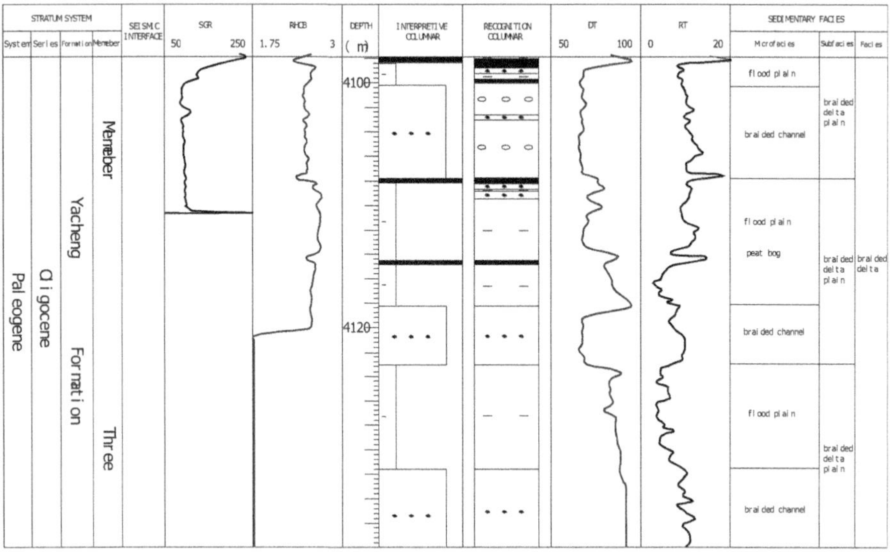

Fig. 5. The result correlation between BP identification and traditional method in Yc13-1-a2 Well

4 Conclusion

BP ANN is an effective way to prediction coal-bearing strata lithology. By studying the Yacheng Formation of the Yc13-1-a2 Well, Qiongdongnan Basin, we can conclude that it is practical for us to predicate the coal-bearing strata lithology of complicated geology area (eg. Sea area of deep water). This work will be helpful to the coal-formed gas exploration.

References

1. Huang, Z., Yang, F., Li, E.: Deconvolution check of gamma-ray log. Logging Technology 1, 38–47 (1982)
2. Huang, Z.: Use the method lecture of The apparent resistivity curve to study the coal-bearing sedimentary environment. Coal Geology & Exploration 2, 1–5 (1984)
3. Huang, Z., Chen, Y.: The application of coal logging information in analysising the sedimentary environment and studying the coal-forming belt. Geophysical and Geochemica Exploration 9(1), 49–57 (1985)
4. Huang, Z.: The application of using geophysical well logging data in anglicizing sedimentary environment, pp. 52–100. Geological publishing company, BJ (1986)
5. Huang, Z.: Analytical method lecture of Logging coal-bearing strata—Lecture One Physical properties of rocks in coal-bearing strata. Coal Geology & Exploration 1, 67–72 (1987)
6. Huang, Z.: Analytical method lecture of Logging coal-bearing strata—Lecture Two Analytical method of Logging coal quality. Coal Geology & Exploration 2, 65–71 (1987)
7. Huang, Z.: Analytical method lecture of Logging coal-bearing strata—Lecture Three Analytical method of Logging lithological characters. Coal Geology & Exploration 3, 62–66 (1987)
8. Huang, Z.: Analytical method lecture of Logging coal-bearing strata—Lecture Four Analytical method of Logging rock strength. Coal Geology & Exploration 4, 63–68 (1987)
9. Huang, Z.: Analytical method lecture of Logging coal-bearing strata—Lecture Five Analytical method of Logging sedimentary environment. Coal Geology & Exploration 5, 69–74 (1987)
10. Baoxun, G.: Research method lecture of the sedimentary environment of coal-bearing series—Lecture Seven Research of Logging curves. Coal Geology & Exploration 5, 67–72 (1986)
11. Heping, P., Huang, Z.: Log interpretation model of determining coalbed caoal quality parameters. Modern Geology 12(3), 447–450 (1998)
12. Duan, X., Huang, W.: Distinguishing Coal Beds and Fixing Thickness by Logging methods. Xinjiang You Se Jin Shu 30(zl)49–52 (2007)
13. Yang, K.: Interpretation of Logging for the Depositional Environment of Coal Formation 3 (1985)
14. Mazheng: Use Logs to determine sedimentary characters and to draw lithofacies map for a bed. Earth Science 11(3), 289–294 (1986)
15. Zhu, Z.: Application of the clustering methodology in the coal logging. Coal Geology of China 7(4), 88–101 (1995)
16. Shen, H., Qin, C., Wang, D.: Distinguishing methods for coal beds in Yacheng Formation of Qiongdongnan Basin. Acta Petrolei Sinica 31(4), 586–590 (2010)
17. Li, Z., He, Y., Liu, H.: Sedimentology characteristics and coal-forming models in Yacheng Formation of Qiongdongnan Basin. Acta Petrolei Sinica 31(4), 542–547 (2010)

The Intrinsic Relationship between Security Mechanisms and Trust Mechanisms

Guo Yimin, Guo Yajun, Peng Fei, and Gao Huidan

Department of computer science, Huazhong Normal University
Wuhan 430079, China
guoyimin333@sina.cn

Abstract. Security and trust are closely related. No trust, no security. The nature relationship between security mechanisms and trust mechanisms in this paper is proposed. Firstly, the existing trust mechanisms are classified, and then the corresponding relations among trust mechanisms and different security mechanisms are analyzed. Finally, a comprehensive trust model for open networks is presented. The model is extensible multi-layer structure, and it is suitable for the establishment of open network security mechanisms.

Keywords: Security mechanism, Trust mechanism, Trust.

1 Introduction

Security mechanism is the approach that can prevent security attacks and restore the system. All security mechanisms have used the different trust mechanisms. If there is no trust mechanism, the security mechanisms are unsafe. The most common security mechanisms such as encryption and authentication are based on trust. In the key management of symmetric cryptography, all entities trust key distribution center (KDC), thus, entities will trust the session key distributed by the KDC.

In asymmetric cryptography technology, the distribution of public key often uses the way of the public key certificate. As long as both sides exchange public key certificates, it will be able to know each other's public key, and believe that the other's public key is really. This is because the public key certificate is encrypted by the private key of certificate authority (CA), and all parties can verify the authenticity of the certificate by the public key of CA. Here there is an implicit trust relationship which all entities trust the certificate authority.

Authentication mechanism also uses the trust implicitly. There are four general methods to user's identity authentication, which are what you know; what you have; who you are and the user's subconscious actions. The four identity authentications are also based on pre-established trust relationship, such as the first case, the system only trusts a password, if the user knows the password, then trusts it. Authentication between devices mainly uses the way of challenge/response. It assumes that *A* expects to get a new message from *B*, *B* first issues a temporary value (challenge), and requests follow-up information received from the *B* (response) that it contains the

D. Zeng (Ed.): ICAIC 2011, Part I, CCIS 224, pp. 566–572, 2011.

correct value of this temporary. If the symmetric cryptography is used to authenticate, when *B* is in response to *A*, *B* often uses the share key between *A* and *B* to encrypt a function of temporary value (such as the temporary value plus 1). If the asymmetric cryptography is used to authenticate, *A* encrypts the temporary value by *B*'s pubic key and sends B. B decrypts it by own private key, and then encrypts a function of temporary value to A. Both authentication methods also exist prior trust relationship. For the first case, if you know the share key, then you can decrypt the temporary value. Obviously the trust is from the share key. For the second case, in the final analysis the trust comes from the trust of the CA.

As there exists the implied inherent relationship between traditional security mechanisms and trust mechanisms, so people often confuse the two concepts. Some researchers often call the traditional security mechanisms, such as cryptography, authentication and access control as the "hard security", and the trust is called as the "soft security" [1]. In fact, this distinction will lose the nature of trust. Trust is the cornerstone of all security mechanisms. If there is no trust, the security mechanisms will no longer work well. Traditional security mechanisms already exist the prior trust relationship in which trust is implied and it is absolute trust. The other is similar to the relative trust of human society. These two types of trust are used to support different security mechanisms. If you want to distinguish between "hard security and soft security", you can call by absolute trust to ensure the security as "hard security," and say the relative trust to ensure the security as "soft security."

2 Trust Mechanism

In this paper, trust mechanisms will be divided into two categories. One is the trust mechanism that adapt to static networks, the other is the trust mechanism that adapt to open networks. Because of there exists different network structure and different security requirement in open networks, researchers also use different trust mechanisms.

2.1 Static Trust Mechanism

Static trust mechanisms are often used for static closed networks which have specific users and organizations. As the user is fixed, it is very easy to set up trust relationship in advance. In this network, the trust relationship among entities is absolute. With the absolute trust, security decision-making becomes relatively simple. For example, in the key distribution of symmetric cryptography, the trusted third party can be established that it is through the master key with the users to set up prior trust relationship. Therefore, the session key distribution among users becomes very easy. We usually say some of the security mechanisms, such as authentication and access control are based on this static trust mechanism.

Public key cryptography trust model is also to use a static trust mechanism, and the trust relationship between entities is established in advance. All of the entities trust the certificate authority (CA), and these certificate authorities trust each other. CA is usually a trusted entity that it can issues certificates. The digital certificate signed by the CA can prove the owner of public key. Another CA can also prove a particular CA, and the system assumes that the user knows the public key of the trusted third party CA, so that user is able to verify the authenticity of the certificate. If the same CA had proved two users, and if they want to communicate securely, they only need to exchange their certificates. If two users are proved by different CA, They need help with a high-level CA, until you find a common CA. The trust relationship of these CA forms a trust tree.

Resurrecting duckling model [2] uses a special static trust mechanism. The trust relationship among entities is established before their interaction, and the trust relationship may not exist after their interaction. It is suitable for wireless networks to establish trust relationship. The entities in a network have an aforehand master-slave trust relationship. The master entity is the mother duck and the slave entity is the duckling. A slave entity is always trust the mother duck.

2.2 Attribute-Based Trust Mechanism

In the open network environment, the trust can not be predetermined, so the static trust mechanism can not solve the security problems. The trust relationship in attribute-based trust mechanism is established by means of entities' attributes [3-5]. If the other party has the necessary attributes, then he trusts, or distrusts. Entity's attributes use credential as a carrier. The request party only shows the credential contained certain attributes which the service party demand to bring forth. Although the trust is absolute "hard trust" relationship, it is completely different with the static trust mechanism. This trust relationship is temporary, if a user visits again, a credential that contained certain attributes must be showed. Attribute-based trust mechanism is suitable for higher security requirements in open network to authorize decision-making.

2.3 Experience-Based Trust Management

The above mentioned two kinds of trust mechanisms are actually "hard-trust mechanism", that is, either trust or distrust. While the experience-based trust mechanism [6-9] is a "soft trust mechanism", which trust is diversified, and it has social features. The establishment of trust relationship usually learns from the subjective trust relationship of human society. In experience-based trust mechanism, the trust relationship establishment between entities is mainly based on entities' direct interaction experience. However, the direct interaction experience is often very limited, and in the unfamiliar environment, the two sides there is no direct experience at the beginning, therefore, experience-based trust mechanism is often through web of trust and reputation systems to build trust. Clearly, this type of trust mechanism is more suitable for open network environment to establish the trust relationship. It is often used to solve access control and service selection, but focus on the service selection. Access control is the assumption that the services provided by service providers are feasible, and the service requestor may be malicious. Service selection considers that the service provider may be malicious, and it may provide services inconsistent with their claim. Because the trust subjectivity in experience-based trust mechanism, it is not suitable for the occasion with high security requirement.

At present, a lot of experience-based trust mechanisms have been proposed, but these trust mechanisms are plane structure, so it is not suitable for some open networks. This paper presents an experience-based multi-layer trust mechanism. Thus, the experience-based trust mechanisms can be divided into two categories, one is an experience-based plane trust mechanism, and the other is an experience-based multi-layer trust mechanism. Experience-based plane trust mechanism often assumes that some level of trust relationship already exist, and only considers the establishment of trust relationship in application layer. However, in some open network, the trust relationship is multilayer.

Experience-based multi-layer trust mechanism believes that the trust relationship between two entities is a multi-level. In some open networks, security threats may come from different levels, we should not only consider the application of security threats that may exist. Mobile ad hoc network systems have not fixed infrastructure, each node can freely move, and it also has the function of the terminal and router. Therefore, the threat can exist at different levels, such as the network connection level and the application level. The trust relationship between entities should be established in a number of levels, different levels express the different points of view of system. For example, the network connection trust layer ensures the connectivity, and application trust layer provides the reliable interaction between applications. The different level trust is mutually independent, and the lower level trust affects the upper level trust. This is because there is no trust in the network connection, the connection no longer exists. Therefore applications can not communicate with each other, and the trust in application level can not be established.

3 Security Mechanism Establishment

In any network, security mechanisms are needed to protect the network security. But different networks have different characteristics, and they use different trust mechanisms. Network security mechanisms need to be established according to the network trust mechanisms. Table 1 is the trust relationship classification in trust mechanism. Table 2 shows the different trust mechanism is suitable the different network. Table 3 shows the relationship of trust mechanism and protected party, security mechanism.

Table 1. The Trust Relationship Classification

Trust Mechanism	Trust Relationship
Static trust mechanism	Absolute trust relationship
Attribute-based trust mechanism	
Experience-based plane trust mechanism	Relative trust relationship
Experience-based multi-layer trust mechanism	

Table 2. Different Trust Mechanisms for Different Networks

Trust Mechanism	Network	Security
Static trust mechanism	Static network	Strong
Attribute-based trust mechanism	Dynamic network	Strong
Experience-based plane trust mechanism	Dynamic network	Weak
Experience-based multi-layer trust mechanism	Dynamic network	Weak

Table 3. The Relationship of Trust Mechanism and Protected Party, Security Mechanism

Trust Mechanism	Protected Party	Security Mechanism
Static trust mechanism	Service provider	Access control
Attribute-based trust mechanism	Service provider	Access control
Experience-based plane trust mechanism	Service provider or service requester	Service selection and access control
Experience-based multi-layer trust mechanism	Service provider or service requester	Service selection and access control

For static networks, the static trust mechanism for traditional security mechanisms has achieved good results. For the dynamic network, we give a comprehensive and scalable open network trust structure (Figure 1)。The number of layers in trust structure is variable. Some dynamic networks need to establish multi-level trust relationship, but some dynamic networks only establish the trust relationship of application layer. Each layer contains the absolute trust relationship or / and relative trust relationship, namely includes attribute-based trust relationship or / and experience-based trust relationship. If security threats only come from the application layer (such as P2P network environment), the comprehensive and scalable open network trust structure will become a plane trust structure. If the security threats come from a number of levels (for example in mobile ad hoc networks), the comprehensive and scalable open network trust structure is a multi-layer trust structure.

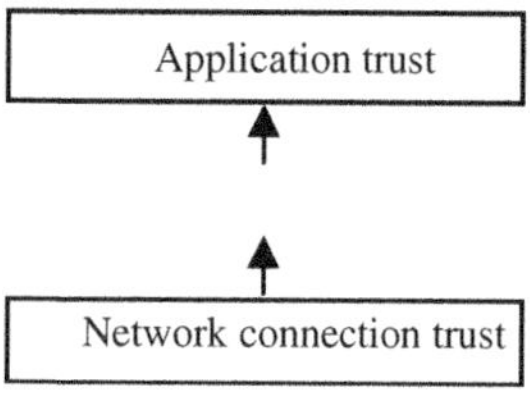

Fig. 1. Multi- layers trust structure

In the development of dynamic network security mechanism, it needs to be determined based on specific situation. Each peer layer needs to be trust evaluated. In a high risk environment, attribute-based trust in each layer is necessary, while in a low risk environment, we may only need to consider the experience-based trust.

Here is a time-based sliding window fuzzy approach to evaluate the experience-based trust. Fuzzy comprehensive evaluation method is to determine the membership degree of principals on trust vector. The results of the evaluation is the trust vector $V=\{v_1,v_2,\cdots v_m\}$. Through fuzzy comprehensive evaluation, the trust vector of a principal is

$$V=\{v_1,v_2,\cdots v_m\}=\{w_1,w_2,\cdots w_l\}\text{o}(r_{ij})_{n\times m}=W\text{o}R$$

Here "o" is the composite operator of fuzzy transform, $v_j=\overset{n}{\underset{i=1}{\vee}}(w_i\wedge r_{ij})(j=1,2,\cdots m)$, $\vee$ and $\wedge$ are Zadeh operators, and they express *max* and *min* operations respectively. $W=\{w_1,w_2,\cdots w_l\}$ is the weight distribution of each evaluation factor, and $R=(r_{ij})_{n\times m}$ is evaluation matrix. As the evaluation factors are too many to affect evaluation efficiency, this paper use time sliding window to separate the time factor from fuzzy evaluation process. In the trust evaluation process, only considers the trust essential factor within the sliding window.

The time sliding window of time (Figure 2.1a) is constituted by the six time units, and all the time units constitute a time series.

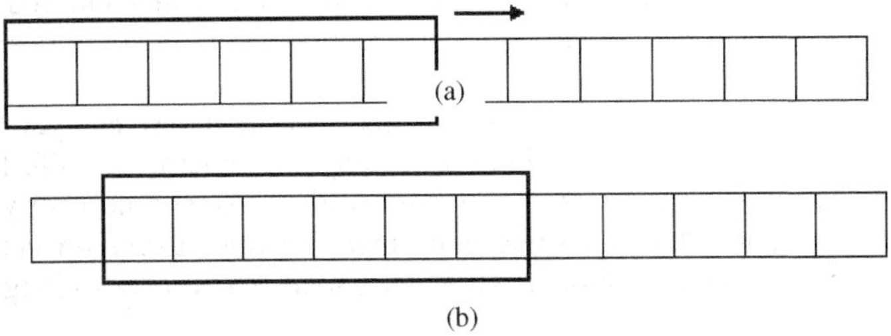

Fig. 2. Time sliding window

When one time fuzzy evaluation is over, the time sliding window moves a time unite to the right ((Figure 2.1b). In each time unite of the window has recorded the transaction events. Each trust evaluation only considers the trust factors of the window. Time sliding window size depends on the user's configuration, and the trust factors mainly include the transaction quality and the transaction size. The evaluation result forms the direct trust to the entity.

4 Conclusion

Security and trust have essential relation. This paper has analyzed the implication relations between security and trust in traditional systems, and their explicit relations in open networks. The development of traditional security mechanisms simply follows the fixed trust relationship, but in open network its development need to be determined by the network structure and security requirements. Some networks only require a level trust relationship, and some networks will need to several levels trust relationship. In each level, the trust relationship includes absolute trust and relative trust. In higher risk situations, the absolute trust relationship must be established, and the relative trust relationship can be a supporting role. In low risk situations, you may only need to establish the relative trust relationship.

References

1. Narula, P., Dhurandher, S.K., Misra, S., et al.: Security in mobile ad-hoc networks using soft encryption and trust-based multi-path routing. Computer Communications 31(4), 760–769 (2008)
2. Stajano, F.: The resurrecting duckling – what next? In: Proceedings of the 8th International Workshop on Security Protocols, pp. 204–214. Springler, Berlin (2000)
3. Blaze, M., Kannan, S., Lee, I., et al.: Dynamic trust management. Computer 42(2), 44–52 (2009)
4. Bandhakavi, S., Winsborough, W., Winslett, M.: A trust management approach for flexible policy management in security-typed languages. In: Proceedings of the 21st IEEE Computer Securituy Foundation Conference, pp. 33–47 (2008)
5. Hess, A., Holt, J., Jacobson, J., et al.: Content-triggered trust negotiation. ACM Transactions on Information and System Security 7(3), 428–456 (2004)
6. Zhou, R., Hwang, K.: PowerTrust: a robust and scalable reputation system for trusted peer-to-peer computing. IEEE Transactions on Parallel and Distributed Systems 18(4), 460–473 (2007)
7. Wang, Y., Vassileva, J.: Bayesian network-based trust model. In: Proceedings of the IEEE International Conference on Web Intelligence, pp. 372–378. IEEE Computer Society Press, Washington (2003)
8. Boukerche, A., Ren, Y.: A trust-based security system for ubiquitous and pervasive computing environments. Computer Communications 31(18), 4343–4351 (2008)
9. Gomez, M., Carbo, J., Benac-Earle, C.: An anticipatory trust model for open distributed systems. In: Proceedings of the 3rd Workshop on Anticipatory Behavior in Adaptive Learning Systems, pp. 307–324 (2007)

Research on Real Estate Monitoring and Forewarning System Based on System Dynamics Model

Demin Wu[1,2], Wenyong Dong[1], Chao Zhou[3], Kai Tang[3], and Aidi Lin[3]

[1] School of Computer
[2] The College of Continuing Education
Wuhan University, Wuhan City, Hubei Province, China
[3] School of Electronic Information, Wuhan University
Wuhan City, Hubei Province, China
Demin_Wu456@126.com

Abstract. This paper concerns the monitoring and forewarning of real estate in China and attempts to establish a simultaneous equation model using housing price factors as its endogenous variables. The study bases itself on system dynamics and an analysis of real estate prices. It aims to set up a real estate monitoring control system, applying Granger causality test on the correspondence between housing and land prices in Shanghai. It discusses theoretical and practical factors involving urban housing prices and their correlations, and also offers corresponding control policy recommendations.

Keywords: Real estate monitoring and forewarning system, Granger causality test, system dynamics.

1 Introduction

The existing real estate monitoring and forewarning system relies on traditional economic theory of forewarning, and, on business fluctuations cycles. The fact that the system presupposes the regularity of market makes it much less applicable in present China as it has to rise to the challenges of the international financial crisis on the one hand and the domestic industrial upgrading and transformation tasks on the other. Moreover, the real estate market is a complex economic system, and a linear model such as based on forewarning has inherent deficiencies in characterizing high-order, nonlinear, and time lagging issues.

2 System Dynamics

System dynamics (it termed as SD) is based on system theory which is derived from Cybernetics. The early SD, then called industrial dynamics, was mostly used in industrial enterprises for business management, dealing with such issues as fluctuations in production and employees, market shares and market volatility and so on. With the continuous expansion of its application deep into social, economic,

D. Zeng (Ed.): ICAIC 2011, Part I, CCIS 224, pp. 573–581, 2011.

resources, agriculture, population, business, finance, and even medical and other fields, industrial dynamics has changed its name to system dynamics, as an important branch of System Theory, studies information feedback through establishing flow positions and flow rates. It describes, as a system analytic technique, system structure by feedback circuit, quantitatively approaching high-order, nonlinear, multiple feedback, complex, and time-varying systems through computer simulation technology. The causal relationship between variables can be pinned down by means of a structural analysis of the real system, and descriptions of the system's future behavioral trend can thus be obtained by way of computer simulation based on information observed from actual workings of the system.

3 The Real Estate Monitoring and Forewarning System Based on System Dynamics

The central idea of SD and the basic economic law of real estate, supported by system dynamic simulations of the real estate market, help to achieve the purpose of the market's monitoring and forewarning. A system so constructed serves as a sub-model of "the real estate forewarning system", functioning as it forecasts running statuses of the real estate market, as it facilitates its dynamic forewarning, and as it provides policy experiments for the government's macro-control policy-making.

3.1 System Structure

With reference to SD, theories of production cost and commodity value, housing prices can be taken to be a system mainly composed of land costs, property costs, and risk profits generated by the market's supply and demand. These factors together constitute a system of real estate prices, which, from the perspective of monitoring and warning, may be divided into the following seven sub-systems: supply, demand, price, land markets, economic development, real estate finance and urban population. Of these sub-systems, the latter four are of great importance, for they each have a direct bearing on the supply and demand of, and therefore on the price and the development of, the urban residential real estate market. Yet the market, as the leading industries of the national economy, also reacts to those sub-systems.

3.2 Real Estate System Monitoring and Forewarning Model Based on System Dynamics

In the real estate market, the impact of population on housing demand comes from its numerical and demographic changes. For one thing, the growth of population will inevitably lead to increased need for housing, and so does floating population. For another, demographic changes stand in direct proportion to housing demand, and the effect of age structure is especially felt.

If the national economy is seen as a large system, the real estate economy is one of its subsystems. The national economy's developmental level, speed and scale, and periodic fluctuations in amplitude and frequency determine the related developmental level, speed and scale of its real estate industry. The growth of urban economy tends to expand the investment scale of fixed assets, and this accordingly steps up residential construction investments, resulting in an increase in the supply of urban housing. Similarly, the raised level of economic development often leads to increased income of urban residents, and with the ability to pay, living standards improve, and so do housing needs (quantitatively and qualitatively) correspondingly.

With this understanding, the real estate market can be seen as a complex dynamic system, and the real estate monitoring system based on system dynamics can thus be established. The model features five major feedback loops as shown below:

(1) Negative feedback loop: Total open space → (+) Government grant → (+)Total land supply → (-) Total open space;

(2) Positive feedback loop: Housing supply → (+) residential vacancy rate → (+) Housing supply;

(3) Negative feedback loop: Total housing supply → (-) Residential vacancy rate → (-) Risks and benefits of the supply and demand → (+) Development volition → (+) Total housing supply;

(4) Negative feedback loop: Housing demand → (-) Residential vacancy rate → (-) Risks and benefits of the supply and demand → (+) Housing prices (-) Housing demand;

(5) Negative feedback loop: Land costs → (+) Housing prices → (-) Housing demand → (-)Risks and benefits of the supply and demand (+) Development volition → (+) Land costs.

3.3 The System Dynamics Equation Model

The impact of factors on commercial housing prices is to be analyzed through a reduced simultaneous equation modeled on changes effected by those influencing the price level of the residential housing market. Variable declarations related to this section are as follows:

Table 1. Main in Factors and Variables Relevant to Changes of the Commercial Housing Price

Variable Name	Instructions	Units
P	The average sales price of commercial housing	Yuan / Square meter
CC	The average cost of completed residential	Yuan / Square meter
SH	Stock Trading residential area	Million square meters
LI	One-year commercial loan rate	%
HI	Residential construction investment	Billion Yuan
AH	Per capita housing area	Square Meter
N	Resident population	Ten thousand
HDI	Household disposable income	Yuan
GDP	Gross domestic product	Billion Yuan

The simultaneous system dynamics equation model has the following characteristics:

1) It facilitates research on the complex relationship between economic variables.
2) It consists of a number of single equation models combined organically.
3) It contains both random and deterministic equation.
4) The various equations in it are fitted with random explanatory variables.

The variable types of the model are:

1) Endogenous variables: Their values are determined by variables within the system.

2) Exogenous variables: Their values are determined by variables outside the system.

3) Given variable: With respect to Endogenous variables for the period, lagged endogenous variable and exogenous variable values are already known (ie predetermined); they are therefore collectively referred to as pre-fixed variables (also known as pre-variables).

The system dynamics equation modeled on the diagram of feedback from the real estate monitoring and warning system and the causal relationship between variables in the dynamics-based forewarning model of the real estate is shown as below:

$$\begin{aligned}\ln P = C_1 \ln CC + C_2 \ln HI + C_3 \ln SH + C_4 \ln LI + C_5 \ln AH + C_6 \ln N \\ + C_7 \ln HDI + C_8 \ln GDP + \varepsilon\end{aligned} \quad . \tag{1}$$

In the system dynamics equation model P are endogenous variables, and the remaining variables are pre-variables. Endogenous variables show a certain probability distribution, the parameters of which are elements to be estimated. These variables not only affect but are also affected by the whole system. Exogenous variables, on the other hand, affect the system but not vice versa.

The log-linear model is selected here is because it enjoys a relatively simple form, and because its independent variable coefficients directly reflect the strain on the elasticity of the independent variable.

4 System Implementation and Simulation

The implementation of the real estate monitoring and forewarning system based on system dynamics consists of the following steps: setting up domestic price system based on the real estate monitoring and forewarning model, taking Shanghai real estate market price system as data samples, making a quantitative analysis of the impact of the main factors of Shanghai primary commercial housing market on price changes, and discerning the causal relationship between the sales price of the primary market and the transaction price of the secondary stock market and that between house prices and land prices.

Based on the historical data (from 1995 to 2008) of the eight regulatory factors, the real estate monitoring and forewarning system based on system dynamics works out the housing prices with land prices excluded by: controlling function and then the natural logarithm function, multiplying the result by the coefficient calculated, and finally summing all. On the right of the simulation system the interaction between land prices and housing prices can be measured, and by the afore mentioned differential equation, the feedback loop can be constructed, which, when amended, may be viewed as a housing price simulation with land prices having been considered.

5 Experimental Results

An analysis of simulation results of the model shows that the impact of demand on prices is more significant than that of supply, indicating that the demand for housing in Shanghai is more vigorous compared to the relevant supply. This means that the current housing prices, in the case of demand-pull, may still have a certain space to rise. The model displays a high degree of fit supported by the value of R^2, which reaches as high as 99.7%, demonstrating the model's relatively strong explanatory power.

It is also evident that financial policies hold a regulatory role on housing demand in Shanghai to a certain extent. They can be employed to stimulate the development of the housing market by lowering the interest rates for housing loans, or to curb it by doing the opposite when the market exhibits excessive speculative or virtual demand.

5.1 Relationship between Housing and Land Prices

Presently warm discussions of the relationship between housing and land prices have focused on two aspects: first, whether the proportion of premium in housing prices is high or low, and second, whether the level of real estate prices depends on land prices or not. Land prices over against those of housing are just as cost prices over against those of commodities. A change in land prices often produces an ascending-or-descending motion in housing prices, and a fluctuation in housing prices also tends to effect a rise-or-fall movement in land prices.

Experimental results are analyzed using Granger causality test, and the relationship between real estate and land prices is examined as a close substitute for the relationship between commercial housing and residential land prices. All the experimental data come from China Monthly Economic Indicators published by the National Bureau of Statistics of China, including real estate sales price index, and land price index. The price indices provided are of the chain type, with those of housing sales price represented as HP, and those of the land transaction price as LP.

5.2 Stationarity Test

In order to avoid spurious regression problems caused by non-stationary time series regression,the ADF unit root test needs to be adopted, for there may be high correlationsin time series. For the results of testing the stability of the variables, see TABLE 2.

Table 2. Unit Root Test Results

Variables	Test Forms (CTK)	Confidences	Thresholds	ADF-t Statistics	Conclusions
HP	C.T.2	99%	-4.5000	-0.3613	Instable
LP	C.T.2	99%	-4.5000	-3.1827	Instable
ΔHP	C.N.2	99%	-4.5348	-4.6356	Stable
ΔLP	C.N.2	99%	-4.5348	-12.9031	Stable

Descriptions: HP and LP expresses the first difference between ΔHP and ΔLP.

Test results show that, in Shanghai, real estate sales prices HP and land prices LP are instable, but the first difference between the two is stable. This means that it is possible to continue to test whether there exists Cointegration relationship between HP And LP.

5.3 Cointegration Test

In this section as in the previous, the same method is used to examine whether the time series HP_t and LP_t are of the cointegration nature. The test method has two steps:

The first step consists of the application of ADF regression following the OLS method.

$$HP_t = \beta_0 + \beta_1 LP_t + \mu_t \,. \tag{2}$$

The second step is to check whether the regression residuals of the equation μ_t is stable or not. The test equation is:

$$\Delta\mu_t = \delta t + \gamma\mu_{t-1} + \varepsilon_1\Delta\mu_{t-1} + \varepsilon_2\Delta\mu_{t-2} + \cdots + \varepsilon_{p-1}\Delta\mu_{t-p+1} + \varepsilon_t \,. \tag{3}$$

In this equation, $\Delta\mu_t$ is the first difference of the sequence y_t; t the time trend term; $\gamma = p-1$, ε_t is white noise, and the value of P is that value of P that guarantees ε_t is the smallest white noise. The test of hypothesis is the same as the ADF test in the section above. Test results are as follows:

$$HP_t = 37.2791 + 0.7605 LP_t \,. \tag{4}$$

Where R_2=0.4196, DW=0.8637, the DW test value of the model is comparatively low, indicating that there is a serious autocorrelation in the regression residual series. Therefore, it is necessary to run a ADF test on the regression residual series μ_t. The value of ADF statistics is -8.8093 while the critical value of the significance level of 1% is -4.500, signaling that the regression residual series μ_t is a stationary one, and that there is a long-term stable relationship between real estate sales prices HP and land prices LP in Shanghai.

5.4 Cointegration Test

This section continues to apply the Granger test to examine the causal relationship between the time series HP_t and LP_t. The model is as below:

$$\begin{cases} HP_t = C_1 + \sum \alpha_i LP_{t-i} + \sum \beta_j HP_{t-j} + \mu_{1t} \\ LP_t = C_2 + \sum \lambda_i HP_{t-i} + \sum \delta_j LP_{t-j} + \mu_{2t} \end{cases} . \tag{5}$$

With F test and P values it can be seen from the above table that in determining the 10% significance level for the demurrage from 2 to 4, there is a reciprocal causation between housing and land prices; at the 1% significance level for the lag period of 5-6 (ie, more than 1 year), housing prices are the main determinant of land prices while land prices had no significant effect on house prices. Thus, it is concluded: for different lag periods there are different Granger causalities between HP and LP.

As Granger causality test only confirms that in different periods there are different causal relationships between housing and land prices, it does not draw specific conclusions. To this end, a further regression analysis is needed. The test results are shown in TABLE 3.

Table 3. LSHP and L NHP Causality Test Results

Null hypothesis	Lag phases	F Statistics	P value (probability)
A	2	4.41381	0.03109
B		21.0554	4.4E-05
A	3	1.93239	0.17823
B		13.3093	0.00040
A	4	2.51797	0.11502
B		8.60911	0.00383
A	5	0.66428	0.66488
B		13.1370	0.00349
A	6	0.48843	0.79118
B		343.591	0.00024

Note: A denotes that the LP to HP Granger causality does not exist.
B denotes that the HP to LP Granger causality does not exist.

(1) The impact of housing prices on land prices

First, to examine the impact of changes of land prices LP on housing prices HP during the previous 4 quarters, a regression equation is constructed as below:

$$HP = C + \lambda_1 LP(-1) + \lambda_2 LP(-2) + \lambda_3 LP(-3) + \lambda_4 LP(-4)\,. \tag{6}$$

Table 4. Impact of changes of land prices LP on housing prices HP during the previous 4 quarters

	Coefficient	Std. Error	t-Statistic	Prob.
C(1)	-71.40595	36.49316	-1.956694	0.0722
C(2)	1.383477	0.284852	4.856829	0.0003
C(3)	-0.082559	0.343144	-0.240596	0.8136
C(4)	1.502977	0.333526	4.506328	0.0006
C(5)	-0.775619	0.381086	-2.035285	0.0627
HP=C(1)+C(2)*LP(-1)+C(3)*LP(-2)+C(4)*LP(-3)+C(5)*LP(-4)				

At the 5% significant level, $LP(-2)$ 、 $LP(-4)$ and the constant term can not pass the t test. With these indicators excluded, the following equation is obtained:

$$HP = \lambda_1 LP(-1) + \lambda_2 LP(-3)\,. \tag{7}$$

For the results calculated on the data, see TABLE 5.

Table 5. Impact of changes of land prices LP on housing prices HP

	Coefficient	Std. Error	t-Statistic	Prob.
C(1)	0.757449	0.150128	5.045370	0.0001
C(2)	0.468505	0.154808	3.026365	0.0076
* HP=C(1)*LP(-1)+C(2)*LP(-3)				

As the equation displays autocorrelation and heteroskedasticity problems, and as the assumed AR (1) random errors are subject to $\mu_t = \rho\mu_{t-1} + \varepsilon_t$, the improved equation is worked out as follows:

$$\begin{cases} HP_t = \beta_1 LP(-1)_t + \beta_2 LP(-3)_t + \mu_t \\ \mu_t = \rho\mu_{t-1} + \varepsilon_t \end{cases} . \tag{8}$$

On calculations of the data, it can be seen that all the indicators are significant, and the adjusted coefficients are of better fit.

(2) The impact of housing prices on land prices

The impact of housing prices on land prices can be examined using the same method. The first regression equation is as follows:

$$\begin{aligned} LP = C + \lambda_1 HP(-1) + \lambda_2 HP(-2) + \lambda_3 HP(-3) \\ + \lambda_4 HP(-4) + \lambda_5 HP(-5) + \lambda_6 HP(-6) \end{aligned} . \tag{9}$$

For the results calculated on the data, see attached TABLE 4.

At the 5% significant level, HP(−1), HP(−3), HP(−6) can not pass the t Test, and when these indicators have been removed, the resulting equation is as follows:

$$LP = C + \lambda_1 HP(-2) + \lambda_2 HP(-4) + \lambda_3 HP(-5) . \tag{10}$$

Through the calculation of the data and by the light of experience, it is found that at the 5% significant level all the indicators are significant.

6 Conclusion

The simulation results from the analysis show that in the next few years or even longer period of time, the main problems facing the Shanghai real estate market are the rapidly rising price and the overheating supply. On the one hand, the supply exceeds the demand; on the other the price continues to rise. The market needs, therefore, urgent and imminent adjustments.

1) To adjust supply and demand. For any product, supply and demand are the most fundamental factors to be considered with reference to its market price. It is precisely because the Shanghai real estate is experiencing a very abnormal process of supply and demand that leads to unprecedented increases in this round of price surges. To keep such a situation under control it is necessary therefore to adjust the supply and the demand of the Shanghai residential housing market in the first place.

2) To adopt a decreasing loan ratio policy. Fast rising costs contribute heavily to high housing prices in Shanghai. First, there are rapid rises in construction and installation costs. These rises are attributed to large increases of real estate raw materials. Secondly, there are many fees of different names attached to building lands before the latter reach the hands of the real estate business. These fees do not create value but are included in housing costs. If developers who want to build higher-priced housing have to bear higher capital costs on their own only to find smaller groups of buyers available, their risk will be greatly enhanced. Leverage loans are used in this way, housing prices will naturally be curbed, and the safety of the banking system will be guaranteed. Government financial regulators can regularly adjust the proportion of such loans formula.

3) To guide the direction of private capital investment. Now that the investment threshold is getting higher and higher, and the government has no effective guidance over private funds, especially small ones, a large number of civil capitals seem to find nowhere to go. Real estate is favored by private capitals as a better project among current available investment selections. It is suitable for funds ranging from tens to hundreds of thousands and to millions, and enjoys an additional edge of relatively stable benefits. In short, the involvement of a large number of private funds also accounts for the rise of residential housing prices in china.

Acknowledgment. The authors gratefully acknowledge the financial support of the National Natural Science Foundation of China under Grant No. 60873114 and 60773009, Post Doctoral Funds number 20080440073 and Tianjin Natural Science Foundation (09JCYBJC27700).

References

1. Wang, X.L., Chen, F.: Misapprehend and Mend of Forewarning Rule in Real Estate. China Real Estate 8, 6–7 (2008)
2. Cai, Y.S., Yang, C., Wang, C.: Research on Forewarning Models of Enterprise finance crisis Based on System Dynamics. Management World 5, 176–177 (2008)
3. Sehlke, G., Jacobson, J.: System Dynamics Modeling of Transboundary Systems,The Bear River Basin Model. Ground Water, Research Library Core 43(5), 722–730 (2005)
4. Mao, L.L., Hu, G.H.: Analysis of the City FinancialEcology Environment Based on System Dynamics. Journal of WUT (Information & Management Engineerng) 30(02), 316–318 (2008)
5. Zhang, D.B., Hu, B., Shao, Z.F.: Research on Enterprise Lifecycle Based on Dynamic System Method. Chinese Journal of Management 2(suppl.), 34–36 (2005)
6. Granger: Testing for Causality: a Personal Viewpoint. Journal of Economic Dynamics and Control 2, 329–352 (1980)
7. Wang, Y.C., Zhang, X.P.: Cointegrated theory, Error Mend model and Granger test. Statistic and Decision-Making 18, 157–158 (2009)
8. Cui, S.T.: Influence Factors Analysis on The Price of City Housing—Taking Shanghai real estate market as an example. Shanxi Journal of Agricultural Sciences 3, 145–148 (2010)

A Novel Method for Fluence Map Optimization with Dose Volume Constraints in IMRT*

Haozheng Ren[1], Yihua Lan[1,**], Cunhua Li[1], Xuefeng Zhao[1], and Zhifang Min[2]

[1] School of Computer Engineering, Huaihai Institute of Technology
Lianyungang, China
[2] Department of system, Huazhong Institute of Optoelectronics, Wuhan, China
renhaozheng86@gmail.com

Abstract. Doctors judge whether the inverse plan can meet the clinical requirements according to their experiences on the dose volume curve, which was used to characterize the dose deposition of each organ in radiation therapy. However, when the dose volume constraints were added to the inverse planning model, the resulting non-convex programming problem needs a complex solving process, which may not lead to a good solution. In order to solving this problem efficiently, a new heuristic algorithm was introduced. In this method, rather than using the traditional dose sorting information, a new geometry distance, getting from the transformed standard quadratic form, was used to guide the constrained voxels' selection. Combining with the effective voxels adding scheme and the quick local optimum searching by quadratic programming, the whole solving process is very fast. Through testing on the head-neck case and prostate case, the results show the new heuristic information is more suitable for adding constraints than the dose dependent way. Therefore, it is a stable solving algorithm for the fluence map optimization process with dose volume constraints.

Keywords: Intensity modulated radiation therapy, fluence map optimization, dose volume constraints, linear constrained quadratic programming model, heuristic algorithm.

1 Introduction

Intensity modulated radiation therapy (IMRT), one of the precise high-energy radiation therapy technology, has been widely used for the treatment of cancers [1-3]. It can deliver controllable dose for target tissues. Additionally, the dose decline rapidly from the target region to the side non-target region, which reduce the irradiation injury of healthy cells.

---

* This work was supported in part by the National Natural Science Foundation of China under Grant No. 40806011, the Natural Science Foundation of JiangSu under Grant BK20082140, the Natural Science Foundation of Huaihai Institute of Technology under Grant Z2009013, and the Construction Found of JiangSu for Key Disciplines in Applications of Computing.

** Corresponding author.

D. Zeng (Ed.): ICAIC 2011, Part I, CCIS 224, pp. 582–589, 2011.

Fluence map optimization of each beam is an important process for the inverse plan[4-5]. A good fluence map should have outstanding performance in two aspects. First, the dose in the targets region should be close to the prescribed dose and distributed evenly. Second, the dose deposition of all tissues surrounding the targets region should be kept as low as possible, especially, the dose deposition of some organs at risk need to be strictly limited to some dose upper bound which appointed by doctors or oncologists.

2 Methods

2.1 The Description of Fluence Map Optimization

In order to describe the radiation impact for each part of the organ, we divide the organ into many cubes, which are called voxels. The voxels' size can be adjusted based on the needs of the plan. Obviously, the smaller the voxels are, the dose measurement is more accurate. At the same time, the scale of data that need considering will increase accordingly.

We divide all the voxels into two parts: A set of target regions $T=\{T_1,T_2,\cdots,T_u\}$, where T_i represents the i-th target region, u represents the number of target regions, the corresponding voxel volumes are $S_{T_1}, S_{T_2}, \cdots, S_{T_u}$; A set of non-target regions $N=\{N_1,N_2,\cdots,N_v\}$, where N_j represents the j-th non-target region, v represents the number of non-target regions (including normal tissues and organs at risk), the corresponding voxel volumes are $S_{N_1}, S_{N_2}, \cdots, S_{N_u}$.

Likewise, the intensity maps of each beam are also discretized into pixels. The pixels size can be determined by the multi-leaf collimator (MLC) used for the dose delivering. We assume all pixels are put into a column vector X.

The relationship between the dose deposition of each voxels and the intensity of each pixel in the column vector X will be expressed by linear matrix. Assume the matrix for the target voxels is $\boldsymbol{F}_T = (\boldsymbol{F}_{T_1}; \boldsymbol{F}_{T_2}; \cdots; \boldsymbol{F}_{T_u})$, and the matrix for the non-target voxels is $\boldsymbol{F}_N = (\boldsymbol{F}_{N_1}; \boldsymbol{F}_{N_2}; \cdots; \boldsymbol{F}_{N_u})$. Consequently, $\boldsymbol{D}_T = \boldsymbol{F}_T \cdot \boldsymbol{X}$ and $\boldsymbol{D}_N = \boldsymbol{F}_N \cdot \boldsymbol{X}$ represent the dose deposition received by the target and non-target voxels with intensity vector X, respectively. The prescription dose values for target regions T are $\boldsymbol{D}_{TP_1}, \boldsymbol{D}_{TP_2}, \cdots, \boldsymbol{D}_{TP_u}$; the dose upper bounds for non-target regions N are $\boldsymbol{D}_{NU_1}, \boldsymbol{D}_{NU_2}, \cdots, \boldsymbol{D}_{NU_u}$.

Then the widely used least square physical dose model can be formulated as follows:

$$\min\left\{\sum_{i=1}^{u}\frac{p_i}{S_{T_i}}\left(\boldsymbol{D}_{T_i}-\boldsymbol{D}_{TP_i}\right)^2\right\}$$
$$S.t.\begin{cases}\boldsymbol{D}_{N_j}\leq \boldsymbol{D}_{NU_j}, for\ j=1,2,\cdots,v\\ 0\leq \boldsymbol{X}\end{cases} \tag{1}$$

Set $\boldsymbol{Q}=\sum_{i=1}^{u}\frac{p_i}{S_{N_i}}\boldsymbol{F}_{T_i}{}^T\cdot\boldsymbol{F}_{T_i}$, $\boldsymbol{c}=-2\sum_{i=1}^{u}\frac{p_i}{S_{N_i}}\boldsymbol{F}_{T_i}{}^T\cdot\boldsymbol{D}_{TP_i}$, $Const=\sum_{i=1}^{u}\frac{p_i}{S_{N_i}}\boldsymbol{D}_{TP_i}{}^T\cdot\boldsymbol{D}_{TP_i}$, the model can be simplified to a linear constrained quadratic programming (LCQP) model:

$$\min\left\{\boldsymbol{X}^T\boldsymbol{Q}\boldsymbol{X}+\boldsymbol{c}^T\boldsymbol{X}+Const\right\}$$
$$S.t.\begin{cases}\boldsymbol{F}_{N_j}\cdot\boldsymbol{X}\leq \boldsymbol{D}_{NU_j}, for\ j=1,2,\cdots,v\\ 0\leq \boldsymbol{X}\end{cases} \tag{2}$$

2.2 The Description of Dose Volume Constraints

To facilitate describing the dose distribution for the irradiation tissues, radiation oncologists often take the dose volume histogram as the plan's evaluation criteria. We give the definition of the dose volume function $\mathrm{H}(d)$ as follows:

For a given tissue in the organ,

$$\mathrm{H}(d)=\frac{\text{volume of the voxels with Dose}\geq d}{\text{volume of all voxels}}\times 100\% \tag{3}$$

The curve of this function was called dose volume curve. Due to the requirement of the dose deposition performance, the dose volume constraint (DVC) is utilized to control the shape of curve. The typical DVC can be expressed as "no more than η % of some tissue should receive λ Gy or higher". Where "Gy" is the shorthand for "Gray", which is the international unit for radiation dose absorption. Intuitively, this constraint just wants that the function curve lies below the point (λ,η) (figure 1).

DVC is very useful in describing a desired dose distribution for tissues, although it brings a high degree of computing complexity to the inverse planning process.

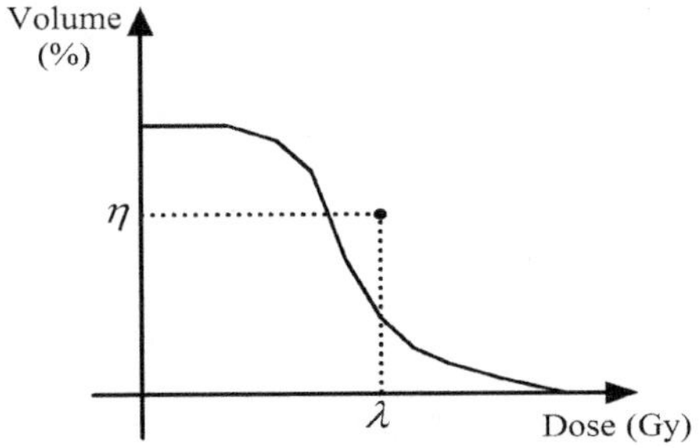

Fig. 1. Dose volume constraints

2.3 The Algorithm for FMO with DVCs

The main idea of the algorithm: we first solve the quadratic programming without any dose volume constraints, then add new constraints and solve the new quadratic programming, repeat this cycle until satisfying the DVCs requirements.

2.3.1 The Flow Chart

The flow chart of the algorithm shows as figure 2.

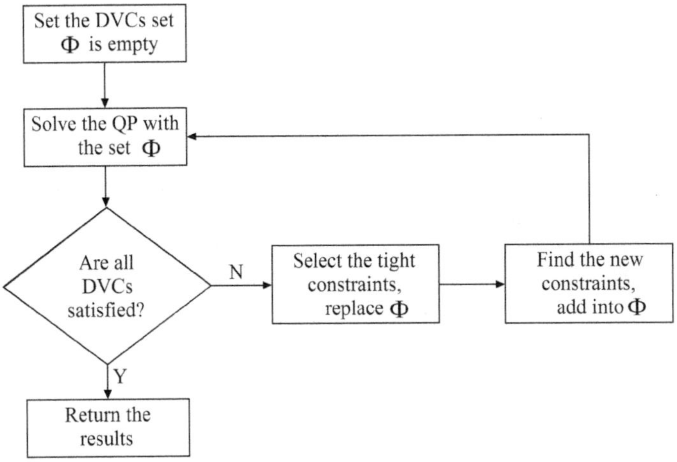

Fig. 2. Flow chart of the algorithm

2.3.2 The Explanation of the Flow Chart

a) Solve the QP with the constraints set Φ

It means to solve the following problem:

$$\min\left\{X^{T}QX + c^{T}X + Const\right\}$$
$$S.t.\begin{cases} 0 \le X \\ \Phi \end{cases} \tag{4}$$

Where the set Φ represents the voxel set which needs dose constraints.

b) Judge the satisfactions of all DVCs

We first compute the dose for each voxels of each tissue, and sort them in descending order. For some tissue i, assuming the dose volume constraint point is (λ,η). Then find out the actual dose which is the dose upper bound for the $\eta\%$ voxels with lowest dose. Finally, we compare the actual dose with λ. If the actual dose is smaller than the dose of DVC, the DVC (λ,η) is not satisfied for this tissue, otherwise it is satisfied.

c) Select the tight constraints

After getting the solution of the QP with the constraint set Φ, we substitute the solution into the constraint set Φ. We will find a number of constraints do not play a role. Therefore, in order to accelerate the optimization process by reducing the constraint dimension; we will delete all the useless constraints and reserve the tight constraints.

d) Find the new constraints

If the DVC of some tissue is not satisfied, we need to add more voxels into the constraint set Φ .The adding voxels are choose from the voxels whose dose deposition is between the actual dose and the dose of DVC. However, to avoid the object function value rising too fast by adding too many constrains one time, and the convergence is too slow by adding too little constrains one time. We will consider the following strategy.

2.4 The Setup of the Experiments

The radiotherapy planning platform used for this project is called CERR (Computational Environment for Radiotherapy Research) which is an opening package [6]. CERR provides the vital features we need for fluence optimization of IMRT, namely clinical data inter face, dose calculation, and visualization.

Table 1. Dose Requirements for the Head and Neck Test Case

Target region	**1**	***Target1***	= 70(Gy)
	2	***Target2***	= 64(Gy)
	3	***Target3***	= 55(Gy)
Non-target region	**1**	***Brain***	≤5%, ≥45(Gy)
	2	***Brain Stem***	≤10%, ≥36(Gy)
	3	***Mandible***	≤20%, ≥50(Gy)
	4	***Parotid Gland***	≤10%, ≥20(Gy)
	5	***Spinal Cord***	≤40%, ≥20(Gy)
	6	***Other Tissue***	≤2%, ≥60(Gy)

3 Results

The results show the objective function value and the actual dose of each organ in each step. The experiment is test by a head-neck case and a prostate case with the same algorithm scheme but different heuristic information.

The dose volume histogram (DVH) is also given for comparing the target dose behaviors solving by different algorithms.

4 Discussion

Looking into table 2 and table 3, in the first step, the objective function have the lowest value 1.9281 in the absence of dose constrain. At this time, all other organs with dose volume constrains did not meet the requirement. In the following iteration steps, with the increasing in the number of constraints, the objective function value is increased gradually, and the actual dose value of each organ is approaching the dose value of the DVCs. The blue color number shows the actual dose value has comply with the corresponding DVCs requirements. Obviously, with the gradual adding voxels to the constrains for each iteration, we hope that the actual dose value of each organ can decline steadily and the objective function value increases slowly. That is to say that a better algorithm should have stable convergence performance. On the other hand, if the actual dose of some tissue declines unevenly or the ultimate objective function value is too large, the algorithm is not a smart choice for getting a good solution. Observing the actual dose performance of each organ in these two tables, we can see after the fist step, the actual dose of brainstem dropped from 65.7704 to 42.8924 when using the dose sorting information, but dropped from 65.7704 to 52.7145 when using geometry distance sorting information; after the second step, the actual dose of spinal cord dropped from 35.9872 to 9.2044 when using the dose sorting information, but dropped from 29.9957 to 20.4541 when using geometry distance sorting information. The latter dose decline is steadier than the former one. For the ultimate objective function value, the latter is 15.0574, which is less than the form 18.1189 significantly.

Table 2. Head-neck Test Case Experiment (Sort by the Dose)

Step	Object value	Brain	Brainstem	Mandible	Parotid gland	Spinal cord	Other issue
1	1.9281	60.4759	65.7704	66.0622	56.4530	52.7350	72.0927
2	3.5467	42.5681	42.8924	62.3208	56.3825	35.9872	69.0440
3	6.2989	42.3475	38.4223	57.4058	43.2828	9.2044	66.6684
4	10.5465	43.5313	37.4331	51.4490	33.4349	9.9007	64.5919
5	14.1371	42.9716	36.0000	50.4078	28.1687	14.9534	61.8035
6	17.2432	41.4892	36.1222	50.3588	24.0108	16.6119	60.9314
7	17.9308	41.9316	36.0000	50.0469	21.4033	17.8090	61.6811
8	18.0945	41.8575	36.0000	50.0933	20.4599	17.9608	60.6487
9	18.1141	41.8108	36.0000	50.0000	20.0000	18.1475	60.3750
10	18.1189	41.7518	36.0000	50.0000	20.0000	18.2591	60.0000

Table 3. Head-neck Test Experiment (Sort by the Heuristic Information)

Step	Object value	Brain	Brainstem	Mandible	Parotid land	Spinal cord	Other tissue
1	1.9281	60.4759	65.7704	66.0622	56.4530	52.7350	72.0927
2	2.7281	45.1200	52.7145	62.3734	53.4588	29.9957	68.9457
3	7.0583	43.1296	40.9559	58.0233	36.5582	20.4541	66.0349
4	12.0005	42.3082	36.2590	52.6641	25.9414	20.0492	62.9025
5	14.8941	43.1964	36.4924	50.5845	20.8191	20.0000	61.0675
6	15.0356	42.6419	36.0122	50.0000	20.0000	20.0000	60.5481
7	15.0502	42.5837	36.0000	50.0000	20.0000	20.0000	60.3341
8	15.0573	42.5705	36.0000	50.0000	20.0000	20.0000	60.0676
9	15.0574	42.5674	36.0000	50.0000	20.0000	20.0000	60.0000

5 Conclusion

This paper presented a voxels selection based heuristic algorithm for solving the combinatorial quadratic programming model formulated in the fluence map optimization with dose volume constrains. We adopt rational geometry distance information rather than the traditional dose sorting information. For the future study, we would consider not only the voxels adding scheme, but also voxels deleting method by the dual solution information.

Acknowledgment. The authors would like to thank Department of Network Engineering, School of Computer Engineering, Huaihai Institute of Technology for supporting us the hardware environment to carry out experiments, and especially to Jian Zhang, a colleague of the first three authors and Jun Shi, the vice dean of School of Computer Engineering, for the very useful discussions in the optimization algorithm at HHIT.

References

1. Bortfeld, T.: IMRT: a review and preview. Physics in Medicine and Biology 51, 363–379 (2006)
2. Hatano, K., et al.: Current status of intensity-modulated radiation therapy (IMRT). International Journal of Clinical Oncology 12, 408–415 (2007)
3. Yu, C.X., et al.: Planning and delivery of intensity-modulated radiation therapy. Medical Physics 25, 5233–5241 (2008)
4. Yang, Y., Xing, L.: Inverse treatment planning with adaptively evolving voxel-dependent penalty scheme. Medical Physics 31, 2839–2844 (2004)
5. Dai, J., Zhu, Y.: Conversion of dose-volume constraints to dose limits. Physics in Medicine and Biology 48, 3927–3941 (2003)
6. Deasy, J.O., et al.: CERR: A computational environment for radiotherapy research. Medical Physics 30, 979–985 (2003)

Existence and Uniqueness of Strong Solution for Predator-Prey System of Three Species with Age-Structure*

Chen Li-Yu and Zhang Qi-Min

Ningxia University, Yinchuan, 750021, People's Republic of China
chen-hy654@tom.com

Abstract. In this paper, existence and uniqueness of strong solution are proved for predator-prey system of three species with age-structure in Hilbert space. Using Gronwall's lemma, some criteria of existence and uniqueness of strong solution are obtained for predator-prey system of three species with age-structure.

Keywords: Existence, Uniqueness, three species.

1 Introduction

The study of age-structured single species was initiated by Rorres and Fair[1]. Since then, the control problem has received many attentions from several authors[2-5]. For the problem of multi-species, Albrecht et al. [6], Lenhart et al. [7]and Crespo et al. [8] considered several system, respectively. However, their results are not concerned with age factor. In [9], the predator-prey system of three species with age-structure can be written in the following form.

$$\begin{cases} \frac{\partial p_1}{\partial t}+\frac{\partial p_1}{\partial a}=-\mu_1(a,t)p_1-\lambda_1(a,t)P_2(t)p_1, \\ \frac{\partial p_2}{\partial t}+\frac{\partial p_2}{\partial a}=-\mu_2(a,t)p_2+\lambda_2(a,t)P_1(t)p_2 \\ -\lambda_3(a,t)P_3(t)p_2, \\ \frac{\partial p_3}{\partial t}+\frac{\partial p_3}{\partial a}=-\mu_3(a,t)p_3+\lambda_4(a,t)P_2(t)p_3, \\ p_i(0,t)=\beta_i(t)\int_{a_1}^{a_2} m_i(a,t)p_i(a,t)da, \\ p_i(a,0)=p_{i0}(a) \\ P_i(t)=\int_0^{a_+} p_i(a,t)da, i=1,2,3 \qquad (a,t)\in Q. \end{cases} \tag{1}$$

* This work is partially supported by NingXia Natural Science Foundation # NZ0935 and CNSF Grant # 11061024.

D. Zeng (Ed.): ICAIC 2011, Part I, CCIS 224, pp. 590–601, 2011.

where $Q=(0,a_+)\times(0,+\infty),[a_1,a_2]$ is the fertility interval , and the other parameters mean as follow: (for the sake of convenience, throughout this paper we suppose that i=1,2,3).

$p_i(a,t)$: the density of i th population of age a at time t, $p_i := p_i(a,t)$;

$\mu_i(a,t)$: the average mortality of I th population;

$\beta_i(t)$: the average fertility of ith population;

$\lambda_k(a,t)$:the interaction coefficients(k=1,2,3,4);

$m_i(a,t)$: the ratio of females in ith population;

$p_{i0}(a)$: the initial of age distribution of I th population;

a_+ : the life expectancy, $0<a_+<+\infty$. Here without loss of generality. we asumme that the three population have the same life expectancy.

In the paper [9], Zhixue Luo, Ze-Rong He and Wan-Tong Li considered optimal birth control for predator-prey system of three species with age-structure. In this paper, existence and uniqueness of strong solution are discussed for predator-prey system of three species with age-structure. Using Gronwall's lemma, some criteria of existence and uniqueness of strong solution are obtained for predator-prey system of three species with age-structure.

2 Preliminaries

Throughout this paper, we always asumme that: (H_1) $\mu_i \in L(Q)$, $0\le \mu_{i0} \le \mu_i(a,t) \le \mu_i^0, \mu_{i0}, \mu_i^0$ are constants, $\int_0^{a_+} \mu_i(a,t+a)da=+\infty,(a,t)\in Q$

(H_2) $0\le B_k \le \lambda_k(a,t) \le A_k,(a,t)\in Q, A_k, B_k$ are constants, (k=1,2,3,4)

(H_3) $0\le m_i(a,t)\le M_i,(a,t)\in Q, M_i$ are constants, and $m_i(a,t)\equiv 0$, when $a<a_1$ or $a>a_2$,

(H_4) $\beta_i \in U_i := \{h_i \in L^\infty(0,\infty): 0\le \beta_{i0} \le h_i(t) \le \beta_i^0, \quad \forall t>0\}$, $U=U_1\times U_2\times U_3$

(H_5) $p_{i0}\in L^\infty(0,a_+), p_{i0}(a)\ge 0, \forall a\in(0,a_+)$.

(H_6) $r_i \le P_i(t) \le R_i, P_i := P_i(t)$. For any given T>0 and $p=(p_1,p_2,p_3)\in C(0,T;L^2(0,a_+;R^3)) \bigcap L^\infty(Q_T;R^3)$, where $Q_T=(0,a_+)\times(0,T)$

3 Existence and Uniqueness of Solutions Uniqueness of Solutions

3.1 Uniqueness of Solutions

Now we shall prove that there exists at most one solution of(1).This result will be deduced mainly from Gronwall's lemma.

Theorem 3.1 Assume the preceding hypotheses hold. Then, there exists at most one solution of (1) in $C(0,T;L^2(0,a_+;R^3)) \bigcap L^\infty(Q_T;R^3)$.

Proof. Suppose that

$p=(p_1,p_2,p_3), q=(q_1,q_2,q_3)\in C(0,T;L^2(0,a_+;R^3)) \bigcap L^\infty(Q_T;R^3)$, and p,q are two solutions of (1). we obtain

$$
\begin{aligned}
& |p_1-q_1|^2 \\
= \quad & -2\int_0^t \langle \frac{\partial(p_1-q_1)}{\partial a}, p_1-q_1\rangle ds \\
& -2\int_0^t \langle \mu_1(a,s)(p_1-q_1), p_1-q_1\rangle ds \\
& -2\int_0^t \langle \lambda_1(a,s)P_2(p_1-q_1), p_1-q_1\rangle ds
\end{aligned}
$$

where $|\cdot|$ is the ordinary norm in $C(0,T;L^2(0,a_+;R^3))$

$\bigcap L^\infty(Q_T;R^3)$.

Since

$$
\begin{aligned}
& -2\langle \frac{\partial(p_1-q_1)}{\partial a}, p_1-q_1\rangle \\
\le \quad & a_+(\beta_1^0 M_1)^2 |p_1-q_1|^2 \\
& -2\int_0^t \langle \mu_1(a,s)(p_1-q_1), p_1-q_1\rangle ds \\
\le \quad & -2\mu_{10}\int_0^t |p_1-q_1|^2\, ds \\
& -2\int_0^t \langle \lambda_1(a,s)P_2(p_1-q_1), p_1-q_1\rangle ds \\
\le \quad & -2B_1 r_1 \int_0^t |p_1-q_1|^2\, ds
\end{aligned}
$$

Therefore, we get that

$$
\begin{aligned}
& |p_1 - q_1|^2 \\
\le\; & a_+(\beta_1^0 M_1)^2 \int_0^t |p_1 - q_1|^2\, ds - 2\mu_{10} \int_0^t |p_1 - q_1|^2\, ds \\
& -2B_1 r_1 \int_0^t |p_1 - q_1|^2\, ds \\
=\; & (a_+(\beta_1^0 M_1)^2 - 2\mu_{10} - 2B_1 r_1) \int_0^t |p_1 - q_1|^2\, ds
\end{aligned} \tag{2}
$$

$$
\begin{aligned}
& |p_2 - q_2|^2 \\
=\; & -2\int_0^t \langle \frac{\partial(p_2 - q_2)}{\partial a}, p_2 - q_2 \rangle ds \\
& -2\int_0^t \langle \mu_2(a,s)(p_2 - q_2), p_2 - q_2 \rangle ds \\
& +2\int_0^t \langle \lambda_2(a,s) P_1 (p_2 - q_2), p_2 - q_2 \rangle ds \\
& -2\int_0^t \langle \lambda_3(a,s) P_3 (p_2 - q_2), p_2 - q_2 \rangle ds
\end{aligned}
$$

Since

$$
\begin{aligned}
& -2\langle \frac{\partial(p_2 - q_2)}{\partial a}, p_2 - q_2 \rangle \\
\le\; & a_+(\beta_2^0 M_2)^2 |p_2 - q_2|^2
\end{aligned}
$$

$$
\begin{aligned}
& -2\int_0^t \langle \mu_2(a,s)(p_2 - q_2), p_2 - q_2 \rangle ds \\
\le\; & -2\mu_{20} \int_0^t |p_2 - q_2|^2\, ds
\end{aligned}
$$

$$
\begin{aligned}
& 2\int_0^t \langle \lambda_2(a,s) P_1 (p_2 - q_2), p_2 - q_2 \rangle ds \\
\le\; & 2A_2 R_1 \int_0^t |p_2 - q_2|^2\, ds
\end{aligned}
$$

$$
\begin{aligned}
& -2\int_0^t \langle \lambda_3(a,s) P_3 (p_2 - q_2), p_2 - q_2 \rangle ds \\
\le\; & -2B_3 r_3 \int_0^t |p_2 - q_2|^2\, ds
\end{aligned}
$$

Therefore, we get that

$$
\begin{aligned}
& |p_2 - q_2|^2 \\
\le\ & (a_+(\beta_2^0 M_2)^2 - 2\mu_{20} + 2A_2R_1 - 2B_3r_3) \\
& \int_0^t |p_2 - q_2|^2\, ds
\end{aligned} \tag{3}
$$

$$
\begin{aligned}
& |p_3 - q_3|^2 \\
= \ & -2\int_0^t \langle \frac{\partial(p_3 - q_3)}{\partial a}, p_3 - q_3 \rangle ds \\
& -2\int_0^t \langle \mu_3(a,s)(p_3 - q_3), p_3 - q_3 \rangle ds \\
& +2\int_0^t \langle \lambda_4(a,s)P_2(p_3 - q_3), p_3 - q_3 \rangle ds
\end{aligned}
$$

Since

$$
\begin{aligned}
& -2\langle \frac{\partial(p_3 - q_3)}{\partial a}, p_3 - q_3 \rangle \\
\le\ & a_+(\beta_3^0 M_3)^2 |p_3 - q_3|^2 \\
& -2\int_0^t \langle \mu_3(a,s)(p_3 - q_3), p_3 - q_3 \rangle ds \\
\le\ & -2\mu_{30}\int_0^t |p_3 - q_3|^2\, ds \\
& 2\int_0^t \langle \lambda_4(a,s)P_2(p_3 - q_3), p_3 - q_3 \rangle ds \\
\le\ & 2A_4R_2\int_0^t |p_3 - q_3|^2\, ds
\end{aligned}
$$

Therefore, we get that

$$
\begin{aligned}
& |p_3 - q_3|^2 \\
\le\ & (a_+(\beta_3^0 M_3)^2 - 2\mu_{30} \\
& +2A_4R_2)\int_0^t |p_3 - q_3|^2\, ds
\end{aligned} \tag{4}
$$

Thus,it follows from (2),(3)and (4)

$$
\begin{aligned}
& |p - q|^2 \\
= \ & |p_1 - q_1|^2 + |p_2 - q_2|^2 + |p_3 - q_3|^2 \\
\le\ & K\int_0^t |p - q|^2\, ds
\end{aligned}
$$

for some positive constant K>0.

Now, Gronwall's lemma obviously implies uniqueness.

3.2 Existence of Strong Solutions

In order to prove the existence of solution for Eq.(1), we shallfirst prove the following Lemmas.

We consider the equations

$$\begin{cases} p_1^1 = p_{10} + \int_0^t \left[-\frac{\partial p_1^1}{\partial a} dt - \frac{a_+ \left(\beta_1^0 M_1\right)^2}{2} p_1^1 \right] ds, \\ p_1^1(0,t) = \beta_1(t) \int_{a_1}^{a_2} m_1(a,t) p_1^1 da, \\ p_1^{n+1} = p_{10} + \int_0^t \left[-\frac{\partial p_1^{n+1}}{\partial a} dt - \frac{a_+ \left(\beta_1^0 M_1\right)^2}{2} p_1^{n+1} \right] ds + \\ \int_0^t \frac{a_+ \left(\beta_1^0 M_1\right)^2}{2} p_1^n ds - \int_0^t \mu_1(a,s) p_1^n ds - \int_0^t \lambda_1(a,s) P_2^n p_1^n ds \\ p_1^{n+1}(0,t) = \beta_1(t) \int_{a_1}^{a_2} m_1(a,t) p_1^{n+1} da, \\ \quad t \in [0,T], \qquad \forall n \geq 1 \end{cases} \tag{5}$$

$$\begin{cases} p_2^1 = p_{20} + \int_0^t \left[-\frac{\partial p_2^1}{\partial a} dt - \frac{a_+ \left(\beta_2^0 M_2\right)^2}{2} p_2^1 \right] ds, \\ p_2^1(0,t) = \beta_2(t) \int_{a_1}^{a_2} m_2(a,t) p_2^1 da, \\ p_2^{n+1} = p_{20} + \int_0^t \left[-\frac{\partial p_2^{n+1}}{\partial a} dt - \frac{a_+ \left(\beta_2^0 M_2\right)^2}{2} p_2^{n+1} \right] ds \\ + \int_0^t \frac{a_+ \left(\beta_2^0 M_2\right)^2}{2} p_2^n ds - \int_0^t \mu_2(a,s) p_2^n ds \\ + \int_0^t \lambda_2(a,s) P_1^n p_2^n ds - \int_0^t \lambda_3(a,s) P_3^n p_2^n ds \\ p_2^{n+1}(0,t) = \beta_2(t) \int_{a_1}^{a_2} m_2(a,t) p_2^{n+1} da, \\ \quad t \in [0,T], \qquad \forall n \geq 1 \end{cases} \tag{6}$$

$$\begin{cases} p_3^1 = p_{30} + \int_0^t \left[-\frac{\partial p_3^1}{\partial a} dt - \frac{a_+ \left(\beta_3^0 M_3\right)^2}{2} p_3^1 \right] ds, \\ p_3^1(0,t) = \beta_3(t) \int_{a_1}^{a_2} m_3(a,t) p_3^1 da, \\ p_3^{n+1} = p_{30} + \int_0^t \left[-\frac{\partial p_3^{n+1}}{\partial a} dt - \frac{a_+ \left(\beta_3^0 M_3\right)^2}{2} p_3^{n+1} \right] ds + \\ \int_0^t \frac{a_+ \left(\beta_3^0 M_3\right)^2}{2} p_3^n ds - \int_0^t \mu_3(a,s) p_3^n ds - \int_0^t \lambda_4(a,s) P_2^n p_3^n ds \\ p_3^{n+1}(0,t) = \beta_3(t) \int_{a_1}^{a_2} m_3(a,t) p_3^{n+1} da, \\ \quad t \in [0,T], \qquad \forall n \geq 1 \end{cases} \tag{7}$$

Lemma 3.1. $\{p^n = (p_1^n, p_2^n, p_3^n)\}$ is a Cauchy sequence in

$$C(0,T;L^2(0,a_+;R^3)) \bigcap L^\infty(Q_T;R^3).$$

Proof.. For n>1

$$\begin{aligned} & \quad | p_1^{n+1} - p_1^n |^2 \\ = & \quad 2\int_0^t \langle -\frac{\partial p_1^{n+1}}{\partial a} + \frac{\partial p_1^n}{\partial a}, p_1^{n+1} - p_1^n \rangle ds \\ - & \quad a_+(\beta_1^0 M_1)^2 \int_0^t |p_1^{n+1} - p_1^n|^2 ds \\ + & \quad a_+(\beta_1^0 M_1)^2 \int_0^t (p_1^{n+1} - p_1^n, p_1^n - p_1^{n-1}) ds \\ - & \quad 2\int_0^t (\mu_1(a,s)(p_1^n - p_1^{n-1}), p_1^{n+1} - p_1^n) ds \\ - & \quad 2\int_0^t (\lambda_1(a,s) P_2^n (p_1^n - p_1^{n-1}), p_1^{n+1} - p_1^n) ds \end{aligned} \tag{8}$$

It is easy to deduce

$$\begin{aligned} & |p_1^{n+1}-p_1^n|^2 \\ \leq\ & |a_+(\beta_1^0 M_1)^2-2\mu_{10}-B_1r_1| \\ & \int_0^t |p_1^{n+1}-p_1^n||p_1^n-p_1^{n-1}|ds \end{aligned} \tag{9}$$

Consequently, (9) yields

$$\begin{aligned} & \sup_{0\le\theta\le t}|p_1^{n+1}(\theta)-p_1^n(\theta)|^2 \\ \leq\ & |a_+(\beta_1^0 M_1)^2-2\mu_{10}-B_1r_1| \\ & \sup_{0\le\theta\le t}\int_0^\theta |p_1^{n+1}(s)-p_1^n(s)||p_1^n(s)-p_1^{n-1}(s)|ds \end{aligned} \tag{10}$$

Now, we estimate the terms on the right-hand side of (9) by using the inequality $2ab\le\frac{a^2}{l^2}+l^2b^2, l>0.$

$$\begin{aligned} & \left|a_+\left(\beta_1^0 M_1\right)^2-2\mu_{10}-B_1r_1\right| \\ & \sup_{0\le\theta\le t}\int_0^t\left|p_1^{n+1}(\theta)-p_1^n(\theta)\right|\left|p_1^n(\theta)-p_1^{n-1}(\theta)\right|ds \\ & \le\frac{1}{4}\left[\sup_{0\le\theta\le t}\left|p_1^{n+1}(\theta)-p_1^n(\theta)\right|^2\right]+ \\ & \left(a_+\left(\beta_1^0 M_1\right)^2-2\mu_{10}-B_1r\right)^2 T\int_0^t\left[\sup_{0\le\theta\le t}\left|p_1^{n+1}(\theta)-p_1^n(\theta)\right|^2\right]ds \end{aligned} \tag{11}$$

If we set

$$\varphi^n(t)=\sup_{0\le\theta\le t}|p_1^{n+1}(\theta)-p_1^n(\theta)|^2, \tag{12}$$

then from (10)-(13), it could be deduced that there exists a positive constant c>0 such that

$$\varphi^n(t)\le\frac{3}{4}\varphi^n(t)+c\int_0^t\varphi^{n-1}(s)ds, \tag{13}$$

and consequently there exists \$k>0\$ such that

$$\varphi^n(t) \le k \int_0^t \varphi^{n-1}(s)ds. \tag{14}$$

By iteration from (16), we get

$$\varphi^n(t) \le \frac{k^{n-1}T^{n-1}}{(n-1)!}\varphi^1(T), \ \forall n > 1, \ \forall t \in [0,T]. \tag{15}$$

Therefore,

$$\sup_{0\le\theta\le T} | p_\theta^{n+1} - p_\theta^n |^2 \le \frac{k^{n-1}T^{n-1}}{(n-1)!}\varphi^1(T), \ \forall n > 1. \tag{16}$$

Obviously, (16) implies that $\{p_1^n\}$ is a Cauchy sequence in $C(0,T;L^2(0,a_+;R^1)) \bigcap L^\infty(Q_T;R^1)$. In a similar manner,we can get $\{p_2^n\} and \{p_3^n\}$ is a Cauchy sequence in

$C(0,T;L^2(0,a_+;R^1)) \bigcap L^\infty(Q_T;R^1)$. Therefore, $\{p^n\}$ is a Cauchy sequence in

$C(0,T;L^2(0,a_+;R^3)) \bigcap L^\infty(Q_T;R^3)$.

By Lemma 3.1, it is easy to deduce that the following theoremis satisfied.

Lemma 3.2 The sequence $\{p^n\}$ is bounded in $C(0,T;L^2(0,a_+;R^3)) \bigcap L^\infty(Q_T;R^3)$.

Now we are in a position to prove the existence of solution to the problem (1).

Theorem 3.2 Assume $(H_1)-(H_6)$ hold.

Then, for each $p_0 \in C(0,T;L^2(0,a_+;R^3)) \bigcap L^\infty(Q_T;R^3)$,

there exists a unique solution of the problem (1) in $C(0,T;L^2(0,a_+;R^3)) \bigcap L^\infty(Q_T;R^3)$

Proof.. Uniqueness hold from Theorem 3.1.

we can use Theorem A and get that there exist a unique process$\{p^n\} \in C(0,T;L^2(0,a_+;R^3)) \bigcap L^\infty(Q_T;R^3)$,

which is the solution of (5)-(7) for n=1. By recurrence, we obtain a sequence of solutions for (5)-(7), $\{p^n\}_{n\ge1} \in C(0,T;L^2(0,a_+;R^3)) \bigcap L^\infty(Q_T;R^3)$.

Now, we want to prove that the sequence p^n is convergent to a p in $C(0,T;L^2(0,a_+;R^3))\bigcap L^\infty(Q_T;R^3)$, which will be the solution of (1).

Firstly, we observe that Lemma 3.1 implies that there exists

$p\in C(0,T;L^2(0,a_+;R^3))\bigcap L^\infty(Q_T;R^3)$

Such that

$p^n \to p$ in $C(0,T;L^2(0,a_+;R^3))\bigcap L^\infty(Q_T;R^3)$.

$$\text{Let } Dp_i=\frac{\partial p_i}{\partial t}+\frac{\partial p_i}{\partial a}, i=1,2,3$$

$$Dp=(Dp_1,Dp_2,Dp_3)\ Dp^n=(Dp_1^n,Dp_2^n,Dp_3^n)$$

So

$$\begin{cases} Dp_1^n=-\dfrac{a_+(\beta_1^0M_1)^2}{2}p_1^ndt-\mu_1(a,t)p_1^{n-1}dt \\ +\dfrac{a_+(\beta_1^0M_1)^2}{2}p_1^{n-1}dt-\lambda_1(a,t)P_2^{n-1}p_1^{n-1}dt \\ Dp_2^n=-\dfrac{a_+(\beta_2^0M_2)^2}{2}p_2^ndt-\mu_2(a,t)p_2^{n-1}dt \\ +\dfrac{a_+(\beta_2^0M_2)^2}{2}p_2^{n-1}dt+\lambda_2(a,t)P_1^{n-1}p_2^{n-1}dt \\ -\lambda_3(a,t)P_3^{n-1}p_2^{n-1}dt \\ Dp_3^n=-\dfrac{a_+(\beta_3^0M_3)^2}{2}p_3^ndt-\mu_3(a,t)p_3^{n-1}dt \\ +\dfrac{a_+(\beta_3^0M_3)^2}{2}p_3^{n-1}dt-\lambda_4(a,t)P_2^{n-1}p_3^{n-1}dt \end{cases} \tag{17}$$

By preceding analysis, we easily obtain that $|Dp_i^n|\le M<\infty . i=1,2,3$

On the other hand, by virtue of lemma 3.2 $\{p_i^n\},(i=1,2,3)$ has a subsequence which is weakly convergent in

$C(0,T;L^2(0,a_+;R^1))\bigcap L^\infty(Q_T;R^1)$.

But, since $p_i^n \to p_i,(i=1,2,3)$ in $C(0,T;L^2(0,a_+;R^1)) \bigcap L^\infty(Q_T;R^1)$, we can assure that $p_i^n \to p_i,(i=1,2,3)$ weakly in $C(0,T;L^2(0,a_+;R^1)) \bigcap L^\infty(Q_T;R^1)$, (in the sequel, we will denote this by $p_i^n \rightharpoonup p_i,(i=1,2,3)$ in $C(0,T;L^2(0,a_+;R^1)) \bigcap L^\infty(Q_T;R^1),$). In conclusion, we have proved:

$$p_i^n \to p_i \ in \ C(0,T;L^2(0,a_+;R^1))\bigcap L^\infty(Q_T;R^1), \tag{18}$$

$$p^n \to p \ in \ C(0,T;L^2(0,a_+;R^1))\bigcap L^\infty(Q_T;R^1), \tag{19}$$

$$Dp_i^n \rightharpoonup h_i. \ in \ C(0,T;L^2(0,a_+;R^1))\bigcap L^\infty(Q_T;R^1). \tag{20}$$

$$Dp^n \rightharpoonup h. \ in \ C(0,T;L^2(0,a_+;R^1))\bigcap L^\infty(Q_T;R^1). \tag{21}$$

Since the differential operator is continuous, so $Dp = h$.

The proof of theorem 3.2 is now complete.

Acknowledgment. The preferred spelling of the word "acknowledgment" in America is without an "e" after the "g." Try to avoid the stilted expression, "One of us (R. B. G.) thanks …" Instead, try "R.B.G. thanks …" Put sponsor acknowledgments in the unnumbered footnote on the first page.

References

1. Rorres, C., Fair, W.: Optimal age specific harvesting policy for continuous-time population model. In: Burton, T.A. (ed.) Modelling and Differential Equations in Biology. Dekker, New York (1980)
2. Chan, W.L., Guo, B.Z.: Optimal birth control of population dynamics. J. Math. Anal. Appl. 144, 532–552 (1989)
3. Chan, W.L., Guo, B.Z.: Optimal birth control of population dynamics. Part 2. Problems with free final time, phase constraints, and mini-max costs. J. Math. Anal. Appl. 146, 523–539 (1990)
4. Anita, S.: Optimal harvesting for a nonlinear age-dependent population dynamics. J. Math. Anal. Appl. 226, 6–22 (1998)
5. Ainseba, B., Langlais, M.: On a population dynamics control problem With age dependent and patial structure. J. Math. Anal. App. 248, 455–474 (2000)
6. Albrecht, F., Gatzke, H., Haddad, A., Wax, N.: On the control of certain interacting population. J. Math. Anal. Appl. 53, 578–603 (1976)

7. Lenhart, S., Liang, M., Protopopescu, V.: Optimal control of boundary habitat hostility for interacting species. Math. Mech. Appl. Sci. 22, 1061–1077 (1999)
8. Crespo, L.G., Sun, J.Q.: Optimal control of population of competing species. Nonlinear Dynam. 27, 197–210 (2002)
9. Luo, Z., He, Z.-R., Li, W.-T.: Optimal birth control for predator system of three species with age-structure. Applied Mathematics and Computation 155, 665–685 (2004)

Reducing Computational and Memory Cost for HMM-Based Embedded TTS System

Rong Fu[1], Zengliang Zhao[1], and Qixiong Tu[2]

[1] Beijing Institute of Applied Meteorology, Beijing 100029, China
[2] Department of Electronic and Engineering, Tsinghua University
Beijing 100084, China
neilruan1@hotmail.com

Abstract. In this paper, we present several methods to reduce the computational and memory cost to embed HMM-based TTS system. We firstly decrease the number of HMMs by applying decision tree based context clustering technique. Secondly propose address-based model compression technique to compress the model size without degradation in synthesis speech quality. Thirdly reduce the feature vector size to decrease computational and memory resources. Finally, fixed-point implementation is taken to fit the TTS system requirements to embedded devices' resource. Experimental results show that the system size can be compressed to 3.61MB from 293MB, memory and computational cost are low enough for real-time embedded application. Subjective evaluation shows that the synthesis speech quality is fairly good.

Keywords: HMM-based speech synthesis, larger speech database, model compression, embedded application.

1 Introduction

Similarly to other data-driven speech synthesis approaches, in the HMM-based TTS system, it appears that the larger the database the better the synthesis speech quality. Study and research of TTS system based on a large database will be more meaningful and convincing. However, from desktop speaking application to incorporating TTS system on hand-held devices, memory limits the size of the TTS system that can be used and severely restricts the synthesis speech quality of the system. It is still a challenging task to develop a high-speed and memory efficient TTS system that works on resource-limited embedded devices.

Several techniques have been described to compress the size of the models in different fields. In automatic speech recognition (ASR), conventional methods to reduce the memory cost of the acoustic models are to reduce HMM (Gaussian distribution) components per state [1]. Other methods such as manipulating floating-point values are also effective. All these methods can be incorporated into TTS system for model compression, However, it will be at the cost of system performance more or less.

In this paper, we study various techniques to limit TTS system requirements for embedded application. we first control the number of HMMs by applying decision

D. Zeng (Ed.): ICAIC 2011, Part I, CCIS 224, pp. 602–610, 2011.

tree based context clustering technique. Then we propose model compression technique we refer to as address-based model compression to compress the developed TTS system trained from a large database of 10,000 sentences to be remarkably small, while it will not degrade the synthesis speech quality.

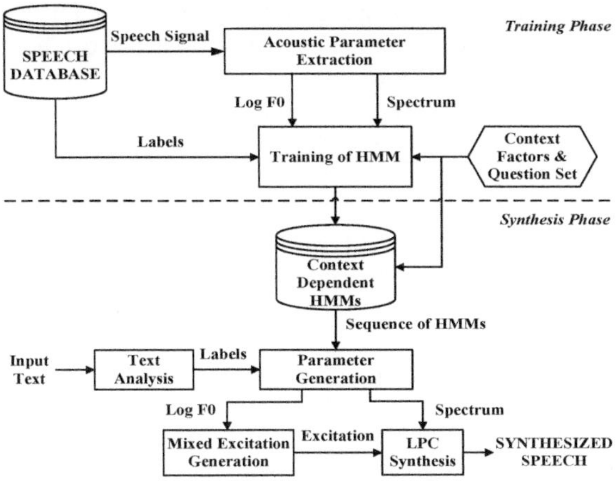

Fig. 1. HMM-based speech synthesis system

Next, we reduce the feature vector size to decrease computation and memory resources with no significant loss of performance. Finally, fixed-point implementation is taken to fit the TTS system requirements to embedded devices' resource.

The rest of this paper is arranged as follows. In Section 2, we briefly review the HMM-based TTS system and the parameter generation algorithm. Section 3 describes the details of the methods we use to reduce the computational and memory cost: decision-tree based clustering, address-based model compression, reducing feature vector size and fixed-point implementation. Next, the experiments to evaluate the effectiveness of the above techniques are presented in Section 4, and concluding reviews and our plans for future work is given in the final section.

2 HMM-Based Speech Synthesis System

The framework of HMM-based speech synthesis system is illustrated in Fig. 1. The system consists of two phases, the training phase and the synthesis phase.

In the training phase, Line Spectral Pair (LSP) coefficients and the logarithm of fundamental frequency (log F0) are extracted from speech database by STRAIGHT analysis, their delta and acceleration coefficients are calculated. The spectrum part is modeled by continuous HMMs. Due to the discontinuity of F0, multi-space probability distribution (MSD) HMMs are introduced to model F0 patterns [2]. In our work, Hidden-semi Markov Model (HSMM), which is an HMM with explicit state duration probability distributions, is applied for state duration modeling. Experiments show that the use of HSMM improved the naturalness of the synthesized speech [3].

In the synthesis phase, a sentence HMM corresponding to the given input text by concatenating the phoneme HMMs is constructed. After that, speech parameter sequence of spectrum and pitch is generated for the given state sequence by the speech parameter generation algorithm based on the maximum likelihood criterion. In order to make the parameter trajectory smoother, dynamic features including delta and acceleration coefficients are adopted in the generation algorithm [4]. Considering the dynamic features, the speech parameter vector sequence can be written as,

$$O = WC \tag{1}$$

where W is the coefficient matrix, C is the speech parameter vector sequence without dynamic features.

After determining the state duration sequence, the parameter generation is to obtain the speech parameter vector sequence C , which maximizes $P(O|Q,\lambda)$ with respect to $O=WC$, i.e.,

$$O = WCW^{T}U^{-1}WC = W^{T}U^{-1}M \tag{2}$$

the following equation are obtained,

$$\frac{\partial \log P(WC|Q,\lambda)}{\partial C} = 0 \tag{3}$$

where λ is a given HMM, Q is the state duration sequence, M and U^{-1} are mean vector and covariance matrix, respectively.

The main processing time of speech parameter generation is to generate spectrum parameter because the parameter vector has many dimensions, while that of F0 has just one. The generation of different dimensions is independent of each other, Eq.3 can be solved for one dimension one time to reduce memory cost.

3 Reducing System's Resource Requirements

In this paper, four techniques used for reducing computational and memory cost are applied to map the TTS system requirements to the limited resource of the embedded platform.

3.1 Decision-Tree Based Clustering

Decision-tree based context clustering technique [5] is originally applied in TTS system to overcome the problem of data sparseness in training phase and improve the robustness. In this technique, the decision tree is built in the model training phase using a top-down sequential optimization procedure and the minimum description length (MDL) criterion is used for node splitting. A context decision tree is a binary tree with a question relating to the left or right child node attached to each non-terminal node. An example of the decision tree is displayed in Fig. 2. In this decision tree, the number of non-terminal nodes and terminal nodes are 127 and 128, respectively. Each non-terminal node of decision trees for spectrum, F0 and state duration consists of 3 parts: question attracted to the node, left child node and right child node, while the terminal nodes stand for the clustered parameter distributions of spectrum, F0 and state duration.

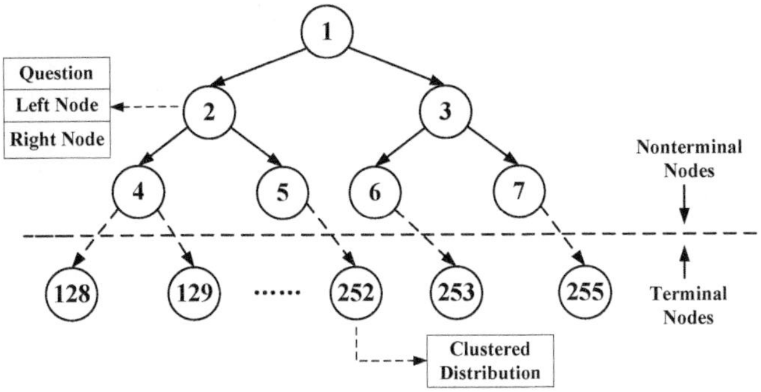

Fig. 2. Construction of decision tree

The acoustic model of TTS system composes of several thousands of HMMs to obtain good performance of speech synthesis, especially when large speech database is used for training acoustic model. However, it does not mean that the more the HMMs the better the synthesis speech quality, the number of HMM states (HMMs) should be controlled in a reasonable scale according to the given training speech database. Consequently, we can use this technique to reduce HMM states (HMMs) by controlling the depth of decision tree and obtain good performance of synthesis speech.

The core speech engine consists of 7 modules, distributions of spectrum, F0 and state duration, decision trees for spectrum, F0 and state duration, and a synthesizer engine which generates waveform from parameter vector of spectrum and pitch. In our TTS system, which is trained from a large speech database of 10,000 sentences, the decision trees for spectrum, F0 and state duration have been controlled to have 9624, 41782 and 3465 leaves in total, respectively. The binary file size of each module of the core speech engine is shown in Table 1.

Table 1. Binary File Size of TTS Core Speech Engine

Module		Size
decision tree	spectrum	798 KB
	F0	3369 KB
	duration	311 KB
distribution	spectrum F0	228 MB
	duration	60.6 MB
synthesizer engine		40 KB
Total		**293 MB**

From Table 1 we can see that the largest components of the TTS system are the acoustic model containing distributions of spectrum, F0 and state duration, they are nearly 99% of total file size. It shows that after embedded clustering training, the file size of the clustered model will be still too big for embedded application if large speech database is used.

3.2 Address-Based Model Compression

In the original TTS system called baseline system, the decision trees for spectrum, F0 and state duration and the distributions of spectrum, F0 and state duration are stored separately. In the acoustic model, there are distributions of spectrum, F0 and state duration which are clustered in the training phase and necessary in the synthesis phase. However, there are also several thousands of language models, these lists consume huge memory.

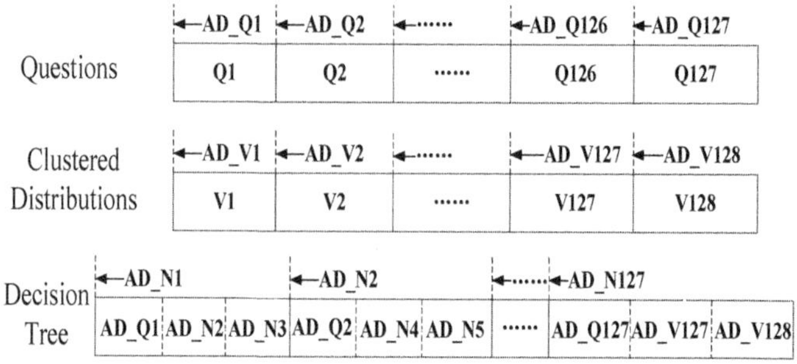

Fig. 3. Address-based storage and search

In this paper, a memory assignment for TTS system is employed, the scheme is address-based storage and search with lossless quality of synthesis speech. Questions attracted to decision tree nodes, distributions of spectrum, F0 and state duration and nodes of decision trees are stored in sequential arrays in question look-up table, clustered distribution look-up table and decision tree look-up table, respectively. Each entry in the look-up tables is mapped onto its address in the memory. The addresses used as indices into the question look-up table, clustered distribution look-up table and decision tree look-up table are stored in nodes of decision tree instead of the detailed information themselves, which is illustrated in Fig. 3. Where $\{Q_1,..., Q_{127}\}$ stand for the 127 questions attracted to the non-terminal nodes of decision tree and $\{AD\_Q_1,..., AD\_Q_{127}\}$ are their addresses in the memory, respectively. $\{V_1,..., V_{128}\}$ stand for the parameter vectors, $\{AD\_V_1,..., AD\_V_{128}\}$ are their addresses, respectively. $\{AD\_N_1,..., AD\_N_{255}\}$ are the addresses of the 255 nodes.

Address-based model compression technique can reduce the model size to be remarkably small by omitting the redundant information. By using the lookup tables it is possible to hold necessary information for speech synthesis in flash rather than main memory and read it in as required, the processing time will be decreased.

3.3 Reducing Feature Vector Size

Among all LPC parameters, Line Spectrum Pair (LSP) has the closest relevance to parameterize the spectral information and has many advantages for speech representation [6].

As discussed in Section 2, the computational and memory cost approximately linearly depend on the dimension of spectral feature, reducing feature vector size to some degrees will help to decrease the computational and memory cost. The spectral feature comprises line spectrum pair (LSP) and log gain. The dimension of LSP is always even because of its symmetry, we use different dimensions of LSP, such as 6, 8,..., 38, 40, to build different TTS systems, and apply subjective listening test to evaluate the results.

The Mean Opinion Score (MOS) test are performed, where 5 means excellent and 1 means bad. 100 sentences out of the 200 sentences synthesized from the developed system were randomly chosen for the same six persons to evaluate the overall quality of synthesis speech. The results are shown in Fig. 4.

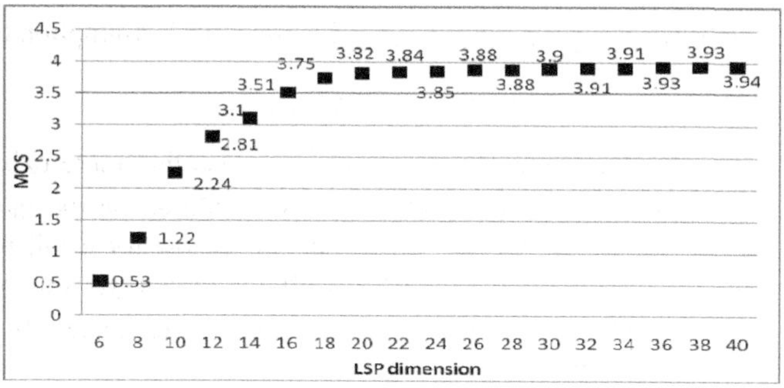

Fig. 4. Subjective evaluation of reducing LSP dimension

From Fig.4 we can see that the MOS score decreases while the LSP dimension decreases from 40 to 6, and an inflection point occurs when LSP dimension is 20. It also means that when the LSP dimension is 20, the synthesis speech quality is still relatively good, while the model size and computational cost will be reduced remarkably. Consequently, we will adopt 20 LSP coefficients instead of 40.

3.4 Fixed-Point Implementation

In order to apply the TTS system to embedded devices, floating point computation for parameter generation should be replaced by fixed-point computation. In our work, 16-bit integer is used as the precision of fixed-point.

Eq.3 can be effectively solved using Cholesky decomposition or LU decomposition. Due to the diagonal covariance matrix U^{-1} we use and the special construction of matrix W depicted in Figure 2, coefficient matrix $W^{T}U^{-1}W$ is a penta-diagonal symmetric positive definite matrix, consequently, pivoting for LU decomposition based on Gaussian elimination is not necessary. The process of solving Eq.3 includes decomposition, forward and backward substitution. Especially, forward substitution can be incorporated into the process of LU decomposition to reduce the computational complexity.

Table 2. Computational complexity of numerical solution

Solution	Decomposition		Substitution	Total	
	+ and *	$\sqrt{}$	+ and *	+ and *	$\sqrt{}$
Cholesky	*8N-13*	*N*	*10N-12*	*18N-25*	*N*
LU	*14N-23*	*0*	*5N-6*	*19N-29*	*0*

The process of parameter generation includes two phases: decomposition and substitution. Assume that the dimension of the coefficient matrix is N, we evaluate the computational complexity with respect to the operation counts. The result is given in Table 2. Where symbols +, * and $\sqrt{}$ stand for addition, multiplication and evolution operation, respectively.

It can be seen that the addition and multiplication operation count of Cholesky decomposition is slightly less than that of LU decomposition. However, the evolution operation of Cholesky decomposition will largely increase the computational complexity because it will be approximated by high-order polynomial in fixed-point computation. In our work, LU decomposition is adopted, it has lower computational complexity in fixed-point computation than Cholesky decomposition.

4 Experiments

4.1 Experimental Setup

The speech database is designed to compose of phonetically and prosodically rich sentences. Training data consists of 10,000 broadcast news style English sentences which are recorded by a male speaker, and the testing data consists of 200 sentences.

Speech signals are sampled at a rate of 16KHz and windowed by a 25ms Blackman window with a 5ms shift. Feature vector consists of spectrum and F0 parameter vector. Spectrum parameter vector consists of 40 LSP coefficients and gain which is obtained by STRAIGHT analysis, their delta and acceleration coefficients. F0 parameter consists of logarithm of F0, its delta and acceleration coefficients. We use language model based on quin-phone and 7-state left-to-right HMMs with single diagonal Gaussian distributions for model training.

4.2 Model Compression and Subjective Evaluation

Four developed systems, which are trained from large speech database, are applied to evaluate the effectiveness of four techniques: HMM model complexity reduction (Baseline System, BS), address-based model compression (System 1, S1), decreasing feature vector size (System 2, S2) and fixed-point implementation (system 3, S3). One thing to note is that the system 1 applies the first two techniques, system 2 applies the first three techniques and system 3 applies all the techniques. The model size compression of the above techniques is compared, and the Mean Opinion Score (MOS) test to evaluate the overall quality of synthesis speech, which is the same as that performed in part C of section 3, are also performed. The results are shown in Table 3.

Table 3. Model Size Comparison and Subjective Evaluation

System's name	BS	S1	S2	S3
Model size(MB)	293	12.8	6.98	3.61
MOS	3.83	3.82	3.67	3.53

It is shown that the model size has been reduced by up to 98.8% of the original size using the method of address-based storage, from 293MB to 3.61MB.

From the MOS test results, we can see that the MOS score of the final system (system 3) decreases about 7.6% of the baseline system, from 3.83 to 3.53. Especially, the high score of the baseline system indicates that the quality of the synthesis speech is fairly good. That is why we want to develop a TTS system trained from large speech database.

4.3 Memory Cost and Processing Time

We apply memory cost and processing time to estimate the resource cost of the developed TTS system (system 3). The memory cost and processing time here stand for the average memory cost and generating time per phoneme, respectively. The experiment is performed on a Celeron 2.13GHz machine (single thread) with 512MB memory.

Table 4. Average memory cost and processing time per phoneme

Memory cost	Processing time
2.56 KB	6 ms

Experimental results are shown in Table 4. It costs about 128 KB memory space and 0.3s processing time to synthesize a sentence with about 50 phonemes. And we can figure out from the table that memory cost is low enough for most embedded devices, and the processing time can also fit the requirements of real-time application.

5 Conclusion

In this literature, We propose four effective techniques to reduce the computational and memory cost of HMM-based TTS system trained from large speech database while minimizing any loss in the quality of synthesis speech. Experimental results show that the developed TTS system can be compressed by up to 98.8% of its original size, from 293MB (baseline system) to 3.61MB (system 3), while the synthesis speech quality will not be degraded significantly. Experimental results also show that the memory cost and processing time of the developed TTS system (system 3) are low enough for real-time embedded application. Future work is to implement the TTS system on embedded devices.

References

1. Levy, C., Linares, G., Nocera, P., Bonastre, J.-F.: Reducing computational and memory cost for cellular phone embedded speech recognition system. In: Proc. ICASSP (2004)
2. Tokuda, K., Masuko, T., Miyazaki, N., Kobayashi, T.: Hidden Markov Models Based on Multi-Space Probability Distribution for Pitch Pattern Modeling. In: Proc. ICASSP (1999)
3. Zen, H., Tokuda, K., Masuko, T., Kobayashi, T., Kitamura, T.: Hidden Semi-Markov Model Based Speech Synthesi. In: Proc. ICSLP, pp. 1180–1185 (2004)
4. Tokuda, K., Kobayashi, T.: S. Imai, "Speech parameter generation from HMM using dynamic features. In: Proc. ICASSP, pp. 660–663 (1995)
5. Shinoda, K., Watanabe, T.: Acoustic Modeling Based on the MDL Principle for speech recognition. In: Proc. EuroSpeech, pp. 99–102 (1997)
6. Wakita, H.: Linear prediction voice synthesizers: line spectrum pair (LSP) is the newest of several techniques. Speech Technol., 17–22 (1981)

A General Survey on Technological Developments of Oil Leakage Detection over the Past Decade*

Zhigang Lou[1], Hongzhao Liu[1], and Mingdu Hu[2]

[1] The Faculty of Mechanical and Precision Instrument Engineering
Xi'an University of Technology, Xi'an, Shaanxi Province, China
[2] Department of Foreign Languages
Ankang University, Anang, Shaanxi Province, China
zhiganglou1818@gmail.com

Abstract. This paper gives a general introduction of the mechanism and hazards of oil and gas pipeline leakage. And it also discusses the major methods, especially the latest developments of oil leakage detection in China and abroad. Furthermore, the trend of future development in the field of oil leakage detection is probed in the paper.

Keywords: leakage of pipelines, fault diagnosis, signal processing, Pattern Recognition, expert system.

1 Introduction

The industry of oil & gas transportation through pipeline has a history of over 100 years. Due to the increased production and consumption of petroleum and natural gas since WW II, the total length of major oil & gas pipelines in the world has reached more than 2.5 million kilometres, which also exceeded the total mileage of railway in the world and has been a major way of energy transportation. All oil & gas transportations are conducted through pipelines in Middle East, USA, and some developed European countries.

Due to corrosion, damage and other factors, pipeline failure becomes inevitable in the increased use of pipelines. Considering its effect on economy, environment and safety, many countries begin to attach more and more importance to pipeline detection and many of them have carried out corresponding regulations. For example, in October 1988, the U.S. Congress passed the Pipeline Safety Re-certification regulations, which requires the Department of Transportation Program Management Office (RSPA) to set a federal minimum safety standard so that all pipelines can be detected by intelligent detectors. What's more, they also detect pipelines regularly according to their different conditions in order to find out the mechanism of pipeline erosion so that the future condition of pipelines can be analysed and predicted. In this way, timely repair work and fault prevention can be done. To minimize the hazards of

* This research was supported by Shaanxi provincial project of special foundation of key disciplines (102-00X903).

D. Zeng (Ed.): ICAIC 2011, Part I, CCIS 224, pp. 611–618, 2011.

leakage and to ensure a safe pipeline transportation, we need to study leakage detection technology so that higher sensitivity of leakage detection and more accurate locating can be achieved. In a sense, the ability of finding out faults of pipeline timely has great significance to economy and society.

2 Overview of Leak Detection

Leak detection of oil & gas pipeline is an interdisciplinary subject, involving pipeline fluid mechanics, thermodynamics, sensor technology, signal detection, signal processing, etc. The research of leak detection and location technology of natural gas pipeline began in the early 1980s, which was based on automatic pipeline control system and data acquisition system and processed pipeline data with the help of modern analytical methods and control theories, making real-time leakage detection and location of pipelines possible.

Currently, there are quite a lot leakage detection and location technologies in the world, which can be divided into two broad categories, namely, hardware-based technologies and software-based technologies [1].

Hardware-based technologies detect leakages directly, such as direct observation, tube smart climbing machine, smell tracing, thermal infrared imaging, ground penetrating radar method, gas imaging, radiation detection, ball detection, fibre optic leak detection method, GPS (Global Positioning System) time labelling, ultrasonic leak detection, etc. [2,3].

Software-based leak detection and location of long-distance pipeline are conducted by using a certain number of sensors installed at the two ends of a pipeline. This technology can be further divided into three major approaches that are separately based on signal processing, model and knowledge.

Signal processing approach mainly uses acoustic method, negative pressure wave method and the pressure gradient method, having no need to establish mathematical models.

Model-based methods mainly include state observation method, system identification method, Kalman filter method, Real-time model method and transient current detection method.

Knowledge-based methods mainly use immune, genetic algorithms, neural networks, fuzzy logic etc.

There are also other methods that are based on pattern recognition and gray theory. The core of pattern recognition is the pattern recognition algorithm or dynamic time warping algorithm used to classify patterns. Grey theory fault diagnosis uses known information to probe the characteristics, state and trends of a system, and to make predictions and decisions.

3 Recent Developments of Detection Technologies

With the development of artificial intelligence, expert systems have been introduced into the field of fault diagnosis. It is a "knowledge-based" artificial intelligence system, and its essence is an artificial intelligent computer program which can solve complex practical problems using a large number of human experts' knowledge and reasoning. There have been some expert diagnosis systems. However, to different extents, these expert systems have some shortcomings, such as high misjudgement rate, low recognition accuracy and poor responsiveness [4].

In recent years, especially since the last decade some of our research institutes and universities have carried on effective research in the fields of stress wave method, negative pressure wave method, real-time pipeline model method and have made a lot of achievements.

3.1 Improving in the Responsiveness and Accuracy of Traditional Real-Time Technology through Combining Software and Hardware

Traditional pipeline leak detection methods, such as negative pressure wave diagnosis method, highly depend on real-time detection. As a result, failure in capturing real-time signal of leakage often causes diagnosis failures. In 2003, Wang Qianlong and Feng Quanke et al(from Xi'an Jiaotong University) accurately located pipeline leakage by using acoustic emission technology and wavelet packet theory of leakage. Test results showed that the accuracy of this method exceeded 94% and it can be used for detecting and monitoring the leakage of experimental pressure pipelines. [5] Ding Hao, from Beijing Jiaotong University, proposed a new method of leak identification - Wavelet correlation analysis in *2004*. [6] Wavelet correlation analysis takes advantage of wavelet analysis and correlation analysis in pinpointing leaks. Field test proved that, if used in leakage monitoring system, this method can gain an alarm response time of less than 2 mins, and the alarm leakage is only ± *1%* of the total flow, leak positioning accuracy ± 1% of the whole pipeline length. In 2009, considering the low SNR in actual testing environments and the time delay caused by noise, Yang Ronggen and his collages(from Nanjing University of Science and Technology) proposed a generalized cross correlation method and gave a fast FFT algorithm[7]. The application of this method in pipeline leakage detection showed that it can effectively calculate the time difference of leakage signals in reaching both ends of a pipeline, and the position error of leakage can be controlled under *2%*, hence the performance of time delay estimation improved.

3.2 The Increase of SNR by Means of Artificial Intelligence Technology

Lun Shu Xian, of Northeastern University, used the denoising method of adaptive fuzzy neural network system to improve the SNR of pressure signals and flow signals in hoping of solving the problem of low SNR in pipeline leakage detection. [8].The adaptive fuzzy neural network system has a nonlinear mapping and self-learning ability, so it can be used for the nonlinear modelling of noise signal. It can not only obtain the best estimate of the signal, but can also overcome uncertainties and incompleteness of existing models and noises. The application results showed that the adaptive noise canceller of adaptive fuzzy neural network is not only workable in saving runtime, and can quickly and effectively eliminate different kinds of noise in flow and pressure signals, thereby enhancing the accuracy of leak detection and location.

In 2005, Chen Huali(from Tsinghua University) proposed a pipeline leak detection and location method based on image processing [9].The method transforms pressure values into gray values of image, and makes the negative pressure on the pressure curve equivalent to the starting point for the positioning of the edge detection image processing gray level histogram calculated using a pressure curve value of the first half of the mainstream. If the latter half of the pressure curve deviated from the mainstream values, then the negative pressure wave is detected. If pressure curve is stretched for gray transformation, the negative pressure wave will be more prominent. Experimental studies have shown that this method can improve the accuracy of positioning, reduce the number of false positioning and failure in positioning.

3.3 The Improved Quality of Sampling by Using New Sensors

Optical fibre sensor was introduced in pipeline fault diagnosis for the first time, the use of which can not only detect physical quantities, but can also transmit signals with a unique advantage in solving signal attenuation and interference, so it can combine hardware and software-based approach better. From *2005 to 2008*,Zhou Yan(from Tianjin University) proposed and improved a distributed optical fiber sensor technology in detecting pipeline leakage, which is based on the distributed optical fiber Raman temperature measurement technique and the Mach2Zehnder fiber optic interferometer [10]. The technology uses optical fiber as the sensor to pick up the vibration signals of leakage along the pipeline and analyses the optical phase change caused by leakage noise, and by analysing the characteristic spectrum, the leakage detection sensitivity can be improved effectively. When the pressure in the gas pipeline is less than *0.2 MPa*, a leakage of *0.4* m^3 / min can be detected and the test distance can reach up to 5km. In *2008*, Hang Lijun(Beijing University of Technology) and others introduced a linear distributed optical fiber pipeline leakage monitoring system, which is based on Sagnac interferometer, to monitor and position real-time pipeline leakage.[11] This system has two sensing optical fiber, which can increase the monitoring distance effectively. They also worked out the expression of optical signal phase changes caused by leakage and analysed the functional mechanism of the interferometer being applied to leakage detection and location, then they carried out a leakage detection experiment at two places with Faraday rotator mirrors of *3990 km* and *4024 km* from the two ends of the sensing fiber. Test results showed that the system accurately identified the leak source location with a positioning error of less than *1.05%*.

3.4 The Improved Detection Accuracy through the Use of a Variety of Algorithms

In *1989*, Wang Guizeng from Tsinghua University proposed a pipeline leakage detection method based on Kullback information measuring. And in 1990, Wang Guizeng proposed to use an extended Kalman filtering method with the help of time-varying noise estimators to assess the state of pipelines, and he also put forward a diagnosis mechanism.[12] In recent years, considering the need of linearizing the nonlinear model when the extended Kalman filter(EKF) is used in assessing nonlinear model, together with the fact that pipeline models are usually strongly nonlinear,

Wang Wei(from Shanghai Jiaotong University) and others proposed a pipeline leak detection and location based on unbiased Kalman filter (UKF) estimation.[13] This method is a kind of approximate nonlinear model by means of sampling strategies, which can avoid linearization and the need of calculating the Jacob matrix. The convergence rate of UKF is obviously superior to that of EKF, and it can quickly find out leaks. Simulation results proved the advantage of UKF over EKF in leakage detection.

As for small scale leakage detection, Xu Jianjun, who is from Daqing Petroleum Institute, raised a statistical decision method of sequential probability ratio test in *2009*. Considering the real-time requirement of leak Detection of long pipelines, he proposed to use the normalized new information sequence generated by Kalman Filter as the input sequence of sequential probability ratio test to satisfy the requirements of it, and he also analysed the method of applying the sequential probability ratio test in detecting and locating small pipeline leakage. Using virtual instruments theory, he designed Kalman filter and LabVIEW program modules using sequential probability ratio test algorithm, which can be embedded directly into existing real-time pipeline leakage monitoring system. Experiments showed that it was very effective in detecting small leakage of less than 3%, and its positioning accuracy was within 2.15%.

As for knowledge-based leakage fault diagnosis methods, Chen Bindeng(from Beijing University of Posts and Telecommunications) presents a pipeline leakage detection method which combined neural network and evidence theory. This method established two sub-node neural network models to simplify the network structure and used leakage characteristic parameters of negative pressure wave and acoustic emission signal as the initial input vector to detect leakage. It also made full use of various redundant and complementary leakage informations by conducting a two-level evidence synthesis at the ordinary node and cluster node with an improved evidence distribution rule. Experiment results showed that this method significantly improved the accuracy of pipeline leakage diagnosis and reduced recognition uncertainty.

Besides, Wu Bin(from Beijing University) designed a wireless intelligent acceleration sensor that can be used for pipeline leakage detection. In *2004*, Shi Ketian(from the Department of Mechanics and Engineering Science of Beijing University) designed a new GPRS-based wireless alarm system for leakage detection and location. Wu Xiaoqin (from Xi'an Jiaotong University) and others proposed an algorithm of correlational analysis method and developed a microcontroller leakage detection system. All the above mentioned methods contributed a lot to the technological development of pipeline leakage detection.

4 The Trends and Prospects of Pipeline Leakage Detection Technology

Owing to the advantages of long-distance pipeline transportation, recent years have seen a rapid development of pipeline application. Correspondingly, an increasingly high standard for leakage detection and location technology is required. Present leakage detection and location technology can hardly solve the problem of low positioning accuracy and false alarms caused by high workplace detection sensitivity, especially in the case of small flow condition. In recent years, with the rapid development of computer technology and the application of SCADA system in pipelines, leakage detection and location technology has shifted from the early hardware-based approach to a software-based approach or an approach combining software and hardware. Integrating different methods with SCADA system represents the future trend, which can make full use of software-based approaches to perform real-time detection and give timely alarm signal. And it can also take advantage of the high positioning accuracy and low false alarm rate of hardware-based approaches to overcome the limitations of a single detection method, hence the operation of pipelines can be further automatized.

In future, we can do more researches in the following areas:

1. To develop software-based and hardware-supplemented methods in detecting gas pipeline accidents.

In recent years, the development of computer technology, control theory, signal processing, pattern recognition, artificial intelligence and other disciplines greatly promoted the advance of the software-based technologies for gas pipeline real-time detection. However, considering the different roles of hardware and software, we should take advantage of both of them. On the one hand, we can improve the reliability of data by improving the detection accuracy and sensitivity of hardware. On the other hand, we can use various detection methods comprehensively to improve the data recognition performance application and reduce the false alarm rate. In this way, real-time online monitoring and timely alarm signalling can be ensured. So this will be the focus of future research. What's more, as pipeline systems have nonlinear time-varying parameters, self-adapting algorithm for detection and location will play an increasingly important role. Hardware-based methods have high positioning accuracy and low false alarm rate, so complementary methods can meet requirements of pipeline leakage detection systems. The purpose of integrating software-based approaches is to improve the leak detection sensitivity and accuracy, solving the conflict between high sensitivity and false alarms. The combination of neural networks, pattern recognition and fuzzy recognition theory can also lay a foundation for the identification of fault types and for the prediction of fault causes.

2. To put emphasis on developing sensor technology, such as ultrasonic sensors, fiber optic sensors.

Optical fiber sensor is also a hotspot in recent years, which can measure physical quantities and transmit signal at the same time with much more advantages than traditional sensors in terms of resisting signal attenuation and interference. In addition, with the development of a variety of distributed optical fiber sensors, temperature, stress and strain, vibration and traffic signals of the medium in oil and gas pipelines can be measured by using a single or a few fibers in future. And by using cross-recognition technology in processing multi sample data, system performance of failure prediction can be improved, thus giving it potential of being applied in pipeline monitoring systems. Therefore, the distributed optical fiber sensor has great prospects in the field of pipeline detection.

3. Hybrid diagnostic system, which combined different intelligent technologies, is an important development in the fault diagnosis of long-distance oil and gas pipeline. Currently, there are a number of such combined intelligent technologies, namely, rule-based expert system and neural network, combined case-based reasoning (*CBR*) and rule-based systems and neural networks, combined information fusion and neural networks, combined wavelet analysis and neural network, combined fuzzy logic and neural network as well as expert system, combined artificial immune and neural network, combined artificial immune and genetic algorithm, combined artificial immune and genetic neural network, among which the combination of artificial immune system, genetic algorithm and neural network is the most promising research direction.

4.With the development of sampling techniques, the detection accuracy of different detection methods is continually improved. With the ever-increasing amount of data, how to extract useful features and rules from these massive detection data for evaluation and prediction becomes an important issue, which is also one of the key technologies to solve in detecting pipeline defects. Therefore, data reduction is vital in improving the ability of fault recognition. For example, compared with the traditional linear dimension reduction methods, manifold learning theory can effectively identify the intrinsic structure of nonlinear high-dimensional data, which is conducive to dimensionality reduction and data analysis. Thus in recent years it has been valued more and more by researchers in fields of machine learning and cognitive science. Jiang Quansheng applied manifold learning method in fault diagnosis [14], which gave new insights into pipeline fault diagnosis. In addition, owing to its support of vector machine in pattern recognition, nuclear methods have gained rapid development. At present, major nuclear methods include support vector machine (*SVM*), kernel principal component analysis (*KPCA*), kernel discriminant analysis (*KDA*), nuclear canonical correlation analysis (*KCCA*), kernel independent component analysis (*KICA*) and so on. The introduction of statistical learning theory will improve the performance in extracting the best fault feature in pipeline fault detection.

References

1. Ellul, I.R.: Advances in Pipeline Leak Detection Techniques. Pipes and Pipelines International 34(3), 7–12 (1989)
2. Hennnigar, G.W.: Advances in Gas Leak Detection. Pipe and Gas Journal 212(11), 39–42 (1985)
3. De Read, J.R.: Comparision Between Ultrasonic and Magnetic Flux Pigs for Pipelines Inspection. Pipes and Pipelines Int. 1, 7–15 (1987)
4. Iron Army, et al.: Of The Development of Oil and Gas Pipeline Transportation. Gas Storage and Transportation 16(7), 1–3 (1997)
5. Wang, Q.: Wavelet packet-based theory of acoustic emission and the pressure of pipeline leak detection. Journal of Xi'an Jiaotong University 05 (2003)
6. Ding, H.: Long-distance oil pipeline leakage detection technique. Journal of Beijing Jiaotong University 06 (2004)
7. Yang, R.r.: GCC TDE in the pipeline leak detection. Computer Engineering 12 (2009)

8. Lun, S.X.: Adaptive fuzzy neural network system in pipeline leak detection. Journal of Petroleum Technology 04 (2004)
9. Chen, H.: Based on image processing pipeline leak detection and location. Journal of Tsinghua University (Natural Science) 01 (2005)
10. Zhou, Y.: Distributed optical fiber pipeline leakage detection and warning technology sensitivity analysis. Nanotechnology and Precision Engineering 05 (2008)
11. Hang, L.-j.: Novel distributed optical fiber pipeline leakage detection and location method. Acta Optica Sinica 01 (2008)
12. Wang, G.-b., et al.: Kullback information measure based on long-distance pipeline leak detection. Information and Control 1, 14–17 (1989)
13. Wei, W.: Unscented Kalman filter based on the fast pipeline leak detection and location. Process Automation Instrumentation 01 (2008)
14. Jiang, Q., Jia, M.P., Hu, J.-Z., et al.: Laplacian feature maps based on the failure pattern recognition method. Journal of System Simulation 20(20), 5710–5715 (2008)
15. Jiang, Q., Jia, M., Hu, J., et al.: Method of fault pat tern recognition based on Laplacian eigenmaps. Journal of System Simulation 20(20), 5710–5713 (2008)

Selecting Principle and Equipment of Valve Tappets

Lian-Hu Xu, Yi-Bao Yuan, and Lei Wang

Department of Automation Measurement and Control Engineering
Harbin Institute of Technology
Harbin, Heilongjiang province, China
xu_lianhu@foxmail.com

Abstract. Valve clearance is crucial to the engine efficacy, so proper valve clearance is required in engine assembly. In this paper we present the definition of valve clearance and the selecting principle of valve tappets, and the equipment called Valve Tappet Selecting Machine. The Valve Tappet Selecting Machine for 3-cylinder overhead camshaft engine has been developed based on the definition of the valve clearance and the selecting principle of valve tappets, which comprises Cylinder Head Measuring Machine and Camshaft Measuring Machine. The errors of the Tappet Selecting Machine were analyzed; the repeatability and the accuracy of the Cylinder Head Measuring Machine and the Camshaft Measuring Machine were tested, the data suggest that the measurement is high precision, and valve clearances will be under control strictly with the Valve Tappet Selecting Machine.

Keywords: engine, valve clearance, valve tappet, selecting principle, equipment.

1 Introduction

For overhead camshaft engine which is in working state, inlet and exhaust valves and other metal parts would expand due to high temperature of the combustion chambers, If there are no valve clearances or valve clearances are too small while the engine is cold, then valves would not be strictly closed due to expanding while the engine is in working state, which would led to valve leak while the engine is in compressing and working stroke, therefore engine power would be declined, furthermore, engine is even difficult to start or parts would be damaged in serious cases; if valve clearances are too large, then valves would not be fully opened, therefore, inlet and exhaust valves would not respire enough, engine power would be declined either [1,2]. In order to keep engine in normal operation, appropriate valve clearance requires being preset.

For engine assembly, in order to obtain appropriate valve clearance, valve clearance adjusting mechanisms or valve gaskets or tappets in different thickness can

D. Zeng (Ed.): ICAIC 2011, Part I, CCIS 224, pp. 619–630, 2011.

be employed [1, 2, 3]. When the valve clearance magnitudes are adjusted with valve gaskets or tappets in different thickness, valve gaskets or tappets known thickness would be pre-loaded, then the actual amount of valve clearances could be measured using feelers, and unsuited valve gaskets or tappets would be replaced. Valves clearances would be adjusted according to the said procedures, one after another. This process may be repeated many times and would be time consuming, it is affected objectively by factors such as parts worn, the experience and methods that operators using feelers, therefore, it's difficult to control magnanimity of every valve clearance, the efficiency is low and the measurement is not accuracy [3, 4]. The Valve Gasket or Valve Tappet Selecting Machine have been self-developed, which are aimed at the requirement of high precise measurement of valve clearances and rapid selecting of valve tappets in automobile engine assembly. This paper researches into the Valve Tappet Selecting Machine for 3-cylinder overhead camshaft engine, the selecting principle and equipment of valve tappets are introduced as below.

2 Selecting Principle of Valve Tappets

2.1 Definition of Valve Clearance

Valve clearance [3] is the distance between the heel of the cam and the top of the valve tappet, or called gap, as shown in Fig.1, where *C(E)* stands for the exhaust valve clearance, and *C(I)* for the inlet valve clearance.

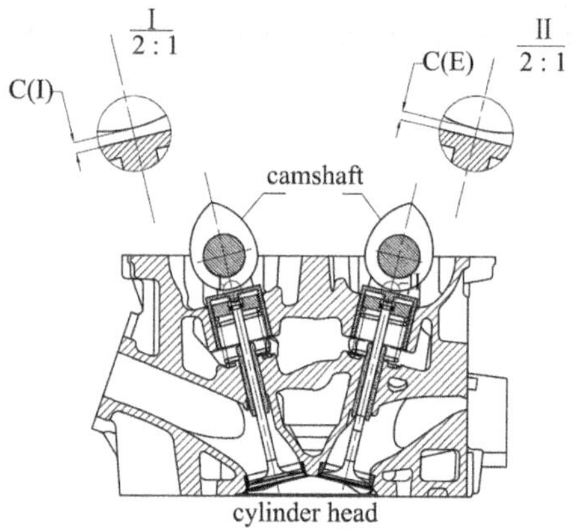

Fig. 1. Valve clearance diagram

2.2 Selecting Principle of Valve Tappets

Selecting principle of valve tappets is shown in Fig.2 below.

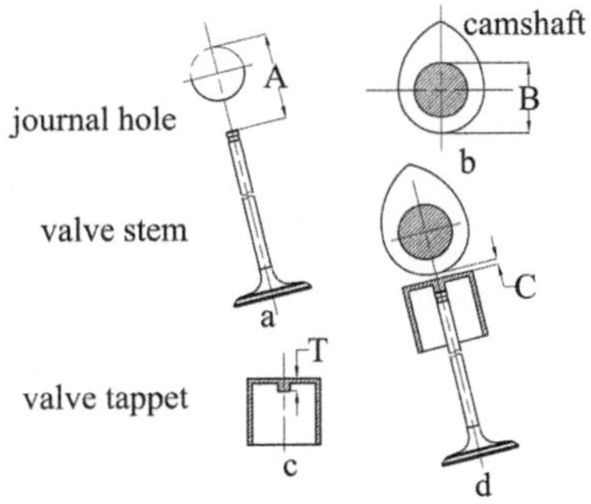

Fig. 2. Selecting principle of valve tappets

- ✧ *A*—the distance from the top of the journal hole to the end of the valve stem
- ✧ *B*—the distance from the heel of the cam to the bus of journal at the side of the cam nose
- ✧ *T*—tappet thickness
- ✧ *C*—valve clearance

In order to control valve clearance C generated after engine assembly, then valve tappets in proper thickness need to be selected, so the tappet thickness T should to be predicted. The tappet thickness T is calculated according to (1).

$$T = A - B - C + K \tag{1}$$

where K is the compensation factor.

Therefore, the distance A that from the top of the journal hole to the end of the valve stem needs to be measured, and the distance B that from the heel of the cam to the bus of journal at the side of the cam nose needs to be measured as well[1, 5-8]. The Camshaft Measuring Machine and the Cylinder Head Measuring Machine are designed to measure the said parameters. The Camshaft Measuring Machine is for measuring the distance A, and measuring results will be send to Computer-aided Measurement System; the Cylinder Head Measuring Machine is for measuring distance B, and measuring results will be send to Computer-aided Measurement System as well; then the Computer-aided Measurement System calculates and predicts proper valve tappet thicknesses based on the said measuring results, finally.

3 Valve Tappet Selecting Machine

Valve Tappet Selecting Machine comprises the Camshaft Measuring Machine, the Cylinder Head Measuring Machine, the Shared Controlling Cabinet and the Shared Computer - aided Measurement System. Measurement system schematic of Valve Tappet Selecting Machine is shown in Fig.3 below.

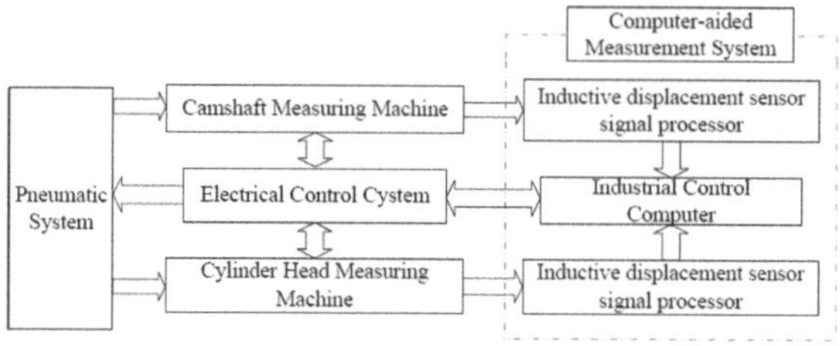

Fig. 3. Schematic of measurement system

3.1 Camshaft Measuring Machine

The Camshaft Measuring Machine comprises the mechanism body, the camshaft master and the Computer-aided Measurement System (shared with the Cylinder Head Measuring Machine), as shown in Fig.3 and Fig.4. For example, in order to measure camshafts for three-cylinder engine, one sensor is arranged for each cam, one sensor is arranged for each bearing Journal, as shown in Fig.5 below. The Camshaft Measuring Machine would measure multiple distances that from the heel of the cam to the bus of the journal at the side of the cam nose, simultaneously.

The Camshaft Measuring Machine is used to measure both inlet camshafts and exhaust camshafts. According to the prompts of the Computer-aided Measuring System, inlet camshaft or exhaust camshaft would be artificially mounted in localizer of the Camshaft Measuring Machine, separately; then the camshaft is rotated 540 degrees driven by electromotor, sensor signals for measuring camshaft bearing journals and cams are sampled simultaneously and respectively while the camshaft rotating, and the sampling data are processed by the Computer - aided Measurement System.

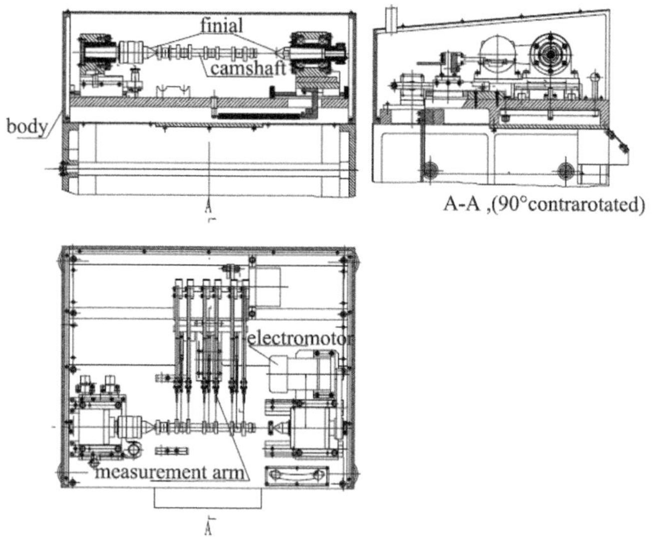

Fig. 4. Schematic of Camshaft Measuring Machine assembly

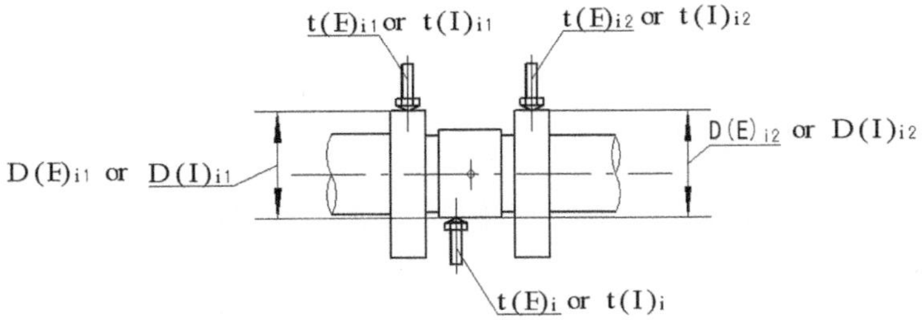

Fig. 5. Schematic of sensor layout for Camshaft measurement

About the Fig.5 is described as follows:

(1) i=1, 2, 3 is the sequence number of camshaft journal;
j=1 stands for the cam at left side of *ith* journal, j=2 stands for the cam at right side of *ith* journal.

(2) $t(E)_i$ stands for the sensor displacement of *ith* exhaust journal, and $t(I)_i$ for inlet journal.

(3) $t(E)_{i,j}$ stands for the sensor displacement of the heel of *jth* cam to the corresponding *ith* journal in exhaust camshaft, and $t(I)_{i,j}$ for the inlet camshaft.

(4) $D(E)_{i,j}$ stands for the distance between the heel of *jth* cam to the bus of corresponding *ith* journal at the side of cam nose in exhaust camshaft, and $D(I)_{i,j}$ for the inlet camshaft.

The Camshaft is rotated 540 degrees driven by electromotor while measuring. $t(E)_i$ and $t(E)_{i,j}$ are got while measuring exhaust camshaft, and $D(E)_{i,j}$ would be calculated according to (2); $t(I)_i$ and $t(I)_{i,j}$ are got while measuring inlet camshaft, and $D(I)_{i,j}$ would be calculated according to (3).

$$D(E)_{i,j} = t(E)_{i,j} - t(E)_i - D_{i,j} \tag{2}$$

$$D(I)_{i,j} = t(I)_{i,j} - t(I)_i - D_{i,j} \tag{3}$$

where $D_{i,j}$ is the distance from the heel of *jth* cam to *ith* journal at the side of the cam nose for camshaft master.

3.2 Cylinder Head Measuring Machine

The assembly drawing of Cylinder Head Measuring Machine is shown in Fig.6 below. The sensors layout of the Cylinder Head Measuring Machine is shown in Fig.7.

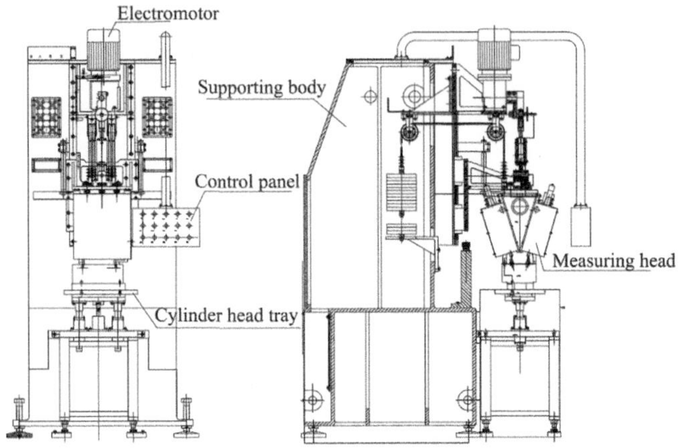

Fig. 6. Cylinder Head Measuring Machine assembly drawing

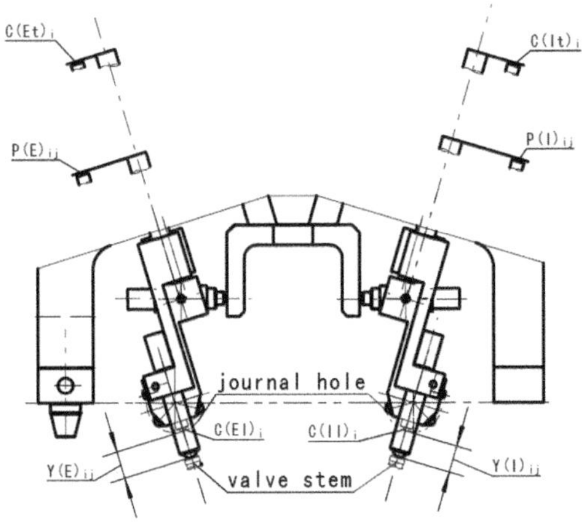

Fig. 7. Schematic of sensors layout for cylinder head measurement

About Fig.7 was described as follows:

(1) i=1, 2, 3 is the sequence number of journal holes

j=1, 2 stands for the valve stem end of left or right side of *ith* journal hole, respectively.

(2) $C(Et)_i$, $C(It)_i$ are the top sensors to determine the center of *ith* journal hole of the exhaust or inlet side; $y[C(Et)]_i$ and $y[C(It)]_i$ are the corresponding sensor displacements, respectively.

$C(El)_i$, $C(Il)_i$ are the bottom sensors to measure the central positions and diameters of *ith* journal hole of the exhaust or inlet side; $y[C(El)]_i$ and $y[C(Il)]_i$ are the corresponding sensor displacements, respectively.

(3) $P(E)_{i,j}$, $P(I)_{i,j}$ are the sensors to measure the positions of *jth* valve stem end at the side of the *ith* exhaust or inlet journal hole, and stand for sensor displacements, simultaneously.
(4) $Y(E)_{i,j}$, $Y(I)_{i,j}$ are the distances from the top of *ith* journal hole to the end of *jth* valve stem at exhaust or inlet side, respectively.
$Y(E)_{i,j}$, $Y(I)_{i,j}$ are the dimensions measured by the Cylinder Head Measuring Machine.

According to the characteristics of cylinder head, $Y(E)_{i,j}$ are calculated by

$$\begin{aligned} Y(E)_{i,j} &= Y[C(E)]_i + P(E)_{i,j} + [Y(E)]_{i,j} \\ &= y[C(El)]_i - y[C(Et)]_i + P(E)_{i,j} + [Y(E)]_{i,j} \end{aligned} \tag{4}$$

$Y(I)_{i,j}$ are calculated by

$$\begin{aligned} Y(I)_{i,j} &= Y[C(I)]_i + P(I)_{i,j} + [Y(I)]_{i,j} \\ &= y[C(Il)]_i - y[C(It)]_i + P(I)_{i,j} + [Y(I)]_{i,j} \end{aligned} \tag{5}$$

3.3 Calculation of the Tappet Thickness

According to the selecting principle of valve tappets, valve tappet thicknesses are calculated based on the measuring results of the camshafts and the cylinder head.

$$T(E)_{i,j} = Y(E)_{i,j} - D(E)_{i,j} - G(E) \tag{6}$$

$$T(I)_{i,j} = Y(I)_{i,j} - D(I)_{i,j} - G(I) \tag{7}$$

where $G(E)$ is the desired valve clearance of exhaust valve, and $G(I)$ is the desired valve clearance of inlet valve, respectively. Thicknesses of valve tappet $T(E)_{i,j}$, $T(I)_{i,j}$ are calculated and given by the Computer-aided Measurement System according to (6) and (7), then valve tappets to be fitted into corresponding valve seats will be selected by operators according to the said valve tappet thicknesses $T(E)_{i,j}$, $T(I)_{i,j}$.

4 Error Analysis

4.1 Systematic Errors

Each major systematic error and its estimation are described as follows:

(1) zero drift of sensor: 0.001mm
(2) calibration errors of parameters $Y(E)_{i,j}$, $Y(I)_{i,j}$ of the cylinder head master are 0.003mm, respectively; calibration errors of parameters $D_{i,j}$ of the camshaft master are 0.001mm.
(3) parameters variations affected by temperature are 0.001mm/5 °C (temperature for calibration is 20 °C)

The total systematic error is

$$\delta_s = \pm\sqrt{0.001^2 + 0.003^2 + 0.001^2 + 0.001^2} = \pm 0.0035\text{mm} \tag{8}$$

4.2 Random Errors

Each major random errors and its estimation are described as fellows:

(1) errors of the sensor's sampling values $y[C(Et)]_i$ or $y[C(It)]_i$: ±0.002mm
(2) errors of the sensor's sampling values $y[C(El)]_i$ or $y[C(Il)]_i$: ±0.001mm
(3) errors of the sensor's sampling values $P(E)_{i,j}$ or $P(I)_{i,j}$: ±0.003mm

The total random error is

$$\delta_r = \pm\sqrt{0.002^2 + 0.001^2 + 0.003^2} = \pm 0.0037\text{mm} \tag{9}$$

5 Analysis of Measurement Repeatability

5.1 Analysis of Camshaft Measurement Repeatability

Using the camshaft master as reference datum for repeatability tests of the Camshaft Measuring Machine, the test data are listed in table 1.

Table 1. Repetitive test data of Camshaft (mm)

1	2	3	4	5	6
27.979	27.977	27.972	27.967	27.976	27.972
27.980	27.977	27.971	27.966	27.976	27.973
27.978	27.976	27.972	27.967	27.975	27.972
27.980	27.977	27.973	27.966	27.977	27.973
27.981	27.976	27.972	27.966	27.978	27.974
27.980	27.977	27.972	27.967	27.977	27.973
27.979	27.976	27.971	27.966	27.978	27.974
27.980	27.977	27.972	27.967	27.976	27.975
27.981	27.977	27.971	27.966	27.977	27.974
27.980	27.976	27.972	27.967	27.977	27.975

Calculating the standard deviation of data in each column of table 1, the maximum standard deviation is 0.0011mm, so the measurement uncertainty of the Camshaft Measuring Machine is ± 0.003mm.

5.2 Analysis of Cylinder Head Measurement Repeatability

Using the cylinder head master as reference datum for repeatability tests of the Cylinder Head Measuring Machine, the test data are listed in table 2 and table 3.

Table 2. Repeatability test data of Exhaust side (mm)

		Exhaust			
E1	*E2*	*E3*	*E4*	*E5*	*E6*
5.228	5.338	5.204	5.300	5.286	5.263
5.229	5.339	5.204	5.300	5.286	5.262
5.229	5.339	5.204	5.300	5.286	5.262
5.227	5.336	5.203	5.300	5.286	5.260
5.227	5.338	5.203	5.300	5.286	5.261
5.228	5.337	5.204	5.300	5.286	5.261
5.228	5.337	5.203	5.301	5.286	5.262
5.226	5.337	5.203	5.300	5.286	2.261
5.226	5.336	5.203	5.300	5.286	5.261
5.227	5.336	5.203	5.298	5.287	5.261
5.228	5.338	5.203	5.298	5.286	5.261
5.226	5.336	5.204	5.301	5.286	5.261
5.227	5.335	5.204	5.300	5.287	5.262
5.228	5.338	5.204	5.300	5.286	5.261
5.226	5.336	5.202	5.298	5.286	5.260
5.226	5.336	5.204	5.301	5.286	5.261
5.226	5.336	5.204	5.301	5.287	5.262
5.225	5.336	5.204	5.301	5.287	5.262
5.227	5.336	5.203	5.298	5.287	5.262
5.227	5.337	5.203	5.298	5.287	5.262

Calculating the standard deviation of data in each column of table 2, the maximum standard deviation is 0. 0011 mm, so the measurement uncertainty of the exhaust side is ± 0.003mm.

Table 3. Repeatability test data of inlet side (mm)

		inlet			
I1	*I2*	*I3*	*I4*	*I5*	*I6*
5.372	5.346	5.449	5.397	5.343	5.304
5.372	5.346	5.450	5.395	5.345	5.305
5.372	5.344	5.452	5.399	5.343	5.305
5.374	5.347	5.451	5.398	5.343	5.306
5.374	5.347	5.450	5.396	5.343	5.304
5.373	5.346	5.450	5.398	5.344	5.305
5.374	5.347	5.450	5.397	5.344	5.303
5.375	5.348	5.449	5.397	5.344	5.303
5.373	5.346	5.451	5.396	5.343	5.304
5.373	5.345	5.450	5.396	5.344	5.304
5.373	5.346	5.449	5.398	5.343	5.303
5.374	5.347	5.449	5.398	5.344	5.304
5.374	5.347	5.449	5.399	5.343	5.303
5.374	5.346	5.451	5.397	5.344	5.304
5.374	5.346	5.449	5.396	5.342	5.304
5.375	5.346	5.450	5.399	5.344	5.303
5.375	5.346	5.450	5.397	5.344	5.304
5.373	5.346	5.450	5.399	5.343	5.303
5.373	5.346	5.450	5.399	5.342	5.305
5.372	5.345	5.450	5.397	5.343	5.305

Calculating the standard deviation of data in each column of table 3, the maximum standard deviation is 0.0012mm, so the measurement uncertainty of the inlet side is ± 0.004mm.

6 Analysis of Measurement Accuracy

6.1 Analysis of Camshaft Measurement Accuracy

Taking the camshaft master for measuring reference, the feeler whose thickness was measured 0.050mm was added to each cam and journal in turn, and the data of measurement accuracy were listed in table 4. The data in the second row of table 4 are the measuring values of the camshaft master, the data of each row under the second row are the measuring data according to characteristics of measuring values changed by adding feeler in turn, the datum where there is only one datum in a column corresponding to adding feeler to the heel of cams, where there are two data in a column corresponding to adding feeler to the camshaft journals.

Table 4. Tests data of Camshaft measurement accuracy (mm)

1	*2*	*3*	*4*	*5*	*6*
27.978	27.977	27.972	27.966	27.975	27.973
28.028					
28.029	28.027				
	28.026				
		28.022			
		28.021	28.016		
			28.017		
				28.025	
				28.024	28.023
					28.024

According to the data in table 4, measurement data of the cam heel and journals feature changes are appreciable the same, the maximum error is 0.003mm.

6.2 Analysis of the Cylinder Head Measurement Accuracy

For accuracy tests of cylinder measuring machine, cylinder head master was regarded as measuring reference, and the feeler whose thickness was measured 0.050mm was added to the end of the valve stem and the bottom of each journal hole in turn. The accuracy tests were carried out and the measuring data were listed in table 5 and table 6. The data in the second row of Table 5 and table 6 are the measuring values of the cylinder head master, the data of each row under the second row are the measuring data while characteristics of measuring values changed by adding the feeler in turn, the datum where there is only one datum in a column corresponding to adding feeler to the end of the valve stem, where there are two data in a column corresponding to adding feeler to the bottom of journal holes.

Table 5. Measuring accuracy testing of exhaust side (mm)

E1	*E2*	*E3*	*E4*	*E5*	*E6*
33.577	33.570	33.574	33. 574	33.565	33.577
33.526					
33.646	33.642				
	33.521				
		33.521			
		33.642	33.646		
			33.521		
				33.517	
				33.634	33.648
					33.526

Table 6. Measuring accuracy testing of inlet side (mm)

I1	*I2*	*I3*	*I4*	*I5*	*I6*
33.645	33.635	33.641	33.649	33.639	33.657
33.596					
33.718	33.706				
	33.587				
		33.589			
		33.711	33.721		
			33.601		
				33.590	
				33.710	33.727
					33.609

According to the data in table 5 and table 6, the measuring data differences of the end of the valve stem feature changes are appreciable the same, the maximum error is 0.003mm; and the journal measuring data differences of the cam feature changes are appreciable the same.

7 Conclusion

The engine valve clearance is a parameter that should be strictly controlled in the process of engine assembly. Predicting valve clearances while the engine assembly, and then selecting valve tappets of appropriate thicknesses, are aimed at strictly controlling valve clearances. In this article the definition of valve clearance and the selecting principle of the valve tappet were introduced, and the Valve Tappet Selecting Machine has been developed according to the selecting principle of valve tappets, and valve tappets selecting errors were analysed, the repeatability and accuracy of the Valve Tappet Selecting Machine were tested and analysed. The application that the valve Tappet Selecting Machine in actual usage in engine assembly workshops suggest that valve tappets can be accurately and quickly selected with the Valve Tappet Selecting Machine, and valve clearances can be under control successfully.

Acknowledgment. We would like to gratefully thank our sponsor Yi-Bao Yuan professor for his guide and support.

References

[1] Yao, C., He, B., Li, W., et al.: Determination and Adjustment for Valve Clearance of Vehicle Engines. Small Internal Combustion Engine 06 (1999)

[2] Huang, J.: Improving the Assembly Process to the Washer for Adjusting the Valve Clearance in Diesel Engine by Measuring Tools. Guangxi Machinery 02 (2001)

[3] Zhu, B., Wang, Q.: Insuring quality of tappet gap adjusting with tappet gap measuring instrument. Diesel Locomotives 08 (2003)

[4] Feng, D.: A Preliminary Exploration on Valve Gasket Choosing and Measurement Machine and Its Perfection. Automobile Technology & Material 08 (2007)

[5] Feng, D.: The online measurement technology of engine manufacture (1). Modern Components 01 (2008)

[6] Feng, D.: The online measurement technology of engine manufacture (2). Modern Components 02 (2008)

[7] Stewart, D.J.: Valve clearance measuring appatatus. United States Patent:3, 829, 979, August 20 (1974)

[8] McCarthy, J.W.: Valve clearance adjusting tool and method for adjusting valve clearance. United States Patent: US 6, 415, 755 B1, July 9 (2002)

Systems Analysis Causes and Countermeasure of Environmental Problems in China

Lu Yali

School of Management and Economy
North China University of Water Resources and Electric Power
Zhengzhou, 450011, China
Luyali_good@126.com

Abstract. In this paper, we analysis the causes for environment pollution. Through a comprehensive analysis of the causes of environment pollution, we recognize the five reasons for the deterioration of environmental quality caused by in China. Then, we propose measures to solve environmental problems. These studies will help solve China's environmental problems. It is may be importance to sustainable development of China and the global.

Keywords: environment problem, causes, countermeasure.

1 Introduction

The process of industrialization in developed countries a century resources and environmental problems arise, in our 30 years of reform and opening up concentration appears, showing the structure, compound, compression-type characteristics. Environmental pollution and ecological damage caused huge economic losses and endanger people's health and affect social stability and environmental security. Environmental Protection and the Chinese nation at the national security strategy for survival and development of highly strengthened.

CPC Plenary Session clearly uphold the scientific concept of development, stressing that "in accordance with the urban and rural development, regional development, economic and social development, balancing development of man and nature, and domestic development and opening-up demand" reform and development; Sixteenth Central Committee of CPC made the first complete "building a socialist harmonious society," significantly improved efficiency of resource use, significant improvement in ecological environment is the goal of building a socialist harmonious society and the main tasks. Seventeenth Party Congress of CPC defined the concept of scientific development, that "We must pursue comprehensive, coordinated and sustainable development", "insist on the development of production and living well off the road of civilized development, building a resource saving and environment friendly society to achieve the speed and structure, quality and efficiency, economic development and population, resources and environment in harmony, so that the people in a good ecological environment and living, Economic and social sustainable development "," congress "further pointed out:" build an ecological civilization, basically forming an energy resources and protect the ecological environment of the industrial structure, growth and consumption patterns."[1]

D. Zeng (Ed.): ICAIC 2011, Part I, CCIS 224, pp. 631–638, 2011.

2 Causes of Environment Problems in China

2.1 The Traditional Model of Economic Growth Facing Constraints of the Resources and Environment

At present the problem of irrational industrial structure in China is economic growth highlighted the second industry, especially over-reliance on heavy industry, but low energy consumption low proportion of tertiary industry, lagging.2003-2007, average annual growth rate of 12% of the secondary industry and tertiary industry average annual growth of only 10.1%., The tertiary industry the proportion of GDP accounted for about 40%, while most developed countries more than 70%, the U.S. is 78%,with similar levels of development in China, Brazil and India were as high as 75.1% and 51.2%. Although in recent years, the rapid development of high-tech industry, but the proportion in the manufacturing sector is still low.

2.2 "Light Pollution, Heavy GDP" Concept of Achievements Affect the Efficiency of Environmental Protection

First, some localities and departments have not really establish the scientific development concept and a correct concept of one-sided pursuit of economic growth, high-speed, eager to engage in face-saving projects performance projects, and even that after pollution Even think that after pollution, destruction of recovery after the first general law of economic development, The result is high growth, paying too much resources and environmental costs and damage to the long-term development.[2]

Second, enterprises intensive awareness of conservation development is not strong. Some companies have neither the energy saving as the inherent requirement of improving competitiveness, and lack of social responsibility, waste of resources freely shift the pollution.

Third, resource conservation, environmental protection has not yet become the conscious action of society as a whole. Consumption patterns and lifestyles is also unreasonable, excessive packaging of many products is not necessary disposable supplies is still quite common, some consumers seeking luxury on ceremony, the formation of resource conservation, environment, social habits cherish long way to go.

2.3 Lack of Environmental Technology Innovation, Environmental Protection, Environmental Protection Investment Is Not Enough Progress Constraints

At present, major technological resource conservation and environmental protection research and development is still relatively weak, and is conducive to efficient use of resources and recycling of common technology, the relative lack of key technologies, promote energy saving, pollution reduction and environmental control technology application is not wide enough ., Renewable energy, clean energy, alternative energy technology development lags behind, which restricts the energy efficiency of resource use, environmental pollution control process.[3]

Whether it is speeding up technological transformation, updating equipment, or improving the ecological environment construction, must have sufficient funding in order to form a solid protection of the environment. At present, the enterprises as energy conservation, environmental protection body, the lack of internal driving force to increase investment and external pressure ; Government at all levels of investment in resource conservation and environmental protection, and generally low, stable support for investment in energy saving mechanisms yet to be formed. According to "the" Eleventh Five-Year "ten key energy conservation projects view" and the urban sewage treatment facilities, such as water pollution prevention plan key measure, "during" the great need of the investment gap, seriously restricting the resources saving and environment-friendly society.

2.4 Environmental Incentive Mechanisms Have Not Yet Formed

Number of resource products pricing mechanism can not fully reflect the scarcity of resources, environmental damage costs and supply and demand is difficult to effectively control waste and irrational use of resources; "Polluter pays" principle is not well implemented, can not effectively act to curb environmental damage. Governments at all levels of financial authority and powers do not match, and adapt to different functional areas have different tax and financial system has not yet formed, in some areas especially county and township government expenditure responsibility and revenue capacity of asymmetry, to alleviate the spending pressures, had to go beyond reality conditions for investment, the project, exacerbated by excessive consumption of resources and environmental pollution; Encourage research and development, production, use energy saving and curb high energy consumption and high pollution products, financial and taxation policy is not perfect, of energy saving technology, equipment, product development and promotion; Performance evaluation system of scientific cadres has not been fully established, the assessment of cadres in many places still focused primarily on economic growth, investment and other content, the completion of energy-saving environmental protection is not enough emphasis.

2.5 Legislative and Oversight Capacity-Building Needs of Environmental Protection Lags Behind

First, gaps in environmental legislation and scientific phenomena. The current laws of environmental resources is not yet complete, mainly in : Environmental resources are still some gaps in legislation, such as lack of soil pollution, chemicals management, biosafety management, genetic resources protection, nuclear safety laws and regulations; Supporting environmental resources behind the law, many environmental resources, laws, regulations, standards, policies, delays in the introduction, the implementation of the law; Environmental resources is often the creation of laws and institutions to "end control" oriented, tend to emphasize individual responsibility for environmental protection, "source control" reflects inadequate; Lack of enforcement of laws and regulations of environmental resources means, weak punishment, illegal, low cost, high compliance costs, enforcement costs are high, hard evidence, hard evidence, the implementation of difficult issues outstanding; The lack of specific binding environmental resources legal requirements of government actions, local protection interfere with the normal law enforcement is widespread; most of the environmental conditions and forms of law enforcement resources are mainly large and medium cities to meet pollution prevention and control of enterprises designed to create, not to seriously study and take adapted to urban construction, rural environment, the legal system and its means of implementation and form. This series of environmental resources has become an important factor in the force of law. [4]

Second, effective monitoring is difficult to boost environmental protection work started. Since 1989, "Environmental Law" enacted, China's environmental resources, constantly improving and perfecting the legal system, the environmental law in general been well implemented, but monitoring of environmental resources has been the soft underbelly of the environmental legal system, a long-term impact on implementation of effective environmental law an important factor, Main features: the supervision and authority is not fully play its role; administrative supervision and less efficient; no system of supervision and protection of the public, "environmental law" does not provide for public participation in the system, "Environmental Impact Assessment Law," Although it has been provided, but guidance does not provide for public participation planning process, the environment does not provide the public the right to administrative proceedings involving the public in monitoring a mere formality.

3 Countermeasure of Environment in China

3.1 Change the Economic Growth Model, the Development of Circular Economy

At present, although China's economic aggregate ranked fourth in the world, but the low level of industrial technology, small scale, serious waste and destruction of resources, coal, steel and cement consumption, emissions of sulfur dioxide and COD, large volume production of ozone-depleting substances exceeding environmental carrying capacity. China's environmental problems arise, there are historical reasons, and natural conditions, but the main period of rapid development of industrialization, the environmental costs, the extensive mode of economic growth is undoubtedly the most prominent reasons. Resolute and effective measures must be taken, otherwise the environment will be putting a heavy debt, and we can not explain these to future generations. [5]

China is at a stage of heavy industrialization, the investment rate is high, heavy pollution in the area of investment, while the small proportion of waste generated resources. Such as scrap recycling accounts for the proportion of consumption in the United States is 50%, China is only 20%.Germany, Japan and other developed countries into the post-industrial society, the development of circular economy have started in the waste recovery and recycling of resources and recycling waste through extended producer responsibility system to promote the business from raw materials selection, product design, production process, etc. production process to achieve waste minimization, waste recycling and for the sound basis.

From now to 2020, is China's national rejuvenation of important strategic opportunities, but also to achieve leapfrog development in environmentally critical period. General Secretary Hu Jintao pointed out: "To speed up the transformation of economic growth, the concept of circular economy through regional economic development, urban and rural construction and production, so that the most efficient use of resources. To minimize waste discharge and gradually the ecological enter a virtuous circle. “Development of circular economy and building a recycling-oriented society, is the current combination of economic development and environmental protection, is to transform the economic growth, an important way to achieve sustainable development. Therefore, China must adhere to both production and consumption and promote the development of circular economy.

3.2 Strengthen Legislative and Market Constraints, Improve Environmental Protection Mechanisms

In legislation, Chairman Wu Bangguo pointed out that "lose focus on development of the socialist legal system with Chinese characteristics play a support role in real life, the urgent needs of more mature legal legislative conditions, changes in time that is incompatible with the laws of economic and social development provisions and urge the parties concerned as soon as possible to enact and amend laws and legal matching. ".Over the years, the NPC Standing Committee has formulated the resources of 28 environmental laws; the State Council promulgated 66 laws and regulations, protection of environmental resources, basically the law, but also continuously improved.

IN the Policy, cut from the level of national development strategies to solve environmental problems. In the development of policy, we must concentrate on the price of the development is conducive to environmental protection, finance, taxation, finance, land and other aspects of economic policy system to encourage the development of policies to promote and encourage the full integration of environmental policy.

In the development layout, to follow the laws of nature, to carry out the work of national ecological function zoning, according to environmental functions in different regions and resource capacity of the environment, in accordance with the optimized development, key development, restricted development to determine the requirements and the prohibition of the development model of development in different regions, reasonable choice to guide around the direction of the formation of distinctive pattern of development. In development planning, to further optimize the layout of the heavy chemical industry, adjusting the industrial structure, change the mode of economic development. [6]

3.3 The Development of Environmental Technology to Improve Environmental Protection Capability

To attach great importance to environmental technology sector ranks, major environmental policy, environmental planning and environmental standards must be conducted before the introduction of full scientific demonstration; to further strengthen the building of scientific and technological personnel, as soon as possible the development of environmental science and technology personnel training plan, establish a conducive incentive independent innovation system of talent evaluation and research awards ;

Further improve the management of environmental technology, focusing on the urgent needs of the current sector management, give prominence to major forward-looking, basic research and key technologies to support macro-policy environment, give prominence to environmental research department for environmental management to provide the necessary technical support, and guide the correct application of technology development, promote environmental protection norms and the rapid application of research and industrialization. To continuously increase the global, regional, basin-wide environmental issues and other major trends in the causes and evolution of the research, and organized scientific and technological, institutional innovation driven environment.

To enhance the environmental technology innovation. Innovation is the soul of environmental technology. Environmental technology and stable investment mechanism, a diversified investment channels for sustainable; promote environmental satellite application system to speed up National Environmental Satellite Application Center, the building and improve the remote sensing information processing, application and development capabilities; rationalize the promotion of new technologies demonstration of the working mechanism, give full play to the role of science and technology sector, improve the quality of screening and assessment technology, promote technological innovation and improve the level of pollution control.

3.4 Strengthen Environmental Protection and Cultural Promotion and Practice of Ecological Civilization

Report of the Seventeenth Party Congress first proposed the "ecological civilization" concept. It is to respect and protect the ecological environment is the theme of sustainable development as the basis for the continued development of the future focus of the human, that human consciousness and self-discipline, emphasizing the human and the natural environment are interdependent and mutually reinforcing, coexistence integration. Ecological civilization with the previous agricultural civilization, industrial civilization has the same point, that is they are advocating the process of transforming the natural development of material productive forces and constantly improve the material standard of living of people, but between them they have obvious differences, that is, ecological highlight the importance of ecological civilization, emphasizing respect for and protection of the environment, emphasizing the transformation of human nature and must respect and love nature, and not arbitrary, blind reckless, do whatever they want. Now, the "ecological civilization" has become the party's congress in 2020 described the report as well-off society in China an important part of the picture. Report, by 2020 achieve the objective of building a moderately prosperous society when China should become "the people are better off and improve the quality of life improved significantly, and a good environment state."[7]

The whole society Mobilized to protect the environment. Environmental protection is the cause of the whole nation must closely rely on the masses to fully mobilize all positive factors, together form a powerful army to protect the environment situation. First, carry out extensive environmental education. Multi-form, multi-faceted, multi-level knowledge of environmental advocacy, policy and laws and regulations, promote the environment, culture, and promote ecological civilization, and create a whole society to care, support and participation in environmental protection, culture, environmental protection and raising the people's consciousness. Second is to strengthen coordination among various departments. Development of environmental protection departments of environmental protection responsibility, environmental protection work in other departments is a common builder. Team and capacity building to further improve the environmental unified supervision and management system. The third is to strengthen social supervision. Public environmental quality, environmental management, corporate environmental behavior and other information, these things is useful to maintain the public's environmental information, participation and supervision. On matters of public interest in development planning and environmental projects, through public hearings, feasibility studies or other forms of public notices, public opinion, to accept supervision. Fourth, public participation is a sound mechanism. Play the role of social organizations; various social forces to participate in environmental protection as a platform to encourage a variety of environmental violations expose the public to promote environmental public interest litigation.

3.5 In Accordance with International Principles, Fulfillment of International Obligations

Further strengthen international cooperation and exchange in a rational manner the successful experience from international environmental protection, actively participate in global and regional environmental activities. As a highly responsible, realistic and pragmatic ruling Communist Party of China before the world in recent years has unequivocally expressed the attitude towards environmental issues, resources and determination. In the scientific concept of development under the guidance of unit GDP energy consumption in China last year fell 2.8% ; Economical and intensive land operations within the context of a larger, land-use and further improve the efficiency and effectiveness; some important development and utilization of mineral resources has improved; Grain for Green Project will continue to implement and promote the Yangtze River, Yellow River Basin Environmental Protection treatment and recovery. However, comparing the level of greenhouse gas emissions in different countries, we must apply the right approach. Can not just volume, but also the per capita emissions; can not just current emissions, but also the historical cumulative emissions; can not just the quantity, depends on the stage of development; can not just local emissions, but also depends on the transfer emissions. "Four can not also" reflects the courage to take responsibility for China, but also distinguish between both the consistent positions of responsibility. If we ignore the reality of China's stage of development and blindly let China take on more responsibility, is bound to affect China's development process, delaying response to climate change capacity-building.

Acknowledgements. This study is supported by the youth teacher training special fund in School of Management and Economy,North China University of Water Resources and Electric Power.

References

[1] UN Commission on Sustainable Development, Indicators of Sustainable Development Framework & Methodologies, vol. 6, pp. 56–74. New York, UN (1996)
[2] Tailor: Respect for nature: a theory of environmental ethics. Princeton University Press, New Jersey (1986)

[3] Odum, H.T.: Environmental Accounting. In: Energy and Evironmental Decision-Making, pp. 48–56. Wiley, NewYork (1996)
[4] Dinda, S.: Environmental Kuznets Curve Hypothesis: A Survey. Ecological Economics 49(4), 431–455 (2004)
[5] van den Bergh, J.C.J.M., Gowdy, J.M.: Evolutionary Theories in Environmental and Resource Economics: Approaches and Applications. Environmental and Resource Economics 9, 37–57 (2000)
[6] Chen, C.J.: Research on the evaluation of sustainable development based on information share. In: Proceedings of the Fourth Asia-Pacific Conference on Industrial Engineering and Management System, pp. 1048–1051 (December 2002)
[7] Unite Nation. Integrated Environmental and Economics Acounting. United Nation, New York (1993)

Academic Emotions Model Based on Radial Basis Function in E-Learning System

Wang Wan-sen, Guo Chun juan, and Liu Shuai

Department of Information Engineering Institute
University of Capital Normal, Beijing, China
wan_sen@sina.cn

Abstract. The traditional e-learning system lack of emotional teaching function，it is an important direction for the development for personalized online education that emotion recognition will be the introduction of interactive e-learning system. Paper to establish e-learning situations learners model of academic emotions using neural network learning in radial basis function (RBF), Experiments show that the method is an efficient method that provides an important theoretical and technical support for personalized e-learning.

Keywords: Emotional model, Radial Basis Function (RBF), Emotion Recognition.

1 Introduction

With the rapid development of Internet, the traditional education has produced great changes. E-learning has become an important method, and all over the world is researching it actively, including China[1]. With the implementing of project of distance education, the system of e-learning collects a large number of learning resources and forms a resource library which is high comprehensive integration. Learners can study through internet in any place.

But the system of traditional e-learning can't perceive and deal with the emotion information of learners. 'A real individuation teaching system is not only intelligent, but must have emotion as well' said Wu Qinglin, an educational psychologist in China. This view reflects the hope of educational psychologists in e-learning and represents the direction of development of e-learning[2].

The development of artificial emotion technology provides a theoretical and technical basis for the individuality e-learning system. This research used for the traditional e-learning system which lacks emotional education. It based on artificial emotion technology and emotional modeling theory. According to radial basis function, it proposes a modeling which is used for the learners' academic emotion in e-learning system. It is academic emotions model based on radial basis function. Experiments show that the method is the network which can be local approximation

D. Zeng (Ed.): ICAIC 2011, Part I, CCIS 224, pp. 639–646, 2011.

and has many advantages, such as, robustness、memory ability、nonlinear mapping and powerful self-learning ability. It is more suitable for real-time system, and has more advantages than traditional linear fit.

2 Emotion Theory and Radial Basis Function

2.1 Emotion Theory

Minsky, the MIT professor of American University said that it should let the computer has the emotional capacity. He asked that 'How to make the machine show emotion when it reflects intelligence.' in his book <The Society Mind> which is published in 1985. Since then, it causes the interest in making computer show emotional capacity and understanding emotion in computer industry, especially artificial intelligence community. In this area, the MIT lab of American University contributed more and more. R.Picad, the professor of the MIT lab of American University gave us a clear definition of affective computing in his book < Affective Computing>, which is published in 1997.It is some calculations about emotion 、from emotional and influence on the emotion[3].

Emotions are psychological tools which are used for human to adapt to survive. It can stimulate the motivation of mental activity and behavior. It is not only an organizer of mental activity, but also important means of interpersonal communication. In the distance learning activities, computers devise and offer joyful and comfortable learning environment through obtaining, classifying, recognizing and responding to human emotion, in order that it can help the learners to get efficient yet warm feeling. It can also effectively reduce the frustration of people in the learning process. Therefore, it is essential to set up the emotion model.

Emotion recognition will measure, analyze and understand the information of a variety of physiological or behavioral characteristics which is reacted by emotion. In the point of physiological psychology, emotion is a complex state of the organism. It not only involves experience and physiological reaction, but contains action as well. Its composition includes emotional experience, emotional expression and emotional physiology at least. So the main methods for emotion recognition include physiological pattern recognition and emotional behavior recognition. The former is objective indicators of emotion which gets by measuring the physiological signals such as skin conductance response, respiration, heart rate, body temperature ate. The latter is also known as facial expression recognition, speech emotion recognition and gesture recognition[4].

2.2 Radial Basis Function

The method of radial basis function is a technology of interpolation in high dimensional space. Broomhead and Love are the first to use this technology to propose the new method of the study in neural network.

Radial basis neuron models

Radial basis neuron models can be seen in figure 1.

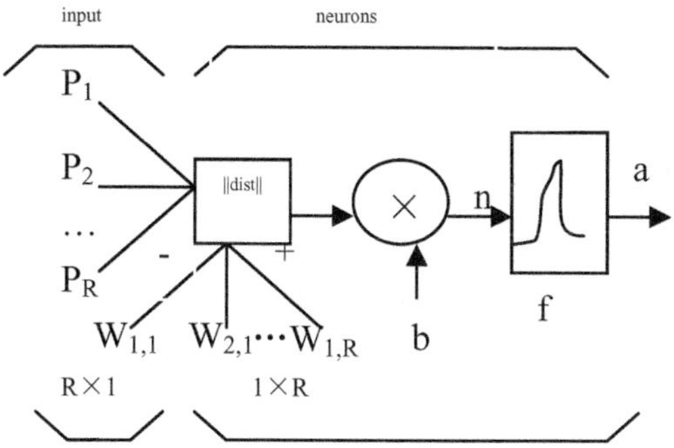

Fig. 1. RBF neuron models

The expression of output is:

$$a=f(\|W-p\|\cdot b)=radbas(\|W-p\|\cdot b) \quad (1)$$

In this expression, radbas is the radial basis function, generally it is gauss function:

$$a(n)=radbas(n)=e--n2 \quad (2)$$

The slickness is very good. It is radial symmetry and the form is simple.

$$\|W-p\|=(\sum i=1R(w1,i-pi)2)1/2=[(W-pT)(W-pT)T]1/2 \quad (3)$$

We call it Euclidean distance.
The graph and sign of the radial basis function can be seen in figure 2.

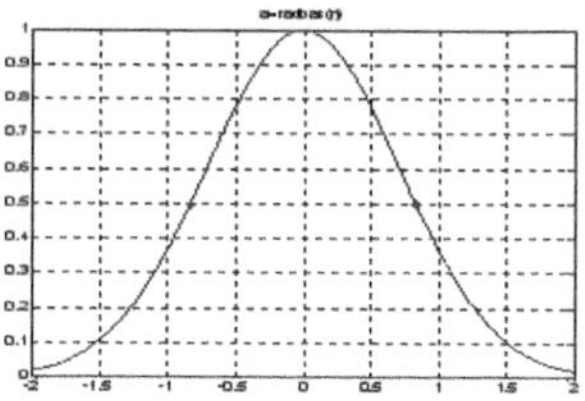

Fig. 2. The transmission characteristic of radial basis output function

The neural network model of radial basis

The neural network model of radial basis is also a neural network which can feed-forward and reverse. There are a couple of network layer: the hidden layer is radial basis layer, the other is linearity layer. Look at figure 3.

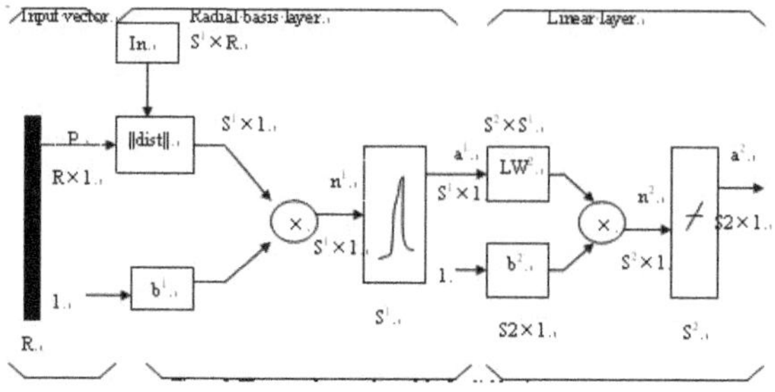

Fig. 3. The neural network model of radial basis

The output of the network is:

$$a2=purelin(LW2a1+b2) \tag{4}$$

$$a1=radbas(n1) \tag{5}$$

$$n1=||IW-P||*b1=(diag((IW-ones(S1,1)*P')(IW- ones(S1,1)*P')'))^\wedge 0.5. *b1 \tag{6}$$

In this expression, diag(x) expresses to get the elements of the leading diagonal of matrix-vector component column vector. ".^" expresses number of power and ".*" expresses product of number. They are the power and product of corresponding element in matrix.

1) Set up the neural network of radial basis
When we set up the neural network of radial basis, there isn't any radial basis neuron at first. We can increase the number of radial basis neuron gradually by following steps.

We can simulate the network with all of the input data;

We can find the sample with the largest error;

We should increase a radial basis neuron, whose weight number equals to the transposition of input vector of this sample. We choose b=[-log(0.5)] 1/2/spread as a threshold value. And the spread is a spreading coefficient of radial basis function. The default is 1.0.

We can use the dot product of radial basis neuron as the input of linear network neurons. We should redesign the linear network neurons in order to minimum the error.

We should repeat the above steps until the mean-square error of network reaches the error property indicator which is ruled before, when the mean-square error misses error property indicator and the number of neurons miss the higher limit which is set before. It can also stop when the number of the neurons reaches the higher limit which is set before.

3 The Mood Model of e-Learning

The OCC model was a evaluation model of cognitive emotion which was proposed by <cognitive structure of emotion>,which was written by Ortony 、Clore and Collins, in

1988. It is the first structuring model which was used in artificial intelligence field. The OCC model possesses some feature as following. (1)It is a model which based on emotion. It includes three main branches, which mirror three kinds of reactive mode that human being reacts to the world. Each reaction contains different emotions, and these emotions are differed by different strength and different induced reason. In the model, there are 22 kinds of affective states. (2)If a person pays attention to the consequence of the event when he is evaluating, the goal is the most important If he pays attention to the action of the object, the standard is most important. But if he pays more attention to the object itself, the attitude is most important. (3)The OCC model contains a whole variable assemblage which can influence the strength of emotion. The variable may be global. It can influence all type of emotion. It also can be local and influence some type of emotion[5]. Besides the above, the OCC model possesses some other feature. Because of these feature, the structuring regulation is easy to realize on computer. This research uses OCC model to imitate the cognize emotion to produce model.

4 Emotions Model Based on Radial Basis Function in e-Learning

4.1 The Model of Degree of Approach-Avoidance

The degree of approach-avoidance can be used to judge learners' attitude to the learning contents by face detection when they are learning. With respect to the normal state, when the face's outline becomes larger, it means the learner's body is forward lean in learning procedure. It indicates that the learner is interested in current study content so that the degree of approach-avoidance becomes larger. When the face's outline becomes smaller, it means the learner's body is backwards lean, even avoids in learning procedure. It indicates that the learner is not interested in current study content so that the degree of approach-avoidance becomes smaller. The model of degree of approach-avoidance is major to get the emotion recognition result about learners' interest level in study contents.

4.2 The Model of Degree of Attention

The degree of attention can be used to judge learners' concentration by detection of eyes space when they are learning. With respect to the normal state, when the eyes space becomes larger, it means that the learner is concentrate in current study contents so that the degree of attention becomes larger. When the eyes space becomes smaller, it means that the learner is not concentrate in current study contents, even tired so that the degree of attention becomes smaller. The model of degree of attention hopes to get the emotion recognition result about learners' concentrate level in study contents. With respect to face detection, the eyes space detection is much harder. The eyes space detective relates to the face detective. If the estimate value of face detective is large, it means that the learner is near to the camera. In that way, the eyes space of detection will be large. If the estimate value of face detection is small, it means that the learner is far from the camera. In that way, the eyes space of detective will be small even can't be detected. Therefore, we should reduce and remove the influence in eyes space detection which is produced by face detection, when we process some data.

4.3 The Model of Degree of Pleasure

The degree of pleasure can be used to judge learners' pleasure by detection of angle of corners of the mouth when they are learning. With respect to the normal state, when the angle of corners of the mouth is upturned and becomes larger, it means that the learner' current mental status in study is very good so that the degree of pleasure becomes larger. When the upturned of angle of corners of the mouth becomes smaller, it means that the learner' current mental status in study is in bad so that the degree of pleasure becomes smaller. The model of degree of pleasure hopes to get the emotion recognition result about learners' pleasure level in study contents.

5 Experiment and the Analysis

This experiment adopts the test data in document[6].This experiment gets the data when learners are over against the camera, and the position of the camera remains unchanged. The learners distance to screen can change throughout the data collection process. And we get the data in the continuous process of learning. Validation results of the degree of approach-avoidance are in figure 4. Validation results of the degree of attention are in figure 5. The results of the degree of pleasure are in figure 6.

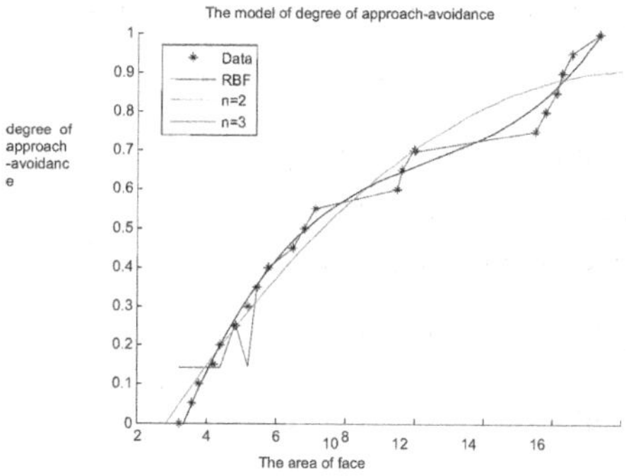

Fig. 4. The experimental result of degree of approach-avoidance

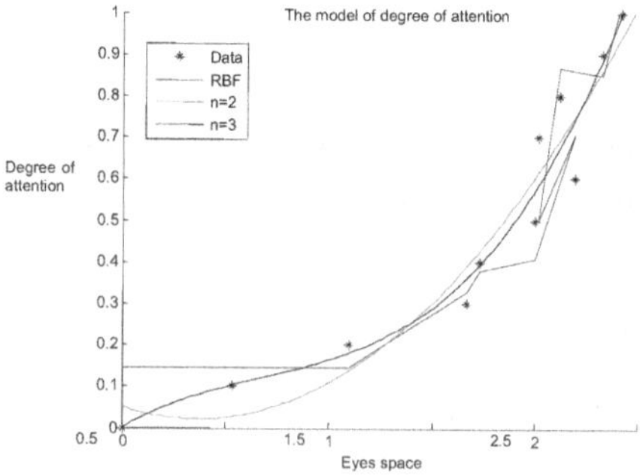

Fig. 5. The experimental result of degree of attention

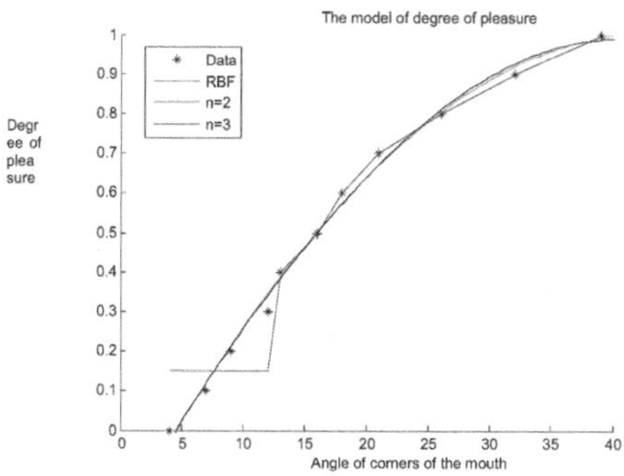

Fig. 6. The experimental result of degree of pleasure

Compared the experimental results of the emotion model which is established by the radial basis function and method of classical linear regression in this experiment, we find that using the emotion model which is established by the radial basis function passes more fitting data points and less error than the linear fit method which is based on the least squares curve. In this experiment we set the linear regression n=2, n=3. It means that we use 2,3 polynomial regression. It proves that the emotion model which is established by the radial basis function possesses higher accuracy.

6 Conclusion

This article is based on the radial basis function in neural network to establish the emotional model. Radial basis function itself has a strong robustness, memory ability, nonlinear mapping ability and strong self-learning ability. It can also make the network train fast. It is fit for the e-learning system which asks for high processing speed. The experiment shows that compared the method of linear fit, the accuracy will gain improvement, if we use the emotion model which is established by the radial basis function. This method is effective when we establish emotional method. However emotional theory is extremely complex. Our knowledge of it is limited now, especially there is some error when we quantize the emotional information. Therefore the emotion-aided teaching capabilities of e-learning are in the research phase. We need to strengthen the study of t emotional theory, improve the method of emotion modeling and improve the proficiency of this system In the follow-up study.

References

1. Meng, X.-y., Wang, Z.-l., Wang, L.-j.: Teaching Assistant System Based on Affective Modeling. Application Research of Computer 4(24), 74–76 (2007)
2. Wang, W.-S., Wen, S.-j., Guo, F.-y.: Study of Intelligent Affective Network Tutoring System Based on Artificial Emotion. Journal of Chinese Computer System 3(27), 569–572 (2006)
3. Wu, Y., Wang, W.-s., Lu, F.: Application of study emotion's research in distance teaching system. Computer Engineering and Design 6(29), 1545–1547 (2008)

4. Wang, G.-j., Wang, Z.-l., Yang, G.-l., Wang, Y.-j., Chen, F.-j.: Survey of Artificial Emotion. Application Research of Computer 3(11), 7–11 (2006)
5. Wang, L., Wang, L.-p.: Research of affective model of Agent based on OCC. Embedded System & Soc. 2(23), 256–258 (2007)
6. Fan, L.-y.: The Research Of Academic Emotions And Modeling Of Stud In E-learning. Master Dissertation In Capital Normal University (2009)
7. Zhou, K.-l., Kang, Y.-h.: The Model Of Neural Network and Matlab Simulation Program Design, pp. 101–106. Tsinghua University Press (2005)

Design and Implementation of Twister Algorithm Based on FPGA

Zhang Lei

Department of Electronic and Information Engineering,
Beijing Electronic Science and Technology Institute, Beijing, China
zhanglei_sunny@yeah.net

Abstract. Recent breakthroughs in cryptanalysis of standard hash functions like SHA-1 and MD5 raise the need for alternatives. The Twister hash function is developed by a team by Ewan Fleischmann in response to the call for proposals for a SHA-3 cryptographic hash algorithm by the National Institute of Standards and Technology. In this paper, introduces the logic structure of Twister algorithm. Using the structure advantage of FPGA hardware devices and give the FPGA Design and Implementation project of Twister algorithm. Final the timing simulation of some modules were given.

Keywords: SHA3, Twister Algorithm, FPGA.

1 Introduction

Cryptographic hash functions are the workhorses of cryptography, and can be found everywhere. Originally created to make digital signatures more efficient, they are now used to secure the very fundamentals of our information infrastructure: in password logins, secure web connections, encryption key management, virus-scanning, and almost every cryptographic protocol in current use. Without hash functions, the Internet would simply not work. Over the past few years, cryptanalysis of these functions has found serious weaknesses. Practical collisions have been demonstrated in MD4 [1-4], MD5 [5-9],and SHA-0 [10]. Known collision attacks against SHA-1 are not yet practical, but they are still more than 10,000 times faster than what was expected [11]. To date, no flaws have been found in SHA-256 and SHA-512 [12], but the common heritage and design principles of all these functions makes them suspect. More seriously, if SHA-256 and SHA-512 were to be broken, the industry would be left without any generally accepted hash functions. To address this undesirable situation, the National Institute for Standards and Technology (NIST) created a design competition for the next generation of hash functions. NIST has asked for proposals and will likely select one as the new SHA-3 hash algorithm sometime in the year 2012. While there is no immediate need to migrate to this new standard, it is assumed that SHA-3 will see widespread use world-wide as applications and standards start using it. The Twister[13] is participate in the SHA-3 open competition.

D. Zeng (Ed.): ICAIC 2011, Part I, CCIS 224, pp. 647–653, 2011.

2 Description of Twister Compression Function

The compression function of Twister consists of building blocks called Mini-Rounds which are grouped into Maxi-Rounds. The instances of the Twister hash function family differ only in their construction of a Maxi-Round.

2.1 A Mini-Round

The Mini-Round is the underlying building-block of any Twister hash function. It's main purpose is to inject the message (Message-Injection) and to take care for the diffusion of the state matrix S. It is visualized in Figure 1. Twister can handle at most 264 Mini-Rounds. This limitation causes by the Add TwistCounter operation where a 64 counter is added. Each Mini-Round can process 64 bit of message data. Therefore, with a native usage of a Mini-Round it is possible to process up to 264 · 64 message bits.

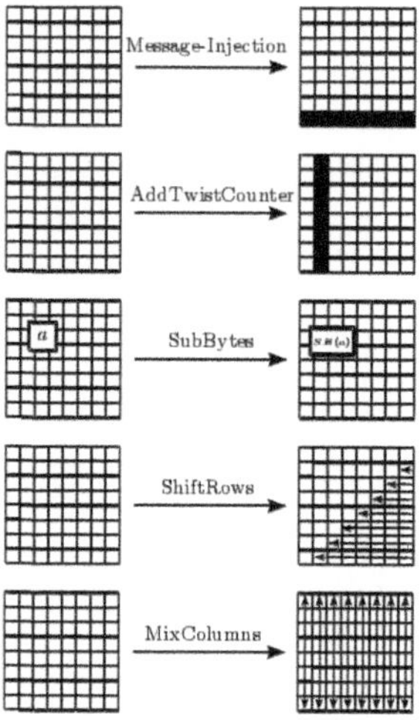

Fig. 1. A Mini-Round

- **Message injection**

A 64 bit message block m is inserted (via XOR ⊕) into the last row. By using the notation m = (m[1], . . . ,m[N]) whereas the length of m[N] is one byte, and $S_{(\to j)} \oplus m := (S_{1,j} \oplus m[1], \ldots, S_{N,j} \oplus m[N])$ we define the message injection process by $S_{(\to 1)} = S_{(\to N)} \oplus m$.

- **Add TwistCounter**

The TwistCounter ϕ is a unsigned 64 bit integer. The initial state is the maximum value (0xFFFFFFFFFFFFFFFF). By using the notation $\phi = (\phi[1], \ldots, \phi[N])$ whereas the length of $\phi[N]$ is one byte, and $\phi[1]$ is the most significant byte of ϕ . The counter is added byte by byte - via the XOR operation-into the second column of the state S. $S_{2,\downarrow} \oplus \phi := (S_{2,1} \oplus \phi[1], \ldots, S_{2,N} \oplus \phi[N])$. We define the TwistCounter addition by $S = S_{2,\downarrow} \oplus \phi$ .After the additon ϕ is decreased by one.

- **SubBytes**

The function is defined as an bijection $SubByte:\{0,1\}^8 \rightarrow \{0,1\}^8$ and is used as an S-box for each byte. It should, among other properties, be highly non-linear. A discussion on how to obtain such cryptographically strong S-Boxes (for 8x8 S-Boxes) can be found in [14]. Twister uses the well known and studied AES S-Box. The S-Box can be found in the Appendix B. We define the SubBytes operation by $S_{i,j} = SB(S_{i,j}) \quad \forall i, j$.

- **ShiftRows**

ShiftRows is a cyclic left shift similar to the ShiftRows operation of AES. It rotates row j by (j-1) mod N bytes to the left. We define the ShiftRows operation by $S_{(i,j-1)} := S_{(i,j)} \quad \forall i, j$.

- **MixColumns**

The MixColumn step is a permutation operation on the state. It applies a N×N-MDS A(a maximum distance separable matrix as defined below) to each column, i.e. performs the operation A · S(j ↓).Definition An [n,k,d] code with generator matrix $G = [I_{k \times k} A_{k \times (n-k)}]$ is an MDS code if every square submatrix of A is nonsingular. The matrix A is called a MDS-matrix.

Our chosen MDS matrix is cyclic, i.e., its i-th row can be obtained by a cyclic right rotation of (02 01 01 05 07 08 06 01) by i entries. It has a branch number of 9 meaning that if two 8 byte input vectors differ in 1≤ k ≤ 8 bytes, the output of MixColumns differs in at least 9 – k bytes. The 8 × 8-MDS matrix used for all proposed instances of Twister is:

$$MDS = \begin{pmatrix} 02 & 01 & 01 & 05 & 07 & 08 & 06 & 01 \\ 01 & 02 & 01 & 01 & 05 & 07 & 08 & 06 \\ 06 & 01 & 02 & 01 & 01 & 05 & 07 & 08 \\ 08 & 06 & 01 & 02 & 01 & 01 & 05 & 07 \\ 07 & 08 & 06 & 01 & 02 & 01 & 01 & 05 \\ 05 & 07 & 08 & 06 & 01 & 02 & 01 & 01 \\ 01 & 05 & 07 & 08 & 06 & 01 & 02 & 01 \\ 01 & 01 & 05 & 07 & 08 & 06 & 01 & 02 \end{pmatrix}$$

All of the byte entries are considered to be elements of $\mathbb{F}_{2^8}$. An element $\sum_{i=0}^{7} a_i x^i \in \mathbb{F}_{2^8}$ is represented by $\sum_{i=0}^{7} a_i 2^i$. The reduction polynomial m(x) of $\mathbb{F}_{2^8}$ is defined as $m(x) = x^8 + x^6 + x^3 + x^2 + 1$.

2.2 A Maxi-Round

A Maxi-Round contains between three and four Mini-Rounds and zero or one blank rounds. A blank round is a Mini-Round with no message input, which is equivalent to the all zero message block. Each Maxi-Round uses also a feed forward operation, i.e., the state before a Maxi-Round is feed forwarded with the state after a Maxi-Round(Figure 2).

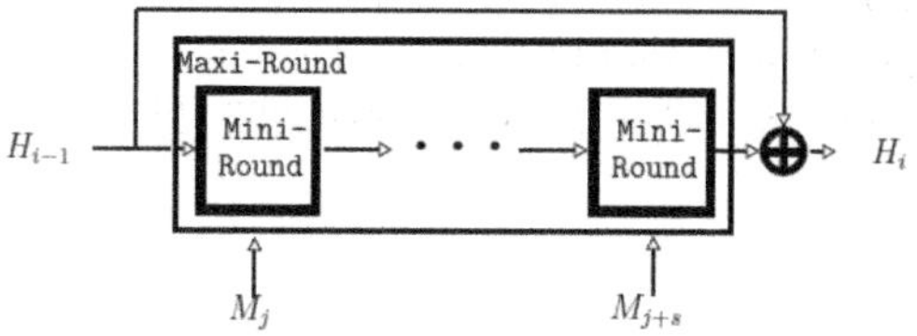

Fig. 2. A Maxi-Round

The compression function of Twister-256 consists of three Maxi-Rounds, where each of them contains three Mini-Rounds. The compression function is displayed in Figure 3. A zero indicates a blank round.

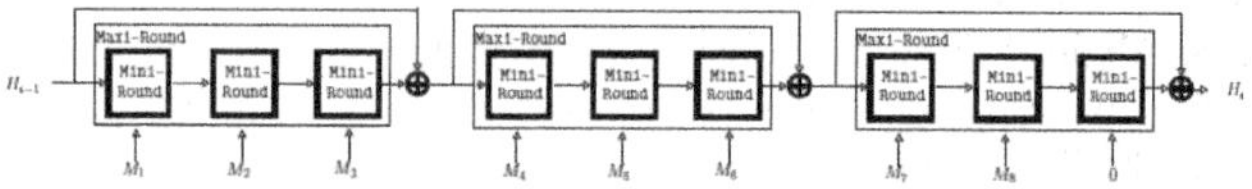

Fig. 3. The compression function of Twister-256

3 FPGA Implementation

Crytographic solutions using software methods can be used for those security applications where data traffic is not too large and low encryption rate is tolerable. On the other hand, hardware methods offer high-speed solutions making them highly suitable for applications where data traffic is fast and large data is required to be encrypted in real time. ASIC and FPGA are two alternatives for implementing cryptographic algorithms in hardware. FPGA offer several benefits for cryptographic algorithm implementations over VLSL as they offer high flexibility. Moreover, basic primitives in most cryptographic algorithms can efficiently be implemented in FPGA. The choice of FPGA as a target platform for hash algorithm implementations appears to be a practical solution for embedded systems.

3.1 The Mini_round Implementation

The Twister algorithm draws on the block cipher AES algorithm ideas. Design the three function of SubBytes (), ShiftRow () and MixColumns (), similar to the operation of AES. Thus build the Mini_Round. According to the data flow diagram(Figure 4), the information into, instead of bytes, add counters, shift rows, columns mixed . Design the program about Mini_round.

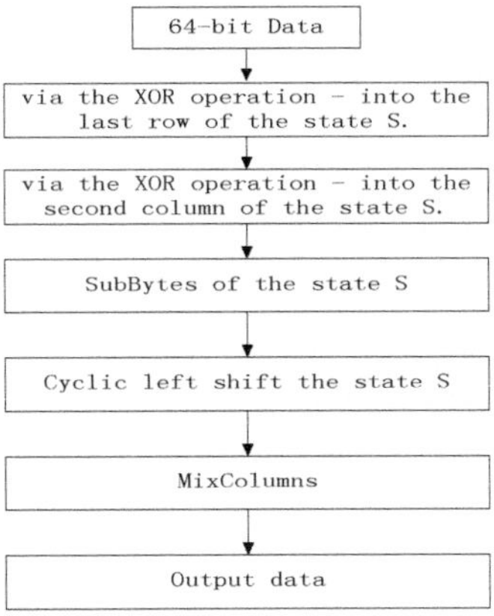

Fig. 4. The data flow of Mini_round

The pipeline method were used to design the Mini_round function. The function set six states(s0, s1, s2, s3, s4, s5). Successive completion information injection, instead of bytes, add counters, shift row, mix column operation. Output the operation result at the state s5. The Mini_round logical structure show in Figure 5.

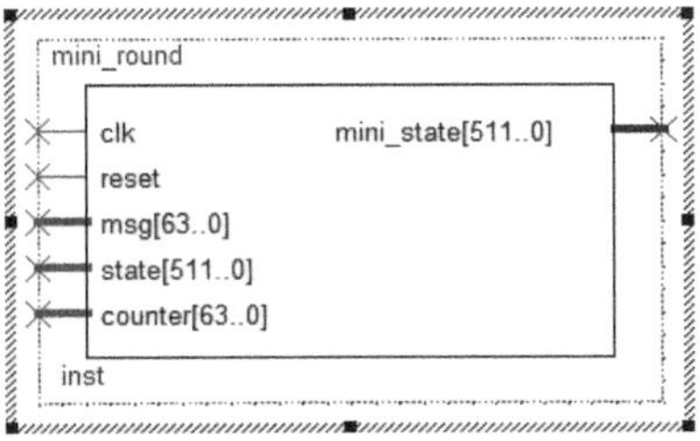

Fig. 5. Mini_round logical structure

Compile the Mini_round function, The use of hardware resources show in Figure 6.

Flow Status	Successful - Wed Jun 03 14:25:18 2009
Quartus II Version	7.2 Build 151 09/26/2007 SJ Full Version
Revision Name	mini_round
Top-level Entity Name	mini_round
Family	Stratix II
Met timing requirements	Yes
Logic utilization	3 %
Combinational ALUTs	4,262 / 143,520 (3 %)
Dedicated logic registers	1,606 / 143,520 (1 %)
Total registers	1606
Total pins	1,154 / 1,171 (99 %)
Total virtual pins	0
Total block memory bits	0 / 9,383,040 (0 %)
DSP block 9-bit elements	0 / 768 (0 %)
Total PLLs	0 / 12 (0 %)
Total DLLs	0 / 2 (0 %)
Device	EP2S180F1508C3
Timing Models	Final

Fig. 6. The use of hardware resources

The establishment of the waveform simulation file for testing the Mini_round (Figure 7), the port as follows:

clk: clock signal;
reset: reset signal;
counter: the counter of Twister;
msg: input message;
state: input state matrix;
mini_state: output state matrix;

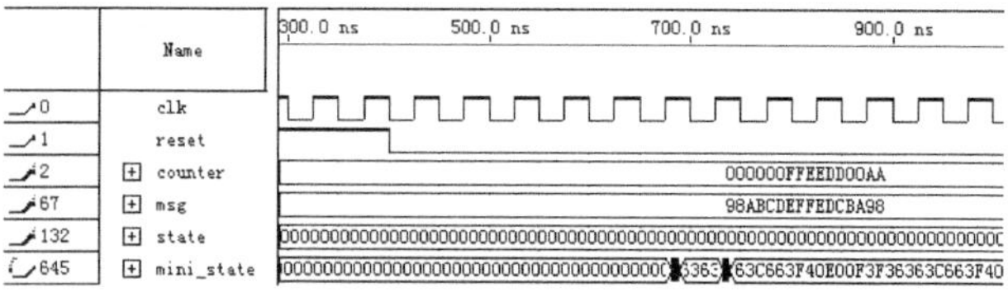

Fig. 7. The waveform simulation of Mini_round

3.2 B The Compression Function Implementation

The compression function of Twister-256 consists of three Maxi-Rounds, each of them contains three Mini-Rounds. The compression function uses the state machine design. It called Mini_round function in each state. The input-data and status matrix operation of the design and implementation:

```
when s1 =>
tempmini <= temp;
temp <= mini(clk,msg(127 downto 64), tempmini, counter);
counter <= counter - 1;
twisterstate <= s2;
```

The XOR operation of the design and implementation:

```
when s3 =>
tempmini <= temp xor tempstate;
tempstate <= tempmini;
twisterstate <= s4;
```

The compression function use of hardware resources show in Figure 8.

Flow Status	Successful - Thu Jun 04 15:30:11 2009
Quartus II Version	7.2 Build 151 09/26/2007 SJ Full Version
Revision Name	Twister
Top-level Entity Name	Twister
Family	Stratix II
Met timing requirements	No
Logic utilization	2 %
Combinational ALUTs	2,578 / 143,520 (2 %)
Dedicated logic registers	0 / 143,520 (0 %)
Total registers	0
Total pins	1,154 / 1,171 (99 %)
Total virtual pins	0
Total block memory bits	0 / 9,383,040 (0 %)
DSP block 9-bit elements	0 / 768 (0 %)
Total PLLs	0 / 12 (0 %)
Total DLLs	0 / 2 (0 %)
Device	EP2S180F1508C3
Timing Models	Final

Fig. 8. The compression function hardware resources

4 Conclusion

In view of that there are some unsafe factors of SHA-1, MD5, and they are broken up, this paper introduces a new algorithm named Twister that participate in the Hash Algorithm open competition, and give the FPGA Design and Implementation project of Twister algorithm. The MD algorithm structure and the pipeline mothered were used to design the VHDL code. Final, the timing simulation of some modules were given. The results show that the algorithm is very easy to implement using FPGA. We will further verify the algorithm's security.

References

[1] Dobbertin, H.: Cryptanalysis of MD4. Journal of Cryptology 11(4), 253–271 (1998)

[2] Kim, J., Biryukov, A., Preneel, B., Lee, S.: On the Security of Encryption Modes of MD4,MD5 and HAVAL. Cryptology ePrint Archive, report 2005/327

[3] Wang, X., Feng, D., Lai, X., Yu, H.: Collisions for Hash Functions MD4, MD5, HAVAL-128 and RIPEMD. Cryptology ePrint Archive, Report 2004/199

[4] Wang, X., Lai, X., Feng, D., Chen, H., Yu, X.: Cryptanalysis of the hash functions MD4 and RIPEMD. In: Cramer, R. (ed.) EUROCRYPT 2005. LNCS, vol. 3494, pp. 1–18. Springer, Heidelberg (2005)

[5] Wang, X., Yu, H.: How to break MD5 and other hash functions. In: Cramer, R. (ed.) EUROCRYPT 2005. LNCS, vol. 3494, pp. 19–35. Springer, Heidelberg (2005)

[6] Stevens, M.: Fast Collision Attack on MD5. Cryptology ePrint Archive, report 2006/104

[7] Klima, V.: Finding MD5 Collisions-a Toy For a Notebook, Cryptology ePrint Archive, Report 2005/075

[8] Klima, V.: Finding MD5 Collisions on a Notebook PC Using Multi-message Modications, Cryptology ePrint Archive, Report 2005/102

[9] Klima, V.: Tunnels in Hash Functions: MD5 Collisions Within a Minute, Cryptology ePrint Archive, Report 2006/105

[10] Chabaud, F., Joux, A.: Differential collisions in SHA-0. In: Krawczyk, H. (ed.) CRYPTO 1998. LNCS, vol. 1462, pp. 56–71. Springer, Heidelberg (1998)

[11] Wang, X., Yin, Y.L., Yu, H.: Collision Search Attacks on SHA1, research summary (2005)

[12] Hawkes, P., Paddon, M., Rose, G.: On Corrective Patterns for the SHA-2 Family, Cryptology ePrint Archive, Report 2004/207

[13] Fleischmann, E., Forler, C., Gorski, M.: The Twister Hash Function Family, October 28 (2008), `http://www.twister-hash.com`

[14] Yi, X., Cheng, S.X., You, X.H., Lam, K.Y.: A Method for Obtaining Cryptographically Strong 8x8 S-boxes. In: IEEE Global Elecommunications Conference, GLOBECOM 1997, vol. 2, pp. 689–693 (1997)

Research on the Forming Mechanism of Multiple Wave in the South Yellow Sea

Tong Siyou, Hao Wei, Liu Huaishan, Zhang Jin,
Wang Linfei, and Wang Shulun

Key Lab of Submarine Geosciences and Prospecting Techniques,
Ministry of Education, Ocean University of China
Qingdao 266100, China
tongsiyou@qq.com

Abstract. The purpose of this paper is to fully understand the forming mechanism of multiple wave of the South Yellow Sea. According to W5-st1 well logging parameters and the processing profiles of the cross-well line,we established a geological model and carried out forward modeling studies.To carry out forward modeling studies by using elastic wave equation and considering the differences by changing conditions of the free surface.With the study results and the actual seismic data,we can fully aware the characteristics and forming mechanism of multiple wave of the sea area.

Keywords: the South Yellow Sea, seismic data, multiple wave, wave equation, forward modeling.

1 Introduction

China has nearly 300×104km^2 blue land, which is rich in oil and gas resources. However, the exploration and development of China's oil and gas resources in the ocean started late. The exploration degree of oil and gas resources in all waters is lower and the proven degree of oil and gas resources is much lower. The South Yellow Sea Basin is particularly special, which is the only sea area without oil and gas (reservoir) in China at present[1]. According to scholars' study, the South Yellow Sea Basin is above the Yangtze block, where the upper Silurian and lower Devonian is missing, and Mesozoic and Paleozoic marine carbonate rocks develop completely. The stratigraphic development is relatively thick, and the distribution of area is wide, which has good oil and gas exploration prospects.

Nevertheless, because of the growth of a variety of multiple waves and the complexity of wave field characteristics, it has a poor seismic data quality currently and it is hard to know the spatial distribution laws and the various structural features in the sea area. So study of oil and gas exploration has been greatly affected. Therefore, to find out the formation mechanism of multiple wave is of great significance.

D. Zeng (Ed.): ICAIC 2011, Part I, CCIS 224, pp. 654–662, 2011.

2 The Formation Mechanism of Multiple Wave

2.1 Wave Field Communication Theory

1) In the case of isotropic medium

In seismic exploration, the source down in the production of elastic wave propagation, non-normal incidence conditions, to reach the surface of elastic boundaries arises reflected P-wave, reflected S-wave, transmitted P-wave and transmitted S-wave. Zoepritz equation can be a good description of the plane wave reflection and transmission. In isotropic medium, P-wave incident, all kinds of wave amplitude to meet the Zoepritz equation[2]:

$$\begin{bmatrix} \sin\theta_{p1} & \cos\theta_{s1} & -\sin\theta_{p2} & \cos\theta_{s2} \\ -\cos\theta_{p1} & \sin\theta_{s1} & -\cos\theta_{p2} & -\sin\theta_{s2} \\ \sin 2\theta_{p1} & \frac{v_{p1}}{v_{s1}}\cos 2\theta_{s1} & \frac{\rho_2}{\rho_1}\frac{v_{p1}}{v_{p2}}\frac{v_{s2}^2}{v_{s1}^2}\sin 2\theta_{s2} & -\frac{\rho_2}{\rho_1}\frac{v_{p1}v_{s2}}{v_{s1}^2}\cos 2\theta_{s2} \\ \cos\theta_{p1} & -\frac{v_{s1}}{v_{p1}}\cos 2\theta_{s1} & -\frac{\rho_2}{\rho_1}\frac{v_{p2}}{v_{p1}}\sin 2\theta_{s2} & -\frac{\rho_2}{\rho_1}\frac{v_{s2}}{v_{p1}}\cos 2\theta_{s2} \end{bmatrix} * \begin{bmatrix} R_{pp} \\ R_{ps} \\ T_{pp} \\ T_{ps} \end{bmatrix} = \begin{bmatrix} -\sin\theta_{p1} \\ -\cos\theta_{p1} \\ \sin 2\theta_{p1} \\ -\cos 2\theta_{s1} \end{bmatrix} \tag{1}$$

By Zoeppritz equation, converted wave is generated only when it is inclined incidence. Converted-wave reflection coefficient is the singular function of incident angle of P-wave.

2) In the case of anisotropic medium

The so-called anisotropic mean: seismic waves spread at one point and that point is not only related to the location, but also the direction of the wave propagation. In general, we have the anisotropic characteristics of the medium called anisotropic media[3]. According to Newton's theorem, wave equation in the non-uniform anisotropic medium can be introduced as follows:

$$\sum_{j,k,l=1}^{3} c_{ijkl}\frac{\partial^2 u_k}{\partial x_l \partial x_j} + \sum_{j,k,l=1}^{3}\frac{\partial c_{ijkl}}{\partial x_j}\frac{\partial u_k}{\partial x_k} = \rho\frac{\partial^2 u_i}{\partial^2 t^2} \quad i,j,k,l = 1,2,3 \tag{2}$$

Under the conditions in the general anisotropic medium, the stress - strain constitutive equations can be written in the following matrix form:

$$\begin{bmatrix} \sigma_{xx} \\ \sigma_{yy} \\ \sigma_{zz} \\ \sigma_{yz} \\ \sigma_{zx} \\ \sigma_{xy} \end{bmatrix} = \begin{bmatrix} c_{11} & c_{12} & c_{13} & c_{14} & c_{15} & c_{16} \\ c_{21} & c_{22} & c_{23} & c_{24} & c_{25} & c_{26} \\ c_{31} & c_{32} & c_{33} & c_{34} & c_{35} & c_{36} \\ c_{41} & c_{42} & c_{43} & c_{44} & c_{45} & c_{46} \\ c_{51} & c_{52} & c_{53} & c_{54} & c_{55} & c_{56} \\ c_{61} & c_{62} & c_{63} & c_{64} & c_{65} & c_{66} \end{bmatrix} \begin{bmatrix} \varepsilon_{xx} \\ \varepsilon_{yy} \\ \varepsilon_{zz} \\ \varepsilon_{yz} \\ \varepsilon_{zx} \\ \varepsilon_{xy} \end{bmatrix} \tag{3}$$

$c_{i,j}$ for the elastic coefficient

In the TI medium, the medium is isotropic elastic along the horizontal, and is changing along in the vertical direction, with unlimited vertical axis of rotation[4]. In transversely isotropic media, SV wave can be formed in P wave propagation, at the same time, the P wave can be formed in SV wave propagation. If a given tensor of anisotropic elastic parameters satisfy the conditions of tensor of isotropic elastic parameters, the wave equation can be simplified into SH, and P-SV wave equations of a homogeneous isotropic medium.

2.2 Multiple Wave Types and Formation Mechanism of Marine Seismic Exploration

The interface between sea level and air (the free surface) is an interface with obvious difference in acoustic impedance, it is a good reflection interface, the reflection coefficient close to -1, reflecting high energy, under it to reach this interface, the reflected wave will continue after reflection down the media, and when faced reflective interface, but also the reflection from happening again return to the sea to form the multiple sets of multiple-wave which relate to free surface; Likewise, the following if there is large differences in the interface reflection coefficient, will produce multiple wave; In this way, it will form a variety of multiples, including the multiple-wave reflection and refraction multiple wave.

Typically, the multiple wave types in the marine seismic survey are generally divided into the following [2]:

1) Whole multiple wave, that means the seabed and its place following a layer interface, the reflected wave return to the sea interface occurred in the dissemination of reflection, but again to the sea the following strata spread down to happen again in the same interface, reflection, back and forth several times to form wave. Also known as simple multiple wave.

2) Short-range multiple wave, is transmitted to a seismic wave reflected back interface, the back surface of the sea and then down the reflection, then a shallower or deeper in a certain place reflected the formation of the interface wave. Also known as the local multiple wave.

3) Peg-leg multiple wave refers to the interface occurred in several multiple reflections, multiple reflections of the path is asymmetrical; or within a thin layer formed by multiple reflection wave.

4) Virtual reflection, refers to the sea below a certain depth excitation, the excitation energy part of the upward spread of the sea and then down the face of the wave formed by reflection is called virtual reflection. Strictly speaking, it is shot virtual reflection,here also have receiver virtual reflection.Usually, shot and receiver have a submergence depth. So,these two phenomena simultaneously exist.

5) Refracted multiple wave, the shock wave down the communication process to achieve critical angle of the incident angle after the seismic refraction occurring at the reflection layer, and the reflection layer interface sliding, then out of reach all parts of the upper medium, to the sea the transmission of the process again strong reflections occur due to different strata reflected or refracted back and forth, several times referred to as refracted wave.

The above classification only considering a single longitudinal wave propagation features of multiple waves in ocean exploration.Because there are many non-normal incidence of waves, usually there will be converted wave generated in the actual spread of medium, in particular the apparent anisotropy of the medium, although the conversion of S-wave can not be produced in sea water to spread, however, in exploration of the sea, converted wave is still received, the received converted multiple-wave is to reach detector after the interface, reflected and converted multiple, the converted wave is not transverse in nature only. (Fig. 1), respectively, when the first wave of S-wave (a) and P-wave (b), converted multiple wave propagation diagram, their common points are the wave propagation to the detector location be the "P" wave in nature.

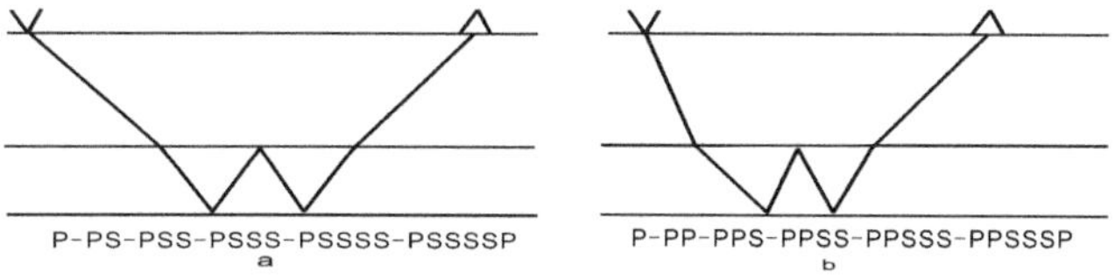

a P_S_P multiple wave b P_P_S_P multiple wave

Fig. 1. Convert multiple wave propagation features

3 The Forming Mechanism of Multiple Wave in the South Yellow Sea by Forward Modeling

The modeling use wave equation finite difference simulation method. In order to ascertain the formation mechanism of multiple wave of the South Yellow Sea, special based on geophysical parameters of a well, establishing a more accurate geological model. Conducting analytical studies using the elastic wave equation.

For the particularity of this free surface, respectively, designed to meet the actual conditions of the free surface existence and the assumptions of the free surface not existence to carry out simulations, the former is gas-liquid interface reflection coefficient of -1, the latter assuming the reflection coefficient is 0. The latter assumption is intended to purify wave field, simulation results does not contain the complex multiple wave formed by the free surface in order to understand conventional wave field characteristics, comparative analysis of the former with the latter, you can better distinguish which wave field is formed by free surface.

Although the water can not transmit S-wave, but in the seabed below the spread around the layer is to follow the mechanism of elastic wave. It will produce S-wave, reflected S-wave back to sea will not spread, but the next wave will form a P-wave formed by complex re-convert S-wave, that is, PSP, PSSP wave, such waves can be spread in the sea and recorded. The elastic wave equation produces results closest to the actual conditions of solid media, including converted wave and S-wave effects. Not only does it take into account the density and P-wave velocity distribution, but also take into account differences of S-wave velocity, S-wave speed of 0 indicated that a liquid medium, so you can in the model taking into account the two kinds of solid and liquid media, analyzing transmission mechanisms of wave field, identifying multiple wave characteristics.

3.1 The Basic Principles of Elastic Wave Simulation with Finite Difference Method

In 2D TI medium, the elastic wave equations expressed with the velocity – stress (assuming the body force is 0) are:

$$\begin{aligned}
&\rho\frac{\partial v_x}{\partial t}=\frac{\partial \tau_{xx}}{\partial x}+\frac{\partial \tau_{xz}}{\partial z},\\
&\rho\frac{\partial v_z}{\partial t}=\frac{\partial \tau_{xz}}{\partial x}\frac{\partial \tau_{zz}}{\partial z},\\
&\frac{\partial \tau_{xx}}{\partial t}=c_{11}\frac{\partial v_x}{\partial x}+c_{13}\frac{\partial v_z}{\partial z}\\
&\frac{\partial \tau_{zz}}{\partial t}=c_{13}\frac{\partial v_x}{\partial x}+c_{33}\frac{\partial v_z}{\partial z},\\
&\frac{\partial \tau_{xz}}{\partial t}c_{14}\frac{\partial v_z}{\partial x}+c_{44}\frac{\partial v_x}{\partial z},
\end{aligned} \tag{4}$$

Among them, v_i is velocity component, τ_{ij} is the stress, ρ is density, c_{ij} is elastic constants of the medium. In the case that the medium is isotropic, $c_{11}=c_{33}=\lambda+2\mu$, $c_{13}=\lambda$, $c_{44}=\mu$.

When use the staggered grid method to numerically solve a first-order elastic wave equation, the velocity and stress, respectively, are calculated in the time $t+\frac{\Delta t}{2}$ and t. In order to improve the accuracy of time difference, using Taylor formula, the time difference approximation of 2M-order accuracy can be obtained[5-6], such as

$$v_x\left(t+\frac{\Delta t}{2}\right)=v_z\left(t-\frac{\Delta t}{2}\right)+2\sum_{m=1}^{M}\frac{1}{(2m-1)!}\left(\frac{\Delta t}{2}\right)\frac{\partial^{2m-1}}{\partial t^{2m-1}}v_x+o(\Delta t^{2M}) \tag{5}$$

3.2 Elastic Wave Equation Modeling

Fig. 2 is simulation records of elastic wave equation without considering the effect of free surface .As shown in the white areas in Fig. 2, incon ① represents interbed multiple.②and③, represents a group of converted refracted waves and reflected-converted-refracted multiples. ④and⑤, represents another group.Their energy are intense, it is difficult to identify the effective wave. The difference of the apparent velocity coming from different strata of the two sets is large. Only the first-order converted multiples is marked, The third-order and even higher order multiples can also be seen to the depth.

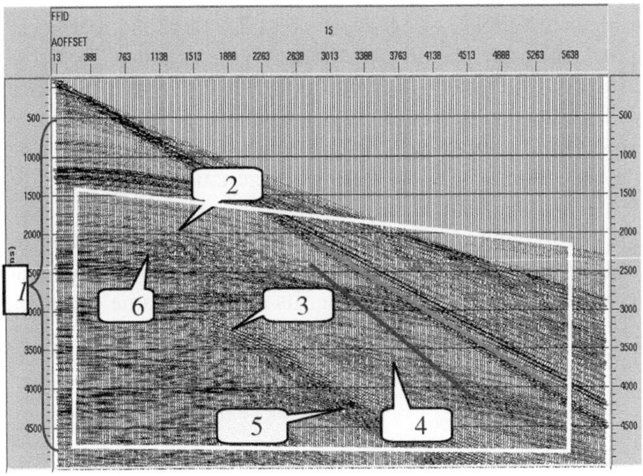

Fig. 2. Simulation records of elastic wave equation without considering the effect of free surface

Fig. 3 is simulation records of elastic wave equation considering the effect of free surface .⑥ represents T_2 multiple. Compared Fig. 3 with Fig. 2, free surface multiples develop and mixed with converted wave. The energy of free surface multiples wave is strong, and the two groups of converted wave characteristics appear relatively weak, but the multiple waves of each convert wave are also strong. The interface of T_2 has obvious multiple wave, as the white areas in Fig. 3. Because of the effort of surface, the refracted wave and the multiple wave produced by refracted wave are obviously enhanced, such as the sings which marked with blue line and red line, mixing with hyperbola performed as group velocity characteristics.

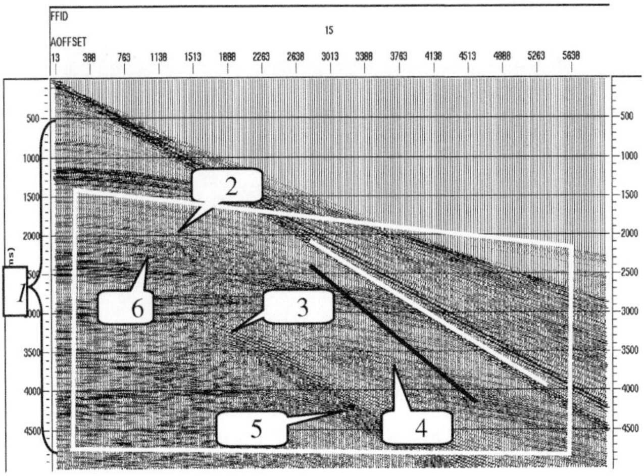

Fig. 3. Simulation records of elastic wave equation considering the effect of free surface

Because of the effort of strong interface as T_2, there is greatly velocity difference between upper and under layer. So it is easily to generate the refracted wave. The reflected-refraction multiple which produced by the strong interface as developed completely. There is an increment of Ts (the arriving time of refracted wave) and an increment of Xs in abscissa (the propagate distance of the refracted wave) when there is a multiple reflection. The wave field characteristics as shown in Fig. 1 and Fig. 4, the refracted wave performed as straight line. The Fig. 4 was the propagation characteristic of refracted wave, because of the large velocity changes greatly between the upper and under ground, the transmission S wave may propagate up and the P wave was easily to achieve critical angle. Its energy became complicated because the incident angle was increased with the increased offset(Fig. 5), and various waves interfered mutually.

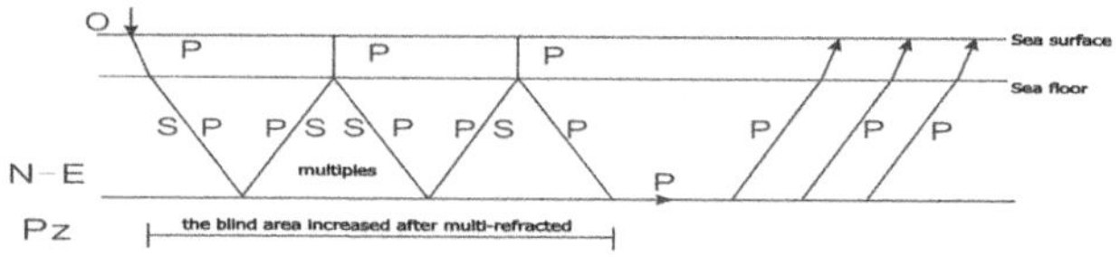

Fig. 4. The mechanism of refracted multiples

4 Multiple Features of the Seismic Data of the South Yellow Sea

Fig. 5 is a single shot records of the actual 2D survey line which is passing the W5-st1 well. Analyze it and the single shot simulation records of elastic wave equation shown in Fig.4, it can be seen that the characteristics of various wave fields are similar, especially the multiples features. This shows that the actual production is close to the elastic wave model with considering the effect of free surface.

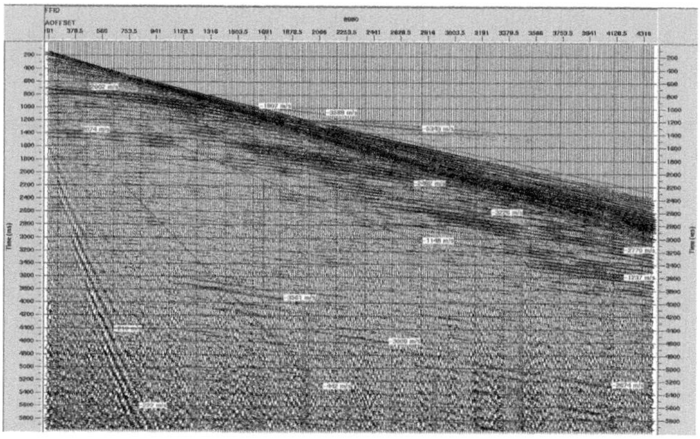

Fig. 5. The actual recording

Fig.5 shows different apparent velocity analysis on account of different phenomena. The multiples in actual data are shown as: singing, interbed multiples, refraction multiples and converted multiples. The actual records have many noises because of the construction environment, which give more negative impact to the already complex multiples wave field. The noise and multiples are dominant, and the strong energy of multiples and singing can be seen in the whole record. The interbed multiples interferes with the wave of deep layers, and the refraction multiples and converted multiples give great impact to the shallow.

5 The Formation Mechanism of Multiple Wave of the South Yellow Sea Seismic Data

Fig. 6 is a single shot and snapshot of the elastic wave equation modeling, which considering the impact of the free surface. Single shot on the left of the simulation is mainly marked with refraction, refracted multiples, converted waves, converting multiple, as in the previous study, during which also includes many other layers formed by high-speed layer multiples, the right corresponding to the main logo analysis of the corresponding reflected wave field, wave field and converted multiple wave field, and reverberation, interbed multiple is clearly visible from the wave field snapshots can clearly see the formation mechanism of the various wave, particularly the formation mechanism of various multiples.

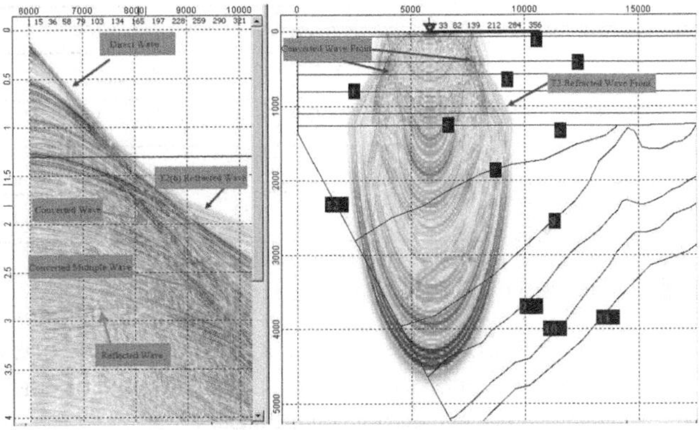

Fig. 6. Considering the role of the free surface elastic wave simulation record and snapshot

Combined with comparative analysis of the actual record, it is clear to know the area multiples the root causes of complex and diverse is the area of special geological and geophysical data closely related to shallow-water environment, we can see many times the South Yellow Sea seismic wave forming mechanism: the free surface and more second wave of strong energy is due to the depth of the sea water caused by the free surface is stronger; strong reflective interface between the layers multiples development is as shallow and deep strata formation causes the great differences between the reflection coefficient; because of the underground waters of vertical and horizontal to the ground rate changes, offset large incident angle change range, and anisotropy of obvious reasons, the formation of significant wave, and then convert multiple wave form; refraction multiples, converted waves and many times more than the free surface second wave and another doped layer multiples, mutual influence, so difficult to identify several waves, leading to the wave field is very complex. To this purpose, to find reasonable and effective handling of multiple suppression technique is very important.

6 Conclusions

Through detailed study, generally we have found out the South Yellow Sea seismic wave forming mechanism: the free surface multiple wave be strong is due to the role of free surface be strong; interbed multiple of strong reflective interface is due to the difference in the reflection coefficient of the shallow and deep formation be large; because of underground stratum of the area of longitudinal and transverse velocity changes, offset large incident angle change range, anisotropic character be obvious and so on,convert wave form and then convert multiple wave form; refraction multiples, converted multiples and free surface multiples and interbed multiples mixed with each other, which cause the entire wave field very complicated.

Acknowledgment. This research was financially supported by, the National High Technology Research and Development Program (863 program) of China(2007AA060502, 2006AA06A108), Undergraduate Education and Teaching Research Subject of Ocean University of China(2009JY16) and Natural Science Foundation of Shandong Province(ZR2010DM012).Thank the support of Qingdao Institute of Marine Geology.

References

[1] Fan, X.: Strategic thinking of Marine areas of the South Yellow Sea Basin oil and gas exploration. Marine Origin Petroleum Geology 6(4), 35–40 (2001)

[2] Lu, J.: Principles of seismic exploration. China Petroleum University Press, Dongying (2009)

[3] Dong, L., Li, G., Yang, Q., et al.: Physical modeling of elastic waves in transversely isotropic medium 38(1), 76–85 (1999)

[4] Li, X.: Multiwave and Multicomponents Numerical Simulation and Processing of Data: [Bachelor Degree Paper]. Chinese Geology University, Beijing (2006)

[5] Virieux, J.: SH-wave propagation in heterogeneous media: velocity-stress finite-difference method. Geophysics 49(11), 1933–1957 (1984)

[6] Dong, G., Ma, Z., Cao, Z., et al.: First-order staggered grid finite difference method. Chinese Journal of Sinica 3(43), 411–419 (2000)

Statistical Modeling for LSB-Based Image Steganalysis: A Systematic Perspective*

Xiaoming Yao, Wencai Du, Taijun Li, Longjuan Wang, Honglei Li, Hanwei Wu, and Zequn Wang

College of Information Science & Technology
Hainan University
Haikou, Hainan Province, China
yao_summer@sohu.com

Abstract. Steganalysis is a science of detecting possible hidden messages in an apparently innocuous cover medium, which is usually modeled as looking for a characteristic function that can discriminate effectively the stego from the cover. In this paper, we investigated the statistical models available for typical tools of LSB-based image steganalysis, focusing on their relations with the statistics of cover images, of secret messages, of operations acted upon the cover image, in an effort to theoretically form a systematic perspective which helps cast better insights into different steganalytic methods of inherent consistence. We proved the equivalence of some statistical models as results and compared the difference of effectiveness among these consistent statistical models.

Keywords: Statistical Modeling, Charateristic Function, Model Equivalence, LSB-based Steganalysis.

1 Introduction

In recent years, a rise of strong and continuing interests on Steganography and Steganalysis with the rapid development of multimedia and networking technologies has been seen among information security researchers. According to literature [1], Steganography is the art of hiding and transmitting data through apparently innocuous carriers in an effort to conceal the existence of the secret data, while Steganalysis as its opponent, addresses the problem of detecting and estimating the possible hidden messages. Steganography actually provides a useful tool for secret communication that cryptography can't provide, giving a very good reason of its current existence.

As one of the earliest researchers, Cachin investigated modeling Steganography based on information theory, and pointed out in [2] that "Steganography is considered perfectly secure if there is no statistical difference between the class of cover messages and the class of stego messages". The possible statistics available is:

* This project is sponsored by the Doctorate Initiation program of Hainan University, 3rd "211 Engineering Construction" Project of Hainan University and Special Expense Support from Hainan Provincial Engineering Technological Research Center under the grant No.2060499.

D. Zeng (Ed.): ICAIC 2011, Part I, CCIS 224, pp. 663–671, 2011.

✧ ***Statistics of the cover medium before and after embedding operation***: the former one must be estimated with some signal processing techniques, while the later is available.

✧ ***Statistics of the cover medium before and after signal processing operations:*** the information for them both must be estimated with some signal processing techniques.

✧ ***Statistics of the hidden messages is usually assumed to be completely random***: Nobody ever considers if the hidden message is not randomized before the embedding process, so we let it as is.

While there are statistical models to go up with novel steganographic or steganalytic methods, no one ever puts them together and sketches them systematically. This work is motivated because different statistical models may have inherent consistence, and consistent statistical models may show significantly different effectiveness of steganalysis in different occasions. In this paper, we investigated the statistical models available for typical tools of LSB-based image steganalysis, focusing on their relations with the statistics of cover images, of secret messages, of operations acted upon the cover image, in an effort to theoretically form a systematic perspective which helps cast better insights into different steganalytic methods of inherent consistence. We have proved the equivalence of some statistical models as results and compared the difference of effectiveness among these consistent statistical models.

The rest of the paper is organized as follows. Section 2 reviews briefly typical statistical models currently available, following the way current steganalysis develops. Section 3 presents discussions on the consistence among some well-known statistical models. Section 4 compares the difference of effectiveness of some consistent statistical models in specific cases. Section 5 gives the summary of the work.

2 A Brief Review of LSB-Based Statistical Models

2.1 LSBs of an Image Modeled as Random Bit Streams

Probably inspired from fundamental image modeling in the field of image processing, famous LSB (least significant bit) substitution steganographic tools (such as Contraband, EzStego, Hide & Seek, PGMStealth, Snow, Steganos, S-Tools, White Noise Storm) are based on the assumption [3] that the least significant bits of pixels in a digital image are independent identically distributed random bit streams, thus replaceable with another random one.

Taking an image as a random sequence, $\{x_1, x_2, \cdots, x_n\}$, the instance of which x_i will randomly take a value between 0 and 255. The first order and higher order statistics, i.e. the sample mean, variance, skewness and kurtosis of the sequence can be estimated directly [4]. Steganographic tools based on the assumption are really featured with high payload and visual imperceptions.

However, Westfeld et al [3] pointed out that this is not true, and went up successfully with the famous Chi-square test as an effective tool of steganalysis to break the LSB substitution image Steganography. The reason is, the secret message is usually randomized with a Key, while LSBs of the cover image are correlated with some structural constraints. This method is especially effective when the secret messages are sequentially embedded with more than 97% payload since in this case the structural constraints among the LSBs have been lost after the replacement and its probability distribution turns to be similar to a randomized one, so by chi-square computation, high probability of embedding is detected. In [5], Westfeld further proposed an enhanced version of chi-square test with some hash functions selected empirically, which fully utilizes both features of hash function and the similarity of neighboring bits or pixels.

The weak point of the methods is also clear. Since LSBs of an image only preserve part of its structural information, once the secret message of payload less than 50% is embedded in a scattered way, chi-square test may fail due to the potential existence of the structural information.

In recent years, many steganalytic techniques based on this assumption of randomness have been proposed, among which the most famous are RS [6] and SPA [7].

Very interestingly, in 2003, Zhang et al [8] proposed a similar statistical assumption of the randomness of the numbers of crossing the odd and even gray-level planes, which observed the similar rules of randomness.

2.2 Kinds of Histograms to Model Relational Randomness

LSB embedding will not only change the randomness of image pixels, but that of their quantitative relations as well.

As an empirical probability mass function, histograms can be a very useful tool for steganalysis. There are several kinds of histograms, roughly categorized into one-dimensional (1D) histogram and high dimensional histogram.

1D histogram: A typical 1D histogram is the frequency of image pixels with the same value of [0,255]. Westfeld et al [3] first noticed the difference between the histograms before and after LSB embedding, i.e. that of the stego image "displays a pronounced 'stair-step' effect" [9]. Based on this observation, known tools like Chi-Square test, can be neatly evaluated mathematically. Details may be referred to [9].

Zhang et al [10] proposed another form of 1D histogram, the DIH derived from subtracting the translated version from its original one, i.e. $D(i,j)=I(i,j)-I(i,j+1)$, which is believed to have a generalized Gaussian distribution.

Obviously, 1D histogram is not necessarily only for image pixels or their random subsets. Actually it can also be built for the transformed coefficients and their random subsets as listed in [11].

2D histogram: Co-occurrence matrix is the most common 2D histogram, as in literatures [12], [13], [14].

For a given gray scale image $I_{x,y}$ with N gray levels, the N×N co-occurrence matrix $M_{r,\theta}$ of the image can be defined as:

$$M_{r,\theta}(i,j)=P\left(I_{x1,y1}=i, I_{x2,y2}=j \left| \begin{matrix} x2=x1+r\cos\theta \\ y2=y1+r\sin\theta \end{matrix} \right. \right) \quad (1)$$

Where r is the step, θ is the direction, and P is the normalized probability (or in discrete form, the frequency), as in [12].

2D co-occurrence matrix is very useful in measuring the neighboring relations, especially in detecting their abrupt changes, thus very powerful for LSB replacement detections.

2.3 Features Derived from Statistical Models

In most of sophisticated steganographic methods proposed, either the first order or the higher order statistics can be preserved [15~18], making the task of detection simply using unique statistics that models one or two kinds of pixel changing behaviors very difficulty. In this case, a joint statistical model is in urgent need. For each model, we got a statistics, which is now called *feature*.

Features by mapping histogram: For a histogram H, a mapping operation f can usually be found to obtain H', which can distinguish better the difference between that before and after LSB embedding. That is to say, $H' = f(H)$.

Harmsen and Pearlman [19] found that modeling the LSB embedding as the addition of noise without regard to the correlation of sampled signals will make the histogram before and after the processing quite different. They choose a cover image with a histogram $h_c[n]$, then add the stego-noise, with a probability mass function of $f_\Delta[n]$, which results in the derived image with a histogram $h_s[n]$. They have shown that this process results in a convolution of their histograms, i.e.

$$h_s[n] = h_c[n] * f_\Delta[n] \tag{2}$$

By taking the discrete Fourier transform (DFT), we have in frequency domain,

$$H_s[k] = H_c[k] F_\Delta[k] \tag{3}$$

The expression of image histogram in the frequency domain is called the histogram characteristic function (HCF). The center of mass (COM) of the HCF can be estimated,

$$C(H_s[k]) = \frac{\sum_{k\in K} k|H[k]|}{\sum_{i\in K} |H[i]|} \tag{4}$$

Where K=$\{0,\cdots,N/2-1\}$, and N is the DFT length. The feature of COM of HCF is useful because it has,

$$C(H_s[k]) \le C(H_c[k]) \tag{5}$$

This can be discriminant function for a classifier if some threshold is obtained by supervised training.

For the histogram of a given image, the local maxima and minima can be easily estimated with a Mask of size 3×1 or 5×1, and the envelope of the histogram can be obtained by separately extrapolating the sets of local maxima and minima. Zhang et al [20] proposed that the area S formed between the upper envelope and the lower envelope of the histogram can be a useful discriminant function since this area for stego-image is usually much smaller than that for cover image, i.e.

$$S_s(h_u[n] - h_l[n]) << S_c(h_u[n] - h_l[n]) \tag{6}$$

Chen et al [12] used a 1D projection of the 2D histogram (the co-occurrence matrix) to reduce the complexity by summing up the equation (2) in a given direction, i.e.

$$H_{r,\theta}(k) = \sum_i M_{r,\theta}(i, i+k), 1-N \le k \le N-1, k \in Z \tag{7}$$

Xuan et al [14] only chose 4 directions (θ =0, 45, 90, 135) to form the detection feature by averaging and normalizing the four co-occurrence matrixes.

Mahdavi et al [21] proposed that the local gradient of the histogram or the difference between the histograms h_{2i} and h_{2i+1} "decreases with the increase of the embedded data".

For DCT or JPEG or DFT coefficients [22], there are similar treatments on histograms of their coefficients or their selected subsets.

Features of image quality metrics (IQMs): As Avcibas et al [23,24] pointed out, "the embedding process on a document leaves statistical artifacts, which could be used to distinguish between stego and cover versions". The basic results they obtained are, filtering an image with no hidden message embedded causes changes in the IQMs differently from that brought about on embedded images. Therefore, selected from many IQMs available by experiments, they built a regressive system by setting the normalized IQM scores respectively to -1 and 1, depending on whether an image did not or did contain a hidden message in the training phase, i.e.

$$y_j = \sum_{i=1}^{q} \beta_i x_{ji} + \varepsilon j \tag{8}$$

where x_{ji} denotes the IQM score, $j = 1, \cdots, N$ means the *j*th test image, $i = 1, \cdots, q$, the *i*th IQM, β the regression coefficients and ε a zero-mean Gaussian noise.

Once the regression coefficients have been obtained in the training phase, the discriminant function can be written as,

$$\hat{y} = \sum_{i=1}^{q} \hat{\beta}_i x_i \tag{9}$$

Noting that here only q IQMs are used, the decision rule is, if $\hat{y} \ge 0$, the image is stego, it isn't otherwise.

Based on the model, they proposed a steganalysis method of binary similarity measures exploiting the correlations between the bit-planes using their binary texture statistics [25]. Readers may refer to [25] for details.

Features as Combinations of statistics: Lots of feature extraction methods using combination of varieties of statistics have been proposed as an integrated discriminant function for this decision, especially in transformed domain, such as the result reported by Farid [26]. New features are continuingly reported for specific steganalysis [27]. Recently, Miche et al even tried to answer what is the minimum set of samples and features that make steganalytic results reliable [28].

New features are also being discovered. As far as we know, it is still an open problem, that among those features, found or being found, which is the most effective and reliable one.

3 Consistence of LSB-Based Statistical Models

For brevity, in this section only a few statistical models are considered for their consistence. Therefore, it's not complete and only for heuristics.

Fridrich et al [6] defined the 'variation' of the group of pixels as the discrimination function:

$$f(x_1, x_2, \cdots, x_n) = \sum_{i=1}^{n-1} |x_{i+1} - x_i| \tag{10}$$

Three types of pixel groups are formed according to (11):

$$\begin{cases} \text{Regular: } G \in R \leftrightarrow f(F(G)) > f(G) \\ \text{Singular: } G \in S \leftrightarrow f(F(G)) < f(G) \\ \text{Unused: } G \in U \leftrightarrow f(F(G)) = f(G) \end{cases} \tag{11}$$

Let the relative number of regular groups for mask M be R_M, and that of singular groups be S_M, we have $R_M + S_M \leq 1$ and $R_{-M} + S_{-M} \leq 1$. The statistical assumption here is:

$$R_M \cong R_{-M} \text{ and } S_M \cong S_{-M} \tag{12}$$

By analyzing the permutations F_1 and F_{-1}, it is obvious that there exists structural symmetry between them, which justifies equation (13). Based on the randomness of the secret messages, after 50% LSB replacement (reasonable for a full payload), the difference between R_M and S_M will be 0. Thus, with these three types of permutations, a RS-diagram is obtained, and the respective parabolas are estimated. If there is any hidden message, its length can be calculated.

Dumitrescu et al [7] have verified with a finite machine the above-stated statistical assumption. Actually in their sample pair analysis (SPA), similar structural features of the so-called *trace multisets* are used, i.e. random LSB flipping will alter the statistical relations between the cardinalities of trace multisets. So is chi-square test.

Therefore, Chi-square test, RS and SPA can be viewed *consistent* according to their statistical assumptions.

Similarly Zhang et al [8] proposed GPC (Gray-level Plane Crossing) using two interlaced families of odd and even gray-level planes, P_O and P_E, parallel to the image plane, each containing planes between 2i+1and 2i+2, or 2i and 2i+1, respectively, where i=0,1,⋯,127. The number of P_O and P_E crossed by all lines connecting adjacent pixels are summed up and denoted as N_O and N_E respectively. They assumed that N_O and N_E should roughly equal. While swapping between 2i and 2i+1 will increase N_E with N_O unchanged. Thus, the ratio between N_O and N_E can be discrminant function.

We point out that the ratio of N_O and N_E will roughly equal to 1 when no hidden bits embedded, simply because in relative smooth regions the variance of the local pixels can be viewed roughly as a random variable. Otherwise, this assumption may not hold.

As adding noise to image corresponds to a low-pass filtering of it, we thus argue that GPC chooses the random component of an image as a feature to detect the structural changes by observing the basic statistical model, while RS, SPA, chi-square test choose the innate structural relations to detect the random changes.

4 Comparison of Consistent Statistical Models

Consistent statistical models may act differently for varieties of cover medium. It is the structural features against the randomness of the embedded bits that make the detection effective. Therefore, we theoretically compare the difference of these methods with two kinds of cover images: one is perfect structural lines, the other random noise. The results are listed in Table 1.

Table 1. Comparison of Consistent Statistical Models

Models	Types of Images	
	Structural Lines	Random noise
Chi-square Test	effective	ineffective
RS Analysis	effective	effective
SPA Analysis	effective	effective
GPC Analysis	Partially effective	effective

5 Conclusions

There are lots of statistical models for steganalysis in literatures without being studied systematically. In this paper, we took a bird-eye-view on those models of random assumption based statistics, histogram-based statistics and feature-based statistics, in an effort to build a systematic connection among their underlying logics. Furthermore, we found that consistent statistical models may act differently depending on randomness of the cover image contents.

References

1. Provos, N., Honeyman, P.: Hide and Seek: An Introduction to Steganography. IEEE Security and Privacy 1(3), 32–44 (2003)
2. Cachin, C.: An information-theoretic model for steganography. Information and Computation 192(1), 41–56 (2004)
3. Westfeld, A., Pfitzmann, A.: Attacks on steganographic systems. In: Pfitzmann, A. (ed.) IH 1999. LNCS, vol. 1768, pp. 61–76. Springer, Heidelberg (2000)
4. `http://en.wikipedia.org/wiki/Kurtosis`
5. Westfeld, A.: Detecting low embedding rates. In: Petitcolas, F.A.P. (ed.) IH 2002. LNCS, vol. 2578, pp. 324–339. Springer, Heidelberg (2003)
6. Fridrich, J., Goljan, M., Du, R.: Reliable Detection of LSB Steganography in Grayscale and Color Images. In: Proc. ACM Workshop Multimedia Security, Ottawa, ON, Canada, pp. 25–30 (October 2001)
7. Dumitrescu, S., Wu, X., Wang, Z.: Detection of LSB steganography via sample pair analysis. IEEE Transactions on Signal Processing 51(7), 1995–2007 (2003)

8. Zhang, X., Wang, S., Zhang, K.: Steganography with Least Histogram Abnormality. In: Gorodetsky, V., Popyack, L.J., Skormin, V.A. (eds.) MMM-ACNS 2003. LNCS, vol. 2776, pp. 395–406. Springer, Heidelberg (2003)
9. Draper, S., Ishwar, P., Molnar, D., Prabhakaran, V., Ramchandran, K., Schonberg, D., Wagner, D.: An Analysis of Empirical PMF Based Tests for Least Significant Bit Image Steganography. In: Barni, M., Herrera-Joancomartí, J., Katzenbeisser, S., Pérez-González, F. (eds.) IH 2005. LNCS, vol. 3727, pp. 327–341. Springer, Heidelberg (2005)
10. Zhang, T., Ping, X.: Reliable detection of LSB steganography based on the difference image histogram. In: Proc. Of IEEE conference on Acoustics, Speech and Signal Processing (ICASSP 2003), vol. 3, pp. 545–548 (2003)
11. Li, Z., Lu, K., Zeng, X., Pan, X.: A Blind Stegananlytic Scheme Based on DCT and Spatial Domain for JPEG Images. Journal of Multimedia 5(3), 200–207 (2010)
12. Chen, X., Wang, Y., Tan, T., Guo, L.: Blind Image Steganalysis Based on Statistical Analysis of Empirical Matrix. In: Proc. Of 18th International Conference on Pattern Recognition (ICPR 2006), vol. 3, pp. 1107–1110 (August 2006)
13. Abolghasemi, M., Aghainia, H., Faez, K., Mehrabi, M.A.: Steganalysis of LSB Matching Based on Co-occurrence Matrix and Removing Most Significant Bit Planes. In: Proc. Of International Conference on Intelligent Information Hiding and Multimedia signal Processing (IIHMSP 2008), pp. 1527–1530 (August 2008)
14. Xuan, G., Shi, Y., Huang, C., Fu, D., et al.: Steganalysis Using High-Dimensional Features Derived from Co-Occurrence Matrix and Class-wise Non- Principal Components Analysis (CNPCA), `http://www.grxuan.org/english/IWDW2006163.pdf`
15. Franz, E.: Steganography Preserving Statistical Properties. In: Petitcolas, F.A.P. (ed.) IH 2002. LNCS, vol. 2578, pp. 278–294. Springer, Heidelberg (2003)
16. Provos, N.: Defending against statistical steganalysis, CITI Techreport 01-4, Center for Information Technology Integration, University of Michigan (2001)
17. Eggers, J.J., BÄauml, R., Girod, B.: A communications approach to image steganography. In: Proc. Of SPIE, Security and Watermarking of Multimedia Contents IV, San Jose, USA, vol. 4675, pp. 1–12 (January 2002), `http://www.lit.lnt.de/papers/EI2002-stego.pdf`
18. Tang, G., Liu, J.: A Secure Steganography Preserving High Order Statistics. Journal of Multimedia 5(2), 189–196 (2010)
19. Harmsen, J., Pearlman, W.A.: Steganalysis of additive noise modelable information hiding. In: Proceedings of the SPIE Security Steganography, and Watermarking of Multimedia Contents VI, vol. 5020, pp. 131–142 (2003)
20. Zhang, J., Hu, Y., Yuan, Z.: Detection of LSB Matching Steganography using the Envelope of Histogram. Journal of Computers 4(7), 646–653 (2009)
21. Mahdavi, M., Samavi, S., Zaker, N., Modares-Hashemi, M.: Steganalysis Method for LSB Replacement Based on Local Gradient of Image Histogram. Iranian Journal of Electrical and Electronic Engineering 4(3), 59–70 (2008)
22. Manjula Devi, T.H., Manjunatha Reddy, H.S., Raja Venugopal, K.B., Patnaik, L.M.: Detecting Original Image Using Histogram, DFT and SVM. International Journal of Recent Trends in Engineering 1(1), 367–371 (2009)
23. Avcibas, I., Memon, N., Sankur, B.: Steganalysis Using Image Quality Metrics. IEEE Transactions on Image Processing 12(2), 221–229 (2003)
24. Prakash Battula, B., Satya Prasad, R.: Essentials of Image Steganalysis Measures. Journal of Theoretical and Applied Information Technology 11(1), 1–9 (2010)
25. Avcibas, I., Kharrazi, M., Memon, N., Sankur, B.: Image Steganalysis with Binary Similarity Measures. EURASIP Journal on Applied Signal Processing 2005(17), 2749–2757 (2005)

26. Farid, H.: Detecting Steganographic Messages in Digital Images. TR2001-412, Dartmouth College, Computer Science, pp. 1–9 (2001), http://citeseerx.ist.psu.edu/viewdoc/summary?doi=10.1.1.2.6548
27. Barbier, J., Filiol, E., Mayoura, K.: New Features for Specific JPEG Steganalysis. International Journal of Mathematical and Computer Sciences 2(3), 119–124 (2006)
28. Miche, Y., Bas, P., Lendasse, A., Jutten, C., Simula, O.: Reliable Steganalysis Using a Minimum Set of Samples and Features. EURASIP Journal on Information Security 2009, Article ID 901381, 13 pages (2009), doi:10.1155/2009/901381

Image Resizing Based on Self-adapting Significant Map

Niu Fenghui and Li Haisheng

Dep. of Computer Science and Technology, East China Normal University,
200241 Shanghai, China
289267183@qq.com

Abstract. The image resizing methods are roughly categoriz-ed into two classes: simple scaling method and content aware resizing. The former is trivial, while the later is able to preserve visually prominent features in the resized image. The measure approach of visual saliency plays an important role in the content aware resizing method. This paper introduces a new saliency measure, self-adapting significant map, which characterizes the prominent features using gradient, saliency map and resizing ratio. Owing to taking resizing ratio into consideration, our computation approach automatically smoothes the significant map when the resizing is highly non-homogenous. Based on this computation approach, we propose a new content-based resizing method, which can reasonably preserve the important and less-important regions according to the resizing ratio. Experimental results show that our method outperforms the similar resizing method when the resizing ratio is bigger.

Keywords: image resizing, self-adapting significant map, prominent feature, resizing ratio.

1 Introduction

The display devices of mobile phones, televisions and computers etc. usually have different aspect ratios. To fit different layout, an image needs to be resized, and the resizing is non-homogeneous when the aspect ratios are different between the source and the target. Simple methods such as scaling and cropping can output resizing result in real time, but they do not provide satisfactory results since they only consider the geometric constraints of the output display. Scaling inevitably causes distortion when the aspect ratio of input image differs from that of the output. Cropping method simply discards unimportant regions to change aspect ratio and easily produces visual artifacts. Therefore, many researchers put more interests in the image resizing with less distortion, and have developed several resizing methods such as seam carving [1, 2] and image warping [3, 4, 5, 6].

Seam carving is a discrete scaling method that supports content-aware image resizing. This method changes the aspect ratio of an image by repeatedly carving out or inserting seams in one direction. As the authors point out, this method failed in processing the image with dense important content or content layout manner that prevents the seams from bypassing important parts. In these cases, this approach often causes noticeable zigzag effect. Image warping supplies a continuous solution for

D. Zeng (Ed.): ICAIC 2011, Part I, CCIS 224, pp. 672–681, 2011.

content-aware resizing. The main idea is to keep the important regions untouched while transferring the distortion to less-important regions. However, the warping method only contributes the distortion along the resizing direction. Consequently, when the width of the important regions is larger than the target size, it would cause evident distortion.

Recently, Wang et al. proposed an optimized scale-and-stretch warping method for image resizing based on mesh parameterization [4]. The warping method takes advantage of local scaling, and can resize an image into arbitrary aspect ratio while preserving prominent regions. However, when the resizing ratio, the ratio of maximum to the minimum between the input aspect ratio and the output, is much bigger, the unimportant regions may be contracted into a line or even a point. This direct cropping leads to discontinuities, as shown in Fig. 1(g). In order to overcome this flaw, we develop a new method for computing the significant map by introducing a stretching function with respect to resizing ratio. This algorithm efficiently smoothes the significant map while the resizing ratio increases, hence avoids cropping result as far as possible. Since the significant map automatically varies with the resizing ratio, we call it self-adapting significant map.

2 Warp-Based Image Resizing

Image warping views the image as a continuous domain and takes the image content into consideration while constructing a continuous geometric deformation As this method takes the image saliency map as weighting of deformation function, it is able to preserve the shape of the salient parts by pushing distortion into regions of less importance. Unlike seam carving, continuous warping redistributes the density of image content instead of removing it, and thus avoids discontinuity artifacts. Among many warping methods, Wang's method [4] is a better one. This method distributes the distortion in all spatial directions, thus fully utilizing the available homogeneous regions to absorb the distortion. The main disadvantage of Wang's method is excessive cropping of unimportant regions. Here, we attempt to figure out this problem by introducing a new saliency measure, and improve performance of warping method.

2.1 Self-adapting Significant Map

In general, content aware warping method is divided into two phases: prominent feature computation and content-based warping. The phase one is the basis of phase two. Gradient, saliency map or the combination of them is usually used to describe prominent features of an image.

Both Avidan and Shamir [1] and Wolf et al. [3] consider pixels with large gradient magnitudes as important. Nevertheless, this method maybe fails when the regions are homogenous but attractive to the human eyes. The majority of prior resizing algorithms employ Itti and Koch [7] to generate their saliency maps based on a heuristic model of low-level human vision. In this paper, we use this visual attention model to determine the saliency map.

Wang et al. [4] have observed that only these regions that are both attractive to the human eyes and contain structured objects should be considered as importance and be protected against distortion. So Wang et al. add structure information into the significant map by combining the gradient with saliency map.

However, when the resizing ratio very large, the resizing algorithm based on this significant map may contract a quad into a line or even a point, therefore resulting in serious distortion, as illustrated in Fig. 1(g). This defect is due to the large value difference between the important and unimportant regions, so that the least important parts are removed. Accordingly, it is necessary to reasonably shorten the distance between the maximum and the minimum in the significant map. We apply an optimally stretching function to pre-process the gradient and saliency map, and then multiply them to generate the significant map that varies with resizing ratio. For clear statement, we introduce some notations as follows.

Denote the four corner points of the input image by A, B, C and D sequentially along the clockwise direction, and let their corresponding points of the output image be A', B', C' and D' individually. Suppose r be the resizing ratio, and then its one formula is

$$r = \max\left(\frac{\|A'B'\|}{\|AB\|}, \frac{\|B'C'\|}{\|BC\|}\right) / \min\left(\frac{\|A'B'\|}{\|AB\|}, \frac{\|B'C'\|}{\|BC\|}\right) \tag{1}$$

Thereafter, the stretching functions of the gradient and saliency map are respectively defined as

$$\begin{aligned} M'_{gradient} &= \frac{255 - a \times r^n}{255} \times M_{gradient} + a \times r^n \\ M'_{saliency} &= \frac{255 - a \times r^n}{255} \times M_{saliency} + a \times r^n \end{aligned} \tag{2}$$

Where a is an integer less than 20, $M_{gradient}$ is the gradient map and $M_{saliency}$ is the saliency map, and n is a positive number that highlights the importance of resizing ratio.

After the pre-processing, the range of the map is changed from [0 , 255] to $[a \times r^n, 255]$. Finally, we normalize the pre-processed gradient and saliency map, which are separately denoted by $NM'_{gradient}$ and $NM'_{saliency}$. Let $SM_{significant}$ be the self-adapting significant map, and then define

$$SM_{significant} = NM'_{gradient} \times NM'_{saliency} \tag{3}$$

Fig. 1 gives the significant map and our self-adapting significant map of an image with obvious prominent features, and corresponding resized results. (e) and (f) show our smoothing operator effectively diminishes the difference of the significant value. Since the excessive removal of unimportant regions affected the important regions around them, the mouth of the duck is removed when the significant map is not smoothed. Compared with previous significant map, this smoothing operation produces more satisfactory result when the resizing ratio is bigger.

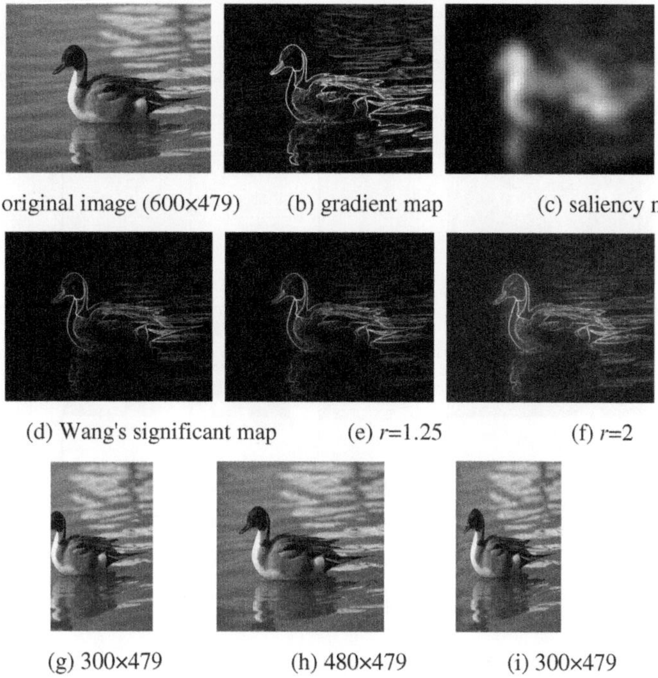

Fig. 1. We get the self-adapting significant map with a=10 and n=3. (d) The original significant map. (e) The self-adapting significant map with r=1.25. (f) The self-adapting significant map with r=2. (g), (h) and (i) The resized results corresponding to self-adapting significant map individually.

To get the optimal transformation, we tested several combinations of a and n on images which uniformly or dominantly layouts prominent features, shortly as uniform feature image or dominant feature image.

Through many experiments, we find that when the important regions are distributed non-uniformly we should assign a bigger value to a, as shown in Fig. 2(a). On the contrary, if important regions are concentrated and proportionally distributed, these two parameters less impact on the results. In general, the ideal parameters are $a = 10$ and $n = 2$.

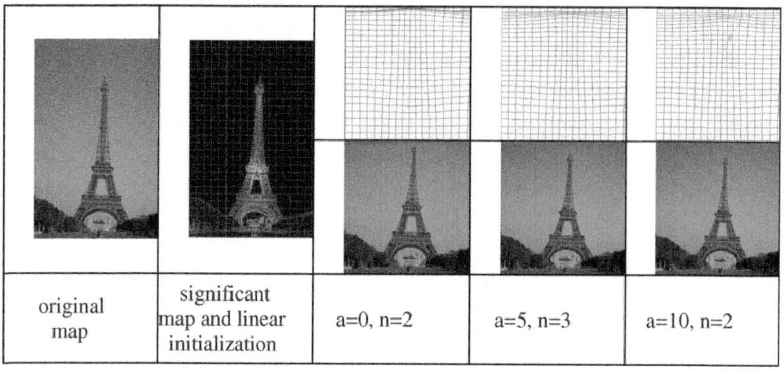

(a) Dominant feature image

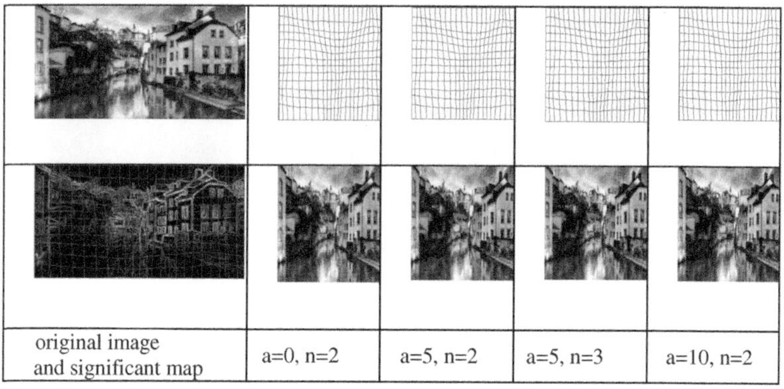

(b) Uniform feature image

Fig. 2. Resized results with different a and n

2.2 Warping Energy Function

The main idea of the algorithm is that important regions should undergo smaller distortion than less-important ones. The image is divided into several quads, and represented as $M = (V, E, F)$, with vertices V ,edges E ,quad faces F , where $V = [v_0, v_1, \ldots, v_n]$ and $v_i \in R^2$ denote the initial vertices positions. The purpose is to find the optimal deformed mesh $V' = [v_0', v_1', \ldots, v_n']$, so as to minimize total distortion energy of the image determined by the distance between the origin and resized vertices.

1) Linear initialization

The simplest method to initialize the mesh is linear initialization, just as $(x, y) \to (ax, by)$. However, it doesn't consider the image content, so the convergence speed and resized result of structure images are generally not ideal.

2) Significant-aware initialization

To enjoy the regular structure, we use the basic idea which is to attract more vertices to the important regions, just as Fig. 2(b). The objective function to achieve the adaptive meshes is

$D_{aware} = \sum_{f\in F}(1+w_i)\left\|v_i^{'}-v_j^{'}\right\|^2$, where w_i is the average of pixel significance of all quads sharing the edge v_iv_j.

3) Shape distortion energy

We formulate the shape distortion energy for each quad-mesh by measuring the distance between the deformed and the original quad-mesh. Ideally, for each $f\in F$ there would be a scale factor s_f such that for each vertex v of the quad, $v^{'}=s_f v+t$, so the distortion energy of f is defined as

$$D_{quad}(f)=\sum_{\{i,j\}\in E(f)}\left\|(v_i^{'}-v_j^{'})-s_f(v_i-v_j)\right\|^2 \quad (4)$$

And then the total distortion energy is defined as the weighting sum of each quad-mesh and its significance weight.

$$D_{quad}=\sum_{f\in F}w_f D_{quad}(f) \quad (5)$$

In most of times, the important regions usually span several quads and the scaling factors are often unequal. To keep the shape of important object similar, we should reduce the difference of the adjacent scaling factors by minimizing the following smooth function. Let us denote the adjacent quads of f by $N(f)$ and the average of all the quad significance values by w_g. Then the smooth function is

$$\sum_{f\in F}\sum_{q\in N(f)}\frac{1}{2}(w_f+w_q)(s_f^{'}-s_q^{'})^2+\sum_{f\in F}w_g(s_f^{'}-s_f) \quad (6)$$

4) Grid line bending energy

Since important objects usually pass through several adjacent quads, we should restrict the bending of the grid lines to prevent their distortion. By preventing the grid lines from serious bending, we can alleviate the flipping problem effectively. We define the length ratios as $l_{ij}=\left\|v_i^{'}-v_j^{'}\right\|/\left\|v_i-v_j\right\|$, and the grid line bending energy is

$$D_{line}=\sum_{\{i,j\}\in E}\left\|(v_i^{'}-v_j^{'})-l_{ij}(v_i-v_j)\right\|^2 \quad (7)$$

Finally, the total warping energy between the original and resized image is defined as

$$D_{total}=D_{quad}+D_{line} \quad (8)$$

5) Boundary conditions

Obviously, the boundary of the target image is fixed, so the warping energy function is subject to the following boundary constrains.

$$\begin{cases} v'_{i,y} = v_{A,y} & v_i \text{ is on the AB boundary} \\ v'_{i,y} = v_{C,y} & v_i \text{ is on the CD boundary} \\ v'_{i,x} = v_{D,x} & v_i \text{ is on the AD boundary} \\ v'_{i,x} = v_{B,x} & v_i \text{ is on the BC boundary} \end{cases} \tag{9}$$

It is difficult to accurately find the nonlinear warping function, so we solve it using iterative method, and in each iterative step, the new vertices are solved by minimizing the distortion energy function. By this, we can cast the problem of obtaining the optimal results between the original and resized image as sparse linear equations on the vertices of x' or y'. The linear equations have the following form.

$$\begin{cases} a_{11}x'_1 + a_{12}x'_2 + \cdots + a_{1n}x'_n = b_1 \\ a_{21}x'_1 + a_{22}x'_2 + \cdots + a_{2n}x'_n = b_2 \\ \vdots \\ a_{n1}x'_1 + a_{n2}x'_2 + \cdots + a_{nn}x'_n = b_n \end{cases} \tag{10}$$

Linear equations on y'_i are the same as x'_i. a_{ij} is decided by the weight of its adjacent quads, and b_i is decided by w_i, sf_i, l_{ij} and v_i.

3 Results and Discussions

We use VC++ to implement our algorithm on a computer with 2.00GHz Core Duo CPU and 1G RAM. Our approach is very efficient and the main computational cost is to solve the sparse linear equations proportional to the number of vertices. In our experiments, the quad size is 20×20 pixels, and the number of iterations is about 10.

3.1 Comparison

Several examples are provided to show our algorithm is effective and better than the previous methods. In Fig. 3, we compare the resized results of simple scaling, seam carving, Wang's method and our method, it can be observed that uniform scaling method inevitably cause serious distortion when undergo non-uniform scaling, while seam carving produces noticeable zigzag on structure objects such as the Eiffel tower and China Pavilion. Wang's method highly curved the gray line between the pavilion and road ((d) bottom), and excessively cut the trees beside the Eiffel tower ((d) top). Our method is able to keep the straight line intact and reasonably preserve less important regions so as to obtain better resized result. Compared with previous methods, our method can diffuse the distortion into less important regions in all spatial directions and the shapes of important objects are well preserved.

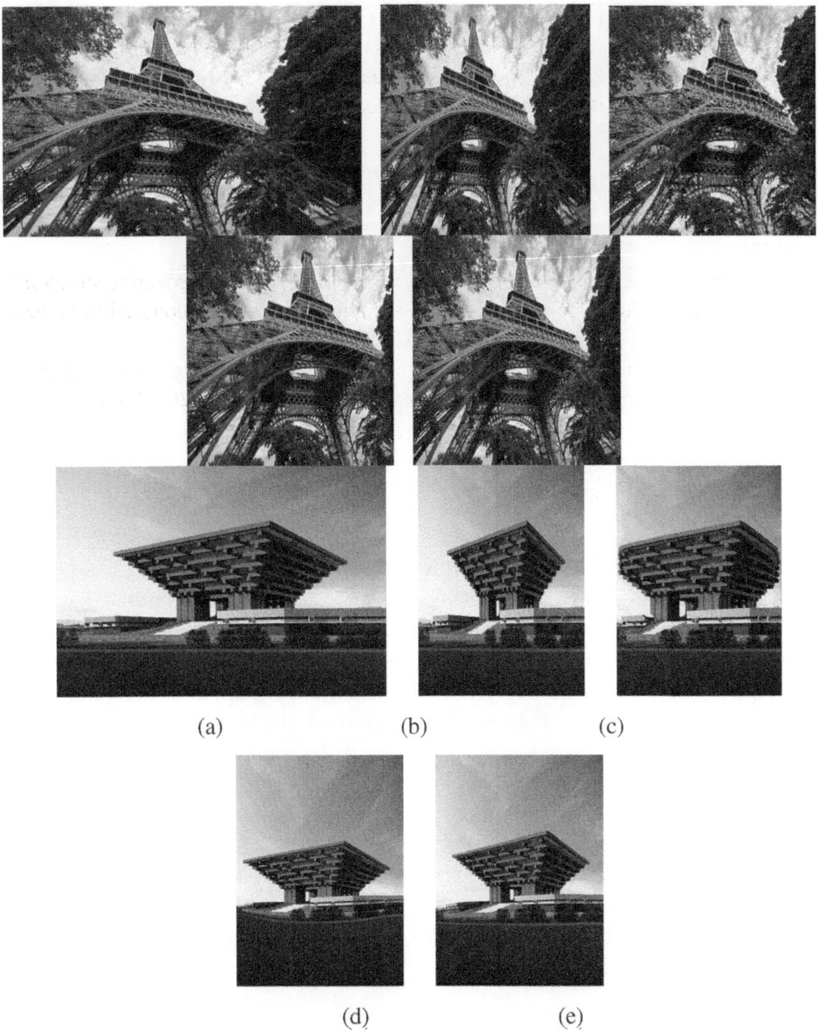

Fig. 3. Experimental results and the comparison with scaling, seam carving and Wang's method. (a) Original image. (b) Scaling method. (c) Seam carving. (d) Wang's method. (e) Result of our method. From the result we can find that our method can reasonably preserve the important and less-important regions with big aspect ratio.

3.2 Limitations

As the distortion amount of each quad is determined by its weight based on the significant map, the result is sensitive to the quality of the significant map. When the significant is poor, the resizing result will not satisfy us. Besides, local self-intersections may occur when having a large aspect ratio resizing, but fortunately, it rarely occurs by using the self-adapting significant map.

Fig. 4. Resized results with different resizing ratio by using our method

4 Conclusion and Future Work

We propose a new image resizing method based on self-adapting significant map, an intelligent description on prominent features. The self-adapting significant map is computed by optimally stretching gradient and saliency map, and it can automatically adjust weighting differences between less-important and important regions according to the resizing ratio. Compared with previous similar methods, our method can have a reasonable reserve on important and less-important regions according to the aspect ratio, and keep object's boundary intact due to the smooth of significant map between important and less important parts.

Future research will focus on extending this approach to video resizing and irregular shape display. It is necessary to design self-adapting significant map considering temporal coherence. Besides, the improvement on the efficiency and quality is another study direction.

References

1. Avidan, S., Shamir, A.: Seam carving for content-aware image resizing. ACM Trans. Graphics 26(3) (2007)
2. Rubinsrein, M., Shamir, A., Avdian, S.: Improved seam carving for video retargeting. ACM Trans. Graphics 27(3) (2008)
3. Wolf, L., Guttmann, M., Cohen-or, D.: Nonhomogeneous content-driven video-retargeting. In: Proceedings of IEEE ICCV (2007)
4. Wang, Y.-S., Tai, C.-L., Sorkine, O., Lee, T.-Y.: Optimized scale-and-stretch for image resizing. ACM Trans on Graphics 27(5), 1–8 (2008)
5. Guo, Y., Liu, F., Shi, J., Zhou, Z., Gleicher, M.: Image retargeting using mesh parameterization. IEEE Trans. on Multimedia 11(5), 856–867 (2009)
6. Zhang, G., Cheng, M., Hu, S., Martin, R.: A shape-preserving approach to image resizing. Pacific Graphics 28(7), 1897–1906 (2009)

7. Itti, L., Koth, C., Niebur, E.: A model of saliency-based visual attention for rapid scene analysis. IEEE Trans. Pattern Analysis and Machine Intelligence 20(11), 1254–1259 (1998)
8. Chen, L.-Q., Xie, X., Fan, X., Ma, W.-Y., Zhang, H.-J., Zhou, H.-Q.: A visual attention model for adapting images on small displays. Multimedia Systems 9(4), 353–364 (2003)
9. Kraevoy, V., Sheffer, A., Shamir, A., Cohen-or, D.: Non-homogeneous resizing of complex models. ACM Trans. on Graphics 27(5), 1–9 (2008)
10. Shi, J., Guo, Y.-W., Du, Z.-L., Zhang, F.-Y., Peng, Q.-S.: A mesh parameterization-based image retargeting method. Journal of Software 19, 19–30 (2008)
11. Igarashi, T., Moscovich, T., Hughes, J.-F.: As-rigid-as-possible shape manipulation. ACM Trans. Graphics 24(3) (2005)
12. Fang, H., Hart, J.-C.: Detail preserving shape deformation in image editing. ACM Trans. Graphics 26(3), 12 (2007)

Research on Intelligence Decision-Making Analysis and Optimization Design Development of Pavement Management System

Dai Xue-zhen, Xing Lei, and Zhang Bo

Key Laboratory for Special Area Highway Engineering of Ministry of Education, Chang'an University
Xi'an Shaanxi 710064, China
Xuezhen_xa@163.com

Abstract. The present research, based on system engineering, information engineering technology, applied mathematics, and the theories and methodology of safety predicative assessment, carried out a thorough and in-depth research into the intelligence decision-making and analysis for optimization design development of road surface maintenance system from the aspects of data support, road performance assessment and optimization and selection scheme for maintenance decision-making and strategies. In addition, the optimization algorithm is provided for data categorization and sifting as well as the division of storage units. Then, an optimization model is constructed based on the load bearing capacity of road structures, road quality for driving, road safety for driving together with road surface damage. At last, based on multi-model predications and the correlation analysis for predicative concepts of decision-making flow for road surface performance, the PPM optimization model is constructed for protective maintenance modules for road surface and the mathematical model and method are offered for the optimization and selection of strategic schemes.

Keywords: Pavement Management System, Model Optimization, Optimization Algorithm, Strategy Optimization and Selection.

1 Introduction

With the rapid development of highway construction, the traffic mileage of high-grade highway is on the continuous increase. Therefore, how to capitalize on the limited capital to maintain the satisfactory service standards and traffic capacity and how to process a large amount of complex information all request a systematic, scientific method to coordinate and control activities pertinent to highway traffic, so as to guarantee a holistic and objective assessment of road surface conditions, to maintain the accurate and stable predictions for highway utilization, to optimize the formulation of counter-strategies, and to bring the benefits of resources into full swing. These aims are the major research contents of the intelligence decision-making and analysis for the optimization design development of road surface maintenance management system.

D. Zeng (Ed.): ICAIC 2011, Part I, CCIS 224, pp. 682–690, 2011.

2 Optimization Construction of Intelligence Decision-Making and Analytic Supportive Data

Supportive data are the basis of assessment, prediction and decision-making, the reasonability of which has a direct impact on the structures of highway use assessment and predictions, hence the great influence on the accuracy and stability of the maintenance decision-making. Therefore, a complete algorithm for data sifting and categorization shall be worked out for the highway surface management system, so as to facilitate the rationalized sifting, selection and the particular categorization of storage units for the data resulting from the assessment and prediction of road surface conditions as well as scheme formulation and optimization. By these efforts, the integrity and objectivity of the assessment of road surface conditions can be ensured, together with the correctness and stableness of the prediction for its use performance.

The following figure is an illustration of the optimization algorithm for data sifting, categorization and division of storage units.

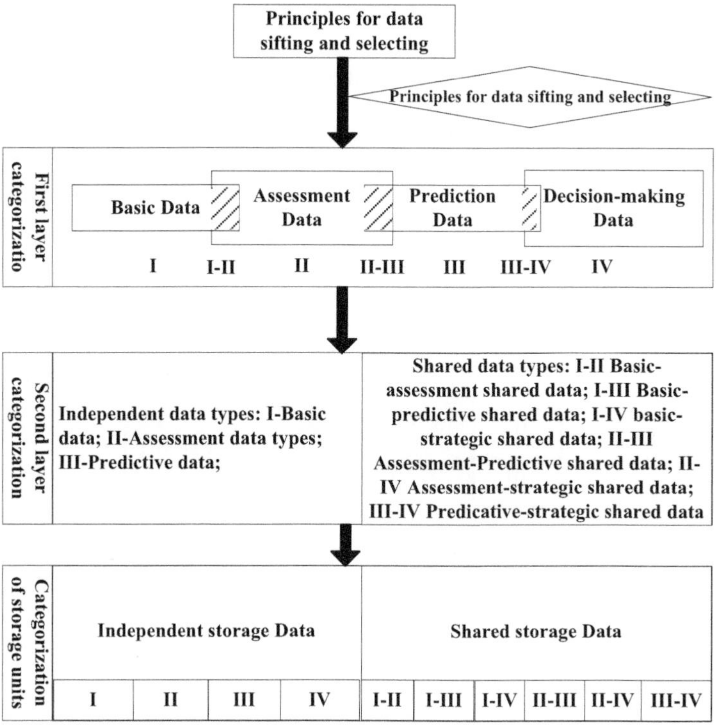

Fig. 1. Optimization Algorithm for Data Sifting, Categorization and Division of Storage Units

2.1 Construction of Storage Data

The storage data shall be the initial sifting and selecting data, which shall guarantee the integrity and accuracy of the data as well as the periodical updating of partial data.

Such data include: The basic data for road surface (road route, road surface, roadbed, construction structures for bridges and tunnels, and the facilities along the route), detecting data for road surface (PCI damage, RQI evenness, RDI tracks, PSSI deflection, SRI lateral force), road surface structure, weather conditions, traffic capacity, maintenance standards and so on.

2.2 Principles for Data Sifting and Selection

The reasonable sifting and selection of data is a key step for their afterward utilization, which is mainly categorized based on the two principles such as the actual data categories and logic types.

The first one is Actual Data Categories. Data, according to their actual types, have been categorized into: Basic data, assessment data, predicative data, and decision-making data, which lay a foundation for the assessment of road surface management system and the future optimization of the algorithm for the predicative models.

The second one is Logic Types. The logics and types of data can be mainly applied to characterize the logic relations between the individual data types. By logic types, data are categorized into independent data and shared data.

2.3 Data Categorization and Division of Storage Units

Firstly, the basic type, assessment data, predicative data, decision-making data and independent data are characterized by I, II, III, and IV respectively while the shared data by I-II, I-III, I-IV, II-III, II-IV, and III-IV respectively. The logical relations between the data types are illustrated by the following matrix.

	I	II	III	IV
I				
II				
III				
IV				

During the process of data categorization and storage, besides the actual types for individual storage, logic management shall also be made referenced to and be provided with particular storage units, so as to offer support to the dynamic updating of data. As the figure illustrates, the gray areas are the particular storage units for the shared data type while the rest areas the particular storage units for the independent data type.

3 Optimization Module Design for Road Surface Performance

Assessment, according to the categorization indicators and certain principles and methods, is meant to comment on the poor and good conditions from one, many or whole aspect. The assessment of road utilization performance, based on the individual storage data and shared storage data of the assessment type in the database of the system, is to judge the suitability degree for utilization needs so as to understand the service capacity and offer support for decision-making maintenance strategies. Therefore, the assessment process is a systematic project.

The assessment of optimization module design for road surface performance is summarized in the following figure.

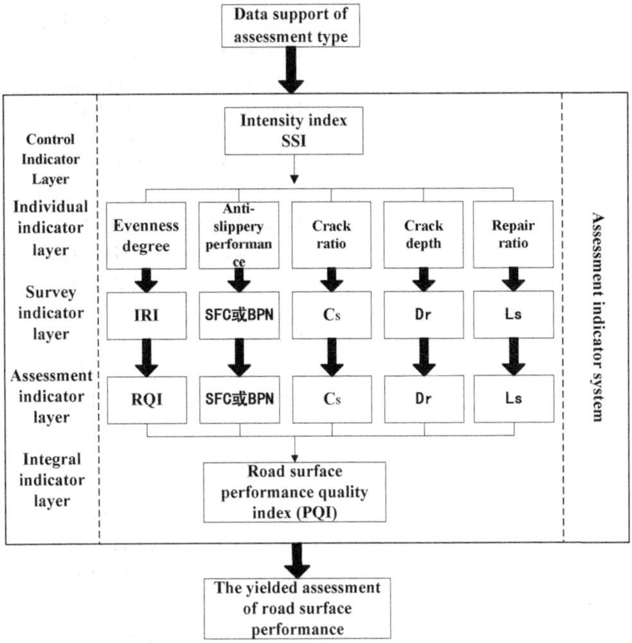

Fig. 2. Road Performance Assessment Optimization Model

3.1 Configuration of Assessment Indicator System

In order to guarantee the good conditions of road surface as well as its excellent service capacity, the corresponding assessment system shall be established for load-bearing capacity, driving quality, and driving safety of the road surface together with surface damage degree.

3.2 Individual and Integral Assessment Indicators

During the actual wearing and tearing process, different degrees of surface deterioration will appear in different sections. Thus, in order to satisfy the use purposes for different degrees, the individual assessment shall be administered to road surface performance. On the other hand, the maintainers and administrators also need an integral assessment of the road performance so as to holistically reflect the general road conditions. At the same time, the integral assessment can provide decision-making support for maintenance strategies. The integral indicators are formulated by the individual ones arranged according to certain methods. The arrangement methods include substitution method, addition method, multiplication method, blending method and vector method.

4 Optimization and Construction of Road Preventive Maintenance Module (PPM)

The optimization and construction of road preventive maintenance module are illustrated in the following figure:

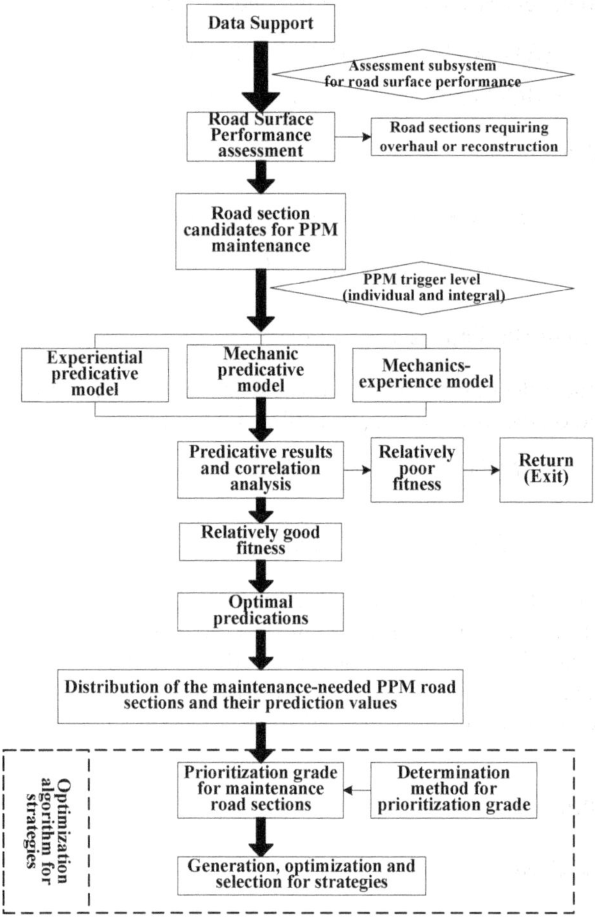

Fig. 3. Road Preventive Maintenance PPM Optimization Module

4.1 PPM Trigger Level (Individual and Integral)

The major guidelines for the obtainment of PPM trigger level are: Mechanism research into road surface diseases, preventive maintenance characteristics and road surface assessment systems, including the trigger values of both individual and integral indicators. During the actual application process, different judging processes shall be accorded to the two stages:

Firstly, initial preventive maintenance implementation stage: With full consideration of the special individual indicator (e.g., surface structural strength indicator (SSI)), the judging process of multi-disease comprehensive assessment with light, medium, and heavy degree and that of maintenance trigger threshold values shall be determined based on the method of fuzzy clustering.

Secondly, as the preventive maintenance has been implemented and certain experience been accumulated, the maintenance administration is able to spot and address, in time, diseases. Then, the preventive maintenance shall be determined and implemented based on both the decision tree of preventive maintenance established by individual detecting indicators and the decision flow formed by the relevant trigger threshold values.

4.2 Selection of Predicative Models

In the establishment of the predicative model for road surface performance, firstly, road networks shall be classified according to the factors influencing road conditions. Then, the predicative models shall be established for different road sections. Common modeling methods include experiential method, mechanic method and mechanic experiential method. And the models thus determined are mainly determinacy model and probability model. The utilization of either model shall satisfy the following conditions:

Firstly, the model is able to reflect the varying tendency of road surface performance.

Secondly, the model curve shall be monotone decreasing.

Thirdly, the model shall satisfy the relevant boundary conditions.

Fourthly, the model is simple in form and easy for program development and application.

4.3 Correlation Analysis of Multi-model Predicative Model and Predicative Results

The actual application demonstrates that unitary predicative model for road surface maintenance management system has both poor accuracy and stability and lacks effective contrast in predicative results. However, the adoption of multi-model predicative model and the establishment of a set of "Correlation analysis mechanism" together with the corresponding decision-making flow can lead to "Optimal predications", which can effectively raise the accuracy and stability provided by the predicative model in terms of the varying tendency of road conditions.

5 Optimization Algorithm for Countermeasure Plan

Certain kinds of diseases with different degrees can appear during the utilization process of road surface. However, due to the limited repair capital, prioritization shall be accorded to different road sections needing repair and maintenance. The development of road surface management system, while providing decision-making support for administrators, shall optimize and select the maintenance plans, so as to guarantee the effectiveness and stableness of decision-making and, at the same time, to effectively reduce the maintenance costs and to optimize the benefit of resources. Here, an algorithm is provided for the optimization and selection of countermeasure plans.

5.1 Basic Hypothesis

During the decision-making process for maintenance, firstly, there are m kinds of road surface maintenance plans, characterized by $\alpha_1, \alpha_2, , \alpha_n)$.

Secondly, set n kinds of indicators for road surface performance, characterized by $\beta_1, \beta_2, , \beta_n)$.

Thirdly, the α maintenance plan satisfies the degree of β_j performance indicator, characterized by γ_{ij} .

Fourthly, the matrix of poor and good coefficients for m kinds road surface maintenance plans is characterized by $F_{m\times n}$;

Fifthly, the matrix of comprehensive poor and good coefficients for m kinds of road surface maintenance plans is characterized by $F_{z(1\times n)}$, among which the comprehensive coefficient is F_{zi} .

Lastly, the matrix of importance degree (subordination relation) for n kinds of performance indicators $\beta_1, \beta_2, , \beta_n)$ is characterized by $W_{1\times n}$.

5.2 Detailed Arithmetic Judging Process

Based on the above-mentioned basic hypotheses, the following matrix can be worked out:

$$
\begin{array}{c} \\ \alpha_1 \\ \alpha_2 \\ \alpha_3 \\ \cdots \\ \alpha_m \end{array}
\begin{array}{c}
\begin{array}{ccccc} \beta_1 & \beta_2 & \beta_3 & \cdots & \beta_n \end{array} \\
\begin{bmatrix}
\gamma_{11} & \gamma_{12} & \gamma_{13} & \cdots & \gamma_{1n} \\
\gamma_{21} & \gamma_{22} & \gamma_{23} & \cdots & \gamma_{2m} \\
\gamma_{31} & \gamma_{32} & \gamma_{33} & \cdots & \gamma_{3m} \\
\cdots & \cdots & \cdots & \cdots & \cdots \\
\gamma_{m1} & \gamma_{m2} & \gamma_{m3} & \cdots & \gamma_{mn}
\end{bmatrix}
\end{array}
$$

As a result, the matrix of poor and good indicators, can be worked out based on, according to experts' experience, the typical strategies of road surface maintenance for the feasibility of all use performance as well as the results of subordination functions of different grading. The good and poor relations between different plans mean that: If, this means that, based on the improvement of road surface performance, the maintenance plan is better than the plan.

The matrix of importance degree (subordination relations) for kinds of performance indicators, with the application of scaling developing method [10], can lead to the corresponding distribution values of the subordination relations and the detailed weighting. As a result, by means of the following formula, the matrix of comprehensive good and poor coefficients can be worked out.

$$F_{z(1\times n)} = W_{1\times m} \cdot F_{m\times n} . \tag{1}$$

To sum up, the corresponding good and poor coefficients for different maintenance plans can be obtained; that is, the corresponding plan α_i for $F_{zi(\max)}$ is the best plan.

During the actual application process, the predicative performance model and cost-benefit analysis model shall be established for every optimized maintenance measure, so as to provide better support for decision-making maintenance strategies.

6 Conclusions

In order to ensure the integrity and objectivity of road surface performance assessment, to rationalize and optimize the accuracy of performance prediction and the stability of measure formulation, to effectively reduce the maintenance cost, and to optimize the benefit of resources, the optimization of intelligence decision-making modules for development of road surface maintenance management system can be carried out from the following perspectives:

Firstly, an algorithm for data sifting and categorization shall be established for the road surface management system in order to assess and predict the road surface conditions and to reasonably sift and categorize the generated strategies and the optimized data, and to set special storage units for them.

Secondly, the assessment of road utilization performance is guided by the independent and shared storage data of the assessment type in the database. Its aim is to judge the suitability for use so as to understand the service capacity and to provide support for decision-making maintenance strategies. In order to guarantee the good conditions of road surface as well as its excellent service capacity, the corresponding assessment system shall be established for load bearing capacity, driving quality, and driving safety of the road surface together with surface damage degree.

Thirdly, based on the multi-model predications and the correlation analysis of decision-making flow for the road surface use performance, the optimized PPM model is established for the preventive maintenance for road surface.

Lastly, the development of road surface management system, while providing decision-making support for administrators, shall optimize and select the maintenance plans. At the same time, based on the implementation of preventive maintenance measures and the accumulated rich data, the predicative performance model and cost-benefit analysis model shall be established for every optimized maintaining measure, so as to provide better support for decision-making maintenance strategies.

References

1. Pan, Y.-l.: Road Management System Theory: a Monograph, pp. 120–354. Renmin Communication Press, Beijing (1998) (in Chinese)
2. Dong, R.-k.: Reserch on Timing of Asphalt Road Maintenance: a Doctoral Dissertation, pp. 56–78. Tongji University (2005) (in Chinese)

3. Shen, J.-a.: The Analysis of Asphalt Road Early Damage and Countermeasures: a Monograph, pp. 213–240. Renmin Communication Press, Beijing (2004) (in Chinese)
4. Yao, H.-n.: Freeway Road Management System Based on Preventive Maintenance: a Doctoral Dissertation, Chang'an University, pp. 36–48 (2008) (in Chinese)
5. Song, D.-d.: Research on Establishing the Present Service ability Index and Predictive Model: a Doctoral Dissertation,Tongji University, pp. 46–78 (2008) (in Chinese)
6. Dai, X.-z., Xing, L.: Consideration and Suggestion about Bridge Management System Software Development structure in China: a case study. Journal of China & Foreign Highway (2008) (in Chinese)
7. Zhong, H.-l.: The Designing Idea of Guangdong Provincial Expressway database system a case study. Journal of South China University of Technology (2000) (in Chinese)
8. Dai, X.-z.: The Research of Highway Tunnel Operation Safety Evaluation and Management System : a Doctoral Dissertation, Chang'an University, pp. 78–96 (2010) (in Chinese)

Laplacian Maximum Scatter Difference Discriminant Criterion

Jun Gao[1] and Lili Xiang[2]

[1] The School of Information Engineering, Yancheng Institute of Technology
Yancheng, Jiangsu Province China
[2] The School of Humanity,Yancheng Institute of Technology
Yancheng, Jiangsu Province China
jungao65@yahoo.cn

Abstract. Linear Laplacian Discrimination (LLD) as a non-linear feature extraction method has obtained very extensive applications. However, LDD suffers from the small sample size problem (SSS) and/or the type of the sample space when it is used. In order to circumvent such shortcomings, in this paper a Laplacian Maximum Scatter Difference Discriminant Criterion (LMSDC) is proposed by using new contextual-distance metric and integrating maximum scatter difference discriminant criterion(MSDC) into LDD. The proposed criterion can obviously decrease the dependence on the sample space and solve small sample size problem. The experimental results indicate the above advantages of the proposed method LMSDC.

Keywords: linear Laplacian discrimination, contextual-distance metric, maximum scatter difference discriminant criterion, samll sample size problem.

1 Introduction

Feature extraction as an effective method of dimension reduction has achieved success in pattern recognition, computer vision and data mining. Recently, two major methods, Principal Component Analysis (PCA) [1] and Linear Discrimination Analysis (LDA) [2], are widely used and studied. Particularly, Zhao and his colleagues proposed a novel method of feature extraction on the basis of LE[3]、LPP[4] and LDA: Linear Laplacian Discrimination (LLD)[5]. LLD, a nonlinear method of feature extracting, lowers the degree of dependence of distance metric on original sample space by weighting the within-class scatter and the between-class scatter respectively, thus upgrading the capability of the feature extraction methods to generalize. However, LLD still requires finding an appropriate distance metric according to the corresponding data space type, but it does not show how to define the type of original sample space. Also, it has the problem of small sample size. In recent years, Contextual-distance Metric as a novel distance metric has been applied successfully[6-9]. In fact, the contextual distance reflects the dissimilarity between samples rather than the true distance between them, that is, the reveal of the degree of samples' contribution to the structure of data clusters, thus showing that contextual-distance metrics are more universal.

D. Zeng (Ed.): ICAIC 2011, Part I, CCIS 224, pp. 691–697, 2011.

Therefore, on the basis of LLD, the Laplacian Maximum Scatter Difference Discriminant Criterion (LMSDC) is proposed, which has the following advantages: (1) Not only does LMSDC inherit the nonlinear feature extracting capability of LLD but also can deal with the small size sample problem; (2) It upgrades the generalizing capability of feature extraction since it uses contextual-distance metrics, which makes LMSDC relatively independent of the space type of input space; (3) By using new form of contextual distance, it has greater adaptability when vectors are used to represent high dimensional data.

2 Laplacian Maximum Scatter Difference Discriminant Criterion: LMSDC

Let M^D denote an input sample space with D dimensions. It has sample sets $\mathbf{X}=[\mathbf{x}_1,\cdots,\mathbf{x}_n]$ with n samples, which is divided into c classes in which the class $s=1,\cdots,c$ is $\mathbf{X}_s=[\mathbf{x}_1^s,\cdots,\mathbf{x}_{c_s}^s]$, thus getting the within-class scatter α and between-class scatter β integrating the contextual-distance metrics of the LMSDC as follows:

$$\alpha=\sum_{s=1}^{c}\alpha_s=\sum_{s=1}^{c}\sum_{i=1}^{c_s}\omega_i^s\left\|\mathbf{y}_i^s-\bar{\mathbf{y}}^s\right\|= \\ \sum_{s=1}^{c}\sum_{i=1}^{c_s}\mathbf{exp}(-\frac{p(\mathbf{x}_i^s\to\bar{\mathbf{x}}^s)^2}{\sigma_w})\left\|\mathbf{y}_i^s-\bar{\mathbf{y}}^s\right\|=\mathbf{U}^T\mathbf{H}_w\mathbf{U} \tag{1}$$

$$\beta=\sum_{s=1}^{c}\omega^s\left\|\bar{\mathbf{y}}^s-\bar{\mathbf{y}}\right\|= \\ \sum_{s=1}^{c}\mathbf{exp}(-\frac{p(\bar{\mathbf{x}}^s\to\bar{\mathbf{x}})^2}{\sigma_b})\left\|\bar{\mathbf{y}}^s-\bar{\mathbf{y}}\right\|=\mathbf{U}^T\mathbf{H}_b\mathbf{U} \tag{2}$$

Note that in the above definition though the same symbols in LLD are used, their contents and intuative meaning are obviously different since the contextual-distance metrics $p(\mathbf{x}_i\to\mathbf{x}_j)$ is used in LMSDC. How to define the contextual-distance metrics in the equations (1) and (2) is to be discussed in Section 3.

Therefore, according to the defined within- class and between-class scatters in the equations (1) and (2), the discriminant method of LMSDC can be gotten:

Definition 1: $\gamma\in[0,1]$ is a parameter, we get LMSDC discriminant criterion:

$$\underset{\mathbf{U}^T\mathbf{U}=\mathbf{I}_d}{\mathbf{arg\,max}}\,J(\mathbf{U})=\underset{\mathbf{U}^T\mathbf{U}=\mathbf{I}_d}{\mathbf{arg\,max}}\,\gamma\beta-(1-\gamma)\alpha \\ =\underset{\mathbf{U}^T\mathbf{U}=\mathbf{I}_d}{\mathbf{arg\,max}}\,\mathbf{U}^T(\gamma\mathbf{H}_b-(1-\gamma)\mathbf{H}_w)\mathbf{U} \tag{3}$$

in which $\mathbf{I}_d=diag\underbrace{(1,\cdots,1)}_{d}$

By using Lagrange multiplier method, we get the corresponding Lagrange function of the equation(3) to calculate it:

$$L(\mathbf{v},\lambda)=\mathbf{v}^T(\gamma\mathbf{H}_b-(1-\gamma)\mathbf{H}_w)\mathbf{v}-\lambda(\mathbf{v}^T\mathbf{v}-1) \tag{4}$$

There must be the following condition if the equation(3) is reasonable.

$$\frac{\partial L}{\partial \mathbf{v}}=0 \tag{5}$$

$$\text{that is, } (\gamma\mathbf{H}_b-(1-\gamma)\mathbf{H}_w)\mathbf{v}=\lambda\mathbf{v} \tag{6}$$

So, the transformed matix $\mathbf{U}$ of LMSDC is a matrix consisting of orthonormal unit eigenvectors $\mathbf{v}_1,\mathbf{v}_2,\cdots,\mathbf{v}_d$ correspongding to d maximum eigenvalues chosen from the matrix $\gamma\mathbf{H}_b-(1-\gamma)\mathbf{H}_w$. From the equation (6), we find that the LMSCD method solves the small size sample problem in LLD.

3 Define the Weights in LMSDC

We use the contextual-distance metric $p(\mathbf{x}_i\to\mathbf{x}_j)$ in LMSDC, thus decreasing to certain extent the level of dependence on the type of input sample space and improving the feature extraction capability of the criterion to generalize. According to the reference books [7] and [8], we learn that the distance metric reflects the internal geometric structure of data clusters through defining the corresponding structural descriptor $f(\Omega)$. That is, if $\mathbf{x}_i$ compiles with the structure of Ω, the structure is not affected much when $\mathbf{x}_i$ is moved away from Ω, whereas if $\mathbf{x}_i$ is an isolated point or a noise sample, the structure is affected greatly when it is moved away. We, in the definition of contextual-distance metric, often use $\delta f_i=\| f(\Omega)-f(\Omega\setminus\mathbf{x}_i)\|$ to denote the contribution degree of $\mathbf{x}_i$ to the internal geometric structure of Ω, thus the contextual-distance metrics is defined as:

$$p(\mathbf{x}_i\to\mathbf{x}_j)=|\delta f_i-\delta f_j| \tag{7}$$

From the above equation, we can know that the contextual-distance metrics indicate the dissimilarity between the samples in the contextual sets. So the smaller $p(\mathbf{x}_i\to\mathbf{x}_j)$ is, the bigger the probability of $\mathbf{x}_i$ and $\mathbf{x}_j$ belonging to the same class is, and vice verse.

There are two ways to define the cluster structural descriptor function $f(\Omega)$ generally when the contextual-distance metrics are use in practices: centroid method and coding length. However, studies show that the former is more applicable to data with spherical structure. The latter, based on information theories, focuses on the effectiveness of the volume changes of information in the contextual sets on the structure. And in the reference books [6] , [7] and [8], it is shown, from theoretical and example respects, that using the contextual-distance metrics constructed by the cluster structure descriptor can maintain the global geometric structure better, which shows better robustness and adaptability. Therefore, we use coding length to define the descriptor $f(\Omega)$.

Definition 2[8,9]**:** there is a data set $\Omega=[\mathbf{x}_1,\cdots,\mathbf{x}_k]$, in which $\overline{\mathbf{x}}=\frac{1}{k}\Omega e$. Let $\overline{\Omega}=\Omega-\overline{\mathbf{x}}e^T$, then the coding length of Ω is:

$$f(\Omega)=L(\Omega)=\frac{k+D}{2}\mathbf{logdet}(\mathbf{I}+\frac{D}{\varepsilon^2 k}\overline{\Omega}\overline{\Omega}^T)+ \frac{D}{2}\mathbf{log}(1+\frac{\overline{\mathbf{x}}^T\overline{\mathbf{x}}}{\varepsilon^2}) \tag{8}$$

in which ε is the allowable distortion and $\varepsilon=\sqrt{10D/(k-1)}$, and D indicates the number of vector dimensions.

3.1 The Definition of Weights

We define the contextual distance and the parameter σ according to the above analysis and the equations (7) and (8) as follows:

$$p(\mathbf{x}_i^s \to \overline{\mathbf{x}}^s)=|\delta f_i^s-\delta\overline{f}^s| \tag{9}$$

in which $\delta f_i^s=\| f(\mathbf{X}_s)-f(\mathbf{X}_s\setminus\mathbf{x}_i^s)\|$, $\delta\overline{f}^s$ and σ_w are the mean and the variance of $[\delta f_1^s,\cdots,\delta f_{c_s}^s]$;

The above equation is similar to the contextual distance in the reference [7] just from the respective of the form, but the contextual sets in the reference [7] were gotten by using nonsupervised k-NN method. The LMSDC method in this paper, a supervised one, takes each class of training samples as a contextual set, which is similar to the reference [6]. But defining the contextual distance $p(\overline{\mathbf{x}}^s\to\overline{\mathbf{x}})$ in the equation (2) is difficult.

The direct way to define is to use the one in [6]: $p(\overline{\mathbf{x}}^s\to\overline{\mathbf{x}})=\|f(\mathbf{X})-f(\mathbf{X}\setminus\mathbf{X}_s)\|$. It indicates the contribution of the internal geometric structure of each class of training samples to maintaining the global structure. However, when dealing with the high dimensional data, such as gene data and image data, we find the definition is likely to lead to infinite $p(\overline{\mathbf{x}}^s\to\overline{\mathbf{x}})$ and infinitesimal weights, thus making it impossible to test. Therefore, it is necessary to discuss how to define $p(\overline{\mathbf{x}}^s\to\overline{\mathbf{x}})$ which is fit for high dimensional data and the LMSDC in this paper.

Following is the algorithm which can be used to calculate the contextual distance $p(\overline{\mathbf{x}}^s\to\overline{\mathbf{x}})$ and the parameter σ_b in (2). Then we are to explain the reasonability of it later.

Alogrithm1: Calculate the contextual distance $p(\overline{\mathbf{x}}^s \to \overline{\mathbf{x}})$ and the parameter σ_b	
Step 1: Input the training sample set $\mathbf{X}$ and the number of classes c. Make $s=1$ to initialize;	
Step 2: Calculate the mean $\overline{\mathbf{x}}^s$ of the s th class of sample set $\mathbf{X}_s$;	
Step 3: Let $\mathbf{X}_k (k=1,\cdots,c \,\&\, k \neq s)$ be the k class training sample set and let $\mathbf{X}_k^{'} = \mathbf{X}_k \cup \{\overline{\mathbf{x}}^s\}$. Calculate $\delta f_k^s = \left\| f(\mathbf{X}_k^{'}) - f(\mathbf{X}_k) \right\| (k=1,\cdots,c \,\&\, k \neq s)$;	
Step 4: Let δf^s be the mean of $[\delta f_1^s,\cdots,\delta f_{s-1}^s,\delta f_{s+1}^s,\cdots,\delta f_c^s]$;	
Step 5: Let $s=s+1$ and when $s \le c$ go back to the step 2, otherwise move to the step 6;	
Step 6: Let $\delta \bar{f}$ and σ_b be the mean and the viarance of $[\delta f^1,\cdots,\delta f^c]$ respectively;	
Step 7: Output $p(\overline{\mathbf{x}}^s \to \overline{\mathbf{x}}) = \left\| \delta f^s - \delta \bar{f} \right\|$ and σ_b。	

We use the mean $\overline{\mathbf{x}}^s$ to represent the s th training sample set $\mathbf{X}_s$ in the algorithm 1, which is the same as in often-used methods. But the calculation of the key **steps 3** and **setp 4** shows us the dissimilarity metric: δf^s between the s th and other data sets. In the **step 3**, the aim of defining new data set $\mathbf{X}_k^{'}$ and calculating δf_k^s is to indicate the dissimilarity between $\overline{\mathbf{x}}^s$ and the k th training samples $\mathbf{X}_k$, that is, to indicate the dissimilarity between the $\mathbf{X}_s$ and the k th sample set $\mathbf{X}_k$, thus showing that δf^s gotten from the calculation in the **step 4** indicates the average dissimilarity between the $\mathbf{X}_s$ and other $c-1$ sample sets, thus also showing that the internal geometric structure of the $\mathbf{X}_s$ is different from that of other $c-1$ sample sets, which shows the contribution of the internal geometric structure of the $\mathbf{X}_s$ to maintaining the global geometric structure. Therefore, the processing principles in the algorithm 1 coincide with the direct meaning of $p(\overline{\mathbf{x}}^s \to \overline{\mathbf{x}})$. Furthermore, many tests show us that this algorithm overcomes the defining difficulties to certain extent in dealing with high dimensional data in [6] although the time complexity increases to certain extent since δf_k^s need calculating more in the **step 3**.

Following is the simplified LMSDC criterion:

Algorithm 2: Laplacian Maximum Scatter Difference Discriminant Criterion (LMSDC)	
Step 1: Input sample set $\mathbf{X}$ and the number of classes c. calculate $p(\mathbf{x}_i^s \to \overline{\mathbf{x}}^s), \sigma_w$ and $p(\overline{\mathbf{x}}^s \to \overline{\mathbf{x}}), \sigma_b$ respectively by using (8) and (9) and also the algorithm 1 ;	
Step 2: Calculate the within-class scatter α and the between-class scatter β according to (1) and (2);	
Step 3: Define γ and get the matrix $\mathbf{U}$ consisting of unit eigenvectors corresponding to d maximum eigen values by using (6) ;	
Step 4: Output the low dimensional embedded set $\mathbf{Y}=[\mathbf{y}_1,\cdots,\mathbf{y}_n]$ corresponding to the input sample set $\mathbf{X}$ according to $\mathbf{Y}=\mathbf{U}^T\mathbf{X}$。	

4 Experiments

In order to show the greater capability of LMSDC in this paper to extract the features, we use LMSDC, LDA, MMC and LLD to test four data subsets in UCI respectively for comparison. During the process of testing, we use 10-fold cross-validation to define the proper parameters in different methods, thus letting $\gamma = 2\wedge(i-20), i = 1,\cdots,20$ in LMSDC and $t = 2\wedge i, i = -4,\cdots,9$ in LLD. Also, the 1-NN is used in the tests. Following shows the results:

Table 1. Recognition Performance Comparison on Ionosphere, Iris, Segment, Glass Datasets

Datasets	**Ionosphere**		**IRIS**		**Segment**		**Glass**	
Algorithm	*Accuracy*	*Dim*	*Accuracy*	*Dim*	*Accuracy*	*Dim*	*Accuracy*	*Dim*
LDA	0.78632	1	0.94	2	0.91948	5	0.77778	4
MMC	0.8974	5	0.94	4	0.95325	11	0.81944	7
LLD	0.92308 ($t=512$)	12	0.96 ($t=0.0625$)	4	0.94805 ($t=8$)	15	0.81944 ($t=16$)	7

From the above table, we find that LMSDC in this paper has better effectiveness in feature extraction and higher classifying accuracy than dose other methods, which shows that it is the introduction of contextural-distanse metrics in the weights of LMSDC that make the method focus on the geometric structure of the input samples, decrease the degree of the dependence on the type of them and thus improve the capability of the method to generalize.

5 Conclusion

After analyzing the problems and the shortcomings of the LLD method, we present a Laplacian Maximum Scatter Difference Discriminant Criterion (LMSDC) by integrating contextual-distance metrics and maximum scatter difference discriminant criterion. The proposed criterion can obviously reduce the dependence on the sample space and solve small size sample problem. Of course, we will go on to solve certain problems in this method, such as how to calculate more properly the contextual-distance metrics from the theoretical and practical aspects.

Acknowledgements. The authors would like to thank the anonymous reviewers for their valuable comments and suggestions to improve the quality of this paper in advance. This work was partly supported by the Jiangsu Provincial Innovation Project of Graduate Students of China (CX09B-175Z) and Yancheng Institute of Technology Project of Applied Basic Research (XKY2009070).

References

1. Jolliffe, T.: Principal component analysis. Springer, New York (1986)
2. Fisher, R.A.: The use of multiple measurements in taxonomic problems. Annals of Eugenics 7, 179–188 (1936)

3. Hsieh, P., Wang, D., Hsu, C.: A linear feature extraction for multiclass classification problems based on class mean and covariance discriminant information. IEEE Trans. Pattern Analysis Machine Intelligence 28(6), 223–235 (2006)
4. He, X.F., Niyogi, P.: Locality preserving projections. In: Advances in Neural Information Processing Systems (NIPS), Vancouver, Canada (2003)
5. Zhao, D.L., Lin, Z.C., Xiao, R., Tang, X.O.: Linear laplacian discrimination for feature extraction. In: IEEE Computer Society Conference on Computer Vision And Pattern Recognition (CVPR), Minnesota, USA (2007)
6. Zhang, W., Lin, Z.C., Tang, X.O.: Tensor linear laplacian discrimination (TLLD) for feature extraction. Pattern Recognition 42(9), 1941–1948 (2009)
7. Zhao, D.L., Lin, Z.C., Xiao, R., Tang, X.O.: Laplacian PCA and its applications. In: IEEE 11th International Conference on Computer Vision (ICCV), Rio de Janeiro, Brazil (2007)
8. Zhao, D.L., Lin, Z.C., Xiao, R., Tang, X.O.: Contextual distance for data perception. In: IEEE 11th International Conference on Computer Vision (ICCV), Rio de Janeiro, Brazil (2007)
9. Ma, Y., Derksen, H., Hong, W., Wright, J.: Segmentation of multivariate mixed data via lossy data coding and compression. IEEE Trans. Pattern Analysis Machine Intelligence 29(9), 1546–1562 (2007)
10. Blake, C.L., Merz, C.J.: UCI repository of machine learning databases. University of California, Irvine, Department of Information and Computer Science (1998), http://www.ics.uci.edu/~mlearn/MLRepository.html

Method of Underwater Autonomous Weapon System Hitting Control Based on PSO*

Pengfei Peng, Zhong Liu, and Jun Xing

Department of Command and Control, Navy University of Engineering
WuHan, HuBei Province, China
Pengpengfei1@live.com

Abstract. Basic makeup and function of underwater autonomous weapon system are introduced, and hitting process model and control parameters are analysed. Concerned with simulation environment of hitting process, a method of underwater autonomous weapon system hitting control based on particle swarm optimization（PSO）is advanced, which makes quick optimization of hitting control parameters come true and improves precise hit of weapon system. It is showed by Lots of numerical values simulation that this method can effectively make optimization control of hitting process, provide credible theoretical basis for study of systemic optimization control, which has good application prospect in future combat use of weapon system.

Keywords: autonomous weapon system, PSO, hitting control, process model.

1 Introduction

Human being's intelligence and action can be imitated by autonomous intelligent system, which can exercise its duties on unknown and complicated environments. It can adapt to environment by environment sense, determination program and intelligent action to change actuality and accomplish scheduled assignments[1][2].

Underwater autonomous weapon system is outcome of integrate autonomous intelligent system and underwater weapon system, which combines attack capability of underwater weapon with action control capability of autonomous intelligent system, and is a complicated intelligent system which can carry out autonomous detection, location and attack for target. So, the advanced underwater autonomous weapon system is integrated with underwater detection, float control, information treatment and etc, acts on autonomous in deep sea, uses passive underwater detection to location, track, recognize and attack underwater target[3][4].

---

* This work is partially supported by defense technology research fund.

D. Zeng (Ed.): ICAIC 2011, Part I, CCIS 224, pp. 698–704, 2011.

On some physics environment, for improving precise attack capability of underwater autonomous weapon system to target, it is necessary to optimize important control parameters in hitting process according to target situation to make probability of hitting target biggest.

Hitting process model of underwater autonomous weapon system is constructed in this article, linked with simulation of hitting control process, method of underwater autonomous weapon system hitting control based on PSO is advanced, which uses PSO[5][6] to optimize hitting control parameters. It is showed by numerical values simulation that hitting control parameters can be quickly optimized by this method, and optimization control of hitting process can be actualized effectively, so precise attack capability of underwater autonomous weapon system can be improved.

2 Analysis of Hitting Process Model and Control Parameters

2.1 Analysis of Hitting Process of Underwater Autonomous Weapon System

Underwater autonomous weapon system can float under water, receive independently information of distance and orientation of target, and attack on autonomous through control system. So, hitting process of this system can be divided as:

(1) autonomous float process

When it detects, locates, tracks, recognizes the target that can be attacked, system switches to stage of weapon hitting attack. It waits to some scheduled time, changes its movement situation, floats to attack position and reaches assigned depth.

(2) launch fighting load

When system reaches assigned depth, control parameters are set to fighting load and it is launched.

(3) autonomous attack

System switches to autonomous attack stage according to assigned parameters and fighting load hits target after three course of going in water, search and guide.

2.2 Control Parameters in Hitting Process of Underwater Autonomous Weapon System

It can be known by analysis of hitting process of underwater autonomous weapon system that there are important control parameters as:

(1)attack time: the whole attack process of system is calculated and right time is chosen for attack.

(2)control parameters of weapon system: According to firepower control theory of weapon system, many assigned control parameters when weapon system launches can be got.

It is showed as Fig.1 that important control parameters are applied in hitting control process of underwater autonomous weapon system. Thereinto, firepower control parameters are decided by factors of tactical target aims and target movement state of weapon system, which can be calculated according to firepower control theory. System attack time is mainly decided by state of adversaries, target movement state and hitting process, and is affected greatly by environment. So, it is an typical optimization control problem of complicated nonlinear system action that how to choose a right attack time to improve hitting probability. It is the reason that system attack time is control parameters required optimization in hitting process of underwater autonomous weapon system.

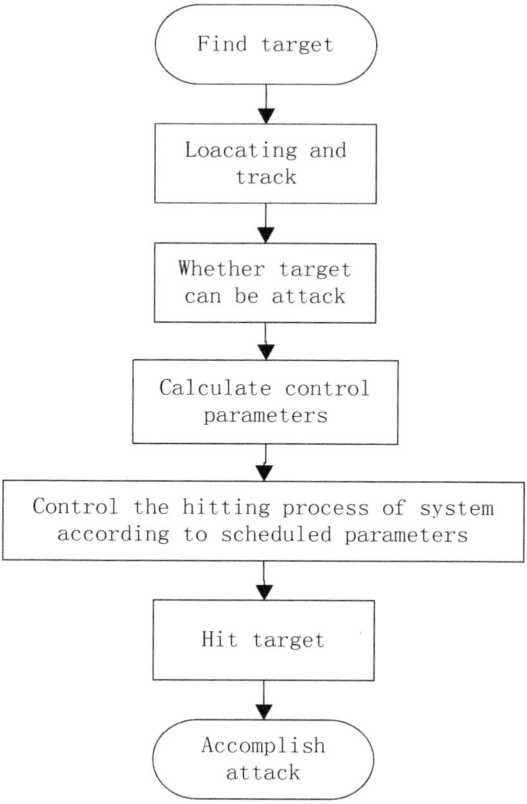

Fig. 1. Hitting control process of underwater autonomous weapon system

3 Particle Swarm Optimization(PSO)

PSO was advanced by Kennedy and Eberhart in 1995, which imitated action of birds flying and looking for food and colony got the best optimization according to collective cooperation among birds. Compare to Genetic Algorithm, it was also based on colony iterative but no cross and variance operators, colony can search in room of random solutions following optimization particles. Strong points of PSO are simple for actualization and concerned with deep intelligent background, which is fit for scientific study and engineering application, and has good application foreground in action optimization control of complicated nonlinear system[7][8].

Initialization of PSO is a group of random particles, and optimization solution can be found by iterative. Particles track two extremum in every iterative as optimization solution Pbest found by particle and Gbest found by colony to update it. Location and velocity of particles are updated by two formulas as followed:

$$V_i = \omega \cdot V_i + c_1 \cdot rand() \cdot (Pbest - X_i) + c_2 \cdot rand() \cdot (Gbest - X_i) \tag{1}$$

$$X_i = X_i + V_i \tag{2}$$

Thereinto, V_i is velocity of the i particle, X_i is location of the i particle, rand() is random number between (0,1), c_1 and c_2 are study gene or accelerating parameter, ω is weighing parameter. The boundary values are get when location X_i and velocity V_i exceed them in iterative process. Iterative ending condition is generally the biggest iterative time according to specific situation or the smallest adaptive threshold value which is searched by particle swarm.

4 Hitting Control Method of Underwater Autonomous Weapon System Based on Particle Swarm Optimization

According to analysis of hitting process and control parameters of underwater autonomous weapon system, it can be known that it is the key problem in hitting control process to optimize system attack time. Because hitting process of underwater autonomous weapon system is a complicated nonlinear one, it is difficult to be solved by method of math resolution. So, a hitting control method of underwater autonomous weapon system based on PSO was advanced. Main idea of this method is that optimization control of system and improvement of integrated fighting efficiency of system are realized by optimization time of system attack based on PSO during the process of system hitting control. The resolution process is showed as Fig.2, and steps of this algorithm as followed:

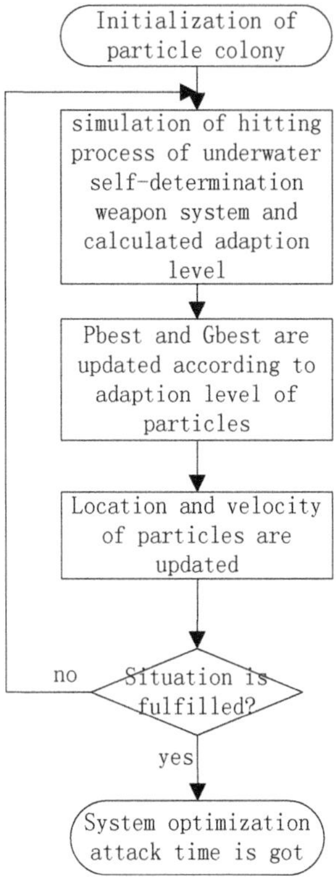

Fig. 2. Parameters optimization for hitting control of underwater autonomous weapon system based on particle swarm

Step 1: particle value is system attack time as for initialization of every particle. Number of particles is n, and initial location (initial solutions) and velocity of n particles are produced randomly.

Step 2: New location of every particle is produced by present location and velocity.

Step 3: Adaptive level of new location of every particle is calculated, and if it is better than Pbest, the present adaptive level is assigned as Pbest.

Step 4: Gbest is found according to Pbest.

Step 5: Particle velocity is updated by formula 1.

Step 6: Present particle location is updated by formula 2.

Step 7: If conditions are satisfied, it turns to step 8, or to step 3.

Step 8: Resolution process ends when optimized hitting control parameters are got.

Thereinto, particle adaptive level is probability of system hitting target. Condition of iterative end is that iterative time is the biggest.

5 Simulation Analysis

According to the advanced method, simulation analysis is conducted to hitting process and optimization control of underwater autonomous weapon system. On conditions of assumed target state, hitting process and attack track can be got as Fig.3, and optimization process of hitting control parameters based on PSO is showed as Fig.4. After several iterative, optimization attack time can be quickly found (466 seconds and 856 seconds), and hitting probability is 0.9.

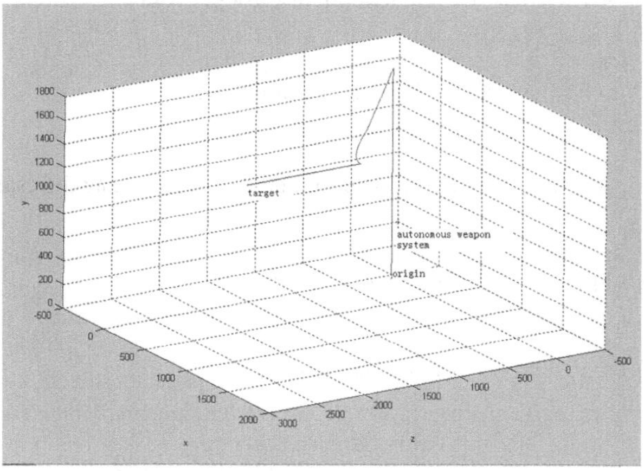

Fig. 3. Simulation of hitting process and attack track of underwater autonomous weapon system

It can be found by simulation test that this method which has little calculation and quick constringency can better make optimization of hitting control parameters, so integrated fighting efficiency of underwater autonomous weapon system is improved.

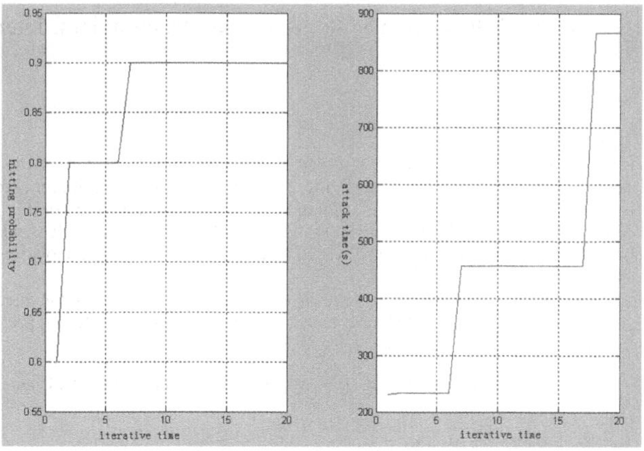

Fig. 4. Optimization process of hitting control parameters (attack time) based on PSO

6 Conclusion

Underwater autonomous weapon system is a specific autonomous intelligent system, also syntheses integrated of many technologies. Hitting process of underwater autonomous weapon system is complicated nonlinear one. It is a problem in system action optimization that how to realize hitting control optimization of underwater autonomous weapon system. In this article, a hitting process model of underwater autonomous weapon system is constructed. A hitting control method based on PSO was advanced on simulation of hitting process to realize quick optimization of hitting control parameters, which has good application foreground in future fighting use of weapon system.

References

1. Wu, G.-q., Jiang, C.-s., Zeng, G.-g.: Several issues about the research and development of autonomous intelligent system. Electronics Optics & Control 9(4), 27–31 (2002)
2. Xu, Y.-r., Pang, Y.-j., Gan, Y., Sun, Y.-s.: AUV state of the art and prospect. CAAI Transactions on Intelligent Systems 1(1), 9–16 (2006)
3. Qu, Y., Liu, Z., Qu, J.-z.: Research on underwater bearings-only target tracking algorithm based on time-delay. System Engineering and Electronics 29(1), 107–109 (2007)
4. Xing, J., Liu, Z., Peng, P.-f.: Analyse of accuracy for passive estimation of target depth in deep sea based on vertical linear array. In: Third International Conference on Innovative Computing, Information and Control, Dalian (2008)
5. Li, N., Fu, G.-j., Ku, S.-p., Chen, M.-j.: Development and prospect of a particle swarm optimization Algorithm. Journal of WUT(Information & Management Engineering) 27(2), 26–29 (2005)
6. Wu, L.-h., Wang, Y.-n., Yuan, X.-f., Liu, Z.-r.: Research and application of compound optimum model particle swarm optimization. Systems Engineering and Electronics 28(7), 1087–1090 (2006)
7. Wang, D.-f., Han, P.: Proportion-integral-derivative chaotic system control algorithm based on particle swarm optimization. Acta Physica Sinica 55(4), 1644–1650 (2006)
8. Li, G.-p., Zhao, H.-h.: Iterative particle swarm optimization algorithm and its application to robust optimization of batch process. Information and Control 36(2), 230–234 (2007)

The Design of the Network Configuration Management Based on NETCONF Protocol*

Jianqun Cui[1], Keming Jia[1], Libing Wu[2], Chuanhe Chen[1], and Mincai Lai[1]

[1] Department of Computer Science, Huazhong Normal University, Wuhan, China
[2] School of Computer, Wuhan University, Wuhan, China
jianqun8585@sina.com

Abstract. NETCONF protocol as a new protocol make up the deficiencies of existing configuration management. It improves network efficiency and automation level. Based on the in-depth study of NETCONF protocol principles, this paper designs NETCONF network management software.

Keywords: NETCONF, Network management, configuration management.

1 Introduction

Continuously, the normative management structure of the Internet has based on the Simple Network Management Protocol (SNMP).There is no statement that the SNMP is international standard protocol for network management, however, it has become the industry standard because of simplicity and practicality. A large number of network device manufacturers integrate the SNMP into the design of product. Due to the simplicity and defects in the data modeling language, the SNMP is the preferred protocol technology in monitoring tasks, but it can not configure complex network effectively. At present, in the area of configuration management the most widely used command mode is CLI (Command Line Interface). This needs input different commands depending on the varied configuration data which is cumbersome and complex. In other aspect, the command mode of CLI doesn't have standard form. It can not configure the network devices congruously, because different suppliers supply different CLI to some extent.

In order to improve the deficiencies of existing configuration management and meet the needs of next generation network configuration management, the Internet Engineering Task Force (IETF) set up a working group of NETCONF. The group combines with the mature technology of XML (Extensible Markup Language). They had passed the RFC4741 [1-2], RFC4742, RFC4743 and RFC4744 in the end of 2006. The working group formulated the next generation configuration management protocol - NETCONF. Then they adopted other new standards such as RFC5277, RFC5381 and

* Supported by the "Dawn" Program of Wuhan (No. 200950431183), self-determined research funds of CCNU from the colleges' basic research and operation of MOE (No. CCNU09A01025) , the Fundamental Research Funds for the Central Universities of WHU and China Postdoctoral Science Foundation funded project.

D. Zeng (Ed.): ICAIC 2011, Part I, CCIS 224, pp. 705–713, 2011.

RFC5539, which improved the NETCONF protocol constantly. Meanwhile, in the aspect of date modeling, IETF founded a special working group of NETMOD studying issues about content layer of NETCONF. The NETCONF protocol and the study about relevant technologies can compensate the deficiencies of existing configuration management. They enhanced the efficiency of network configuration management and the degree of automation.

The paper is structured as follows. Section 2 provides an overview of NETCONF protocol and section 3 introduces the related works. Section 4 gives the design of the network configuration management. Finally, we conclude the paper with a summary of conclusion.

2 Netconf Protocol

NETCONF protocol is a new configuration management agreement that bases on XML [3-4]. XML is used for configuring data and date encoding. Its transmission includes SSHv2, SOAP, BEEP and so on. The NETCONF protocol uses the simple RPC (Remote Procedure Call) mode to access and update some or all of the management information. NETCONF protocol can support multiple platforms. Firstly, it provides a standard configuration database; secondly, it separates different conceptual layer, sending the request and response by remote invocation; thirdly, it provides configuration lock to ensure accessing units of the configuration database at a certain moment. Furthermore, it supports a variety of transformation model and conceptual models, providing a simple set of protocol operations.

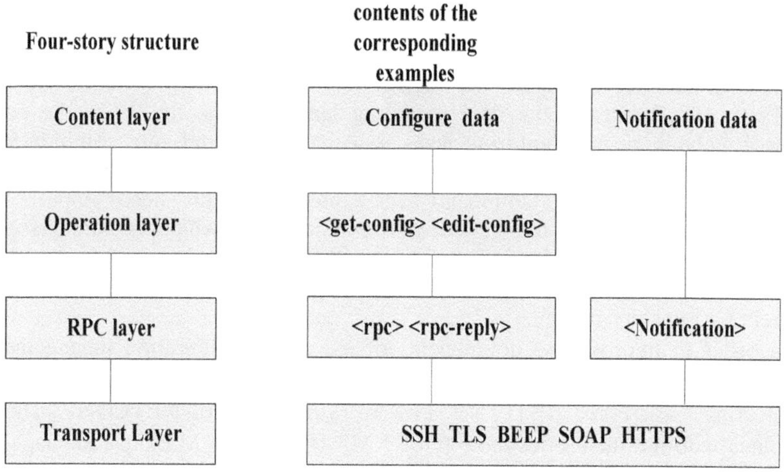

Fig. 1. The improved algorithm flowchart

NETCONF protocol is divided into four layers-- transport layer, RPC layer, operation layer and content layer (see Fig. 1). The four layers of NETCONF protocol are independent, realizing separately. The lower layer provides interface to upper layer when the services invoke. The implementation of internal layer is diversiform.

3 Related Works

Reference 5 proposes a network management system based NETCONF protocol. The model ensures configuration operations reliability [5]. Reference 6 also gives a network configuration management system. It has good scalability, allowing developers to extend the configuration operations and management information easily [6]. This paper combines the advantages on the basis of their design, designing a new system.

NETCONF network configuration management software use B/S architecture. Its interface design uses the current popular Ajax framework—extjs, the tiring-room use struts frame to interact contextually. It uses open source framework-- Dom4j to package and handle message, linking agency side securely and effectively.

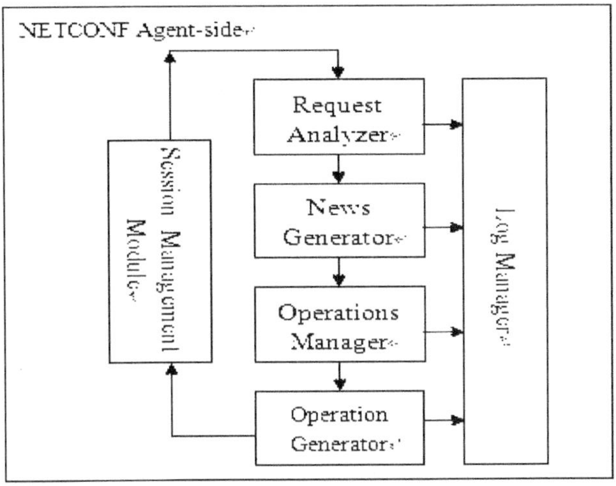

Fig. 2. System Architecture

Fig. 2 shows the system architerture. There are mainly five modules. In the management--side, managers send out relevant configuration commands in order to access and modify the relevant configuration information of devices. The management-side takes charge of launching operation request and receiving the result of configuration operations. Agency side, running on a managed network device, is responsible for responding the requirements of configuration-side. Device management information can be configured to operate. For instance, it extracts and modifies the information and returns the result to management-side.

4 System Design

Features of this network configuration management software can be summarized as follows: firstly, it discovers and manages network devices, packaging the user's various operations to the required format. Then it sent them to the designated agent; secondly, the messages returned by agency side are parsed to required format by interface display. Management-side mainly includes operation interface, device management module, requesting packet encapsulation module, returning the message parsing module and the session management module.

4.1 Equipment Management Module

When management-side starting, it will read a proxy configuration file named AgentConf.xml. The file contains the entire agents managed by management-side. Accordingly, users can select the corresponding device and manage it. Definitely, users can increase new proxy devices by inputting the new IP and password in the interface. Simultaneously, the management-side updates the file called AgentConf.xml, writing new proxy information to the configuration. Fig. 3 and Fig. 4 show the detailed design of class and mutual calling relationships.

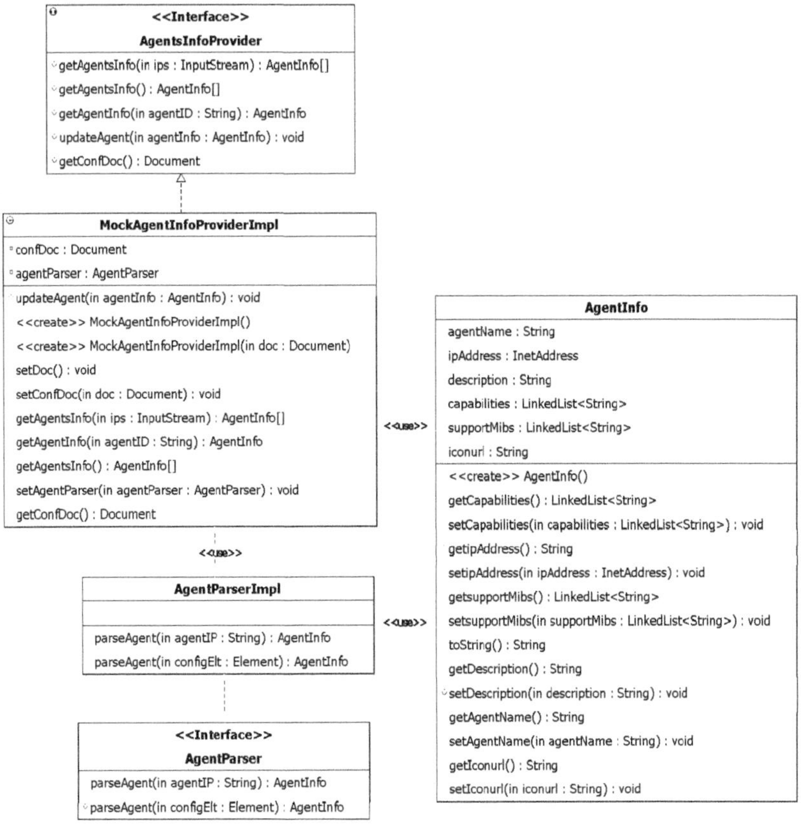

Fig. 3. Device Management Module

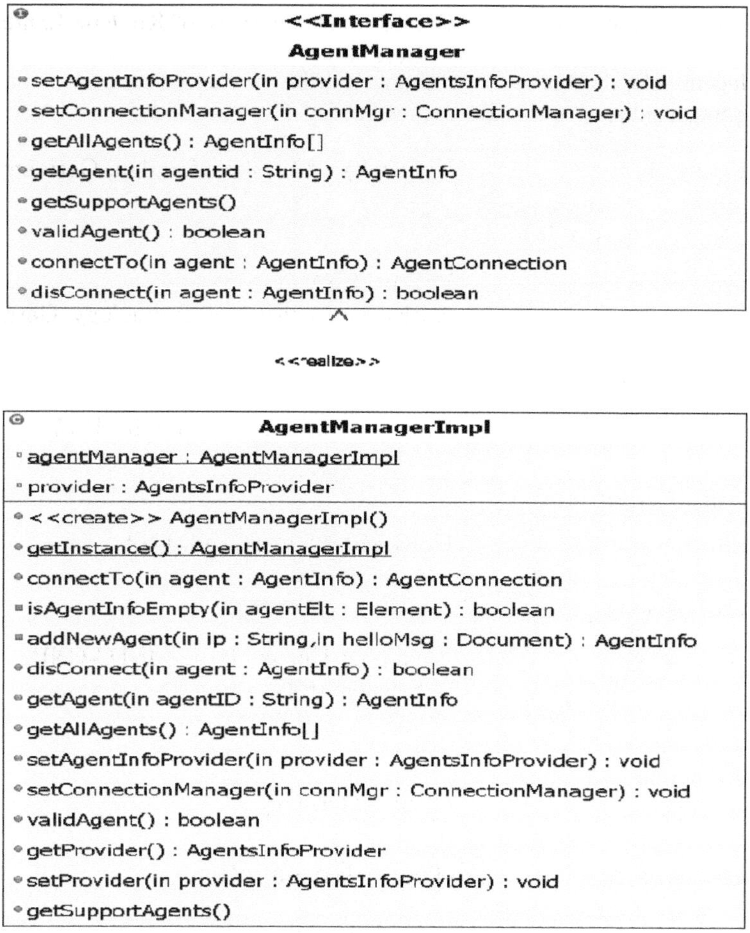

Fig. 4. Device Management Module

4.2 Session Management Moudle

The main task of the session management module is the communication between management-side and agent-side. When there is RPC request in RPC message processor, session management module packages this message to the agent-side. Session management module waits for the response message sent from the agent-side, extracting RPC response message when the response message arrives. Then, it transmits to RPC message processor.

It clearly defined that the implementation of NETCONF must support the SSH transfer protocol in RFC4741. With the help of open source tools--Openssh management-side takes the secure authentication mechanism of key-based. Management-side must generate a pair of public/private key, and send the public key to agent-side. Agent-side copies the file's content to the authorized keys file located under Openssh. Only with above steps, can management-side establish SSH tunnel with agent-side. In the end, it connects with Socket. The connection between management side and agent side is shown in Fig. 5.

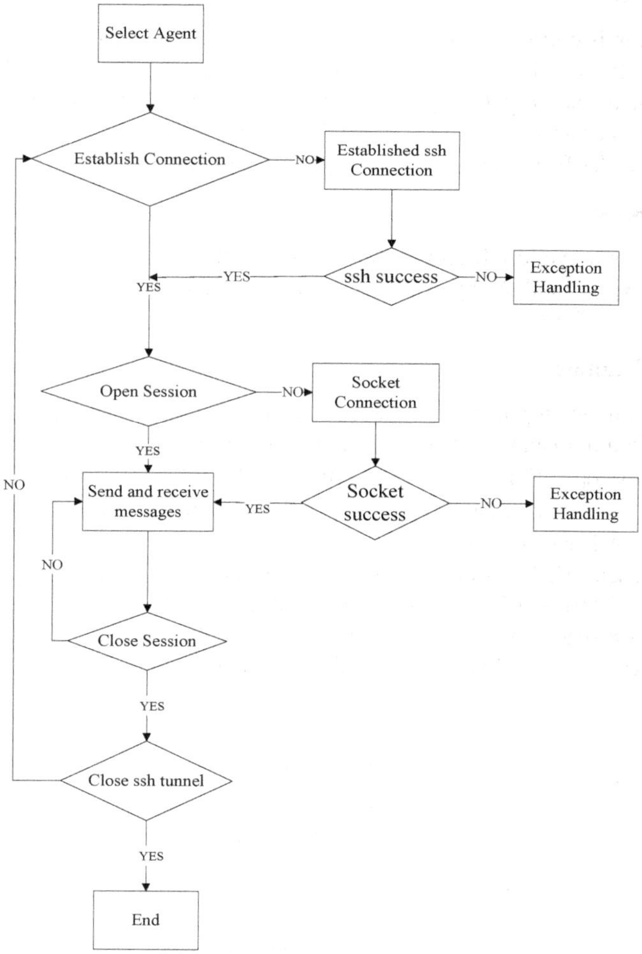

Fig. 5. Flow chart of communication to agent-side

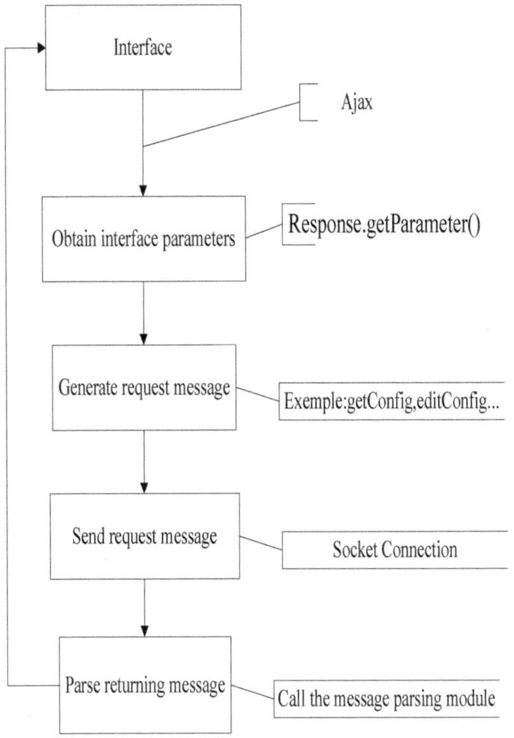

Fig. 6. Flow chart Packaging and packet analysis module

4.3 Session Packaging and Packet Analysis Module

When users configure the specific equipment, all operations will be created varied message meeting the RFC4741 specification. They will be sent to agent side. Then agency side will return message that contains needed information, and the message will be parsed to the json format and sent to user interface. Management side of the package back request message package and return packet parsing module's flow char is shown in Fig. 6.

In allusion to specific requests message for the management side, the agency side return a corresponding response message, may be normal message, OK message, or an error message, all these meet the specifications of the document—xml. Management-side use open source tools named dom4j to determine the returning message's type. Then, management-side parses message according to the different types by calling different packet parsing module. At last, management-side will return json strings. The flow chart of parsing module is shown in Fig. 7.

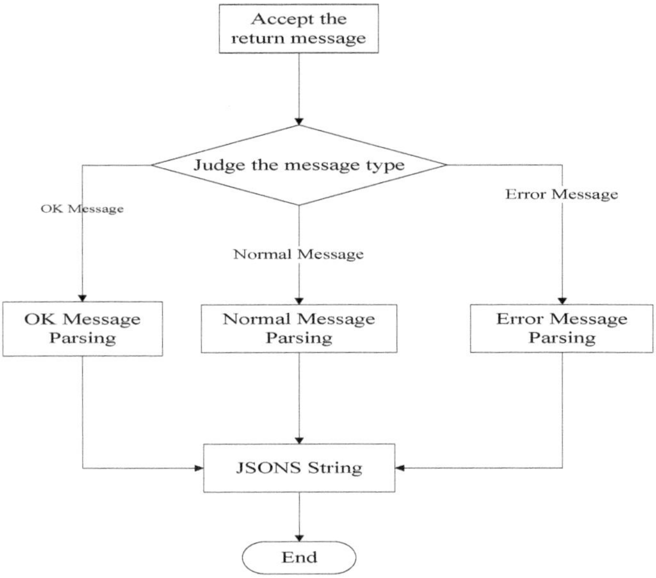

Fig. 7. The flow chart of parsing module

5 Conclusion

We implement network configuration management software using JAVA language based on NETCONF protocol. The software's testing environment is as follows: Management-side runs on client servers in WINDOWS platform, agent-side runs on the managed device which are simulated by PC.

The paper analyzes the advantage and disadvantage of traditional network configuration management. A network configuration management system which bases on NETCONF protocol has been designed. The system follows the principle about NETCONF protocol. In addition, the paper analyses NETCONF network configuration management function module and the design process. Furthermore, it illuminates relevant details and implementation technology about management-side.

References

1. RFC4741. NETCONF configuration protocol
2. Mi, J.C., Hyoun, M.C., Hong, J.W., et al.: XMl-based configuration management for IP network devices. IEEE Communications Magazine 7, 84–91 (2004)
3. Qu, Z., Zhang, M., Xu, M., Deng, H.: Survey of XML-based Network Management, Journal of Chinese Computer Systems 29(2) (2008)
4. Wang, X., Dong, X.: Design of an NETCONF-based Network Management System. Journal of Nanjing University of Posts and Telecommunication (Natural Science) 26(3), 62–68 (2006)

5. Wang, C., Wang, W., Zhang, L.: Design and Implementation of NETCONF-based Configuration Management System. Computer and Moderation 10 (2009)
6. Xu, H., Ai, X., Xiao, D.: New Generation Network Management Based on the NETCONF Protocol. Journal of Beijing University of Posts and Telecommunications 32(suppl.)
7. Xiao, D., Chen, L., Ai, X.: Research and implement on next generation network configuration protocol NETCONF. Journal of HuaZhong Normal University (Nat. Sci.) 42(4) (December 2008)

Resource Allocation: An Optimum-Seeking Approach under the Uncertainty for PERT*

Li Changqing[1] and Zhang Mang[2]

[1] Inner Mongolia University School of Management Dean, PhD Tutor
Research Interests: management under uncertainty
School of Management, Inner Mongolia University of Technology
Huhhot, 010051, P.R. China
[2] Inner Mongolia University School of Management Graduate
Research Interests: management under uncertainty
School of Management, Inner Mongolia University of Technology
Huhhot, 010051, P.R. China
li52048976@163.com

Abstract. on the basis of Resource optimum-seeking approach, the article estimate earliest finish time, optimistic time and pessimistic time and calculate expectation and variance of each process. The resource allocation problem can be resolved by using the "branch-and-bound" algorithm. The article explores how to choose path with the different expectation and variance, Especially, the problem can be resolve by coefficient of variation. The method can overcome the subjectivity which comes from personal preference options.

Keywords: Indeterminacy, Resource allocation, Coefficient of variation, An optimum-seeking approach.

1 Introduction

The resource allocation problem can be resolved by using the "branch-and-bound" algorithm, here, the resource is certain. If the resource is under the condition of indeterminacy, what should do to optimize the resources. The article uses a simple example to explain the problem. The complex problems demand a computer to solve. Here, only one resource is under the condition of indeterminacy.

To illustrate circumstances, the activity-on-node (AON) convention will be used here. The method is identical if the activity-on-arrow (AOA) display is used. Two basic rules will be followed:

(1) The basic logic of the network is always maintained
(2) An activity once started will always be finished

Initial network that under the condition of indeterminacy will be followed:

* This paper was supported by Inner Mongolia Natural Science Foundation under Grant No.2009zd13, the National Social Science Foundation of China under Grant No.05BJY043 and the National Natural Science Foundation of China under Grant No.70640008.

D. Zeng (Ed.): ICAIC 2011, Part I, CCIS 224, pp. 714–725, 2011.

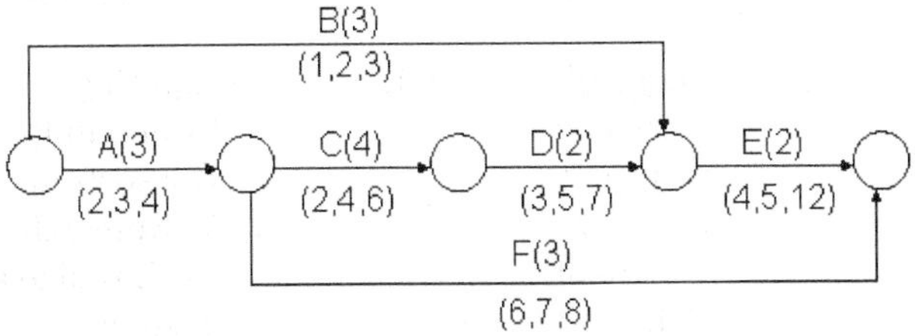

Fig. 1. Initial network

the number in bracket at the back of the letter represents the men of each process, below the arrow, the three letters representative the earliest finish time、optimistic time and pessimistic time.

The article will be demonstrated here by using PERT, using the formula $t_e = \frac{a+4m+b}{6}$ to calculate the expectation of each process, using the formula $V_{t_e} = (\frac{b-a}{6})^2$ to calculate the variance of each process. In the two formulas, a represents the optimistic time, m represents the possible time, b represents the pessimistic time. The expectation and variance using the two formulas will be followed:

Table 1. The Expectation and Variance

activity	a	m	b	expectation	variance
A	2	3	4	3	**1/9**
B	1	2	3	2	**1/9**
C	2	4	6	4	**4/9**
D	3	5	7	5	**4/9**
E	4	5	12	6	**16/9**
F	**6**	**7**	**8**	**7**	**1/9**

Hence, initial network in fig.1 can be turned into initial network that using the branch-and-bound algorithm.

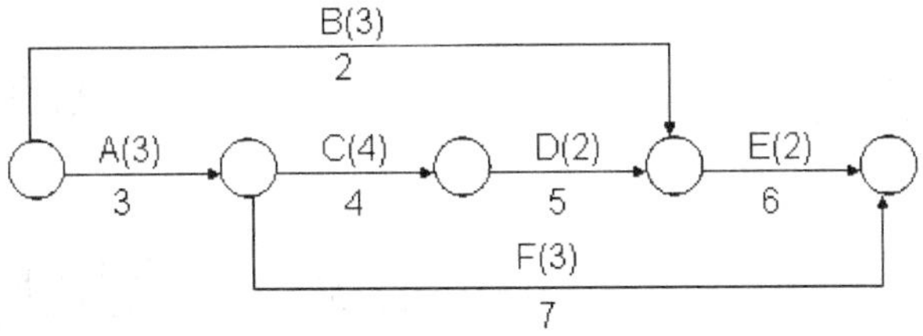

Fig. 2. The adjusted initial network

Here, it can use as many as 5 men, and all activities can start as early as possible. The situation that the men is constrained can be shown by the Gantt chart(fig.3). In the fig.3, some parts has exceeded the resource ceiling, thus not all activities can start as early as possible.

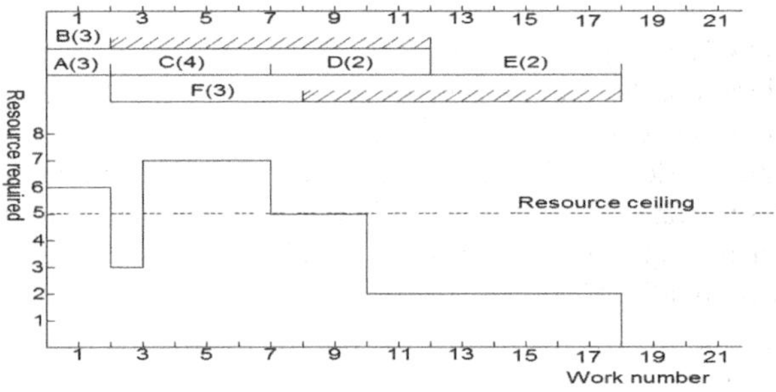

Fig. 3. Gantt chart(all activities start as early as possible)

2 Branching

In order to solve the problems, the article branch initial node of the initial network using the "branch-and-bound" algorithm, three alternatives present themselves, and the first two alternatives are acceptable.

Table 2. The Choices of the Initial Nodes

Serial number	Start	resource requirement(men)	feasible
1	A	3	Yes
2	B	3	Yes
3	A+B	3+3=6	No

Because of the constraint of the men, only the first two are acceptable. Here, a "tree" can "grow" from an initial node (node 1) with two branches. Where a branch represents a course of action. Each branch terminating in a node representing the results of that action. Thus the branch between nodes 1 and 2 represents activities A being carried out, while the branch between nodes 1 and 3 represents activities B being carried out.

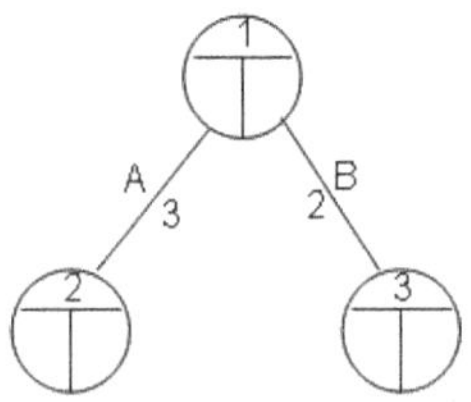

Fig. 4. Initial growth of the tree

Now, consider the situation represented by node 2. the network would be as in fig.5, with a total project time(TPT) of 18 weeks. While node 3 represents the network of fig.6, with a TPT of 20 weeks.

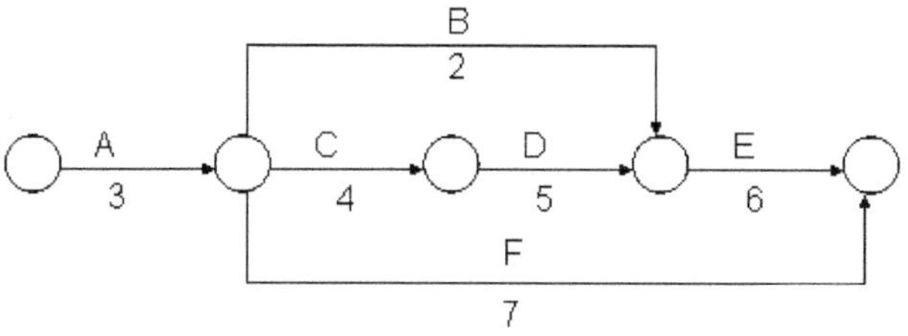

Fig. 5. Situation represented by node 2 (TPT=18 weeks)

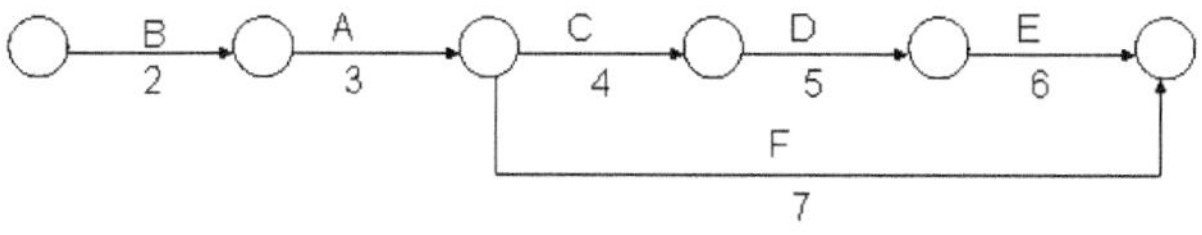

Fig. 6. Situation represented by node 3 (TPT=20 weeks)

3 Bounding

At the node 2 the only decision that has been taken is that activity A is fixed into position with the result that the minimum possible duration time. The figure can never be reduced no matter how subsequent activities are deployed. Indeed it is possible that later resource allocation decision may cause this time increase. Since this is the lowest possible TPT for this decision it is known as the lower bound for this node. Similar considerations show that node 3 has a lower bound of 20 weeks.

Here, there is no guarantee that the future TFP as many as the now TFP. Only that the TPT from that node can never be less than the lower bound.

The committed time at a node(2 weeks for node 3,3 weeks for node 2) is enter into the bottom left-hand side of the node, and the lower bound for the TPT is entered in the bottom right-hand side, the node number appearing in the top of the node.

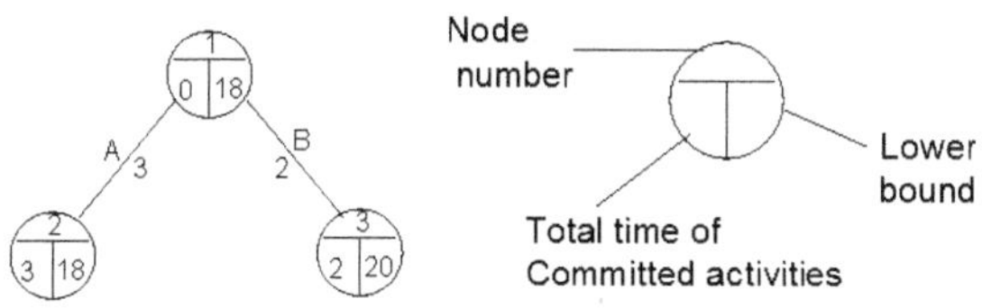

Fig. 7. First branches of the resource tree

4 Further Branching and Bounding

The resource tree of fig.7 shows two nodes from which further growth may take place. The article chooses node 2. node 2 has the least lower bound and 7 actions could follow:

Table 3. The Choices of Node 2

Serial number	The fixed activities	resource requirement(men)	feasible
1	B	3	Yes
2	C	4	Yes
3	F	3	Yes
4	B+C	3+4=7	No
5	B+F	3+3=6	No
6	C+F	4+3=7	No
7	B+C+F	3+4+3=10	No

Here, only the first three are feasible as far as resources are concerned, so that three further branches will grow from node 2, ending in node 4, 5 and 6 respectively. For each activity, activity A is fixed. Consider node 4. Here, the node 4 are represented by fig.8, Node 5 are represented by fig.9, Node 6 are represented by fig.10.

Branching again takes place from the node present themselves as fig.11.

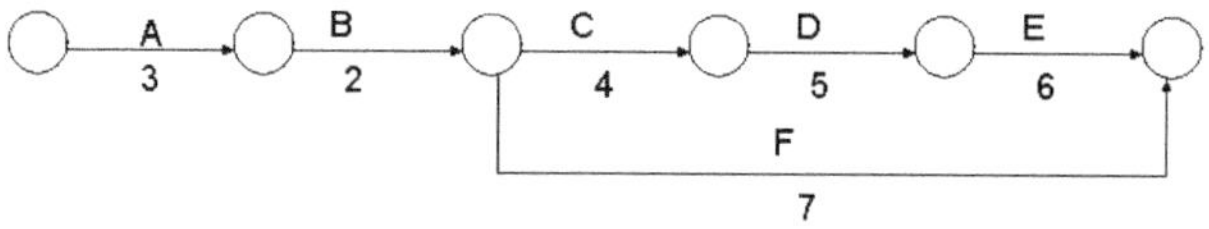

Fig. 8. Situation represented by node 4(TFP=20 weeks)

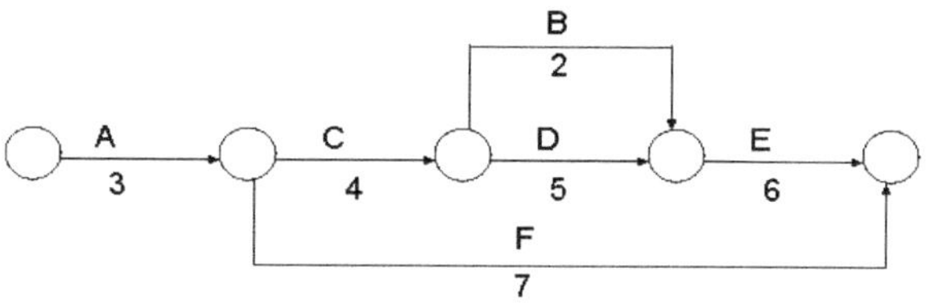

Fig. 9. Situation represented by node 5(TFP=18 weeks)

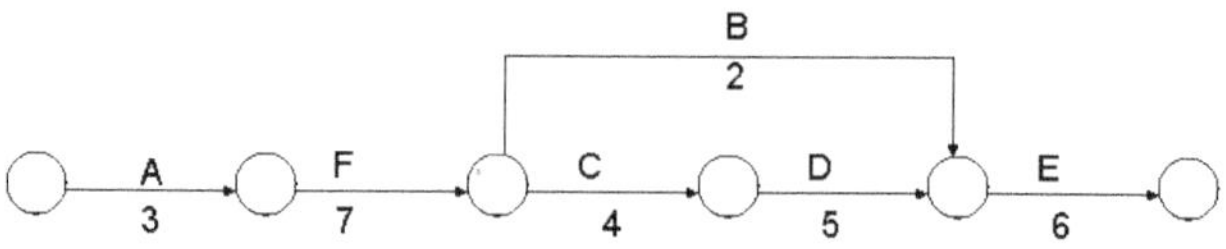

Fig. 10. Situation represented by node 6(TFP=25 weeks)

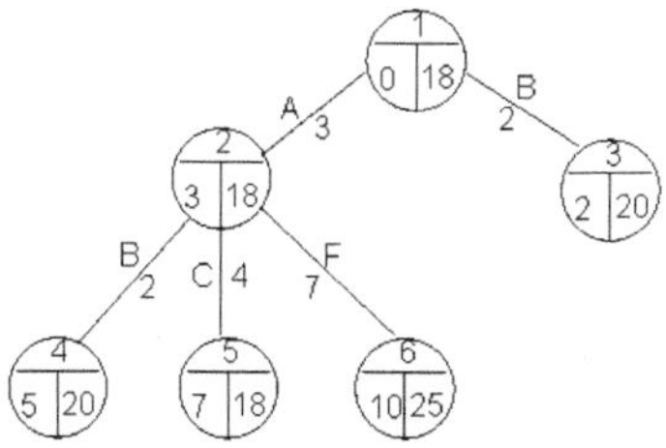

Fig. 11. Situation represented by node 2

It can be seen from fig.11, branching and bounding takes place from many nodes, if branching and bounding takes place each nodes, it will be complex. Therefore, one node will be chosen. Consider node 4. In the fig.8, three alternatives present themselves.

Table 4. The Choices of Node 4

Serial number	Commit activity(s)	resources required(men)	feasible
1	C	4	Yes
2	F	3	Yes
3	C+F	4+3=7	No

Here, only the first two are feasible as far as resources are concerned, so that two further branches will grow from node 4, ending in node 7 and 8 respectively. Node 7 and 8 are represented by fig.12, the resource tree has now grown to fig.13.

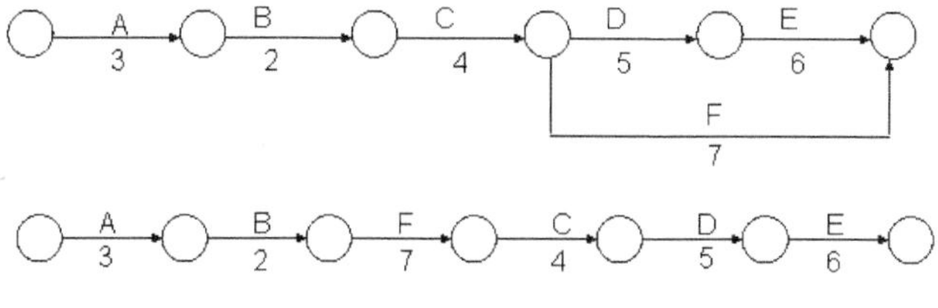

Fig. 12. Situation represented by node 7 and 8(TFP=20 weeks TFP=27 weeks)

According to the above the steps, the forth branching present themselves as fig.14, and the total branching and bounding of initial network will be presented. Due to the limited space, the part of the branching and bounding of initial network could follow as fig.15, according to the above method, the branching and bounding of the other nodes can be shown.

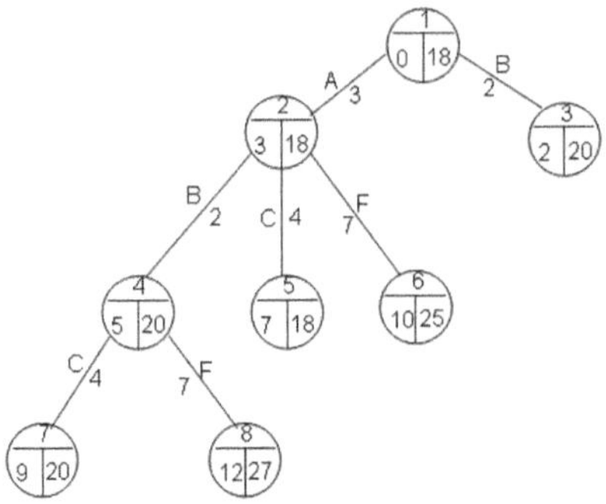

Fig. 13. Situation represented by node 4

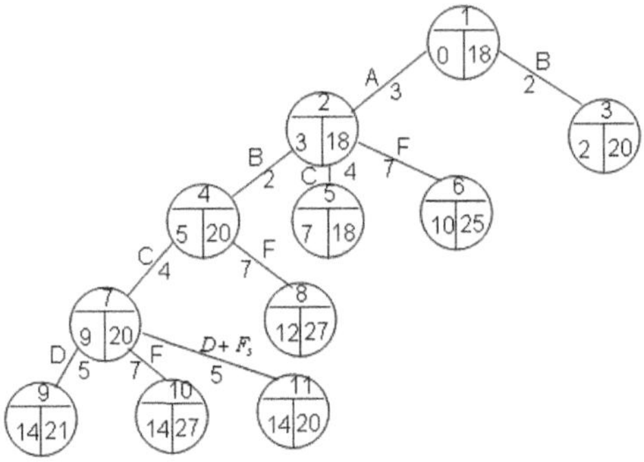

Fig. 14. Situation represented by node 7

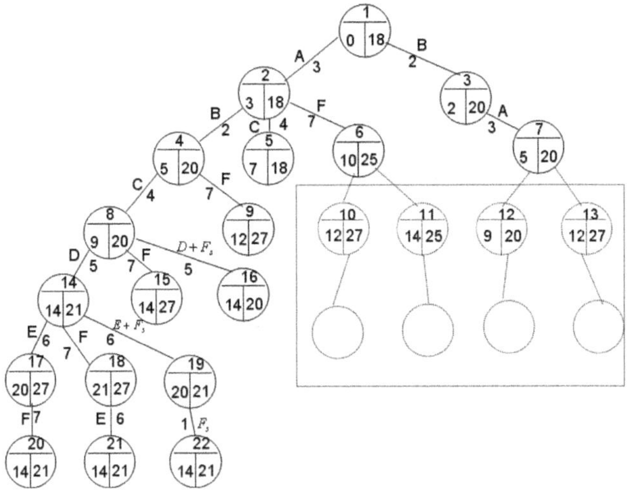

Fig. 15. The final resource tree

5 Selecting the Different Path

From the end figure of the branching and bounding, we can get the initial network diagram which satisfy the constraint conditions, these paths not only meet the constraint condition of the number of workers, and satisfy the basic rules of the network diagram. This article put the paths which corresponding the fig.15 in the following list, as shown in table 5: the 37 paths Corresponds to the fig.15.

Table 5. The 37 Paths Corresponds to the Fig.15

1	A,B,C,D,E,F
2	A,B,C,D,F,E
3	$A,B,C,D,(E+F_s),F_f$
4	A,B,C,F,D,E
5	$A,B,C,(D+F_S),F_f,E$
6	$A,B,C,(D+F_s),(F_f+E_s),E_f$
7	A,B,F,C,D,E
8	A,C,B,D,E,F
9	A,C,B,D,F,E
10	$A,C,B,D,(E+F_s),F_f$
11	A,C,B,F,D,E
12	$A,C,B,(D+F_s),F_f,E$
13	$A,C,B,(D+F_s),(F_f+E_s),E_f$
14	A,C,D,B,E,F
15	A,C,D,B,F,E
16	$A,C,D,B,(E+F_s),F_f$
17	A,C,D,F,B,E
18	A,C,F,B,D,E
19	A,C,F,D,B,E
20	$A,C,F,(B+D_s),D_f,E$
21	$A,C,(B+D_s),D_f,E,F$
22	$A,C,(B+D_s),D_f,F,E$
23	$A,C,(B+D_s),D_f,(E+F_s),F_f$
24	$A,C,(B+D_s),(D_f+F_s),F_f,E$
25	$A,C,(B+D_s),(D_f+F_s),(E_s+F_f),E_f$
26	$A,C,(D+F_s),F_f,B,E$
27	A,F,B,C,D,E
28	A,F,C,B,D,E

Table 5. (*continued*)

29	A,F,C,D,B,E
30	$A,F,C,(B+D_s),D_f,E$
31	B,A,C,D,E,F
32	B,A,C,D,F,E
33	$B,A,C,D,(E+F_s),F_f$
34	B,A,C,F,D,E
35	$B,A,C,(D+F_s),F_f,E$
36	$B,A,C,(D+F_s),(E_s+F_f),E_f$
37	B,A,F,C,D,E

Satisfying the basic rules of network diagram, this article do not consider the order of each activity in the path. So, we can put the 37 paths for eight paths. The 8 representative paths are shown in table 6, those network diagrams of 8 paths are shown in fig.16.

Table 6. The Representative Paths

Serial number	Path
1	A,C,B,D,F,E
2	$A,C,B,D,(E+F_s),F_f$
3	$A,B,C,(D+F_S),F_f,E$
4	$A,B,C,(D+F_s),(F_f+E_s),E_f$
5	$A,C,F,(B+D_s),D_f,E$
6	$A,C,(B+D_s),D_f,(E+F_s),F_f$
7	$A,C,(B+D_s),(D_f+F_s),F_f,E$
8	$A,C,(B+D_s),(D_f+F_s),(E_s+F_f),E$

In the above figure, the number on the front of each network diagram corresponding to the number in the table 6. Considering expectation and variance of each activity in the table Ⅰ, we can calculate expectation and variance of the above eight representative path. Here, it is important to note that:

(1) Assuming that each activity is independent, the expectation and variance of every network diagram is the sum of expectation and variance of each activity, these activities are critical one.

(2) For a activity is divided into two parts, how to compute their variance? This article use the approach is that pro rata variance based on each segment part time. For example, in the network diagram which Corresponds to the eighth path, D is divided into two parts, which are D_S and D_f, the calculation process of variance Corresponds to the D_S and D_f as follows:

$$V_{D_s} = \frac{2}{2+3} \times \frac{4}{9} = \frac{8}{45}$$

$$V_{D_f} = \frac{3}{2+3} \times \frac{4}{9} = \frac{12}{45}$$

(3)For two activity (or a part of the activity) showing side-by-side. In this article, select a larger variance represents the two processes (or part of the activity) of variance. For example, in the network diagram which Corresponds to the eighth path, B and D_s are side-by-side, we use the variance of D_s On behalf of their variance. The expectation of each path is the sum of completion time of every activity. Follow the above rules, we can get expectations and variance of eight paths, as shown in the table 7:

Table 7. Expectations and Variance of Eight Paths

Serial number	Expectations	Variance	Serial number	Expectations	Variance
1	27	27/9	5	25	26/9
2	21	61/21	6	19	176/63
3	22	34/21	7	22	179/63
4	20	26/9	8	18	25/9

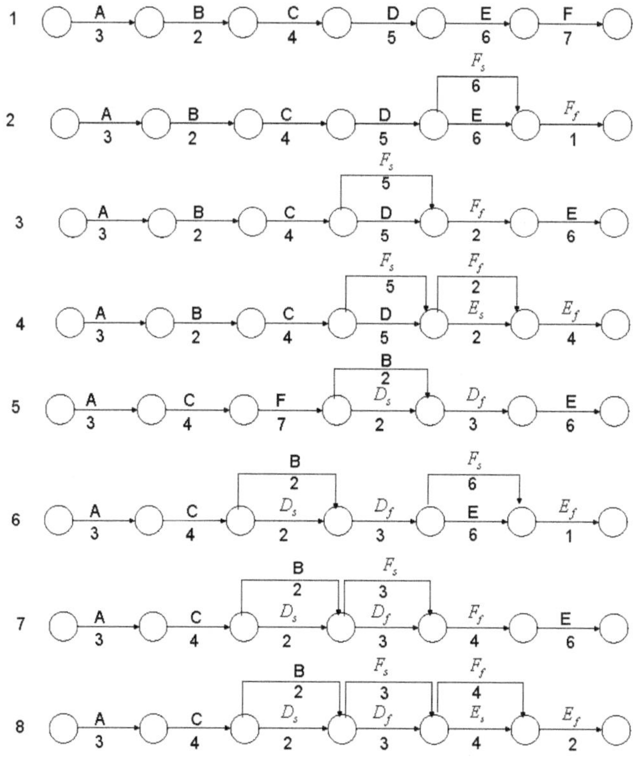

Fig. 16. Network diagram represented by eight paths

On the various paths of expectations and variances listed above, what decision should project management personnel make? It is possible that person with various preferences may have unlike choices: person with risk preference would like those of low expectation and big variance; person with risk aversion could want those owning path of huge expectation in order to get rid of the risk. Whatever the choice is made, they will not prefer paths possessing huge expectations and variances at one time. Hence, some paths can be rejected according to the rules, that is, under the circumstances of same expectation, delete the one with huge variance; under the circumstances of same variance, wipe out the one with huge expectation. On the basis of this rule, the former 8 paths can be shorten into 2, which is Path 3 and Path 8. Then, what to do is just selecting from the two. However, in the realistic setting, only one is needed to be picked up, how to solve this problem? Maybe the readers say, just do it in the light of project management personnel's preference, but that is quite subjective. For the sake of removing the influence of subjectivity, the notion of coefficient of variation is brought into this article. Formula of coefficient of variation is as follow:

$$C.V = \frac{S}{t_e} \times 100\%$$

In the formula, $C.V$ means coefficient of variation, S is for standard deviation of path, t_e marks expectation of path. One issue could be noticed: normally speaking, the bigger the mean value of coefficient of variation, the better is, but that is not valid in this article. A constant is drawn in to meet the situation, then coefficient of variation is marked as $C.V1$, whose formula is written below. Meanwhile, to avoid 0 or negative number appearing in denominator of coefficient of variation, the constant wanted should be bigger than expectations of all paths, constant is 28 here.

$$C.V1 = \frac{S}{28 - t_e} \times 100\%$$

From the above formula, coefficient of variation of Path 3 and Path 8 would be calculated as follow:

$$C.V1_3 = \frac{1.27}{28 - 22} \times 100\% = 21.21\%$$

$$C.V1_8 = \frac{1.67}{28 - 18} \times 100\% = 16.67\%$$

Through comparing values of coefficient of variation in Path 3 and Path 8, it can be obtained that Path 8 is the best choice.

Suppose exponential time with mean value in construction duration is 18, variance normal distribution is 25/9 in Path 8, project's the completion time can be forecasted, probability values of different completion time are confirmed. Such as, if construction duration is 18 to 22 days in Path 8, what is the probability to accomplish it? Assume T is project construction duration, depending on probability:

$$P(X \leq A) = \phi(\frac{A-\mu}{\delta})$$

In the formula, μ is mathematical expectation, A is random event. Due to

$$P(T \leq 22) = \phi(\frac{22-18}{\sqrt{25/9}}) = \phi(2.4)$$

searching the standard normal distribution table, then $P(T \leq 22) = 0.9918$ is gotten. That means the probability of finishing the building project within 22 days is 99.18%.

6 Further Discussion

On talking about optimization method of resource constraint in the background of uncertain conditions, this article uses programme evaluation and review technique (PERT) to dispose expectation and variance in each working procedure. And when the time of drawing up plan and that of actual construction are far apart, expectation and variance of working procedure may be related to time. At that moment, random process is introduced to deal with uncertainty under the circumstance. About this issue, hope the capable readers can do further research.

References

1. Montalbamo, M.: High-Speed Calculation of the Cvitical Paths of Large Networks. IBM System Research and Development Center Technical Report (1990)
2. Davis, E.W.: An Algorithm for Optimal Project Scheduling under Multiple Resource Constrains. Management Science (1993)
3. Lawrence, J.A., Pasternack, B.A.: Applied Management Science:Spredsheet Analysis and Communication for Decision Making. John Wiley & Sons, Inc., Chichester (2002)
4. Lockyer, K.: Critical Path Analysis and other Project Network Techniques. Pitman Publishing Inc. (1984)

Influencing Factors Research of Phenol Wastewater Treatment by Cathode Electro-Fenton Method*

Yafeng Li, Yuzhuo Guan, and Cuicui Tao

Department of Municipal and Environmental Engineering
University of Shenyang Jianzhu
Shenyang, Liaoning Province, China
Yafeng545@qq.com

Abstract. In this paper, the method of cathode electro-Fenton was used to study the influence of different controlling factors on phenol wastewater treatment and reaction kinetics of phenol oxidative degradation. The experiment was made in homemade three-dimension electrode reactor. The effect of the phenol wastewater treatment was studied by changing pH, electrolysis voltage and dosage of Fe^{2+}, while the other reaction conditions were fixed. When pH was 3, electrolysis voltage was 15V and dosage of Fe^{2+} was 0.6mmol/L, the effect of phenol wastewater treatment was the best, phenol removal rate reached to 91.85%, the effect reached the first level of reaction kinetics.

Keywords: cathode electro-Fenton method, three-dimension electrode, phenol, reaction kinetics.

1 Introduction

Phenol wastewater mainly comes from petrochemical industry、plastic and synthetic resin factories. Along with the development of industrial and agricultural production, more and more phenol wastewater is let out, the phenomenon makes a bad influence to environment. Phenol wastewater is one of industrial wastewater which is understood as the special consideration and solution in the field of water pollution control. While traditional water treatment technique which is taken to treat phenolic wastewater has the shortcomings of bad effectiveness、large investment and long working time [1-4], etc.

Cathode electro-Fenton method can be effectively applied to phenolic wastewater treatment. Compared to the other advanced oxidation degradation technology, cathode electro-Fenton method has more advantages of no extra H_2O_2、complete organic matter degradation、fast reaction、easy for operation、automatically flocculation [5-7], etc. Cathode electro-Fenton method is worth to propagate in actual application [8-9].

---

* Liaoning province education department scientific research projects(2009A600).

D. Zeng (Ed.): ICAIC 2011, Part I, CCIS 224, pp. 726–733, 2011.

The method of cathode electro-Fenton which was used in this paper took active carbon fibre (ACF) which is tied to a titanium line as cathode, and anode is ruthenium iridium titanium.

2 Materials and Methods

2.1 Test Device

Fig. 1 is test device. The device is homemade three-dimension electrode reactors, its measurements are 25 by 20 by 25 cm. In the electrolytic cell of experimental device, ACF which is tied to a titanium line is cathode, and ruthenium iridium titanium is anode. Area of each electrode is 15 by 15cm. Specific surface area of ACF is 1450m^2/g. Use small air compressor to the reactor bottom and cathode aeration simultaneously. Specially, the third electrode is 3mm columnar activated carbon which is adsorption satisfied in treated wastewater.

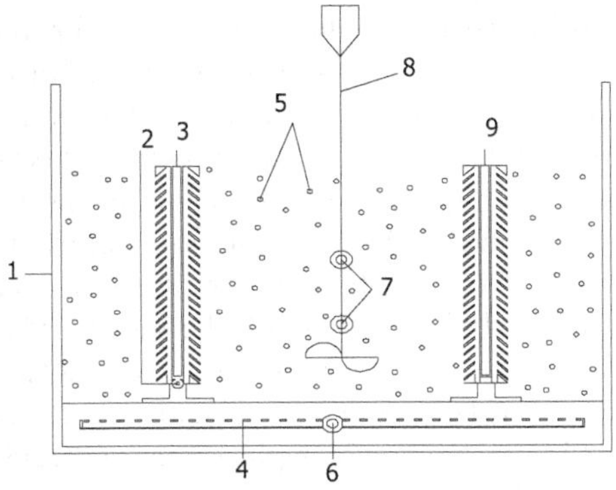

1 electrolytic cell	2 cathode aeration tube
3 cathode	4 the bottom of the aeration panel
5 the third electrode	6 the bottom of the aeration tube
7 sampling ports	8 the blender
9 the anode	

Fig. 1. Test device

2.2 Pretreatted Electrodes and Active Carbon

ACF were washing three times in deionized water before they are used, and drying at 120℃ for two hours, then saving in the dryer. To ward off adsorption between ACF and activated carbon particles, soaked several times with the coking wastewater before each use, then made activated carbon particles and ACF adsorption basically saturated, so eliminating the effect of adsorption on the test.

2.3 Test Water Samples

In the experiment, self-made synthetic phenol wastewater was chosen as research object.

2.4 Test Methods

Taking 10L of simulated phenol wastewater whose concentration was 300mg/L into the three-dimensional electrode reactor. pH value was adjusted by sulfate and sodium hydroxide, then added a certain amount of Fe^{2+} and Sodium sulfate, from time to time for sample analysis.

Determination of phenol concentration took 4-amino antipyrine direct spectrophotometric method.

3 Test Results and Discussions

3.1 Established Primary Relation of Different Factors

Taking phenol solution whose concentration was 300mg/L, fixed other test conditions: the reaction time 90min, aeration quantity was $0.6m^3/h$, Na_2SO_4 dosing quantity was 1g/L, electrode spacing was 10cm, then processed static orthogonal experiment. Orthogonal experiment factors level design were shown as Tab. 1, orthogonal test results were shown as Tab. 2.

Table 1. Orthogonal Experiment Factors Level Design

Level	A	B	C
	pH value	Electrolysis voltage (V)	Dosage of Fe^{2+} (mmol/L)
1	2.5	12	0.4
2	3.0	15	0.5
3	3.5	18	0.6

Table 2. Type Size for Papers

Experiment number	A	B	C	90min removal rate (%)
1	2.5	12	0.4	80.27
2	2.5	15	0.5	86.43
3	2.5	18	0.6	86.03
4	3.0	12	0.5	85.80
5	3.0	15	0.4	90.30
6	3.0	18	0.6	90.65
7	3.5	12	0.6	86.21
8	3.5	15	0.5	88.10
9	3.5	18	0.4	85.68
K_1	84.243	84.093	85.417	
K_2	88.917	88.277	86.777	
K_3	86.663	87.453	87.630	
Pole difference R	4.673	4.183	2.213	

As were shown in Tab. 2, fixed other reaction conditions, the primary relation of the different factors which affect phenol degradation rate was pH value>electrolysis voltage>dosage of Fe^{2+}. Based on the nine groups phenol wastewater treatment experiments, preliminary established the optimizing reaction condition was: pH was

3, electrolysis voltage was 15V, and dosage of Fe^{2+} was 0.6mmol/L. To further determine the best reaction conditions, on initial optimum reaction conditions, made single factor experiment, then modify the initial optimum reaction conditions.

3.2 Analysis of Single Factor

1) The Influence of pH on phenol Removal Rate: When electrolysis voltage was 15V and dosage of Fe^{2+} was 0.6mmol/L, the relation between phenol removal efficiency and pH value which was 2、3、4、5、6、7、8、9 respectively was shown in Fig. 2.

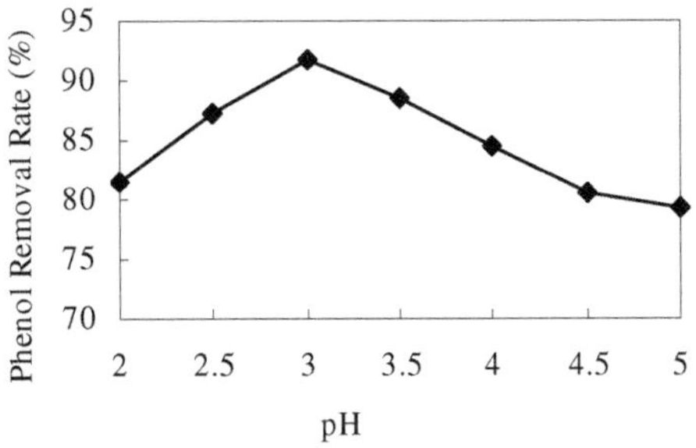

Fig. 2. The effect of pH on phenol removal rate

As were shown in Fig. 2, the phenol removal efficiency increased firstly, then decreased afterwards with increasing of pH. When the pH was 3, the phenol removal efficiency was the biggest, then phenol removal efficiency significantly decreased.

Some reasons could account above phenomenon. Cathode electro-Fenton reaction must be carried out under acidic conditions, so that a large number of H_2O_2 could be generated. Equation (1) is Fenton reagent reaction.

$$Fe^{2+}+H_2O_2+H^+\rightarrow Fe^{3+}+\cdot OH+H_2O \quad (1)$$

As were shown in (1), low pH value favored to happening positive reaction. When pH value was too low, H_2O_2 generation capacity would be reduced, hydrogen evolution side- reaction would happen, equation as follow:

$$2H^++2e^-\rightarrow H_2\uparrow \quad (2)$$

Fenton reaction was inhibited, so that removal rate was poor.

2) The Influence of Electrolysis Voltage on Phenol Removal Rate: When the pH was 3, the Fe^{2+} dosage was 0.6mmol/L, the relation between phenol removal efficiency and electrolysis voltage which was 6、9、12、15、18、21V respectively was shown in Fig. 3.

As were shown in Fig. 3, when the electrolysis voltage was less than 15V, the phenol removal efficiency increased significantly, while the electrolysis voltage was more than 15V, removal efficiency began decreased.

Some reasons could account above phenomenon. As the electrolytic voltage increases, making the electrode surface degradation of organic pollutants accelerated,

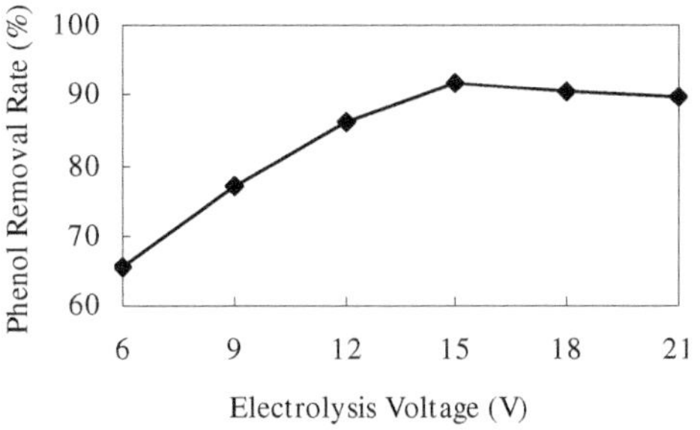

Fig. 3. The effect of electrolysis voltage on phenol removal rate

and increasing particle electrode complex electrode polarization level, then growing the number of working electrode; at the same time, the increase of electrolytic voltage made an augmentation of difference for the main potential of the electrode and the conductive particles and the electrolyte, improved an impulsive force of electrochemical oxidation reaction, accelerated the direct and indirect oxidation rate, so that phenol treatment effect was better. While electrolytic voltage was more than 15V, the system energy consumption increases, the temperature rise, so electrolytic voltage was too high was not good.

3) The Influence of Dosage of Fe^{2+} on Phenol Removal Rate: When the pH was 3, electrolysis voltage was 15V, the relation between phenol removal efficiency and dosage of Fe^{2+} which was 0.3、0.4、0.5、0.6、0.7mmol/L respectively was shown in Fig. 4.

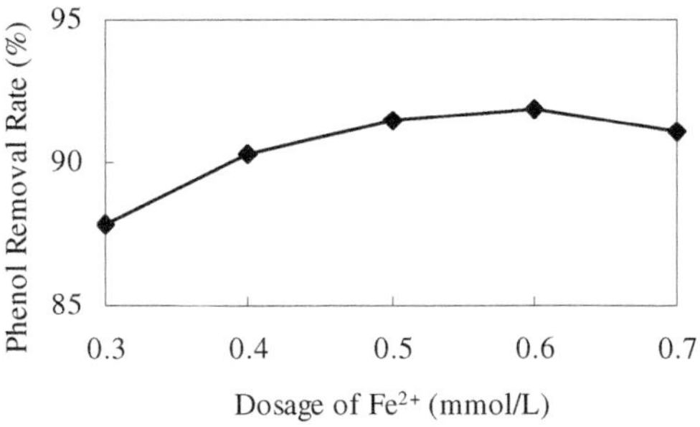

Fig. 4. The effect of Fe2+ dosage on phenol removal rate

As were shown in Fig. 4, the phenol removal rate increased firstly, and decreased afterwards with increasing Fe^{2+} dosage. When the Fe^{2+} dosage was 0.6mmol/L, the phenol removal rate was the biggest.

Some reasons could account above phenomenon. With increasing Fe^{2+} dosage, Fenton reagent reaction began to happen, Fe^{2+} as catalytic agent reacted with H_2O_2 to form stronger oxidizing ·OH. At the same time, Fe^{2+} was also an electrolyte, increasing the conductivity of the solution, so that Fenton reagent reaction was easy to happen. Then the phenol removal rate increased. When Fe^{2+} dosage exceet 0.6mmol/L, the phenol removal rate decreased. Firstly, a large number of Fe^{2+} could catch on ·OH, ·OH reaction equation as follow:

$$OH+Fe^{2+}\rightarrow Fe^{3+}+OH^{-}O \tag{3}$$

The amount of ·OH would reduced, so affectted Fenton reagent reaction. Secondly, when Fe^{2+} dosage was too large, making ·OH quickly generated, reaction equation as follow:

$$2\cdot OH+2\cdot OH\rightarrow 2H_2O+O_2 \tag{4}$$

The decrease of ·OH amount made the phenol removal rate declined.

3.3 Kinetics Studying

Taking phenol solution whose concentration was 300mg/L, when aeration quantity was $0.6m^3/h$、Na_2SO_4 dosing quantity was 1g/L、 electrode spacing was 10cm、pH was 3、 electrolysis voltage was 15V and dosage of Fe^{2+} was 0.6mmol/L, analysis the effect of reaction time on the phenol removal rate. Results were shown as Fig. 5.

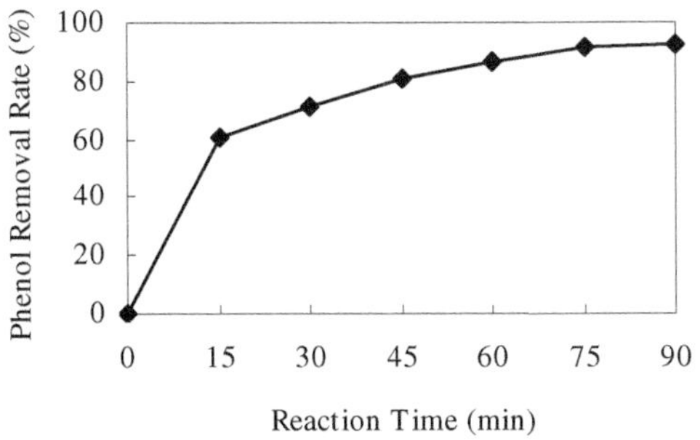

Fig. 5. The effect of reaction time on phenol removal rate

According to the rate equation, the kinetics equation of phenol oxidation and decomposition could be expressed as:

$$V = d(C_t)/dt = kC_t n \tag{5}$$

Where: V is reaction rate, C_t is phenol concentration in water samples when reaction time is t, t is reaction time, k is the rate constant, n is the reaction order.

From Fig. 5, the phenol degradation reaction could be described as first kinetics equation model. Definite integral to (5), the result could be expressed as:

$$Ln(C_0/C_t) = kt \tag{6}$$

$Ln(C_0/C_t)$ fitting with the reaction time curve was Fig. 6.

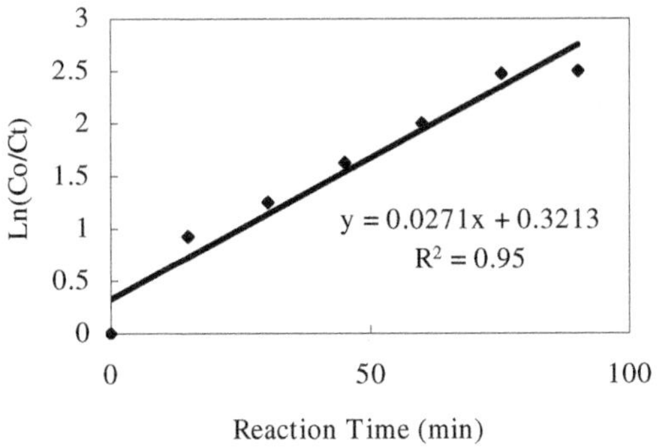

Fig. 6. Fitting curve of $Ln(C_0/C_t)$ along with reaction time

As were shown in Fig. 6, the phenol degradation reaction fit the first kinetics equation mode. $Ln(C_0/C_t)$ and t is the relationship of linear, slope of the line is the reaction rate constant k that is 0.0271min^{-1}. Based on Fig. 6, when the reaction time is 90min , phenol removal rate is 91.85%. Assume phenol removal rate is 92%, based on fitting equation, the reaction time is 93.20min. It is proved that dynamic model consistent with the actual test result, the reaction rate constant fitting error is small.

4 Conclusions

1) The orthogonal experiment results showed that the primary relation of the different factors which affect phenol degradation rate was pH value> electrolysis voltage> dosage of Fe2+.

2) The optimizing reaction condition of phenol wastewater treatment by cathode electro-Fenton method was: pH was 3, electrolysis voltage was 15V, and dosage of Fe^{2+} was 0.6mmol/L. At the optimizing condition, phenol removal rate reached to 91.85%.

3) The process of phenol degradation by cathode electro-Fenton method was in line with first reaction kinetics, and the dynamic model consistent with the actual test results, fitting out of the reaction rate constant error was least, fitting effect was good.

References

1. Chen, M.: Actuality and developping trend in the treatment of phenolic waste water. Chemical Engineer 2, 48–51 (2003)
2. Yin, Y., Xiao, Y., Zhu, Y.: Process of refractory waste water treatment by electro-Fenton method. Technology of Water Treatment 35(3), 5–9 (2009)
3. Liu, Q., Li, T.: The study progress in innocuous treatment of phenolic waste water. Technigues and Equipment for Enviro. Poll. Cont. 3(2), 62–66 (2002)
4. Wang, H., Xi, H.: Present situation and future development of phenol containing waste water treatment. Industrial Water Treatment 6, 6–9 (2002)

5. Zhang, N., Zheng, W., Peng, Y.: Study progress on treatment of refractory-degraded organics by electro-Fenton method. Shanghai Environmental Sciences 21(7), 440–441 (2002)
6. Cai, J., Shi, H., Li, A.: Study progress in treating industrial effluents by catalytic oxidation method. Jiangsu Environmental Science and Technology 16(4), 39–42 (2003)
7. Fu, J., Zhai, J., Wang, B.: Design and application of beer wastewater treatment by CAST. China Water & Waste water 19(11), 90–92 (2003)
8. Zhang, S., et al.: CASS process to treat wastewater of beer brewing. Water & Wastewater Engineering 24(3), 30–32 (1998)

Numerical Simulation Reaseach on Stress Field Distribution of Coal Bed Fault Structure Formation and Evolution

He Jun, Zhai Pei jie, Chen Xin sheng, and Jing Fu xing

Henan Polytechnic University,
School of Safety Science and Engineering, Jiaozuo
Jiaozuo 454003, China
hejun_good@sohu.com

Abstract. Using finite element numerical simulation software, ADINA, the formation of a fault structures under the action of tectonic stress was simulated. With the formation of coal-bed fault under a modern tectonic stress field, the destruction conditions of coal and the distribution of stress were simulated. Simulation results show that a tectonic fault structures under the action of the formation of coal seam, in the footwall near the fault plane of the seam and near the bottom of the fault plane of the plate at the top, coal vulnerable to damage; fault structure after the formation of lead in different Direct stress and horizontal stress combinations, are in reverse fault footwall fault plane exist in the vicinity of stress concentration phenomena, reverse fault stress field in the direction of maximum stress from the direction of the main decisions, and normal faults only in the level of stress and vertical stress closer, the stress field in the direction of the major decisions by the vertical stress. Conclusion of the study for the coal and gas outburst prevention and control has important theoretical guidance.

Keywords: fault, Tectonic evolution, numerical simulation, gas outburst.

1 Introduction

In ancient tectonic stress field, the tectonic evolution of the coal structure play a role in the deformation and failure, it affects mainly the coal structure and mechanical properties, and gas generation and preservation[1-4]. Geological structures that already exist in the present tectonic stress field[5-6], the coal and gas outburst for a direct control effect. Through the process of mining coal and gas outburst occurred in instances of statistical analysis, highlighting the geological structure with the seam zone is closely related. Gas content, emission size and the occurrence of coal and gas outburst conditions by the tectonic evolution of the control, and there were obvious regional, sub-band features. During the formation of geological structure, the original morphology of the coal seam a strong transformation of tectonic evolution of shear compression not only destroyed the structure of coal, but also changed the stress field

D. Zeng (Ed.): ICAIC 2011, Part I, CCIS 224, pp. 734–740, 2011.

of coal seams, which for the seam gas generation, storage and transport have a major impact. Geological structure is coal seam gas, the stress and the physical and mechanical properties of the three coal-linked bonds[7-9]. Carried out with the mechanical characteristics of geological structure and stress distribution characteristics of the study, with coal and gas outburst prediction and prevention of direct importance.

Currently existing in geological formation may be experienced hundreds of years. experienced a number of tectonic movement result,The mechanical properties of coal throughout the long process of structural evolution is not easy to determine, in order to facilitate the analysis, only the initial assumption that the known morphology and mechanical properties of coal under the premise of the fault structure of the coal formation and structure generated by again under the action of tectonic forces seam deformation and stress distribution law of the numerical simulation.

2 The Formation Process Numerical Simulation of Seam Fault Structure

The first simulation assumes that coal is in the horizontal position, The fault has been formed, Then make seam two under the stress of dislocation formation is, reverse faults, Analysis of faults in the formation of the stress field characteristics, Fault in the vicinity of coal structure destruction. For the normal faults and reverse faults are the same model with size model coal values of the physical and mechanical parameters are the same, but the stress and constraints imposed by the boundary conditions change.

2.1 Test Model

Contact friction coefficient set to 0.55. Model constraints as boundary conditions, under the plate only in the y = 0 and y = 250 two-plane y displacement constraint, the model of other surface to free surface, the plate in the z = 0 plane z displacement constraint, in the y = 0 and y = 250 2 y plane displacement constraint, the constraint x = 0 plane displacement x, ie, movement under the plate, but remain at rest on the plate (Figure 1). Model of load conditions, the model 2 z direction, the compressive stress side 5MPa imposed on behalf of the stress on the weight of overlying strata, corresponding time function 1, from 0 to the last moment remained constant; corresponds to the z axis under the bottom plate coercive displacement load, displacement direction of the fault plane in the same direction, set the vertical drop is 10m, corresponding to a function of time 2 times its size in the 0 time its size 0.000001 times, 30s when times its size 1. Calculated by static analysis, time step of 0.5, calculation of 20 steps; time step 1, 20 steps; the total computing time for the 30s. Solution set to open automatically solve the time-step switches and low power option switch, the other control parameters according to the default values. Reverse faults and normal faults similar to the test model, is set to a relatively stationary lower plate, the plate is relatively increased (Figure 2).

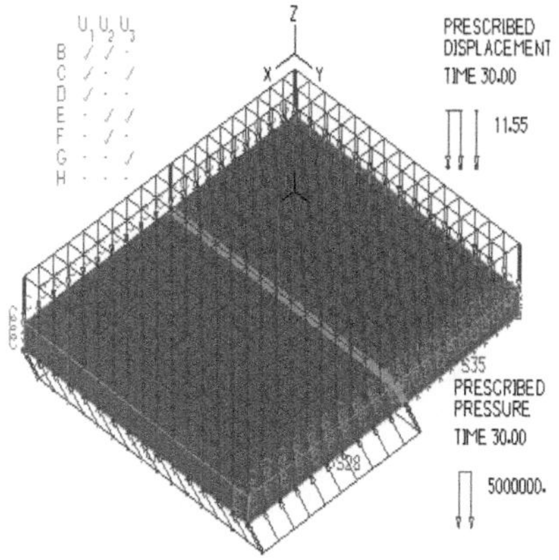

Fig. 1. Normal fault testmodel

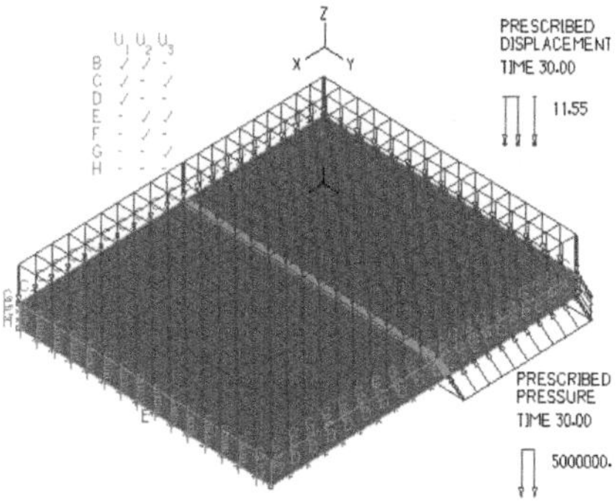

Fig. 2. Reverse fault test model

Table 1. Materialsmechanical Parametr

Rock name	Elastic modulus / MPa	Poisson's ratio	density / kg • m^{-3}	Uniaxial compressive strength / MPa	Uniaxial tensile strength / MPa
Coal	*9.8×10^3*	*0.1*	*1980*	*40*	*4*

2.2 Test Results and Analysis

Mainly from the equivalent stress distribution and the results of the three principal stress, we analyzed the fault of the coal formation damage. Figure 3 shows the fault to form the final moments of the effective stress diagram and the three-vector, such other time graphics slightly. By observing the faults in the formation of equivalent stress distribution and the distribution of three dimensional stress vector can be, the next set up process, the maximum normal stress to stress the main movement in the floor plate is only around the next principal tensile stress will be generated from the fault plane and the more recent, the greater the tensile principal stress.

Tensile strength of rock is often many times lower than the compressive strength, so the next plate in the bottom seam area around the same time close to the fault plane is easily broken. Most of the time during exercise, Seam equivalent stress plate changing, different positions of increasing stress from time to time, sometimes reduced, until the movement to the specified displacement, under the roof plate in favor of office equivalent stress away the distance from the fault plane increases, in favor of floor in the equivalent stress from fault plane with the increases.

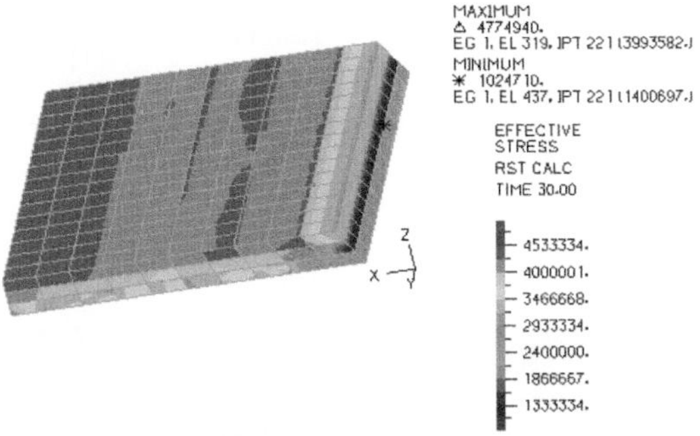

(a) Next plate

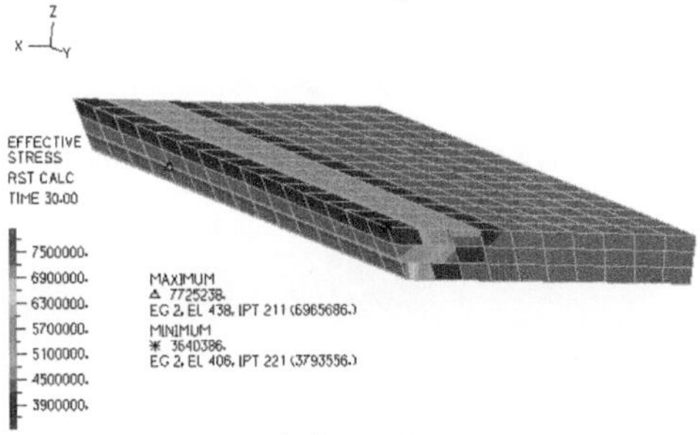

(b) On plate

Fig. 3. Efficetive stress of normal fault model footwall and hanging wall at last minut

3 Seam Rupture Tectonic Stress Field in the Numerical Simulation Under

3.1 Test Model

Symmetry in geometry and mechanical condition of symmetry conditions, plane strain stress analysis can be used to replace the three-dimensional simulation, to facilitate the computer to solve. Normal fault and reverse fault geometry and material parameters, the sety ∈ (0,200), z ∈ (0,80) into the roof, seam and bottom layer, seam thickness of 10m. Roof, floor and coal use Adina defined in the concrete, filling layer between the use of fault weakening the media to deal with the elastic material to define, the main mechanical parameters of materials, such as Table 2. The crustal stress being going against fault without exception under fixed constraint of basal plane, and then trial two kinds loading way, imitates: (1) y axis exerts level pressure on two sides being 14 MPa, z pushes down self-respect loading to exerting 8 erect pressure of Mpa , By weight loading of coal rock.(2) axial y two flanks exert level pressure to be 4MPa , z pushes down self-respect loading to still being 8 erect pressure of MPa , By weight loading of coal rock.

Table 2. Materils Mechanical Parametres

Rock stratum name	Flexible modulus/ MPa	Poisson's ratio	Density / kg • m-3	Uniaxial compressive strength / MPa	Uniaxial tensile strength / MPa
Roof	36.7×10^3	0.12	2750	100	20
Coal seam	9.8×10^3	0.1	1980	40	4
Bottom board	24.5×10^3	0.15	2600	70	10
Fill a tier	1×10^3	0.3	1300		

Fig. 4. The effective stress of normal fault under the first load pattern

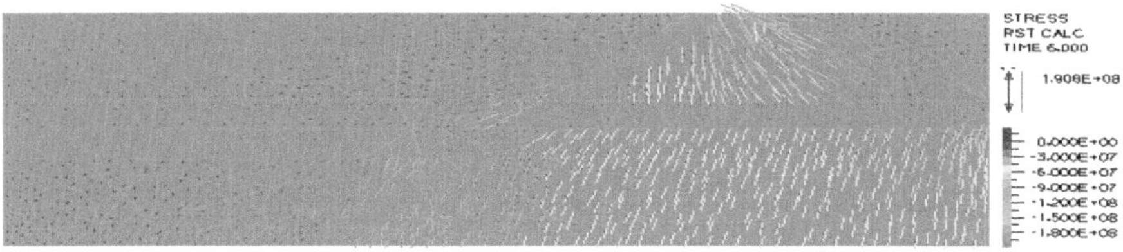

Fig. 5. The stress vector of normal fault under the first load pattern

3.2 Numerical Value Simulates Result and Analysis

1) Normal fault: To concentrate phenomenon comparatively nearby face to face, (if pursuing 7); Main strain major part are pressure strain (if pursuing 8) in coal rock stratum , main maximal coal rock stratum strain direction basic and fault incline to parallel face to face within an inch of approximation fault face. Under second kinds loading way, except equivalent strain is worth size besides different to some extent, the distribution condition that strain is worth is same as the first kind loading reaction basic (if pursuing 9) , coal gives first place to in the rock stratum in being to betoken pressure strain basically under the coal seam, in order main at present maximal strain direction erecting straight direction (if pursuing 10).

2) Thrust fault: Load analysis thrust fault mainly is the equivalent stress and the principal stress vector, analysis, and is the same fault, in this directly, the conclusion is Tulio.While horizontal strain is controlled by almost double times of plumb strain about, the contrary fault gets along in approximation fault coal seam soft and floury footwall roof having strain to concentrate phenomenon , the most maximum betokens the main pressure strain that strain shows in order lead straightens direction, the maximum betokens strain direction basic and fault face inclination within an inch of fault of equal rank within coal rock stratum; Main most maximal strain behaviour is horizontal pressure strain within contrary fault , direction tilts to some extent only within an inch of fault , the footwall has strain to concentrate a phenomenon within an inch of fault face. The Mechanics behaviour basic rectifying a fault does not change , effective strain in going against fault coal seam is bigger than top bottom board but , this is different from the behaviour that the first kind adds when being loaded with way, main maximal strain becomes main plumb direction pressure strain when plumb strain is double times of horizontal strain, give first place to, direction changes Only change in the direction near the fault and the fault plane bias.

4 Conclusions

Nature of the geological structure changing shape, its formation and evolution are extremely complex, through the normal fault and thrust fault formation and the situation of the modern tectonic stress field numerical simulation, the preliminary draw the following conclusions:

1) Normal faults and reverse faults during the formation of coal in general is in compression, integrity well preserved, but the fault plane near the bottom of the lower plate seam (large range) and close to the fault plane of the plate at the top (range small), coal vulnerable to damage, easy to accumulate a large number of gas occurrence.

2) In the modern tectonic stress field, different levels of vertical stress and stress combinations, the reverse fault stress field mainly by the largest force in the direction of the decision, the relative size of the coal strata of the stress changes, the normal fault performance The abnormal level of pressure in the pressure difference of less than vertical, the coal strata in the main stress direction decided mainly by the vertical stress. Reverse fault is the fault in the vicinity under the disc stress concentration exists.

3) Under modern structural strain field effect, different plumb strain and horizontal strain constitute the neighbouring footwall fault area being going against fault under condition, all existence strain concentrates a phenomenon.

References

1. Yu, B.F.: Comment on the control action that crustal stress lays stress on to coal and the gas. World Coal Technologies 7, 28–31 (1990)
2. Zhang, Z.M., Zhang, Y.G.: Gas geology law and the gas forecast, 9th edn., vol. 9, pp. 77–83. Coal industry press, Beijing (2005)

3. Zhu, X.S., Xu, F.Y.: The controlling effect of tectonic stress field and its evolution on coal and gas outburst. Journal of China Coal Society 19(3), 304–313 (1994)
4. Wan, T.F.: Chinese earth tectonics outline, p. 214. Geology press, Beijing (2007)
5. Han, J., Zhang, H.W., Song, W.H.: In-situ stress field of coal and gas out burst mining area. Chinese Joumal of Rock Mechanics and Engineering 27(2), 3840–3852 (2008)
6. He, J., Sheng, C.: A Research state and its development trends for control function of geological structure to coal and gas outburst. Journal of He nan Polytechnic University Natural Science 28(1), 1–7 (2009)
7. Lin, g., Zhao, c.b., Zhang, Y.H.: The principle method and related research progress on the numerical modeling of geological structural deformation. Advance in Earth Sciences 20(5), 549–555 (2005)
8. Xu, Z.B.: Early phase goes against Beijing west coal field Yan Shan covering structural cause of formation according to pushing the mechanism finite element method simulates. Journal of China University of Mining & Technology 19(3), 78–84 (1990)
9. He, J., Liu, M.J., Yan, A.H.: Fractal research of relation between geological tectonic coal fields and gas outburst. Journal of China Coal Society 27(6), 623–626 (2002)

Author Index

GPSR Compliance

The European Union's (EU) General Product Safety Regulation (GPSR) is a set of rules that requires consumer products to be safe and our obligations to ensure this.

If you have any concerns about our products, you can contact us on ProductSafety@springernature.com

In case Publisher is established outside the EU, the EU authorized representative is:

Springer Nature Customer Service Center GmbH
Europaplatz 3
69115 Heidelberg, Germany

Batch number: 10615007

Printed by Printforce, the Netherlands